THE OXFORD ENCYCLOPEDIA OF THE Modern Islamic World

The graphic device that appears on the title page and elsewhere in the encyclopedia is an example of Arabic calligraphy in traditional angular script. The dark area spells the name of the prophet Muḥammad, while the white area spells the name of his son-in-law and successor, ʿAlī. Each name is repeated in all four directions.

THE OXFORD ENCYCLOPEDIA
OF THE
Modern Islamic World

John L. Esposito
EDITOR IN CHIEF

VOLUME 1

New York Oxford
OXFORD UNIVERSITY PRESS
1995

Oxford University Press

Oxford New York
Athens Auckland Bangkok Bombay
Calcutta Cape Town Dar es Salaam Delhi
Florence Hong Kong Istanbul Karachi
Kuala Lumpur Madras Madrid Melbourne
Mexico City Nairobi Paris Singapore
Taipei Tokyo Toronto

and associated companies in
Berlin Ibadan

Published by Oxford University Press, Inc.,
200 Madison Avenue, New York, NY 10016

Oxford is a registered trademark of Oxford University Press

Library of Congress Cataloging-in-Publication Data

The Oxford encyclopedia of the modern Islamic world
John L. Esposito, editor in chief
p. cm.
Includes bibliographic references and index.
1. Islamic countries—Encyclopedias. 2. Islam—Encyclopedias.
I. Esposito, John L.
DS35.53.095 1995 909'.097671'003—dc20 94-30758 CIP
ISBN 0-19-506613-8 (set)
ISBN 0-19-509612-6 (vol. 1)

Grateful acknowledgment is made to grantors of permission to use the following written and illustrative materials in this volume. Aesthetic Theory: *photographs by Walter B. Denny.* African Languages and Literatures, *article on* West Africa: *permission to reprint translations by Jan Knappert published in the* Journal for Islamic Studies *granted by Jan Knappert.* Architecture, *article on* Traditional Forms: *figure 1 © the Walt Disney Company; figure 5, courtesy of American Institute of Indian Studies, Center for Art & Archaeology; figures 2-4, 6-7, photographs by Irene A. Bierman.* Architecture, *article on* Contemporary Forms: *figures 3-6, courtesy of the Aga Khan Award for Architecture.* Carpets: *photographs by Walter B. Denny.*

EDITORIAL AND PRODUCTION STAFF

SENIOR PROJECT EDITOR: Jeffrey P. Edelstein
DEVELOPMENT EDITOR: Mark D. Cummings
COPYEDITORS AND PROOFREADERS: Jane McGary, Carl D. Rosen, Philomena Mariani, Karen Fraley, Donald Spanel
BIBLIOGRAPHIC AND TECHNICAL RESEARCHERS: Yaḥyá Monastra, Philomena Mariani
ILLUSTRATIONS COORDINATOR: Paul Arthur
INDEXER: Stephen R. Ingle
PRODUCTION COORDINATOR: Donna Ng
MANUFACTURING CONTROLLER: Sara Connell
BOOK DESIGNER: Joan Greenfield

Printing (last digit): 9 8 7 6 5 4 3 2 1

Printed in the United States of America
on acid-free paper

CONTENTS

EDITORIAL BOARD

PREFACE

EVENTS IN RECENT decades have underscored the need for a major reference work that provides immediate access to current scholarship on the presence and influence of Islam on a global scale. *The Oxford Encyclopedia of the Modern Islamic World* has been designed to meet that need.

The lack of such a work became particularly apparent following the Iranian revolution of 1978-1979, which dramatically highlighted the reassertion of Islam in politics and society. The revolution proved to be a watershed not only in the politics of the Middle East but also in the study of Islam and Muslim societies. However one evaluates its ultimate significance and impact, the Iranian revolution revealed many of the limitations in our understanding of Islam and the Islamic world and served as a catalyst to redress them.

Islam is the second largest of the world's religions. Almost one billion Muslims live in more than forty-eight Muslim countries from Africa to Asia, and there are significant Muslim minorities in the nations of Europe and the Americas. Despite these facts, in the aftermath of the Iranian revolution the West discovered how little it knew or understood about Islam and the dynamics of religion in Muslim societies. Ignorance and stereotypes of Islam and Muslim societies were matched by an astonishingly limited coverage of them in the media, university and school curricula, publications, and political analysis. In many ways, the Iranian revolution shocked many Westerners out of their ignorance and complacency. It served to generate an interest in Islam and the Islamic world; it increasingly shed light on the faith of Islam, its unity and diversity, and in particular on the global reassertion of Islam.

Since the late 1960s, much of the Islamic world has experienced a resurgence of Islam in personal and public life. Greater attention to religious observances (prayer, fasting, dress, family values) has been accompanied by a reassertion of Islam in state and society. Islamic rhetoric, symbols, and actors have become prominent fixtures in Muslim public life, often used by rulers to buttress nationalism or by their opponents to challenge the legitimacy of rulers and secular forms of nationalism and socialism. A backlash against political and cultural dependence on the West, the westernization and secularization of society, has reawakened and reinforced a sense of pride in past glories and a quest for identity that has emphasized authenticity and a return to, or reappropriation of, indigenous values. Whatever the vast differences among Muslim societies, a return to the past has meant for many a reclaiming of their Islamic history and heritage and a turning to Islam as a source of personal guidance and as an ideological alternative for state and society.

Commensurate with this new-found vitality in the Islamic world has been an explosion of scholarship in religion, history, and the social sciences. A proliferation of studies and coverage of Islam has contributed toward redressing earlier imbalances and in some instances has challenged the "wisdom of the past," arguing that modernization and religious self-assertion are not necessarily incompatible and that the secularization of society is not a precondition for social, economic, and political change or development.

Origins and History of the Project

As useful as many studies have been in correcting the conventional wisdom and expanding our knowledge and coverage of Islam and the Islamic world, there has been no reference work that focuses on the modern period and that treats the Islamic world in a comprehensive, comparative, and systematic manner. Scholars, students, journalists, analysts who seek information on beliefs, events, movements, and leaders have lacked a readily accessible resource and guide. While some existing reference works are dated, others emphasize history, language and literature, and texts rather than modern contexts. The *Encyclopaedia of Islam* (1st ed., 5 vols, Leiden, 1908-1938; new ed., 7 vols. to date, Leiden, 1960-) has largely relied on classical texts and on classical and medieval history. Moreover, it is a grand project whose production has extended over decades, with volumes appearing from time to time. It will remain unfinished and incomplete for some time to come.

The Oxford Encyclopedia of the Modern Islamic World complements the *Encyclopaedia of Islam*. It concentrates on the ways that Muslims have expressed themselves in the modern period through political and social action as well as formal texts. It draws heavily on the insights of the social sciences as well as religion, history, and literature.

The Cambridge History of Islam (Cambridge, 1970), completed more than two decades ago, provides a major historical treatment that ranges from pre-Islamic times to the era of independent nation states. Its geographical organization or focus utilizes a center-periphery dichotomization ("The Central Islamic Lands" [vol. 1] and "The Further Islamic Lands" [vol. 2]). The *Oxford Encyclopedia* is more comparative in approach, less self-consciously tied to geographical region, and includes extended coverage of contemporary interpretations, events, and movements.

This assessment of available resources was supplemented by experiences in dealing with students, members of the media, and political analysts who commented about their frustrations in finding readily available and succinct information on contemporary Muslim politics and societies. These realities informed our conviction that there was a pressing need for an easily accessible major reference work on the modern Islamic world. In general, three characteristics were meant to make *The Oxford Encyclopedia of the Modern Islamic World* distinctive and timely. First, it focuses on the modern period, roughly from the end of the eighteenth century, when direct and indirect encounters with European imperialism and Western technology and ideologies precipitated a profound self-examination among Muslims and an inevitable process of cultural change, to the present. Second, it relies heavily on the methodologies of the social sciences. The insights of sociology, anthropology, economics, and political science are combined with those of religion, history, and literature to explain the changing realities of Muslim life. Third, the *Oxford Encyclopedia* balances an essentialist approach with the empirical realities of the Islamic world. It documents the complexity and diversity of belief, practice, and loyalties, relying heavily on comparative studies. Thus, this encyclopedia emphasizes the practice as well as the theory of Islam, political and social action as well as formal texts. It accentuates the context, the public and private cultures, in which Muslims live their lives and interpret and devise their texts.

The challenge in writing a book is often magnified by an awareness that colleagues and reviewers will have their own ideas on what should be included or excluded. An author's concerns can become an encyclopedia editor's nightmare, given the breadth and magnitude of the project. The number of countries, groups, individuals, institutions, issues, and conflicts to be found in the Islamic world are truly overwhelming. To develop an effective outline (to draw up a final list of articles), faced with the need to be selective while remaining within the bounds of four volumes, is an experience not to be fully appreciated until one has had to meet the challenge.

At the very beginning, we spent a great deal of time debating possibilities for the precise title of our work. In particular, the discussion focused on the use of the terms "Islamic world" versus

"Muslim world" and the word "modern." Realizing that academic critics would probably not be pleased with any resolution, the present title was accepted. "Islamic world" was used instead of "Muslim world" because "Muslim world" is a more generic term whereas this encyclopedia would be focusing on the "Islamic dimension" of its topics. The term "modern" was selected as an inclusive reference to the past three centuries.

The encyclopedia offered an exciting possibility to commission articles that provided new information and fresh perspectives. However, it also brought to our attention the limitations and lacunae in our scholarship, the number of areas that lack the specialists and sufficient research necessary to produce those articles. The situation is compounded when the scope is the entire Islamic world, not just the Arab world or the Middle East. Because Islam in sub-Saharan Africa and Southeast Asia, for example, have attracted fewer scholars, the resources to address this imbalance were often quite limited. Another major challenge was our desire to provide as comparative a perspective as possible both within articles and among clusters of articles. Much of our past scholarship has been focused on a specific country (e.g., Iran or Turkey) or region (e.g., the Arab world). Only recently has there been a major emphasis on comparative studies. Thus, it was often difficult to find numbers of colleagues who not only work with several countries within a region but also across regions. Where possible, clusters of articles around a particular topic or theme were used to overcome this difficulty.

To ensure comprehensive coverage of all facets of Muslim social and religious life, we organized the 750 articles in the encyclopedia into five major categories: Islamic thought and practice, Islam and politics, Muslim communities and societies, Islam and society, and Islamic studies. The entries hinge on a number of major essays that seek to provide geographical, conceptual, and chronological balance. Articles range from major interpretive and synthetic essays of up to ten thousand words (e.g., "Ethnicity," "Human Rights," "Islamic State") to briefer entries, generally five hundred to one thousand words long, on religion, law, politics, economics, international relations, and culture and society (e.g., "Ayatollah," "Contract Law," "Ḥijāb," "Sainthood"). They explicate the relevant history, ideas, doctrines, institutions, contending schools of thought, and contentious issues or controversies. Related entries include coverage of social and political movements, women, Muslim minorities, human rights, Islam in the West, and interreligious affairs. In addition, biographical entries treat a limited number of influential figures. Keeping in mind our comparative focus, we encouraged contributors to provide as many country-specific examples as possible. We also asked them to write in clear and, as far as feasible, nontechnical language and to provide a brief select bibliography for each of their articles.

More than four hundred and fifty authors have been drawn from the international community of scholars, reflecting the breadth and depth of contemporary scholarship in Islamic studies. Our authors represent not only different disciplinary perspectives (historians, sociologists, anthropologists, economists, political scientists) but also diverse national and religious traditions. European, Middle Eastern, South and Southeast Asian, and African experts (Muslim as well as non-Muslim scholars) on Islamic societies have been involved in the planning as well as writing of the articles. The inclusion of a significant number of scholars raised in diverse Muslim environments reflects the breadth and complexity of "Islam observed" and guards against the potential pitfalls of Orientalism.

The Oxford Encyclopedia of the Modern Islamic World has been designed to become the primary reference not only for scholars and students of religion, history, and the social sciences but also for general readers seeking to understand the background of current events. For the academic community, the encyclopedia provides a breadth of coverage that will supplement and enhance research and be useful in teaching; graduate and undergraduate students will be able to find a concise and accessible summary of major concepts, trends, and perspectives. We trust, however, that the usefulness of the work will not be limited to scholars and students. We designed the encyclopedia to appeal as well to a more general audience of government and corporate analysts, political consultants, journalists, lawyers, interfaith organizations, and secondary school teachers interested in the faith, institutions, movements, personalities, and issues of the modern Islamic world.

Editorial Practices

Entries in the encyclopedia are alphabetically arranged, strictly letter by letter. In order to make use of the specialized expertise of individual scholars while ensuring that all aspects of larger topics were fully covered, "composite entries" group together several articles under one headword. For example, the entry "Marriage and Divorce" includes two articles, one on legal foundations and one on modern practice. Each composite entry begins with a headnote explaining its division.

To guide readers from one article to related discussions elsewhere in the work, there is an extensive system of cross-references within the articles. In addition, "blind entries" of alternate spellings and synonyms occur throughout the alphabetical range of headwords, providing cross-references to the articles they seek. For example, the reader looking up "Blasphemy" will be directed to the entry "Kufr." A comprehensive index is a further resource, especially for topics that are not headwords themselves. Readers interested in finding all of the articles on a particular subject (e.g., economics, Sufism) are encouraged to consult the Synoptic Outline of Contents in volume 4.

Of particular concern as manuscript editing began was the establishment of a consistent policy on the romanization of languages not using the Latin alphabet, primarily Arabic, Persian, and Urdu. As this is a scholarly work, it did not seem prudent to omit the proper diacritical marks that indicate pronunciation, and the decision was made to follow the United States Library of Congress systems for all of these languages. Because the encyclopedia deals with the modern world, however, it was necessary and sensible to make exceptions for well-known figures where the use of the Library of Congress spelling would render obscure a name that is commonly recognized. Thus, the reader will find Gamal Abdel Nasser rather than Jamāl ʿAbd al-Nāṣir, Ruhollah Khomeini rather than Ruḥollāh Khumaynī, and Mohammad Mossadegh rather than Muḥammad Muṣaddiq. Variants are frequently given parenthetically on first mention in an article as well as being listed in the index. Most problematic were Iranian names and terms. As the subfield of Iranian studies has long employed a variant system of romanization (chiefly involving a shift in vowels from *i ī u ū* to *e i o u*), spellings of some names according to this system were permitted where contributors preferred them (e.g., Maḥmud Ṭāleqāni, not Maḥmūd Ṭāliqānī; Abol-Qāsem Kāshāni, not Abū al-Qāsim Kāshānī). Once again, alternate spellings are frequently provided parenthetically throughout the articles and index.

Acknowledgments

It was clear from the beginning that the ultimate success of this project would hinge on its board of supervising editors. I knew that the editorial board should not be a group of distinguished scholars who merely lent their names to the project. They had to be convinced of the value of the project and committed to achieving its goals. I was fortunate enough to assemble such a group. Each of the editors of this encyclopedia, though representing a disciplinary affiliation, is noted for his or her interdisciplinary research and often for work in more than one geographic area. From our first meeting at the offices of Oxford University Press in New York to the end of the project each member remained deeply involved. The editors assisted me in devising the general and specific entries for the encyclopedia, suggested names of potential contributors, and reviewed and edited the specific manuscripts that were within their areas of responsibility.

Given the magnitude of the project and in order to ensure both broad and comparative coverage, a second body of experts was created. It seemed unimaginable that such a project would not benefit from the advice of the late Albert Hourani, who graciously agreed to be senior consultant. With his advice and that of the editorial board, our consultants and advisers were drawn from the full range of disciplines and areas covered in the encyclopedia and was composed of scholars from the United States, Europe, and the Islamic world. They suggested additional topics and possible contributors unknown to or overlooked by the editors, and, in many cases, served as authors themselves.

This project owes its origins and realization to Oxford University Press and to a core of unusually committed academic colleagues. Elizabeth Maguire of Oxford had the foresight to realize that there might well be a need and a market for a reference work on Islam. The task of serving as editor in chief, although initially daunting, was made infinitely easier by the professionalism of Oxford's Academic Reference Department under the leadership of Claude Conyers. Those who fear the organizational and logistical nightmares of producing an encyclopedia need only see the superb systems that Oxford has in place—from the materials provided during the planning and development of the contents to the database used during the administrative and editorial stages—to be reassured. Mark Cummings and then Jeffrey Edelstein epitomized the best that one could imagine in terms of their professional skills and commitment to the project. Mr. Edelstein's sense of quality, eye for detail, and close monitoring of deadlines kept the project under control and on schedule.

From its inception, the prospect of an encyclopedia of the modern Islamic world was received with great enthusiasm, both by the scholars in the United States and Europe initially queried by Oxford's representatives and by colleagues and friends when I agreed to serve as editor in chief. However, congratulations were mixed with condolences as some recounted tales of similar projects that confirmed and reinforced my own apprehensions about the potential headaches and aggravations. In addition, the already tight schedules of editors and authors alike would be strained and, in some cases, pushed to their limits. There were in fact the usual frustrations associated with large projects—authors who were unconscionably late or who, after a year or more, simply backed out or did not deliver promised manuscripts. But these were the exception. I was struck by how many colleagues not only agreed to join the project but were also remarkably committed and cooperative at every stage, meeting deadlines, making revisions, responding to queries. Many proved the maxim that the best and busiest are often the most productive. The few who declined did so often with genuine regrets. Although previous commitments precluded their participation, they welcomed the project and were eager for its successful completion. Throughout the years, the interest and response of colleagues in the field regarding the progress of the encyclopedia and the need for its publication have strengthened our resolve and maintained our spirits. The combination of dedicated professionals at Oxford and the members of the editorial board, who seemed always there and prepared to do whatever it took to assure quality and stay on schedule, made this a remarkable experience.

We all undertook this project in the belief that *The Oxford Encyclopedia of the Modern Islamic World* was timely and necessary. We were contributing to an endeavor whose scope was beyond our individual capabilities and whose usefulness and impact would, "in shā' Allāh" (God willing), stand for some time to come. Given past history and the increasing interdependence of nations and cultures around the world, there has never been a greater need for better understanding of the faith and practice of Islam.

John L. Esposito
Wayland, Massachusetts
August 1994

A

ʿABBĀSID CALIPHATE. Succeeding the Umayyad Caliphate in 750, the ʿAbbāsid dynasty ruled the caliphate until 1258. Descendants of the Prophet's uncle al-ʿAbbās, the ʿAbbāsids claimed membership in the family of the Prophet or Banū Hāshim. This relationship enabled them to attract some support in the last three decades of the Umayyad Caliphate, from 720 to 750, when many Muslims were searching for an alternative to that regime. While the ʿAbbāsid family remained in Syria, their most active and militant supporters were to be found in Khurasan. In 747 these supporters began a military rebellion in the province under the leadership of Abū Muslim. After taking Khurasan, they advanced on Iraq, which they occupied in 749, and proclaimed a member of the ʿAbbāsid family caliph as al-Saffāḥ (r. 750–754).

The early ʿAbbāsids faced opposition from supporters of the Umayyads, notably in Syria, and from those who looked to the house of ʿAlī for leadership and felt that the ʿAbbāsids had usurped their rights. The supporters of the ʿAlids were most numerous in Iraq; they staged a number of uprisings, notably that led by Muḥammad the Pure Soul in Medina and his brother Ibrāhīm in Basra in 762, and abandoned any real attempt to rule Spain and the Maghrib, which now became independent. ʿAbbāsid power was made effective throughout the Middle East by al-Manṣūr (r. 754–775), who built up a powerful state apparatus based on the army, most of whose members were of Khurasani descent, and on a bureaucracy, led by the Barmakid family, who continued the Sassanian traditions of financial administration. The state was based in Iraq; in 762 al-Manṣūr founded a new capital at Baghdad, which soon developed from a palatial and governmental complex into a thriving metropolis.

The apogee of ʿAbbāsid power was reached under Hārūn al-Rashīd (r. 786–809), but, probably in order to appease provincial discontent about the rising burden of taxation, he divided the caliphate between two of his sons, al-Amīn (r. 809–813) in Iraq and the West and al-Ma'mūn (r. 813–833) in Iran. The agreement began to break down almost immediately after his death in 809; a decade of destructive civil war ensued before al-Ma'mūn was able to establish himself in Baghdad. His reign was a period of great intellectual activity, and the caliph himself played an important part in the translation of Greek learning into Arabic. The government was less strong; to his brother and successor, al-Muʿtaṣim (r. 833–842), was left the task to develop a new and effective army based on a corps of Turkish cavalry. Meanwhile, the Ṭāhirid family were allowed a free hand in eastern Iran. In order to accommodate his new army, al-Muʿtaṣim transferred the capital to Samarra, and it was here, from 861 to the mid-870s, that the caliphs were kept as virtual prisoners by their Turkish guards.

When ʿAbbāsid authority was restored by al-Muʿtaḍid (r. 892–902), the political influence of the caliphs was virtually confined to Iraq, although Egypt was temporarily regained in 905. Even this limited authority was lost during the reign of the incompetent al-Muqtadir (r. 908–932), a period that saw the virtual collapse of state finances and the impoverishment of much of Iraq. In 945 the caliphate was effectively taken over by the Būyids (also referred to as the Buwayhids), military adventurers from northern Iran. The ʿAbbāsid remained as ornamental figures in their Baghdad palace.

In the early eleventh century, Būyid control crumbled and the ʿAbbāsids returned to the life of the Muslim community. In opposition to the Shīʿī Būyids and their supporters, al-Qādir (r. 991–1031) put himself at the head of the emerging Sunnī movement, publishing the *Risālat al-Qādirīyah,* which established the bases of Sunnī doctrine. This influence grew after 1055 when Baghdad was taken by the Seljuk Turks, professed Sunnīs who accepted the religious leadership of the family. However, it was not until Seljuk power in turn began to collapse after the death of Sanjar in 1157 that this prestige could be translated into political power. Caliph al-Nāṣir (r. 1180–1225) reestablished ʿAbbāsid control over most of Iraq with the support of popular *futūwah* movements. His successors failed to maintain this momentum. When the ʿAbbāsids were faced by the still pagan Mongols, who had no respect for their religious status, they were unable to put up an effective resistance. Baghdad fell to the invaders in 1258, and the last caliph, al-Mustaʿsim (r. 1242–1258) was put to death.

The ʿAbbāsid Caliphate enjoyed a certain afterlife in Cairo, where members of the family continued as titular caliphs, although, in effect, they were members of the Mamlūk court, kept to confer legitimacy on the sultanate but without any independent power. With the Ottoman conquest of Egypt in 1517, even this small survival of their ancient glory was swept away.

[*See also* Caliphate; Umayyad Caliphate.]

BIBLIOGRAPHY

Bowen, Harold. *The Life and Times of ʾAlí ibn ʾÍsʿa, the "Good Vizier"*. Cambridge, 1928. Classic that still gives a good impression of political and artistic life in the tenth century.

Kennedy, Hugh. *The Prophet and the Age of the Caliphate*. London and New York, 1986. Introduction to the political history up to the mid-eleventh century.

Le Strange, Guy. *Baghdad during the Abbasid Caliphate*. London, 1909. Historical geography closely based on Arabic sources.

Shaʿbān, Muḥammad ʿAbd al-Ḥayy. *Islamic History: A New Interpretation*. Vol. 2. Cambridge, 1976. Interesting insights, but not wholly reliable on detail.

Sharon, Moshe. *Black Banners from the East*. Leiden, 1983. Meticulously researched account of the build-up to the ʿAbbāsid revolution of 747–750.

Sourdel, Dominique. *Le vizirat ʿabbāside*. 2 vols. Damascus, 1959–1960. Still the best history of the ʿAbbāsid bureaucracy.

Yarshater, Ehsan, ed. *The History of al-Tabari: An Annotated Translation*. Vols. 27–38. Albany, N.Y., 1984–. English translation of the classic Arabic history, from 750 to the beginning of the tenth century.

HUGH KENNEDY

ʿABD AL-ʿAZĪZ, SHĀH (1746–1824), Indian Islamic scholar. In northern India, ʿAbd al-ʿAzīz was a prominent Ṣūfī *ʿālim* of his time, a powerful orator *(khaṭīb)*, an effective preacher *(wāʿiẓ)*, and an expert on *ḥadīth* and the Qurʾān. He left a deep imprint on Islamic learning through his writings and through the students who came to the Madrasah-i Raḥīmīyah from all over India. He was also a connoisseur of Indian vocal music and Urdu and Persian literature as well as an accomplished calligrapher and horseman.

At the age of sixteen, following the death of his father Shāh Walī Allāh (d. 1762), the foremost *ʿālim* of eighteenth-century India, Shāh ʿAbd al-ʿAzīz assumed responsibility for administering and teaching at the *madrasah*, which had been founded by his grandfather. Author of twenty-two known works, ʿAbd al-ʿAzīz wrote on topics ranging from Islamic philosophy, *ḥadīth*, *tafsīr*, and the spirit of Sunnism to rhetoric, genealogy, music, and Persian literary styles. In the Qurʾānic studies, his *Fatḥ al-ʿAzīz* (translation and exegesis of the first two chapters and the last two parts of the Qurʾān in Persian, in 3 volumes) is a major contribution in its methodological framework and interpretation. He witnessed the disintegration of the social and political order, the transfer of political power into Shīʿī hands (and the subsequent ascendancy of Shiism in northern India), and the British takeover of Delhi in 1803. Against this backdrop, his other two important Persian works *Malfūẓāt-i ʿAzīzī* and *Fatāwā-i ʿAzīzī*, along with *Fatḥ al-ʿAzīz*, serve as comprehensive sources for religious and social reconstruction. They reflect the concerns of the Muslim community in a period of transition and expound his views on how to deal with such issues as the legal status of India under British rule, social intercourse with the British, the adoption of Western dress, learning English and joining the British service, interest on loans or deposits under British rule, the marriage of Muslim women with Christians, Shīʿī-Sunnī intermarriage, abortion, and the use of contraceptives.

ʿAbd al-ʿAzīz's major preoccupation, however, was to restore the superiority of Sunnism by refuting aspects of Shiism. Although he wrote several epistles on aspects of Shiism, his most comprehensive and controversial work was *Tuḥfah-i isnā ʿasharīyah*, completed in 1789–1790. His concern with the "right religion"—explaining beliefs and rituals and correcting misconceptions of historical realities such as the caliphate of the first three caliphs—may be seen as an attempt to preserve the Sunnīs' social identity in the changing sociopolitical order. ʿAbd al-ʿAzīz accepted Shiism as an important sect of Islam but rejected some Shīʿī practices.

ʿAbd al-ʿAzīz did not assume any title that might suggest that God had designated him for a specific role in the community. His contemporaries and posterity, however, bestowed upon him such titles as *sirāj al-Hind* (lamp of India) and *muḥaddith* (expert on *ḥadīth*). Posterity acknowledged ʿAbd al-ʿAzīz's erudition and placed him in the ranks of religious reformers (Sayyid Abū al-Aʿlā Mawdūdī, *Tajdīd va iḥyaʾ-i dīn*, Lahore,

1966, pp. 114–115). Among ʿAbd al-ʿAzīz's writings, the *Tuḥfah* (also translated into Arabic and Urdu) should be singled out for its lasting impact. This work not only demonstrates his profound knowledge and understanding of authentic sources of the Shīʿī and Sunnī law but also epitomizes the linear development of sectarian polemics written by Sunnī *ʿulamāʾ* in the seventeenth and eighteenth centuries. His contemporaries among the Shīʿī *ʿulamāʾ* in the state of Awadh vehemently refuted each chapter of the *Tuḥfah*. In the wake of sectarian strife and polemical discussions in Pakistan in the early 1990s, the Sunnī *ʿulamāʾ* have often referred to the *Tuḥfah* as a source.

[*See also* Islam, *article on* Islam in South Asia; *and the biography of Walī Allāh.*]

BIBLIOGRAPHY

Mushir-ul-Haq. "Shāh ʿAbd al-ʿAzīz al-Dihlawī and His Times." *Hamdard Islamicus* 7.1–2 (1984): 51–96, 77–103. Insightful overview of ʿAbd al-ʿAzīz's response to the Muslim community's specific concerns over social and political problems.

Rizvi, S. A. A. *Shāh ʿAbd al-ʿAzīz: Puritanism, Sectarian, Polemics, and Jihad*. Canberra, 1982. Comprehensive study of Shāh ʿAbd al-ʿAzīz's thought and of polemical discussions between Shīʿī and Sunnī *ʿulamāʾ* in India from a Shīʿī perspective.

SAJIDA SULTANA ALVI

ABDALĪ DYNASTY. *See* Durrānī Dynasty.

ʿABD AL-NĀṢIR, JAMĀL. *See* Nasser, Gamal Abdel.

ʿABD AL-QĀDIR (1808–1883), Algerian independence leader, Ṣūfī mystic, and poet. Born Muḥyī al-Dīn al-Ḥasanī at Wādī al-Ḥammām, some 20 kilometers west of Mascara in Algeria, into a family of northern Moroccan origin who claimed descent from the prophet Muḥammad, Amīr ʿAbd al-Qādir entered history after the French occupation of Algiers on 5 July 1830. This invasion led ʿAbd al-Qādir's father Sīdī Muḥyīʾ al-Dīn to proclaim a *jihād* against European colonization in the region of Oran. Ill health forced him in November 1832 to hand over control of the anticolonial resistance to his son, who was proclaimed "Sultan of the Arabs" by the tribes of Hāshim, Banū ʿĀmir, and Gharābah. Despite mixed results on the battlefield, this tactic prevented the "pacification" of Algeria and led the French to enter into negotiations with ʿAbd al-Qādir on 26 February 1834. Now officially recognized as "commander of the faithful" *(amīr al-muʾminīn)*, ʿAbd al-Qādir was able to extend his authority to the gates of Algiers itself by the middle of 1835.

The amir's continued agitation for Algerian autonomy led to a resumption of hostilities. After an Algerian victory at Macta (28 June 1835), the French generals Clauzel and Bugeaud counterattacked, burning Mascara, occupying Tlemcen, and scoring a victory against ʿAbd al-Qādir's army at Wādī Sikkāk (6 July 1836). Although abandoned by his troops three times, the amir successfully regrouped his tribal forces and continued to inflict heavy losses on the French. The desire to protect their western flank while pursuing the conquest of Constantine led the government of King Louis-Philippe to negotiate once again. The resulting Treaty of Tafna (30 May 1837) divided western Algeria into two spheres of influence; the urban areas remained in French hands, while the interior portions of the province of Oran, the *beylik* of Titteri, and part of the province of Algiers were given over to ʿAbd al-Qādir. Disputes over secret codicils to the treaty—as well as the "Iron Gates" expedition in which the Duke of Orléans opened a corridor between Constantine and Algiers—led to the resumption of hostilities and the amir's invasion of the Mitidja in November 1839.

In the face of ʿAbd al-Qādir's threat, Bugeaud was appointed governor-general of Algeria on 29 December 1840. By sending mobile columns into the Algerian hinterland, he succeeded in occupying the major towns of Orania and Tlemcen (1841–1843). The capture of the Amir's "traveling capital" *(smālah)* on 16 May 1843 caused the Arab tribes to surrender to the French and forced ʿAbd al-Qādir to flee to Morocco. Although French attacks on the Moroccan cities of Tangier and Mogador (1844) compelled the Moroccan sultan, Mawlay ʿAbd al-Raḥmān, to declare the amir an outlaw, he appeared again in Algeria in 1846 at the head of numerous clandestinely organized uprisings. Despite a major victory at Sīdī Brāhīm (23 September 1846), the French counterattack crushed this revolt and forced him back across the Moroccan border. ʿAbd al-Qādir surrendered to the French on 23 December 1847.

After pledging not to resist the French in Algeria, he was released from prison in 1852 and given a pension by Napoleon III. Choosing exile in the Muslim-ruled Ottoman Empire, he settled first in Brusa (1853), and finally in Damascus (1855). His final *beau geste* came in

July 1860, when he personally protected the French consul in Damascus and several thousand Christians from massacre by Druze rebels. After his death on the night of 25–26 May 1883, his body was interred next to the tomb of the great Andalusian mystic Ibn ʿArabī (d. 1240).

Although initiated into the Qādirīyah Ṣūfī order by his father, Amīr ʿAbd al-Qādir joined the Naqshbandīyah in Damascus. He also remained associated with the unofficial Akbarīyah tradition throughout his life, a link which led to the amir's burial next to his father's intellectual eponym, Muḥyī al-Dīn Ibn ʿArabī. His penultimate "opening" *(fatḥ)* into Sufism was at the hands of a master of the Akbarīyah, Muḥammad al-Fāsī al-Shādhilī, whom he met in Mecca in 1863. ʿAbd al-Qādir's major Ṣūfī works are *Kitāb al-mawāqif* (Book of Stages), an extended discourse on the doctrines of Ibn ʿArabī, and a *Diwān* or collection of mystical poems.

[*See also* Algeria.]

BIBLIOGRAPHY

ʿAbd al-Qādir ibn Muḥyī al-Dīn. *Écrits spirituels*. Translated by Michel Chodkiewicz. Paris, 1982. Translation of ʿAbd al-Qādir's *Kitāb al-Mawāqif*. Chodkiewicz's introduction is the best discussion of the amir's Sufism available in a European language.

Blunt, Wilfrid. *Desert Hawk: Abd el Kader and the French Conquest of Algeria*. London, 1947. Biography of the amir, based primarily on French sources.

Danziger, Raphael. *Abd al-Qadir and the Algerians: Resistance to the French and Internal Consolidation, 1832–1839*. London and New York, 1977. Detailed account of the first phase of the Algerian resistance.

Jazā'irī, Muḥammad ibn ʿAbd al-Qādir al-. *Tuḥfat al-zā'ir fī ma'āthir al-Amīr ʿAbd al-Qādir wa-akhbār al-Jazā'ir*. Damascus, 1964. Biography of ʿAbd al-Qādir and the Algerian resistance, written by the amir's son. This is the primary source for the "Algerian side" of the issue.

Rouina, Karim. *Bibliographie raisonnée sur l'émir Abdelkader*. Oran, 1985. Indispensable bibliography for anyone attempting a serious study of ʿAbd al-Qādir and the Algerian resistance against colonialism in the nineteenth century.

VINCENT J. CORNELL

ʿABD AL-RAḤMĀN, ʿĀ'ISHAH (b. 1913), Egyptian writer and professor of Arabic language and literature and Qur'ānic studies. Under the pseudonym Bint al-Shāṭi' ʿAbd al-Raḥmān was the author of more than sixty books on Arabic literature, Qur'ānic interpretation, the lives of women of the early Muslim community (especially members of the Prophet's family), contemporary social issues, and fiction.

Raised in the Delta port city of Dumyat (Damietta), she was taught the Qur'ān and classical Arabic literature by her father, an al-Azhar-educated teacher at a mosque-based religious institute. Although he educated her in the traditional style at home, mosque, and Qur'ānic school *(kuttāb)*, he objected to her attendance at public schools. With the assistance of her mother and maternal great-grandfather, she managed to get a secular education despite her father's objections. ʿAbd al-Raḥmān began her literary career by writing poems and essays for *Al-nahḍah*, a women's magazine, and became a literary critic for the semiofficial newspaper *Al-ahrām* in 1936, the same year she entered the Faculty of Letters at Fu'ād I University. At this time she assumed the pen-name Bint al-Shāṭi' ("Daughter of the Shore") in order to conceal her identity from her father. Her first articles for *Al-ahrām* focused on conditions in the Egyptian countryside, but she is best known for her later works on religious and literary topics. She received her doctorate in 1950 with a thesis on the poet Abū al-ʿAlā' al-Maʿarrī (d. 1058). In 1951 she became professor of Arabic language and literature at ʿAyn Shams University in Cairo. Throughout the 1960s she participated in international literary conferences, served on several government-sponsored committees on literature and education, and was a visiting professor at the Islamic University in Ummdurman (Sudan), the University of Khartoum, and the University of Algiers. After retiring from her position at ʿAyn Shams University, she became professor of higher Qur'ānic studies at al-Qarawīyīn University in Fez, Morocco. Her regular articles for *Al-ahrām*, her biographies of the women of the Prophet's household, and especially her exegesis of the Qur'ān have brought her recognition and distinction in Egypt and throughout the Arab world.

ʿAbd al-Raḥmān's pursuit of public education offered her little challenge after her early education at the hands of her father, until she met Professor Amīn al-Khūlī when she was a student at Fu'ād I University (later Cairo University). He introduced her to the literary analysis of the Qur'ān that became her trademark. In *ʿAlā al-jisr* she describes her entire life as a path to this encounter with Amīn al-Khūlī, whom she married in 1945. Her work is seen as the best exemplification of his method, and she has been much more prolific than her teacher, who died in 1966.

ʿAbd al-Raḥmān's "rhetorical exegesis of the Qur'ān" makes a plea for removing the Qur'ān from the exclusive domain of traditional exegesis and placing it within literary studies. Whereas some earlier exegetes allowed for a multiplicity of interpretations of any single Qur'ānic verse, seeing in this multiplicity a demonstration of the richness of the Qur'ān, ᶜAbd al-Raḥmān argues that every word of the Qur'ān allows for only a single interpretation, which should be elicited from the context of the Qur'ān as a whole. She rejects extraneous sources, particularly information derived from the Bible or Jewish sources *(Isrā'īlīyāt)*, the inclusion of which in traditional Qur'ānic exegesis she sees as part of a continuing Jewish conspiracy to subvert Islam and dominate the world. She also argues that no word is a true synonym for any other in the Qur'ān, so no word can be replaced by another. Whereas many scholars believe certain phrases in the Qur'ān were inserted to provide the text with its characteristic rhythm and assonance, ᶜAbd al-Raḥmān insists that every word of the Qur'ān is there solely for the meaning it gives.

ᶜAbd al-Raḥmān is both deeply religious and very conservative, despite her active public life. On the subject of women's liberation, she affirms the principle of male guardianship over women but firmly rejects male responsibility for the behavior of women. She insists that a proper understanding of women's liberation does not abandon traditional Islamic values. She has been consistently supported and honored by successive Egyptian regimes.

BIBLIOGRAPHY

Works by ᶜĀ'ishah ᶜAbd al-Raḥmān (Bint al-Shāṭi')

Umm al-nabī (Mother of the Prophet). Cairo, n.d. (1961?).

Nisā' al-nabī (Wives of the Prophet). Cairo, n.d. (1961?). Translated into Persian, Urdu, and Indonesian.

Al-Tafsīr al-bayānī lil-Qur'ān al-Karīm (The Rhetorical Exegesis of the Noble Qur'ān). 2 vols. Cairo, 1962–1969. Her most important work, reprinted in a number of editions.

Banāt al-nabī (Daughters of the Prophet). Cairo, 1963.

Al-Sayyidah Zaynab, baṭalat Karbalā' (Sayyida Zaynab, Heroine of Karbalā'). Cairo, n.d. (1965?). Life of the granddaughter of the Prophet, who is credited with heroism at the battle of Karbala in which her brother Ḥusayn and other male relatives were killed.

ᶜAlā al-jisr: Usṭūrat al-zamān (On the Bridge: A Legend of Time). Cairo, 1966. Autobiographical work that centers on the author's education, culminating in her encounter with Amīn al-Khūlī. Written in the year of his death, her entire life is seen as a path leading to this meeting, as a result of which she is "born again."

Al-Qur'ān wa-al-tafsīr al-ᶜaṣrī (The Qur'ān and Modernist Exegesis). Cairo, 1970. Written against a book on "modernist" or "scientific" exegesis by the physician and television personality Muṣṭafā Maḥmūd.

Al-Isrā'īlīyāt fī al-ghazw al-fikrī (The Israelite Tales in the Intellectual Conquest). Cairo, 1975.

Works on ᶜĀ'ishah ᶜAbd al-Raḥmān (Bint al-Shāṭi')

Boullata, Issa J. "Modern Qur'an Exegesis: A Study of Bint al-Shāṭi''s Method." *Muslim World* 64 (1974): 103–113. Positive evaluation of Bint al-Shāṭi''s contribution to Qur'ānic exegesis.

Hoffman-Ladd, Valerie J. "Polemics on the Modesty and Segregation of Women." *International Journal of Middle East Studies* 19 (1987): 23–50. Analyzes Bint al-Shāṭi''s stance on women's social roles.

Jansen, J. J. G. *The Interpretation of the Koran in Modern Egypt*. Leiden, 1974. Chapter 4, on "philological exegesis," deals primarily with Bint al-Shāṭi''s exegesis, which he believes to be the best example of contemporary exegesis focusing on language analysis.

Kooij, C. "Bint al-Shāṭi': A Suitable Case for Biography?" In *The Challenge of the Middle East*, edited by Ibrahim A. A. El-Sheikh et al., pp. 67–72. Amsterdam, 1982. Critical description of Bint al-Shāṭi', which includes impressions gained from personal interviews with her, as well as interviews in Arabic literature. The author depicts her as both charming and domineering, and stresses Bint al-Shāṭi''s self-centeredness, claiming that her autobiography, *ᶜAlā al-jisr*, romanticizes and distorts reality.

VALERIE J. HOFFMAN-LADD

ᶜABD AL-RĀZIQ, ᶜALĪ (1888–1966), Egyptian *sharīᶜah* (divine law) judge, controversial intellectual, and author of *Al-Islām wa-uṣūl al-ḥukm: Baᶜth fī al-khilāfah wa-al-ḥukūmah fī al-Islām* (Islam and the Bases of Political Authority: A Study of the Caliphate and Government in Islam). Published in Cairo in 1925, ᶜAbd al-Rāziq's book challenged the notion that Islam legislated a specific type of political authority or, for that matter, that it legitimated any form of government at all. In addition to creating a constitutional crisis in Egypt, ᶜAbd al-Rāziq's ideas generated violent controversy throughout the Muslim world. The Egyptian Higher Council of ᶜUlamā' brought ᶜAbd al-Rāziq to trial and expelled him from both their ranks and his position as a *sharīᶜah* judge.

ᶜAlī ᶜAbd al-Rāziq was a member of a famous and powerful landowning family from the village of Abū Girg (Jirj) in al-Minyā Province. A graduate of al-Azhar and Oxford universities, he rose to the position of judge in the al-Mansūra *sharīᶜah* court. In addition to writing *Islam and the Bases of Political Authority*, ᶜAbd al-Rāziq edited a study of the life and work of his brother, a rector of al-Azhar, entitled *Min āthār Muṣṭafā ᶜAbd al-Rāziq* (From the Legacy of Muṣṭafā ᶜAbd al-Rāziq, Cairo, 1957) and *Al-ijmāᶜ fī al-sharīᶜah al-Islāmīyah* (Consensus in Islamic Law, Cairo, 1947).

Along with Ṭāhā Ḥusayn's 1926 volume, *Fī al-shiᶜr al-jāhilī* (On Jāhilīyah Poetry), ᶜAbd al-Rāziq's work was seen by the *ᶜulamā'* and many Muslims as presenting a fundamental challenge to Islam's legitimacy as a religion. The specific event that precipitated ʿAbd al-Rāziq's study and gave it such significance was the abolition of the caliphate by the Turkish government of Mustafa Kemal Atatürk in 1924. Following World War I, many Muslims felt particularly vulnerable to increased colonial penetration by Western powers, such as Great Britain and France, with the fall of the Ottoman Empire. In their minds, the abolition of the caliphate was a prominent symbol that underlined their political weakness.

What angered many Muslims was ʿAbd al-Rāziq's assertion that the prophet Muḥammad was sent by God only to preach a spiritual message and not to exercise political authority. Although Muḥammad did establish *al-ummah al-islamīyah* (an Islamic community), he never mentioned or promulgated a specific form of government. For ʿAbd al-Rāziq, the unity of the Islamic community did not constitute a unitary Islamic state. "The Prophet's leadership . . . was religious and came as a result of his Message and nothing else. His Message ended with his death as did his leadership role" (ʿAbd al-Rāziq, 1925, p. 90).

ʿAbd al-Rāziq's thesis that the Islamic *ummah* is purely spiritual and bears no relation to politics or forms of government effectively separated religion and politics in Islam. Furthermore, it denied that the caliphate was an integral and necessary part of Islam or that it maintained any special religious status. Rather than part of Islamic law, the caliphate was to ʿAbd al-Rāziq simply a matter of custom.

To many Muslim thinkers, these arguments were anathema, as they seemed to undermine the very essence of Islam. Since such thinkers viewed a key part of Muḥammad's prophetic mission as implementing a system of laws, Islam was political by definition. In denying the Prophet's political role, ʿAbd al-Rāziq implicitly called for a redefinition of Muḥammad's prophetic mission and, by extension, the very nature of Islam.

From one perspective, *Islam and the Bases of Political Authority* can be seen as part of the Islamic reform movement that began in Egypt during the nineteenth century. Most strongly influenced by Shaykh Muḥammad ʿAbduh (1849–1905), this movement sought to revitalize Islam by emphasizing the role of human reason and by seeking to reconcile Islamic and Western notions of science and social organization. For many reformers and disciples of ʿAbduh, such as ʿAbd al-Rāziq, reason, not revelation, determined the form of government that rules a particular community. [*See the biography of ʿAbduh.*]

The overt dispute over ʿAbd al-Rāziq's book was cast in theological terms, but political considerations also motivated its publication. As were many other native-born landowning families, the ʿAbd al-Rāziq family was closely associated with the Ḥizb Aḥrār al-Dustūriyīn (Liberal Constitutional Party), which, in turn, was the successor to the secularly oriented and antimonarchical Ḥizb al-Ummah (People's Party) founded in 1907. With Turkey's abolition of the caliphate, a number of Arab leaders, including King Fu'ād of Egypt, indicated a desire to wrest the title for themselves. Many Liberal Constitutionalists opposed such a move.

A number of factors point to the political dimensions of *Islam and the Bases of Political Authority*. Certainly ʿAbd al-Rāziq himself was aware that even many of his supporters believed that he had exaggerated his arguments. This raises the distinct possibility that he purposely overstated his case for political reasons. It also seems highly doubtful that the Misr Printing Company, a Bank Misr company under the tight control of Muḥammad Ṭalʿat Ḥarb, a devout Muslim, would have published a text consciously intended to undermine Islam. Without denying the sincerity of his arguments, it seems highly plausible that ʿAbd al-Rāziq's treatise was intended less as a major contribution to Islamic thought than as an effort to deny King Fu'ād the ability to appropriate the title of caliph.

Without detracting from its intellectual stature, ʿAbd al-Rāziq's book should also be seen as part of a patchwork of efforts by reformist elements within an increasingly assertive native-born Egyptian bourgeoisie to bring about significant changes in Egypt's political and cultural identity. This stratum sought to assert its power against the monarchy and its supporters among the *ʿulamā'*. ʿAbd al-Rāziq's treatise, however, did not represent an overt conspiracy among the Liberal Constitutionalists and their wealthy supporters, as many within the party opposed it. Rather, ʿAbd al-Rāziq's work was one of many thrusts and parries by members of the indigenous bourgeoisie intended to circumscribe the powers of the king. The Egyptian bourgeoisie sought to hasten the transformation of Egypt's cultural identity from one that had been dominated by a Turco-Egyptian elite and an emphasis on Pan-Islamism to one that was dominated by an Egyptian- and, to a lesser extent, Arab-centered nationalism.

On yet another level, the fierce opposition to ʿAbd al-

Rāziq's book reflected the pervasive fear among many social strata of further fragmentation of both the Muslim world and Egyptian society. For many Muslims, the book represented another effort by the West (in this instance at the hands of a westernized Muslim) to fragment the Muslim world, so as to facilitate its subjugation to colonialism, by undermining Islam's traditional value structure from within. The fact that *Islam and the Bases of Political Authority* continues to stimulate debate indicates the extent to which the issues that ʿAlī ʿAbd al-Rāziq raised in 1925 still dominate Islamic discourse today.

[*See also* Islamic State; Modernism; Secularism.]

BIBLIOGRAPHY

ʿAbd al-Rāziq, ʿAlī. *Al-Islām wa-uṣūl al-ḥukm: Baʿth fī al-khilāfah wa-al-ḥukūmah fī al-Islām*. Cairo, 1925.

ʿĀlim, Maḥmūd Amīn al-. "Thawrah fikrīyah . . . wa-lākin: Ḥadīth maʿa ṣāhib *Al-Islām wa-uṣūl al-ḥukm*" (An Intellectual Revolution . . . with Qualifications: A Conversation with the Author of *Islam and the Bases of Political Authority*). *Al-muṣawwar* 2191 (7 October 1966): 32–33. Interview with ʿAbd al-Rāziq shortly before his death that highlights the inspirational effect of his work on the secular Left in Egypt in its struggle against the Islamist movement both within and outside the country.

Berque, Jacques. *Egypt: Imperialism and Revolution*. New York, 1972. Insightful commentary on some of the sociopolitical motivations behind the publication of *Al-Islām wa-uṣūl al-ḥukm*.

Binder, Leonard. *Islamic Liberalism: A Critique of Development Ideologies*. Chicago, 1988. Chapter 4 contains a comprehensive analysis of ʿAbd al-Rāziq's arguments and the major criticisms of them.

Ḥaqqī, Mamdūḥ. *Al-Islām wa-uṣūl al-ḥukm: Baʿth fī al-khilāfah wa-al-ḥukūmah fī al-Islām: Naqd wa-taʿlīq*. Beirut, 1966. Contemporary critique of ʿAbd al-Rāziq that argues for his faulty grasp of Islamic doctrine and corruption by the West.

Hourani, Albert. *Arab Thought in the Liberal Age, 1798–1939*. London, 1962. Offers an excellent summary of the main arguments of *Al-Islām wa-uṣūl al-ḥukm* and its relationship to ʿAbduh and the Islamic reform movement in Egypt (pp. 183–192).

Ḥusayn, Muḥammad al-Khiḍr. *Naqd kitāb al-Islām wa-uṣūl al-ḥukm*. Cairo, n.d. One of the main critiques of ʿAbd al-Rāziq's work by a contemporary.

ʿImārah, Muḥammad. *Al-Islām wa-uṣūl al-ḥukm li-ʿAlī ʿAbd al-Rāziq*. Beirut, 1972. Classic critique of ʿAbd al-Rāziq's work that faults the author for a lack of understanding of Islamic history and for having fallen under the influence of Western liberalism.

Eric Davis

ʿABD AL-RAZZĀQ AL-SANHŪRĪ (1895–1971), Egyptian jurist, legal scholar, and architect of civil codes in several Arab countries. The academic and professional life of Sanhūrī is a reflection of the time during which the need for legal reform arose. For some Muslim countries, this meant the codification and modernization of the *sharīʿah*, and for others the replacement of imported legislation by national and Islamic laws. Sanhūrī drafted the modern civil codes of various Arab countries and attempted to reinvigorate the *sharīʿah* in light of contemporary legal developments and to incorporate it in the study of comparative jurisprudence.

Born in Alexandria, Egypt, in 1895, Sanhūrī received a modern education and graduated from the Khedevial School of Law in Cairo in 1917. He was appointed assistant prosecuting attorney and by 1920 had joined the School of *Sharīʿah* Judges as a lecturer. The following year he went to France for postgraduate studies. He wrote two theses, *Les restrictions contractuelle à la liberté individuelle de travail dans la jurisprudence anglaise* and *Le Califat*, obtaining dual doctorates in law and political science from the University of Lyon. He was also awarded a diploma from the Institut des Hautes Études Internationales in Paris.

In 1926, Sanhūrī returned to Egypt and began teaching civil law at the Law School, where he became dean a decade later. His involvement in politics led to his dismissal in 1936. He then served as dean of the Law College in Baghdad and began drafting the Iraqi civil code. Sanhūrī went back to Egypt in 1937 and served in various cabinet posts, becoming president of the Council of State in 1949.

He supported the movement of the Free Officers in 1952, and in his capacity as president of the Council he provided the legal advisory opinion that gave a constitutional basis for the Revolutionary Command Council's (RCC) exercise of power. Following a falling-out among RCC members, Sanhūrī was forcibly ousted from the Council of State in 1954 and was later deprived of his political rights. He devoted the rest of his life to teaching, research, and writing.

Sanhūrī articulated his theoretical approach of legal reform in *Le Califat: Son evolution vers une société des nations orientale* (Paris, 1926). Unlike ʿAlī ʿAbd al-Rāziq, who claimed that political authority was not an integral part of Islam, Sanhūrī considered the restoration of the caliphate a necessity, signifying the unity of Muslims and the preservation of the law. To reflect prevailing conditions, he made a distinction between an irregular (temporary) and a regular caliphate. He proposed that the caliphate develop into an Eastern League of Nations, with the caliph presiding over a body exercising only religious authority until a similar body with executive functions could be established. The exercise of executive and legislative authority would be the prerogative of individual governments and heads of state.

The restoration of the regular caliphate, Sanhūrī maintained, must be preceded by an evolution of Islamic law. Despite his genuine belief in the relevance and significance of the *sharīʿah* to the judicial and social institutions of the Muslim world, he was more concerned with maintaining the stability of legal practices and relationships. In an effort to make legal reforms acceptable to all citizens, he differentiated the immutable and temporal parts of the *sharīʿah* and claimed that only the variable rules of the temporal portion were subject to change. His proposed modernization of Islamic law would pass through two phases. The first would be that of scientific research, during which the *sharīʿah* would be thoroughly studied in light of modern comparative law. The second, the legislative phase, would include the gradual revision of existing codes. These new legislative reforms would take into account the historical, social, and legal experience of each country.

Sanhūrī put these ideas into practice in the revisions of the Egyptian and Iraqi codes, enacted in 1949 and 1951 respectively. He selected provisions—Islamic or Western—according to their merit, but he often concluded that the *sharīʿah* was more effective. In Egypt, where the existing code was based on foreign laws, he added provisions that made it more Islamic. In Iraq, however, the code was based largely on the *Mecelle*, and he introduced Western provisions that made it more modern. His final objective was a modern comparative legal system that would gradually come to emphasize Islamic rather than Western values and thus would become the basis for a unified Arab code.

Sanhūrī was responsible for laying the foundation for modern legislation in the Arab world. The codes he drafted for Egypt and Iraq have become models for other countries: they were adopted with minor modifications by Syria, Libya, and Jordan. His voluminous work on civil codes and Islamic law remains the main reference for Islamic scholarship in comparative law and codification to this day.

BIBLIOGRAPHY

Hill, Enid. *Al-Sanhūrī and Islamic Law.* Cairo, 1987. The most thorough study to date in English on al-Sanhūrī's life and work, with an extensive bibliography of his works.

Hill, Enid. "Islamic Law as a Source for the Development of a Comparative Jurisprudence, the 'Modern Science of Codification': Theory and Practice in the Life and Work of ʿAbd al-Razzāq Aḥmad al-Sanhūrī (1895–1971)." In *Islamic Law: Social and Historical Contexts*, edited by Aziz al-Azmeh, pp. 146–197. London and New York, 1988. Insightful analysis of al-Sanhūrī's contribution to codification and legal reform.

Khadduri, Majid. *Political Trends in the Arab World: The Role of Ideas and Ideals in Politics.* Baltimore and London, 1970. See pages 239–244.

Sanhūrī, ʿAbd al-Razzāq al-. "Wujūb tanqīḥ al-qānūn al-madanī" (The Necessity of Revising the Civil Code). *Majallat al-Qānūn wa-al-Iqtiṣād* 6.1 (January 1936): 3–144.

Sanhūrī, ʿAbd al-Razzāq al-. "ʿAlā ayyi asas yakūnu tanqīḥ al-qānūn al-madanī al-Miṣrī?" (On What Basis Will the Egyptian Civil Code Be Revised?). *Al-kitāb al-dhahabī lil-maḥākim al-ahlīyah* 2 (1938): 106–143.

Sanhūrī, ʿAbd al-Razzāq al-. "Al-qānūn al-madanī al-ʿArabī" (The Arab Civil Code). *Majallat al-Qaḍāʾ* (Baghdad) 20.1–2 (1962): 7–33.

Sanhūrī, ʿAbd al-Razzāq al-. ʿAbd al-Razzāq al-Sanhūrī min khilāl awrāqihi al-shakhṣīyah (ʿAbd al-Razzāq al-Sanhūrī through His Journals). Edited by Nādiyah al-Sanhūrī and Tawfīq al-Shāwī. Cairo, 1988. Collection of al-Sanhūrī's personal journals and his views on various issues, arranged chronologically.

Ziadeh, Farhat. *Lawyers, the Rule of Law, and Liberalism in Modern Egypt.* Stanford, Calif., 1968. See pages 137–147.

EMAD ELDIN SHAHIN

ABD EL-KRIM (1882–1963), more fully, Muḥammad ibn ʿAbd al-Karīm al-Khaṭṭābī, Moroccan leader of the Rif Rebellion (1921–1926) and Islamic reformer. Abd el-Krim was the eldest son of ʿAbd al-Karīm ibn Muḥammad al-Khaṭṭābī, a notable of the Ait Warayaghar, a Tamazight-speaking Berber tribe of the Rif Mountains in northeastern Morocco. In 1921, Rifian troops under Abd el-Krim's command defeated Spanish forces under General Silvestre at the battle of Anual. The Spanish losses may have numbered as many as nineteen thousand killed, making this battle the greatest defeat suffered by a European force in one battle in the colonial history of North Africa. Thus began the Rif Rebellion, a major insurrection against the Spanish and French protectorate authorities in Morocco.

The Rif Rebellion was the most important anticolonial uprising in Morocco until the emergence of the Istiqlāl party and modern mass nationalism in 1943 [*see* Istiqlāl]. In retrospect it can be seen as a transitional political phenomenon, at once the last *jihād* and the first modern political movement. The Rif Rebellion and the *ripublik* established by Abd el-Krim was a major political and strategic challenge to colonial rule. To understand its significance, the history of the family of Abd el-Krim and of Morocco from 1900 to 1925 must be examined.

Between 1900 and 1912, when the French and Spanish protectorates were established, large areas of Morocco, including the Rif Mountains, escaped the rule of the *makhzan* (the central government). In the early twentieth century *makhzan* control of northern Morocco was shaken by a series of rebellions, culminating in the uprising of Abū Ḥimārah (1902–1909) in northern Morocco. In 1907 and 1908 a popular insurgency overthrew ʿAbd al-ʿAzīz, the French-supported sultan, and brought to power his brother, ʿAbd al-Ḥafīẓ. From 1909 until the establishment of the French and Spanish protectorates in 1912, Morocco was in many respects already a colonized territory. This was especially the case in the Moroccan Rif area around the Spanish enclave of Melilla, which became the center for ambitious mining schemes by Spanish and German capitalists. By 1912, the Spanish presidio of Melilla had become one of the largest port cities in Morocco. For Rifians, these changes created enormous risks as well as opportunities.

The family of Abd el-Krim was well placed to take advantage of this rapidly changing situation. Abd el-Krim himself was the scion of a successful *aʿyān* (notable) family based in Ajdir, a community on the Mediterranean near the Spanish base at Alhuecemas. Around 1902 both Abd el-Krim and his brother studied for several years at the Qarawiyin mosque university in Fez, where they received a thorough grounding in Islamic law. After his return to the Rif around 1906 Abd el-Krim was employed by the Spanish government in Melilla as a teacher and subsequently as editor of the Arabic-language page in the Spanish newspaper, *El Telegrama del Rif*. While his father served as Moroccan-government-appointed *amīn* (customs agent) and (after 1912) as representative of the Spanish protectorate authorities in the district around Melilla, Abd el-Krim held an appointment from the Moroccan sultan as *qāḍī* (religious judge) for the same district, and his brother was studying to be a mining engineer in Spain. By playing off the *makhzan,* the local tribes, and the Spanish and French imperialists in the preceding decade, Abd el-Krim and his family were well positioned by 1912 to gain from the gradual collapse of the Moroccan state.

Abd el-Krim was able to increase his power and influence after 1912, following the simultaneous establishment of Spanish and French protectorates in northern Morocco. After the outbreak of World War I, his balancing act became more difficult to sustain. Although Abd el-Krim secretly supported the efforts of the Ottomans to foment a rebellion, he was denounced by some Moroccans as a collaborator because of his public role as a Spanish functionary. By 1921, in response to the increasing harshness of Spanish policy, Abd el-Krim launched his rebellion.

The Rif Rebellion was accompanied by the proclamation of a *ripublik* in 1923 by Abd el-Krim. It sought a far-reaching transformation of Rifian society based on the suppression of the feud, which was endemic, and the application of *sharīʿah* in place of Berber customary law. Religiously, Abd el-Krim sought to introduce the ideas of the Salafīyah movement and opposed the Ṣūfī brotherhoods, whom he regarded as the source of internal division and backwardness [*see* Salafīyah]. Refusing the label of rebel, Abd el-Krim sought to present his rebellion as a modern state, a Dawlat al-Jumhūrīyah al-Rifīyah, or Rifian Republic. The *ripublik* invoked the language of national self-determination and human rights in an effort to win support among European liberals. Headed by Abd el-Krim as president, it had a national assembly composed of the heads of the Berber tribal councils.

At its height, the Rifian state embraced most of the Spanish protectorate zone, excluding the cities of Melilla, Alhuecemas, and Tetouan, and a portion of the French protectorate zone north of Fez. New methods of military organization, added to exceptional fighting qualities, made the Ait Warayaghar a formidable opponent even to modern European armies. Only in 1926, after the full military might of France and Spain was brought to bear (including massive artillery and aerial bombardments), was Abd el-Krim defeated.

The legacy of Abd el-Krim is an ambiguous one. His brave and resourceful struggle served as an inspiration to Moroccan contemporaries, notably the young nationalists, but the idea of a Rifian republic has also been seen as a potentially divisive one in independent Morocco. Perhaps because of this, Abd el-Krim played no role in the nationalist movement that overthrew the Spanish and French protectorates in 1956. Abd el-Krim himself died in exile in Cairo in 1963.

[*See also* Morocco.]

BIBLIOGRAPHY

Fāsī, ʿAllāl al-. *Independence Movements of Arab North Africa*. Translated by Hazem Zaki Nuseibeh. Washington, D.C., 1954.

Hart, David Montgomery. *The Aith Warayaghar of the Moroccan Rif: An Ethnography and History*. 2 vols. Tucson, 1976.

Pennell, C. R. *A Country with a Government and a Flag: The Rif War in Morocco, 1921–1926*. Wisbech, England, 1986.

Roger-Mathieu, J. *Mémoires d'Abd-el-Krim*. Paris, 1927.

Shinar, Pessah. " ʿAbd al-Qadir and ʿAbd al-Krim: Religious Influences on Their Thought and Action." *Asian and African Studies* 1 (1965): 139–174.

Woolman, David S. *Rebels in the Rif: Abdel Krim and the Rif Rebellion*. Stanford, Calif., 1968.

EDMUND BURKE, III

ABDEL RAHMAN, OMAR (b. 1938), more properly spelled ʿUmar ʿAbd al-Raḥmān, Egyptian religious scholar and Islamic fundamentalist leader. Born to a poor rural family in the village of al-Jamālīyah in Lower Egypt, Omar Ahmed Ali Abdel Rahman was accidentally blinded at ten months of age. He received a traditional religious education in regional urban centers, memorizing the Qur'ān. In 1960 he entered the faculty of Fundamentals of Religion at al-Azhar University in Cairo, where he graduated first in his class in 1965. Although he had hoped to become a teaching assistant at the university, he was appointed by the state as a mosque preacher in a poor rural village in the Fayyum, Upper Egypt. He soon returned to al-Azhar, however, obtaining a master's degree in 1967 and a faculty appointment in 1968. He continued both his graduate studies and occasional preaching in the Fayyum.

Abdel Rahman made the pilgrimage to Mecca in 1968 and there met Saʿīd Ramaḍān, an expatriate leader of the Egyptian Muslim Brotherhood who opposed the government of Gamal Abdel Nasser. Ramaḍān persuaded him to transport funds back to Egypt for the families of jailed brotherhood members; Abdel Rahman was arrested in the process and, although he was soon released, he lost his faculty position. He was appointed to a bureaucratic post in late 1969, but he saw this as a shameful demotion.

Abdel Rahman continued to preach in the Fayyum. At a public ceremony after Nasser's death on 28 September 1970, he condemned Nasser as an infidel and prohibited prayers for him. As a consequence, he was detained by the government for eight months.

The new regime of Anwar el-Sadat declared an amnesty for jailed Islamic fundamentalists with the aim of enlisting them as a counterweight to leftist forces. Abdel Rahman was reappointed as a teaching assistant at the Azhari Institute in Fayyum, but he was still the subject of controversy among university administrators. After completing his doctorate in 1972 he briefly held a professorship at al-Azhar before being transferred to the religious faculty in Asyut, a center of Islamic fundamentalist activity. Both the regional and national governments supported the establishment there of the Jamāʿah al-Islāmīyah, the Muslim Brotherhood's student organization, to which Abdel Rahman was strongly sympathetic.

In 1977 Abdel Rahman married ʿIshā' Ḥasan Jūdah, daughter of a brotherhood member, and left Egypt to spend four years in Saudi Arabia as a professor of Qur'ānic interpretation at Saud University. Soon after his return, he was arrested for his involvement in the fundamentalist Jihād Organization accused of assassinating President Sadat. He was accused of leading the organization and of participating in the assassination but was acquitted on both counts and released in 1984.

During this protracted trial (1981–1984), three factors led to Abdel Rahman's emergence as the leading figure in his Islamist movement. The first was his book *Mīthāq al-ʿāmil al-Islāmī* (Charter of Islamic Action), an explanation of his view of correct Islamic life; it marked his departure from the more moderate wing of the brotherhood and affiliation with the radical forces informed by the concept of *jihād* and the necessity to overthrow the secular state in order to restore the principles of the Qur'ān. Second, he married again, this time to Fātin Shuʿayb, a kinswoman of several important activists, affirming his solidarity with the Jamāʿah al-Islāmīyah in Upper Egypt and lending weight to his religious status as *muftī al-jihād*. Third, most of the major leaders of the *jihād* organization were executed or imprisoned for life, leaving a power vacuum that Abdel Rahman readily filled.

During the decade that followed Abdel Rahman came to be portrayed by his political opponents and the media as the high priest of radical fundamentalism both in and outside Egypt. In 1990 he emigrated to the United States, where he was alleged to have inspired his followers to bomb the World Trade Center in New York City in 1993. He has in fact been acknowledged by the Jamāʿah al-Islāmīyah as its spiritual guide, and he has assumed great importance to radical Islamists in much of the Muslim world.

[*See also* Egypt; Jamāʿat al-Islāmīyah, al-; Jihād Organizations; *and* Muslim Brotherhood, *article on* Muslim Brotherhood in Egypt.]

BIBLIOGRAPHY

Abu Lughod, Janet. "Rural Migration and Politics in Egypt." In *Rural Politics and Social Change in the Middle East*, edited by Richard Antoun and Ilyia Harik, pp. 315–334. Bloomington, 1972.

Auda, Gehad. "An Uncertain Response: The Islamic Movement in

Egypt." In *Islamic Fundamentalisms and the Gulf Crisis*, edited by J. P. Piscatori, pp. 109–130. Chicago, 1991.
Auda, Gehad. "Islamic Movement and Resource Mobilization: A Political Culture Perspective." In *Political Culture and Democracy in Developing Countries*, edited by Larry Diamond, pp. 379–407. Boulder, 1993.
Auda, Gehad. "The Normalization of the Islamic Movement in Egypt." In *Accounting for Fundamentalisms*, edited by Martin E. Marty and R. Scott Appleby, pp. 374–412. Chicago, 1994.
Fawzī, Muḥammad. *ʿUmar ʿAbd al-Raḥmān*. Cairo, n.d.

GEHAD AUDA

ʿABDUH, MUḤAMMAD (1849–1905), Egyptian scholar and reformer regarded as the architect of Islamic modernism. The birth year of Muḥammad ʿAbduh coincided with the death of Muḥammad ʿAlī, the Albanian adventurer and creator of modern Egypt. ʿAlī's regime, in political terms, generated the issues of modern change associated in intellectual terms with ʿAbduh's pioneer leadership as a journalist, theologian, jurist and—in the last six years of his life—grand *muftī* of Egypt. The initial factors in his career were his traditional studies at al-Azhar University and an early commitment to Sufism with the Shādhilī order of mystical discipline and the practice of *dhikr* and *taʿwīdh*. His university studies ensured not only his grounding in the skills of an *ʿālim* but also his awareness of the inhibitions of *taqlīd* (adherence to tradition), against which his reforming energies were later directed. Although he intellectually renounced his Ṣūfī background, it continued to impart a quality of piety to his academic concerns for liberation from the harmful effects of *taqlīd*.

The crucial influence in his development was the impact of Jalāl al-Dīn al-Afghānī (1839–1897), a strenuous advocate of a unitary Islam who emphasized the concept of *ummah* (community) against the regionalism that in the next century was to break up allegiance to the Ottoman empire into nationalism and the nation-state. Pan-Islam was al-Afghānī's response to British rule in Egypt and to European domination in general. ʿAbduh was drawn into the cause and became editor of the journal *Al-ʿurwah al-wuthqā* (Firm Handhold), which took its title from a Qur'ānic phrase (surahs 2.256 and 31.22); despite the brevity of its publication in the 1880s, the journal kindled the enthusiasm of a generation of writers, including Rashīd Riḍā, ultimately ʿAbduh's biographer and his chief literary legatee.

ʿAbduh was exiled from Egypt between 1882 and 1888, when he made wide contact with kindred minds in Syria and North Africa, with a short sojourn also in France. After his return to Cairo, his thoughts and efforts were drawn increasingly toward education and a renewal of Islamic theology. Given the ambiguities implicit in Arab Ottomanism and the actualities of British power in Egypt, he sensed that political activism had to be accompanied, if not overtaken, by the invigoration of the Muslim mind. Western influences had taken hold ever since Napoleon's intrusion into the Arab East, but largely in practical forms—arms, trade, travel, and finance. A response to modernity had to be made in the way Islam perceived itself. ʿAbduh's training in the familiar scholastic patterns of *tafsīr* (Qur'ānic exegesis or commentary) and *fiqh* (jurisprudence) had made him aware of the impediment to critical self-awareness in those habits and attitudes. The zest he had acquired from al-Afghānī he now harnessed to intellectual ends. The attitude and training of the *ʿulamā'*, as he saw them, had entrenched them in the citation of authority, the appeal to sacrosanct exegesis, and a supine satisfaction with static norms. This *taqlīd*, or "hideboundness" (to adopt a harsh translation), had its origins in the bases of Islam's concept of *waḥy* ("revelation") in the Qur'ān and in the assumptions of *isnād* ("reliance") on which its handling of tradition had long relied. Once an instinct of loyalty to the past and as such characteristic of Muslim scholarship, *taqlīd* had come to sap the genuine articulation of Islam's meaning and quality. [*See also* Taqlīd.]

To achieve emancipation from the mentality of *taqlīd* and yet retain Islamic authenticity was therefore a formidable task. ʿAbduh shouldered it with admirable tenacity, patience, and resilience, corroborating his scholarly credentials by earning increasing personal stature, despite the toll on his health and resources caused by pressure from reactionary forces. The idea that the *sharīʿah* could be subject to wise discretion and that even theology could be flexible within limits served to enliven theological education, to increase student initiative, and to give scope to existing ideas of *istiḥsān* and *istiṣlāḥ* (considerations of equity through appeal to well-being and good sense).

The main ground of ʿAbduh's "liberal-loyal" equation was the conviction that revelation and reason, each rightly perceived, were inherently harmonious. Was not reason one with that *fiṭrah* (creation) by which, the Qur'ān affirms (30.30), God had made human nature fit religion, the two being combined in the very word *Islam?* In *Risālat al-tawḥīd* (The Theology of Unity), his most popular work, he expounded his conviction that "every sound speculation led to a belief in God as He is described in the Qur'ān" (p. 10). ʿAbduh held that the premise on which this belief rested was such as to make proof unnecessary: despite the word "described," the being of God was incomprehensible. There were things about which it was not permissible to inquire, where curiosity could lead only to "confusion of belief." Nevertheless, what was given in revelation should be rationally possessed—a task incumbent on every generation. There was no need to raise questions of theodicy, but sound exegesis should avoid crudely reading into the Qur'ān anticipations of new discoveries and inventions. The purpose of revelation was essentially religious; what reason as science could achieve on its own, God had left it to do, and faith must respect its methods. ʿAbduh sustained the traditional case for the *ʿijāz* (matchlessness) of the Qur'ān as conclusive evidence of its divine origin. He identified as a form of *shirk* ("associationalism," or more broadly "not letting God be God") any reluctance to apply rationality to issues of society or to refuse its scientific fruits. Such reluctance would be a disavowal of divine creation. *Sharīʿah* law was to be interpreted by the same principle of divinely created status and human custody in harmony.

At the time of his death ʿAbduh was in his middle fifties. The bitter opposition he suffered from both academic and legal foes was proof of the measure of his influence and the range of his vision for a renewed Islam. His ideas found some continuing expression through the pages of the influential journal *Al-manār* (Lighthouse), but his disciples lacked his stature, and there is evidence of an adverse reaction to his legacy soon after his demise. At longer range, however, he came to epitomize an incipient modernism, opening up a fresh viewpoint yet leaving many issues unresolved.

[*See also* Modernism.]

BIBLIOGRAPHY

ʿAbduh, Muḥammad. *The Theology of Unity*. Translated by Ishaq Musaʿad and Kenneth Cragg. London, 1966. Translation of *Risālat al-tawḥīd*.

Adams, Charles C. *Islam and Modernism in Egypt*. London, 1933. Pioneering study focusing on ʿAbduh.

Amīn, ʿUthmān. *Muḥammad ʿAbduh*. Translated by Charles Wendell. Washington, D.C., 1953.

Cragg, Kenneth. *Counsels in Contemporary Islam*. Edinburgh, 1965.

Hourani, Albert. *Arabic Thought in the Liberal Age, 1798–1939*. London, 1962.

Rahman, Fazlur. *Islam and Modernity*. Chicago, 1982.

KENNETH CRAGG

ABDÜLHAMID II (1842–1918), thirty-fourth Ottoman sultan (r. 1876–1909). A profound political and economic crisis brought Abdülhamid II to the throne. Since 1839 the open-door policy of the government, the commercial and legal privileges granted to European powers, and the westernizing reform attempts—the Tanzimat—had ruptured the Ottoman social fabric. Trade and budget deficits soared. Heavy government borrowing abroad and at home delayed the inevitable financial crisis, but in 1875 the Treasury declared insolvency. European creditors protested. Unrest mounted everywhere, fanning nationalist revolts among Christians in the Balkans and anti-Tanzimat movements among Muslims. [*See* Tanzimat.]

The government in Istanbul lost control of events. Since the death of the last powerful Tanzimat minister Mehmed Emin Âli Pasha in 1871, senior statesmen had been engaged in a struggle to control the government. In 1876 a group of ministers led by Midhat Pasha provoked the armed forces to effect a coup d'état and deposed the reigning sultan Abdülaziz. His successor Murad V suffered a mental collapse and was deposed within three months. On 31 August 1876, Abdülhamid II succeeded him on the throne.

Meanwhile, nationalist uprisings in the Balkans turned into bloody ethnic and religious confrontations. The European powers put pressure on the Ottoman government to grant autonomy to the Christian population. Midhat responded by promulgating a constitution (23 December 1876) that assured basic civil liberties, including the equality of all subjects before law, and provided for a parliament.

Forestalling foreign intervention was only one objective of the constitution, and in this it failed. A disastrous war with Russia nearly brought the end of the Ottoman state in 1877. In a series of difficult negotiations that lasted until 1882, the Ottomans surrendered large tracts of territory not only to the Balkan states and Russia but also to other major powers.

The constitution was also intended as a solution to the crisis of authority afflicting the Ottoman state. As such, it reflected a consensus among the Ottoman political elite. The constitution set certain limits on executive authority but left the sultan with great powers vis-à-vis both the cabinet and the parliament. Indeed, Abdülhamid dismissed and exiled Midhat in February 1877 and suspended the parliament in February 1878 on the basis of his constitutional prerogatives. He did not meet any opposition, for the most influential Ottoman elite viewed him as a sensible sovereign capable of providing the leadership necessary to deal with the grave problems facing the government. In 1878 he began to establish an authoritarian regime that eventually breached the spirit of the constitution and brought his downfall.

In the meantime, however, his reign saw respectable accomplishments in the construction of highways, waterways, railroads, the telegraph, and other infrastructural public works. Judicial and public security services improved and expanded significantly. Institutions were formed to supply credit and technical advice to agricultural producers. General public education and literacy improved. Many specialized schools were established and the old ones expanded with the specific purpose of training a corps of technical government personnel and better public administrators and jurists.

Abdülhamid made an effort to concentrate government investments and reforms in the predominantly Muslim parts of the empire. He emphasized Islam as a basis of internal social and political solidarity. Pan-Islamists such as Jamāl al-Dīn al-Afghānī viewed him as the symbol or focus of Islamic solidarity [*see* Pan-Islam *and the biography of Afghānī*]. Recent territorial losses and the immigration of large numbers of Muslims from the Balkans and Russia had rendered the Ottoman population overwhelmingly Muslim and had raised religious sentiments. Abdülhamid responded to this situation. He did not breach the principle of legal equality, because he believed in it, and he did not want to create pretexts for foreign intervention. He staunchly resisted, however, any attempt or pressure to obtain additional concessions and autonomy for the Christian population. He maintained that European protection had already put the Christians in an unduly advantageous position over the Muslims, who were in his mind the truly loyal subjects of the Ottoman state.

Abdülhamid's resistance to intervention in favor of Christians, particularly in eastern Anatolia and Macedonia, remained a sensitive issue in the government's relations with European powers. In this and other international problems, Abdülhamid tried to hold his ground by taking advantage of the rivalries among the powers and by resorting to delaying tactics. He hoped to gain time until the Ottoman government attained a stronger position to defend its interests, relying on a better-educated and unified population and a more prosperous economy.

His hopes were in vain. The state of Ottoman finances was a major problem: around thirty percent of the government revenue went directly into the coffers of the foreign-controlled Public Debt Administration, and an additional forty percent was devoured by military expenditures. Given the consequent dearth of funds, the government awarded many of the planned projects and important mines to European concerns as monopolistic concessions. To a certain extent, Abdülhamid was able to use European vested interests to perpetuate his own policies; but the commercial and legal capitulations enjoyed by the European powers, backed by threats of force, left him with little room to maneuver.

The Ottoman regime looked increasingly helpless in defending local interests at a time when limited but real achievements aroused expectations, and nationalistic sentiments therefore gained momentum even among Muslims, undermining Abdülhamid's appeal to Islamic solidarity. There also developed a Muslim religious opposition to the sultan, not least because of his emphasis on modern secular schools at the expense of traditional religious ones. It was, however, among the graduates of the modern schools that the most formidable opposition to Abdülhamid's regime took form. Demanding a more institutionalized and participatory regime, a large group of Ottoman officials, officers, and intellectuals organized the Committee of Union and Progress (CUP), the indigenous organization of the Young Turks [*see* Young Turks].

In 1908 sporadic mutinies broke out among the army corps in Rumelia and Macedonia and rapidly evolved into a popular movement that forced Abdülhamid to call for elections and to agree to serve as a parliamentary-constitutionalist monarch. Supporters of the CUP won the majority in the parliament. But as the parliament and the cabinet became bogged down in a struggle over their respective rights, and as the separatist movements in the Balkans intensified, the political situation remained tense. On 13 April 1909, a popular revolt broke out in Istanbul, led by certain religious groups and army units alienated by the CUP. An army of loyal units and volunteers rushed to Istanbul to crush the rebellion. Abdülhamid was falsely accused of having instigated the rebellion and was dethroned on 27 April. He spent the rest of his life under house arrest, until his death on 10 February 1918.

[*See also* Ottoman Empire.]

BIBLIOGRAPHY

There are numerous books on Abdülhamid II and his reign; see the works listed in A. H. Ongunsu, "Abdülhamid II," in *İslâm Ansiklo-*

pedisi, vol. 1, pp. 76–80 (Istanbul, 1940), and J. Deny, " ʿAbd al-Ḥamīd," in *Encyclopaedia of Islam*, new ed., vol. 1, pp. 63–65 (Leiden, 1960–). Most of these works are based on Western sources and nationalistic accounts. Research on the vast collection of contemporary Ottoman documents has just begun, but it is already evident that this new source of information will significantly revise our perceptions of Sultan Abdülhamid II. For examples of recent works that make use of contemporary Ottoman documents, see Stanford J. Shaw and Ezel Kural Shaw, *The History of the Ottoman Empire and Modern Turkey*, vol. 2, *Reform, Revolution, and Republic: The Rise of Modern Turkey, 1808–1975*, pp. 172–272 (Cambridge, London, and New York 1977); William Ochsenwald, *The Hijaz Railroad* (Charlottesville, Va., 1980); Donald Quataert, *Social Disintegration and Popular Resistance in the Ottoman Empire, 1881–1909* (New York, 1983); Kemal Karpat, *Ottoman Population, 1830–1914* (Madison, Wis., 1985); and articles by Donald Quataert, Selim Deringil, Engin Deniz Akarlı, and Butrus Abu-Manneh, in the *International Journal of Middle Eastern Studies, Middle Eastern Studies*, and other journals.

ENGIN DENIZ AKARLI

ABDURRAHMAN WAHID (b. 1940), Indonesian Islamic thinker, writer, and politician. One of the most influential Muslim intellectual leaders in Indonesia today, Abdurrahman Wahid is also a popular columnist on cultural, social, and political affairs, urging Islam's contribution to pluralism, social justice, and democracy. He currently serves as chairperson of the Executive Council (Tanfidziyah) of the Nahdatul Ulama (NU), an association of traditionalist *ʿulamāʾ* with a reported thirty million supporters, mostly among the rural population, is widely called "Gus Dur"; Gus is an honorific for a young man from a respected Javanese family, and Dur is a diminutive of Abdurrahman.

Gus Dur was born in 1940 in Tebuireng, Jombang, East Java. His grandfather was Hasyim Asyʿari (1871–1947), a great *ʿālim* (Islamic scholar) of the Shāfiʿī schools, who founded a *pesantren* (rural Islamic boarding school) at Tebuireng in 1899 and established the NU in 1926 as a federation of *pesantren* leaders. His father was Wahid Hasyim (1914–1953), a leader of the NU and minister of religion of the Republic of Indonesia. His mother, Shalihah, was the daughter of Bisri Syamsuri, the head of a *pesantren* at Tambakberas, Jombang, and a cofounder of the NU.

In spite of his family's background in *pesantren*, Gus Dur received his primary education at a government school (*sekolah rakyat*) in Jakarta (1947–1953) and went on to a secular secondary school in Jogjakarta, graduating in 1956. He then studied at the *pesantren*s of Tegalrejo (1956–1958) and Tambakberas (1958–1963). From 1963 to 1970 he went abroad to study at the Department of Higher Islamic and Arabic Studies of al-Azhar University in Cairo and the Faculty of Letters at the University of Baghdad. Upon returning to Indonesia, he taught first as a lecturer and then as dean of the faculty of *ushuluddin* at the University of Hasyim Asyʿari in Jombang from 1972 to 1974. He served as the secretary at the *pesantren* of Tebuireng from 1974 to 1979.

By the end of the 1970s Gus Dur had become widely known outside *pesantren* circles through his contributions to major newspapers and journals. He participated actively in a number of seminars, symposia, and conferences on national development. Through these opportunities he attracted public attention to the *pesantren*'s role as an agent for the development of the rural community and the growth of a democratic society at the grassroots level. He also become known as a spokesperson for the nongovernment organizations (NGOs) of Indonesia, among which development-oriented *pesantren*s occupied an important position.

Gus Dur represents the trend of neomodernism among the new generation of Muslim intellectuals in Indonesia. He strives for the liberation of the Muslim community from the restrictions of traditionalist as well as modernist scripturalism. He endeavors to reconstruct socio-ethical guidelines for Muslims today through thorough reinterpretation of the Qur'ān and *sunnah* in historical perspective. He argues that principles for such values as basic human rights, social justice, fair development, and democracy are inherent in Islam; thus contemporary Muslim pursuit of those values is not an ideological compromise or cultural mixture with Western liberalism, but an undertaking genuinely grounded in Islamic teachings. However, the preoccupation of traditionalist *ʿulamāʾ* with ritual correctness and that of modern Islamicists with legal formalism have both hindered the rediscovery of these principles, leaving the Muslim community in a state of ignorance, backwardness, and poverty.

Gus Dur finds sufficient potential in the NU's traditionalism for its self-renewal. There is a dynamism in its Shāfiʿī worldview, and its methodology of Islamic jurisprudence provides ample room for adaptation to new situations. He first joined the NU's national leadership in 1979 as a junior secretary to the Syuriyah or Consultative Council of Ulama. At the *muktamar* (congress) of the NU in 1984, he was elected chairperson of its executive council for the period 1984–1989, and again in 1989 for another five-year term.

Since 1984 Gus Dur, in collaboration with Ahmad Siddiq, new president of Syuriyah, has initiated a bold turnaround in the direction of the NU. Under their leadership the NU accepted the state philosophy of Pancasila (Five Pillars) as the sole foundation of its organization, reconfirming its loyalty to the present regime. It withdrew from party politics, severing its relationship with the PPP (Development Unity Party), a coalition of four Islamic parties. It decided to return to its original identity as a social, religious, and educational movement, working for the wellbeing of the rural population under its influence and for the consolidation and rationalization of its organization.

Gus Dur opposes making Indonesia a secular state, but he stands firm against that form of Islamic fundamentalism that claims Islam to be a comprehensive way of life superior to existing secular regimes. He believes that Islam, as a revealed religion, should not be degraded to the level of an alternative to any human-made ideology, but should be regarded as an eternal source of moral and ethical inspiration for Muslims in any regime. In the Pancasila pluralism of Indonesia, neither Islam nor any other religion should be in confrontation with the state or with another religion. In practice, he established the Democratic Forum in 1991 as an interreligious coalition, mostly with Christian intellectuals, intending it to be a move to counterbalance the recent tendency of exclusivism within the Muslim community.

Gus Dur is more an independent intellectual than a conventional Islamic scholar or organizational functionary. He is widely read in history, philosophy and literature in Arabic and English, as well as Indonesian, and has many friends among academics, writers, and artists. He is a sociable person, at ease with people from all walks of life, foreign as well as domestic. He is bold in criticism and brave in dissent, often inviting controversy, but always full of humor and he maintains a simple, egalitarian lifestyle. He was presented with the 1993 Raman Magsaysay award, the "Asian Nobel prize," for "his guiding Southeast Asia's largest Muslim organization as a force of religious tolerance, fair development, and democracy in Indonesia."

[*See also* Indonesia; Nahdatul Ulama.]

BIBLIOGRAPHY

The reader may consult the following works by Abdurrahman Wahid:

"Pesantren sebagai sub-kultur" (Pesantren as a Subculture). In *Pesantren dan Pembaharuan* (Pesantren and Reformation), edited by M. Dawam Rahardjo, pp. 39–60. Jakarta, 1974. One of the earliest writings of Abdurrahman Wahid, introducing the *pesantren* as a distinct subculture with significant implications for Indonesia's national development.

"Making Islamic Law Conducive to Development." *Prisma* (English edition) 2 (November 1975): 87–94. Delineation of his idea of the innovative adaptability of *fiqh* methodology.

"Menetapkan pangkalan-pangkalan pendaratan menuju Indonesia yang kita cita-citakan" (Setting Up Landing Bases towards an Indonesia We Hope For). In *Dialog: Indonesia kini dan esok* (Dialogue: Indonesia Today and Tomorrow), edition by Imam Walujo and Kons Kleden, pp. 103–129. Jakarta, 1980. Discussion of his strategy for constructing Muslim community gradually as a basis for democracy, social justice, and fair development.

"Religion, Ideology and Development." *Prisma* (English edition) 19 (December 1980): 56–65.

"Hukum pidana Islam dan hak-hak asasi manusia" (Islamic Criminal Law and the Basic Human Rights). In *Muslim di tengah pergumulan* (Muslims in the Midst of Struggle), pp. 94–100. Jakarta, 1983. Explicit argument for the contribution of Islamic law to basic human rights.

"The Islamic Masses in the Life of State and Nation." *Prisma* (English edition) 35 (March 1985): 3–10. Justification of the acceptance of Pancasila as the state ideology of the Republic of Indonesia.

"The Nahdlatul Ulama and Islam in Present Day Indonesia." In *Islam and Society in Southeast Asia,* edited by Taufik Abdullah and Sharon Siddique, pp. 175–186. Singapore, 1986. Excellent summary of his vision on the role of the Nahdatul Ulama in contemporary Indonesian society.

NAKAMURA MITSUO

ABIM. The Muslim organization Angkatan Belia Islam Malaysia or the Malaysian Islamic Youth Movement was officially registered on 17 August 1972 in Selangor state, after operating as a loose forum of concerned Muslim activists from 1969 to 1971. Its major objectives, as contained in its Articles of Association, were as follows: to establish and propagate Islamic tenets and principles as enshrined in the Qur'ān and the *sunnah;* to spread and defend, in a progressive manner, the Islamic message, in particular its universalistic dimension; and to mobilize Muslim youth to collaborative endeavors in all fields, including the economy, society, education, culture, and technology.

The man most instrumental in the establishment of ABIM was Anwar Ibrahim. Born in Bukit Mertajam in Penang state, Anwar was an active student leader while studying at the Universiti Malaya from 1968 to 1971. In 1968 he was president of both the National Association of Muslim Students and the Muslim Students Association of Universiti Malaya; in 1969 he became president of the Malay Language Society at the university. He held these appointments until 1970/1971.

While a student leader, Anwar and his group were often very critical of government policies, particularly on the role of the Malay language, and other policies regarded as prejudicial to Malay *(bumiputra)* interests. At that time, Anwar supported Malay nationalist figures such as Dr. Mahathir Mohamed in their criticisms of Prime Minister Tunku Abdul Rahman, whose leadership style and policies were said to be responsible for the worsening plight of the Malays. The Tunku was also blamed for the racial riots on 13 May 1969, which pitted the Malays against the Chinese. When Anwar and his activist friends were about to graduate from the university, they realized the need to form an association to enable them to continue their Islamic activities. Hence ABIM came into being in 1972, and Anwar became its first secretary-general. He later assumed the presidency of the movement in 1974.

Helping him to establish ABIM were Kamaruddin Mohammad Nor, who later became one of ABIM's vice presidents and the official representative of the World Assembly of Muslim Youth (WAMY); Ahmad Hajj Ismail, a secretary in the Defense Ministry; Fauzi Abdul Rahman, the parliamentary secretary of the Ministry of Information; and Zakaria Hashim, a successful businessman. At the time of its formation, ABIM had only forty members; in 1992, the membership reached more than fifty thousand nationwide. In its first decade of existence, a large proportion of the members were schoolteachers and university students. Today, many are also executives in both the government and private sectors. Although the president is significant in projecting the image of the movement, ABIM's leadership is known to operate under the Islamic principle of *shūrā* (consultation) in its decision-making process.

ABIM's relationship with the government has undergone change over the years. In the first decade of its existence, the relationship was tense: Anwar was arrested without trial under the Internal Security Act in 1974 on the charge of instigating Malay farmers against the government; in turn, ABIM criticized the government openly on issues such as corruption, abuse of power, and exploitation of workers, and called upon the authorities to abolish the Internal Security Act, which ABIM regarded as "repugnant to the Islamic spirit." ABIM also charged that the nationalist-secularist orientation of the government would never solve the nation-building problems of multiracial Malaysia; only an "Islamic solution" would do so. However, since Anwar was coopted by the UMNO (United Malays National Organization) party a year after Mahathir Mohamed became prime minister in 1981, the government seems to have somewhat tolerated ABIM's many criticisms and has accommodated some of its demands and representations.

Anwar's successors continue the foundations and philosophical orientations set by him. Siddiq Fadhil, who assumed the presidency of the movement from Anwar, was a former neighbor whom Anwar had invited to join ABIM. Lacking the charisma of Anwar, Siddiq compensated that by his deeper knowledge of Islam and the Arabic language, amply demonstrated by his frequent quotations from the Qur'ān and the *sunnah*. Siddiq vacated the position in August 1991 on the occasion of ABIM's twentieth convention (Muktamar Sanawi) in Kuala Lumpur. Having been Anwar's deputy for many years prior to his elevation as president in 1983, Siddiq had served ABIM longer than Anwar. His wife Zulaikha was also, during his term as president, the head of ABIM's women's wing.

Since 1991 ABIM's fourth president has been Dr. Muhammad Nur Manuty. Dr. Manuty received his early Islamic education in Perak state before becoming a staff member of the National University of Malaysia in 1970. He continued his postgraduate education at Temple University in Philadelphia, where he met the renowned Muslim scholar Ismāʿīl Rājī al-Fārūqī. He secured his Ph.D degree from Temple in the field of contemporary Islamic thought and movements and began teaching at the International Islamic University in Petaling Jaya, Malaysia. Dr. Manuty began his active involvement in ABIM in 1978, when he was appointed assistant secretary-general, and later was vice president for international relations from 1989 to 1991.

As previously, Manuty's leadership is characterized by the policy of maintaining close relations with Muslim organizations and movements overseas. In 1980 ABIM had established formal relations with twenty-four international Muslim groups, especially with nongovernmental Muslim bodies such as the Jamāʿat-i Islāmī in the Indian subcontinent, the Ikhwān al-Muslimīn in the Gulf region, and the Muhammadiyah organization in Indonesia; by 1993 the number of bodies had reached more than thirty-five. Locally, ABIM's dealings with other Muslim *dakwah* (Ar., *daʿwah;* Islamic propagation) organizations are cordial. While the movement does not seem to approve of the propagation methods of movements like PERKIM and Dar ul Arqam, it often collaborates with them, for example with Perkim in recruiting non-Malay converts to Islam. [*See* Dar ul Arqam; Muhammadiyah; PERKIM.]

ABIM's role in Malaysian life is considerable. First, it has on many occasions acted as the voice or conscience of Muslims in Malaysia in matters affecting Islam and the Muslim community. Second, with its systematic and comprehensive approach to Islamic propagation, the movement has educated many Malaysian Muslims about the relevance and efficacy of the Islamic faith in confronting the perennial problems faced by an increasingly open and modern Malaysia. Third, among all contemporary Muslim bodies and groups in the country, ABIM is the most organized force, instrumental in the birth of Islamic revivalism in Malaysia since the late 1970s. Finally, because many ABIM activists continue to occupy key leadership positions in the religious, social, educational, and political arenas, the movement has not only access to the decision-making channels of government and the bureaucracy, but also the ability to affect policy directions as well as the intensification of the Islamic ethos in the country. With the recent elevation of Anwar Ibrahim as the deputy prime minister of Malaysia (and deputy president of the UMNO party), it now remains to be seen whether or not such an active role of ABIM in Malaysian society will increase further.

[*See also* Daʿwah, *article on* Modern Usage; Malaysia; *and the biography of Ibrahim.*]

BIBLIOGRAPHY

Chandra Muzaffar. *Islamic Resurgence in Malaysia.* Petaling Jaya, Malaysia, 1987. Insightful interpretation that links the *dakwah* phenomenon to the wider sociopolitical context of Malaysian politics.

Hussin Mutalib. *Islam and Ethnicity in Malay Politics.* New York and Singapore, 1990. The most comprehensive treatment of Malay politics in Malaysia post-1980, as well as a detailed examination of the dialectical relationship between Islam and Malay nationalist sentiment.

Hussin Mutalib. *Islam in Malaysia: From Revivalism to Islamic State?* Singapore, 1993. An original and probing study of the feasibility of Malaysia becoming an Islamic state in the future.

Nagata, Judith. *The Reflowering of Malaysian Islam: Modern Religious Radicals and Their Roots.* Vancouver, B.C., 1984. One of the earliest penetrating studies about the sources of the contemporary *dakwah* phenomenon in Malaysia, approached primarily from a sociological-anthropological perspective.

Zainah Anwar. *Islamic Revivalism in Malaysia: Dakwah among the Students.* Kuala Lumpur, 1987. Revealing study of the role of Muslim students in the regeneration of the Islamic ethos in Malaysia.

Hussin Mutalib

ABLUTIONS. *See* Ṣalāt.

ABORTION. The expelling of the fetus from the womb before the period of gestation, abortion has ethical and legal implications in practically all societies, irrespective of prevailing religious traditions. Muslim and Western conceptions of abortion differ, both with respect to unplanned and unwanted pregnancies. Within the Islamic system, procreation of the human species is regarded as one of the most important aspects of marriage. A Muslim may not terminate pregnancy on the grounds of it being unplanned or unwanted as the trend seems to be in the West. The question for Muslims is not whether it is right or wrong, from an ethical standpoint, to engage in abortion. Rather, Muslims ask whether the *sharīʿah* (Islamic law) sanctions abortion, and proceed accordingly.

Muslim jurists (*fuqahā'*), in attempting to determine the legal implications of abortion, engage in what is termed *ijtihād* (intellectual deliberation) in order to deduce laws from the broad teachings of the Qur'ān and the *ḥadīth* (sayings, practices, judgments, and attitudes) of the prophet Muḥammad (570–633 CE). The Qur'ān places a high premium on life and its preservation. Punishment for the unlawful killing of a human being is imposed in this life and in the Hereafter (surah 4.93). Moreover, it propounds that neither poverty nor hunger should cause one to kill one's offspring (surah 17.31). Insofar as the *ḥadīth* is concerned, mention is made of an incident wherein a woman approached the prophet Muḥammad, informing him that she had committed adultery. He commanded that the punishment for adultery (stoning to death) be effected only after she had delivered and weaned the baby (Karim, 1939, vol. 2, pp. 538–540).

From these original sources, Muslim jurists deduce the sanctity of human life and unanimously hold abortion to be blameworthy (Naciri, 1973, p. 144). They then face the problem of determining the gravity of the crime, hence the appropriate punishment. Their deliberations on this matter revolve around the quality of personhood contained in the fetus. The word janīn ("fetus"; pl. *ajinnah*) literally stands for "that which is veiled or covered" (Lane, 1955, vols. 1–2, pp. 463). The Qur'ān refers to *janīn* as the procreated being inside the woman's body, irrespective of the stage of its development (surah 53.32). However, commentators on the

Qur'ān *(mufassirūn)* hold that the words *khalqan ākhar* ("another act of creation"), which appear in surah 23.13, signify the ensoulment of the fetus (Musallam, 1983; p. 54). The *ḥadīth* contain at least two vital citations relating to the fetus. In one it is stated that organ differentiation occurs forty nights after fertilization. In another, ensoulment of the fetus is said to occur 120 days after conception (Muslim [trans. Siddiqi], 1976, vol. 4, pp. 1391–1392).

Thus, Muslim scholars differ in their definition of the fetus. Some maintain simply that the fetus stands for that which is in the womb (Ebrahim, 1989 , p. 73). Others, including the Islamic jurist al-Shāfiʿī, hold that the "fetus" is initiated after the stages of *al-mudghah* ("the chewed lump") and *al-ʿalaqah* (something that clings) have been completed; only then can a human possessing differentiated characteristics, such as fingers, nails, or eyes, be clearly identified (al-Būṭī, 1976, p. 197). A third group uses the word *janīn* to mean that which exists in the womb after the ensoulment has taken place (Madkūr, 1969, p. 32). However, despite these differences in interpretation, there is consensus among scholars that, after the ensoulment of the fetus, abortion constitutes homicide and is thus liable to penalty (al-Qaraḍāwī, p. 201).

Legal Rights of the Fetus. The schools of Islamic jurisprudence allot certain rights to the fetus. First, the fetus is accorded the right to life, that is, the right to be born and to live as long as God permits. Thus, in the event of the death penalty being passed on a pregnant woman, the sentence may only be carried out after delivery and provisions have been made for the child to be suckled by a wet nurse. The Shāfiʿī school provides that the belly of a pregnant woman who has died be cut open in order to give the fetus a chance to survive (Ebrahim, 1989, p. 76).

Second, the fetus has a right to inheritance. The fetus cannot, according to the *sharīʿah*, inherit while still in the womb, but the law provides that the inheritance be kept in abeyance for various practical reasons until birth occurs (Madkūr, 1969, pp. 287–288). In the case of a fetus being stillborn, there is no question of existence (Ibn ʿĀbidīn, 1979, vol. 2, p. 228). Shares of the inheritance are determined after birth, on the basis of the infant's sex.

Third, the *sharīʿah* provides that a stillborn baby or miscarried fetus has the right to a burial. Babies who die before uttering any sound should be given the ceremonial bath *(al-ghusl)* and a name, placed in a white cloth *(kafan)*, and then buried. These provisions apply to both formed and unformed fetuses (Ibn ʿĀbidīn, 1979, vol. 2, p. 228). The only difference between the burial of a human being and that of a stillborn or miscarried fetus is that no prayer is said for the latter.

Concept of "Therapeutic Abortion." The Ḥanafī jurists render abortion permissible up to 120 days after conception and only for a juridically valid reason (Khan, 1979, p. 101). "Therapeutic abortion" before the fourth month of pregnancy may be sanctioned in the following cases: (1) if the doctors fear that the pregnant mother's life is in danger; (2) if the pregnancy may result in causing a disease to the mother; and (3) if a second pregnancy severely reduces the mother's ability to lactate while her infant is completely dependent on her milk for survival (al-Būṭī, 1976, pp. 96–99).

Although the mother's life takes precedence over that of the fetus, priorities change should the mother's life be in danger after the fourth month of pregnancy. Muslim jurists hold that, since ensoulment occurs after 120 days, the fetus has a right to life equal to that of the mother. This dilemma is resolved through application of a general principle of the *sharīʿah*: choosing the lesser of the two evils. Rather than losing both lives, the life of the mother should be given preference over that of the fetus. For the mother is the origin of the fetus, established in life, with duties and responsibilities, and is also a pillar of the family (al-Qaraḍāwī, p. 202).

[*See also* Family Law; Family Planning; Surrogate Motherhood.]

BIBLIOGRAPHY

ʿAlī, ʿAbdallāh Yūsuf, trans. *The Holy Qur'ān: Text, Translation, and Commentary*. New rev. ed. Brentwood, Md., 1989.

Būṭī, Muḥammad Saʿīd Ramaḍān al-. *Taḥdīd al-Nasl*. Damascus, 1976.

Ebrahim, Abul Fadl Mohsin. *Abortion, Birth Control, and Surrogate Parenting: An Islamic Perspective*. Indianapolis, 1989.

Ibn ʿĀbidīn, Muḥammad Amīn Ibn ʿUmar. *Ḥāshiyat Radd al-Muḥtār ʿalā al-Durr al-Mukhtār*. 8 vols. Beirut, 1979.

Karim, Fazlul. *Al-Hadis*. 4 vols. Lahore, 1939.

Khan, M. E. *Family Planning among Muslims in India: A Study of the Reproductive Behaviour of Muslims in an Urban Setting*. New Delhi, 1979.

Lane, Edward William. *Arabic-English Lexicon*. 8 vols. New York, 1955.

Madkūr, Muḥammad Salām. *Al-Janīn: Al-Aḥkām al-Mutaʿalliqah bihi fī al-Fiqh al-Islāmī*. Cairo, 1969.

Musallam, Basim F. *Sex and Society in Islam*. London, 1983.

Muslim ibn al-Ḥajjāj al-Qushayrī. *Ṣaḥīḥ Muslim*. 4 vols. Translated by ʿAbdul Hamid Siddiqi. Lahore, 1976.

Naciri, Mohamed Mekki. "A Survey of Family Planning in Islamic

Legislation." In *Muslim Attitudes toward Family Planning*, edited by Olivia Schieffelin, pp. 129–145. New York, 1973.

Qaraḍāwī, Yūsuf al-. *The Lawful and the Prohibited in Islam*. Indianapolis, n.d. (1980?).

ABUL FADL MOHSIN EBRAHIM

ABŪ DHARR AL-GHIFĀRĪ (d. 652), companion of the prophet Muḥammad and focus of modern ideological debate. As in the case of many other companions of the Prophet, we have a few reports about Abū Dharr's life and his relation to the early Islamic community. Most of these reports, however, reflect the early schisms of Islamic history. Abū Dharr Jundub ibn Junādah al-Ghifārī reportedly came to meet the prophet Muḥammad in Mecca. He was one of the earliest converts to Islam and brave enough to announce this to the Quraysh. The Quraysh seized him and would have killed him had they not been reminded of his clan's strategic position on their trade route. This may have been the reason that the prophet Muḥammad asked him to return to his home and call his people to the new religion. Consequently, Abū Dharr did not participate in the early battles between the Muslims and the Quraysh until the conquest of Mecca. Later, after the death of the Prophet, he participated in the early Islamic conquests as an ordinary solider. He became prominent again when he advocated the sharing of the increasingly overflowing Syrian treasury with the poor. He was recalled to Medina by ʿUthmān and exiled sent to Rabdhah, a village near Medina. Abū Dharr died two years before ʿUthmān's assassination (Cameron, 1973, pp. 26–49).

Even though Abū Dharr was not involved in the first great political and religious dissension in Islam, his criticism of ʿUthmān's rule was fertile ground for later Islamic interpretation. The Sunnīs in particular admire his asceticism and piety but play down his criticism of ʿUthmān's rule and the detail of his final exile. Furthermore, they extol his bravery both on the occasion of his conversion in a hostile Mecca and later during the battles. In contrast, the Shīʿīs emphasize his early liaison with ʿAlī and posit him as the ideal supporter of the ʿAlīd cause after the death of Muḥammad. For the latter, Abū Dharr becomes a symbol of an ideal Muslim loyal to the family of the Prophet (Haarman, 1978, p. 285).

In modern times, Abū Dharr has been reincarnated in the debate between Islam and contemporary sociopolitical ideologies. An Egyptian scholar, Muḥammad Sharqāwī, has posited him as the ideal Muslim socialist on the basis of his criticism of hoarding wealth. However, both Shīʿī and the Sunnī *ʿulamā'* have rejected this radical association with a companion of the Prophet. In order to deflect the radicalization of the early Islamic period, the shaykh of al-Azhar, ʿAbd al-Ḥalīm Maḥmūd, even suggested that Abū Dharr was not a companion (Haarman, 1978, p. 286).

Among the Shīʿī *ʿulamā'*, Abū Dharr's status has not been threatened so seriously, but ideological battles also rage over his Islamic and socialist inclinations. ʿAlī Sharīʿatī (d. 1977) translated an Arab biography of Abū Dharr and introduced his Iranian Shīʿī audience to the modern conception of Abū Dharr. Sharīʿatī's Abū Dharr remained the ideal Shīʿī model but now took on the radical dimensions of modern thought, including a rejection of established religion (Sachedina, 1983). Quite expectedly, Iranian *ʿulama'* have rejected this overly material and radical interpretation of the personality of Abū Dharr (Muṭahharī, 1986, pp. 117–118).

[*See also the biography of Sharīʿatī.*]

BIBLIOGRAPHY

Abrahamian, Ervand. "Ali Shariati: Ideologue of the Iranian Revolution." In *Islam, Politics, and Social Movements*, edited by Edmund Burke, III, and Ira Lapidus, pp. 289–297. Berkeley, 1988.

Cameron, Archibald J. *Abû Dharr al-Ghifârî: An Examination of His Image in the Hagiography of Islam*. London, 1973. Exhaustive outline of Abū Dharr in Islamic thought.

Haarman, Ulrich. "Abū Dharr: Muḥammad's Revolutionary Companion." *Muslim World* 68 (1978): 285–289. Critical review of Cameron.

Muṭahharī, Murtaẓā. *Social and Historical Change*. Berkeley, 1986.

Sachedina, A. A. "Ali Shariati: Ideologue of the Iranian Revolution." In *Voices of Resurgent Islam*, edited by John L. Esposito, pp. 191–214. New York and Oxford, 1983.

ABDULKADER I. TAYOB

ʿADĀLAH. *See* Justice.

ADAT. One of the most important structural elements of Islamic society in Southeast Asia is *adat* (Ar., *ʿādāt*), which denotes refined culture and more specifically local custom and indigenous law, established through practice and repeated precedent. In the Malay world *adat* should first of all be viewed as a cultural concept that can be understood only within the context of the historical process of islamization. During this process, largely oral traditions were written down and somewhat reformulated.

From the perspective of those within the culture, *adat* usually has two overlapping meanings. First, *adat* is perceived as an all-embracing term for the rules of behavior and social institutions that the society holds to be legitimate and right. *Adat* is "natural" because its basic foundation is consistent with sacred law. Attachment to Islam as a system of belief is an inseparable part of *adat*. This aspect of *adat* is revealed mostly in traditional historiographies, *adat* aphorisms, and popular sayings. It deals with questions of sacred permanency and unavoidable change.

The second meaning of *adat* refers to local traditions, rules and regulations, and institutional remnants from pre-Islamic times. Like *ʿurf*, it may be a valid legal foundation in Islamic jurisprudence as provided for in the Qur'ān (7.199) and in a *ḥadīth* narrated by Ibn ʿAbbās, to the effect that "those things that are considered good by the *ummah* are also good in the eyes of God."

The numerous local sayings and codified *adat* regulations reflect not only attempts to harmonize the universal religion with local customs, but also the stages by which Islam has penetrated the social fabric of local communities. The early phase of the harmonizing process involved a separation of jurisdiction between secular rulers and religious authorities—as in the seventeenth-century sultanate of Aceh—or between spheres of social activities, as in the case of the matrilineal Minangkabau. The process was complete after a satisfactory principle of unification was found. Thus Acehnese tradition holds that "*Adat* and *hukum* (Ar., *ḥukm;* legal ruling) cannot be separated; their relationship is like the essence *(dzat)* and its characteristics." As the Minangkabau and the Malay in the Malay Peninsula would put it, "*Adat* is based on the religious law; the religious law is based on *Kitabullah* (Ar., *Kitāb Allāh;* "the book of Allāh," i.e., the Qur'ān)." Somewhat different utterances with similar meanings can be found in other communities. The unifying principle might also be found, as in Java, in the integrative power held by the king as the ruler and also the *khalīfah* and the "regulator of religion." In the final analysis, attachment to Islamic doctrine should take precedence over attachment to *adat*.

Structural changes, either originated from within or imposed from without, posed serious challenges to the concept of the integrated harmony of Islamic and *adat* laws and to the continuing validity of the latter regulations. Questions as to the locus of legitimate power in the community, the relationship between the kinship system and inherited property, and the legal right to ancestral and communal land—each with economic and political implications—have been the most crucial issues and the likeliest to be affected by any type of structural change.

The so-called "reception theory," an inseparable part of colonial policy toward Islam, was introduced by the Orientalist Christiaan Snouck Hurgronje in what is now Indonesia. This policy not only sharply redivided jurisdictions between secular rulers and religious authorities but also rather artificially separated those elements of Islamic law that were thought to have been adapted by *adat* and those that remained as in the *fiqh* or jurisprudence books. This theory reached its maturity after "the discovery of *adat*-law" (the title of his book) by the legal scholar Cornelis van Vollenhoven. The "discovery" revealed that the Indonesian communities had always been living under their respective *adat* laws and that there were several *adat* groupings in the Indonesian archipelago. On the basis of these findings, the Dutch colonial government decided that the jurisdiction of the long-established religious court should be sharply curtailed and that the state courts should take *adat* law, instead of Islamic law, as the basis of judicial judgments in civil cases.

With one stroke the colonial government hoped to curb the ethnically integrative appeal of Islam and to slow the penetration of Islam into local communities. It also created a situation in which Indonesian communities continued to live under a multiplicity of legal systems, each with its own defenders and literati. This situation may have contributed to the deepening of the gap between the *ʿulamā'* with their community of *santri* (religious students and, by extension, the devout social groups) and the bureaucratic aristocracy, the heirs of the *kraton* (the palace as the center of power). In Minangkabau, indigenous matriliny and devotion to Islam, with its patrilineal legal bias, have long constituted the two, often competing, pillars of society. On the practical level, the call to integrative harmony has thus had to face the attraction of whatever advantages the multiplicity of legal systems might offer. Despite an ideological attachment to the notion of *Kitabullah* as the overriding legal foundation, the major source of internal conflict has been the varying rules governing inherited property.

The British colonial government in the Malay Peninsula never had a chance to "discover *adat*-law." From the beginning it left "Malay religion and custom," as stated by the Pangkor Agreement (1872) and successive agreements with other Malay rulers, in the hands of the Malay sultans. In theory, at least, the application of either the *adat perpatih,* the matrilineal inheritance law of Negri Sembilan, or the *adat temenggong,* the patrilineal inheritance law of other states, was left to the dynamics of interaction between the *adat* authorities and the changing economic and political realities. As a consequence of this legacy, *adat* may still become a sensitive issue in contemporary local politics.

[*See also* Indonesia; Islam, *article on* Islam in Southeast Asia and the Pacific; Law, *article on* Legal Thought and Jurisprudence; Malaysia; Popular Religion, *article on* Popular Religion in Southeast Asia.]

BIBLIOGRAPHY

Geertz, Clifford. *The Religion of Java.* Glencoe, Ill., 1960. Classic anthropological study on Java in the aftermath of the national revolution and during the young Indonesian republic's experiments with Western-inspired parliamentary democracy. The empirical validity of Geertz's classifications of Javanese cultural orientations as "priyayi," "santri," and "abangan" has been criticized, but because of its analytical rigor, the work remains influential in Indonesian studies.

Hooker, M. B. *Adat Laws in Modern Malaya: Land Tenure, Traditional Government, and Religion.* Kuala Lumpur, 1972. Thorough examination of the workings of *adat* law, dealing with not only all known *adat* digests and the history of respective *adat* communities, but also with the dynamics of the law as reflected in judicial cases.

Josselin de Jong, P. E. de. "Islam versus Adat in Negri Sembilan (Malaya)." *Bijdragen tot Taal-, Land- en Volkenkunde* 116 (1960): 158–203. Interesting study by an anthropologist on a political competition at the local level which took *adat* as the central issue.

Siegel, James T. *The Rope of God.* Berkeley and Los Angeles, 1969. Anthropological study of Aceh, which takes the question of *adat*'s relationship to Islam as one of its central issues. Highly critical of C. Snouck Hurgronje's classic study, *The Achehnese* (Leiden, 1906), on this crucial issue.

Taufik Abdullah. "Adat and Islam: An Examination of Conflict in Minangkabau." *Indonesia* 2 (1966): 1–24. Short introduction to the problems of *adat* and Islam in the Minangkabau region (West Sumatra).

TAUFIK ABDULLAH

ADOPTION.

See Inheritance.

AESTHETIC THEORY.

The absence of a body of written aesthetic theory in Islam before the nineteenth century may be attributed in part to the traditional Islamic disapproval of visual arts and music, but primarily to the lack in Islam of a parallel to the artist's role as it emerged in Europe at the time of the Renaissance. With the exception of great calligraphers, traditional Islamic artists were for the most part anonymous, or their reputations existed within very limited circles of the court or local bazaar. Treatises on music, calligraphy, and painting do exist, but these are mainly technical and pedagogical works. Although there exists in many epochs of Islamic art an implied and widely accepted aesthetic standard, it is very rarely expressed in theoretical writings. Without a theater tradition and with its own distinctive poetic forms, classical Islam ignored Aristotle's *Poetics* and other pre-Islamic formulations of aesthetic theory.

In the nineteenth century this situation gradually changed, primarily in response to contacts with the West and under the impact of European colonialism, but this impact was uneven across the Islamic world. The primary spokesmen for the arts of Islam were at first the colonizers themselves, or, in the case of the Ottoman Empire, Western specialists working for Ottoman patrons. The early works by Europeans dealing with the art of Islamic lands were largely descriptive and often lavishly illustrated with engravings. Some stressed the exotic or picturesque aspects of Islamic art, and expressed the European view that aspects of Islamic art were primitive—primarily its lack of a tradition of sculpture and easel painting, and its use of a high point of view in preference to linear perspective. At the same time, the serious collecting of Islamic art by Europeans began at a time when Europe was granting new status to art forms traditionally among the foremost in Islamic society—the so-called "decorative arts"—through the foundation of the Union des Arts Decoratifs in France and the Arts and Crafts movement in Britain and through the establishment of new museums devoted to such art forms.

Both new and old European art theories influenced the Islamic world profoundly. From the Ottoman Empire artists were sent to Europe to learn Western techniques of painting and means of depicting pictorial space, primarily as an adjunct to military training; at the same time, the establishment of European museums of decorative arts where Islamic works figured prominently caused Islamic artists and writers to look at their own early traditions with new respect. By the turn of the twentieth century various movements to renew or "purify" Islamic art began to emerge in various parts of the Islamic world. In the Ottoman Empire this movement grew out of a nationalist ideology, especially in

FIGURE 1. *Lobby, Safir Hotel, Rabat.* New Moroccan laws require that a certain percentage of construction expenses for all buildings with public areas must be spent on traditional crafts such as wood carving, tile mosaic, and textiles, all seen here in this hotel lobby.

FIGURE 2. *Contemporary Turkish Paper Marbling.* The old Turkish art form of *ebru,* with its ties to traditional music and Ṣūfī mysticism, has been reborn with new technical innovations and a new sense of scale in the work of a number of talented artists. In this work the contemporary master Feridun Özgören has used a series of complex paper masks to create a calligraphic inscription on a richly colored and patterned ground.

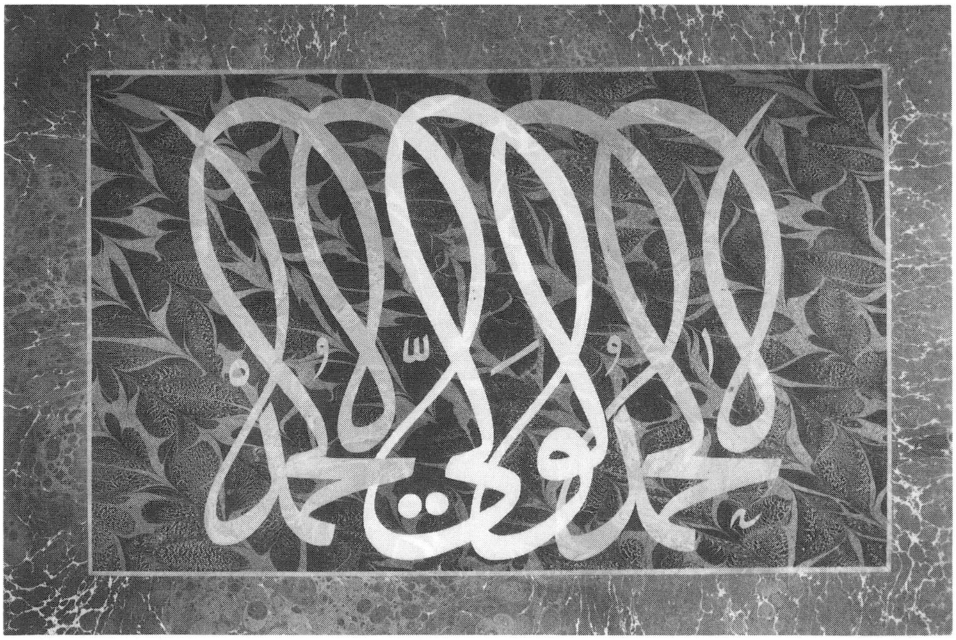

architecture, and resulted in a body of writing that sought the establishment of a true national style in architecture by rejecting the europeanized taste of the nineteenth century and returning to the classical Ottoman style of the fifteenth and sixteenth. In Iran a somewhat similar movement, incorporating historicism and a revival of past glories and applied to many artistic media, arose under the Qājārs. Nationalist writers in the Arab world and to a lesser extent in India decried the artistic influence of the colonial masters, but the structure of colonial educational systems and patronage meant that few artists or architects were able to express the new theories. Between the two World Wars, little changed in the Islamic world; in the meantime, however, European Orientalists had taken a fresh look at early texts, and a more comprehensive view of Islamic aesthetic practice, if not theory, began to emerge in the works of such scholars as Thomas Arnold and Ernst Kuehnel.

Following World War II, with the emerging independence of many Islamic nations, a revolution in aesthetic theory has occurred all over the Islamic world. European converts to Islam and scholars from the Islamic world have sought a new centrality and universality of meaning in Islamic art under the concept of *tawḥīd* or unity, while wrestling with the traditional Islamic proscription against figural images. The emergence of the printing press, television, the cinema, and political democracy with its attendant political imagery have prompted tentative attempts to tackle the theological issues around *taṣwīr* (representational painting). Some have proposed that representation of the human form is not necessarily anti-Islamic, but in fact an important and vital part of Islamic cultural traditions. Islamic religious art has been viewed in new perspectives by European Muslims such as James Dickie, Martin Lings, and Titus Burckhardt, and in the Islamic world by Seyyed Hossein Nasr in Iran and Tharwat ʿUkāshah in Egypt. State-supported "reislamization" of artistic traditions has been attempted with varying degrees of success across the Islamic world, most notably in Morocco, where with the strong backing of King Ḥasan II, laws supporting traditional arts and crafts and even a national movement toward the wearing of traditional clothing have become fundamental pillars of national policy as well as of artistic theory (see figure 1). By contrast, secular Islamic regimes such as Turkey or Baʿthist Iraq have seen the broad development of responses to international artistic styles such as abstract expressionism; Atatürk promoted the study of Western art theory and public art, and today's Turkish students can read Wolfflin, Panofsky, and Umberto Eco in Turkish translation.

The varieties of contemporary aesthetic theory in the Islamic world are enormous, ranging from traditional interpretations of Islamic values on one hand to contemporary international literary theory on the other, and from reinterpretations of traditional Islamic calligraphy, paper marbling, and arabesque to the study of life-drawing with nude models (see figure 2). The resulting conflicts profoundly reflect the deeper dialectic of modern Islamic society and culture. In one area, however, something like consensus may be emerging. Under the aegis of programs established by the Aga Khan Foundation, architects and architectural historians from all over the Islamic world are beginning to communicate with each other and share ideas on what constitutes an Islamic architecture, both as a phenomenon of style and technology and as a response within a unique cultural framework to basic human needs.

[*See also* Aga Khan Foundation; Architecture; Carpets; Painting; Tawḥīd.]

BIBLIOGRAPHY

Arnold, Thomas. *Painting in Islam.* Oxford, 1928. The first major study of the religious environment of Islamic pictorial art.

Beg, Muhammad Abdul Jabbar, ed. *The Fine Arts in Islamic Civilization.* 2d ed. Kuala Lumpur, 1981. Collection of essays on various aspects of art theory and practice in Islam.

Burckhardt, Titus. *Art of Islam: Language and Meaning.* London, 1976. Examines the theoretical and aesthetic principles of Islamic art.

Nasr, Seyyed Hossein. *Islamic Art and Spirituality.* Albany, N.Y., 1987. Discussion of the aesthetics and spirituality of Islamic visual art, music, and literature.

Schimmel, Annemarie. *Calligraphy and Islamic Culture.* New York and London, 1984. Aesthetics and symbolism of the most important Islamic art form in the context of the Islamic mystical tradition.

ʿUkāshah, Tharwat. *The Muslim Painter and the Divine.* London, 1981. Deals with the phenomenon of figural representation of religious themes in Islamic art.

WALTER B. DENNY

AFGHĀNĪ, JAMĀL AL-DĪN AL- (1838/39–1897), writer and Pan-Islamist political activist. Controversial during his lifetime, al-Afghānī has become since his death one of the most influential figures in the Muslim world, even though his written output was rather small. His influence, especially in the twentieth century, may be seen as owing primarily to three factors: he reflected ideas that have become increasingly popular in the Muslim world since the late nineteenth century, including nationalism, Pan-Islamism, and the identification of many new ideas with Islam; he was a charismatic speaker and teacher; and he traveled so widely in the Muslim world that he was able to have a direct impact in several countries.

Life and Activities. Despite his claim to Afghan origin—whence his name—overwhelming evidence shows that al-Afghānī was born and raised in Iran of a Shīʿī family. Among this evidence are several documents in the papers he left in Tehran when expelled from Iran in 1891, of which a catalog was published in 1963. Here and elsewhere there are letters to his Iranian nephews, but no such early documentation is found for Afghanistan, where the first published reference to him dates from World War I and consists of a paraphrase of an Egyptian biography. His passport also identified him as Iranian. Primary documents from Afghanistan in the 1860s, when he was there, speak of him as a foreigner, previously unknown in Afghanistan and speaking Persian like an Iranian.

Sunnī Muslims are often reluctant to admit that al-Afghānī was raised in Shīʿī Iran and did not tell the truth about it. In fact, however, he was operating in a Shīʿī tradition of self-protection and apparently feared repercussions from an Iranian identification. Moreover, he knew he would have less influence in the Sunnī world if he were thought to be from Shīʿī Iran. There is no evidence that he internally identified himself as a Shīʿī, and his Pan-Islamic thinking involved the reduction or removal of Shīʿī-Sunni conflicts.

Documents indicate that after his education in his home town of Asadabad in northwest Iran, and in Qazvin and Tehran, he went for higher education in the 1850s to the Shīʿī shrine cities in Ottoman Iraq. In these cities there was considerable intellectual ferment, with some religious figures following the Shaykhī school of Islam and a few its heretical Bābī offshoot. The earliest treatises found among al-Afghānī's papers and dated from this period are Shaykhī treatises; he annotated them in a way that makes it clear that he followed, at least for a time, this innovative and philosophically oriented school of thought. [*See* Shaykhīyah.] Al-Afghānī's books and papers also confirm the influence of the rationalist Islamic philosophers, especially such Iranian thinkers as Avicenna (Ibn Sīnā) and Naṣīr al-Dīn Ṭūsī.

In his late teens al-Afghānī traveled to India and was almost surely there at or near the time of the Indian Mutiny of 1857. It seems likely that his lifelong hatred of the British, and especially of their power in colonized countries, dates from his contact with them in India. It is also possible, as one later account says, that he was in Iranian Bushire at the time of the British-Persian War of 1857.

Al-Afghānī then seems to have embarked on a slow journey that probably included Mecca, and certainly a trip across Iran into Afghanistan in the early 1860s. According to the Indian who was the British newswriter from Afghanistan at this time, al-Afghānī came to Afghanistan with secret papers (which the newswriter thought were from the Russians) that gained him rapid access to the *amīr*. He was reported as speaking Persian like an Iranian, and also Turkish (widely spoken in northwest Iran), and he was believed to be from Anatolia (he was therefore called Rūmī). His conversations of this period, the earliest ones documented, already have the fiercely anti-British ring that characterizes his whole life. A change in *amīrs* brought a pro-British ruler to the throne, and al-Afghānī's attempts to keep his position failed; he was expelled in late 1868.

In 1869 he went briefly to Cairo and then to the Ottoman capital Istanbul. His intelligence and personality quickly brought him into high circles—those of the Tanzimat reformers then in power. He was involved in the council of education and the new university, where he gave one of a series of public lectures. What he said has been distorted by his followers; a text with quotations from his talk indicates that the main charge against him—that he compared philosophy with prophecy and referred to prophecy as a craft—is true. This is a theme close to those in Iranian philosophy, which was still taught in Iran but considered heretical in Muslim countries to the west of Iran. This speech gave conservative *ʿulamāʾ* an excuse to attack the new university, which they disliked, and the head of the university was compelled to resign, while al-Afghānī was expelled from the country.

From 1871 to 1879 al-Afghānī lived in Cairo, supported by a grant from government funds paid by the statesman Riyāḍ Pasha. He spent most of this time teaching, introducing an interpretation of Islamic philosophy that included restricting rational inquiry to the elite while encouraging orthodoxy among the masses. As Egypt entered a political and financial crisis in the late 1870s, al-Afghānī encouraged his disciples to publish political newspapers; he himself gave speeches and carried out political activities as head of a secret society. His followers included several young men who later became the leaders of Egyptian political and intellectual life, notably his closest disciple, the young Muḥammad ʿAbduh, as well as ʿAbd Allāh Nadīm, Saʿd Zaghlūl, and Yaʿqūb Ṣannūʿ. Al-Afghānī blamed Egypt's plight on both the British and Khedive Ismāʿīl, whom he talked of assassinating. When Ismāʿīl was replaced by Tawfīq in 1879, however, it was the work of the British and French, and Tawfīq responded to al-Afghānī's continued fiery anti-British speeches by expelling him from Egypt. There is no evidence for the common view that the British instigated this expulsion.

Al-Afghānī returned to India, going to the Muslim state of Hyderabad. Here he did much of his important writing, an activity he generally disliked; many of his writings are actually transcriptions of talks. He wrote a series of articles and his most famous treatise, known in English under the title *The Refutation of the Materialists.* It was intended mainly to refute the work of the pro-British (though liberal) Sayyid Aḥmad Khān. The writings from this and the Egyptian period include a great deal on nationalism (both local Egyptian and Indian, Hindu-Muslim nationalisms), and nothing of the Pan-Islamism with which his name is now associated. That entered his published writings only later. [*See the biography of Aḥmād Khān.*]

At the time of the ʿUrabī revolt in Egypt (1881–1882), al-Afghānī took steps to leave India. Muḥammad ʿAbduh joined him in Paris, where they edited an Arabic newspaper, *Al-ʿurwāh al-wuthqā* ("The Strongest Link," i.e., the Qur'ān). This was sent free throughout the Muslim world; it seems to have been subsidized, evidently partly by the English Arabophile Wilfrid Scawen Blunt. The paper lasted only a year but was very influential; its main themes were Pan-Islamist and anti-British, and it also included theoretical articles. While in Paris al-Afghānī published in the *Journal des débats* a famous "Answer to Renan," in which he appeared at least as skeptical about religion as did Ernest Renan, with whom he disagreed only in saying that Islam and Arabs were no worse than others.

In 1884 al-Afghānī went to Britain, where Blunt presented him to high governmental figures. He became involved in an abortive plan to accompany Sir Henry Drummond Wolff to Istanbul with the aim of inducing Britain to end its occupation of Egypt. Ironically, Blunt's writings on these events persuaded some Muslims to consider al-Afghānī a British spy.

In 1886 al-Afghānī went to Iran, where he gathered liberal disciples, and thence to Russia, where he tried but failed to arouse Russian leaders to go to war against Britain. Returning to Iran in 1890–1891, he encouraged growing activity against the shah's economic concessions to foreigners. A pamphlet against these concessions probably inspired by al-Afghānī brought his expulsion to Iraq in early 1891. Here he wrote a famous anticoncession letter to the leader of the Iranian *ʿulamā'*, Shīrāzī, who later entered the nationwide movement against a tobacco concession to the British. From Iraq al-Afghānī went to Britain, where he joined another reformer, Malkom Khān, in written and spoken attacks on the Iranian government. [*See the biography of Malkom Khān.*]

The Ottoman sultan Abdülhamid II invited al-Afghānī to Istanbul but became increasingly suspicious of him; he was kept in comfort but prevented from publishing or giving speeches. In 1895 he encouraged an Iranian disciple, Mīrzā Riẕā, to kill Nāṣir al-Dīn Shāh. This Mīrzā Riẕā did near Tehran in May 1896. The assassin and three innocent Iranian progressives were executed, but the Iranian government failed in its efforts to extradite al-Afghānī; the Ottomans claimed, though they knew better, that he was an Afghan. In 1897 al-Afghānī died of cancer of the jaw. The illness is well-attested, and no evidence exists for the story that he was poisoned by the sultan.

Al-Afghānī's unusual life was the source of much mythmaking, some of it based on stories that he himself told. Most biographies of al-Afghānī written before his papers became available in 1963 (and many since) derive from biographies by his disciples based on what al-Afghānī wanted people to believe—especially ʿAbduh's biography prefaced to his version of *The Refutation of the Materialists*. Only recently have scholars sought and found independent early documentation.

Contributions to Modern Islam. Whatever the facts of his biography, one cannot deny the importance of al-Afghānī or his contributions to modern Islamic thought and events. It is true that he was not the kind of intellectual who did extensive writing or tried to work out a complex theoretical system. He was rather one who picked up, combined, and developed a number of existing themes to create a novel whole. The following important points may be identified.

From traditional Islamic philosophy al-Afghānī drew a belief in reason and natural law, and a deity who did not contradict these. His background in Muslim philosophy, well documented in texts marked for his teaching in Egypt, allowed al-Afghānī to give his modernizing teaching an Islamic base. He taught what Muslim philosophers advocated: preaching orthodox religion to the masses and a kind of rationalist, natural-law deism to the elite.

His political thought was impelled by hostility to British rule in foreign, especially Muslim lands. Although al-Afghānī expressed himself in friendlier terms toward the French and Russians, his anti-British speeches and writings could be, and were, extended to a more general anti-imperialism that has increased in the Muslim world since his time.

Al-Afghānī is strongly associated with two movements that he did not originate, but that he expressed lucidly and propagated widely. One is nationalism, supported in Egypt with references to the glories of ancient Egypt and in India with praise of the ancient Hindus. The other is Pan-Islamism, which started with the nineteenth-century Ottoman sultans and was then voiced in more progressive, anti-imperialist forms by the Young Ottomans, especially Namık Kemal. As al-Afghānī's works on this subject were written in Arabic, he had more influence internationally than did the Young Ottomans. Nationalism and Pan-Islamism were seen as different but not necessarily contradictory strategies for communal unity and anti-imperialism. [*See* Arab Nationalism; Young Ottomans; *and the biography of Kemal.*]

In keeping with his stress on anti-imperialism and his desire to maintain the independence of Muslim countries, al-Afghānī stressed pragmatic aspects of internal reform and self-improvement, including technical and scientific education. Although some admirers point to al-Afghānī's rare proconstitutional remarks, these were largely limited to Egypt in the late 1870s, when a constitution was a practical issue. He frequently worked with autocratic rulers, and only near the end of his life did he express regret and speak rather of the need to awaken the people.

Al-Afghānī was one of the first modern Muslim figures to be involved in a wide variety of activist political undertakings, accounting for much of his lasting influence. In Egypt he made public speeches, encouraged and wrote in newspapers, and used a masonic lodge for political purposes. In Iran he encouraged opposition to foreign concessions, as well as the formation of secret opposition organizations and the publication of leaflets, and even the assassination of the shah.

It is clear that al-Afghānī's reputation has continued to grow since his death. His chief disciple Muḥammad ʿAbduh, even though he renounced al-Afghānī's political activism, carried on one aspect of al-Afghānī's work when he tried to elaborate modern and pragmatic interpretations of Islam. ʿAbduh's pupil Muḥammad Rashīd Riḍā specifically stressed al-Afghānī's influence, even though Riḍā's more conservative emphasis on Islam was rather different. Together ʿAbduh, Riḍā, and others, chiefly in North Africa, are often characterized as the Salafīyah, those who wanted to go back to the ways of Muḥammad's early followers. Although al-Afghānī occasionally spoke in this way, his ideas did not have a specific Salafī emphasis. He was, however, probably congenial to the Salafīyah because he identified himself as a reforming and activist Muslim. [*See* Salafīyah *and the biographies of ʿAbduh and Rashīd Riḍā.*]

Pan-Islam, in the sense of either a political or a more general unity of Muslim countries as a barrier to further European conquest of Muslim territory, became especially strong after the British conquest of Egypt in 1882, the French protectorate of Tunisia in 1881, and the European taking of Muslim territories in the Russo-Turkish war and the Congress of Berlin in 1877–1878. In the more general sense of Muslim solidarity against the Christian and imperial West, Pan-Islam has continued to be popular to the present. This, combined with his anti-British activities, is one reason al-Afghānī has remained popular in the Muslim world at a time when reformers associated with Westerners, such as ʿAbduh, have lost much popularity.

More generally, al-Afghānī may be said to have had his finger on the pulse of modern Muslim thought, especially that concerned with politics. His status keeps him popular with a variety of sometimes contradictory groups and individuals. Those who stress political reform can cite his few articles on this subject from Egypt; those who stress Islamic principles and values can cite his 1880s articles on Pan-Islamism. Although he was not at all what would now be called an Islamist or fundamentalist, his belief in using certain aspects of Islam to promote a primarily political program shows a temper of thought shared by many Islamists. Nationalists can similarly find support in his program. Thus he is one of the few Muslim thinkers who have retained considerable popularity both in the liberal age of the interwar and immediate postwar years and in the current age of Islamism. He is popular and much discussed, for example, in the Islamic Republic of Iran. Naturally, Islamists do not cite the evidence that he was less than a true believer and that his use of Islamic themes was not only philosophical and rationalist but also largely instrumental.

Al-Afghānī's deliberate use of different arguments in different conditions encourages a variety of interpretations. His legacy of reinterpretation of Islam in a modernist, pragmatic, anti-imperialist direction and his political activism have been of great importance to the modern Muslim world.

[*See also* Modernism; Pan-Islam.]

BIBLIOGRAPHY

ʿAbduh, Muḥammad. *The Theology of Unity*. Translation of *Risālat al-tawḥīd* by Ishaq Musaʿad and Kenneth Cragg. London, 1966. Treatise of modern Islam that reflects the influence of al-Afghānī's philosophical rationalism.

Afghānī, Jamāl al-Dīn al-. *Réfutation des matérialistes*. Translated by Amélie-Marie Goichon. Paris, 1942. French translation, with an intelligent introduction, of al-Afghānī's most important book-length treatise.

Berkes, Niyazi. *The Development of Secularism in Turkey*. Montreal, 1964. The first work to use primary material to demythologize al-Afghānī's first stay in Istanbul.

Browne, Edward G. *The Persian Revolution of 1905–1909*. Cambridge, 1910. Contains important primary documents in translation, although this account contributed to the exaggerated al-Afghānī myth.

Cole, Juan R. I. *Colonialism and Revolution in the Middle East: Social and Cultural Origins of Egypt's Urabi Movement*. Princeton, 1993. The only work to make good use of the Arabic material in al-Afghānī's papers and other early primary sources in Egypt.

Hourani, Albert. *Arabic Thought in the Liberal Age, 1798–1939*. London, 1962. The most intelligent presentation of al-Afghānī before the publication of his papers.

Keddie, Nikki R. *Sayyid Jamāl al-Dīn "al-Afghānī": A Political Biography*. Berkeley, 1972. Biography of al-Afghānī making extensive use of his papers and other primary sources.

Keddie, Nikki R. *An Islamic Response to Imperialism: Political and Religious Writings of Sayyid Jamāl al-Dīn "al-Afghānī."* 2d ed. Berkeley, 1983. English translation of the "Refutation" and of al-Afghānī's most important articles, preceded by an analysis of his life and influence.

Kedourie, Elie. *Afghani and ʿAbduh: An Essay on Religious Unbelief and Political Activism in Modern Islam*. London, 1966. Perhaps overly skeptical, but deserves to be read for its use of new material.

Kudsi-Zadeh, A. Albert. *Sayyid Jamāl al-Dīn al-Afghānī: An Annotated Bibliography*. Leiden, 1970. Thorough bibliography; needs updating.

Mahdavī, Aṣghar, and Īraj Afshār, eds. *Documents inédits concernant Seyyed Jamal al-Din Afghani*. Tehran, 1963. Excellent catalog of the papers and books left by al-Afghānī in Tehran when he was expelled in 1891, covering his adult life to the beginning of exile. In Persian, Arabic, and French.

Smith, Wilfred Cantwell. *Islam in Modern History*. Princeton, 1957. Classic and still useful analysis.

NIKKI R. KEDDIE

AFGHANISTAN. In the nineteenth century Afghanistan emerged as a buffer state between the contending British Indian and tsarist Russian colonial empires. This overwhelmingly Muslim (more than 99 percent), landlocked nation covers an area of 647,500 square kilometers consisting primarily of rugged mountains, deep valleys, deserts, and arid plateaus. Situated in the heart of Asia, it has been an important crossroads for diverse peoples and their cultural and religious traditions. Neither the actual size nor the ethnic composition of the population is known because no complete national census has ever been taken. In 1986/87 the United Nations High Commission for Refugees (UNHCR) estimated the total population at 16.7 million, with 11 million living inside Afghanistan, and 5.7 million who were then refugees (2.4 million in Iran, 3.2 million in Pakistan, and .1 million in other parts of the world). Since April 1992, following the collapse of the Soviet-installed Communist regime in Kabul, some refugees have returned to rural areas and provincial towns. However, continuing factional fighting among the Afghan Mujāhidīn (Islamist resistance groups) for control of Kabul has resulted in further displacement of hundreds of thousands of people, most of them to Pakistan.

Estimates of the proportions of ethnic groups (based on language and sectarian affiliation) in Afghanistan are highly contested and increasingly politicized. In the early 1970s, Louis Dupree (*Afghanistan*, Princeton, 1973, pp. 58–64), offered the following estimates: Pashtun, 47 percent; Tajik-Farsiwan-Aimaq, 35 percent; Uzbek, Turkmen, and Kirghiz, 8 percent; Hazara, 7 percent; Baluch-Barahui, 2.5 percent; and other Muslim and non-Muslim groups, including Hindus, Sikhs, and Jews, 0.5 percent. Based on Dupree's estimates, Sunnīs constitute 88 percent and Shīʿīs (primarily Imāmī and some Ismāʿīlī) 12 percent of the Muslim population. Dupree used official information provided by the Pashtun-dominated government and assumed the total population to be about 14 million. At present, by contrast, the Shīʿī political groups claim that Shīʿīs constitute 20 to 25 percent of the national population and are demanding proportional representation.

Historically, Muslim Arab armies penetrated the region at the turn of the eighth century CE. Many Muslim empires rose in the area during the following centuries and expanded the frontiers of Islam into Central and South Asia. Modern Afghanistan is the remnant of one of the last such great Muslim empires in the region, the Durrānī empire founded by Aḥmad Shāh Durrānī (r.

1747–1772). The Durrānī empire began to disintegrate at the turn of the nineteenth century owing to bloody struggles over succession as well as growing external military and political pressures. The prolonged fratricidal wars (1800–1880) encouraged British and Russian colonial encroachments, resulting in two Anglo-Afghan Wars (1839–1842 and 1879–1880) and considerable territorial losses. These civil wars and colonial interventions left powerful legacies, notably the increasing economic, military and technological dependence of Afghan governments on European colonial and postcolonial powers.

The effects of foreign assistance and interventions began immediately after the Second Anglo-Afghan War (1879–1880), when Britain installed Amīr ʿAbd al-Raḥmān Khān (1880–1901), a member of the Muḥammadzai branch of the Durrānīs. With substantial annual British subsidies and technical assistance, Amīr ʿAbd al-Raḥmān, the "Iron Amīr," consolidated power over the entire country. Unlike his predecessors, Amīr ʿAbd al-Raḥmān believed that his power as amir emanated directly from God rather than from the support of the people or tribal khans. He took the title Ziʾul Millati wal-Dīn (Light of the Nation and the Faith) and claimed that God's purpose in honoring him with his "vice-regency" was to avert the threat of foreign aggression against Afghanistan and to safeguard it from further internal disturbances. He forcibly converted the peoples of Kafiristan, the only remaining indigenous non-Muslims in the country, and renamed their territory Nuristan (Land of Light). In an attempt to pacify the recalcitrant Hazara Shīʿīs of central Afghanistan, he labeled them "infidels" and declared a *ghazawāt* or *jihād* against them.

The Iron Amir justified his cruel policies by systematically dressing the monarchy in an Islamic cloak. As head of an Islamic state, the amir claimed to be the sole interpreter of religious doctrine and proclaimed that "whether just or despotic, the king must be obeyed, provided his commands do not violate the *sharīʿah*." Suspected enemies were killed, forced to exile, or detained in the capital, or their young sons were held hostage as *ghulām bachagān* (court page boys). The amir's disingenuous use of Islam in this manner was not without precedent. His policies differed only in the rigorous articulation and effective utilization of the main operative principles of Afghan political culture—ideals of kingship, kinship, and Islam, buttressed by patron-client and patrimonial practices and by politics of fear and favor (*zūr wa zar*). He weakened the pervasive role of *ʿulamāʾ* and *mashāyikh* (Ṣūfī leaders) in the management of Islamic education and civil society and claimed these tasks for the state. Administration of *awqāf* (Muslim endowments; sg., *waqf*) and Muslim education were incorporated into the state apparatus. *Sharīʿah* courts were set up throughout the country and settlement of disputes outside the state courts forbidden. For the first time in the history of the country, books of sermons and guidelines for preaching were published and widely disseminated; many of these are still used in the *masājid-i jāmiʿ* (great mosques) in Afghanistan today. Tribal stratification among the Pashtun, as well as sectarian inequalities favoring Sunnīs over Shīʿīs and Pashtun over non-Pashtun, were institutionalized. The peasantry in general and those in non-Pashtun areas in particular suffered oppressive taxation. Villages replaced tribal and ethnic communities as principal units of administration. These policies produced alienation and resignation among large segments of the rural population, giving rise to the development of smaller, village-based, parallel power structures that enabled the villagers to limit costly contact with state authorities. Amīr ʿAbd al-Raḥmān's policies were maintained unchanged during the reign of his son, Amīr Ḥabīb Allāh (r. 1901–1919).

Toward the end of Ḥabīb Allāh's reign, however, owing to the introduction of modern schools and the press, such new political ideals as constitutionalism, nationalism, liberal secularism, reformism, and Islamic modernism entered the political culture of Afghanistan, both to complement and to compete with the traditional ideals of kingship, kinship, and Islam. These ideals found adherents among the nascent intelligentsia, members of the royal family, the court page boys, and some *ʿulamāʾ*. King Amānullāh (r. 1919–1929), a grandson of Amīr ʿAbd al-Raḥmān and a supporter of modernist-nationalist thought, introduced the first constitution of Afghanistan (1923). He attempted to promote the idea of equality and the development of a national ideology based on traits common to all citizens of Afghanistan, but he failed. His rule was challenged by a popular armed rebellion supported by some conservative *ʿulamāʾ* and *ruḥānī*s (spiritual or Ṣūfī dignitaries), under the banner of a *jihād* against an "infidel king," and he was forced into exile in 1929.

Muḥammad Nādir Shāh (r. 1929–1933), who succeeded King Amānullāh after a nine-month interregnum, attributed his success to "the exclusive help of the Almighty God" and the "sacrifices of the peoples of Afghanistan." Nādir Shāh abandoned many of Amānullāh's western-inspired reforms, but he attempted to legitimize his own dynastic rule by constitutional means. He called a Grand Assembly (Loya Jirga) of the tribal elders, religious dignitaries, and local aristocrats to ratify a new constitution (1931). [*See* Loya Jirga.] He established a Jamʿīyatul ʿUlamā' (Supervisory Council of Muslim Scholars), ordered the country's first printing of the Qur'ān, removed restrictions on the role of the mullahs and *mawlawīs* (Muslim scholars) in education, reaffirmed the absolute primacy of Ḥanafī *sharīʿah* in the country, closed girls' schools, and formally sanctioned gender inequalities. Reverting to Amīr ʿAbd al-Raḥmān's practices, both civil and criminal cases were brought within the domain of *sharīʿah* courts, making them the most important vehicles of centralization. Southeastern frontier Pashtun tribes that had helped him in his bid for power were granted exemptions from taxes and conscription, and members of the influential Mujaddidī family of *ruḥānīs* were awarded cabinet posts for their support. Discrimination against non-Pashtuns became rampant in the allocation of economic, educational, and developmental resources. Many rural aristocrats were coopted by the Musahiban monarchy by being either elected to or selected for the newly established rubber-stamp bicameral parliament (Majlis-i Shūrā wa A'yān).

The Musahiban rulers (1929–1978) pursued ambivalent policies toward Islam, especially in the expanding modern educational system. Islam was presented in the curriculum simply as a body of rituals and legal injunctions rather than as a vibrant religious doctrine compatible with modern living. The educational system had a secularist agenda devoid of any coherent or viable moral and political ideology aside from Pashtun-based nationalism. In the absence of a clearly articulated and commonly held moral purpose to guide state policies and political processes, nation-building and the so-called modernization programs in the form of Demokrasi-i Now (New Democracy) turned out to be nothing more than a few staged "democratic" procedures, such as voting for rubber-stamp parliaments, and a "free" press. Therefore, during the crucial decades of the 1960s and 1970s, when economic development programs were failing and development-related corruption was rampant, Afghan leaders became preoccupied with introducing Western-style governance to appease their foreign patrons, instead of extending social services and equitably meeting the needs of all citizens.

After the promulgation of the liberal constitution of 1964 and the onset of New Democracy in Afghanistan, Marxist and Maoist parties were formed. In response, Islamist movements began to emerge, not only to address the potential communist threat but also to challenge the legitimacy of the Musahiban monarchy. The rise of both communist and Islamist parties and movements—each with ideological ties and financial patrons (actual or potential) outside the country—was without precedent in the political history of Afghanistan. The government's dependence on foreign assistance for economic development programs and the maintainance of its large military and police forces had also reached new heights.

Specifically, the Afghan state depended overwhelmingly on Soviet patronage for its survival. Hence the government strongly opposed the Islamist movements, while the communist groups, especially the pro-Soviet Marxist parties, were given free rein. As a consequence, in July 1973 Prince Muḥammad Dā'ūd, a former prime minister (1953–1963) and paternal first cousin of King Zāhir Shāh (r. 1933–1973)—also a long-time royal supporter of the pro-Soviet Marxists—staged a military coup, abolished the monarchy, and proclaimed himself president of the Republic of Afghanistan (1973–1978). Only five years later Dā'ūd himself fell victim to a coup led by the People's Democratic Party of Afghanistan (PDPA) that ended Durrānī dynastic rule by establishing a communist government (1978–1992). The Islamist movements, already seriously weakened by the monarchy and Dā'ūd's regime, suffered devastating new attacks from the Marxist government. Ironically, however, the usurpation of state power by the PDPA and the direct military intervention of the former Soviet Union (1979–1989) offered the fledgling Islamist movements a new lease on life.

Islamist revolutionary ideas were brought to Afghanistan from Egypt in the 1950s by a few Afghan scholars studying at al-Azhar University in Cairo and by al-Azhar shaykhs teaching at the Faculty of Sharāʿīyāt (Islamic Studies) at Kabul University. The Islamist political movement emerged on the campus of Kabul University, initially with an underground faculty wing and a public student branch, the Nahẓat-i Javānān-i Musulmān (Muslim Youth Movement). Unlike earlier rural-centered *jihād* movements mobilized exclusively to oppose outside colonial forces or the allegedly un-Islamic policies of a particular ruler, the new Islamist movement was urban-centered, organized and led by educated youth who questioned the legitimacy of the existing political system, and it called for the positive radical transformation of power relations through the establishment of an Islamic government. The Islamist movement attracted mostly provincial and rural youth who were studying in Kabul and other major towns. Before the Marxist coup they had few active supporters among traditionally educated *ʿulamāʾ* and *mashāyikh,* especially in the rural areas. However, following the PDPA coup, elements of the Islamist groups living in exile in Pakistan and elsewhere quickly joined with traditional tribal and religious leaders in rural areas to launch a nationwide popular armed struggle, a *jihād,* that eventually drove out the invading Soviet army (1989), defeated the Afghan communists, and declared Afghanistan an Islamic state (April 1992).

Their apparent military triumph, however, has gradually deteriorated into humiliating and bloody interethnic and sectarian warfare. The vastly popular Islamist armed struggle, despite its remarkable military success, did not produce a coherent Islamic ideology or political unity. The manner in which an Islamist victory by Afghan Mujāhidīn has turned into a spectacular political and ideological defeat raises serious doubts about the future viability of militant Islamist political struggles. This is especially true in the minds of those educated Muslim youth who saw a ray of hope after the Afghan Mujāhidīn triumphed.

The tensions currently undermining the Muhājidīn are rooted in the recent history of Islamist movements in Afghanistan. The *jihād* struggle was spearheaded and sustained by two major factions of the original Islamist movement: the Jamʿīyat-i Islāmī (Islamic Society) headed by Burhanuddin Rabbani, an al-Azhar-educated former professor of Islamic studies; and the Ḥizb-i Islāmī (Islamic Party) led by Gulbuddin Hekmatyar, a former undergraduate engineering student at Kabul University. This factional difference mirrored in part the split in the Ikhwan al-Muslimūn (Muslim Brotherhood) movement in Egypt. Rabbani favored Ḥasan al-Bannā's moderate populist approach seeking to effect change from the bottom up. Hekmatyar, by contrast, favored the more radical strategies of Sayyid Quṭb and his more militant followers, the Hijrat wa al-Takfīr faction led by Omar Abdel Rahman (ʿUmar ʿAbd al-Raḥmān), that called for change from above through capturing state power. [*See* Muslim Brotherhood, *article on* Muslim Brotherhood in Egypt; *and the biography of Abdel Rahman.*]

The impact of these differences in Rabbani's and Hekmatyar's political outlooks—combined with their distinct ethnic affiliations (Rabbani is Tajik and Hekmatyar Pashtun) and serious interpersonal tensions—became evident when the two leaders took refuge in Pakistan. In the economically and politically volatile environment of the Afghan exile community in Peshawar, animosities and factional conflicts flourished.

Two other developments also played a significant role in the creation and perpetuation of factional divisions within the *jihād* movements in Afghanistan. First, the Pakistan government created or officially recognized five additional, primarily Pashtun-dominated resistance organizations. These groups included two led by traditional *ʿulamāʾ* (Mawlawī Yūnus Khāliṣ and Mawlawī Muḥammad Nabī Muḥammadī), two led by *ruḥānī* families (Ṣibghat Allāh Mujaddidī and Sayyid Aḥmad Gīlānī) with strong ties to the defunct monarchy, and one led by another al-Azhar-educated former Kabul University professor, ʿAbd al-Rabb Rasūl Sayyāf. In addition, at least eight Shīʿī resistance groups were organized in Iran and one in Pakistan. The Iranian groups have formed an alliance called Waḥdat-i Islāmī (Islamic Unity), led by Muḥammad ʿAlī Mazārī. Scores of other nonofficial Mujāhidīn groups active in the resistance complemented these groups.

Second, nearly all these groups were or still are headquartered in neighboring Pakistan and Iran and are completely dependent on outside sources, both Muslim and non-Muslim, for money and arms. Because of direct Soviet intervention, there were no shortages of foreign supporters, both covert and overt, especially during the Reagan era, to help defeat and destroy the former USSR. Mujāhidīn parties and organizations representing many diverse (ideological, sectarian, ethnolinguistic, tribal, regional, and local) interest groups competed with one another for the patronage of numerous international aid organizations.

The reason for the political and ideological failure of the Mujāhidīn was the fact that their numerous foreign patrons gradually but systematically subordinated the Islamist ideological purpose of *jihād* to their own anti-communist and anti-Soviet military objectives. Therefore, as soon as Soviet troops withdrew, external sponsors drastically reduced support to the Mujāhidīn and even encouraged factional fighting to undermine their Islamic "fundamentalist" objectives.

Undoubtedly, both Islam's role in Afghan politics and the Mujāhidīn commitment to Islamist ideology faced their most serious test at the moment of their military victory. Specifically, when an arrangement between the forces of Aḥmad Shāh Masʿūd, a Tajik Mujāhidīn commander, and ʿAbd al-Rashīd Dūstam, a powerful Uzbek leader of a militia force in northern Afghanistan, brought about the collapse of Dr. Najibullah's Marxist government in Kabul, the Mujāhidīn had a chance to end the war and establish a credible Islamic government. They failed because of powerful feelings of mistrust, encouraged by their foreign patrons, among the factions.

On the fall of the communist regime, the forces of the Iranian-backed Islamic Unity coalition of eight Shīʿī and other predominantly Hazara groups had occupied significant areas of Kabul. Dūstam, forming and leading the National-Islamic Movement of Northern Afghanistan (Junbush-i Millī-i Islāmī-i Shimālī Afghānistān), demanded a role in the new Islamic State of Afghanistan. Similarly, other armed and newly empowered ethnic and sectarian minorities, such as the traditionally oppressed Shīʿī Hazaras, asked for fair representation in the new government.

Pashtun groups, notably those led by Sayyāf and Hekmatyar, responded by armed attacks against Masʿūd, Dūstam, and the Shīʿī coalition forces in and around Kabul. Sayyāf, who enjoys the support of powerful Saudi patrons and has introduced controversial Wahhābi practices, began armed attacks against the pro-Iranian Shīʿī Islamic Unity group. Hekmatyar, formerly willing to recruit Pashtun communist officers for his failed military coups against the communist regime, condemned Aḥmad Shāh Masʿūd's alliance with Rashīd Dūstam's militia. He opposed the inclusion of members of Dūstam's militia in the government while welcoming numerous high-ranking communist Pashtun military officers into his own camp. Hekmatyar's devastating rocket attack against Kabul was apparently motivated by fear that non-Pashtun minorities might dominate the central government.

The present succession crisis has extensive historical precedents. Many Afghan leaders have employed Islam to manage kingship, kinship, and ethnicity, to further two often contradictory state goals. That is, Islam has been utilized both to universalize, homogenize, and integrate the diverse elements of society and also to differentiate and divide groups. Leaders used Islam as a unifying force most effectively in confrontations with non-Muslim forces—offensively in the Durrānī empire's expansionary wars in northern India, and defensively in *jihāds* against the encroaching Sikhs and the British in the nineteenth century, and more recently against the Afghan communists and their invading Soviet sponsors. From these experiences, a positive and constructive relationship between Islam and the political independence and integrity of the country has emerged, albeit with heightened feelings of xenophobia. At the same time, these conditions have offered *ʿulamāʾ* and *ruḥānīs*, as well as local khans, opportunities for political and military leadership. This development has generally worked against the domestic centralizing aims of the state.

Domestically, monarchs who deployed Islam to legitimize a policy of divide and rule found their efforts did not help to consolidate power and were harmful to nation-building. At the national level, the most significant examples are the Shīʿī-Sunnī riots in Kabul in the first decade of the nineteenth century and Amīr ʿAbd al-Raḥmān's wars against the Shīʿī Hazara of central Afghanistan. On the local level, conflicts among tribal and ethnic communities (and at present among rival Mujāhidīn political parties and factions), or even among individuals, often escalate to moral conflicts justified on Islamic grounds, arousing intense emotion. Conflicts between Pashtun and Hazara, as well as among Hazara and Sunnī Tajiks and Uzbeks in northern Afghanistan (Turkistan) during the nineteenth century, provide additional examples of ethnic wars that escalated to *jihād*. Afghan governments and the outside patrons of recent *jihād* alike have perpetuated communal tensions in pursuit of political advantage.

From the perspective of Afghan citizens, the legitimacy of governments (*ḥukūmat*) and the state (*dawlat*) has always depended, in the first place, on the responsibility of the state as the defender of Islam and the homeland, and secondarily on the peoples's perception of the personal piety and dignity of the rulers and government officials. Periods of popular support coincide with the reigns of kings who were considered pious and just (such as Aḥmad Shāh Durrānī) or of leaders who were directly engaged in defense of Islam and the nation. By contrast, popular opposition arose when the personal integrity and piety of the ruler and his officials were questioned, and when the sincerity and ability of the government to defend Islam were in doubt. The revolt against Amānullāh and the recent *jihād* against Khalq-Parcham Marxists and their Soviet protectors are the most obvious examples.

The participation of so many international actors, Muslim and non-Muslim, during the armed resistance against the Soviets has had a mixed outcome for the Islamist movements of Afghanistan. Although outside patrons of *jihād* helped the Mujāhidīn win a military victory, these patrons also engaged, directly or indirectly, in fanning the flames of ethnic and sectarian conflicts in post-communist Afghanistan. Sadly, the flames of factional war have consumed not only Kabul but also the credibility of the Islamist ideology, and with it the cherished hopes of millions of Muslims worldwide.

[*See also* Durrānī Dynasty; Ḥizb-i Islāmī Afghānistān; Mujāhidīn, *article on* Afghan Mujāhidīn; *and the biography of Hekmatyar.*]

BIBLIOGRAPHY

ʿAbd al-Raḥmān Khān. *The Life of Abdur Rahman, Amir of Afghanistan* (1900). 2 vols. Edited by Sultan Mahomed Khan. Oxford and New York, 1980. Alleged autobiography of the *amīr*, informative about his views on Afghan society and polity.

Arnold, Anthony. *Afghanistan's Two-Party Communism: Parcham and Khalq*. Stanford, 1983. Well-researched and documented account of the history and development of pro-Soviet Communist parties.

Banuazizi, Ali, and Myron Weiner, eds. *The State, Religion, and Ethnic Politics: Afghanistan, Iran, and Pakistan*. Syracuse, N.Y., 1986. Part 1 of the volume consists of four analytical essays on state-building, ethnicity, and Islam in Afghanistan.

Bradsher, Henry S. *Afghanistan and the Soviet Union*. Durham, N.C., 1985. Serious examination of Soviet involvements in Afghanistan before and after the intervention.

Dupree, Louis. *Afghanistan*. Princeton, 1980. Valuable reference on the general history and ethnography of the country.

Gregorian, Vartan. *The Emergence of Modern Afghanistan: Politics of Reform and Modernization, 1880–1946*. Stanford, Calif., 1969. Excellent and thorough analysis of the rise and development of the Afghan state.

Kakar, M. Hasan. *Government and Society in Afghanistan: The Reign of Amir ʿAbd al-Rahman Khan*. Austin and London, 1979. Fine documentation of the *amīr*'s policies, based on vernacular and Western sources.

Poullada, Leon B. *Reform and Rebellion in Afghanistan, 1919–1929: King Amanullah's Failure to Modernize Tribal Society*. Ithaca, N.Y., and London, 1973. Useful but conventional interpretation of Amānullāh's disastrous attempt at political reform.

Roy, Olivier. *Islam and Resistance in Afghanistan*. 2d ed. Cambridge, 1991. Insightful analysis of the role of Islam and Mujāhidīn in the armed resistance against the Soviets.

Shahrani, M. Nazif, and Robert Canfield, eds. *Revolutions and Rebellions in Afghanistan: Anthropological Perspectives*. Berkeley, 1984. Collection of essays examining the social and historical contexts of the local-level armed resistance, in various parts of the country, to Communist coup and Soviet intervention.

Tapper, Richard, ed. *The Conflict of Tribe and State in Iran and Afghanistan*. London, 1983. Contains several excellent articles on Afghanistan.

M. NAZIF SHAHRANI

AFGHAN MUJĀHIDĪN. *See* Mujāhidīn, *article on* Afghan Mujāhidīn.

AFRICAN LANGUAGES AND LITERATURES. [*This entry articulates the themes and values in the languages and literatures of Muslims in sub-Saharan Africa. Reflecting major linguistic divisions, it comprises two articles:* East Africa *and* West Africa. *For discussion of the literatures of North Africa, see* Arabic Literature. *See also* Islam, *article on* Islam in Sub-Saharan Africa.]

East Africa

Islam was brought to the peoples of eastern Africa mainly by settlers who arrived either by land, traveling up the Nile, or by sea, crossing the Red Sea or the Indian Ocean. Since the Arab conquest of Egypt (641 CE), the cultures of many East African peoples have become entirely Islamic. Some nations were only partially islamized because Islam became dominant only in part of their territory, or only in the cities; examples are the speakers of Amharic, Gurage, and Oromo in Ethiopia. Apart from a few examples, most African ethnic groups have been islamized wholly, or not at all. This demonstrates that individual conversions to Islam are, or were, rare, although they are the rule in Christianity. Most conversions of a nation or tribe probably took place after the king or chief was converted to Islam. Some nations, such as the Nubian kingdom of the Middle Ages, were fragmented under the impact of Islam; others, such as the Nilotic peoples, have resisted Islam throughout history. Unlike the hard-hit Nubians, most African peoples retained their cultural identity and individuality after islamization; for example, the Somali and the Swahili, though neighbors and both adherents of the Shāfiʿī school, are very different in culture and cosmology.

Languages. The islamized peoples of East Africa speak the following major languages, from north to south.

Nubian was the literary language of the Nubian kingdom, which survived until around 1400 CE. Manuscripts in Coptic script on Christian subjects are still being discovered. At present the Nubians are islamized, but no Islamic literature is known to have been composed in Nubian; the scribes write Arabic.

Bedawiye or Beja is a Cushitic language spoken on the Red Sea coast of the Sudan. The Beja were islamized well before the Nubians, but they are not known to have developed a literary language.

The languages of the eastern Sahara, Teda (Tubu), Zaghawa, Masalit, and Tama-Mararit are only spoken languages. Their speakers use Arabic for all literary purposes.

In the northern three-quarters of Eritrea Tigré is spoken. It is a Semitic language with no significant tradition of writing in either Arabic or Ethiopic script. Afar, spoken in the triangle between the Red Sea, the Awash River, and the escarpment of the Ethiopian High Plateau, also lacks a written tradition in either script.

A number of Bantu languages are spoken south of the Equator by populations including some Muslims. A few Muslim tracts have appeared in Kituba, spoken in Brazzaville. Kingwana is spoken by the Zairean Muslims in Kivu, Shaba, and Kisangani provinces, who write literary Swahili. Yao is spoken in northern Mozambique, extending into Tanzania and Malawi; for literary purposes Swahili is used. Nyanja, the chief language of Malawi, is written by Christians and Muslims using roman script; some tracts have appeared. In Shona, the chief language of Zimbabwe, a life of Muḥammad has been published in roman script by the Zimbabwe Islamic Youth Council.

At least two dialects of the Malagasy language of Madagascar were used for works written in Arabic script before the beginning of the twentieth century. Today the orthography of Merina, the dialect of the capital Tananarive and surrounding districts, is so well established that all writers, Christian and Muslim, write their works in it.

The Bantu language Makua is spoken in northern Mozambique along the coast near the Tanzanian border. The Makua have been islamized for several centuries. A few manuscripts in Makua in Arabic script are known to exist. The so-called Zanzibaris, the Muslims of Natal, numbering about five thousand, speak Makua among themselves.

Literature. The contents of Islamic literatures of eastern Africa are fairly similar in Ethiopia and Somalia as well as along the Swahili coast. The prose works comprise chronicles and other history texts, such as biographies of the prophet Muḥammad, the Biblical prophets, ʿAlī, Ḥusayn, and Ṣūfī saints; there are also works on *fiqh, sharīʿah, tawḥīd,* and astrology.

As in all Islamic literatures, East African poetry is a splendid contribution to art. Verse translations of Arabic poems have been made in many languages; for example, the *Burdah* of al-Buṣīrī is popular in both Fulani and Swahili. In Swahili, there are half a dozen poetic versions of the Miʿrāj, Muḥammad's journey to heaven, but none has been traced to an external origin. This type of popular religious poetry, composed by scholars, helps to spread Islamic ideas among all segments of the population.

Egyptian influence. Ever since Arabic and Islam came to dominate Egypt it has played a leading role in Africa, radiating Islamic culture and literature in all directions. The great jurist and theologian ʿAbdallāh al-Shāfiʿī (d. 820) spent the last years of his life in Egypt; his legal school spread after his death to most of Egypt, all along the Red Sea and the East African coast, and as far as Malaysia and Indonesia. Even today a large number of the books and pamphlets on *tawḥīd, fiqh,* poetry, or fiction sold in bookstores in Mombasa or Singapore are printed in Egypt. The great Egyptian poet Sharaf ud-Dīn al-Buṣīrī (d. 1296) wrote two long poems in praise of the prophet Muḥammad that became famous throughout Africa—the *Burdah* and the *Hamzīyah,* still recited from Morocco to Indonesia. Both have been translated into Swahili.

Apart from a few classical authors, the vast majority of Arabic literary works that have influenced the Islamic nations of eastern Africa are popular tales, some in poetic form, but most in prose, and not in classical Arabic but in modern colloquial or postclassical written Arabic. These prose works are nearly all printed in Cairo, while the colloquial poetic texts usually circulate in local editions. These printed booklets (only a few can be called books) are of two kinds. The first comprises Islamic legends beginning with the Creation, Adam and Eve, the *Qiṣaṣ al-anbiyāʾ*, the *Sīrah* and the *Qiyāmah,* and ranging to the *Qatl al-Ḥusayn* and lives of the saints *(awliyāʾ).* The other type are popular works on Islamic duties.

Amharic. Amharic is the chief Semitic language of Ethiopia. It is called Amara or Amarinya by its speakers who number well over twenty million people. It is not known when Islam began to penetrate the Ethiopian Highlands, the heartland of the Amharic language, but it appears that at least the eastern part of the country was influenced by Islam from the thirteenth century on. The capital Addis Ababa was founded by the Emperor Menelik II only about a century ago. Its citizens, including more than fifty thousand Muslims, came from various parts of the country and its sixty-seven language groups; they use Amharic as a common language. The

Islamic religious leaders, most of whom are shaykhs of the Qādirīyah order, have learned Arabic, but most of the population know only Amharic. Learned works on Islamic law and theology are in Arabic; the liturgical works in Amharic can be obtained in the three Islamic bookshops of Addis Ababa. Fewer than a dozen such books have been printed; the majority exist only in manuscript form, always in the Amharic script. Here are some fragments of Islamic liturgy, called *zikr* in Amharic (Ar., *dhikr*), intended for recitation.

The Merits of Friday
When the dawn arrives on Friday,
Hell turns into glowing embers.
For the Muslims in the Fire
punishment will be suspended.
Even for the unbelievers
punishment will be much lighter.
Whosoever dies on Friday
will not suffer in the Fire.
On the Friday, by God's favour
will the souls converse together.
On the night preceding Friday
Muslims should perform the *zikr*.
(Freely adapted after Drewes, 1968, p. 15)

Zikr for the Holy Prophet
Prophet whose neck is like a golden flask
whose eyes adorned with black antimony
shine like the moon shines in the darkest night
you are my medicine, my amulet
come quickly, help me, a true slave of God.

Prophet whose fingers shine like stars at night
who leads the faithful into Paradise
we all who say Muḥammad is our guide
we all who make perfection our high goal
may we be safe when Resurrection comes.

Prophet whose calves resemble golden cups
our hearts are pure of sensuality
for soon our bodies will fall into dust
we love you, we are yearning like dry land
for your own love, may it soon fall like rain.

To you God has assigned His Paradise
where virgins clothed in silk, rest on divans
Oh ruler of the world, oh king of kings
you are for me like trousers, like a shirt,
please help me when my soul feels overcome.

You are my shield, my shelter and my sword!
You are my food, my needed beverage.
Please help me when my grave is filled with dirt
to find my words, to answer as I should
the dark and frightening angels of the tomb.
(Freely adapted after Drewes, 1968, pp. 15–16)

Oromo. Also called Galla, Oromo is spoken over a large part of central, western, and southeastern Ethiopia and in northern Kenya; it is a Cushitic language related to Somali. The millions of Oromo speakers are divided by religion: many are Christians; those who live in the Ethiopian province of Arusi are Muslims; and the vast majority still adhere to their indigenous religion.

There is a wealth of oral traditions in Oromo, but very little of this has yet been published. The Islamic traditions in particular are poorly represented; only two publications by B. W. Andrzejewski (1972, 1974) give oral Islamic texts. These are all connected with the veneration of the Islamic saints, whose lives are narrated by the Oromo storytellers in tales full of morals and miracles; praise poems are also recited about the saints' virtues and holiness.

Harari. The Harari language is used for literary works in Arabic script in the city of Harar, eastern Ethiopia. Its chief prose work is the *Kitāb al-Farā'id,* which contains the basic doctrinal and moral precepts of Islam. Much of the poetry in Harari is liturgical, called *zikri* and intended to be recited during nocturnal prayer meetings, often under the supervision of the local leaders of the Qādirīyah. Here are a few of the almost six hundred lines of the *Zikri* of ʿAbd al-Mālik.

Oh Prophet may God's blessing be upon you
we seek our refuge with you from our problems.
You are a medicine for all diseases.
Praying to God for you will be salvation.

Oh Prophet whom the Lord of light created
from light that is more radiant than sunshine.
Oh Prophet who revealed the hidden knowledge,
whose name was first of all the names God mentioned.

Oh God admit the people who have studied
and love the humble servants who implore Thee.
Open for us the shining gate of mercy,
as Thou hast showered mercy on Thy Prophet.

Oh Prophet who hast filled our hearts with splendour,
pray God for us that He may give us blessing.
His blessings have no end and no beginning.
May you guide us towards the gate of Heaven.
(Freely adapted after Drewes, 1976, p. 181)

Gurage. Living in central Ethiopia between the Awash and Omo rivers, the Gurage form a dialect cluster within the subfamily of the Ethiopian Semitic languages. One of their seven tribes, the Silt'e, is islamized. They use their own language for their Islamic literature, as well as Amharic, which at least the educated among them speak well. All are conservative Shāfiʿīs. The men migrate to Addis Ababa once a year after the harvest to earn a supplementary income, and there they learn more about Islam than in their own mountainous countryside.

Islam may have been introduced in east Gurage by missionaries from Harar some three hundred years ago. One female saint, Makkula, is particularly venerated, especially in the Makkula mosque near her grave, where *zikr* is recited every Thursday night. The present leader of the Gurage Muslims is Sayyid Budala Abbaramuz, known as Getoch or Shekhoch, the head of the Qādirīyah order for all the Gurage and the Quṭb (spiritual center) of the age who was created before Adam, so his followers say. He writes his own *zikr* hymns, all in Arabic, which are printed as a liturgy for his followers. Here follows the last stanza of a long poem in praise of Shekhoch, written by a Silt'e Gurage (after Drewes's translation):

> By God's good grace this poem is complete.
> Your faithful follower is drunk with love
> with love for you who were created first.
> Lord may our end be good on the Last Day.
> May his light shine upon us. Bless Muḥammad.

Somali. The Somali language is spoken in the Horn of Africa, the eastern corner of the continent, roughly east of a line running north to south from Djibouti to the point where the Equator meets the Indian Ocean. The Somalis were probably islamized in the late Middle Ages when they still lived in what was to become British Somaliland, whence they expanded south and west during the centuries that followed.

Somali literature was unwritten until 1972 when an orthography based on the roman script was accepted. Numerous books were soon published containing traditional Somali prose and poetry. Originally, the Islamic literature of the Somali was written exclusively in Arabic. Although Andrzejewski (1964) has said that there is no truly Islamic literature in the Somali language, the influence of Islam is well illustrated by the following love poem, composed by a caravan guide.

> No oryx will expose her young one to the hunter's eye;
> then why do you so shamelessly expose your thigh?
>
> A flash of lightning, which thirst can it satisfy?
> How can my heart be happy, when you just pass by?
>
> When I am being carried to the grave
> come to my bier and whisper a sweet word.
>
> I strained my eyes to get a glimpse of you.
> It was like lightning flashing in the distance.
>
> My heart is single: no one can divide my love.
> Alas! The object of my love is distant like the moon.
>
> Until I die I will continue singing songs.
> With my last breath my last verse will go out.
>
> (Freely adapted after Andrzejewski, 1964, p. 146)

The poem betrays its Arabian inspiration in several elements: the oryx occurs frequently in Arabic poetry; and the description of repeated lightning preceding long-awaited rains is found in the poetry of many people of eastern Africa, with an early Arabic example quoted by A. J. Arberry (*Arabic Poetry,* Cambridge, 1965, p. 19).

The following poem was composed in the late Middle Ages, when Islam started expanding.

> No house can hold a saint, a friend of God.
> He does not own a building nor a field.
> He leaves the fields and travels to the hills.
> The desert weeps when he has gone away.
> The saint will pray to God while shedding tears:
> Oh Lord my heart is broken and distressed!
> What I will ask of Thee is not a house,
> Nor precious stones, nor buxom concubines;
> Not even any of those gardens high
> Where all the trees are full of scented fruits.
> I only want your presence near my soul
> For ever after may I see Thy light.

The author of this poem, Shaykh Abdurrahmaan Ismaa'uul (Ar., ʿAbd al-Raḥmān Ismāʿīl; d. 1491), was an important figure in the history of what is now northern Somalia. His work in the Djibouti region preceded the great expansion of Islam that was checked only by the Portuguese coming to the aid of the Ethiopian emperor in 1541.

South Africa. There are some 25 million people in South Africa, of whom fewer than 2 percent are Muslims; fewer than ten thousand of these are black Muslims, whose languages are Zulu and Makua. The Qur'ān has been translated into Zulu. The largest Muslim group are Indians, mainly from Gujarat and the Punjab; they number some 160,000. Most of them are fluent in English and use Gujerati only as a home language. Young Indian Muslims learn Urdu in school as their language of culture and literature, but they read all their

Islamic literature in English, including *fiqh*-books, prayer manuals, and theology.

The only original Islamic literature in South Africa arose in the nineteenth century and was written in Afrikaans in Arabic script, making Afrikaans the only European language to have been regularly used for a literature in Arabic script. Afrikaans literature in Arabic script is extant in a large number of manuscripts, all dating from after 1860; the oldest were written by and for Ḥanafī Afrikaans-speaking Muslims. (Knappert, 1980, p. 189). Today the Afrikaans-speaking Muslims can all write Afrikaans in the modern roman orthography. These Muslims of the Cape Province used to be referred to as the "Cape Malays" because some of their ancestors were brought to South Africa three hundred years ago from Java. They therefore belong to the Shāfiʿī school, whereas the Indian Muslims of Natal belong to the Ḥanafī school; the two groups have very different customs.

Swahili. Of all the Islamic literatures of Africa the Swahili contribution is by far the most extensive, even though numerically Swahili speakers come well behind the Berber, Fulani, Galla, Hausa, Mande, and Somali nations. Swahili literature is also the oldest: the first datable text comes from 1652. The history of Swahili literature is closely linked to the geographical position of the Swahili coast between Mogadishu and Mozambique, a thousand miles long and only forty miles wide. The poetic activity was the fruit of the commercial towns, which all date from the Middle Ages: Barawa, Kisimaiu, Siu, Pate, Lamu, Malindi, Mombasa, Tanga, Bagamoyo, Dar es Salaam, Kilwa, Mikindani, and Zanzibar. Commercial ties with the Islamic Middle East existed from the early eighth century, mainly with the port towns along the Gulf, the Red Sea, and the South Arabian coast, and later also with the towns on the west coast of India.

Swahili territory was occupied by the Portuguese from 1498 to 1729. Reislamized after 1729, the Swahili towns flourished, and so did their literature, especially the Islamic epic, the *Kasidas* (Ar., Qaṣīdah; hymns to Muḥammad), and the *Waadhi* or admonitions to believers. The tradition of writing Islamic poetry continued throughout the nineteenth century and is alive today. Muslim scholars write hymns and prayers *(dua,* Ar., *duʿā')* to be sung in the mosque. Especially popular is the celebration of the prophet Muḥammad's nativity, during which specially composed *kasida*s and epic legends are recited or sung; both the feast and the recital are called *maulidi* (Knappert, *Mi'raj and Maulid;* Leiden, 1971). Perhaps the finest religious poems in Swahili are the elegies *(malalamiko,* Ar., *marthiyah)* in honor of recently deceased men of merit (rarely of women).

Wedding songs *(nyimbo za ndoa)* are composed freely by local poets, often using lines from traditional songs, and are sung at every wedding, wishing God's blessing and a fruitful marriage for the couple. Lyrical songs, if in one of two traditional meters, are often referred to as *tarabu* songs (the form *taarab* is incorrect; the Arabic word is *ṭarb,* "entertainment"). Their theme is love for a sweetheart, for parents, or for a child. A frequent topic is a man's complaint about his girlfriend's unfaithfulness.

By far the most frequent meter in Swahili is the *utenzi (tendi)* with stanzas of four times eight syllables. It is much in use for didactic poems, easy for boys to memorize, concerning the duties of of *ṣalāt, ṣawm,* obedience to parents or to one's *mu'allim,* and so on. More interesting are the seventy-two epic songs in Swahili, more than half of which recount historic legends and didactic chronicles of the sacred history of Islam in verse, extolling the exploits of ʿAlī ibn Abū Talīb and his heroic contemporaries. This Islamic epic poetry is a strong living tradition, written down only to be memorized and recited or sung by trained singers *(waimbaji).*

BIBLIOGRAPHY

Allen, John W. T. *Tendi: Six Examples of a Swahili Verse Form.* London, 1971.

Andrzejewski, B. W. "Allusive Diction in Galla Hymns in Praise of Sheikh Hussein of Bale." *African Language Studies* 13 (1972): 1–31.

Andrzejewski, B. W. "Sheikh Hussēn of Bālī in Galla Oral Traditions." In *Il quarto congresso internazionale di studi etiopici.* Vol. 1. Rome, 1974, pp. 463–480.

Andrzejewski, B. W., and I. M. Lewis. *Somali Poetry.* Oxford, 1964.

Bakari, Mtoro bin Mwinyi. *Desturi za Waswahili.* Göttingen, 1903.

Büttner, Carl G. *Anthologie aus der Suaheli-Literatur.* Berlin, 1894.

Cerulli, Enrico. "The Folk-Literature of the Galla of Southern Abyssinia." *Harvard African Studies* 3 (1922): 9–228.

Cerulli, Enrico. *La lingua et la storia di Harar.* Rome, 1936.

Dammann, Ernst. *Dichtungen in der Lamu-mundart des Suaheli.* Hamburg, 1940.

Drewes, A. J. "Islamic Literature in Central Europe." Paper read at SOAS. London, 1968.

Drewes, A. J. *Classical Arabic in Central Ethiopia.* Leiden, 1976.

Knappert, Jan. "Miiraji, the Swahili Legend of Mohammed's Ascension." *Swahili* (Dar es Salaam) 36 (1966): 105–156.

Knappert, Jan. *Traditional Swahili Poetry.* Leiden, 1967.

Knappert, Jan. *Swahili Islamic Poetry.* 3 vols. Leiden, 1971.

Knappert, Jan. *Swahili Songs of Love and Passion.* Los Angeles, 1972.

Knappert, Jan. "Swahili Tarabu Songs." *Afrika und Übersee* 60.1–2 (1977): 116–155.
Knappert, Jan. *Myths and Legends of the Swahili*. Nairobi, 1978.
Knappert, Jan. *Epic Poetry in Swahili and Other African Languages*. Leiden, 1983.
Knappert, Jan. "Swahili Sailor Songs." *Afrika und Übersee* 68.1 (1985): 105–133.
Knappert, Jan. "Songs of the Swahili Women." *Afrika und Übersee* 69.1 (1986): 101–137.
Knappert, Jan. "The Islamic Poetry of Africa." *Journal for Islamic Studies*, no. 10 (1990): 91–140.
Samatar, Said S. *Oral Poetry and Somali Nationalism: The Case of Sayyid Maḥammad ʿAbdille Ḥasan*. Cambridge, 1982.
Selms, Adriaan van. *Arabies-Afrikaanse Studies*. Amsterdam, 1951.

JAN KNAPPERT

West Africa

There are two levels of Islamic literature in African Islam, as Knappert (1990) points out. First is the scholarly level of the learned African *ʿulamāʾ*, fully literate in classical Arabic, who compose in that language. This literature is not essentially different from its counterparts elsewhere in the Islamic world. It probably began in copying directly from classical Arabic sources imported from North Africa and Egypt, then by making extracts and summaries. Gradually the African *ʿulamāʾ* began to compose original works in classical Arabic in which they attempted to interpret the *sharīʿah* in the light of African conditions and to explain Islamic theology against a background of prevailing African animism. Typical of such endeavors in West Africa were the Arabic works of the nineteenth-century Fulani Islamic reformers of Hausaland (see Musa, 1992). Local historical chronicles in classical Arabic were also written by West African *ʿulamāʾ* from the seventeenth century onward.

In addition to this indigenous classical Arabic literature—and no doubt arising out of it—there also developed in the Fulfulde and Hausa languages what may be considered a subclassical or vernacular tradition of African Islamic literature. It deals exclusively with Islamic themes and is written in these vernacular languages using a modified form of the Arabic script known as *ajami*, (from the Arabic root *ʿ-j-m*, "foreign"). Various diacritical marks were evolved, in addition to those already existing in the classical Arabic script, to serve the phonetic needs of these African tongues; the process in Hausa is described by Hiskett (1975).

It is uncertain when these subclassical scripts and the literatures they record first emerged. Paper perishes rapidly in the African climate, especially in the storage conditions of earlier times. Written Islamic verse in Zenaga, a language of the Saharan Berbers, can be traced back to about AH 1112/1700 CE, although it may have been extant much earlier. A written Islamic literature in Fulfulde probably emerged somewhat later, in the eighteenth century, perhaps under the influence of neighbouring Zenaga (see Haafkens, 1983, and Seydou, 1972). Hausa written literature is believed to have arisen later still, during the nineteenth century, as the Hausa peasantry were drawn more closely into Islam; it gathered force after the successful *jihād* in Hausaland in the early nineteenth century. The peasants were illiterate in the Arabic script in which this vernacular Islamic material was written, but they could understand it when it was read to them by the literate *ʿulamāʾ*, which would have been impossible if the material had remained in Arabic. A similar situation applied among the Fulani nomadic herders, for whose Islamic instruction the Fulfulde material was largely composed. Once it began, this vernacular written literature burgeoned, especially in Hausa, which now has a voluminous corpus of *ajami* composition.

Fulfulde and Hausa written vernacular literatures are almost exclusively in verse. Both derive from the classical Arabic genre of *naẓm*, didactic or instructional verse. Their content is drawn from the Qurʾān and from *tafsīr*, the classical Arabic Qurʾānic commentary. They consist typically of descriptions of divine punishment and reward (Hausa *waʾazi*, from the Arabic root *w-ʿ-ẓ*, "warn," "admonish"). Frequent in this category are poems about *dunyā* (Arabic and Hausa, "'world"), which are Islamic *memento mori*. They personify the world as a painted harlot or as a fractious mare that throws her rider. The poet dwells on the transitory nature of worldly pleasures and on the untrustworthiness of the world. Here is an example from Hausa of this well-known genre:

> We know, by God, that we shall go,
> On the day that death befalls us
> There is no doubt that she will attack us
> For our women and our riches.
> Woe to us on the day it shall be said,
> 'What of So-and-so? Today he has passed away'.
> Everything of his has passed away,
> All the heirs now drink the soup.
> When the day of your death comes,
> You will forget son and grandchild,
> That wealth you have hidden away,
> Will not ransom you, you hear?
>
> (Hiskett, 1975, p. 29)

Equally popular in both vernacular written traditions is a category known in Hausa as *madahu* (Ar., *madīḥ* or *madḥ,* "panegyric"). This consists of praise poems to the prophet Muḥammad that closely follow the format, imagery, and content of classical Arabic verse compositions such as the *Burdah* of al-Buṣīrī, the *ʿIshrīnīyah* of al-Fāzāzī, and other North African and Egyptian panegyrics. Such prophetic panegyric is closely associated with the spread of Sufism in West Africa. The following are examples of this genre, the first from Fulfulde and the second from Hausa.

More shining than all the pearls or rubies is Muḥammad,
More beauty than all gold and silver has Muḥammad,
More splendour than all moonshine or sunlight has Muḥammad,
More sweetness than the purest honey has Muḥammad,
More quenching for the thirst than water is Muḥammad.
(Knappert, 1990, after Seydou)

Heaven is lofty but you know it does not reach
So high as to equal the glory of Muḥammad.
The throne of Heaven is beneath him in respect of glory.
Because of his glory, our Prophet Muḥammad,
His light exceeds the light of the moon on the fourteenth day of the month,
Because there is no light like the light of Muḥammad.
(Hiskett, 1975, p. 45)

Among the most popular categories of Islamic verse in both these West African languages are poems describing the prophet Muḥammad's *isrā'*, his fabulous night journey from Mecca to Jerusalem upon the mythical riding beast al-Burāqah, and his subsequent *miʿrāj* (ascension) through the seven heavens to the throne of God. The following extract is taken from a long Hausa poem that tells the story of this event.

In the night, on a Monday Gabriel came to Aḥmad [he said]
'The king greets you, He says He is calling,
You are to mount al-Burāqa, O Prophet Muḥammad',
And Gabriel it was who led him on to hear the call
To the palace where no other had been before, Aḥmad.
. . .
There at Jerusalem he dismounted, we have heard,
. . .
And Gabriel brought water so that they might perform their ablutions a second time,
Then Gabriel said, 'Ascend, O Muḥammad',
And a ladder had been placed there for him to ascend to heaven.
. . .
At the farthest lote tree Gabriel stopped,
And Muḥammad said, 'O Gabriel, do you leave me here alone?'
Gabriel said, O Trustworthy One, Muḥammad,
Do not fear, you shall not fear today,
Go to the palace, the king calls you, Muḥammad',
Then he crossed screens and rivers of light
And came before the king who had created Muḥammad.
(Hiskett, 1975, pp. 53–55)

Both languages also feature didactic verse on theological subjects, known in Hausa as *tauhidi* (Ar., *tawḥīd*). Here is an example from Hausa:

The Lord God is One, the Unique,
Wherever you seek Him you will find Him,
Say He, Allah, is One,
Allah is He on whom all depend,
He begets not nor is He begotten,
And there is none like Him.
(Aliyu, 1983, p. 6)

Astrology is also a popular theme for this verse, often intended for an agricultural or pastoral audience. Thus a poet writes charmingly in Fulfulde:

Have patience! Patience, soon there will be change:
The dori-stars are not yet in the sky;
The geese from Egypt have not yet returned;
The first warm drops of rain have yet to fall;
The last green grass is drying in the sun;
The sand is hot like ashes in the hearth;
No cloud, no plume or feather in the sky;
No mist that rests upon the sandy hills.
Patience, my cow with copper-coloured back;
Patience, white-bellied bull with twisted horns.
(Knappert, 1990, after Seydou)

This delightful piece is strikingly reminiscent of the pre-Islamic *qaṣīdah*s of Arabia, which reflect nomadic pastoral life in a desert environment. A Hausa poet writes, in a more pedestrian vein:

The sun remains in each lunar mansion
For a period of eighteen days; then it goes to another lunar mansion.
This is the reckoning of the non-Arabs, you hear.
. . .
On the seventeenth of May is the coming in of summer,
On the seventeenth of August is the coming of the harvest season,
The cold season comes in on the sixteenth of November,

> The spring is on the fifteenth of February,
> Each lunar season, its lunar mansions are seven,
> Start with their advent, know that they go seven, seven.
> (Hiskett, 1975, p. 121)

The apparent purpose of such verse is to assist Hausa farmers to plan their planting and harvesting, though it is probably read more widely for pleasure.

There is also a tradition of unwritten vernacular Islamic literature in Fulfulde and particularly in Hausa. This consists of oral versions, often highly localized, of major Islamic folkloric cycles such as the romance of Banū Hilāl, the saga of Sayf ibn Dhī Yazan, and the Islamic version of the Alexander cycle. The *Maqāmāt* stories and the classical Arabic collection *Qiṣaṣ al-anbiyā'* are also common sources for oral tales. This oral literature appears mainly to have been acquired by contacts with popular Cairene Muslim storytellers by Hausa and Fulani pilgrims and other travelers passing through Egypt in the Middle Ages. The tales were then taken up by native storytellers and adapted for Hausa and Fulani audiences. Unlike the Swahili case, such material was seldom if ever recorded in verse in these West African languages. Verse, and the expensive paper it was written on, were reserved strictly for religious and didactic purposes, and the tales therefore continued as a purely oral tradition. Later, during the colonial period, they were written down in Hausa in the *boko* (English, "book") roman script introduced by the colonial administration, not in *ajami;* they were then published in volumes printed and bound in European fashion. Similar recordings in Fulfulde are not known, though some may exist. Typical examples are the Alexander cycle, in Hausa *Ruwan bagaja;* the *Maqāmāt* tales, Hausa *Gan doki,* and the Islamic version of the Cid, Hausa *Iliya Dan Maikarfi.* These stories are now commonly referred to as "Hausa novels," an inappropriate term that disguises their ancient Islamic folkloric origin.

In addition to these cycles of Arabic origin, there is also a vast corpus of Hausa and Fulfulde oral narrative that is clearly of pre-Islamic folkloric origin but has picked up Islamic accretions. These color the stories but go no deeper. The genre is thus typical of the level of Hausa and Fulani society characterized by "mixed" Islam—an attenuated form of Islam syncretized with pre-Islamic animist culture. One example, from Hausa, is the ancient story of the monstrous pumpkin. This fantastic vegetable grew and grew, to the initial delight of the Hausa villagers who looked forward to endless supplies of pumpkin soup. But when it reached a certain size, it began to devour all the beans, then all the corn, then all the goats and cattle, and finally all the virgins. At this point the desperate villagers called in the local cult hero to save them. He drew his sword, exclaimed "There is no god but Allāh," and struck the pumpkin a mighty blow that split it asunder. At once all the goats, cattle, and virgins emerged, safe and sound. He then revealed that he was the prophet Muḥammad! The story appears to be an early African wisdom tale, with the moral "Nothing is for nothing," that acquired its prophetic twist after the introduction of Islam to West Africa. There are many such examples of pre-Islamic folkloric tales now featuring such Islamic characters as Iblīs, the Mahdi, and the companions of the Prophet, especially his son-in-law ʿAlī.

Certain other major West African languages exhibit similar Islamic traces in their otherwise essentially African folkloric traditions, for instance Mande, Songhay, and Yoruba. These languages, spoken in the part of West Africa that was broadly dominated by the medieval Islamic empire of Mali, are characterized by the "weak" Mali tradition of Islam, which largely escaped the rigors of Islamic reformism that influenced the faith in Hausaland. The early tradition of composing Islamic literature in classical Arabic certainly flourished among the Mali *ʿulamā'* of the Middle Ages; however, owing perhaps to the lack of a sustained reformist tendency, a vernacular written tradition never developed, and no significant *ajami* literature exists in these languages. Their folklore is tinged with Islam in much the same way as that of Hausa, but not to the extent that it should be regarded as a fully Islamic literary tradition.

There are at least three hundred minor vernacular languages in West Africa. Many of these, especially those adjacent to Muslim-majority areas, contain Arabic loan words, usually in fully adapted form; most also contain Hausa loans. There is little doubt that many of these loans entered the languages during the Middle Ages through trading contacts with Muslims, especially Muslim Hausas. The Islamic reform movement in Hausaland and the *jihād* of the nineteenth century left behind a further accumulation of Arabic and Hausa loans. Thus the Gwaris of west central Nigeria, who remained animists until quite recently, nonetheless worship a deity they call "Allāh Bango," "Allāh of the writing board," reflecting their contacts with itinerant Hausa Muslim literates who carry the *bango,* a wooden slate inscribed with Qur'ānic texts from which they recite; they also worship a deity they call "Mamman," apparently derived from "Muḥammad." The oral traditions of many animist peoples of West Africa have also acquired minor tinges of Islam, but no written Islamic vernacular literatures of any significance have developed among them.

Hausa is the West African language that exhibits the richest deposits of Arabic loans. Its grammar places it unmistakably in the Chadic group, as does its native vocabulary; however, it has acquired several strata of Arabic loans that now make up a substantial proportion of its total lexicon. The first layer is an ancient one that appears to have come into the language through very early contacts with Islam via North Africa and Borno. These words are often so phonologically altered that it is difficult, at first sight, to recognize their Arabic origin. Later, as the trade of the Sahara developed and encompassed Hausaland, this vocabulary of Arabic loans was enriched with words relating to commerce and associated activities. Finally, around 1112/1700, the growth of literary activities in Hausaland and the rise of centers of Islamic learning in such towns as Katsina and Kano appear to have released further Arabic vocabulary into both Hausa and Fulfulde. It seems probable that the scholarly practice of lection and commentary in these schools was responsible for this additional accretion of Arabic loans. The Muslim *ʿālim* would read his Arabic text—Qurʿān, *tafsīr, fiqh,* or whatever other branch of Islamic learning he might specialize in—to his assembled students. He would then deliver his commentary in a learned variety of Fulfulde or Hausa generously larded with Arabic theological, literary, and legal terms. In time these exotic Arabic words became integrated into scholarly varieties of the indigenous languages, bequeathing to them yet another Arabic lexicon. Fulfulde in particular acquired a sacerdotal status because it was the language of the Fulani reformers of the nineteenth century; for this reason it came to be especially favored as the language of commentary in the schools of higher Islamic learning in Hausaland.

BIBLIOGRAPHY

Aliyu, Muhammad Sani. "Shortcomings in Hausa Society as Seen by Representative Hausa Islamic Poets from ca. 1950 to ca. 1983." Master's thesis, Bayero University, 1983.

Haafkens, J. *Chants musulmans en Peul.* Leiden, 1983. Study of the Fulfulde written vernacular tradition.

Hiskett, Mervyn. *A History of Hausa Islamic Verse.* London, 1975. Detailed account of the Hausa written vernacular tradition.

Knappert, Jan. "The Islamic Poetry of Africa." *Journal for Islamic Studies,* no. 10 (1990): 91–140.

Musa, Sulaiman. "The Main Objectives of the Literary Works of Shaykh ʿUthman b. Fudi." Selly Oak Colleges, Centre for the Study of Islam and Christian-Muslim Relations, Papers, no. 9. Birmingham, 1992. Lists the Arabic works of the Muslim reformer of Hausaland.

Seydou, Christiane. *Silâmaka et Poullôri.* Paris, 1972. Covers the Fulfulde written vernacular tradition.

Mervyn Hiskett

AFSHĀRID DYNASTY. A Turcoman line ruling in Iran from 1736 to 1796 was known as the Afshārid dynasty. The empire established by the dynasty's founder, Nādir Shah Afshār (r. 1736–1747), stretched from Iraq to northern India; Nādir's successors reigned only in northeastern Iran (Khurasan province). Nādir Shah began his career as commander-in-chief for Ṭahmāsp II, claimant to the throne of the Ṣafavid dynasty, which had been ousted from Isfahan by the invading Ghilzai Afghans in 1722. In 1732 he deposed Ṭahmāsp in favor of his infant son and, in a series of military and diplomatic offensives, drove the Afghans from Iran and obliged the Ottoman Turks and Russians to withdraw from territory that they had occupied. In Azerbaijan in 1736 he convened a *quriltāy* (national assembly of tribal chiefs, provincial governors and religious leaders). Backed by his large army, containing strong contingents of Sunnī Afghans, he engineered the deposition of the Ṣafavid dynasty and his own acclamation as shah. Moreover, he obtained nominal consent to the abolition of the ritual cursing of the first three caliphs and other distinctive practices of the Twelver Shīʿa, established by the Ṣafavids as the national cult of Iran.

Nādir Shah had been brought up a Shīʿī and twice embellished the shrine of Imam ʿAlī Riẕā at his capital, Mashhad. His religious volte-face was evidently political in motivation: he wished to conclude a stable treaty with the Ottoman Empire, leaving him free to invade India, and explicitly regarded Iran's religious dissidence as an obstacle to this. He may also have planned to challenge the Ottoman claim to leadership of the Muslim world, although in his correspondence he was careful to acknowledge the sultan as caliph, and stressed their ethnic ties. After subjugating the Mughal emperor and the khan of Bukhara in 1739–1740 and recruiting more Sunnī Afghan and Uzbek troops, Nādir again advanced on Ottoman Iraq. Having made pilgrimages to both Sunnī and Shīʿī shrines, he called a council of clergy at Najaf in December 1743 and forced a compromise: the Shīʿī *ʿulamāʾ* agreed to renounce explicitly anti-Sunnī practices, and the Sunnī *ʿulamāʾ* agreed to recognize certain legal precepts of Imam Jaʿfar al-Ṣādiq as a fifth *madhhab* (school of orthodox Islamic law). The sultan, however, refused to recognize the Jaʿfari *madhhab;* a peace treaty was signed in 1746 without mention of the religious question.

The next year Nādir Shah was assassinated by Shīʿī Turcoman officers who feared a plot against them by the shah and his Afghan officers. His immediate successors, his nephew ʿĀdil Shah (r. 1747–1748) and the latter's younger brother Ibrāhīm Shah (r. 1748), failed to hold western Iran during their struggle for power. Shāhrukh Shah (r. 1748–1796), Nādir's teenage grandson by a Ṣafavid princess, was for most of his "reign" a puppet of tribal chieftains, his own sons Naṣr Allāh and Nādir Mīrzā, and the Afghan monarch Aḥmad Shah Durrānī, who invaded Khurasan three times. Shāhrukh was briefly deposed during 1750 in favor of Mīr Sayyid Muḥammad, the *mutawallī* (*waqf*-administrator) of the shrine at Mashhad, who was also of Ṣafavid descent; Nādir Shah's attempts, both political and religious, to demolish the Ṣafavid tradition had obviously failed. Shāhrukh was deposed and killed by Āghā Muḥammad Khan, the first Qājār ruler, during his reconquest of Khurasan in 1796. Although Mashhad retained its prestige as Iran's preeminent place of pilgrimage, the internecine power struggles and looting of the treasury (even the shrine) during the later Afshārid period plunged the province into an economic depression that lasted well into the nineteenth century.

[*See also* Iran.]

BIBLIOGRAPHY

Lockhart, Laurence. *Nadir Shah: A Critical Study Based Mainly upon Contemporary Sources.* London, 1938.

Perry, John R. "Afsharids." In *Encyclopaedia Iranica,* vol 1, 587–589. New York and London, 1982–.

JOHN R. PERRY

AFTERLIFE. The reality of the afterlife is integral to an understanding of the Islamic views of both the individual life cycle and the flow of human history. It is also the basis for the structure of ethical responsibility in Islam: one's condition in the afterlife, felicitous or painful, is determined by the degree to which one has affirmed the unity and justice of God and, because of that affirmation, has acted with justice and mercy toward one's fellows.

In the sociocultural context of Arabia where the prophet Muḥammad received his revelations, belief in an afterlife was virtually nonexistent. Thus the preaching of the Prophet concerning the day of resurrection and the accountability of every individual at the time of judgment was met with scorn and rejection, as attested to by the Qur'ān itself. Integral to the message of the Qur'ān, however, and providing the content of the earliest revelations, is the affirmation that God will indeed raise the dead on the day of judgment and that resurrected bodies and souls will be joined for the definitive and inevitable time of assessment and recompense. The very moment of resurrection and judgment, therefore, epitomizes the ultimate and absolute power of God over human destiny, the crucial nature of responsible human interaction, and the fact that the arena of life and afterlife is one over which God alone is judge and master.

The Qur'ān is replete with descriptive details concerning the cataclysmic events that will signal the end of time and the coming of the day of resurrection, the judgment process itself, and the abodes of recompense. Afterlife in that context refers both to the ultimate dissolution of this world and to the process of final determination in which all individuals of all ages will share. *Barzakh* (literally, "interval" or "partition"), mentioned in the Qur'ān only fleetingly, came to be understood in popular imagination as both the period of time between individual death and resurrection and the barrier signaling that the deceased can no longer return to the realm of the living. Some eschatological manuals, supported by traditions of often dubious authenticity, suggest a variety of temporary circumstances in the *barzakh* that are conditioned by the quality of life lived by the deceased. According to the detailed descriptions of popular belief, the judgment to be experienced at the end of time is also presaged in such things as the mode of death itself, the ability or inability of the dead person in the grave to answer correctly the questions posed by the fearsome angels Munkar and Nakīr immediately after death, and the degree of comfort or discomfort he or she experiences while awaiting the resurrection.

It is in the depiction of that dread day when resurrected bodies are joined with their souls and brought before the throne of God's judgment that the Qur'ān becomes most eloquent. Among the elements of the Qur'ānic narrative are the signs of the hour and the events that herald the end of time and of the world, the terrifying moment when the trumpet is blown, the resurrection itself, the ingathering of all persons for judgment, the actual reckoning *(ḥisāb)*, the crossing of the Ṣirāṭ bridge, the possibility of intercession *(shafāʿah)*, and the preparation for final consignment to the fires of hell *(al-nār)* or the gardens of bliss *(al-jannat)*. Among the indicators of the circumstances of one's final resting place, good or ill, none is more graphic than the Qur'ānic description in surah 9.19–31 of the accounting of one's book of deeds. The person who is given his or her book in the right hand is destined for a blissful condition. But woe to the one to whom it is given in the left hand, for that person will be seized and bound and exposed to the burning of the fire.

Many of the details of the fire and the gardens are reminiscent of biblical references; some reflect the tone of early Arabian poetry. In general, however, the Qur'ānic images are unique and awe-inspiring. The fire, sometimes referred to as Jahannam, is often interpreted as having seven gates, leading to the understanding common to several religious traditions that hell has seven layers. By putting together scattered Qur'ānic passages, one can determine that these gates are intended for different categories of sinners, although there is no consistent picture provided. The bridge of Ṣirāṭ is said to stretch over the layers of the fire; those who have lived good lives pass across this bridge easily, but evildoers find it thin as a razor and plunge from it into the flames below. According to the Qur'ān, the tortures of the fire are fearful—it has crackling and roaring flames, fierce boiling waters, scorching wind, and black smoke. The inhabitants sigh and wail, wretched in their torment, their scorched skins exchanged for new ones so that they can experience the pain again and again; they drink foul liquids in the hopeless effort to assuage their thirst; boiling water is poured over their heads, melting their insides; iron hooks drag them back if they try to escape.

Those whose fate is happier find themselves in the gardens of paradise. The Qur'ān identifies clearly those who are destined to enjoy this bliss: they do no evil but only good works; they are dutiful, truthful, contrite, and penitent; they feed the needy and orphans; and they have faith in the revelations of God. While there is no indication of seven layers in the garden (in fact, some commentators have argued that the Qur'ān suggests four), later tradition has come to suggest a sevenfold division to parallel that of Jahannam. In any case, the descriptions of life in the garden are as graphic as those of the tortures of the damned. The faithful there are peaceful and content, enjoying gentle speech, pleasant shade from dark green foliage, fruits, cool drink, and meat as they desire. They are treated to delicious wine from a shining stream from which they will suffer no ill effects. They recline on couches, adorned in armlets of gold and pearls and wearing green and gold robes of embroidered silk, waited on by menservants.

Among the pleasures afforded to the male inhabitants of the garden are the ministrations of the *ḥurīs*, young virgins said to have eyes like guarded pearls. Some commentators have attempted to identify the *ḥurīs* with the wives of believers, but there is no Qur'ānic justification for such an equation. Later traditions elaborated greatly on the descriptions and functions of the *ḥurīs*, who have been the subject of derision by some Western critics of Islam. The traditions also added a myriad of detail to the Qur'ānic descriptions of the joys of paradise, including such things as choirs of angels singing in Arabic, the ability of the inhabitants to eat and drink one hundred times more than their bodies would normally hold, Friday market days where they can buy new apparel to make themselves more beautiful, immunity to bodily ailments, and eternal youth.

A range of theological issues has been addressed by those who have contemplated the reality of human responsibility and divine judgment. One is the difficult dilemma of individual freedom versus the recognition of divine omnipotence and omniscience, generally couched as the issue of free will and predestination. Another is the matter of God's justice in balance (or tension) with God's mercy. The Qur'ān makes it clear that justice decrees that those who are in the fire will remain there eternally; later commentary has softened that reality by interpreting it to mean that they will remain only as long as the fire itself lasts, and that God in his mercy will at last bring all souls back into his presence in paradise.

One matter about which there has been considerable difference in interpretation throughout the history of Islamic thinking is whether the details of the process of resurrection and judgment—as well as the Qur'ānic descriptions of life in the abodes of recompense—should be understood literally or symbolically. It is clear that for the great mass of the faithful the particulars given in the sacred scripture, and often those added by eschatological narratives, are to be taken at face value. Certainly in terms of exegesis of the Qur'ān, this has also been the position of Muslim traditionalists over the centuries, with the exception of some who have written from a more mystical orientation. Many recent exegetes and commentators, however, have attempted to see the details of these descriptions of the afterlife as metaphorical and symbolic rather than literal and factual; their interpretations have often been influenced by Western rationalism.

The fact is that until recently, most Muslims writing about Islam over the past century have not dealt in much detail with the subject of the afterlife as such, choosing rather to affirm the reality of human accountability and of the day of judgment with little elaboration of the specific consequences of that judgment. They stress rather the linkage between this world and the next, *al-dunyā* and *al-ākhirah,* and focus on the importance of ethical achievement in the present. Those who do comment on the afterlife tend to treat the subject under several different rubrics. Some follow the general pattern of the traditionalists of past centuries, repeating the details that have been outlined above and affirming the writings of earlier scholars as definitive and valid. Others discuss both the *barzakh* and the afterlife in light of contemporary concerns with such issues as reconciling the Qur'ān with modern scientific discoveries, supporting the idea of continuing human development, and reaffirming the Qur'ānic emphasis on individual and corporate ethical responsibility. Still others, writing primarily in the early and middle part of the twentieth century, have been deeply influenced by movements of Western spiritualism; particularly in their elaboration of the period between individual death and resurrection, they have tried to adapt to the Islamic context some of these notions concerning the world of the spirits and the activities of the immediately deceased.

In the more contemporary writings it is often difficult to make the distinction, possible in earlier materials, between discussions of the immediate period after death and those dealing with the post-resurrection time. Even the classical distinction between *dīn* and *dunyā* can become blurred precisely because of the recent emphasis on the continuity of life in this world with that of the next, and the direct cause and effect on which contemporary authors want to insist between what is done now and the consequences of such action for the future life. The signs of ethical decay portending the coming of the day of resurrection, which the traditions spell out more clearly than the Qur'ān, are often brought to bear in an analysis of what is perceived as the moral degradation of modern society. Less frequently, the interpretation is positive rather than negative, suggesting that humans have made such progress in the advancement of civilization that the day of resurrection must certainly be near.

One issue that has engaged a number of twentieth-century writers is the way in which the resurrection of the body is to be understood. Some deny that this can be a physical resurrection, much as the early Meccans scorned the idea when it was first preached by the Prophet. Others argue that as God has created once he will be able to create again, underscoring the divine power and will. Sometimes the findings of modern science and medicine are called on as proof of the resurrection of each individual intact: as we know that foreign cells are rejected by the human body, so the resurrected body will reject anything that was not originally of its own constitution. One prominent line of interpretation insists that the resurrected body will have affinities with the original one, but that it will be essentially different from it as the afterlife is essentially different from life in this world.

This discussion is extended into an understanding of the nature of the rewards and punishments in the abodes of recompense. A considerable number of twentieth-century commentators have chosen to maintain a kind of middle position between literal (or physical) and allegorical (or spiritual) interpretations of the afterlife. Some say that rewards and punishments are sometimes physical and sensual, and at other times more abstract and spiritual. The suffering of the fire, for example, may at times be a psychological condition. Or it is possible that the joys or sufferings may be at once spiritual and sensual. The great majority of commentators, if they venture to speculate on the nature of afterlife realities at all, acknowledge that the world to come is beyond our clear comprehension precisely because of its differentiation from the present world. They avoid taking sides on the issue of whether afterlife realities are to be understood in literal or allegorical terms and rely on the conclusion that such matters ultimately are known only to God. All that we humans need to know is that the judgment itself is inevitable and that God's justice will prevail.

One of the strong affirmations of traditional Islam has been that those who earn the felicity of the garden will have as an important measure of their reward the opportunity to gaze on the face of God. Most contemporary writers do not dwell on this possibility in specifics, in part because it engages again the ancient, anthropomorphic question of whether or not God has a face. The literalist interpretation continues to insist on this vision, while others are more esoteric in their understanding. A common theme is that the ultimate reward of a life of obedience is the supreme pleasure in the afterlife of dwelling in the presence of the divine. Vision is interpreted as the finally inexplicable possibility of basking in the radiance of God's divine oneness, however this is to be understood.

In twentieth-century commentary through the 1970s, then, the primary themes stressed in the interpretation of the afterlife in Islamic thought are that human accountability is inextricably bound up with divine justice; that human action in the context of this world is meaningful only in light of the life of the next; and that the primary reason for any attempt to interpret or explain the afterlife is to provide the rationale and the impetus for moral rectitude in the here and now. For the most part, these have been ingredients in the extensive reinterpretation of Islam by modernists, socialists, liberals, humanists, and secularists. Since the Islamic resurgence beginning in the 1980s, scores of texts have been written by revivalists, especially Salafīs, on the theme of the afterlife. They have engaged this genre of literature as a tool for enlisting people into the Islamist cause. The same familiar images of the abodes of reward and recompense are used, but they now are presented in modern Arabic accessible to the everyday reader. Verbal descriptions accompanied by graphic illustrations and jacket covers warn of the horrors of hell awaiting those who are not working for the islamization of the world and hold out the hope of eternal bliss for those who are active participants in the Islamist movement.

[*See also* Cosmology; Eschatology; Satan.]

BIBLIOGRAPHY

Blair, Sheila S., and Jonathan M. Bloom, eds. *Images of Paradise in Islamic Art*. Hanover, N.H., 1991.

Eklund, Ragnar. *Life between Death and Resurrection According to Islam*. Uppsala, 1941.

Gardet, Louis. *Dieu et la destinée de l'homme*. Paris, 1967.

O'Shaughnessy, Thomas. *Muhammad's Thoughts on Death*. Leiden, 1969.

Qāḍī, ʿAbd al-Raḥīm ibn Aḥmad al-. *The Islamic Book of the Dead*. Translated by ʿĀ'isha ʿAbd al-Raḥmān. Norwich, 1977.

Saleh, Soubhi El-. *La vie future selon le Coran*. Paris, 1971.

Smith, Jane I., ed. *The Precious Pearl: Al-Durra Al-Fakhira*. Missoula, 1979.

Smith, Jane I., and Yvonne Y. Haddad. *The Islamic Understanding of Death and Resurrection*. Albany, N.Y., 1981.

JANE I. SMITH

AGA KHAN. The Nizārī Ismāʿīlī imams since the time of Ḥasan ʿAlī Shāh (d. 1881) have borne the title Aga Khan. The present imam, Prince Karīm al-Ḥusaynī, Aga Khan IV, is according to this tradition the forty-ninth hereditary imam of the community worldwide, representing direct lineal descent and succession from the first Shīʿī imam ʿAlī and his wife Fāṭimah, the prophet Muḥammad's daughter.

The first Aga Khan served as Governor of Qom and Kirman in Iran before intrigues and conflicts at court caused him to leave in 1841. He went first to Afghanistan and then to British-ruled India, where he settled in Bombay. He and his successor Aga Khan II (d. 1885) represent the phase of transition to the modern period of Ismāʿīlī history.

Aga Khan III, Sir Sulṭān Muḥammad Shāh (d. 1957) during his seventy-two-year imamate initiated major developments in Ismāʿīlī institutions, guiding and organizing the community through periods of significant transition in world and Muslim history. He was an international statesman and was appointed president of the League of Nations in 1937. He was a strong advocate of Muslim interests, a supporter of modern education for women, and an activist for global peace.

The present Aga Khan, born in 1936, spent his early childhood in Kenya and after school in Switzerland attended Harvard University, from which he graduated in 1959 with a degree in Islamic history. His headquarters are in France near Paris, where he is in constant contact with various communities, many of whom he visits regularly. Since becoming imam in 1957, he has consolidated and further developed community institutions, adapting a complex system of administration to a world of nation-states. Several hundred health, educational, social welfare, and economic institutions exist today to serve the worldwide Ismāʿīlī community and others among whom they live. The Aga Khan's teachings emphasize intellectual inquiry and social commitment in order to solve problems of faith, modernity, and continuity through institution building; they also emphasize partnership with others in the countries in which Ismāʿīlīs live and cooperation among Muslims.

The Aga Khan has also sought to give expression to his view that Islam is an all-encompassing faith that gives direction to every aspect of human life by creating major new institutions. In 1967 he established the Aga Khan Foundation, now a highly regarded international development agency, and in 1977 he launched the Aga

Khan Award for Architecture to stimulate concern for a contemporary built environment drawing upon the diverse resources of Islamic culture. He inaugurated the Aga Khan University in 1985 as a center for higher education and research on the health-care needs of Pakistan and the developing world in general. The existence of the Aga Khan Development Network reflects the growing role of the imam in contextualizing the Muslim faith according to the circumstances of time and place and in balancing spiritual needs with material concerns. The emergence of Muslim and Ismāʿīlī communities in Central Asia, China, and the Western world presents new opportunities for the Aga Khan, as a Muslim leader, to continue the role of mediating between the spiritual and ethical ideals of Islam and changing worldly contexts.

[*See also* Aga Khan Foundation; Ismāʿīlīyah; Khojas.]

BIBLIOGRAPHY

Aga Khan III, Sulṭān Muḥammad Shāh. *The Memoirs of Aga Khan: World Enough and Time.* London, 1954. Autobiographical account of his life as imam and international statesman.

Daftary, Farhad. *The Ismāʿīlīs: Their History and Doctrines.* Cambridge, 1990. Excellent and detailed survey up to modern times.

Nanji, Azim A. "Sharīʿat and Ḥaqīqat: Continuity and Synthesis in the Nizārī Ismāʿīlī Muslim Tradition." In *Sharīʿat and Ambiguity in South Asian Islam,* edited by Katherine Ewing, pp. 63–76. Berkeley, 1988. Explores the organizing principles and their relation to Ismāʿīlī thought in the policies of the Aga Khans.

AZIM A. NANJI

AGA KHAN FOUNDATION. A private, nondenominational, philanthropic institution established by the Aga Khan, the Ismāʿīlī imam, in 1967 to translate "the Muslim ethic of care and compassion for those of the society in greatest need," the Aga Khan Foundation (AKF) was conceived as an extension and outreach to the developing world by way of relating Islam's humanitarian philosophy to issues of modern development that arose in the diverse contexts in which Ismāʿīlīyah and other Muslims live. In this way, the ideals and ethics of Islam could act as a springboard to address economic and social needs in an integrated manner for the benefit of Muslims and non-Muslims. The Ismāʿīlī community has been the catalyst for the development of the AKF's program, building on its traditions of voluntary service, self-reliance, and commitment to the leadership of the imam. Funding for AKF's activities is provided by the imam, the community, as well as by international and local donor agencies, foundations, partners, and many other individuals.

Since its inception, AKF has become a recognized international development agency with programs in four continents: Africa (Kenya, Tanzania, and Uganda); Asia (India, Pakistan, and Bangladesh); Europe (Portugal and the United Kingdom); and North America (Canada and the United States). Its global presence has become one of its greatest strengths, enabling it to bridge the developed and developing worlds. The AKF's headquarters are in Geneva, and the various country units pursue common objectives under the guidance of a board of directors chaired by the Aga Khan.

Although it is a funding agency, AKF also involves itself in the formation, development, and replication of projects, enabling local populations to create and manage sustainable institutions that are sensitive to cultural values as well as development needs. The current portfolio of projects reflects the following major thematic concerns:

1. *Health:* improving the health status of the poor and providing financial support and access to primary health care. AKF helped finance studies that led to the development of the now widely used cereal-based oral rehydration solutions to treat diarrhea among newborn infants and is focusing on developing health systems that address the needs of underserved and poor communities.

2. *Education:* the emphasis has been on addressing the needs of young children and improving the quality of schools through better teacher training and involvement of families and communities. Its approach integrates physical, cultural, spiritual, and cognitive dimensions into the learning process.

3. *Rural Development:* such programs in Pakistan, India and Bangladesh have been among AKF's major initiatives, transforming degraded environments while generating income and institutional development and alleviating poverty in rural areas. These models have been judged by various international agencies to be suitable for replication in other developing countries.

The thematic areas attempt to integrate concerns that cut across all of the projects: community participation, strengthening of nongovernmental organizations, women's and family development, the environment and human-resource development and sustainability. One of AKF's foremost goals is to build what the Aga Khan has called "an enabling environment," where individuals as volunteers and the private and public sectors contribute jointly to create favorable conditions for building permanent capacities in developing societies.

The following examples of projects in Asia and Africa, respectively, illustrate the nature of AKF's approach to program development and to improving socioeconomic status by action at the grassroots level.

The highly successful rural development program in the mountainous northern areas of Pakistan has been internationally recognized for its innovative and effective approach. In its first phase, the program was able to motivate diverse Muslim communities in the area to form village organizations and women's organizations on a nonsectarian basis, to build consensus on program development, to act as a channel for the use of collective savings, to utilize grants for the building of small infrastructures, and to train men and women in farming techniques, organization, and fiscal responsibility. Over a decade, this model of participatory community organization has transformed dramatically the economy and the lives of the people of the region, creating a framework for genuine grassroots development and strong community structures for its pioneering efforts to alleviate poverty among a million people in the rural areas of South Asia.

Another example involves the development of preschool programs on the East African Coast (primarily in Kenya and Zanzibar). In cooperation with parents and religious leaders, hitherto underutilized Muslim learning centers for children, which served as places for the instruction of the Qur'ān, popularly known as *madrasah*s, are now equipped to also provide children with educational skills that are aimed at not simply complementing religious education but are responsive to their cultural, spiritual, cognitive, and total health needs. The integrated curriculum has facilitated entrance to and competence in primary school education. A teacher-training program and a resource center have been created to disseminate materials developed by Muslim women teachers, thereby playing an important leadership role in linking families and communities in education.

AKF has been particularly committed to improving the health of the poor through comprehensive primary health-care programs. By working through the Aga Khan University, it has been able to develop programs in squatter settlements in Karachi, Pakistan. A new generation of health-care professionals are specifically trained to work in such poor neighborhoods. Primary health-care programs also exist in India, Kenya, and Bangladesh. Particular attention is also paid to environmental factors in health, such as clean drinking water and sanitation.

Although AKF is an autonomous institution, it is now a partner in the emerging Aga Khan Development Network, with which it shares a common philosophy and approach to development. Among the other major institutions with which it collaborates actively in the development network are the Aga Khan University, the Trust for Culture, the Fund for Economic Development, and the Health and Education Services. Their differing but complementary programs, reflect a breadth of interest that has given the network and the AKF the reputation of a unique and extremely effective global Muslim philanthropic organization.

[*See also* Aga Khan.]

BIBLIOGRAPHY

Aga Khan Foundation Canada: An Institutional Review. Toronto, 1991.

Aga Khan Foundation International Strategy, 1991–1999. Geneva, 1992. Overview of the history, mission, and program directions.

The Aga Khan Rural Support Program in Pakistan: A Second Interim Evaluation. Washington, D.C., 1990.

Khan, S. S., and M. H. Khan. *Rural Change in the Third World: Pakistan and the Aga Khan Rural Support Program.* New York, 1992.

Azim A. Nanji

AGRICULTURE. There are thirty-four countries with both significant agricultural sectors and majority Muslim populations. They form a broad band running from west to east across the tropics and northern subtropics of Africa and Asia, spanning a diversity of natural environments from the verdant rain forests of West Africa and the East Indies to the barren deserts of the Sahara, Rub' al-Khali, and Kara-Kum. Elevations and temperatures range from the glacial peaks of the Hindu Kush mountains to the torrid depression of the Jordan River Valley. The Islamic countries may be divided into four broad agro-ecological regions, each defined principally by climatic conditions, characteristic systems, and historical development. The Tropical Asia region is a noncontiguous area comprised of Bangladesh, Malaysia, and Indonesia. The Central Asia region includes the former Soviet republics of Kazakhstan, Kyrghyzstan, Tajikistan, Turkmenistan, and Uzbekistan. The West Asia and North Africa region includes Afghanistan, Azerbaijan, Iran, Pakistan, Turkey, and the Arab countries. The Sub-Saharan region is the belt of countries between Senegal and Guinea in the west to Somalia in the east, excluding Ethiopia.

In total, the Islamic countries account for some 21 percent of the world's land surface, 15 percent of its cropped area, and 25 percent of its irrigated area. They are equal to 49 percent of the combined Afro-Asian land mass, 34 percent of its cropped area, and 37 percent of its irrigated area. The estimated 1991 agricultural population of the Islamic countries was 412 million people, about 47 percent of their combined population of close to 900 million. The agricultural proportion of the Islamic population compares with the respective world and Afro-Asian agricultural population ratios of 45 percent of and 60 percent. Countries in Asia and Africa, with substantial Muslim minorities, India and Nigeria among them, could reasonably add 100 to 120 million Muslim farmers to those in Islamic states.

Islamic agriculture is an important contributor to world food production, encompassing some 22 percent of world wheat area, 18 percent of world rice area, and 12 percent of world maize and other coarse grains area. Islamic countries contained some 490 million sheep and goats in 1990, or about 46 percent of the total small ruminant population in Africa and Asia. Despite the preponderance of agricultural resources in the Islamic world being devoted to food production, there remain substantial food deficits that must be overcome by massive importation. Of all the Islamic countries, only Indonesia and Turkey have a consistent record as net food exporters. The average annual trade deficit in food for the Islamic world, excluding the former Soviet republics, during 1987–1991 was almost $15 billion, with the value of food imports being 2.5 times that of exports. This situation shows no sign of improvement in the near future, given the severely limited agricultural resource base and the high rates of population increase.

At the dawn of the nineteenth century the Islamic lands were agrarian societies, dominated by the particularism of village life and the seasonality of agricultural rhythms. Perhaps 90 percent or more of the total population were engaged in producing their own food. The annual cereal harvest was the key to survival. Rice was the predominant food grain in tropical Asian areas, where it was often combined with labor-intensive irrigation techniques to produce high yields per unit area. In Central and West Asia and in North Africa, wheat occupied the greater part of the arable land, while barley was used in marginal areas with less rainfall. Yields were low and a high proportion of the land was left fallow each year to store moisture. In the semiarid tropics south of the Sahara and in southern Arabia, sorghum and millets were the staples. Outside the human tropics, animal husbandry, either in combination with extensive cereal cultivation or as nomadic pastoralism, was a method of utilizing crop residues and native grasslands for human food production.

Most production was consumed locally, but wherever political authority had enforcement power, significant amounts of grain and animals were collected and sent to administrative centers and towns as payment of taxes and rent. The great empires of the Ottomans, Ṣafavids, and Mughals were based on this form of expropriation. Medium- and long-distance trading in agriculturally based commodities had existed side-by-side with subsistence production and surplus extraction for centuries, and Muslim traders from Mughal India were largely responsible for the spread of Islam into Southeast Asia, while North African merchants introduced their religion into the West African Sudan.

The most important trade crops trade were fibers: silk, cotton, and flax. A wide variety of tree crops, including olives, dates, fruits, and nuts, also produced marketable commodities, although in fairly small quantities. In tropical Asia, coffee, black pepper, cloves, nutmeg, mace, and cinnamon became important items in transcontinental trading from the sixteenth century onward, largely as a result of the arrival of Europeans in the Indian Ocean. European traders were largely responsible for introducing New World crops such as maize, tobacco, and a range of vegetables that spread rapidly in the Islamic world.

European involvement in Islamic agriculture moved from the indirect influences of merchants to the direct interventions of government and landlord. The movement began in Tropical Asia, where the English and Dutch established monopolistic trading companies that evolved into military and political traditional agricultural sector, either as in-kind taxes or as forced deliveries of produce, but as European economies expanded during the Industrial Revolution and market demand both grew and deepened in the late eighteenth and early nineteenth centuries, the old trading companies gave way to direct colonial administration by European governments, and European capital directly intervened to encourage the production of crops exclusively for export. This entailed new forms of production, particularly capital-intensive large plantations specializing in a single crop and using hired or coerced labor. Jute and tea plantations, for example, were established in what later became Bangladesh, while the Dutch moved from the less direct arrangement of the "culture system," in which each village was made to set aside one-fifth of its land to produce designated export crops for the colonial administration, to the "liberal policy" that allowed Europeans the right of long-term leasehold over village lands, allowing them therefore to organize vast estates producing single crops for export where formerly village communities had pursued food production. In Malaya, rubber plantations using imported labor from China and the Indian subcontinent were established by British investors soon after British political control was extended over the native states. Large plantations producing export crops juxtaposed with communities of small farmers eking out a subsistence from rice and other tropical crops continues to characterize the agricultural landscape of Indonesia, Malaysia, and, to a lesser extent, Bangladesh.

The years since 1960 have witnessed both expansion and intensification of the agricultural sectors in the Tropical Asian countries, particularly in Bangladesh and Indonesia where huge increases in population have created enormous economic and nutritional pressures. The specter of mass hunger due to insufficient land resources has been dispelled by the so-called Green Revolution of new, higher-yielding rice technologies. Rice yields indeed increased in Bangladesh by 47 percent per hectare between 1961–1965 and 1987–1991, and in the same period by 133 percent in Indonesia. In both countries the area of rice cultivation was increased substantially; irrigated area doubled in Indonesia and jumped fivefold in Bangladesh, a country so densely populated that it has almost reached the limits of areal agricultural expansion. The two East Asian countries, however, continue to clear natural forests in an alarming rate, and almost 6 million hectares have been added to their arable land in the past three decades. Deforestation is encouraged by the profitability of timber exports and developing oil palm plantations.

Russian penetration of Central Asia began in the eighteenth century with military incursions into the Kazakh khanates. By 1876 the tsar had absorbed the Khanate of Khoqand, and by 1900 the Uzbeks and Turkmens were under imperial protection. Military conquest was followed by agricultural colonization. Vast areas of grazing land were expropriated from the Kazakh pastoralists for the purpose of settling peasants from European Russian and the Ukraine. By the end of the nineteenth century close to one million settlers had come from the West, and the economies of Central Asia were being gradually realigned to meet the Russian need for raw materials and new markets. Agricultural settlement was followed by industrialization under the Soviet regime, and during the same period there was the almost complete abandonment of nomadism and individual farming. Both were replaced by forced state collectivization of animal and crop production. During the 1950s the Soviet government embarked on gradiose irrigation schemes and the mechanization of production. Wheat continues to be the principal food crop, covering some 35 percent of the cropped area, but this is mainly grown under rainfed conditions in Kazakhstan. Barley, used to feed the important livestock sector, covers another 17 percent. Cotton is by far the most valuable crop, and occupies 3 million hectares of irrigated land, primarily using the waters of the Amu Darya and Syr Darya rivers. In fact, the emphasis on cotton has, since the 1970s, contributed to a growing ecological disaster as precious water resources are being overburdened. In part, this explains why only 65 percent of the irrigation-equipped area was sown in the early 1990s, and why the once vast reservoir of the Aral Sea is rapidly drying up.

The agrarian history of West Asia and North Africa since 1800 has been characterized by three dominant themes: commercialization of production, capital investment, and state intervention. The first half of the nineteenth century witnessed European economic penetration of the old Ottoman and Persian Empires that at least nominally ruled over most of the region, and eventually foreign commercial interest came to control the majority of the trade with the outside world. New industrial crops, notably cotton, were introduced for domestic industry and export in the early nineteenth century. In some areas, most notably Egypt under Muḥammad ʿAlī Pasha, local dynasts sought to stave off foreign control by organizing monopolistic state production, processing, and export enterprises. In the Egyptian case this included substantial state investment in improving the irrigation system by converting the traditional seasonal basin flooding to perennial canal irrigation. This technical advance was replicated over the next century and a half in the major river valleys in Sudan, Syria, Iraq, Turkey, and Morocco. Similarly, there has been a phenomenal growth in tube well irrigation throughout the region since the 1950s as a result of advances in deep-well drilling technology. The tendency for state-sponsored commercialization coupled with irrigation investments continued both under the colonial regimes established by the European powers and in the successor states to the Ottomans and Qājārs, and it is still a principal feature of the postcolonial states.

Since World War II and the demise of the colonial regimes, state intervention in agriculture has gained the added dimensions of land reform and central planning. Partly as a means of creating incentives for cultivators to increase production, and partly as a means of reducing the power of large landlords while gaining the loyalty of the rural masses, reforming governments enacted measures that set limits on the amount of land that could be owned by an individual or family and usually also set a minimum farm size. Land in excess of the specified limits was subject to expropriation and, at least in theory, redistribution to landless farmers. The first major land reform took place in Egypt in the 1950s, but similar legislation was later promulgated in Syria, Iraq, Iran, and Pakistan. In former French North Africa, the large estates that were created by colonists were either as state farms or as cooperatives (especially in Algeria, but to a limited extent in the other two countries also). On the whole, the land reform movement in West Asia and North Africa has been praised for helping to alleviate, if not eliminate, inequalities inherited from the past.

West Asian and North African governments have generally followed policies to encourage self-sufficiency in staple foods, particularly cereals and animal products, while at the same time guaranteeing inexpensive food supplies for urban consumers. In essence, this has meant massive subsidies for both food production and food consumption. To help offset these costs, governments have sought to profit from the production of traditional export crops (such as cotton in West Asia and the Nile Valley) through regulations, quota systems, and national marketing organizations. Despite the achievement of impressive yield gains in cereals and other food crops, most countries with their limited arable land and water resources have not been able to keep pace with their burgeoning populations. Consequently, it is characteristic for the region that most national agricultural sectors are usually in deficit.

Since the 1960s, agriculture in West Asia and North Africa has become increasingly dependent on irrigation. About 10.5 million hectares were added between 1965 and 1991, making irrigated area about one-third of the cultivated area. All countries showed at least modest gains, but Pakistan, with the largest irrigated area by far, increased by a further 50 percent as massive projects in the Indus Valley were completed. Iraq, Iran, and Turkey each added about a million hectares. Tapping underground water, Saudi Arabia extended its irrigated area by a half-million hectares. Throughout the region there were innumerable individual investments in tube wells, especially for irrigated production of high-value fruit and vegetable crops. By the end of the 1980s, these crops had surpassed cotton and other traditional export crops both in volume and in value. But at the same time the region began to reach the limits of expansion. There were growing limitations on water availability, competition for nonagricultural uses, and negative environmental impacts, most notably salinization of soils and groundwater.

In Islamic Africa south of the Sahara, agriculture changed little until the establishment of European colonial regimes in the last decades of the nineteenth century. In the late 1850s, the French began to extend their control up the Senegal River and to foster local African production of peanuts (groundnuts) to help meet the growing European demand for vegetable oils. This emphasis continued for a century in the more humid areas of Senegal, Gambia, and Guinea. In the first half of the twentieth century the French encouraged cotton production in Chad and Mali, but its expansion was hindered by the need to invest in irrigation facilities and by the long distances involved in moving the harvest from the interior to the coast for export. Since independence, economic dependence on single export crops has continued, although there has been some progress toward diversification, including the introduction of other pulses, vegetables, oil palm, and cashews. In Somalia, colonial rule by Italy in the south and Britain in the north had little direct impact on agriculture. Nomadic pastoralism continued to be the way of life for the overwhelming majority of people. There has been a limited development of irrigation infrastructure in Somalia's two river valleys, and until the disruptions of the civil war in the early 1990s, bananas had become the second largest export earner after live animals. Settled agriculture, particularly that dependent upon irrigation, is only slowly recovering from the civil war. Echoing precolonial patterns of the last century, the export of live animals is the largest agricultural money-earner in both Niger and Somalia, with 80 percent of export value for both countries in 1991.

The sub-Saharan region continues to be plagued by the poverty of the people and the lack of public or private investment in the infrastructure necessary for agricultural development. In contrast to West Asia and to North Africa, a region that shares similar limitations on arable land and water resources, irrigated agriculture has only a minor role in most Islamic states south of the Sahara, despite the presence of a number of major rivers flowing in and through the semiarid and humid zones.

The overwhelming importance of agriculture to the livelihood of the people is indicated by the fact that the agriculturally active population is actually larger than the rural population, with many people living in the comparatively small urban centers commuting to work on farms. The small percentage of arable land, however, when combined with the high dependence on agriculture, results in their being only about one-half hectare of productive land available per capita of the agricultural population. In contrast to the Tropical Asian countries, where small farm size is compensated by high productivity per unit area, and to the Central Asian, West Asian, and North African regions, where there are many nonagricultural employment opportunities and governments are rich enough to subsidize much of the agricultural sector, the sub-Saharan countries have few internal resources that can be invested in improving conditions for the agricultural population. As a group, these countries are the poorest in the Islamic world, with a regional gross national product per capita for 1990 of just $332.

As the Islamic world moves toward the twenty-first century, it faces perhaps insurmountable threats to its nonrenewable natural resource base. In Tropical Asia, the rain forests that have served as natural preserves for biodiversity and recycling are disappearing at an accelerating rate. In the vast expanses that sustained nomadic pastoralists for millennia are all but gone too, replaced by plowed land subject to intense erosion from wind and water. Desertification is a widespread phenomenon. Expanded irrigation facilities have been followed by depleted water reserves and salinization of both soil and aquifers. In the African savannahs south of the Sahara, overexploitation of a fragile environment aggravated by drought, appears to have reduced long-term agricultural potential. There are bright spots, however. Since the 1970s there have been spectacular improvements in productivity that have not been at the expense of the environment, but rather through improved management of existing resources and utilization of improved technology. We can anticipate that future farmers and governments will build on these achievements to improve productivity while conserving the resources on which sustainable improvements depend.

BIBLIOGRAPHY

There are no works specifically covering agriculture in all the Islamic countries. Essential quantitative information for individual countries is available in international databases prepared and maintained by the United Nations and other organizations. Among the most useful and easily accessed are those listed below.

Food and Agriculture Organization of the United Nations (FAO). *Agrostat-PC Database and Software*. Rome, 1994. Essential starting place for any quantified evaluation of agriculture in the Islamic world. The annually issued FAO *Production Yearbook* and Food Balance Sheets are also useful.

Jazairy, Idriss, et al. *The State of World Rural Poverty: An Inquiry into Its Causes and Consequences*. New York, 1992. Benchmark study sponsored by the International Fund for Agricultural Development (IFAD) that concentrates on social and economic factors contributing to rural poverty and their causes.

World Bank. *World Development Report 1992*. New York, 1993. See as well reports from previous years and the periodically issued *World Table* of social and economic indicators. These studies place agricultural sectors in their national and global development contexts.

World Resources Institute. *World Resources 1992*. Washington, D.C., 1993. Similar in format to the World Bank economic reports, this valuable annual includes major sections on agricultural populations and natural resources used in agricultural production, highlighting conservation and sustainability issues.

Interpretive and synthesizing studies of individual countries or regional issues in agriculture include the following:

Amin, Samir. *L'Afrique de l'ouest bloquée: L'économie politique de la colonisation, 1880–1970*. Paris, 1971. Although dated and no longer in print in English, this seminal study introduced the concept of economic neocolonialism to Islamic West Africa, and is still useful for understanding the agricultural problems of the Sahel today.

Beaumont, P., and Keith McLachlan, eds. *Agricultural Development in the Middle East*. New York, 1985. Contains useful review articles and case studies of several countries seldom covered elsewhere.

Franke, R. W., and B. H. Chasin. *Seeds of Famine: Ecological Destruction and the Development Dilemma in the West African Sahel*. Montclair, N.J., 1980. Environmental approach to the region's agricultural problems.

Geertz, Clifford. *Agricultural Involution: The Processes of Ecological Change in Indonesia*. Berkeley, 1963. Classic study applying ecological and sociological principles to the interpretation of agricultural systems in the humid tropics.

Issawi, Charles. *An Economic History of the Middle East and North Africa*. New York, 1984. The chapter on agricultural expansion and intensification in the nineteenth and early twentieth centuries is the best synopsis of the subject available for the region.

Lewis, Norman N. *Nomads and Settlers in Syria and Jordan, 1800–1980*. Cambridge, 1987. Fascinating historical account of the advance of cultivation and settlement in the great Syrian steppe.

Mears, L. A. *The New Rice Economy of Indonesia.* Yogyakarta, Indonesia, 1981. Examines the implications of the Green Revolution in Indonesia, providing useful contemporary counterpoint to the thesis elaborated by Geertz.

Richards, Alan, and John Waterbury. *A Political Economy of the Middle East: State, Class, and Economic Development.* Boulder, 1990. Contains an important chapter on agriculture summarizing the impact of land reform movements in various countries of the region.

Swearingen, Will D. *Moroccan Mirages: Agrarian Dreams and Deceptions, 1912–1986.* London, 1987. Excellent case study of Morocco's fitful agricultural progress and its roots in the colonial era.

Tully, Dennis, ed. *Labor and Rainfed Agriculture in West Africa and North Africa.* Dordrecht, 1990. *Labor, Employment, and Agricultural Development in West Asia and North Africa.* Dordrecht, 1990. The best collection available, including regional and national overviews and local case studies, covering the complex relationships among labor, mechanization, and agricultural intensification in the region.

Wennergren, E. Boyd, et al. *Agricultural Development in Bangladesh: Prospects for the Future.* Boulder, 1984. Useful review for this important country.

RICHARD N. TUTWILER

ʿAHD. *See* Covenants.

AHL AL-BAYT. Literally "people of the household," *ahl al-bayt* refers to the family of the prophet Muḥammad and his descendants. Shīʿī Muslims are particularly devoted to the family of the Prophet—his cousin and son-in-law, ʿAlī ibn Abī Ṭālib (d. 661), his daughter, Fāṭimah (d. 632), and their sons, Ḥasan (d. 669/70) and Ḥusayn (d. 680)—and the other imams, succeeding leaders of the community and descendants of the Prophet. The Shīʿī believe that these figures embody special holiness and spiritual power and knowledge through their blood relationship with the Prophet and his attachment to them.

After the death of the prophet Muḥammad in 632, the Muslim community experienced conflict over the means by which to determine a successor. One party argued for election and the other, the *shīʿat ʿAlī* (the "party of ʿAlī"), was convinced that leaders could only come from among the *ahl al-bayt,* the immediate family of the Prophet and his descendants. The Shīʿīs believed ʿAlī to have been designated by the Prophet, guided by divine inspiration, as his successor, and they looked on him as the first imam, leader of the Shīʿī community. However, ʿAlī did not become caliph, head of the entire Muslim community, until three others had held the position, and then only for five years before he was murdered. ʿAlī's son Ḥasan, the second Shīʿī imam, was coerced into giving up the caliphate to Muʿāwiyah (r. 661–680), governor of Damascus and Syria. After the death of Ḥasan and then of Muʿāwiyah, Ḥusayn was urged by ʿAlī's supporters in Kufa (in present-day Iraq) to lead a revolt against Yazīd, successor to Muʿāwiyah. Accepting the call, Ḥusayn, the third Shīʿī imam, set out from Mecca for Kufa with his family. He was intercepted on the plains of Karbala near the Euphrates River by Yazīd's forces. From the second until the tenth of the month of Muḥarram in 680, Ḥusayn and his followers battled Yazīd's army. On the tenth, Ḥusayn was killed. The females of his group were taken as captives to Damascus. There, Ḥusayn's sister, Zaynab, held the first *majlis* (mourning ceremony), setting a model for the many rituals of lamentation to follow, keeping the story of Ḥusayn's martyrdom alive and providing a means for believers to share in the passion of Ḥusayn and his family.

The Twelver Shīʿīs see the twelve imams, successors to the prophet Muḥammad, as the true leaders of the Muslim community. They believe that each was persecuted by the reigning caliph and prevented from taking his rightful position. The twelfth imam is believed to have been taken into occultation by God in 873 or 874 to protect him from enemies. Concealed thus, the Hidden Imam or Mahdi will return for the final judgment.

In the temporary period of unavailability of the twelfth imam, the Shīʿī have other means of connection with the venerated *ahl al-bayt.* Believing in the spiritual powers of the Prophet's family and the imams, obtained through their suffering on behalf of God and the religious community, the Shīʿīs aim to gain closeness with these religious figures in order to share in their rewards from God. They are thus encouraged in a number of practices and rituals to form special relationships with the family and descendants of the Prophet and to join in their pain. People make pilgrimages to the shrines of the imams and to the tombs of their descendants where they profess their devotion, plead their causes, and provide donations in thanks for the granting of requests. Women are most active, particularly in local shrine visitation, as is clear from the research of Anne Betteridge (1985). Likewise, women are active in organizing and funding feasts in honor of the *ahl al-bayt* and hold readings or performances of the stories about Ḥusayn and his family at Karbala. During the month of Muḥarram, Shīʿī Muslims commemorate the martyrdom of Ḥusayn by donating refreshments for other mourners and hosting or attending the mourning rituals to weep, chant mourning couplets, and practice self-flagellation. Believers can thereby join the family of the Prophet through participation in their anguish.

During the period of inaccessibility of the twelfth imam, the Shīʿīs rely on his representatives, the *ʿulamāʾ* (religious scholars), for guidance. Ideally, each believer is to choose a living religious leader to provide direction in all areas of life. In following the models set by these representatives of the Hidden Imam, such as the ayatollah, Shīʿī Muslims can feel assured of maintaining indirect contact with the holy line of imams, successors to the Prophet.

Relationships with the *ahl al-bayt* are intense and highly personal. Time and space are eliminated as believers think of the *ahl al-bayt* as their own brothers, sisters, mothers, fathers, sons, and daughters. In sharing their sorrows through intense, repetitious interactions and demonstrations of loyalty, believers become related to them and thus expect their consideration.

The Shīʿīs accept the events of Karbala as a central paradigm of the religion and honor the Prophet's family and the imams and their representatives as the spiritual leaders provided by God for his people. However, the related beliefs and practices of Shīʿī Muslims are not uniform or static. Rather, they are subject to controversy and questioning (see Betteridge, 1989; Friedl, 1989; and Loeffler, 1988). individually variable (see Loeffler), and dynamic (see Ayoub, 1978; and Hegland, 1983). The interpretation and political implications of the Karbala events can evolve. As Mahmoud Ayoub points out (1978, p. 19), the martyrdom of Ḥusayn provides the means of redemption for Shīʿī Muslims either through the intercession of those who suffered at Karbala or through their example of self-sacrifice. For the first, believers attempt to join in the company of those who suffered at Karbala by commemorating their persecution and sharing their suffering, thus gaining their favor and assistance. For the second, believers attempt to follow their examples of sacrificing self for God, the cause of justice, and the religious community. They enlist in Ḥusayn's party by performing like actions. Both interpretations can carry potent impetus for political behavior (see Hegland, "Two Images of Husain: Accommodation and Revolution in an Iranian Village," in Keddie, 1983, pp. 218–235). In viewing Ḥusayn's martyrdom as providing him and his family with the power to intercede, people perceive connection with those in positions of power as the best route to fulfilling needs. They are prompted to turn also to secular figures of power, striving to gain their favor and patronage. To demonstrate their devotion to Ḥusayn and thus their political legitimacy, political leaders have sponsored mourning performances and rituals. If their supporters which to renew vows of loyalty to the imam and to their political leader, they will attend.

During the Iranian Revolution of 1979, believers saw Ḥusayn as an example to follow and thus were willing to become martyrs on behalf of justice. Believers could see themselves as powerful and active, able to resist inappropriate leaders and to bring about positive changes in society. Shīʿī Muslims have often united for political action at different levels through their connections as joint participants in the passion of *ahl al-bayt*. Fāṭimah and Zaynab are held up as models for the perfect Muslim woman and examples to follow in political action. The organization "Sisters of Zaynab" in Iran recruits women to political causes. The ayatollahs, as representatives of the Hidden Imam, and thereby of the beloved *ahl al-bayt* as well, can exert strong political persuasion through their counsel to followers.

Today, many Shīʿī believers in various locations continue to feel themselves members of the *ahl al-bayt* through their own sense of persecution. They share in the suffering of the family of the Prophet and of the imams through the wrongs done to themselves as well as through remembrance of Karbala. Whether in quiet, personal devotion and the seeking of intercession, or by courageously joining the party of Ḥusayn through taking up his cause of justice, practicing Shīʿī Muslims find comfort and strength through their relationship with the revered *ahl al-bayt*.

[*See also* Imam; Karbala; Mahdi; Muḥammad, *article on* Life of the Prophet; Muḥarram; Shīʿī Islam, *historical overview article; and the biographies of* ʿ*Alī and Ḥusayn*.]

BIBLIOGRAPHY

Ayoub, Mahmoud M. *Redemptive Suffering in Islam: A Study of the Devotional Aspects of ʿĀshūrāʾ in Twelver Shīʿism*. The Hague, 1978. Excellent presentation of popular piety surrounding the Martyr of Karbala and his family, based on research in Iran on the oral tradition of the suffering of the Holy Family.

Betteridge, Anne. "Ziarat: Pilgrimage to the Shrines of Shiraz." Ph.D. diss., University of Chicago, 1985.

Betteridge, Anne. "The Controversial Vows of Urban Muslim Women in Iran." In *Unspoken Worlds: Women's Religious Lives*, edited by Nancy Auer Falk and Rita M. Gross, pp. 102–111. Belmont, Calif., 1989.

Chelkowski, Peter, ed. *Taʿziyeh: Ritual and Drama in Iran*. New York, 1979. Collection of articles about Muḥarram performances in Iran and elsewhere.

Cole, Juan R. I., and Nikki R. Keddie, eds. *Shīʿism and Social Pro-*

test. New Haven, 1986. Eleven case studies by researchers in several disciples on the interaction of Shīʿī belief and practice resulting in political activism.

Fernea, Elizabeth W. *Guests of the Sheik*. New York, 1989. Delightful portrayal of the religious beliefs and practices of southern Iraqi Shīʿī women, through an intimate view of their ongoing, everyday lives.

Fischer, Michael M. J., and Mehdi Abedi. *Debating Muslims: Cultural Dialogues in Postmodernity and Tradition*. Madison, Wis., 1990. Personal perspectives on Shīʿī Islam, including memoirs of participation in Muḥarram rituals and discussion of religious beliefs and practices among Iranian immigrants in the U.S.

Friedl, Erika. "Islam and Tribal Women in a Village in Iran." *Unspoken Worlds: Women's Religious Lives*, edited by Nancy Auer Falk and Rita M. Gross, pp. 125–133. Belmont, Calif., 1989.

Hegland, Mary Elaine. "Ritual and Revolution in Iran." In *Culture and Political Change*, edited by Myron J. Aronoff, pp. 75–100. New Brunswick, N.J., 1983.

Keddie, Nikki R., ed., *Religion and Politics in Iran: Shiʿism from Quietism to Revolution*. New Haven, 1983. Collection of articles tracing the political developments in Shīʿī Islam leading to the Iranian Revolution.

Loeffler, Reinhold. *Islam in Practice: Religious Beliefs in a Persian Village*. Albany, N.Y., 1988. Stresses the diversity and creativity of Shīʿī beliefs and how they relate to existential conditions through the words and lives of twenty-one individuals.

Momen, Moojan. *An Introduction to Shiʿi Islam: The History and Doctrines of Twelver Shiʿism*. New Haven, 1985. Thorough presentation of the development and theological aspects of the religion.

Mottahedeh, Roy P. *The Mantle of the Prophet: Religion and Politics in Iran*. New York, 1985. Outstanding work on the history of Shīʿī Islam and its contemporary directions, told through the training, thoughts, and life of one modern ayatollah.

Norton, Augustus Richard. *Amal and the Shiʿa: Struggle for the Soul of Lebanon*. Austin, 1987. Political scientist traces the development of the Shīʿī Amal Militia and the group's interactions with other powers in the area.

Pinault, David. *The Shiites: Ritual and Popular Piety in a Muslim Community*. New York, 1992. Fine study of the history of Shīʿī Islam and its practice in Hyderabad, India, based on observation of the Muḥarram rituals and interviews.

Ṭabāṭabāʾī, Muḥammad Ḥusayn. *Shiʿite Islam*. Translated by Seyyed Hossein Nasr. Albany, N.Y., 1975. Significant introduction to Shiism written by a contemporary, learned Shīʿī scholar.

MARY ELAINE HEGLAND

AHL AL-ḤALL WA-AL-ʿAQD. Those who are qualified to act on behalf of the Muslim community in electing a caliph are known as *ahl al-ḥall wa-al-ʿaqd* (less frequently, *ahl al-ʿaqd wa-al-ḥall*). In medieval political theory, their main function was contractual, namely, to offer the office of caliphate to the most qualified person and, upon his acceptance, to administer to him an oath of allegiance (*bayʿah*). They were also entrusted with deposing him should he fall short in fulfilling his duties. They must be Muslim, of age, just, free, and capable of exercising *ijtihād* (interpretation of religious sources). The implication of the last requirement is that *ahl al-ḥall wa-al-ʿaqd* are jurists of the highest caliber, whose consensus is binding.

In the absence of any revealed text stipulating the number of *ahl al-ḥall wa-al-ʿaqd*, scholars were in disagreement concerning this issue. Some argued that they must be sufficient in number to represent all regions of the Islamic empire. The prevailing opinion, however, seems to have been that one person suffices; this reflects the historical reality in which a caliph normally designated his successor. Since the caliph appointed by *ahl al-ḥall wa-al-ʿaqd* must enjoy the same qualifications required of the members of the appointing body, the caliph himself was deemed a most qualified member, who might alone designate a successor. This is perhaps why some Muslim political theorists, such as the eleventh century Shāfiʿī jurist al-Māwardī, maintain that the *bayʿah* of *ahl al-ḥall wa-al-ʿaqd* is a subsidiary process, resorted to when the preceding caliph fails to appoint an heir.

Theory diverged from practice in at least one respect. In later times, military commanders played the role of *ahl al-ḥall wa-al-ʿaqd*, although they did not fulfill the qualifications of theory. Most notably, they were not deemed *mujtahids* (interpreters of the law), and thus they were not empowered to form a consensus on behalf of the Muslim community. Their assumption of this role was finally justified on the basis of public interest (*maṣlaḥah*), mainly in terms of the doctrine that however objectionable the appointments of military commanders may be, they are preferable to a situation wherein the community is left without leaders.

In modern political thought the title *ahl al-ḥall wa-al-ʿaqd* has gained particular significance. The title is now intimately connected with an expanded meaning of the concept of *shūrā*, a term that previously meant consultation among the oligarchs on political matters, including the appointment of a caliph. In nineteenth- and particularly twentieth-century political thought, the *ahl al-ḥall*, through the medium of *shūrā*, speak for the full community. Khayr al-Dīn al-Tūnisī (d. 1889), a Tunisian reformer, equates *ahl al-ḥall* with a European-style parliament, and Muḥammad Rashīd Riḍā (d. 1935) entrusts them with powers to elect and depose rulers by virtue of their influential status in the community and of their mutual consultation. Their decisions, though they may be at variance with those of the ruler, are binding upon him because *ahl al-ḥall* are the deputies of the community and express its will. For Rashīd Riḍā the ruler thus becomes subservient to *ahl al-ḥall,* who express through their consultation the will of the community on matters of public law and policy. More recent political thinkers deem the ruler a servant of the people, elected by a process of consultation whose medium is *ahl al-ḥall.* No rule, they argue, can be legitimate unless it is based on this process.

[*See also* Bayʿah; Ijtihād.]

BIBLIOGRAPHY

Faḍl Allāh, Mahdī. *Al-Shūrā: Ṭabīʿat al-Ḥākimiyah fī al-Islām.* Beirut, 1984.

Kerr, Malcolm H. *Islamic Reform: The Political and Legal Theories of Muḥammad ʿAbduh and Rashīd Riḍā.* Berkeley and Los Angeles, 1966, pp. 34–36, 159–165, 183.

Lambton, Ann K. S. *State and Government in Medieval Islam.* New York and Oxford, 1981. Summarizes the theories of various medieval scholars on the subject. See pages 18, 73, 89, 105, 111–114, 139, 141, 184, 311.

Māwardī, Abū al-Ḥasan ʿAlī ibn Muḥammad al-. *Al-Aḥkām al-Sulṭānīyah.* Edited by M. Engri. Bonn, 1853. French translation by Léon Ostrorog, *Le droit du Califat.* Paris, 1925. Well-known classical work on constitutional theory. See pages 6–7, 21–22.

Shaltūt, Maḥmūd. *Min Tawjīhāt al-Islām.* Cairo and Beirut, 1983, pp. 471ff.

WAEL B. HALLAQ

AHL AL-KITĀB. *See* People of the Book.

AḤMAD BARELWĪ, SAYYID. *See* Barelwī, Sayyid Aḥmad.

AḤMADĪYAH. A messianic movement in modern Islam, the Aḥmadīyah has been one of the most active and controversial movements since its inception in British India in 1889. It has sustained its activities for more than a century and has been unrivaled in its dedication to the propagation of the faith. Aḥmadī mosques and missionary centers have been established not only in the Indian subcontinent but also in numerous cities of the Western world, Africa, and Asia.

The core of Aḥmadī thought is prophetology, which draws its inspiration from the great medieval Muslim mystic Muḥyī al-Dīn ibn al-ʿArabī (1165–1240), who postulated an uninterrupted succession of nonlegislative prophets following Muḥammad. Claiming for its founder messianic and prophetic status, the Aḥmadī movement aroused the fierce opposition of Sunnī Muslims and was accused of rejecting the dogma according to which Muḥammad was the last prophet. While India was under British rule, the controversy remained a doctrinal dispute among private individuals or voluntary organizations, but when the Aḥmadī headquarters moved in 1947 to the professedly Islamic state of Pakistan, the issue became a constitutional problem of major importance. Religious scholars belonging to the Sunnī mainstream demanded the formal exclusion of the Aḥmadīs from the Islamic fold and achieved that objective in 1974. The history of the Aḥmadī movement thus affords a unique example of the intricate relationship between religion and state in Islam, an example in which secularly elected members of political institutions arrogated to themselves the authority to determine the religious affiliation of a group of citizens, and to draw constitutional conclusions from this determination.

History. Mirzā Ghulām Aḥmad, the founder of the Aḥmadī movement in Islam, was born in the late 1830s in Qādiān, a village in the Punjab. His claim to special spiritual standing was first announced in the early 1880s. The movement was established in March 1889, when Ghulām Aḥmad accepted a pledge of allegiance from a number of his followers in the Punjabi city of Ludhiana. He devoted the following years to prolific literary activity, to the organization and expansion of the new community, and to many polemical encounters with Sunnī *ʿulamāʾ,* Christian missionaries, and members of the Hindu revivalist movement of Ārya Samāj. A number of periodicals were launched in Qādiān: including the monthly *Review of Religions,* the main English organ for the propagation of the Aḥmadī view of Islam.

Ghulām Aḥmad died on 26 May 1908. He was succeeded in the leadership of the community by Nūruddīn, one of his first supporters, who became the first "Successor of the Messiah" *(khalīfat al-masīḥ).* During his leadership, the unity of the movement began to be threatened by differences of opinion on issues such as the relationship with non-Aḥmadī Muslims and the nature of the community's leadership.

Nūruddīn died in 1914 and was succeeded by Ghulām Aḥmad's son Bashīruddīn Maḥmūd Aḥmad. The differences in the movement now came to a head, and the Aḥmadīyah split into two factions, known as the Qādiānī and the Lāhorī. The Qādiānī faction, which was larger and retained control of the movement's headquarters and of its main publications, was headed by Maḥmūd Aḥmad, now known as *khalīfat al-masīḥ* II; the prominent personalities among the Lāhorīs were Muḥammad ʿAlī and Kḥvājah Kamāluddīn. In addition to personal friction among members of the two groups, the focal points of disagreement were the nature of Ghulām Aḥmad's religious claim, the extent of Maḥmūd Aḥmad's authority in community affairs, and the attitude to be adopted toward non-Aḥmadī Muslims. The Qādiānīs stressed Ghulām Aḥmad's claim to prophethood, maintained that Maḥmūd Aḥmad's religious authority was not less than that of Ghulām Aḥmad, and left little doubt that they considered non-Aḥmadī Muslims infidels. The Lāhorīs, on the other hand, held that Ghulām Aḥmad never claimed to be more than a "renewer" *(mujaddid)* of religion; they suggested that the community leadership be entrusted to a group such as the Supreme Council of the Aḥmadīyah (Ṣadr Anjuman-i Aḥmadīyah) rather than to one successor of the messiah; and they deemed infidels only those Muslims who regarded the Aḥmadīs the same. This attitude toward non-Aḥmadīs was intended to minimize friction with other Muslims.

Following the split, the Aḥmadīs continued their missionary and literary activity. The two factions renounced any connection with each other. The Lāhorī publications deal almost exclusively with familiar themes of Islamic modernism. They contain few references to ideas that distinguish the Aḥmadīyah from the Islamic mainstream. The Qādiānī *Review of Religions*, however, continued to stress the crucial role of Ghulām Aḥmad in the spiritual history of mankind. Its pages provide translations from Ghulām Aḥmad's works and details of such Aḥmadī missionary activities as the establishment of mosques and centers and cases of conversion to Islam. Several new institutions were established in Qādiān by order of Maḥmūd Aḥmad in order to coordinate the worldwide missionary and literary endeavors of the movement.

Following the partition of the subcontinent in 1947, the headquarters of the movement moved to Pakistan, where a town called Rabwa (after Qur'ān 23:51) was built in order to serve as the new center of the Aḥmadīyah. In Pakistan the movement faced increasing difficulties. Various Islamic groups, led by the Jamāʿat-i Islāmī, insisted that the Aḥmadīs be declared a non-Muslim minority and excluded from public office. In the early 1950s, this agitation was directed primarily against Muhammad Zafaru'llah Khan, a prominent Aḥmadī, who served at that time as Pakistan's foreign minister. The demand was accompanied by widespread anti-Aḥmadī riots in the Punjab, but the government stood its ground. The Aḥmadī issue came to the fore again in 1974. Following a clash between Aḥmadī and non-Aḥmadī students in Rabwa, pressure to exclude the Aḥmadīs from the fold of Islam was renewed; it was accompanied by riots and threats of a general strike by the religious leadership. After some initial resistance, Prime Minister Zulfiqar ʿAli Bhutto's government gave way and the National Assembly decided "to discuss the status in Islam of persons who do not believe in the finality of the prophethood of Muḥammad (peace be upon him)." After lengthy deliberations behind closed doors, the Assembly met in open session on 7 September 1974 and unanimously decided to amend the constitution of Pakistan by adding a clause stipulating that

> a person who does not believe in the absolute and unqualified finality of the prophethood of Muḥammad (peace be upon him), the last of the Prophets, or claims to be a Prophet, in any sense of the word or of any description whatsoever, after Muḥammad (peace be upon him), or recognizes such a claimant as a Prophet or a religious reformer, is not a Muslim for the purposes of the Constitution or Law.

In April 1984, in the context of intensifying the Islamic characteristics of public life in Pakistan, President Muhammad Zia ul-Haq promulgated an ordinance making Aḥmadī religious observance a punishable offense. Among other things, the Aḥmadīs were forbidden to refer to their faith as Islam, to preach or propagate it, or to call their places of worship mosques. All these offenses were made punishable by three years of imprisonment and a fine. In the wake of this ordinance, Mirzā Ṭāhir Aḥmad, the present head of the Aḥmadīyah, moved to London, where he still resided in the early 1990s.

Religious Thought. The religious thought of the Aḥmadīyah until 1914, and of its Qādiānī branch since then, revolves around Ghulām Aḥmad's persistent claim to be a divinely inspired religious thinker and reformer. The many ways in which Ghulām Aḥmad expressed his convictions enabled both his supporters and his rivals to make diverse and often contradictory interpretations of his claim to spiritual eminence. As has often been the case with Muslim revivalist and messianic movements, the starting point of Ghulām Aḥmad's thought was the assertion that Muslim religion and society had deteriorated to a point where divinely inspired reforms were essential in order to arrest the process of decline and restore the purity of Islam. It was against this background that Ghulām Aḥmad claimed to have been chosen by Allāh for the task of revitalizing Islam.

Ghulām Aḥmad's mission is described in his writings in diverse terms. The definition of his spiritual claim that was most acceptable to the Sunnī point of view was his declaration that Allāh appointed him to be the renewer *(mujaddid)* of Islam in the fourteenth century AH. More controversial was his claim to be the Mahdi and the Promised Messiah *(masīḥ-i mawʿūd)*. He supported this claim by an elaborate Christology arguing that Jesus did not die on the cross but only swooned; that he was taken down and cured of his wounds; and that he went to India and died a natural death at the age of 120 in the city of Srinagar. The Christian belief in the resurrection of Jesus and his return in glory at the end of days is, according to Ghulām Aḥmad, groundless. It is incontrovertibly refuted in several verses in the Qur'ān (e.g., 3:55) and is a Christian invention designed to prove that the living Jesus is superior to the deceased Muḥammad, and that Christianity is consequently superior to Islam. Whenever a Muslim tradition seems to suggest the second coming of Christ, it should be taken to indicate not the coming of Jesus himself, but that of a person similar to him. This person is Ghulām Aḥmad, whose spiritual role bears complete affinity with that of Jesus, in that both Jesus and Ghulām Aḥmad appeared when their people were subjected to foreign rule; both were rejected by their religiously decadent communities; both repudiated *jihād;* and neither brought a new law but rather vowed to revive laws brought by Moses and Muḥammad, respectively.

Ghulām Aḥmad's repeated assertion that Allāh made him a prophet was the most controversial formulation of his claim. Since it contradicted the Muslim dogma of Muḥammad as the last prophet, it brought upon Ghulām Aḥmad and his followers the most vociferous denunciations by the Sunnī *ʿulamā'*. However, Ghulām Aḥmad was able to maintain that his theology was compatible with the Muslim belief in the finality of Muḥammad's prophethood. He divided prophets into two categories: *tashrīʿī*, legislative prophets, who are entrusted with bringing a new book of revealed divine law and are usually founders of new communities; and *ghayr tashrīʿī*, nonlegislative prophets, who do not receive a new book of divine law but are sent to an existing community to urge it to implement the divine law brought by an earlier, legislative prophet. According to Ghulām Aḥmad, the belief in the finality of Muḥammad's prophethood applies only to the first, legislative category. This classification of prophets enabled Ghulām Aḥmad to attest that Muḥammad was, indeed, the seal of the prophets and to claim at the same time that Allāh could not possibly leave Muslims without prophetic guidance after the death of Muḥammad, a condition that would make Muslims an accursed and abandoned community. Therefore, while it is true that no law-giving prophet can appear after Muḥammad, prophetic perfections are continuously bestowed upon his most accomplished followers, such as Ghulām Aḥmad, to whom Allāh speaks and reveals his secrets. However, since Ghulām Aḥmad attained this position only by his faithful following of Muḥammad, his prophethood does not infringe upon Muḥammad's status as the seal of the prophets. Rather, the fact that the Prophet of Islam was capable of bestowing prophetic perfections on his accomplished followers proves Muḥammad's superiority over his predecessors in the prophetic office. Muslims are thus the only community privileged with divine communication and prophethood after the completion of Muḥammad's mission. Although this prophethood does not involve the revelation of new laws and is given only as a shadow of the prophethood of Muḥammad, its existence is a decisive indication of Islamic superiority over other religions.

Ghulām Aḥmad's claim to be the Mahdi is closely related to his view of *jihād*. The classical tradition according to which the Mahdi "will break the cross, kill the swine, and abolish war" is interpreted in a way that transforms the Mahdi into an entirely peaceful figure. The statement that the Mahdi will "abolish war" is understood literally, and great stress is laid on it; on the other hand, the killing of the swine and the breaking of the cross are understood metaphorically and are said to indicate the Mahdi's victory over Christianity by means of argument and spiritual power. *Jihād* with the sword has thus come to an end with the advent of the Mahdi. Even before that, however, it was far from all-out aggressive war; it was allowed only in response to persecution by infidels. This interpretation rejects the traditional view that the idea of *jihād* developed from a total prohibition in Mecca to a command of unrestricted validity in Medina. According to the Aḥmadīs, Islam has always been a religion dedicated to peace. Ghulām Aḥmad repeatedly denounced Muslims who preached violent *jihād:* not only did they distort an essential part of Islamic teaching, they also assisted Christian missionaries in misrepresenting Islam as a religion committed to expansion by violent means; the only *jihād* sanctioned by Islam is spreading the faith by preaching and persuasion.

Summary. The dispute between the Aḥmadīyah and mainstream Sunnī Islam stems from different approaches to the question of religious authority. As a messianic movement claiming a certain kind of prophethood for its founder and continuous divine inspiration for his successors, the Aḥmadīyah was bound to clash with the *ʿulamāʾ*, who felt that their authority as custodians of Islamic learning and interpreters of Islamic law was being undermined. The dispute was exacerbated by the fact that the *ʿulamāʾ* focused their opposition to the Aḥmadīyah on the emotional issue of Muḥammad's honor, which was said to have been tarnished by Ghulām Aḥmad's claim to be a receiver of divine revelation after the completion of Muḥammad's mission.

As far as the Aḥmadī struggle within Islam is concerned, the main point of contention is thus the religious claim of Ghulām Aḥmad, which is couched in terms derived from medieval Sufism. In its relationship with the non-Muslim world, however, the Aḥmadīyah is primarily engaged in defending Islam and depicting it as a liberal, humane, and progressive religion that has been systematically slandered by non-Muslims. This aspect of Aḥmadī teaching is well in line with that of modernist Muslim thinkers, though in other matters—for example, in their support for *pardah* and polygamy—the Aḥmadīs follow the traditional point of view. One of the essential differences between them and other contemporary Muslim movements is that the Aḥmadīs consider the peaceful propagation of their version of Islam among Muslims and non-Muslims alike to be an indispensable activity; in this they are persistent and unrelenting.

[*See also* India; Indonesia; Pakistan; Prophethood.]

BIBLIOGRAPHY

Aḥmadī Works

Aḥmad, Bashīruddīn Maḥmūd. *Invitation to Aḥmadiyyat.* Rabwa, 1961. The most comprehensive description of Aḥmadī beliefs in English, translated from the Urdu original of Ghulām Aḥmad's son and second successor.

Ghulām Aḥmad. *Jesus in India: Jesus' Escape from Death on the Cross and Journey to India.* London, 1978.

Khan, Muḥammad Ẓafrullah. trans. *Tadhkira: English Translation of the Dreams, Visions, and Verbal Revelations Vouchsafed to the Promised Messiah on Whom Be Peace.* London, 1976.

Khan, Muḥammad Ẓafrullah. *Aḥmadiyyat: The Renaissance of Islam.* London, 1978. History of the movement from the Aḥmadī point of view.

Non-Aḥmadī Works

Binder, Leonard. *Religion and Politics in Pakistan.* Berkeley and Los Angeles, 1961. The Aḥmadī controversy during the first years of Pakistan's existence.

Brush, Stanley E. "Aḥmadiyyat in Pakistan: Rabwa and the Aḥmadīs." *Muslim World* 45 (1955): 145–171.

Fisher, Humphrey J. *Aḥmadiyya: A Study of Contemporary Islam on the West African Coast.* London, 1963. Excellent study of the Aḥmadīyah in an African setting.

Friedmann, Yohanan. *Prophecy Continuous: Aspects of Aḥmadī Religious Thought and Its Medieval Background.* Berkeley, 1989. History of the Aḥmadīyah and its expansion. Includes analysis of the prophetology of both factions. The chapter on Aḥmadī *jihād* surveys relevant beliefs in medieval Muslim tradition. Extensive bibliography.

Pakistan National Assembly. "Verdict on Finality of Prophethood of Ḥaźrat Muḥammad (Peace Be Upon Him)." Islamabad, 1974.

Smith, Wilfred Cantwell. "Aḥmadiyya." In *Encyclopaedia of Islam*, new ed., vol. 2, pp. 301–303. Leiden, 1960–.

YOHANAN FRIEDMANN

AḤMAD KHĀN, SAYYID (1817–1898), Indian Islamic modernist writer and political activist. The family of Sir Sayyid Aḥmad Khān claimed lineal descent from the prophet Muḥammad; his ancestors had settled in Herat in Afghanistan and then migrated to Mughal India in the seventeenth century. Despite their residence in India for nearly two hundred years, Sir Sayyid's family retained a consciousness of their foreign origin. This extraterritorial consciousness determined their outlook, and that of other upperclass Muslims, in the Indian environment. They viewed the culture and political problems of Muslims from this particular perspective, generally detaching themselves from the indigenous Muslim masses but associating with them closely in periods of political crisis.

Sir Sayyid's formal education was strictly traditional and was never completed; he ceased formal schooling at eighteen. What traditional education he had acquired was neither comprehensive nor intensive, and this later exposed him to the ridicule of conservative critics, who considered him unqualified to undertake his bold modernization of Islam. Yet his weakness was his real strength: unfettered by the discipline of rigorous traditional education, through personal study and independent investigation he reached out to new horizons of intellectual creativity and laid the groundwork for a modern interpretation of Islam.

Sir Sayyid was loyal to the British colonial regime, which appointed him *sarishtahdār* (recorder) in the criminal department of a lower court. In 1839 he was appointed deputy reader in the office of the divisional commissioner in Uttar Pradish province, eventually rising to the position of subjudge. In 1855 he was transferred to Bijnore, where he participated in the upheavals of 1857. He emerged from this ordeal as both a loyal functionary of the British Government and a staunch Muslim nationalist.

Immediately after 1857 Sir Sayyid undertook three projects: to initiate an ecumenical movement in order to create understanding between Muslims and Christians; to establish scientific organizations that would help Muslims understand the secret of the West's success; and to analyze objectively the causes for the 1857 revolt. He was the only Muslim scholar ever to venture a commentary on the Old and New Testaments, in his *Mahomedan Commentary on the Holy Bible* (1862).

In order to refute the British view that the rebellion of 1857 was led by Muslims, he advanced the thesis that a large number of Muslims had remained loyal to the British government. Between 1860 and 1861 he published a series of articles, collected in *Risalah khair khawahan Musalmanan: An Account of the Loyal Mahomdans of India,* attempting to show that the majority of influential Muslims remained loyal to the British government and that they were by no means inveterate enemies of the British. At the same time Sir Sayyid continued to urge Muslim loyalty to the British in order to elicit British support for a fair Muslim share in the Indian political system. His mission also fostered respect and understanding between Muslims and Christians.

In May 1869 Sir Sayyid arrived in London and remained in Britain for fifteen months. There he internalized positive aspects of British culture, including the value system of modern scientific education and the capitalistic form of economy characterized by social and political *laissez-faire*.

In London he published twelve essays on the life of the prophet Mohammed, *A Series of Essays on the Life of Mohammad* (1870). In order to study British educational institutions he visited the universities of Cambridge and Oxford, as well as private preparatory schools including Eton and Harrow. These educational models enabled him to develop the blueprint for the Mohammedan Anglo-Oriental College, which he established in 1875 at Aligarh; in 1920 the college became Aligarh Muslim University.

Equipped with modern ideas and orientations, Sir Sayyid returned to India on 2 October 1870 and initiated his movement of religious and cultural modernism among Muslims. He resigned his position in the judicial service in 1876 and until his death in 1898 devoted his life to modernizing the life of Muslims in the Indian subcontinent.

Sir Sayyid devoted most of his energies to promoting modern education among Muslims, especially through the All-India Mohammedan Educational Conference, which existed from 1886 to 1937. From 1886 to 1898 the Educational Conference was pitted against the All-India National Congress, which espoused secular Indian nationalism. Sir Sayyid, on the contrary, promoted a form of Muslim nationalism that accentuated separatist Muslim politics in India; this gave rise to the All-India Muslim League, which in the 1930s and 1940s spearheaded the movement for the creation of Pakistan.

In the field of religion Sir Sayyid promoted an Islamic modernism that drew inspiration from the writings of Shāh Walī Allāh (1703–1762) and emphasized a rational approach to Islam and social reforms in Muslim culture. What made Sir Sayyid controversial was his emphasis on religious modernism that rejected the traditional practices and orientations of the orthodox, and his advocacy of modern education, which lured young Muslims from orthodox religious seminaries into Western-style schools and colleges. In recognition of his accomplishments, the British Government knighted him in 1888.

[*See also* Aligarh; All-India Muslim League.]

BIBLIOGRAPHY

Abd Allah, Doctor Sayyid. *The Spirit and Substructure of Urdu Prose Under the Influence of Sir Sayyid Ahmad Khan.* Lahore, 1940.

Baljon, J. M. S. *The Reforms & Religious Ideas of Sir Sayyid Ahmad Khan.* Lahore, 1958.

Dar, Bashir Ahmad. *Religious Thought of Sayyid Ahmad Khan.* Lahore, 1957.

Graham, George F. Irving. *The Life and Work of Sir Sayyid Ahmad Khan.* London, 1909.

Malik, Hafeez. *Sir Sayyid Ahmad Khan and Muslim Modernization in India and Pakistan.* New York, 1980.

Malik, Hafeez. ed. *Political Profile of Sir Sayyid Ahmad Khan: A Documentary Record.* Islamabad, 1982.

Malik, Hafeez, ed. *Sir Sayyid Ahmad Khan's Educational Philosophy: A Documentary Record.* Islamabad, 1989.

Malik, Hafeez, and Morris Demb, trans. *Sir Sayyid Ahmad Khan's History of the Bijnore Rebellion.* Delhi, 1982.

Troll, Christian W. *Sayyid Ahmad Khan: A Reinterpretation of Muslim Theology.* New Delhi, 1978.

HAFEEZ MALIK

AḤMAD SIRHINDĪ. *See* Sirhindī, Aḥmad.

AKHBĀRĪYAH. An emphatically traditionalist tendency in Shīʿī jurisprudence, Akhbārīyah first crystallized into a distinct school in the twelfth century. Its designation comes from the word *akhbār* (traditions of the Twelve Imams). Qom was an early stronghold of the traditionalists, but the opposing rationalist tendency (which came to be known as Uṣūlīyah) prevailed for many centuries. The rise of the Akhbārīyah came relatively late in Islamic history, its positions being formulated systematically for the first time by Mullah Muḥammad Amīn Astarābādī (Akhbārī; d. 1624). He rejected the teachings of most jurisprudents after the tenth century, insisting that principles of law accepted by them, such as *qiyās* (analogical reasoning), were unacknowledged borrowings from Sunnī jurisprudence. According to Astarābādī, the *akhbār* were the single most important source of law, enjoying precedence over both the apparent meaning of the Qur'ān and the traditions of the Prophet; this position was grounded in the Shīʿī belief that the imams are the infallible and indispensable interpreters of both Qur'ān and prophetic tradition. Indeed, the permissibility of a given action depends on the availability of a tradition from an imam sanctioning it; in the absence of such a tradition, the action is dubious and best omitted. (This contradicts the principle, found in both Uṣūlī and Sunnī jurisprudence, that every action is licit unless expressly forbidden.) This heavy reliance on *akhbār* had as its corollary a simple division of all traditions of the imams into *ṣaḥīḥ* (sound) and *ḍaʿīf* (weak); the more numerous and precise categories used by the Uṣūlīs were denounced as another borrowing from Sunnism.

Among prominent Akhbārīs of the seventeenth century were two figures who combined Ṣūfī proclivities with the strict traditionalism of their legal school, Muḥammad Taqī Majlisī (d. 1660) and Mullah Muḥsin Fayḍ Kāshānī (d. 1680); the compiler of a vast collection of the traditions of the imams, al-Ḥurr al-ʿĀmilī (1624–1693); and the jurist Sayyid Niʿmat Allāh Jazā'irī (1640–1700). During much of the eighteenth century, Akhbārī scholars, principally from Bahrain, exercised near-complete dominance of the *ʿatabāt,* the shrine cities of Iraq, which were the chief centers of Shīʿī learning after the collapse of the Ṣafavid dynasty (1501–1722) in Iran; such was their power, it is said, that adherents of the Uṣūlī school did not dare show their books in public. The situation was reversed through the efforts of the Uṣūlī scholar Āqā Muḥammad Bāqir Bihbahānī (1704–1793), who was able both by argumentation and vehemence of conduct to overcome his chief Akhbārī rival, Yūsuf Baḥrānī (1695–1772), whose adherence to the Akhbārīyah was in any event less dogmatic than that of his predecessors. The completeness of Bihbahānī's triumph enabled him to declare the Akhbārīs nonbelievers. The last Akhbārī of note was Mīrzā Muḥammad Akhbārī (1765–1818), who is said to have gained a promise of support from the Iranian ruler, Fatḥ ʿAlī Shāh (r. 1797–1834), in exchange for his obtaining by magical means the death of a Russian commander besieging Baku. The shah broke his word, forcing Mīrzā Muḥammad to leave for the *ʿatabāt,* where he met his death in a riot in 1818. The eclipse of the Akhbārīs is to be attributed ultimately to the greater flexibility and realism of the Uṣūlīs, whose tenets enabled them to offer the Shīʿī community a living source of guidance in the continued absence of the Twelfth Imam.

Today, Akhbārīs are to be found only in Khuzistan and in the Shīʿī communities of Bahrain and the southern littoral of the Persian Gulf.

[*See also* Uṣūlīyah.]

BIBLIOGRAPHY

Cole, Juan R. I. "Shiʿi Clerics in Iraq and Iran, 1722–1780: The Akhbari-Usuli Conflict Reconsidered." *Iranian Studies* 18.1 (Winter 1985): 3–34.

Kohlberg, Etan. "Akhbārīya." In *Encyclopaedia Iranica,* vol. 1, pp. 716–718. London and New York, 1982–.

Kohlberg, Etan. "Aspects of Akhbari Thought in the Seventeenth and Eighteenth Centuries." In *Eighteenth-Century Renewal and Reform in Islam,* edited by Nehemia Levtzion and John Obert Voll, pp. 133–160. Syracuse, N.Y., 1987.

Madelung, Wilferd. "Akhbāriyya." In *Encyclopaedia of Islam,* new ed., Supplement, fasc. 1–2, pp. 56–57. Leiden, 1960–.

Scarcia, Gianroberto. "Intorno alle controversie tra Aḫbārī e Uṣūlī presso gli imamiti di Persia." *Rivista degli Studi Orientali* 33 (1958): 211–250.

Hamid Algar

ĀKHŪND. Several meanings for *ākhūnd,* a Persian word meaning "religious scholar" or "leader," have been proposed by Iranian, Turkish, and Western writers. One states that the prefix *a* is actually a corrupted form of *āghā,* meaning "lord" or "master." Focusing on the *khūnd,* another source states that this is derived from the Persian *khāndān,* meaning "to read." However, Iranian scholar ʿAlī Akbar Dihkhudā states that *khūnd* is an abbreviation of Khudāvāndigār, (Almighty God). The Turkish researcher, Ahmed Zeki Velidi Togan, rejects all Persian etymologies. Instead, he argues that *ākhūnd* is a transposition of the Greek *arkūn* (or *argūn*), which was a common title for the Nestorian priests in pre-Islamic Asian regions. These etymological discrepancies point to the fact that no agreement exists as to the derivation of this term; what can be stated with certainty is the fact that it connotes a title given to religious personalities. (Among the Chinese Muslims, the imam in the mosque is also called *ahung*.)

The first usage of *ākhūnd* in Iran can be traced to the Timurid period (1409–1506), when personalities of distinguished accomplishments were called *ākhūnd*. A Timurid prince by the name of Amīr ʿAlīshāh Navā'ī refers to his mentor Mawlānā Faṣīḥ al-Dīn Niẓāmī (d. 1513) as *ākhūnd* for his broad knowledge of traditional and contemplative sciences. Niẓāmī also directed *madrasahs* (seminaries), which again may explain the usage of this word for religious scholars or leaders. We can state with certainty that *ākhūnd* was used as an honorific reserved for scholars of distinguished accomplishments during the Timurid period. The word maintained this connotation during the Ṣafavid period (1501–1722) as well. Two great philosophers of this period, Mullā Ṣadrā (d. 1640), and Mullā Naṣr Allāh Hamadānī (d. 1632), were referred to as *ākhūnd*.

In the Qājār period (1796–1925), the usage of *ākhūnd* became more frequent, and the term was used interchangeably with mullah. Even teachers of the old-fashioned elementary schools (*maktabkhānahs*) were sometimes referred to as *ākhūnds*. In spite of this wider usage, the term still continued to have an elevated honorific meaning, and the most distinguished religious scholar of the Qājār period, Kāẓim Khurāsānī (1839–1911), was called *ākhūnd*. Ākhūnd Khurāsānī's books are still required readings in the *madrasahs* of Iran and Iraq. His *Kifāyat al-uṣūl* has been endorsed by over a hundred leading *mujtahids*. However, according to Hamid Algar (*Encyclopaedia Iranica*), the expanded application of the term resulted in a "devaluation, and came gradually to signify not a religious leader, but on the contrary one who had failed to reach the degree of *ijtihād* and whose competence was restricted to the leading of prayers and the teaching of children."

During the Pahlavi period (1925–1979), the usage of *ākhūnd* as a pejorative term was encouraged by the monarchy, whose distaste for the religious hierarchy was anything but subtle. The secular antireligious forces gave a contemptuous ring to the term. In the government-sanctioned press, the term was applied to those who were anachronistic and opposed to "modernization." The legacy of this has been the entry of several pejorative derivations of *ākhūnd* into the Persian language. These are *ākhūndzādah* (one whose father is an *ākhūnd*), *ākhūndbāzī* (those who commit illegal acts), and *ḥukūmat-i ākhūndhā* (rule of the clergy). Aside from these, one can use the term *ākhūnd* to simply mean a religious leader.

[*See also* Mullah.]

BIBLIOGRAPHY

Algar, Hamid. "Ākūnd." In *Encyclopaedia Iranica*, vol. 1, pp. 731–732. London, 1982–.

Dā'irat al-maʿārif-i buzurg-i Islāmī (The Great Encyclopaedia of Islam). Edited by Kāẓim Mūsavī Bujnūrdī. Tehran, 1988–. The most comprehensive use of original sources in Persian and Arabic.

Dihkudā, ʿAlī Akbar. *Lughat'nāmah*. Tehran, 1947–. Well-known etymological reference for the Persian language.

Qazvīnī, Muḥammad. *Yād'dāsht'hā-yi* (Notes of Qazvīnī). Edited by Īraj Afshār. Tehran, 1953–. Contains several references to certain religious scholars as *ākhūnd*.

Bahman Baktiari

AL-. *See under following element of name or term.*

ʿALAWĪ, AḤMAD AL-, (1869–1934), more fully Abū al-ʿAbbās Aḥmad ibn Muṣṭafa al-ʿAlawī, Algerian Ṣūfī and poet. Characterized by the French Orientalist Emile Dermenghem as "one of the most celebrated mystic shaikhs of our times," al-ʿAlawī overcame humble origins and lack of formal education to create a substantial religious clientele with disciples and affiliated *zāwiyahs* throughout the Maghrib, Mashriq, East Africa, Yemen, and even Europe. His story is one of remarkable spiritual renewal within the idiom of Sufism in an era when Ṣūfīs and Sufism were under attack by the reformist Salafīyah movement.

Aḥmad al-ʿAlawī was born in Mostaganem in western Algeria during the period of intense colonization. The popular appeal of his teachings and the response they elicited were in part linked to the travails of the Muslim population under the French civilian administration. Al-ʿAlawī's great-grandfather had been a local notable; however, the family had fallen on hard times, and his father's death when the young man was only sixteen forced him into the profession of cobbler, ending what minimal Islamic education he had received. Al-ᶜAlawī's first association with formal Sufism came in the 1880s when he joined the ᶜĪsawī *ṭarīqah*. After attending Isawīyah *dhikr* gatherings and participating in their more extravagant practices, such as snake-charming, al-ᶜAlawī began to doubt the spiritual merit of the *ṭarīqah*. By the time he encountered the celebrated Darqāwī Shādhilī shaykh Muḥammad al-Būzīdī (d. 1909), al-ᶜAlawī had already distanced himself from the ᶜĪsawīyah.

Received into the Darqāwā *ṭarīqah* at the hands of al-Būzīdī, who also instructed the novice, al-ᶜAlawī was a *muqaddam* (one authorized to initiate members into a particular *ṭarīqah*) by the age of twenty-five, with authority to initiate others into the order.

Al-ᶜAlawī apparently remained in the Oran until 1909, the year his spiritual master al-Būzīdī died. Then he embarked on a journey to Tunis, Tripoli, and Istanbul, where he lingered until 1910. The Ottoman Empire was at that time rent by the political upheavals of the Young Turk revolution that deposed the sultan in April 1909. His experiences in the Ottoman capital during the Committee of Union and Progress's rule appear to have reinforced al-ᶜAlawī's conservative orientation. He returned to his native land shortly thereafter and only returned to the Mashriq for the *ḥajj* to Mecca and Medina, visiting Jerusalem and Damascus on the way, just before his death in 1934.

In the Oran, al-ᶜAlawī's followers persuaded him after 1909 to serve as head shaykh; some five years later he established an order independent from the Moroccan Darqāwā. In Tidgitt, Mostaganem's purely Muslim quarter, a great *zāwiyah* was constructed overlooking the sea and drew growing numbers of disciples. The master's position on the Muslims' relationship with the colonial regime and on Salafīyah teachings caused conflict with both the Europeans and fellow Muslims. Denouncing Algerians who had become naturalized French citizens, the shaykh also decried westernization, secularism, and modernization. As a riposte to the reformist publication *Al-shihāb*, al-ᶜAlawī created a weekly newspaper to defend Sufism against its detractors. By his death, al-ᶜAlawī had written some fifteen works, mostly on Sufism, as well as a *dīwān* of poetry. Some of these works exist only in manuscript form even today and are found at the Tidgitt *zāwiyah*, where the shaykh was buried in 1934.

[*See also* Algeria; Sufism, *article on* Ṣūfī Thought and Practice.]

BIBLIOGRAPHY

Berque, Augustin. "Un mystique moderniste: Le Cheikh Benalioua." *Revue Africaine* 79 (1936): 691–776. Biography by a French colonial official, based on the his friendship with al-ᶜAlawī from 1921 to 1934.

Lings, Martin. "Ibn ᶜAlīwa." In *Encyclopaedia of Islam*, new ed., vol. 3, pp. 700–701. Leiden, 1960–. Concise version of Lings's full-length biography, containing a short bibliography of additional sources on the ᶜAlawīyah and its founder.

Lings, Martin. *A Sufi Saint of the Twentieth Century: Shaikh Ahmad al-Alawi. His Spiritual Heritage and Legacy*. 2d ed. Los Angeles, 1971. The fullest English-language treatment of al-ᶜAlawī's life and works, including selections from his writings and poetry.

JULIA CLANCY-SMITH

ᶜALAWID DYNASTY. A family of religious notables, the ᶜAlawīs gained political dominion and the status of a royal house in Morocco during the seventeenth century and have ruled there continuously since that time, playing a significant, formative role in its development as a modern nation-state. The dynasty is also known as the Fīlālīs or Filalians because of its long association with the region of Tāfīlālt.

Like the Saᶜdīs who preceded them as rulers and state-builders (1509–1659), the ᶜAlawīs are *sharīf*s, descendants of the prophet Muḥammad. In circumstances and stages that remain obscure, they migrated from the Arabian Peninsula to the Tāfīlālt in southeastern Morocco during the early thirteenth century. There they settled near Sijilmassa (present-day Rissani), the region's capital and an important terminus of the trans-Saharan trade. As *sharīf*s they soon prospered in this new setting, where veneration of the Prophet and the exaltation of his descendants were emerging as particularly salient forms of popular social and religious practice, giving those who claimed descent from him increasing access to economic and political power. Very little is known concerning the ᶜAlawīs' activities in the Tāfīlālt before the seventeenth century, but clearly by then they had evolved into a political movement with dynastic ambitions. Between 1631 and 1664 they established themselves as sovereign rulers of this region and began to expand their control into adjacent territories.

Under the able leadership of sultans Mawlāy (literally "my lord", a title given to *sharīf*s) al-Rāshid (r. 1664–1672) and his half-brother Mawlāy Ismāᶜīl (r. 1672–1727), the ᶜAlawīs extended their political dominion over all the Atlantic, Mediterranean, and Saharan territories that together make up Morocco, appropriating their revenues and human resources to strengthen the new dynasty's military forces, to reestablish permanent structures of government, and to finance the *jihād* against Christian forces still in possession of strategic points along the Atlantic and Mediterranean coasts. By the beginning of the eighteenth century they had won significant victories in the last cause and had imposed a degree of internal control unmatched until the twentieth century.

After the death of Mawlāy Ismāʿīl the power and authority of the sultanate was seriously weakened by a prolonged succession struggle (1727–1757) among his numerous heirs and by widespread rebellion against continuation of the imperious, arbitrary, and economically burdensome regime he had sought to enforce throughout the country. Despite the upheavals of this interregnum, the ʿAlawīs preserved their role as ruling dynasty and after 1757 gradually reasserted their political control under the astute guidance of Mawlāy Muḥammad ibn ʿAbd Allāh (r. 1757–1790), who defused political discontent by implementing a more decentralized system of government and by relieving the tax burden on agricultural producers through increasing the *makhzan*'s (government) dependence on revenues from Morocco's growing commerce with Europe.

Nonetheless, relations between state and society remained contentious, the *makhzan*'s financial resources limited, and its military forces weak and unreliable. These difficulties were exacerbated throughout the nineteenth century by the damaging effects of European military, political, and economic intervention. ʿAlawī sultans, especially Mawlāy Muḥammad ibn ʿAbd al-Raḥman (r. 1859–1873) and Mawlāy al-Ḥasan I (r. 1873–1894), responded to these conditions by initiating military, administrative, and fiscal reforms intended to provide the *makhzan* with European technology and expertise, modern armed forces, and a more efficient and centralized government. At considerable cost these reforms enhanced the scope and power of the state but could not provide it with means sufficient to repulse European invasion or to prevent the imposition of a Franco-Spanish protectorate in 1912.

The protectorate powers retained the ʿAlawī sultanate and elements of its government as legitimizing symbols and structures and as a buffer against popular resistance. ʿAlawī sultans reluctantly accepted this subservient role until the 1930s, when Mawlāy Muḥammad ibn Yūsuf (r. 1927–1961) began to reassert royal authority and lent his support to the movement for national unification and independence that emerged under religious and secular leadership during this period. His defiance of protectorate authorities became a powerful symbol of the national will to resist foreign rule and played a crucial role in the sultanate's political revival. His exile in 1953 by the French administration precipitated widespread popular unrest and gave decisive impetus to the culminating stage of Morocco's struggle for political independence. At the same time, it consolidated the dynasty's identification with that struggle and confirmed Muḥammad ibn Yūsuf's leadership role in it. After his triumphant return to Morocco on 17 November 1955 he led its delegation in the final negotiations for independence, which was granted on 2 March 1956. He ruled the country as King Muḥammad V until his death in 1961 and was succeeded by his son, the present King Ḥasan II.

The ʿAlawī sultans have drawn religious authority and prestige from a variety of sources to legitimate and promote their political objectives. As *sharīfs* they were believed to be possessed of a special grace (*barākah*), a privileged access to divine favor that empowered them to be effective intermediaries in spiritual as well as material affairs. As such they were strategically placed in Morocco's predominantly tribal society to accumulate the symbolic and material capital essential to their larger political and dynastic goals. Their functions and status converged in practice and public perception with those of the popular saint (*murābiṭ*, *ṣāliḥ*, or *sayyid*), effectively fusing the power and prestige of their sacred lineage with the latter's reputed ability to work miraculous deeds and broker divine assistance in day to day affairs. They also drew authority and legitimacy from asserting their role as *ʿulamāʾ* interpreters of the *sharīʿah*, scrupulous adherents to the Sunnī interpretation of Islam, and ardent patrons of Islamic scholarship and education. Similarly, they claimed leadership of the faithful in the duty of *jihād* against Christian adversaries and achieved renown in this cause, although their credibility in this role diminished during the nineteenth century when military operations against vastly superior European armies and navies became impracticable and nonbelligerence toward Europe became a compelling state interest.

Combined, these overlapping roles provided enormous symbolic and practical power to the monarch as person and institution. By themselves, however, they were never sufficient in practice to sustain a broad and lasting acceptance of ʿAlawī political legitimacy or to secure their political dominion. This was realized only with the simultaneous deployment of military force and the apparatus of a temporal state, which alone could guarantee their continuing access to material resources, security against internal opposition, and a measure of success against European intervention.

Over the centuries the history of the ʿAlawī dynasty has become inextricably intertwined with the history of modern Morocco. Although opposition to the method and legitimacy of their political dominion persists, they continue to embody and unite the Arab, Islamic, and Moroccan traditions that are essential constituents in the modern nation's identity and to provide an important link between contemporary society and these historical and religious traditions.

[*See also* Mawlāy; Morocco.]

BIBLIOGRAPHY

Abun-Nasr, Jamil M. *A History of the Maghrib in the Islamic Period.* 3d ed. Cambridge, 1987. The most comprehensive historical survey available in English.

Brown, Kenneth L. *People of Salé: Tradition and Change in a Moroccan City, 1830–1930.* Cambridge, Mass., 1976. Rich source on religion, culture, and society, seen through a perceptive account of the life of one urban community.

Burke, Edmund, III. *Prelude to Protectorate in Morocco: Precolonial Protest and Resistance, 1860–1912.* Chicago, 1976. Important discussion of the internal and external factors that led to the imposition of European protectorates.

Eickelman, Dale F. *Moroccan Islam: Tradition and Society in a Pilgrimage Center.* Austin, 1976. Examines the role of an influential lineage of religious notables, the Sharqawa, in Moroccan culture, society, and politics.

El Mansour, Mohamed. *Morocco in the Reign of Mawley Sulayman.* Wisbech, Cambridgeshire, 1990. Informative, in-depth study of the sultan and his time, based on extensive use of Moroccan archival and manuscript sources.

Entelis, John P. *Culture and Counterculture in Moroccan Politics.* Boulder, 1989. A political scientist explores the sources of national identity and political legitimacy in modern Morocco.

Geertz, Clifford. *Islam Observed: Religious Development in Morocco and Indonesia.* New Haven, 1968. Ground-breaking effort that focuses substantially on the relationship between religion and temporal power in Morocco.

Gellner, Ernest. *Saints of the Atlas.* London, 1969. Seminal work on the function and status of Muslim holy men in the tribal society of the High Atlas Mountains in Morocco.

Julien, Charles-André. *History of North Africa: Tunisia, Algeria, and Morocco from the Arab Conquest to 1830.* Translated by John Petrie. Edited by C. C. Stewart. London, 1970. Volume 2 of a standard historical survey by the late dean of French historians of North Africa.

Laroui, Abdallah. *The History of the Maghrib: An Interpretive Essay.* Translated by Ralph Manheim. Princeton, 1977. New perspective on Moroccan history by one of that country's most important historians.

Munson, Henry, Jr. *Religion and Power in Morocco.* New Haven, 1993. Thoughtful reinterpretation of this theme by an anthropologist well versed in Moroccan textual sources.

Waterbury, John. *The Commander of the Faithful: The Moroccan Political Elite—A Study in Segmented Politics.* London, 1970. Insightful application of segmentary theory to Morocco's political system.

Zartman, I. William. *Morocco: Problems of a New Power.* New York, 1964. Reliable introduction to the challenges facing monarchy and nation since independence.

WILFRID J. ROLLMAN

ʿALAWĪYAH. A term derived from the name of the cousin and son-in-law of the prophet Muḥammad, ʿAli ibn Abī Ṭālib (d. 661), ʿAlawīyah was applied originally to those who supported ʿAlī's exclusive right to lead the Muslim community after the death of the Prophet in 632. The tenth-century Shīʿī writer al-Nawbakhtī called them al-Shīʿah al-ʿAlawīyah in his *Firaq al-Shīʿah* (The Shīʿah Sects, Najaf, 1969, p. 66). These Shīʿī (Partisans of ʿAlī) were also called ʿAlawīyūn. According to a Shīʿī source, the Prophet is reported to have told ʿAlī, "At the Day of Resurrection you and your partisan [Shīʿah] shall come riding on she-camels of light shouting: We are the followers of ʿAlī [ʿAlawīyūn]!" (Al-Shaykh ʿAbbās al-Qummī, *Safīnat al-biḥār* [The Ship of Seas], Qom, 1935, vol. 2, p. 253). Throughout history the term *ʿAlawīyah* has been generally used to include all the Shīʿah, whether orthodox or heterodox, who place ʿAlī and his descendants the imams at the center of their religious system. Thus, there is no contradiction in the fact that the Zaydīyah of Yemen, an orthodox school of thought, and the Ithnā ʿAsharīyah (Twelvers), considered moderate Shīʿī, are both ʿAlawīyah. Likewise, heterodox Shīʿī groups, such as the Kizilbash, Takhtajīs, and Çepnîs of Turkey, the Mutāwilah (Mutawallīs) of Lebanon, the Shabak and Sarlīyah-Kaka'īyah of Iraq, and the ʿAlī Ilāhīs or Ahl-i Ḥaqq (People of the Truth) of Iran, are considered ʿAlawīyah. However, in modern times the terms ʿAlawīyah, ʿAlawīyūn, ʿAlawites, and ʿAlids exclusively denote the Nuṣayrīyah, an extremist Shīʿī school of thought whose adherents live in the northwestern mountain range of Syria (al-ʿAlawīyūn Mountain). The major city of al-ʿAlawīyah district is al-Lādhiqīyah (Latakia), famous for its choice tobacco. The term Nuṣayrīyah is derived from the name Muḥammad ibn Nuṣayr, a follower of the eleventh Shīʿī imam, al-Ḥasan al-ʿAskarī (d. 873). At first, Ibn Nuṣayr claimed to be the *bāb* ("gate") of this imam and privy to the divine mysteries of the twelve Shīʿī imams. But he went further, proclaiming the apotheosis of al-ʿAskarī, who therefore condemned him. The teachings of Ibn Nuṣayr led to the growth of a school of thought originally called al-Namirīyah because of Ibn Nuṣayr's association with the Arab tribe of this name. But since the time of Abū ʿAbd Allāh al-Ḥusayn ibn Ḥamdān al-Khuṣaybī (d. 957), the great propagandist of this school, it has been known as Nuṣayrīyah.

In the nineteenth century, because of harsh living conditions, the ʿAlawīyah, who were mostly farmers, began to leave their mountain abode and seek employment in other parts of Syria. Many of them engaged in menial work and were despised by the Sunnī Muslim majority. In the wake of World War I, the French occupied Syria, and in 1922 they established Dawlat al-ʿAlawīyīn (the ʿAlawīyūn State) for the ʿAlawīyah, whom they called ʿAlawīyūn (Followers of ʿAlī). Under the French mandate, young ʿAlawī men readily enlisted in the newly established Syrian army, while the Sunnī majority, who hated the French imperialists, shunned military service. When the Arab Socialist (Baʿth) party was established in the 1940s, many ʿAlawīs joined. By the middle 1960s they occupied key positions in both army and government; in 1970, Hafez al-Assad, a high-ranking ʿAlawī military officer, overthrew the government in a coup d'état, and in February 1971 he became the first ʿAlawī president of Syria.

The ʿAlawīyah are extremist Shīʿīs, known as *ghulāt* (exaggerators), whose religious system separates them from Sunnī Muslims. The fundamental article of their religion is the absolute oneness of God, but they do not attempt to define his existence or attributes either philosophically or theologically. Like another group of *ghulāt*, Ahl-i Ḥaqq, they believe that God appeared on earth seven times in human form, and that ʿAlī is the last manifestation of the deity and the consummate reality in whom all previous manifestations found their ultimate end and completion. But this God who appeared in seven forms has three personalities, corresponding to a trinity comprised of ʿAlī, also called the Maʿnā (Meaning or Causal Determinant), Muḥammad (God's *ism*, or "name"), and Salmān al-Fārisī (God's *bāb*). This God ʿAlī, the creator of heaven and earth, also created Muḥammad and charged him to preach the message of the Qur'ān. Thus, Muḥammad cannot be homologous with ʿAlī in his divinity; he occupies an inferior position in the trinity. Like the Ithnā ʿAsharīyah the ʿAlawīyah believe that the twelve imams possess divine knowledge and have *bābs* who transmit this knowledge to the faithful of their generation. When the twelfth and last imam, Muḥammad (the Mahdi), disappeared at the end of the ninth century, Ibn Nuṣayr claimed to be his *bāb*, as he had done before with his father al-Askarī. The ʿAlawīyah maintain that every generation should have an imam to uphold the Shīʿī faith.

Worship of light forms is an essential part of the ʿAlawīyah religious system, which probably has its origin in the astral religion of the Sabaeans. This light, symbolized by the sun, is the mystery of God; thus ʿAlī is surrounded by light and dwells in the sun *(shams)*. Those who hold this belief are called Shamsīs. The Qamarīs, however, believe that the God ʿAlī dwells in the moon *(qamar)*, and that the black spots which appear on the moon are the embodiment of the worshiped ʿAlī, who carries his famous sword Dhū al-Fiqār (that which has splitting power).

One of the unique doctrines of the ʿAlawīyah concerns spiritual hierarchies. They believe that there are countless worlds known to God, chief among them al-ʿĀlam al-Nūrānī (World of Light), inhabited by spirits of many ranks, including the Aytām (Incomparables), Naqībs (Princes), Najībs (Excellent Ones), Mukhtaṣṣūn (Peculiars), Mukhliṣūn (Pure in Faith), and Mumtaḥanūn (the Tried), who correspond to the ranks of angels. They also acknowledge al-ʿĀlam al-Turābī (Earthly World), where men reside. They believe in the metempsychosis of human beings, animals, and plants. At death the soul of a good ʿAlawī will pass into another human body, while that of a wicked one will pass into an unclean or predatory animal. The ʿAlawīyah are very secretive, refusing to divulge their beliefs to strangers. They resort to *taqīyah* (dissimulation) to preserve their ancient religion, especially the belief in the principles of good and evil, symbolized by light and darkness, which depends on an allegorical interpretation of the Qur'ān and the traditions of the prophet Muḥammad. For this reason, initiation into the mysteries of this school is an extremely important ceremony which may have its origins in Sufism and Ḥikmat al-Ishrāq (Neoplatonism). [*See also* Taqīyah.]

The ʿAlawīyah celebrate many of the Muslim festivals, like ʿĪd al-Fiṭr and ʿĪd al-Aḍḥā. Like the rest of the Shīʿah, they observe ʿĀshūrā' to commemorate the martyrdom of the imam al-Ḥusayn, whom they regard as divine and liken to Jesus Christ. They also celebrate Persian festivals, chiefly the Nawrūz (New Year), because of their belief in the superiority of the Persians over the Arabs. They believe that after the Arabs rejected ʿAlī, he appeared as the Maʿnā in the person of the Persian Sassanian kings. They also celebrate some Christian festivals including Epiphany, Pentecost, Palm Sunday, and the feasts of St. John the Baptist, St. John Chrysostom, St. Barbara, and St. Mary Magdalene. The ʿAlawīyah also celebrate Mass, including consecration of bread and wine, albeit in a Shīʿī context. In the Mass the great mystery of God is the sacrament of the flesh and blood which Christ offered to his disciples at the Last Supper, but the ʿAlawīyah maintain that the mystery of faith is ʿAlī the light, who is manifested in the wine. This indicates that they may have Christian origins; at the least, they were greatly influenced by their Christian neighbors.

[*See also* ʿAlī ibn Abī Ṭālib; Ithnā ʿAsharīyah; Shīʿī Islam, *historical overview article*.]

BIBLIOGRAPHY

Dussaud, René. *Histoire et religion des Nosairis*. Paris, 1990.

Goldziher, Ignácz. *Vorlesungen über den Islam*. Heidelberg, 1910.

Hasluck, F. W. *Christianity and Islam under the Sultans*. 2 vols. Oxford, 1929.

Jurji, Edward J. "The ʿAlids of North Syria." *Moslem World* 29 (October 1939): 329–341.

Lammens, Henri. "Au pays des Nosairis." *Revue de l'Orient Chrétien* 4 (1899): 572–579; 5 (1900): 99–117, 303–318, 423–444.

Luschan, Felix von. "The Early Inhabitants of Western Asia." *Journal of the Royal Anthropological Institute* 41 (1911): 221–244.

Luschan, Felix von. "Die Tahtadji und andere Reste des alten Bevolkerung Lykiens." *Archiv für Anthropologie* 19 (1918): 31–53.

Lyde, Samuel. *The Ansyreeh and Ismaeleeh*. London, n.d.

Lyde, Samuel. *The Asian Mystery*. London, 1860.

Madelung, Wilferd. "Bemerkungen zur imamitischen Firaq-Literatur." *Der Islam* 43 (1967): 37–52.

Massignon, Louis. "Nuṣairī." In *Encyclopaedia of Islam*, vol. 3, pp. 963–967. Leiden, 1913–.

Molyneux-Seel, L. "A Journey in Dersim." *Geographical Journal* 44 (July 1914): 49–68.

Moosa, Matti. *Extremist Shiites: The Ghulat Sects*. Syracuse, N.Y., 1988.

Salisbury, Edward. "The Book of Sulayman's First Ripe Fruit Disclosing the Nosairian Religion." *Journal of the American Oriental Society* 8 (1864).

Strothmann, Rudolf. "Die Nusairi im heutigen Syrien." *Nachrichten der Akademie der Wissenschaften, Gottingen, Philosophische-Historische Klasse* 4 (1950): 29–64.

Trowbridge, Stephen V. R. "The Alevis, or Deifiers of Ali." *Harvard Theological Review* 2 (1909): 340–352. Republished as "The ʿAlevis." *Moslem World* 11 (July 1921): 253–266.

White, George E. "The Shiah Turks." *Faith and Thought* 43 (1908): 225–239.

White, George E. "The Alevi Turks of Asia Minor." *Contemporary Review Advertiser* 104 (November 1913): 690–698.

White, George E. "Some Non-Conforming Turks." *Moslem World* 8 (July 1918): 242–248.

Matti Moosa

ALBANIA. The only European country with a Muslim majority, Albania emerged in 1992 from nearly half a century of communism and state-sponsored suppression of religious beliefs. The Balkan nation, which borders Serbia, Macedonia, and Greece, is the poorest and most isolated country in Europe. The rugged Albanian countryside is dotted with hundreds of thousands of concrete bunkers—a bizarre legacy of Enver Hoxha, the Marxist leader who feared foreigners and who in 1967 declared Albania the world's first atheist state.

No reliable census has been taken since 1945, but experts say an estimated 70 percent of Albania's 3.3 million people either practice Islam or come from Muslim families. Another 20 percent are Orthodox Christians, and the remaining 10 percent are Roman Catholic.

Archaeological excavations at Butrint, along the Adriatic Sea near Albania's border with Greece, show that the country was first inhabited by the Kaon tribe, who lived in the area from around 800 to 600 BCE. Albania, known in ancient times as Illyria, was invaded by the Greeks, Romans, Byzantines, and Turks. A beautifully preserved Roman amphitheater at Butrint dates from the second century CE; nearby are Ottoman tombstones with markings in Arabic script dating from the fifteenth century.

In addition to the spread of Islam's influence into Albania, the Middle Ages also saw the birth of the Bektāshīyah, a Shīʿī-influenced liberal Ṣūfī order based on the teachings of Shaykh Ḥajjī Bektāsh, a thirteenth-century scholar who built a large following in Anatopia.

Today an estimated 800 mosques can be found throughout Albania, in addition to 360 Bektāshī holy places or *tekke*s. Albania's oldest mosque was built in 1380 in the town of Berat, around the time the Ottoman Empire began setting its sights on the territory. In Korçë can be found Albania's second oldest Muslim site, the Mosque of Ilias Mirahori, constructed in 1494. The Shkoder mosque is the only one in Albania influenced by the imperial style of Istanbul. The Abdurrahman Pashi mosque near Peqini is considered one of the most important examples of Islamic culture in Albania; built in 1822, its clock tower and minaret are connected by the main section.

The medieval warrior Skanderbeg, whose statue dominates the main square of Tirana, is still revered in Albania for having held the Turks at bay for thirty-six years. He was ultimately defeated by Sultan Mehmed II in 1479. Except for the beginning of the nineteenth century, when Ali Pasha of Tepelena established a short-lived principality in the southern half of the country, Albania was little more than a backwater of the vast Ottoman Empire. That status continued until 1912, when another patriot, Ismail Kemal, rose up to declare Albania's independence.

Through the long years under Ottoman rule many Albanians came to practice Islam; others were won over by the Orthodox Church of neighboring Greece, and still others—influenced by the Vatican—chose Roman Catholicism. As Lord Byron once said of the Albanians, "The Greeks hardly regard them as Christians, or the Turks as Muslims; and in fact they are a mixture of both, and sometimes neither."

In a biography of Ismail Kemal, the Italian historian Renzo Falaschi wrote, "With their indomitable and adamantine character, the Albanians imposed even more adaptations to Islam than vice versa. It could be said that [the Albanian Muslims] have accepted Baha'ism spiritually, Illuminism philosophically and, practically, the European nationalism of the nineteenth century. On the whole, they have created an Islam that has the meditation of the East and the dynamism of the West" (*Ismail Kemal Bey Vlora,* Rome, 1985, p. 346).

That combination of meditation and dynamism persisted into the early twentieth century, when Albania unexpectedly became the world headquarters of the Bektāshīyah. In 1928, when Kemal Atatürk's secular reforms forced the Bektāshīs out of Turkey, their leader Salih Dedei came to Albania and established himself in Tirana.

In fact, until the Communist takeover in 1944 Albania was noted for its religious tolerance. During the Fascist and Nazi occupation of World War II, Albania refused to turn over its 300-member Jewish community to the Germans. Because of the shelter provided by their Muslim and Christian neighbors, only five Albanian Jews perished.

Following the Communist victory over the Nazis and the declaration of an Albanian People's Socialist Republic, however, Hoxha warned Muslim, Orthodox, and Catholic clergymen alike not to preach against his hard-line government. Two prominent Bektāshī leaders, Baba Fajo and Baba Fejzo, were killed in March 1947 in circumstances that still are unclear. Other Muslim clerics who disappeared included Mustafa Effendi Varoshi, mufti of Durres, Hafez Ibrahim Dibra, former grand mufti of Albania, and Sheh Xhemal Pazari of Tirana. By 1968 the New York-based Free Albania Committee reported that the Communists had executed or sentenced to labor camps some two hundred clergymen of all faiths.

In 1967 Hoxha took his views a step further and declared Albania the world's first officially atheist state. By May of that year 2,169 mosques, churches, monasteries, and other houses of worship had been either closed, converted to other uses, or destroyed. Believers caught wearing religious symbols risked up to ten years' imprisonment. The regime proudly announced that "the last and most parasitical form of exploitation of the masses has been swept away."

In 1985 Hoxha died, and by late 1990 the democratic reforms sweeping across eastern Europe reached Albania. In the face of unprecedented student demonstrations, Hoxha's hand-picked successor Ramiz Alia was forced to reverse the ban on religion, allow freedom of speech, and permit the formation of new political parties.

In 1991, shortly after religious worship was allowed once again, more than fifteen thousand onlookers crowded into and around the Ethem Bey Mosque in downtown Tirana for Albania's first legal Muslim service in twenty-four years. Shortly after that the Bektāshī mosque, surrounded by crumbling apartment buildings on the city's outskirts, was rededicated; precious Islamic works of art were brought out and displayed after years in hiding. By early 1992, Albania had announced its intention of joining the forty-five-nation Organization of the Islamic Conference, a move welcomed by Saudi Arabia and other Muslim states.

In addition to the dominant Sunnīs and the Bektāshīs, Albania also has members of the Rifāʿīyah, the Khatwatīyah, and at least six other small Muslim groups—some of them numbering fewer than one hundred adherents. Prominent Muslims estimate that there are only two hundred practicing imams throughout Albania, and that fewer than three thousand Albanian Muslims can read Arabic.

This situation is rapidly changing. Since March 1992, with the inauguration of cardiologist Sali Berisha as the country's first democratically elected president, Pope John Paul II has visited Albania, and Mormons, Bahā'īs, Baptists, Jehovah's Witnesses, and Protestant evangelicals have flocked to Albania, bringing food, clothing, and medicine along with new religious ideas. Likewise, Muslim missionaries from Saudi Arabia, Kuwait, and the United States have set up offices in Tirana to promote Islam and provide funds for the restoration of mosques. Thanks to Arab charities, new mosques are also being built throughout the country, though they rarely follow traditional Albanian architectural styles.

Arab companies are also becoming prominent in business. One of the country's first private lending institutions, the Arab-Albanian Islamic Bank, was established in 1993 as a joint venture between Albania's state-owned National Commercial Bank and a group of investors from Bahrain and Saudi Arabia. The bank, which occupies a former Communist Party office, has $100 million in authorized capital and promotes investment within the guidelines of Islamic banking principles. Another company, from Kuwait, is building Albania's first five-star luxury hotel on the outskirts of Tirana.

[*See also* Bektāshīyah.]

BIBLIOGRAPHY

Biber, Mehmet. "Albania, Alone against the World." *National Geographic* 158 (October 1980). Unusual account of Albania during the Hoxha regime.

Brewer, Bob. *My Albania: Ground Zero*. New York, 1992. Anthology of essays and photos chronicling the fall of communism in Albania.

Doder, Dusko. "Albania Opens the Door." *National Geographic* 182 (July 1992).

Prifti, Peter R. *Socialist Albania since 1944*. Cambridge, Mass., 1978. Political appraisal of the Hoxha dictatorship.

Sidoma, Michel. "Le pays qui a chassé l'Islam." *Jeune Afrique*, no. 1097 (13 January 1982). French journalist's report, one of the first published, on Albanian Islamic life under Marxism.

LARRY LUXNER

ALCHEMY. Viewed from the perspective of the history of science, alchemy can legitimately be considered an Islamic creation. Indeed, notwithstanding some development in ancient China, it was in the Islamic world that alchemy developed from a dark craft with its mysterious recipes into a systematic discipline founded on well-defined cosmological and metaphysical principles; and it was here that we find for the first time a body of alchemical literature largely (though not invariably) written in a clear scientific language unobscured by the veils of esoteric figurative terminology. Muslim alchemists deserve yet further credit: while they themselves had drawn on various foreign and indigenous sources, including Indian and possibly Chinese sources, it was their ideas and doctrines that served as the point of departure for the alchemists of the medieval West. Thus Islamic alchemy should be recognized as the springboard of that complex process that led to the birth of the modern science of chemistry.

As for the philosophical matrix of Islamic alchemy, it is possible to glean from a vast body of largely unstudied Arabic alchemical literature two of its fundamental aspects: a cosmology, and a theory of elements. The cosmology of Muslim alchemists is thoroughly non-Aristotelian. In a highly enigmatic but equally influential Arabic text available to Islam from the earliest phases of its alchemical tradition, one finds unmistakable indications of the belief that there is an immutable cosmic correspondence between "what is above" and "what is below," and between the inner world of the soul and the outer world of phenomena, and that the manifold forms in which matter occurs have a single and unique origin. This doctrine of an essential unity in diversity discards Aristotle's fateful distinction between the terrestrial and celestial worlds; furthermore, it implies a naturalistic possibility of transmutation and accommodates astrology. In addition, it renders the process of purifying matter inseparable from that of the purification of the soul. The text in question, the celebrated *Al-lawḥ al-zumurrud*, is an apocryphal collection of aphorisms; in its Latin translation, *Tabula smaragdina*, it was an avidly studied document throughout the later European Middle Ages.

As for the Islamic alchemical theory of elements, it seems to have been derived from the standard Greek sources. All Muslim alchemists accept, as Aristotle does, the Empedoclean doctrine of four primary bodies—earth, water, air and fire—and all of them recognize Aristotle's four primary qualities—hot, cold, moist and dry. Yet some of them profoundly violate the familiar Aristotelian doctrine of elements that claims that all material things are ultimately composed of the Empedoclean primary bodies, which are distinguished from one another by their qualities, but that these qualities do not exist independently of the bodies in which they inhere; qualities were *forms*—that is, conceptual rather than real entities. In contrast, for example, Jābir ibn Ḥayyān believed that the four qualities, called natures (*ṭabā'iʿ*), were indeed independently existing real entities; it was these natures—and not the Empedoclean bodies—that were the true *material* elements of things. Nonetheless, many alchemists of Islam appear here to follow Aristotle faithfully.

This appears to be the theoretical framework of Islamic alchemy. Fundamental themes of this enterprise include not only the transmutation of base metals into gold, but also the artificial generation of living beings, even of new forms of life not existing in nature. Believing that all varieties *(anwāʿ)* of metals belong to the same genus *(jins)*, the alchemists differentiated them only in terms of "accidents" *(aʿrāḍ)*. Accidents were changeable; therefore, one metal could be changed into another. This transmutation could be carried out in many ways, but the best method was that of the elixir *(al-iksīr)*. Likewise, given the universal relationship between the macrocosm *(al-ʿālam al-kabīr)* and the microcosm *(al-ʿālam al-ṣaghīr)*, all grand biological processes occurring in nature could be replicated, and in principle improved upon, in the alchemical laboratory. Thus all kinds of monsters and strange birds, and all kinds of novel human beings, could be generated artificially. Another fundamental theme of Islamic alchemy is the prolongation of human life by means of the elixir; here alchemy is directly related to medicine.

It seems ironic that despite their fantastic claims and tantalizing discourses, it was the Muslim alchemists—and not the sober, hellenized sages of Islam—who made lasting theoretical and material contributions to the science of chemistry. For example, the Islamic alchemical theory that all metals (in some cases all substances) were composed of sulphur and mercury proved fateful, leading to the celebrated phlogiston theory of early modern chemistry. Likewise, sal ammoniac *(nūshādir)*, a substance that played a highly productive role in the development of chemistry, was introduced into the repertoire of alchemy by Muslims. Two varieties of this substance were known to them, natural *(al-ḥajar)* and derived *(mustanbaṭ)*—ammonium chloride and ammonium carbonate. The latter was obtained by the dry distillation of hair and other animal substances. Again, the use of organic materials in chemical procedures, in addition to the inorganic, was a historic contribution of the alchemists of Islam.

By far the most luminous name in the history of Islamic alchemy is Jābir ibn Ḥayyān, but this giant figure remains wrapped in mystery, with historians since an early period doubting his very historical existence. The large encyclopedic corpus attributed to him indicates that he was a disciple of the sixth Shīʿī imam Jaʿfar al-Ṣādiq, and this would place him in the eighth century. If Jābir was the first historical alchemist of Islam, a possibility we cannot rule out definitively, then he is the pioneer of all that is important and characteristic of Islamic alchemy: the sulphur-mercury theory, the use of organic substances, the introduction of sal ammoniac, the production (though not recognition) of mineral acids, the quantification of qualities, and the conceptual distinction between heat and temperature. Jabirian ideas were known to the European alchemists, and at least three of his treatises were translated into Latin. The great physician of Islam, Abū Bakr Muḥammad ibn Zakarīyā al-Rāzī (known also by his Latin name Rhazes, d. 925) used to refer to Jābir as "our Master."

Rāzī himself is another outstanding alchemical figure. In his works we find for the first time a systematic classification of carefully observed facts regarding chemical substances, reactions, and apparatus described in an unambiguous language. He too managed to produce mineral acids, although it is again doubtful if he recognized them as isolated substances. Rāzī's clear language stands in sharp contrast to the obscure alchemical discourses of his younger contemporary Ibn Umayl (c. 900–960), a favorite of medieval European writers who read his *Al-Māʾ al-waraqī wa-al-arḍ al-nujūmīyah* (Silvery Water and Starry Earth) as *Tabula chemica*, just as they read in Latin translation his *Risālat al-shams ilā al-hilāl* (Epistle of the Sun to the New Moon). The Islamic West too contributed some celebrated alchemists: a familiar name is Maslamah ibn Aḥmad al-Majrīṭī (tenth century), from whose original writings were developed the *Rutbat al-ḥakīm* (The Sage's Step), containing precise instructions for the preparation of gold and silver by cupellation, and the *Ghāyat al-ḥakīm* (The Aim of the Wise), known in Latin as *Picatrix*. Finally, among the last prominent figures of Islamic alchemy are Abū al-Qāsim of Iraq, a contemporary of Roger Bacon, and Ibn Aydamir al-Jildakī, living in Egypt in the fourteenth century. The latter, a great admirer of Jābir, was both an alchemist and a historian of alchemy; but by his time the hub of scientific activity had already begun to shift from the Islamic world to the Latin West.

In the contemporary Islamic world there exists no institutional or organized practice of alchemy. Still, a traditional belief in the alchemical transmutation of base metals into gold continues in the popular culture, and individuals are still searching for the ever-elusive elixir.

[*See also* Science.]

BIBLIOGRAPHY

By far the best English-language survey of Islamic alchemy is still that of Joseph Needham, "Arabic Alchemy in Rise and Decline," in his

Science and Civilisation in China, vol. 5, part 4 (Cambridge, 1980). My short article, "Chemistry and Alchemy," in *Cambridge Encyclopedia of the Middle East,* edited by T. Mostyn and Albert Hourani, pages 389–491 (Cambridge, 1988), covers the same ground as the present essay and is useful for the nonexpert. Eric J. Holmyard wrote prolifically, though sometimes uncritically, on the subject. His many articles are nevertheless worthy of serious consideration (see a bibliography of his work in my *Names, Natures, and Things,* cited below); see, in particular, *Alchemy* (Harmondsworth, 1957). H. E. Stapleton made an important contribution to the history of Islamic alchemy in several studies published with his colleagues in the *Memoirs of the Asiatic Society of Bengal* (MASB). Of special interest is his "Three Arabic Treatises by Muḥammad ibn Umail (Tenth Century AD)," written in collaboration with M. T. ʿAlī and M. H. Ḥusain in *MASB* 12.1 (1933): 1–127. Stapleton, Ḥusain, and R. F. Azo also completed a rigorous textual study of Rāzī in "Chemistry in Iraq and Persia in the Tenth Century AD," *MASB* 8 (1927): 315–417. For Jābir, see Paul Kraus's monumental, unparalleled study, "Jābir ibn Ḥayyān: Contributions à l'histoire des idées scientifiques dans l'Islam," *Mémoires de l'Institut d'Égypte* 44 (1942) and 45 (1943). The only full-scale English-language study of Jābir is my *Names, Natures, and Things* (Boston, 1994), which contains as well an annotated selected text and translation of a Jābirian treatise. Scholarly readers will find my extensive bibliographic references highly useful.

S. Nomanul Haq

ALGERIA. At the beginning of the nineteenth century Algeria had been a province of the Ottoman Empire for four centuries. Like other provinces it evolved through the cycles of Turkish imperial conquest, increasing administrative autonomy from Istanbul, and integration of the Turkish ruling class with the local Arab and Berber leadership. During the first two periods the country had acquired a heroic history of *jihād* against the Habsburg Empire and corsair exploits against Christian shipping. Ruling-class integration, however, was far from complete; local leaders, often claiming religious legitimation, periodically revolted, as in 1805–1808 when shaykhs of the Darqāwīyah brotherhood rebelled against central government control. Although Algeria possessed a shared, heroic history and basic central administrative institutions before 1830, when the French conquest began, its ruling class remained divided, leaving it an imperial, not a national state.

Sparsely populated, primarily rural Algeria lacked the institutions of learning that in other Islamic areas undergirded political centralism. Legal scholarship (*fiqh*), the leading field of intellectual activity in the early modern age, was far less prominent in Algiers than it was, for example, in Fez, Tunis, or Cairo. (An exception was the Mzab, an oasis cluster in the Sahara that was the refuge of the Ibāḍī Khawārij, a minority branch distinct from the Mālikī Sunnī mainstream in North Africa [*see* Ibāḍīyah].) Given a comparatively low level of literacy and the absence of large libraries, Algerian popular Islam was a largely oral religion in which communal mnenomic practices tended to take the place of literary studies.

The central figure in this oral Islam was the saint (*walī* or, locally, marabout), a person endowed with charisma (*barakah*) and often descended (or claiming descent) from the Prophet or his companions. In his lodge (*zāwiyah*) the saint was the master (*mawlāy*) who instructed his followers in sacred litanies. The recitation of these litanies, requiring repetitive breathing and prayer movements, induced a communal trance (*wajd*) in which the saint wrought miracles for his followers, such as exorcism or healing. Over the centuries Algeria acquired hundreds of saints whose tombs, administered either by descendants or by new saints, were often places of local pilgrimage and veneration. Some Ṣūfī lodges established branch lodges; others, equipped with small libraries, engaged in a measure of scholarship. Saintly Islam was thus highly differentiated, ranging from the shaykh at the head of a large regional brotherhood to the local mystic (Ṣūfī) with his handful of adepts. [*See* Sainthood; Barakah; Zāwiyah; Mawlāy; *and* Sufism, *article on* Ṣūfī Shrine Culture.]

Among noteworthy recent shaykhs was the Fez-educated Arab Abū Ḥamīd al-Darqāwī (d. 1823) whose followers sided with the sultan of Morocco in the latter's struggle with the dey of Algiers for control of western Algeria after Spain had relinquished Oran in 1803. Another was ʿAbd al-Raḥmān al-Gushtūlī (d. 1793), a Kabyle Berber who studied in Cairo and after his death became so famous that he manifested himself in two tombs, one in Algiers and the other for his following, the Raḥmanīyah, in his native Kabylia. [*See* Kabylia.] A third notable saint was Aḥmad al-Tijānī (d. 1815), a scholarly mystic who taught in Tlemcen and Fez before returning to his native ʿAyn Māḍī in the Sahara. [*See the biography of Tijānī.*] Saints could be well-traveled and highly educated but still strongly committed to the preaching of oral Islam. In sum, the Algeria the French invaded in 1830 was a centrally—if weakly—governed country with strong countervailing traditions of communal autonomy, both political and religious.

The conquest of Algiers occurred after France had lost its old overseas empire and before it entered the European scramble for African territories. A minor dispute over French payments for Algerian wheat deliveries during the Napoleonic wars had escalated into a military confrontation, lost by a militarily inept dey. The French were initially reluctant to commit themselves to a costly conquest of the rest of the country, and their hesitancy enabled leaders—such as the Turkish-descended Aḥmad Bey of Constantine or the Arab leader of the Qādirīyah in the Oranais, Emir ʿAbd al-Qādir Muḥyī al-Dīn—to establish temporary regimes. [*See* Qādirīyah *and the biography of ʿAbd al-Qādir.*]

Even after being defeated in the north in 1857, the Algerians continued to resist the French, albeit sporadically. The most dangerous uprising occurred in 1871–1872 when a regional administrator, Muḥammad al-Muqrānī, together with Shaykh al-Ḥaddād of the Raḥmanīyah brotherhood, mobilized large areas of eastern Algeria against the French. In the south, the French conquest was completed only in 1882 with the retreat to Morocco of Bū ʿAmāmah, a saintly leader of the Awlād Sīdī Shaykh who traced his descent to Caliph Abū Bakr.

The French exacted merciless retribution against the vanquished Algerians. By the end of the century the colonial government had settled some 200,000 immigrants from France, Italy, and Spain on 2.3 million hectares—or nearly 40 percent of the agricultural land—after either expropriating or buying the land at nominal prices. The most fertile, irrigable lands were turned over to European commercial farming enterprises for the cultivation of grapes, vegetables, and citrus fruits. Around 400,000 other European immigrants settled in the newly founded urban network of about fifty towns and cities.

In spite of all colonial settlement efforts the indigenous population remained the majority; in fact, it more than tripled during 1830–1914, from 1.5 to 4.8 million, owing mostly to the decline of cholera and famine cycles after 1867. At first the traditionally extensive wheat and barley agriculture provided sufficient work and income to all, but since the land of rural Algerians could not be irrigated and they could not afford chemical fertilizers, eventually a large landless proletariat emerged (from 360,000 to 600,000 persons in 1901–1914). At the same time, rural-urban migration began to pick up (urban population increased 8 percent above that of the countryside in 1901–1914), as did labor migration to France (rising from 200 to 15,000 persons in 1906–1914). Thus the combination of indigenous population increase and French colonialism created the impoverishment of the traditional rural population as well as the emergence of a new urban society.

The elite of this urban society, highly literate and therefore at some remove from the enchanted world of oral religion, embraced the two typical forms of disenchantment—secularism and fundamentalism. Secularism gained its first recruits between 1900 and 1914 from among some 25 Muslim Algerian doctors, lawyers, engineers, and professors and 200 high-school teachers who were fully assimilated to French culture, as well as perhaps another 1,000 intellectuals with some French education. Their political engagement was directed toward the abolition of the discriminatory penal laws, taxes, and voting rights to which the indigenous population was subjected, as well as toward the establishment of full equality with the European settlers. These demands acquired urgency in 1908 when Paris began to consider military conscription for Muslim Algerians (which became a reality during World War I). Although the metropole was willing to grant concessions in return for war service, the European settlers were not, even after the war. The Young Algerians, as the politically minded secularists called themselves, had minimal success.

At roughly the same time an even smaller handful of religious scholars, graduates of mosque schools in Algiers, Constantine, and Tlemcen, were publishing ephemeral journals in Arabic. They were inspired by the visit to Algiers in 1903 of Muḥammad ʿAbduh, the Egyptian representative of the Salāfīyah movement that promoted a spiritual return to the foundations of Islam. Accordingly, they criticized the representatives of saintly Islam for indulging in what they called blameworthy doctrinal innovation *(bidʿah)* and un-Islamic practices, such as ecstatic union with God, saintly mediation between believers and God, and pilgrimages to saints' tombs. In their opinion religion was determined by scripture and early Islamic practice alone—hence the fundamentalism of their faith.

During the interwar period Algeria's secularists, led by the pharmacist Ferhat ʿAbbās (d. 1985), remained committed to a future for the country as an equal part of France, even after 1938 when a major reform bill proposing improved voting rights failed in Paris. By contrast, the fundamentalist Association of Algerian ʿUlamāʾ, founded by ʿAbd al-Ḥamīd ibn Bādīs (d. 1940) in 1931, favored the early Islamic framework in which the status of believers and unbelievers, as well as that of men and women, was differentiated under the law. [*See the biography of Ibn Bādīs.*] By implication, no common future could exist for France and Algeria. The colonial authorities were quite aware of the radicalism hidden in the ʿ*ulamā*'s position and severely restricted the latter's efforts to disseminate their ideas in the mosques and private schools where they offered courses in Qur'ānic exegesis *(tafsīr)*, prophetic tradition *(ḥadīth)*, and legal scholarship. But given the fact that the colonial system provided schools for fewer than 9 percent of Muslim children of school age during the interwar period, neither secularists nor fundamentalists had much chance of finding mass audiences, even had the French been less repressive.

The great majority of new indigenous urban dwellers, with severely limited access to French or Arabic education, stayed in the enchanted world of oral Islam. They often had to practice it without much saintly guidance, especially if they were among the Algerian industrial workers in France (300,000 by 1936). Because they lacked extensive exposure to literary culture, secularism as well as fundamentalism passed them by. They remained at bottom the Darqāwīs or Raḥmanīs they had been in their villages before moving to town or across the Mediterranean, even though as emigrant workers in France many of them acquired the practical abilities to function in an industrial society well before independence.

A characteristic example is Messali al-Ḥajj (Messali Hadj, d. 1974), founding father in 1926 of Algerian nationalism. Messali was the son of a Turkish-descended laborer and later guardian of the tomb of Sīdī Bū Madyān (Shuʿayb Abū Madyan) in Tlemcen. He graduated from both the local Darqāwī lodge and French primary school, did his army service in France, and stayed on as an unskilled worker. Although he took evening courses in French and Islamic cultural topics and married a French labor militant, he did not abandon his roots—nor did he later repudiate his acquired French culture. Because his Islamic oral culture and modest Islamic and French literary acquisitions were of such vastly different natures and hence in no serious competition, he experienced no cultural conflicts. Only people divorced from oral culture and brought up in the two competing universes of written Arabic and French letters were apt to suffer the cultural Manichaeism of which Frantz Fanon speaks in his books on Algeria. Like many other nationalists prior to Algerian independence, Messali al-Ḥajj (according to his autobiography) was thoroughly at ease with his eclectic cultural makeup.

In spite of having attracted some 10,000 party members by 1940, Messali al-Ḥajj's Party of the Algerian People was just as powerless as the assimilationists and ʿ*ulamā*' in bringing about political reforms—not to mention independence—for the country: the European settlers considered the colony an irrevocable part of France. During World War II nationalists began envisaging violence as a means to attain independence. On 8 May 1945, Messali al-Ḥajj was apparently ready to step forward as the liberator of the country when nationalists turned the victory celebrations in Setif into riots. Savage French repressions resulting in the death of at least fifteen thousand Muslims ended the dream of independence through spontaneous mass uprisings. [*See the biography of Messali al-Ḥajj.*]

In the postwar years a serious split between a secret military underground and a central committee that considered any further violence suicidal immobilized nationalist action. It was only on 1 November 1954 that the underground cut the Gordian knot by reconstituting itself as a National Liberation Front (known by its French initials FLN) separate from Messali al-Ḥajj and the nationalists, launching a carefully prepared guerilla war for independence. Initially the FLN was able to exploit serious weaknesses in a French army demoralized from the loss of Vietnam, but in the long run it was no military match. The FLN survived politically only because French president Charles de Gaulle realized that France would benefit more from an independent Algeria, paying its own bills, than from continued colonialism.

When Algeria became independent on 18 March 1962 it was an impoverished, overwhelmingly rural country. Two-thirds of the population still depended on subsistence agriculture, which only one-quarter of it was able to do without resorting to part-time urban labor or depending on remittances from relatives working in cities or abroad. One million Muslim Algerians, of a population of nine million, had died in the struggle, and two million had lost their homes. Three-quarters of urban Algerians were jobless because nearly all settlers, including most professionals and administrators, had left the country. The FLN faced a hopeless task; it was three years before Colonel Houari Boumédienne was able to establish the first stable government.

The nationalists of the FLN were largely (77 percent) primary-school graduates from small towns and villages whose vocational or university careers had been interrupted by the war. As such they formed the vanguard of the new urban population, a sizable but nevertheless minority group in a mass of farmers. However, they did not hesitate to regard themselves as representatives of rural Algerians, assuming the role of preceptors of the nation. On the basis of ample oil and gas revenues an ambitious program of state-controlled heavy industrialization was adopted to provide the basis for a modern consumer society.

The cultural underpinnings for the achievement of industrialization were to be provided by an educational system that borrowed from the fundamentalist *ʿulamā'* of a generation earlier as well as from the French secular system once supported by the assimilationists. Accordingly, children were educated in the literary Islam of the religious scholars (constitutionally sanctioned as the state religion), the heroic history of Muslim North Africa, and also the modern languages and scientific-technical fields inherited from France. An ambitious plan to arabize the entire administrative and educational structures was set in motion. Saintly Islam was officially vilified in the National Charter of 1976 as archaic and tainted by collaboration with colonialism, destined to die away under the onslaught of modernity.

By the 1990s the mission of national reeducation had been largely accomplished. The initial successes of the industrialization program resulted in a rapid urbanization that shrank the percentage of the population depending on agriculture from two-thirds to one-quarter. This shrinkage is all the more impressive if one takes into account the high birthrate (rising from 2 percent to over 3 percent from 1962–1992), which nearly tripled the overall population in the thirty years of independence (about 27 million in 1992). Nearly all these new urbanites, and 84 percent of all those between the ages of six and fifteen, received at least a primary-school education. By the mid-1980s the majority of the population born since independence was acculturated into the new Arabic culture officially decreed by the nationalists and possessed little emotional attachment to the oral culture of saintly Islam. Literary Islam has become the new popular religion of Algeria—the large numbers of secularists excepted.

Unfortunately, by the mid-1980s the industrialization process had also gone sour. The worldwide decline of oil prices forced drastic reductions in the program of heavy industrialization that was still an integral part of the state socialism proclaimed in the 1976 Charter. In the absence of private light industries geared toward satisfying urban consumer demand, unemployment and inflation were rampant. After widespread riots in October 1988, Colonel Benjedid Chadli, a former FLN fighter who had succeeded Boumediène in the presidency after the latter's death in 1978, decided to replace the single-party rule of the FLN with a multiparty system.

Almost overnight the fundamentalist Islamic Salvation Front (known by its French initials FIS; Ar., Jabhat al-Inqādh al-Islāmī) became the strongest challenger of the FLN, demanding the establishment of an Islamic state and the privatization of the economy. However, Chadli continued to cling to state socialism; his only concession was the transfer of industrial management from the state ministries to a complicated system of trusts staffed by the ministries. Only in March 1990, with the passing of a first set of laws, did the government finally bow to the inevitability of a private industrial sector if economic collapse was to be avoided. [*See* Islamic Salvation Front.]

The crisis that began in 1988 highlighted the grave danger of a major split in present Algerian society. Since a majority of Algerians have left the enchanted culture of the spoken word for that of the written word or scientific formula, the inescapable disenchantment seems to impose a necessary choice between secularism or fundamentalism. The entrenched technocrats of the bureaucracies, state industries, and army, as well as the FLN functionaries born after independence, are faced by angry Islamists without jobs but in possession of the true word of the Qur'ān. Cultural reconciliation is essential but a saint-led reenchantment no longer seems possible.

BIBLIOGRAPHY

Religion and religious practices of the Ottoman period are covered by J. Spencer Trimingham, *The Sufi Orders in Islam* (London, 1971). Jamil M. Abun-Nasr studied one of these "orders," which rose concomitantly with the French conquest, in *The Tijaniyya: A Sufi Order in the Modern World* (London, 1965). A comprehensive bibliography on the topic of modern Islam in Algeria is Pessah Shinar, *Essai de bibliographie sélective et annotée sur l'Islam maghrébin contemporain: Maroc, Algérie, Tunisie, Libye (1830–1978)* (Paris, 1983).

The history of modern Algeria is authoritatively studied by John Ruedy, *Modern Algeria: The Origins and Development of a Nation* (Bloomington, 1992). Alternatively, see also Mahfoud Bennoune, *The Making of Contemporary Algeria, 1830–1987* (Cambridge, 1988). Two classics on the nineteenth century are Charles-André Julien, *Histoire de l'Algérie contemporaine*, vol. 1, *La conquête et les débuts de la colonisation, 1827–71* (Paris, 1979), and Charles-Robert Ageron, *Histoire de l'Algérie contemporaine, 1871–1919*, 2 vols. (Paris, 1964). For an extension of the latter, see *Histoire de l'Algérie contemporaine, 1871–1954*, vol. 2, *De l'insurrection de 1871 au déclenchement de la guerre de libération* (Paris, 1979).

The classic works on the history of the first half of the twentieth century (nationalism, Islamic reform) are André Nouschi, *Les origines du nationalisme algérien* (Paris, 1979) and Ali Merad, *Le réformisme musulman en Algérie de 1925 à 1940* (Paris, 1967). The best biography on the founder of Algerian nationalism is by Benjamin Stora, *Messali Hadj, 1898–1974: Pionnier du nationalisme algérien* (Paris, 1986). On Algerian society during the interwar period, see Germaine Tillion, *The Republic of Cousins: Women's Oppression in Mediterranean Society* (London, 1983), and Pierre Bourdieu and Sayad Abdelmalek, *Le déracinement: La crise de l'agriculture traditionelle en Algérie* (Paris, 1977).

The most detailed study in English of the war of independence is Alistair Horne, *A Savage War of Peace* (New York, 1987). The definitive work on Algeria's political institutions after independence is Jean Leca and Jean-Claude Vatin, *L'Algérie politique, institutions et régimes*, vol. 2 (Paris, 1975). The social evolution of the country after 1962 is expertly discussed by Bruno Étienne, *Algérie: Cultures et révolution* (Paris, 1977). The outstanding critic of Islamic religion, and one of the few thinkers outside the Islamist current, is the Algerian (teaching in Paris) Mohammed Arkoun, best known for his *Pour une critique de la raison islamique* (Paris, 1984).

PETER VON SIVERS

ALIGARH. This large town in western Uttar Pradesh, India, in the district of the same name, has been associated with major Muslim educational, political, and ideological movements since the late nineteenth century. Situated 79 miles south of Delhi, the town, also known as Koil, in 1865 became the headquarters of the Aligarh Scientific Society and ten years later of the Mahomedan Anglo-Oriental College. Both were established under the leadership of Sayyid Aḥmad Khān (1817–1898), with the goal of making contemporary European learning available to a relatively privileged public that included Hindus but was primarily Muslim. In 1920 the college was reconstituted as the autonomous, degree-granting Aligarh Muslim University. After the partition of India and the creation of Pakistan as a separate nation-state for South Asian Muslims, Aligarh Muslim University remained in India as one of a small group of national universities.

Sir Sayyid Aḥmad Khān or "Sir Syed," the major figure in what became known as the Aligarh movement, founded the Scientific Society in Ghazipur in 1863. It shifted to Aligarh when Sayyid Aḥmad himself was transferred there as a subordinate judge. Although the society included Hindus as well as Muslims, a trip Sayyid Aḥmad made to England in 1869 persuaded him to devote the rest of his life to the establishment of an educational institution particularly for Indian Muslims. His unorthodox religious ideas created some opposition from the outset, but Sayyid Aḥmad was able to gather support from a diversity of Muslims, combining prominent Sunnī and Shīʿī leaders in an effort to create a new generation of Muslims who would be well educated in European learning but safely committed to Islam. With support from the British government, reinforced by Sayyid Aḥmad's opposition in 1887 to the newly founded Indian National Congress, the Aligarh College succeeded in its goal of creating a new generation of leaders for what Sayyid Aḥmad conceived as the aggregate Muslim *qaum*, or in Indian English, "community." As government officials, lawyers, and journalists, Aligarh graduates became prominent figures in early twentieth-century Indian public life.

After the death of Sayyid Aḥmad Khān, Aligarh became an arena for social and political controversy. In 1906 the Aligarh Zenana Madrasah provided separate education for girls, becoming a college in 1925. Although most prominently associated with Muslim separatism, Aligarh always had important figures associated with Indian nationalism and Marxism. The movement to transform the college into an autonomous, all-India educational system for Muslims foundered on British opposition and internal factionalism; the university was established in 1920 only after Mohandas K. Gandhi and two Aligarh graduates, Shaukat and Muḥammad ʿAlī, had led a noncooperation campaign that established an alternative nationalist institution, the Jāmiʿah Millīyah Islāmīyah, outside the campus gates. In the final years before independence and partition, many Aligarh students devoted themselves to the cause of Pakistan, but many others remained staunch advocates of a united and secular India.

Under the leadership of its first post-independence vice chancellor, Zakir Hussain, later President of India, Aligarh Muslim University sought to retain its special role as a center of Muslim culture, including Urdu, and in preparing Muslims for full participation in national life. Particularly prominent for its Urdu writers and historians of Mughal India, many of them Marxist, the university has been a battleground with regard to its special character as an institution for Muslims.

[*See also* India *and the biography of Aḥmad Khān.*]

BIBLIOGRAPHY

Graff, Violette. "Aligarh's Long Quest for 'Minority' Status: AMU (Amendment) Act, 1981." *Economic and Political Weekly* 25.32 (11 August 1990): 1771–1781. Status of Aligarh Muslim University within the Republic of India since independence.

Hasan, Mushir ul-. "Nationalist and Separatist trends in Aligarh,

1915–47." *Indian Economic and Social History Review* 22.1 (January–March 1985): 1–34. The best study of the history and ideological conflicts at Aligarh in the context of the nationalist movement and the creation of Pakistan.

Lelyveld, David. *Aligarh's First Generation: Muslim Solidarity in British India*. Princeton, 1978. History of Aligarh College in its first twenty-five years in its wider social and cultural context.

Minault, Gail. "Shaikh Abdullah, Begam Abdullah, and *Sharif* Education for Girls at Aligarh." In *Modernization and Social Change among Muslims in India*, edited by Imtiaz Ahmad, pp. 207–236. New Delhi, 1983. Study of the foundations of women's education at Aligarh.

Troll, Christian W. *Sayyid Ahmad Khan: A Reinterpretation of Muslim Theology*. New Delhi, 1978. The most thorough study of the religious ideas of the major figure in the Aligarh movement.

David Lelyveld

ʿALĪ IBN ABĪ ṬĀLIB (c. 597–660), the cousin and son-in-law of the prophet Muḥammad, the fourth caliph of the Sunnī Muslims, and the first imam of all the Shīʿīs. ʿAlī was ten or eleven years old when he embraced Islam and is considered to be the first Muslim after Khadījah, Muḥammad's wife. He grew up in Muḥammad's household, and during the night of Muḥammad's emigration (the Hijrah) from Mecca to Medina in 622, he occupied the Prophet's bed, facilitating the latter's escape. Following this event, he joined the Prophet after restoring to their owners the objects that Muḥammad was holding as trust. Some months later he married Muḥammad's daughter Fāṭimah, and of their marriage were born two sons, Ḥasan and Ḥusayn, and two daughters, Zaynab and Umm Kulthūm, the latter two known through their roles in the Battle of Karbala [*see* Karbala]. During the Prophet's lifetime, ʿAlī participated in almost all the expeditions, except that of Tabūk, during which he had the command at Medina. The description of ʿAlī's bravery as the standard-bearer and sometimes as the commander in these expeditions has become legendary.

After Muḥammad's death in 632, a dispute arose between ʿAlī and other associates of the Prophet on the question of succession. It was this dispute that divided the Muslims into two major factions: the Shīʿah (partisans of ʿAlī), those sympathetic to ʿAlī's claim as having been specifically appointed by the Prophet as his successor during his farewell pilgrimage; and the Sunnī, those who denied ʿAlī's claim and acknowledged the caliphate of Abū Bakr, ʿUmar, and ʿUthmān in succession and placed ʿAlī as the fourth caliph, following ʿUthmān's assassination in 656. The period of ʿAlī's rule was marked with political crisis and civil strife. ʿAlī had inherited events which he could not avert as a caliph, and under the pressure of circumstances he had to submit to these events and the constraints of his partisans. In the month of Ramaḍān in 660, a member of the Khawārij (a sect that had seceded from ʿAlī in the battle against the Umayyad governor of Syria, Muʿāwiyah, in 656) struck ʿAlī with a sword while he was in prostration in the mosque of Kufa. He died about two days later. ʿAlī's burial place was at a spot some miles from Kufa, Najaf, where his mausoleum subsequently arose and which has become an important site for the Shīʿī pilgrimage and a center for Twelver Shīʿī learning. [*See* Najaf.]

The personality of ʿAlī is difficult to assess, since so much controversial and tendentious material has grown up around his person. Although his stature as a distinguished judge, a pious believer, and an ardent warrior for Islam is accepted by Muslim biographers, historians, and jurists, the idea of ʿAlī alongside God and the Prophet as the pivot around which religious belief revolves, which the Shīʿīs developed after ʿAlī's death, is rejected altogether by the Sunnīs. Even among subdivisions of the Shīʿīs there has been much conflict on the status of ʿAlī in personal piety. The deification of ʿAlī by extremist Shīʿīs, such as the ʿAlawīyun of present-day Syria, stands at one end of the spectrum; whereas the most moderate views about him are those held by the major Shīʿī school of thought, the Twelvers (Ithnā ʿAsharīyah). [*See* ʿAlawīyah; Ithnā ʿAsharīyah.] In the Shīʿī and Sūfī hagiographical literature, where ʿAlī's profoundly religious spirit is emphasized, he is raised to the status of the *walī* ("friend") of God and is regarded as the saint in whom the divine light resided. His *wilāyah* (in the meaning of "friendship" as well as "stewardship") is esteemed as the fundamental requirement of faith on which the entire spiritual edifice of the Shīʿah was built. Faith was conceived in terms of personal devotion to ʿAlī and what he symbolized, as far as Islamic piety was concerned. [*See* Walī; Wilāyah.]

In the context of Iran (and to some extent Iraq, where Shīʿīs constitute a majority), the only modern nation-state that promulgates Twelver Shiism as its official religion, the figure of ʿAlī provides the downtrodden with the paradigm for a political activism that can be used to redress social and political injustices. In this connection, political discourse, sermons, letters, and wise sayings ascribed to ʿAlī and compiled in the eleventh-century collection, *Nahj al-balāghah* (The Peak of Eloquence), with detailed commentaries by Sunnī and Shīʿī scholars, have served as the ideological groundwork for the establishment of Islamic government.

One of the most important Islamic celebrations in the Shīʿī calendar is the Festival of Ghadīr on 18 Dhū al-Ḥijjah—the day of *wilāyah* (ʿAlī's appointment by the Prophet as his successor). This festival is given even more importance than the Festival of Sacrifice commemorating the event of *ḥajj* in the Islamic world.

[*See also* Imam; Shīʿī Islam, *historical overview article.*]

BIBLIOGRAPHY

Ḥusayn, Ṭāhā. *Al-Fitnah al-Kubrā,* vol. 1, *ʿUthman;* vol. 2, *ʿAlī wa-banūh.* Cairo, 1947–1956.

Vaglieri, Laura Veccia. "ʿAlī b. Abī Ṭālib." In *Encyclopaedia of Islam,* new ed., vol. 1, pp. 381–386. Leiden, 1960–. Valuable revisionist outline of ʿAlī's biography.

ABDULAZIZ SACHEDINA

AL-KHOEI BENEVOLENT FOUNDATION.

Established in the late 1980s, the Al-Khoei Benevolent Foundation has centralized religious centers and institutions for Islamic education that were acquired through pious donations managed by the late Ayatollah Abol-Qāsem al-Kho'i (Abū al-Qāsim Khūʾī, d. 1992) in his position as the *marjaʿ al-taqlīd* (supreme juridical authority) of the majority of Shīʿī Muslims. Practical considerations prompted lay and religious leaders among al-Kho'i's Persian and Arab followers in Europe and North America to seek the establishment of the foundation to supervise the large number of religious endowments and other tangible and intangible assets that had been managed by al-Kho'i's *wukalāʾ* (personal representatives). Shīʿī religious law recognizes the *marjaʿ* as the superintendent of religious assets as long as he lives. In the absence of any established legal procedure for the succession of juridical authority, there is no provision to ascertain legal conveyance of these assets to the subsequent *marjaʿ* acknowledged by the Shīʿīs. The convention is to treat these assets as pious endowments supervised by appointed trustees or by the newly created ministry of *awqāf* (sg., *waqf;* pious endowments) in various Muslim countries.

An additional concern that prompted the advisers of al-Kho'i to venture into this innovative idea of creating a multinational foundation in the name of the *marjaʿ* himself, who was not the actual owner of the trust, was that foreign assets were registered in accordance with laws in nations that did not recognize the jurisdiction of Islamic law or the supervisory role of the ayatollah in governing them. This left the Shīʿī public trust in the West open to embezzlement by even the ayatollah's close family members.

The trustees appointed by al-Kho'i himself included highly successful businessmen. They expanded the mandate of the foundation by registering it as a nonprofit corporation, empowering it to solicit, raise, accept, hold and administer, invest and reinvest, the funds and other property. Hence, the foundation has expanded its activities in many parts of the world and has successfully established centers and schools in London and New York. It has also engaged in humanitarian activities that include feeding Afghani war victims and digging wells in East Africa, as well as voicing concerns related to the violation of the human rights of Shīʿīs in Iraq with the UN.

The danger of the foundation turning into a family empire was not unforeseen by the community in general. Following a dispute in the New York branch of the foundation in 1990–1992, which led to a court case in the County of Queens, New York, the board amended the foundation's constitution to protect its charitable nature, recognizing the need to hand over its supervision to the next leader in the event of al-Kho'i's death. However, this new leader had to be recognized and confirmed by three-quarters of the foundation's trustees. Such a provision implied a clear departure from the traditional role of the supreme juridical authority as the trustee of the Hidden Imam, as conceived in Shīʿī jurisprudence. The trustees of the foundation thus reserved the legally and traditionally recognized supervisory role for themselves while assigning the ceremonial role of a patron to the *marjaʿ*. From the viewpoint of the Shīʿī community, this development in the empowerment of the trustees raises serious questions regarding the limited authority invested in the *marjaʿ* by the *sharīʿah* and the ever-expanding mandate claimed by the foundation in the name of the *marjaʿ*. There is also an increasing awareness among Shīʿīs (whose donations the *marjaʿ* merely manages) about their right to know how their pious donations are being distributed among competing needs and priorities of various sectors of the transcultural and transnational followers of the ayatollah. The Western notions of public accountability and democratically created institutions in management of religious donations are not part of the traditional religious endowments among Muslims.

Al-Kho'i's death in 1992 left the Shīʿī community with an evident vacuum in religious leadership. It also created a crisis for the board of trustees, who were caught between a traditional autocratic vision and modern public accountability. After much deliberation and in order to establish its credibility among the followers of the late Ayatollah Kho'i, the board decided to acknowledge the next *marjaʿ* as its ceremonial patron in August 1993. In the absence of any other universally recognized leader of the Shiʿis, the board requested Ayatollah Muḥammad Riẕā Gulpaygānī (d. 1993) of Iran to assume the newly created post of "patron of the Foundation." However, Gulpaygānī's death has once again left the foundation without a legitimating patron. It is likely that Ayatollah Muḥammad al-Sistānī of Najaf, a disciple of Kho'i and the board's favored candidate for the post, will assume the patronage. Public accountability to the plurality of Shīʿīs in the West still remains a disputed matter. So far, following the traditional method of the *marjaʿ* (who never publicized accounts because of the extreme trust in which he was held by his followers), the foundation has not made accounts public. The only thing to date made public in the organ of the foundation, *Al-Noor Magazine* (August 1993), is the list of centers and schools, both secular and religious, that it has established in various cities around the world. Moreover, although the foundation has as its objective representation of Shīʿī interests worldwide, its exclusive goals are defined and executed by the board, which is made up of the followers of the late Ayatollah Kho'i from Iran and Iraq, including his two sons.

[*See also* Marjaʿ al-Taqlīd; Waqf; *and the biography of Kho'i.*]

BIBLIOGRAPHY

The constitution of the Al-Khoei Foundation is contained in Petition No. 18915/90, filed with the Supreme Court of the State of New York, Eleventh Judicial District, County of Queens. For other information on the foundation, consult the following:

Al-Khoei Foundation: Concepts and Projects. London, 1992. Informational publication distributed by the head office of the foundation.

Al-Noor [*Al-Nūr*], no. 27 (August 1993). Arabic-language journal issued by the Al-Khoei Foundation in London. This particular issue lists all the centers and schools founded and administered by the foundation.

ABDULAZIZ SACHEDINA

ALLĀH. Islam knows no creed, no formal profession of faith that every Muslim is required to proclaim as a sign of membership in the Islamic community. A number of Muslims have attempted to elaborate such an *ʿaqīdah* (creed) to supply the immediate doctrinal needs of some moment of Islamic history, but none has won the ecumencial support enjoyed by the simple and powerful *shahādah* ("testimony"), the first of the so-called Pillars of Islam, and the only one of the five that has to do with faith and belief. "I testify," the Muslim says, "that there is no god but The God . . ." ("Ashaduan lā ilāha illā Allāh"), "and Muḥammad is His envoy." The God of that testimony, in Arabic Allāh (a contraction of *al-ilāh*), is the same God worshiped, to the exclusion of all others, by the Jews and the Christians, and the deity is described clearly and succinctly in the famous "Throne Verse" (surah 2.255) of the Qur'ān:

> God! There is no god but He, the Living, the Self-Subsistent. Slumber seizes Him not, no, nor sleep. To Him belong all that is in the heavens and upon the earth. Who is there who interecedes with Him except with His permission? He knows what has appeared as past and as yet to come, and there is no share in His knowledge except by His will. His throne extends over the heavens and the earth, and their preservation wearies Him not. He is the All-sublime, the All-glorious.

The cult of a deity termed simply "the god" *(al-ilāh)* was known throughout southern Syria and northern Arabia in the days before Islam—Muḥammad's father was named ʿAbd Allāh ("Servant of Allāh")—and was obviously of central importance in Mecca, where the building called the Kaʿbah was indisputably his house. Indeed, the Muslims' *shahādah* attests to precisely that point: the Quraysh, the paramount tribe of Mecca, were being called on by Muḥammad to repudiate the very existence of all the other gods save this one. It seems equally certain that Allāh was not merely a god in Mecca but was widely regarded as the "high god," the chief and head of the Meccan pantheon, whether this was the result, as has been argued, of a natural progression toward henotheism or of the growing influence of Jews and Christians in the Arabian Peninsula. The most convincing piece of evidence that it was the latter at work is the fact that of all the gods of Mecca, Allāh alone was not represented by an idol.

How did the pagan Meccans view their god Allāh? The Qur'ān provides direct and primary evidence: "And if you ask them [i.e., the Quraysh] who created them, they will certainly reply, "Allāh" (Qur'ān 43.87).

> Say: Who is it that sustains you from the sky and from the earth? Or who is it who has power over hearing and sight? And who is it who brings out the living from the dead and

> the dead from the living? And who is it who rules and regulates all affairs? They will soon answer, "Allāh."
>
> (Qur'ān 10.31)

> If you ask them who created the heavens and the earth, they will certainly say "Allāh." Say: Those (female) things you call upon apart from Allāh, do you think that if God wills evil to me, they can remove this evil, or, if He wills mercy to me, they can hold back this mercy? (Qur'ān 39.38)

In this latter verse Allāh appears quite clearly as the "high god" of Mecca. On the one hand, there is Allāh, the creator, sustainer and ruler of the universe, and on the other, a host of minor deities—the "daughters of Allāh" among them—who intercede with the lord of the gods, and this is precisely the view that is attacked in the Qur'ān:

> They serve apart from Allāh that which what neither harms nor benefits them, and they say "These are our intercessors with Allāh." Say: Are you informing God of something He knows not in the heavens or on earth? Glory be to Him! He is far above any partners. (Qur'ān 10.18)

The Qur'ān is our most certain testimony to the religious life in Mecca before the appearance of Islam, since at the least in the beginning of his career Muḥammad's concern was not, as it was later in Medina, with regulating the life of a community of believers but rather in reforming the beliefs and practices of his fellow Meccans. "Reforming" is a more appropriate term than "converting," since the Qur'ān also reveals, as we have seen, that the worship of Allāh was already well established there before Muḥammad. What was at question, then, was not simply belief in or worship of Allāh, which the Quraysh certainly did, but the Meccans' "association," as the Qur'ān calls it, of other deities with Allāh, an issue that seemed to accept the existence of other gods in the "exalted assembly," while at the same time denying that they had any autonomous power, though perhaps they could help men if God so willed (Qur'ān 34.22–23).

Some verses of the Qur'ān seem openly to concede the existence of such gods, simply pointing to the fact that they are Allāh's creatures (surah 25.3), and that rather than being Allāh's partners, they are his servants (surah 7.191–195). Those deities falsely associated with Allāh will even appear at the Judgment Day to disavow the worship of their devotees (surah 10.28–29). Finally, Allāh's position in regard to the other gods is illuminated by one of the epithets applied to him, together with a self-gloss, in surah 112, itself a basic statement of Qur'ānic monotheism:

> Say: He is Allāh: One;
> He is Allāh: the Eternal.
> He has neither begotten, nor was He begotten,
> And no one is equal to Him.

Thus Allāh was neither an unknown nor an unimportant deity to the Quraysh when Muḥammad began preaching his worship at Mecca. What is equally certain is that Allāh had what the Qur'ān disdainfully calls "associates," other gods and goddesses who shared both his cult and his shrine. On the prima facie witness of the Qur'ān, it was Muḥammad's preaching that introduced a new monotheistic urgency into the Meccan cult: the Quraysh are relentlessly chastised for "partnering God," and from what we otherwise know of Muḥammad's Mecca, the charge is not an unjust one. But a closer look reveals that the matter was by no means so simple. While he was still at Mecca, Muḥammad had begun to invoke the example of Abraham, as in this verse that establishes the continuity of the "religion of Abraham" through the line of the prophets to his own monotheism:

> He has established for you the same religion that He enjoined on Noah—and which We revealed to you—and that He enjoined on Abraham, Moses and Jesus—namely, that you remain steadfast in the religion and make no divisions in it. (Qur'ān 42.13)

Whatever his beliefs before his prophetic call, the Muḥammad who began to preach the "warning" and the "good news" of Islam in Mecca had a bold new understanding of God, which unfolds in the early surahs of the Qur'ān. Muḥammad's God was no longer the Allāh of the pagan Quraysh, to be sure, but what is chiefly remarkable, perhaps, is that in those same surahs Muḥammad almost invariably refers to the deity not as "Allāh" but as "Lord," or since God is often the speaker, "your Lord." It is patently not the name of some new divinity, some god whose presence at Mecca was previously unknown; rather, it is an appellative, a reference to a familiar. Who is Muḥammad's "Lord"? It is not at all clear, not at this point, although later it is unmistakably the Allāh of the Quraysh, and, of course, of the Jews and Christians.

Sometime after the beginning of his preaching, Muḥammad also began to use the name *al-Raḥmān* ("The Merciful One") for his God, and conspicuously, in surahs 56, 68, 78, 89, and 93, "Lord" and "Raḥmān" are used together, with no mention of Allāh. Unlike "Lord," Raḥmān appears to be a proper name, always used with the article and quite different from the other appellatives applied to God in the Qur'ān. The name *al-Raḥmān* appears more than fifty times in the surahs of the so-called "second Meccan period," and often with explicit reference to the fact that the Meccans found the name strange or the deity somehow unacceptable (21.36; 25.60; 13.30). Thus Muḥammad's choice of the name *al-Raḥmān* to designate the "Lord" who was sending him revelations caused confusion and objections among the Quraysh. Some may have thought that Muḥammad's Raḥmān and their own Allāh were two distinct gods, and we can see the beginnings of a reconciliation in 17.110 ("Pray to Allāh or pray to al-Raḥmān; whichever you call upon, to Him belongs the beautiful names."), but after that, there are no more mentions of al-Raḥmān, not as the unique name of God. Thenceforward that name was the familiar Allāh of Mecca, and Raḥmān became one of his characterizations, enshrined in the formula which stands at the head of 113 surahs of the Qur'ān: "In the name of Allāh, the Merciful, the Compassionate."

Muḥammad apparently had a direct experience of God (53.1–18; 81.19–27), but the Muslims' understanding of Allāh is based not on that personal experience, which the Prophet did not share with his followers, but on the Qur'ān's public witness. Allāh is Unique, the Creator, Sovereign and Judge of humankind. It is Allāh who directs the universe through his direct action on nature and who has guided human history through his prophets, Abraham, with whom he made his covenant, Moses, Jesus, and Muḥammad, through all of whom he founded his chosen communities, the "Peoples of the Book," his Book. Indeed, His guidance descends even to the most particular actions: "He turns astray whom He wishes and guides whom He wishes" (14.14; 16.93; etc.). From the Qur'ānic portrait Muslim piety later extracted the scriptural ninety-nine "beautiful names of Allāh" (7.180; 17.110; 20.8), which became in turn the ground for prayer, particularly of the repetitive Ṣūfī type known as *dhikr* ("remembrance"), and of theosophical speculation on which of the ninety-nine was the "true" name of Allāh that might reveal the divine essence.

The Qur'ān provided the revealed base on which later Muslims built their own expanded understanding of God, and in two different directions. Under the clear influence of Greek and Christian prototypes, there came into existence in the ninth century the Muslims' own version of sacred theology, what they called *kalām* ("dialectical discourse"), and it was one of the objectives of this science to investigate the nature, attributes, and operations of God. The traditionists, who wanted to affirm all the scriptural predicates of Allāh, held for the reality of God's attributes (knowledge, power, speech, etc.); the early theologians, however, saw this as compromising *tawḥīd* (the divine unity) and reduced the Qur'ānic attributes to nominal or created status. Thus God's speech, that is, the Qur'ān, was for the rational theologians something created, while the traditionists regarded it as uncreated and eternal, no matter what the theological consequences, and it was their view that eventually prevailed.

One attribute, God's power, led off into another debate on divine omnipotence vs. human free-will. The Qur'ān asserts the first on many occasions ("It is God who has created you and all that you have done" [surah 37.96]), but at the same time insists on human responsibility for moral acts ("Every good which comes to you comes from God; every evil which comes to you comes from yourself" [surah 4.79]). Neither side ceded, and the issue remained *non liquet,* though with an inclination to assert the appearance of human liberty: the human agent "acquires" the sense of responsibility. There followed from this another dispute, with perhaps more profound consequences, on the efficacy of all secondary causality, with philosophers asserting the existence of natural causes and the traditionists arguing against them for both a moral and a physical universe under the immediate control of, if not actually determined by, God alone.

The mystics too got caught up in speculation about God, though more often in the wake of an experience of the divine than as the term of a logical demonstration. Many Ṣūfīs claimed to have experienced oneness with Allāh—one, the notorious al-Ḥallāj (d. 922), was executed for the boldness of his claim—which they described in a variety of metaphors and attempted to explain by a number of technical terms ("vision," "infusion," "identity"). And some Ṣūfīs, notably Ibn al-ʿArabī and his school, announced, on the basis of this experimental insight, a kind of existential monism under the rubric "the oneness of being," God's, that is, and the universe's. These Ṣūfī insights into the nature of God often stood in explicit opposition to the traditionalist theologians' more reasoned discourse and even the simple piety of the ordinary believer. According to Abū Ḥāmid al-Ghazālī (d. 1111), the great medieval standard-bearer of Islamic orthodoxy, it was the Ṣūfīs' approach to God that finally brought a healing certitude to his doubting heart, but others were abashed and scandalized by the freedom—almost the licentiousness—of the mystics' language in describing that totally transcendent Other.

Sufism's legacy remains deeply embedded in Muslim spirituality. Although Muslims no longer argue the question of the relationship between Allāh's essence and attributes, and the profound debate between God's omnipotence and man's creative freedom to act has been stilled for many centuries, the devotion to the "beautiful names of God" still has an important place in Islamic devotion, and the Muslims' primary virtue is *tawakkul* (total trust and reliance on God). And despite the energetic and devoted attempts of Muslim theologians, theosophists, lawyers, and mystics to enlarge, enhance, or simply explain, the Muslim's portrait of that God besides which there is no other is still the Qur'ān's, drawn in its opening verses: "Praise be to Allāh, the Lord of the Worlds, the Merciful, the Compassionate, the Sovereign of the Day of Judgment. Truly, it is You we worship and You whose aid we seek" (Qur'ān 1.1–5).

[*See also* ʿAqīdah; Pillars of Islam; Shahādah; Tawḥīd; Theology.]

BIBLIOGRAPHY

Ibn al-ʿArabī. *The Bezels of Wisdom.* Translated by R. W. J. Austin. New York, 1980. Easily accessible version of Ibn ʿArabī's meditations on God and man.

Peters, F. E. *Muhammad and the Origins of Islam.* Albany, N.Y., 1993. The Meccans' notion of God and that announced in the Qur'ān.

Schimmel, Annemarie. *Mystical Dimensions of Islam.* Chapel Hill, N.C., 1975. See especially "Theosophical Sufism," which describes the main line of mystics' speculations about God.

Watt, W. Montgomery. *Free Will and Predestination in Islam.* London, 1948. The Qur'ānic evidence and later discussions on the omnipotence of God and human free will.

Watt, W. Montgomery. *The Formative Period of Islamic Thought.* Edinburgh, 1973. Continuing Muslim discussions on the nature and attributes of God.

F. E. PETERS

ʿALLĀL AL-FĀSĪ, MUḤAMMAD. *See* Fāsī, Muḥammad ʿAllāl al-.

ALL-INDIA MUSLIM LEAGUE. Established in 1906, the All-India Muslim League had a somewhat limited role until it came under the leadership of Mohammad Ali Jinnah in the mid-1930s. In his hands it became the vehicle for the Pakistan movement. After independence and partition in 1947 and Jinnah's death the following year, it became one among several political parties in Pakistan, where it has continued intermittently to play a significant political role.

The origins of the Muslim League are to be found in what is commonly called the Aligarh Movement. India's leading Islamic modernist of the nineteenth century, Sir Sayyid Aḥmad Khān, had in 1875 founded a college (later a university) in the town of Aligarh, with the intention of providing Western education to the upper strata of Indian Muslim society, especially the Urdu-speaking landlords and professionals of North India. From the beginning the college and its graduates sought to provide a political lead to the country's Muslims, although there was rarely unanimity. The initial forum for this task was the Muhammadan Educational Conference, and at its Dhaka meeting in December 1906 it transformed itself into the Muslim League. The political context was provided by the election in Britain of a Liberal government and subsequent moves toward limited representative institutions in India. In October 1906, with thc hclp of thc British principal of Aligarh, a delegation of Muslim notables called on the viceroy, Lord Minto, in Simla, and presented a petition asking for various forms of special protection for the Muslim population, notably separate electoral rolls. These were in fact incorporated into the 1909 Indian Councils Act. [*See* Aligarh.]

Founded initially as a loyalist organization, the Muslim League a few years after its creation was taken over by a different group of Aligarh graduates, most prominently Muḥammad ʿAlī and his brother Shaukat ʿAlī, who emphasized Pan-Islamic themes on the one hand and cooperation with the Indian National Congress on the other. In 1916 the League leaders, including Mohammad Ali Jinnah, who had joined in 1913, negotiated an agreement with the Congress that secured separate electorates in return for support for a common program of constitutional change. After the end of the war, however, the League as an institution was temporarily swept aside by the force of the Khilāfat movement, although several of its leaders played prominent parts in the latter. Muslim politics during the 1920s and early 1930s were dominated by provincial leaders and parties, such as Sir Fazli Husain in the Punjab. Jinnah himself had retired to London in 1931 following the failure of efforts to negotiate new agreements or understandings with the Congress, and Muslim interests at the national level were represented by conservative loyalists. [*See* Khilāfat Movement.]

By the mid-1930s, however, the political environment had changed substantially following the civil disobedience campaign by Congress, and the 1935 Government of India Act appeared to presage an elected government at the all-India level. The possibility that the government in India might represent Congress' views and attitudes and emphasize either secular or Hindu values forced a rethinking of the Muslim position. Jinnah, seen as having the negotiating skills and contacts to represent the Muslim cause, was called back from London in 1935 and took on the presidency of the League. His first task was to contest the initial elections under the 1935 Act, which were held in early 1937. An electoral organization had to be created from scratch, and the overall League performance was poor compared to both Congress and regional parties such as the Unionists in the Punjab. A further setback came when the Congress refused to allow Muslim League representatives in the United Provinces, where the League had won a number of seats, to join the Congress government there. This confirmed Jinnah's view that the Congress was unwilling to allow the Muslim League political space in any future constitutional arrangements.

From the middle of 1937 Jinnah succeeded in projecting the League as the representative agent of the Muslims. In September 1937 he persuaded the premiers of the Muslim-majority provinces of the Punjab and Bengal to join the League, while maintaining their provincial party structures. Simultaneously the League launched a sustained attack on the Congress, portraying it as fundamentally hostile to Muslim interests. In March 1940 the Muslim League at a meeting in Lahore passed what has become known as the Pakistan Resolution, calling for independent states in Muslim-majority areas. Jinnah's own speech at this meeting set out his view of the Muslims of India as a separate nation. Although the resolution apparently called for the partition of the subcontinent into separate states, there has been much controversy over whether this was in fact Jinnah's aim. Some writers have argued that it was primarily intended as a bargaining counter.

During World War II Jinnah and the Muslim League made progress on various fronts. The League moved from being mainly an agent of other groups to being a principal actor. In the Punjab and elsewhere it began to attract the support of prominent landlords and of some sections of the *ʿulamāʾ* and Ṣūfī pirs. An unbroken string of by-election victories paved the way for a landslide result in the 1945 and 1946 elections. With solid political support from the Muslim community, Jinnah then moved into the final stage of tripartite negotiations with the Congress and the outgoing British. Against a background of increasing violence, the only solution that could be found involved the partition of India and also the partition of the provinces of Punjab and Bengal, which formed the bulk of the new state of Pakistan. Millions of the League's members and supporters from all over North India were forced to abandon their homes and move to the unfamiliar setting of Sindh or the Punjab. Although a homeland had been created for the Indian subcontinent's Muslims, it was far from ideal.

After independence and Jinnah's death in September 1948, the League found difficulty in establishing a separate role for itself. Within a short time the army and bureaucracy came to dominate the political process, and the only role for the League was as a vehicle for rival groups of provincial politicians. Splits occurred from time to time along factional lines. It has, however, been a convenient label for politicians to adopt, and in 1988 it formed the core of the Islāmī Jumhūrī Ittiḥād (Islamic Democratic Alliance). This coalition won the 1990 elections and formed the government under the leadership of Mian Nawaz Sharif, himself a member of the League.

[*See also* India; Pakistan; *and the biography of Jinnah. For the post-partition history of the League as a political party in Pakistan, see* Muslim League.]

BIBLIOGRAPHY

Hardy, Peter. *The Muslims of British India*. Cambridge, 1972. Masterly synthesis.

Jalal, Ayesha. *The Sole Spokesman: Jinnah, the Muslim League, and the Demand for Pakistan*. Cambridge, 1985. The most important study of Jinnah's tactics and long-term aims, although considered controversial by some critics.

Pirzada, Syed Sharifuddin, ed. *Foundations of Pakistan: All-India Muslim League Documents, 1906–1947*. 2 vols. Karachi, 1969–1970. Includes presidential addresses and other important material relating to the annual sessions of the League and to the League Council in the years leading up to independence.

Qureshi, Ishtiaq Husain. *The Muslim Community of the Indo-Pakistan Subcontinent, 610–1947: A Brief Historical Analysis*. 2d ed. Karachi, 1977. Standard Pakistani account of the history of the Subcontinent.

Robinson, Francis. *Separatism among Indian Muslims: The Politics of the United Provinces' Muslims, 1860–1923*. London, 1974. Discusses the dynamics of politics among the elite Muslim groups of northern India, from whom emerged the initial League leadership.

Shaikh, Farzana. *Community and Consensus in Islam: Muslim Representation in Colonial India, 1860–1947*. Cambridge, 1989. Challenges the widely accepted view that the Muslim League's demands can be interpreted primarily in terms of the immediate political interests of its elite leadership.

Talbot, Ian. *Provincial Politics and the Pakistan Movement: The Growth of the Muslim League in North-West and North-East India, 1937–47*. Karachi, 1988. Brief look at the rise of the Muslim League at provincial level.

Wolpert, Stanley A. *Jinnah of Pakistan*. New York, 1984. Thoroughly researched biography that deals with both his political and personal life.

DAVID TAYLOR

ALMSGIVING. *See* Zakāt.

AMAL. A populist movement of Lebanese Shīʿī Muslims that first emerged in 1975, Amal has become an important political force in Lebanon.

Political Mobilization of the Shīʿah. Against a background of social exclusion and economic deprivation, the Shīʿah of Lebanon have emerged as major political actors on the Lebanese scene. Well into the twentieth century, the Shīʿah were only bit players in Lebanon. They were unnoticed by other Lebanese, given scant attention by scholars, and presumed insignificant by Lebanese politicians. Socialized into a religious tradition that extolled sacrifice and presumed temporal injustice, the Shīʿah found ready confirmation for their beliefs in their mundane surroundings. Lebanon's confessional (sectarian) political equation—in which privilege, office, and political rights were allocated according to sect—operated to the disadvantage of the Shīʿah. This became pronounced as their population grew disproportionately to the country's other major sects. In a political system dominated by Maronite and Sunnī politicians, the Shīʿah were trapped by their confessional identity.

Although they lagged behind non-Shīʿīs, the Shīʿah were still very much affected by the rapid modernization that had marked Lebanon since independence in 1943. Access to education produced a growing pool of individuals who were no longer content to confine their horizons to subsistence farming. Improved transportation eroded the geographic isolation of the community. A rapidly growing communications network, both within and outside of Lebanon, brought the outside world—with its political ideologies and its modern ideas and technologies—into even the most remote village.

Modernization of the agricultural sector, including an increasing emphasis on cash crops and farm mechanization, led to underemployment and unemployment. Many of the Shīʿah were forced to move off the land in order to survive. As the modernization process began to have an effect, and as the Shīʿah gained from exposure to horizons wider than the village, they became more aware of the disparities between them and their relatively affluent neighbors. Fleeing the poverty of the village and the drudgery of farm labor, many Shīʿah took work where they could find it in Beirut, usually as petty laborers or peddlers. This migration of labor led to the swelling of the population of the Lebanese capital by the 1960s. The Shīʿah made their homes in the squalid suburbs; although some actually escaped from poverty, most remained dreadfully poor. Not surprisingly, these migrants from the country became a fertile pool for recruitment by radical parties that claimed to have answers to their difficulties.

More important, the dearth of economic opportunities within Lebanon factored into the movement of many Shīʿī men overseas, where opportunities in the Gulf states, and especially West Africa, provided a way out of poverty. Some made their fortunes and thereby gained the wherewithal to support political movements in their image. Later, the money earned by these Shīʿī migrants would play a crucial role in financing the growth of Shīʿī political activism within Lebanon. Though the Shīʿah as a whole are still relatively impoverished, many Shīʿīs have done well as merchants, building contractors, and professionals. Yet, even among the affluent, there is an ethos of deprivation, a lingering memory imparted by a lifetime of accumulated grievances and slights.

The 1960s and 1970s also exposed the Lebanese Shīʿah to the vibrant and dynamic leadership of Sayyid Mūsā al-Ṣadr. Although born in Iran, Ṣadr traced his ancestry back to southern Lebanon and the village of Marakah. He moved to Lebanon in 1960 from Najaf, Iraq, where he had been studying Islamic *fiqh* (jurisprudence) under the sponsorship of several of the most important ayatollahs of the day. He was a looming presence in the pre-civil war period, and it was under his direction and leadership that the Ḥarakat al-Maḥrūmīn (Movement of the Deprived)—the forerunner of the Amal movement—emerged in 1974. Ṣadr was a populist leader with an agenda of reform, not destruction and revolution.

Although the Movement of the Deprived claimed to represent all of the politically dispossessed Lebanese, regardless of confession, it was transparently a party of the Shīʿah. The charismatic Ṣadr skillfully exploited Shiism's potent symbolism to remind his followers that they were people with a heritage of resistance and sacrifice. He revitalized the epic martyrdom of Imam Ḥusayn (the grandson of the prophet Muḥammad) at Karbala in 680, and he inspired his followers to emulate the imam's bravery.

Despite his magnetic appeal for many Shīʿah, Ṣadr's movement was only one in a field of organizations that successfully mobilized the Shīʿah into political action. In Lebanon, as in Iraq among the Shīʿah, the Communist Party was the party of prominence in the 1970s. Only later, and under bizarre circumstances, did Ṣadr's movement assume center stage for the Shīʿah. With the civil war that began in 1975, Ṣadr's popular following was challenged by a number of militia organizations, including the Palestinian Fidāʿīyān, which recruited many Shīʿah youths. Ṣadr's appeal diminished in a setting where guns became commonplace adornments and the rhetoric of hatred and cruelty overwhelmed his rhetoric of reform.

War's exuberance faded predictably, and in the south, the heartland of Shiism in Lebanon, the conflict destroyed villages, took lives and livelihoods, and alienated many Shīʿīs from their political alliances. Increasingly, throughout 1977 and 1978, Shīʿīs often found themselves in the crossfire between the Palestine Liberation Organization (PLO) and Israel. This was a period of heightened suffering, especially in southern Lebanon, where a heavy price was paid for the armed Palestinian presence.

Development and Activities of Amal. By the late 1970s many—but by no means all—of the politicized Shīʿah deserted the political left and joined or supported the rejuvenated Amal movement. *Amal* means hope, but it is also an acronym for Afwāj al-Muqāwamah al-Lubnānīyah (Lebanese Resistance Detachments). In 1978 the Israelis increased their military pressure on south Lebanon, thereby helping to stoke the tensions between the Shīʿah and the PLO, although subsequent Israeli errors would indicate that theirs was a very incomplete understanding of what was taking place among the Shīʿah. Amal began to take shape as a loose grouping of village homeguards, intent on circumscribing the influence of the PLO and thereby reducing the exposure of the Shīʿah to Israeli preemptive and retaliatory strikes.

With the Iranian Revolution gathering momentum in 1978, many Lebanese Shīʿah took inspiration from the actions of their Iranian coreligionists. If the Islamic Revolution was not a precise model for Lebanon, it was still an exemplar for action, and Amal, as an authentically Shīʿī movement, was the momentary beneficiary of this enthusiasm. Ṣadr was known to be a key supporter of Ayatollah Ruhollah Khomeini (1902–1989) and an adversary of the shah (although his opposition had been tempered by a good dose of realism). Moreover, several key Amal officials, including the Iranian Muṣṭafā Chamrān, took up key positions in the new regime.

Ironically, it was also Ṣadr's disappearance in 1978 that helped to retrieve the promise of his earlier efforts. In August 1978 he visited Libya with two companions, Shaykh Muḥammad Shihādah Yaʿqūb and journalist ʿAbbās Badr al-Dīn. The party has not been heard of since. Ṣadr became a hero to his followers, who revere his memory and take inspiration from his works and his plights. The symbol of a missing *imam*—reminiscent of the central dogma of Shiism—is hard to assail, and even blood enemies were heard to utter words of praise for the missing leader. The reform movement Ṣadr founded became the largest Shīʿī organization in Lebanon. By 1982, when Israel launched its invasion of Lebanon, Amal was arguably the most dynamic force in Lebanese politics.

Amal's calls for the reformation of the Lebanese political system went unheeded, however. The Maronite Christians, who have enjoyed the dominant role in the politics of modern Lebanon, were intent to preserve their power, not to share it. The Sunnī Muslims, the Maronites' junior partner, were also little interested in seeing the diminution of their privileges to the advantage of the Shīʿah. Thus, the answer to Amal's demands was calculated intransigence. The predictable result was increased anger and frustration among the Shīʿah.

True to its reformist origins, the Amal leadership sought a role in the Lebanese political system in the exuberant second half of 1982. Although Lebanon's civil war did not definitively end until 1990, the expulsion of the bulk of the PLO's fighters from Lebanon and the energetic engagement of U.S. diplomacy seemed to signal that the worst was over. Amal leader Nabih Berri, the Sierra Leone-born son of a Shīʿī trader, waited in vain for a call that never came. Meanwhile, though Israel earned the gratitude of many southern Shīʿah for expelling the widely disdained Palestinian gunmen, Israel remained in occupation of much of Lebanon, including all of the south.

By 1983, the hopes of 1982 were in tatters. U.S. diplomacy proved to be clumsy and poorly conceived, and Syria, defeated soundly by Israel in 1982, was determined to undermine Israel's gains and America's ambitions in Lebanon. An increasingly potent Lebanese resistance emerged, based initially in the parties of the left, but by the autumn of 1983 Amal was deeply implicated in the resistance. From 1982 onward, the Shīʿī community became increasingly militant, in no small measure because of an arbitrary campaign of intimidation and arrests by the Maronite-led government.

The high point of Amal's organized military power was in 1984. Amal fighters were heavily engaged against the Israeli occupation of Lebanese soil, and, in Beirut, Amal confronted the central government. After terrible shelling of the heavily populated southern suburbs by the army, Nabih Berri called successfully on Shīʿī soldiers to lay down their arms, whereon Amal became the dominant force of the moment in West Beirut.

Shortly thereafter, in early 1984, U.S. marines withdrew from their positions in Beirut. Following the disastrous attack on the marine barracks in 1983 that killed more than two hundred marines, the departing marines left their positions to Amal militiamen. Amal moved to solidify its power position, while also maintaining pressure on Israel in the south, where the invading army consolidated its positions. Deadly, intense attacks prompted Israel to extricate most of its forces from Lebanon, while, in 1985, retaining a foothold in a self-proclaimed "security zone."

For a time, the Amal leaders had some faith in U.S. promises, but, by 1985, those promises rang hollow and Amal was heavily influenced by Syria. Given the extant hatreds, Amal did not need much prodding to move to suppress surviving PLO positions in the environs of Beirut, but Syria was a generous supplier of arms and ammunition for Amal's bloody war of the camps, which lasted until 1988.

Amal's ascendancy, however, was promptly checked. A tactical alliance with the Druze leader Walid Jumblatt crumbled, and among the Sunnī Muslims fears of Shīʿī suzerainty sparked a variety of organizational ripostes. Amal's moment of singular power was over.

Competition with Ḥizbullāh. Amal, which promised in the early 1980s to become the dominant organizational voice for the Shīʿah, faced a serious erosion in its following. Ineffective and even incompetent leadership, corruption, and more than a modicum of arrogance have undermined its support, especially in the environs of Beirut.

Ḥizbullāh (or "the Party of God"), the Iranian-funded alternative to Amal, emerged since 1982 as a competent, dedicated, and well-led challenger. Although young Shīʿī clerics dominate the leadership of Ḥizbullāh, it is noteworthy that Ḥizbullāh has been especially effective in recruiting among well-educated Shīʿah from secular professions, many of whom have lost confidence in Amal. In May 1988, fighting in Beirut suburbs, which saw the Ḥizbullāh triumph over the Amal militia, underlined Ḥizbullāh's steady success in enlisting the Shīʿah, many of whom are ex-Amal members.

As the overall situation grew worse, Ḥizbullāh gained supporters, although Amal remained a force with which to be reckoned. The persistent insecurity, the stalling of political reform, and the near total collapse of the Lebanese economy have made religion a refuge, skillfully manipulated to be sure, in a situation where there were no other answers. Taking its cue from Iran, Ḥizbullāh has exploited the symbolism of Shiism to enlist support. For instance, ʿĀshūrāʾ, the day on which the Shīʿah commemorate the martyrdom of Imam Ḥusayn more than thirteen hundred years ago, and certainly the most significant day of the Shīʿī calendar, has become not just a plea for intercession or an act of piety, but a revolutionary statement.

Ḥizbullāh has enjoyed much less success in south Lebanon, where about one-third of the Shīʿah live (the total population of Shīʿah in Lebanon is usually estimated to be at least one million, or 30–35 percent of the total Lebanese population, but it may be even higher). Anti-PLO animosity runs deep in the south, and Amal's staunch stance against the restoration of an armed PLO presence in the area accurately reflects popular sentiment and distinguishes Amal from Ḥizbullāh.

The civil war ended in 1990, generally along the lines of the 1989 Ṭāʾif Accord, which called for Muslim-Christian parity in parliament and increased, marginally, the influence of the Shīʿī Muslims in the Lebanese political system. In agreement with the accord, Amal was disarmed in 1991 and the movement's militia phase ended.

Amal's rival, Ḥizbullāh, however, did not disarm and continued to enjoy the toleration of Syria and the support of Iran. In addition, although Amal leaders had long railed against the corruption and arrogance of the *zuʿamāʾ* (political bosses), senior Amal figures were susceptible to the same charges. Amal maintained an important core of support, especially in the south, but Ḥizbullāh continued to siphon off members, who were attracted by Ḥizbullāh's network of social services and its reputation for integrity.

With the resumption of "normal" politics in Lebanon, Amal's raison d'être had to be modified radically. Although the killing stopped, for the most part, the aftermath of the civil war was a national economic crisis in which the real standard of living of the Lebanese declined dramatically. Amal's capacity for conversion into a widely encompassing political movement has thus been limited.

Nonetheless, Nabih Berri, long a political outsider, ascended in 1991 to the position of parliamentary speaker, the highest political position allotted to a Shīʿī, signifying both a personal success and a marker of Amal's accomplishments since its creation in 1974. Popular movements tend to offer more than they can reasonably be expected to deliver, otherwise they would lose their populist base, and Amal is no exception. Yet, in the quest of the Shīʿah of Lebanon for dignity and political power, Amal's role was central. The movement authentically symbolized the moderation and the project of reform that defines the vast majority of this community.

[*See also* Ḥizbullāh, *article on* Ḥizbullāh in Lebanon; Lebanon; *and the biography of* Ṣadr.]

BIBLIOGRAPHY

Collings, Deidre, ed. *Peace for Lebanon? From War to Reconstruction.* Boulder, 1994.

Crighton, Elizabeth, and Martha Abele MacIver. "The Evolution of Ethnic Conflict: Group Dynamics and Political Underdevelopment in Northern Ireland and Lebanon." *Comparative Politics* 23.2 (January 1991): 127–142.

Fisk, Robert. *Pity the Nation: The Abduction of Lebanon.* New York, 1990.

Hanf, Theodor. *Coexistence in Wartime Lebanon: Decline of a State and Rise of a Nation.* Oxford, 1993.

Mallat, Chibli. *Shiʿi Thought from the South of Lebanon.* Oxford, 1988.

Norton, Augustus Richard. *Amal and the Shiʿa: Struggle for the Soul of Lebanon.* Austin, 1987.

Piçard, Elizabeth. *Liban, état de discord: Des fondations aux guerres fratricides.* Paris, 1988.

Sirriyeh, Hussein. "Lebanon: Dimensions of Conflict." *Adelphi Paper* 243 (August 1989).

Theroux, Peter. *The Strange Disappearance of Imam Moussa Sadr* [sic]. London, 1988.

United States. Congress. House of Representatives. Committee on Foreign Affairs. Subcommittee on Europe and the Middle East. "Islamic Fundamentalism and Islamic Radicalism." Hearings before the 99th Cong., 1st sess., 24 June, 15 July, and 30 September 1985.

Augustus Richard Norton

AMĀN. *See* Diplomatic Immunity.

AMEER ALI, SYED (Amīr ʿAlī, Sayyid; 1849–1928), Indian jurist and author of Islamic modernist apologia. Syed Ameer Ali was born in Chinsura, Bengal into a Shīʿī family with a history of service to Persian and Mughal rulers and to the nawabs of Awadh, as well as to the British East India Company. He was educated at Hooghly College outside Calcutta, then studied law in London and was called to the Bar in 1873. Returning to Calcutta to practice law, he also lectured in Islamic law at Presidency College of Calcutta University. In the 1870s he served as presidency magistrate. In 1881 he was appointed to the Bengal Legislative Council, and in 1883 to the Viceroy's Legislative Council. In 1890 he was named a judge of the Bengal High Court, where he served until his retirement in 1904. Thereafter he settled in England, his wife's home, serving as a member of the Judicial Committee of the Privy Council from 1909 until his death in 1928.

Ameer Ali's distinguished public career was punctuated by frequent writings on Islamic topics for such British journals as *Nineteenth Century*. His books on Islamic religion and history were written in English with a Western readership in mind and established his reputation as a modern apologist for Islamic culture. His best-known works are *A Short History of the Saracens* (1889) and *The Spirit of Islam* (1891). He viewed Islam as the vehicle of rationality and dynamism during the age of European barbarism, and the Prophet Muḥammad as a messenger of moral humanism and progress entirely in tune with the modern age. These works had considerable influence on the thinking of Western-educated Muslims in India in their efforts to refute British or Christian missionary criticisms of their faith, and in their sense of an emerging political and religious identity.

Ameer Ali's position and politics allied him with the British, but throughout his career he endeavored to represent Indian Muslim opinion, as he saw it, to the government. In 1877 he founded the Central National Muhammadan Association with the purpose of petitioning the British government to safeguard Muslim interests. He also established the London branch of the All-India Muslim League in 1908; he lobbied for the establishment of separate electorates for Muslims, a provision of the Morley-Minto constitutional reforms of 1909. Ameer Ali also lobbied the British government for fair treatment of the Ottoman sultan-caliph in the treaties ending World War I, even though he took no part in the Khilāfat movement in India [*see* Khilāfat Movement]. His efforts on behalf of the Ottoman caliph included a letter that he and the Aga Khan wrote to the prime minister of Turkey in 1923, urging a restoration of the caliph's temporal powers. Ironically, this letter from the two Indian Shīʿī leaders had the opposite effect: the Turkish National Assembly, indignant at this foreign meddling, voted to abolish the caliphate early in 1924.

BIBLIOGRAPHY

Ahmad, Aziz. *Islamic Modernism in India and Pakistan, 1857–1964.* London, 1967. Good general guide to intellectual modernism in Indian Islam.

Ameer Ali, Syed. *The Spirit of Islam: A History of the Evolution and Ideals of Islam with a Life of the Prophet.* Reprint, London, 1965. Ameer Ali's best-known work of apologetics.

Aziz, K. K. *Ameer Ali: His Life and Work.* Lahore, 1968. A brief biography, plus reprints of many of Ameer Ali's articles from scattered journals; a very helpful compendium together with Wasti's, listed below.

Hardy, Peter. *The Muslims of British India.* Cambridge, 1972. The best short intellectual history of Muslims in nineteenth- and twentieth-century India.

Wasti, Syed Razi, ed. *Memoirs and Other Writings of Syed Ameer Ali.* Lahore, 1968.

Wasti, Syed Razi, ed. *Syed Ameer Ali on Islamic History and Culture.* Lahore, 1968. Collected articles by Ameer Ali, some also contained in the Aziz work, listed above.

GAIL MINAULT

AMĪR. From the Arabic root *amara* ("to command") *amīr* is traditionally defined as military commander, leader, governor, or prince. Although the word *amīr* is not found in the Qur'ān (its root appears once as *ulū'al-amr* (those in authority) in surah 4.59, 83), it does have Islamic origins. Although different shades of the meaning of *amīr* can be gleaned from the rich prophetic traditions, all converge on the importance of leadership in Islam, both to an individual and on a social level. More importantly, many of these *ḥadīth*s draw a direct link between leadering *(amara)* and consulting *(shāwara)*, suggesting that those who are sought for consultation should be in a position of leadership. This link falls in tandem with the linguistic usage of *amīr*, for it is a synonym of *mushāwar* ("the consulted one"). This conceptual relationship was evidenced particularly in the early period of Islam.

Historically, *amīr* was used as a title for the caliphs—first by the second rightly guided caliph ʿUmar ibn al-Khaṭṭāb, as "Amīr al-Mu'minīn," ("Commander of the Faithful"). This title did not imply a separation of Islamic affiliation from political leadership. In fact, Islamic religious piety was the principal prerequisite for the leader of the Islamic *ummah* (community). Both the Umayyad and ʿAbbāsid caliphs followed suit in styling themselves with this title, as did their successors and some of their dynastic opponents (e.g., ʿAlids and Fāṭimids) who also laid claim to the caliphate.

The title of *amīr*, on the other hand, was bestowed on an *ʿamīl* (delegate) appointed with the approval of the caliph, as well as on those who excelled in the military, such as commanders of armies (and occasionally of divisions of an army), and governors who were initially the conquering generals. The *amīr*'s governance was generally restricted to a province, and his *bayʿah* (allegiance) was to the ruling caliph. His authority was substantially enhanced as a result of the increased bureaucratic complexities introduced initially by the seventh-century Umayyad dynasty and further developed by the ʿAbbāsids.

Consequently, the duties of the amirate were expanded to incorporate affairs outside the military, allowing *amīr*s to distinguish themselves in both their administrative and financial duties. These included organizing the army, conducting expeditions, concluding agreements, appointing officials to various posts (e.g., *ʿārif*s who kept registers of their units, *qāḍī*s [judges], the police, the postmaster), distributing pay, levying or abolishing taxes, leading prayer, and building mosques and other public works. This full ruling power caused many *amīr*s to amass such wealth and power that some established dynasties, thereby reducing their relations with the caliph to receiving his *ʿahd* (decree of appointment) and reciting his name in the Friday *khuṭbah* (sermon). The military rule of the Seljuks, the Ayyūbids, and the Mamlūks illustrates the military orientation of the *amīr* throughout the tenth and eleventh centuries.

In modern times, the title *amīr* denotes membership in the ruling families of the many monarchies governing Muslim countries (e.g., Saudi Arabia, the Gulf countries). The function of the amirate has basically been reduced to that of executive, and the title has come to mean prince.

BIBLIOGRAPHY

Bukhārī, Muḥammad ibn Ismāʿīl al-. *The Translation of the Meanings of Sahih al-Bukhari.* 9 vols. Translated by M. M. Khan. 3d rev.

ed. Chicago, 1979. The premier authoritative Sunnī compilation of *ḥadīth.*
Dūrī, ʿAbd al-ʿAzīz al-. "Amīr." In *Encyclopaedia of Islam,* new ed., vol. 1, pp. 438–439. Leiden, 1960–. Treats the concept in the context of classical and medieval Islam.
Al-munjid fī al-lughah wa-al-aʿlām. 28th ed. Beirut, 1986.
Zabīdī, Muḥammad Murtaḍā al-. *Tāj al-ʿarūs min jawāhir al-qāmūs.* 10 vols. Cairo, 1889.

HIBBA ELTIGANI ABUGIDEIRI

AMĪR AL-MU'MINĪN. A title created early in Islamic history and adopted by a series of Muslim polities to the present day, *amīr al-mu'minīn* means "Commander of the Faithful." Early medieval Muslim historians report that the term was used in reference to those in positions of command over Muslim forces during the initial period of conquest, both during and after the life of the Prophet. According to separate anecdotes reported by al-Ṭabarī (*Ta'rīkh,* 1:2748) and al-Yaʿqūbī (*Ta'rīkh,* 2:171–172), among others, the second of the Rāshidūn caliphs, ʿUmar ibn al-Khaṭṭāb, adopted it as a title. Neither passage explicitly supports the assertion (Gibb, 1960) that the adoption of the title was connected to the Qur'ānic injunction (4.58, 62) to obey not only God and the Prophet, but "those among you who are charged with authority *(al-amr)*" as well.

Under Umayyad rule, beginning with Muʿāwiyah, the title appears to have taken on increasing ideological weight; along with Hijrī dates and the Basmalah ("in the name of God" invocation), the title was used on coins minted by the Islamic state. Early Arab-Sassanian coins bear the legend "Muʿāwiyah, Commander of the Faithful" in Pahlavi script, although a change to the use of Arabic on coins appears to have occurred by the end of the seventh century. On at least two occasions in the later part of that century, the title was claimed by rivals to the Umayyad caliphate: ʿAbd Allāh ibn Zubayr in the second civil war and a Khārijī leader, ʿAbd Allāh ibn Qaṭarī ibn al-Fujā'ah, over the years 688–699.

The anecdote concerning ʿUmar ibn al-Khaṭṭāb suggests that from early on the title was used more commonly than its complex companion term, *khalīfah.* Like *khalīfah,* it did not refer to a clearly delineated set of powers or the possession of absolute authority; in this sense, then, its meaning evolved as the scope and nature of the caliphal office were defined and debated by Muslim political and religious writers over the course of Islamic history. Generally speaking, *amīr al-mu'minīn* referred to the temporal powers of the sovereign, whereas *khalīfah* connoted "deputyship," either to the Prophet or to God. A third term, *imām,* often used for caliphs or caliphal aspirants, connoted religious authority.

In the Sunnī Islamic world, the adoption of the title implied the claim either to the caliphate, as during the Umayyad and ʿAbbāsid dynasties, or to autonomous political authority over a region of the Islamic world, as used by the Umayyad rulers of Spain, beginning with ʿAbd al-Raḥmān III in 928. Its use by the Fāṭimid state, a Shīʿī dynasty with Ismāʿīlī roots, was a rival claim to the universal sovereignty of the caliphate. In Yemen, in the early tenth century, the founder of the Zaydī Imamate, which was only overthrown in 1962, laid claim to the title as well. The use of the title by the various branches of Shiism generally reflects their respective conceptions of authority; the Twelvers, for example, apply it exclusively to ʿAlī ibn Abī Ṭālib.

The use either of titles bearing the component *amīr al-mu'minīn* (as in the sultanate dynasties of the Seljuks and Ghaznavids and others such as the Ayyūbids in Syria and Rasūlids of Yemen) or of a new title, for example, *amīr al-muslimīn,* adopted by the Almoravid (al-Murābiṭūn) state in the western Maghrib in the early twelfth century, implied primarily a symbolic recognition of ʿAbbāsid sovereignty. The Almohad (al-Muwaḥḥidūn) ruler, ʿAbd al-Mu'min, successor to the founder of the dynasty, Ibn Tūmart, assumed the title around 1132, thereby directly challenging the claim of the ʿAbbāsids (by that point a badly weakened dynasty) to the caliphate. The Almohad claim was then taken up by the Ḥafṣid dynasty in the thirteenth century; in the following century, in Morocco, the Marīnids pushed the Ḥafṣids aside and assumed the title and its accompanying claim to authority for themselves. The two succeeding dynasties of Morocco, the Saʿdīs and ʿAlawīs, refined a Marīnid idea of combining caliphal-like authority, expressed in the use of *amīr al-mu'minīn,* with Ṣūfī doctrines and the claim of descent from the Prophet. While the current Moroccan king, Ḥasan II, a member of the ʿAlawī dynasty, may draw some support from his assertion of a combined spiritual and temporal authority, his authoritarian regime relies to a great extent upon backing from the military and security services.

The use of *amīr al-mu'minīn,* quite unlike that of *khalīfah,* appears to have waned in the Middle East following the Mongol invasions of the thirteenth century. The Ottoman rulers, even at the height of their power in the sixteenth century, do not appear, with several rare exceptions, to have laid formal claim to the title, a change that has been linked to later developments in the theory of the caliphate (Gibb, 1962, pp. 145–149). The title retained, however, a strong ideological resonance in West African Muslim communities. In the late seventeenth century, in Mauritania, ethnic and religious tensions sparked the formation of a primarily Berber socioreligious movement under the leadership of Nāṣir al-Dīn. He announced himself to be both the *imām* and *amīr al-mu'minīn,* and bringing together messianic and militant reformist ideas, led his followers against local Arab tribal forces. The movement was effectively crushed by 1677, following the death of Nāṣir al-Dīn in 1674. Messianic and reformist ideas also fueled the more successful movement led by Usuman dan Fodio (1754–1817) in what is today northern Nigeria. Drawing on his training as a Sunnī *ʿālim,* and responding to what he perceived as the corrupt and irreligious ways of the rulers of the Gobir state, don Fodio announced a *jihād* against them in 1804–1805. Among his titles was that of *amīr al-mu'minīn.* Military victories led to the creation of the Sokoto Caliphate, which survived until its defeat by the British in 1903.

[*See also* Caliph *and the biography of Dan Fodio.*]

BIBLIOGRAPHY

Berchem, Max van. "Titres califiens d'Occident." *Journal Asiatique* 10.2 (1907): 245–335.

Crone, Patricia, and Martin Hinds. *God's Caliph: Religious Authority in the First Centuries of Islam.* Cambridge, 1986.

Gibb, H. A. R. "Amīr al-Mu'minīn." In *Encyclopaedia of Islam,* new ed., vol. 1, p. 445. Leiden, 1960–.

Gibb, H. A. R. "Some Considerations on the Sunni Theory of the Caliphate." In his *Studies on the Civilization of Islam.* Boston, 1962.

Lapidus, Ira. *A History of Islamic Societies.* Cambridge, 1988.

Morony, Michael. *Iraq after the Muslim Conquest.* Princeton, 1984.

MATTHEW S. GORDON

ANAVATAN PARTİSİ. Turkey was governed from 1983 to 1991 by the Anavatan Partisi (Motherland Party), better known by the Turkish acronym Anap. It was formed in April 1983 after the military regime that had seized power on 12 September 1980 allowed the return of electoral politics. The junta, which had ruled as the National Security Council (NSC), had dissolved all parties and banned their leaders from political activity for periods of five to ten years. The generals thus hoped to introduce "new politics" involving people who had little or no prior political experience. Anap's founder Turgut Özal (1927–1993) was such a figure; Anap soon became identified with him and the vehicle for his ambitions.

Özal was born in Malatya in eastern Turkey into a humble provincial family, his father a minor bank official and his mother a primary-school teacher. His mother, Hafize Hanım, was the stronger influence. She emphasized the importance of education and may have initiated her sons into the Naqshbandī order, to which she was attached. (When she died on 10 May 1988, the cabinet issued an edict permitting her to be buried in the courtyard of the Süleymaniye mosque near the grave of Mehmed Said Kotku Efendi, a Naqshbandī shaykh.)

After completing his schooling Turgut Özal entered Istanbul Technical University, where he met future politicians like Süleyman Demirel, prime minister in the 1960s and 1970s, and Necmettin Erbakan. He graduated in 1950 and entered the bureaucracy as a technocrat. Özal rose through the ranks and in 1966 became Prime Minister Demirel's technical adviser. The following year he was appointed undersecretary at the State Planning Organization, where he formed around him a team of like-minded conservatives, many of whom became prominent in Anap. When Demirel was ousted by the coup of 12 March 1971, Özal also lost his position. He worked at the World Bank in Washington from 1971 to 1973; there he became infatuated with American technology and know-how. Meanwhile his younger brother Korkut Özal joined the Islamist National Salvation Party (Millî Selamet Partisi, MSP), was elected to parliament in 1973, and became a minister in the 1974 coalition of the Republican People's Party (Cumhuriyet Halk Partisi) and the MSP. Turgut Özal stood for election on the MSP ticket in 1977 but lost; had he been elected, he too would have been disqualified from politics by the NSC. In November 1979 he was appointed Demirel's economic adviser, a post he continued to hold under the junta until July 1982, when the "Bankers' scandal" forced him to resign.

Anap, Özal claimed, had brought together all the ideological tendencies represented in the recently dissolved parties. The influence of the NSP and the neofascist Nationalist Action Party (Milliyetçi Hareket Partisi, MHP) was especially strong and was reflected in the attempt to reconcile ultranationalism and Islam with the so-called Turkish-Islamic synthesis. Anap was a center-right party that appealed largely to provincial elements most comfortable with the traditional cultural values generally associated with Islam; for example, Anap women tended to prefer modest attire, including the head scarf or *türban,* over fashions imported from the West. Such people had had a peripheral political role in the old system; now they filled the vacuum created by the NSC's policies. Many of the new politicians were technocrats (like Özal himself) whose familiarity with the modern world did not go beyond their field of expertise, and they had little appreciation of Western mores or culture; such people formed the Islamist faction. There was also a secular faction to which Özal belonged, with his wife Semra, an important role model for Turkish women. Özal mediated between these factions and manipulated them to safeguard his own hegemony in the party.

Anap won the November 1983 elections largely because only parties approved by the NSC were allowed to run, and Anap seemed to be the one least tied to the military. However, the policies the Anap government pursued were virtually laid down by the NSC. In economic matters, Özal as prime minister continued to favor free-market and supply-side economics. Ever-rising prices and low wages curbed consumption, enabling Turkey to export its goods and improve its balance of payments. Inflation remained very high, hovering between 60 and 85 percent through the 1980s. In order to stay in power Anap used patronage with great skill and manipulated the electoral laws to its advantage.

Anap adopted most of the policies inherited from the NSC in other areas as well. Despite its promise to restore Kemalism, and thus secularism, as the nation's ideology, the NSC had promoted Islamic indoctrination in schools as the antidote to social democracy and socialism. It went further than any previous government in making religious lessons a statutory part of the curriculum, countering the previous stress upon critical thinking. The Higher Education Law of 1981 even legislated a dress code for students, forbidding beards for men and head scarves for women; this led to protests in the universities. The Saudi-financed organization Rabita ül-Alem ül-Islamî (Ar., Rābiṭat al-ʿĀlam al-Islāmī) was permitted to subsidize the activities of Turkey's Directorate of Religious Affairs in Europe so as to isolate Turkish workers from foreign ideologies. At home, Saudi influence is thought to have worked through the agency of the Intellectuals' Hearth (Aydınlar Ocağı). This body, founded in the mid-1970s, planned political strategies for Islamist parties and factions and attempted to reconcile nationalism and Islam by proposing a synthesis of the two.

The Islamist faction in Anap, led by Vehbi Dinçler and Mehmed Keçeciler, fought hard to further the NSC's policies in education. They challenged the theory of evolution, claiming that it served only materialism; like the creationists in America, they wanted "the errors of the theory of evolution exposed and what the Holy Books said about creation to be taught." The Istanbul daily *Cumhuriyet* (9 September 1985) noted that islamization of education was causing confusion: "Religion speaks of creation, science of evolution: the students are confused as to what to believe."

For Anap, state support for religious education was also part of its strategy of remaining in power. Qur'ānic schools run by orders like the Naqshbandīyah and the Qādirīyah were patronized in return for political support. State-run schools for chaplains and preachers (the Imam-Hatip schools) also flourished under Anap, so that in the 1980s religious education had overtaken secular education—especially in English—and the latter became the preserve of the upper classes.

This strategy failed to bring political rewards in an atmosphere of economic stagnation and high inflation. The voters refused to elect Islamist parties. Despite its generous use of patronage, Anap's vote in the 1987 elections declined to 36 percent from 45 percent in 1983. The Welfare Party (Refah Partisi, the MSP reincarnated) failed to win even the 10 percent necessary to enter parliament. Thereafter Anap's fortunes declined until its popularity had slipped below 20 percent. A struggle between the nationalist and Islamist factions followed Özal's election as Turkey's eighth president in October 1989. Mesut Yilmaz's election as Anap's leader in June 1991 suggested that the modern wing had won, but the party's defeat in the October 1991 elections leaves its future hanging in the balance.

[*See also* Cumhuriyet Halk Partisi; Refah Partisi; Turkey; *and the biographies of Erbakan and Özal.*]

BIBLIOGRAPHY

Ahmad, Feroz. "The Transition to Democracy in Turkey." *Third World Quarterly* 7.2 (April 1985): 211–226. Useful for the Anavatan party's founding and first years in power.

Ahmad, Feroz. "Islamic Reassertion in Turkey." *Third World Quarterly* 10.2 (April 1988): 750–769.

Ahmad, Feroz. *The Making of Modern Turkey*. London and New York, 1993. Reinterpretation of Turkey's history, emphasizing the dynamic, human factor.

Ergüder, Üstün. "The Motherland Party, 1983–1989." In *Political Parties and Democracy in Turkey*, edited by Metin Heper and Jacob Landau, pp. 152–169. London and New York, 1991. Article full of insights by a Turkish political scientist.

Tapper, Richard, ed. *Islam in Modern Turkey: Religion, Politics, and Literature in Secular Turkey*. London and New York, 1991. Some excellent articles on Islam in Turkey, on topics not often discussed elsewhere.

FEROZ AHMAD

ANGELS. Angels are mentioned in the Qur'ān both as individuals and as a group and appear to have been known to Muḥammad's listeners. They are described in the Qur'ān (35.1) as having two, three, or four wings, as having hands (6.93), and not eating (25.7). They are sent as messengers from God, and may intercede with God, but only with his permission (53.25). Besides acting as messengers, individual angels have specific functions. Gabriel (Jibrīl) is the bringer of divine revelation to Muḥammad, while death is brought by an angel unnamed in the Qur'ān but known in post-Qur'ānic Islamic tradition as ʿIzrā'īl. Mīkāʿīl is the same rank as Gabriel. Joseph is thought to be an angel because of his beauty, and evidently some expected Noah to be an angel, implying that angels have human form.

Both the concept of angels and the names for them are related to the larger Semitic tradition. The Arabic word for angel, *malak* (sg.), *malā'ikah* (pl.), appears to be a loan word from Hebrew or Aramaic, possibly through Ethiopic, although Muslim philologists have assumed one of several Arabic roots (**mlk, *lʿk, *ʿlk*). Individual names like Jibrīl, Mīkāʿīl, and Isrāfīl appear also to be derived from the same linguistic source assimilated into Arabic phonological patterns. The process of assimilating angels into the Arabic language and culture of northwestern Arabia seems to have happened in the pre-Islamic period before the birth of Muḥammad. By the time of the rise of Islam, Jews, Christians, and polytheists in the Arabic cultural sphere each had their own view of angels.

The Qur'ān does not set forth a systematic description of the different varieties and classes of angels but gives enough information that commentators were able to propound various theories. As well as messengers, angels are guardians over humans and keepers of the inventory of good and bad deeds (82.10–12), although the recording is also ascribed to God (21.94). The Qur'ān does not name the two angels, Munkar and Nakīr, who visit the dead in the grave and test the person for entry into paradise or hell. Some believe that these angels inflict punishment on those in the grave, making that period before the day of judgment a kind of purgatory. This was denied by the Mu'tazilīs and various rationalists, prompting a counterreaction among some traditionists that made belief in these angels an article of faith. The angel Mālik rules over hell (43.47), apparently commanding the Zabāniyah, nineteen angels who thrust people into torment (96.18, 74.30). According to tradition, angels are made of light but in the view of some Qur'ān scholars are not impeccable, as Iblīs, who is sometimes ranked as an angel and sometimes as a *jinn,* rebelled when God commanded the angels to worship Adam. Scholastic traditions are careful to distinguish between satans (*shayṭāns*), *jinn,* and angels. In Shīʿī traditions, the imams can see angels that surround and protect them and their families. In Ismāʿīlī traditions, each hierarchical order of the universe has an angel associated with it. Some modernist commentators have rejected the existence of angels as nonscientific, but this has been a minority view. Most modern commentators accept the existence of angels as part of the physical universe created by God.

[*See also* Satan.]

BIBLIOGRAPHY

Kisā'ī, Muḥammad ibn ʿAbd Allāh al-. *The Tales of the Prophets of al-Kisā'ī.* Translated by Wheeler M. Thackston. Boston, 1978. Good translation of extra-Qur'ānic stories about prophets, angels, devils, etc.

Macdonald, J. "The Creation of Man and Angels in the Eschatological Literature." *Islamic Studies* 3 (1964): 285–308. Sound discussion of early Muslim ideas about angels.

Schwarzbaum, Haim. *Biblical and Extra-Biblical Legends in Islamic Folk-Literature.* Walldorf-Hessen, 1982. Thorough treatment of Islamic folklore and methodology, with a good bibliography.

Welch, Alford T. "Allah and Other Supernatural Beings: The Emergence of the Qur'anic Doctrine of Tawḥīd." *Journal of the American Academy of Religion* 47.4 (1979): 739, 749, and *passim.*

GORDON D. NEWBY

ANGKATAN BELIA ISLAM MALAYSIA. *See* ABIM.

ANGLO-MUHAMMADAN LAW. A system of law founded on interpretation of Islamic texts and practice and applied in the courts of colonial British India, Anglo-Muhammadan law was often referred to simply as "Muhammadan" law. The system's roots lay in the earliest colonial legal structures established by the British after their conquest of Bengal in the late eighteenth century. Initially, Anglo-Muhammadan law included both criminal and civil law. For civil cases involving Muslims, and for all criminal cases, Muslim religious specialists were attached to British East India Company courts to expound the technicalities of Muslim law for British judges as they rendered their decisions. A welter of government regulations gradually superseded Muslim criminal law in the early nineteenth century, and with the official promulgation in 1860 of a comprehensive, Benthamite penal code for British India, "Muhammadan" criminal law disappeared.

More lasting was the application of Anglo-Muhammadan personal law in civil cases (involving marriage, adoption, inheritance, endowments, etc.) in which Muslims and Hindus were each, in theory, subject to their own law. The interpretation of Anglo-Muhammadan law was dependent not just on Muslim specialists who continued to have an advisory role in law courts until 1864, but also on a limited number of English translations of and commentaries on Arabic sources of Muslim law. More important, a growing body of case law provided precedents which dominated Anglo-Muhammadan law in the nineteenth century, and a large number of digests and commentaries, written by both Indian Muslim and British lawyers and judges, proved increasingly influential by the second half of the century.

The importance of Anglo-Muhammadan law for the history of the Muslim community is considerable. As Gregory Kozlowski has argued, the development of the law rested on several British (and ultimately Indian) assumptions about Muslims in India: that they constituted a single community, that that community was defined by acceptance of a single, systematic set of personal laws, and that the original sources of those laws were, at least in theory, fixed and unchanging. In practice, Anglo-Muhammadan law did not apply equally to all Indian Muslims, as in certain areas and for certain Muslim sects, the British courts were willing to apply distinctive Islamic or "customary" law. At the same time, important groups of reform-minded Indian *ʿulamāʾ* (religious scholars) disseminated *fatwā* (formal legal opinions) independently of the British court system, thus maintaining an arena for the operation of *sharīʿah* (divine law) distinct from the British legal system.

Nevertheless, the development of the Anglo-Muhammadan law exerted a profound influence on Muslim ideas about the nature of law, for it brought personal law—and issues of family, inheritance, and the status of women—to the center of Muslim legal identity. It also assumed an important place in the political definition of the Muslim community in India, as indicated by the passage in 1937, with considerable Muslim support, of the Muslim Personal Law (Shariat) Application Act, which sought to universalize the application of the Anglo-Muhammadan law for Indian Muslims as a statement of common political identity. The legacies of the Anglo-Muhammadan law have continued to influence strongly not only the legal systems of the postcolonial states of the Indian subcontinent, but also debates about the meaning of the law (and of *sharīʿah*) in contemporary South Asian societies.

[*See also* Islam, *article on* Islam in South Asia; Law, *article on* Legal Thought and Jurisprudence.]

BIBLIOGRAPHY

Ameer Ali, Syed. *Principles of Mohammadan Law.* Rev. ed. Allahabad, 1983. The author (1849–1928), a judge of the Calcutta High Court, was among the most important of those Indian Muslims who aided the development of Anglo-Muhammadan law.

Fyzee, Asaf A. A. *Outlines of Muhammadan Law.* 3d ed. Oxford, 1964. Important summary of the substance of "Muhammadan law" as it developed in British India.

Kozlowski, Gregory C. *Muslim Endowments and Society in British India.* Cambridge, 1985. In examining endowments, Kozlowski interprets the context and the political significance of the British development of Anglo-Muhammadan law.

Wilson, Roland Knyvet. *An Introduction to the Study of Anglo-Muhammadan Law.* London, 1894. Concise history of the nineteenth-century development of Anglo-Muhammadan law from a British barrister who was among the law's systematizers.

David Gilmartin

ANJUMAN. Meaning assembly, meeting, or association, *anjuman* has played in important role in the political and cultural life of twentieth-century Iran. It gained currency during the Constitutional Revolution (1905–1909), when many political action groups emerged to support different ideologies. The *anjuman*s were modeled on a semi-secret society founded by Malkom Khan in 1858 which aimed to introduce modern ideas and rule of law in Iran. But this society was banned in 1861, since it aroused the suspicion of the ruler, Nāṣir al-Dīn Shāh (1848–1896).

Political *anjuman*s appeared during the last years of Nāṣir al-Dīn's reign. They were formed by a few government officials and intellectuals who discussed the need to emulate European concepts of government to overcome Iran's backwardness. Some *anjuman*s, such as Anjuman-i Makhfī (Secret Society), which later played a leading role during the Constitutional Revolution, initially advocated and opened modern schools and libraries in order to disseminate European ideas among Iranians.

At the start of the twentieth century, the country's conditions worsened—czarist Russia's influence grew, foreign debt mounted, and corruption became rampant. This prompted a growing number of bureaucrats, courtiers, merchants, and *ʿulamāʾ* (religious scholars) to form secret societies to try to change the way the country was governed. Early *anjumans* were small—for example, the Mujtamaʿ-i Āzādigān founded in 1903 had forty-two members—but they helped generate the demand for constitutional government among the larger public. Their members wrote articles in antigovernment, Persian-language newspapers published abroad, in such cities as Cairo, Istanbul, Baku, Calcutta, and London. These were distributed clandestinely in Iran. As the movement for constitutional government grew, the *anjumans* coordinated activities of various groups seeking political change.

Following the promulgation of the constitution in August 1906, *anjumans* proliferated openly throughout the country and in cities outside of Iran with large Iranian communities, such as Najaf, Iraq, Istanbul, and Baku. In Tehran alone, about two hundred *anjumans* were founded between 1905 and 1909. Their ideologies ranged from republican to anticonstitutional, and membership sometimes overlapped. Guilds and professional groups had their own *anjumans*. Women formed at least one *anjuman*, Anjuman-i Nisvān (Women's Anjuman), which raised the question of the franchise for women.

The Fundamental Law ratified on 30 December 1906, required the creation of provincial *anjumans* in cities, small towns, and even some villages across the country to supervise the election of provincial candidates to the first Parliament. Even though they were meant to be temporary, some *anjumans*, especially Anjuman-i Tabriz or Azerbaijan, began to function as a provincial parliament. It published a newspaper called *Anjuman* to promote its views.

However, the activities of radical *anjumans* alarmed the new king, Muḥammad ʿAlī Shāh (1907–1909). In the crisis and eventual civil war that erupted between the majlis (parliament) and the king, some of the *anjumans* provided leadership to supporters of the constitution and prevented the disintegration of the Constitutional movement. Anjuman-i Azerbaijan led the way in defending Tabriz against the king's forces. But a large number of *ʿulama* joined anticonstitutional *anjumans*, such as Anjuman-i Āl-i Muḥammad (Society of the House of Muḥammad), because they feared that constitutional government would undermine *sharīʿah* (the divine law). The crisis was resolved by the king's abdication and the restoration of the constitution in 1909. But the radicalism of some of the *anjumans* disillusioned many political activists, who then channeled their energies into other areas, such as literary and cultural activities.

During the authoritarian rule of Reza Shah Pahlavi (1925–1941), political activism almost ceased. Although during the first decade of the reign of Muhammad Reza She Pahlavi (1941–1979), new political parties were formed, the regime became more hostile to dissent after the coup d'état of 1953. Consequently, internal opposition to the regime expressed itself increasingly in religious terms. Small underground cells also challenged the regime by engaging in guerrilla war. The Marxist Fidāʾīyān-i Khalq and the quasi-Marxist Mujāhidīn-i Khalq are important examples of the latter development.

Interest in religious associations among opposition groups, especially university students, grew slowly. The earliest groups, Anjuman-i Islāmī-yi Dānishgāhīyān (Society of Islamic Students), was founded in 1942 at the University of Tehran by an engineering professor, Mehdi Bāzargān, who later became the first prime minister of the Islamic Republic of Iran. Bāzargān's goal was to offer religion as an alternative to secular ideologies, to which many students were flocking. Similar associations were formed in other universities, but only after 1963 did they begin to appeal to a growing number of educated members of the lower and middle classes. Interest in religion was spurred by disillusionment with Western ideologies, the increased authoritarianism of the regime, and its strident hostility to traditional culture. The writings of ʿAlī Sharīʿatī (1933–1977), a Sorbonne-educated sociologist, convinced many that Islam offered a viable solution for change and even revolution. By 1974, 12,300 religious associations had formed in Tehran.

As the regime became less tolerant of political expression, the initiative for religiopolitical activity shifted abroad. The presence of large numbers of Iranian students in Europe and the United States introduced a new chapter in the history of political activism in Iran. Initially, religiously oriented students expressed opposition to the regime under the umbrella of the secular Confederation of Iranian Students, founded in 1958. However, they eventually became an independent organization, known as Anjuman-i Islāmī-yi Dānishjūyān-i Fārsīzabān (Islamic Association of Persian-Speaking Students) and joined the Muslim Students Association of the United States and Canada. The association also founded chapters in European universities. Many members of this association were among Ayatollah Ruhollah Khomeini's earliest supporters. After the overthrow of the monarchy, some members, such as Ibrāhīm Yazdī and Ṣādiq Quṭbzādah, assumed posts in the Bāzargān cabinet, and Abol-Hasan Bani Sadr was elected president. Others continued to be active in parliament and other government posts.

The political ferment of the Constitutional period also prompted the creation of associations whose main focus was literary and cultural activities. The upheaval and civil war that preceded the restoration of the constitution in 1909 dampened the enthusiasm of many participants in politics. Some disillusioned intellectuals, literati, and bureaucrats turned their energies to literary and cultural activities. They met informally to discuss the need for modern education, the dissemination of European literary ideas and literature, and the degree of innovation and borrowing permissible in poetry and other classical forms.

Literary *anjumans* continued their activities under Reza Shah, but they steered clear of politics. However, during the reign of Muhammad Reza Shah, political themes began to influence literature, and some literary *anjumans* provided protection and support to their members against political harassment. The most important of these, Kānūn-i Nivīsandigān-i Īrān (Writers Association of Iran), was founded in 1968. It did not receive official recognition and kept a low profile. However, in 1977 this association openly challenged the regime by demanding an end to censorship and respect for human rights. Despite its important role in undermining the monarchy in 1979, the association fell out of favor with the Islamic Republican regime and ceased its official activities.

[See also Iran.]

BIBLIOGRAPHY

Abrahamian, Ervand. *Iran between Two Revolutions*. Princeton, 1982. Excellent account of the social and political causes of the Constitutional and Islamic revolutions.

Ādamīyat, Farīdūn. *Fikr-i Āzādī va Muqaddamah-yi Nahẕat-i Mashrūṭīyat dar Īrān*. Tehran, 1340/1961. Contains valuable information on the Farāmūshkhānah and Anjuman-i Ādamīyat.

Ādamīyat, Farīdūn. *Īdi'ūlūzhī-yi Nahẕat-i Mashrūṭīyat-i Īrān*. 2 vols. Tehran, 1976–. Both volumes, along with other works by the authors, the leading historian of the period, constitute important sources on the political history of the Constitutional Revolution, and provide useful information on various *anjumans*.

Algar, Hamid. *Mirzā Malkum Khān*. Berkeley, 1973. Detailed and somewhat negative discussion of the Farāmūshkhānah, the earliest secret society formed in Iran, and its founder.

Arjomand, Said Amir. *The Turban for the Crown*. New York and Oxford, 1988. Insightful analysis of the role of religion in Iran and the Islamic Revolution, with some discussion of religious associations.

Aryānpūr, Yaḥyā. *Az Ṣabā tā Nīmā, Tārīkh-i 150 Sāl-i Adab-i Fārsī*. Vol. 2. Tehran, 1350/1971. Useful information on literary societies, particularly during the early decades of the twentieth century.

Bayat, Mangol, et al. "Anjoman." In *Encyclopaedia Iranica*, vol. 2, pp. 77–83. London, 1985.

Bayat, Mangol. *Iran's First Revolution: Shi'ism and the Constitutional Revolution of 1905–1909*. New York, 1991. Thoughtful and important study of the role of the *'ulama'* in the Constitutional Revolution, with reference to various *anjumans*.

Karimi-Hakkak, Ahmad. "Protest and Perish: Commitment of the Writers' Association of Iran." *Iranian Studies* 18.2–4 (1985): 189–231. Thorough account of the history of the association.

Khānbābā Tihrānī, Mahdī, and Ḥamīd Shawkat. *Nigāhī az darūn bih junbish-i chap-i Īrān*. 2 vols. Saarbrücken, 1989. Detailed interview with a leader of the Confederation of Iranian Students on the activities of this organization and other opposition student groups in Europe and the United States.

Lambton, Ann K. S. "Secret Societies and the Persian Revolution of 1905–06." *St. Anthony's Papers*, no. 11 (1956): 43–60. Reprinted in *Qājār Persia*. Austin, 1987. Earliest study of *anjumans* by a leading historian of Iran.

Malikzādah, Mahdī. *Zindagānī-yi Malik al-Mutakallimīn*. 5 vols. Tehran, 1325/1946. Excessively laudatory account of the role played by a major constitutionalist and founding member of several *anjumans*, written by his son. The work contains important information on *anjumans* of the period.

Martin, Vanessa. *Islam and Modernism: The Iranian Revolution of 1906*. London, 1989. Detailed analysis of the role of the leading *'ulama'* in the Constitutional Revolution, and a useful discussion of *anjumans*.

Mustawfī, 'Abd Allāh. *Sharḥ-i zindagānī-yi man*. 2 vols. Tehran, 1945. Conveys some information on the Constitutional period, with discussion of the role of radical and literary *anjumans*.

Nāẓim al-Islām Kirmānī. *Tārīkh-i Bīdārī-i Īrāniyān*. 5 vols. in 2. Edited by Sa'īdī Sirjānī. 4th ed. Tehran, [1983]. Important source for the Constitutional period, by an active participant, with much useful information on the various *anjumans*.

Rafī'ī, Manṣūrah. *Anjuman: Urgān-i anjuman-i ayālatī-i Āzarbayjān*. Tehran, 1362/1985. Brief discussion of Anjuman-i Tabriz, with a facsimile of most issues of the newspaper *Anjuman*.

GUITY NASHAT

ANṢĀR. The religio-political movement known as Anṣār ("companions") was named after the supporters of the Sudanese Mahdi, Muḥammad Aḥmad ibn 'Abdallāh (d. 1885), who were disbanded in 1898 following their defeat by the Anglo-Egyptian army. Their surviving commanders were imprisoned, and the children of the Mahdi and of Khalīfah ʿAbdallāhi were kept under surveillance. The Mahdi's *rātib* (prayerbook) and other Mahdist writings were banned.

In 1908 ʿAbd al-Raḥmān al-Mahdī, the Mahdī's posthumous son, started to regroup the Mahdists as a religious order *(ṭarīqah),* first building the family's mosque in Omdurman with a loan from the government. In the same year he was permitted to cultivate lands on Aba Island, where Muḥammad Aḥmad had announced his Mahdist mission in 1881. This enabled him to proclaim the imamate of the newly organized Anṣār and to create the spiritual, political, and economic center of the movement on Aba. To overcome government suspicions he emphasized peaceful aims and denounced every Mahdist antigovernment action. He proclaimed that the Mahdist *daʿwah* was not opposed to the government and hence should not be forbidden as illegal.

The movement came into the open in 1915 when Governor-General Sir Reginald Wingate sought Muslim allies against the Turks. ʿAbd al-Raḥmān traveled to meet Mahdist supporters, thousands of whom demonstrated the depth of their loyalty as, armed with swords as in earlier days, they greeted their Mahdi's son wherever he appeared, claiming that "the day had arrived" *(al-yawm atā).* Although ʿAbd al-Raḥmān was explicitly forbidden from organizing the Anṣār, this was in effect taking place. Thenceforth his agents, though not recognized by the authorities, represented him in the provinces, collected *zakāt,* and spread the banned prayerbook *(rātib al-Mahdī)* among his followers. Agents were appointed first in the Blue Nile and Funj provinces in 1916, and later in Kordofan and Darfur. In 1921 ʿAbd al-Raḥmān presented to the government a list of his provincial agents, including six in the White Nile, four in Kordofan, two in the Funj, four in the Blue Nile, three in Darfur, and one each in five other provinces, for a total of twenty-four. Many of the agents were merchants and tribal shaykhs rather than religious leaders.

In 1917 Shaykh Muṣṭafā al-Marāghī, the Sudan's Qaḍī al-Quḍāt, was asked to give a verdict as to whether the Mahdi's writings should be legalized. He proclaimed the Mahdi's letters and proclamations *(manshūrāt)* as unacceptable but said that there was nothing wrong with the *rātib,* except that the words *al-Mahdī ʿalayhi as-salām* ("the Mahdi, peace be upon him") should be replaced by *al-Mahdī raḥmatu Allāh* ("the Mahdi, [the] mercy of God [Be upon him]). The *rātib*'s acceptance as a legitimate prayerbook signified the legitimacy of the Anṣār. In 1923 an edition of five thousand copies was published under the title *Al-rātib as-sharīf li-sayyidinā wa-malādhinā al-imām al-Mahdī ibn ʿAbdallāh* (The Holy Prayerbook of Our Master and Protector the Imām al-Mahdī ibn ʿAbdāllah) and distributed to the Anṣār throughout the Sudan.

Despite the government's inconsistency in its dealings with ʿAbd al-Raḥmān and the Anṣār since the 1920s—when it forbade their payment of *zakāt,* their pilgrimage to Aba, and the activities of ʿAbd al-Raḥmān's agents—the movement continued to flourish. Between 5,000 and 15,000 Anṣār made the pilgrimage to Aba Island annually, and many of them stayed there and supplied cheap labor for ʿAbd al-Raḥmān's agricultural ventures. Thus when the Sudan achieved independence in 1955, the Anṣār was its largest Muslim sect.

Politically the Anṣār provided the core of the Ummah party and most of its leaders. Whenever the independence of the Sudan seemed to be threatened, there were thousands of armed Anṣār to come to the rescue. In March 1954 they demonstrated against unity with Egypt; in the attempted coup of July 1961 against General ʿAbbūd, it was proposed to use the 7,000 Anṣār stationed in Omdurman to overthrow the regime. Ṣiddīq al-Mahdī, then the imam, refused, saying, "I do not wish to meet God with the blood of Muslims on my hands." During the regime of Jaʿfar al-Nimeiri (or al-Numayrī, 1969–1985) the Anṣār first resisted on Aba Island, led by their imam al-Hādī al-Mahdī, and stopped Nimeiri from landing. The subsequent bombardment of the island and its 40,000 Anṣār on 22–24 March 1970 led to an estimated five to ten thousand casualties. Other Anṣār died in fierce battles in their quarter in Omdurman. In Anṣār folklore the Aba Island massacre has been compared to the battle of Kararī against the Anglo-Egyptian forces in 1898, in which 11,000 were killed.

Later the Anṣār, led by Ṣādiq al-Mahdī, participated in several attempted coups, notably in July 1976. Finally, in the April 1986 elections, the Anṣār gave the Ummah party massive support and made it the single biggest political power in the country with some two million supporters. Since the assassination of Sayyid al-Hādī in 1970 the Anṣār have remained without an imam. Elections were postponed several times and were scheduled for March 1988, with Ṣādiq al-Mahdī and Aḥmad al-Mahdī, as the only contenders. Since the

June 1989 coup, there have been attempts to promote alternative Mahdist leaders, notably from among the offspring of the Khalīfah ʿAbdallāhi.

The Anṣār, though regarded by many as a Ṣūfī order, is in fact an activist, revivalist Islamic political movement seeking to convert Muslims to its concept of an Islamic state through political rather than spiritual means. They aim at the puritanical reestablishment of the Mahdīyah and regard themselves as purer and more representative of true Islam than any Ṣūfī order. They pray and study in their own mosques and use their own prayerbook. They regard their political struggle as part of their religious duty in which tribal, ethnic, and regional boundaries are irrelevant. For most of their adherents, especially the tribal elements in Darfur and Kordofan and the West African pilgrims *(fallātah),* Mahdism expresses their Islamic beliefs; it is therefore a blueprint for the future Islamic state in the Sudan, should the Anṣār come to power.

[*See also* Mahdi; Mahdīyah; Sudan; Ummah-Anṣār; *and the biography of (al-Ṣādiq al-) Mahdī.*]

BIBLIOGRAPHY

Daly, Martin W. *Empire on the Nile: The Anglo-Egyptian Sudan, 1898–1934.* Cambridge, 1986.

Ibrāhīm, Ḥasan Aḥmad. "The Development of Economic and Political Neo-Mahdism in the Sudan, 1926–1935." Unpublished ms., Khartoum, 1980.

Ibrāhīm, Ḥasan Aḥmad. "Imperialism and Neo-Mahdism in the Sudan: A Study of British Policy towards Neo-Mahdism, 1924–1927." *International Journal of African Historical Studies* 13.2 (1980): 214–239.

Ibrāhīm, Ḥasan Aḥmad. "Al-Sayyid ʿAbd al-Raḥmān al-Mahdī wabarā'at al-munawwarāt al-siyāsīyah." In *Dirāsāt fī ta'rīkh al-mahdīyah,* pp. 193–202. Khartoum, n.d.

Mahdī, al-Ṣādiq al-, ed. *Jihād fī sabīl al-istiqlāl.* Khartoum, n.d. (1965).

Vincent, Andrew. "Religion and Nationalism in a Traditional Society: Ideology, Leadership, and the Role of the Umma Party as a Force of Social Change in the Northern Sudan." Ph.D. diss., University of Pennsylvania, 1988.

Warburg, Gabriel R. "From Anṣar to Umma: Sectarian Politics in the Sudan, 1914–1945." *Asian and African Studies* 9.2 (1973): 101–153.

GABRIEL R. WARBURG

APOSTASY. *See* Kufr.

ʿAQĪDAH. The Islamic creed *(ʿaqīdah)* as found in the Qur'ān is quite simple: the so-called five articles of faith—belief in God, angels, prophets, scriptures, and the Last Day—sum up that creed, and it was only later that more detailed formulations began to appear. Three of the five articles—the first, third, and fifth—are the principal articles; the second (belief in angels as the servants and worshipers of God) is a corrective to the pre-Islamic view of angels as daughters of God, and the fourth (belief in scriptures) is an important supplement to the third. Thus modern as well as classical scholars frequently maintain that the triad of God–Prophet–Judgment Day constitutes the essential belief system of Islam.

The origin of the more elaborate statements of *ʿaqīdah* is to be sought in the polemical environment of the period beginning within half a century of Muḥammad's death. The polemics were both internal and external. Internally, certain theological and political developments led scholars to produce creeds that were meant to refute allegedly heterodox doctrines. The insistence of the Khārijīs that one guilty of a grave sin ceases to be a Muslim was predicated on the view that faith and works are inseparably linked, and that one who commits a gross violation of Islam dissolves that link. The reaction, in the form of Murji'ism, based itself on the view that it is faith that is crucial to salvation. The Sunnī-Shīʿī conflict was also reflected in the creeds. The Shīʿīs proposed the notion of imamate by designation (the view that the head of the Muslim community after the Prophet's death was designated by God, the community having no right to elect one), and the Sunnīs responded by laying it down that the imam was to be elected by the community, and that the historical order of the caliphates of Abū Bakr, ʿUmar, ʿUthmān, and ʿAlī was in fact the right order. The debate between the Muʿtazilah and the Ashāʿirah led to further additions to the doctrine. The Muʿtazilah, although not a homogenous group holding a common set of doctrines, generally denied that the eternity of the attributes of God could be distinguished from the being of God; they argued in favor of strict divine justice; they insisted on the createdness of the Qur'ān on the grounds that the Qur'ān was a manifestation of the divine attribute of speech, which was noneternal; and they maintained that humans possess the freedom of the will. The Ashāʿirah, so named for their chief spokesman, Abū al-Ḥasan al-Ashʿarī (d. 941 or 945), opposed the Muʿtazilah on all these counts. A synthesis of the Muʿtazilī and Ashʿarī positions was attempted by al-Māturīdī (d. 944) of Central Asia.

External factors also influenced the content and language of the creeds. The need to respond to Greek philosophic thought led Muslim dogmatists to adapt their arguments using the categories and terms of a foreign thought-system. The confrontation with Christian theology led them to explain their positions with reference to such doctrines as Trinitarianism.

Abū Ḥanīfah's *Al-fiqh al-akbar I* is taken to be the first formal statement of the Islamic creed, and in it he tries to rebut what he regarded as deviations from standard Islamic dogma. For example, the very first clause says that commission of a grave sin does not make one an unbeliever—an obvious attack on the Khārijī position. More detailed and also more complex treatments are to be found in the works of al-Ashʿarī, al-Bāqillānī, al-Juwaynī, and al-Ghazālī.

Three points should be kept in mind about the discussions of *ʿaqīdah* in the early centuries. First, the discussions represented the attempts of Muslim scholars to come to terms with their past religious, political, and intellectual history. This was especially true in the case of formulas used about the distinguished companions of the Prophet, their status relative to one another, and the disagreements (which later led to wars) that occurred among them beginning in the latter half of ʿUthmān's caliphate. Second, the issues raised had not only an abstract, theoretical character but also practical and ethical dimensions. For example, the question of the relationship between faith and works had a direct bearing on religious conduct and attitudes, for if faith is sufficient for salvation, then the importance of deeds is diminished. Again, if salvation depends on faith, then it becomes unlawful—or at least difficult—to revolt against an oppressive ruler, for oppression, one could argue, does not greatly hurt the ruler's standing as a Muslim. Third, if there was an eagerness to state clearly and effectively the correct dogma, there also was a tendency, especially in statements about God, to use the "negative approach." Thus on the issue of whether God has a face and hands, as the Qur'ān says he does, the majority view (while accepting the Qur'ānic statements at their face value) insisted that this belief must be held "without asking how" *(bi-lā kayfa)*.

The trend in the Islamic world in modern times to reject *taqlīd*, adopt an attitude of *ijtihād*, seek solutions to the pressing issues of practical life, and look to pristine Islam for guidance has led to scrutiny of the Islamic creed in its medieval formulation. Already in the eighteenth century Muḥammad ibn ʿAbd al-Wahhāb expressed dissatisfaction with the sterile intellectualism of the Muslim medieval period, but his stance was more rejectionist than critical in an objective way. In the last century Muḥammad ʿAbduh, eager like his mentor Jamāl al-Dīn al-Afghānī to reform the traditional Muslim educational system, called for a new synthesis of reason and revelation. In so doing, he not only disagreed with a number of Ashʿarī positions (e.g., determinism), but also pointed out the historical character of the early theological dogma. Thus in his *Risālat al-tawḥīd* (Treatise on the Unity of God) he refuses to get involved in metaphysical discussions (e.g., on the relationship between the essence and attributes of God) and is content to argue that reason can discover, either on its own or with the help of revelation, proofs for the validity of the essential Islamic doctrines. More recently, Ḥasan Ḥanafī, in his multivolume *Min al-ʿaqīdah ilā al-thawrah* (From Dogma to Revolution; see especially volume 1), has made a scathing critique of the medieval formulation of the Islamic creed, calling many of its articles dead weight.

[*See also* Pillars of Islam.]

BIBLIOGRAPHY

Arabic Sources

ʿAbduh, Muḥammad. *Risālat al-tawḥīd.* Translated by Isḥaq Musāʿad and Kenneth Cragg as *The Theology of Unity.* London, 1966.

Āl-Kāshif al-Ghiṭā', Muhammad Ḥusayn. *Aṣl al-Shīʿah wa uṣūluhā.* Najaf, 1961. Translated into English as *The Shia: Origin and Faith.* Karachi, 1982.

Ashʿarī, Abū al-Ḥasan al-. *Al-ibānah ʿan uṣūl al-diyānah.* Hyderabad, 1903.

Ashʿarī, Abū al-Ḥasan al-. *Maqālāt al-Islāmīyīn wa-ikhtilāf al-muṣallīn.* 3 vols. Edited by Helmut Ritter. Istanbul, 1929–1933.

Bāqillānī, Muḥammad ibn al-Ṭayyib al-. *Kitāb tamhīd al-awā'il wa-talkhīṣ al-dalā'il.* Edited by ʿImād al-Dīn Ḥaydar. Beirut, 1987.

Ghazālī, Abū Ḥāmid al-. *Kitāb qawā'id al-ʿaqā'id.* Beirut, 1983. Translated by Nabih A. Faris as *The Foundations of the Articles of Faith.* Lahore, 1963. Part 1, Book 2 of *Iḥyā' ʿulūm al-dīn.*

Ḥanafī, Ḥasan. *Min al-ʿaqīdah ilā al-thawrah.* Vol. 1. Beirut, 1988.

Ibn Babūyah (Bābawayh) al-Qummī, Muḥammad ibn ʿAlī. *A Shīʿite Creed.* Translation of *Iʿtiqādāt al-Imāmīyah* by Asaf A. A. Fyzee. Rev. ed. Tehran, 1982.

Ibn Ḥazm, ʿAlī. *Kitāb al-fiṣal fī al-milal wa-al-ahwā' wa-al-niḥal.* Cairo, 1928.

Ibn Ṭāhir al-Baghdādī, ʿAbd al-Qāhir. *Kitāb al-farq bayna al-firaq.* Edited by Muḥammad Badr. Cairo, 1910.

Juwaynī, ʿAbd al-Malik al-. *Kitāb al-irshād ilā qawāṭiʿ al-adillah fī uṣūl al-iʿtiqād.* Edited by Asʿad Tamīm. Beirut, 1985.

Shahrastānī, Muḥammad ibn ʿAbd al-Karīm al-. *Kitāb al-milal wa-al-niḥal.* Beirut, 1982.

Taftāzānī, Masʿūd ibn ʿUmar al-. *Sharḥ al-ʿAqā'id al-Nasafīyah.* Edited by Maḥmūd Ḥijāzī al-Saqqā. Cairo, 1988. Translated by E. E.

Elder as *A Commentary on the Creed of Islam*. New York, 1980. Based on the *ʿAqāʾid* of ʿUmar al-Nasafī.

Other Sources

Adams, Charles C. *Islam and Modernism in Egypt*. London, 1933.

Goldziher, Ignácz. *Introduction to Islamic Theology and Law*. Translated by Ruth Hamori and Andras Hamori. Princeton, 1981.

Macdonald, D. B. *Development of Muslim Theology, Jurisprudence, and Constitutional Theory*. New York, 1903.

Watt, W. Montgomery. "ʿAḳīda." In *Encyclopaedia of Islam*, new ed., vol. 1, pp. 332–336. Ledien, 1960–. Includes a detailed bibliography.

Wensinck, A. J. *The Muslim Creed*. Cambridge, 1932.

MUSTANSIR MIR

ARABIC. Although the Arabic language existed long before the inception of Islam, it has been closely associated with this religion ever since the Qurʾān, its holy scripture, was revealed in Arabic to the prophet Muḥammad ibn ʿAbd Allāh in seventh-century Arabia. As a cosmopolitan religion, Islam carried Arabic to all peoples who became Muslims. Those in the regions nearest to Arabia whose languages were originally Semitic—Mesopotamia and Syria—eventually became Arabic speaking, as did those whose languages were originally Hamitic in Egypt and North Africa. Together with Arabia itself, these regions constitute the Arab world today, which also includes non-Muslim religious minorities who speak Arabic (e.g., Christian Arabs) and non-Arab Muslim minorities who have retained their original languages but use Arabic as a second language (e.g., Kurds and Berbers). Peoples who adopted Islam in other regions of the world have kept their ethnic or national languages but have borrowed many words from Arabic and often also the Arabic writing system (e.g., Persian, Ottoman Turkish, and Urdu). During the heyday of Islamic civilization, Arabic was the lingua franca of a vast Islamic empire and its universal language of learning. Muslim scholars of non-Arab origin, like the historian and theologian al-Ṭabarī (d. 923), the philosopher and physician Ibn Sīnā (d. 1037), the astronomer and encyclopedic scientist al-Bīrūnī (d. 1048), and many others wrote their works in Arabic. Arabic today is not so widespread a language of scholarship as it was earlier, but it continues to be the common language of worship for Muslims all over the world and, of course, the living language of the Arab people themselves.

Despite its long history and great geographical spread, Arabic has retained its identity and distinctive characteristics. Its flexible structural system has continuously absorbed the cultural differences it encountered, and it has adapted itself in order to serve the needs of its new speakers. Perhaps in no period of its history has Arabic faced a greater challenge than in the modern age with its dizzying advances in science and technology and its seemingly endless cultural flux; yet Arabic continues to adapt to modernity and to retain its flexibility and adaptability despite claims that it cannot cope with the pace of change, particularly in specialized scientific and technological disciplines and in areas of complex societal organization.

Translators of Western works into Arabic and Arab journalists in the burgeoning Arabic press of the nineteenth century were perhaps the first to feel the necessity of adapting the language creatively to modern needs. Their success in updating Arabic depended on their grasp of the intricacies of Arabic morphology and grammar, as well as on their knowledge of the history of the language, its adaptability, and its wealth. Efforts to modernize Arabic remained more or less individual, and the process was not organized, but as new knowledge kept pouring in from the West, the necessity of organizing academic institutions for language development and of adopting planning principles was increasingly felt. In 1892 a circle of scholars was founded in Cairo to discuss linguistic matters, and in 1907 scholars at Dār al-ʿUlūm in Cairo established a similar circle; but these efforts remained limited and did not achieve continuity. *Lughat al-ʿArab* (The Language of the Arabs), a journal founded in 1911 in Baghdad by Anastase-Marie al-Karmilī (1866–1947), was devoted to issues related to the Arabic language and was an effective inter-Arab forum on the subject.

In 1919 the first academy for the Arabic language was founded in Damascus, thanks to the organizing efforts of Muḥammad Kurd ʿAlī (1876–1953) and the support of King Fayṣal and his government. Called al-Majmaʿ al-ʿIlmī al-ʿArabī (The Scientific Arabic Academy), it concerned itself with linguistic and literary matters as well as with problems in the arts and sciences related to Arabic. In 1921 it founded a journal that is still published. In 1932 scholars in Egypt succeeded in founding another academy with government support. Originally called Majmaʿ al-Lughah al-ʿArabīyah al-Malakī (The Royal Academy of the Arabic Language) and, since the abolition of the monarchy in 1952, renamed Majmaʿ al-Lughah al-ʿArabīyah (The Academy of the Arabic Language), it publishes a journal and the minutes of its meetings; the academy concerns itself with preserving the purity of Arabic and with rendering Arabic a capable vehicle of modern communication. In 1947 an Iraqi academy was established in Baghdad with government support and called al-Majmaʿ al-ʿIlmī al-ʿIrāqī (The Scientific Iraqi Academy). Since 1950 it has published a journal reflecting its concerns and contributing to keeping the Arabic language abreast of cultural and civilizational developments. The Arab League has worked to unify the academies of Damascus, Cairo, and Baghdad so that they can coordinate their work, and a conference of academies of the Arabic language was held in Damascus in 1956, attended by representatives from all over the Arab world. Pan-Arab efforts still continue, but the formation of a united Arabic academy is still an unfulfilled hope.

These Arabic academies have been implemental in updating Arabic and enriching it with new words, although at times they have been the butt of popular jokes for their pedantry and snail-like pace. With their help and the continuing creative efforts of individual Arab translators, journalists, linguists, scientists, poets, novelists, essayists, and other Arab literati, the Arabic language today has become adequately modernized. Cutting across the boundaries of the Arab countries, each with its own spoken dialect or dialects, an overarching modern standard Arabic is now used, mainly in written communications but also in formal oral presentations and in radio and television broadcasts. It is understood by the general Arab public and is a functional vehicle of communication in any field of knowledge. It has been declared one of the official languages of the United Nations. Based on classical Arabic *(al-ʿArabīyah al-fuṣḥā)*, it has retained the latter's syntax and morphology to a large degree but has acquired a renewed phraseology and many additional lexical elements.

In modern standard Arabic one may find words like *barlamān* (parliament), *tilifūn* (telephone), and *tilifizyūn* (television), directly borrowed from Western languages and assimilated into Arabic. This arabicization is not usually the Arab academicians' preferred method of updating the language, although it is a practice of scholars of the ʿAbbāsid period and earlier: witness, for example, old Arabic words like *falsafah* (philosophy) and *iqlīm* (climatic region), arabicized from Greek. With common usage, verbs have been derived from some of the recently arabicized words, for example, *talfana* (to telephone) and *talfaza* (to televise); one further finds participles like *mutalfaz* (televised) and substantives like *tilfāz* (television set)—very much as past scholars treated Greek loanwords in *tafalsafa* (to philosophize) and *faylasūf* (philosopher). Such arabicized words have been usually made to agree with the rules of Arabic morphology and phonology.

Modern Arabs, however, prefer to form new words by deriving them from existing Arabic roots whenever possible. Thus the word *sayyārah* (automobile) is derived from the verb *sāra* (to walk); *thallājah* (refrigerator) from the noun *thalj* (snow, ice); *miṣʿad* (elevator) from the verb *ṣaʿada* (to ascend); and *maṭār* (airport) from the verb *ṭāra* (to fly). These neologisms follow Arabic morphological rules and have been smoothly assimilated into the language. Modern Arabs also derive new meanings from old Arabic vocabulary by figurative extension or semantic approximation; thus *qiṭār* (train) in old Arabic meant a string of camels, and *jarīdah* (newspaper) meant a stripped palm-branch once used for writing. They do not mind translating Western expressions—for example, *majlis al-nuwwāb* (chamber of deputies), *markaz al-thiqal* (center of gravity), and *mukayyif al-hawā'* (air-conditioning)—but with due respect to heaven, they have translated "skyscraper" as *nāṭiḥat al-saḥāb* ("cloud-scraper"). Some Western idiomatic expressions have been literally translated in modern Arabic usage, like *laʿiba dawran* ("he played a rolc"), *ṭalaba yadahā* ("he asked for her hand"), or *qatala al-waqt* ("he killed time"). In the manner of European languages, prefixes have been used in some words—successfully in *lāsilkī* (wireless), *lānihāya* (infinity), *lāshuʿūrī* (unconscious), and *lāmubālāh* (indifference), which are now common words, and not so successfully in *ghibjalīdī* (postglacial), *qabtārīkh* (prehistory), and *taḥshuʿūrī* (subconscious), which have been suggested by Sāṭiʿ al-Ḥuṣrī (1880–1968).

On the whole, modern standard Arabic has retained the basic characteristics of classical Arabic. Reformers who wanted to modify its writing system or adopt Latin characters for it have been vehemently resisted; so were those who called for replacing it with vernacular dialects. This continuing resistance is based in part on the political need of Arab nationalists to preserve Arab cultural unity and historical continuity, for they consider the use of dialects to be divisive, and they fear that the adoption of Latin characters will alienate Arabs from their heritage. Islamic religious fervor strengthens this resistance, considering it a duty to preserve the language of the Qur'ān and all the Islamic culture that has flowed from it.

[*See also* Arabic Literature.]

BIBLIOGRAPHY

Beeston, A. F. L. *The Arabic Language Today*. London, 1970. Good general survey.

Blau, Joshua. *The Renaissance of Modern Hebrew and Modern Standard*

Arabic: Parallels and Differences in the Revival of Two Semitic Languages. Berkeley, Los Angeles, and London, 1981. Good comparative study of modern developments in Hebrew and Arabic.

Chejne, Anwar G. *The Arabic Language: Its Role in History*. Minneapolis, 1969. Comprehensive survey of Arabic and of scholarly studies in the language from earliest times to the present.

Saʿid, M. F. *Lexical Innovation through Borrowing in Modern Standard Arabic*. Princeton, 1967. Focuses on one method of language extension.

Stetkevych, Jaroslav. *The Modern Arabic Literary Language: Lexical and Stylistic Developments*. Chicago, 1970. Thorough examination of modern developments in Arabic, treated analytically and historically.

Wehr, Hans. " ʿArabiyya." In *Encyclopaedia of Islam*, new ed., vol. 1, pp. 561–603. Leiden, 1960–. See section entitled "Modern Written Arabic."

ISSA J. BOULLATA

ARABIC LITERATURE. [*This entry comprises two articles on Islamic themes and values in modern Arabic literature. The first presents a general overview; the second focuses specifically on issues of gender in fiction and poetry.*]

An Overview

From the beloved pre-Islamic odes, the *muʿallaqāt,* to the contemporary novel, literature written in Arabic spans centuries, continents, and historical periods. Although Arabic literature began during the Jāhilīyah (pre-Islamic period), Islam has had a profound influence on its development. The Qur'ān itself is a literary tour de force, and down to the present day Islamic texts forming part of the centuries-long *turāth* (the textual tradition of the Arabo-Islamic world) continue to play an important role in the development of contemporary literature. With the award of the Nobel Prize in Literature in 1988 to the Egyptian Naguib Mahfouz (Najīb Maḥfūẓ), Arabic literature became poised to play a larger role on the world literary scene.

The literature of the Jāhilīyah was that of a partly Bedouin society and was dominated by poetry; the poet often acted as the oracle of his tribe. The premier art form was the *qaṣīdah* or ode. The poet was conventionally inspired to compose an ode by the sight of animal droppings that signaled an abandoned encampment. The critic and anthologist Ibn Qutaybah (d. 889) links the creation of the ode to the remnants of this encampment and elucidates the ode's structure. Although twentieth-century critics have questioned Ibn Qutaybah's classification of the *qaṣīdah,* this has by no means detracted from the significant role that poetry played in the codification of the Arabic language and Arabic grammar by medieval grammarians and lexicographers. Both the male and the female poetic voices existed in the pre-Islamic period; the female poet al-Khansā' has entered the annals of Arabic literature with the elegies she composed for her brother.

With its powerful imagery and its often incantatory style, the Qur'ān joined the pre-Islamic poetic corpus as a literary and aesthetic model as well as a religious one. For Muslims the Qur'ān is the direct, unmediated word of God; therefore it is as perfect from a literary standpoint as it is from a religious one. The speech of God is not normal speech, and its inimitability *(iʿjāz)* becomes a topic of central concern for later theorists, both grammatical and literary.

The Arab-Islamic conquests of the seventh and eighth centuries created a multinational empire from Spain to Afghanistan. This cosmopolitan society drew virtually without prejudice from the previous cultures of local regions, spawning a sophisticated literature far exceeding in richness and quantity the literatures of either the classical Mediterranean world or of medieval Europe. Paper had recently been invented in China, and its dissemination through the lands of Islam had much to do with this literary florescence; so too did the opening of cultural channels and the circulation of ideas across an unprecedented geographical expanse. Scholars and writers might begin their careers in what is today Portugal and end them on the banks of the Red Sea or the borders of the Hindu Kush.

Most critics associate classical Arabic literature with poetry. A formalized and detailed metrical system was codified by al-Khalīl (d. 791). The panegyric became a highly refined art form, as did the lighter *ghazal,* a shorter ode. The *qaṣīdah* survived the passage of time, although its erotic prologue was transformed and adapted to new needs, such as the pastoral and the ascetic. The neoclassical duo of Abū Tammām (d. 845) and al-Buḥtūrī (d. 897) became familiar literary names, as did that of the heroically inclined al-Mutanabbī (d. 965). Not all poets, however, felt constrained to obey the sacred rules of the poetic genre; thus Abū Nuwās (d. 815) mocked the erotic prologue by addressing the opening of one of his poems to a tavern.

Numerous works have come down to us from the classical period of this highly sophisticated culture. One of the literary genres dominating the Arabic prose corpus is an anecdotal form designed to be at once edifying and entertaining, known as *adab*. To characterize it as prose can be, however, misleading. In its discourse *adab* can include Qur'ānic verses, poetry, and traditions of the Prophet. These traditions, called *ḥadīth,* are collections of the sayings and actions of the Prophet intended to serve as guides for the daily life of the Muslim. Generally recognized as the greatest master of Arabic *adab* is the ninth-century writer al-Jāḥiẓ. His *Book of Misers (Kitāb al-bukhalā')* has survived the centuries, and its anecdotes circulate in children's literature in the contemporary Arab world. The characters who populated medieval Arabic anecdotal works ranged from rulers and judges to misers and party-crashers.

Medieval anecdotal literature had close family relations to two other literary products, the *maqāmah* and *The Thousand and One Nights*. The *maqāmah* is an indigenous Arabic form invented by Badīʿ al-Zamān al-Hamadhānī (d. 1008). His *Maqāmāt* (loosely translated as "Séances"), executed in rhymed prose, featured a sort of picaresque hero whose narrative existence centered around his eloquence and his ability to outwit his listeners and gain from them. Al-Ḥarīrī (d. 1122) also made his name by writing in this genre, although his literary constructions are more rhetorically fanciful than those of his predecessors. It is his *Maqāmāt* that would serve as the model for nineteenth-century writers anxious to reenergize Arabic literature.

The Thousand and One Nights is a much more amorphous literary text whose stories were collected over centuries. The *Nights* is now as much a classic of Western literature as of Arabic. Magic, sexuality, flying carpets, questions of the body: all were part and parcel of the stories associated with the *Nights*. Shahrazād and her sister Dunyāzād, Shahriyār and his brother Shāhzamān, are the two couples whose lives set the narrative in motion. Shahrazād weaves the tales that will immortalize her in the annals of world literature, at the same time as she will help resolve the dilemma of the heterosexual couple whose instability opens the narrative. Many of the story cycles from the *Nights,* like that of Sindbad, reappear in modern guises in twentieth-century Arabic writings. In these rewritings, the personality of Shahrazād holds pride of place as the female hero who can play in two arenas—classical and modern Arabic literature.

Literature flourished in the Islamic West as it did in the Islamic East. Although the *maqāmah* was invented in the Eastern part of the Arabo-Islamic world, examples of it appeared in Islamic Spain. The hybrid literary population of that region gave birth to a new poetic form, *muwashshaḥāt,* a complex poem combining Arabic and local linguistic elements. These *muwashshaḥāt* can be set to music, and one can still hear them sung in the Arab world today. The Andalusian author ʿAlī Ibn Ḥazm (d. 1064), displays another dimension of anecdotal prose literature in his treatise on the psychology of love, *Ṭawq al-ḥamāmah* (The Dove's Neckring). The special development given to courtly love themes in Hispano-Arabic literature has often been linked to the rise of the troubadours in neighboring Provence.

From quite early in the development of Islamic orthodoxy, echoes of asceticism and mysticism could be heard. Generally these came from individuals dissatisfied with what they perceived to be the loss of the personal dimension in the religious experience, buried under legalistic discussions and ritualized practice. A different sort of mystical and philosophical narrative was woven in Andalusia by the physician-philosopher Ibn Ṭufayl (d. 1185–1186). His great allegory *Hayy ibn Yaqzān* (Alive Son of Awake) had medieval relatives in the Arabo-Islamic philosophical tradition; it is a masterpiece whose literary echoes, from gender to philosophy, can be heard across the centuries down to the contemporary Middle East, where it resurfaces in children's literature from Egypt to Tunisia. Its appeal lies partly in its plot: an abandoned infant grows up alone on an island and discovers science and mysticism on his own. He then meets another young man who also seeks shelter from his own society, and the two, after an aborted attempt at setting this society on the right path, live happily on their own island.

The competing trends of the mystical and the legal were harmonized by the great thinker Abū Ḥāmid al-Ghazālī (d. 1111), whose autobiography, *Al-munqidh min al-ḍalāl* (The Rescuer from Error), talks about this dilemma. Al-Ghazālī's autobiography, like that of St. Augustine, recounts a religious quest. But the premodern period also boasted other autobiographical sagas, among them that of the great twelfth-century Syrian warrior-writer Usāmah ibn Munqidh. His story takes place during the Crusades, and some of his observations of Western combatants in his *Kitāb al-iʿtibār* are by now classic. As an Arabic writer living through the occupation by Western invaders, Usāmah has great appeal to modern-day Palestinian writers such as Emile Habiby, who do not hesitate to draw parallels spanning the centuries.

The medieval autobiographical form coexisted with a

well-developed indigenous Arabo-Islamic literary form, the biography. The genesis of the biographical dictionary has been linked by some to the science of *hadīth* criticism and by others to Arab genealogical storytelling and poetic traditions. The arrangement of biographical compendia is linked to the concept of *ṭabaqāt* or classes. In *ṭabaqāt* collections the biographies were divided into groups that could be arranged according to generations (as with *hadīth* transmitters) or on levels of merit or skill (as with poets). In a possibly later development, this term was also applied to compendia limited to a given type. Biography developed into a diverse and sophisticated historical and literary genre that saw its golden age under the Mamlūks (c. 1250–1500) and included works devoted to persons with particular physical characteristics, such as the blind. [*See* Biography and Hagiography.]

To read Usāmah's autobiographical text in which he discusses the Crusaders or the biographical compendia is to realize that Arabic literature is an inherent part of the political and cultural processes in the region. This becomes clearer in the modern period. In the nineteenth and twentieth centuries the West had a more profound influence on the Middle East than that of mere politics. With Western imperialism came new literary genres, the novel and the short story. Poetry, which has always been one of the mainstays of Middle Eastern culture, continues to be promoted and promulgated in a spirit different from that of prose.

It is generally considered that the first Arabic novel is *Zaynab* by the Egyptian Muḥammad Ḥusayn Haykal, published in 1913. But this point is the culmination of a process that started in the nineteenth century and involved the revitalization of the Arabic literary scene. Here the name of the Syrian Nāṣīf al-Yāzijī (d. 1871) looms large; he penned *maqāmāt* in imitation of those of his medieval predecessor al-Harīrī. Modern-day travelers who walk the Cairo streets and pick up a copy of the Egyptian monthly magazine *Al-hilāl* may not know that this long-lived periodical owes its existence to this early revitalization movement, in which its founder, Jirjī Zaydān (d. 1914), was quite prominent. Other nineteenth-century intellectuals, such as Rifāʿah Rāfiʿ al-Ṭahṭāwī (d. 1873), traveled in Europe (al-Ṭahṭāwī was imam of the Egyptian educational mission in France) and wrote about it in their native Arabic. This early phase of modern Arabic literature also saw other literary experiments, including the early twentieth-century neoclassical prose works of Muḥammad al-Muwayliḥī (d. 1930), Aḥmad Shawqī (d. 1932), and Ḥāfiẓ Ibrāhīm (d. 1932). Drawing on the traditional form of the *maqāmah*, these authors composed texts that were literary masterpieces functioning as well as social criticism. Shawqī and Ibrāhīm were also famed for their neoclassical odes.

This early twentieth-century neoclassical experiment in poetry was not to last, however. The classical *qaṣīdah* was doomed to fade away, except among old-fashioned poets. Free verse invaded the Arabic poem, from Iraq and North Africa, and dominated it. Prose poems did not lag behind, and today the field of Arabic poetry is as complicated as the political face of the region. Writers such as Ṣalāḥ ʿAbd al-Ṣabūr (d. 1981), Adonis, Maḥmūd Darwīsh, and Aḥmad ʿAbd al-Muʿṭī Ḥijāzī are those who give Arabic poetry a prominent place on the regional (and world) scene.

The distance that twentieth-century Arabic literature has traveled from the days of neoclassicism to the present postmodern narratives is enormous. The names and works that loom large fill library catalogs. Drama as an independent literary genre (and not as a modern rewriting of the *maqāmah*, as some critics would have it) appears. Because Arabic literature has traditionally been considered to be written in the literary language *(fushā)*, vigorous debates arise over the possibilities of using the vernaculars in this high-cultural product; both authors and audiences must appreciate the artificiality of having a peasant appear on the stage speaking in literary Arabic.

One of the foremost proponents of the pure Arabic language was himself a man of letters. Ṭāhā Ḥusayn (d. 1973), an Egyptian scholar and writer, was one of the Arab world's leading modernizers. He penned an autobiography, *Al-ayyām* (The Days), that remains one of the most beloved works of twentieth-century literature as well as being a landmark in Arabic letters. The saga it recounts forms part of its appeal: a blind Egyptian boy conquers social and educational barriers to become a professor at the modern university in Cairo. Along the way, he becomes part of the student delegation to France and returns to his native Egypt with a French doctorate and a French wife. His visual handicap only accentuates the drama of this text and the cultural differences it raises between tradition and modernity, East and West. It is no accident that schoolchildren from Syria to the Sudan and from Saudi Arabia to North Africa still read this work. This most dramatic of Arabic stories, the tale of "the Conqueror of Darkness," has also been made into a film and broadcast for millions of Arab viewers. [*See the biography of Ḥusayn.*]

Ṭāhā Ḥusayn lived through the traumatic days of Egypt's battle for independence, that precious contemporary commodity that was to spread throughout the Arab region. With newfound independence, critics of Arabic literature could now begin to speak of Egyptian literary production in comparison with Syrian or Sudanese; but in fact, tempting as these national categories might be, the major driving force behind literary categories is linguistic. Does a writer write in Arabic, or does he or she write in the colonizer's language? Literature written in Arabic now stands alongside Franco-Arab literature or Anglo-Arab literature (to take but two examples) that comprise texts written by Arab authors, not in Arabic. The fact that many contemporary Arab writers, whether writing in Arabic or in a Western language, live in exile—combined with the transnational nature of cultural production in the world—generally means that writers from one Arab country are read in many. For example, the prominent Lebanese woman writer Ḥanān al-Shaykh lives in London, but her novels are available to Arabophone readers the world over. The same is true for the verse of the important Palestinian poct Maḥmūd Darwīsh.

Naguib Mahfouz is undoubtedly the name that most Westerners today associate with Arabic literature. The Nobel Prize is crucial here, as are Mahfouz's novels and short stories portraying Egyptian life, sometimes at its seediest. At the time Mahfouz won the coveted prize, however, there were many other writers whose fame might have suggested that they too should have been laureates. Yusūf Idrīs (d. 1991), considered by many younger writers to be the *shaykh* of the short story, is one such writer. Some of Idrīs's narratives are among the most powerful in world literature, rife with sexuality and exploitative male-female relationships.

In the modern period more than genres have changed. The female voice is much more important in the contemporary literary production of the Middle East than it was in the premodern period. The male dominance of most classical Islamic literary genres has been replaced by a far greater balance between male and female voices. This is true not only in poetry (where women contributed even in classical times) but also in the novel and short story.

With women's writings have come women's concerns, and often feminism. Both male and female literature, of course, also often reflects the political and social issues in contemporary Middle Eastern societies. Many women writers have distinguished themselves, from Morocco to Saudi Arabia, but undoubtedly the most visible Arab woman writer is the Egyptian feminist physician Nawāl al-Saʿdāwī. Among women writers al-Saʿdāwī stands out by virtue of her uncompromising texts, from fiction to autobiography and didactic essays and studies (e.g., *The Hidden Face of Eve*). She comes closest to her male colleagues in her outspoken fiction, dealing as it does with sexuality and woman's exploitation. Hers is a searing gender critique added to the class critique, familiar to Arabic readers from the work of Yūsuf al-Qaʿīd. Al-Qaʿīd exposes the less savory aspects of government bureaucracies, imbuing his narratives with a bleak vision that allows his characters no escape (e.g., *War in the Land of Egypt*). In this al-Qaʿīd is not too dissimilar from the Palestinian Ibrāhīm Naṣr Allāh, whose postmodern fiction (for instance, *Prairies of Fever*) is a desperate commentary on Arab political and social dilemmas. [*See the biography of Saʿdāwī.*]

Arabic literature today is undergoing profound changes. Metafictional narratives and narratives rich in intertextuality are invading contemporary prose, as they havc that of thc Wcst. But the new Middle Eastern literary experiment is different. Contemporary writers, whatever their religious or political allegiance, are turning toward the classical tradition, redigesting it, redefining it, and recasting it. The name most often associated with this development is that of the Egyptian Jamāl al-Ghīṭānī. He draws on the rich Arabo-Islamic textual heritage, including historical, biographical, and mystical texts, to create modern narratives, demanding that his reader intertextually link his literary universe with that of his medieval antecedents. The intertextual use and reuse of classical Arabo-Islamic materials is not restricted to al-Ghīṭānī; practitioners of the contemporary Arabic metafictional narrative cover the entire geographical range of Arabic letters and include the brilliant Palestinian writer Emile Habiby and the innovative Tunisian author al-Misʿadī, to cite but two.

This attempt to return to the classical heritage and to exploit it in new narrative ways was predominantly, and until recently, the domain of Arabic male writers. Once again it is Nawāl al-Saʿdāwī who has made the breakthrough: Her two recent novels, *The Fall of the Imam* and *The Innocence of the Devil*, are attempts at a redefinition of the rich Arabo-Islamic tradition in both its more secular and its more religious manifestations.

It is one of the ironies of literature that it can be manipulated to various ends. One of the most important international developments to date, the religious revival, has played a significant role in literary developments, changing the face of Arabic literature. Despite its image in the West, the Islamist movement is not just a matter of street demonstrations or sermons in the local mosque. At stake is the control of various forms of cultural production, some of which—such as literature and the arts—have long been in the hands of more secularized and leftist intellectuals. The transnational nature of Islamism means that its ideas and advocates know no borders. Books may be printed in Cairo and Beirut, but one is as likely to find them in bookstores in other Middle Eastern cities as well as in European capitals with large Muslim populations.

This literary movement has been dubbed "Adab Islāmī," or "Islamic literature." Islamic literature is a parallel Islamic literary production that encompasses all the genres hitherto promulgated by more secularly minded intellectuals—plays, novels, short stories, and poetry. Even the terms of the debate are clearly laid out. "Committed" literature is no longer the prerogative of one group. One must extend it, we are told, to the religiously engaged text.

The nexus of literature and the religious revival has still to be fully explored. Oddly enough, this critical occultation comes about because of the unwitting collusion of different academic specialists. On the one hand, most studies of religious movements concern themselves with political and theological questions. On the other hand, Western specialists in Arabic and other literatures of the Middle East confine themselves to the enormous secularized literary production of the region, perceived as it is to be artistically serious and hence more worthy of study.

The Islamist movement is teaching us that literature is as political today as it was in the medieval period. The deep influence of the dual and complementary processes of islamization and arabization is perhaps most visible in North Africa, where many writers once consciously employed the language of the colonizer; now, in an equally conscious move, many of them are switching to Arabic.

Islamic literature is, of course, not neutral. It advocates a way of life—the religious way. (Statistically, in Arab countries, sales of Islamic books far outnumber those of secular ones.) One of the favored modern Islamic literary genres is the autobiography. The major figures of the Islamist movement have indulged themselves here, from the popular television preacher Muḥammad Mutawallī al-Shaʿrāwī to the equally colorful blind Shaykh ʿAbd al-Ḥamīd Kishk. Kishk's *Story of My Days* chronicles not only his religious development but also his saga as a visually handicapped young man. In an ironic twist of literary fate, it calls to mind Ṭāhā Ḥusayn's *The Days*. [*See the biography of Kishk.*]

The Islamist movement has also given rise to many female literary voices. The classic example here remains that of Zaynab al-Ghazālī, whose *Days from My Life* recounts her religious activism and her dramatic imprisonment. In recent years, as veiling has become more popular among the educated elite of the Arab world and North Africa, many women writers are taking the occasion to exhibit not their bodies but their narratives of salvation. These spiritual autobiographies, not too distant in their aim from that of al-Ghazālī, now abound on the shelves of Islamic bookstores all over the world. [*See the biography of Ghazālī.*]

Nonetheless, the contemporary autobiography, like its other contemporary generic prose relatives, differs in spirit from its classic antecedent. Whereas it can be argued that classic literary text (be it anecdote or biography, to take but two examples) is more an expression of collective norms, the modern literary text expresses and centers more deeply on the individual. Genres may be superficially similar, but their cultural bases alter their articulation.

Examining this recent literary production that is Islamic literature alongside the intertextual postmodernism of someone like al-Ghīṭānī will show that contemporary Arabic literary discourse is being transformed. The new Arabic discourse is one that synchronically telescopes centuries of previous Arabic literary production. When verses from the Qur'ān, sayings from the *ḥadīth*, or historical incidents from Usāma's chronicle are transposed and embedded into a twentieth-century Arabic creation, a new literary product emerges. Present-day Arabic literature is to be characterized as a complex discourse that partakes of cultural elements from both the rich Arabo-Islamic past and the equally rich Western tradition.

Arabic literature, whether in its more secular or in its more religious guises, is today a major cultural force in the Middle East. Through its relations with other contemporary literatures, especially Western, it participates in an emerging world literary culture. At the same time, through its frequently self-conscious relation to its own immense Arabo-Islamic textual inheritance, it adds its own distinctive flavor.

BIBLIOGRAPHY

Allen, Roger. *The Arabic Novel: An Historical and Critical Introduction*. Syracuse, N.Y., 1982.
Beard, Michael, and Adnan Haydar, eds. *Naguib Mahfouz: From Regional Fame to Global Recognition*. Syracuse, N.Y., 1993.
Hamori, Andras. *On the Art of Medieval Arabic Literature*. Princeton, 1974.
Malti-Douglas, Fedwa. *Structures of Avarice: The Bukhalāʾ in Medieval Arabic Literature*. Leiden, 1985.
Malti-Douglas, Fedwa. *Blindness and Autobiography: Al-Ayyām of Ṭāhā Ḥusayn*. Princeton, 1988.
Malti-Douglas, Fedwa. *Woman's Body, Woman's Word: Gender and Discourse in Arabo-Islamic Writing*. Princeton, 1991.
Malti-Douglas, Fedwa. *Men, Women, and God(s): Nawal El Saadawi Writes Arab Feminism*. Berkeley, 1995.
Monroe, James T. *The Art of Badīʿ az-Zamān al-Hamadhānī as Picaresque Narrative*. Beirut, 1983.
Stetkevych, Jaroslav. *The Zephyrs of Najd: The Poetics of Nostalgia in the Classical Arabic Nasīb*. Chicago, 1993.
Stetkevych, Suzanne Pinckney. *Abū Tammām and the Poetics of the ʿAbbāsid Age*. Leiden, 1991.
Stetkevych, Suzanne Pinckney. *The Mute Immortals Speak: Pre-Islamic Poetry and the Poetics of Ritual*. Ithaca, N.Y., 1993.

FEDWA MALTI-DOUGLAS

Gender in Arabic Literature

Most twentieth-century Arabic fiction is informed by an Islamicate consciousness, yet relatively few authors have chosen specifically Islamic themes. Many writers question the place of tradition in a rapidly modernizing world, but few examine the religion as a social, symbolic system. Those novels and poems that have dealt with Islam specifically have three foci: criticism of the institutions of orthodox Islam; the spiritual role of Islam and of the prophet Muḥammad as a counterproject to westernization; and Islamicist activism. Such texts tend to exaggerate traditional conceptions of gender roles and behaviors. Gender is here used to refer to the images, values, interests, and activities held to be important to the realization of men's and women's anatomical destiny. As women have added their voices to the corpus of literature on Islam, so have the understandings of gender changed.

It was in the first quarter of the twentieth century that Muslim intellectuals began to write fiction that reflected political and socioreligious concerns. Members of the Egyptian Madrasah Ḥadīthah exposed the oppressive treatment of women and the unchallenged power of religious authorities. Maḥmūd Ṭāhir Lāshīn's 1929 short story "Bayt al-ṭāʿah" ("House of Obedience") criticizes men who use what they consider to be an Islamic institution to crush women's will; the "house of obedience" authorizes the husband of a woman who wants a divorce to become his wife's jailer. One of the earliest Arabic novels is Ṭāhā Ḥusayn's autobiographical *Al-ayyām* (published serially in 1926–1927 and as a book in 1929). In this *Bildungsroman* that traces the triumphs of Egypt's blind doyen of letters, the pro-Western Ṭāhā Ḥusayn criticizes the all-male, tradition-bound al-Azhar system and its hypocritical *ʿulamāʾ*. He constructs himself as a strong man in defiance of social expectations that blind men should be as marginal to society as are women.

While some intellectuals were attacking the corrupt institutions and agents of modern Islam, others were invoking the power at the core of a well understood, timeless faith. The neoclassical court poet Aḥmad Shawqī was one of the first to write long poems on Muḥammad; his *Alhamzīyah al-nabawīyah* and *Nahj al-burdah* inspired others to write about Islamic history and the life of the Prophet. The 1930s in Egypt saw the publication of fiction and drama by leading modernist writers lauding the Islamic exemplar and showing that Islam is no obstacle to progress, for example Tawfīq al-Ḥakīm's unwieldy play *Muḥammad* (1936), Muḥammad Ḥusayn Haykal's *Ḥayāt Muḥammad,* and Ṭāhā Ḥusayn's *ʿAlā hāmish al-sīrah* (1937–1943). During the post-Revolution period two more important works focusing primarily on Muḥammad were published. In 1959 the Egyptian Nobel laureate Najīb Maḥfūẓ (Naguib Mahfouz) published *Awlād ḥāratina,* an allegory based on the lives of several Islamic prophets that was considered blasphemous and was censored. Qāsim-Muḥammad is the revolutionary with the widest vision, the toughest foe whom the unruly gangs of the alley had yet confronted, yet he like his predecessors was doomed to find his revolution coopted. ʿAbd al-Raḥmān al-Sharqāwī's Marxist study *Muḥammad rasūl al-ḥurrīyah* (1962) presents the prophetic mission as an exploitative obsession. Each Muḥammad is at once an ordinary man and a driven reformer. The women characters in the Prophet's life are presented as at best foils to his greatness.

One of the first attempts to consider Islam in tandem rather than in mutually exclusive competition with modernity was *Qindīl Umm Hāshim* (1945) by the Egyptian *adīb* Yaḥyā Ḥaqqī. It tells the by now paradigmatic tale of the rejection of Islam in favor of Western science, the failure of this science, and the recognition of the need to meld the spiritual and the material. Women act as vehicles of each culture's values and shape Ismail's decisions.

During the globally troubled decade of the 1960s Arab men and women began to question the role of religion in the rapidly changing life of the modern individual. While Saudi poets like ʿAbd al-Raḥmān Ṣāliḥ al-ʿAshmāwī and Ṭāhir Zamakhsharī were writing pious poetry, Egyptian secularists were targeting religion. Najīb Maḥfūẓ laments the transformation of Islam into an ideology and the concomitant loss of soul in society. Several characters search in vain for an absent father-figure, a transparent symbol for God. These desperate quests involve Ṣūfī masters and chaste prostitutes, the latter often providing greater solace than the former. The Sudanese al-Ṭayyib Ṣāliḥ seems less pessimistic: in *Urs al-Zayn* (1966), Zayn, the saintly fool, wins the love of the village beauty and assumes his real persona when he becomes united with her. Both writers create women who merely facilitate a man's access to the spiritual realm.

While some women were writing overtly feminist texts, others turned to Islam to find a legitimate space for women as active agents. In 1966 the leader of the Egyptian Association of Muslim Ladies, Zaynab al-Ghazālī, published *Ayyām min ḥayātī*, her memoir of six years in prison under Nasser. She describes torture so great that only she, and not the men, could bear it. In a kind of gender reversal, she cites men only to demonstrate her spiritual superiority. At about the same time in Iraq, another pious woman was producing religiously didactic yet also arguably feminist literature. In the 1960s and 1970s Bint al-Hudā, also known as Amīnah Ṣadr, participated in the Islamicist revivalism in Najaf; in 1980, the Baʿth regime executed her. She wrote several novels (notably *Liqāʾ fī al-mustashfā*, c. 1970), short stories, and poems in which she created models of ideal behavior for Muslim women. These women are anti-Western; they embrace domesticity and advocate the veil, yet they are not subservient to men; and they may work in the public sphere as long as they follow correctly understood Islamic prescriptions. They may even bear arms should the Islamic mission require it.

With the rise of Islamicist movements during the 1970s and 1980s, a few women have chosen to devote their literary talents to Islam. These women do not try to support or oppose gender bias in Islam or its texts. They see rather the hand of patriarchy at work in the misappropriation of scripture to oppress women. The Egyptian feminist physician and novelist Nawāl al-Saʿdāwī has written more than twenty novels, of which two concentrate on Islam. The heroine of *Suqūṭ al-Imām* (1987) is called Bint Allāh, or Daughter of God; not only is her name a blasphemy, but she also has dreams of being raped by God. *Jannāt wa-Iblīs* (1992) delves into the psyche of the Islamicist movement to expose men's expedient uses of religion. When God declares Satan to be innocent, the transcendent binary of good and evil is undermined. Saʿdāwī's fearless condemnations of those who abuse religious privilege have earned her a place on the death list of a powerful fundamentalist group. Another Egyptian, but of the next generation, is Salwā Bakr. Her 1986 novella *Maqām ʿAṭīyah* explores the relationship between Islamic sensibilities and the pharaonic heritage. Should the shrine of Lady ʿAṭīyah be removed to give access to archaeological remains that hold a secret that will transform modern Egypt? Her next novel, *Al-ʿarabah al-dhahabīyah lā taṣʿadu ilā al-samāʾ* (1931), takes place in the women's prison, by now a familiar place for readers of Egyptian women's writings, where a "madwoman" assesses her companions' eligibility to join her in the golden chariot that will whisk them all off to heaven.

Men and women have both extolled and criticized Islamic texts and institutions throughout the twentieth century. Men have depicted the Prophet as the perfect man who might serve as a model for all, and women have looked into the scriptures for right guidance in their search for power and position in society. However, many have recognized that unscrupulous individuals have used Islam to further their own ambitions. Those who have dared to speak out against such distortions have often had to pay a dear price.

[*See also the biographies of Ḥusayn, Ghazālī, and Saʿdāwī.*]

BIBLIOGRAPHY

Bakr, Salwā. *Al-ʿarabah al-dhahabīyah lā taṣʿadu ilā al-samāʾ*. Cairo, 1991.

Bakr, Salwā. *Maqām ʿAṭīyah*. Cairo, 1986.

Bint al-Hudā. *Liqāʾ fī al-mustashfā*. Beirut, ca. 1970.

Ghazālī, Zaynab al-. *Ayyām min ḥayātī*. Cairo, 1966.

Ḥakīm, Tawfīq al-. *Muḥammad*. Cairo, 1936.

Ḥaqqī, Yaḥyā. *Qindīl Umm Hāshim*. Cairo, 1945.

Haykal, Muḥammad Ḥusayn. *Ḥayāt Muḥammad*. Cairo, 1938.

Ḥusayn, Ṭāhā. *ʿAlā hāmish al-sīrah.* Cairo, 1937–1943.
Ḥusayn, Ṭāhā. *Al-ayyām.* Cairo, 1926–1927.
Lāshīn, Maḥmūd Ṭāhir. "Bayt al-ṭaʿah." Cairo, 1929.
Maḥfūẓ, Najīb (Mahfouz, Naguib). *Awlād ḥāratinā.* Beirut, 1967.
Religion and Literature 20.1 (Spring 1988). Special issue devoted to Middle Eastern literature, with an Islamic focus.
Saʿdāwī, Nawāl al-. *Suqūṭ al-Imām.* Cairo, 1987.
Saʿdāwī, Nawāl al-. *Jannāt wa-Iblīs.* Beirut, 1992.
Ṣāliḥ, Al-Ṭayyib. *ʿUrs al-Zayn.* Beirut, 1967.
Sharqāwī, ʿAbd al-Raḥmān al-. *Muḥammad rasūl al-ḥurrīyah.* Cairo, 1962.

MIRIAM COOKE

ARAB-ISRAELI CONFLICT. The origins of the Arab-Israeli conflict can be traced back more than a century, when Jews, disillusioned with prospects for integration into European societies, began to immigrate to Palestine in 1882, not as individuals seeking to pray and die in Jerusalem but as a part of a political movement. In 1897, this political trend was further inspired by the First Zionist Congress, which called for the creation of a Jewish homeland in Palestine, thus spawning the modern Jewish national movement, Zionism. The land, which the Jews considered theirs by virtue of God's will and historic rights, was, however, inhabited by another people, the Palestinians who had been living there for centuries, albeit not until recently as a political entity.

Yet the first Jewish immigrants to Palestine did not encounter resistance from the local population. It was only a few decades later that the Zionist movement began to be perceived as a threat by the indigenous Palestinian population, as well as by other Arabs. The turning point in the relationship between the two national movements, the Arab and Palestinian on the one hand and Zionism on the other, was the Balfour Declaration of 2 November 1917, in which British Foreign Minister Arthur Balfour promised a "national home for the Jewish People" in Palestine, adding that the British Government would pursue its "best endeavors to facilitate the achievement of this object. . . ."

This move by the British Government, which acquired mandatory power in Palestine in 1920, following the end of World War I, angered the Palestinians and resulted in an eruption of violence that was to continue, intermittently, to the present day. The Palestinians were further alienated by the massive Zionist immigration to Palestine, which had brought the number of Jews from 24,000 in 1881 (less than 5 percent of the population) to 85,000 by 1914 (12 percent of the total population). Immigration intensified further following the Balfour Declaration and the rise of Nazism in Germany in 1933, swelling the number of Jewish immigrants to 368,845 between the years 1921 and 1945. In Jerusalem alone, the most significant city in Palestine for both Jews and Arabs (Muslims and Christians alike), the number of Jews grew from 53,000 to 70,000 during the four years from 1931 to 1935.

Consequently, in 1936 the Palestinians began a revolt against British policy in Palestine which was to last until 1939. One of the leaders of this revolt was al-Ḥājj Amīn al-Ḥusaynī, *muftī* of Jerusalem and president of the Supreme Muslim Council in Mandatory Palestine (appointed to these posts by the British in 1920). When the revolt began, al-Ḥājj Amīn assumed the presidency of the Arab Higher Committee, thus becoming a pivotal figure in the Palestinian national movement.

Several years before the revolt began, al-Ḥājj Amīn had sought to bring the Palestinian national struggle against Zionism to the attention of the international Muslim community by (1) raising funds to refurbish the two revered mosques on al-Ḥaram al-Sharīf ("the Noble Sanctuary") in Jerusalem, al-Aqṣā and the Dome of the Rock (Qubbat al-Ṣakhrah); (2) holding an international congress of *ʿulama'* in November 1928, attended by delegations of Damascus, Beirut, and Transjordan; and (3) holding an international Muslim conference in Jerusalem in December 1931. This conference, attended by 150 Muslim scholars from all over the Islamic world, passed a resolution on the importance of Palestine and the holiness of Jerusalem for Muslims. [*See the biography of Ḥusaynī.*]

The *muftī*'s drive to refurbish the Muslim holy sites in Jerusalem occasioned a strong reaction from the Jewish populace, which claimed that this reconstruction would adversely affect the Western Wall, the ancient site of the first and second Jewish temples, and Jewish access to it. Thus, the national conflict took a religious turn in the Holy Land, the struggle over competing national goals assuming at times the shape of a religious war over holy places and symbols. This trend was reinforced by unfortunate events in another holy city for both Jews and Muslims, Hebron (al-Khalīl). Sixty-four unarmed Orthodox Jews were massacred in Hebron on 28 August 1929 by Arabs in riots, which had erupted in several cities, echoing growing tension surrounding the refurbishment of al-Ḥaram al-Sharīf.

During the late 1920s and early 1930s, there were intermittent calls for *jihād* by some groups—most notably by the imam of Haifa, Shaykh ʿIzz al-Dīn al-Qassām (1882–1935), and his followers. Likewise, during the 1936–1939 revolt, Syrian, Iraqi, and even the remote but active Indian and other Muslim religious authorities issued *fatwās* (religious legal opinions) endorsing *jihād* for the sake of Palestine as a duty. Conspicuous by their silence, however, were the *ʿulama'* of Egypt's al-Azhar University.

Britain's regional strategic considerations in the wake of the rise of German military power and its fear of losing credibility with the Arabs, forced it in subsequent years to balance its policy in Palestine. This led to the White Paper of 17 May 1939, in which the British government seemed to accept the Palestinian demand for national independence with an Arab majority (within ten years), restricting Jewish immigration to Palestine as well as land sale to the Jews. Naturally, this move angered the Jews, who were meanwhile building a formidable military force and a complex social infrastructure.

Clashes were inevitable between the Palestinians and the Jewish immigrants. With 1.2 million indigenous Palestinians and more than 650,000 Jews in the Yeshuv, the prestate Jewish settlement in Palestine, facing one another at such close quarters and each group holding fast to its claims in Palestine, the stage was set for further conflict when, in September 1947, Britain announced its intention to depart from Palestine on 15 April 1948.

Resolution 181 of the United Nations, issued on 29 November 1947, recommended the partition of Palestine into two states—one Arab and the other Jewish—but failed to avert a conflict. David Ben-Gurion (one of the founders of the Jewish state and later to become the first prime minister of Israel) and the other Zionist leaders accepted the UN resolution, because they understood that this was the best the Jewish community in Palestine could achieve under the given circumstances. The Arabs, however, elected to fight in an attempt to reverse what they viewed as an injustice that forced them to relinquish parts of their homeland.

After approximately six months of fighting between Arab and Jewish forces (December 1947–May 1948), the Palestinian and Arab volunteer forces were defeated. Following this major round of the military conflict, Ben-Gurion, on 14 May 1948, announced the establishment of the Jewish state of Israel on parts of historic Palestine. As a result of the war in Palestine between Jews and Arabs, approximately 20,000 out of 27,000 square kilometers of the Palestinian land came under the control of the state of Israel; the remaining portions—the West Bank and the Gaza Strip—came under the control of the Jordanians and Egyptians, respectively. More than one million Palestinians either fled or were forced to leave by the Israeli forces. Many Palestinian cities, such as Haifa, Akka, Jaffa, Lidda, and Ramlah, and, above all, the western part of Jerusalem, as well as about four hundred villages, were virtually abandoned by the Arab Palestinian population as a result of this war. Those who left their homes became refugees in Lebanon, Jordan, Syria, and in the West Bank and Gaza Strip. Some Palestinians sought refuge in other Arab countries, including the Persian Gulf countries (Saudi Arabia and Kuwait in particular). Most, however, continued to feel like and be treated as foreigners in the countries where they took up residence, a mirror image of the situation of the Jews in Europe, at least in the last century. The Palestinian situation had the additional dimension that the Arab countries, with the exception of Jordan, and to a lesser extent Lebanon, as a matter of policy refused to grant the Palestinians citizenship in order to prevent any possibility of assimilation.

The defeat of the Arab armies, the massive immigration of the Palestinian population to neighboring Arab countries, and above all, the loss of a major part of Palestine to the Jewish forces (led by the Haganah), sent a shock wave through the Arab world, then in the throes of the early stages of decolonization. Many questions surfaced about the Arab regimes and their inability to deal with vital questions, such as foreign occupation of Arab/Muslim countries. Even the sincerity and commitment of the leaders of the Arab world were questioned, and a crisis of legitimacy soon developed. Consequently, several coups d'état and revolutions were staged, most notably the 1952 revolution in Egypt, in search of better leadership and a brighter future for the Arab nations.

During this time, Israel was growing stronger militarily, economically, and demographically. In the late 1940s and early 1950s, a massive Jewish immigration from the Arab countries added a new social and demographic dimension to Israeli society. Although the perceived Arab threat became a major factor in uniting, and indeed strengthening, the fabric of this society, the enormous support of world Jewry accelerated the advancement and extension of technology, agriculture, and medicine. Israel became an industrialized country complete with a military industry. It continued to rely on Western powers (France, Britain, and the United States), but sought to develop its own defense systems, including nuclear weaponry.

From Suez to the June 1967 War. Nine years after winning its first battle against Palestinian and Arab forces, Israel collaborated with France and Britain in defeating the Egyptian army in the Suez War of October–November 1956, during which Israeli forces occupied the Sinai and the Gaza Strip. One of the reasons for this war was the nationalization of the Suez Canal (on 26 July 1956) by the four-year-old Free Officers Revolution, which had brought about the demise of the monarchy in Egypt.

The main figure among these revolutionary leaders was Gamal Abdel Nasser, who became president of Egypt in 1954 and eventually became the leader of modern Arab nationalism until his death in September 1970. Ironically, Nasser's military defeat in the 1956 war strengthened him politically and morally, as the occupying forces were ordered by the United Nations to evacuate the Sinai, mainly because of the active role of the United States and the Soviet Union. With the Arab world expressing strong solidarity with Egypt, Nasser used the crisis to galvanize the Arabs, as well as the Muslim world, in his struggle against imperialism and Zionism.

Nasser's commitment to Arab unity was put to the test in May 1967, however. Soviet and Syrian intelligence reports indicated that Israel was mobilizing massive troops on the border with Syria in preparation for an attack on Syria. Nasser, whose troops were busy in bloody battles in Yemen in support of the revolutionary forces against the imam, rushed to mobilize the remainder of his troops and station them along the southern borders of Israel. Nasser acted on the principle that aggression against any Arab country would be considered aggression against Egypt.

Three weeks of high military and political tension erupted into war early on the morning of 5 June 1967, when Israel attacked and destroyed the air forces of Egypt, Syria, and Iraq, thus disabling the Arabs in less than two decades. This defeat, in what become known as the Six-Day War or the June War of 1967, was a major turning point in Middle East history. Within six days the Israelis occupied the remaining 20 percent of the Palestinian lands, which were then in the hands of Jordan and Egypt (the West Bank, including the eastern side of Jerusalem, and the Gaza Strip, respectively). They also reoccupied the Sinai peninsula and the portion of Syrian land known as the Golan Heights, which the Likud Government of Menachem Begin annexed in 1981, considering it a vital security zone. Nasser took full responsibility for the defeat and submitted his resignation as president of Egypt. Because of enormous public pressure, however, he remained in power until his death in 1970. [*See the biography of Nasser.*]

Ascendance of Local Nationalism. The Arab defeat gave the Palestinians an opportunity to become more active and indeed to take their fate into their own hands. Thus, the Palestinian Liberation Organization (PLO), founded in 1964, gradually gained recognition among the Palestinians and the Arab nations and their leaders. Taking advantage of the Arab defeat, the PLO began to assert itself as an independent organization within the complex arena of Arab politics and became the champion of the Palestinian cause. Palestinian nationalism replaced Arab nationalism. The Palestinian issue, despite the efforts of Israel and its supporters, regained its status as the crux of the Arab-Israeli dispute and once again took center stage in Middle East politics. The Arab countries continued as players, but a sense of realism, supported by a growing sense of local patriotism, supplanted Arab nationalism and began to prevail throughout the Arab world, including among the Palestinians.

Anwar el-Sadat's Egypt (1970–1981) led the way in this direction. Egypt continued to see itself and to be seen by others as the heart of the Arab world, but now the notions of Arab unity and Pan-Arabism were relegated to a back burner. Even the War of October 1973 against the Israeli forces in the Sinai and Golan Heights was intended above all to put Egypt and Syria in a better position to negotiate a political settlement. Sadat's trip to Jerusalem in November 1977 and the subsequent Camp David Accords (signed in September 1978), which brought about a "cold peace" between Israel and Egypt, demonstrated the point. Solving Egypt's economic problems was Sadat's main goal during his presidency, something for which he was willing to go the extra mile, including signing a peace treaty with Israel. Although not high priority of his, the Palestinian problem was clearly one Sadat wanted to solve; he even negotiated an autonomy plan with the Israelis for the Palestinians, although his formula was not accepted by the Palestinians or by the rest of the Arab world, and dissatisfaction with it brought about Egypt's isolation for several years. Nor was the nation accepted by most Egyptian people, and it eventually led to Sadat's assassination by a member of the Egyptian Islamic Jihād on 4 October 1981.

Widening of the Conflict. Since the 1967 War, the Palestinians have been the main advocate of their own cause. Politically, they have established diplomatic relations with most countries of the world, and militarily, they have launched guerrilla attacks from any Arab country that has allowed them to do so (or could not prevent them from doing so), mainly Jordan and Lebanon. In Jordan, however, the PLO lost its bases following the September 1970 civil war, which the king and forces loyal to him launched against the Palestinian organizations. Consequently, the focus of military activity moved to Lebanon, a militarily weaker northern neighbor of Israel. With 300,000 Palestinians living there in refugee camps, a weak central government, and sympathy for the Palestinian cause from several political and religious factions, the conditions in Lebanon were conducive to establishing a Palestinian military and even a social infrastructure.

Responding to repeated attempted Palestinian raids on Israel, most of which had no military value, Israel occasionally launched massive counterattacks (such as the Litani River Operation in March 1978) or carried out fullscale military operations. With the cooperation of a military Christian faction led by Saʿd Ḥaddād and his successor, Anṭūn Laḥd, the Israelis created a "security zone" in southern Lebanon to protect their northern settlements from repeated shelling and raids by Palestinian forces and their supporters in Lebanon. The Israeli counterraids on Palestinian positions disrupted the life of the southern Lebanese, many of whom fled to the northern parts of Lebanon to seek shelter and food in a country already devastated by civil war since 1975. Consequently, support for the Palestinians in that country eroded and the presence of Palestinian military force of any significance was finally eradicated following the June 1982 Israeli invasion of southern Lebanon (in Operation Peace for Galilee) and the eventual takeover of Beirut, the first Arab capital to be occupied by Israeli forces. Although PLO forces held out for eighty-two days against the strongest army in the Middle East, they were ultimately forced to leave Lebanon and move their headquarters to another Arab capital, Tunis.

Crystallization of Opposing Trends. The move to Tunis marked the beginning of the end of Palestinian attempts to confront Israel militarily. The failure of the Palestinian guerrilla movement to liberate any part of Palestine through military operations necessitated a shift in political attitudes among many Palestinians, a shift that was on the minds of many long before the move to Tunis. Already in 1974, Palestinian intellectuals close to the PLO chairman Yasir Arafat wrote several articles hinting at a willingness of the part of the Palestinian leadership to live side by side with a Jewish state. They first proposed a solution based on a secular democratic state in which all parties, Palestinians and Israelis, could live together. When Israel reacted very negatively to this proposal, the Palestinians eventually moved toward a compromise solution, acceptable to at least some Israelis, which became known as the two-state solution.

The harsh reality of more than 1.5 million Palestinians living under Israeli occupation since the 1967 war contributed to this compromising trend. A sense of realpolitik replaced the maximalist views of many Palestinians (i.e., demanding creation of an independent Palestinian state on the entire Palestinian land). Almost simultaneously, however, an opposing process developed among the occupiers.

In the early stages of Israel, the Arabs were blamed for their lack of willingness to reach a peace agreement with the Jewish state. After the 1967 war, however, Israel began to feel more secure and less threatened and began to see itself as the military superpower of the region. When the maximalists in Israel, the Likud Government and the right-wing political parties, gained power in 1977, the desire to trade land occupied during the 1967 war for peace decreased. The formula "land for peace" was replaced under the various Likud Governments (1977–1992) by another, "peace for peace." The land occupied in 1967, according to this view, is part of the Holy Land, indeed the heart of the Holy Land. It is "liberated," rather than "occupied," land and, therefore, should remain under Israeli control. Israel essentially offered the Palestinians in the Occupied Territories two choices: (1) a limited autonomy if they wished to stay in the "land of Israel"; or (2) movement to Jordan where, some prominent Israelis argued, they could establish their Palestinian state, since the majority of the population living in the Hashemite Kingdom of Jordan were already Palestinians.

In order to assert their presence in the Occupied Territories, a number of Jewish settlements were built throughout the Occupied Territories with the support of Israeli governments (including the Labor government, which initiated the process before losing the 1977 elections). About 150,000 Jews currently live on that land as settlers and control about 50 percent of the Palestinian land, thus complicating the possibility of settling the dispute and reaching a formula for coexistence between the two nations. During the fifteen years (1977–1992) when the Israeli right wing had the upper hand in Israel, a spirit of defiance, indeed a Jewish fundamentalism, developed among many Israelis, often new immigrants from the United States and other Western countries. In view of Arab and Islamic impotence, coupled with strong political and generous financial and military support from the United States, the Israeli government felt no pressure to relinquish its claim to the entire Palestinian land. The Palestinians, although in many ways a major player in the Middle East conflict, had limited political or military options; they were the weakest link. Or so it seemed until 9 December 1987, when a unique combination of circumstances contributed to the eruption of an uprising against the occupying forces.

After more than twenty years of discrimination, the jailing of tens of thousands of Palestinian men and women by the Israeli forces, the confiscation of land, and the building of Jewish settlements in the heart of Arab towns and cities, the Palestinians launched their uprising or *intifāḍah.* This sociopolitical endeavor represents one of the major landmarks in Palestinian history. The Palestinians have fought their powerful occupiers with all means available, including stones, knives, boycotts, and strikes. The Palestinian people decided, once again, to take their fate into their own hands and not wait for salvation from the outside, not even from the PLO, their national symbol and, by Arab consensus since 1974, sole political representative. The Israelis, in an attempt to contain this phenomenon, adopted even harsher measures than those they had been practicing against the Palestinians since the occupation began in 1967.

In November 1988, in the midst of the *intifāḍah,* the Palestinians, through the PLO, expressed their desire to reach a historic compromise with the state of Israel, a compromise that would be based on a two-state solution. Once again Israel felt under no obligation to respond positively to the proposal. The Palestinian Declaration of Independence and the verbal declarations associated with it, which laid out the new attitude of the Palestinians and their desire to reach a compromise, were then overshadowed by more significant political events.

In August 1990, after Iraqi forces invaded Kuwait, many Palestinians, for psychological and political reasons, expressed sympathy with Iraq, and the PLO was perceived as having followed popular sentiment in this matter. Along with the Iraqi people, the PLO and the Palestinian people paid a heavy price, as the rich Arab Gulf states halted financial aid to the Palestinians. The consequences of this for the Palestinians, individually and institutionally, have been severe, contributing to further decline in the ability of the Palestinians to withstand the pressures of the occupation and the conditions of the *intifāḍah,* which has brought about daily clashes between the Palestinians and the Israeli army.

Islamic Dimensions of the Conflict. In Palestine, most people have perceived the struggle as mainly a nationalist, secular one. Many prominent Christian Palestinians have taken part in the struggle alongside Muslim Palestinians, imparting to the Palestinian and Arab national movements a secular, rather than a religious, fervor. Indeed, in the 1920s, Palestinians even formed the Muslim-Christian Associations in a combined effort to combat Zionism.

The doctrine of *jihād* was not invoked throughout the Arab-Israeli conflict by any official government until an arson attack on al-Aqṣā mosque took place in 1969. Following this event, King Fayṣal of Saudi Arabia called for *jihād* to liberate Jerusalem. He also organized the first summit of Muslim states in Rabat in September 1969, which was attended by representatives of twenty-six states. In subsequent years, several summit meetings were held at which the issues of Palestine and Jerusalem were inevitably addressed, reflecting the broad sympathy and support these issues command in the Islamic world.

Subparagraph 5 of article 2 (A) of the charter of the Organization of Islamic Conference (OIC) shows the centrality of Palestine to the Muslim countries: one of the organization's goals is, "To co-ordinate efforts for safeguard of the Holy Places and support of the struggle of the people of Palestine, and help them to regain their rights and liberate their land." The suspension of Egypt from the OIC was justified by Egypt's material breaching of this article of the charter when it concluded the Camp David Accords with Israel in 1978. In January 1981, the third summit of the OIC was held in Saudi Arabia, entitled "The Session on Palestine and Holy Jerusalem." At the conclusion of this conference, the participants agreed to adopt *jihād* to save Jerusalem and to liberate the Occupied Territories.

Although the struggle has more commonly been seen as a national one, and although the PLO continues to be viewed as the sole representative of the Palestinians and Yasir Arafat the symbol of their struggle, Palestinians have been losing faith in their political leadership. The inability of this organization to solve political, social, and economic problems has led many people in the Occupied Territories to opt for an Islamic solution.

More and more are becoming convinced that the secular national movement of the Palestinians is doomed to fail to achieve the goals of the Palestinian people, just as the Arab national movements in the rest of the Arab world have failed to solve the sociopolitical and economic problems facing their respective peoples. The Islamists in the Occupied Territories have enhanced their position by capitalizing on the weaknesses of the PLO. At the same time, they are working at the grassroots level to help people under the increasing economic difficulties resulting from prolonged occupation and lack of sufficient assistance from outside sources.

In the aftermath of the collapse of the Soviet Union, the cooperation between the West and the majority of the Arab world to expel Iraq from Kuwait, the United States and Russia jointly sponsored a peace conference dealing with the Middle East problem. The parties (Israel, the Palestinian representatives, Syria, Lebanon, and Jordan) held their first meeting in Madrid on 30 October 1991. The process led nowhere, however, and once again the Palestinians lost hope for a peaceful, let alone just, solution. In addition, the PLO lost further credibility.

Meanwhile, however, some Israelis and Palestinians, working on the assumption that the open negotiations were not about to yield any immediate results, met secretly in Oslo, Norway, and struck an agreement on certain principles for the first stage of Palestinian-Israeli conflict resolution. This agreement was signed by Israel's prime minister and the PLO chairman in Washington, D.C., on 13 September 1993, leading to a major breakthrough in Middle East politics. Yet the Declaration of Principles (DOP) is only a first step in the direction of a political solution for a century-old conflict, and there are many aspects of this conflict that have still to be addressed and were deliberately set aside for future negotiations, as they present major difficulties in the process of trying to reach a historic solution.

One of these issues is the question of Jerusalem. Jerusalem is the spiritual capital of both the Palestinians (Muslims and Christians) and the Israelis (and Jews all over the world), and it is inconceivable for either of them not to have Jerusalem as part of their political identity. For Jews, Jerusalem is the site of their ancient temple and their historical capital, and in 1980 they passed a law considering the entire city the undivided capital of Israel; for Christians, the city is the site of the Church of the Holy Sepulcher where Jesus was crucified and buried; for Muslims, the city is their third holiest (after Mecca and Medina), the site of the rock from which the prophet Muḥammad is said to have ascended to heaven in the Night Journey (*miʿrāj*) and where the Dome of the Rock was built in 691 by an Umayyad caliph. This rock, according to rabbinic authorities, is the same rock, Rock Morieh, on which Abraham prepared to sacrifice his son Isaac. A second mosque, al-Aqṣā, also shares the site of the Temple Mount. This is why Jerusalem is called in Arabic al-Quds (the holy [city]). Indeed, all previous plans for solving the Palestinian-Israeli conflict suggested the internationalization of this city, precisely because of its importance of both nations, religiously and hence politically.

Since the signing of the DOP, however, the situation on the ground has not improved. In fact, acts of hostility between Israelis and Palestinians have increased, as many groups from both sides to sabotage the agreement by committing acts of violence against the other side. Leading the resistance wave against the DOP are political Islam and political Judaism. The Ḥamās (acronym for the Arabic Ḥarakat al-Muqāwamah al-Islāmīyah, Islamic Resistance Movement), which began as a political wing of the Palestinian Muslim Brotherhood at the end of 1987, and Islamic Jihād are leading the struggle against the agreement on the Palestinian side, whereas the religious-nationalist settlers in the Occupied Territories are leading the Israeli resistance.

It is ironic, however, that this conflict, which has until now been a conflict mainly between two secular movements, might end as a conflict between two religious communities. The present trend is in that direction. This was illustrated in most unfortunate terms on 25 February 1994, when a Jewish settler acting on his religious beliefs entered the Ibrāhīmī Mosque in Hebron (where Muslims pray at the Tomb of the Patriarchs, a site of the graves of the prophets Abraham, Isaac, and Jacob) and massacred more than thirty Muslims at Friday morning prayer during the month of Ramaḍān, the holiest month for Muslims. This act instantly brought the political negotiations to a halt.

In the Middle East, the two worlds of religion and politics cannot be entirely separated, and the dialectical relationships between them will continue. The majority of people, however, will persist in perceiving the struggle as a national struggle over territory and self-determination. To these people, the holy places are symbols for the existence and continuation of national life, whereas for others these symbols become the essence of the struggle.

[*See also* Arab Nationalism; Ḥamās; International Relations and Diplomacy; Israel; Jerusalem; Organization of the Islamnic Jihād; Palestine Liberation Organization; West Bank and Gaza.]

BIBLIOGRAPHY

Facts and Figures about the Palestinians. Information Paper No. 1. Center for Policy Analysis on Palestine. Washington, 1992.

Flapan, Simha. *The Birth of Israel: Myths and Realities*. New York, 1987.

Hourani, Albert. *A History of the Arab People*. Cambridge, Mass., 1991.

Hourani, Albert, et. al., eds. *The Modern Middle East: A Reader*. Berkeley, 1993.

Kimmerling, Baruch, and Joel Migdal. *Palestinians: The Making of a People*. New York, 1993.

Mansfield, Peter. *A History of the Middle East*. New York, 1991.

Moinuddin, Hassan. *The Charter of the Islamic Conference and Legal Framework of Economic Co-operation among its Member States*. New York, 1987.

Muslih, Muhammad. *The Origins of Palestinian Nationalism*. New York, 1988.

Peters, Rudolph. *Islam and Colonialism: The Doctrine of Jihad in Modern History*. New York, 1979.

Polk, William. *The Arab World Today*. Cambridge, Mass., 1991.

Smith, Charles. *Palestine and the Arab-Israeli Conflict*. New York, 1988.

A Survey of Palestine. Volume 1. Reprint, Washington, 1991.

Tannous, Izzat. *The Palestinians: Eyewitness History of Palestine under British Mandate*. New York, 1988.

Shukri B. Abed

ARAB LEAGUE. Until the mid-twentieth century, the Arabs of modern times were under foreign domination, mainly Ottoman, British, and French. Their first opportunity to regain their independence and unity came when the Hashemite *sharīf*, Ḥusayn ibn ʿAlī, ruler of the Hejaz (d. 1931) launched the famous Arab revolt in 1916 against the Ottoman Empire, which at the time dominated most of the Arab East. Although Britain promised Ḥusayn its support in his quest for Arab unity, the British had secretly signed the Sykes-Picot Agreement a month earlier with France, dividing the Arab East between the two countries.

The Arab revolt accelerated Arab demands for independence and unity. Sharīf Ḥusayn's sons, particularly Emir Fayṣal of Iraq (d. 1933) and Emir ʿAbd Allāh (Abdullah) of Jordan (d. 1951), joined several Arab Muslim groups in pressuring London for Arab independence and unity. The British foreign minister, Anthony Eden, responded to Arab pressure by declaring to the House of Commons in May 1941 Britain's support for the Arabs in achieving their unity through an institution that looked after their interests and tightened their ties. Emir ʿAbd Allāh, who opposed the partitioning of Syria in the Sykes-Picot Agreement, was the first Arab leader to endorse Eden's statement. Iraq envisaged an "Arab League" that would include Syria, Lebanon, Palestine, Jordan, and Iraq, but owing to Egyptian, Saudi, and Syrian opposition and British hesitation, the Hashemite endeavors were unsuccessful.

Britain tilted toward Egypt, the center for British activities in the region. Egypt was also viewed as a bridge between Christian Western Europe and the Arab Muslims. Throughout 1943 and 1944 Egyptian leaders discussed with officials and representatives from Iraq, Transjordan, Saudi Arabia, Syria, Lebanon, Yemen, and Palestine the Arab proposals for some form of union. These officials consented to an Egyptian proposal for the establishment of an Arab League. Representatives of the Arab states met in September 1944 in Alexandria, Egypt, and eventually agreed on a structure in which member states would retain their sovereignty, and resolutions would be binding on all member states only when voting was unanimous. Majority decisions would be binding only on those states that accepted them. The league would strive to achieve cooperation among the Arab states and to maintain their independence and sovereignty.

Arab representatives met in Cairo and signed the Pact of the League of Arab States on 22 March 1945. The founding members were Egypt, Saudi Arabia, Syria, Iraq, Lebanon, Yemen, and Transjordan. In addition to the original members, the following states have joined the League: Libya (1953); Sudan (1956); Tunisia and Morocco (1958); Kuwait (1961); Algeria (1962); South Yemen (1967, united in 1990 with Yemen); Bahrain, Qatar, Oman, and the United Arab Emirates (1971); Mauritania (1973); Somalia (1974); Palestine (1976); and Djibouti (1977).

The Arab League comprises six major bodies: the League Council, the supreme body of the organization composed of the representatives of the member states; Permanent Commissions, which include the important Political Committee; the General-Secretariat, comprising the Secretary-General, assistants, and other officials; the Common Defense Council; the Social and Economic Council; and the Specialized Arab Organizations. The goals of these bodies have been extensive, including encouraging close cooperation of the member states in political, security, economic, communications, cultural, social, and financial matters.

The provisions of the pact outlawed the use of force for the settlement of disputes between member states, and the league is responsible for dealing with any dispute that may arise between members. Any threatened state has the right to request the league's council to take the necessary steps to repel aggression.

There have been a number of achievements, particularly through the specialized organs of the league. In the area of social and economic welfare numerous agreements have been signed between member states, including joint ventures like the Arab Potash Company, the Arab Maritime Companies, the Arab Satellite Communications Organization, the Arab Monetary Fund, and the Arab Fund for Economic and Social Development. The last two institutions have extended considerable financial assistance for social and economic development in the Arab world, especially in the poorer states. Other specialized organizations prepare studies and present recommendations to help member states in solving their social and economic problems. The Arab Bank for Economic Development in Africa extends financial assistance to several African Muslim states. In the area of cultural cooperation, the specialized Arab Organization for Science, Culture, and Education has organized numerous educational conferences and publishes extensive studies on science and education.

The league has also played an important role in political issues at the regional and international levels, as in championing the Palestinian cause. It continuously raises Arab and Islamic issues in international conferences such as the United Nations, the Non-Aligned Conference, and summits of the Organization of the Islamic Conference. The league has contributed to solving inter-Arab conflicts and helps in strengthening Arab relations with foreign states such as those of Europe, Africa, and Latin America. To facilitate its work outside the Arab countries the league has opened more than twenty offices around the world.

Nevertheless, the league has been viewed by several Arab states as an instrument of Egyptian foreign policy. To counter Egypt's domination of the league, Saudi Arabia, supported by other Arab and Muslim states, founded the Muslim World League (1962), followed by the Islamic Pact (1965) and the OIC. [*See* Muslim World League *and* Organization of the Islamic Conference.] In 1979, when Egypt signed a peace treaty with Israel, Arab leaders met in March in Baghdad, expelled Egypt from the league, moved the league's headquarters to Tunis, and appointed a Tunisian as the new secretary-general.

Soon after the Baghdad summit Iraq found itself at war with Iran (1980–1988), which contributed more to Arab divisions and rivalries and further weakened the league. Several Arab leaders, notably King Hussein of Jordan and King Ḥasan of Morocco, attempted to "reestablish" Arab solidarity. King Hussein was instrumental in the return of Egypt to the Arab League during the Arab summit of 1987 in Amman. Several Arab summits were organized by the league between 1988 and 1990, resulting in the return of the league to Cairo, although a "second center" remains in Tunis. The newfound solidarity was shattered by the Iraqi invasion of Kuwait in August 1990. The league was divided as never before; the Tunisian secretary-general resigned his post, and an Egyptian was appointed in his place.

It is often said that the league is a mirror of Arab politics. Today more than ever, *waṭanīyah* and *iqlimīyah* (local and regional nationalism) rather than *qawmīyah ʿarabīyah* (Pan-Arabism) are the main driving forces in Arab politics. This portends a negative impact on the effectiveness of the Arab League in the near future.

BIBLIOGRAPHY

Gomaa, Ahmed M. *The Foundation of the League of Arab States*. London and New York, 1977. Covers the colonial and inter-Arab politics that produced the Arab League.

Hasou, Tawfiq Y. *The Struggle for the Arab World: Egypt's Nasser and the Arab League*. Boston and London, 1985. Study of Egypt's role in the Arab League during the Nasser era, showing how the league was used as an instrument of Egyptian foreign policy.

Hassouna, Hussein A. *The League of Arab States and Regional Disputes*. Dobbs Ferry, N.Y., 1975. Written by the son of the former secretary-general of the league, ʿAbd al-Khāliq Ḥasūnah. Detailed work on the mechanism of the league and its utilization in attempting to solve Arab conflicts.

MacDonald, Robert W. *The League of Arab States: A Study in the Dynamics of Regional Organization*. Princeton, 1965. The first major English-language study on the Arab League.

Maddy-Weitzman, Bruce. *The Crystallization of the Arab State System, 1945–1954*. Syracuse, N.Y., 1993. Study of inter-Arab politics in the first decade after the formation of the Arab League.

Muḥāfaẓah, ʿAlī, et al. *Jāmiʿat al-Duwal al-ʿArabīyah: Al-wāqiʿ wa-al-ṭumūḥ* (The League of Arab States: The Reality and the Aspiration). 2d ed. Beirut, 1992. Publication of a symposium organized by the league in Tunis, April 1982. Excellent and exhaustive collection of papers by League officials and Arab experts on the league.

Riyāḍ, Maḥmūd. *The Struggle for Peace in the Middle East*. London and New York, 1981. Riyāḍ, Egypt's foreign minister under Nasser and Sadat and secretary-general of the Arab League, discusses the

Egyptian-Israeli conflict, the road to peace, and his role in the league.

TAWFIQ Y. HASOU

ARAB NATIONALISM. Like other strands of third-world nationalism, *qawmīyah ʿarabīyah* or Arab nationalism cannot be understood apart from its anticolonial ethos and its glorification of the collectivity's origins and history in the face of Western dominance. These general components of nationalist doctrine raise, however, important issues in the case of Arab nationalism. For instance, can anticolonial movements based on Islamic reformism (like those of al-Afghānī or Abduh) or regional empire-builders (Egypt's nineteenth-century ruler Muḥammad ʿAlī and his son Ibrāhīm) be considered precursors of the doctrine? Some have looked even further back to emphasize the role of eighteenth-century Salafīyah Islamic movements, such as Wahhābism that preached a pure, "uncontaminated" Islam.

The view adopted here is that Arab nationalism as a political movement is essentially a twentieth-century product. Its bases and components may, however, originate with the presence of the Arabic language itself or with the Arabs' social, intellectual, and political culture. Arab nationalism has been centered on "Arabness" and hence on the important question "Who is an Arab." At present there is consensus around the view of Sāṭiʿ al-Ḥuṣrī (1882–1962) that Arabs are identified by their language, having Arabic as their mother tongue and consciously identifying with it. Indeed, al-Ḥuṣrī defined nationalism as love of the nation and organic identification with it, and the bases of such a national collectivity are language and common history. To these bases some have added common traditions and interests as well as common culture shaped by the same environment. In its most modern form (with Nasser, the Baʿth, or Muʿammar al-Qadhdhāfī), Arab nationalism aims at the political reunification of all Arabic-speaking states from the Persian Gulf to the Atlantic Ocean, and their transformation from a *Kulturnation* into a *Staatnation*. [*See the biography of Ḥuṣrī.*]

This interplay between the doctrine's cultural and political phases attracts attention to the sequences in its evolution, for the movement acquired its present form only gradually. Its vicissitudes are a function of various factors: intervention of external powers in the region; defining events or political upheavals that shook the area; the type of leadership at the head of the movement; and its competition with two other loci of people's loyalty—the territorial state and Pan-Islamism. The movement's evolution may be divided into four phases.

Nineteenth Century to World War I. Ottomanism and Islamic solidarity were challenged by modernizing forces at the empire's center and by the provinces' demand for Arab distinctiveness. Though interest in Western science and technology united the Young Turks and many Arabs, the drive of the Committee of Union and Progress for turkification alienated the Arabs and accelerated their demand for autonomy. Cultural clubs—organized by Lebanese Christians in collaboration with American missionaries—proliferated (al-Yāzijī, 1819–1871; al-Shidyaq, 1805–1887). When the Syrian Buṭrus al-Bustānī (1819–1883) pleaded for girls' education or the Egyptian Rifāʿah Rafīʿ al-Ṭahṭāwī (1801–1873) emphasized *waṭan* (fatherland), they constituted secularist challenges to the Islamic establishment of the Turkish caliph. ʿAbd al-Raḥmān al-Kawākibī (1848–1902) tried to find a compromise and suggested in his *Umm al-Qurā* the return of the caliphate to its originators, the Arabs. The first Arab nationalist conference, limited to Asian Arabs, was held in Paris in 1913. World War I marked the beginning of an explicitly political phase. Sharīf Ḥusayn and his sons, in collaboration with Britain and France and with the active help of T. E. Lawrence, revolted against the empire to establish a single Arab kingdom in its Arab provinces. [*See* Young Turks; Waṭan; Congresses; *and the biographies of Kawākibī and Ḥusayn.*]

Interwar Period to the Establishment of Israel. Rather than forming a unified Arab kingdom, however, the Arab provinces were divided between France and Britain according to the secret 1916 Sykes-Picot agreement. In November 1917 as well, Lord Balfour promised Palestine as a national home for the Jews. Directed against European domination (rather than as before against Muslim authority), the basic We/They dichotomy of nationalism facilitated the movement's politicization. African Arabs were still excluded (as Najib Azouri shows in *Le réveil de la nation arabe dans l'Asie turque*, Paris, 1905). Given the predominantly hereditary leadership at the time and the increasing imposition of European-type administrative divisions, Arab nationalism was locally rather than regionally oriented. Pan-Arab writings such as al-Ḥuṣrī's, with their secularist orientation and objective of a unified Arab state, compensated for this localism.

Revisionist and Mass-Oriented Movements, 1945–1967. Increasingly dominated by a new middle class (military or otherwise), this period was dense with major political events including the establishment of the Arab League in 1945, which, with its exclusive Arab membership, institutionalized the Arab/non-Arab distinction in the region. In addition, the disastrous end of the 1948 Arab-Israeli war made Palestine a core issue in inter-Arab politics and in the Arabs' relations with outside powers. Moreover, disillusioned young officers soon toppled corrupt civilian regimes (three coups in Syria alone in 1949) and came to be the region's new leaders as Gamal Abdel Nasser did after the 1952 Egyptian coup. Nasserist charisma, whether or not in alliance with the Baʿth, aimed at the establishment of a unified Arab state, nonaligned and with its own development model of Arab socialism. This "third road" policy represented a consensus among different nationalist forces, from revolutionary Algeria to opposition forces in the Gulf. [*See* Baʿth Parties *and the biography of Nasser.*]

Another, more activist conceptualization, distinct from that of Michel ʿAflāq and the Baʿth establishment, was also in the making. Its reading of unification experiences in history resulted in the distinction between secondary and primary determinants. Secondary determinants such as language and history are necessary but not sufficient, whereas primary determinants are both necessary and sufficient. The latter include a base-region or pole of attraction (e.g., Egypt), and a transnational charismatic leadership (e.g., Nasser), and an external threat (e.g., Israel and Western encroachment.). Unity between Egypt and Syria, which produced the United Arab Republic between 1958 and 1961, seemed to confirm this theory. But its dissolution and the failure of unity negotiations in 1963, which also included Baʿthī Iraq, cast doubt on the theory's immediate applicability. A protracted civil war in Yemen following Imām Badr's overthrow, with Egypt and Saudi Arabia championing opposite camps, deepened Arab divisions. Regionally, opposition intensified between radical Arab nationalism and a conservative Pan-Islamic strategy that emphasized the convening of Islamic conferences promoted by Saudi Arabia, Jordan, and Morocco. In this context, the region was shaken to its roots in 1967 by the third Arab-Israeli war. The magnitude of Arab defeat restructured regional leadership, culminating in the decline of revisionist forces and the rise of the oil-producing powers. The Khartoum Arab Summit of August 1967 sealed the withdrawal of Egyptian forces from Yemen and resulted in Egyptian dependency on oil-state subsidies.

Arab Territorial State and Militant Pan-Islam, 1968–1992. Influential leadership bases shifted from *thawrah* (revolution) to *tharwah* (wealth), from ideologists and officers to rich royalty and "wealthy merchants who flitted between East and West, between royal palaces and the offices of oil companies (examples are Kamāl Adham, Mahdī al-Tājir, and Adnan Khashoggi)." The public was more tempted by the riches of the oilfields than by the hardships of the battlefields.

Neither the 1969 coup of the young and fiery al-Qadhdhāfī nor the revolutionary but stateless Palestinians could stop the decline of the radical pole. Quantitative indicators confirm this. By 1979, 55 percent of the capital of inter-Arab economic joint ventures was contributed by oil-rich Saudi Arabia, Kuwait, the United Arab Emirates, Qatar, and Libya. The country that contributes the most capital is usually the host country for the project's headquarters; thus the oil states were becoming the locale of an increasing number of new Arab organizations. In 1970 Cairo was host to twenty-nine, or 65 percent, of these organizations, Iraq hosted none, and Saudi Arabia only one. Eight years later, Baghdad had become the locale for twelve organizations, thereby occupying the second place after Egypt. Saudi Arabia was in third place with eight organizations. In addition, fewer Arab League meetings were held in Egypt and more in the oil states. The proportion of meetings held in Cairo decreased from 70.5 percent in 1977 to 42.2 percent in 1978. Egypt's share in the Arab League budget also dropped; it was above 40 percent until the late 1950s but declined until 1978—the year the Arab League moved to Tunis—when it was only 13.7 percent, equivalent to that of Kuwait.

It might be supposed that the movement of migrant labor from densely populated Egypt or the West Bank to the Gulf, and the transfer of capital in the form of remittances and investments in the opposite direction, would promote Arab integration. Economic activities, however, are usually pragmatic and hence may serve to dampen and subordinate the revolutionary ethos, promoting stability rather than revolutionary change. Nasser's death in 1970 amid the ashes of the Jordanian-Palestinian civil war concretized the change by eliminating one of the postulated primary determinants of political unification—charismatic leadership. Egyptian rapprochement with Israel, culminating in the 1978 Camp David Accords, seemed to take away the second primary determinant, the existence of a threat. This rise of independent diplomacy concerning one of the most sacred causes of the Pan-Arab ideal confirmed—if the need existed—the primacy of *raison d'état* over *raison de la nation*. Moreover, hindsight tells us, it presaged the integration of Israel as a member of the regional system. This diluted Arab regional exclusiveness and promoted an enlarged Middle East. Ironically, the radical pole was engaged from quite a different direction in an equally diluting process when, in the Iran-Iraq war (1980–1988), Syria, Libya, and Algeria sided with non-Arab revolutionary Islamic Iran against Arab Iraq. Harassed on two fronts by territorial *raison d'état* and revolutionary Islamism, Arab nationalism was wounded but not dead. Its troubles still reflect both its own weakness as a political program and the disappearance of the simple world of heroic politics and categorical formulas.

To acquire control over a complex situation, Arabs tried subregional groupings: the Gulf Cooperation Council (GCC, including Saudi Arabia, Kuwait, Bahrain, Qatar, the United Arab Emirates, and Oman) in the early 1980s, the Union du Maghreb Arabe (Morocco, Algeria, Tunisia, Libya, Mauritania), and the Arab Cooperation Council (Egypt, Jordan, Iraq, and Yemen) in the late 1980s. This was a way of escaping the double bind of nation versus state and replacing it with a sequential logic. But this *étapiste* strategy (with the exception of the GCC) did not survive the political upheaval of the second Gulf War following Iraq's invasion of Kuwait. In its discourse Iraq appealed to the opposition of many Arabs to artificial colonial frontiers and the division of the Arab nation, and to their demand for a fairer redistribution of Arab wealth between haves and have-nots. Though tempted, many Arabs also mistrusted Saddam Hussein's cynical exploitation of Pan-Arabism and Pan-Islamism. Arabs both at the state level and in the transnational civil society were seriously divided and traumatized, with the Arab League (now back in Cairo) paralyzed and foreign troops stationed around their holy places in Saudi Arabia poised to decide the issue for them.

By invoking a *jihād* against the presence of foreign troops in the area of the Muslim holy places, Iraqi strategy was to show that Arab nationalism and revolutionary Islam could be united in their opposition to the status quo and outside powers. In fact, the two movements are overlapping rather than identical, hence their occasional mutual tension. Increased dialogue between the representatives of the two show both the potential and the difficulty of consensus on such issues as the bases of citizenship in an Arab-Islamic polity. Accumulated state, regional, and world complexities have dwarfed Arab nationalism's Ottoman legacy. Indeed, this dizzying complexity stirs nostalgia for the simplicity of Arab nationalism as the counterforce to Ottomanism of a century earlier.

[*See also* Arab League; Pan-Islam.]

BIBLIOGRAPHY

Despite the ubiquity of Arab nationalism, many essential aspects of its analysis are lacking. For instance, the debate is still unsettled about the relative importance to the rise of Arab nationalism of such external factors as the role of the European powers in weakening the Ottoman empire and such internal factors as increasing Ottoman decline, growing social change, and modernization within the Arab provinces. Concentration on the caliphate system or alternatively on the territorial state (a Kuwait, a Morocco, or an Egypt) has drawn energies away from more focused analysis of Arab nationalism.

Another characteristic of the existing literature is the scarcity of social science conceptualization. We do not know whether the rise of Arab nationalism is best explained by Karl Deutsch's social communication theory, Michael Hechter's theory of internal colonialism (e.g., by Turks over Arabs), Stein Rokkan's theory of regionalism (increasing politicization of the Arab periphery against the Turkish center), Ernest Gellner's industrialization thesis of nationalism as part of modernization and the drive for a nation-state Benedict Anderson's theory of nationalism's psychological appeal (e.g., "what makes people love and die for nations, as well as hate and kill in their name"?), or Anthony Smith's ethnic origin of nationalism thesis. We also need a classification of the mode of nationalist expression in different subregions. For instance, in the Fertile Crescent Ottoman rule was direct and centralized, but much less so in Saudi Arabia, Egypt, and Tunisia. In the last two countries opposition was mainly to European imperial authority, whether British or French.

The basic works on Arab nationalism have been dominated until now by historians. The few political scientists who have ventured into the field have dealt with Arab nationalism as part of the evolution of Arab political thought rather than applying empirical political science methods. The Centre for Arab Unity Studies in Beirut has pioneered the empirical approach by commissioning two sociological research teams. One team applied content analysis to the study of historical material of Arab ideologues to dissect the emergence, evolution, and components of Arab nationalism. The second team applied survey methods and interviews to measure the state of public opinion toward Arab nationalism and unity in at least ten Arab countries.

Literature in Arabic

What characterizes the present literature is the growing number of studies in Arabic, not limited to historical analyses. The basic studies—from the works of Sāṭiʿ al-Ḥuṣrī to various primary sources—come from the Centre of Arab Unity Studies. In addition to its monthly periodical *Al-mustaqbal al-ʿArabī* (The Arabic Future), a sample of its most notable publications follows. *Bībliyūgrāfīya al-waḥdah al-ʿArabīyah, 1908–1980* (Bibliography of Arab Unity, 1908–1980; Beirut, 1983), a two-volume, 2,300-page listing of books and articles; volume 1 concentrates on Arabic sources, and volume 2 on

English and French, each with a detailed index. *Yawmīyāt wa-wathā'iq al-waḥdah al-ʿArabīyah* (Chronology of Arab Unity; yearly); chronicles both Pan-Arab organizations and the different Arab countries. *Al-qawmīyah al-ʿArabīyah fī al-fikr wa-al-mumārasah* (Arab Nationalism: Thought and Practice; Beirut, 1980); the fifteen chapters deal with historical and social science aspects by established authorities. Includes a summary of the two projects (mentioned above) by S. Ibrahīm and S. Yasīn, using survey research and content analysis, dissecting the historical evolution of Arab nationalism and its status at the end of the 1970s. *Al-qawmīyah al-ʿArabīyah wa-al-Islām* (Arab Nationalism and Islam; Beirut, 1981) and *Al-ḥiwār al-qawmī al-dīnī* (The Nationalist-Religious Dialogue; Beirut, 1989). Thirteen scholars in the first and eight in the second (including five of the first meeting) try to achieve consensus in this open-ended discussion. The 1989 volume is much more of a dialogue, and faces up to such thorny issues as the bases of citizenship, the application of *sharīʿah* and the status of non-Muslims. The Centre is in the process of completing the publication of a multivolume collection of al-Ḥuṣrī's dispersed writings.

Western Literature

Antonius, George. *The Arab Awakening*. London, 1938. Early and detailed analysis of the origins of the movement in the Fertile Crescent. Almost a primary source.

Cleveland, William L. *The Making of an Arab Nationalist*. Princeton, 1971. Exhaustive analysis of the life, works, and ideas of al-Ḥuṣrī, considered the father of the movement.

Farah, Tawfic E., ed. *Pan-Arabism and Arab Nationalism*. Boulder, 1987. Except for a previously unpublished postscript by Fouad Ajami (pp. 192–201), the book republishes nine articles announcing, or contesting, the end of Pan-Arabism, beginning with a very useful bibliographic essay by E. Chalala (also previously unpublished).

Flory, Maurice, and Pierre-Sateh Agate, eds. *Le système régional arabe*. Paris, 1989. Based on a joint French–North African research project, authors accept Arab specificity as the basis of an identifiable regional system. A happy marriage of legal, economic, and political science approaches.

Haseeb, Khair el-Din, et al. *The Future of the Arab Nation: Challenges and Options*. London and Beirut, 1991. Synthesis of a five-year, multivolume investigation of the different scenarios of evolution of the "Arab homeland." At one point, the project involved as many as two hundred Arab scholars and assistants. A mine of data.

Kerr, Malcolm H. *The Arab Cold War*. 3d ed. London and New York, 1971. Detailed analysis of the unity negotiations between Nasserist Egypt and Baʿthist Iraq and Syria, situating the differences within the context of the 1960s.

Kerr, Malcolm H., and El Sayed Yassin, eds. *Rich and Poor States in the Middle East*. Boulder, 1982. Analysis of different facets of regional restructuring in the 1970s, based on a collaborative research project between Arabs and Americans.

Khalidi, Rashid, et al., eds. *The Origins of Arab Nationalism*. New York, 1991. The most recent and complete guide to the state of (historical) research on Arab nationalism. Its thirteen chapters include analysis of some neglected regions (e.g., Libya, Saudi Arabia).

Korany, Bahgat, et al. *The Foreign Policies of Arab States: The Challenge of Change*. 2d ed. Boulder, 1991. Since an identifiable foreign policy is the criterion of state sovereignty, the analysis concentrates on the multiplicity of state roles at the regional and international levels. While Arab states converge on some core issues in their foreign policy conceptions, they have shown diversity in foreign policy practice and concrete decisions.

Piscatori, J. P. *Islam in a World of Nation-States*. Cambridge, 1986. Faces up to a controversial issue: does Islam adapt to a multistate world? Demonstrates systematically that both Muslims' doctrinal evolution and their practice indicate that the answer is yes. *Dār al-Islām* is increasingly—and will continue to be—part of the post-Westphalian interstate system.

Porath, Yehoshua. *In Search of Arab Unity, 1930–1945*. London, 1986. Analytical history of the bases of Arab nationalism in different countries of the Mashreq, with discussion of the British role and the influence of the Palestinian problem. Devotes almost sixty pages to the establishment of the Arab League.

Salamé, Ghassan, ed. *The Foundations of the Arab States*. London, 1987. First of a four-volume international project on "Nation, State, and Integration in the Arab World." Its eight chapters show clearly the challenge represented by the existence and persistence of the territorial state in the face of Pan-Arabism, both in the recent past and at present.

Tibi, Bassam. *Arab Nationalism: A Critical Enquiry*. Edited and translated by Marion Farouk-Sluglett and Peter Sluglett. London and New York, 1981. The most thorough analysis of al-Ḥuṣrī's views, tracing their German origins.

BAHGAT KORANY

ARAB SOCIALISM. The notion of Arab socialism was never articulated precisely, but it can be taken as representing the economic and social aspirations of Nasserism and Baʿthism, the state ideologies of Egypt in the late 1950s and 1960s and of Iraq and Syria from the 1960s until the early or mid-1980s (although officially until the present time). During the years following World War II, a widespread consensus developed among the educated middle classes and among the largely unofficial opposition in each of these states to the effect that the country's most urgent needs were national independence and economic development, and that the *state* was the natural vehicle to carry out the necessary transformations. After the revolutions of the 1950s and 1960s, this notion became an important part of the political discourse of the various successor regimes.

In practice, the word *socialism* is something of a misnomer in the sense that neither a socialist revolution nor exclusive state ownership of the means of production was envisaged. The postrevolutionary economies of Egypt, Iraq, and Syria might have had some superficial similarities with the command economies of the contemporary eastern European states, but it was no accident that all three countries continued to maintain substantial and indeed often buoyant private sectors. Thus the "socialism" in Arab socialism is best understood as state-sponsored economic development.

Apart from the various land reforms of the 1950s (1952 in Egypt, 1958 in Iraq and Syria) and the nationalization of the Suez Canal in 1956, it was not until the early 1960s that the nationalization of large private and foreign-owned companies took place, and the governments of all three states began to act more determinedly to bring the various sectors of the economy under state control. More stringent land reforms were introduced, and banking, insurance, foreign trade, and large industrial enterprises were all nationalized. This took place in Iraq under ʿAbd al-Salām ʿĀrif in 1964. In spite of its socialist rhetoric, the Baʿth's only further step in this direction after 1968—admittedly a particularly crucial one—was the nationalization of the Iraq Petroleum Company and its various subsidiaries in 1972. In fact, the considerable enhancement of Iraqi state power which the oil nationalization facilitated was only the most extreme example of what would turn out to be one of the salient features of Arab socialism, namely, that the concentration of economic power in the hands of a largely unaccountable political authority facilitated the emergence of increasingly repressive and dictatorial state structures.

Alongside this economic *dirigisme* came a very considerable expansion in social, welfare, health, and educational services. Naturally, the quality of provision varied considerably both between and within states and was generally much better and more comprehensive in the larger cities than in the countryside, but, at least in theory, free education, for example, was available from primary school through university for every child. At the same time, most basic foodstuffs were either or both subsidized or made available in exchange for coupons from special government establishments, and there were also government stores selling such items as clothing, footwear, and furniture at subsidized prices.

Insofar as it had ideological underpinnings, the notion of Arab socialism was probably most clearly articulated in some of the writings of Michel ʿAflaq, one of the founders and principal ideologues of Baʿthism. It is important to stress, however, that ʿAflaq formulated his ideas in the 1950s and did not significantly modify them when Baʿth parties came to power in Syria and Iraq in the 1960s. It is also important to note that, although socialism is the third member of the Baʿthist trinity (unity, freedom, socialism), it was far less important to ʿAflaq, and the object of much less of his attention, than either (Arab) unity or (Arab) nationalism. Article 26 of the party constitution says: "The Party of the Arab Baʿth is a socialist party. It believes that the economic wealth of the fatherland belongs to the nation." Article 34 reads: "Property and inheritance are two natural rights. They are protected within the limits of national interest." The only other reference to socialism in the Baʿth Party constitution is the expression of the belief that "socialism is a necessity which emanates from the depth of Arab nationalism itself," and that it "constitutes the ideal social order which will allow the Arab people to realize its possibilities." There is no exposition of the meaning of these assertions, although it is clear from ʿAflaq's other writings, and also from the Nasserist version of Arab nationalism, that socialism is essentially non-Marxist and in fact anti-Marxist, in that it stresses the primacy of ethnic and national identity and rejects the notion of antagonistic social classes. Once the Arabs are liberated and united, it is asserted, class conflict will somehow melt away.

In general, some of the vogue enjoyed by Arab socialism and Islamic socialism probably reflected a need to incorporate some of the more unexceptionable aspects of socialist ideology (the extension of state power as an expression of the transfer of power to the people, the introduction of comprehensive social reform and welfare measures) into the nationalist and Islamic religious discourse of the time. Naturally, such a synthesis produces its own contradictions, such as the coexistence of the notion of the sanctity of private property with the notion of equality and equality of opportunity. It is clear, however, from the writings and speeches of Arab nationalists and Muslim Brothers in the 1950s that invocations of socialism were necessary for both groups to assert their progressive credentials and intentions; the aspiration for social justice, together with the sense that the state was the appropriate vehicle to spearhead social and economic development, was almost universally shared at the time. It was also the case that the Arab communists had their own much more precise and elaborate version of socialism. Arab socialism and Islamic socialism, because of their allegedly "home-grown" nature, could thus be useful weapons in blunting or deflecting the appeal of communism at the time of its greatest popularity in the Middle East, which coincided with the height of the Cold War.

[*See also* Arab Nationalism; Baʿth Parties; Nasserism; *and* Socialism and Islam.]

BIBLIOGRAPHY

Baker, Raymond William. *Egypt's Uncertain Revolution under Nasser and Sadat.* Cambridge, Mass., 1978. Interesting analysis of the balance of continuity and change in Egypt between 1952 and the mid-1970s.

Batatu, Hanna. *The Old Social Classes and the Revolutionary Movements of Iraq: A Study of Iraq's Old Landed and Commercial Classes and of Its Communists, Baʿthists, and Free Officers.* Princeton, 1978.

Beinin, Joel. "Labour, Capital, and the State in Nasserist Egypt, 1952–1961." *International Journal of Middle East Studies* 21.1 (February 1989): 71–90.

Carré, Olivier. "Le mouvement idéologique baʿthiste." In *La Syrie d'aujourd'hui,* edited by André Raymond, pp. 185–224. Paris, 1980. Subtle and considered analysis of Baʿthism, with particular reference to its development in Syria.

Farouk-Sluglett, Marion. "Socialist' Iraq, 1963–1978: Towards a Reappraisal." *Orient* 23.2 (1982): 206–219.

Farouk-Sluglett, Marion, and Peter Sluglett. "The Iraqi Baʿth Party." In *Political Parties in the Third World,* edited by Vicky Randall, pp. 57–74. London, 1988.

Haim, Sylvia G., ed. *Arab Nationalism: An Anthology.* Berkeley, 1962. Contains useful extracts from the writings and speeches of ʿAflaq and Nasser.

Hinnebusch, Raymond A. "Syria under the Baʿth: State Formation in a Fragmented Society." *Arab Studies Quarterly* 4.3 (Summer 1982): 177–199.

Sayegh, Faiz. "The Theoretical Structure of Nasser's Socialism." In *St. Anthony's Papers,* no. 17, *Middle Eastern Affairs,* no. 4, edited by Albert Hourani, pp. 9–55. London, 1965.

PETER SLUGLETT

ARCHITECTURE. [*To survey the architectural forms characteristic of Islamic societies, this entry comprises two articles. The first presents an overview of the development of traditional forms of building with attention to regional styles; the second assesses contemporary architecture in various parts of the modern Islamic world. For related discussions, see* Gardens and Landscaping; Urban Planning.]

Traditional Forms

Traditional forms provide images of the past: they enable a group to envision its origins, and they display its descent. The preservation of some forms and the alteration or obliteration of others are part of the ongoing fabrication, transformation, and maintenance of national, regional, and ethnic identities. The selection of past architectural forms creates a visually complex historical layering of shapes, materials, forms, and functions. "Traditional" is thus a relational term, from a given present moment to a directed understanding of the past.

Now as in the past, governments are often the most active social force in deciding what forms are to be identified as traditional. What is built and where, which buildings are preserved and which are incorporated into the urban fabric, and the aesthetic judgments affecting the quality and use of materials, have all been the prerogative of rulers. Each ruling group makes such decisions about the architectural forms of the previous period in its turn. Forms preserved in this manner over time can serve as emblems of identity, and fabricating national, regional, or ethnic identities in the contemporary world often requires different means depending on the audience being addressed.

Traditional Forms and International Audiences. The idea of emblematizing a nation's visual history in an amalgam of traditional forms addressed specifically to an international audience is best understood through the architecture of World's Fairs. Beginning in the second half of the nineteenth century, these encapsulations of a nation's traditional forms have revealed how such forms represent a nation, as well as how the actual buildings function in the society. In the case of the Moroccan Exhibition recently built at Epcot Center in Orlando (figure 1), the entire ensemble might be understood as an amalgam of forms emblematic of larger constructions, bringing together historically significant elements associated with Morocco and its history. Chosen by the Moroccan government, this ensemble of traditional forms flanks a courtyard on two sides. The entrance to the courtyard (left, figure 1) is a lobed arch portal similar to ones in Tlemcen and Rabat that date to the twelfth-century Almohad period. The next structure, which begins the second side of the courtyard, is a replica of the minaret of the Kutubīyah Mosque in Marrakesh, dating to the same dynasty. Detailing is precise on the replica: lambrequin, lobate, and interlaced arches frame the windows as on the minaret in Marrakesh. Juxtaposed is a pavilion similar to that in the courtyard in the Qarawīyīn mosque in Fez, from the sixteenth-century Saʿdian dynasty. The structure on the far right is a Berber house similar to those built in villages and towns until the twentieth century.

This amalgam of traditional forms presents a visual story that links the buildings, the cities from which they come, and the dynasties that supported them with the modern nation of Morocco. Forming a facade framing a courtyard, these traditional forms are assembled in a spatial relationship not found in Morocco itself: urban forms built by ruling dynasties are combined with domestic housing from towns and villages; interior forms,

FIGURE 1. *Moroccan Exhibition, Epcot Center.* Florida, U.S.A. (©The Walt Disney Company).

such as the pavilion, are combined with exterior ones such as the minaret. In what sense is this amalgam an effective complex symbol of the ongoing architectural tradition of Morocco?

The Epcot forms are effective because they are parts which stand for whole structures. The pavilion, a structural feature of the courtyard inside some of the most famous mosques and *madrasah*s in Fez, represents the whole mosque and *madrasah* and symbolizes the important role of these structures in housing major centers of Islamic learning in both medieval and modern times. The minaret, in indexing a mosque, reminds the viewer of the call to prayer as fundamental to the practice of Islam in Morocco, a Muslim country.

The styles of the portal, minaret, and pavilion in Orlando are evocative of periods in the past when Marrakesh and Fez were the center of rule in the western Mediterranean. The forms also make visual reference to similar forms outside Morocco, in particular on the Iberian peninsula, recalling a time when Islam flourished there. The minaret from Marrakesh, and what is now known as the Giralda tower (the bell tower of the cathedral in Seville) were built by rulers of the same dynasty and bear unmistakable formal similarities. The pavilion also relates to the porticos in the palaces of the Alhambra in Granada.

These forms function well as an emblem of Moroccan architectural tradition because they indicate the essential relationship of the material and manner of production to the form itself, and to its categorization as traditional in Moroccan terms. The relationship of material to form is most obvious: the Kutubīyah minaret in Marrakesh and the replica in Orlando are made of stone of similar size; green tile roofing, multicolored tile mosaics, and stucco patterning, which are characteristic of the premodern *madrasah*s and mosques of Fez, were used in the pavilion and the room behind it. Less obvious is the association of traditional methods and tools for stucco-carving and achieving tile patterns with the production of the final form. In this case, Moroccan artisans skilled in earlier methods of production were brought in to make the stucco and tile patterns. Patterns and forms achieved by other processes, or of similar design but executed in different materials, would not be perceived as traditional. In these instances, the process, the material, and the form are inextricably linked. The amalgam of forms in Orlando serves as an icon of Moroccan traditional architecture; it acts like a travel poster intended for an external audience, combining in a single image items gathered from various places.

Traditional Forms and Internal Audiences. Within Morocco, the buildings to which these forms relate function in their own settings as historical layers in complex urban fabrics. Although the Kutubīyah mosque itself is not well preserved, its frequently restored minaret serves as a memorial of earlier times. The minaret also links the city of Marrakesh with Rabat, where the tower of the twelfth-century Ḥasan mosque is similar in style. Also built by the Almohads, the *ḥaram* (sanctuary) of the Ḥasan mosque was never completed, but its size—one of the largest in the Muslim world when it was under construction—makes it a powerful visual presence in the city. This mosque and minaret were linked to the present in 1973 when the mausoleum of King Muḥammad V was built adjacent to it. Likewise, the medieval *madrasahs* still function in the cities of Morocco. Some of the structural conventions associated with them, such as roofing tiles and the carved stucco and tile mosaic that richly pattern their walls, have served as models for newer, nineteenth- and twentieth-century buildings in the same cities. The forms in Morocco are not simply facades acting as icons of national traditions; they relate to the interior spaces with which and within which people interact.

In the process of creating traditional forms addressed primarily to an internal audience, publicly visible architectural elements are appropriated and assigned new meanings or connotations. Recreated old forms are used to establish visual relationships with the past, linking newer structures and areas with older ones and transforming the identities of others. Possibly because so many are extant—in Cairo, for example—the most consistent and visually prominent sources for the appropriation of old forms have been the buildings of the Mamlūk period (1250–1517), in particular the *madrasah* complex of Sultan Ḥasan (figure 2). Finished in 1363, the *madrasah*-mosque-mausoleum complex in its time was the most prominent large-scale project in the city. Built on a highly visible site at the foot of the citadel where the government resided and on the road to the Qarāfah cemetery, outstanding in design, workmanship, and quality of materials, the complex of Sultan Ḥasan has been the building to be emulated for 450 years.

In 1568, fifty years after Egypt became an Ottoman province, Mahmud Paşa built a new complex, appropriating significant elements of the form as well as the function of the Sultan Ḥasan complex (figure 3). Mahmud Paşa built his mosque-mausoleum complex on the hill rising toward the citadel, somewhat northeast of the earlier complex. It had the same silhouette as that of Sultan Ḥasan, although substantially smaller in scale and supporting fewer functions; anyone walking in the area of the citadel could not fail to notice the resonance of forms. The later building continued the form of the earlier one, placing the mausoleum behind the *miḥrāb* wall. Yet in altering one significant element, it signaled the transformation of rule. To a viewer descending from the citadel, the difference in scale between the two buildings allows the later building to superimpose itself visually on the earlier one. The Ottoman-style minaret on Mahmud Paşa's complex, a slender shaft with a conical top, different from the Mamluk minaret with triple balconies and bulbous top, was a significant formal modification and signaled the change in dynastic rule and visually linked the newer complex with the ruling tradition outside Egypt.

More than 350 years later, the complex of Sultan Ḥasan again served as the source for a new structure. Completed in 1915, the Rifāʿī mosque-mausoleum, across the street from that of Sultan Ḥasan, echoed many of its external structural aspects, including the shape of the minarets (figure 2). Much of the ornamental detailing on the newest structure was taken from various Mamlūk structures throughout the city, visually linking the area with its Mamlūk past. Even many of the functions of the original building were maintained; in addition to provide a place for daily prayer, it was also intended as a mausoleum for members of the royal family.

Domes. Architectural elements, such as domes and minarets, are appropriated and assigned new meanings and connotations more frequently than entire buildings. In Cairo in the twentieth century, a neo-Mamlūk dome has become a visual emblem of an Egyptian national style in Islamic congregational structures. Recognizable by its distinctive silhouette marked by a high drum, pointed dome, and patterned surface, this architectural element consciously links new constructions with those of the past. In contemporary Cairene use, silhouette and surface pattern rather than materiality refer to the Mamlūk past: Mamlūk domes were mainly stone while many late twentieth-century neo-Mamlūk domes are reinforced concrete (figure 3). From the exterior the new domes resonate with Mamlūk domes across the wide expanse of the city, linking areas of new urban growth with those of the past. New meanings and uses, however, have been assigned to these traditional forms. Mamlūk domes covered mausoleum spaces, serving as memorial markers; the new domes cover mosques and signal spaces of communal prayer. As a Cairene emblem, the shape of the neo-Mamlūk dome has been adopted by many Muslim communities in the United States and throughout the world, reminding people

FIGURE 2. *Complex of Sultan Ḥasan, the Rifāʿī Mosque, and Complex of Mahmud Paşa in the Foreground.* Cairo, Egypt.

FIGURE 3. *Complex of Mahmud Paşa and Sultan Ḥasan.* Cairo, Egypt.

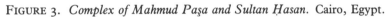

FIGURE 4. *Gur-i Mir*. Samarkand, Uzbekistan, sixteenth century.

of Cairo's role as a major center of Islamic learning.

The profile of the Timurid domes of Samarkand (1370–1506) has also served later groups in the fabrication of their dynastic and regional identities (figure 4). Its distinctive shape, a bulbous pointed dome surmounting a high drum narrower than the dome in circumference, became emblematic of the splendor of Timurid Samarkand. Its brick and glazed tile surfaces and the plain color juxtaposed with writing in high-contrast colors functioned to heighten the visual impact of the domes. The splendors of the buildings, the height of the domes, and their visibility from afar all contributed to the renown of the city and its rulers. They were an especially powerful reminder to subsequent rulers in adjacent lands of the efficacy of architecture in memorializing the name of Timur and his dynastic successors.

Two centuries later, the dome of the Taj Mahal (figure 5), with its profile reminiscent of Timurid forms, was an intentional visual link from Agra to Samarkand and the dynasty from whom the Mughals claimed descent. The silhouette of the Taj Mahal's dome was a sharp contrast to the domes of structures sponsored by previous Muslim rulers in that area.

The Timurids built structures throughout their empire in cities such as Herat and Mashhad, and thus their characteristic dome was spread farther west. The silhouette, with modified proportions, was maintained by the victorious Ṣafavid rulers (1501–1732), most noticeably in the Masjid-i Shāh in Isfahan, completed in 1637 (figure 6). In this dome both the form and materiality of the earlier domes were maintained; what is noticeably different is the pattern and balance of color of the dome's glazed tile skin.

In the late twentieth century, all these domes and the structures they surmount represent national or ethnic identities—Uzbekistan, India, and Iran. These forms have become part of the articulation of the collective memory of each nation. In Uzbekistan, they refer to the Turkic past; in India, the Taj Mahal represents not only a time and place when Muslims ruled, but also the romantic legends that Europeans attached to the structure, ensuring its place in international memory. Identifying these forms as traditional and imbuing them with new meaning is an active, ongoing social process.

Minarets. One of the most ubiquitous symbols of Islam throughout the world is the minaret—although in some places, such as Djenne and Namou, minarets are not a consistent feature of Friday mosques (i.e., mosques in which Friday prayers are conducted). Over time, the specific shape and profile of the minaret has come to indicate different dynasties and different regional practices. In historically complex areas, different styles of minarets represent the sequential history of a place. The tall, square tower with ornamental arches and latticework indexes the presence of Almohad rule in the twelfth century in both the western Maghrib and the

Iberian peninsula (see figure 1). The external spiraled minaret on Aḥmad ibn Ṭūlūn's mosque linked that structure with the extraordinary spiraled towers the ʿAbbāsid caliphs built in Samarra in the ninth century. The most ubiquitous basic form, a tapering, rounded shaft, is found throughout Turkey, Iraq, Iran, Afghanistan, India, Pakistan, and Uzbekistan. Ruling dynasties modified the proportions of this basic form, varied its number of balconies and their placement, and its materiality and surface ornamentation. The minarets of Ṣafavid Isfahan are similar yet recognizably different from those of Mughal Agra (see figures 5 and 6).

The minaret is more than a clear index of Islam; its shape can be a powerful symbol of political domination. Ottoman building practices offer a rich view of the complex issues raised by the concept of traditional forms. In the fourteenth and fifteenth centuries the Ottomans developed a distinctive style of minaret, a tall, tapering tower with a conical top. Usually two, but as many as six, minarets associated with a mosque indicated the Sultan's patronage and construction of the mosque. As the empire expanded into areas that were predominantly Christian, as well as into areas ruled by other Muslim groups, the distinctive Ottoman minaret on the skyline of a city indicated the presence of Ottoman rule.

When Ottoman governors or the sultan himself sponsored mosque-building, the style of the mosque as well as of the minaret was often similar to those in the capital cities. Thus Ottoman-style mosques and minarets were built in Mostar, Acre, and Tunis. That the form of the minaret was sufficient to symbolize Ottoman power is indicated by other practices. In some cities, such as Cairo, where the mosque the Ottoman governor sponsored was local in form, the Ottoman-style minaret was a clear signal of Ottoman patronage. In Damascus, the Ottomans added the distinctive top portion of the minaret (the shaft and conical top) to the square Umayyad-period base of the Great Mosque. In still other cities where the populations were predominantly Christian—Athens, Heraklion, and Thessaloniki—the Ottoman-style minaret also signaled the conversion of a church into a mosque (figure 7).

In the nineteenth and twentieth centuries, as the lands once part of the Ottoman empire became individual nations and began to articulate their own collective social memory, the presence of the Ottoman minaret was handled in varying ways. It was sometimes obliterated, but elsewhere preserved and inscribed in the new national tradition. In almost all places, including Istanbul itself, the use of the traditional Ottoman minaret has changed over the past century.

This variation is apparent in Greece. In Thessaloniki (figure 7) the highly visible Ottoman minaret was preserved on the rotunda, a state church dating to the late

FIGURE 5. *Taj Mahal.* Agra, India, completed c.1645.

FIGURE 6. *Masjid-i Shāh.* Isfahan, Iran, completed 1637.

Roman period and made a mosque by the Ottomans, who added the extremely tall minaret. At the end of the twentieth century, as a museum of the history of the city, this structure encapsulates its long and varied history. In Athens and Heraklion, by contrast, the Ottoman minarets were removed from both converted churches and structures originally built as mosques.

In Damascus, the minarets of the Friday mosque indicate the succession of rule. Ayyubid and Mamlūk as well as Ottoman portions of minarets were maintained on the mosque and are visible on the skyline today. In Cairo, in the late nineteenth and early twentieth centuries, Ottoman minarets were removed from many highly visible mosques, such as al-Azhar and Ṣālīḥ al-Talā'ī. Built by the Fāṭimid dynasty (969–1171), neither of these mosques has Fāṭimid-period minarets; only Mamlūk-style minarets are attached to al-Azhar, and no minaret was replaced on Ṣāliḥ al-Talā'ī. Ottoman-style minarets were, however, retained on buildings constructed by the Ottomans. The national styles of the twentieth century in both Syria and Egypt rely heavily on the traditions of Mamlūk forms, and in Syria the traditions also include Ayyubid forms.

Mosque Form. Anywhere in the world in the twentieth century, the Friday mosque with a minaret indicates the presence of a Muslim community. It is the institution that supports Muslim life in all its aspects, from communal worship to education for children and adults. Most Friday mosques have until recently been built following one of three general models. Historically, these forms appeared at specific times and places, but all three, or a combination of their elements, are contemporary today. Each type combines covered and open spaces. In the early Islamic centuries, most Friday mosques were large enclosed areas that combined a flat-roofed, hypostyle sanctuary (*ḥaram*) with an unroofed courtyard (*sahn*). Friday mosques of this type were found from the Iberian peninsula to Central Asia. In approximately the eleventh century, an *īwān*-style mosque was built combining vaulted *īwāns* (galleries) on two, three, or four sides of a central courtyard, usually unroofed. Friday mosques of this type are found from Egypt and Turkey eastward to India and Pakistan. The third type, a domed central prayer space with a courtyard, developed later still and is usually associated with Ottoman practice; it is found from the Balkans to Saudia Arabia and Algeria. Mosque forms in other areas, such as in China and Mali, were more localized, differing from city to city.

In the later part of the twentieth century, Friday mosques throughout the world, from New York to Jakarta and London to Sydney, have been built that combine mosque forms from before the eighteenth century with purely contemporary elements. In alluding to traditional forms, the builders of these mosques look to the local area as well as to mosque-building traditions elsewhere in the world. The Friday mosque commissioned by the Muslim community in Vosoko, Bosnia, and completed in 1980 is an example: thoroughly modern in its reinforced concrete construction, outward appearance, and many aspects of the inside space, its quiet interior, ambient lighting, and the form and presence of the writing flanking the *miḥrāb* and on the side wall, are all related to mosques in that area built before 1700.

In Europe, in North and South America, and in countries of the Pacific Rim, the question of the form of the mosque and minaret is especially complex. No local traditions for mosque-building exist. For these new communities where Islam is an emerging religion, the Friday mosque is more than a congregational center of the community. The mosque and minaret present Islam in a visual and social context where other religious traditions and their associated building practices predominate. In these instances, the bases for selecting

FIGURE 7. *View of the Rotunda with Ottoman Minaret.* Thessaloniki, Greece.

appropriate traditional forms rest on questions of identification and linkage. They involve a range of considerations, including identification with a particular Muslim community in another country, with a particular tradition of Islamic learning and the forms associated with it, or with the wishes of the patron. In some instances, the choice is to link the new structure visually with a selection of traditional forms from a broad range of mosque-building traditions. Modern Egyptian mosque design has served as an inspiration for the design of mosques in Seattle, Los Angeles, and Chicago, in recognition of the role of that city as an Islamic learning center. The new Friday mosque complex in Rome combines elements from several traditions of the Mediterranean, particularly the Umayyad mosque of tenth-century Cordoba and the sixteenth-century Ottoman mosques in Istanbul. In these new structures old forms are not replicated as they were in the Moroccan exhibition, but rather translated and expressed in new materials in ways that allude to but do not copy the earlier forms.

Although most Muslim communities in these new lands have looked to the urban building traditions of Muslim dynasties of the past, the Dar al-Islam complex in Abiquiu, New Mexico, was built with a different tradition as a model. Adobe connects this new project with nonurban building practices throughout the Muslim world, particularly the Nubian, and with the local pueblo-building tradition. Two Nubian masons were brought to work with local architects and craftsmen in the construction of the large complex, which includes a mosque, school, dormitories, housing for families, and a clinic. The domes in this complex are built without wooden roof timbers, concrete, or steel. The community operates a school for maintaining these building traditions.

Tombstones, Screens, Mausolea, and Cenotaphs. Some *ḥadīth*s and the writings of many Islamic jurists disapprove of marking graves. Nevertheless, throughout the history and world of Islam, graves have been marked in various ways. Simple tombstones are known as early as the mid-seventh century in Egypt. Later, in Ottoman areas, more elaborate tombstones marked the graves of members of the ruling group; these had sculptural tops in the form of the headdress of the deceased, indicating his rank in the ruling society.

Screens were put around burial sites beginning in the first century after the Hijrah. In the first decade of the eighth century CE, an irregular masonry screen was put around the Prophet's tomb in Medina by order of Umayyad Caliph al-Walīd. Subsequently, putting a screen around a gravesite became a widely paracticed tradition. Screens vary in material and design; for example, the screen in the late thirteenth-century tomb of Mamlūk Sultan Qalā'ūn is a wooden *mashrabīyah.* In the twentieth century screens are often made of elaborately worked metal, such as that used in the restoration of the tomb of Sayyidah Nafīsah in Cairo. Screens keep people away from the cenotaph except at specific times. In some places supplicants leave remembrances on these screens, tying strips of cloth or fastening locks of hair on them. Screens are also used around commemorative areas that are not burial sites, for example in the Dome of the Rock. Early records indicate that wooden beams supported drapery that served as a screen around the rock in the center of that commemorative structure.

Mausolea are the most elaborate form of grave marking. These enclosed structures are usually built to commemorate people of special status or holiness, such as members of the Prophet's family, great religious scholars, saints, or members of a ruling group. Mausolea have been built as parts of larger complexes, where the mauseoleum is combined with other institutions such as mosques, *khānqāh*s, hospitals, or *madrasah*s. In the complexes of Sultan Ḥasan and Mahmud Paşa, the mausoleum is under the dome on the side of the complex facing Mecca, as the deceased is placed in the grave on his side facing Mecca. The elaborate complex of Sultan Ḥasan also includes a mosque and a large *madrasah* housing scholars of the four Sunnī schools of law. That of Mahmud Paşa combines a mosque with the mausoleum. Such associations continue into the late twentieth century. Thus the mausoleum of King Muḥammad V of Morocco was built adjacent to the twelfth-century Almohad Ḥasan mosque in Rabat; this new mausoleum was itself a complex including a museum and a new mosque.

Mausolea equally often stand alone. Tomb towers in Khurasan dating to the twelfth century seemed to attest to a practice of building mausolea to punctuate the landscape, standing in relative isolation. Most often, however, mausolea are found in cemeteries outside a city, whereas the mausolea complexes are often within the city. Notable exceptions to this generalization exist. Ottoman sultans and their families were usually buried in mausolea on the grounds of the mosque, as the faithful are today in parts of Indonesia. In the Mamlūk period, mausolea complexes with *khanqah*s and mosques were built in the northern cemetery outside Cairo. In the countryside, single mausolea as well as mausolea complexes commemorating revered teachers are often found along well-traveled roads and bring people to the site for prayer or study.

Materials and shape vary by region and level of patronage. In cities, stone and marble as well as other expensive and permanent materials are used in construction. The complexes of Sultan Ḥasan and Mahmud Paşa (figure 3) as well as the Taj Mahal (figure 5) are notable examples. These are complexes for rulers, but equally elaborate and permanent complexes exist at shrines for members of the Prophet's family, such as those at Mashhad, Qom, and Karbala. In the countryside, mausolea for revered teachers are often built of mud brick and adobe, materials which require regular renewal. The fact that many have existed for centuries is testimony to the constant reverence of the believers.

Mausolea also vary in shape. In Cairo, for instance, regardless of how elaborate the complex, the mausoleum chamber was usually square. In Ottoman practice the chamber was round or octagonal. The mausoleum of the Il-khanid Mongol ruler Öljeitü (r. 1304–1316) in Sultaniya and the Taj Mahal are more elaborate structures with side chambers off a central room. Regardless of materials, shape, and scale, most mausolea have been domed.

The shape of the dome was characteristic of its time and place. In general, high-profile domes in varying silhouettes and materials topping a drum of narrower circumference than the base of the dome are common from Iraq eastward. More rounded domes on drums of approximately equal circumference are found in more western regions. In both areas, conical domes appear in Khurasan in the twelfth century, in Anatolia in the thirteenth, and in Morocco in the twentieth.

Found throughout the Muslim world, cenotaphs have a similar boxlike shape. Some also have head and/or foot stones. They vary widely in material: the cenotaph of Imām Shāfiʿī (1178) in Cairo is wood, that of the Tughluq governor Zakī al-Dīn ʿUmar (1333) in Cambay is stone, and that of Mehmet I (1421) in Bursa is glazed tile. Often Qur'ānic verses are displayed on the cenotaph, as well as the name of the deceased. While cenotaphs are usually placed in the center of mausolea under the dome, the burial vault in the ground, below the floor of the mausoleum, is not necessarily centered under the cenotaph itself.

Ḥammāms. Before the late twentieth century, when water-delivery systems to individual houses rendered them obsolete, *ḥammām*s or baths were located near congregational mosques to serve the requirement of bathing for ritual purity before the Friday prayer. The technology of steambaths made the *ḥammām* form, particularly the steam room, recognizable throughout the Muslim world. Steam, generated by heating water, flowed through double, pierced walls into a steam room. Usually smaller than the other rooms of the bath, these rooms were roofed by a round dome which encouraged the circulation of the hot, moist air. Domes were punctuated with glass inserts enabling daylight to enter the room. These functional glass inserts were often made decorative by their shape, color, and pattern of placement. From the outside, it is the glass inserts of the dome that immediately distinguish the *ḥammām* from other domed structures. In addition to the steam room, changing rooms and hot and tepid water rooms are provided. Towels are often dried on the roofs of these buildings that, aside from the dome, are usually flat.

Public *ḥammāms* were usually supported by the patron of the mosque or by the local governor. Fuel was costly, and the fire necessary to provide continuous steam often served the double purpose of cooking food for distribution to the poor.

Unless two separate structures were provided, as they were near the Sultan Ahmet mosque in Istanbul, men and women used the *ḥammām* at different times. In some places flags of differing color were flown outside the *ḥammām* to indicate whether men or women could use the bath; in other places specific days of the week were set aside for each gender.

Khans, Caravanserais, and Marketplaces. These traditional forms were part of the trade network and were located in major cities, and between them on the major trade routes. They have modern counterparts in airport terminals, warehouses, and shopping malls, which maintain some of their functions if not forms. Referred to by different terms in different areas, khans and caravanserais mainly served to store goods and to provide temporary housing for traveling merchants. For this reason most khans and caravanserais were double storied, with animals stabled on the ground floor. These structures also served to safeguard the merchants, their goods, and their animals, and for this reason they were built around a central courtyard, usually with one main entrance. Especially when these structures were situated between cities, but often within the city, a prayer space and small *ḥammām* were part of the structure.

Covered marketplaces with formal entrances that can be closed and locked are a traditional form throughout most of the Islamic world. Most of these markets consisted of shops selling expensive goods, such as silver, gold, silks, and jewels. The market was closed at night. In Cairo, however, owners and workmen lived in the marketplace, behind and above the shops. Near such marketplaces the great warehouses were located. Today, in many cities such as Isfahan, Cairo, Edirne, or Bursa, some of these traditional buildings have been preserved and incorporated into the modern marketplace. The form of the medieval and premodern two-storied warehouses served a function that has been taken over by other forms and by machinery; these structures, with rare exceptions, are disappearing.

Domestic Space. The dynastic building traditions for communal structures that serve the Muslim population are richly varied, but domestic architecture is even more richly textured, varying by region, time, and communal group. Regardless of the specific shape, scale, and materials, the space within all these structures throughout the Islamic world was used similarly. The use if not the form of the space separated public from private—that is, the communal, male activities from those of the family. In great houses there were separate rooms to serve these functions, and separate entrances for males and famales. In less elaborate dwellings, hanging curtains served to distinguish different social spaces. The space designated as private was for women and children and close male relatives, as well as female visitors. The public or communal areas were for men and their male visitors. The area immediately outside the covered dwelling often served as part of the social space of the house.

The tradition of separating these spheres of life did not preclude using the same room or outdoor place at different times for different social activities. For example, a courtyard or area immediately outside a door could be family space in the morning, and communal or male space in the afternoon or evening. In the late twentieth century, while some of these social practices have been modified, many remain in place.

[*See also* Gardens and Landscaping; Houses; *and* Mosque, *article on* Mosque Architecture.]

BIBLIOGRAPHY

Abu-Lughod, Janet. *Cairo: 1001 Years of the City Victorious.* Princeton, 1971. A concise history of a city.

Anderson, Benedict R. *Imagined Communities: Reflections on the Origin and Spread of Nationalism.* London and New York, 1991. A thoughtful introduction to the concept of identity as fostered by nationalism. It raised issues particularly relevant to the concept of a traditional past.

Architecture as Symbol and Self-Identity. Aga Khan Awards, 1980. The publication of the proceedings of Seminar Four of the Aga Khan Award for Architecture, the essays deal specifically with the question of identity and the symbolism of form. The articles by Mahdi and Grabar in this slim volume are included in the volume edited by Holod (see below).

Asher, Catherine B. *Architecture of Mughal India.* The New Cambridge History of India, vol. 1, pt. 4. Cambridge, 1992. Excellent introduction to the architecture of India with a full and useful bibliography.

Bierman, Irene A., Rifaʿat A. Abou-El-Hah, and Donald Preziosi, eds. *The Ottoman City and its Parts*. New York, 1991. A wide-ranging analysis of Ottoman cities taken as a whole, and examined in part.

Çelik, Zeynap. *Displaying the Orient*. Berkeley, 1992. An excellent fulsomely illustrated study of the architecture of Islam in nineteenth century World Fairs.

Golombek, Lisa and Donald Wilber. *The Timurid Architecture of Iran and Turan*. Princeton, 1988. With contributions by several authors this two-volume work is a compendium of Timurid practice.

Goodwin, Godfrey. *A History of Ottoman Architecture*. London, 1971. A fulsome survey of Ottoman architecture, mainly in the cities of Turkey. Ottoman architecture elsewhere is not included.

Grabar, Oleg. *The Formation of Islamic Art*. New Haven and London, 1973. An excellent study of the making of a tradition or category called Islamic.

Hoag, John. *Islamic Architecture*. New York, 1975. A useful general introduction to the major monuments of Islamic architecture from the eastern Mediterranean to India. No color reproductions.

Holod, Renata, and Darl Rastorfer, eds. *Architecture and Community Building in the Islamic World Today*. New York, 1983. A collection of essays related to the series of seminars on Islamic architecture sponsored by the Aga Khan Award for Architecture. It catalogs the first Aga Khan Awards as well as reissuing some essays published in the Proceedings of the Seminars for the Aga Khan Award. It is an excellent introduction to the issues involved with the concepts of traditional Islamic forms.

Iranian Studies 7.1–2 (1974). Studies on Isfahan. Proceedings of a colloquium on Isfahan, the articles offer a wide ranging study of this city.

Michell, George, ed. *Architecture of the Islamic World*. New York, 1978. An excellent introduction to a broad range of types of architecture, from palaces and citadels and houses. Most useful is small compendium with plates of key monuments of Islamic architecture. Monuments from the western Mediterranean to the Far East are included.

Mimar; Architecture in Development. This journal focuses on contemporary architecture in Islamic lands. It has a glossy format, with ample color illustrations. It highlights new designs and contemporary architects, as well as vernacular traditions. The articles are aimed at a general audience. The lack of footnoting is made up for by the inclusion of images of little known areas.

Mitchell, Timothy. *Colonizing Egypt*. Cambridge and New York, 1988. A thoroughgoing analysis of the effects of an international audience on a communal identity.

Rogers, Michael. *The Spread of Islam*. Oxford, 1976. A useful thematic introduction to Islamic architecture. Good photographs and broad coverage.

IRENE A. BIERMAN

Contemporary Forms

Any study of the evolution of nineteenth- and twentieth-century architecture in the Islamic world should consider a number of factors. The varied regions of the Islamic world have produced a wide variety of architectural traditions, and these traditions cannot be treated as a monolithic architectural heritage. Furthermore, the amount of published information available for recent architecture in the Islamic world remains relatively limited. Although the development of architecture during the modern period in some Muslim regions, such as Turkey, is well documented, information about other areas—for example, the newly formed countries of Central Asia—is only now becoming accessible. Finally, although the architecture of areas in North Africa, Egypt, Turkey, the Indian subcontinent, and Indonesia has shown effects of contact with the West since the first half of the nineteenth century, parts of the Arabian Peninsula, for example, remained immune to these until the mid-twentieth century.

A number of common themes have nonetheless characterized the development of modern architecture throughout the Islamic world. These themes are strongly connected to the processes of interaction with (and in some cases, reactions to) Western approaches toward architecture during the past two centuries. As a result of these processes, the continuity of the autonomous premodern architectural traditions of the Islamic world ended, and its architectural production started referring to Western models.

Studying the Architectural Heritage of the Islamic World. An important development in the modern period has been the invention of the idea of "Islamic architecture." It was Westerners who began studying the architectural heritage of various Muslim regions. A few rudimentary attempts at providing some information about the Islamic architectural heritage had appeared as early as the first half of the eighteenth century. Thus a general history of architecture by the Viennese architect Johann Bernhard Fischer von Erlach, published in 1721, identifies Arab, Turkish, and Persian architecture, and discusses buildings from Istanbul, Mecca, Medina, and Isfahan. The British artists William Hodges, Thomas Daniell, and his nephew William published drawings of works of architecture from the Indian subcontinent during the second half of the eighteenth century.

One of the earliest systematic attempts to study the architecture of a Muslim region is found in the *Description de l'Égypte*, compiled by the French scholars who accompanied Napoleon during his expedition to Egypt (1798–1801), and published between 1809 and 1823. Part of this multivolume work deals with Islamic Egypt and addresses, among other things, its architectural heritage. It contains perspectives and measured plans, elevations, and sections of some important Egyptian Muslim monuments.

A significant number of works dealing with the Muslim architectural heritage appeared during the first half of the nineteenth century, a number of them treating the architecture of Islamic Spain. These include James Cavannah Murphy's *Arabian Antiquities of Spain* (1813) and *Plans, Elevations, Sections, and Details of the Alhambra,* which Jules Goury and Owen Jones published in the 1840s. The French architect M. A. Delannoy published a book on the architecture of Algiers (*Études artistique sur la régence d'Alger*) during the 1830s. Another French architect, Pascal Coste, published works on the Islamic architecture of Cairo (*Architecture arabe ou monuments du Kaire,* 1818–1825) and of Iran (*Monuments modernes de la Perse,* 1851–1867). Many of these works contain numerous inaccuracies, and their authors, who were primarily architects, lacked adequate knowledge of the languages and history of the regions they were studying. Still, by the middle of the nineteenth century, a relatively comprehensive set of publications addressing the architectural heritage of a number of Muslim regions had come into being.

By the end of the nineteenth century, authors with a better command of the languages and history of the Islamic world began to study its architectural heritage. At the same time, the various Muslim architectural traditions, originally categorized according to their geographic locations, began to be grouped under the headings of "Islamic" or "Muhammadan" architecture, as evident in Julius Franz's *Die Baukunst des Islam* (1896), Henri Saladin's 1907 volume on architecture in the *Manuel d'art musulman,* and G. T. Rivoira's *Muslim Architecture* (1919).

Until very recently, the Islamic world did not participate in studying and defining its architectural heritage; it only provided the monuments that were studied. Scholars and architects from the Islamic world have begun to participate effectively in studying their own architectural traditions only during the past few decades. Even now, most scholarship in the field of Islamic architecture is carried out in Western institutions and by Western scholars.

Publications such as those mentioned above have defined the Muslim architectural heritage in both the West and the Islamic world. They have also provided architects from the Islamic world with more detailed information about their architectural heritage and introduced them to the architecture of other Muslim regions.

Growth of the Architectural Profession. Another important development in the modern period has been the gradual replacement of traditional master builders by professional architects, that is, those with some formal education in architecture. Although professional architects working in the Islamic world were originally from the West, they were eventually joined or replaced by local architects. Schools of architecture and university departments developed in the various countries, as did professional associations and journals devoted to architecture.

Western architects in the Islamic world. The earliest professional architects to practice in the Islamic world were generally Westerners who worked either for the local ruling elite or for colonial powers. Western architects practicing in the Islamic world provided a crucial link through which Western approaches to architecture reached the Islamic world. They played a major role in introducing Muslim regions to architectural vocabularies prevalent in the West, and they even introduced the idea of reviving the Muslim architectural heritage. The idea of the Islamic revival originated in Europe; it can be traced, in its earliest forms, to the first half of the eighteenth century.

Western architects reached the various parts of the Islamic world at different periods, depending on the arrival of Western political, economic, and cultural influences. Many of these architects had tremendous influence on the architectural development of the regions in which they practiced. In Morocco, for example, more than 120 French architects were practicing during the 1920s, when the country was a French protectorate. Among the best-known of these is Henri Prost, who was responsible for organizing the growth of Moroccan cities between 1914 and 1923.

A number of Western architects left their mark on the development of architecture in Egypt. They include Julius Franz, who participated in designing Cairo's first Islamic-revival structure, the 1863 Jazīrah palace (now the Marriott Hotel) for the Egyptian ruler Ismāʿīl (r. 1863–1879). (See figure 1.) The Italian architect Antoine Lasciac worked in Egypt from 1882 to 1936 and was the chief architect for the royal palaces between 1907 and 1917. Another Italian, Mario Rossi, designed a number of mosques in Cairo and Alexandria during the 1940s.

Western architects who practiced in Turkey include the Frenchman Antoine Vallaury, the chief instructor at the School of Fine Arts and the imperial architect for

FIGURE 1. *Dolmabahçe Palace.* Istanbul, 1853. Architect: Karabet Balyan.

the palace. The structures he designed in Istanbul include the massive Neorenaissance Ottoman Bank structure, built during the 1890s, and the 1907 Neoclassical Archaeological Museum. A German architect usually identified as Jachmund Effendi designed numerous structures in Istanbul, including one of its earliest Islamic revival structures, the 1890 Sirkeci railroad station. The well-known Italian Art Nouveau architect Raymond D'Aronco served as chief architect to the imperial court between 1896 and 1908.

In Iraq, a group of architects accompanied the British forces who occupied the country in 1915. A number of British architects, including J. M. Wilson, H. C. Mason, and J. B. Cooper, initially worked for the British authorities, serving the Iraqi government after the country achieved nominal independence in 1922. These architects introduced modern idioms to Iraq and worked on incorporating local traditions in their work. Wilson, who had been an assistant to the renowned British architect Sir Edwin Lutyens in New Delhi, became the first Director of Public Works in Iraq. His numerous structures include Āl al-Bayt University in Baghdad (1922–1924). He also cooperated with Cooper on a number of designs, including the 1931 Basra Airport and the Baghdad International Railway Station (1947–1951).

In the Indian subcontinent, the British government appointed Sir Edwin Lutyens as architect to the New Delhi Planning Commission. Beginning in 1912, he participated in developing the city plan for New Delhi; he also designed a number of important buildings in the new city, including the Viceroy's House Complex, combining Neo-classical and Mughal elements.

Numerous Dutch architects worked in Indonesia, where Dutch control extended from the late sixteenth century to the end of World War II. Notable was Henri Maclaine Pont, in Indonesia from 1911 until the end of Dutch colonial presence. His work aimed at incorporating local architectural traditions, as evident in the 1920 Institute of Technology in Bandung, which relies heavily on Javanese architectural elements.

Western architects reached even relatively isolated Muslim regions such as Afghanistan. During the late nineteenth and early twentieth centuries, architects from Germany, Austria, Britain, Italy, and France designed buildings for the Afghani ruling elite.

With time, indigenous architects trained in the West or in local institutions based on Western models began to participate in the development of architecture in their regions. Colonialism, however, kept the role of local architects to a minimum, and many had to wait until independence before they could affect the architectural evolution of their countries.

Even during the postcolonial period, Western architects, many of international stature, have maintained an effective presence in the Islamic world. During the 1950s, the Iraqi government invited some of the West's most influential architects, including Alvar Aalto, Le Corbusier, Walter Gropius, and Frank Lloyd Wright, to design a series of public buildings in Baghdad. The American architect Louis Kahn designed the National Assembly complex in Dhaka, Bangladesh; planned in the 1960s but not completed until 1983, this is considered one of the masterpieces of twentieth-century architecture. The mausoleum of King Muḥammad V in Rabat, Morocco (r. 1963–1973), which borrows heavily from traditional Moroccan architecture, was designed by Vo Toan, a Vietnamese-born French architect. The celebrated American architect Paul Rudolph has carried out numerous projects in Southeast Asia, including the 1986 Dharmala Sakti office building in Jakarta, Indonesia.

Major international architectural firms have established a strong presence in the Islamic world. The American firm of Hellmuth, Obata, and Kassabaum designed a number of projects, including the 1975 King Saʿūd University Campus and the 1976 King Khālid International Airport, both in Riyadh. Another major American firm, Skidmore, Owings, and Merrill, designed the 1982 Ḥajj Terminal at ʿAbd al-ʿAzīz International Airport in Jeddah. These two airports in Saudi Arabia are among the largest in the world.

Japanese architects have also been active in the Islamic world since the 1970s. Kenzo Tange has designed public buildings throughout the Islamic world, including university campuses in Oran, Algeria (1972–1974), Irbid, Jordan (1979), Ṣakhir, Bahrain (1987), and al-Qāsim, Saudi Arabia (1983).

Architects from the Islamic world. It took some time before professional architects from the Islamic world began to participate effectively in building their countries, and published information on these pioneers is scanty. In the parts of the Islamic world that had remained isolated from the West, the local professional architect often did not exist, and the traditional master builder continued to dominate the building process. In the regions under direct Western domination, Westerners also dominated the architectural profession. The Islamic world's earliest indigenous professional architects appeared in Turkey and Egypt, both of which had established strong early contacts with the West but had managed to maintain a degree of (often nominal) political autonomy.

In Ottoman Turkey, the most important group of local professional architects to appear during the nineteenth century were members of the Armenian Balyan family, who served as architects to the Ottoman court for much of the nineteenth century. Their eldest members, Kirkor Balyan and his son Karabet, did not receive any formal training, but Kirkor's three grandsons, Nikogos, Sarkis, and Agop, studied architecture in France. Members of the family worked as a team on the design of numerous buildings. Kirkor Balyan's earliest major work is the 1826 Nusretiye mosque in Istanbul, commissioned by the Ottoman Sultan Mahmud II (r. 1808–1839). Karabet Balyan's major work is the massive 1853 Empire style Dolmabahçe palace that replaced the Topkapı palace as the new imperial residence (see figure 2).

Mehmet Vedad and Ahmet Kemalettin are usually viewed as the first professional Muslim Turkish architects. Vedad was the son of a high official in the court of Sultan Abdülhamid II (r. 1876–1909). Against the wish of his father, who considered architecture an inferior profession, Vedad completed his architectural education at the École des Beaux Arts in Paris and returned to Istanbul in 1897, where he opened a private practice and taught at the Academy of Fine Arts. His first major building is the 1909 Central Post Office. Ahmet Kemalettin came from a more modest background and studied at the School of Civil Engineering in Istanbul. After graduating in 1891, he became an assistant to Jachmund. In 1896 he went to Germany, where he studied architecture for two years and worked before returning to Turkey in 1900. He held a number of professional governmental positions and taught at the School of Civil Engineering, as well as designing many religious, residential, commercial, and institutional buildings. Both architects worked on developing a national architectural idiom that combined Classical Revival vocabularies with

FIGURE 2. *Jazīrah Palace.* Cairo, 1863. Architects: Julius Franz and Carl von Diebitsch.

traditional Ottoman ones. They are credited with developing what is referred to in Turkey as the First National Style.

One of Egypt's first professional architects was Maḥmūd Fahmī, who received a diploma from the Cairo Polytechnic School in 1858. Like Kemalettin, he held a number of professional government positions, becoming chief architect for the Ministry of Waqfs. His designs include the Ministry of Waqfs building, of which the first phase was completed in 1896. Maḥmūd Fahmī's son, Muṣṭafā, is considered the founder of the modern Egyptian architectural profession. He studied at the École des Ponts et Chaussées in Paris and held various government positions, including minister of Public Works. His many buildings include the 1928 Mausoleum of the Egyptian nationalist leader Sa'd Zaghlūl and the 1930 headquarters of the Egyptian Society of Engineers. Like the Balyan family, the Fahmīs formed an architectural dynasty: in the early 1940s one of Muṣṭafā's nephews was head of the University of Alexandria's newly formed department of architecture; another nephew headed the department of architecture at the University of Cairo, and a third was head of the Government School of Design.

By the 1930s, a group of local architects trained in both local institutions and abroad had emerged in Turkey and Egypt. In Turkey, among the best known of this new generation of architects is Sedat Hakki Eldem. Eldem belonged to a wealthy, upper-class Turkish family and graduated from the Fine Arts Academy in Istanbul in 1928. During his long professional career, he concentrated on developing a Modern national style that combined modernist approaches with Turkey's premodern architectural traditions. One of his better-known buildings is the Social Security Complex in Istanbul (1962–1964).

An Egyptian contemporary of Eldem is Sayyid Kurayyim. Kurayyim received his first architectural degree from the Cairo Polytechnic School in 1933 and continued his education in Switzerland. After returning to Egypt in 1938, he established an architectural practice that became one of the most active in the Arab world. Soon after his return, he also founded *Al-ʿimārah*, the Arab world's first journal devoted to architecture, which appeared until the 1950s; it promoted twentieth-century architectural modernism, of which Kurayyim was a strong advocate.

The twentieth-century architect from the Muslim world to receive the most international recognition is another Egyptian, Hassan Fathy (Ḥasan Fatḥī). Although Fathy started practicing architecture immediately after graduating from the University of Cairo in 1926, his work did not receive much attention until the 1970s, when the University of Chicago Press published his *Architecture for the Poor* (1973). The book discusses his experience of designing the village of New Gourna for displaced villagers in the Egyptian countryside during the 1940s. In his design Fathy relied on local traditional architectural forms, materials, and construction techniques, and the villagers built most of the structures themselves. Unlike Kurayyim, who strongly advocated a Modernist approach to architecture, or Eldem, who attempted to combine Modernist and traditional forms, Fathy rejected imported Modernist forms and construction techniques and instead relied heavily on local vernacular ones. [*See the biography of Fathy.*]

Although local professional architects had established themselves in Egypt and Turkey by the 1930s, most Muslim countries had to wait until the middle of the century for similar development, often only after these countries achieved independence from colonial rule. For example, when the state of Pakistan came into existence in 1947, it had fewer than ten local professional architects. Up to the mid-1950s, more than three decades after Iraq had achieved nominal independence from the British, the country had only about twenty professionally trained Iraqi architects. As Muslim countries gained their independence around the middle of the twentieth century, a strong need emerged for local professional architects who would replace Western ones and participate in constructing the residential, institutional, commercial, and industrial structures that these emerging states embarked on creating. Consequently, many students began to study architecture in both local and foreign institutions. These architects have followed varying approaches, from strict International Style Modernism to literal historicism.

Architectural teaching institutions. An important phenomenon that has contributed to forming the architectural profession in the Islamic world since the late nineteenth century has been the founding of university-level architectural schools based on Western models. Many of the important architects of the Islamic world have studied or taught in these institutions.

The earliest such institutions appeared in Turkey and Egypt. In Turkey, the School of Fine Arts was established in 1882, and soon after that began to offer training in architecture. The School of Civil Engineering, founded in 1884, also provided teaching in architecture but subordinated it to civil engineering. In Egypt, the Cairo Polytechnic School began graduating architects in 1886 and had started to provide training in architecture even earlier. The School of Fine Arts in Cairo was established in 1908. At the beginning of World War II, the Islamic world had only five university-level schools of architecture, the fifth being at Tehran University in Iran, founded by the French architect André Godard, who had visited Afghanistan during the 1920s and carried out some architectural work there.

A number of centers that trained draftsmen and assistants to architects were also established in the nineteenth century. One is the Mayo School of Arts in Lahore, founded in 1875 (its first director was John Lockwood Kipling, Rudyard's father), which began offering classes in architectural drafting in the early twentieth century. In 1958, it was upgraded to a university-level institution and renamed the National College of the Arts.

Other university-level departments of architecture were established in the 1950s in Lebanon, Iraq, and Indonesia, along with additional institutions in Egypt and Turkey. Departments of architecture multiplied during the following decades, and by the mid-1980s, the Islamic world had more than sixty such schools.

Professional associations, journals, and awards. The earliest professional associations for architects appeared in Egypt and Turkey: the Society of Egyptian Architects was founded in 1917, and a similar Turkish association in 1927. Professional architectural associations came much later in other Muslim countries; the Pakistani Institute of Architects was founded in 1957. Architects were often grouped with engineering associations, as in Iraq, whose Union of Engineers was established in 1959.

In 1931, a few years before Sayyid Kurayyim started *Al-ʿimārah*, the Turkish architect Zeki Sayar established the Islamic world's first journal devoted to the profession of architecture, *Mimar;* in 1935, its name was changed to *Arkitekt*. The journal was published by Sayar until his retirement in 1980. From 1944 to 1953 the Association of Turkish Architects published a biweekly journal, *Mimarlik*. Between 1981 and 1992, another journal called *Mimar* appeared; addressing an international readership, it was published in English from Singapore and later from London and concentrated on the contemporary architecture of the Islamic world. The departments of architecture and professional architectural associations of the Islamic world have published other architectural journals, but these usually have only local circulation. The architectural journals of the Islamic world have played an important role in presenting the works of local and foreign architects to their readers and have provided a forum for discussing important issues.

More recently, architectural awards have played an important role in promoting architecture in the Islamic world. The best known is the Aga Khan Award for Architecture, which had its first cycle in 1980. Every three years, up to $500,000 in prizes are awarded to architectural and urban projects that serve Muslim communities, making it the largest architectural prize in existence. Other awards include the Organization of Islamic Capitals and Cities Award, established in the mid-1980s.

Building Types. One of the most important changes to affect the architecture of the Islamic world during the modern period has concerned building types. Some preexisting building types were no longer built, others were heavily modified, and new types were imported from the West. In residential architecture, for example, the villa and apartment building replaced the traditional inward-looking courtyard house, in institutional architecture, the modern school replaced the traditional *madrasah,* and the hospital the *māristān*. The introduction of new building types has been often perceived as a sign of technological, cultural, political, economic, and political progress.

A wide variety of new building types have been imported from the West. Many of the earliest examples began to appear in Cairo and Istanbul around the mid-nineteenth century. Just as the Dolmabahçe palace replaced Topkapı as the new official imperial residence of the Ottoman rulers, the Egyptian ruler Khedive Ismāʿīl moved his official residence from the Cairo Citadel, from which Cairo had been ruled since the twelfth century, to ʿĀbdīn palace, an Empire style structure built between 1863 and 1874.

During the 1860s Cairo acquired an opera house, and in 1893, a large railway station. Around the turn of the century, the French architect Marcel Dourgnon built a monumental Classical Revival structure to house the collection of the Egyptian Museum. Cairo's Heliopolis Hotel, built by the Belgian architect Ernst Jaspar during the early twentieth century, was for a while the largest hotel in the world. The previously mentioned Antoine Lasciac designed the headquarters of Bank Misr in Cairo (1927), Egypt's first wholly national bank. Similar changes took place in Istanbul, which acquired a railroad station in the 1870s and an archaeological museum around the turn of the century; its early bank buildings include that of the Ottoman Bank.

Although during the nineteenth century Tehran was relatively insulated from Western influences, especially in comparison to Cairo and Istanbul, it also acquired new imported building types during that period. The newly built westernized part of the city included European hotels, embassy buildings, a telegraph building, and the imposing Imperial Bank of Persia.

Along with these new building types came new construction materials and techniques. New materials such as steel, reinforced concrete, and wide panes of glass allowed for the construction of larger and higher buildings with wider openings.

By the middle of the twentieth century, a new set of building types and complexes, also imported from the West, had appeared. Two that were constructed in large numbers are the airport and the university campus. As the airplane replaced the train as the primary means of long-distance travel, airports appeared throughout the Islamic world. In many cases, relatively small airports built earlier have been replaced by much larger ones. Besides the already mentioned Saudi Arabian airports in Jeddah and Riyadh, new airports and airport terminals include the 1984 Jakarta International airport and the 1991 Jinnah Terminal at Karachi airport. Vast sums have gone into the construction of these airports: King Khālid International Airport in Riyadh cost over $3 billion.

Expansive university campuses have also been constructed since the 1960s, at costs of hundreds of millions or even billions of dollars. Many are in the Arabian Peninsula, but some have been built in North Africa, the Indian subcontinent, and Southeast Asia.

New types of mosques have even emerged during the twentieth century, in association with new political, demographic, and economic developments. One example is the large state or national mosque, often built as new countries have come into existence or gained their independence. In some ways, these state mosques, each of which functions as the official mosque of its country, hark back to the great congregational mosques of early Muslim cities, and to the subsequent great imperial mosques of Islam, and can be seen as twentieth-century nationalist versions of those.

An early example is the National Mosque in Kuala Lumpur, Malaysia, completed during the 1960s; it was the largest mosque in Southeast Asia at the time of its construction (see figure 3). Another national mosque from the same period and region is the Independence Mosque in Jakarta. Since the 1970s, such mosques have proliferated throughout the Islamic world, notably in Morocco, Jordan, Saudi Arabia, Kuwait, and Pakistan (see figure 4). Some national mosques have not been realized: in 1982, the Iraqi government organized a competition for the design of an enormous Baghdad State Mosque, in which internationally known architects such as Robert Venturi and Ricardo Bofill participated. If built, this mosque would have been one of the largest in existence.

FIGURE 3. *National Mosque.* Kuala Lumpur, 1967. Architect: Dato Baharuddin Abu Kassim.

These large mosques, airports, and university campuses are among the numerous large-scale projects that have been built in the Islamic world since the 1970s. Such construction activity is partly the consequence of the dramatic rise in oil prices during that decade. Many of the world's oil-exporting countries are Muslim and saw their national incomes rise significantly. Even non-oil-exporting Muslim countries benefited from these rising revenues because of their economic ties with oil-producing countries.

Another mosque type that has emerged during the twentieth century is that built for a Muslim community outside the Islamic world, usually as the nucleus of an Islamic cultural center. Among the earliest of these is the mosque and cultural center which the French government built in Paris during the 1920s for the city's Muslim community. Since then, sizable similar complexes have been built in a number of Western capitals, including Washington, D.C., London, and Rome. Muslim communities in other Western cities and towns have built smaller Muslim religious centers, such as the 1981 Dar al-Islam mosque, which Hassan Fathy designed for a Muslim community living near Abiquiu, New Mexico (see figure 5).

Architectural Vocabularies. An important aspect of the development of architecture in the Islamic world during the past two centuries has been the replacement of traditional premodern architectural vocabularies by a wide variety of Western ones. Classical Revival vocabularies were usually the first to appear, reaching Ottoman Turkey in the early eighteenth century, when the Ottoman elite began to show a fondness for European, and especially French, products. European architectural details made their way into the architecture of the era referred to as the Tulip Period. By the mid-eighteenth century, this importing of European architectural details culminated into the phase called the Ottoman Baroque. In both periods, however, the integrity of Ottoman systems of architectural expression was maintained, and there was no break with Ottoman traditions.

During the nineteenth century, the importation of architectural vocabularies from the West reached new levels. Not only architectural details, but also building types complete with their organizational systems were imported. Local ruling elites and colonial powers initiated the importing of these systems that gradually replaced traditional ones, especially at the upper levels of patronage. Important examples of structures that local ruling Muslim elites built include the above-mentioned Dolmabahçe palace in Istanbul and the ʿĀbdīn palace in Cairo; structures built by colonial powers include the 1830 Neoclassical Saxe-Weimar house in Jakarta, which later became the People's Council building.

Beginning in the second half of the nineteenth century, other architectural revivals appeared, among them Neorenaissance buildings such as the Ottoman Bank building in Istanbul, and Gothic Revival buildings such as the Mosque of al-Ḥusayn in Cairo as rebuilt during the 1870s, and Nikogos Balyan's 1886 Hamidiyc Mosque in Istanbul. Cairo even had its own Neo-Hindu structure, the early twentieth-century villa of the Belgian developer Edouard Empain, designed by his compatriot Alexandre Marcel, in Heliopolis, the new Cairene suburb Empain developed.

The most significant revivalist vocabularies imported

FIGURE 4. *State Mosque.* Kuwait, 1986. Architect: Mohamed Makiya.

FIGURE 5. *Dar al-Islam Mosque.* Abiquiu, New Mexico, U.S.A., 1981. Architect: Hassan Fathy.

into the Islamic world, however, were those of the Islamic Revival. By the time these vocabularies arrived in the Islamic world, Western architectural vocabularies had displaced premodern traditional ones at the upper levels of patronage. In Europe, the vocabularies of the Islamic Revival had been used since the eighteenth century. European Islamic Revival structures incorporated an eclectic variety of details and organizational features borrowed from both Islamic and non-Islamic traditions. Western architects practicing in the Islamic world later transferred these vocabularies to the areas in which they were working.

Islamic Revival buildings built in a region of the Islamic world often introduced that region to the architecture of other Muslim areas. This is evident in one of the earlier Islamic Revival works in the Islamic world, the 1863 Jāzirah palace in Cairo, designed by Julius Franz and Carl von Diebitsch. The structure employs Moorish features rather than ones taken from Cairo's Islamic architectural heritage. In a similar manner, Indian and Middle Eastern influences reached the mosque architecture of Southeast Asia through colonial architects working in the area; before the colonial period, the mosques of Java, for example, did not have minarets or domes.

Since the arrival of Islamic Revival vocabularies in the Islamic world, a debate has emerged concerning the degree to which contemporary architecture of the Islamic world should establish connections with its premodern past, and the manner in which such connections could be achieved. However, attempts at articulating a theoretical framework discussing contemporary architectural production in the Islamic world remained few and lacked intellectual rigor. During the late nineteenth century, some documents appeared in Turkey that aimed at defining the characteristics of classical Ottoman architecture, tried to differentiate it from other architectural traditions, and discussed how architects could revive it.

An example of this broad debate took place during the 1920s concerning the design of the mausoleum of the Egyptian nationalist leader Saʿd Zaghlūl. The Egyptian press presented this debate between those who advocated a Neo-Mamlūk mausoleum and those who advocated an Egyptian Revival one. Advocates of an Egyptian Revival design argued that this vocabulary better expressed the unity of the Egyptian people, both Christian Copts and Muslims. Eventually their opinion prevailed, and the mausoleum was built as an Egyptian Revival structure. The popularity of the Egyptian Revival in Egypt, however, did not extend beyond the 1920s.

Since the 1930s, Modernist movements rejecting architectural historicism began to play an increasingly important role in the architectural development of the Islamic world. Modernist vocabularies became increasingly popular as the Islamic world began to achieve political independence, especially around the middle of the twentieth century. Revivalist vocabularies were associated with colonialism; in contrast. Modernist vocabularies, which called for the creation of universal architectural forms inspired by images of technology rather than geographic or historical factors, were associated with the idea of progress.

Architects who transferred principles of twentieth-century Modernism to the Islamic world include Sayyid Kurayyim, who was greatly influential not only in Egypt but throughout the eastern Arab world. In Turkey, Modernist architecture began to replace revivalist vocabularies after the 1920s. Initially, Western architects such as the Austrian Clemens Holzheimer carried out most Modernist designs in the country; the Turkish government commissioned Holzheimer to design a number of large-scale public buildings in Ankara. Turkish architects such as Sedat Hakki Eldem soon began to participate effectively in the introduction of Modernist architecture to Turkey. By the 1950s, Modernism, especially the International Style, predominated in Turkey. The better-known examples of International Style Modernism in Turkey include the 1952 Hilton Hotel in Istanbul, which Eldem designed with Skidmore, Owings, and Merrill.

Modernism did not achieve complete victory in the architecture of the mosque. Throughout the modern period, the mosque predictably maintained higher levels of continuity with the traditional architectural heritage of the Islamic world than did other building types. The dome and minaret became standard features in most mosques, even in regions where they were not traditionally common. A degree of simplification affected the architecture of the mosque as a result of Modernist influences, so that elaborate decorative details such as *muqarnaṣ* (or stalactite) vaults were abandoned, highly simplified, or abstracted. Nonetheless, mosque architecture remained historically defined, looking at past forms for models. A relatively small number of mosques that reject historical references, however, have been designed during this period. One is Sherefuddin's White Mosque in Visoko, Bosnia-Herzegovina, which Zlatko Ugljen designed in 1967, but which was not completed until 1980 (see figure 6). Some architects have combined highly abstracted forms with historical references in mosque designs; this approach has included an unusual reference to the cube-shaped Kaʿbah in Mecca in the early 1970s mosque at the University of Kerman in Iran.

By the 1970s, a reaction against the ahistoricism of Modernism and its lack of cultural specificity began to set in, and architects started searching for architectural vocabularies that established contacts with perceived notions of the Islamic heritage. These changes are partly the result of a rise in religious sentiment during that period, and partly connected to the critique of Modernism that had been evolving internationally since the 1960s.

The search for new architectural forms initially avoided the nineteenth- and early twentieth-century examples of the Islamic Revival; the connection between architectural revivalism and the colonial period was still alive. Moreover, architects were involved in a critique, rather than a rejection, of Modernism, and therefore were searching for vocabularies that would modify but still incorporate it. Numerous architects turned to local vernacular traditions, which many had been examining long before the 1970s. Sedat Hakki Eldem had attempted to incorporate regional vernacular features within a modernist context since the 1940s, as evident in his Taşlik Coffee House in Istanbul, which makes references to traditional residential Turkish architecture.

Colonial architects had also worked with local architectural idioms in areas such as North and West Africa. Examples include the 1940s Controle Civil building in Bizerte, Tunisia, which Jacque Marmay designed, using traditional building techniques and local building forms,

FIGURE 6. *Sherefuddin's White Mosque*. Visoko, Bosnia-Herzegovina, 1980. Architect: Zlatko Ugljen.

as well as various administrative structures that French architects built in Mali during the 1920s and 1930s. The Dutch architect Henri Maclaine Pont also carried out similar attempts in Indonesia, as evident in his design for the Institute of Technology in Bandung.

The architect whose work with traditional vocabularies has emerged as a powerful guiding and inspirational force for architects throughout the Islamic world is Hassan Fathy. Fathy too had been working with vernacular traditions since the 1940s, when he designed the village of New Gourna. His work showed a commitment to improving the quality of life for villagers, an uncompromising dedication to local rural architectural traditions, and a firm rejection of Modernist approaches to architecture on both the technological and formal levels.

More recently, the negative memories of colonialism began to fade, a younger generation of architects born since the 1940s have returned to the revivals of the nineteenth and early twentieth centuries and their literal reproduction of past forms. For example, the Tunisian architect Tarek Ben Miled (Tāriq ibn Mīlād) persuaded a client not to tear down a 1922 Classical Revival villa in Carthage, and instead renovated it and built an extension that maintained the villa's original character. The Egyptian architect Abdel Wahed El-Wakil (ʿAbd al-Wāḥid al-Wakīl) has relied on an eclectic combination of Islamic Revival vocabularies for the numerous mosques he designed in Saudi Arabia, such as the 1986 King Saʿūd Mosque in Jeddah. The mosque combines elements taken from Mamlūk Egyptian and Iranian Ṣafavid architecture.

Within this pluralism that has characterized the evolution of architecture in the Islamic world since the 1970s, a strong current has emphasized the need to develop regional vocabularies within the context of modern technologies and forms. The Iraqi architect Rifat Chadirji (Rifʿat Chādirjī) has most effectively articulated a theoretical framework for this view. Chadirji began practicing architecture in the early 1950s, but since the late 1970s he has devoted himself to writing on architectural theory and criticism in both English and Arabic. In his writings, he has explored the connection of architecture to themes including technology, aesthetics, and the role of the past.

BIBLIOGRAPHY

A.A.R.P. Environmental Design: Journal of the Islamic Environmental Design Research Centre. 1985. Issue devoted to the theme "Maghreb: From Colonialism to a New Identity." Contains articles discussing the evolution of architecture in North Africa during the nineteenth and twentieth centuries.

al-Asad, Mohammad. "The Re-invention of Tradition: Neo-Islamic Architecture in Cairo." In *Artistic Exchange: Acts of the XXVII International Congress for the History of Art. Berlin, 15–20 July 1992,* edited by Thomas W. Gaehtgens, pp. 425–436. Berlin, 1993. Discusses the evolution of the discipline of "Islamic architecture," the development of Islamic-Revival architecture in the West, and its transfer to Egypt.

Cantacuzino, Sherban, ed. *Architecture in Continuity: Building in the Islamic World Today.* New York, 1985. Documents winning projects for the second cycle of the Aga Khan Award for Architecture. Also includes articles on contemporary architecture in the Islamic world.

Çelik, Zeynep. *The Remaking of Istanbul: Portrait of an Ottoman City in the Nineteenth Century.* Seattle, 1986.

Chadirji, Rifat. *Concepts and Influences: Towards a Regionalised International Architecture.* London, 1986. Provides a theoretical framework for discussing the relationships between technological developments and architectural form. Discussion includes sections dealing with non-Western settings.

Evin, Ahmet, and Renata Holod, eds. *Modern Turkish Architecture.* Philadelphia, 1984.

Evin, Ahmet, ed. *Architecture Education in the Islamic World.* Singapore, 1986.

Goodwin, Godfrey. *A History of Ottoman Architecture.* London, 1971. Includes sections dealing with Ottoman architecture during the nineteenth century.

Head, Raymond. *The Indian Style.* Chicago, 1986. Discusses Indian influences on Western architecture.

Holod, Renata, with Darl Rastorfer, eds. *Architecture and Community: Building in the Islamic World Today.* New York, 1983. Documents winning projects for the first cycle of the Aga Khan Award for Architecture. Also includes articles on contemporary architecture in the Islamic world.

Lotus International 26(1980). Issue devoted to the theme "Hybrid Architecture." Discusses the influence of Western architecture on non-Western regions during the late nineteenth and early twentieth centuries.

Mimar. Various issues.

Rastorfer, Darl, J. M. Richards, and Ismail Serageldin. *Hassan Fathy. A Mimar Book.* Singapore and London, 1985.

Sakr, Tarek Mohamed Rifat. *Early Twentieth-Century Islamic Architecture in Cairo.* Cairo, 1993.

Salam, Hayat. *Expressions of Islam in Buildings: Proceedings of an International Seminar Sponsored by the Aga Khan Award for Architecture and the Indonesian Institute of Architects held in Jakarta and Yogyakarta, Indonesia, 15–19 October 1990.* Geneva, n.d. Includes papers on contemporary mosque architecture.

Serageldin, Ismail, ed. *Space for Freedom: The Search for Architectural Excellence in Muslim Societies.* London and Geneva, 1989. Documents winning projects for the third cycle of the Aga Khan Award for Architecture. Also includes articles on contemporary architecture in the Islamic world.

Steele, James, ed. *Architecture for a Changing World.* London and Geneva, 1992. Documents winning projects for the fifth cycle of the Aga Khan Award for Architecture. Also includes articles on contemporary architecture in the Islamic world.

Steele, James, ed. *Architecture for Islamic Societies Today*. London and Geneva, 1994. Documents winning projects for the fourth cycle of the Aga Khan Award for Architecture. Also includes articles on contemporary architecture in the Islamic world.

Volait, Mercedes. *L'architecture moderne en Egypte et la revue al-ʿImara (1939–1959)*. Cairo, 1987. Discusses the founding and development of the architectural journal *Al-ʿimārah*, and the evolution of modern architecture in Egypt.

Wright, Gwendolyn. *The Politics of Design in French Colonial Urbanism*. Chicago, 1991. Includes a detailed discussion of French urban policies in Morocco.

Yamada, Sohiko, ed. "Medinat al Salaam: Baghdad 1979–1983." *Process: Architecture* 59 (1985). Contains articles and documentary information on Baghdad's architectural development during the modern period.

MOHAMMAD AL-ASAD

ARKĀN. *See* Pillars of Islam.

ARKOUN, MOHAMMED (b. 1928), Algerian Islamic scholar and writer. One of today's leading Arab Muslim intellectuals, Arkoun is involved in the sensitive task of reinterpreting and recasting the classical religious, legal, and philosophical traditions through a sophisticated hermeneutical system inspired by contemporary Western critical methodologies, a task that has made him a controversial participant in the creation of a modern Arabo-Islamic critical discourse.

Arkoun was born on 2 January 1928 in the Berber village of Taourirt-Mimoun in Kabylia. From his modest beginnings as the son of a spice merchant, Arkoun went on to become a highly successful international scholar and thinker. He began Arabic studies in his native country and completed them in Paris. He is presently attached officially to the Sorbonne as Professor of the History of Islamic Thought and was formerly Director of the Institute of Arab and Islamic Studies there. He has also been editor in chief of the French scholarly journal *Arabica* for many years. Arkoun's international visibility has brought lectures and visiting appointments at academic institutions worldwide, including the Institute for Advanced Study in Princeton. His adopted homeland has appointed Arkoun Chevalier de la Légion d'Honneur and Officier des Palmes Académiques.

What distinguishes Arkoun from many other contemporary Arab and Muslim intellectuals is precisely what qualifies him to be Editor of *Arabica*—his serious training as a medievalist. Arkoun established himself as a foremost student of medieval Islamic thought with his work on the philosopher and thinker Miskawayh (d. 1030). He edited two treatises by Miskawayh and translated his *Tahdhīb al-akhlāq*, a work whose close relationship to Aristotle's *Nichomachean Ethics* forces anyone dealing with the Arabic text to grapple with Greek philosophy.

With this solid philosophical background combined with the resources of French criticism, Arkoun began his own intellectual crusade. His rereadings of the rich Islamic religious and legal traditions are an extension of this dual intellectual allegiance to the modern humanities and social sciences and to medieval studies. Arkoun has also written widely on topics ranging from the twelfth-century Andalusian philosopher and physician Ibn Ṭufayl to Orientalism.

Arkoun's *Lectures du Coran* is perhaps his most challenging and important work. The author pleads eloquently and passionately for clear analytical distinctions in dealing with the Muslim holy book. According to Arkoun, too many levels of production of the sacred text are amalgated under the title of the Qur'ān. There is the word of God, the Logos, of which the revelations of the three monotheistic religions are but fragments. There are also the Qur'ānic discourse, the actual written text of the Qur'ān, and the commentaries on this text. These distinctions permit a much more sophisticated reading of the scriptures.

Arkoun's ideas have not gone unchallenged by the intellectual leaders of the contemporary Islamist movement. An impassioned debate occurred between Arkoun and the Egyptian Shaykh Muḥammad al-Ghazālī in Algeria; almost as quickly as the works of al-Ghazālī are becoming available to an international audience, so Arkoun's works are being reedited in French in North Africa, translated into Arabic, and published in London. [*See the biography of Ghazālī.*] Arkoun's impact on the contemporary Arab Muslim intellectual scene will become increasingly important as the Islamist movement grows in strength. Arkoun defines the Islamic concept of the *jihād al-nafs* (personal *jihād*) as the work of the intellectual who feels a sense of solidarity with the society to which he belongs. This *jihād al-nafs* is Arkoun's mission.

BIBLIOGRAPHY

Arkoun, Mohammed. *Lectures du Coran*. 2d ed. Tunis, 1991. Essential work that brings together various studies ranging from close readings of Qur'ānic surahs to an essay on Islam and politics.

Arkoun, Mohammed. *Ouvertures sur l'Islam*. Paris, 1989. Fascinating essay on Islam and Islamic thought; essential for understanding Arkoun's interpretive system.

FEDWA MALTI-DOUGLAS

ʿAṢABĪYAH. Derived from the root *ʿaṣab* ("to bind") and *ʿaṣabah* ("union") ʿaṣabīyah refers to a sociocultural bond that can be used to measure the strength of social groupings. It was a familiar term in the pre-Islamic era and became a popular concept when Ibn Khaldūn (1332–1406) used it in his work *Muqaddimah.* ʿAṣabīyah, then, can be understood as social solidarity, with emphasis on group consciousness, cohesiveness, and unity.

ʿAṣabīyah is a social as well as psychological, physical, and political phenomenon; it is neither necessarily nomadic nor based on blood relation. Its meaning is close to Émile Durkheim's idea of the "conscience collective." The *ʿaṣabīyah* that unites a group of people against strangers simultaneously reinforces the values and norms of the group. Strong spirit and strong morals seem to go hand in hand, especially in nomadic societies. Here, Ibn Khaldūn's *ʿaṣabīyah* may be compared with Durkheim's "mechanical solidarity." Whereas Durkheim believed that suicide rates rise as a result of the weakening of mechanical social solidarity, Ibn Khaldūn believed that the weakening of the *ʿaṣabīyah* among civilized people indicates the approaching suicide of the society as a whole.

Pre-Islamic nomadic *ʿaṣabīyah* was condemned to a great extent by the prophet Muḥammad, because it was used generally in intertribal wars and raids. *ʿAṣabīyah,* like any other human trait, can be "good" or "bad," depending on the purpose for which it is used; Islamic history provides many examples that illustrate this point, especially from the period of the caliphate. To Ibn Khaldūn, Muʿāwiyah's rebellion against the legitimate caliph, ʿAlī, and the takeover of the caliphate by force was a result of Muʿāwiyah's strong *ʿaṣabīyah.* By the same token, the rebellion of Ḥusayn (ʿAlī's son) did not succeed because of Yazīd's strong *ʿaṣabīyah.* The Ikhwān al-Ṣafāʾ (Brethren of Purity) and subsequently, Ibn Khaldūn witnessed the rise and fall of many states during the Islamic empire. Ibn Khaldūn was specific in analyzing the change in the mode of living from *badāwah* (nomadic or primitive life) to *ḥaḍārah* (sedentary life); the clash between nomadic invaders and urban people results in a cyclical rise and fall of dynasties, and each new stage arises from the conflicting contradictions of the previous stage. It should be noted that *ʿaṣabīyah* is too vague a factor to be useful in political and social affairs. Islamic history shows that the same *ʿaṣabīyah* may increase or decrease in power according to a change in situation. Many leaders lost their own *ʿaṣabīyah* after suffering a defeat; others gained strong *ʿaṣabīyah* after some accidental victory or sudden rise in fortune.

Throughout Islamic history, a strong relationship has existed between *ʿaṣabīyah* and religion. The Ikhwān al-Ṣafāʾ, Ibn Khaldūn, and other Muslim thinkers believed that religion strengthens group cohesiveness. This social function of religion to unify people can be seen in the achievement of the Arabs after they became Muslims. When Arab tribal *ʿaṣabīyah* coincided with certain aspects of religion, the Arabs became extremely religious. They showed amazing zeal and devotion to Islam when, after the Prophet's death, their *ʿaṣabīyah* was directed against the "unbelievers" outside Arabia.

In the nineteenth and twentieth centuries the Arabs, who were subjected to foreign rule, felt the need for unity, solidarity, and self determination: the major elements of *ʿaṣabīyah.* Hence the rise of Arab national consciousness. *ʿAṣabīyah* and nationalism may be considered analogous. Both emphasize identity, loyalty, a sense of belonging, and aspiration. Specifically, the invasion of Egypt by Napoleon, the Italian seizure of Tripoli, the Ottoman policy of Turkification, the European betrayal of the Arabs by the 1916 Sykes-Picot Agreement, the 1917 Balfour Declaration, and the subsequent creation of Israel led to Arab dissatisfaction and resentment. Their awakening, sense of unity, and aspiration for self-determination and constructive social reforms gave rise to modern Arab nationalism.

[*See also* Arab Nationalism; Nation; *and the biography of Ibn Khaldūn.*]

BIBLIOGRAPHY

Baali, Fuad, and Ali Wardi. *Ibn Khaldun and Islamic Thought-Styles.* Boston, 1981. Detailed interpretation of Ibn Khaldūn's ideas on idealism versus realism, right versus might, and Islam versus nomadism.

Hitti, Philip K. *The Arabs: A Short History.* Chicago, 1956. Introduction to the history and accomplishments of the Arabs through many centuries.

Ismael, Tareq Y. *Government and Politics of the Contemporary Middle East.* Homewood, Ill., 1970. Excellent collection of ideas relating to nationalism and other aspects of Middle East politics.

Jabara, Abdeen, and Janice Terry. *The Arab World from Nationalism to Revolution.* Wilmette, Ill., 1971. Thorough analysis of the social structure and social problems of the Arab World.

FUAD BAALI

ASADĀBĀDĪ, JAMĀL AL-DĪN AL-. *See* Afghānī, Jamāl al-Dīn al-.

ʿĀSHŪRĀʾ. The tenth day of the Muslim month of Muḥarram, ʿĀshūrāʾ had been considered by early Muslims to be a very auspicious and joyous day, as many important and happy events, such as the landing of Noah's ark, took place on it. This perception was changed forever on ʿĀshūrāʾ in the year 680 when Ḥusayn, the beloved grandson of the prophet Muḥammad and third imam of the Shīʿīs, brutally perished in the Battle of Karbala. The tragic death of Ḥusayn on ʿĀshūrāʾ is viewed by the Shīʿīs as the greatest suffering and redemptive act in history. In fact, to the Shīʿīs it has transcended history to become metahistory, having acquired cosmic proportions. This places the ʿĀshūrāʾ passion of the imam Ḥusayn at a time that is "no time" and in a space that is "no space." In any Shīʿī community that regards itself as deprived, humiliated, and abused, what happened thirteen hundred years ago is looked on as if it were taking place now.

The timeless quality of this tragedy allows Shīʿī communities to measure themselves against the paradigm of Ḥusayn in the fight against any injustice, tyranny, or oppression of the day. By doing so, they hope to be considered worthy of the sacrifice of the Prince of Martyrs (Ḥusayn). That is why one of the main slogans during the Islamic Revolution in Iran, chanted by the crowds or scribbled in graffiti on town and village walls, was "Every day is ʿĀshūrāʾ; every place is Karbala; every month is Muḥarram." This same slogan was intoned on radio and television broadcasts, as well as being graphically depicted on posters and even postage stamps, during Iran's long, bloody defensive war against Iraq (1980–1988).

The commemoration of the imam Ḥusayn's passion and martyrdom is charged with unusual emotions throughout the world's Shīʿī communities. Even the Sunnīs and the members of other religions that live among the Shīʿīs are greatly affected by these commemorative rituals. The belief that participation in the annual observance of Ḥusayn's suffering and death is an aid to salvation on the Day of Judgment is an additional incentive to engage in the many mourning rituals. In the words of Nobel laureate Elias Canetti, the suffering of Ḥusayn on ʿĀshūrāʾ and its commemoration "becomes the very core of the Shīʿī faith, . . ." which is "a religion of lament more concentrated and more extreme than any to be found elsewhere. . . . No faith has ever laid greater emphasis on lament. It is the highest religious duty, and many times more meritorious than any other good work" (1978, pp. 146, 153).

Elaborate ʿĀshūrāʾ observances were being carried out in Baghdad during the reign of Muʿizz al-Dawlah of the Shīʿī Būyid dynasty (932–1055)—bazaars closed and men circumambulated the city weeping, wailing, and striking their heads while dressed in torn black clothing; women appeared disheveled as well (Ibn Kathīr, *Al-bidāyah wa-al-nihāyah,* Cairo, 1977, vol. 11, p. 243). Many ʿĀshūrāʾ rituals are still developing in various Shīʿī communities, and although they might differ in form, the passionate participation within them is universal. These rituals can be divided into two categories, ambulatory and stationary, and they are primarily performed during the first ten days of Muḥarram; the greatest discharge of emotion and the greatest number of rituals occur on the day of ʿĀshūrāʾ. As a result of Shīʿī Islam becoming Iran's state religion in the sixteenth century and the subsequent spread of Shiism and its popular beliefs throughout the country, Iran has come to be the sine qua non of ʿĀshūrāʾ observances.

Among the ambulatory ʿĀshūrāʾ rituals of Iran one finds processions as well as floats with live tableaux representing the scenes from the Karbala tragedy. The procession participants are divided into different groups of self-mortifiers: *sināḥzan,* those that beat their chests with the palms of their hands; *zanjīrzan,* those who beat their backs with chains; and *shamshīrzan,* those who wound their foreheads with swords or knives. Some also mortify themselves with stones. Others carry the *ʿalam,* which signifies the standard of Ḥusayn at Karbala. In some processions, *nakhl* (date palm) is carried, because according to tradition, Ḥusayn's beheaded corpse was carried on a stretcher made of date-palm branches. Some *nakhl* are so large that they require more than 150 people to carry them. Processions are accompanied by bands of martial and mournful music. The grandest procession takes place on ʿĀshūrāʾ itself. The processions join in a succession unique to each district of a town or city and end in a specific locality.

To the stationary rituals belong *rawẓah khvānī,* a recitation and singing of the story of Ḥusayn, his family, and followers at the bloody Battle of Karbala. The storyteller of the Shīʿī martyrology *(rawẓah khvān)* sits above the assembled crowd on a *minbar* in a black tent, under an awning, or in a special edifice called *ḥusaynīyah* or *takīyah* and brings the audience to a state of frenzy with recitation, chanting, crying, sobbing, and body language. *Pardah-dārī* is another one-man show of visual and verbal narrative in which a storyteller carries a huge rolled-up canvas oil painting depicting scenes of the Battle of Karbala in a cartoon-strip-like series. As the storyteller travels from one locality to the next, he hangs up the painting, sings, and recites the story using a pointer to elucidate the scenes. The most famous stationary ritual of Iran, however, is the *taʿziyah,* the only serious drama ever developed in the Islamic world, in which the martyrdom of Ḥusayn is performed on ʿĀshūrāʾ. [*See* Rawẓah Khvānī; Ḥusaynīyah; Taʿziyah.]

In India and Pakistan, the ʿAshūrāʾ rituals follow the Iranian patterns with some exclusions and additions. The *taʿziyah* as a dramatic theatrical form is not known there. The Shīʿī painting recitation is not performed. What is interesting, however, is the fact that Sunnīs and even Hindus actively participate in many ʿĀshūrāʾ rituals. The Sunnīs even have separate rituals. The most characteristic features of ʿĀshūrāʾ commemoration on the Indo-Pakistani subcontinent are the huge artistic interpretations of Ḥusayn's mausoleum carried or wheeled in the ʿĀshūrāʾ procession. At the end of ʿĀshūrāʾ, these structures, called *taʿziyah (sic),* are either buried at the local cemetery, called "Karbala," or immersed in water. The *rawẓah khvānī* type of commemoration of Ḥusayn's martyrdom, called *majlis* or *majālis* in India, is carried either in the open or in special buildings called *imāmbārah* or *ʿāshūrkhānah.* Many of the Indian ʿĀshūrāʾ rituals were introduced by Indian Muslims to the Caribbean basin in the first half of the nineteenth century. The ʿĀshūrāʾ observance is, after Carnival, the most important event in Trinidad today. The ʿĀshūrāʾ observance there is called Hosay and goes on for three nights and one day. The final night of ʿĀshūrāʾ is the most spectacular; colorful replicas of Ḥusayn's tomb called *taja*s, which stand up to fifteen and a half feet high, are paraded to the accompaniment of *tāssah* and bass drums. In southern Iraq, the procession and the *majlis* are common features of the first ten days of Muḥarram, coming to a peak on ʿĀshūrāʾ itself. The ʿĀshūrāʾ observances seem more elaborate in those countries located at a greater distance from Karbala: this pattern of observances at the periphery being more spectacular than those at the center is a familiar one in many religions.

The ʿAshūrāʾ processions also served as prototypes for the massive demonstrations in Ṭehran and other Iranian cities during the 1978–1979 revolutionary upheavals. The mixing of ʿAshūrāʾ mourning slogans with political ones is an old Muḥarram tradition. The Iranian Revolution utilized the Ḥusayn/ʿĀshūrāʾ paradigm and was carried out in accordance with the Shīʿī calendar. Ayatollah Ruhollah Khomeini's revolution started the afternoon of ʿĀshūrāʾ, 5 June 1963, when he delivered a speech at the Fayẓīyah Madrasah in Qom in which he criticized the internal and external policies of the shah and his government. In the book *Islamic Government,* written in exile in Najaf, Khomeini states: "Make Islam known to the people, then . . . create something akin to ʿĀshūrāʾ and create out of it a wave of protest against the state of the government" (1981, p. 131). A week before Muḥarram on 23 November 1978, in order to accelerate the revolution, Khomeini issued from Neauphle-le-Château, France, the declaration called "Muḥarram: The Triumph of Blood over the Sword," which was taped and distributed in Iran through its network of mosques. The opening paragraph of the declaration states:

> With the approach of Muḥarram, we are about to begin the month of epic heroism and self sacrifice—the month in which blood triumphed over the sword, the month in which truth condemned falsehood for all eternity and branded the mark of disgrace upon the forehead of all oppressors and satanic governments; the month that has taught successive generations throughout history the path of victory over the bayonet. (1981, p. 242)

Less than two months later, the shah left Iran, enabling Khomeini to return from fourteen years of exile.

When Iran was invaded by Iraq in the fall of 1980, the Ḥusayn/ʿĀshūrāʾ paradigm was again used. Many of the Iranian combatants on the front lines in the war with Iraq had the following inscriptions written on their helmets and headbands or combat fatigues: "The epic makers of ʿĀshūrāʾ " or " ʿĀshūrāʾ is the epic of faith, the epic of blood."

[*See also* Karbala; Muḥarram.]

BIBLIOGRAPHY

Alserat 12 (Spring–Autumn 1986). Proceedings of the Imam Ḥusayn Conference held July 1984, London, which contain a wealth of information on ʿĀshūrāʾ.

Ayoub, Mahmoud M. *Redemptive Suffering in Islām: A Study of the Devotional Aspects of ʿĀshūrāʾ in Twelver Shīʿism.* The Hague, 1978. The most important study of ʿĀshūrāʾ.

Canetti, Elias. "The Muharram Festival of the Shiʿites." In his *Crowds and Power.* New York, 1978. Masterpiece of psychological interpretation of ʿĀshūrāʾ crowds.

Chelkowski, Peter. *Taʿziyeh: Ritual and Drama in Iran.* New York, 1979.

Khomeini, Ruhollah. *Islam and Revolution.* Translated and annotated by Hamid Algar. Berkeley, 1981. Contains writings and declarations of Imam Khomeini.

Von Grunebaum, G. E. *Muhammadan Festivals.* London, 1958.

PETER CHELKOWSKI

ASTROLOGY. To say that a belief in astrology is a feature of the popular culture of the modern Islamic world is to make a trivial statement, for this is true of practically all world cultures. It is a nontrivial exercise, however, to study the distinguishing features of the Islamic astrological tradition, the role it has played in blending and modifying and then transmitting outward all the various elements in drew from a host of classical foreign cultures, and the attitudes Islam displayed toward astrological doctrines and practices. A study of this kind suffers from an inherent limitation—a large number of primary Arabic astrological sources are no longer extant; moreover, a large number of those that are preserved still await scholarly examination. Many of our present views and conclusions must thus remain tentative, and this discussion is no exception.

By the eighth century CE, astrology had emerged as a distinct discipline in Islam—a discipline born out of a creative blending of the Hellenistic traditions of Iran, India, Mesopotamia, and the eastern Mediterranean. All these traditions share certain fundamental features. They all presuppose a geocentric finite universe in which celestial bodies exercise an influence on the terrestrial world. They all accept some version of Aristotelian physics, believing variously that astral influences determine all motions of the four sublunar elements—Earth, Water, Air, and Fire—and that these influences signify trends that may be altered by future influences, or by supernatural or human intervention, or that these influences simply manifest divine will.

Eastern Emphases. With these characteristic features, astrology is evidently a Hellenistic invention, a system based on Greek astronomy and physics mixed with elements drawn from Babylonian celestial omens and Egyptian demigods. This Hellenistic astrology reached India in the second century CE, and here it received local treatments and was then transmitted as a transformed entity to Sassanian Iran in the following century. Through an assimilative process in Iran the Greco-Indian astrological tradition underwent further modifications, now integrated with both indigenous Iranian as well as additional Greek elements. Thus developed a Greco-Indo-Iranian astrological tradition that finally became part of the cultural booty of conquering Islam.

In Islamic civilization this complex phenomenon of transmission becomes even more intricate: texts were translated into Arabic not only from Pahlavi and Sanskrit, but also from Syriac and directly from Greek. Thus the Islamic astrological tradition displays not only certain characteristically Hellenistic features but also elements contributed locally by India and Iran. Unlike what occurred in many other sciences, Eastern elements remained strong in Islamic astrology. Thus despite their intimate relationship and similar routes of transmission, the science of astronomy underwent in Islam a thorough Hellenization, whereas astrology continued to show a dominance of characteristically Indo-Iranian features, with emphases on interrogational, military, and political astrology.

Categories. Experts recognize four broad categories of astrological practice: genethlialogy, which relates all aspects of an individual's life to the situation of the heavens at the moment of his nativity; catarchic astrology, which consists in determining on the basis of the celestial configurations whether a given moment is auspicious (*saʿd*) or inauspicious (*naḥs*) for a particular activity; general astrology, which is concerned with periodic heavenly situations (eclipses, planetary conjunctions, equinoxes, etc.), relating them to events affecting large numbers of people, nations, or the whole world; and interrogational astrology, which answers specific questions on the basis of the heavenly configuration at the time of the query.

Genethialogy (*mawālīd*) had already reached its high point in the work of Dorotheus of Sidon, written in about 75 CE. In this work we find a number of historic innovations in the techniques of horoscope casting, horoscopes being diagrams of the signs of the zodiac based on the aspects of celestial bodies at a given moment. One of the Dorothean innovations is the system of lots (Ar., *sihām*, sg. *sahm*)—points whose distance from some specified points in the horoscopic diagram equals the distance between two planets. Another is the introduction of the prorogator (Ar., *al-haylāj*, whence Lat. *alhyleg*), a point on the ecliptic that determines the life of the native. Dorotheus had spoken also of continuous horoscopy; this assumes that even though an individual's basic natal horoscope is generally valid, new horoscopes must be cast at periodic intervals and compared with the base horoscope to generate specific predictions for the next period.

All these Dorothean features are found in Islamic astrology; but here they are further fortified by the Harrānian version of the Neoplatonic doctrine of astral influences cast in terms of Aristotelian physics, and creatively blended with Indian and Iranian elements. An outstanding example of this blending is found in the writings of Abū Maʿshar (d. 886), Islam's most influential astrologer. For example, as compared to the two principal lots of the Greeks—the Lot of Fortune and the Lot of the Demon—Abū Maʿshar could enumerate well over a hundred lots. Similarly, the complicated rules governing the prorogator are here made even more elaborate. A variation on or adjunct to the prorogator was the Lord of the Year, the strongest planet in the horoscope. Again, the techniques of determining this planet are further refined by Arabic astrologers.

It is interesting to note the grafting of Iranian political and continuous astrology onto the Hellenistic base of the Islamic tradition. For example, among the thirteen lots employed by the astrologer Māshā'allāh (d. c.815) in his *Kitāb al-mawālīd al-kabīr* (Great Book of Nativities), one finds also the Lot of Political Power *(sahm al-sulṭān),* taken from the Sassanian tradition. Similarly, Arabic horoscopes frequently include the Lot of Warfare (or Soldiering)—a lot that had received a distinct emphasis and development in India, growing into a whole field of military astrology *(yātrā)* and reaching Islam through circuitous routes. Indian as well as Harrānian features of Islamic astrology are evident also in the elaborate rituals Arabic writers devised to avert or alter the influences of the planets; these rituals include mysterious invocations, prayers, and animal sacrifices.

Islamic catarchic astrology is likewise a combination of the Dorothean and Indian systems. Treated under the general classification of *aḥkām al-nujūm* ("judgments of the stars," hence the term "judicial astrology"), a whole genre of *ikhtiyārāt* ("choices") literature exists in the Arabic astrological tradition. Indeed, "choices" is a happy title for this activity, since it presupposes free will on the part of the subject: he is free to choose the best time for commencing on activity, with the time being judged from the horoscope. This may be one reason why catarchic astrology enjoyed a relatively wider acceptance in Islam. In one notable instance, the ʿAbbāsid caliph al-Manṣūr consulted as many as four astrologers—Nawbakht, Māshā'allāh, al-Fazārī, and ʿUmar ibn al-Farrukhān—to determine an auspicious moment for the founding of his new capital Baghdad; they chose 30 July 762.

The credit of developing techniques of applying horoscopy to general astrology, the third broad category of astrology, belongs to Sassanian Iran. It arose out of the blending of Hellenistic continuous astrology with the Zoroastrian belief in the twelve-thousand-year cycle of the creation and destruction of the material world, thereby becoming a potent device for all kinds of chiliastic propaganda. Indeed, many an Arabic astrological history culminates in an absolute future victory for the author's chosen party. Given the millennial aspects of general astrology, it carried a particular appeal for the Ismāʿīlīs, who predicted the emergence of the hidden imam at the moment of certain planetary conjunctions, and even the revelation of a new *sharīʿah* and the beginning a new cycle of seven imams. The chiliastic writings attributed to the alchemist Jābir ibn Ḥayyān (probably eighth century) constitute a tantalizing example of this kind of astrology.

Interrogations *(masā'il),* the final category of astrology, saw its greatest development in Islam. This astrological practice determines the answer to the question from the horoscope of the moment when the query is formally presented to the astrologer. Experts believe that interrogational astrology first appeared in India, where it developed as an extension of divination, and then reached Islam via Sassanian versions. An outstanding Arabic work in this field is that of Abu Maʿshar's pupil Shādān, a collection of examples called *Mudhākarāt* (Studies), which constitutes a rich sample of the highly developed interrogational activities of Islamic astrologers.

Recently a few interrogational texts of Mashā'allāh have been subjected to a critical analysis which throws into relief the eclectic nature of the astrologer's enterprise. Their topics include the intention of the querist, finding buried treasure, travel, marriage, debts, clipping nails and hair, cutting out new clothes, manumission of slaves, childbirth, political power, and many more. Here all topics, except political power, are derived from the catarchic aspect of the Greek astrological tradition. Thus one notes that, following the Indians, a Greek technique is appropriated for a different purpose and mixed with Sassanian elements.

From the 10th century Arabic innovations in all four categories of astrology began to travel outward to other cultural areas: first to Byzantium, then to the Latin

West, and finally to India. A great many Arabic astrological texts were translated into Latin: the Europeans knew Abū Maʿshar as Albumasar, ʿAlī al-ʿImrānī as Haly Imrani, Abū ʿAlī al-Khayyāṭ as Albohali, Sahl ibn Bishr as Zahel, and Abū Bakr al-Khāṣibī as Abubather. Indeed, Islamic astrology has profoundly influenced the astrological traditions of both India and the West.

Attitudes toward Astrological Practices. According to a *ḥadīth* in al-Bukhārī, the Prophet had denounced the astral cults of the pre-Islamic Arabs; this must have created in Islam an ethos unfavorable to the growth of an astrological tradition. But a tradition did grow, and it came under heavy fire from religious circles. Genethlialogy and general astrology in particular were the targets of opposition, primarily because they were considered to offend the idea of free will and human responsibility on the one hand, and God's infinite power on the other. Although these astrological practices received strong support from the Shīʿīs, especially those of the Ismāʿīlī persuasion, they were eventually abandoned by sober thinkers and now survive only in the popular culture. Catarchic and interrogational astrology do leave room for free will; therefore, these enjoyed a longer and flourishing career in the Islamic world.

Nonetheless, general attacks on all things astrological have never ceased in the Islamic world. The great sage Ibn Sīnā wrote a whole work against astrology in the eleventh century; some nine hundred years later, the modern poet-philosopher Muhammad Iqbal elegantly mocked the very enterprise of the astrologer:

How can it transmit my fate?
A star!
Humiliated, helpless
In the infinite vastness of the heavens!

[*See also* Astronomy; Divination; Geomancy; Magic and Sorcery; Numerology.]

BIBLIOGRAPHY

David Pingree is a leading contemporary scholar of Islamic astrology. The present entry draws heavily on some of his works, which are strongly recommended to the serious reader. A general and lucid account is to be found in his "Astrology," in *Dictionary of the History of Ideas*, edited by Philip P. Wiener, vol. 1, pp. 118–126 (New York, 1968). His articles on Abū Maʿshar and Māshā'allāh in the *Dictionary of Scientific Biography*, edited by Charles Coulston Gillespie, vol. 1, pp. 32–39 and vol. 9, pp. 159–162 (New York, 1970–), constitute important studies and deserve particular attention. *The Astrological History of Māshā'allāh* (Cambridge, Mass., 1971), coauthored by Pingree and E. S. Kennedy, is another valuable work based on primary material. An article by Pingree, "Māshā'allāh: Greek, Pahlavī, and Latin Astrology," will be published in *Arabic Science and Philosophy* and presents many original reflections on the fortunes of the Hellenistic astrological tradition in the Islamic world.

C. Nallino's "Astrologia e astronomia presso i Musulmani. 1. Astrologia," *Raccolta di scritta editi e inediti* 5 (1944): 1–41, is still the best standard source for the history of Islamic astrology. The reader should also consult relevant articles in the new edition of the *Encyclopaedia of Islam* (Leiden, 1960–) including "Ikhtiyārāt" (vol. 3, pp. 1063–1064), "Kihāna" (vol. 5, pp. 99–101), and "Nudjūm" (vol. 8, pp. 105–108), all by Toufic Fahd, as well as D. B. Macdonald's "Siḥr," in *E.J. Brill's First Encyclopaedia of Islam*, vol. 7, pp. 409–417 (Leiden, 1987). Numerous references to Arabic astrological sources are given in volume 7 of Fuat Sezgin's *Geschichte des arabischen Schrifttums* (Leiden, 1979). For sources, see as well Manfred Ullmann's *Die Natur- und Geheimwissenschaften in Islam* (Leiden, 1972).

S. NOMANUL HAQ

ASTRONOMY. One of the greatest astronomers of Islam, al-Battānī (the Albatenius, Albategni, or Albategnius of the Latin West, d. c.929 CE), declares that astronomy is the most noble of the sciences, elevated in dignity, and second only to the science of religious law (Sayili, 1960, p. 15). This praise of the discipline is not merely a practitioner's claim; embodies a historical truth.

Indeed, astronomy is the only natural science that escaped the censure of the medieval Muslim opponents of secular sciences (*ʿulūm al-awā'il*) and found a home in mosques, receiving the blessing of mainstream religious circles; and it is virtually the only Islamic hard science that lasted well into the modern period, continuing vigorously and fruitfully long after the Mongol sack of Baghdad, when much of Islamic scientific activity began to decline. Moreover, because of its traditional link with astrology and its utility in matters such as calendar reform, the determination of the direction of Kaʿbah, and the calculation of the times of daily prayers, Islamic astronomy enjoyed throughout its history the enthusiastic and undiminished patronage of rulers and nobles. In the internal perspective of the science, astronomy is owed credit for the birth of trigonometry, a remarkable creation of Islam; due to astronomy too are numerous other important developments in mathematics, particularly in quantitative techniques and geometry, for all these mathematical disciplines were for a long time subservient to the needs of astronomers. Finally, it should be noted that astronomy was a truly international enterprise of Islam, a collaborative effort involving people from all over the Islamic world, including experts from China and India. It is evident, then, that al-Battānī's claim is hardly exaggerated.

Origins to Ptolemaicization. The origins of Islamic astronomy are intricately eclectic. The earliest Arabic treatises on this subject, sets of astronomical tables known as the *zīj* (Pers., *zīk*), were written in the first half of the eighth century CE in Sind and Qandahār. These treatises were based on Sanskrit sources, but they have been found to incorporate some Pahlavi material as well. Such derivations from Indian and Iranian works, which constitute the first phase of Islamic astronomy, introduced to the Arabic world many concepts of Greek mathematical astronomy—concepts that were largely non-Ptolemaic, having already reached India and Iran through circuitous routes and having been modified by local traditions. A further infusion of Indian and Iranian material marks the second phase of Islamic astronomy, but this was also the time when the works of the famous Greek astronomer Ptolemy (second century CE) and the Pahlavi *Zīk-i Shahryārān* (Ar., *Zīj al-Shāh*) were translated into Arabic. This activity took place during the reigns of ʿAbbāsid caliphs al-Manṣūr (r. 754–775 CE) and Hārūn al-Rashī (r. 786–809), a period that also saw the emergence of a sustained *Sindhind* Arabic tradition growing out of the translation of a Sanskrit astronomical text, presumably entitled *Mahāsiddhānta*.

During the early ʿAbbāsid period, thus, three astronomical systems were pursued concurrently: the Indian (*Sindhind*); the Iranian (*Zīj al-Shāh*); and the Ptolemaic. These systems were at many points in conflict, and the Islamic astronomical activity of this period is characterized by perpetual efforts to reconcile them. Astronomers soon concluded that the Ptolemaic system was superior to all others known to them. Thus—with al-Battānī marking the turning point—by the beginning of the tenth century Islamic astronomy had undergone a complete ptolemaicization: available now was a newer and better Arabic translation of Ptolemy's *Almagest* made by the Nestorian Christian Isḥāq ibn Ḥunayn (d. 910/11) and the "pagan" Thābit ibn Qurrah (d. 901); Ptolemy's *Planetary Hypothesis* too was now rendered into Arabic by Thābit; and the *Sindhind* and *Shāh* traditions were finally relegated to history. The story of Islamic astronomy from this point is characterized by what Thomas Kuhn would describe as "puzzle-solving" within a Ptolemaic paradigm.

Theoretical Innovations. Let us now, following the lead of contemporary historians, set up the theoretical problem to which these different systems had offered different solutions. Consider two rotating wheels. A larger wheel (the deferent, *al-ḥāmil*) has a stationary center E and a point S on its rim. Let S, namely the point rotating on the circumference of the deferent, be the center of a smaller wheel (the epicycle, *al-tadwīr*). Let P be a point on the rim of the smaller rotating wheel. Then, if P's rate of rotation is properly adjusted, it will appear to an observer at E, the center of the deferent, as periodically advancing and receding as the wheels spin, now coming forward, now sliding back. If in this arrangement S represents the sun, E the earth, and P a planet, then this ancient geocentric model of wheels upon wheels provides a valid if simplified explanation of the looped paths of the planets as seen from the earth.

In practice, however, this mechanism needs adjustments to bring it in accord with the observed planetary motions. Indeed, Ptolemy managed to make a drastic improvement in the correspondence between theory and observation by introducing into the arrangement a geometric device known as the equant (*muʿaddal al-masīr*). What Ptolemy did was to shift the earth a small distance from the center of the deferent E to, say, E_g—thereby making the deferent eccentric with respect to the earth. Furthermore, from E he displaced the center of the uniform motion of S to a rigorously calculated point O. Thus the motion of S was uniform with respect neither to E nor to E_g, but with respect to an imaginary point O, and this O was Ptolemy's fateful equant.

Ibn al-Haytham (Latin, Alhazen, d. 1039), the scientific giant of Islam, wrote an attack on Ptolemy's planetary theory: if Ptolemy's system was not merely an abstract geometrical model but represented the real configuration of the heavens—as Ptolemy had claimed it did—then it violated the accepted classical principle of uniform velocity for all celestial bodies, a principle the Greek astronomer had himself espoused. Indeed, in his *Planetary Hypothesis* Ptolemy had conceived of the observed motions of the planets as produced by the combined motions of corporeal spherical shells in which the planets were embedded. The idea of an eccentric celestial shell was unacceptable to Ibn al-Haytham, as it was to many astronomers who shared his views.

The subsequent history of Islamic mathematical astronomy is a chronicle of attempts to modify the Ptolemaic system so that it would accord more accurately with observations while at the same time preserving the principle of uniform circular motion. It was more than two centuries after Ibn al-Haytham that Naṣīr al-Dīn al-Ṭūsī, the head of the celebrated Marāghah observatory built by Hülegü in 1259, inaugurated outstandingly successful efforts along these lines. Ṭūsī appears to have been the first to recognize that if one circle C_1 with a diameter D rolls inside another circle C_2 with a diameter $2D$, then any point on the circumference of C_1 describes the diameter of C_2. In modern terminology this device can be considered a linkage of two equal and constant-length vectors with constant angular velocity (one moving twice as fast as the other); this is the famous "Ṭūṣī couple." By means of this device the observed phenomena were explained by Marāghah astronomers solely in terms of a combination of uniform circular motions. The apex of these Marāghah techniques is embodied in the work of Quṭb al-Dīn al-Shīrāzī (d. 1311), who, eliminating the Ptolemaic equant, constructed a highly accurate geometrical model for Mercury, by far the most irregular planet visible to the naked eye. In the middle of the fourteenth century the astronomer Ibn al-Shāṭir, a *muwaqqit* (timekeeper) at a mosque in Damascus, further refined the Ṭūsī innovations and managed to develop for the Moon and Mercury new models that were far superior in accuracy to those of Ptolemy.

Historians have pointed out that the mathematical devices created by the Marāghah, scientists and the planetary models constructed by the *muwaqqit* reappear two centuries later in the work of Copernicus. In particular, Copernicus's models of the Moon and Mercury have been found to be identical with those of Ibn al-Shāṭir; moreover, both astronomers employ the Ṭūsī couple, and both eliminate the equant in essentially the same manner. Here the possibility of historical transmission has not been ruled out.

Observational Astronomy. A characteristic feature of the Islamic astronomical tradition is the separation of theoretical exercises from observational activity. Thus observational astronomy took its own independent course, guided by the Ptolemaic concept of testing (*miḥnah* or *iʿtibār),* which requires constantly renewed corrections of the observational data collected by preceding generations. Thus from the early ʿAbbāsid period, astronomical observation remained an intensely pursued activity in Islam, with numerous observatories built over the centuries throughout the Islamic world from Baghdad to Samarra and Damascus, and from Egypt to Persia and Central Asia. Lunar and solar eclipses, meridian transits of the sun, transits of fixed stars, planetary positions and conjunctions—these were all part of the observational repertoire of Islamic astronomy.

Among the observatories that at Marāghah stands out. Indeed, it is regarded as the first observatory in the full sense of the word. It employed a staff of about twenty astronomers, including one from China; it was supported by a library; and it had a workshop for storing, constructing, and repairing astronomical instruments. These instruments included a mural quadrant and an armillary astrolabe, as well as solistical and equinoctal armillaries; also included in the holdings was a new instrument constructed by the Damascene al-ʿUrḍī, which had two quadrants for simultaneous measurement of the horizon coordinates of two stars. Historians have noticed striking similarities between al-ʿUrḍī's observational devices and those of the Danish astronomer Tycho Brahe (d. 1601), even though the results of the latter are unprecedentedly precise.

Long after the Copernican Revolution, Islamic observational astronomy continued in the geocentric Ptolemaic tradition. In the 1570s a major observatory was built in Istanbul. Then, in imitation of the Samarkand observatory founded by Ulugh Beg in 1420, the Indian Mahārāja of Amber (1693–1743) built as many as five different observatories—at Jayapura, Ujjayinī, Delhi, Mathurā, and Vārāṇasī—with the purpose of harmonizing Indian astronomy with the Islamic Ptolemaic tradition. Nonetheless, the alter Islamic observatories were not altogether fruitless exercises, for they contributed to European astronomy many of their observational techniques instruments, and organizational features. Even though Islamic astronomy did not take the daring philosophical step of breaking out of the geocentric Ptolemaic system, it has to its credit numerous impressive achievements: it gave to the world of science the astronomical observatory; it created trigonometry; at Marāghah it developed new instruments and powerful mathematical techniques; and it perpetually improved and corrected astronomical parameters. By consensus of historians, Islamic astronomers were the best of their age.

[*See also* Astrology; Mathematics; Science.]

BIBLIOGRAPHY

David Pingree's "ʿIlm al-Hay'a," in the *Encyclopaedia of Islam,* new ed., vol. 3, pp. 1135–1138 (Leiden, 1960–), is a lucid and comprehensive survey of Islamic astronomical tradition. The early history of the field is covered in Pingree's highly scholarly essay, "The Greek Influence on Early Islamic Mathematical Astronomy," *Journal of the American Oriental Society* 93 (1973): 32–43, which includes an extensive survey of literature. A very useful account of an early astronomer is Pingree's "Māshā'allāh," in the *Dictionary of Scientific Biography*, edited by Charles Coulston Gillispie, vol. 9, pp. 159–162 (New York, 1970–). E. S. Kennedy provides much technical information in readable articles such as "The Arabic Heritage in the Exact Sciences," *Al-Abḥāth* 23 (1970): 327–344; "The Exact Sciences," in *The Cambridge History of Iran*, vol. 4, *The Period from the Arab Invasion to the Saljuqs*, edited by Richard N. Frye, pp. 378–395 (Cambridge, 1975); and "The Exact Sciences in Iran under the Saljuqs and Mongols," in *The Cambridge History of Iran*, vol. 5, *The Saljuq and Mongol Periods*, edited by J. A. Boyle, pp. 659–679 (Cambridge, 1968). For the question of the transmission of Islamic astronomical theories to the West, see Kennedy's classic paper, "Late Mediaeval Planetary Theory," *Isis* 57 (1966): 365–378. A fuller account of the history of trigonometry may be found in Kennedy, "The History of Trigonometry," *Yearbook of the National Council of Teachers of Mathematics* 31 (1969). Aydın Sayılı's *The Observatory in Islam* (Ankara, 1960) is a comprehensive social and intellectual history of the subject. A. I. Sabra's "The Andalusian Revolt against Ptolemaic Astronomy," in *Transformation and Tradition in the Sciences: Essays in Honor of I. Bernard Cohen*, edited by Everett Mendelsohn, pp. 133–153 (Cambridge, 1984), is an important work on the attempts of Spanish Muslim astronomers to improve upon the Ptolemaic system. A brief but rigorous account of Islamic astronomy is Sabra's "The Scientific Enterprise," in *The World of Islam*, edited by Bernard Lewis, pp. 181–199 (London, 1976). D. A. King's "The Astronomy of the Mamluks," *Isis* 74 (1983): 531–555, is a rich and very useful work on the state of the subject during the period under consideration.

S. NOMANUL HAQ

ʿATABĀT. The Shīʿī shrine cities of Iraq, Najaf, Karbala, Kazimayn, and Samarra—comprising the tombs of six of the imams—are important centers of devotion, pilgrimage, scholarship, and political activism known as *ʿatabāt* ("thresholds").

Primacy among the *ʿatabāt* is held by Najaf, 150 kilometers to the south of Baghdad; it is generally held to be the site of burial of ʿAlī ibn Abī Ṭālib, first of the imams, the origins of whose shrine go back to the late ninth century. Karbala, 90 kilometers southwest of Baghdad, the place of martyrdom and burial of ʿAlī's son Ḥusayn, the third of the imams, was first endowed in the mid-eighth century but was temporarily destroyed a hundred years later by the ʿAbbāsid caliph al-Mutawakkil. Both Najaf and Karbala benefited substantially from patronage by the Shīʿī Būyid dynasty during the tenth and eleventh centuries. Similarly, both escaped the depredations of the Mongol conquest of Iraq in the mid-thirteenth century and prospered under the Il-khānid dynasty founded by the Mongols. By contrast, Kāẓimayn, the site of the burial of the seventh and ninth imams, Mūsā al-Kāẓim (d. 802) and Muḥammad al-Taqī (d. 834), being situated on the left bank of the Tigris opposite Baghdad, was extensively damaged by fire when the Mongols sacked that city. Timur, who conquered Iraq in 1400, settled endowments on Najaf, Karbala, and Kāẓimayn. Samarra, being situated 107 kilometers northwest of Baghdad, lies somewhat apart from the remainder of the *ʿatābat* and has generally played a less important role than the other shrine cities: it differs from them in having a largely Sunnī population. It contains the tombs of the tenth and eleventh imams, ʿAlī al-Naqī (d. 868) and Ḥasan al-ʿAskarī (d. 873), and additionally is believed to be the site of the occultation, in 873, of Muḥammad al-Mahdī, the twelfth imam (but not of his anticipated return). The shrines of Samarra owe their architectural origins to Būyid patronage.

In the sixteenth century, Iraq became an object of dispute between the Ottomans and the Ṣafavids, and the *ʿatabāt* accordingly changed hands several times. The veneration of the imams being a part (although admittedly a minor one) of Sunnī religiosity, the Ottomans lavished patronage on the *ʿatabāt* almost to the same degree as their Ṣafavid rivals; thus, projects inaugurated by the Ṣafavid shah Ismāʿīl during his visit to Iraq in 1506 were completed by Sultan Sulaymān Qānūnī ("the Magnificent") after the Ottoman conquest of Iraq in 1534. Iraq and with it the *ʿatabāt* passed definitively into Ottoman control in 1638, their rule being interrupted only by Nādir Shāh during the years 1743 to 1746, an interlude notable primarily for the coerced Sunnī-Shīʿī dialogue that took place under his auspices in Najaf. The *ʿatabāt* remained nonetheless part of the spiritual geography of Iran, and Iranian patronage of the shrines continued throughout the nineteenth century; this accounts for the largely Iranian appearance of the shrines in the present age (or at least down to the time of the Shīʿī uprising that followed the Gulf War of 1991 and its suppression, with the attendant damage to both Najaf and Karbala). In the nineteenth century, Muḥammad Shāh provided for the repair of the damage inflicted on Karbala by the Wahhābīyah during their incursion of 1801, and his successor, Nāṣir al-Dīn Shāh, commissioned much substantial work in all the *ʿatabāt* during his visit to Iraq in 1870. Indian Shīʿī potentates, notably the rulers of Oudh, also settled endowments on the *ʿatabāt;* when their principalities came under British rule, British officials in Iraq sought to make the administration of these endowments a means for gaining influence among the *ᶜulamā'* (religious scholars) of the shrine cities.

Pilgrimage to the *ᶜatabāt* has always formed an important part of Shīᶜī piety, being attested, in the case of Karbala, as early as 684. Such pilgrimage, consisting essentially of circumambulating the tombs while reciting a series of traditional prayers, serves such purposes as the expiation of sins, the making of vows, the accumulation of merit, and gaining the intercession of the imams in the hereafter. Karbala has been particularly favored for pilgrimage, not least because of the special qualities its soil, once moistened with the blood of Ḥusayn and his followers, is believed to possess; it is often used to fashion the clay tablets on which Shīᶜīs place their foreheads when prostrating in prayer. Likewise, diluted in water, the soil of Karbala yields a beverage that is sometimes given to the dying to ease their passage from this world. Burial at the *ᶜatabāt* has traditionally been regarded as highly desirable, particularly at Najaf, in light of the tradition that whoever is buried there will be spared the torment of the grave and questioning by interrogating angels. Accordingly, to the northwest of Najaf, on the road leading to Karbala, there has grown up a vast cemetery known as Wadi al-Salam ("The Valley of Peace"). Despite the general recommendation of swift burial for the deceased, Shīᶜīs from Iran and even India would often send their dead for burial at the *ᶜatabāt* as recently as the 1950s.

The *ᶜatabāt* have also been important in the intellectual life of Shiism; for example, Najaf is known as Dār al-ᶜIlm ("the Abode of Learning"), enjoying preeminence in this respect. The cultivation of scholarship in Najaf, going back to the time of Shaykh al-Ṭā'ifah Abū Jaᶜfar al-Ṭūsī (d. 1067), has been uninterrupted until recent times; teaching would be conducted in the courtyard of the shrine itself as well as in *madrasahs* (Islamic schools) of varying size and prominence, of which thirty-three were to be counted in 1975. Nonetheless, Najaf was occasionally overshadowed by other centers of Shīᶜī learning, such as Ḥillah in Iraq, the Jabal ᶜĀmil in Syria, and, during the Ṣafavid period, by Isfahan in Iran. The primacy of the *ᶜatabāt* was restored in the eighteenth century when chaos and insecurity in Iran prompted many scholars to seek refuge in Iraq, and it was in Karbala that a development of capital importance took place toward the close of the century: the triumph of the Uṣūlī school of Shīᶜī jurisprudence over its Akhbārī adversary, primarily through the exertions of Sayyid Muḥammad Bāqir Bihbahānī (d. about 1791).

With the establishment of relative stability in Iran by the Qājār dynasty in the closing decades of the eighteenth century, scholarly life began to revive in Iran, above all in Isfahan, and many of the pupils of Bihbahānī took up residence there, fulfilling important political as well as religious functions. The *ᶜatabāt* nonetheless retained their importance throughout the nineteenth century; many leading scholars, of both Arab and Iranian origin, spent their entire careers there, and a period of study at the *ᶜatabāt* was essential even for those whose ultimate goal was power and influence in Iran. Comparable to Bihbahānī in their accomplishments were three scholars resident in Najaf: Sayyid Muḥammad Mahdī Bahr al-ᶜUlūm Ṭabāṭabā'ī (d. 1797), a jurist remarkable for his gnostic inclinations; Shaykh Jaᶜfar Kāshif al-Ghiṭā' (d. 1812), author of an important text on the methodology of Shīᶜī jurisprudence; and Shaykh Muḥammad Ḥasan Najafī (d. 1850), who trained a whole generation of influential *ᶜulamā'*. Leading scholars of the *ᶜatabāt* were, moreover, able to play a political role of some significance on several occasions in the early decades of the nineteenth century. Thus, in 1804, ᶜAli Pasha, the governor of Baghdad, sought the intervention of Shaykh Jaᶜfar Najafī to dissuade an Iranian army from advancing on Baghdad. A similar role was played in 1818 by Aqa Aḥmad Kirmānshāhī of Karbala and in 1821 by Shaykh Mūsā Najafī, son of Shaykh Jaᶜfar. When the Shīᶜī inhabitants of Russian-occupied Azerbaijan began to suffer persecution, it was to the *ᶜulamā'* of the *ᶜatabāt* that they turned for relief, and in 1826 Sayyid Muḥammad Iṣfahānī of Karbala issued a *fatwā* (formal legal opinion) calling on the Iranian government to go to war against Russia, traveling personally to Iran to ensure its implementation.

The continuing centrality of the *ᶜatabāt* for the Shīᶜī world was made fully apparent by the emergence in Najaf in 1850 of the first scholar to be universally recognized as the supreme authority *(marjaᶜ al-taqlīd)* in matters of law, Shaykh Murtaḍā Anṣārī (d. 1864). Since Anṣārī was a quintessentially quietist scholar, this development had no immediate political consequences, but the enhancement of *ᶜulamā'* authority it implied was soon to impinge on the political life of Iran. Anṣārī's successor as sole *marjaᶜ al-taqlīd*, Mirzā Ḥasan Shīrāzī, left Najaf for Samarra in 1875, and it was there in 1891 that he issued the celebrated *fatwā* calling for a boycott of tobacco in Iran that was almost universally followed and led to the cancellation of the tobacco concession that had been granted to a British consortium. Fearful of the emergence of a new center of Shiism in a traditionally Sunnī city, and mindful, perhaps, of the way in which Karbala had almost become a semiautonomous enclave in the 1830s, the Ottoman sultan Abdülhamid II took measures to counter Shīrāzī's influence in Samarra and established a Sunnī *madrasah* there under the direction of Shaykh Muḥammad Saʿīd Baghdādī. For whatever reason, the prominence of Samarra was short-lived; significantly enough, Shīrāzī was buried in Najaf on his death in 1895, and it was there that his successors resided and taught. Important among them was Mullā Muḥammad Fāḍil Sharabiyānī (d. 1904), who in contrast to Shīrāzī enjoyed collaborative relations with the Ottomans and benefited from their support in his efforts to curb the growth of Russian influence in Iran.

The importance of the *ʿatabāt* as a center of religio-political direction beyond the reach of the Iranian government came clearly to the fore during the Constitutional Revolution of 1905–1909. The cause of the constitutionalists was powerfully supported by three of the leading scholars of Najaf, all of them pupils of Shīrāzī: ʿAbd Allāh Mazāndarānī (d. 1912), Mirzā Ḥusayn Khalīlī Tihrānī (d. 1908), and Ākhūnd Muḥammad Kāẓim Khurāsānī (d. 1911), the foremost among them in scholarly achievement. Their proclamations equating the constitutionalist struggle with *jihād* were regularly conveyed to Iran by telegraph, and it was from their circle that there emerged the most detailed vindication of constitutionalism in terms of Shīʿī doctrine, Muḥammad Ḥusayn Nāʿīnī's *Tanbīh al-ummah*. When Russian forces entered Iran in 1909 in support of the absolutist monarch, several scholars of Najaf prepared to leave for Iran in order to direct popular resistance; however, they did not proceed beyond Karbala. The activities of the constitutionalist *ʿulamāʾ* were opposed throughout by another senior scholar of Najaf, Sayyid Muḥammad Kāẓim Yazdī (d. 1919). When Russian troops occupied several Iranian cities in 1911, the pro- and anticonstitutionalist *ʿulamāʾ* buried their differences and jointly issued *fatwā*s calling for resistance to the Russians. Some of the *ʿulamāʾ* again planned to leave for Iran, but as before the movement was aborted, largely because of the sudden demise of Khurāsānī. [*See* Constitutional Revolution.]

During World War I several scholars of Najaf, including Yazdī and Shaykh al-Sharīʿah Iṣfahānī (d. 1920), as well as Mīrzā Muḥammad Taqī Shīrāzī (d. 1920) of Karbala, issued *fatwā*s calling for *jihād* against the foes of the Ottomans; in this, they were motivated both by feelings of Pan-Islamic solidarity and by hostility to Britain and Russia, enemies of Iranian independence for a whole century. Certain *ʿulamāʾ*, including Shīrāzī and Sayyid Muṣṭafā Kāshānī, went so far as to participate personally in the fight against the British invaders of Iraq, notably in the battle at Kut al-ʿAmarah in 1916. The *ʿulamāʾ* of the *ʿatabāt* continued their resistance to the British after the defeat of the Ottomans; *fatwā*s were now issued, by Shīrāzī and Shaykh Abū al-Ḥasan Iṣfahānī (d. 1946), against the appointment of Sir Percy Cox as the governor of Iraq and were influential in causing the British to abandon their plans for imposing a mandatory regime on Iraq. The establishment of the Hashemite monarchy in Iraq also met with opposition from scholars of the *ʿatabāt,* notably Iṣfahānī, Nāʾīnī, and Shaykh Muḥammad Mahdī Khāliṣī. Their campaign climaxed in a protest demonstration at Karbala in 1922, attended by some 300,000 people, which led to the exiling of Khāliṣī to Hejaz and the banishing of Nāʾīnī and Iṣfahānī to Iran. Once the agitation had subsided, the two were permitted to return to Iraq in April 1924.

Coincidentally with the foundation of the Hashemite regime in Iraq and, three years later, the replacement of the Qājārs by the Pahlavi dynasty in Iran, Qom began its rise to ascendancy as a center of religious scholarship and direction comparable to the *ʿatabāt*. However, Shaykh ʿAbd al-Karīm Ḥāʾirī Yazdī (d. 1937), the main force behind this development, was not the sole *marjaʿ al-taqlīd*, and all the other principal authorities of the day continued to reside in Najaf. These included Nāʾīnī, Shaykh ʿAbd Allāh Mamāqānī (d. 1936), and Iṣfahānī, who came to enjoy unchallenged supremacy during the last ten years of his life. Roughly a year after the death of Iṣfahānī in 1946, Qom supplanted Najaf as the chief center of religious guidance in the Shīʿī world through the universal acknowledgement of Ayatollah Moḥammad Ḥosayn Borujerdi (d. 1962) as sole *marjaʿ al-taqlīd*. Even during the period of his leadership, however, most Arab and Indian Shīʿīs preferred to study in Najaf, and after his death there were as many claimants to his mantle in Najaf as there were in Qom. Chief among these were Ayatollah Abol-Qāsem Khoʾi (d. 1992), Ayatollah ʿAbd al-Hādī Shīrāzī (d. 1962, a few months after Borujerdi), and Ayatollah Muḥsin al-Ḥakīm (d. 1970). The Shīʿī *ʿulamāʾ* of the *ʿatabāt* had been largely quiescent since the turmoils of the early 1920s, but the changes that followed the overthrow of the Iraqi monarchy in 1958 prompted them to resume comment on political affairs. Thus, in April 1960 Shīrāzī issued a *fatwā* condemning the Iraqi Communist party, one of the principal supports of the regime of ʿAbd al-Karīm Qāsim, and in 1968 al-Ḥakīm protested publicly against the hostility shown to the Shīʿī *ʿulamāʾ* by the Baʿthist regime that had succeeded Qasim in 1963, a hostility that was to take on murderous dimensions in later years.

In October 1965, Ayatollah Ruhollah Khomeini (d. 1989) arrived in Najaf, after a period of forced residence in Turkey, for an exile that was to last almost exactly thirteen years. In consenting to this move, the shah's regime had hoped either that Khomeini would be silenced or overshadowed by senior scholars in Najaf, such as Kho'i and Muḥsin al-Ḥakīm, or that his revolutionary views would inevitably lead him to clash with them and create dissension among the *ʿulamāʾ*. However, Khomeini conducted his relations with the leading figures of Najaf with great discretion, and he appears in any event to have taught and lectured almost exclusively to Iranian students (the celebrated lectures on Islamic government were, for example, delivered in Persian to an Iranian audience). It is also not without significance that Khomeini was the first major religious leader who had received his training entirely in Iran; Qom rather than Najaf was his spiritual home. Despite occasional harassment by the Baʿthist authorities, intermittently eager to improve their relations with the shah's regime, Khomeini was able to conduct from Najaf an effective campaign of opposition to the shah, receiving visitors from Iran itself and from the Iranian oppositional diaspora and issuing political declarations that greatly increased in frequency and effect during the Islamic Revolution of 1978–1979. It can thus be said that under his auspices Najaf came to play a role analogous to that which it had exercised during the Constitutional Revolution seven decades earlier. [*See* Iranian Revolution of 1979.]

By the time that Saddam Hussein deported Khomeini from Iraq in October 1978, at the request of the Iranian government, tensions between the Baʿthist regime and the *ʿulamāʾ* of the the *ʿatabāt* had already been growing for several years. Since the early 1970s the annual celebrations of Muḥarram in the shrine cities had begun to assume a markedly political character, and in 1972 Ayatollah Muḥammad Bāqir al-Ṣadr of Najaf, a gifted political organizer and prolific author whose outlook was in many ways close to that of Khomeini, was arrested for the first time. Riots in Najaf and Karbala, first in 1974 and then in 1977, were brutally suppressed and led to the execution of numerous Shīʿī activists. The triumph of the Islamic Revolution in Iran in February 1979 and the fear that the movement might be replicated in Iraq inspired a still harsher policy in Saddam Hussein, and in June of the same year he had al-Ṣadr placed under house arrest. When it became apparent that Shīʿī revolutionary potential was nonetheless growing, Saddam Hussein had al-Ṣadr executed in April 1980, together with his sister, Bint al-Hudā. (This measure might also be regarded as part of Saddam Hussein's preparations for the war he unleashed on Iran in September 1980). From then on, the *ʿatabāt*—especially Najaf and Karbala—were subjected to unceasing waves of repression that took the lives of hundreds, including, in 1983, three of the sons of Muḥsin al-Ḥakīm, as well as many other religious scholars. In addition, numerous families of Iranian origin (including those who had been settled in Iraq for generations and held Iraqi nationality) were uprooted from the *ʿatabāt* and pushed across the Iranian frontier.

After the defeat of Iraq in the Gulf War of 1991, the Shīʿīs rose in full-scale revolt, and Najaf and Karbala were freed from the control of the Baʿthist regime. But this triumph was short-lived, and when government forces retook the two cities, the reprisals were massive; in addition, numerous mosques and libraries were destroyed in the course of the fighting or sacked after its termination. Ayatollah Kho'i, who had studiously avoided all comment on the tempestuous events of the preceding two decades, was briefly arrested in April 1991 and coerced into appearing on Iraqi television at the side of Saddam Hussein. The death of Kho'i in August 1992 left the *ʿatabāt* without any leading Shīʿī authority, and it is now in Iran, through a reversal of historical roles, that the scholarly traditions of Najaf are being preserved by refugee Iraqi *ʿulamāʾ*, notably Muḥammad Bāqir al-Ḥakīm, a son of Muḥsin al-Ḥakīm. This circumstance, together with the material and demographic devastation that has been visited on Najaf and Karbala and the continuous repression practiced by the Baʿthist regime, has reduced the *ʿatabāt* to a state of unprecedented debilitation, recovery from which will be slow and difficult if at all possible.

[*See also* ʿAlī ibn Abī Ṭālib; Ḥusayn ibn ʿAlī; Karbala; Najaf; Marjaʿ al-Taqlīd; *and* Shīʿī Islam, *historical overview article. In addition, many of the figures mentioned are the subjects of independent biographical entries.*]

BIBLIOGRAPHY

Algar, Hamid. " ʿAtabāt." In *Encyclopaedia of Islam,* new ed., supplement, pp. 94–96. Leiden, 1960–.

Algar, Hamid. " ʿAtabāt." In *Encyclopaedia Iranica,* vol. 2, pp. 902–904. New York, 1987.

Batatu, Hanna. *The Old Social Classes and the Revolutionary Movements of Iraq.* Princeton, 1978.

Hairi, Abdul-Hadi. *Shiʿism and Constitutionalism in Iran: A Study of the Role Played by the Persian Residents of Iraq in Iranian Politics.* Leiden, 1977.

Ḥakīm, Muḥammad Bāqir al-. *Qatl al-ʿUlamāʾ fī al-ʿIrāq.* Tehran, 1404/1984.

Khalīlī, Jaʿfar al-. *Mawsūʿat al-ʿatabāt.* 4 vols. Baghdad, 1382–1385/1969–1972.

Maghnīyah, Muḥammad Jawād al-. *Maʿa ʿulamāʾ al-Najaf al-ashraf.* Beirut, 1984.

Mallat, Chibli. "Religious Militancy in Contemporary Iraq." *Third World Quarterly* 10.2 (April 1988): 699–729.

Momen, Moojan. *An Introduction to Shiʿi Islam.* New Haven and London, 1985.

HAMID ALGAR

ATATÜRK, MUSTAFA KEMAL (1881–1938), founding father of the Turkish Republic. Born of modest Turkish parentage in the cosmopolitan Ottoman port of Selânik (now Thessaloníki in Greece) into a markedly Muslim environment, Atatürk opted for a military education, passing out as an infantry staff-captain in 1905. A participant in the Young Turk movement, his early military career ran concurrently with his secret, illegal political activities against the despotism of Sultan Abdülhamid II—itself a misconstrued attempt to invigorate the empire against slow throttling by the Great Powers. Atatürk and his fellows diagnosed the grievous condition of their society as caused by its political structure and prescribed political restructuring as the cure.

Atatürk's obsession with partisan politics was typical of the Young Turk officers who secured the restoration in 1908 of the 1876 Constitution and thereby the transfer of the center of power to the officer corps. He saw no contradiction between his military profession and his founding, joining, and propagating of various revolutionary societies in the Arabian and Macedonian provinces. Only when he perceived that factionalism based on military membership in political societies would undermine the discipline, and therefore the fighting capacity, of the armed forces did he advocate that the military disengage from partisan politics and the officer corps thus assume an autonomous position and hence a commanding role. Unheeded, somewhat excluded, and overshadowed by more glamorous officers in the tumultuous aftermath of 1908, Atatürk devoted himself to military writing and fighting. He was active in quelling domestic uprisings in the capital (1909) and Albania (1910), as well as in the defense of Ottoman Libya against Italy (1911–1912); but it was the disastrous Balkan War of 1912–1913 that really accelerated his conversion to Turkish nationalism, not yet wholly negating his Ottomanism but salving his wounded *Volksgeist.*

Atatürk emerged from World War I a brigadier-general, acknowledged as one of the youngest and most outstanding commanders among the combatants and accorded prestige and popularity at home. Yet the finality of their defeat faced the Turks with the problem of preserving their very existence against the victorious Allies' attempts to dismember what remained of the empire. Atatürk shared the officers' prevalent belief in the efficacy of the regular military to resist such pressures and so in their own indispensability to the life of the nation; he therefore assumed decisive military and political leadership. His supervision and centralization of spontaneous and widespread local resistance, establishing an alternative national assembly to represent the resisting Turkey, was founded upon his conviction that a nation's right to full independence is fought for, not granted—a postulate central to the National Struggle of 1919–1922 and demanding the absolute loyalty of the professional soldiers to it.

With the foundation of the Republic of Turkey in 1923, President Atatürk concentrated on the furtherance of his nationalist revolution. Through a series of predominantly political reforms, relentlessly pursued despite some internal and international opposition, Atatürk, from 1927 a retired field-marshal, endeavored to establish an inherently capitalist nation-state based on the principle of popular sovereignty; the state's moral substance would be a conscious synthesis of indigenous and universal elements. His envisaged social order for Turkey was fashioned out of long reflection on the Ottoman disorder he had lived through. This social order assumed a modern state inclining toward social democracy, in which ideas that had taken root in Reformation Europe would be grafted onto the liberated Turkey through the complementary concepts of contemporaneity and nationalism.

Atatürk considered contemporaneity to derive from the rationalist essence of civilization, holding contemporary civilization as equivalent to, but not identical with, civilization in western Europe. He strove to cultivate rational enquiry as the ultimate authority in society, to gain individual self-awareness and thence national unity. Linking civilization with the idea of progress as both technological development and moral improvement, his view of contemporary world civilization to which all nations might contribute involved recognition of the multiplicity of its origins, including medieval Islamic civilization. Simultaneously, he sought to nurture that sense of loyalty to country, already beginning to overtake traditional loyalty to sultanate during the National Struggle, into an intense Turkish nationalism, whether combined with the traditional bond of Muslim society or, preferably, replacing it; nationalism would be the Turks' rediscovery and reassertion of their Turkishness—based on assimilation no less than birth. To Atatürk, contemporaneity, fostering the integrative tendency of contemporary world civilization, involved a break with the past, while nationalism with its self-assertive tendency served as a counterbalance, providing continuity with the past through even the most drastic social change. The conjunction of contemporaneity and nationalism thus forms the core of his holistic view of the political universe, underpinning all the reforms he initiated, and it relates directly to his belief in the power of ideas—developing the individual so that the individual can change the society. He aimed to educate individuals toward control of their own affairs, to stimulate a nationalist economy free from foreign dominance, and, significantly, to secularize the polity; for this, he would extricate the state from the cumbersome dichotomous structure whereby social institutions were regulated in part according to *şeriat* (Ar., *sharīʿah*), and unify those institutions under state authority alone.

The depth of Atatürk's religious conviction is still unclear; what is certain is that his drive to secularism (called *lâyiklik* or *lâiklik,* a misappropriation of the term *lâicisme*) in Turkey was not conceived as an attack on Islam, which he considered the most rational, natural, and therefore final religion. He held the decay of the Muslim world and its falling under oppression to be the fault of Muslims, dominated by their wrong thinking. His idealist philosophy ascribed this to Muslims' retreat over the centuries from rationalism to implicit acceptance, rendering themselves submissive and defenseless. As he argued, the weight of rigid orthodoxy that had turned Islam from a reasoned belief to blind faith must be lifted from society, not just so that Muslims might advance but for Islam itself, which needed to be cleansed of irrational and inflexible accretions. Then, too, since Islam is essentially a rational religion in which knowledge preponderates, individuals might reach the divine by using their intellect. Atatürk's persistent attempts to have the Qur'ān and the language of worship rendered into an authorized Turkish version for general use were thus aimed at religious enlightenment. He wanted for Turkey a secular society of Muslims wherein the maintenance and advancement of Islam would rest upon the voluntary adherence of individual believers: nonreligious government for the religious rather than religious government, in what would inevitably be a secular state.

Atatürk lived his life determining how to impose the possible but not attempting rigidly to impose the not-yet-possible. Given the dearth of religious scholars of sufficiently revolutionary caliber, he abandoned his earlier feeling that a secular state must nevertheless provide some kind of infrastructure for the regulation and instruction of Islam. His consequent withdrawal in the 1930s to the thesis that the government of such a state has no role in the people's religious development, and to the legal implementation of this, was perhaps misconceived. It created the paradox of the unlettered *hoca* (religious teacher), who lacked adequate state-supported education yet was blamed for perpetuating ignorance and bigotry among the faithful.

Atatürk's attempted reform of Turkish religious life comprises, with his other social reforms, a consistent political philosophy. His ultimate objective, in a formula admitting of general application, was the achievement of a genuine and modern nationhood, responsible for and answerable to its citizens individually and collectively, which would survive, conscious and assured, in the contemporary world.

[*See also* Kemalism; Ottoman Empire; Turkey; Young Turks.]

BIBLIOGRAPHY

Atatürk, Mustafa Kemal. *A Speech Delivered by Ghazi Mustapha Kemal, President of the Turkish Republic, October 1927*. Leipzig, 1929. English version of Atatürk's famous six-day speech, covering the years from the 1918 Armistice (without the original documents). Essential for an understanding of the man and the period.

Aydemir, Şevket Süreyya. *Tek Adam: Mustafa Kemal*. 3 vols. Istanbul, 1963–1965. The most perceptive life of Atatürk in print ; the book still awaits a critical editing and translation into English.

Gökman, Muzaffer. *Atatürk ve Devrimleri Tarihi Bibliyografyası/Bibliography of the History of Atatürk and His Reforms*. 3 vols. Ankara, 1981–1983. Comprehensive bibliography that includes works by Atatürk, comprising speeches, statements, declarations, treatises, diaries, letters, handwritten and dictated notes, and unsigned articles, together with secondary material in numerous languages.

İğdemir, Uluğ, et al. *Atatürk: Biography* (1963). Translated by Andrew J. Mango. Reprint, Ankara, 1981. Published by the Turkish National Commission for UNESCO, this is a complete translation of the entry "Atatürk, Gazi Mustafa Kemal" in *İslâm Ansiklopedisi* (13 vols.), vol. 1, fasc. 10, pp. 719–807 (Istanbul, 1949–1986). The authorized biography, an encyclopedic compendium of information; dated but factually sound.

Kazancıgil, Ali, and Ergun Özbudun, eds. *Atatürk: Founder of a Modern State*. London, 1981. Informative, though somewhat uncritical, example of collected scholarship on Atatürk.

Kinross, Lord (John Patrick Douglas Balfour). *Atatürk: The Rebirth of a Nation* (1964). Nicosia, 1981. Still the most readable biography in English. While there have been numerous workaday lives of Atatürk, he still has not found his much-needed scholarly biographer.

Tongas, Gérard. *Ataturk and the True Nature of Modern Turkey*. Translated by F. F. Rynd. London, 1939. Though long out of print, this study by a contemporary is still one of the most incisive in its approach to Atatürk's revolution. Nevertheless, the ideas behind the revolution continually require further examination. The author of the present article, for example, has already written elsewhere (in English) on the political thought of Atatürk, and is currently preparing a book-length study.

Turfan, M. Naim. "Mustafa Kemal Atatürk, 1881–1938." In *The Routledge Dictionary of Twentieth-Century Political Thinkers*, edited by Robert Benewick and Philip Green, pp. 12–14. London and New York, 1992. Readily accessible and recent example.

M. NAIM TURFAN

AUSTRALIA AND NEW ZEALAND. Although there have been Muslims in Australia and New Zealand for more than a century, the present small but active Muslim communities have developed since 1950. The first Muslims in Australia were camel drivers who helped open up the interior of the country in the late nineteenth and early twentieth centuries, but they did not establish a continuing Muslim community. This occurred only in the 1950s when some Muslims came as part of the considerable postwar immigration from Mediterranean countries. More arrived in the following years, including Turks who came with the support of their government and a large number of Lebanese Muslims fleeing the civil war after 1975. Numbers nearly tripled from 1976 to 1986. Lebanese are now the largest national group and with the Turks account for more than 80 percent of the Muslim population. There are also Muslims from other Arab countries, South and Southeast Asia, ex-Yugoslavia, and elsewhere. According to government figures there were 109,500 Muslims in Australia in 1986, representing 0.7 percent of the total population. Other estimates, however, put the number as high as 250,000. Some 87 percent are in the urban centers of New South Wales and Victoria in the southeastern part of the country.

Local Islamic associations were first organized in the mid-1950s, and by the 1970s several were quite well established. They largely follow ethnic lines and have established mosques and provide a variety of religious, educational, cultural, welfare, and community services relevant to their immigrant constituencies. There are also several organizations for Muslim women.

In 1965 a national organization was formed, and this developed by 1975 into a three-tiered structure consisting of local associations, eight state councils, and a new national organization, the Australian Federation of Islamic Councils (AFIC). AFIC and the state councils provide a number of educational, cultural, and religious services, but local associations retain their autonomy. Other AFIC functions include representing Australian Muslims to both Australian and overseas agencies and certifying the *ḥalāl* slaughter of animals.

Local associations select their own imams (congregational leaders), but these are often supported by AFIC and overseas agencies. The Turkish government plays a major role in choosing and supporting imams for Turkish mosques. Financial assistance for building mosques often comes from Saudi and other sources, channelled through AFIC. Partly for these reasons there has been some tendency toward centralization in recent years. Although the local associations are still strongly ethnic in character, awareness of broader Islamic identity has been increasing.

New Zealand Muslims are predominantly of Fijian Indian and other South Asian origin, but a number are from other countries, including some overseas students and a small but active group of Western converts. At least half live in Auckland, New Zealand's largest city. According to the 1991 census they numbered 5,277, about 0.15 percent of the total population, although estimates by Muslims run as high as 9,000. The roots of the present community go back to a handful of Gujarati men who arrived after 1906, but only after 1950 did Muslim families began to settle in New Zealand. Significant growth began in the late 1960s, with more than a tenfold increase from 1966 to 1991. The 1987 coup d'état in Fiji has caused a considerable recent influx.

The first Muslim association was formed in Auckland in 1950, and between 1964 and 1989 five others were founded. The mosque in Christchurch, completed in 1985, is furthest from Mecca of the world's mosques.

Depending on resources, the associations provide for religious, educational, and social activities, including *ḥalāl* food and publicity. Some have separate women's and youth groups, and many have *usrah* (family) groups. *Tablīgh* activity (similar to revival missions, deriving from Mawlānā Ilyās's movement in India) is important. Some associations are served by fulltime imams, but policy control is largely in the hands of lay leaders. As in Australia, outside financial assistance, often from Saudi Arabia, has been necessary for both the construction and maintenance of buildings and the payment of imams. New Zealand associations are not divided along ethnic or sectarian lines, mainly because of their small numbers, but partly also because of the efforts of local and national leaders. In 1979 a national organization, the Federation of Islamic Associations of New Zealand (FIANZ), was formed to coordinate financial requests and other dealings overseas and to provide other services. It offers a *ḥalāl* certification service, although much of New Zealand's considerable meat export to the Muslim world is certified in other ways.

Australian Muslims are mainly working-class immigrants and economically disadvantaged, although some, especially South Asians, are white-collar and middle-class. In New Zealand the Auckland community has a large working-class component, but the average income of New Zealand Muslims is close to the average for the country. In both countries Muslims have suffered from some discrimination, negative stereotyping, and conflicts between Muslim customs and local ways, such as difficulties in getting time off for religious services, insensitivity of health agencies and schools to Muslim concerns, and legal problems with marriage and divorce. Such problems seem to be greater in Australia than in New Zealand. There is also negative publicity and hostility arising out of events overseas, such as the Iranian revolution, the Rushdie affair, and the the Gulf War of 1990–1991. All these issues have been confronted with some success in both countries by the Islamic councils and associations and also by agencies such as the Human Rights Commissions. In both countries Muslims have made considerable progress in establishing themselves and learning to function in their new environments.

[*See also* Islam, *article on* Islam in Southeast Asia and the Pacific.]

BIBLIOGRAPHY

Humphrey, Michael. "Is This a Mosque Free Zone? Islam and the State in Australia." *Migration Monitor* 3.12 (January 1989): 12–17.

Humphrey, Michael, "Islam, Immigrants, and the State: Religion and Cultural Politics in Australia." *Islam and Christian-Muslim Relations* 1.2 (December 1990): 208–231.

Islam in Australia. Sydney, 1985. Articles from a 1984 seminar held at the MacArthur Institute of Higher Education.

Islamic Communities in N.S.W. [Sydney?, 1985]. Articles giving thorough coverage of Muslims in the Sydney area.

Shboul, Ahmad, "Muslims." In *Many Faiths, One Nation*, edited by Ian Gillman, pp. 217–234. Sydney, 1988.

Shepard, William E. "The Islamic Contribution." In *Religion in New Zealand Society*, 2d ed., edited by Brian Colless and Peter Donovan, pp. 181–213. Palmerston North, N.Z., 1985.

WILLIAM E. SHEPARD

AUTHORITY AND LEGITIMATION. Most Muslim rulers try to legitimize their authority through Islam; however, there are today only two regimes in Sunnī Islamic countries in which the king claims a religious title associated with his political authority—Morocco and Saudi Arabia (Tibi 1985). The title of the Moroccan king is *amīr al-mu'minīn* ("commander of the faithful"), and the Saudi king is *khādim al-ḥaramayn al-sharīfayn* ("custodian of the holy shrines" of Mecca and Medina). In Saudi Arabia the Qur'ān is considered the constitution, in contrast to Morocco, which has a modern constitution.

In August 1992 the Moroccan king showed willingness to amend the constitution to enhance the power of his prime minister, who is constitutionally fully subservient to royal authority. The amendment also refers to human rights mentioned in the constitution. When the constitutional change was submitted to a referendum on 4 September 1992, the king responded to opposition criticism by emphasizing the authority of an Islamic ruler. He said, "Islam does not permit a constitutional monarchy like the one that exists in western Europe. As a Muslim ruler, I am entitled to temporarily delegate some of my authority to others, but I have no right to give up on my own power privileges." This poses the question whether the king's view represents an authentic perspective on authority and legitimacy in Islam. The al-Azhar scholar ʿAlī ʿAbd al-Rāziq, in *Islam and the Principles of Government* (1925), held that Islam does not entail a system of government. ʿAbd al-Rāziq argued further that Islam historically has been abused to legitimize unjust rule. [*See the biography of* ʿ*Abd al-Rāziq*.]

Islam is characterized by a holistic view of the world in which politics, law, and all other spheres of life are intimately and organically merged into one unity (Tibi 1990, chapter 3). The governing principle of this totality is *tawḥīd* (the oneness of God). *Tawḥīd* means that the world and consequently the lives of Muslims are wholly governed by the oneness of God, the supreme authority. It follows that Muslims in principle see no separation between political and religious authority. The corollary of this is that political authority has to be religiously grounded; that is, its legitimation has to be related to the principle of *tawḥīd*. No Muslim ruler can therefore claim to have sovereign authority, because that is God's alone. The ruler has to base his authority on the precept that he executes the divine will of God as fixed in Islamic revelation. It is this provision to which the Moroccan king's statement refers. [*See* Tawḥīd.]

The medieval Islamic theologian Ibn Taymīyah (d. 1328) coined the term *taʿṭīl* for claims by humans to govern the world. In his authoritative pamphlet *Maʿālim fī al-ṭarīq* (Milestones), the spiritual father of Islamic fundamentalism, Sayyid Quṭb (1906–1966), reactivated this precept in his challenge to democratic legitimacy and the idea of popular sovereignty. [*See the biographies of Ibn Taymīyah and Quṭb.*]

Although this characterization of the basic concept of authority and legitimacy is shared by most Muslims, Islamic history reveals a multiplicity of competing patterns of authority and legitimacy related to sectarian developments. Historians of Islam have described this civilization in terms of a conflict over identifying the true imam or authority for Muslims (Hartmann 1944). The wide range of political rulers who have been Islamically legitimized shows that Muslims have disagreed about legitimacy. In classical Islam, Sunnī and Shīʿī rulers as well as their opponents have legitimized their authority based on their specific understanding of Islam. The lack of a tradition of a consensually accepted pluralism has contributed to the growth of religious controversies regarding Islamic authority and legitimacy, as Watt (1968) has shown. All Muslim rulers refer to the Qur'ānic commandment, "Oh ye who believe, obey Allāh, obey the Prophet and those in authority [*al-amr*] among you" (4.59); it is open to interpretation whether authority here means power.

In modern times, the disintegration of the Ottoman Empire and the subsequent abolition of the caliphate in 1924 smoothed the way for the introduction of the European concept of popular sovereignty among Muslims (Enayat, 1982, pp. 111f.). In the Arab lands the concept of an Islamic *ummah* (community) has been superficially secularized to refer to an Arab *ummah* that unites Muslims and Christians in a modern nation-state based on popular sovereignty (Tibi, 1991). The rise of Islamic fundamentalism has greatly challenged this new secular concept of the *ummah* (Choueiri, 1990, pp. 63ff.) and has contested the assumption that in the modern state legitimacy is secularly grounded. [*See* Ummah.]

In his general monograph *The Legitimation of Power* (1991), David Beetham devotes a chapter to Islam, in which he points out that the politicization of Islam presents a challenge to Western notions of the exclusively secular basis of political legitimacy. The core of this challenge is the idea of the Islamic state. Fundamentalists argue that the Islamic state (see Kurdi, 1984) can only be based on a specific pattern of authority and legitimacy. Given that Islamic fundamentalists are not traditionalists—they themselves are both a product of modernity and a reaction to the process of modernization—the question is whether the concept of an Islamic state is based on a new rather than a traditional type of legitimacy.

Departing from the *tawḥīd* principle and thus from the belief that God governs the entire world, all spheres of life in the Islamic state are expected to be organized in consonance with Islamic revelation. In other words, political authority in Islam has to be constantly grounded in divine legitimacy. In classical Islam, the caliph's authority was based on his submission to the *sharīʿah*. Although he is the absolute political chief of the Islamic community, he has no right to legislate. His authority is restricted to administrating *sharīʿah*. In practice, however, Islamic rulers have deviated from this principle by introducing the autonomous realm of *siyāsah* (administration), in which the caliph retained some sovereignty. As Joseph Schacht writes in his introduction to Islamic law, "This *siyasa* is the expression of the full juridical power which the sovereign . . . can exercise whenever he thinks fit . . . a double administration of justice, one religious and exercised by the Kadi [*qāḍī*] on the basis of the shariʿa, the other secular and exercised by the political authorities" (1964, p. 54). This system of authority was practiced by the caliphs from the Umayyad period onward.

Contemporary Islamic rulers who base their political authority on Islamic legitimacy draw on a tradition embedded in the political history of Sunnī Islam. Classical and contemporary Islamic societies share a low degree of institutionalization in their political systems. According to Samuel P. Huntington's *Political Order in*

Changing Societies (1968), one of the consequences of this lack of highly institutionalized structures and processes is the personalization of political power. Thus the authority of the political ruler in Islam, classical and contemporary alike, has been highly personal, not institutional, and has been legitimized in an arbitrary manner by the *ʿulamāʾ* and jurists submissive to the ruler. This fact explains the lack of continuing institutional power in Islamic history.

Among the sectarian religious divisions with regard to authority and legitimacy, the most pertinent one is that differentiating the doctrines of the caliphate in Sunnī Islam and the imamate in Shīʿī Islam. For Sunnī Muslims the caliph is equally an imam in the double meaning of being both the symbolic leader of congregational prayers and the political leader, but the Shīʿī imam does not embody temporal political leadership. Whereas Sunnīs believe that prophecy ended with the death of the Prophet, Shīʿīs believe in the continuation of prophecy through the imams; however, they conceive the imamate not as temporal leadership but as religious guidance "for preserving and explaining the Divine Law" (Momen, 1985, p. 147). Thus the legitimacy of the Shīʿī imam is not only based on the interpretation of Divine Law, "the Imam's knowledge is co-extensive with that of the prophets. . . . Thus the Imam as a result of his knowledge is perfectly able to give judgement on all matters of religious law" (p. 156). Some Shīʿī scholars interpret the authority of the imam as political insofar as he is "a person who takes the lead in a community in a particular social movement or political ideology" (Ṭabāṭabāʾi, 1975, p. 173). However, until the advent of Ayatollah Ruhollah Khomeini, this was not a common view among Shīʿīs. Khomeini's revisionist interpretation of *vilāyat-i faqīh (wilāyat al-faqīh)* "obliterates some of the most important differences between Sunnis and Shiʿis. He minimizes the extent of the rift by . . . his appeal to the Shiʿis to . . . install an Islamic state [that] indicates his denunciation of . . . Shiʿi practices that have become staple themes of Sunni polemics against Shiʿism" (Enayat, 1983, pp. 174–175). [*See* Wilāyat al-Faqīh.] It is not surprising that current treatises by Sunnī fundamentalists have recourse to Khomeini's ideas of authority and legitimacy, which endorse harmony and reconciliation between Sunnīs and Shīʿīs. The Sunnī writer Muḥammad Salīm al-ʿAwwā, in his book *Fī al-niẓām al-siyāsī lil-dawlah al-Islāmīyah* (The Political System of the Islamic State, 1983), published seven times in Arabic, presents such a case.

In the period between the abolition of the Ottoman Empire in 1924 and the rise of Islamic fundamentalism in the early 1970s, the idea of the nation-state and its secular legitimacy seemed to have superseded the idea of an Islamic order. In the nineteenth century ʿAbd al-Raḥman al-Kawākibī (d. 1903) was the most significant Muslim Arab author seeking to revive the caliphate under Arab rule against the Sunnī Turks. Muḥammad Rashīd Riḍā's (d. 1935) book *The Caliphate or the Supreme Imamate* (1922/1923) was the last significant Islamic work to defend the caliphate. The scholar Shaykh ʿAlī ʿAbd al-Rāziq held that those who have legitimated political authority by recourse to Islam have abused Islam for political ends. ʿAbd al-Rāziq's argument, which provoked his dismissal from al-Azhar, was that Islam is a religion and ethical system, but not a system legitimizing political authority. Despite his dismissal, ʿAbd al-Rāziq's argument had already come to represent the spirit of the times. [*See the biographies of Kawākibī and Rashīd Riḍā*].

The two Arab Muslim monarchies, Morocco and Saudi Arabia, are legitimized by Islam, and although they differ considerably, both do in some measure reflect Islamic political culture. In his book on legitimacy in Arab politics, Michael Hudson writes:

> The ideal Arab monarchy, perfectly legitimized, entirely congruent with the values of the traditional political culture, would be an Islamic theocracy governed by the ablest leader of a tribe tracing its lineage to the prophet. The ruler would be guided by the substantive ethic of Islam and by the patriarchal consultative procedures of tribal decision-making. The ruler's authority would rest not only on his coercive power but in the respect of his people for a leader on the right path (the Sunna). . . . By this legitimate behavior alone, he would earn the deference of his people and thus acquire authority (1977, p. 167).

Morocco and Saudi Arabia, however, ran counter to the dominant pattern of secularization throughout the period of early decolonization until 1967. Between the 1930s and early 1970s, the secular nation-state was the most accepted form of legitimacy in the Arab world, even though the processes of secularization and structural differentiation needed as underpinnings for the nation-state had not taken place in the Islamic world (Tibi, 1980). In the world of Islam secularization has been normative rather than structural in nature and thus has failed to take root.

The turning point for the resurgence of political Islam

and its views on authority and legitimacy was the Arab defeat in the Six-Day War in 1967. The Arab hub of the Muslim world was the center of the recent Islamic revival long before the Islamic revolution in Iran drew the attention of the West to this process. One of the main features of this revival has been the renewed focus on authority and legitimacy in Islam and their relevance for the crisis of the secular Muslim state (Khoury, 1983, pp. 213ff.). The redefinition of these ideas is meant to establish a religious order in place of the existing secular ones. This is the content of the new concept of the Islamic state. As exemplified in the case of ʿAlī ʿAbd al-Rāziq, debates on these issues have never ceased in modern Islam, even in the period when secular ideologies prevailed (Tibi, 1986). During the 1950s and 1960s, some important publications revived these debates and reopened the arguments against ʿAbd al-Rāziq's views; significant among them were the works of al-Rayyis (1953), Mūsā (1962), and Mutawallī (1964).

In terms of dissemination and popularity, however, these books could not compete with prevailing secular positions, such as that of Khālid Muḥammad Khālid's *Min hunā nabda'* (From Here We Start). Khālid's book was reprinted ten times between 1950 and 1963 and distributed far beyond Egypt. Khālid's strong argument against what he called *kahānah Islāmīyah* (Islamic theocracy) culminates in a clear commitment against the use of Islam as a legitimation of political authority:

> We should keep in mind that religion ought to be as God wanted it to be: prophecy not kingdom, guidance not government and preaching, not political rule. The best we can do to keep religion clean and pure is to separate it from politics and to place it above it. The separation between religion and the state contributes to keeping religion away from the shortcomings of the state and from its arbitrariness (1963, p. 184).

Such views have been superseded since the early 1970s. Even Khālid, having recanted, is now among those who support the idea of the Islamic state (see Khālid, 1988). [*See the biography of Khālid.*] The strongly articulated plea of Islamic fundamentalists for an Islamic solution began to replace the secular writings of the enlightened Arab Muslim authors. In 1953 Muḥammad Ḍiya' al-Dīn al-Rayyis assured readers that Islam provides a pattern of legal rule because political authority is bound to the *sharīʿah* as a legal framework. Those who disagree with him, in particular those whom he calls Orientalists, are blamed for viewing Islamic governments as despotic: "The Orientalists, in their allegation that the government of Islam is despotic, are mistaken. . . . The source of their mistake is that they look at the Caliphate that really existed in history. . . . Thus they confuse Islam as a legal idea with what really happened in the Muslim world" (1953, pp. 225–226). Al-Rayyis thus sees Islam as a pure idea to be kept apart from the dirt of history; the implementation of the idea remains a pious call. This is also the case in the most authoritative book of ʿAbd al-Ḥāmid Mutawallī, *Mabādi' nizām al-ḥukm fī al-Islām* (1964), where he writes, "As far as the science of government is concerned, Islam provides general principles valid for every time and place." These principles, he says, guarantee equally the practice of the "Islamic constitutional norms" justice, freedom, participation *(shūrā)*, and equality (p. 548).

Another authority, Muḥammad Yūsuf Mūsā, states that in Islam the relationship between the ruler and the ruled is based on a type of social contract called *bayʿah*. The author is thus reading into Islam the Rousseauian idea of social contract. *Bayʿah* means "oath of allegiance" as a source of legitimacy; however, it is not a social contract based on the unbreakable, institutionally controlled commitment of the ruler to the practice of Islamic law. [*See* Bayʿah.] The historical record shows that no Islamic ruler has ever been legally accountable, and norms not substantiated in history have no meaning. Mūsā insists that an Islamic ruler is democratic insofar as, by accepting the *bayʿah*, he commits himself "to rule and to cast his policy in accordance with Islamic law as fixed by the Qur'ān and the *sunna* of the Prophet." To define Islamic rule, Mūsā writes:

> Islam is not theocratic because it denies the ruler a divine character . . . nor is it a monarchy since Islam does not allow succession by inheritance . . . nor is it despotic because an Islamic ruler is subject to the law, and thus it guarantees the citizens all kinds of freedom. . . . It cannot however be called democracy in the old Greek or modern Western sense since in Islam the will of the people counts only if it is in line with the shariʿa. The shariʿa has the highest sovereignty in Islam (1962, pp. 142–145).

Besides the fact that "citizenship" is a modern concept that did not exist in classical and medieval Islam, we are still confronted with the questions, what is the legitimate Islamic system, and what is Islamically unique in the authority it incorporates? Mūsā answers, "The system differs from all others known to mankind in classical, medieval, and modern history as well as in the present. . . . In recognizing the unique character of this system, we ought to say that it is an incomparable system. It is the Islamic system and that is sufficient" (pp. 146–147).

The truth is that all attributes denied to have characterized political rule in Islam have existed in actual Islamic history. Despite this, al-Rayyis, Mūsā, and Mutawallī, who published their fundamentalist views of political Islam in the 1950s and 1960s, and who have ignored the historical record, are extensively quoted in the contemporary writings of Islamic revivalism.

The political literature of Islamic revivalism during the 1970s and 1980s, with its focus on authority and legitimacy, does not go beyond the arguments highlighted above. This revival is related to the crisis of legitimacy in existing political regimes. The acid test of the legitimacy of rulers is acceptance by the ruled, but absence of any popular legitimizing basis is the reality in most current regimes in the Islamic world. The envisaged return to Islam is presented in the guise of an Islamic state as a solution to perceived moral decline. Even though the proponents of the Islamic state derive the legitimacy of their model from the distant past, the pattern of authority and legitimacy they propose is an artifact of the modernity they rhetorically reject.

The most sophisticated authors of current, broadly disseminated books on authority and legitimacy are Muḥammad Salīm al-ʿAwwā (1983) and Muṣṭafā Abū Zayd Fahmī (1981). They emphasize the legal and participatory meanings of Islamic political norms and so provide an Islamic model of authority and legitimacy seemingly compatible with modernity; but even they fail to tell us why Islam has never achieved the specifically democratic, legal, and participatory Islamic values they present. From the early history of Islam (Mottahedeh, 1980; Dabashi, 1993) until the present, the political authority of imams and emirs has been based on personal rule, and Islam was used to justify the ruler's status as an imam. The historical context of authority and legitimacy has changed, but not the principle of personal rule.

[*See also* Caliph; Imam; Islamic State.]

BIBLIOGRAPHY

Ahmed, Ishtiaq. *The Concept of an Islamic State*. London, 1987. Presents the argument that Islamic authority and legitimacy are components of the idea of an Islamic state, focusing on Pakistan.

ʿAwwā, Muḥammad Salīm al-. *Fī al-niẓām al-siyāsī lil-dawlah al-Islāmīyah*. Cairo, 1983.

Beetham, David. *The Legitimation of Power*. London, 1991. Excellent overall study of the legitimacy issue, with a chapter on Islam.

Choueiri, Youssef M. *Islamic Fundamentalism*. Boston, 1990. Critical study of the claim that political Islam represents true Islamic legitimacy.

Dabashi, Hamid. *Authority in Islam*. New Brunswick, N.J., 1993. Social science–oriented inquiry into authority in Islam, from Muḥammad to the Umayyad period.

Enayat, Hamid. *Modern Islamic Political Thought*. Austin, 1982. Excellent study by the late Iranian Oxford scholar in which tensions in Islam between classical and modern political concepts are reviewed.

Enayat, Hamid. "Iran: Khomeini's Concept of the Guardian of the Jurisconsult." In *Islam in the Political Process*, edited by J. P. Piscatori, pp. 160–180. Cambridge, 1983. Excellent chapter on Khomeini's revisionist interpretation of authority and legitimacy in Shīʿī Islam.

Fahmī, Muṣṭafā Abū Zayd. *Fann al-ḥukm fī al-Islām*. Cairo, 1981.

Hartmann, Richard. *Die Religion des Islam* (1944). Reprint, Darmstadt, 1987. Concise and knowledgeable classic survey of Islamic history, with a discussion of Islamic debates on "who is the true imam."

Hudson, Michael. *Arab Politics: The Search for Legitimacy*. New Haven, 1977. Overview of the legitimacy problem in the modern Middle East, with reference to Islamic history and case studies on all Arab states.

Khālid, Khālid Muḥammad. *Min hunā nabda'* (1950). 6th ed. Cairo, 1963. Translated from the third edition by Ismāʿīl R. al-Fārūqī as *From Here We Start*. Washington, D.C., 1953.

Khālid, Khālid Muḥammad. *Al-dawlah fī al-Islām*. Cairo, 1988.

Khoury, Philip S. "Islamic Revival and the Crisis of the Secular State." In *Arab Resources*, edited by Ibrahim Ibrahim, pp. 213–236. London, 1983. Analysis of the legitimacy crisis of the secular state and its implications for the repoliticization of Islam.

Khūrī, Fu'ād Isḥāq. *Imams and Emirs: State, Religion, and Sects in Islam*. London, 1990. Study of sects in Islam as an opposition to prevailing authority.

Kurdi, Abdulrahman A. *The Islamic State*. London, 1984. Effort to trace the concept of the Islamic state to the Qur'ān, laden with grand projections.

Momen, Moojan. *An Introduction to Shīʿi Islam*. New Haven, 1985. Includes information on the Shīʿī concept of authority and legitimacy.

Mottahedeh, Roy P. *Loyalty and Leadership in an Early Islamic Society*. Princeton, 1980. In-depth historical inquiry into acquired loyalties and loyalties of category in early Islam.

Mūsā, Yūsuf Muḥammad. *Niẓām al-ḥukm fī al-Islām*. Cairo, 1962.

Mutawallī, ʿAbd al-Ḥamīd. *Mabādī' niẓām al-ḥukm fī al-Islām*. Alexandria, 1966.

Rayyis, Muḥammad Ḍiyā' al-Dīn al-. *Al-naẓarīyah al-siyāsīyah al-Islāmīyah*. Cairo, 1953.

Schacht, Joseph. *An Introduction to Islamic Law*. Oxford, 1964. Authoritative study on the juridical bases of authority and legitimacy in Islam.

Ṭabāṭabā'ī, Muḥammad Ḥusayn. *Shīʿite Islam*. London, 1975. Includes important information on Shīʿī views on authority.

Tamadonfar, Mehran. *The Islamic Polity and Political Leadership*. Boulder, 1989. Important social science study on the legitimacy of Islamic leadership, past and present.

Tibi, Bassam. "Islam and Secularization: Religion and the Functional Differentiation of the Social System." *Archives for Philosophy of Law and Social Philosophy* 66.2 (1980): 207–222. Presents the idea that secularization of legitimacy and authority in Islam failed because it lacked a structural underpinning and was restricted to normative change.

Tibi, Bassam. "A Typology of Arab Political Systems: Arab Monarchies Legitimized by Islam." In *Arab Society,* edited by Samih Farsoun, pp. 48–64. London, 1985. Analysis of Islamic legitimacy in Morocco and Saudi Arabia.

Tibi, Bassam. "Islam and Modern European Ideologies." *International Journal of Middle East Studies* 18.1 (1986): 15–29.

Tibi, Bassam. *The Crisis of Modern Islam.* Salt Lake City, 1988. Social and cultural roots of tension between Islam and modernity.

Tibi, Bassam. *Islam and the Cultural Accommodation of Social Change.* Boulder, 1990. Analysis of the gap between normative and actual levels of legitimacy and authority in Muslim societies.

Tibi, Bassam. *Arab Nationalism.* New York, 1991. Critical inquiry into the rise, development, and decline of secular Arab nationalism.

Tibi, Bassam. "The World View of Sunni Arab Fundamentalists." In *Fundamentalisms and Society,* edited by Martin E. Marty and R. Scott Appleby, pp. 73–102. Chicago, 1993. Analysis of the holistic view of the Islamic world, as revived by contemporary Islamic fundamentalists. Their views merge with politics and religion and thus move authority and legitimacy issues to center stage.

Watt, W. Montgomery. *Islamic Political Thought: The Basic Concepts.* Edinburgh, 1968. Overview of the basic political concepts in Islam, including those on authority and legitimacy.

BASSAM TIBI

AVRUPA MİLLÎ GÖRÜŞ TEŞKİLATI. In the early 1970s the first branches of the "National Vision" (Millî Görüş) organization were founded by Turkish labor migrants in Europe. These groups had close connections to the National Salvation Party (Millî Selamet Partisi [MSP]). The name "Millî Görüş" stands for a philosophy as well as for the organization and is derived from the programmatic book *Millî Görüş*" (Ankara, 1973) of party leader Necmettin Erbakan. In 1976 the various groups joined together in the Turkish Union in Europe, which changed its name in 1982 to the Islamic Union in Europe and in 1985 to the Organization of the National Vision in Europe (Avrupa Millî Görüş Teşkilatı [AMGT]). With its headquarters in Cologne, Germany, about twenty-five to thirty centers and 145 mosques in different parts of Germany, 150 to 220 affiliated organizations, about seventy thousand members and the Organization of Islamic Youth in Europe (Avrupa Islamci Gençlik Birliği), the AMGT is the largest nongovernmental organization of Muslims in Germany.

The AMGT also runs centers in Denmark, the Netherlands, Belgium, France, Switzerland, and Austria. It cooperates with other Islamist organizations, such as the Syrian Muslim Brotherhood, the Afghan Party of God (Ḥizbullāh), the Filipino Moro National Liberation Front, and the Libyan Islamic Call Society. After the Islamic Revolution in Iran in 1979 and the military takeover in Turkey in 1980, severe ideological and political conflicts erupted within the organization. In 1984, a group of radical fundamentalist and antisecular Muslims around Cemalettin Kaplan left the AMGT and founded the Iran-oriented Federation of the Islamic Unions and Communities. In 1986 three members of AMGT were accused at the State Security Court in Ankara of attempting to establish a theocratic state in Turkey. They were also suspected of working as a connecting link between AMGT, the Kaplan group, and Iran.

The ideological orientation of AMGT is Islamist. It is based on the Qur'ān, the *sunnah* (traditions of the Prophet), and *sharīʿah.* The Qur'ān ranks as the only legitimate constitution. The political developments in Iran are considered to be an important step toward the liberation of Islam and as a model for the reislamization of Turkish society. AMGT advocates the bipartite division of the world in accordance with Islamic international law *(dār al-Islām/dār al-ḥarb).* Living in Western societies means living in societies alien and hostile to Islam. Integration into Western societies and adaptation to the Western way of life is strictly rejected and is regarded as a treason to Islam. Consequently AMGT is also opposed to the integration of Turkey into the European Community. Since the end of the 1980s, however, there have been indications of a new dialogue with trade unions, churches, and the media. But it is too early to tell if this portends a change in policy or if this is mainly a tactical move. Like other Muslim organizations, AMGT has applied for the legal status of "body of public law," but no Muslim organization in Germany has yet been granted this status.

[*See also* Germany *and the biography of Erbakan.*]

BIBLIOGRAPHY

Binswanger, Karl, and Fethi Sipahioğlu. *Türkisch-islamische Vereine als Faktor deutsch-türkischer Koexistenz.* Munich, 1988. Insightful study of religious and political organizations among Turks in Germany.

Gerholm, Tomas, and Yngve Georg Lithman, eds. *The New Islamic Presence in Western Europe.* London and New York, 1988. Collection of essays on the institutionalization of Islam in various European countries and on the changes in the religious experience through migration.

Landau, Jacob. "The National Salvation Party in Turkey." *Asian and African Studies* 11.1 (1976): 1–57. Overview of the early years of the party and the political background of the AMGT.

HANNS THOMÄ-VENSKE

AWAMI LEAGUE. As one of Bangladesh's two major political parties, the Awami ("people's") League led the country's war of independence against Pakistan in 1971, under the charismatic Shaikh Mujībur Raḥmān (1920–1975), affectionately called the Banglabandhu or "Friend of Bengal." It is a secularly oriented, left-leaning political organization. Its party symbol, the boat, symbolizes the river-based life of the region.

The Awami League, originally called the East Pakistan Awami Muslim League, was founded in Dhaka (Dacca) in 1949. Articulate Bengali Muslims of East Pakistan had become increasingly resentful of the Muslim League leadership because of its failure to transform that party into a representative organization. Bengalis resented the domination by a new political elite composed mostly of expatriate Muslims from India and the civil-military bureaucracy of West Pakistan. The founding of the Awami League thus reflected the growing sense of frustration of the indigenous Bengali elite with central authority in Pakistan. By 1966 the party had emerged as the embodiment of a Bengali political community.

Although widely associated with the name of Huseyn Shaheed Suhrawardy (1893–1963), a former prime minister of united Bengal and Pakistan, the organization owed its origin to Maulānā Bhasanī (1885–1976), a pro-Beijing peasant leader. Dubbed the "Red Maulana," Bhasanī's goal was to transform the structure of Pakistani politics by radically democratizing political institutions and involving the masses. The leadership of the party was, however, taken over by the centrist leader Suhrawardy, who began molding it as an organization of the nascent Bengali Muslim bourgeoisie. It was renamed the Awami League, dropping the word "Muslim" to emphasize its secular character. Soon Bhasanī and his socialist confidants were pushed out of the party.

The watershed in the Awami League's development as a mass organization occurred under Shaikh Mujīb. The Language Movement of 1952 that had urged recognition of Bengali as one of Pakistan's official languages, the dismissal of a popularly elected government in East Pakistan in 1954, and the subsequent imposition of martial law in 1958 that had specifically disadvantaged the Bengali political elite had all been perceived as indications of the rulers' hostility toward the political, economic, and cultural aspirations of Bengalis. As a consequence, the assertion of Bengali linguistic-cultural identity, in sharp contrast with the closer identification with Islam during the Pakistan movement, became the dominant theme of East Pakistani politics, especially during the 1960s. The Awami League under the leadership of Shaikh Mujīb emerged as the voice of this movement.

Beginning in 1964 Shaikh Mujīb played a dominant role in reorganizing and revitalizing the Awami League, attracting mass support, and gaining control of the political movement in favor of greater regional autonomy. He formulated the famous Six-Point Program in 1966, which demanded, *inter alia,* the formation of a federation in Pakistan with the federate units enjoying a large measure of political and economic power. Mujīb was charged with treason by the government in the same year and imprisoned in the Dhaka army cantonment. An upsurge in popular support soon made him a symbol of Bengali nationalism and forced the government to drop the case.

Elections held in 1970 under a new military regime gave the Awami League 160 of the 162 seats allotted to East Pakistan, ensuring an absolute majority in the 300-seat national parliament. The military junta, however, refused to hand over power to the elected representatives, leading to a popular uprising in the province in February 1971. Shaikh Mujīb launched a noncooperation movement against the central government on 7 March, urging people to fight for freedom and democracy. The independence movement had begun.

Although mass mobilization was central to the Awami League's political strategy, the control of rural elites severely restricted its ability to initiate meaningful reforms once in power. For example, the Eleven-Point Program of the students (1968) demanded nationalization of banking, insurance, and major industries, reduction of taxes on farmers, and better wages for workers. Although these were incorporated into the League program in order to broaden its base of support, a section of the party hierarchy opposed them.

One of the notable achievements of the Awami League was to enact a constitution for Bangladesh in 1973, less than two years after independence. But this exercise in democracy soon became academic when Mujīb amended the constitution in 1975, introducing a one-party system under the banner of BAKSAL (Bangladesh Peasants and Workers Awami League). Gross mismanagement of the economy, corruption, and the highhandedness of party cadres created mounting problems for the government and eroded its popular support.

Questions were also raised as to the Awami League's loyalty to Islam, although it is doubtful that the party leadership, despite its ambivalent commitment to secularism and socialism, has ever underrated the strength and appeal of Islam in a predominantly Muslim country. Earlier, in October 1970, Shaikh Mujīb had clearly asserted his "commitment to the constitutional principle that no law should be enacted or imposed . . . which is repugnant to the injunctions of Islam" (1972, p. 11). There is no evidence to suggest that his position ever changed. His government imposed a ban on religious parties after independence, basically as a reaction to the excesses they had committed during the war in 1971. Mujīb recognized the need for closer ties with other Muslim countries and became gradually more receptive to Islamic issues. He even attended the summit meeting of the Organization of the Islamic Conference in Lahore, Pakistan, in 1974.

The Awami League government was overthrown in August 1975 in a coup staged by a group of young army officers, who killed Shaikh Mujīb, most of his immediate family members, and a number of his close associates. The party has since suffered from factionalism and defections. It has equally had to confront its political opponents, backed by the army and the armed cadres of the fundamentalist Jamāʿat-i Islāmī. However, it has successfully consolidated its position in recent years, reemerging as one of the largest political parties in the country. Shaikh Hasīnah Vājid, one of the surviving daughters of Shaikh Mujīb, was made leader of the party in 1979; she was elected to parliament in 1990 and has since led the opposition there.

Although Shaikh Hasīnah Vājid and her party embody the spirit of Bengali nationalism and democratic government popularized by her father, her affiliation with Islam appears more pronounced. The party has moved closer to an Islamic posture despite efforts to project a secular-socialist image. However, its old stereotype as an un-Islamic party persists among its opponents.

[*See also* Bangladesh.]

BIBLIOGRAPHY

Bhuiyan, Md. Abdul Wadud. *Emergence of Bangladesh and Role of Awami League*. Delhi, 1982. Highly informative account of the rise of the Awami League as a mass political organization and its role in Bangladesh's War of Independence.

Jahan, Rounaq. *Pakistan: Failure in National Integration*. New York, 1972. Balanced view of the origins of Bengali nationalism in Bangladesh.

Mujibur Rahman, Sheikh. *Bangladesh My Bangladesh*. Delhi, 1972. Selection of speeches by Shaykh Mujīb and relevant documents on Bangladesh (compiled by Ramendu Majumder).

O'Donnell, Charles P. *Bangladesh: Biography of a Muslim Nation*. Boulder, 1984. Excellent overview of society and politics in Bangladesh.

Sen, Rangalal. *Political Elites in Bangladesh*. Dhaka, 1986. Socialist view of politics and political elites in Bangladesh.

Umar, Badruddin. *Politics and Society in East Pakistan and Bangladesh*. Dhaka, 1974. Marxist analysis of political developments in the region.

Westergaard, Kirsten. *State and Rural Society in Bangladesh*. London, 1985. Study in the dynamics of regional and rural society and politics in Bangladesh.

RAFIUDDIN AHMED

AYATOLLAH. Derived from the terms *āyat* (sign, testimony, miracle, verses of the Qur'ān) and Allāh (God), *ayatollāh* ("sign of God"), is an honorific title with hierarchical value in Twelver Imamite Shiism, bestowed by popular usage on outstanding *mujtahid*s, with reference to Qur'ān 41.53. The sense of this title can be traced to the need for legitimacy sought by the Shīʿī *ʿulamā'* during the absence of the twelfth imam, the Master of the Age, in the end of the greater occultation, from 940 to the end of time. Its attribution reflects the socioreligious environment prevailing in the Qājār period (1796–1925). The title was not in use among the Shīʿīs of Lebanon, Pakistan, or India and remained restricted in Iraq to *mujtahid*s of Iranian origin. An imitation of the title *ẓill Allāh* ("shadow of God") traditionally applied to Persian Islamic rulers, which was confirmed by the use of *āyat Allāh zādah* ("son of ayatollah"), a counterpart of *shāh zādah* ("son of the shah"), has also been proposed as the origin of the title (Matīnī, 1983).

The attribution of this title seems to have coincided with crucial moments of influence of Twelver Shiism in Iran. Its first reputed bearer, Ibn al-Muṭahhar al-Ḥillī (d. 1325), converted the Mongol Il-khān Öljeitü Muḥammad Khudābandah (r. 1304–1317) to Twelver Shiism. He was styled *āyat Allāh fī al-ʿālamayn* (ayatollah in the two worlds), in addition to his best-known title of *al-ʿAllāma'* (i.e., "the most learned"; this became an essential requisite for a *marjaʿ al-taqlīd,* a "source of emulation" in the Qājār period). But this case remained an exception. Although the modern bio-hagiographical Shīʿī literature sometimes applies retrospectively titles such as *marjaʿ al-taqlīd* or ayatollah to pre-Qājār *ʿulamāʾ*, this is historically groundless. Former Ṣafavid and even Qājār Shīʿī titles were styled differently. Most titles were related to the functions of the *mujtahid,* such as: *mujtahid al-zamān* (*mujtahid* of the age); *khātam al-mujtahidīn* ("seal of *mujtahidīn*"); *shaykh al-mujtahidīn* ("dean of *mujtahidīn*"), and so forth. Except for the functional title of *marjaʿ al-taqlīd,* other titles were related to Islam, such as *thiqat al-Islām* ("trustee of Islam") and *ḥujjat al-Islām* ("proof of Islam").

The general use of the title appears in the late Qājār period. It is mentioned in a pamphlet against the *ʿulamāʾ* (see Ḥājj Sayyāh, *Khāterāt,* Tehran, AH 1346/1930 CE, p. 338; text written between the 1870s and 1910s). Among its earlier modern bearers one may find religious/political leaders of the constitutional revolution of 1905 to 1911, Sayyids ʿAbd Allāh Bihbahānī (d. 1910) and Muḥammad Ṭabāṭabāʾī (d. 1918). But anti-constitutionalist *mujtahids* were also called ayatollah, and a spiritual leader, ʿAbd al-Karīm Ḥāʾirī-Yazdī (d. 1937), founder of the new theological center of Qom, is said to be the first *mujtahid* to bear this title. Titles such as *āyat Allāh fī al-anām* ("ayatollah among mankind"), or *fī al-ʿālamayn* ("in the two worlds"), or *fī al-warā* ("among mortals") also appeared from the time of the constitutional revolution.

Besides being a fully qualified *mujtahid,* an aspiring ayatollah must assert his authority over both his peers and his followers. As shown by recent research on Shīʿī leadership (Amanat, 1988), to the prerequisite notion of *aʿlamīyat* ("superiority in learning") must be added the often overlooked concept of *riyāsat* ("leadership") that is solidified by popular acclamation and payment of religious taxes. Although contributing to centralizing clerical authority, *riyāsat* also meant clerical leadership over specific communities (e.g., Arab, Turkish, or Persian-speaking groups in Iraqi Shīʿī sanctuaries, the *ʿatabāt* [*see* ʿAtabāt]).

With the appearance of such outstanding figures as Moḥammad Ḥosayn Borujerdi (d. 1962), who emerged as the sole *marjaʿ al-taqlīd,* and the religious political leader Abol-Qāsem Kāshāni (d. 1962), the title ayatollah became increasingly common and ubiquitous. Losing its initial prestige, it even came to be applied, against their own usage, to Sunnī religious dignitaries. The leading ayatollah of his time came to be designated by the elative *āyatullāh al-ʿuẓmā* ("grand ayatollah", i.e., the supreme *mujtahid* or *marjaʿ al-taqlīd*), the first bearer of the title being Borujerdi. A kind of restricted college of ayatollahs, in Qom, decided on his nomination. A further debasement of even this higher title occurred with the application of the title imam to Ayatollah Ruhollah Khomeini (d. 1989), quite unusual for Twelver Shīʿī (see Matīnī, 1983, p. 603f.).

At the time of Borujerdi's death there was a great discussion among prominent *mujtahids*, ayatollahs, and Shīʿī laymen regarding the role of the *marjaʿ al-taqlīd* and his function. Among the views discussed was the idea, formerly favored by ʿAbd al-Karīm Ḥāʾirī-Yazdī, that the concept of a sole *marjaʿ al-taqlīd* be abandoned. Each *mujtahid* should then specialize in a field and be followed in that field. Another idea was that a council of *mujtahids* should be sharing leadership. In practice, there was a split in the leadership, outstanding ayatollahs and *marājiʿ al-taqlīd* being established in the main centers of learning (Mashhad and Qom in Iran; Najaf in Iraq). After rivaling Qom from the 1960s until the mid-1970s, Mashhad declined in importance. After the events of 1963, Ayatollah Khomeini emerged as one of the top-ranking *marājiʿ al-taqlīd,* although Muḥsin al-Ḥakīm (supported by the shah) had a large following in Iraq.

Although Shīʿī *ʿulamāʾ* were traditionally reluctant to structure their leadership, as a result of the Iranian Islamic Revolution, by 1980 a sort of seven-degree hierarchy was established: *ṭalabah* ("student"); *thiqat al-Islām* (title formerly given to higher ranking *mujtahids*); *ḥujjat al-Islām; ḥujjat al-Islām wa al-muslimīn; āyatullāh; āyatullāh al-ʿuẓmā; nāyib-i imām* ("lieutenant of the Imam"). The latter title reflects the assumption of both temporal and spiritual power by Khomeini. The concept of *niyābat* (general vicegerency of the Hidden Imam) was until then purely theoretical in Twelver Shiism. Despite its devaluation, a growing number of *mujtahids* bore the title ayatollah. A decree from Khomeini (September 1984) stated that certain persons calling themselves ayatollah should henceforth be called *ḥujjat al-Islām.*

With the establishment of the Islamic Republic of Iran (1979), a leading role was attributed to prominent ayatollahs. But some of them reluctantly accepted or even objected or opposed the application of Khomeini's theory of *vilāyat-i faqīh* (*wilāyat al-faqīh;* mandate of the jurist), the most prominent opponent being Sharīʿat

Madārī (d. 1986), demoted from the rank of grand ayatollah in 1982. One of the leading opponents, Ayatollah Abol-Qāsem Kho'i (Abū al-Qāsim Khū'ī, d. 1992) had many followers. After Khomeini's death, Sayyid ʿAli Khamene'i became the *valī-i faqīh* (leading theologian), while Ayatollah Ḥusayn ʿAlī Muntaẓirī, initially nominated by Khomeini as his spiritual heir (and ratified by the Assembly of Experts, or *shūrā-yi khibrigān*, in 1985), only to be dismissed by Khomeini in 1989, is still waiting a general acknowledgment of his title of *āyatullāh al-ʿuẓmā* at the top of the hierarchy.

[*See also* Ijtihād; Marjaʿ al-Taqlīd; Mujtahid; *and* Iran; *in addition, many of the figures mentioned are the subjects of independent entries.*]

BIBLIOGRAPHY

Akhavi, Shahrough. *Religion and Politics in Contemporary Iran*. New York, 1980.

Algar, Hamid. "Āyatallāh." In *Encyclopaedia Iranica*, vol. 3, fasc. 2, p. 133. New York and London, 1982–. See related bibliography.

Amanat, Abbas. "In Between the Madrasa and the Marketplace: The Designation of Clerical Leadership in Modern Shiʿism." In *Authority and Political Culture in Shiʿism*, edited by Said Amir Arjomand, pp. 98–132. New York, 1988.

Arjomand, Said Amir. *The Shadow of God and the Hidden Imam*. Chicago and London, 1984.

Arjomand, Said Amir. "Ideological Revolution in Shiʿism." In *Authority and Political Culture in Shiʿism*, edited by Said Amir Arjomand, pp. 178–209. New York, 1988.

Arjomand, Said Amir. *The Turban for the Crown: The Islamic Revolution in Iran*. New York and Oxford, 1988.

Bakhash, Shaul. *The Reign of the Ayatollahs: Iran and the Islamic Revolution*. London, 1986.

Calmard, Jean. "Āyatullāh." In *Encyclopaedia of Islam*, new ed., Supplement, pp. 103–104. Leiden, 1960–. See related bibliography.

Calmard, Jean. "Mardjaʿi-taḳlīd." In *Encyclopaedia of Islam*, new ed., vol. 6, pp. 548–556. Leiden, 1960–. See related bibliography.

Calmard, Jean. "Mudjtahid." In *Encyclopaedia of Islam*, new ed., vol. 7, pp. 295–304. Leiden, 1960–. See related bibliography.

Fisher, M. M. J. *Iran: From Religious Dispute to Revolution*. Cambridge, Mass., and London, 1980.

Matīnī, J. "Spiritual Titles in Iranian Shiʿism" (Persian). *Iran Nameh* 1.4 (1983): 560–608.

Momen, Moojan. *An Introduction to Shiʿi Islam*. New Haven and London, 1985.

JEAN CALMARD

ĀZĀD, ABŪ AL-KALĀM (1888–1958), Urdu journalist and stylist, Islamic thinker, and religious universalist symbolizing the Muslim option for composite Indian nationalism. Mawlānā Āzād was born in Mecca, where his father Khairuddīn Dihlawī (1831–1908) had migrated in 1858 and later married the daughter of a mufti of Medina. The ancestors of Āzād had intellectual and spiritual links with Shaykh Aḥmad Sirhindī (d. 1624), Shah Walī Allāh Dihlawī (d. 1762), and Shah ʿAbd al-ʿAzīz (d. 1824). Khairuddīn was an influential *ʿālim-pīr* (learned Ṣūfī authority) with outspoken anti-Wahhābī leanings. The family moved to Calcutta around 1898.

Āzād was taught at home under the strict supervision of his father and completed, at the age of fifteen, the *dars-i Niẓāmī* course of higher Islamic studies. His phenomenal memory, as well as his public preaching, prose, and verse, made him famous as a child prodigy. Very early, however, he became critical of his father's bitter opposition to the scripturalist Wahhābīs and of his practices of *taqlīd* (reliance on tradition) and *pīrī-murīdī* (the relation between spiritual guide and disciple). For some time Āzād fell under the spell of Sayyid Aḥmad Khān's (1817–1898) reformist ideas and rationalistic theology. This was followed by a period of doubts, unbelief, and sensuous living. A deep experience of mystic love induced by earthly love led him back to faith in God by the end of 1909.

Āzād's journalistic career started with his launching in 1903 of the short-lived reformist journal *Lisān al-ṣidq*. Thereafter he worked for short periods with *Al-nadwah*, the organ of the Nadvat al-ʿUlamā' academy in Lucknow, under the guidance of Muḥammad Shiblī Nuʿmānī (d. 1914), and with the renowned newspaper *Vakīl* in Amritsar. He was familiar with the contemporary writing of the Arab world in the vein of Jamāl al-Dīn al-Afghānī and those associated with the influential journal *Al-manār* with its roots in neo-Ḥanbalī theology. On a visit to western Asia in 1908–1909 he met Iranian nationalists in Iraq, and in Cairo Arab nationalists and Turkish revolutionaries, followers of Mustafa Kemal (Atatürk, d. 1938). He synthesized their ideas with his own experience of contact with the Bengal Hindu revolutionaries in the wake of the 1905 partition of Bengal.

In 1912 Āzād, through his widely influential weekly journal *Al-hilāl* (The Crescent), set out first to revive among the Muslims of India the true spirit of Qur'ānic Islam as the only solution to the nation's problems, and second to move them to political revolt through participation in the struggle of the Indian Congress Party for self-government. The fight for independence was a religious duty for Muslims, but they had first to be freed of their "pathological fear of the Hindus." Āzād emerged as a forerunner of Mohandas Gandhi, who was to launch his anti-British noncooperation agitation in 1919. However, nonviolence for Āzād was a matter of policy, not of principle.

When the government forced *Al-hilāl* to close down, upon the outbreak of war between Turkey and Britain, Āzād started another journal, *Al-balāgh*. But soon, exiled from Bengal, he was to spend three and a half years in internment near Ranchi. Immediately upon his release in January 1920, he joined the nationwide struggle for political freedom led by Gandhi. The address that Āzād delivered in February 1920, as president of the Bengal Provincial Khilāfat Conference, served as a strong inspiration and theoretical basis for the Khilāfat movement. Referring to the covenant concluded in 622 between Muḥammad and the people of Medina, including Jews and pagans, Āzād described Muslim together with non-Muslim parties as a single community *(ummah wāḥidah)*.

Āzād was again arrested toward the end of 1921 and formally put on trial. His defense, later published under the title *Qaul-i fayṣal,* occupies an eminent place in both the political history of India and the history of Urdu literature. In 1929 Āzād, in cooperation with thirty other nationalist Muslim leaders, convened the Nationalist Muslim Conference, but his real field of political activity was within the Congress. During the 1930s and 1940s he was imprisoned four times; he eventually spent one-seventh of his life in either internment or jail. In 1940 Āzād was elected president of the All-India National Congress and held this position until 1946. He failed to prevent the partition of India, which was for him a lasting tragedy overshadowing the achievement of independence. In 1947 he joined the interim government of India as minister of Education. This post, as well as that of deputy leader of Congress, he held until his death.

Āzād's overall religious perspective is marked by the unique blending in his temperament of aesthetic experience and religious consciousness. The charming letters to his friend from the British prison at Ahmadnagar (*Ghubār-i khāṭir,* edited by Malik Ram, New Delhi, 1967; rev. ed. 1983) provide insight into his multifaceted Islamic sensitivity. Earlier, in his fragmentary autobiography *Tazkirah* (edited by Fazluddin Ahmad, Calcutta, 1919; rev. ed. Malik Ram, New Delhi, 1968), Āzād had offered a passionate discussion of such moral and religious issues as the eternal validity of the Word of God, the affinity between earthly and sacred love, and the appreciation of beauty in its varied forms, including music, which he held to be compatible with the Qur'ān. All of Āzād's writings had a deeply religious tenor and were marked by his artistic, highly personalized diction, appealing to intuition rather than discursive reason.

Āzād's mind accommodated conflicting elements without any attempt to reconcile them in a conceptual whole. His countless writings and speeches all refer to a few fundamental attitudes and options sponsored by his interpretation or *tafsīr* of the Qur'ān. However, in *Tarjumān al-Qur'ān*, Āzād's annotated Urdu rendering of surahs 1–23, and especially in his commentary on the opening verses of the Qur'ān, his main concern is to let the Qur'ān speak for itself. The Qur'ān is a spiritual text concerning God and humanity, enjoining good and prohibiting evil. Pseudoscientific attributions of medieval or modern provenance must not distort its divine beauty and simplicity.

In their essence all faiths are one *(dīn);* their distinctiveness, expressed in different laws, is neither original nor inherent. Islam as the religion of the Qur'ān does not have to be politically and nationally separatist to be viable and effective in history. Moreover, God's attributes are readable in their qualities of nurture, harmony, and guidance as imprinted on the created universe. The Qur'ān indicates the middle path between transcendentalism and anthropomorphism. Praise, gratitude, and universal brotherhood are the obvious human responses. Although Āzād believed that human obduracy generates destructive "groupism," he preferred not to probe the depths of sinful perversion in individuals or societies.

A basic lacuna in Āzād's religious scholarship is the absence of an updated hermeneutics of the fundamental sources of Islam—the Qur'ān and *ḥadīth*—and, based on that, a reformulation of the principles of legal construction. However, although he did not initiate a school of thought, his vision of Islam as Qur'ān-based universal humanism continues to inspire Muslim sensitivity, especially in the Urdu-speaking world.

BIBLIOGRAPHY

Āzād, Abū al-Kalām. *Tarjumān al-Qur'ān*. 2 vols. Delhi, 1931–1936. Critical edition by Malik Ram. 4 vols. New Delhi, 1964–1976. Translated and edited by S. A. Latif, *The Tarjumān al-Qur'ān*. 3 vols. Bombay, 1962–1967.

Āzād, Abū al-Kalām. *Speeches of Maulana Azad, 1947–55*. New Delhi, 1956.

Āzād, Abū al-Kalām. *Khuṭubāt-i Āzād*. New Delhi, 1981. The chief public speeches of Āzād, 1914–1948, in the Urdu original.

Āzād, Abū al-Kalām. *India Wins Freedom* (1959). Edited by Humayun Kabir. Reprint, Madras, 1988. Reprint containing thirty pages originally withheld from publication.

Datta, V. N. *Maulana Azad*. New Delhi, 1990. Places Āzād more firmly than Douglas in the context of Indian politics.

Douglas, Ian Henderson. *Abul Kalam Azad: An Intellectual and Religious Biography*. Edited by Gail Minault and Christian W. Troll. New Delhi, 1988. The most penetrating study of Āzād's life and works. Comprehensive bibliography.

Faruqi, I. H. Azad. *The Tarjuman al-Qur'an: A Critical Analysis of Maulana Azad's Approach to the Understanding of the Qur'an*. New Delhi, 1982. Elucidates the links of *Tarjumān* with earlier Qur'ān exegesis and brings out its distinguishing features.

Hameed, Syeda Saiyidain, ed. *India's Maulana: Abul Kalam Azad*, vol. 1, *Tributes and Appraisals;* vol. 2, *Selected Speeches and Writings*. New Delhi, 1990. Volume 1 adds to Humayun's memorial volume (below) on the occasion of Āzād's centenary. Volume 2 presents a number of key texts by Āzād (for the first time in English) and offers a comprehensive bibliography of the primary and secondary sources.

Hasan, Mushir ul-, ed. *Islam and Indian Nationalism: Reflections on Abul Kalam Azad*. New Delhi, 1992. Delineates Āzād's political trajectory in the context of nationalist struggles in West Asia and India.

Kabir, Humayun, ed. *Maulana Abul Kalam Azad: A Memorial Volume*. Bombay, 1959. Remains the most important collection of views and analyses of Āzād's personality and work by contemporaries.

CHRISTIAN W. TROLL

AZERBAIJAN. Northern or Caucasian Azerbaijan is situated on the western shore of the Caspian Sea. Conquered by the Russian Empire early in the nineteenth century, it remained under Russian rule until the collapse of that empire in 1918. The first Republic of Azerbaijan existed from 28 May 1918 until 28 April 1920, when it was reconquered by the Red Army. The country remained under Soviet rule as the Azerbaijan Soviet Socialist Republic until declaring its independence on 30 August 1991.

At the time of the Russian conquest, the population of Azerbaijan was approximately 80 percent Shīʿī and 20 percent Sunnī Muslim; the latter lived mainly in the north near Daghestan. The Azerbaijani Turks were thus the only Turks to be mainly Shīʿī, a result of direct Iranian rule since the founding of the Ṣafavid dynasty under Shah Ismāʿīl I (r. 1501–1525). The Russians conquered the independent khanates in Caucasia in two wars with Iran, ending in the Treaties of Gulistan (1813) and Turkmanchai (1828). Direct military rule was in force until the early 1840s.

With the establishment of Russian imperial rule, the power of the Muslim *ulema* (Ar., *ʿulamāʾ*) began to diminish sharply. Russian imperial law supplanted the mix of religious *(sharīʿah)* and customary *(ʿādāt)* law, and religious properties *(awqaf;* sg., *waqf)* were seized. Thus the legal and administrative functions of the *ʿulamāʾ* were taken over by tsarist administrators, and their economic power was undercut.

The key tsarist policy that destroyed the *ulema* was the creation in the 1840s of Sunnī and Shīʿī ecclesiastical boards. These were meant to bring the Muslim "church" and its believers under state control as the Holy Synod had done with the Russian Orthodox Church. Each board consisted of a state-appointed president (called *muftī* for the Sunnī, and *shaykh al-Islām* for the Shīʿī), its supporting administration,and a judicial administration for each province—Tiflis, Erevan, Elizavetpol (Ganje), and Baku. The apparatus was under the control of the Russian imperial ministry of internal affairs and the personal authority of the viceroy of Transcaucasia. The mullahs in each province were under the legal jurisdiction of the civil authorities.

Regulations established parameters within which mullahs and qāḍīs could act but also granted them rank in the government system and a range of privileges. Before a cleric could occupy any post, he was required to pledge loyalty to the tsar. He was to "fulfill unswervingly the laws and instructions of the government," and to inspire in his coreligionists "steadfast loyalty and devotion to the sovereign Emperor" and "obedience to authorities."

State regulations concerning religious properties fundamentally altered the Islamic legal definition of *waqf*, to include any properties or capital used by religious institutions or the religious classes. All "religious properties" could be sold by public auction, and disputes concerning them were decided according to the civil law established for state administration.

The relationship between the religious establishment and the modernizing secular elite was complex. By the early twentieth century, when the national movement was in flower, the Islamic establishment was greatly weakened after a century of Russian rule. In the face of Russian pressure, sectarian peace prevailed among the Shīʿī and Sunnī of the Russian Empire. At the All-Russian Muslim Congresses of 1905–1906, the Sunnī *ulema* in the Russian Empire, in an unprecedented move, accepted Shiism as a fifth *madhhab* or legal school, the Jaʿfarī. Furthermore, a reform movement within Islam (Jadīdism) divided the religious classes along "traditionalist" (Qadīmist) and "reformist" (Jadīdist) lines, and therefore did not constitute a single monolithic body.

Finally, secular elites, though anticlerical, never rejected Islam. Even a 1907 school reform program designed by a committee of secular intellectuals called for native Azerbaijani Turkish students to be taught, in their native Turkish dialect, a mixed program of language, literature, religious studies, and various secular subjects; Russian would be taught and used as the language of instruction for other subjects. A mullah, presumably a reformer, would oversee the program.

After the fall of the Russian Empire, when the first Republic of Azerbaijan was declared, secular and religious forces had achieved a modus vivendi in a primarily secular framework. The republic's constitution guaranteed religious freedom but separated religion from the state. Christian churches continued to operate. The Bolshevik conquest of Azerbaijan and the creation of a soviet socialist republic there subjected Azerbaijan to the antireligious campaigns of the Communist regime.

The antireligious campaigns of the 1920s were brutal. Along with clergymen of all other denominations, Muslim *ulema* in Azerbaijan were beaten, arrested, deported to Siberia, or shot. Mosques and other religious institutions were closed; some were destroyed and their materials used for public buildings, school dormitories, or factories.

Efforts to purge religious and national elements from Azerbaijani culture lasted throughout the 1920s and 1930s. From 1926, a concerted effort to displace existing literature with "proletarian literature" gathered momentum. In the following years, native novels, poetry, music, and the visual arts were vilified and replaced by socialist realist works. Education was a crucial target for antireligious campaigns: teachers were accused of "spreading religious (and/or nationalist) propaganda," removed from their jobs, and sometimes arrested or exiled; textbooks were replaced; their authors were often removed from their posts, and some were exiled.

The German invasion of Russia in June 1941 led Stalin's regime to grant numerous cultural concessions to the various peoples of the USSR. Among these was the reestablishment of Muslim ecclesiastical boards on the imperial model. These represented some loosening of the official policy on religion but kept institutions under state control. Training was only possible in Bukhara (lower level seven-year *madrasahs*) and in Tashkent (upper level, four-year *madrasahs*).

In the postwar decades antireligious efforts, more often called "scientific atheist" education, addressed the popular notion that religious practices and beliefs were part of the national heritage. Atheist propaganda stressed the separation of religious and national traditions, arguing the harmful nature of the former and the positive nature of the latter—as long as it remained at the level of folkdancing and handicrafts.

The regime's policies had limited success. The urban population at least had little idea of Islam by the 1970s. The ancient celebration of the beginning of spring, Novruz, was widely thought to be an Islamic holiday. Few people knew the difference between Sunnī and Shīʿī Islam. Many openly expressed the belief that the official mullahs were "KGBers." Much surviving religious practice descended to the level of superstition. In rural areas, pilgrimages to tombs continued and occasional "holy men" or "holy women" were said to have miraculous healing powers. Still, the word "Muslim" continued to be associated with decency and morality. It became a group marker to indicate those who shared certain moral and social values, as opposed to outsiders like Russians who, though traditionally Christian, were believed to have lost their morality under communism. Even members of the Azerbaijan Communist Party routinely practiced religious rituals in connection with circumcision, marriage and burial.

Azerbaijanis, like the Soviet Central Asians, experienced a demographic resurgence since the 1960s, and for the first time since the start of industrialization in the 1880s, they are again a majority in their republic and its capital Baku. The head of the ecclesiastical board (which has not been abolished by the new republic), Shaykh al-Islām Allahshukur Pashazade, came to prominence for speaking out against Russian repression of the national movement in 1990. He subsequently played a lesser political role, though he cultivated relations with Iran and Saudi Arabia. He participated in the presidential inauguration of Azerbaijan Popular Front leader Abulfez Elchibey in June 1992. Elchibey included kissing the Qur'ān in the ceremony. One year later, in a coup of June 1993, former communists returned to power. Pashazade appeared also at the swearing-in ceremony of Heydar Aliyev, former Communist Party first secretary, as president.

Religious parties are virtually unknown in Azerbaijan and religion plays no role in political mobilization. Elchibey's government had pledged itself to religious freedom and other civil liberties, and the separation of church from state. In the first months of Aliyev's rule, despite repressions of political rivals and critics, Aliyev made no changes in laws regarding religion.

BIBLIOGRAPHY

Altstadt, Audrey L. "The Forgotten Factor: Shiʿi Mullahs of Pre-War Baku." In *Passé Turco-Tatar, Présent Soviétique,* edited by Gilles Veinstein et al. Louvain and Paris, 1986. Provides more detail on Russian imperial ecclesiastical boards and the economic position of mullahs.

Altstadt, Audrey L., *Azerbaijani Turks: Power and Identity under Russian Rule.* Stanford, Calif., 1992. History of Azerbaijan from the Russian conquest to 1991; includes detail on religion and religious policies.

Atkin, Muriel. *Russia and Iran, 1780–1828.* Minneapolis, 1980. Includes coverage of the religious repressions that accompanied Russian conquest.

Bennigsen, Alexandre, and Chantal Lemercier-Quelquejay. *Islam in the Soviet Union.* Translated by Geoffrey E. Wheeler and Hubert Evans. London, 1964. Historical overview covering tsarist and Soviet times.

Bennigsen, Alexandre, and S. Enders Wimbush. *Mystics and Commissars: Sufism in the Soviet Union.* London, 1985. Includes some information on pilgrimage places in Azerbaijan.

Khadzhibeili, Dzheikhun [Jeyhun Hajibeyli]. *Antiislamskaia Propaganda i ee Metody v Azerbaidzhane.* Munich, 1957. The only comprehensive treatment of antireligious propaganda in Azerbaijan.

AUDREY L. ALTSTADT

AZHAR, AL-. Situated in the heart of premodern Cairo, al-Azhar is the greatest mosque-university in the world today. Reluctantly adjusting to modern times over the last century, the millennium-old Azhar remains a focal point of Islamic religious and cultural life for Egypt and the entire Islamic world.

The First Nine Centuries (to 1872). Jawhar al-Ṣiqillī conquered Egypt for the Fāṭimid caliph al-Muʿizz in 969, founded Cairo as the new capital, and in 970 began constructing al-Azhar as the official assembly mosque. Al-Azhar has been enlarged and much remodeled since. Organized instruction began there in 978. The mosque's name, "the brilliant," may allude to the prophet Muḥammad's daughter Fāṭimah "al-Zahrā'," the eponymous ancestor of the Fāṭimids. Al-Azhar became one of several Cairene missionary centers for the Fāṭimids, Ismāʿīlī Shī'īs who claimed to be the true imams.

Ṣalāḥ al-Dīn and his Ayyūbid heirs downgraded al-Azhar when they restored Egypt to Sunnī Islam in 1171. Sultans and emirs of the Mamlūk dynasty (1250–1517) patronized and restored the now Sunnī mosque, but it was as yet only one among many seats of Islamic learning in Cairo. Cairo's situation on the Nile, the road to Syria, and Maghribi pilgrimage routes to Mecca made it a natural cultural hub. The Mongol sack of Baghdad (1258) and the loss of Islamic Spain enhanced Cairo's religious and cultural centrality.

The Ottoman conquest of 1517 diverted power and patronage to Istanbul, but al-Azhar weathered the storm and emerged as the preeminent seat of Arabic-Islamic learning. It also provided a vital link between the Arabic-speaking population and the Turkish-speaking military elite. By the late seventeenth century, the shaykhs of the mosque were choosing their own head—the shaykh al-Azhar. Shaykhs of the Shāfiʿī school of law, predominant in Cairo and the Delta, monopolized the post from 1725 to 1870. This suggests considerable autonomy, for the Ottomans themselves were Ḥanafīs.

During the French occupation (1798–1801), Azharī shaykhs continued as intermediaries between the people and foreign military rulers, but al-Azhar also became a rallying point for revolt against the French, who bombarded, occupied, and desecrated the mosque. In 1805, the Azharī *ʿulamā'* sanctioned the ouster of Egypt's Istanbul-appointed governor by Muḥammad ʿAlī and his Albanian troops. But Muḥammad ʿAlī soon felt strong enough to begin the long campaign to subordinate al-Azhar to the state. He ignored the ruler's obligation to consult the *ʿulamā'*, chose the shaykhs al-Azhar himself, played Ṣūfī leaders off against the shaykh al-Azhar, and confiscated many religious endowments.

As usual in premodern Islamic schools, al-Azhar had no formal admissions procedures, classrooms, desks, grade-levels, academic departments, required courses, written examinations, grades, or degrees. Professors lectured from a favorite pillar of the mosque, the students gathering at their feet. Memorization and commentary, often on epitomes and commentaries rather than on the original classics, were the means of instruction. Qur'ānic exegesis, *ḥadīth,* and jurisprudence were taught in the morning; grammar, rhetoric, and other "auxiliary sciences" after the noon prayer; and various nonessential subjects after the sunset prayer. Many Azharīs were active Ṣūfīs as well as *ʿulamā'*.

Students from outside Cairo joined groupings called *riwāq*s, which were supported by religious endowments. Each *riwāq* had its shaykh and bread allowance, and larger ones had libraries, lavatories, and living quarters. Around 1900, there were three *riwāq*s for Lower Egyptian students and one each for students from the Fayyum, central Egypt, and Upper Egypt. There were *ri-*

*wāq*s for Kurds and Berbers, and for students from Java, India, Afghanistan, Iran, the Sudan, Chad, Bornu, Somalia, the Hejaz, Yemen, Iraq, and Syria. The Upper Egyptian and Maghribi *riwāq*s were fiercely Mālikī, the Lower Egyptian ones Shāfiʿī, and the Syrians Ḥanafī. The few Ḥanbalīs had a *riwāq* of their own, and several *riwāq*s were open to all. In 1876, al-Azhar had 5,651 Shāfiʿī students with 147 shaykhs, 3,926 Mālikīs with 99 shaykhs, 1,270 Ḥanafīs with 76 shaykhs, and 25 Ḥanbalīs with 3 shaykhs.

Resistance and Reform from Ismāʿīl to Nasser, 1872–1952. State reformers found it easiest to bypass al-Azhar in founding schools, a printing press, an official journal, and Western-inspired courts. The departure of progressive Azharīs like Rifāʿah Rāfiʿ al-Ṭahṭāwī, Muḥammad ʿAbduh, and Saʿd Zaghlūl to work for the state reinforced al-Azhar's conservatism. Beginning in 1872, state reformers tried to overhaul al-Azhar despite conservative resistance. Eventually the necessity of competing with state school graduates for government jobs fostered a reformist minority within al-Azhar itself.

Khedive Ismāʿīl prepared the ground for reform by installing the first non-Shāfiʿī in 145 years as shaykh al-Azhar. Muḥammad al-ʿAbbāsī al-Mahdī, a Ḥanafī, also served concurrently as grand *muftī* of Egypt. In 1872, Ismāʿīl instituted an oral examination (the *ʿālimīyah*) as a prerequisite for teaching at al-Azhar. When the ʿUrābī revolt of 1881–1882 broke out, al-Azhar was a rallying point for national resistance to European interference. A Shāfiʿī shaykh al-Azhar replaced al-Mahdī, who was identified with the palace and the Turkish elite. With the arrival of the British army of occupation, al-Mahdī reclaimed his post.

Cooperation between ʿAbbās II and the great Islamic modernist Muḥammad ʿAbduh, then a Sharīʿah Court judge, ushered in another reform attempt in the 1890s. ʿAbbās installed a Ḥanafī shaykh al-Azhar and named ʿAbduh to a new supervisory council for al-Azhar. Innovations included the establishment of a central library, a standardized salary scale, and a nationwide network of preparatory religious "institutes" under al-Azhar. The reforms bogged down when ʿAbbās and ʿAbduh quarreled. ʿAbbās then installed a conservative shaykh al-Azhar, and, shortly before his death in 1905, ʿAbduh resigned in frustration from the Azhar council.

In 1908, a sweeping decree added new subjects, required yearly examinations, and regularized a primary-secondary ladder in the institutes, but student and faculty protests forced the cancellation of these measures. In 1911, a cautious substitute decree shrewdly exempted a Council of Senior ʿUlamāʾ (today's Academy of Islamic Research) from reformist regulations imposed on other professors.

Ismāʿīl had opened a School of Law (originally Administration and Languages) and the Dār al-ʿUlūm teachers' college to bypass al-Azhar. The opening of the School for Qāḍīs (1907) and the state-run Egyptian University (1925) dealt a further blow to job prospects for the unspecialized Azharī graduates. The two elderly Mālikī shaykhs al-Azhar between 1909 and 1927 responded not with reform but with pressure on the state to hire Azharīs. King Fu'ād agreed to do so, for he needed Azharī endorsement of his caliphal ambitions and a counterweight to Saʿd Zaghlūl's and the Wafd Party's following among secondary and Egyptian University students.

The Wafdist-Liberal Constitutionalist cabinets of 1926–1928 canceled the state's commitment to hire Azharīs, seized the prerogative of naming the shaykh al-Azhar, and brushed aside the king's candidate, Muḥammad al-Aḥmadī al-Zawāhirī, in favor of Muḥammad Muṣṭafā al-Marāghī. But King Fu'ād soon turned the tables on al-Marāghī, a Ḥanafī and an admirer of ʿAbduh. Fu'ād suspended the constitution, reclaimed the prerogative of appointing the shaykh al-Azhar, and put in Zawāhirī.

Nevertheless, the Azhar decree of 1930 and follow-up decrees in 1933 and 1936 implemented much of al-Marāghī's program. Al-Azhar was pressed more firmly into the Western-inspired mold of the Egyptian University and the state schools. It became a university *(jāmiʿah)* as well as a mosque *(jāmiʿ)*, with colleges of theology, *sharīʿah,* and the Arabic language, each with a state-appointed dean. The three colleges occupied temporary quarters until moving in the 1950s to a new quadrangle behind the mosque. Only public lectures were still given in the mosque itself.

Fu'ād's bid for autocracy failed, and al-Marāghī returned as shaykh al-Azhar in 1935. He sent Azharīs to study in Europe and encouraged dialogue with Shīʿīs, but his exile had taught him caution. He took care to cultivate young King Fārūq. Muṣṭafā ʿAbd al-Rāziq accomplished little as shaykh al-Azhar (1945–1947), for Azharīs distrusted him as a disciple of ʿAbduh, a graduate of the Sorbonne, and a professor of philosophy from the Egyptian University.

New Directions under Nasser. Disappointed in Shaykh al-Azhar ʿAbd al-Raḥmān Tāj's (1954–1958) conservatism despite his Sorbonne education, Egyptian President Gamal Abdel Nasser found the reformist shaykh he wanted in Maḥmūd Shaltūt (1958–1963). Disappointed by his master al-Marāghī's latter-day royalism and conservatism, Shaltūt immediately had welcomed the 1952 revolution. In June 1961 Nasser had Speaker Anwar el-Sadat ram a bill for radical al-Azhar reform through a surprised parliament in a single night. A withering press attack on the *ʿulamā'* followed.

The Azhar law of 1961 provided for a Supreme Council under the shaykh al-Azhar, an Islamic Research Academy, a Department of Cultural and Islamic Mission, al-Azhar University, and the precollegiate institutes. The existing colleges of theology, *sharīʿah,* and the Arabic language (renamed Arabic Studies) were further reformed. The College of Arabic Studies drifted farthest from its old moorings; in 1974, 93 percent of its contact hours were in "secular" subjects. The College of Sharīʿah added Qānūn (non-*sharīʿah* law) to its name and curriculum, and even the College of Theology now requires social sciences and a Western language. Opening the College of Islamic Women (literally "Girls") was a radical step, as was the addition of colleges of engineering, medicine, commerce, science, agriculture, and education. Azharī old-timers resented the newcomers, and students in such subjects as medicine and engineering grumbled about the extra preparatory year of religious studies required of them. The location of the new colleges in the suburb of Madīnat Naṣr separated them psychologically as well as physically from al-Azhar.

Students from poor, provincial, rural, and illiterate families had long mingled at al-Azhar with those from privileged urban backgrounds. But from the late nineteenth century onward, privileged families deserted al-Azhar for state or private schools and better career opportunities. A survey of seniors at al-Azhar and Cairo universities in 1962 shows that Azharīs were generally poorer, more provincial, more rural, and from less educated families than their Cairo University counterparts. They were also far more conservative on such issues as coeducation and family planning.

Al-Azhar in Contemporary Perspective. The balance of numbers shifted away from the Azhar system and toward the state schools as the twentieth century wore on. By 1970–1971 only 1 percent of Egyptian primary school students, 2 percent of secondary students, and 5 percent (al-Azhar's three original colleges) of college students were in religious schools. Al-Azhar's 1,263 university students in 1935 paled beside the Egyptian University's 7,021. By 1960 al-Azhar had grown to 6,145 students, but Cairo (formerly the Egyptian) University had 27,973 students, and there were three new state universities as well. By expanding its range of subjects and opening branch campuses, al-Azhar had 160,000 university students taking year-end examinations in 1990 compared to 600,000 in the state universities. Standards in both systems plunged in the face of inadequate support and overwhelming numbers of students.

Al-Azhar's Preaching and Guidance section sent preachers and lecturers throughout Egypt. Al-Azhar acquired its own press. Its *Majallat al-Azhar* (Journal of al-Azhar, originally *Nūr al-Islām,* Light of Islam) was established in 1930, its Voice of al-Azhar radio program in 1959, and Azharī preachers increasingly saturate Egyptian radio and television airwaves.

Outside Egypt, al-Azhar is prized as a champion of Sunnī Islam and the Arabic language. Students returning from studies at al-Azhar and Azharī professors and preachers on mission abroad are in demand throughout the Islamic world. Everywhere they have helped establish and improve Islamic schools and communal institutions.

Al-Azhar had 639 foreign students enrolled in 1903, and 999 in 1948. Foreign student enrollments at both al-Azhar and the state universities increased rapidly under Nasser, reflecting his ambitions in the Arab, African, and Islamic worlds. Al-Azhar's foreign student enrollments in the Nasser era peaked at 4,291 in 1955, then tapered off to 2,500 in 1972 just after his death. In 1990, al-Azhar campuses hosted about 6,000 foreign students from seventy-five countries. The Institute of Islamic Missions offered foreign students, who were often poorly prepared, a less rigorous program.

Arabs from east of Egypt (particularly Palestinians, Jordanians, and Syrians) came in substantial numbers throughout the twentieth century. With 1,534 students in 1972, they comprised 61 percent of all foreign students. Nearly a third of these were Palestinians. The once substantial Maghribi contingent declined in the 1960s because of independence and educational expansion at home. Only modest numbers of Sudanese came before midcentury (214 in 1948), but by 1955 there were 2,441, 57 percent of all foreign students. By 1972 the figure had dwindled to 124. Students from elsewhere in Africa, barely noticeable in 1903, reached 1,300 in 1964 but fell to 400 in 1972.

Stereotypes of al-Azhar as a rigid institution frozen in time persist among its secularist detractors, but Muḥammad ʿAbduh or his feminist disciple Qāsim Amīn would not recognize it today. Al-Azhar takes the education of women, albeit in a separate college, for granted and offers such areas of concentration as commerce and engineering. The Assembly Hall even bears ʿAbduh's name. Al-Azhar requires a Western language, often adds an English section to its *Journal,* and has had shaykhs al-Azhar who hold French and German degrees. Western experts and a Ford Foundation grant helped it establish an Institute of Languages and Translation.

Nevertheless, al-Azhar is indeed conservative. It held Islamist activists at arm's length, from Jamāl al-Dīn al-Afghānī, Muḥammad ʿAbduh, and Muḥammad Rashīd Riḍā, to Muslim Brotherhood leaders Ḥasan al-Bannā' and Sayyid Quṭb. It is significant that Bannā' and Quṭb were products of Dār al-ʿUlūm, not al-Azhar, and that in Egypt most leaders of today's "Islamic groups" are not Azharīs. Azharī shaykhs may dismiss radical Islamists as extremists only superficially familiar with Islam, and many Islamists disparage Azharīs as "official *ʿulamā'*," cravenly subservient to the state which pays them. [*All of the figures named in this paragraph are the subject of independent entries.*]

Islamists generally approve, however, of the condemnation of controversial books by al-Azhar's Islamic Research Academy, which sees itself as guardian of true Islam. In the 1920s, al-Azhar stripped ʿAlī ʿAbd al-Rāziq of his degree and drove him from his judgeship for reinterpreting the caliphate in secular fashion, and it hounded Ṭāhā Ḥusayn for his provocative book *On Pre-Islamic Poetry*. Certain books by Nobel Prize-winner Najīb Maḥfūẓ (Naguib Mahfouz) and literary critic Louis ʿAwaḍ are banned in Egypt, and al-Azhar has condemned Salman Rushdie's *Satanic Verses* and works by outspoken secularist Saʿīd ʿAshmāwī. Not a few Azharīs privately agree with Shaykh ʿAbd al-Ḥamīd Kishk, the blind Azharī graduate whose radical, populist sermons drew an enthusiastic Islamist following in the 1970s and 1980s. Kishk chided his alma mater for accepting Western-educated shaykhs al-Azhar, demanded elections to fill that office, and called for the elimination of the colleges added since 1961. [*See the biographies of ʿAbd al-Rāziq, Ḥusayn, and Kishk.*]

For a decade, President Hosni Mubarak and Shaykh al-Azhar ʿJād al-Ḥaqq ʿAlī Jād al-Ḥaqq have maintained the uneasy state-Azhar symbiosis. Al-Azhar walks a tightrope between provoking another state assault like Nasser's and discrediting itself in popular eyes through subservience to the state. Azharī authorities issued *fatwās* endorsing family planning, the Egyptian-Israeli peace treaty, and Egypt's participation in the Gulf War of 1990–1991. Jād al-Ḥaqq condemned terrorism by Ayatollah Ruhollah Khomeini's Iranian partisans. Yet he refused to sanction the payment of interest on funds invested for national development, as the government wanted. The balancing act goes on.

[*See also* Education; Egypt; Universities; *and the biographies of ʿAbduh, Marāghī, Shaltūt, and Nasser.*]

BIBLIOGRAPHY

Creswell, K.A.C. *The Muslim Architecture of Egypt*. 2 vols. Oxford, 1940–1959. See volume 1, pages 36–64.

Delanoue, Gilbert. *Moralistes et politiques musulmans dans l'Egypte du XIXe siècle, 1798–1882*. 2 vols. Cairo, 1982. Painstaking and profound study of intellectual life in nineteenth-century Egypt. Nothing remotely comparable in English exists.

Dodge, Bayard. *Al-Azhar: A Millennium of Muslim Learning*. Washington, D.C., 1974. Readable if pedestrian account, ending on the eve of the 1961 reform.

Eccel, A. Chris. *Egypt, Islam, and Social Change: Al-Azhar in Conflict and Accommodation*. Berlin, 1984. A mine of information and stimulating interpretation. Despite organizational problems and excessive sociological jargon, the fundamental work in English on al-Azhar.

Gran, Peter. *Islamic Roots of Capitalism: Egypt, 1760–1840*. Austin, 1979. Biographical study of Shaykh al-Azhar Ḥasan al-ʿAṭṭār, with a controversial interpretation of the relationship of culture to society and the economy.

Heyworth-Dunne, James. *An Introduction to the History of Education in Modern Egypt*. London, 1968. Fundamental work in English on nineteenth-century Egyptian education.

Hussein, Taha (Ḥusayn, Ṭāhā). *The Stream of Days: A Student at the Azhar*. Translated by Hilary Wayment. London, 1948. Highly personal reminiscences of student days at al-Azhar in the early twentieth century by one of Egypt's leading writers.

Jomier, Jacques. "Al-Azhar." In *Encyclopaedia of Islam,* new ed., vol. 1, pp. 813–821. Leiden, 1960–.

Reid, Donald Malcolm. *Cairo University and the Making of Modern Egypt*. Cambridge, 1990. Views al-Azhar's evolution as background to the development of Cairo University and the state school system.

Shafshak, Mahmoud. "The Role of the University in Egyptian Elite Recruitment: A Comparative Study of al-Azhar and Cairo University." Ph.D. diss., University of Chicago, 1964. Valuable social background and attitudinal data, unavailable elsewhere, from a 1962 survey of students.

Vollers, Karl. "Azhar." In *Encyclopaedia of Islam,* vol. 1, pp. 532–539. Leiden, 1913–.

DONALD MALCOLM REID

B

BĀB. In the middle of the nineteenth century, Iranian Shiism underwent radical changes. Among these was a marked improvement in the status and power of the clerical leadership—a development which began in the late eighteenth century and culminated in recent times with the Islamic Revolution, which placed full political authority in the hands of the clergy.

Shīʿī Islam has always emphasized the superiority of individual, "inspired" leadership over political power or consensus and has, throughout its history, given rise to numerous messianic movements. Even with the emergence since the sixteenth century of an officially recognized clerical establishment within Twelver Shiism in Iran, the tension between spontaneous leadership empowered from "above" and routine authority elaborated through a consensus with political power has been a constant element in the religious life. This is the context for appreciating the popular support accorded a nonclerical messianic religious leader, Sayyid ʿAlī Muḥammad Shīrāzī (1819–1850), better known as the Bāb.

Neither the parentage nor upbringing of the Bāb indicated a religious career. His family was part of a wealthy merchant class which traded from Shiraz and the Persian Gulf port of Bushire, and the Bāb's schooling was designed to prepare him for a mercantile career. After an elementary education, he began work in the family business and was sent to the Bushire offices in 1835. However, natural piety and an inclination toward philosophy, mysticism, and theology led him to engage privately in religious studies and even to compose short works on theological topics.

Around 1840, he spent a year at the Shīʿī shrine cities in Iraq, where he came into direct contact with Sayyid Kāẓim Rashtī, the head of the Shaykhī school, a semiorthodox branch of Shiism in which esoteric ideas were emphasized. The Bāb's family already had Shakyhī connections, and it would seem that he found here a potential outlet for frustrated clerical aspirations.

Following Rashtī's death in early 1844, the Bāb, now back in Shiraz, was visited by a number of the sayyid's disciples. Whether encouraged by them or on his own initiative, the young merchant now declared himself Rashtī's successor and the gate (Ar., *bāb*) to the Twelfth Imam, the expected messiah of the Twelver Shīʿīs. What is significant is that a number of younger Shaykhī clerics from Iraq and parts of Iran readily accepted his claims and began to preach the imminent advent of the imam. Shīrāzī was not the only individual to make prophetic claims around this time, but he was by far the most successful, mainly because of the existing structure of the Shaykhī sect, from which his first followers were drawn. [*See also* Shaykhīyah.]

The Bāb was the first individual in Islamic history to make a serious attempt to break away from Islam in order to found a separate religion with distinct books and laws. What is not clear is how he came to adopt such a radical position. In the earliest phase of his preaching, no such development seems to have been envisaged. His earliest writings are concerned with the reinforcement of Islamic law, and, if anything, the early Bābīs were most noted for the zeal of their adherence to it. Much hinges on the vexed question of whether the Bāb saw himself as the recipient of direct divine inspiration from the beginning or whether such ideas only came much later, while in prison in Azerbaijan. Both cases can be argued, with modern Bahāʾī writers taking the view that the Bāb knew his "true station" from an early age. What cannot be denied is that his own writings show a development through several stages, from that of claiming to be a gate to the Hidden Imam and an interpreter of the Qurʾān, to that of being the imam in person, to a final stage in which he proclaimed himself the latest manifestation of the Primal Will and the bearer of a new divine revelation.

Most of the Bāb's prophetic career was spent either under house arrest or in prison in northwest Iran, leaving the actual leadership of his sect in the hands of a group of young clerics. His claim in 1848 to be the returned Hidden Imam resulted in violent clashes between some of his followers and government troops and, by 1850, the defeat of the movement. He himself was shot by firing squad in Tabriz in July 1850. His remains were recovered and later removed to Palestine, where they were interred in a mausoleum built by the Bahā'īs on Mount Carmel. The late nineteenth century saw a brief cult of the Bāb in some European literary circles.

During his confinements, the Bāb busied himself with the composition of a large body of writing in Persian and Arabic, much of which has survived and some of which has been published (although it has been much overshadowed by the texts of the Bahā'ī prophet, Bahā' Allāh). The central text of this canon is an unfinished Persian book known as the *Bayān,* which sets out the main laws of the new dispensation. The later works of the Bāb in particular are original, often eccentric to the point of obscurity, and frequently prolix. They reflect the concerns of a small religious sect whose members explored the more recondite avenues of Shīʿī esotericism. It is by the merest chance that they have come to have any wider significance, on account of the much greater accessibility and relevance of the scriptures of the Bahā'ī movement which grew out of Bābism in the 1860s. The Bāb's vision was very much the product of a subculture within a wider culture itself under threat from rapid change. But in one major respect it was to acquire lasting significance: it challenged the consensus of immutability within Islam and raised the specter of wholesale legal and religious change.

[*See also* Bābism; Bahā'ī; Imam.]

BIBLIOGRAPHY

Amanat, Abbas. *Resurrection and Renewal: The Making of the Babi Movement in Iran, 1844–1850.* Ithaca, N.Y., and London, 1989. See chapter 3, "The Merchant-Saint of Shiraz" and later references. Very full account of the Bāb's background and early life.

Balyuzi, H. M. *The Báb: The Herald of the Day of Days.* Oxford, 1973. Hagiographical study from the Bahā'ī perspective.

MacEoin, Denis. "Bāb, Sayyed ʿAlī Moḥammad Šīrāzī." In *Encyclopaedia Iranica,* vol. 3, fasc. 3, pp. 278–284. London and New York, 1982–. Comprehensive article.

DENIS MACEOIN

BĀBISM. In the eighteenth and nineteenth centuries, several important revivalist movements appeared throughout the Islamic world. Only one of these—but by no means the least important—emerged within the confines of Twelver Shiism. This was a militant messianic movement centered around the person of a young Iranian merchant, Sayyid ʿAlī Muḥammad Shīrāzī (1819–1850), the Bāb, which was at its height during the late 1840s.

Nowadays, it is possible to consider Bābism from two distinct perspectives. For historians of Iran and modern Shiism, it represents a doomed attempt to effect radical social and religious change within an essentially medieval worldview that was itself about to give way before more powerful external forces. To members of the modernizing Bahā'ī religion, it begins a new era of religious aspiration, providing the matrix from which their own faith emerged in the last decades of the century.

In 1844, a dispute occurred over the question of leadership in an esoteric school of Shīʿī thought known as Shaykhīyah, which had adherents in both Iran and Iraq. Among the various claimants, the most unlikely was the above-mentioned Shīrāzī (then twenty-five), who lacked formal training in the religious sciences. He and the group of mostly younger clerics who formed the core of his movement emphasized the priority of "innate" knowledge over that available in the Shīʿī seminaries. This eventually produced a mass movement which, although clerically led, had much of its support from merchants, government officials, and other social groups normally passive in religious matters.

The Bāb originally advanced only limited claims for himself. His function was, he maintained, to provide an esoteric interpretation of the Qur'ān, to intensify observance of Islamic religious law, and to prepare men for the imminent appearance of the Hidden Imam, the Mahdi or Shīʿī messiah (hence his own title of Bāb ["Gate"], a traditional term for an individual acting on behalf of an imam). To this latter end, the first Bābīs made and purchased arms in readiness for the Holy War that would inevitably follow the imam's earthly reappearance, expected in 1845 or 1846.

Things did not go smoothly. Clerical opposition to the new teachings was encountered in several places, and the Bāb decided to postpone the day of the Parousia and to play down his public claims. He himself was placed under house arrest in his hometown of Shiraz and later (from 1847) imprisoned in the northwestern province of Azerbaijan. In spite of this, the activities of several provincial clerics won large numbers to the Bāb's cause, and pressure for military action grew.

In early 1848, the Bāb announced that he was himself the Hidden Imam and that he had initiated a new religious era. This radical departure was formalized at a meeting of Bābī activists in July, when the laws of the Qur'ān were declared abrogated. The Resurrection had come, and throughout Iran Bābīs anticipated the coming of a new heaven and earth. In the next two years, a series of bloody clashes between bands of armed Bābīs and state troops convulsed the country. Grossly outnumbered, in spite of stiff resistance, the Bābīs succumbed. Much of the leadership was wiped out, and the movement's central promise of a new order was torn to shreds.

The Bāb was executed in Tabriz in July 1850, leaving behind a substantial body of writing deemed by his surviving followers to be divine revelation. To many, this proved the final blow; to a remnant of diehard believers, some form of reassessment and restructuring became inevitable. Following a slapdash attempt on the life of Nāṣir al-Dīn Shāh in 1852, a group of survivors was expelled from Iran and chose to take up residence in Baghdad.

Here, two strands of what can be termed "Middle Bābism" emerged under the leadership of two brothers, Mīrzā Ḥusayn ʿAlī Nūrī (Bahā' Allāh) and Mīrzā Yaḥyā (Ṣubḥ-i Azal).The latter was the designated successor of the Bāb and the original focus for what life remained in the sect. He emphasized an obscurantist approach, basing his own teaching firmly on the later, post-Islamic doctrines of the Bāb. Curiously enough, the rather introspective group centered on Yaḥyā (and known later as Azalīs) produced several important figures in the democratic and social reform movement in Iran around the turn of the century.

In contrast to Ṣubḥ-i Azal, Bahā' Allāh was a worldly wise leader who in time attracted to himself the majority of living Bābīs and, later, a growing following from outside the sect. During the 1850s and 1860s, Bahā'ī Bābism had succeeded in playing down the more militant and occult side of the Bāb's teachings. In the late 1860s Bahā' Allāh began to advance claims of a quasi-divine nature, claiming to be the author of a new revelation, with the Bāb his forerunner. In association with these claims, he developed a much simpler and more accessible theological system, bringing the movement directly within reach of lay persons. In consequence, Bahā'ī Bābism and the larger Bahā'ī religion which emerged from it ceased to be clerically dominated and attracted large numbers of the new educated classes in the Iranian cities.

Although its direct impact on the Islamic world or on Iran was small, Bābism is important for a number of reasons. To use rather loose terminology, it was the last of the "medieval" Islamic movements, with values drawn from a world already threatened by the penetration of the West. Unlike later reformist movements, it was not a response to the challenges of modernism. But, whereas earlier extremist Shīʿī movements of its type had vanished or continued in the marginalia of orthodox Islam, Bābism hung on just long enough to refashion its teachings and to move, in its Bahā'ī form, entirely beyond Islam. It was the first and only Islamic sect to do so, and the implications have not been lost on the large numbers of Muslim writers who have portrayed Bābism and Bahā'ism as ideal types of modern heresy.

[*See also* Bahā'ī; Imam; Mahdi; *and the biographies of the Bāb and Bahā' Allāh.*]

BIBLIOGRAPHY

Amanat, Abbas. *Resurrection and Renewal: The Making of the Babi Movement in Iran, 1844–1850.* Ithaca, N.Y., and London, 1989. Authoritative and detailed history of the sect up to the execution of the Bāb. Excellent analysis of the social and political background. Some carelessness in the use of sources.

Browne, Edward G. "The Bābīs of Persia. I. Sketch of Their History, and Personal Experiences amongst Them. II. Their Literature and Doctrines." *Journal of the Royal Asiatic Society* 21 (1889): 485–526, 881–1009. Reprinted with annotations in *Selections from the Writings of E. G. Browne on the Bābī and Bahā'ī Religions,* edited by Moojan Momen, pp. 145–315. Oxford, 1987. Early accounts by the first serious Western scholar to study the subject, still of great value for Browne's observations, based on contact with survivors of the earliest period.

MacEoin, Denis. "Babism: i. The Babi Movement," and "Babism: ii. Babi Executions and Uprisings." In *Encyclopaedia Iranica,* vol. 3, fasc. 3, pp. 309–317. London and New York, 1982–. The most comprehensive encyclopaedia entry currently available.

MacEoin, Denis. *The Sources for Early Bābī Doctrine and History: A Survey.* Leiden, 1992. Specialized study that provides the broadest overview of the literature of Bābism as well as a full discussion of the many controversies over historical sources.

Momen, Moojan. "The Social Basis of the Bābī Upheavals in Iran, 1848–53." *International Journal of Middle East Studies* 15 (1943): 157–183. One of a number of intelligent studies locating Bābism in its social context.

Momen, Moojan. *The Bābī and Bahā'ī Religions, 1844–1944: Some Contemporary Western Accounts.* Oxford, 1981. The first part of this book contains numerous documents on Bābism, taken mainly from European diplomatic archives. The editor's summaries of Bābī history are helpful, if biased in favor of a modern Bahā'ī interpretation.

Momen, Moojan, and Peter Smith. "The Bābī Movement: A Resource Mobilization Perspective." In *In Iran,* edited by Peter Smith, pp. 33–93. Studies in Bābī and Bahā'ī History, vol. 3. Los Angeles, 1986. Comprehensive overview of the movement, representing a fruitful collaboration between two Bahā'īs, one a historian, the other a sociologist.

Zarandī, Muḥammad Nabīl. *The Dawn-Breakers: Nabīl's Narrative of the Early Days of the Bahā'ī Revelation*. Translated and edited by Shoghi Effendi. New York, 1932. Standard Bahā'ī account of the period to 1852, written by a contemporary of the Bāb's. This is the most detailed source for Bābī history, although the author's religious bias must be taken into account constantly.

DENIS MACEOIN

BAHĀ' ALLĀH (1817–1892), title by which Mīrzā Ḥusayn ʿAlī Nūrī, the prophet-founder of the Bahā'ī faith is best known. It is from the title Bahā' Allāh (often seen as Bahā'u'llāh, "Glory of God") that the religion takes its name (Bahā'ī means "follower of Bahā'," or "of Bahā' Allāh"). Other titles by which he is frequently referred are Jamāl-i Mubārak ("the Blessed Beauty") and Jamāl-i Qidam ("the Ancient Beauty"). He was born into a well-to-do family attached to the Qājār court with vast holdings of land in Mazandaran. He was inclined to pacifism at an early age and later became a follower of the Bāb (1819–1850), whom he never met. His association with the Bābī movement led to his arrest in August 1852 when certain Bābīs made an attempt on the life of the shah to avenge the execution of the Bāb. He emerged in the post-Bābī period as one of the leaders of the movement and was exiled first to Baghdad, then Istanbul, Edirne, and finally ʿAkkā (Acre), Palestine.

During the Baghdad period (1853–1863) Bahā' Allāh's prestige within the Bābī community continued to grow, causing difficulties between himself and his half-brother, Mīrzā Yaḥyā (Ṣubḥ-i Azal), who had been appointed head of the Bābīs by the Bāb. From 1854 to 1856 he removed himself from that community to lead the life of a wandering dervish in the mountains of Sulaymānīyah and was finally persuaded to return to Baghdad by his followers. Although as early as 1853 Bahā' Allāh had become apprised of his calling through visions experienced during his incarceration, it was not until 21 April 1863 that he made this calling known to a group of followers. The occasion was a further exile from Baghdad to Istanbul brought about by the intervention of the Persian authorities in the Shīʿī shrine centers of Iraq. Later, in Edirne (1863–1868), he would announce his mission through a series of letters addressed to the crowned heads of Europe and other heads of state throughout the world. At this time the community of exiles began to distinguish themselves as either followers of Bahā' Allāh (Bahā'ī) or followers of Ṣubḥ-i Azal (Azalī). He and his followers were moved to 'Akkā in 1868. Bahā' Allāh would remain in this region until his death in 1892 at Bahjī, the *qiblah* of the Bahā'ī world.

Bahā' Allāh's literary legacy, considered divine revelation by Bahā'īs, is preserved in works in Persian and Arabic too numerous to list here. Many of the most important of these have been translated into numerous languages, but several remain in manuscript. A number of works date from the early Baghdad period including the *Haft vādī* (Seven Valleys) and what in some ways may be considered his most important work, the *Kitāb-i īqān* (The Book of Certitude). It is in the *Kitāb-i īqān* that one of the most significant aspects of his thought as a son of Islamic culture can be found clearly and uncompromisingly set forth, namely, that divine revelation did not end with Muḥammad but had occurred quite recently with the Bāb. The main feature of his later work is his claim to be the future divine messenger foretold by the Bāb, *man yuẓhiruhu Allāh* (he whom God will manifest).

The central message of Bahā' Allāh is that the establishment of the unity of the world is the foremost religious duty of humanity and that he, as the *maẓhar-i ilāhī* (divine manifestation) for this time and for all people is empowered by God to provide the means to achieve it. The chief means are the laws, verities, and admonitions contained in several works but most importantly outlined in the *Kitāb-i aqdas* (Most Holy Book), which dates from 1872–1873. The *Kitāb-i aqdas* calls for the establishment of a world tribunal, the adoption of a universal auxiliary language, and the cultivation of the belief that all religions come from the same God and teach the same essential truth, varying only in their articulations as a result of historical, linguistic, and social factors (an idea first put forth from within an Islamic milieu by the tenth-century philosopher al-Fārābī). He also taught that other divine manifestations would come after him to educate the world, as there is no end to the potential for the progress and perfection of the human spirit. His ideas were received with varying degrees of enthusiasm by Muslim thinkers, ranging from condemnation by, for example, Muḥammad Rashīd Riḍā to admiration by Muhammad Iqbal. His religion can be seen as a response to the challenges that the nineteenth century posed to the Islamic world; the manner in which his teachings both arose from within the parent religion and acquired their own distinct identity is unique in the history of modern Islam.

[*See also* Bāb; Bābism; Bahā'ī.]

BIBLIOGRAPHY

Bahā' Allāh [Mīrzā Ḥusayn ʿAlī Nūrī]. *The Kitāb-i-Aqdas: The Most Holy Book*. Haifa, 1992.

Balyuzi, H. M. *Bahá'u'lláh: The King of Glory*. Oxford, 1980. Standard biography.

Cole, Juan R. I. "Iranian Millenarianism and Democratic Thought in the Nineteenth Century." *International Journal of Middle East Studies* 24 (1992): 1–26. Illuminates Bahā' Allāh's place in later nineteenth-century Islamic intellectual discourse.

Collins, William P. *Bibliography of English-Language Works on the Bábí and Bahá'í Faiths, 1844–1985*. Oxford, 1990. The result of meticulous bibliographic industry replacing all earlier attempts. Contains a guide to virtually every significant English-language work on the subject, including a lengthy section on anti-Bahā'ī polemic. Many of the entries are annotated.

Smith, Peter. *The Babi and Baha'i Religions: From Messianic Shīʿism to a World Religion*. Cambridge, 1987. Highly informative study written from a sociology of religion perspective.

B. TODD LAWSON

BAHĀ'Ī. The word *bahā'ī* is the adjectival form of the Arabic word *bahā'*, which means "glory" or "splendor." From early times this was recognized as one of the extra-Qur'ānic attributes of God, as is evident, for example, in a *tafsīr* attributed to the sixth Shī'ī Imam Jaʿfar al-Ṣādiq (d. 765) in which the *bā'* of the *basmalah* is glossed as standing for the glory of God *(bahā' Allāh)*, or in a *ḥadīth* of the prophet Muḥammad: "The red rose is of the glory of God *(al-ward min bahā' Allāh)*." At present the word is most usually associated with a religion that arose out of the rubble of the collapsed Bābī movement of mid-nineteenth-century Iran. As such, Bahā'ī refers to a follower of Bahā' Allāh (Bahā'u'llāh; Mīrzā Ḥusayn ʿAlī Nūrī, 1817–1892) a title he assumed during an important meeting of Bābīs convened by him near the hamlet of Badasht, not far from Alamut in northwestern Iran, in 1848. The purpose of the meeting was to discuss the affairs of the movement associated with the name of the Bāb, who was at the time, as a result of his messianic activities, imprisoned by order of the Qājār state in the mountains of Azerbaijan. Present also was Ṭāhirah, the famed Bābī heroine whose daring behavior scandalized many of the ardent religionists gathered there.

Origins. To speak of the origin of the Bahā'ī faith, the designation for the movement preferred by its present leadership and adherents—although one sometimes encounters "the Bahā'ī religion" (but never "Bahaism")—is not an altogether easy task, even if we were to concentrate only on the historical origins. We must also address the problem of essential origins, for in the Bahā'ī answer to this question much of the true nature of the religion is revealed. In a sense it is easier to deal with this second question, whose answer, like all good religious dogma, is completely innocent of irony and ambiguity.

We do not know the occasion of the first usage of the term "Bahā'ī" to describe a follower or the teaching of Bahā' Allāh, but we can be reasonably sure in setting the date at around the years 1866–1868. These years found the exiled Bābī community, resident in Edirne since December 1863, divided in its loyalty between the two half-brothers Bahā' Allāh and Mīrzā Yaḥyā Ṣubḥ-i Azal ("Morn of Eternity," a title with deep roots in Shīʿī Islam). The title was bestowed upon the latter by the Bāb, who had also designated him as the head of the Bābī religion. He seems to have been universally regarded as such for a few years after the execution of the Bāb in 1850. The split was the result of differing interpretations of the Bāb's prophecy of the coming of one who would have the authority to alter the Bāb's laws. Ṣubḥ-i Azal and his followers put the event far into the future, but in 1866 an event known in Bahā'ī sources as "the Most Great Separation" was instigated by Bahā' Allāh; as a result, those who were loyal to Azal were separated from those who were loyal to Bahā'. It was at this time that Bahā' Allāh publicly and unambiguously (in contrast to his first announcement to a small group of intimate friends prior to his departure from Baghdad for Constantinople in 1863) claimed to be *man yuẓhiruhu Allāh* or "he whom God shall manifest," the figure mentioned in numerous places in the Bāb's writings, especially his *Persian Bayān,* and interpreted by Bābīs to be the focus of the Bāb's eschatology. There is no question that Bahā' Allāh was the more able leader and the more popular and charismatic of the two, as is evidenced by the undisputed fact that most of the Bābīs chose to be designated as "the people of Bahā' " *(ahl-i Bahā')*. It was now that the Bahā' Allāh proclaimed the obsolescence of Bābism and promulgated a new and distinct religion. The exact nature of this break may be seen by comparing the basic teachings of the Bahā'ī Faith with those of Bābism. The fact that both latter-day religions are variations on a basic revealed ethical monotheism—Islam—and that monotheism's distinctive articulation by the Twelver Shīʿī community, will also be evident.

Bahā' Allāh died in May 1892 near the prison city of ʿAkkā (Acre) in Ottoman Syria, where he and his followers had been sent by the Ottoman authorities in 1868 in response to the conflicts brought about in the community between the two half-brothers. (Ṣubḥ-i Azal and his comparatively few followers had been sent to Famagusta.) Although the first two years of this exile were passed in intense hardship in wretched prison conditions, eventually Bahā' Allāh and his family were permitted to take up residence outside the city, although technically remaining prisoners. We do not know the exact number of Bahā'īs surrounding Bahā' Allāh at this time; certainly the majority of the community remained in Iran. Most of the affairs of the community and the religion (usually referred to as the Cause of God, *amr Allāh*) were entrusted to the care of Bahā' Allāh's eldest son, ʿAbbās, known as ʿAbd al-Bahā' ("Servant of Bahā'," 1844–1921), leaving his father free to attend to a huge correspondence and the composition of religious works, all of which is considered by Bahā'īs to be divine revelation. ʿAbd al-Bahā' was appointed by his father in his will to be the "center of the Covenant." (On the basic Bahā'ī teaching of the Covenant, see below.) ʿAbd al-Bahā' had already distinguished himself as a tireless disciple of his father and commanded enormous respect both within an outside the Bahā'ī community. At his death in Haifa, it is estimated that his funeral was attended by over "ten thousand people including dignitaries of the Muslim, Roman Catholic, Greek Orthodox, Jewish, and Druze communities as well as the British High Commissioner and the Governors of Jerusalem and Phoenicia" (Hatcher and Martin, 1984, p. 61). In 1892, however, a conflict arose in which another son of Bahā' Allāh, Muḥammad ʿAlī, disputed his father's will. As a result, most of Bahā' Allāh's relatives were effectively excommunicated, and for a while the fledgling religious movement was divided. Those who recognized ʿAbd al-Bahā's authority were in the majority, while those who followed his brother eventually dwindled to insignificance (see Eric Cohen, "The Baha'i Community of Acre," *Folklore Research Centre Studies* (Jerusalem) 3 [1972]: 119–141)—despite the fact that it was one of the latter who was responsible for bringing Bahā'ī teachings to the United States in 1894. ʿAbd al-Bahā' came to be the focus of devotion for the community, and his rank is that of perfect exemplar of the Bahā'ī life. His authority was absolute in all matters of belief and interpretation of his father's writings. He himself wrote several works, such as *The Secret of Divine Civilization*, a critique of modern (especially Persian) society, and *A Traveler's Narrative*, a history of the Bābī movement. In addition, a number of transcriptions of his talks have been published, including *The Promulgation of Universal Peace* and *Some Answered Questions*. It is as a result of his stewardship that the Bahā'ī Faith came to be firmly established in the West through his correspondence with the small Bahā'ī community that had been established in Chicago in 1894, and through an eighteen-month visit to North America in 1912. This was to have a dramatic effect on the fortunes of the new religion:

> The emergence of small communities of Baha'is in North America and Europe during the 1890s marked a profoundly significant advance in the development of the Baha'i religion. Although comprising no more than a few thousand individuals, these early Western communities represented a major expansion beyond the existing cultural boundaries of the Baha'i community, demonstrating the cultural adaptability of the religion and securing a fresh base for further expansion (Smith, 1987, p. 100)

With this foundation the Bahā'ī Faith began consolidating in earnest its identity as a world religion distinct and separate from the parent Twelver Shīʿī Islam and its heresy, Bābism. The writings of Bahā' Allāh had laid the groundwork for a kind of cosmopolitanism/universalism, distinguished by a lack of ambiguity and concern with recondite Islamic Shīʿī theosophical arcana, which prepared his followers for the ever-expanding vision represented first by the religious liberalism of ʿAbd al-Bahā and later by the consolidation and systematization of this liberal vision by the latter's grandson Shoghi Effendi Rabbānī (1897–1956), known as the Guardian of the Cause of God *(valī-yi amr Allāh)*, terminology still fresh from the Shīʿī matrix. With the expansion of the vision also came an expansion of numbers. It is difficult to know exactly, but current statistics place the worldwide Bahā'ī population at around 5 million (see Smith and Momen, 1989, p. 72). The vast majority of Bahā'īs are found in the so-called "Third World," the largest national community being in India, where one of seven existing Bahā'ī temples (*mashriq al-adhkār*, "dawning place of the remembrances [or praises, of God]") was recently dedicated on the outskirts of Delhi.

Basic Teachings. A starting point for a discussion of Bahā'ī belief is the doctrine or principle (the preferred term) known as "progressive revelation." In its basic structure, the idea is not substantially different from similar "theologies of progress' advanced during the latter half of the nineteenth century from certain Christian quarters (cf. George W. Stocking, *Victorian Anthropol-*

ogy, New York and London, 1987, p. 189ff.). It is as follows: God, the eternal and unchangeable utterly transcendent, has from the beginning that has no beginning made "his" will known to his creation through chosen beings, in human form, who are known to history as prophets and messengers. Indeed, these figures, inasmuch as they have revealed divine laws and verities and inasmuch as their lives and persons are qualitatively different from others, that is to say holy, may be considered personifications of the divine will (a specific teaching which owes much to the theosophical synthesis known as *ḥikmat-i ilāhī,* dating from the Ṣafavid period). It is, in short, a further elaboration of a distinctively Islamic logos doctrine. The main difference is that the series of prophets that began with Adam and ended with Muḥammad represents, in the Bahāʾī view, a completed cycle of prophecy. With the proclamation of the Bāb in 1844 a new cycle was inaugurated, known as the "cycle of fulfillment." Students of Islamic religious movements may see here a variation on the basic Shīʾī view which sees revelatory prophecy *(nubūwah)* as having ended with Muḥammad but nonetheless maintains the continuance of absolute religious authority in the institution of the imamate through the spiritual prerogatives and dignities represented by the word *walāyah* (guardianship), which was passed on to each of the twelve imams in succession and which rendered them infallible *(maʿṣūm)* in all matters. The distinctive Ismāʿīlī teaching of cycles *(adwār)* is also of interest here; it may have left its influence indirectly through the metaphysical synthesis of the Shaykhīyah, a Twelver Shīʿī movement intimately connected with the rise of the Bābī religion. It is important to observe that in the Bahāʾī teaching the finality of Muḥammad's prophethood *(khātam al-nabīyīn,* Qurʾān 33.40) is maintained, while room is made for the appearance of a new revelator of God's will. The terminology changes accordingly. Rather than referring to themselves by the Qurʾānic words "prophet" *(nabī)* or "messenger" *(rasūl),* the two recent figures are most commonly called divine manifestations *(maẓhar ilāhī),* a term that derives from the *waḥdat al-wujūd* ("oneness of being") school associated with Ibn al-ʿArabī (d. 1240). It may be laboriously, though accurately, translated as "place where divinity is caused to appear." In the Bahāʾī view, all previous prophets and messengers were divine manifestations; those whom we know about include all those recognized by the Qurʾān, together with Zoroaster, Gautama Buddha, and presumably others such as Krishna. The continuance of this divine contact with humanity represents God's fulfillment of a great covenant or promise never to leave his creation alone and without divine guidance. Many of these ideas are unobjectionable to Islam or Shiism as such; however, it was the Bāb's propagation of a new *sharīʿah* and the eventual supplanting of this by an even newer code of holy laws, together with the claim that both the Bāb and Bahāʾ Allāh were, despite the different terminology, functionally of the same status as the prophet Muḥammad, which has caused the movement to be seen as heretical and ultimately non-Islamic.

The primary purpose of life is to know and love God. This can be done most perfectly by knowing and loving his most recent manifestation. It is most perfectly expressed through obedience to the laws and principles revealed by the same. Thus the Bahāʾī teaching that God has created humanity in order to carry on an ever-advancing civilization is directly and inextricably related to prophetic history. While it is certainly possible to read the Qurʾān as propounding such a view (indeed, both the Bāb and Bahāʾ Allāh were Muslims), the revelatory authority acknowledged by Bahāʾīs for this interpretation makes it binding and not open to debate. Bahāʾīs expect other divine manifestations to appear. There also seems to be no special hierarchy among the manifestations: they are essentially or ontologically equal. Bahāʾ Allāh uses the example of the sun and its rising at different places on the horizon: in reality, it is always the same sun, but nonetheless it makes sense to refer to the sun of yesterday, the sun of today, and so on (Bahāʾ Allāh, 1931, pp. 21, 43–44, 161). The Bahāʾī Faith is the ancient religion of God whose exact historical origin none knows. History makes sense only when seen as the gradual unfolding of the divine plan, or the revelation of the mind of God.

Bahāʾ Allāh wrote numerous works in Arabic and Persian, all of which are considered divine revelation and as abrogating the Bāb's revelation, which had already, according to Bahāʾī belief, abrogated the Qurʾān and the Islamic *sharīʿah.* Among the most important of these are the *Kitāb-i īqān* and *Al-kitāb al-aqdas,* the *Most Holy Book.* In addition, Bahāʾ Allāh revealed numerous prayers. Not all of his approximately one hundred works have been translated.

From the early twentieth century a number of principles have been put forth as an answer to the question "What do Bahāʾīs believe?" They include the oneness of God; the oneness of humanity; the oneness of religion; independent investigation of truth; abandonment of prejudice and superstition; harmony of science and religion; equality of men and women; universal education; social/economic justice; the spiritual basis of society; and an auxiliary international language.

These principles were articulated in this form in the West and as a result of ʿAbd al-Bahā's stewardship of the new community. The question of how much this formulation was influenced through dialogue with Christian leaders is an important but as yet little-studied one. But the purpose of these principles and others, such as the abolition of holy war and any notions of exclusivity—such as the "chosen people" or "people of the Book" *(ahl al-kitāb)*—is the establishment of world unity, the achievement of which represents "the coming of age of the entire human race . . . marking the last and highest stage in the stupendous evolution of man's collective life on this planet" (Shoghi Effendi, 1938, p. 163). Bahā Allāh is reported to have said, during one of the four interviews conducted with him in 1890 by E. G. Browne:

> That all nations should become one in faith and all men as brothers; that the bonds of affection and unity between the sons of men should be strengthened; that diversity of religion should cease, and differences of race be annulled—what harm is there in this? . . . Yet so it shall be; these fruitless strifes, these ruinous wars shall pass away, and the 'Most Great Peace' shall come. . . . Do not you in Europe need this also? Is not this that which Christ foretold? . . . Yet do we see your kings and rulers lavishing their treasures more freely on means for the destruction of the human race than on that which would conduce to the happiness of mankind. . . . These strifes and this bloodshed and discord must cease, and all men be as one kindred and one family. . . . Let not a man glory in this, that he loves his country; let him rather glory in this that he loves his kind. (Quoted in Smith, 1987, p. 76.)

Taking a lesson perhaps from Islamic religious history, Bahā' Allāh sought to ensure the doctrinal and administrative unity of his religion by explicitly appointing his successor and outlining the basic components of Bahā'ī institutions. The doctrine or principle of the Covenant is central to this and consists of two major parts. The first is the great covenant, mentioned above, representing God's promise never to leave humanity alone and without guidance to carry forward an "ever-advancing civilization." That this promise has been honored is seen in the succession of prophets and messengers who have been responsible for particular stages in this mighty development. The most recent proof of this covenant is Bahā' Allāh, whose life and message have the special purpose of establishing a universal theology of history and giving humanity the necessary moral, ethical, and spiritual guidance to realize the unit of the human race. The second is a series of "lesser" covenants that have functioned within this framework and pertain directly to the laws and teachings of each of the divine messengers and the obligation of their audience to recognize their divine authority and to follow their laws. In the case of the Bahā'ī Faith, the covenant has become a distinctive religious institution because it is through this that the unity of the religion has been safeguarded: fulfillment of the covenant entails recognition of the transmission of authority first to ʿAbd al-Bahā', then to Shoghi Effendi, and finally to the Universal House of Justice.

Bahā'ī Administration and the Covenant. The Bahā'ī view is that all religions have been promulgated to establish and affirm unity but have only partially achieved their goal because these religions have themselves fallen prey to disunity. Through the Covenant, for which ʿAbd al-Bahā is the recognized Center, the unity of the Bahā'ī Faith has with few exceptions been impressively maintained. Despite localized activities by "covenant breakers" (*nāqidīn*, another term from Shiism), the vast majority of Bahā'īs recognize the infallible authority of the Universal House of Justice, the governing body of the Bahā'ī world community established in 1963 with headquarters in Haifa, Israel. This institution is provided for in Bahā' Allāh's *al-Kitāb al-Aqdas* and more specifically in ʿAbd al-Bahā's *Will and Testament.* It was originally to have functioned as the supreme body in conjunction with another institution, the Guardianship, after his death. Although ʿAbd al-Bahā died in 1921, Shoghi Effendi postponed calling an election for a Universal House of Justice in order first to establish a broader basis of local and national communities. Between 1921 and 1963 two international bodies were established under the direct guidance of Shoghi Effendi: an International Bahā'ī Bureau, based in Geneva from 1925 to 1957, and the International Bahā'ī Council with eight members appointed in 1950 by Shoghi Effendi, which is seen as the precursor for the eventual establishment of the Universal House of Justice. Between December 1951 and October 1957 twenty-seven Hands of the Cause of God were appointed, as further discussed below.

The Bahā'ī Faith puts much emphasis on what it calls "the administrative order." The institutional features of this order include, at the top, the Universal House of Justice, which is infallible and divinely inspired in its rulings and legislative activity. Beneath this supreme body are two distinct but interrelated hierarchies of administrative authority known respectively as "the rulers" and "the learned." The institutions of the rulers consist of National Spiritual Assemblies and their respective committees and conventions and Local Spiritual Assemblies. In the future these Assemblies will come to be called Houses of Justice as well. Since the 1920s it has been the practice that wherever nine or more adult Bahā'īs reside, a Local Spiritual Assembly should be formed, either by a vote of the entire community or through acclamation. In countries and other broader jurisdictions where a sufficient number of Local Assemblies exist, a National Assembly should be formed by means of election through delegates to a National Convention held every year in April. By 1983 there were 135 National Spiritual Assemblies and 24,714 Local Spiritual Assemblies. In addition, there were 112,776 localities where Bahā'īs resided but where there were not yet sufficient numbers to form Assemblies (Smith 1987, pp. 168–169). The institutions of the "learned" also proceed from the Universal House of Justice (in the absence of a Guardian); the first rank here is the Hands of the Cause. As only the Guardian can appoint these, this institution will end when the last of these die. Continental Boards of Counselors at present assist the Hands of the Cause (in 1993 only three of the original twenty-seven appointees were living). These boards are in turn assisted by Auxiliary Boards and their assistants. The Universal House of Justice and all national and local Spiritual Assemblies are elected, the first body every five years, the remaining two yearly. All elections take place on the first day of the festival Riẕvān. For a clear discussion of the relationship between the "rulers" and the "learned," including the existence of these institutions notwithstanding the Bahā'ī ban of the clerical class, see Smith and Momen (1989).

Bahā'ī Calendar: Feasts and Holy Days. An integral factor in the establishment of a Bahā'ī identity has been the adoption of a new calendar that had been put forth by the Bāb in his *Persian Bayān*. This is a solar calendar of nineteen nineteen-day months. On the first day of each of these months Bahā'īs observe their feasts, a time when the community gathers to read or listen to the sacred word, to consult on local activities and plans, and to associate with each other in fellowship. The names of these months are taken from a well-known Ramaḍān prayer, the Duʿā' al-Bahā', ascribed to the fifth Shīʿī imam, Muḥammad al-Bāqir.

In addition there are several Holy Days observed throughout the year, usually through commemorative meetings or community-minded events. Both non-Bahā'īs and Bahā'īs participate together at Holy Day functions (non-Bahā'īs are prohibited from attending the nineteen-day feast). New Year's Day is the ancient Iranian Nawrūz, which becomes the first day of the first Bahā'ī month. The Bahā'ī Era began with the Bāb's declaration, which has been precisely fixed as having occurred at 2 hours and 11 minutes after sunset on 23 May 1844. The nine Holy Days on which work is suspended are the Feast of Nawrūz (Bahā'ī New Year), 21 March; the Feast of Riẕvān (Declaration of Bahā' Allāh), 21 April–2 May; the Declaration of the Bāb, 23 May; the Ascension of Bahā' Allāh, 29 May; the Martyrdom of the Bāb, 9 July; the Birth of the Bāb, 20 October; the Birth of Bahā' Allāh, 12 November; the Day of the Covenant, 26 November; and the Ascension of ʿAbdu'l-Bahā', 28 November.

Although Bahā'īs have no dietary restrictions, they do observe a yearly fast which takcs place for the entire month of ʿAlā'. During these nineteen days Bahā'īs who have attained the age of majority (fifteen) are required to abstain from food and drink between dawn and sunset. Other laws and prohibitions for Bahā'īs include obligatory prayer, abstention from the nonmedical use of drugs and alcohol, and the prohibition of backbiting. These and other laws are established in the *Kitāb al-aqdas*, an authorized English translation of which was published for the first time in 1993.

Current Status. According to the most recent statistics, the worldwide Bahā'ī community includes approximately 6 million people. There are 165 National Spiritual Assemblies, while the total number of countries, significant territories, and island where Bahā'īs reside is 233. Worldwide there are approximately 20,000 local Spiritual Assemblies. Bahā'ī literature has been translated into 802 different languages, and there are 2,112 different minority and ethnic groups represented. Throughout the world there are seven Houses of Worship, and sites are owned by Bahā'īs for another 125. There are approximately 950 schools or other educational projects, seven radio stations, and 670 social and economic development projects. In the United States there are roughly seven thousand localities where Bahā'ī reside, 1,700 local Spiritual Assemblies, and five schools and institutes serving an approximate population of

120,000 (figures from the Canadian Bahā'ī Office of Public Information, March 1994.) The largest Bahā'ī community is in India.

[*See also* Bābism; *and the biographies of the Bāb and Bahā' Allāh.*]

BIBLIOGRAPHY

ʿAbdu'l Bahā' [ʿAbbās Effendi]. *A Traveller's Narrative Written to Illustrate the Episode of the Bāb*. Translated by Edward G. Browne. Cambridge, 1892.

ʿAbdu'l Bahā' [ʿAbbās Effendi]. *The Secret of Divine Civilization*. Translated by Marzieh Gail. Wilmette, Ill., 1970.

ʿAbdu'l Bahā' [ʿAbbās Effendi]. *The Promulgation of Universal Peace* (1922). 2 vols. in 1. Wilmette, Ill., 1982.

The Bāb [ʿAlī Muḥammad Shīrāzī]. *Le Bèyán persan*. 4 vols. Translated by A. L. M. Nicolas. Paris, 1911–1914. French translation of the Bāb's book of laws.

The Bāb [ʿAlī Muḥammad Shīrāzī]. *Selections from the Writings of the Bāb*. Translated by Habib Taherzadeh et al. Haifa, 1982.

Bahā' Allāh [Mīrzā Ḥusayn ʿAlī Nūrī]. *The Kitāb-i-Iqān: The Book of Certitude, Revealed by Bahā'u'llāh*. Translated by Shoghi Effendi. Wilmette, Ill., 1931. Bahā' Allāh's most influential work, clarifying the Bahā'ī principle of "progressive revelation" and the deep influence of Shīʿī Islam (especially its theosophic dimension) on the formation of Bahā'ī belief. For other important works, such as *The Hidden Words, The Seven Valleys*, and others available in English, see Collins, below.

Bahā' Allāh [Mīrzā Ḥusayn ʿAlī Nūrī]. *The Kitāb-i-Aqdas; The Most Holy Book*. Haifa, 1992.

Balyuzi, H. M. *ʿAbdu'l-Bahā: The Centre of the Covenant of Bahā'u'llāh*. Oxford, 1971. *The Bāb: The Herald of the Day of Days*. Oxford, 1973. *Bahā'u'llāh: The King of Glory*. Oxford, 1980. Biographies written in the finest tradition of scholarly hagiography and essential reading for the early history of the Bahā'ī Faith and its central figures as perceived by followers.

Collins, William P. *Bibliography of English-Language Works on the Bābī and Bahā'ī Faiths, 1844–1985*. Oxford, 1990. Meticulous bibliographic guide with many annotated entries, containing virtually everything of any importance to do with the subject in English, including a lengthy section on anti-Bahā'ī polemic. Replaces all earlier attempts.

Effendi, Shoghi. *The World Order of Bahā'u'llāh: Selected Letters* (1938). 2d rev. ed. Wilmette, Ill., 1974. Perhaps the best statement on the current religious vision held by the worldwide Bahā'ī community, written in a distinctively elevated and luxurious English.

Hatcher, William S., and J. Douglas Martin. *The Bahā'ī Faith: The Emerging Global Religion*. New York, 1984. Concise and reliable introductory description of current Bahā'ī belief and practice, written by proponents.

Nabīl-i-Aʿẓam [Muḥammad Nabīl Zarandī]. *The Dawn-Breakers: Nabīl's Narrative of the Early Days of the Bahā'ī Revelation* (1932). Translated and edited by Shoghi Effendi. Wilmette, Ill., 1974. Standard history of the Bābī religion written by an early convert to the religion of the Bāb who would become one of the more illustrious disciples of Bahā'u'llāh. Edited, translated, and annotated with introductory material, appendices, bibliographies, and photographs by the first and only Guardian of the Bahā'ī Faith. Invaluable resource for scholars of the movement, as well as a kind of sacred history for the Bahā'īs.

Rabbānī, Rūhiyyih. *The Priceless Pearl*. London, 1969. Biography of Shoghi Effendi by his widow, lovingly told with consummate grace and humanity, providing a wealth of detail not found elsewhere.

Smith, Peter. *The Babi and Baha'i Religions: From Messianic Shiʿism to a World Religion*. Cambridge, 1987. The first detailed examination of the subject, from a sociology of religious perspective. Smith announces his commitment to the Bahā'ī Faith and at the same time raises questions that might disturb unreflected belief in the religion.

Smith, Peter, and Moojan Momen. "The Baha'i Faith, 1957–1988: A Survey of Contemporary Developments." *Religion* 19 (1989): 63–91.

Stockman, Robert. *The Bahā'ī Faith in America*. Wilmette, Ill., 1985. The first scholarly discussion of the subject, illuminating the profound relationship between American Protestantism and the development of Bahā'ī thought.

Universal House of Justice. *Wellspring of Guidance: Messages, 1963–1968*. Wilmette, Ill., 1969. Important collection of documents from the first term of the supreme authority of the Bahā'ī Faith, resolving several potentially controversial issues.

Universal House of Justice, comp. *A Synopsis and Codification of the Laws and Ordinances of the Kitāb-i-Aqdas, the Most Holy Book of Bahā'u'llāh*. Haifa, 1973. Apart from those who read Arabic, the Bahā'īs have been without a canonical edition of their most holy book until 1993. This book was the only indication of its contents until that time.

Universal House of Justice. *The Promise of World Peace*. Haifa, 1985. The most recent articulation of the Bahā'ī approach to world peace by the supreme religious authority, addressed to the non-Bahā'ī world and marking the beginning of the United Nations International Year of Peace in 1985.

B. Todd Lawson

BAHRAIN. *See* Gulf States.

BAKKĀ'Ī AL-KUNTĪ, AḤMAD AL- (c. 1803–1865), Sudanese religious and political leader. Aḥmad al-Bakkā'ī inherited the religious and economic influence of the Kunta confederation in the Timbuktu region of the West African Sudan in the years 1847–1865 and was titular head of the Qādirīyah *ṭarīqah* in West Africa during that period. He was a grandson of Sīdī al-Mukhtār al-Kuntī (d. 1811), patriarch of the Kunta Awlād Sīdī al-Wāfī to whom most strains of the Qādirīyah in West Africa are traced. He worked closely with his elder brother, Sīdī al-Mukhtār al-Saghir ibn Sīdī Muḥammad, who succeeded at his father's death in 1824 as principal *shaykh* of the Kunta until his own death in 1847. During this period the autonomy of Timbuktu and environs came under threat from the Masina *mujāhid* Aḥmad Lobbo, whose forces were initially welcomed in Timbuktu in 1824 as a counter to the Tuareg extractions of tribute that were blamed for a half-century decline in the city's fortunes. A revolt by the urban elite of Timbuktu in 1833 set the stage for a thirty-year effort by Sīdī al-Mukhtār al-Saghir and then Aḥmad al-Bakkā'ī to negotiate the city's autonomy with the Masina rulers. In the 1850s al-Bakkā'ī initially sought the support of al-Ḥājj ʿUmar Tal, whose *jihād* eclipsed Masina in 1860, but thereafter he directed a coalition of Kunta, Tuareg, and Fulbe forces that took control of the city while launching a general offensive against ʿUmar's control over Masina. This warfare led to the deaths of both al-Ḥājj ʿUmar (in 1864) and Aḥmad al-Bakkā'ī in 1865.

Aḥmad al-Bakkā'ī's career and voluminous correspondence focus upon his efforts to assert Kunta control over the Timbuktu region, his objections to efforts in Masina to restrict the sale and use of tobacco (not unconnected to Kunta commercial interests), and his mounting antipathy toward the Tijānīyah and its adherents. Al-Bakkā'ī visited Sokoto before 1837 while al-Ḥājj ʿUmar was in residence there. Correspondence between al-Bakkā'ī and the Tijānī reformer a decade later gives no indication of the virulent attacks against al-Ḥājj ʿUmar and the Tijānīyah that were to come, despite contemporaneous heated debate between al-Bakkā'ī and the Masina Tijānī leader, ʿUmar's disciple al-Mukhtār ibn Yirkoy Talfī. From the early 1850s until his death, however, al-Bakkā'ī's correspondence reveals a growing hostility toward the Tijānīyah that led him to write to *ʿulamā'* in Marrakesh warning of the dangers posed by the *ṭarīqah*. At the same time, an issue that set al-Bakkā'ī at odds with the Masina authorities was the hospitality he offered the explorer Heinrich Barth, who visited Timbuktu in 1853. The event marked both the nadir of al-Bakkā'ī's formerly cordial relations with Masina's ruler Ahmadu III and the beginning of his efforts, which continued to 1860, to attract British assistance against the French advance (and control over commerce) in the central Sahara. Al-Bakkā'ī's defense of his hospitality for the Christian traveler reveals his sophisticated grasp of contemporary Mediterranean and European politics and his self-appointed role as a representative of both Ottoman and Moroccan authority in the region.

Aḥmad al-Bakkā'ī's correspondence provides a rare, detailed glimpse into political and religious thought in the West African Sudan relating to three overriding concerns in the mid-nineteenth century: the nature of the imamate/caliphate in Sahelian and Sudanese communities; the problem of coming to terms with encroaching Christian powers; and the growing politicization of *ṭarīqah* affiliation. The nature of the imamate had long preoccupied southern Saharan savants in the *zāwiyah* tradition out of which al-Bakkā'ī arose. Two positions had emerged by the early nineteenth century. One legitimated the acquisition of authority by force in times of *fitnah* (conflict, by which Saharan society, in the absence of a state, defined itself). The second, which was earlier argued by al-Bakkā'ī's father, was that a sovereign is only an agent of corruption on earth, and that to seek the authority of the imamate is to challenge the established powers ordained by God. Al-Bakkā'ī used the latter argument to question the legitimacy first of the Masina *jihād* and then of al-Ḥājj ʿUmar's movement, pointing up the fact that religious suzerainty in the region was owed to the ʿAlawī sultan in Morocco and/or the Ottoman sultan, because that was the largest Islamic polity of the time. The imam, he argued, must be a descendant of Quraysh Arabs in any event, and Fulani claims to this title represented innovation (*bidʿah*). In advice he ignored during the last three years of his life, al-Bakkā'ī summarized this position in his reply to Muḥammad Bello's suggestion that the Kunta *shaykh* declare a *jihād* himself. Al-Bakkā'ī warned, "*Jihād* . . . leads to kingship, and kingship to oppression, and our condition as it is now is better for us than *jihād*, and safe from the error to which it leads" (Robinson, 1985, p. 305).

European visitors to the Muslim communities of the West African Sudan from the 1820s, growing European commercial interests along the West African coast by mid-century, and French colonial ventures in Algeria posed new religious and economic issues for West Africa's Islamic leaders. For al-Bakkā'ī, Barth's visit crystallized these issues. His response was to assert himself as an enlightened defender of Christians and Jews as people of the book, against his less informed critics who sought scriptural justification for detaining them. In correspondence with Ahmadu III of Masina he argued that since the only enemy of the Muslim peoples at the time was Russia (the Crimean War had just begun), Barth, a German under English sponsorship, could not be detained but rather deserved *aman* (safe passage).

Al-Bakkā'ī's hostility toward the Tijānīyah *ṭarīqah* was closely linked to the political implications of al-Ḥājj ʿUmar Tal's movement. It was a threat to the longstanding Kunta religious hegemony symbolized by the Qādirīyah, and al-Bakkā'ī was further scandalized by the authority granted to persons from the lower classes in the ʿUmarian state. Al-Bakkā'ī increased his attacks on the Tijānīyah during the 1850s, and by the time he was leading armed attacks on the ʿUmarian forces he was labeling Tijānīs as infidels and atheists *(zandaq)*. This confrontation effectively marks the beginning of a politicization of *ṭarīqah* affiliation in the Western Sudan that was to gain even greater momentum in the years following his death.

Aḥmad al-Bakkā'ī was one of the last principal Muslim spokesmen in the Western Sudan in the precolonial era for an accommodationist stance vis-à-vis the threatening Christian European presence and, until the last years of his life, an exponent of noninvolvement in temporal matters. He was also the last of the great Kunta shaykhs, whose prestige and religious influence were interwoven with the Qādirīyah and the economic fortunes of the Timbuktu region. His significance lies in his wide range and voluminous correspondence documenting these issues.

[*See also* Mauritania; Qādirīyah; Tijānīyah; *and the biography of* ʿ*Umar Tal.*]

BIBLIOGRAPHY

Bâ, Amadou Hampaté, and Jacques Daget. *L'émpire Peul de Macina.* Mouton, 1962. Provides oral tradition of al-Bakkā'ī's career as it touched on Masina politics after 1848.

Robinson, David. *The Holy War of Umar Tal.* Oxford and New York, 1985. By far the best account of al-Ḥājj ʿUmar's movement and al-Bakkā'ī's career from an ʿUmarian perspective.

Saad, Elias N. *A Social History of Timbuctu.* Cambridge and New York, 1983. Surveys al-Bakkā'ī's career from the perspective of Timbuktu history.

Zebadia, Abdelkader. "The Career of Ahmed al-Bakkay." *Revue d'Histoire Maghrébine* 3 (1975): 75–83. Summarizes his 1974 University of London Ph.D. thesis, which is the most thorough compilation of al-Bakkā'ī's correspondence to date.

CHARLES C. STEWART

BALKAN STATES. The Islamic communities of the Balkan states and southeastern Europe in general (all Sunnīs of the Hanafī school) comprise a relatively large number of ethnic groups speaking about ten different languages. They have lived and continue to live under social and political conditions that vary widely from one state to another, according to their numbers on the one hand and according to the ideology professed by the successive regimes of each state on the other. Despite these differences, the Balkan Muslim communities have much in common. They share a common history beginning with the invasion and occupation of the region by Ottoman forces beginning in the fourteenth century. Their populations can be traced to the same three origins—Turkish-speaking settlers who arrived in the wake of the invasion or some time later, Muslim settlers from other parts of the Islamic world who were established in the region by Ottoman power, and indigenous people who converted to Islam. Conversion was most common in Albania, Bosnia-Herzegovina, Bulgaria (the Pomaks of the Rhodopes, whose mountain lands also extend into the modern states of Greece and Macedonia), and Crete. During the Ottoman era these groups enjoyed privileged status, since non-Muslims were denied full citizenship. After the Christian reconquest they were reduced everywhere except in Albania to the status of an inferior religious and/or ethnic minority. Today, in all the countries of the region except Albania, Muslim communities remain minorities—sometimes very small ones—in predominantly Orthodox Christian or Catholic societies. This history has affected different Muslim communities in different ways, depending on the regime in power, the historical period, and the group's ethnic origins.

Hungary. Two distinct Islamic communities have existed in Hungary. The first was formed there between 1526 and 1699 as a result of the Ottoman conquest and occupation of many Hungarian territories. It disappeared immediately after the reconquest, when those Muslims who did not flee with the retreating armies were either massacred or forced to convert to Christianity.

A new Islamic community was created, beginning in 1878, by the immigration of a small number of Muslims from Bosnia-Herzegovina (occupied at the time by Austria-Hungary), as well as an influx of Ottoman Turkish craftsmen, traders, and students. Over time, however, these groups shrank as their members were assimilated into the general population. Today in Hungary there is no organized Islamic community, although a few hundred—perhaps a few thousand—individuals adhere to the faith; they include Arabs, Turks, Pakistanis, Iranians, and other immigrants, along with a handful of local converts.

Romania. Two small Islamic communities have existed on Romanian territory in modern times. The first was built on Ada Kale, a small island in the Danube conquered by the Ottomans late in the fifteenth century. At the end of World War II the island's population numbered about one thousand, but the community was dispersed in 1968 when the island was submerged by the construction of the Iron Gate hydroelectric dam.

The second community is in Dobroudja, a region conquered by the Ottomans in the fourteenth and fifteenth centuries but ceded to Romania in 1878, an event that triggered a mass exodus of Muslims to Turkey. Today the population numbers about fifty thousand Turks and Tatars, mostly farmers. Under Communist rule this small community found itself in a difficult situation: Turkish and Tatar schools were closed, as was the country's only Muslim seminary at Medjidiya; Muslim religious publications were banned; and travel restrictions made pilgrimage to Mecca impossible. Beginning in 1972 the changing international situation and the country's enormous economic difficulties forced the authorities to grant a few concessions to the Muslims in a clear effort to improve Romania's image with wealthy Arab and other Muslim states. Today there is little information available on the Muslims of Dobroudja or on the ties they must have developed over the past four to five decades with religious bodies in Turkey, the Arab states, and other Islamic countries.

Greece. The regions that comprise modern Greece were conquered by the Ottomans in the mid-fourteenth century (some islands were not seized until the sixteenth or seventeenth century) and underwent a long occupation until they were liberated during the War of Independence and subsequent campaigns from 1821 to 1912. Much of the Muslim population then fled; those who did not were expelled from their lands, massacred, or forced to convert. After Greece and Turkey exchanged populations in 1923, the only Muslims left in Greece were three small communities with a total of 130,000 to 150,000 inhabitants, about 2 percent of the national population. These groups include the Turks (and Gypsies) of western Thrace (numbering 100,000 to 120,000), the Bulgarian-speaking Pomaks in the Rhodopes (about 25,000), and a handful of Turks (perhaps 3,000) in the Dodecanese islands, primarily Rhodes and Kos.

The Dodecanese group is gradually disappearing as its aged members die. The Pomaks, who live in the Rhodope Mountains along the Bulgarian border, form a virtually closed village society, self-reliant and isolated from the outside world by both rugged terrain and strategic considerations: the Greek government has declared the area a military zone and closed it to all outside civilians.

The principal Muslim group is thus that in western Thrace, a community that is alive but restricted by local authorities and very much at the mercy of day-to-day changes in relations between Greece and Turkey—relations that are in turn influenced by its presence. At present there is no sign of improvement in the religious, political, social, or economic conditions of this disadvantaged community, which the Greek government wishes would simply disappear.

Bulgaria. The lands of modern Bulgaria, like those of Greece, were under Ottoman occupation for a long period, from the fourteenth-century conquest until 1878 in northern Bulgaria and until 1908 in the south. Here, however, the number of Muslims was so large that despite the dislocations of war, subsequent massacres, forced and voluntary migration, and some incidents of forced conversion, the 1946 census found that 13.35 percent of the Bulgarian population still identified itself as Muslim. The Bulgarian Islamic community is composed of four distinct and quite different ethnic groups.

The islamized Bulgarians (numbering about 150,000) are known as Pomaks. They speak Bulgarian, know nothing of Turkish, and live in the Rhodope Mountains and in the southwestern part of the country in a region centered on Razlog. Mostly illiterate until relatively recent times, they have never really had a local intelligentsia. Since Bulgaria regained its independence, civil and military authorities have sought to weaken the Pomaks' distinctive identity—a campaign pushed to extremes by the Communists in the past few decades. In the 1980s, for instance, the government forced all minorities to "bulgarianize" family and given names. Nevertheless, since the fall of the Communists it has become clear that both the ethnic identity and the religious traditions of the Pomaks are far from eradicated, and that they continue to pose a problem to the country's present rulers.

Turks are the largest Muslim group in the country. Their number has varied widely over the years since 1878 and today stands at 500,000 to 600,000, by conservative estimate. They are scattered through various regions (Deli Orman, Dobroudja, along the Danube, and in the Western Rhodopes), and it is impossible to say how many of them are actually practicing Muslims. The split between religious and nonreligious Turks has come into the open with the recent emergence of two rival political groups: the Movement for Rights and Freedom is a secular political party with ties to official organizations in Turkey; the followers of the grand *muftī* (in 1993 there were two rival grand *muftī*s in Bulgaria) form a party that maintains strong ties to Islamic religious organizations in the Arab world. The drive to bulgarianize names, and the xenophobic policies it heralded, brought about a massive exodus, with some 300,000 refugees reaching Turkey in 1989. Some of them have since returned, while many others eventually resettled in third countries.

Tatars number a few thousand (they were 6,000 in 1946). Practicing Muslims make up an indeterminate portion of this population. The Tatars are being gradually absorbed into the larger Turkish minority.

The last group is the Gypsies, whose number is uncertain, perhaps 100,000. Most consider themselves Muslims, although religion does not appear to play a very large part in their lives.

A notable aspect of the Turkish-Tatar community in Bulgaria is that it is divided into two distinct religious groups. The vast majority are Sunnī of the Hanafī school, but there is a minority of Alevis (Ar., ʿAlawīyah; locally called Alijani or Kizilbash) in Deli Orman, who are devoted to the veneration of ʿAlī.

Albania. The region of modern Albania was conquered by the Ottomans during the fourteenth and fifteenth centuries. The conquest was followed by the spread of Islam through the local population to such an extent that by the time an Albanian state was created in 1912, 70 percent of the country's population was Muslim. This large community has two noteworthy characteristics: it is completely homogeneous, since virtually all the Muslims in the country are Albanian by ethnic origin and by language; and it consists of two parallel communities, one Sunnī (about 80 percent of the country's Muslims) and the other comprising followers of the Bektāshīyah.

These two communities have consistently pursued independent and autonomous courses. In the period between the two world wars the Albanian Sunnī community separated itself from the caliphate by a decision taken at its first Congress, held in Tirana in 1923. In the beginning of the Communist period, the Bektāshīs gained recognition as the fourth official religion of the country, on an equal footing with Sunnīs, Orthodox Christians, and Roman Catholics. In 1967, however, the Communist authorities banned all religious organizations in the country and closed all houses of worship.

The recent fall of this repressive regime has brought about, as might be expected, the reopening of the mosques, the churches, and the *tekke* of the Bektāshīs and other Ṣūfī brotherhoods. Albania today is witnessing a sweeping religious revival that is being watched with great interest in religious circles of the Islamic world eager to see their faith established as firmly as possible on the European continent.

Former Yugoslavia. It is in the former Yugoslavia—home to the largest number of Balkan Muslims, more than three million—that the situation has been most complex, reflecting the turmoil of history and the existence of several ethnic and linguistic groups. The Ottoman occupation of what became the Yugoslav republics took place over many decades from the late fourteenth century to the late sixteenth. Islam took root among some of the local populations, especially in Bosnia-Herzegovina and in Macedonia, while Ottoman military and administrative officials settled in many parts of the country. Other Muslim immigrants established themselves in parts of the country, among them seminomadic Turks and non-Turkish Muslims, like the Albanians who came to Kosovo beginning in the late seventeenth century.

Following the reconquest Muslim populations were expelled from some regions and concentrated in others, creating today's distinct ethnic and geographic pattern. In Bosnia-Herzegovina, a region occupied by Austria-Hungary from 1878 to 1918, the Islamic population consists of Slavic Muslims speaking Serbo-Croatian; in Kosovo, it consists of Albanians and a small number of Turks who remained after Yugoslav independence; and in Macedonia, Slavic Muslims, Turks, and ethnic Albanians, both recent immigrants and longtime residents, live side by side.

It is clearly impossible to recount even briefly the eventful history of each of these large groups, let alone describe the experience of many smaller ones, like the one-time Turkish *sanjak* of Novi Pazar. The seventy-five-year history of the country as a whole falls into four main periods: the Kingdom of Yugoslavia (1918–1941), World War II (1941–1944), the Communist dictatorship (1945–1989), and the present dissolution of the federation. Each of these eras has had its own impact on the region's Muslim populations. Under the kingdom, Yugoslavia had two very different Islamic groups: the well-organized Muslims of Bosnia-Herzegovina, whose leaders were the de facto heads of an ill-defined "Yugoslav Muslim community," and the Muslims of "South Serbia" (i.e., Kosovo and Macedonia), much less unified because of their ethnic diversity (Albanians, Turks, Macedonian Slavs, and Gypsies). During World War II Bosnia was annexed by the puppet Croatian fascist state, and some Bosnian Muslims joined the Ustashe terrorists, often against their better judgment. Both during and after the war, ties to the Ustashe had tragic consequences. Under the Tito regime, the situation became even more complex. Beginning in 1960 the government decided to favor the Yugoslav Muslim community by granting them significant freedom of action and material advantages. In 1967 a Muslim Nation was recognized as one of the country's constituent peoples, although this recognition extended only to Muslims in Bosnia-Herzegovina. This privileged status rapidly deteriorated, however, as ethnic and religious tensions grew following the sharp downturn in the Yugoslav economy and the collapse of the Communist regime. Recent events in the former Yugoslavia have affected the three main Muslim groups in different ways.

In Macedonia local Muslims are seeking to build stronger ties with their non-Muslim neighbors. Above all, they seek to free themselves from the grip of Albanian Muslims from Kosovo, who continue to migrate to western and southern Macedonia in large numbers.

In Kosovo the situation is explosive owing to the longstanding enmity between the Serbs and the Albanians, which was raised to a fever pitch during the Communist era. It is virtually impossible to say anything precise about the current religious situation of the Albanian community because the assertion of Albanian nationalism monopolizes public discourse, making it difficult to analyze the actual influence of both the mosque and the mystical brotherhoods.

Bosnia-Herzegovina has seen Islam politicized by the Democratic Action Party of Alija Izetbegović, whose theories are clearly presented in two books, *The Islamic Declaration* (1970) and *Islam between East and West* (1980; English translation, 1984). Izetbegović has pushed the various Bosnian Muslim communities toward a "holy union," even though many of them had previously shown little enthusiasm for any sort of religious activism. The country's Orthodox Serbs and Catholic Croats have similarly retreated into hard-line nationalism, bolstered by their respective churches. Exploited by leaders who are all former members of the Titoist political elite, this communal division has led to the gruesome combat that began in the spring of 1992.

[*See also* Albania.]

BIBLIOGRAPHY

Clayer, Nathalie. *L'Albanie, pays des derviches: Les ordres mystiques musulmans en Albanie à l'époque post-ottomane, 1912–1967*. Berlin and Wiesbaden, 1990.

Kalionski, A. "The Pomak Dilemma." In *La transmission du savoir dans le monde musulman périphérique, Lettre d'information*, no. 13, pp. 122–130. Paris, 1993.

Lederer, G. "Islam in Hungary." *Central Asian Survey* 11.1 (1992): 1–23.

Popovic, Alexandre. *L'Islam balkanique: Les musulmans du sud-est européen dans la période post-ottomane*. Berlin and Wiesbaden, 1986. Provides an overall view of the Muslim communities of Southeast Europe, with an extensive annotated bibliography arranged by country and period.

Popovic, Alexandre. *Les musulmans yougoslaves, 1945–1989: Médiateurs et métaphores*. Lausanne, 1990.

ALEXANDRE POPOVIC

Translated from French by Harry M. Matthews, Jr.

BANGLADESH. The identity of Bangladesh as a modern nation-state is derived from a cohesive ethnic and regional base in which Islam has long been a key element. Nearly all of the country's 114 million people are speakers of the Bengali language, and, minor sectarian variation aside, some 85 percent are also Sunnī Muslims governed by the Ḥanafī school of Islamic law. Most of the remaining 15 percent are Hindus.

Islam in Bengal dates from the arrival of Turkic invaders in 1200 CE. In 1576 the region was incorporated into the Mughal Empire, which retained hegemony until 1757 and the onset of the British empire in India. Military and political domination do not by themselves produce mass conversion; thus one mystery of South Asian history is how the territory today comprising Bangladesh came to contain some 40 percent of the Muslims counted in British India at its first census (1872), and to become home to around 30 percent of all South Asian Muslims today.

In explanation of this phenomenon, the British scholar-administrators who devised and interpreted the early censuses, notably H. H. Risley, concluded that massive conversion had occurred among low-caste Hindus seeking refuge from caste oppression in the egalitarian fold of Islam. Seen as an insult to Islam, this conclusion was vigorously opposed by English-educated Muslim intellectuals such as Khondkar Fazli Rubbee, whose *Origins of the Musalmans of Bengal* (Calcutta, 1895) attempted to show that the Muslim population of Bengal was mainly descended from Arab, Mughal (Turkic), and Afghan invaders. Muhammed Abdur Rahim (1963, 1967) has more recently sought to reiterate the argument, but with statistical evidence that few other historians accept. A contrasting view has it that Bengal was the last bastion in India of a corrupt and effete Buddhism, and so its people were ripe for the appeal of Ṣūfī mystics who followed the first Muslim rulers.

In one way or another, historians universally emphasize the role of Sufism in the initial stages of Bengali conversion to Islam. Current explorations of Bengali Muslim history link the earliest phase of islamization to the deforestation of the Bengal Delta by land-hungry peasants of no discernibly stable religious commitment, spurred on by the revenue-famished rulers of both pre-Mughal and Mughal Bengal. In Richard Eaton's (1993) analysis, Ṣūfī adepts also figure prominently as charismatic pioneer leaders or *ghāzī-pīrs* ("warrior saints") who organized the spread of farming, protected cultivators from the natural and supernatural hazards of the forest, and spearheaded development of rural communities, linking them to the Muslim rulers. Over time, devotional cults initiated by these Ṣūfī pioneers came to focus on them as "saints," and their religious ideology, Islam, thus embryonically embedded itself in the deltaic countryside. This amalgam of agriculture and religion might be seen as the first stage of islamization in Bengal. Its legacy lives on in the myth of creation found today among Bengali Muslim cultivators, who, as described by John Thorp (1978), see themselves as descendants of a primordial Adam, the first Prophet of Islam and also the First Farmer, created by God for the express purpose of mastering the earth.

A second stage of islamization in eastern Bengal may be witnessed in the development of a tradition syncretizing popular forms of Islam and Hinduism. Asim Roy (1983) argues that the formal doctrines of Islam were at first absorbed only lightly by the largely rural Bengali population. Their folk religious culture mingled beliefs in the fantastic with perceptions of the natural world, and mixed superstition, myth, and magic with faith. This was no less true of Bengali Hinduism, since it was Vaishnavism (Krishna-focused worship) and not orthodox Brahminical codes that captured the imagination of rural people who identified themselves as Hindus, providing forms of religious devotion as emotionally satisfying and evocatively mystical as the Ṣūfī pirism that had enthralled converts to the Muslim fold.

The result was a syncretic folk religion in which Ṣūfī pirs and Vaishnavite saints were worshiped interchangeably by both Hindus and Muslims. Worship itself commonly took form (and to this day often occurs) in didactic narrative exposition by local or itinerant charismatics, or it featured folk music whose devotional lyrics were imbued with spiritual metaphor and allegory intelligible to Hindus and Muslims at once, and whose performers might claim to be either or both. Indigenous healers and shamans might proffer curatives whose power was derived from Qur'ān and Krishna alike.

There was, however, a considerable gap between the popular religion of most rural Muslims—descendants of indigenous converts known as the *ajlāf* or *aṭrāf* ("low ranked") social classes—and Muslim elites or *ashrāf* ("noble") classes who claimed Middle Eastern descent and espoused a version of Islam that looked to North India, Persia, and Arabia for its inspiration and its linguistic expression (in Persian and Urdu, not in Bengali). That gap was bridged by religious guides, preceptors, philosophers, and poets whose writings introduced orthodox Islamic dogma by seeking its broad parallels in Hinduism. For example, accounts of the life of the Prophet might be couched in terms accommodating to the Hindu belief in divine incarnations, and descriptions of Fāṭimah might evoke the Mother Goddess of popular Hinduism. There developed a "Muslim-Vaishnavite" synthesis in lyric poetry; similar efforts at harmonizing Hindu and Muslim cosmological, mystical, and esoteric traditions arose. Thus was constructed a syncretic version of Islam that aimed at accommodating elite, Perso-Arabic versions as well as the devotional, pir-focused folk traditions of rural non-elites who had identified themselves with the Islamic faith. This may be seen as the second stage in the islamization of eastern Bengal.

A third stage may be posited with the rise of several strains of revivalism confronting the homegrown, syncretic Bengali variety of Islam in the early nineteenth century. Among the most important was the Farā'iẕī (Farā'iḍī) movement (from Arabic *farḍ*, recalling the obligatory duties of Islam), founded in 1818 by Ḥājjī Sharīʿatullāh (1781–1840), an East Bengali whose twenty years in the Arabian Muslim heartland had imbued him with Meccan standards of belief and practice. Spreading rapidly throughout eastern Bengal down to 1900, this movement called upon the local Muslim faithful to abandon pirism and eschew Hindu-tainted customs and beliefs. The Farā'iẕīs presented what they considered orthodox models of Islamic credo and conduct and insisted that belief and behavior be shaped in conformity with the Five Pillars. They also became active in agrarian struggles, which often pitted Muslim peasants against Hindu and European landlords, thus adding a religiously communal element to the social and political antagonisms spreading in the Bengali countryside at this time.

Another movement, the Ṭarīqah-i Muḥammadīyah, an Indian counterpart to the Wahhābī movement of eighteenth-century Arabia, had been initiated in Delhi in 1818 by Sayyid Aḥmad Shahīd (1786–1831). Introduced into western Bengal by Titu Mīr (1782–1831) in 1827, it also became involved in peasant struggles. A key feature of this movement was its emphasis on strict adherence to the *sharīʿah;* one of its offshoots, the Ahl-i Ḥadīth ("people of *ḥadīth*") movement, was vehement in stressing *ijtihād*. The Ahl-i Ḥadīth movement is the most visible remnant of the last century's reformist movements in Bangladesh today, with a reported two thousand local branches and two million adherents in the mid-1980s, especially in the northern districts of the country. Its local groups display distinctive variations in ritual performance but otherwise avoid exclusive, sect-like behavior and are open to relationships with Muslims of other persuasions. The Ahl-i Ḥadīth is led by highly educated and articulate spokespersons, such as its long-standing *amīr,* Professor Muḥammad ʿAbdul Bāri, a respected Islamic scholar and top university administrator; these leaders have developed the original movement's doctrines toward progressive social reform along Islamic lines.

The revivalist "purification" of Bengali Islam undermined its earlier syncretism by stressing the differences between Islam and Hinduism. As Rafiuddin Ahmed (1981) has argued, these militant movements deepened Islamic consciousness in late nineteenth-century East Bengal and paved the way for effective mobilization of its Muslim peasantry by the Muslim elites who would lead the Pakistan movement in the twentieth century. Such elites included in their number many belonging to an Islamic modernist tradition, begun in the late nineteenth century and similar to its counterparts elsewhere in the Muslim world, which advocated Western education and stressed the utility of European science in harmonic combination with classical Islamic scientific and humanistic learning and moral ideals. Thus, in its Islamic dimension, by 1947 the maturing national identity of East Bengal not only retained remnants of Sufism and syncretism but also contained elements of orthodox fundamentalism and modernism.

From a large survey she has recently conducted of Bangladeshi Muslims claiming an active faith, Razia Akter Banu (1992) has identified three basic tendencies in present-day Bangladeshi Islam, all of which have their roots in these historic movements. Nearly half of her rural and a quarter of her urban respondents evinced the syncretism of folk belief and practice described above. Followers of popular forms of Islam most often represent lower levels of income, education, and occupation.

Attribution of supernatural power to pirs is an especially salient feature of popular Bangladeshi Islam. Commemorative gatherings *(ʿurs)* at the ubiquitous tombs *(mazār)* of the pirs occur year-round, and major shrines are located throughout the country. At least one major Ṣūfī order *(ṭarīqah),* the Qādirīyah, has a large following, with a national center in the Chittagong district village of Maijbhandar. These Maijbhandari, as they are called, meet in weekly gatherings *(maḥfil)* where religious folk music forms the centerpiece of devotional worship, and they have an annual conclave at their national center. The nature and extent of Ṣūfī activity in Bangladesh needs much further study, but it is widespread and attracts persons of all social, educational, and occupational backgrounds.

Another 50 percent of Banu's rural sample, and more than 60 percent of her urban respondents, claimed adherence to orthodox forms of Islam: literality in acceptance of Qur'ān and *ḥadīth,* strictness in observing the obligatory duties, and total obedience to the Ḥanafī school of law. Both urban and rural people of moderate educational background register among the ranks of the orthodox; in the rural areas orthodoxy is associated with relatively higher levels of land ownership, in contrast to its correspondence with middle levels of income in the cities.

Finally, while very few rural Bangladeshi Muslims espouse an Islamic modernist point of view, with its emphasis on rationalism and scientism and rejection of literalistic determinism, Banu found that 12 percent of the urbanites in her sample adopted this perspective. Not surprisingly, espousal of this viewpoint was associated with high levels of Western education as well as with higher occupation and income.

Banu's study also suggests that adherents to both the popular and orthodox versions of Islam hover between high and moderate levels of actual practice, as measured by the degree to which they claim to carry out the daily and annual obligatory duties of the faithful. Modernists tend toward moderate and lower levels of practice, as one might surmise. In my observation, the daily and weekly requirements of prayer and the mandate of the annual fast are widely met by rural Bangladeshis, and a good deal of social pressure is exerted via shaming mechanisms and fear of embarrassment toward the maintenance of Muslim propriety in public conduct. In urban areas, where normative conformity is more difficult to exact, performance in these areas is more varied.

The Islamic component of East Bengal's regional identity was at the forefront of its people's political consciousness during their struggle for an independent Pakistan until 1947. Thereafter, however, the Bengalis in what became East Pakistan became disillusioned as they perceived their economic, political, and cultural interests increasingly subordinated to those of their confrères in non-Bengali West Pakistan. Accordingly, the ethnolinguistic element of their national identity, especially pride in their language and its associated cultural traditions, took political primacy, and although their religious commitment to Islam by no means waivered, it no longer shaped their immediate political goals. By the mid-1950s Bengali enthusiasm for the Muslim League, which had spearheaded Pakistani independence, became deeply eroded. The growing rift between Pakistan's eastern and western wings broke into rebellion in 1971, and, led by the secular nationalist Awami League, an independent Bangladesh was born. [*See also* Muslim League; Awami League.]

In part because members of Islamic political parties had—sometimes violently—opposed separation from Pakistan, the first constitution of Bangladesh (1972) proclaimed secularism as a principle of state policy and prohibited political parties based on religious affiliation. Individuals thought to have stood against independence on religious or other grounds were stigmatized, and, not uncommonly, ordinary Muslims visibly observant in dress and ritual performance could find themselves shunned or mocked by supporters of the party in power.

A great many Bangladeshi Muslims, however, were uncomfortable with official secularism. Daily religious practice went on unabated, as did the expressions of popular and orthodox Islam noted above. The Delhi-based Tablīghī Jamāʿat, which aims at strengthening Islamic faith and practice among believers, became highly active in the country, attracting large numbers and presaging an Islamic resurgence. In 1975 the increasingly dictatorial Awami League was overthrown; a more favorable domestic climate for the political expression of Islam was ushered in.

Against this domestic background, one should also note that Bangladesh was receiving mounting proportions of its foreign aid from the oil-rich and conservative Arab states, where Bangladeshis were working in massive numbers, especially in Saudi Arabia. The post-coup government of Ziaur Rahman (1975–1981) became prominently active in Islamic international organizations, and increasing ties to the wider Muslim world may have prompted it in 1977 to replace the secularism clause of the constitution with a proclamation of "absolute faith and trust in almighty Allāh," mandating that government strengthen "fraternal ties with the Muslim states on the basis of Islamic solidarity." The Zia government began to sponsor Islam as well, in its establishment of a cabinet-level Division of Religious Affairs, creation of an Islamic Foundation for research, and plans for a new Islamic University. Under a separate directorate in the Ministry of Education, since 1975 the number of *madrasahs* in Bangladesh has increased by 50 percent, their teachers by one-third, and students by well over two-thirds. The subsequent government of H. M. Ershad (1982–1991) continued in this vein; the president and members of his cabinet publicly associated themselves with a famous and politically active pir. In 1988 the National Assembly passed a constitutional amendment declaring Islam the "state religion" of the country.

The intent and import of this change remain unclear. It did not, however, result in institution of the *sharīʿah*. Bangladeshis have not recently been prone toward fundamentalist government. In the first post-independence National Assembly election (1979) that permitted Islam-oriented parties to compete, the conservative but non-theocratic Muslim League won 19 of 300 seats and 10 percent of the popular vote; no fundamentalist parties contested. But in the parliamentary election of 1986, the Muslim League's mere four seats were surpassed by ten that went to the Jamāʿat-i Islāmī (Islamic Assembly), which advocates a fullfledged Islamic state. Harbinger of things to come, the Jamāʿat's student front, the Islamiya Chhatra Shibir (Islamic Student Group), emerged as a major force in Bangladesh's politically volatile universities. Not surprisingly, then, the Jamāʿat garnered nearly 12 percent of the popular vote in the 1991 National Assembly elections, winning 18 (6 percent) of all 300 seats, and 8 percent of the 221 it contested.

It remains to be seen whether Bangladesh will ever become an Islamic state. Its past has shown, however, that Islam seeks perennial renewal in the dynamic interplay between Bengali nationalism and Muslim universalism that lies at the heart of its national identity.

[*See also* Islam, *article on* Islam in South Asia; Pir.]

BIBLIOGRAPHY

Ahmad Khan, Muin-ud-din. *History of the Fara'idi Movement in Bengal, 1818–1906.* Karachi, 1965. Definitive work to date on the Farā'iẕīs and their relations with other movements; essential reading on Islamic revivalism in nineteenth-century Bengal.

Ahmed, Rafiuddin. *The Bengal Muslims, 1871–1906: A Quest for Identity.* Delhi, Oxford, and New York, 1981. Best general study of nineteenth-century Bengali Muslim society, covering religious, social, and political development in an integrated manner. See also his *Islam in Bangladesh: Society, Culture, and Politics* (Dhaka, 1983), and *Religion, Nationalism, and Politics in Bangladesh* (New Delhi, 1990), both collections of original essays on social and political aspects of Islam in Bangladesh since 1971.

Ahmed, Sufia. *Muslim Community in Bengal, 1884–1912.* Dhaka, 1974. Comprehensive study with chapters on educational, social, economic, and political development, focusing on elites.

Banu, U. A. B. Razia Akter. *Islam in Bangladesh.* Leiden and New York, 1992. Unique and highly imaginative social science survey research study of current attitudes and beliefs, with informative historical background chapters.

Eaton, Richard Maxwell. *The Rise of Islam and the Bengal Frontier, 1204–1760.* Berkeley, 1993. Path-breaking reassessment of the spread of Islam as seen in the context of Bengali agrarian and economic history.

Haq, Muhammed Enamul. *A History of Sufi-ism in Bengal.* Dhaka, 1975. Detailed, if not particularly critical, history through the medieval period, with an outline of major beliefs and biographical notes on saints.

Karim, Abdul. *Social History of the Muslims in Bengal, Down to A.D. 1538.* Dhaka, 1959. Covers intellectual development, social organization, and daily life in the early Islamic period.

Mallick, Azizur R. *British Policy and the Muslims of Bengal, 1757–1856.* Dhaka, 1961. Focus on educational policy and its impact on Muslim society; background on religious syncretism and revivalist reaction to it.

Rahim, Muhammed Abdur. *Social and Cultural History of Bengal.* 2 vols. Karachi, 1963–1967. *Tour de force* survey of Bengal's medieval history from a Muslim nationalist perspective; covers all aspects, including both Hindu and Muslim societies.

Raychaudhuri, Tapan. *Bengal under Akbar and Jahangir: An Introductory Study in Social History.* Delhi, 1953. Seminal study of the early Mughal period, with important chapters on religious development.

Roy, Asim. *The Islamic Syncretistic Tradition in Bengal.* Princeton, 1983. The best study of beliefs and practices in the prerevivalist medieval period; essential for the study of popular Islam in Bangladesh today.

Thorp, John P., Jr. "Masters of Earth: Conceptions of 'Power' among Muslims of Rural Bangladesh." Ph.D. diss., University of Chicago, 1978. Pioneering anthropological study of community organization and religious culture among Bangladeshi Muslim peasantry.

PETER J. BERTOCCI

BANKS AND BANKING. Modern banking was first established in the Islamic world in the mid-nineteenth century. Financial intermediaries of course were not new to the region, as the sophisticated Moslem trading economies had long used specie as a means of exchange, and money changers and moneylenders carried out their business in most urban centers. Money changers were especially active in the cities of the Hejaz, such as Mecca and Medina, catering for needs of the pilgrims, demonstrating that there was no Islamic objection to currency dealings and the exchange of precious metals. The prohibition of *ribā* ("interest") in the Qur'ān, however, meant that there was much suspicion of conventional commercial banking in the form in which it had developed in Europe.

The Penetration of Colonial Banking. The early commercial banks were all European owned, the Imperial Ottoman Bank being an Anglo-French venture, and the Imperial Bank of Persia was British owned and managed. Much financial intermediation in the Ottoman territories was in the hands of Greek Christians or Jews rather than Muslims. The latter were keen traders, and indeed the prophet Muḥammad had been a trader, but there was a reluctance on religious grounds to get involved in the collection and lending of money. Muslim traders granted credit in kind on a deferred-payment basis rather than charging interest. Advances were covered from personal and family equity rather than from savings attracted from strangers by the promise of interest.

The Imperial Banks served the government and the trade of the European empires rather than the local Muslim business community or the wealthy landlord class. The management of Ottoman debt was a major undertaking, and the Imperial Ottoman Bank acted on behalf of the sultan in arranging bond issues in London and Paris. The Imperial Bank of Persia was closely involved with the Anglo-Iranian oil company, later to become British Petroleum. The National Bank of Egypt, a wholly British-owned institution, was mainly involved in the finance of cotton exports, on which the Lancashire textile industry depended. This trade was controlled by Greek and Levantine merchants rather than Egyptian Muslims. In Malaya the Hong Kong and Shanghai Bank was active in the finance of the rubber trade, but even the plantation workers were immigrants rather than indigenous Muslims.

Muslim-owned Commercial Banks. It was not until the 1920s that groups of Muslim businessmen began to realize that traditional financial intermediation was of limited value in modern economies. For large-scale deals, especially with foreigners, letters of credit, guarantees, and acceptance of bills were indispensable. Such facilities significantly reduced transactions costs and could result in deals being made which might otherwise be missed opportunities. Yet moneylenders and money changers were unable to provide such facilities. At the same time potential Muslim clients often experienced difficulties in obtaining credit from the European-owned banks. The only answer was for Muslim businessmen to found banks themselves. It was these pressures that resulted in the establishment of Bank Misr of Egypt, the Arab Bank, a Palestinian institution, the Habib Bank in British India, and other similar commercial banks in many Muslim countries and communities.

Banks had been kept out of Saudi Arabia by King Abdul Aziz (ʿAbd al-ʿAzīz), who believed that only infidels patronized Western banks, whose practices could never be Islamically acceptable. With the kingdom's development and the discovery of oil, there were strong pressures to admit foreign banks, and even Bank Misr applied for a banking license, as its directors thought that their Muslim credentials might impress the king. Permission to establish a branch was refused, but when two well-respected local money changers, the Bin Mahfouz (Ibn Maḥfūẓ) and Kakī families, applied for a banking license, the king agreed, after consultations with some prominent Jeddah merchants.

The license was conditional on the bank operating in a way which was acceptable to the majority of the Muslim faithful. This meant avoiding interest payments or receipts. The institution established, the National Commercial Bank, charged fees for its services and provided current accounts for its customers on which no interest was paid. Lines of credit had to be agreed in advance, and contracts between the bank and its clients were set out clearly, according to the prescribed Qur'ānic rules on just trading practice. *Sharīʿah* (religious law) would apply to banking in Saudi Arabia, as it was this that governed all commercial practice.

Nationalization and Muslim Nationalism. The political revolutions in Egypt, Syria, and Iraq in the 1950s resulted in both the colonial banks and the private Muslim banks being taken into state ownership. In Pakistan the banking system was nationalized a decade later, and in most Muslim countries the state was to play a significant role in the financial system. The intervention by the state was not due to Islamic ideology; indeed *sharīʿah* is concerned with inheritance matters in the context of the private ownership of property. Rather the nationalization measures reflected the adoption of a planned approach to economic development and an attempt to introduce heavy industry following a Soviet type of model.

The nationalized banks mainly advanced funds to the new state-run industries, the allocation being determined by the priorities set out in the development plans. Quotas were set for each industrial sector and even individual plants, which meant that there was scarcely any flexibility to allow for changing circumstances or indeed new opportunities. In practice the funding available was often less than had been anticipated, which meant across-the-board reductions in lending ceilings rather than selective cutbacks on which it might have proved difficult to get agreement.

One problem was that the nationalized banks failed to attract new depositors. Ordinary citizens appeared unimpressed by the fact that their deposits were more secure, as government-owned banks were unlikely to go out of business. Interest was paid on savings deposits, but the rates were low and scarcely compensated for inflation. Financial repression prevailed in the sense that savings were not harnessed by the formal banking system. Instead there continued to be much hoarding of gold and, to a lesser extent, silver. Money changers and moneylenders continued in business, catering for needs which the nationalized banks clearly did not cover.

Evidence of the failure of the nationalized banks is easy to find. Bank deposits were worth less in Syria and Iraq, for example, than they were in Jordan, a much smaller country, where there had been no nationalization measures. The ratio of bank assets to gross domestic product was static in Egypt, and fell in Pakistan, indicating financial shallowing rather than the deepening that might be expected with development. The bureaucratic nature of the nationalized banking business put off many potential clients. There was a reluctance to widen the range of financial services on offer, and no competitive pressures to innovate through the introduction of modern technology.

In some Muslim countries, notably the Gulf states, Malaysia, and Indonesia, governments have favored privately owned banks in the form of publicly quoted joint-stock companies. There has nevertheless been a desire to see a majority ownership stake in the hands of local Muslims. Following independence in Kuwait the branches of the British Bank of the Middle East were sold to indigenous investors, and the bank became the

Bank of Kuwait and the Middle East. In Saudi Arabia 60 percent of Citibank's operation was offered to the public, and a new institution created, the Saudi American Bank. The injection of Saudi Arabian capital into the hitherto foreign-owned banks enabled them to expand, creating a more-competitive financial environment.

An Islamic Financial Alternative. There was considerable dissatisfaction with conventional commercial banking in most Islamic countries, both on the part of Muslim scholars and intellectuals and among the general public, who were aware of the Qurānic position on *ribā*. Merely having fees and service charges instead of interest was not seen by many as a satisfactory solution, and in many Muslim countries *ribā* was quite open. Some thought that only usury was *ribā*, and in any case charging interest to business borrowers could not be a problem on religious grounds, if the aim of the prohibition on *ribā* was to protect the poor private borrower from suffering hardship. In the United Arab Emirates a court ruling outlawed compound interest but permitted simple interest.

In Turkey, where inflation has long been a problem, it was argued that nominal interest to compensate for price rises was justifiable, as long as there was not a real interest burden on borrowers. Such arguments, however, did not impress fundamentalist thinkers. Their concern was not merely with the prohibition of interest, but with the introduction of participatory finance as a real Islamic alternative. Earning a predetermined return for merely hoarding could not be justified. Profit as a result of risk sharing was not only legitimate, however, but highly desirable.

Profit Sharing. The principle of profit sharing, which was well established in Islam, was known as *muḍārabah*. Depositors could earn a share in either the bank's profits or the profits from a specified investment. Usually profit-sharing deposits are described as investment accounts, with the depositor required to give a minimum period of notice for withdrawals, usually from one month up to a year. The rate of profit is declared by the bank at the end of the financial year after the accounts are audited, and the depositors profit share is greatest for the longer-notice accounts.

If the bank is making a loss, no profit share may be offered, although profit pay-outs to depositors generally take precedence over dividend payments to shareholders. The value of deposits is usually guaranteed, unlike bank equity, the price of which depends on stock-market conditions. There is less risk therefore for holders of investment accounts than for equity investors, but the latter have voting rights at the annual general meeting of the bank, whereas depositors do not.

Islamic banks also offer current account facilities for transactions balances, which can be instantly withdrawn by check or automatic teller machine. No return is offered to current account holders, but in some cases international charge cards such as Visa are offered to depositors, though these are managed on a direct-debit basis rather than as credit cards. Usually only current account holders can apply for credit.

Credit Facilities. The use of bank funds reflects the demands of their clients and the environment in which the institutions operate. As much of the finance required in Muslim countries is to fund trading activity, Islamic banks are not surprisingly most active in this field. Islamic trade financing is offered on a *murābaḥah* basis whereby the bank purchases a good on behalf of the client and later resells it to the client at a markup. The bank charges the markup to cover its costs and to allow a return for the risk it takes on during the period it owns the good being traded. The Islamic bank usually does not take delivery of the good itself, but it has the responsibility of ownership, unlike a conventional commercial bank.

Islamic banks also offer longer-term credit facilities through leasing or *ijārah*, especially for items of capital equipment. In some cases this may involve hire purchase or installment sale, where the customer eventually acquires ownership of the equipment. Longer-term participatory finance is also provided by an Islamic bank becoming a partner in the business according to the principle of *muḍārabah*. The bank may provide all of the funding, acting as *ṣāḥib al-māl* (the financier), and the *muḍārib* (the active manager) provides the entrepreneurial skills and management.

Under a *mushārakah* equity-sharing arrangement funding may be provided to an existing company. Alternatively a new company can be established as a financing vehicle which may be wound up after an agreed period.

The Spread of Islamic Banking. The first modern Islamic banking institutions were farmer credit unions in Pakistan in the 1950s and the Mit Ghamr Savings Bank, a small rural institution founded in Egypt in 1963. The latter was modeled on the German local savings banks, which had impressed Aḥmad al-Najjār, the bank's founder. Influential elements in Nasser's political party, the Arab Social Union, and some of the senior managers in the country's nationalized banks disliked al-Najjār's initiative and the Islamic nature of the institution. In 1971 it was incorporated into a new government-controlled institution, the Nasser Social Bank, which had responsibility for the collection of *zakāt,* the Islamic wealth tax. Many saw this new institution as a state agency rather than a bank.

The major expansion in Islamic banking came in the 1970s with the establishment of the Dubai Islamic Bank in 1975, the Fayṣal Islamic Banks in Egypt and Sudan in 1977, the Kuwait Finance House the same year, the Jordan Islamic Bank in 1978, and the Bahrain Islamic Bank in 1979. The impetus was partly the oil-revenue boom in the Persian Gulf and the growing economic muscle of the more-conservative Muslim states of the gulf at the expense of the more-secular Arab nationalist movement. There was in any case a growing dissatisfaction with Arab socialism, especially among the young, and a feeling that there should be a greater emphasis on Islamic values in all spheres, including the economic and financial.

Gulf business interests strongly supported the new Islamic banking movement. Prince Muḥammad ibn Fayṣal of Saudi Arabia was the instigator of the Fayṣal Islamic Banks. Shaykh Ṣāliḥ Kāmil's Dallah group based in Jeddah aided the Jordan Islamic Bank and funded the al-Barakah Islamic Banks, which spread from Turkey to Tunisia, and even to London. The al-Rājiḥī money-changing group applied for an Islamic banking license in Saudi Arabia and offered Islamic financial services internationally through their London-based investment company. Prince Muḥammad founded Dār al-Māl al-Islāmī, the house of Islamic funds, as an international financing body in Geneva.

The new Islamic banks had to compete with the conventional *ribā*-based banks in most Muslim countries, and they appear to have been particularly successful in attracting deposits. The Kuwait Finance House accounts for one-fifth of total deposits in its home country, and the Jordan Islamic Bank has succeeded in attracting deposits from poorer people who had not previously used banks. Financial deepening has been helped by the new banks, which often compliment rather than serve as a substitute for existing banks. Islamic banking has now spread to Malaysia and Indonesia, and Bank Islam Malaysia has funded many promising industrial ventures, including those run by Chinese-speaking non-Muslims. Bank Muamalat Indonesia would appear to have enormous potential in a rapidly industrializing country with 160 million Muslims.

Some commercial banks have started offering Islamic banking facilities, including the state-owned banks in Egypt and the National Commercial Bank in Saudi Arabia. Even some European banks offer Islamic financial products, including Kleinworth Benson of London and the Swiss Banking Corporation. Islamic financial instruments are increasingly accepted internationally, even in non-Islamic countries, and the basic principles are generally understood.

In Iran and Pakistan the entire financial system was Islamized in the 1980s, and all banks in those countries operate under *sharīʿah.* Not only is *ribā* prohibited, but all deposits are accepted on a participatory basis and financing is entirely through Islamic instruments. It is too early to assess the success of these experiments, as Iran's economy was severely damaged in the lengthy war with Iraq, and Pakistan has been subject to political instability and ethnic tensions.

It is clear, however, that Islamic banking is no mere passing phenomenon. Ethical concerns are perfectly consistent with profitability, and the Islamic banks have been able to harness long-term savings on more favorable terms than secular institutions. The substitution of equity for debt finance is advocated by many development agencies. Participatory finance is especially suited for small business, and there is a venture-capital gap in many Muslim countries. Islamic finance can meet these needs, and provide a workable alternative to conventional lending. Of course teething problems have inevitably occurred, but the experience so far is encouraging. The best motivation is moral rather than merely financial, and Islamic financial intermediation has been welcomed by many with considerable enthusiasm.

[*See also* Economics, *article on* Economic Institutions; Interest.]

BIBLIOGRAPHY

Beauge, Gilbert. *Les capitaux de l'Islam.* Paris, 1990. Major French-language source on the subject.

Chapra, Mohammed Umar. *Towards a Just Monetary System.* Leicester, 1985. Discussion of money, banking, and monetary policy in the light of Islamic teaching.

El-Ashker, Ahmad. *The Islamic Business Enterprise.* London, 1987. The Egyptian experience, including the calculation of financial ratios.

Iqbal, Zubair, and Abbas Mirakhor. *Islamic Banking.* Washington, D.C., 1987. First detailed account of the experiences of Iran and Pakistan.

Kazarian, Elias. *Finance and Economic Development: Islamic Banking in Egypt*. Lund, 1991. Well-written treatment from an economic development perspective.
Mallat, Chibli, ed. *Islamic Law and Finance*. London, 1988. Especially interesting on Malaysia and Turkey.
Meyer, Ann Elizabeth. "Islamic Banking and Credit Policies in the Sadat Era: The Social Origins of Islamic Banking in Egypt." *Arab Law Quarterly* (London) 1.1 (November 1985): 32–50. Well-researched article based on interviews with participants.
Presley, John, ed. *Directory of Islamic Financial Institutions*. London, 1988. Useful reference volume.
Shirazi, Habib. *Islamic Banking*. London, 1990. Legal aspects of Iran's Islamic financing practices.
Siddiqi, Muhammad Nejatullah. *Muslim Economic Thinking*. Leicester, 1981. Survey of contemporary literature on the subject.
Siddiqi, Muhammad, Nejatullah. *Partnership and Profit Sharing in Islamic Law*. Leicester, 1985. Covers contracts and business liability.
Wilson, Rodney. *Islamic Business: Theory and Practice*. London, 1985.
Wilson, Rodney. *Islamic Financial Markets*. London, 1990. Experiences of Islamic banking in Kuwait, Iran, Jordan, Pakistan, and Turkey.
Wilson, Rodney. "Islamic Financial Instruments." *Arab Law Quarterly* (London) 6.2 (April 1991): 205–214. Considers Islamic bonds, certificates of deposit, and equities.

RODNEY WILSON

BANNĀ', ḤASAN AL- (1906–1949), founder of the Muslim Brotherhood and author of *Majmūʿat al-rasā'il* (Letters) and *Mudhakkirat al-daʿwah wa-al-dāʿ iyah* (Memories of the Message and the Messenger). Born in Maḥmudīyah near Alexandria, Egypt, Bannā', from his youth onward, took part in the Ḥaṣāfīyah Ṣūfī brotherhood with his friend Aḥmad al-Sukkarī. After attending the Damanhūr teachers' training college from 1923 to 1927, he went to the Dār al-ʿUlūm in Cairo, founded by Muḥammad ʿAbduh (d. 1905) and made famous by Muḥammad Rashīd Riḍā, who taught there until his death in 1935. By his own account, Bannā' read Spengler, Spencer, and Toynbee while a student there. In September 1927, he began teaching primary school in Ismāʿīlīyah. There, he continued to be a correspondent of the Cairo Muslim Youth magazine *Al-fatḥ (The Beginning)* and pursued his relationship with Riḍā's Maktabah Salafiyah (Fundamentalist Library) group and with his scholarly journal *Al-manār (The Lighthouse)*, which Bannā' took over from 1939 to 1941.

Political Activities. In Ismāʿīlīyah in March 1928, Bannā' and six friends founded a "religious association devoted to the promotion of good and the rooting-out of evil," a branch of the Ḥaṣāfīyah (perhaps until 1933). By 1929, the organization was already being referred to as the "Muslim Brotherhood" (Jamʿīyat al-Ikhwān al-Muslimūn) in the semi-official *Al-ahrām* newspaper, where a photograph of the group was shown. Bannā' received donations, in particular five hundred books from the Suez Canal Company, which had its headquarters in Ismāʿīlīyah, and he obtained permission to build offices and a mosque for the Muslim Brotherhood. The growth of the movement, which moved its base to Cairo in 1933, was rapid, numbering four branches in 1929, fifteen in 1932, three hundred in 1938, and eventually two thousand branches in 1948, according to its own journals. In 1945, Bannā' made mention of a half million "active members" in Egypt. There were also branches in Palestine, Sudan, Iraq, and Syria beginning in the period of 1946 to 1948. By 1930, the organization of the movement had been established by Bannā', and it was publicized in 1933, confirmed at the Third Congress in 1935, and codified in a "Fundamental Law" at the Eighth Congress in 1945. Bannā' was the author of the law, which conferred absolute personal authority on him. The "oath of obedience" of the active member, according to this law, stipulates "absolute trust in the leader and total obedience in all circumstances, good or ill."

In 1933, Bannā' transformed the Muslim Brotherhood into a political movement, excluding nonpolitical elements, but he kept the title of *murshid* ("guide"). He chose from twelve to twenty members to be his personal assistants, who made up the organization's governing body. Decisions made by the executive committee required unanimity, and Bannā' alone had final decision-making power. Parallel to the organization defined by these statutes was a Special Organization (al-Tanẓīm al-Khāṣṣ), referred to outside of the brotherhood as a "secret organization" or "military machine." This body answered directly to Bannā's authority at first, but perhaps as early as 1938 it was controlled by Ṣāliḥ ʿAshmāwī, an activist who became increasingly autonomous and who was even to maintain contact with the 1939 secessionist group Muḥammadan Youth (Shabāb Muḥammad) whose journal *Al-nadhīr* (The Warner) belonged to him. The armed units of this Special Organization demonstrated their ability and their stock of weaponry when they took part in the Arab revolt in Palestine in 1936, and later in the Arab-Israeli war of 1948–1949.

From 1944 to 1948, the armed units of the Muslim Brotherhood were the same as the Secret Organization of the Free Officers commanded by Gamal Abdel Nasser within the army, according to the account of Ḥasan al-ʿAshmāwī in *Al-ikhwān wa-al-thawrah* (The Brotherhood and the Revolution, Cairo, 1977). Anwar el-Sadat met Bannā' in 1940, and Nasser and Bannā' had contact in 1944, thanks to Sadat and to the Free Officer Muslim Brother Kamāl al-Dīn Ḥusayn. In 1948, the two secret armed organizations of the Muslim Brothers and the Free Officers separated, but they continued to cooperate. Bannā's "Letter of Teachings" (c. 1943) explicitly addresses the "fighting" brothers, ranked fourth after the assistant brothers, the affiliated brothers, and the active brothers.

All developments in Egypt, especially from 1940 to 1952, were necessarily affected, in one way or another, by Bannā', who was wooed by the government from 1933 to 1941 and from 1945 to 1948. Between 1941 and 1945, and from 1948 until his assassination in February 1949, he was active in the underground movement. In order to explain this success of the "idea," as Bannā' called it, one must take into account the fact that after the euphoria in Egypt of the 1920s, the 1930s were marked by deep disappointment. The formal independence of Egypt that was declared in 1922 and the 1923 constitution were both attributable to the Wafd party, a popular movement born in 1919 during nationalist demonstrations and riots; both were eroded by the 1936 Anglo-Egyptian treaty that confirmed Egyptian dependence. From that time onward, the Wafd party increasingly lost its credibility and popularity. The enthronement of the young King Fārūq in 1937 gave Bannā' the opportunity to acclaim him enthusiastically, in hopes of being able to manage him and to replace the Wafd party with the Muslim Brotherhood. In 1939, Bannā' stated that he was both separate from and yet close to the Muslim Youth and Young Egypt (Miṣr al-Fatāh; the future Socialist party), from which Nasser and several Free Officers were later to emerge. During these years he was courted by King Fārūq as well as Muṣṭafā al-Marāghī, head of the Islamic university al-Azhar, who wished him to compete with parliament and the political parties, especially the Wafd party.

World War II brought about further internal conflicts. In addition to Egyptian neutrality as provided for in the 1936 treaty, in 1942 Great Britain demanded general support for the Wafdist government that it had installed in February of that year. The Wafd party found itself discredited by Egyptian political public opinion and was harshly criticized by the Muslim Brotherhood. Bannā', who was a personal friend of the respected Arab Muslim nationalist ʿAzīz al-Miṣrī, like all the members of the Egyptian nationalist movement, felt sympathies for the Nazis and fascists, Britain's enemies. However, his politics were inconsistent, and he was criticized by the political parties on that account. At the beginning of the war, he relied on the support of King Fārūq and his prime minister ʿAlī Māhir. When the king was forced to submit to British authority in 1941–1942, Bannā' found himself harassed and even incarcerated briefly in Cairo in 1941, and again in 1945. This did not, however, prevent him from maintaining close contact during these years with the government. During the 1930s and 1940s, he founded Muslim schools and started a publishing house, which put out the newspaper *Al-ikhwān al-muslimūn* from 1933 to 1938 and from 1942 to December 1948, as well as the weekly *Al-taʿāruf* (Knowledge) from 1940 to 1942. In addition, it published *Al-manār,* inherited from Rashīd Riḍā, from 1939 to 1941. In these publications, Bannā' argued against the Christian schools of the missionaries.

In his letter to the Fifth Congress of the Muslim Brotherhood in 1939, Bannā' was already advising the king to dissolve the parties and to form a "People's Union" that would "work for the good of the nation in conformity with the principles of Islam." In 1945, he again made this suggestion and refused to join with the Wafd party as his friend Sukkarī had suggested. Sukkarī then broke with him and censured him for his nepotism, particularly for enriching his uncle ʿĀbidīn. Sukkarī left the Muslim Brotherhood in 1947. Rather than coinciding precisely with the Muslim Brotherhood, the People's Union was to form its own nucleus. Bannā' reassured the king and the British that there was no threat of military action by the Muslim Brotherhood against the government.

Bannā's movement, which had weakened in the 1940s, faltered. He withdrew from the 1943 elections in favor of the Wafd party, and having lost the king's support, suffered an outright defeat in the 1945 elections. Nevertheless, in 1946 the Muslim Brotherhood's militia (scouts and the Special Organization) served to back up demonstrations in favor of the king against the "blue shirts" of the Wafd and even against the "green shirts" of Young Egypt. In the same year, the Muslim Brotherhood organized student demonstrations and independent workers' strikes.

A crisis with the government developed in 1948, after Bannā' tried in vain, apparently with secret help from the British embassy, to regain the favor of the king and Prime Minister Nuqrāshī Pāshā, who were unpopular.

The volunteer units of the Muslim Brotherhood in the Palestine-Israel war of 1947–1948 were compelled to become part of the Egyptian army and to observe the ceasefire against their will. Although Bannā' submitted, not all of the fighting members of the Muslim Brotherhood followed him. They kept their weapons, and under the leadership of Shaykh Farāghlī they withdrew to the Suez Canal until 1952, with the intention of guerrilla warfare against the British. Faced with the Wafd party and the Socialist party (formerly Young Egypt) in 1948, Bannā' even allied himself with the Communist groups, participating in demonstrations and writing tracts against the British and the government, but not the king.

The assassination on 22 March 1948 of a judge by a young Muslim Brother seems to have been completely independent of Bannā's authority. In November 1948, a large student demonstration of brotherhood members ended in the death of two British officers, and a jeep loaded with explosives and weapons on its way to brotherhood members was intercepted in Cairo. A military decree dissolved the Muslim Brotherhood on 6 December 1948. On 28 December, Prime Minister Nuqrāshī, who had issued the decree, was assassinated by a student affiliated with the brotherhood. Bannā' denied responsibility for any of these actions in three papers that were only printed after his death. These were: *Al-qawl al-faṣl* (The Conclusive Word), *Al-bayān* (Declaration), and *Laysū ikhwānan wa-laysū muslimīn* (They Are Neither Brothers Nor Muslims). The secret police assassinated Bannā' in the street on 12 February 1949. The funeral ceremonies took place under heavy military escort and without a procession. The founder of the Muslim Brotherhood was regarded as a martyr, and a 1951 trial found him innocent of the criminal actions of 1948.

Replacing Bannā' was to prove difficult, for the movement, still secret in 1951, was moving in three different directions. One school of thought, that of the Bannā' family (expressed in Bannā's son-in-law Saʿīd Ramaḍān's journal, *Al-muslimūn*), was moderate and loyal to the reformist wait-and-see policy of the majority of Bannā's writings. Another more activist and combative group was led by Ṣāliḥ ʿAshmāwī, who was Bannā's de facto successor in the underground movement and who in 1951 started the publication *Al-daʿwāh* (The Call). The third branch saw itself as moderate and was led by Shaykh Bāqūrī (a future minister in Nasser's government) and Kamāl al-Dīn Ḥusayn, the Free Officer. The new guide of the Muslim Brothers, Ḥasan al-Huḍaybī, appointed in 1951 after the relegalization of the movement, represented the moderate tendency.

Sayyid Quṭb, who officially rejoined the Muslim Brotherhood in 1951, was to inspire extremist groups from the 1970s to the 1990s. The ideologue of the Islamic Jihād Organization, Muḥammad ʿAbd al-Salām Faraj, in his 1981 tract *The Missing Precept (Al-farīḍah al-ghaybah),* deemed Bannā' and the Muslim Brotherhood to have compromised with "the pagan power" and become an enemy of the "minority of activist believers." However, the brotherhood's traditional adversaries mistakenly believed that violent extremism was contained in letters written by Bannā' himself, in particular the "Letter of the Jihād" and the "Letter of Teachings," and that his disavowal of the 1948 crimes was only tactical. Nasser and his associates, who were at first respectful of Bannā' and his memory, after 1954 wrongfully imputed the 1945 assassination of Prime Minister Aḥmad Māhir to him. The beliefs held about Bannā' and his movement by Nasser and his circle were often echoed in general works on contemporary Egypt.

Ideas and Philosophy. Two main themes dominate Bannā's doctrine, aside from his traditional dogmatic beliefs concerning faith in a single God and in his book as revealed to the Prophet. Four terms dominated his discourse—nation, state, social justice, and society. If we add the qualifier "Islamic" to these four terms, we will have characterized Bannā's "idea," the key to which is the view of Islam as a comprehensive system of life. According to Bannā', it was this conviction, this intimate and illuminating discovery in the face of Western intrusions, which specifically defined the Muslim Brotherhood as an active political movement. The slogans that the Muslim Brotherhood took up from Bannā' were: "The Qur'ān is our Constitution," "No other Constitution but the Qur'ān," and "The Qur'ān is our Law and Muḥammad is our model." And yet, an analysis of existing trends in the Islamic world shows Bannā' as accommodating and much more "westernized" than he would have acknowledged.

Bannā' rejected the movement for secularization begun in the nineteenth century, and also the secular Arab nationalism mapped out by Sāṭiʿ al-Ḥuṣrī (d. 1968) in the 1920s and systematized by Michel ʿAflaq (d. 1989) in Damascus in the 1940s. ʿAflaq launched the secret Arab Baʿth ("Renaissance") party in 1941 and founded it publicly in 1947, explaining that "Islam is the soul; Arabism is the body." For Bannā', however, "The Arabs are the backbone of Islam, and its guardians. The

Muslim Brotherhood speaks about Arabism in the same terms as the Prophet. In effect, just as Islam is a faith and a religion, it is also a country and a citizenship that erases differences of background between men: 'The faithful are brothers.' Thus Islam knows no geographical frontiers, nor 'racial or civic differentiations' " ("Letter to the Fifth Congress"). Bannā' considered all Muslims to exist in a sole *ummah* (nation-community) and felt that the Muslim country is one country, no matter how physically distant its provinces might be. He did not hesitate to condemn expressly modern nationalisms, especially European fascism or Nazism.

On the subject of war, or "combat for God," Bannā's texts do not demonstrate that he preached terrorist violence. However, he asserted that war was an obligation at the time that Egyptians faced British colonial power. He interpreted the *jihād* tradition by making it a present-day individual obligation (*farḍ ʿayn*) for all, rather than a collective obligation (*farḍ kifāyah*) in which some could represent the whole. To the "fighting" brothers, the elite that was militarily trained and armed, Bannā' explained the stages of combat, especially that to which those who are part of the "first rank," the Special Organization, are normally called. The fact that they went to fight in Palestine and then, against Bannā's decision, in the Suez Canal Zone against the British, was according to "the engagement that the first line of Muslim Brothers undertook on the 5 Rabīʿ al-Awwal 1359 [13 April 1940]" ("Letter of Teachings").

Finally, Bannā' advocated certain major principles of Islamic social justice. These were to be expanded on and specified, in the 1950s, by the socialist-leaning branch of Bannā's disciples. This group included Quṭb, Muḥammad al-Ghazālī, ʿAbd al-Qādir ʿAwdah, and especially the Syrian Muṣṭafā Sibāʿī, who were part of the pro-Nasser segment of the Muslim Brotherhood in 1952–1953 and later. Bannā' envisioned a radical Islamic reform of the Egyptian economic and social situation. Out of *zakāt* ("alms"), one of the pillars of Islam, Bannā' constructed a rigorous fiscal system: "Islam consecrates the *zakāt* entirely to social expenses. This is used to help the insolvent and the destitute, which all the best sentiments in the world could not do. Thus we must at all costs attend to establishing social taxes by stages, taking into account wealth and not profits. The poor, naturally, will be exempt. Taxes will only be levied on the rich, and will be used to raise the standard of living" ("Letter on Our Problems in Light of the Islamic System"). Bannā' also rejected the modern system of interest in banking, and he condemned bonds (at a fixed interest rate) but not stock dividends. He was firmly opposed to speculative interest, which he called *ribā* (usury).

An Islamic society will thus be a society of social justice, said Bannā', not through righteous thinking and good works alone, but through institutions, the intervention of the state, and taxes on income and wealth, including progressive taxation. This interpretation is not explicitly traditional; it reflects a modernist and quasi-socialist reading of the Qur'ān and the *ḥadīth*s. But this theoretical reflection was the product of the daily concrete experience of a man of the people who traversed Egypt for almost twenty years, and who knew his countrymen better than many liberal or Marxist Egyptian intellectuals. We have as evidence this extract from a text serving as the Muslim Brotherhood's political program in 1943: "Remember, brothers, that more than 60 percent of Egyptians live in conditions worse than those in which animals live; they can only get their food by breaking their backs. Egypt is threatened with deadly famine, exposed to economic problems which have no solutions except through God" ("Letter on From Yesterday to Today").

As to Islamic criminal law, in particular the *ḥudūd* (Qur'ānically prescribed penalties), Bannā' advocated its application only on the condition that an Islamic society with social justice was established, with appropriate legal interpretations required by present and future situations. The Muslim Brothers of the 1980s, in particular in Sudan, were disloyal to Bannā' in this regard and inverted his priorities. However, it is true that Bannā' wanted to see the implementation of all the Qur'ānic laws in the proper circumstances.

[*See also* Egypt; *and* Muslim Brotherhood.]

BIBLIOGRAPHY

Carré, Olivier, and Gérard Michaud. *Les Frères Musulmans, 1928–1982*. Paris, 1983.

Delanoue, Gilbert. "Al-Ikhwān al-Muslimūn." In *Encyclopaedia of Islam*, new ed., vol. 3, pp. 1068–1071. Leiden, 1960–.

Harris, Christina. *Nationalism and Revolution in Egypt: The Role of the Muslim Brotherhood*. The Hague, 1964. Informative, in particular on the connections between al-Bannā' and the Free Officers.

Husaynī, Isḥāq Mūsā al-. *The Moslem Brethren*. Beirut, 1956. Detailed information on Bannā' and his relations and actions throughout the Arab East.

Imām, ʿAbd Allāh. *ʿAbd al-Nāṣir wa-al-Ikhwān* (Nasser and the Brethren). Cairo, 1981. Well-documented, pro-Nasserist view.

Mitchell, Richard P. *The Society of the Muslim Brothers.* London, 1969. Classic, well-informed study of Bannā' and the organization of his movement up to 1955.

Sa'īd, Rif'at al-. *Ḥasan al-Bannā'.* Cairo, 1977. Open-minded, Marxist biography; includes the last three writings by al-Bannā'.

OLIVIER CARRÉ

Translated from French by Elizabeth Keller

BARAKAH. The concept of *barakah* is invested with a multitude of implicit or explicit religio-cultural meanings depending on historical and social context. It encapsulates Islamic spirituality and spiritual sensibilities, particularly in relation to mysticism, sainthood, holy persons and spaces, and in some cases the local popular understanding of Islam. Thus *barakah*'s diverse connotations are at once an expression of universal Islam and a manifestation of Islamic particularism. The word *barakah* is derived from the Arabic root *b-r-k* and is found in the Qur'ān, though only in the plural *(barakat).* Its most fundamental meaning is "blessing," "beneficent force," or "supernatural power," conferred by the Almighty upon humankind.

Uncommonly pious individuals—prophets and especially Muḥammad and his house—are privileged with *barakah,* as is the Qur'ān, God's word. In turn, those blessed with *barakah,* either living or dead, can transmit it to ordinary mortals who thereby benefit in both material fortune and spiritual rewards. As Islam spread and evolved, *barakah* came to play a significant role in the social construction of holy persons, whether saints or mystics, and sacred places, and entered the practices of pilgrimage *(ziyārah)* and the veneration of saints. For the *awliyā'* (those close to God), *barakah* represented a sort of badge of saintly status. In this context, *barakah* signified an ineffable supernatural substance—grace, blessings, superabundance, purity, and piety—communicated from God to the believers via those who, in this life and the next, were endowed with heroic *iḥsan* (virtue). Yet mere possession of *barakah* was not sufficient to enter the ranks of holy persons: the possessor had to be able to convey it to others. In short, *barakah* helped to create the saint or mystic because it confirmed his or her privileged relation to God and thus conferred a special niche within the socioreligious order. Communal recognition of an individual's (or group's) access to *barakah* created a spiritual clientele that sought their favor as mediators, patrons, and intermediaries. One of the most visible, singular manifestations of *barakah* was the ability to perform miracles *(karāmāt)* signaling a temporary suspension of the natural order through divine intervention. Thus the social recognition of *barakah* and its unequal distribution were fundamental in the elaboration of saints, saint cults, and sainthood.

In the Maghrib and elsewhere from the fifteenth century onward, *barakah* came to be viewed as hereditary. Certain lineages, invariably of Sharīfī origins (descended from the prophet Muḥammad), claimed to be depositories of divine powers passed on through especially worthy individuals. Indeed in Morocco, *barakah* became conflated in the popular mind with extraordinary political wisdom and the 'Alawī dynasty, with the sultan seen as a *barakah*-endowed figure.

Barakah was associated not only with beings but also with specific places, things, and acts, such as certain foods, animals, plants, events, words, and gestures. *Barakah*'s mysterious, wonder-working qualities were often concretized in charms, amulets, and other means of protection from evil spirits. Folk medicine and healing were also connected with *barakah,* which in the hands of extraordinary individuals could cure illness, bestow fertility, and ward off harm. In this way *barakah* as an ideology as well as a set of diverse cultural practices spanned the fluid, uneasy boundaries between scripturalist, mosque-centered Islam and the more popular or local Islamic beliefs.

[*See also* Sainthood; Ziyārah.]

BIBLIOGRAPHY

Coulon, Christian. "Women, Islam, and Baraka." In *Charisma and Brotherhood in African Islam,* edited by Donal B. Cruise O'Brien and Christian Coulon, pp. 113–133. Oxford, 1988. First-rate study of African Muslim women's relationship to popular religion, Ṣūfī *ṭarīqahs*, saint cults, and *barakah.*

Eickelman, Dale F. *Moroccan Islam: Tradition and Society in a Pilgrimage Center.* Austin, 1976. Anthropological study of Islam as locally lived and understood in Morocco, particularly as regards North African beliefs and traditions surrounding saints, sainthood, and pilgrimage centers.

Trimingham, J. Spencer. *The Sufi Orders in Islam.* Oxford, 1971. While somewhat dated, this is still the only comprehensive study of the historical development of Ṣūfīs and Sufism in the entire Muslim world. The diverse cultural understandings and uses of *barakah* as it concerns Ṣūfī orders and related matters, particularly saint veneration, are considered.

Westermarck, Edward A. *Ritual and Belief in Morocco.* 2 vols. London, 1926. Still unsurpassed classic in anthropology with a detailed consideration of the notion of *barakah* in North Africa during the first decades of the twentieth century.

JULIA CLANCY-SMITH

BARELWĪ, SAYYID AḤMAD (1786–1831), North Indian activist and leader of *jihād*. Born in Rai Bareilly in the old Mughal province of Awadh in north India, this dynamic visionary died in battle on the mountainous frontier of the Northwest. Three strands of experience in his life came together in this utopian military endeavor. First, he was born into a family of sayyids, known for their piety and learning but, like many of the educated and well-born, now impoverished and frustrated in finding employment in a princely court. Second, in Delhi from 1806 to 1811, he entered into the circle of the family of Shāh Walī Allāh with its program of the dissemination of scripturalist norms. Third, at about the age of twenty-five, he left Delhi to spend some seven years as a cavalryman for Amīr Khān (1768–1834) in central India, immersing himself in the world of local state-building so characteristic of this period.

Back in Delhi, Sayyid Aḥmad rejoined the reformist *ʿulamāʾ* but rapidly distinguished himself by more far-reaching and stringent reform, for example in opposing certain Ṣūfī practices and enjoining such aspects of family behavior as the remarriage of widows. His teachings were written down in two works, the *Ṣirāṭ mustaqīm*, compiled by Maulānā Muḥammad Ismāʿīl, and the *Taqwiyat al-īmān;* both circulated in the vernacular language of Urdu thanks to the newly available lithographic press. The texts identified practices derived from false Sufism, Shīʿī doctrine, and local customs; these were said to compromise God's unity *(tawḥīd)*. It is notable that Sufism as such was not opposed (as it was by the Wahhābīs in Arabia and the Farāʾiẓī [Farāʾiḍī] in Bengal); it is also noteworthy that reformers rarely attributed deviations to Hindu influence, but rather blamed Muslims themselves.

With a small group of followers, Sayyid Aḥmad toured northern India in 1818–1819. In 1821 he undertook the *ḥajj* as a prelude to *jihād*, traveling downriver to Calcutta, preaching, and collecting a band of some six hundred for a journey whose very practice had long been neglected. In 1823 he returned to Rai Bareilly where he spent two years teaching and preparing for *jihād*.

His followers regarded him as the *mujaddid* of the age; some considered him the Mahdi. They were prepared to abjure customs that had defined and given honor to personal and family status; many were prepared to leave their homes and even to die. The model for *jihād*, while seen as following Prophetic precedent, took its shape from the quest for new states in the post-Mughal period.

In 1826 Sayyid Aḥmad left for the frontier, an area of Muslim population as precedent required, to launch warfare on the Punjab, then under Sikh rule. Although he was called *amīrulmuʾminīn* (Ar., *amir al-muʾminīn;* "commander of the faithful") by his followers, many of the local tribes disliked the reforms of the *mujāhidīn* and had their own quarrels to prosecute. Sayyid Aḥmad was trapped in Balakot with some six hundred followers and killed in 1831. Many cherished the idea that he was still alive because his body was not found. Followers kept the embers of the *jihād* alive until the 1860s; Sayyid Aḥmad's example and teachings inspired reformers long after his death.

[*See also* Islam, *article on* Islam in South Asia; Messianism.]

BIBLIOGRAPHY

Ahmad, Mohiuddin. *Saiyid Ahmad Shahid: His Life and Mission.* Lucknow, 1975. A detailed biography that also provides information on both primary and secondary sources available in Urdu and Persian.

Hardy, Peter. *The Muslims of British India.* Cambridge, 1972. The best overall survey, providing a good context for this and other religious movements.

Metcalf, Barbara D. *Islamic Revival in British India: Deoband, 1860–1900.* Princeton, 1982. Although focusing on a later Islamic movement of the colonial period, also provides material on the first half of the nineteenth century as background.

Muḥammad Ismāʿīl. "Translation of the *Takwiyat-ul-Iman,* preceded by a Notice of the Author, Maulavi Ismaʿil Hajji." Translated by Mir Shahamat Ali in *Journal of the Royal Asiatic Society* 13 (1832): 479–498. An influential tract of Sayyid Aḥmad's movement.

Muḥammad Ismāʿīl. "Notice of the Peculiar Tenets Held by the Followers of Syed Ahmad, Taken Chiefly from the 'Sirat-ul-Mustaqim,' a Principal Treatise of that Sect, Written by Moulavi Mahommed Ismaʿil." Translated by J. R. C. *The Journal of the Asiatic Society of Bengal* 1 (1832): 479–498.

BARBARA D. METCALF

BARELWĪS. The Barelwī movement emerged during the 1880s in the North Indian town of Bareilly, in the Rohilkhand region of the United Provinces. The movement is so called because of its close association with the writings of Maulānā Aḥmad Riẓā Khān (1856–1921), who, as a resident of Bareilly, had the toponymic *(nisbah)* name "Barelwī." Followers of Maulānā Aḥmad Riẓā, however, have always identified themselves as the Ahl al-Sunnat wa-al-Jamāʿat or "people of the (prophetic) way and the majority (community)." The significance of this nomenclature is clear: they believe themselves to be the true representatives and heirs in

South Asia of the earliest Muslim community, the companions and followers of the prophet Muḥammad.

The late nineteenth-century emergence of the Barelwī movement is significant. The failure of the Indian revolt of 1857 was followed by the formal colonization of India by the British, leading to the final dissolution of the Sunnī Muslim Mughal Empire. This sequence of events, traumatic from the Indian Muslim point of view, led to a period of lively religious debate among the scholars of Islamic law (the *ʿulamāʾ*) in North India. They could all agree that Indian Muslims had lost political power because of internal moral weakness and decay (because, in other words, they had neglected to be good Muslims), but they differed widely in their understanding of what constituted a "good" Muslim and how renewal *(tajdīd)* and reform should proceed. The Barelwī movement emerged in this context of internal debate about identity and action deemed necessary to reverse a politically unfavorable situation.

Maulānā Aḥmad Riẕā Khān was born into a well-to-do family of Pathan origin. His ancestors had been associated with Mughal rule and had become local notables *(ruʾasāʾ)* with land holdings and trading interests in and around Bareilly. Aḥmad Riẕā's grandfather, Maulānā Riẕā ʿAlī Khān (1809–1865/66), breaking with family tradition, devoted his life to jurisprudential *(fiqh)* scholarship and the Ṣūfī way of life *(taṣawwuf)*. There is no evidence that he was involved in the 1857 revolt; the suggestion in Aḥmad Riẕā's biography *Ḥayāt-e aʾla hazrat* (1938) that Riẕā ʿAlī's piety protected him from falling prey to a British punitive expedition can be variously interpreted as complicity or as covert opposition, depending on one's perspective. Naqī ʿAlī Khān (1831–1880), Aḥmad Riẕā's father, developed close ties with the nawab of Rampur, a ruling family of largely Shīʿī persuasion.

In scholarly terms, Aḥmad Riẕā had a strong orientation toward the "rational" *(maʿqūlāt)* sciences, and jurisprudence. His voluminous writings, estimated by some at one thousand, consist for the most part of *fatwās*, decisions on specific aspects of the law delivered in response to questions posed by Muslims from all parts of the country and even outside (including the Ḥaramayn in Arabia). The rapid growth of telecommunications and railway networks in late nineteenth-century British India facilitated the wide dissemination of Aḥmad Riẕā's views.

Aḥmad Riẕā and his followers were also Ṣūfī shaykhs or pirs (masters of select circles of disciples), owing particular though not exclusive allegiance to the Qādirī order. In this capacity, Aḥmad Riẕā enjoyed close relations with a number of prominent Qādirī Ṣūfī families in the Rohilkhand region, particularly those of the Barakatīyah Sayyids in the rural town *(qaṣbah)* of Marahra (Etah district) and the ʿUthmānī pirs of Badayun. The impact of these ties on Aḥmad Riẕā was twofold: a strong emphasis that a "good" Muslim accord primacy to the *sharīʿah* (Islamic law) over *tarīqah* (the Ṣūfī path); and an insistence that being a "good" Muslim was contingent on personal devotion to the prophet Muḥammad as a loving guide and intercessor between Allāh and the individual through a chain of pirs ending in the living pir to whom each individual was bound by an oath of loyalty or *bayʿah*.

Barelwī ritual practice reflected this interpretation of correct belief and practice in its emphasis on activity centered on Ṣūfī shrines, particularly the periodic observance of the death anniversaries *(ʿurs)* of the founder of the Qādirī order, Shaykh ʿAbd al-Qādir Jīlānī Baghdādī (d. 1166) and of one's own personal pir. The Barelwī observance of the *ʿurs* sprang from the insistence (based largely on Aḥmad Riẕā's interpretation of medieval *fiqh* works) that individual believers needed the Prophet's intercession with Allāh if they hoped for Allāh's forgiveness. Those who denied the importance of intercession on the grounds of the equality of all believers before Allāh were deemed by Aḥmad Riẕā to be guilty of arrogance.

What brought the Barelwīs into conflict with other Sunnī Muslim reform movements of the late nineteenth century, particularly with the *ʿulamāʾ* associated with the Dār al-ʿUlūm at Deoband, was primarily the Barelwī vision of the prophet Muḥammad's attributes. These attributes included his ability to see into the future, to have knowledge of the unseen *(ʿilm al-ghayb)*, to be spiritually—and perhaps physically, if the Prophet so wished—present in many places simultaneously, and to be invested with Allāh's preeminent light. Aḥmad Riẕā argued on the basis of certain verses of the Qurʾān, as well as *ḥadīth* and *fiqh* scholarship, that the prophet Muḥammad had been invested with these and other qualities by God, with whom his relationship was that of a beloved. Denial of these prophetic attributes was interpreted by Aḥmad Riẕā as denial of some of the "fundamentals of the faith" *(ḍarūrīyat al-dīn)*. These fundamentals, which fall under the rubric of *ʿaqāʾid* (articles of faith), broadly interpreted, were indivisible: one could not accept some and reject others, as some *ʿulamāʾ* in his view had done, for denial of even one of these fundamentals was tantamount to apostasy from

Islam, or *kufr* (unbelief). Such denial, to Aḥmad Riẓā's mind, was implicit in the position taken by those he designated as "Wahhābīs," a term he applied variously to Sayyid Aḥmad Barelwī (d. 1831), leader of the early nineteenth-century *jihād* against the Sikhs; to Sayyid Aḥmad Khān (d. 1898), the founder of the Muhammadan Anglo-Oriental College at Aligarh; and to various Deobandī *ʿulamā'* of his own time. In *Ḥusām al-ḥaramayn*, a *fatwā* written in 1906, he specifically designated a handful of Deobandī *ʿulamā'* as "Wahhābīs" and *kāfirs* (infidels). [*See* Deobandīs *and the biographies of Aḥmad Khān and Barelwī.*]

During Aḥmad Riẓā's lifetime, the Barelwī movement centered on a small core of followers personally loyal to him. These followers, returning to their own towns after receiving *khilāfat* (the right to accept students of their own), carried his vision beyond the confines of learned *ʿulamā'* circles into a wider arena. Since Aḥmad Riẓā's death in 1921, "Barelwī" leaders (most of them from towns other than Bareilly)—among them Maulānās Naʿīmuddīn Murādābādī (d. 1948), Shāh Aulād-i Rasūl Marharvī (d. 1952), Ẓafaruddīn Bihārī (d. 1950s), Aḥmad Riẓā's son Muṣṭafā Riẓā Khān Barelwī (d. 1981), and Burhānulḥaqq Jabalpūrī (d. 1984)—have led the movement in varying directions in terms of the leading political issues of twentieth-century British India, most importantly that of partition in 1947. Although the movement has been viewed as largely rural in terms of its following, it is currently in the throes of a resurgence among urban, educated Pakistanis and Indians. Schools and *madrasahs* identifying themselves as "Ahl al-Sunnat wa-al-Jamāʿat" are to be found in South Asian cities and towns including Lahore, Karachi, Bareilly, Mubarakpur, and Hyderabad (Deccan). Beyond South Asia, the movement also has followers in Great Britain and South Africa.

[*See also* Islam, *article on* Islam in South Asia.]

BIBLIOGRAPHY

Aḥmad Riẓā Khān. *Al-ʿAṭāyā lil-nabawīyah fī al-Fatāwá al-Riḍawīyah.* Vols. 1–7, 10–11. Saudagaran, Bareilly, 1981–1987.

Aḥmad Riẓā Khān. *Malfūẓāt-i Aʿlā Ḥaẓrat.* 4 vols. Gujarat, Pakistan, n.d.

Metcalf, Barbara D. *Islamic Revival in British India: Deoband, 1860–1900.* Princeton, 1982. See pages 296–314.

Sanyal, Usha. "In the Path of the Prophet: Maulana Ahmad Riza Khan Barelwi and the Ahl-e Sunnat wa Jamaʿat Movement in British India, c. 1870–1921." Ph.D. diss., Columbia University, 1990.

Ẓafaruddīn Bihārī. *Ḥayāt-i Aʿlā Ḥaẓrat.* Vol. 1. Karachi, 1938.

USHA SANYAL

BASMACHIS. The term "Basmachi" was applied by Russians to opponents of the Bolsheviks who were active in Central Asia between the Russian Revolution and the early 1930s. This name—as the character of the movement—parallels the case of the Mujāhidīn forces opposing the Soviet invasion of Afghanistan in the 1980s, whom the Russians referred to by the Persian word *dushman,* meaning "enemy"; "Basmachi" is similarly a pejorative term, meaning "bandit." Like the Afghan "Dushmany," those whom the Bolsheviks called "Basmachi" included a great variety of people who did not call themselves by this name, nor did they operate as a unified movement. The Soviet government was able to exploit internal divisions within the Basmachi movement to quell it fairly rapidly, once the Red Army had consolidated power elsewhere in Russia and Central Asia.

The roots of the Basmachi movement extend to the Russian conquest of Central Asia. Most of the region now comprised by the former Soviet republics of Kazakhstan, Kyrghyzstan, Uzbekistan, Turkmenistan, and Tajikistan came under Russian domination between the 1830s and the 1880s. The native, overwhelmingly Muslim population strongly opposed the "infidel" conquest, but the Russians exploited military superiority and rivalries within the region to subjugate all opposition. Sporadic outbreaks during the tsarist period, such as the Andijan Uprising of 1898 under the leadership of a Naqshbandī Ṣūfī Īshān, were quickly suppressed. A more significant uprising occurred in 1916 when, hard pressed by the war with Germany, the tsarist government instituted military conscription of Central Asians. This, combined with a range of humiliating and impoverishing policies of the colonial administration, was decisive in mobilizing Central Asian opposition to rule from Moscow.

When the Bolsheviks seized power in Saint Petersburg in 1917, their counterparts from among the very narrow Russian immigrant proletariat established a "Soviet" government in Tashkent in Russian Central Asia. In spite of the Bolsheviks' affirmed support for "national self-determination," this self-declared regional government included only Russians. Some Central Asian intellectuals and reformers had considered alliance with the Communists in hopes that this would lead to autonomy within the new Soviet framework; however, the Qoqand government established in December 1917 by such Central Asians was quickly crushed by Tashkent Communists with support from Moscow. The Russian Bolsheviks in Central Asia entered on a campaign of seizing lands, looting the native population, and generally affirming their intention of maintaining Russian domination.

The leadership of the Basmachi movement, which derived its widespread popular support from the resulting hostility toward the Russians, was composed of the most diverse elements: reformists, including Jadīdists and "Young Bukharans"; the traditional Islamic leadership, whose authority had been severely undermined by the colonial government; Central Asian rulers such as Said Alim Khan, emir of Bukhara; and even brigand-leaders of outlaw groups that had preyed on the Russian colonists and Central Asians alike. In 1921 Enver Pasha, leader of the deposed Young Turk government in Turkey, appeared in Central Asia, seeking to unify the opposition under his opportunistic leadership; however, the movement remained divided by leadership rivalries, and Enver Pasha was killed in a skirmish in 1922. [*See* Jadīdism; *and the biography of Enver Pasha.*]

At its height (1920–1922), the Basmachi movement was in control of the entire Ferghana Valley, aside from Russian railroad and military installations, as well as most of what is now Tajikistan and some other areas. During this same period, however, the Moscow government established control over the Central Asian Bolsheviks and began to conduct a policy in the region that was friendlier to the Muslim population, reopening markets, returning seized lands, and encouraging native participation in state institutions. Support for the opposition was thus undermined, and military action was intensified now that other regions such as Bukhara and Khiva were under Red Army control. By 1924 the movement was largely crushed. The Soviet government was successful in encouraging substantial defections from Basmachi ranks and in winning over the populace simply by promoting stability and allowing prosperity under the reforms of the New Economic Policy of the 1920s. Basmachi resistance persisted only in the mountains of the southeasternmost region of Central Asia bordering on Afghanistan until the early 1930s.

The legacy of the Basmachis is the legacy of opposition to foreign rule in Central Asia generally: it has always been highly disorganized, deeply divided, and readily susceptible to manipulation by outside forces. The call for unity under Islam has not proven to be sufficiently attractive to a population that, when pressed by economic hardship, can rise up against the perceived oppressor, but that ultimately prefers compromised stability and prosperity.

[*See also* Islam, *article on* Islam in Central Asia and the Caucasus.]

BIBLIOGRAPHY

Fraser, Glenda. "Basmachi." *Central Asian Survey* 6.1 (1987): 1–73, and 6.2 (1987): 7–42.

Olcott, Martha. "The Basmachi or Freeman's Revolt in Turkestan, 1918–24." *Soviet Studies* 33 (July 1981): 352–369.

Park, Alexander G. *Bolshevism in Turkestan, 1917–1927*. New York, 1957.

Pipes, Richard. *The Formation of the Soviet Union: Communism and Nationalism, 1917–1923*. Rev. ed. Cambridge, Mass., 1964.

JOHN S. SCHOEBERLEIN-ENGEL

BAʿTH PARTIES. The Arab Socialist Baʿth Party (Ḥizb al-Baʿth al-ʿArabī al-Ishtirākī) was founded in Syria in the early 1940s by militants of the Iḥyāʾ al-ʿArabī (Arab Revival) movement, which was led by the two Damascene teachers Michel ʿAflaq and Ṣalāḥ al-Dīn Bayṭār, in conjunction with followers of the philosopher Zakī al-Arsūzī of Antioch. At its first congress in Damascus in April 1947, the Baʿth promulgated the *Dusṭūr* (constitution) as its fundamental text. In reaction to Ottoman domination and European colonization, the party took as its rallying cry the revitalization, reunification, and liberation of "one Arab nation with an eternal mission"—an expression inspired by Fichte—and advocated a revolutionary process of reversing *(inqilāb)* the course of history. The Baʿth nationalist ideology developed in opposition to European nationalisms, but it also drew on German and Italian fascism. This ideology rests on the concept of an Arab nation defined not by race but by cultural reality.

Three elements underlie the notion of a common Arab identity "from the Persian Gulf to the Atlantic Ocean." The first is the history, and even the prehistory, of the Middle East and above all the modern history of imperialism and the installation of Israel at the center of the Arab East. The Second is the Arabic language—the natural language of humanity, according to al-Arsūzī (Antūn Maqdisī. "Fīʾl-ṭarīq ilāʾl-lisān," *Al-Nawqif al-Adabī* 3–4 [July–August 1972), pp. 15–55). Finally there is Islam, which is seen not as a religion—since the Baʿth respects the freedom of religion (*Dusṭūr* II.1) and rejects religious fanaticism (*Dusṭūr* III.2)—but as a culture and spiritual experience unique to Arabs through the language and the revelation of the Qurʾān. According to ʿAflaq, who himself was an Orthodox Christian, the key to Arab identity lies in the sacred experience of the

Muslim revelation to Muḥammad, the Arab prophet. The Baʿth aims to instill the sacred and mobilizing mission of Islam into the secular mystique of nationalism.

From its inception the Baʿth has advocated a moderate form of anticommunist socialism. After World War II and decolonization the party adopted a report inspired by Yāsīn al-Ḥāfiẓ entitled *Baʿḍa al-munṭalaqāt al-naẓarīyah* (Some Theoretical Points of View) at the Sixth National Pan-Arab Congress in October 1963 in Damascus. The report recommended the immediate adoption of socialism in the form of agrarian reform, nationalization, and economic planning in those countries where the party was in power, Iraq and Syria. However, its doctrine has been marked rather by populism and corporatism, and it challenges the class struggle within the nation.

Begun as an underground movement, the Baʿth party developed a hierarchical structure and a method of functioning inspired by democratic centralism, which was officially adopted by the Eighth National Congress in April 1965. Party members are grouped into categories ranging from the cell *(khalwah)* and the local section *(firqah)* to the division *(shuʿbah)* of the departmental branch *(farʿ)*, and finally to the participants in the Congress who elect the members of the Command and the secretary-general. It is distinctive in that it has developed a double structure and a double hierarchy. The national structure *(qawmī)* groups together adherents from the entire Arab homeland, while a regional structure *(quṭrī)* exists in each Arab state where the party is active, particularly in Syria and Iraq.

The Baʿth party came to power in Iraq in February 1963 for a period of nine months; in Syria it has ruled since March 1963. Before that year the party functioned as a Pan-Arab party in which Jordanians, Palestinians, Lebanese, Iraqis, and even Tunisians were represented along with the Syrian majority. The 1963 National Congress marked the high point of Pan-Arabism in the organization; certain Syrian leaders led by ʿAflaq intervened in an internal struggle of Iraqi Baʿthists in November 1963. Their intervention failed to prevent a de facto rupture between the Syrian and Iraqi elements of the party. This rupture crystallized in February 1966 with the triumph of the neo-Baʿthist leftists of Ṣalāḥ Jadīd in Damascus. From July 1968, when the party returned to power in Baghdad, it was officially divided and had two rival national Commands, one under Syrian influence and the other Iraqi-influenced, with ʿAflaq serving as secretary-general until his death in 1990.

The conflict between Baʿth factions is not ideological; during the 1970s the two nations where the party was in power evolved toward state capitalism and *infitāḥ*, or the opening up to private national entrepreneurs and Western partners. In part the conflict concerns the concept of Arab unity, which Syria envisions as developing in stages with an initial regrouping in the Mediterranean Arab region ("Greater Syria") around Damascus. Baghdad, however, wishes to make Iraq the Arab nation's federative state, following the example of Prussia in relationship to the German nation. This conflict is above all a conflict of competing ambition between two leaders, Hafez al-Assad of Syria and Saddam Hussein of Iraq, both of whom are regional secretaries of the Baʿth party and derive legitimation of their power from the party. This explains the failure of the attempt at reunification from October 1978 to July 1979.

In Syria and Iraq, the Baʿth party rules without sharing any of its power, having learned from the painful experience during the period of the United Arab Republic (1958–1961), when Egyptian President Gamal Abdel Nasser had forced the party to dissolve itself in Syria. After eliminating its rivals and reducing the number of likely candidates for leadership in the 1960s, the party allied itself with the Communists and other small parties of the left in a Progressive National Front (Syria, 1972; Iraq, 1973), where it was in the majority while retaining exclusive influence over the youth and the army. Formerly the party of the avant-garde, on coming to power the Baʿth in Syria and Iraq transformed itself into the party of the masses by taking control of trade unions and popular organizations. As an apparatus of recruitment and mobilization, it also became the privileged channel of social advancement and of redistribution of the advantages associated with positions of power.

Despite its unitarian and social agenda, the Baʿth progressively changed into a coterie of minority solidarity. The non-Sunnī Arab minorities, especially the ʿAlawīyah, are overrepresented in the party in Syria, which permits leaders of the ʿAlawī community to dominate in the name of party ideals; President Assad, an ʿAlawī, is also head of the party. Opposition to the authoritarian and military-dominated Baʿth regime has been voiced in the name of Palestinian liberation and the defense of Arab Lebanon. This opposition was silenced in the political sphere but mobilized around Islamist themes and leaders who denounced the Baʿth's atheism (1965, 1973) and waged a civil war from 1979 to 1982, followed by terrible repression.

In Iraq, the Sunnīs of the Tikrīt region progressively garnered more party representation, controlling the executive, the Revolutionary Command Council, at the expense of the Kurds and especially of the Arab Shīᶜī majority. As in Syria, Baᶜthist Iraq makes explicit reference to Islam, and the *sharīᶜah* is recognized as the principal source of legislation. Yet in controlling the mosques and the *ᶜulamā'* the Baᶜth imposes the domination of politics over religion. The opposition has rallied around the Shīᶜī *ᶜulamā'* since the beginning of the 1980s, the time of the Iranian revolution and the Iran-Iraq war, and calls for a reislamization of society. Based on an ideology that fosters Arab unity and modernity, the Baᶜth has become the sole party of two authoritarian regimes.

[*See also* Arab Socialism; Iraq; Socialism and Islam; *and* Syria.]

BIBLIOGRAPHY

Batatu, Hanna. *The Old Social Classes and the Revolutionary Movements of Iraq: A Study of Iraq's Old Landed and Commercial Classes and of Its Communists, Baᶜthists, and Free Officers*. Princeton, 1978. Exhaustive study of the social structure and politics of Iraq up to the second Baᶜthi regime.

Choices of Texts from the Baᶜth Party Founder's Thought. Florence, 1977. Collection of essays and articles written in Arabic by intellectuals of the Baᶜth's first generation.

Devlin, John F. *The Baᶜth Party: A History from Its Origins to 1966*. Stanford, Calif., 1976. Well-informed and reliable study of the party before its seizure of power.

Farouk-Sluglett, Marion, and Peter Sluglett. "Iraqi Baᶜthism: Nationalism, Socialism, and National Socialism." In *Saddam's Iraq: Revolution or Reaction?*, edited by CARDI (Campaign Against Repression and for Democratic Rights in Iraq), pp. 89–107. London, 1986. Critical assessment of the Iraqi case.

Hinnebusch, Raymond A. "Syria under the Baᶜth: Social Ideology, Policy, and Practice." In *Social Legislation in the Contemporary Middle East*, edited by Laurence O. Michalak and Jeswald W. Salacuse, pp. 61–109. Berkeley, 1986. Balanced assessment of the Syrian case.

Kienle, Eberhard. *Baᶜth v. Baᶜth: The Conflict between Syria and Iraq, 1968–1989*. London, 1990. Useful study of intra-party conflict and political rivalries.

Party of the Arab Baᶜth. "Constitution." In *Arab Nationalism: An Anthology*, edited by Sylvia G. Haim, pp. 233–241. Berkeley, 1962. Translation from the Arabic of the party's fundamental document.

Rabinovich, Itamar. *Syria under the Bath, 1963–66: The Army-Party Symbiosis*. Jerusalem, 1972. Insightful study of a critical period.

Springborg, Robert. "Baathism in Practice: Agriculture, Politics, and Political Culture in Syria and Iraq." *Middle Eastern Studies* 17.2 (1981): 191–209. Thoughtful reflection on the relation between ideology and practice in Baᶜthist regimes.

ELIZABETH PICARD

Translated from French by Elizabeth Keller

BAYᶜAH. An unwritten contract or a pact, a *bayᶜah* involves a recognition of, and an oath of allegiance to, a caliph, a ruler, a king, or an emir. This oath is usually given on behalf of the subjects by the leading members of the tribe, or the important members of a family or a clan. When these tribal representatives (or "electors") make the pact with the ruler, they do so with the understanding that as long as the ruler abides by certain responsibilities toward his subjects, they are to maintain their allegiance to him. Usually, the representatives include religious scholars *(ᶜulamā')*, political leaders within the community, and sometimes family elders. The *bayᶜah* involves also a bestowing of God's blessings or felicity *(riḍwān)* on the ruler by the representatives of his subjects.

The Arabic phrase expressing these blessings, "Raḍiya Allāh ᶜanhu" ("May God be pleased with him"), is traced to the time of the prophet Muḥammad and his companions. The same phrase was used also during the time of the caliphs. In the Qur'ān, *riḍwān* means that God looks with favor upon the ruler who is given the *bayᶜah* by his subjects and is pleased with him. The ruler is essentially receiving God's "good pleasure." Sūrat al-Fatḥ gives an illustration of God's *riḍwān* on the faithful: Allāh's good pleasure was on the Believers when they swore fealty to Thee under the tree: He knew what was in their hearts, and He sent down tranquility to them; and He rewarded them with a speedy victory (48.18). As a final, complete, and unequivocal acceptance by God, the *riḍwān* is cited again in the *Sūrat al-Fajr* (8.27–30).

The prophet Muḥammad himself received individual oaths of fealty from his followers in 628 at al-Hudaybīyah, a place on the road from Jeddah to Mecca, where he was preparing to make a pilgrimage to Mecca, in accordance with the Qur'ānic revelation (48.27) that he would pray there. The oath given to the Prophet was known as the "Pact of Felicity" or *bayᶜat al-riḍwān*.

The *bayᶜah* is still practiced in such countries as Saudi Arabia, especially at the time of the ascension to the throne. In 1964 during the dispute between King Saᶜūd ibn ᶜAbd al-ᶜAzīz and his brother, the heir apparent Fayṣal, the latter was able to secure the throne as a result of the *bayᶜah* that he received from the *ᶜulamā'* and other community leaders. Following the assassination of Fayṣal in 1975, his brother Khālid received a similar *bayᶜah* from the *ᶜulamā'*, as did Fahd in June 1982 upon the death of King Khālid.

The social, economic, and political challenges facing

modern Muslim states, the rise of political Islam as a political movement, and the increasing demands by both Islamic and secular elites for political participation suggest that Muslim leaders are increasingly unlikely to receive *bayʿat al-riḍwān* unconditionally. Several important questions remain unanswered: what would an aspirant to the throne do if the representatives of the subjects refuse to extend the *bayʿah* to him? What would happen if a segment of the population decides to withdraw its *bayʿah?* Would such a person rely on the military to bring him to office and secure him there? *Bayʿah,* like other concepts of classical tribal Islam, is experiencing enormous change as traditional tribal communities transform themselves into modern administrative states.

[*See also* Authority and Legitimation.]

BIBLIOGRAPHY

Khadduri, Majid, et al., eds. *Law in the Middle East,* Vol. 1. Washington, D.C., 1955. Scholarly anthology on the origin and development of Islamic law.

EMILE A. NAKHLEH

BAYRAMIYE. Established in the early fifteenth century, the Bayramiye (Ar., Bairamīyah) is a Turkish Ṣūfī order. Its eponym, Hacı Bayram Veli, was born near Ankara around the middle of the fourteenth century. In conformity with a pattern typical in Sufism, he abandoned a successful career as a teacher of the law to become a disciple of Hamidüddin Veli Aksarayî, remaining with him for at least three years until his death in 1412. Hacı Bayram thereupon returned to Ankara and began, with great success, to propagate the order that became known after him. Either because of the size of his following or because of his master's links to the Ṣafavid order in Ardabil, which was then in the process of transition to Shiism, Hacı Bayram Veli was summoned to the Ottoman court in Edirne for interrogation by Murad I. He favorably impressed the sovereign, who not only permitted him to return to Ankara but also provided for the establishment of a Bayrami hospice in Edirne. By the time of Hacı Bayram Veli's death in 1429, the order had spread to Gelibolu, Karaman, Beypazarı, Balıkesir, Bursa, Larende, Bolu, İskilip, Kütahya, and Göynük.

The central hospice of the Bayramiye remained that established in Ankara by Hacı Bayram Veli himself, and its administration became vested in his descendants. Nonetheless, the most important of his successors was Akşemsettin of Göynük, a Syrian who had joined his following in 1426. Although Akşemsettin gained the favor of Sultan Mehmed the Conqueror by participating in the conquest of Istanbul in 1453, he chose not to settle in the new capital, remaining in Göynük until his death in 1457. Akşemsettin had a number of successors, the most influential of whom were İbrahim Tennuri (because of whose prominence one branch of the order became known as Bayramiye-Tennuriye) and Şamlı Hamza, active in the region of Adana. The line of Tennuri continued for at least three generations, but it was eclipsed in the seventeenth century by the Himmetiye, founded by Himmet Efendi, a descendant by initiation of Şamlı Hamza. The Tennuriye and the Himmetiye were classified together as Bayramiye-Şemsiye because of their shared descent from Akşemsettin.

In radical opposition to both stood the Bayramiye-Melamiye, going back to a certain Ömer Dede Bıçakçı, who had disputed Akşemsettin's succession to Hacı Bayram Veli. The Bayramiye-Melamiye rejected, for the most part, all forms of *dhikr* (invocation of the divine name), the wearing of distinctive garb, and most of the other external appurtenances of Sufism; this line may be thought of as perpetuating antinomian tendencies that had been suppressed in the first Bayrami congregation. Its adherents followed a cult of devotion to the Twelve Imams of Shiism and cultivated an extreme interpretation of the doctrine of the unity of being *(waḥdat al-wujūd).* The combination of these characteristics earned execution for several prominent representatives of the Bayramiye-Melamiye. The two varieties of the Şemsiye were largely restricted to Anatolia (particularly its western regions), but the Bayramiye-Melamiye became widespread in the Balkans, especially in Bosnia, where its best known figure, Şeyh Hamza Bali (executed in Istanbul in 1573) originated a branch of the order known as the Hamzevi.

Bayramis of the two Şemsi lines also adhered to *waḥdat al-wujūd,* although in more circumspect fashion, and this may well have furnished the basis for an unspoken rapprochement with the Bayramiye-Melamiye during the nineteenth century. The authority of two Istanbul shaykhs, Hafız Seyyid Ali Efendi (d. 1838) and İbrahim Efendi (d. 1898), was accepted by all existing branches of the Bayramiye. Despite this reunification, the order failed to produce any leader of significance in early modern times, with the possible exception of Seyyid Abdülkadir Belhi (d. 1921), an immigrant to Istanbul from Balkh in Afghanistan, who combined a Hamzevi affiliation with an inherited loyalty to the Naqshbandīyah. [*See* Naqshbandīyah.]

In 1840 the Bayramiye had only nine hospices in Istanbul, far fewer than several other Ṣūfī orders. By 1889, the number had sunk to four; these appear still to have been functioning when in 1925 the Turkish Republic banned all the Ṣūfī orders. By that time, the Bayramiye existed outside Istanbul only in İzmit, Kastamonu, and Ankara, where the central hospice was presided over by Şemseddin Bayramoğlu (d. 1945), a descendant of Hacı Bayram Veli in the twenty-seventh generation. Unlike other Ṣūfī groups, the Bayramiye was unable to survive the official proscription of the orders and the closure of its hospices. Although the subterranean cells used for retreat at the shrine of Hacı Bayram Veli in Ankara are still frequented, it is primarily Naqshbandīs who make use of them.

There are traces of the Bayramiye in the twentieth-century Balkans. They were one of the orders represented in the Savez Islamskih Derviških Redova Alijje u SFRJ, a federation of the Ṣūfī orders existing in Yugoslavia, established at Prizren in Kosovo in 1974. A Hamzevi hospice (led in 1986 by Abdulkadir Orlović) survived through many generations in Zvornik, northeastern Bosnia, until the pillage of that city by Serbian forces in the spring of 1992.

[*See also* Sufism, *articles on* Ṣūfī Thought and Practice *and* Ṣūfī Orders.]

BIBLIOGRAPHY

Aynî, Mehmed Ali. *Hacı Bayram Veli.* Istanbul, 1343/1924.

Bayramoğlu, Fuat. *Hacı Bayram-ı Veli.* 2 vols. Ankara, 1983.

Bayramoğlu, Fuat, and Nihat Azamat. "Bayramiye." In *Türkiye Diyanet Vakfı İslam Ansiklopedisi,* vol. 5, pp. 269–273. Istanbul, 1988–.

Ćehajić, Džemal. *Derviški rodovi u jugoslovenskim zemljama.* Sarajevo, 1986. See pages 185–204.

Gölpĭnarlĭ, Abdülbâki. *Melâmîlik ve Melâmîler.* Istanbul, 1931. See pages 33–228.

Gölpĭnarlĭ, Abdülbâki. "Bayramiye." In *İslam Ansiklopedisi,* vol. 2, pp. 423–426. Istanbul, 1943.

Kissling, Hans Joachim. "Zur Geschichte des Derwischordens der Bajramijje." *Südost-Forschungen* 15 (1956): 237–268.

HAMID ALGAR

BAZAAR. The Persian word for "market" *(bāzār)* refers to a range of economic and architectural forms from covered bazaars, periodic rural markets, and small neighborhood strips of shops in alleys to abstract understandings of markets as sectors of the economy involved in trade, especially those not under the control of the state banking system. As an occupational structure, the traditional bazaar contains a differentiated network of commission agents, jobbers, hawkers, peddlers, wholesalers, long-distance merchants, brokers, moneychangers, craftsmen and shop assistants (see especially Rotblat, 1972). The bazaar also has a variety of social meanings ranging from class style or outlook (*tājir*s [large merchants] are often distinguished from *bāzārī*s [small shopkeepers]) to modes of social control (located partly in the bazaar's credit system; partly in the bazaar's social institutions, such as guilds, mosques, *hay'at-i maẕhabī* [religious circles; on which see Thaiss, 1973], *zūrkhānah*s [traditional gymnasia], and *ḥammām*s [bathhouses]; and partly in the style of the enforcers of internal policing, who are spoken of in terms of character types—*dāsh, gardankuluft, jāhil, awbāsh, javānmard, āghā, ustāẕ, and shāgird*) and finally to the moral codes of Islamic discourse—the bazaar as a place of personal *jihād* (ethical struggle), where services on behalf of the *farḍ al-kifāyah* (communal good) are performed, and where Islamic codes of commerce at times can be enforced by judicial officers called *muḥtasib*s as well as *qāḍī*s (judges) or *mujtahid*s (experts in religious law).

These interlocking economic, social, and moral arenas can be elaborated in a variety of ways, given changing social and political circumstances. Many of the covered bazaars were built under the patronage of kings or governors as places where taxes as well as rents could be collected with ease. Some smaller covered bazaars were also constructed by groups of merchants, but the economic form of providing facilities and then charging rents to *bāzārī*s is a general one extending to shopping strips along modern streets and boulevards. Rents might often be designated as *waqf* (revenue for religious endowments), and this has provided one link between the bazaar and the religious establishment. Kings and governors also periodically tried to formalize and use the guild structure as a way of collecting rents and taxes and enforcing political controls. But this was variably successful, with the term for guild *(ṣinf)* often decaying into simply a term meaning craft or occupation but not necessarily implying any organization. More often guild structures, when they existed, were autonomous of the state and attempted to regulate competition and disputes among their members. Bakers guilds, for instance, appeared quite frequently, regulating where new shops might be located and which immigrants into a community might be allowed to open a bakery. Bread shops and a few other businesses like butchers or grocers need to be distributed not only in the central bazaar but throughout the city. Other businesses tend to cluster together, so that one gets a cloth bazaar, a blacksmith's bazaar, and so on. At the center of most traditional bazaars was the banking bazaar, the so-called Qayṣarīyah (from Caesar), where the *ṣarrāfs* (money-changers), and credit suppliers were located. Often the Qayṣarīyah had heavy doors that could be closed at night to provide added security. The credit supplied was a mechanism that enforced a hierarchy of control: small merchants would get loans guaranteed by larger merchants. To default on a loan was the ultimate sin; better to get yet another loan even at a usurous rate, because to default is to then be excluded from the system entirely. This hierarchy of control spilled over into social affairs as well through the various religious organizations funded by and manned by the *tājirs*, *bāzārīs*, and craftsmen. For this reason the state would often try to influence or control these organizations. Periodically, in Iran, the Pahlavi regime would attempt to regulate the guilds, the prices, and the traditional gymnasia and their followings of young men. The last time this was tried in any large scale by the Pahlavis was in 1975 during the institution of the single (Rāstākhiz) party state, and it lead to an intensification of hostility to the state, a precursor of the mobilization that fed into the revolution of 1977–1979. More successful efforts to regulate the bazaar and the economy affected by the bazaar occurred in periods when the government was willing to consult with producers and traders on costs; other efforts at control proved to be punitive and generated reactions. *Bāzārīs* funded not only the mosques and *hay'ats* within the physical confines of the bazaar, but also religious leaders who would speak out against state policies that negatively affected the bazaar (this was often done to keep alive the various oppositional counters). The *hay'ats* took various forms, ranging from weekly poetry and Qur'ān reading circles to young men's groups which practiced chants and pious exercises for the religious processions during the month of Muḥarram. These latter groups, *dāstah,* formed an organization which could be mobilized on need and utilized for political purposes as well.

Both under the Pahlavis and today under the Islamic Republic, the bazaar and its credit systems are a major part of the Iranian economy. There was an attempt by the Pahlavi Government to provide alternative credit and distribution systems through state banks and cooperatives, but modern formal banks required too much collateral and were unable to provide credit as flexibly as the bazaar. The fact that banks in Pahlavi Iran had bad loan rates of one-tenth of one percent (versus 3 to 4 percent in the United States) indicates this lack of flexibility. So while the banking system was central to the state and large industrial sector, for commercial loans, the bazaar remained central to the economy, and therefore also central to much of the political maneuvering around economic issues. The bazaar was also central to the traditional agricultural and craft systems, both as outlet and for credit. Cloth and carpet weaving was often organized through the bazaar on a putting out system using village craft labor (on the Kirman example, see Dillon, 1976; English, 1966).

The moral discourse of the Islamic bazaar is built around a series of notions about fair price and negotiated justice. The main Shīʿī commercial code for the bazaar is still the century-old *Makāsib* (On Trade), the manual of Shaykh Murtaẓā Anṣārī of rules for exchange in the bazaar, and the sections on commerce in the various *Risālat tawḍīḥ al-masā'il* (Explanatory Text on Problems [of Religion]) issued by each of the *marjaʿ al-taqlīd* (highest rank of the *ʿulamā'*). There have been a few attempts at updating mainly through ideological arguments about social justice and progressive politics, rather than through case examples as in the traditional manuals (e.g., Sadr, 1961; Ṭāleqāni, 1962; Shirazi, 1973; for the Arab world and a Muslim Brotherhood perspective, translated into Persian, see Quṭb, 1981; for the Urdu world, see Mawdūdī, n.d.; also more generally Mannan, 1986), or through the attempts by the Islamic Republic of Iran to rewrite the legal code of Iran. The main concern in the moral discussions about bazaar economics is with ensuring the conditions of knowledge and volition to the parties in an exchange of buying or selling. For instance, children may not buy and sell, but may only be agents of competent adults; goods may be returned if the buyer finds he bought them above the fair price or if the seller is uncertain of the price and finds he sold for too little. There are rules about what must be said for a transaction to be counted as a *bayʿ* (final sale) and arguments about the status of other transactions which are not so formalized *(muʿāṭāt)*. Of these rules, those on *ribā* (interest and usury) are most central and problematic (particularly given the credit structure of the bazaar mentioned above, with its highly differentiated interest rates, which often seem very high by standards of more integrated economies. In medieval and early modern Europe, both Christians and Jews eventually came to terms with the biblical injunction against usury by differentiating between unjust return on money (usury) and just return (interest), thereby bringing the religious law into harmony with commercial practice and commonsense economic morality (see Nelson, 1969). In Islam this distinction is also argued, but it has not yet gained universal acceptance. Indeed, the majority opinion among conservative *ʿulamāʾ* remains that all interest is usury. The result is the use of *ḥiyal-i sharʿī* or *kūlah-i sharʿī* (lawful deceits), *qarẕ-i ḥasanah* (loans of goodness) or *mihrabānī* (kindness), and *mukhāṭirah* (contracts)—ways of calculating interest as if it were something else. There have also been various experiments in the past two decades, and especially now under the Islamic Republic, with so-called Islamic banks which do not charge interest but treat all deposits as pooling of shared risk in business gain and loss. From the legal history of the word *ribā*, and its use in the early traditions, it seems clear that the prohibition of *ribā* was intended to counter excessive interest rates, and especially the debt enslavement that resulted from the practice of doubling the principle if a debtor asked for an extension of time to repay. It was also intended to make explicit equalities and inequalities of exchange and to reduce the uncertainties of speculation, such as in buying pregnant animals or crops that were not yet ripe.

Apart from the rules of fair price and the prohibition on biting usury, there are also principles of the public good and those of substituting something better *(tabdīl)* used to modify endowment contracts. Bazaar exchanges provide a recognized arena of tension between individual rights and the good of the community, which is but vaguely regulated by personal morality and litigation. This vagueness is recognized in al-Ghazālī's metaphor that the bazaar is an arena of *jihād*, an internal holy war to maintain one's morality when there is temptation to take unfair advantage. Other commentators speak of the role of the merchant as an occupation taken up as a service to the community but not for its own sake *(farḍ al-kifāyah);* it is something dangerous to one's own morality, but the risk is shouldered, because it is a task the community must have performed. Another formulation is that the bazaar should be regulated under *ḥisbah* (the religious obligation to avoid evil), and at times there were officials, *muḥtasib*, who helped maintain order, set prices, and collect taxes. This is a role that was already institutionalized in Greco-Roman markets, and it is an office still so named in Saudi Arabia, in the Berber *sūq*s of Morocco (where prices are adjudicated by the *muḥtasib* after consulting on production prices with the wholesalers), and a few other places. Finally, there is a notion that although Islam protects private property, such property is ultimately only usufruct and stewardship ownership on behalf of God and the community, which thus provides the community the right to intervene and establish rules of just use, exchange, and taxation.

In Iran, the Islamic Revolution nationalized banks, insurance, large industries, undeveloped land, and some trade. This was all done in the name of the public good, of the defense of the revolution or Muslim community, of rooting out unjust corrupt practices (banking interest, excessive profiteering by large companies controlling large shares of a market), and of ensuring equitable circulation of God's wealth. Trouble came with land reform, where the redistribution of wealth was pursued not by expropriating to the state or community but by taking from one individual and giving to another. Although various efforts have been made to extend the terms of traditional Islamic discussions about the market to a modern national economy, the bazaar itself remains in place as a semiautonomous realm, with powerful economic and political interests that even the Islamic Republic must respect and negotiate with.

Finally, in addition to the moral codes embedded in Islamic law and speculations on social justice, there are the social institutions located in the bazaar which extend their own cultural forms of moral discourse. Of these the *hayat*s, *zūrkhānah*s, and *ḥammām*s (as places where people gather, gossip, and discuss communal affairs) have been mentioned. It is of cultural and historical interest that the *zūrkhānah* draws on both pre-Islamic and Islamic traditions and that it cultivates a particular style of the youthful heroic sense of responsibility. The exercises are done to the chant of the national epic, the *Shāhnāmah*, or also to songs about ʿAlī, the first Shīʿī imam. The name for the athletic champions of the *zūrkhānah* is the same word used for the heroic warriors of the *Shāhnāmah: pahlavān* (on *zūrkhānah* in English, see further Fischer, 1973, pp. 252–258). There is a range of other moral statuses for young and older men who assume responsibility in the community which begin with this notion of *pahlavān* (see further Bateson *et al.*, 1977). For young men there is the chivalrous notion of *javānmard*. It is paired with the negative, tough, hooligan: the *gardankuluft, jāhil, awbāsh*, or *lūṭī*. Middle-aged men who maintain their physical prowess and enforce community peace are called *dāsh;* while older men who can only exert moral influence are called and attempt to live by a code of being *darvīsh* (simple, honest, direct, unconcerned with the games of social pretension). Unlike the hierarchies of the religious youth who grow beards of varying styles (three day growth for believers, full beards for leaders), these moral types grow mustaches. The ideology draws on Ṣūfī mystical teachings, drawing on internal spiritual powers increasingly as one moves toward the role of *darvīsh*. The ideologies encoded in these character types have been generalized and disseminated, among other ways, through the Iranian cinema (Fischer, 1984). The last great *lūṭī*s of the Tehran bazaar were Ṭayyib, who collected a tax on goods moving in and out of a fruit bazaar near Ayatollah ʿAbd Allāh Bihbahānīs house; and his rival and successor, Shaʿbān Bimukh ("The Brainless") Qummī, who led royalist toughs in the 1950s and 1960s, being rewarded by the shah with a grand showplace *zūrkhānah* at City Park. The theme of men protecting neighborhood morality was a frequent one in "B" or working-class films (so-called *ābgūshtī* films, named after the workingman's soup-stew, *ābgūsht*): tension is heightened in the plots by the need to achieve revenge for injury before the police and civil legal system can intervene. Factory managers and even occasionally bureaucrats and academics refer to a *lūṭī* or *dāsh* style as the only effective authority pattern (i.e., tough, no-nonsense, paternalistic, but moral and fair and doing right both behind the scenes and publicly).

Descriptive accounts of bazaars are potentially inexhaustible: their local forms, social, economic, political, and cultural inflections vary from the *sūq*s of the "West" or Maghrib (North Africa) to the Hindu-complemented bazaars of India and beyond in all directions (e.g., Geertz, 1979, 1965, 1963; Fox, 1969; Goitein, 1973, 1969; Ostor, 1984; Rudolph, 1987). If the Persian bazaar is given focal attention here, it is because its structure illustrates that of a variety of bazaars. But even for Persian bazaars one could go on in ever more detail, about the secret languages of various guilds (Fischer, 1973; chap. 6), about the specializations of different crafts in different places (Centlivres, 1972; Centlivres-Demont, 1971), about the differences in relative numbers of wholesalers to retailers in different bazaars (and the implications for social control), about the relations between the bazaar and the public and large industrial sectors, and so forth.

Analytic theories of bazaars (the evolution of trade forms, location theories of economic spatial arrangements, sociological forms of exchange and their ritualization, economic theories of capital fragmentation) also have large literatures. Most of these literatures, however, see the bazaar as but one phase in the transition and/or complexity of trade forms. There is also a naive literature on the "Islamic City," which usually restricts itself to observing that the public spaces of the Islamic city are constructed around the triad of mosque, bazaar, and castle, and that the streets are labyrinthian; but little real knowledge of the workings of the bazaar is demonstrated. Occasionally Max Weber's sociological observations are cited about the differences between cities founded in Western Europe with autonomous charters (and thus as important players in the evolution of political forms of the state) and patrimonially embedded Asian cities lacking such autonomy; these are now supplemented by a small but growing literature by social historians on the formation of local elites in urban centers and their relations to landownership, bazaars, control of regional trade and taxation, and imperial structures. There also are now a large number of descriptive accounts by geographers of many cities with bazaars, including maps and sometimes statistical information on numbers of shops and kinds of shops. Novels as well occasionally provide rich insight into both the social worlds and the economic structures of the bazaar (e.g., Hedayat, 1979; Narayan, 1953).

[*See also* Guilds; Interest; Khums; Zūrkhānah.]

BIBLIOGRAPHY

Abedi, Mehdi, and Gary Legenhausen, eds. *Bibliography on Islamic Banking*. Houston, 1988.

Anṣārī, Murtaẓā. *Kitāb al-Makāsib*. Najaf, 1972.

Bateson, Mary Catherine, et al. "Ṣafā-yi Bāṭin: A Study of the Interrelations of a Set of Iranian Ideal Character Types." In *Psychological Dimensions of Near Eastern Studies,* edited by L. Carl Brown and Norman Itzkowitz, pp. 257–273. Princeton, 1977.

Centlivres, Pierre. *Un bazaar d'Asie centrale: Forme et organisation du bazaar de Tāshqurghān (Afghanistan)*. Wiesbaden, 1972.

Centlivres-Demont, Micheline. *Une communauté de potiers en Iran: Le centre de Meybod (Yazd)*. Wiesbaden, 1971.

Dillon, Robert. "Carpet Capitalism and Craft Involution in Kirman, Iran." Ph.D. diss., Columbia University, 1976.

English, Paul. *City and Village in Iran.* Madison, Wis., 1966.

Fischer, Michael M. J. "Zoroastrian Iran between Myth and Praxis." Ph.D. diss., University of Chicago, 1973. See especially chapter 6.

Fischer, Michael M. J. "Persian Society: Transition and Strain." In *Twentieth-Century Iran,* edited by Hossein Amirsadeghi and R. W. Ferrier, pp. 171–195. London, 1977.

Fischer, Michael M. J. *Iran: From Religious Dispute to Revolution.* Cambridge, Mass., 1980.
Fischer, Michael M. J. "Towards a Third World Poetics: Seeing through Iranian Short Stories and Films." *Knowledge and Society* 5 (1984): 171–241.
Fischer, Michael M. J., and Mehdi Abedi. *Debating Muslims.* Madison, Wis., 1990. See pages 143–146.
Fox, Richard G. *From Zamindar to Ballot Box: Community Change in a North Indian Market.* Ithaca, N.Y., 1969.
Geertz, Clifford. *Peddlers and Princes.* Chicago, 1963.
Geertz, Clifford. *The Social History of an Indonesian Town.* Cambridge, Mass., 1965.
Geertz, Clifford. "Suq: The Bazaar Economy in Sefrou." In *Meaning and Order in Moroccan Society,* edited by Clifford Geertz et al. Cambridge, 1979.
Goitein, S. D. *A Mediterranean Society,* Vol. 1, *Economic Foundations.* Berkeley, 1968.
Goitein, S. D. *Letters of Medieval Jewish Traders.* Princeton, 1973.
Hidāyat, Ṣādiq. *Hājī Āghā.* Austin, 1979.
Ḥijāzī, ʿAbd al-Riẕā. *Sīstim-i iqtiṣādī-yi Islām.* Qom, 1970.
Khūrī, Fu'ād Isḥāq. "Etiquette of Bargaining in the Middle East." *American Anthropologist* 70.4 (1968): 698–706.
Mannan, Muhammad Abdul. *Islamic Economics: Theory and Practice.* Boulder, 1986.
Mawdūdī, Sayyid Abū al-Aʿlā. *Capitalism, Socialism, and Islam.* Kuwait, n.d.
Mines, Mattison. *The Warrior Merchants: Textiles, Trade, and Territory in South India.* Cambridge, 1984.
Narayan, R. K. *The Financial Expert.* New York, 1953.
Östör, Ákos. *Culture and Power: Legend, Ritual, Bazaar, and Rebellion in a Bengali Society.* Beverly Hills, 1984.
Quṭb, Sayyid. *Tafsīr āyāt al-ribā* (Commentary on the Verses about Interest). Beirut, [197–?].
Quṭb, Sayyid. *Maʿrakat al-Islām wa-al-ra'smālīyah* (Islam versus Capitalism). Beirut and Cairo, 1983.
Rotblat, Howard J. "Stability and Change in an Iranian Provincial Bazaar." Ph.D. diss., University of Chicago, 1972.
Rudner, David. "Caste and Commerce in Indian Society: A Case Study of Nattokottai Chetiars." Ph.D. diss., University of Pennsylvania, 1985.
Rudolph, Lloyd I. *In Pursuit of Lakshmi: The Political Economy of the Indian State.* Chicago, 1987.
Ṣadr, Muḥammad Bāqir al-. *Iqtiṣādunā.* New rev. ed. Beirut, 1977. Translated into English as *Our Economics.* 2 vols. in 4. Tehran, 1982–1984.
Shīrāzī, Ṣādiq. *Rāhī bih sū-yi Bank-i Islāmī.* Qom, 1393/1973.
Ṭāleqāni, Maḥmud. *Islām va mālikīyat.* Tehran, 1965. Translated into English by Ahmad Jabbari and Farhang Rajaee as *Islam and Ownership.* Lexington, Ky., 1983.
Thaiss, Gus. "The Drama of Husain." Ph.D. diss., University of Washington, St. Louis, 1973.

MICHAEL M. J. FISCHER

BĀZARGĀN, MEHDI (b. 1907), Iranian Muslim modernist and reformer, regarded as one of the major voices of Islamic opposition in the pre- and postrevolutionary eras. Mehdi Bāzargān was born into a religious family of bazaar merchants. His elementary and secondary education in Tehran combined traditional Qur'ānic learning with a modern curriculum. In 1928 he was one of the few students chosen by the government to study abroad. He studied engineering at the École Centrale in Paris, returning to Iran in 1935 after receiving his doctorate. After a year of military service, he worked at the National Bank and joined the engineering faculty of Tehran University. Later in the 1930s he began a lifelong collaboration with Sayyid Maḥmud Ṭāleqāni, one of the leading oppositionist clergy, spreading the message of progressive Islam. In 1939 he was imprisoned for opposing the shah's religious policies. Since 1941, Bāzargān has been instrumental in establishing various professional Islamic organizations, including Muslim student associations and the Association of Engineers.

As an ardent nationalist Bāzargān was also drawn to Mohammad Mossadegh's nationalist cause. After World War II he collaborated with Mossadegh and the National Front. Known for his honesty and integrity, he was named deputy minister in 1951, heading a committee that supervised the nationalization of Iranian oil. Subsequently he became the first chairman of the board of directors of the National Iranian Oil Company.

After the downfall of Mossadegh in the CIA-backed coup d'état of 1953, he joined the nationalist resistance movement, Nahẓat-i Muqāvamat-i Millī (NMR). The NMR was crushed in 1957 and many of its leaders, including Bāzargān, were imprisoned. In 1961, with Ayatollah Ṭāleqāni and Yadollah Ṣaḥābi, he founded the Liberation Movement of Iran (LMI), which called for an end to foreign domination and the restoration of constitutional and democratic rights. Their political activities brought all three men prison terms. Between 1963 and 1977, Bāzargān was sentenced to several short prison terms for his political activities.

In the 1950s and 1960s Bāzargān also collaborated with Ayatollah Murtaẕā Muṭahharī, another prominent cleric, by contributing to the monthly Religious Society Lectures. Muṭahharī, Ṭāleqāni, and Bāzargān were among the founders of the Islamic Association of Teachers and organized its first and second national congresses.

Shortly before the emergence of massive antishah political activism in the late 1970s, Bāzargān cofounded the Human Rights Association in 1977 to defend the democratic rights of the opposition. Bāzargān also played an active role in the revolution that toppled the shah, when Ayatollah Ruhollah Khomeini sent him to organize the oil workers' strikes in mid-1978. In February 1979 Khomeini appointed him as the first prime minister of the provisional government, but in November of that year he resigned complaining of powerlessness and multiple centers of power and more specifically over the seizure of the American embassy on 4 November 1979. Bāzargān was also a member of the Council of the Islamic Revolution and was elected to the first parliament in 1980 as a representative for Tehran. In the early 1980s when the Islamic Republic launched a major assault on the opposition, Bāzargān's LMI was the only political group that escaped suppression. Although tolerated as a loyal opposition, LMI members were often imprisoned and harassed. Disillusioned with the policies of the Islamic Republic in general and the suppression of democratic rights in particular, Bāzargān cofounded the Association for the Defense of the Freedom and Sovereignty of the Iranian Nation (ADFSIN) in 1984. In the early 1990s Bāzargān was active in both the LMI and ADFSIN.

Throughout his political career Bāzargān has attempted to reconcile Shīʿī theology with the modern world and his own democratic aspirations. His politics represent a synthesis of nationalism, gradualism, liberalism, and Islam. These attributes distinguished him from the traditionalist clergy, such as Khomeini, and the radical Islamists, such as ʿAlī Sharīʿatī. Whereas Sharīʿatī's firebrand rhetoric galvanized the youth and Khomeini articulated the resentment of the underprivileged and the traditional social groups, Bāzargān's appeal was confined to more enlightened members of the traditional middle class. By the time the revolutionary mass movement erupted, Bāzargān's political reformism was out of step with the revolutionary fervor of the masses. Bāzargān's liberalism and gradualism had a wider appeal in the 1950s when Mossadegh's liberalism and his parliamentary method of political struggle captured the imagination of the postwar generation. But by the mid-1960's and early 1970s, because of the radicalizing impact of such global events as the Chinese, Vietnamese, and Cuban revolutions on Iranian youth, Bāzargān's reformist political program and his liberal rendition of Islam seemed increasingly irrelevant to them. The generation of the 1960s had no memory of Mossadegh's liberal nationalism; rather, it was inspired by a radical vision that attributed the defeat of Mossadegh to his parliamentary method of political struggle. Some of the founding members of Mujāhidīn-i Khalq, a guerrilla organization that fought against the shah's regime and the Islamic Republic, began their political careers as members of the LMI, many joining the party in 1963; by 1965, inspired by the example of armed struggle, they founded their own political party. Therefore, the moderate LMI did not greatly grow in strength throughout the Iranian Revolution of 1979. This, however, did not prevent some of its leaders from occupying influential positions in the early years of the Islamic Republic.

Whereas Bāzargān's attempt to develop a scientific basis for his Islamic modernism made him popular among the educated middle classes, his polemics against Marxists and his political gradualism were akin to the conservative predispositions of the bazaar merchants. During the shah's rule, Bāzargān's attempt to modernize and politicize Islam was intended to create an Islamic alternative to monarchy, but the monopolization of power by the traditional clergy since 1980 and the restrictions on democratic rights that characterized the early years of the revolution put him in the opposition camp once again. This time his pluralist interpretation of Islam opposed the totalitarian tendencies of the traditional Islam of the clergy. Prior to the 1979 revolution, in his attempt to politicize Muslims, Bāzargān emphasized the unity of politics and religion; in the postrevolutionary era, however, his interpretation increasingly depicted Islam as a private faith. Calling for separation of religious institutions from the state, he asserted that interference of the state in matters of personal faith would lead to theocratic despotism. Bāzargān opposed any monolithic interpretation of Islam and advocated popular participation and public sovereignty. These ideological attributes establish him as one of the major voices of Islamic liberalism in post–World War II Iran.

[*See also* Iranian Revolution of 1979; Liberation Movement of Iran; *and the biographies of Muṭahharī and Ṭāleqāni.*]

BIBLIOGRAPHY

Bāzargān, Mehdi. *Mudāfaʿāt dar dādgāh-i ghayr-i ṣāliḥ-i tajdīd-i naẓar-i niẓāmī*. Tehran, 1971. Good biographical source on Bāzargān's personal life and political career.

Bāzargān, Mehdi. *Rāh-i Ṭayy shudah*. Houston, 1977. Reflects on the political problems of Iranian society, including the role of opposition groups under the Pahlavis, and proposes remedies to overcome them.

Bāzargān, Mehdi. *Bāzyābī-i arzishhā*. Tehran, 1983. Provides an interesting perspective on the evolution of Bāzargān's Islamic modernism.

Bāzargān, Mehdi. *Inqilāb-i Īrān dar dū ḥarakat.* Tehran, 1984. Analysis of the Iranian Revolution and the postrevolutionary situation, from the political perspective of the Liberation Movement of Iran.

Chehabi, H. E. *Iranian Politics and Religious Modernism: The Liberation Movement of Iran under the Shah and Khomeini.* Ithaca, N.Y., 1990. One of the best studies available to date on Bāzargān and the Liberation Movement of Iran.

MANOCHEHR DORRAJ

BEKTĀSHĪYAH. This Ṣūfī order became widespread in the Ottoman Empire and today has communities in Turkey, in Albanian regions of the Balkans, and among Albanian immigrants in North America; *Bektāshīyah* is the Arabic form of its name, while in Turkish it is *Bektaşi.* The Bektaşi order traces its origin to central Anatolia in the thirteenth century. It takes its name from Haji Bektash Veli, a religious leader from Khurasan in northeast Iran, who, according to tradition, was sent by command of the famous Ṣūfī of western Turkestan, Ahmed Yesevi, to Anatolia where he settled in a village near the present city of Kırşehir. The organization of the Bektaşi order, however, is credited to a later personage, Balım Sultan, known as the "Second Pir" (patron saint) of the order, who became head of the Bektaşis in 1501. Balım Sultan was born of at least partly Bulgarian parentage near the city of Edirne, now in European Turkey. In addition to centralizing authority at the Bektaşi headquarters in Anatolia, Balım Sultan instituted the celibate branch of the order that has continued to coexist with the married branch.

Central to Bektaşi teachings is the importance of the spiritual teacher (Ar., *murshid;* Tk., *mürşit*). One cannot progress in spiritual growth without a spiritual teacher, and prayer and blessings are mediated by the teacher. Unlike orthodox Muslims, Bektaşis believe in intercession. This intercession can also be through earlier spiritual teachers, including the two pirs of the order, the saints, the twelve imams, and ʿAlī, whom the Bektaşis as well as many other Ṣūfī orders view as the one who revealed mystic understanding of the Qur'ān. Thus the Bektaşis are ʿAlid in orientation, professing strong love and loyalty to Ehli Beyt, the "household of the Prophet." They have been called Shīʿīs but theologically they differ from many Shīʿīs in their emphasis on the mystic path, as well as in their understanding of Muḥammad and ʿAlī, which includes reference to "Muḥammad ʿAlī" as a single personage; thus they both raise the status of ʿAlī and emphasize the complementarity and unity of the word of God and its mystical dimension. Practices that reflect the ʿAlid orientation of the Bektaşis are their two main annual holidays: Aşure (Ar., ʿĀshūrā'), which commemorates the martyrdom of ʿAlī's son Ḥusayn; and Nevruz (Nawrūz), which is celebrated at the spring equinox and is understood as the birthday of ʿAlī.

Further practices that are distinctively Bektaşi include their initiation rites. These rites are private, reserved for other initiated members, and include ceremonial use of candles, sheepskins, and sweet drink. What is striking about these rites, in the context of Islamic society, is the presence of unveiled women. Bektaşis have always accepted women as initiated members, thereby sanctioning their participation in these ceremonies.

Another Bektaşi practice is their communal praise of God *(dhikr),* which involves the alternation of the chanting of spiritual poetry *(nefes)* with formalized sharing of food and drink. Much of the teaching of the order is in these spiritual poems. Also distinctive is a disregard for certain basic practices of Islam; for example, Bektaşis pray twice daily rather than five times. Finally, during the ten-day period before Aşure, Bektaşis engage in a special fast and each evening read aloud from the sixteenth-century Turkish poet Fuzulî's account of the suffering of the prophets and martyrs.

Throughout their history the Bektaşis have been criticized by Sunnī Muslim authorities for a range of offenses, from laxness in following standard Muslim practices and immorality in including women in their private rites, to heresy in elevating ʿAlī to the level of the prophet Muḥammad or above him, and in comparing both to God. (These last allegations of heresy reflect nonmystic Sunnīs' inability to deal with the mystic expression.) Yet despite these criticisms, the order flourished in the Ottoman Empire among townspeople (in contrast to the Mevlevî order (Ar., Mawlawīyah), which drew more urban intellectuals), in frontier regions in the Balkans, and among the Janissaries, the elite troops of the empire. Estimates of the number of Bektaşis in 1900 range from one to seven million. Careful sources (Birge, 1965; Rexhebi, 1972) see 10 percent of the population of Turkey (with modern boundaries) and 15 percent of the population of Albania as directly or indirectly influenced by the order at that time. The popularity of the Bektaşi order may be partly explained in that it embodied and also shaped popular Turkish piety, and that it was syncretistic in its inclusion of pre-Islamic pagan and Christian elements, thus appealing to populations that were formerly Christian. Certainly it provided a broader range of religious expression than the mosque; socially, it added communal networks of interaction at a local level and across the empire.

In addition to its religious and social roles in more settled communities, the Bektaşi order was a source of missionaries of Islam who traveled with Ottoman forces into the Balkans. The mobility and simplicity of Bektaşi organization, its relaxed attitude toward the letter of Muslim law, and its tolerance of non-Muslim peoples were all well suited to facilitating the gradual conversion of people in these regions.

The Bektaşis also had a longstanding special relationship with the Janissaries, many of whom had been born of Christian parents. Scholars have debated the onset of this relationship, but it was in place at least by the end of the fifteenth century (the Janissaries were founded in the fourteenth). The Bektaşis officially blessed the troops, provided an ideology of bonding among them, and traveled with them as chaplains. This relationship was also a source of political power for the Bektaşis within the empire.

The connection of the Bektaşis with the Janissaries was such that in 1826, when Sultan Mahmud II abolished the Janissaries as part of his campaign to modernize the military, the Bektaşis were also targeted. Bektaşi *tekke*s, or centers, were destroyed; some Bektaşi leaders were executed, some were exiled, and some refigured themselves as Nakşibendis (Ar., Naqshbandīyah) to ride out the persecution. Yet by the second half of the nineteenth century, the Bektaşis had regained their *tekke*s and were publishing numerous books. Politically, many Bektaşis of this period were progressive and included members of the Young Turks as well as Albanian patriots. Nonetheless, the Bektaşis again suffered the closing of their *tekke*s when in 1925 Atatürk abolished all Ṣūfī orders in the Republic of Turkey. In response, the Bektaşis moved their headquarters from Anatolia to Albania.

With the Communist takeover of Albania in 1944 the Bektaşis again began to suffer restrictions. In 1945 all property of religious institutions was confiscated in Albania, and in 1947 an attempt was made to force celibate Bektaşi clerics to marry. The 1967 proclamation of Albania as an atheist state was followed by more destruction of Bektaşi tombs and mausoleums (*türbe*s), along with mosques and churches. Countering this, Albanian immigrants and refugees in America established a Bektaşi *tekke* in Michigan in 1953. Yet another blow to the Bektaşis followed in 1957, when the government in Egypt under Nasser closed the Bektaşi *tekke* in the Muqaṭṭam outside Cairo, which since the nineteenth century had been led by Albanian *baba*s.

In the 1990s, the situation in both Albania and Turkey has improved somewhat for Bektaşis. The Communist regime in Albania fell in 1990–1991, and the Bektaşi headquarters there reopened in April 1991. In Turkey there has been recognition of the contribution of the Bektaşis to Turkish culture through their extensive spiritual poetry that is largely in Turkish. After great decline in the early part of the century, there has recently been some growth in Bektaşi fellowships in Turkey and among Turkish guest workers in Europe. Further, in the second half of the twentieth century there has been public acknowledgment by Bektaşis that the village Alevîs (Ar., ʿAlawīyah; including the Kizilbash) and the Bektaşis have much in common in terms of practice and belief (Noyan, 1985).

Overall, the Bektaşi order was an important expression of and influence on Islam among Turkish people in Anatolia and an important agent of Islam in the Balkans. Its practices, theology, and link with the Janissaries attest to the wide range of variation in Islam. The spiritual poetry produced and preserved by its adherents is a valued contribution to Turkish and Albanian culture.

It appears unlikely, however, that the Bektaşis will regain the popularity and political power they once held. In Turkey there remain laws limiting the order, and the Islamic political parties are not favorable toward them. In Albania, in the Muslim Albanian regions of the former Yugoslavia (Kosova and Macedonia), and in Albanian communities in North America, there is a critical lack of trained Bektaşi clerics, partly reflecting the secularization of the times but also exacerbated by the direct suppression Bektaşis have suffered in the twentieth century.

BIBLIOGRAPHY

Birge, John Kingsley. *The Bektashi Order of Dervishes*. London, 1937; reprint, 1965. Still the most comprehensive overview (history, beliefs, practices) on the Bektaşi order to date. It is clearly written and well documented.

Clayer, Nathalie. *L'Albanie, pays des Derviches: Analyse due rayonnement des ordres msytiques musulmans en Albanie à l'époque post-ottomane, 1912–1967*. Berlin, 1990. An interesting analysis of the spread of Ṣūfī orders in Albania in this century, including much on the Bektaşis.

De Jong, Frederick. "Problems concerning the Origins of the Qizilbaş in Bulgaria: Remnants of the Safaviyya?" In *La Shi'a nell'Impero Ottomano*. Accademia Nazionale dei Lincei, Fondazione Leone

Caetani, Rome, 15 April 1993. One of the few references to Bektaşis in Bulgaria, based partly on ethnographic work conducted in the early 1980s.

Faroqhi, Suraiya. *Der Bektaschi-Orden in Anatolien (from the late 15th century to 1826)*. Vienna, 1981. An economic and social history of the Bektaşi order in Anatolia, based largely on archival material. Includes maps of the location of Bektaşi *tekkes* in Anatolia in the seventeenth, eighteenth, and nineteenth centuries.

Noyan, Bedri. *Bektaşîlik Alevilik: Nedir?* (Bektashism and Alevism: What are They?). Ankara, 1985. A thorough description of Bektaşi beliefs and practices by a scholarly Bektaşi leader in Turkey, whose father was also a high-ranked Bektaşi.

Nüzhet, Sadettin. *Bektaşi Şairleri* (Bektashi Poets). Istanbul, 1930. An anthology of selections of poets along with brief biographies. The nineteenth- and twentieth-century Bektaşi poets are particularly well represented.

Rifat Efendi. (The Mirror of Retaliation in the Refutation of Villainies). Istanbul, 1876. The Bektaşi response to a bitter attack on the order by the the Sunnī Ishak Efendi in 1873.

Rexhebi, Baba. *Misticizma Islame dhe Bektashizma* (Islamic Mysticism and Bektashism). New York, 1972. A contextualization of mysticism in Islam, and Bektashism in Islamic mysticism by the *baba* of the Bektaşi *tekke* in Michigan. Includes biographies and poetry of otherwise inaccessible Balkan Bektaşis.

Trix, Frances. *Spiritual Discourse: Learning with an Islamic Master*. Philadelphia, 1993. A sociolinguistic study of learning in the Bektaşi master-student relationship, based on extensive research with Baba Rexheb of the Michigan Bektaşi *tekke*.

FRANCES TRIX

BEN BADIS. *See* Ibn Bādīs, ʿAbd al-Ḥamīd.

BIDʿAH. In modern Islamic religious discourse the meaning of the term *bidʿah* (lit., "innovation") can be understood from the saying attributed to the Prophet: "Any manner or way which someone invents within this religion such that that manner or way is not a part of this religion is to be rejected." The statement of the Qur'ān usually quoted in this context further explicates the rationale behind the prohibition: "Today I have perfected your religion [*dīn*] for you . . . and I have chosen Islam as your religion" (surah 5.3). Innovation in matters of religion is an implicit statement that religion as revealed to the Prophet was not complete.

A minimal interpretation of *bidʿah* would restrict it to innovation in religious ritual or belief—since only in these fields is there the sense that one is attempting to "improve on" what God gave the Prophet. The core of the concept is that a practice which has no precedent in the practice of the Prophet or his companions be performed with the intention of gaining religious merit; the anticipation of religious merit makes the innovation reprehensible, for it suggests that there are ways of pleasing God which were not available to the Prophet. As this basic concept is elaborated, more actual practices from the daily lives of Muslims come under the threat of being considered *bidʿah,* and one finds more disagreement within the modern discourse regarding each elaboration.

Innovation in religious matters includes both modification and invention of ritual and practice. Specifying times, places, or manners of performing religiously prescribed acts can turn an act of worship into an innovation. For example, reciting the Qur'ān, gathering together for its recitation, and reciting it in order to ask God to bless a dead person by means of one's recitation are all acts of worship. But proponents of this first understanding of *bidʿah* object to the common practice of gathering together forty days after the death of a relative to recite the Qur'ān in order to invoke God's blessings on the deceased. They argue that by joining these acts together one has created an entirely new ritual. Furthermore, if this practice were useful one would find examples of it in the *sunnah* (practice) of the Prophet and his companions.

Prohibition of "proto-innovation" to avoid potential corruption of religious practice expands the scope of the concept. Participants in a Qur'ān-recitation gathering of the type described above might have a clear understanding that no merit is to be gained in the fact of the manner and time of this gathering. But even their participation would be considered *bidʿah,* since the distinctions they make between the organizational arrangement and the source of the anticipated religious merit might be lost on an observer.

A second interpretation extends the prohibition against innovation beyond strictly religious matters to social practice. Such a broader understanding requires Muslims to conduct ceremonies relating to marriage, death, birth, and the like in the manner in which the Prophet had conducted such ceremonies. The rationale for such an extension of the concept is that *dīn* covers one's way of life in its entirety. To think that we are able to improve on the ways in which the Prophet taught his companions to conduct themselves on social occasions is to question the fact that the religion he was given had been perfected.

To follow the ways of the Prophet in all dealings is an undisputed ideal among Muslims. The distinctive feature of this interpretation of *bidʿah* is that not to act in conformity with *sunnah* is not merely to forego performing a meritorious act; rather, it is to sin by committing *bidʿah.* Those who define *bidʿah* more narrowly than the proponents of this second interpretation also condemn the failure of Muslims to follow the example of the Prophet in social dealings, but they condemn it on grounds other than it being *bidʿah.*

A third understanding of *bidʿah* brings the word close to its literal meaning. *Bidʿah* is seen as divided into as many legal categories as human actions, and it can thus be obligatory, approved of, frowned on, or forbidden. According to this understanding, disapproval of *bidʿah* is seen as referring to reprehensible *bidʿah* only, that is, acts that are disapproved. One of the reasons for this watering down of the concept is found in an explicit saying of the second caliph, ʿUmar ibn al-Khaṭṭāb (d. 644), who is reported to have approved of an act he saw by saying, "What a good *bidʿah* this is!"

Another reason for this conception of *bidʿah* might relate to the difficulty in establishing a distinction between *bidʿah* and the type of religious reasoning used, for example, in *qiyās* (analogical argumentation). In the case of analogical reasoning, a jurist is presented a case not covered by an explicit saying of the Qur'ān or the Prophet. The jurist attempts to come to a ruling by searching for an appropriate analogy from among the cases actually dealt with in the Qur'ān and the sayings of the Prophet. In formal terms, however, the jurist seems to introduce into religion something which is not apparently present before his ruling.

The distinction between the first definition of *bidʿah* and the third is primarily one of terminology. In the first definition, the reprehensibility of an act is seen as turning on its being an "addition" to the types of acts of which a life based on *sunnah* is composed. But this "life based on *sunnah*" consists of both the explicit practice of the Prophet and things incorporated in it by analogical extension. In this last definition of *bidʿah,* the domain of permissibility is expanded explicitly by allowing "good *(ḥasanah) bidʿah*" a place alongside the practice of the Prophet and by leaving the realm of *sunnah* narrowly defined.

[*See also* Sunnah.]

BIBLIOGRAPHY

Memon, Muhammad Umar. *Ibn Taymīya's Struggle Against Popular Religion, with an Annotated Translation of His Kitāb iqtiḍā' aṣ-ṣirāṭ al-mustaqīm mukhālafat aṣḥāb al-jaḥīm.* The Hague and Paris, 1976. Ibn Taymīyah is the source for many modern Muslims' conception of *bidʿah.* In addition to providing a full translation of Ibn Taymīyah's work on *bidʿah,* Memon's work is useful in placing the issues surrounding *bidʿah* in the context of everyday life in Muslim society.

Shāṭibī, Ibrāhīm ibn Mūsá al-. *Al-'iʿtiṣām.* Beirut, 1988. Because of its organization and its coverage of the issues surrounding *bidʿah,* no other single Arabic work rivals its discussion of the topic.

IFTIKHAR ZAMAN

BIGI, MUSA YARULLAH (1874–1949), Volga-Ural Muslim philosopher and religious scholar. Born 24 December 1874 in Rostov on Don, Bigi was the son of the mullah Yarullah Devlikam, originally from the Kikine village of Penza Gubernia, and of Fatma, the daughter of Imam Habibullah of the same village. He attended the Külbüe *madrasah* in Kazan but left without graduating and returned to Rostov to enroll in the Russian science gymnasium from which he graduated in 1895, when he left for Bukhara to continue his Islamic studies. After four years, he returned to Rostov only to leave again for an extended Middle Eastern trip.

Bigi traveled to Istanbul and then to Cairo, where he studied at al-Azhar and attended classes offered by Muḥammad ʿAbduh. After four years studying Islamic philosophy, theology, and jurisprudence, he returned to Rostov and married, but instead of seeking employment as a mullah or *madrasah* teacher and settling down, he left his wife Äsma in his mother's care and went to St. Petersburg to attend classes at the Law Faculty. As a scholar interested in *tafsīr* (Qur'ānic exegesis) and *fiqh* (law), he wanted to acquire the knowledge necessary to compare the Islamic and Western legal systems. Bigi's closer acquaintance with Russian society during his stay in St. Petersburg resulted in a politicization of his thought and a deeper appreciation of Islam as a political force. While in St. Petersburg (1905–1917), he contributed eighteen essays to the Pan-Islamist journal *Ulfät.* He continued, however, to dedicate most of his time to research and scholarly writing, and his only active involvement in politics was the contribution he made as secretary to the Muslim Congress.

In 1910 and 1911 Bigi was employed as teacher of Arabic, Islamic, history, and theology at the Khösäeniya *madrasah* in Orenburg. As a scholar and teacher, Bigi was an exemplary practitioner of *ijtihād* (interpretation of Islam), but some of his interpretations were considered so far-fetched by the religious establishment that he was forced to leave Orenburg, despite the support of the well-respected scholar Rizaeddin Fakhreddin. [*See the biography of Fakhreddin.*]

The revolutions of 1917 triggered Bigi's hope for the beginning of an era of freedom for Muslims, and he chose not to leave Russia. Soon, however, he was to face bitter disappointment. In response to Bukharin's *ABC of Communism,* Bigi wrote in 1920 an "ABC of Islam" *(Islam älifbasï),* which he presented to the Congress of Scholars in Ufa. Of the work's 236 points, 68 concerned the situation of the Muslims in Russia, and the remainder were devoted to Muslims elsewhere. The government retaliated with arrest and imprisonment, but after three months Bigi was released owing to a press campaign launched in Turkey and Finland on his behalf. Despite this experience, Bigi chose to stay in Soviet Russia and in 1926 participated in the Muslim Congress at Mecca representing his country; a year later he received permission to perform the pilgrimage. Bigi returned to Russia after this trip as well, because he still believed that he could serve his people by fighting to keep their heritage alive.

By 1930, however, even the idealist Bigi understood that all doors had been closed and neither political nor cultural pluralism was acceptable to the leaders of Soviet Russia. Consequently, he left his wife and six children behind and fled Russia. He stopped in Chinese Turkestan and then went to Afghanistan and India; in 1931 traveled to Egypt and Finland; and in 1932 took part in the first Congress of Turkish History in Ankara. The years of 1933 to 1937 took Bigi to Finland, Germany, and the Middle East, while in 1938 he traveled to China and Japan. In 1939 he went to India and Afghanistan with the intention of settling in the latter, but after being imprisoned by the British for eighteen months, he went to India instead. Bigi remained there until 1947, when he went to Egypt. He died there on 25 October 1949, having spent his last days in poverty in a charitable hospice.

Musa Yarullah Bigi left 122 works. The majority were written in Arabic and were devoted to issues of Islamic theology and jurisprudence; others addressed the social, political, and religious life of the Muslims of Russia and were written in Tatar. Several of his scholarly endeavors should be noted as illustrations of Bigi's qualities as *mujtahid.* In *Sherhu'l-luzumiyat* (Kazan, 1907), a volume of commentaries on the work of the tenth-century Islamic poet and philosopher al-Ma'ari, he argued, sharing al-Ma'ari's skepticism, that none of the existing religions could be pleasing to God because they all contained moral if not physical oppression.

Bigi pursued the same iconoclastic line of thought in *Rähmät-i ilahiyä burhannarï* (The Storms of God's Clemency; Orenburg, 1910), which challenged the official dogma that God's mercy and forgiveness were not extended to unbelievers, arguing that on the contrary, God extended his forgiveness to everyone. Bigi was attacked by conservative *ʿulamā'* through their publication *Din vä magishät* (Religion and Life), as well as by liberal mullahs and *jadīd* (modernist) intellectuals. One of the most vocal criticisms coming from the *jadīd* reformers was articulated by Ismail Gasprali̇ (Gasprinskii) in his article "Woe from Philosophy." Fakhreddin was among the few defenders of Bigi, but he stated the issue from a different perspective, pointing to the historical precedents for the same interpretation. [*See* Jadīdism *and the biography of Gasprinskii.*]

When he discovered editorial changes in one of the copies of the Qur'ān, Bigi was relentless in his criticism of mullahs, arguing that the changes reflected the ignorance of those who had tampered with the original text, whom he attacked in *Tarikhu'l Qur'an vä'l-masahif* (A History of the Qur'ān and Qur'ānic Texts). Bigi also advocated translation of the Qur'ān into Tatar, which he felt would contribute to making individual religious experience a more meaningful and conscientious act. He stressed that in a civilized world, it was the duty of the community to translate the Qur'ān into the languages of the people and to ascertain the accuracy of existing translations. Bigi himself worked on a Tatar translation of the Qur'ān, but it may have been destroyed together with his personal archives after his departure from Russia.

Bigi wrote extensively on issues concerning the position of women in Islam *(Khatun, Ailä mäsäläläre, Hukuku'n-nisa fi'l-Islâm); Sunnah* and *sharīʿah* *(Kitabu's-sunnä;* Bhopal, 1945; *Shariat esaslarï,* St. Petersburg, 1916); and the social and political life of Russian Muslims (*Islahat esaslarï,* St. Petersburg, 1914; *Khalq nazarïnda bir nichä mäsäle,* Kazan, 1912). His most important contributions to Islamic thought, however, are his *ijtihād* works, of which two more deserve attention: *Uzun künlärde rüzä* (Fasting during Long Days; Kazan, 1911), and *Büyük mevzularda ufak fikirlär* (Small Thoughts on Big Issues; St. Petersburg, 1914). In the first essay he discusses the ritual obligation of fasting with regard to Muslims living in the far north where the length of daylight and darkness does not coincide with that of the Islamic heartlands and renders a sharp criticism to dogmatics. In the second he criticizes those who opposed Sufism and Ṣūfī brotherhoods. Bigi valued the philosophical message of mysticism and was interested in the Ṣūfī orders, and even in Christian monasticism.

Despite the breadth and originality of his thoughts and writings, Bigi did not have a strong impact on either Islamic thought in Russia or elsewhere, probably in large part because the door to Islamic studies was closed in Russia after 1917, and his works remained unknown. After leaving his country, he was socially and intellectually an outsider; although he was respected for his knowledge, his wanderings prevented him from planting the seeds of his *ijtihād* thought firmly in the soil of any Muslim country.

BIBLIOGRAPHY

Binark, Naile. "Musa Carullah Bigi." *Kazan*, no. 16 (1975): 27–29.

Kurat, Akdes N. "Kazan Türklerinin medeni uyanış devri." *Ankara Üniversitesi Dil Tarih-Coğrafya Fakültesi Dergisi*, no. 3–4 (1966): 94–196.

Rorlich, Azade-Ayşe. *The Volga Tatars: A Profile in National Resilience.* Stanford, Calif., 1986. See pages 53–61.

Uralgiray, Y. *Filozof Musa Carullah Bigi: Uzun günlerde oruç; İctihad Kitabı.* Ankara, 1975.

AZADE-AYŞE RORLICH

BINT AL-SHĀṬI'. *See* ʿAbd al-Raḥmān, ʿĀ'ishah.

BIOGRAPHY AND HAGIOGRAPHY. Religious biography has held great importance in Islamic civilization from the earliest period, when works in various genres enumerated the virtues of the Prophet's associates, established priority in joining the Muslim community, and traced tribal genealogies and affiliations. Particularly important is the relationship between early biography and the *ḥadīth* collections. The *ʿilm la-rijāl*, or "science of men," was a branch of Islamic historiography verifying the reliability *(taʿdīl)* of *ḥadīth* transmitters according to such criteria as their direct acquaintance with the Prophet or other transmitters and their virtues and activities as individuals. Shīʿī writings also elaborated these proofs of piety and authority.

The virtuous qualities *(faḍā'il)* of important persons constitutes a subsection of most *ḥadīth* collections and reveals early concepts of charisma, character, or religious authority. A related genre lists the special merits *(khaṣā'iṣ)* of prophets or companions. Both types demonstrate a pattern of virtue established through relationship and contiguity. A further theme in the *ḥadīth* that blossomed into a genre of biographical literature is found in the books on asceticism *(kutub al-zuhd)*, which provide insight into the early development of Sufism and how ascetic practices established rankings of merit and authority.

Traditional Genres. Biographical information is widely dispersed in Islamic writings, but there also exist a significant number of specifically biographical genres. Religious biography and hagiography often took the form of one of the following major genres.

The term *sīrah* (pl. *siyar*) connotes a certain manner of conduct. *Sīrah* usually refers to the biography of the prophet Muḥammad, but the lives of saints may also be termed *siyar;* in this case they are often collective biographies.

The *ṭabaqāt* is the form usually referred to as the "biographical dictionary." The designation *ṭabaqāt* ("ranks" or "classes") refers to the system of arranging the biographical entries in these often voluminous works. The earliest extant example is the *Kitāb al-tabaqāt al-kabīr* of Ibn Saʿd (d. 845), which contains some 4,250 biographical entries for men and women of the first Islamic generations, ranging from two lines to a number of pages. The general pattern of an entry includes the person's genealogy, marriage(s), children, acceptance of Islam, declaration of allegiance to the Prophet *(bayʿah)*, and various reports about the person in *ḥadīth* form (with a chain of transmitters narrating a specific event, comment, or saying of the person), ending with the death and funeral and a list of the mourners. The inclusion of ordinary persons in the classical biographical dictionaries indicates that the history of the Islamic community was understood in this period as being constituted to a large extent by the contributions of individuals to building up and transmitting its specific worldview and culture.

Recent Western concepts of what a life is tend to be diachronic and linear, stretching from birth to death, and the life is related so as to reveal character development. In contrast, the typical life in Ibn Saʿd's *Ṭabaqāt* begins far back in genealogy and may extend into the afterlife by establishing a rank in or promise of paradise. From the earlier material up to the present time, the telling of lives in much Islamic biographical material does not present a series of events or cumulative reflections as contributing to character development. Rather, biographical entries serve to establish origins and display a person's type or example by presenting his or her discrete actions and sayings. The *ṭabaqāt* genre, which is most popular in Arabic, may focus on a certain religious profession, collecting, for example, the biographies of jurists, judges, Qur'ānic reciters and memorizers, or Ṣūfīs. Other *ṭabaqāt* chronicle individuals from a particular city or region, and some are "centennial" biographies that record all prominent Muslims who died in a particular Islamic century.

Tadhkirah means "memorial." These collections of the lives of poets, mystics, or scholars are more common in later periods, especially in Iran, the Ottoman Empire, and South Asia. *Tadhkirāt* are similar to *ṭabaqāt* in presenting lives through anecdotes, although they may also offer further narrative biographical material on the person. They do not necessarily incorporate ranking systems, although in the Persian context, generational, alphabetical, or other types of ordering by affinity or family relationship may be used. Both the *ṭabaqāt* and *tadhkirah* forms were also used for prominent persons in nonreligious fields, such as poets or calligraphers.

Malfūẓāt are records of audiences and the question-and-answer sessions of notable scholars or Ṣūfīs. These sessions may be presented chronologically and dated, rather like a dairy. This genre is indigenous to South Asian Islam, where the early Indian Ṣūfīs are known through records preserved in this form. Issues raised in the scholarly study of early *malfūẓāt* collections include the authenticity of these works and the principles of selectivity used by the compiler. *Malfūẓāt* often provide a more spontaneous, authentic impression of the subjects and their circles than do the more idealized portrayals of the *tadhkirāt*. Although their topoi are less obvious than those of more formally structured biographies, the *malfūẓāt* are a valuable source for their historical context and for information about teachings and attitudes—if not of the purported originator, at least of a subsequent but still early period.

Manāqib is the genre recording the merits and miraculous actions of sacred persons. Their emphasis on the miraculous as a source of authority means that the social and doctrinal context of the period shaped the presentation of saintly lives. For example, Muslim saints may be variously portrayed in these narratives as opposed to non-Muslim detractors, other saints, or doubting Muslims. At the same time, the types of miracles recounted reflect specifically Islamic symbols of the sacred. Thus a distinction is made between *karāmāt* (ways in which the saint confirms his high rank) and *barakāt* (blessings emanating from the saint), indicating refinements in the concept of saintly charisma. Notions of saintly hierarchy, territory, and patronage are often embedded in these texts.

Individual biographies *(tarjamah)* and autobiographies were less common in early periods, although a small number may be found. One should not neglect to mention the biographical significance of related genres—for example, travel accounts like those of the famous Ibn Baṭṭūṭah (d. 1368). Early Muslim autobiographies in Arabic were thoroughly studied by Franz Rosenthal (1937), who proposed that a Greek model had been transmitted to the Arabs through Ḥunayn ibn Isḥāq (d. 877). In the medieval period biographical or autobiographical notices were sometimes prefaced or appended to a scholar's works in the form of a curriculum vitae including the individuals' teachers, places visited, and works studied, transmitted, or composed. The *isnād*s or chains of transmission established through this or related material, such as *ijāzah*s (certificates that the holder had a teacher's permission to give instruction about a specific work or a general body of knowledge), have proved valuable sources in tracing Muslim scholarly networks for the transmission of ideas.

The subjects of religious biography include Sunnī and Shīʿī scholars, the early personages of Islam, and Ṣūfī saints. The concept of thc Prophct as a model for all Muslims is to a degree extended by the biographical tradition so that all learned and pious persons are potential exemplars and instantiators of the tradition. This is explicit in the idea of the *shajarah* or lineage tree, which may be scholarly or saintly as often as genealogical. Diagrams of these lineage relationships figure prominently in Ṣūfī biographical compendia and are frequently displayed in the form of posters on the walls of Ṣūfī lodges. They are also used performatively in the form of group recitations of the lineage.

The form of the collective biography was especially popular among the Ṣūfīs in the classical and premodern period; some of the best-known examples are ʿAṭṭār's (d. 1220) *Tadhkirat al-awliyā'*, Jāmī's (d. 1492) *Nafaḥāt al-uns*, and ʿAbd al-Ḥaqq Dihlavī's (d. 1642) *Akhbār al-akhyār*. These Ṣūfī compendia often memorialize Ṣūfīs of a particular order or region, but they were also appreciated as edifying moral literature by a wider public and were often abridged, imitated, and translated into regional languages.

The influence of the biographical genre in traditional settings was much broader than the presence of manuscripts or printed texts might indicate, because the lives of the saints and the prophets comprised a major category of folk literature and performance that sustained popular knowledge of Islam, especially in rural areas. In such settings bards, those with religious status, or any literate persons might perform aspects of biography for this wider audience.

Modern Developments. Western literature has increasingly influenced biographical and autobiographical writing in many Islamic societies. Most academic studies by scholars in Muslim societies who deal with contemporary biographical writing focus on works written under the influence of Western models rather than on the traditional forms.

In South Asia innovations in the tradition of religious biography were related to the development of Urdu as a modern prose language in the late nineteenth century and to the efforts to combine Islamic and modern learning embodied in the Aligarh movement. Most significant in this trend are the writings of Shiblī Nuʿmānī (1857–1914), who prepared a series of monographs on "Heroes of Islam" including studies of ʿUmar, Abū Ḥanīfah, Rūmī, and al-Ghazālī, as well as of the Prophet. This new style of biography was marked by critical evaluation and a rationalist treatment of the subject matter influenced by the biographical canons of European and in particular English literature.

While many of the traditional genres of religious biography still persist as the dominant forms in religious contexts and in more traditional segments of Muslim societies, in the modern period, a number of new developments have occurred. Among the most striking are the increasing use of religious biography for personal edification and its use to reinforce symbols of national or regional identity and to inspire or legitimate political action.

In the postcolonial period in Pakistan, for example, many medieval and premodern Persian compendia of saints' lives have been translated into Urdu, published, and widely distributed. In addition to reflecting the importance of saint-veneration among the majority of Pakistanis and the social and political importance of the Barelwī interpretation of Islam there, such publications may indicate the new role of the saints as symbols of Pakistani nationalism. Since many of these publications, from inexpensive chapbooks to gold-embossed tomes, are subsidized by the hereditary custodians of the various Ṣūfī shrines, additional motives for their publication and distribution seem to include the legitimization of the authority of the current shrine custodians and the affirmation of family and social linkages among affiliated groups of individuals. It is not unusual for a living Ṣūfī master or his immediate successor to publish lists of authorized deputies and prominent disciplines, a practice that suggests an additional social and economic basis behind the current production of biographical literature. Successive governments of Pakistan have also taken an interests in portraying popular saints' lives in such a way as to reinforce their specific policy objectives—for example, by distributing pamphlets or encouraging journalism that emphasizes biographical elements that confirm a particular saint as either an Islamic activist or a social reformer and populist.

In Shiism the lives of the imams have always been a source of inspired poetry and performances of commemoration. A recent significant trend in the use of biography was evident during the prerevolutionary period in Iran, when the focus of Ḥusayn's biography shifted from his role as tragic martyr to portraying him as an activist challenging an unjust social order. During the same period the biographical genre was strategically employed by the influential Iranian intellectual ʿAlī Sharīʿatī (d. 1977), who composed inspiring biographies of early Islamic figures such as Fāṭimah, Zaynab, ʿAlī, and Abū Dharr, in order to make the role models of the past more relevant to the younger generation. These biographies, which combined the use of traditional Islamic sources with a more Western existential focus, deliberately linked the events and challenges of the past to the problems facing contemporary Iranians.

Female biographies were featured even in the earliest *ṭabaqāt* compendia, where they were usually grouped in a separate section at the end of the collection. The modern period has seen increased attention given to the lives of early Muslim women in heroic roles. Bint al-Shāṭi' is an Egyptian woman religious writer who specializes in retelling the biographies of early Muslim heroines. Traditional Muslim scholars such as Ashraf ʿAlī Thānvī (1864–1943), Sayyid Sulaimān Nadvī in *Heroic Deeds of Muslim Women* (New Delhi, 1985), and Muḥammad Zakarīyā Kāndhalavī, *Stories of the Sahaabah* (Johannesburg, 1987) have presented early Muslim heroic women in ways that honor their contributions to Islamic history while reinforcing traditional patterns of female behavior. In contrast, the Moroccan feminist historian Fatima Mernissi has presented a revisionist look at the lives of a number of prominent early Muslim women that attempts to recover their independence of action and their defiance of supposed cultural norms. [*See the biography of Mernissi.*]

The importance of the biographical pattern is evidenced by the fact that today's Islamist leaders have begun to participate in the biographical and autobiographical tradition. Although one biographer of the reformer Abū al-ʿAlā Mawdūdī (d. 1979) explicitly eschewed the sanctification of his subject in his extensive study of Mawdūdī's life, the preexisting model of saintly lives has inevitably influenced many biographical treatments. Similar developments have occurred in both formal and informal Iranian tellings of Ayatollah Ruhollah Khomeini's story, which increasingly assimilate his role to that of the the Shīʿī imams. Zaynab al-Ghazālī, a contemporary Egyptian female activist in the Muslim Brotherhood, offered her prison memories in *Hayātī* (My Life) in the form of a heroic narrative with noticeable hagiographic undertones. [*See the biography of (Zaynab) al-Ghazālī.*]

As the forces of westernization have increasingly penetrated many Muslim societies,the canons of modern literature have tended to favor the novel, short story, and free verse over biographical forms. With the decline in the popularity of Sufism, the audience for collective memorials and devotional biographies has also decreased. In Turkey and the Arabic-speaking world the traditional Islamic biographical forms have declined in importance while secular, literary, and even English-language biographies are now being produced, albeit in relatively small numbers. Religious biography has adapted to these new circumstances in the ways discussed above.

[*See also* Muḥammad, *article on* Biographies; Sainthood; *and* Sufism, *article on* Ṣūfī Shrine Culture.]

BIBLIOGRAPHY

Auchterlonie, Paul. *Arabic Biographical Dictionaries*. Durham, N.C., 1987. Useful survey of the best known Arabic biographical dictionaries. Includes an annotated bibliography of classical works and relevant Western scholarship.

Eickelman, Dale F., and J. P. Piscatori, eds. *Muslim Travellers: Pilgrimage, Migration, and the Religious Imagination*. Berkeley and Los Angeles, 1990. Collection of recent scholarly articles.

Ewing, Katherine. "The Politics of Sufism: Redefining the Saints of Pakistan." *Journal of Asian Studies* 42.2 (February 1983): 251–268. Describes successive governments' use of Ṣūfī biography to legitimize policy.

Farīd al-Dīn ʿAṭṭār. *Muslim Saints and Mystics*. Translated by A. J. Arberry. Chicago, 1966.

Hafsi, Ibrahim. "Recherches sur le genre *Ṭabaqāt* dans la littérature arabe." *Arabica* 23 (1976): 227–265, and 24 (1977): 1–41. Review article of sources.

Hermansen, Marcia K. "Interdisciplinary Approaches to Islamic Biographical Materials." *Religion* 18.4 (1988): 163–182. Review article on biographical genres and critical scholarship, with an extensive bibliography.

Hermansen, Marcia K. "The Female Hero in the Islamic Religious Tradition." *Annual Review of Women in World Religions*, no. 2 (1992): 111–143. Material on traditional and recent treatments of heroines in religious literature and folklore.

Hoffman, Valerie J. "An Islamic Activist: Zaynab al-Ghazzali." In *Women and the Family in the Middle East*, edited by Elizabeth W. Fernea, pp. 233–254. Austin, 1985.

Kooij, C. "Bint al-Shāṭi': A Suitable Case for Biography." In *The Challenge of the Middle East*, edited by Ibrahim A. A. El-Sheikh et al., pp. 67–72. Amsterdam, 1982.

Lawrence, Bruce B. *Notes from a Distant Flute: Pre-Mughal Indian Sufi Literature*. Tehran, 1978.

Mernissi, Fatima. *Women and Islam*. Oxford, 1991. Revisionist look at the role of women in early Islamic history, by a Moroccan feminist.

Metcalf, Barbara D. *Perfecting Women: Maulana Ashraf ʿAlī Thanawi's Bihisti Zewar*. Berkeley, 1990.

Niẓāmuddīn Auliyā. *Nizam ad-Din Awliya: Morals for the Heart; Conversations of Shaykh Nizam ad-Dim Awliya Recorded by Amir Hasan Sijzi*. Translated and annotated by Bruce B. Lawrence. New York, 1992.

Roded, Ruth. *Women in Islamic Biographical Collections: From Ibn Saʿd to Who's Who*. Boulder, 1994. Roded surveys the historical development of the genre using both quantitative and qualitative approaches to assess women's roles in kinship, seclusion, and Islamic religious life.

Rosenthal, Franz. "Die Islamische Autobiographie." *Studia Arabica* 1 (1937): 1–40.

Zaidi, Mujahid Husain. "Biography in Modern Urdu Literature." *South Asian Digest of Regional Writing* (Heidelberg) 5 (1976): 99–120. Survey plus an extensive bibliography.

MARCIA K. HERMANSEN

BIRTH RITES. [*To articulate religious values and traditions reflected in birth rites in modern Islamic societies, this entry comprises two articles:* Legal Foundations *and* Modern Practice.]

Legal Foundations

Islam has relatively few birth rites compared to other Near Eastern religions, and those that exist are recommended *(sunnah)* rather than obligatory. Structurally, this may be accounted for by the Muslim belief that Islam is the natural religion *(dīn al-fiṭrah)*. As the *ḥadīth* says, "the child is born according to its nature; it is his parents who make him a Jew or Christian" (Ṣaḥīḥ Muslim, *Kitāb al-qadr*). Since humans are born Muslim, it makes sense that there is no need for a rite of initiation such as baptism or circumcision.

Works of piety are filled with supplications to be uttered during the act of conception, such as this *ḥadīth*. "If you intend to go to your wife, say: In the name of God, O God, protect us against Satan and keep Satan from the one you have beestowed upon us and if He has ordained a male child for them Satan will never be able to do any harm to him" (Ṣaḥīḥ Muslim, *Kitāb al-nikāḥ*). The pious are also enjoined to orient the marital bed toward the *qiblah* and the like.

The most notable birth rite attested in legal sources is the *ʿaqīqah,* a ritual substitution in which the child's hair is shaved on the seventh day, and money, gold, or silver is given to the poor of value equal to the weight of the hair. As part of the ritual complex an animal is sacrificed (one for a girl child, two for a boy), and the child is named. It is best to give a child a "good Muslim name" like Aḥmad or Muḥammad, or a name compounded with a name of God like ʿAbd al-Qādir, "bondsman of the Powerful-One"; but any name is acceptable as long as it is not heathenish, for example, ʿAbd Shams, "slave of the sun." At the time of the *ʿaqīqah* it is also recommended to speak the call to prayer in the child's right ear and the summons to prayer *(iqāmah)* in the left ear. The sacrifice should be of a one-year-old sheep or a two-year-old goat. The bones must not be broken even in cooking, and the meat is in part to be distributed to the poor. Also recommended is *taḥnīk,* a rite in which a parent or pious person of either sex chews dates until they are soft and puts them into the mouth of the newborn child.

Circumcision is quite significant from the popular perspective, but it receives relatively little space in legal texts. The schools range from regarding it as recommended for men, to obligatory; for women, the assessments range from "it is a kindness" to seeing it as obligatory. It is significant that the Shāfiʿī school, the school historically identified with Egypt, is most emphatic in requiring circumcision for both men and women. For most schools the matter is of less theoretical significance: thus one who converts to Islam and fears circumcision may forego it. For both men and women the ritual takes place between the age of one week and fifteen years, depending on local custom. In fact, it is local custom that determines the significance of the ritual, its timing, and the manner of its observance. Where it is observed as a rite of passage into manhood circumcision often involves parading the subject, dressing him elaborately (sometimes as a girl, to deflect the evil eye), and feasting. Female genital excision, surrounded by the taboos of female sexuality, is almost always performed with less fanfare. [*See* Circumcision; Clitoridectomy.]

Popular culture includes many other rituals connected with childhood and birth, but most of these have no foundation in normative Islamic sources. The announcement of the birth to the father is often the occasion for celebration and gift-giving. Special foods are cooked for the child and mother and the afterbirth and umbilical cord are often disposed of ceremonially.

[*See also* Rites of Passage.]

BIBLIOGRAPHY

Most legal works have a discussion of the *ʿaqīqah* ceremony in the section on sacrifice in the book on pilgrimage. If the book contains a discussion, it is usually in the section on purification preceding the section on ritual prayer.

Granqvist, Hilma. *Birth and Childhood among the Arabs*. Helsingfors, 1947.

Wensinck, A. J. "Khitān." In *Encyclopaedia of Islam,* new ed., vol. 5, pp. 20–22. Leiden, 1960–.

Zwemer, Samuel M. "The ʿAkika Sacrifice." *Moslem World* 6.3 (1916): 236–252.

A. KEVIN REINHART

Modern Practice

Rites surrounding birth operate at the interface of social, cultural, and religious systems. Muslim communities are not only aware of the formal doctrinal requisites of Islam at such a moment but are also particularly sensitive to family and kin values. Intersecting these are local cultural concerns, many of which operate in loose relationships to Muslim law and norms. Hence the birth of a child activates many of the intangibles that support a Muslim community.

The inadequacy of modern information on this topic probably reflects both a lack of sustained male interest and the paucity of women researchers. In addition, what is available concentrates on practices in specific countries or locales. Although scholarship is not yet able to give a comprehensive picture, enough is known to identify four critical areas that may roughly be called rites of proper production of children, rites of proper protection of birth, rites of validating the existence and personhood of the child, and rites of integrating the child into the Muslim community. Islamic norms impinge upon and sometimes specify these rites, even if outward practice may appear quite foreign to formal Islamic thought.

The Qur'ān is quite explicit that the creation of a human is an act of God (40.68–69, 22.6, 96.2–3); it follows that the entire process of bringing a child to be has sacred content. The primary reason for the sex act is procreation, and a traditional Muslim prayed before the critical first intercourse with his new bride. Among some Muslim men it still is the practice to say "Bismillāh" ("in God's name") upon ejaculation, expressing the hope and belief that the seed will be subject to God's overarching plan. An infertile woman in Brunei may seek out a *dukun* (indigenous practitioner of medicine) to recite *bacha-bacha* (potent Qur'ānic verses) while blowing upon her; a barren woman in Egypt may go on a pilgrimage to a saint's shrine and leave a note with an explicit vow should the saint successfully intercede for her. Modern Ismāʿīlī women having problems conceiving, including many residing in the West, seek to be present at a ceremony in which the Aga Khan gives a special fertility blessing. Moroccan women may visit the shrine of the *marabout,* leaving a piece of clothing as a binding vow. Once a woman is pregnant, a wide range of protections come into play, including special foods and satisfying the whims of the mother-to-be.

Perceived defilement must be remedied with ritual ablutions by both partners after intercourse and by a woman after her period. The origins of the notion of defilement are associated with the fall of Adam and Eve; Turkish villagers hold that menstruation is woman's curse for Eve's disobedience against God in the Garden, and blood, even the blood of birth, is the primary symbol of mortality. In Iran, as elsewhere, the potency of women's menses is such that it can cause a defect in another woman's unborn fetus.

A number of rites are performed at the end of pregnancy to ensure safe birth. South Asian Ismāʿīlī expectant mothers attend the *jamāʿatkhānah* between the seventh and eighth month for a special prayer by the *mukhi* (religious leader). In Marrakesh, there are rites of confinement, signaling that birth is vulnerable to evil; the mother and child remain in the same room for forty days lest crossing the threshold lead to an encounter with malevolent powers. Restoration of safety occurs only following the visit of the mother to an important saint's shrine. Egyptians customarily whisper the *adhān* (call to prayer) in the ear of the newborn child to thwart lingering negative influences. This is also the reason for painting kohl around the child's eyes. Villagers in Iran hold that a child may be born with the evil eye, in part because of astrological influences, so a range of incantations are utilized to free the child, including the names of the "Five" (Muḥammad, ʿAlī, Fāṭimah, Ḥasan, and Ḥusayn); such an incantation is held to be *ʿāṭil wa bāṭil* (offensive and defensive). In Lebanon about one-third of Sunnīs utilize incense or fumigation to dispel evil from a newborn infant; in the latter practice, incense obtained from a shaykh is thrown into an open fire, and the child is passed through the fumes three (or seven) times while an incantation or prayer is recited. Other villagers in Lebanon believe there are special powers attached to the placenta and do not cut the cord for twelve hours so that the child will not be weakened. In Syria, there is also significant use of amulets for protection, including tiny Qur'āns in pendants suspended around girls' necks. While some may contend that none of these practices are overtly Muslim, they are loosely allied with notions of the presence of the *jinn* and "evil envy" among humans noted in the Qur'an, surahs 113–114, or with the need to protect the newborn child from Satan.

Important rites establish the identity and position of the child in Muslim society. Some of these, like circumsion, are more properly community events; a few are designed specifically for the child. Ismāʿīlīs take the newborn to the *jamāʿatkhānah* for the official *bayʿah* ceremony, in which the child becomes a true member of the faith through swearing allegiance to the imam of the time. [*See* Bayʿah.] Naming rites are obviously significant for personal reasons, but they differ widely across the Muslim world in terms of complexity and emphasis. They usually take place when the child is officially registered, an act that is necessary so a child's kin relationships are firmly established under religious law.

From the standpoint of the community, the birth of a child is a positive, celebratory event, validating God's continued beneficence to believers. The first child is particularly important because it demonstrates the fertility of the mother. The Malay Muslims have a feast forty days after birth, with the mother and father dressed in finery and seated in state as at their wedding and the community joyously participating. In Aceh both husband and wife participate in visiting rituals before and after birth, while Muslims in Java carefully perform household food rituals on days governed by the thirty-five-day Javanese calendar after the child is born.

Sons are evidently preferred among heartland Muslims because they ensure the family's economic and genealogical continuity, but daughters are protected by Muslim law and can make marriage alliances that enhance the family's prestige. However, because they can endanger the family's honor through inappropriate sexual behavior, girls must be ritually protected, restricted, and trained. First sons are particularly admired; in Lebanon, such a son is called *ma'rūth* ("the treasured one").

Sexual distinctions are affirmed very early and are drawn with the shedding of blood: among the *fellahin* of Egypt, a ceremony of subincision for girls may take place before they reach the age of ten, while in modern Cairo, boys delivered in hospitals are circumcised within seven days. Traditionally, both these rites are community centered. In Egypt, with the birth of a boy, a ceremony called *ʿaqīqah* occurs within the forty-day period, involving shaving the boy's head, weighing, and giving gold or silver to charity. Community feasting is likely to include the killing of two lambs for a boy and one for a girl.

Men, except for physicians, take no part in the delivery of children; the process is exclusively a female responsibility. Usually older relatives assist midwives in the delivery. Children are swaddled throughout the Muslim world, and the child sleeps near the mother in her room. The Western practice of a separate nursery is held to run counter to the baby's need for close ties with its mother's body. The result is that women and children spend far longer in more intimate proximity, at least until the time of puberty, and this provides a close, secure environment that is a hallmark of the Muslim family and that has been held to be the direct result of Islamic notions of the proper structure of human society.

[*See also* Circumcision; Clitoridectomy; Names and Naming; Rites of Passage.]

BIBLIOGRAPHY

Classical understandings of birth rites are found throughout the *Encyclopaedia of Islam,* 4 vols. and supplement (Leiden, 1913–1938), along with the more recent edition (Leiden, 1960–). Dale F. Eickelman provides a general overview in "Rites of Passage," in *The Encyclopedia of Religion,* edited by Mircea Eliade, vol. 12, pp. 380–403 (New York, 1987), with bibliography. Material on human sexuality is found in Basim F. Musallam, *Sex and Society in Islam* (Cambridge, 1983). Also helpful is the section on Islamic societies in Erika Bourguignon et al., *A World of Women* (New York, 1980), especially Linda A. Kimball's "Women of Brunei" (pp. 43–56). The religious assumptions behind the pollutions of menses are explored in an important article by Carol Delaney, "Mortal Flow: Menstruation in Turkish Village Society," in *Blood Magic,* edited by Thomas Buckley and Alan Gottlieb, pp. 75–93 (Berkeley, 1988), and in the books she mentions throughout. A dramatic presentation of the different worlds of men and women is found in M. E. Combs-Schilling, *Sacred Performance: Islam, Sexuality, and Sacrifice* (New York, 1989). Two recent local studies are Linda A. Kimball, *Borneo Medicine: The Healing Art of Indigenous Brunei Malay Medicine* (Ann Arbor, 1979), and Judith R. Williams, *The Youth of Haouch el-Harimi: A Lebanese Village* (Cambridge, Mass., 1968). Bess Allen Donaldson, "The Evil Eye in Iran," and Jamal Karam Harfouche, "The Evil Eye and Infant Health in Lebanon," in *The Evil Eye: A Folklore Casebook,* edited by Alan Dundes, pp. 66–77 and 86–106 (New York, 1981), as well as Alexander Fodor, "The Evil Eye in Today's Egypt," *Folio Orientalia* 13 (1971): 51–65, provide material on birth and the evil eye. Also helpful are Edwin T. Prothro, *Child Rearing in the Lebanon* (Cambridge, Mass, 1961), and Hilma Granqvist, *Birth and Childhood among the Arabs* (Helsinki, 1947).

EARLE H. WAUGH

BLACK MUSLIMS. *See* Nation of Islam.

BLASPHEMY. *See* Kufr.

BOHRĀS. This Muslim community of Gujarat in western India traces its spiritual ancestry to early conversions to Ismāʿīlī Shiism during the reign of the Fāṭimid caliph-imam al-Mustanṣir (AH 427–487/1036–1094 CE). When schisms occurred in the Ismāʿīlī *daʿwah* (mission) in the eleventh and twelfth centuries in Egypt, the Ismā'īlīs in India followed the Fāṭimī Ṭayyibi *daʿwah* of Yemen. Subsequently, this community split a number of times to form the Jaʿfarī Bohrās, Dā'ūdī Bohrās, Sulaymāni Bohrās, ʿAlīyah Bohrās, and other lesser-known groups.

The word Bohrā (also spelled Boharā or Vohrā) is derived from the Gujarati *vohorvū* or *vyavahār,* meaning "to trade." This has sometimes caused Hindus, Jains, and Muslims of trading communities other than those related to the Ṭayyibi Ismāʿīlīs to list themselves on census forms as Bohrās. The early Hindu converts of the eleventh century comprised a single group of Ismāʿīlī Bohrās owing allegiance to the *dāʿī muṭlaq* in Yemen. A number of them seceded in 1426 to form the Jaʿfarī Bohrās, who adopted the Sunnī Ḥanafī school. The modern Jaʿfarī Bohrā community comprises mainly cultivators residing in Patan, Gujarat, who revere descendants of the sixteenth-century Sunnī missionary Aḥmad Jaʿfar al-Shīrāzī. After the Jaʿfarī schism, the Ismāʿīlī Bohrās were subject to severe persecution by local rulers. However, by the late sixteenth century, they had grown strong enough to enable the transfer of the mission's headquarters and the residence of the *dāʿī muṭlaq* to India. The *dāʿī muṭlaq* operates as the sole representative of the secluded Ismāʿīlī imam, and as such has had a great influence on the history, faith, and practices of the Ismāʿīlī Bohrās.

The term "Bohrā" applies most commonly to the

Dā'ūdī Bohrās, who are reputed to be the best organized and wealthiest of all Bohrās. The Dāū'dī Bohrā community has largely been molded into its present form by the two *dāʿīs* who have led the community in the twentieth century. The fifty-first *dāʿī*, the celebrated Ṭāhir Sayf al-Dīn (1915–1965), was an accomplished scholar, a prolific writer and poet, a capable organizer, and a man of vision. During his period of fifty years he revitalized the community, fostered strong faith, modernized the mission's organization, promoted welfare and education in the community, and guided it through the tumultuous period of world wars and independence of nations. A doctrinal dissent that had severely disturbed the community for sixty years prior to his accession was successfully challenged and reduced during his period to a less significant anti-*dāʿī* social reform movement. As much as 2 percent of the community belongs to this movement, whose demands are regarded as heretical by the rest of the Bohrās. The reformists were particularly active in the 1970s and early 1980s, but their efforts failed to win legal recognition and only amounted to bad press and distress for the Bohrā community.

The present *dāʿī*, Muḥammad Burhānuddīn, has continued his predecessor's endeavors with particular emphasis on strengthening the community's Islamic practices and on the promotion of its Fāṭimid heritage.

The religious hierarchy of the Dā'ūdī Bohrās is essentially Faṭimid and is headed by the *dāʿī muṭlaq* who is appointed by his predecessor in office. The *dāʿī* appoints two others to the subsidiary ranks of *ma'dhūn* (licentiate) and *mukāsir* (executor). These positions are followed by the rank of shaykh and mullah, both of which are held by hundreds of Bohrās. An *ʿahīl* (usually a graduate of the order's institution of higher learning, al-Jāmiʿah al-Sayfīyah) who leads the local congregation in religious, social, and communal affairs, is sent to each town where a sizable population exists. Such towns normally have a mosque and an adjoining *jamāʿatkhānah* (assembly hall) where socioreligious functions are held. The local organizations which manage these properties and administer the social and religious activities of the local Bohrās report directly to the central administration of the *dāʿī* based in Bombay, called al-Daʿwah al-Hādiyah.

At the age of puberty every Bohrā, or *mu'min* (believer) as sectarians call each other, pronounces the traditional oath of allegiance which requires the initiate to adhere to the *sharīʿah* and accept the leadership of the imam and the *dāʿī*. This oath is renewed each year on the 18th of Dhū al-Ḥijjāh (ʿId Gadīr al-Khumm). The Bohrās follow the Fāṭimid school of jurisprudence, which recognizes seven pillars of Islam. *Walāyah* (love and devotion) for Allāh, the Prophets, the imam, and the *dāʿī* is the first and most important of the seven pillars. The others are *ṭahārah* (purity and cleanliness), *ṣalāh* (prayers), *zakāh* (purifying religious dues), *ṣawm* (fasting), *ḥajj* (pilgrimage to Mecca), and *jihād* (holy war). Pilgrimages to the shrines of the saints are an important part of the devotional life of Bohrās, for the facilitation of which resthouses and assisting organizations have been set up. The martyrdom of Imam al-Ḥusayn is commemorated annually during the first ten days of Muḥarram. The Dā'ūdīs use an arabicized form of Gujarati, called *lisān al-daʿwah,* which is permeated with Arabic words and written in Arabic script. Another distinctive feature is their use of a Fāṭimid lunar calendar which fixes the number of days in each month. There is a strong religious learning tradition among the Dā'ūdī Bohrās, their *dāʿīs* usually being prolific writers and orators. The Dā'ūdī Bohrās number about a million and reside in India, Pakistan, the Middle East, East Africa (since the eighteenth century), and the West (since the 1950s). They are easily recognizable by their dress: men wear beards and white gold-rimmed caps, and women wear a colorful two-piece head-to-toe dress called a *ridā'*.

Dā'ūdī Bohrās are named after their twenty-seventh *dāʿī* Dā'ūd ibn Quṭbshāh (d. 1612). Sulaymānī Bohrās acknowledge a different line of *dāʿīs* ensuing from their twenty-seventh *dāʿī*, Sulaymān ibn Ḥasan (d. 1597). Similarly, ʿAlīyah Bohrās follow ʿAlī ibn Ibrāhīm (d. 1637) as their twenty-ninth *dāʿī* having seceded from the Dā'ūdīs in 1625. Neither have significant doctrinal differences with the Dā'ūdī Bohrās, though their religious organizations are different. The ʿAlīyah Bohrās are led by their forty-fourth *dāʿī*, Ṭayyib Ḍiyā' al-Daimin, residing in Baroda, India, and number about five thousand. The Sulaymānī leadership reverted to Yemen soon after the Dā'ūdī-Sulaymāni split and in the main has remained there. Their current leader, Sharaf al-Ḥusayn ibn Ḥasan al-Makramī, is the forty-ninth *dāʿī* in the Sulaymānī series; his chief representative in India, called the *manṣub,* resides in Baroda. The Sulaymānīs number about four thousand in India and about seventy thousand in the Yemenite region of Najran.

[*See also* Ismāʿīlīyah; Jāmiʿah al-Sayfīyah, al-; *and the biography of Burhānuddīn.*]

BIBLIOGRAPHY

Amiji, Hatim. "The Bohras of East Africa." *Journal of Religion in Africa* 7.1 (1975): 27–61.

Buhānpūri, Quṭb al-Dīn. *Muntazaʿ al-akhbār*. Vol. 2. N.p., 1884.

Burhānuddīn, Sayyidnā. *Istiftāh Zubad al-Maʿārif*. Bombay, 1965.

Constitutions. Governing local Dā'ūdī Bohrā organizations in India and East Africa, these documents provide a summary of their beliefs and practices.

Daftary, Farhad. *The Ismāʿīlīs*. Cambridge, 1992.

Davoodbhoy, T. A. A. *Faith of the Dawoodi Bohras*. Bombay, 1992.

Fyzee, Asaf A. A. "Bohorās." In *Encyclopaedia of Islam*, new ed., vol. 1, pp. 1254–1255. Leiden, 1960–.

Fyzee, Asaf A. A. *Compendium of Fatimid Law*. Simla, 1969.

Fyzee, Asaf A. A. *Outlines of Muhammadan Law*. 4th ed. Oxford, 1974.

Habibullah, Abdul Qaiyum. *Syedna Taher Saifuddin Saheb: Dai-ul-Mutlaq of Dawoodi Bohras*. Bombay, 1958.

Hodgson, Marshall G. S. "Dāʿī." In *Encyclopaedia of Islam*, new ed., vol. 2, pp. 97–98. Leiden, 1960–.

Hollister, J. N. *The Shiʿa of India*. London, 1953.

Jhaveri, K. M. "A Legendary History of the Bohoras." *Journal of the Bombay Branch of the Royal Asiatic Society* 9 (1933).

Jīvābhāi, Muḥammad ʿAlī ibn Mullā. *Mausam-i bahār*. Vol. 3. Bombay, 1882.

Khān, ʿAlī Muḥammad. *Mir'āt-i Aḥmadī*. Translated by S. N. ʿAlī. Baroda, 1924.

Khān, Najmulghanī. *Madhāhib al-Islām*. Lucknow, 1924.

Lokhandwalla, Sh. T. "The Bohras: A Muslim Community of Gujarat." *Studia Islamica* 3 (1955): 117–135.

Madelung, Wilferd. "Makramids." In *Encyclopaedia of Islam*, new ed., vol. 6, pp. 191–192. Leiden, 1960–.

Misra, S. C. *Muslim Communities in the Gujrat*. Bombay, 1964.

Najafʿalī, ʿAbbāsʿalī. *Law of Marriage Governing the Dawoodi Bohra Muslims*. Bombay, 1943.

Nuʿmān, Qāḍī al-. *Daʿā'im al-Islām*. 2 vols. Edited by Asaf A. A. Fyzee. 2d ed. Cairo, 1963–1965. The principle text of jurisprudence followed by the Bohrās.

Poonawala, Ismail K. *Bibliography of Ismāʿilī Literature*. Malibu, Calif., 1977.

Roy, Shibani. *The Dawoodi Bohras: An Anthropological Perspective*. Delhi, 1984.

Saifiyah Educational Trust. *A Golden Panorama*. Bombay, [1961].

Sayf al-Dīn, Ṭāhir. *Rasāʿil al-Ramaḍānīyah*. 48 vols. Bombay, 1912–1963. Along with Burhānuddīn above, the most authoritative exposition of the faith and practices of contemporary Dā'ūdī Bohrās.

Ṣaḥīfat al-Ṣalāt wa-al-ʿibādāt. Bombay, 1989. Dā'ūdī prayer book containing information on religious practices.

Walīd, ʿAlī ibn Muḥammad al-. *Tāj al-Aqā'id*. Thirteenth-century manuscript. An english summary by W. Ivanow titled "A Creed of the Fāṭimids" (Bombay, 1936) gives a good summary of the creed of the Bohrās.

MUSTAFA ABDULHUSSEIN

BOOK PUBLISHING. A distinction must be maintained between printing and publishing in Islamic countries, and Islamic printing and publishing. The former comprises Christian printing from the seventeenth century to our own day, publication of books on secular subjects such as textbooks, belles-lettres, and popular magazines, all of which trace their roots to eighteenth-century Istanbul and to the nineteenth-century press at Būlāq in Cairo. The latter, Islamic publishing, the subject of this article, developed in the middle to late nineteenth century. From modest beginnings it has grown to assume an overwhelming presence in today's publishing in the Middle East.

One of the reasons for the delay of Islamic printing was the traditional disdain of the religious establishment for the printing press. The famous İbrahim Müteferrika (c. 1674–1754), pioneer of printing in the Middle East, spent more than a decade trying to persuade the Ottoman sultan and his shaykhs that the printing press was not a danger to Islamic culture, but would instead lead to advances beneficial to the Ottoman state in confronting the European powers. In his treatise on printing of 1726 he argued that Muslims had been better at preserving their scripture than Christians or Jews, but books had been lost in political cataclysms such as the Mongol invasions and the expulsion from Spain. Printing had many advantages that would spread learning among Muslims: books would become cheaper and thus more widespread among the populace; they would be easier to read and more durable. The Ottoman sultan could take credit for introducing these benefits to Muslims, while eliminating from circulation the corrupt and ugly texts printed in Europe. The following year Müteferrika received permission to print on condition that he avoid works on religion, a stipulation he honored. This explicit restriction on the printing of religious works such as the Qur'ān, *ḥadīth*, and jurisprudence restrained Muslim printers and publishers for more than a hundred years.

Confident of their control of the infrastructure of traditional education, the shaykhs saw no reason to improve communication by means of the printing press. The Friday sermon, the *madrasah*, and the manuscript preserved the learned sciences and formed a vehicle for popular piety. It was a culture confident in itself, unselfconsciously Muslim, where new religious ideas such as those of Ibn Taymīyah (1263–1328) or Muḥammad ibn ʿAlī al-Sanūsī (1787–1859) percolated slowly via influential preachers or Ṣūfī conclaves to a largely illiterate populace.

In general, printing in the Islamic subjects did not

appear in the core Muslim region (the Ottoman Empire and Iran) in the core languages of Islam (Arabic, Persian, and Turkish) until the latter half of the nineteenth century. In Istanbul, Müteferrika and his immediate sucessors did not print any books in Islamic subjects. During the nineteenth century publishing in Istanbul retained its secular character, although there is evidence of an underground reaction to europeanization in the form of lithographed tracts against Western innovations such as the telegraph and the steamship.

In Egypt the case was not much different, in that the emphasis was on modern technical subjects, with history and belles-lettres also represented. Muḥammad ʿAlī Pasha (c. 1770–1849) founded his famous Būlāq Press in 1822. Virtually independent of Istanbul and a man of practical rather than theological inclination, Muḥammad ʿAlī used the press to further the goal of building a modern state capable holding both the European powers and the sultan at bay. The Būlāq printshop therefore concentrated on works of practical value during its heyday, 1822 to 1840. The press produced few books of Islamic content.

Iran is quite a different case. There the printing press was introduced, according to some scholars, as early as 1812 in the western city of Tabriz. Although the impetus to printing was largely secular, religious publishing began earlier than it had in Istanbul or Cairo. There is evidence that one Manūchihr Khān printed religious books in Tehran in the 1820s. *Zād al-maʿād*, a guide to prayer and ritual by the prolific seventeenth-century Shīʿī religious leader Muḥammad Bāqir al-Majlisī, was printed nearly twenty times during the nineteenth century in Tehran and Tabriz in Iran, and Lucknow in India. Nevertheless the publishing industry developed very slowly, even after the founding in 1851 of the first school employing the European curriculum, the Dār al-Funūn, or Institut Polytechnique. Textbooks, class notes and translations from European languages were required for this school, but the techniques and methods of printing afforded private persons the opportunity to produce books in a wide range of subjects, religious books among them. To be sure, the clergy constituted a large cadre of literate and influential persons. Slow to adopt the press as an instrument of propagating the faith, they had certainly become aware of its potentialities by the time of the Tobacco Rebellion of the 1890s. Although we understand little of what caused this transformation, we know that by the turn of the century religious works were the steadiest sellers in the country.

Exactly when printing turned into publishing in the region is difficult to say—first, because the distinction between the two activities is subtle, and second, because more research is needed on cultural life between 1860 and the turn of the century. Government printers seemed to have had no knack for getting what they printed into the hands of readers. In this sense none of the early government printshops were truly publishers. Publishing is above all the commerce in books, and successful publishers require a steady supply of titles from authors or from the stock of available classics, a mastery of production machinery and methods (i.e., printing), marketing, and the development of readership where none existed before.

The case of Egypt under ʿAbbās and Ismāʿīl may demonstrate the point. The climacteric between printing and true publishing seems to have occurred during the reigns of Khedive ʿAbbās (r. 1849–1854) and Khedive Saʿīd (r. 1854–1863). This was a turbulent era in Egyptian publishing. The Būlāq press, moribund during the last years of Muḥammad ʿAlī's reign, began to rely heavily on contract work. Moreover, rival presses both governmental and private competed for business. Individuals contracted with these presses to produce Turkish and Arabic religious and literary classics. By this time the clergy had abandoned their former reservations about printing. Numerous examples attest to their enterprise in investing in book production for moral and financial uplift. A best-seller of the time was *Badr al-munīr*, along with other works by the tenth century Shāfiʿī scholar ʿAbd al-Wahhab al-Shaʿranī; fourteen of his works were printed between 1858 and 1861, some privately and some at Būlāq under private contract. It was in this period too that the first attempts were made to print the Qur'ān, but this complex venture was doomed. Other books central to Islamic theology were printed: Bukhārī's *Ṣaḥīḥ* (1863), a canonical collection of the Prophet's sayings; Ibn al-ʿArabī's *Futūḥāt al-Makkīyah* (1857); and *Rūḥ al-bayān fī tafsīr al-Qurān*, a popular work by Ismāʿīl Ḥaqqī, an edition of which was published in 1859. The vitality of printing makes a comprehensive bibliography of what was printed very difficult. Adding to the problem was the introduction of the lithographic press around 1850. Because of this cheap printing technology, Egypt, Iran, and Turkey witnessed widespread popular religious publishing. These presses produced volumes on religious topics whose subject matter and crude format made them consumables, in contrast to the heftier tomes coming from the presses of the governments, which were sought after for permanent retention in libraries.

Modern publishing can be said to grow out of the desire of Muslims to propagate the faith where they saw the population was weak in its knowledge and practice of Islam. Regardless of when the turning point occurred, it resulted in an outpouring of books so broad in subject matter and so widespread geographically that it is impossible to review the phenomenon briefly. The distinction can be drawn between *turāth* (heritage) and *daʿwāh* (piety or propaganda). Publishers began to specialize in one or the other. Yūsuf al-Bustānī, a leading Cairo bookseller, in his catalog for 1934 displays few if any of the latter but a decided interest in the former. *Turāth* works are most often reprints of classic works in the Islamic sciences. Sometimes hot topics broke into print, such as Muṣṭafā al-Karīmī's polemical work of 1921 against the Wahhābīs, *Risālat al-Sunnīyīn.*

In succeeding years private publishers in Cairo and Beirut began publishing both kinds of books for the mass market. As literacy increased, profits could be made from the two kinds of Islamic literature. Egyptian publishers also prospered from their proximity to al-Azhar and its associated academies, turning out cheap editions of classics for use by students. Works in all branches of Islamic learning are kept in print and make up the stock at kiosks and colorful book markets in the al-Azhar quarter of Cairo. These editions are eagerly sought after in all Islamic countries.

Government publishing houses continue to issue in this field. Some publishers, such as Egypt's General Egyptian Book Organization, market their books through government bookshops or through private booksellers. Others, such as the ministries of culture or religious endowments in Oman, Morocco, and Iran, continue the time-honored practice of distributing their publications only to scholars and learned societies.

Of greater technological sophistication are the works of *turāth* reprinted at Beirut by publishers such as Dār al-Gharb al-Islāmī and Dār al-Jīl. The tragic war in Lebanon from 1975 to 1985 did little more than inconvenience these commercial publishers of Islamic reprints. A vast market in the Gulf and the Arabian Peninsula opened up for titles that had formerly been rare manuscript treasures or available only in long-out-of-print editions. These titles, many in multiple volumes—generally bound in imitation leather and adorned with gilt calligraphy—are familiar to anyone who has visited bookstores in any Muslim country, or Mideastern specialty stores in the United States and Europe.

Works of *daʿwāh* too have their specialist publishers and readership. This large category of works includes sophisticated intellectual commentary on spiritual and cultural life of Islam, such as works by the Egyptians Muḥammad al-Ghazālī and Muḥammad ʿAmmārah published by Dār al-Shurūq. This prominent publishing firm was founded in Cairo in 1961 by Muḥammad al-Muʿallim, a graduate of Cairo University's prestigious Dār al-ʿUlūm. At the outset the company was called Dār al-Qalam and was immediately profitable; its success caught the attention of authorities in the socialist administration of Gamal Abdel Nasser, who nationalized the firm. Al-Muʿallim directed the state-owned company for a short time, after which he invested in a new, independent publishing house which he named Dār al-Shurūq. He was imprisoned for a short period for his audacity. Upon his release he left Egypt for Beirut, where he continued to publish provocative Muslim writers such as Sayyid Quṭb, returning to Egypt after Nasser's death. Dār al-Shurūq now publishes in Egypt, Lebanon, and Saudi Arabia, bringing out books of *daʿwah* as well as *turāth.*

Today each Arab and Islamic country has its publishing houses for *turāth* and *daʿwah.* Each also has a selection of popular religious magazines and incorporates religious topics into general-interest periodicals. Examples range from *Majallat al-Azhar* (Journal of al-Azhar) in Egypt to political comment from an Islamic viewpoint in all the major Egyptian dailies. In Turkey religion once again is a popular subject, and a profitable one for publishers and booksellers. Works translated into modern Turkish from Arabic fill bookshops in Istanbul. Turkish Muslims now have access to the writings of the Egyptian Islamic martyr Sayyid Quṭb, while they are still waiting for translation of the Egyptian Nobel laureate Naguib Mahfouz.

Statistics on publication of religious books as a percentage of all publishing in Islamic countries are not available or usefully accurate, but it is unanimously agreed by publishers in the region that religious subjects have dominated trade publishing for the past fifteen years. It is no exaggeration to say that it is the income from their religious books that pulls many a publisher and bookseller into profitability.

Translation of classical books of the Islamic faith into English, as well as translation of didactic and pietistic works, has been a common recent development. Classics currently available in English include several translations of the Qur'ān along with commentaries by leading figures such as the late Abū al-Aʿlā Mawdūdī of Pakistan and the Egyptian preacher Muḥammad Mutawallī al-Shaʿrawī. Also available are selected works from the corpus of Islamic literature—the life of the Prophet, *ḥadīth*, principles of jurisprudence, and books to guide prayer, pilgrimage, and other rituals. These works are available thanks to the effort of Western Orientalists and Muslim scholars, principally from the Indian subcontinent. Works by Sayyid Quṭb and the Iranian teacher and writer ʿAlī Sharīʿatī, Muslim thinkers of the mid-twentieth century, once proscribed in their own countries and their authors martyred, are also available in English.

Finally, a review of Islamic publishing today must take account of video and audio publications. Muslim religious practice is documented in these relatively new formats. Documentary filmmakers have sought to portray the richness and variety of Muslim spiritual and cultural life from Southeast Asia to West Africa to English-speaking audiences. There is no doubt that these media can be highly effective; their role in transmitting Ayatollah Khomeini's message to his countrymen from exile has been widely noted. Similarly, Muslims are making use of cable television and small commercial and public-service channels in the United States. All this must be recognized as the newest form of what began modestly 150 years ago in small printshops.

[*See also* Children's Books and Cartoons; Communications Media; Newspapers and Magazines; Pamphlets and Tracts.]

BIBLIOGRAPHY

Aboussouan, Camille, ed. *Le livre et le Liban jusqu'à 1900*. Paris, 1982. Contains several essays on printing and publishing in Lebanon.

Albin, Michael W. "The Iranian Publishing Industry: A Preliminary Appraisal." *Libri* 36.1 (1986): 1–23.

Albin, Michael W. "The Survival of the Bulaq Press under Abbas and Said (1848–63)." *International Journal of Orientalist Librarians* 30–31 (1987): 11–17.

Berkes, Niyazi. *The Development of Secularism in Turkey*. Montreal, 1964. Treatment of Müteferrika and early Ottoman printing.

Faruqui, Jalees A. *Reading Habits in Pakistan*. Karachi, 1974. Unique empirical study in English on reading preferences.

Heyworth-Dunne, James. *An Introduction to the History of Education in Modern Egypt*. London, 1939. Covers the early years of modern education and printing; never superseded in English.

Peters, Rudolph. "Religious Attitudes towards Modernization in the Ottoman Empire: A Nineteenth-Century Pious Text on Steamships, Factories, and the Telegraph." *Die Welt des Islams* 26 (1986): 76–105.

Rypka, Jan. *History of Iranian Literature*. Dordrecht, 1968. Comprehensive history of Persian literature, with important coverage of printing and publishing.

"Maṭbaʿa" (Printing Press). In *Encyclopaedia of Islam*, new ed. vol. 6, pp. 794–807. Leiden, 1960–. Starting point for historical research on printing in Turkey, Iran, and the Arab countries.

Michael W. Albin

BORUJERDI, MOḤAMMAD ḤOSAYN (also rendered Muḥammad Ḥusayn Burūjirdī; 1875–1962), Iranian theologian and religious leader who by the time of his death became the sole source of emulation *(marjaʿ al-taqlīd)* for all Iranian Shīʿīs. Born in Borujerd (Burūjird) Province in western Iran, Ayatollah Borujerdi came from a family known for its religious learning and piety. At twelve he enrolled in Borujerd's *madrasah* (Islamic seminary), where his father, Sayyid ʿAlī Ṭabāṭabā'ī, was one of his main mentors. At eighteen he went to Isfahan to study jurisprudence and philosophy. In 1901 he left Isfahan for Najaf, where he studied with Ayatollah Muḥammad Kāẓim Khorāsāni and ʿAllāmah Muḥammad Kāẓim Yazdī. After ten years, he returned to Borujerd, where, apart from brief interruptions, he stayed for the next thirty-seven years. While in Borujerd, he taught jurisprudence and was *marjaʿ al-taqlīd* for the people of Khorasan and southwestern Iran. In 1945 he left Borujerd for Tehran to receive medical treatment, and, by invitation of the city of Qom's *ʿulamā'*, he settled there. Borujerdi's arrival at the Iranian center of Shīʿī learning filled the vacuum created by the death of two leading *ʿulamā'* of that city: Shaykh ʿAbd al-Karīm Ḥā'irī Yazdī and the chief source of emulation, Sayyid Abu al-Ḥasan al-Iṣfahānī. These events paved the way for Ayatollah Borujerdi's ascendence as the new *marjaʿ al-taqlīd* of Iranian Shīʿīs.

Because of his lack of political ambition and conservatism, Ayatollah Borujerdi maintained a quietist attitude toward politics, refraining from using his powerful position to mobilize his vast following. On several important occasions, however, Borujerdi abandoned his political quietism.

On his initiative, after the attempted assassination of the shah at Tehran University on 4 February 1949, a gathering of clergy in Fayẓīyah Madrasah in Qom passed a resolution calling on their colleagues to stay aloof from political involvement and partisan politics. While Mohammad Mossadegh, the nationalist leader, was in power (1951–1953), Borujerdi and Ayatollah

ʿAbd Allāh Bihbahāni opposed most of his policies, most notably the bill on female enfranchisement. Borujerdi agreed to mediate the conflict between Mossadegh and the shah in April 1953. Fearing a communist takeover, however, he tacitly supported the August coup of 1953 that brought the shah back to power, welcoming him on his return to Iran. Borujerdi was also prominent in the anti-Bahāʾī campaign of 1955. By accusing the Bahāʾīs of secret activities against the monarchy and state, Borujerdi elicited the support of the shah in the campaign. He called on the shah to purge Bahāʾīs from all government positions and to seize their assets in order to build more mosques and *madrasahs*. He instructed, however, that this should be done without the shedding of blood. He also issued a *fatwā* (religiously binding authoritative statement) to boycott the consumption of Pepsi Cola, because the Iranian franchise was owned by Sabet Pasal, a wealthy Bahāʾī. Borujerdi also opposed the government's 1959 land reform bill. This bill, among other things, affected religious endowments, diminishing the clergy's means of subsistance and their financial independence from the state.

Borujerdi's contribution to Shīʿī theology is primarily in the domain of *ḥadīth* (deeds and words attributed to the Prophet) and the reinvigoration of the practice of independent investigation. He also displayed interest in Sunnī-Shīʿī rapproachment and worked to establish closer ties with the Egyptian Sunnī *ʿulamāʾ* of al-Azhar.

BIBLIOGRAPHY

Akhavi, Shahrough. *Religion and Politics in Contemporary Iran: Clergy-State Relations in the Pahlavi Period*. Albany, N.Y., 1980. Provocative analysis of clergy-state relations in twentieth-century Iran.

Algar, Hamid. "The Oppositional Role of the Ulama in Twentieth-Century Iran." In *Scholars, Saints, and Sufis*, edited by Nikki R. Keddie, pp. 231–255. Berkeley, 1972. Good autobiographical essay on Iranian clergy in the twentieth century.

Keddie, Nikki R. *Roots of Revolution*. New Haven, 1981. Comprehensive historical study of religion and politics in Iran.

Rāzī, Muḥammad Sharīf. "Āyat Allāh Burūjirdī." In *Ganjīnah-ʾi Dānishmandān*. Tehran, 1973–. Provides some useful autobiographical information on the life of Borujerdi; in Persian.

MANOCHEHR DORRAJ

BOUHIRED, DJAMILA (b. 1937), Algerian Front de Libération Nationale (FLN; National Liberation Front) militant whose role in the 1957 Battle of Algiers gained her international notoriety as a symbol of resistance to French rule and of the more active role anticipated for women in independent Algeria. Through members of her family involved in the nationalist movement, Djamila Bouhired (Jamīlah Būḥrayd) came to the attention of Saadi Yacef, the FLN commander of the Algiers Qasbah. Yacef recruited her and other young Algerian women who could pass as Europeans when dressed in Western garb to plant bombs in cafés and other gathering places frequented by the French. The devastating bombings, which began in September 1956, sparked a concerted effort by the French army to round up FLN activists in Algiers. In April 1957, Bouhired was arrested and savagely tortured by French soldiers, but refused to divulge information about FLN leaders.

At her military trial in July, Bouhired acknowledged belonging to the FLN, but denied participating in the fatal bombing with which she was charged. In a trial marred by irregularities, Jacques Vergès, her French communist attorney, was denied access to essential documents and prohibited from making a final plea in her defense. The most incriminating testimony came from a woman accused of planting bombs with Bouhired, despite the fact that her behavior showed clear signs of mental instability. Bouhired was found guilty and sentenced to death. Yacef ordered a new round of bombings and threatened to engulf the city in violence if the sentence were carried out, but the French had been systematically uncovering FLN cells in Algiers, and he was captured in August.

Outraged by both the conduct of the trial and the increasingly commonplace resort to torture by the authorities, Vergès and fellow communist Georges Arnaud published a pamphlet entitled *Pour Djamila Bouhired*. Her case became a *cause célèbre* as French leftists, and many others distressed by the dehumanizing aspects of the Algerian conflict, organized rallies on her behalf, as did FLN sympathizers elsewhere in Europe. Bouhired's story was also widely publicized throughout the Arab world, where she was portrayed as a heroine of the revolution and a symbol of Algerian women.

The demonstrations reached a crescendo in March 1958, with the termination of the appeals process. Under considerable international pressure, and with the FLN threatening to reopen its bombing campaign if Bouhired were executed, French president Coty commuted her sentence to life imprisonment. She was transferred to France and remained incarcerated until the war's end.

Thereafter, she married Vergès and ran unsuccessfully for a seat in Algeria's first National Assembly. With her husband and Zohra Drif (another of Yacef's former agents), she edited *Révolution africaine* until a purge of communists forced them from their positions in 1963. She subsequently divorced Vergès and pursued an entrepreneurial venture in Algiers, but did not return to public life. Bouhired's opportunity to follow a nontraditional lifestyle and choose a career option not generally open to women before the revolution was, however, more closely related to her own personality than to any genuine change in the status of Algerian women, few of whom experienced any significant improvement in their socioeconomic status with independence.

[*See also* Algeria.]

BIBLIOGRAPHY

Arnaud, Georges, and Jacques Vergès. *Pour Djamila Bouhired*. Paris, 1958. Important primary source, but this impassioned account of Bouhired's case is no longer readily available.

Courrière, Yves. *Les temps des léopards*. Paris, 1969. This book, one in a four-volume study of the Algerian War, provides useful and detailed background information on the Battle of Algiers.

Horne, Alistair. *A Savage War of Peace: Algeria, 1954–1962*. Rev. ed. New York, 1987. The best account in English of the Algerian War, with several pages devoted to Bouhired.

"Jamilah Buhrayd." In *Middle Eastern Muslim Women Speak*, edited by Elizabeth W. Fernea and Basima Qattan Bezirgan, pp. 251–262. Austin, 1977. Two interviews with Bouhired conducted by Lebanese journalists in 1971.

Lebjaoui, Mohamed. *Bataille d'Alger, ou, bataille d'Algérie?* Paris, 1972. Struggle for control of Algiers from the perspective of an FLN militant.

KENNETH J. PERKINS

BRAZIL The history of Islam in Brazil begins in Portugal, which conquered and colonized Brazil from 1500 to 1822. Colonial customs such as the seclusion of women and their wearing of the veil have been traced to Muslim influence in Portugal. However, a deepseated anti-Muslim sentiment was expressed by the Portuguese crown in its determination to bar descendants of Muslims from filling posts of authority either at home or in its colonies. Moors—like Jews, Indians, and blacks—were considered an "infectious race." The Inquisition persecuted Islam as well as Judaism and other non-Christian beliefs, although there is no record of the arrest of Muslims in Brazil.

The first important Muslim migration to Brazil originated not in the Mediterranean but in tropical Africa. These Muslim Africans were probably islamized Mandinka slaves, brought to Brazil in small numbers over the sixteenth to eighteenth century. Very little is known about their religious practices beyond the fact that they gave name to the famous *bolsas de mandinga* (Mandinka pouches or amulets). The great wave of African Muslims came in the first half of the nineteenth century. They were primarily Hausas and Yorubas and less frequently Bornus, Nupes, and Fulanis brought as slaves to work in mines, on cotton and coffee plantations, in cities, and above all on sugar plantations. Historians have estimated that at least 354,100 slaves, including a significant number of Muslims, were imported from the Bight of Benin between 1791 and 1850. Most had been taken prisoner during political and religious conflicts within present-day Nigeria, including successive revolts that led to the demise of the Yoruba empire of Oyo and the *jihād* initiated by Usuman Dan Fodio in 1804, followed by Islamic expansion into Yorubaland.

In Brazil, Muslim slaves were initially known by the Hausa term *musulmi* and later by the more popular Yoruba term *imale* or *malê*, indicative of the greater number of Yoruba in the Muslim community in the 1820s and 1830s. These slaves' religious culture became interwoven with their political history. They remain known for their involvement in a series of more than twenty revolts in Bahia, then a sugar-producing province in northeastern Brazil that received the majority of Muslim slaves.

In 1814 slave fishermen from whaling warehouses on the coast revolted with the help of runaway slaves and freedmen from the Bahian capital city Salvador. More than two hundred men set fire to nets and warehouses, attacked a nearby village, and tried to reach the plantation area, killing more than fifty people before being overpowered by troops. The rebel ranks were overwhelmingly Hausa but included a few Nupe, Bornu and Yoruba. Their principal leader, a man called João, was described as "*malomi* or priest", the term *malomi* being certainly derived from *malam*, a Hausa word for a Muslim priest. The Muslim contribution to the episode is confirmed by confiscated papers written in Arabic.

A more serious episode occurred on 25 January 1835, the so-called "Malê revolt." For nearly four hours, about five hundred African rebels fought in the streets of Salvador. They were mostly Yoruba and Hausa slaves and freedmen, who paid bitterly for their actions, receiving punishments that varied from the death penalty to whippings and hard labor.

The movement was led by Muslim preachers, most of them elders who had promised to protect their followers with Islamic amulets. Although there is no reason to believe they sought to establish an Islamic state or saw the movement as a *jihād* of the sword, the uprising did not lack a ritual dimension. For instance, it was planned to occur at the end of Ramaḍān, probably after the *Laylat al-Qadr* festival of AH 1250 (25 January 1835). The trial that followed revealed, through the testimony of participants, a network of Muslim practices: the celebration of Muslim holy days, daily prayers, the observance of food and sexual taboos, initiation rites, Qur'ānic reading meetings, the teaching of the Arabic language, and the making of Muslim clothes and amulets. There is evidence that a strong process of conversion to Islam was under way at the time of the rebellion, particularly among Yoruba slaves and freedmen.

The brutal repression disrupted and dispersed the Muslim community. Hundreds of freedmen were deported back to Africa, and others willingly crossed the Atlantic to avoid continued police violence and ethnic discrimination; numerous slaves were separated and sold south to coffee plantations. Any blacks found with Muslim writings were immediately viewed as suspect. Following the abolition of slavery in 1888, in Bahia and elsewhere in Brazil, Muslim ex-slaves could still be found as isolated practioners of their faith; some of them became famous for making amulets, which they sold to a clientèle immersed in magical beliefs. But beyond this, Islam was unable to penetrate the African-Brazilian community, who developed a syncretism of Catholicism and African ethnic religions.

As the last African Muslims were disappearing at the turn of the century, Middle Eastern Muslims were arriving to Brazil in small numbers along with Christian immigrants from the Ottoman territories of Syria and Lebanon. Today, however, the great majority of Muslims in Brazil are descendants of Sunnī Muslims who left Lebanon after World War II. Mostly engaged in commerce, some two hundred thousand (estimates vary widely) are concentrated in the greater São Paulo area, the economic heart of Brazil, where they continue to follow Muslim ways through mosques, Islamic centers, periodicals, and social clubs.

[See also Islam, *article on* Islam in the Americas.]

BIBLIOGRAPHY

Kent, Raymond. "African Revolt in Bahia, 24–25 January 1835." *Journal of Social History* 3.4 (1970): 334–356.

Nina Rodrigues, Raimundo. *Os africanos no Brasil.* 4th ed. São Paulo, 1976.

Reis, João José. *Slave Rebellion in Brazil: The Muslim Uprising of 1835 in Bahia.* Translated by Arthur Brakel. Baltimore, 1993.

JOÃO JOSÉ REIS

BRUNEI. Islam is the national religion of the tiny but oil-rich sultanate of Brunei on the northwest coast of Borneo. An estimated 65 percent of the population of about 230,000 is Muslim, virtually all Sunnīs of the Shāfiʿī school, with most of these being Brunei Malays (55 percent of the population). Most of the other Muslims are traditionally Muslim Kedayans, converted members of small indigenous tribal groups, and converts from among Chinese immigrants (the second largest ethnic group with about 25 percent of the population).

Brunei Malays adopted Islam during the fifteenth century, or possibly as early as the fourteenth, after one of their leaders was installed as sultan (according to oral traditions) by the sultan of Johore. As head of the faith, the sultan has always been responsible for upholding the Islamic way of life, but he has traditionally delegated this responsibility to appointed nonnoble officials.

Islam provided a unifying theocratic and political base that allowed Brunei, a trading center for jungle produce, to attain the status of empire during the sixteenth century. However, internal dissension and European encroachment led to disintegration, and Brunei probably would have disappeared entirely had not the British taken it on as a protectorate in 1888. In 1906 Brunei yielded control of internal affairs to a British Resident, with the sultan retaining responsibility only for matters related to Islam.

During the nineteenth century and through the mid-twentieth, the status and institutions of Islam continued to reflect traditions broadly shared with the sultanates of the Malay Peninsula. The available literature on this period contains little to suggest that there were any significant movements or events focusing on Islam. Brunei was truly a backwater, untouched by the religious controversies that occasionally flared elsewhere in the region. The British accepted Islam as the established way of life, while most Bruneians respected the British as akin to saviors of their country.

The situation began to change after World War II. The British promoted experimentation with democracy even as control of internal affairs was returned to the sultan with the adoption of the constitution of 1959. The socialist Brunei People's Party (BPP) emerged as dominant by playing on the disaffections of commoners over the hereditary privileges of the nobility and by proposing Brunei as the power center of a new Pan-Islamic state that would recover territories in Borneo lost to private British interests during the nineteenth century. The BPP was never allowed a share of power and staged a short-lived rebellion in 1962, which proved so traumatic to the ruling elite that they reversed course on democracy. Revenues from oil exports, which began during the 1930s, were fortuitously climbing, allowing the late Sultan Sir Omar Ali Saifuddin to address the disaffection of his poorer subjects through an extensive social welfare system and the promotion of Islam. He built one of Asia's largest mosques, greatly expanded the Department of Religious Affairs established in 1954, and subsidized performance of the *ḥajj* to make it the norm rather than the exception for Brunei Malays.

Sultan Omar abdicated in favor of his eldest son Hassanal Bolkiah (the twenty-ninth sultan) in 1967, but he remained the power behind the throne until his son began asserting himself in the early 1980s. The resulting power struggle between them was often played out along religious lines, reflecting a rift within the royal family and the government between what have been called "ideologues" who want a theocratic Islamic state and "pragmatists" who are secularly oriented and open to Western values.

Sir Omar, who died in 1986, was allied with the ideologues, many of whom attended Cairo's al-Azhar University and hold top positions in the Ministry of Religious Affairs and the Ministry of Education (a ministerial form of government was introduced at full independence from Britain in 1984). Sultan and Prime Minister Hassanal, who often warns of the dangers of religious extremism, is considered a pragmatist. Yet, to the dismay of many pragmatists, he has promulgated the concept of Malay Islamic monarchy as a national ideology that would entrench what the pragmatists see as an anachronistic system of governance. Some believe the Islamic monarchy is meant to preclude demands for an Islamic theocracy by mollifying the ideologues and keeping the general populace focused on religion rather than politics. The most prominent pragmatists are Western educated and tend to come from wealthier, higher-ranking sectors of the nobility, which strongly suggests that the social class tensions underlying the 1962 rebellion remain unresolved and that the place of Islam in Brunei society will continue to be contested for some time.

[*See also* Islam, *article on* Islam in Southeast Asia and the Pacific.]

BIBLIOGRAPHY

Bartholomew, James. *The Richest Man in the World: The Sultan of Brunei*. London, 1989. Biography includes discussion of how Sultan Hassanal Bolkiah has grappled with the sultanate's most critical political issue: the relationship of Islam to government and society.

Brown, Donald E. *Brunei: The Structure and History of a Bornean Malay Sultanate*. Bandar Seri Begawan, 1970. In-depth study of historical influences underlying the structure of modern Brunei Malay society.

Leake, David. *Brunei: The Modern Southeast-Asian Islamic Sultanate*. Jefferson, N.C., 1989. The only comprehensive overview of Brunei's history and current society.

Singh, D. S. Ranjit. *Brunei, 1839–1983: The Problems of Political Survival*. Oxford, 1984. Describes how Brunei sultans have used international diplomacy to maintain the sultanate as a distinct entity.

Tarling, Nicholas. *Britain, the Brookes, and Brunei*. Kuala Lumpur, 1971. Highly detailed treatise on early British involvement in northern Borneo; Islam was rarely a contentious issue.

Weaver, Mary Anne. "In the Sultan's Palace." *The New Yorker* (7 October 1991): 56, 63–78, 80–86, 88–90, 92–93. Author's conversations with Bruncians and officials up through the sultan provide rare insights into the ongoing rift between Islamic "ideologues" and "pragmatists."

DAVID LEAKE, JR.

BUKHARA KHANATE. This important Central Asian state existed for nearly four centuries until 1920. It had its roots in the conquest of Ma Warā' al-Nahr (Mawarannahr, Transoxiana) by the Uzbeks under Muḥammad Shaybānī Khān around 1500. Ousting the Timurid dynasts from Central Asia, the Uzbeks initially formed a decentralized polity based in several cities (the most important being Bukhara, Samarkand, Tashkent, and Balkh), dominated by a ruling clan descended from Chinggis Khan and by chieftains of the still nomadic Uzbek tribes. By the second half of the sixteenth century, Bukhara had emerged as the effective "capital" of a more centralized state, and while the Shaybānid dynasty soon gave way to a collateral Chinggisid lineage (the Jānid or Ashtarkhānid house), Bukhara retained its central status through the political and economic decline that plagued Central Asia into the eighteenth century. By the middle of that century, the steady rise in the power of the tribal aristocracy, at the expense of the khans' authority, that had characterized the entire Ashtarkhānid era culminated in the killing of the last Chinggisid khan and his replacement by Muḥammad Raḥīm, chief of the Uzbek Manghït tribe. The Manghït dynasty ruled Bukhara until the khanate's transformation into a Soviet puppet state in 1920.

The founder's grandson Shāh Murād (r. 1785–1800) expanded his realm at the expense of Iran and Afghanistan; internally his reign brought a restructuring of the khanate's central bureaucracy and provincial administration. Preferring the title *amīr* over that of *khan,* he and his son Ḥaydar (1800–1826) cultivated the support of the urban population and the *ʿulamāʾ* in an effort to curtail the power of the Uzbek tribal aristocracy and forge a centralized state; it was left to Ḥaydar's son Naṣr Allāh (1827–1860) to crush virtually all potential challenges to his authoritarian rule. Naṣr Allāh also reorganized the Bukharan army to reduce his dependence on tribal levies, but his attempts at military expansion were generally unsuccessful, with virtually constant warfare against the khanate of Khoqand weakening both states on the eve of the Russian advance.

Under Naṣr Allāh's son and successor Muẓaffar (1860–1885), longstanding commercial and diplomatic ties with Russia gave way to armed conflict as Russian troops, soon after their conquest of Tashkent in 1865, engaged Bukharan forces. A string of defeats induced the Amīr to sign a treaty with Russia in June 1868, ceding the region of Samarkand to direct Russian rule but retaining formal sovereignty as a vassal of the Russian tsar within the remainder of the khanate. Russian domination brought few changes under Muẓaffar, but under his son ʿAbd al-Aḥad (1885–1910) the completion of a rail line through the khanate in 1887 led to increased Russian influence in Bukhara's internal economic, social, and political development.

Both ʿAbd al-Aḥad and his son Sayyid ʿĀlim (1910–1920) effectively suppressed internal opposition in the form of liberal reformist circles inspired by Western political and social thought. Following the Bolshevik revolution of 1917, however, Bukharan reformists who had fled the khanate turned for support to Soviet officials in Tashkent, for whom the Bukharans provided the "internal" revolutionary legitimation for the seizure of Bukhara by Soviet troops in September 1920. The amīr fled, and from then until 1924 the former khanate existed as the Bukharan People's Soviet Republic; this was dissolved in the "national delimitation" of Central Asia in 1924, with most of its territory allotted to the new Soviet republic of Uzbekistan.

[*See also* Islam, *article on* Islam in Central Asia and the Caucasus; Khan; *and* Uzbekistan.]

BIBLIOGRAPHY

Allworth, Edward, ed. *Central Asia: 120 Years of Russian Rule.* Durham, N.C., 1989. Rev. ed. of *Central Asia: A Century of Russian Rule.* New York, 1967. Well-balanced collection of chapters covering all of Central Asia and both Tsarist and Soviet eras, but useful for political and cultural history of Bukhara since the Russian conquest.

Becker, Seymour. *Russia's Protectorates in Central Asia: Bukhara and Khiva, 1865–1924.* Cambridge, Mass., 1968. Still the best general history of the two khanates that "survived" the Russian conquest, down to their incorporation into the Soviet state; like all available surveys, however, it is based almost exclusively on Russian sources, ignoring indigenous Persian and Turkic works.

Carrère d'Encausse, Hélène. *Islam and the Russian Empire: Reform and Revolution in Central Asia* (1966). Translated by Quintin Hoare. Berkeley, 1988. Fine study focused on the reform-minded *Jadīdī* and their cultural and political agenda, but with minimal attention to economic and political issues affecting those outside the modernist elites.

Holdsworth, Mary. *Turkestan in the Nineteenth Century: A Brief History of the Khanates of Bukhara, Kokand and Khiva.* Oxford, 1959. Short survey, but one of the few English-language treatments of the khanates' political, economic, and cultural development before the Russian conquest.

DEVIN DEWEESE

BUNYĀD. *Dehkhoda's Dictionary of Persian Vocabularies* defines the term *bunyād* as "base, root, origin, and foundation." In this article, *bunyād* refers to a certain type of grassroots, putatively nonprofit institutions that were organized for particular purposes after the Iranian Revolution in 1979. A few *bunyād*s antedated the revolution but never acquired the immense size or social significance that postrevolutionary *bunyād*s accumulated. Although all claim nonprofit status, some certainly make money. Most also engage in functions such as trade, manufacturing, banking, and social services. Some also function as vehicles for patronage, mass mobilization, ideological indoctrination, and even repression. Three types of *bunyād* exist in contemporary Iran: public, private and *waqf* (endowment). They are basically unregulated, exempt from taxes, and organized into an elaborate network of functional and spatial offices.

Endowment *bunyād*s, which were in fashion before the revolution, have hardly grown in number or importance since. Bunyād-i Āstān-i Quds (The Eighth Imam

Foundation), formed decades ago, is among the country's largest *bunyāds*; it owns and controls an immense amount and variety of properties, ranging from land, hotels, and trading companies to industries and social service delivery centers. It also employs several thousand people and sponsors many poor families. Although no definite figure exists for its annual budget, it may be close to $2 billion. A significant part of the organization's financial resources is drawn from daily cash vows donated by pilgrims to the tomb of the Eighth Imam.

The other two important *bunyāds* of the endowment type are Bunyād-i Pānzdah-i Khurdād (The Fifteenth of Khurdad Foundation) and the Mu'assasah-yi Nashr-i Āṣār-i Haẕrat-i Imām Khumaynī (Institute for Publication and Distribution of the Grand Imam Khomeini's Writings). Both these institutions were established after the revolution, the first immediately following it in memory of the 1963 uprising led by the late Ayatollah Ruhollah Khomeini (d. 1989), and the second after Khomeini's death to propagate his teachings. They also supervise Khomeini's mausoleum in a Tehran suburb. Bunyād-i Pānzdah-i Khurdād has offered more than $2 million in bounty to anyone who kills Salman Rushdie, the author of *The Satanic Verses* [*see* Rushdie Affair]. It had 805,722 families under its tutelage in 1991, including the poor and the households of martyrs, the disabled, POWs, and MIAs.

Private *bunyāds* were established by various factions within or outside the Islamic ruling elite. Allegedly they are nonprofit organizations, but they make money. Some have become major economic institutions, such as Sāzman-i Iqtiṣad-i Islāmī (Islamic Economic Organization), Bunyād-i Jāvid (Eternal Foundation), Bunyād-i Rajā' (Foundation for Growth of Islamic Republic), Bunyād-i Rafāh (Welfare Foundation), Bunyād-i Taʿāvun (Coop Foundation). To give an indication of their size, in 1987, the loanable fund of the Sāzman-i Iqtiṣad-i Islāmī stood at 50 billion Iranian rials, roughly equal to 5 percent of the country's total liquidity.

Other private *bunyāds* are involved in controlling cultural matters such as cinemas. Examples include Bunyād-i Fārābī (Farabi Foundation) and Sāzman-i Tablīghāt-i Islāmī (Organization for Islamic Propagation). Many also support electoral candidates with money and propaganda, control important economic and extraeconomic institutions, and publish newspapers, magazines, books, and occasional reports. Principal among these is Bunyād-i Risālat (Foundation for Prophetic Mission), which publishes the economically conservative daily *Risālat*. Relationships between these private institutions and the government has not always been easy, and some, including the Sāzman-i Iqtiṣād-i Islāmī and the now defunct Nubūvat Foundation (Prophetic Foundation), have been charged with corruption, misuse of public funds, and interference with government policies.

Public *bunyāds* were established by the Islamic Republic in the first few years of its existence. In theory, these are separate and independent entities; in reality, however, they are mainly dependent on the government, and this dependency has increased over time as popular material support for them has declined. They were allocated some 20,000 million rials from the public budget in 1980, the figure increased to 230,000 million rials by 1987. A few *bunyāds* came into being to replace institutions of the previous regime or to honor certain individuals. Examples include Bunyād-i ʿAlavī, which replaced Bunyād-i Pahlavī (Pahlavi Foundation), and Bunyād-i Shahīd Chamrān (Martyr Chamran's Foundation).

Most public *bunyāds*, however, were established to act as executive arms of the new regime in areas of special social and economic concern to the Islamic government. Sometimes, however, they have duplicated the work of the more traditional ministries or institutions. These include Bunyād-i Shahīd (Martyr's Foundation), originally established to look after the families of the martyrs of the revolution, and Bunyād-i Mustaẕʿafān (Foundation for the Oppressed), formed to assist the poor. More will be said about these two very important *bunyāds* below. The Bunyād-i Maskan-i Inqilāb-i Islāmī (Housing Foundation of the Islamic Revolution) was established on 26 May 1979 to provide housing for the poor, particularly in rural areas; its initial funding came from the previously established Account Number 100 of Imam (Khomeini), among other private donations.

Jihād-i Sāzandigī (Reconstruction Crusade), which is now a ministry, was originally established by a group of Muslim university students on 17 June 1979 to undertake grassroots development projects in rural areas. Bunyād-i Umūr Muhājirīn-i Jang-e Taḥmīlī (Foundation for the Affairs of the Imposed War Migrants) was organized on 4 June 1979 to assist war-afflicted families and areas damaged in Iran-Iraq war. In 1982, some 120,162 families, or about 40 percent of all war-afflicted households, were under the care of this *bunyād*. Finally,

Kūmītah-i Imdād-i Imām Khumaynī (Imam Khomeini's Relief Committee) was formed immediately following the revolution to help disadvantaged people. By 1991, this organization had brought some 994,000 needy people and 309,300 students under its care.

Public *bunyāds* have been established using primarily the expropriated properties of wealthy Iranians who had supposedly acquired their wealth illegitimately by cooperating with the shah. Although they were initially organized as nonprofit public institutions, over time some have become profit-oriented and are becoming increasingly removed from government control. Nevertheless, they continue to receive funds from the public budget, and their leadership is appointed by the president and confirmed by the spiritual leader of the Islamic regime.

As governmental organizations have become institutionalized, some *bunyāds* have also changed their form and structure. More specifically, a process of "ministerialization" and integration has gradually occurred. Thus, the Revolutionary Guards Corp and the Reconstruction Crusade have both become ministries; Bunyād-i Umūr-i Muhājirīn-i Jang-i Taḥmīlī has joined the Ministry of Labor; the Jihād-i Savād Āmūzī (Mobilization for Literacy) has become part of the Ministry of Education; and the Kūmītah-i Inqilāb-i Islāmī (Islamic Revolution Committee) has been integrated with the regular police force. Meanwhile, a process of "fiefdomization" has brought certain *bunyāds* under control of given families, restricting their effectiveness.

To provide a more focused analysis of postrevolutionary *bunyāds* the remainder of this article will focus on Bunyād-i Mustaẕʿafān and Bunyād-i Shahīd. On 1 March 1979, Ayatollah Khomeini issued a decree confiscating properties of the shah, his family, and their associates. Two days later the Bunyād-i Mustaẕʿafān was formed to consolidate, control, and manage the confiscated wealth in the interests of the poor, especially their housing conditions. The magnitude and value of the confiscated assets are not precisely known. In 1982, the organization controlled a total of 3,423 economic units, of which 1,049 were industrial, mineral, agricultural, commercial, development and construction related, and cultural; and 2,786 were real estate and housing units. Only a year later, during an interview with the daily newspaper *Kayhān* on 21 November 1983, the organization's director claimed that "the organization is one of the largest conglomerates in the world and the largest Islamic entity in Iran."

According to its 1986 annual report the foundation employed 42,095 people and produced 136.7 billion rials worth of goods and services, equal to 14.1 percent of total production by large industrial units in the country. At the time, the *bunyād* also controlled 113 large industrial units. By 1990, its activities and economic capabilities had significantly grown. In an interview with *Kayhān*, Mohsen Rafiqdust, the present director of the foundation, revealed that it was planning to build an oil refinery, construct 5,000 low-cost houses for the urban poor in Tehran, and import large quantities of steel. Currently, the *bunyād* is the sole official representative of Mercedes, BMW, Volkswagen, and Toyota cars in the country. In 1992, the *New York Times* reported that the total annual budget for the foundation was about $10 billion.

Bunyād-i Shahīd was established in March 1980, following a decree from Khomeini on 12 March 1980 calling for care for veterans of the revolution and the dependents of those who had died in it. After September 1980, responsibilities of the *bunyād* were expanded to care for disabled Iran-Iraq war veterans and the families of war martyrs, POWs, and MIAs. Currently the organization is under the supervision of Iran's president, but its director is confirmed in office by Khomeini's successor. In 1985, it had an income of 50 billion rials and an expenditure of 56 billion rials (about $3.8 billion at the current market rate of 1,580 rials to a dollar).

The *bunyād*'s major functions include: giving priority to student admission to all educational institutions and to obtaining basic needs and provision of employment through establishment or acquisition of factories; reduced fares on state-owned transport; medical insurance, hospitalization, prescription drugs, and provision of protheses; provision of housing at subsidized prices or rentals; and assistance in marriage and purchase of startup household appliances.

By March 1987, some 1,382 families had reportedly received housing in 19 housing complexes. The *bunyād* also assigns land to families able to build their own houses and assists them in obtaining mortgages. By 1989 more than a thousand families had been aided in this way. The Marriage Unit facilitates the marriage of war widows and veterans by providing loans, cash grants, and household goods gratis or at a reduced price. By 1987, the number of marriages arranged by the *bunyād* had reached 420.

Like Bunyād-i Mustaẕʿafān, the Bunyād-i Shahīd is funded by confiscated properties. Additionally, it has established a number of new companies. In early 1985, the total number of firms and factories under its control included 68 industrial units, 75 commercial companies and agencies, 21 construction companies, and 17 agricultural units. The *bunyād* also owns more than 6,000 units of real estate in Tehran, including villas, apartments, shops, malls, schools, hospitals, and hotels, the majority of which it uses to house the families of war dead. It also has 140 orchards and plots of land at its disposal.

Postrevolutionary *bunyād*s have become powerful organizations. They have very large sums at their disposal and represent major vehicles for extending patronage in ways that rival the state bureaucracy. Although it is difficult to tell what the future has in store, there is reason to believe that *bunyād*s will continue to be salient features of the national landscape in the Islamic Republic of Iran for some time to come.

[*See also* Iran.].

BIBLIOGRAPHY

This article is based on field research in Iran and the following sources:

Amirahmadi, Hooshang. *Revolution and Economic Transition: The Iranian Experience*. Albany, N.Y., 1990. Details the political-economic changes in Iran from 1976 to 1990, with extensive statistical and other information on the economy. Researchers interested in postrevolutionary Iran will find this book indispensable.

Āyinah-yi Āmār 1364 (Mirror of Statistics, 1985). Tehran, 1986. Discusses the Mustaẓ῾afān Foundation, with detailed statistics on its holdings and an explanation of its various functions.

Barrasī-yi taḥavvulāt-i iqtiṣādī-yi kishvar ba῾d az inqilāb (An Analysis of Economic Changes after the Revolution). Tehran, 1982. Major source of information on developments during the first three years of the Islamic Republic. Gives extensive tables on the economy and lists some of the major policies and nationalization laws passed by the Revolutionary Council.

Kayhān, 21 November 1983. Semi-official daily newspaper published in Tehran.

Majmū῾ah-yi qavānīn-i avvalīn Dawrah-i Majlis-i Shūrā-yi Islāmī (A Collection of Laws from the First Islamic Consultative Assembly) (7 Khūrdād 1359 to 6 Khūrdād 1363). Document published by the Majlis, covering laws and regulations passed in the Iranian parliament during the period noted. The table of contents lists bills by title and date of approval.

Majmū῾ah-yi qavānīn-i duvumīn Dawrah-i Majlis-i Shūrā-yi Islāmī (A Collection of Laws from the Second Islamic Consultative Assembly) (7 Khurdād 1363 to 6 Khurdād 1367). Document published by the Majlis, giving laws and regulations passed in the Iranian parliament during the period noted. The table of contents lists bills by title and date of approval.

Sālnāmah-yi āmārī-yi kishvar 1370 (Statistical Yearbook of Iran, 1991). Tehran, various years. Major annual publication on sectoral and territorial developments in Iran; indispensable research tool for those interested in Iranian studies.

HOOSHANG AMIRAHMADI

BURHĀNUDDĪN, SAYYIDNĀ MUḤAMMAD

(b. AH 1333/1915 CE), head of the Dā'ūdī Bohrā Ismā῾īlī community and fifty-second occupant of the office of *dā῾ī muṭlaq* ("absolute summoner"). The office held by Burhānuddīn originated in Yemen in AH 532/1138 CE when the heir to the Fāṭimid caliphate, the twenty-first imam al-Ṭayyib, chose seclusion. The Ismā῾īlī community believes that since then the imamate has continued in seclusion in the progeny of al-Ṭayyib and that prior preparations had been made by his predecessors to ensure that the Fāṭimid Ismā῾īlī mission would continue through the *dā῾ī muṭlaq*. The *dā῾ī* thus represents the secluded imam and operates with the imam's authority. He carries out virtually all the imam's religious and juridical functions and sustains the social structure of the community of believers. The present *dā῾ī* resides in Bombay, the headquarters of the mission having been transferred to India from Yemen in 974/1567. Like his predecessors, he is greatly revered by his followers.

Burhānuddīn received his religious and administrative training during the leadership of his renowned father and predecessor, Ṭāhir Sayf al-Dīn (1915–1965) and succeeded him in 1965. He has led his community into an era of fresh vibrancy and renewed zeal by devoting his efforts to the preservation of the Fāṭimid Ismā῾īlī heritage in a number of ways: he has ushered in a spiritual reawakening by requiring his followers to adhere closely to Qur'ānic injunctions in their everyday lives. He has emphasized adherence to Islamic business ethics that include the prohibition of interest and institutionalized interest-free loan schemes to cater for the community's borrowing needs. He has strengthened the age-old Shī῾ī practice of lamenting the martyrdom of Imam al-Ḥusayn; the annual gatherings to mourn the martyrdom during the first ten day of Muḥarram (῾Āshūrā') has become the major spiritual expression of the community, with thousands of Bohrās attending the sermons of the *dā῾ī*, which are relayed live to Bohrā centers all over the world. He has promoted the blending of secular and religious studies by initiating Islam-oriented schools which attempt to provide an integrated education in an Islamic atmosphere. Finally, he has undertaken the restoration of Fāṭimid relics and has promoted Fāṭimid architecture and design in the construction of a large number of mosques, mausolea, and other public buildings all over the world. The most important of such works has been the restoration in 1980 of al-Jāmiʿ al-Anwar, the grand mosque in Cairo built by the Fāṭimid caliph al-Ḥākim (996–1021).

Sayyidnā Burhānuddīn is an accomplished scholar. He personally supervises the curriculum of the Arabic academy al-Jāmiʿah al-Sayfīyah where his followers receive religious training. He is the author of several books on Ismāʿīlī religious thought and has composed thousands of verses in Arabic on supplication and in praise of the Prophet, imams and *dāʿīs*. He has received honorary doctorates from al-Azhar University (1966) and from Aligarh Muslim University (1966).

He has frequently visited Dā'ūdī Bohrā centers all over the world to personally imbue Islamic values in his followers, a practice he has continued even at an advanced age. He spends many hours each day in attending to the needs of the Dā'ūdī Bohrās, who seek his advice on all aspects of life, even on mundane matters such as the choice of name of a newborn. His charitable endeavors, promotion of institutes and trusts for educational and economic welfare, support of projects on environmental issues, and renovation activities have earned him international recognition, including the highest civilian honors of Egypt (1976) and Jordan (1981).

[*See also* Bohrās; Fāṭimid Dynasty; Ismāʿīlīyah; Jāmiʿah al-Sayfīyah, al-.]

BIBLIOGRAPHY

Sayyidnā Burhānuddīn's annual commemorations of the martyrdom of Imām al-Ḥusayn are recorded in publications of the Bohrā community where the commemorations are held, for instance, *Dhikr al-Safar al-Jamīl* (Bombay, 1993) and *The Mombasa Experience* (Bombay, 1993). Examples of Burhānuddīn's published works include *Istiftāh Zubad al-Maʿārif* (Bombay, 1965) and *Al-munājāt al-sharīfah al-Ramaḍānīyah* (Bombay, 1990), a compendium of poetic supplications for Ramaḍān written from 1965 to 1990. The secretariat of Al-Dāʿī al-Muṭlaq publishes a series of pamphlets providing statistical and historical information, including the following titles: *A Golden Chapter in Islamic Economy* (Bombay, 1985); B. H. Zaidi, *From Strength to Strength* (Bombay, 1991), T. A. A. Davoodbhoy, *Day of Thanksgiving* (Bombay, 1992); and Kauser Niyāzī, *Heir to a Great Spiritual Heritage* (Bombay, 1992). The reader may also consult the following works:

Najmuddin, Y. *Fifty-Second El-Dai el-Fatimi: Seventy-Five Momentous Years in Retrospect*. Bombay, 1985.

Quarashī, ʿIdrīs ʿImād al-Dīn. *ʿUyūn al-akbār wa-funūn al-āthār*. Vol. 7. Beirut, 1974.

Sayf al-Dīn, Ṭāhir. *Dhu'ī Nūr al-Ḥaqq al-Mubīn*. Bombay, 1917. Doctrinal exposition on the transfer of authority from the imam in Fāṭimid Egypt to the *dāʿī muṭlaq* in Yemen which quotes from the fourth/ninth-century work by Jaʿfar ibn Mansūr al-Yaman, *Kitāb al-shawāhid wa-al-bayān*.

Sayf al-Dīn, Ṭāhir. *Al-Mashrab al-Kawtharī*. Bombay, 1920.

Souvenir Akhbār Nūr. London, 1982.

A Treasury of Reminiscences. Bombay, 1967. Informative pictorial book charting the early life of Sayyidnā Burhānuddīn.

MUSTAFA ABDULHUSSEIN

BURMA. *See* Myanmar.

C

CALENDAR. *See* Islamic Calendar.

CALIPH. The Arabic word *khalīfah* (vicegerent, deputy, or successor) is one of the titles—others included *imām* (leader, particularly of prayer) and *amīr al-mu'minīn* (commander of the faithful)—given to those who succeeded the prophet Muḥammad as real or nominal rulers of the Islamic world. The full title is *khalīfah rasūl Allāh* (caliph of the messenger of God). Some later rulers, at a time when pre-Islamic Persian concepts of absolute monarchy were infiltrating the more democratic practices of the early Muslims, attempted to glorify themselves by shortening the title to *khalīfah Allāh* (caliph of God), but the early caliphs as well as the classical jurists rejected this.

The caliphate *(khilāfah)* emerged spontaneously immediately after the Prophet's death when leaders of the Muslim community elected Abū Bakr to succeed him. (The Shīʿīs believe that Muḥammad had actually designated his son-in-law ʿAlī for the succession.) The first four caliphs—Abū Bakr, ʿUmar, ʿUthmān, and ʿAlī—succeeded to the office on a nonhereditary basis by acclamation of the community, preceded in the first three cases by designation made by a few leading people or the preceding caliph. These four are known as the Rāshidūn (Rightly Guided) caliphs. Some Muslim writers have argued that the real caliphate ended here, degenerating thereafter into *mulk* (kingship) as it became hereditary and as many holders of the office demonstrated a lack of piety. In any case, the practices of the Rāshidūn era provided precedents for later theories of the caliphate. [*See* Rightly Guided Caliphs.]

Succession was the basic issue that divided Muslims into sects. The caliphate that prevailed in the early Islamic period was accepted by those who came to be known as Sunnī Muslims, while the Shīʿī branch is based on rejection of the legitimacy of these rulers in favor of a series of hereditary imams starting with ʿAlī. A third branch of Islam, the Khawārij, originally supported ʿAlī but later broke with him and argued that the caliphate is an optional institution.

With Damascus as their capital, caliphs of the Umayyad dynasty generally ruled the Islamic world from 661 to 750. The ʿAbbāsids (descendants of ʿAbbās, the Prophet's uncle), with their seat in Baghdad (or nearby), continued the caliphate in the face of occasional rivals until the Mongol conquest in 1258. The Mamlūk Sultanate subsequently kept members of the ʿAbbāsid family as titular caliphs in Cairo until the Ottoman conquest of Egypt in 1517. [*See* Umayyad Caliphate; ʿAbbāsid Caliphate; Mamlūk State.]

Long before this time it had become commonplace for rulers in various parts of the Islamic world—including the Ottoman sultans—to style themselves loosely as "caliphs," without necessarily claiming the universal dominion that the title originally implied. Most Muslims long considered the true caliphate a thing of the past, but the Ottoman sultans came to be widely recognized as the holders of the office prior to its abolition by the Turkish government in 1924.

Role in the Muslim Community. The caliph is not the Muslim equivalent of the pope, that is, the head of a Muslim Church, for Islam has no such institution that may be differentiated from the state. It is misleading to think of the caliphate as a spiritual office; it is a religious office mainly in the sense that the purpose of the state itself is religious in Islam.

The functions of the caliph (the term "imam" was more commonly used) according to classical writers largely corresponded to the powers of rulers in other societies. Thus the list of ten functions provided by al-Māwardī (d. 1058) in perhaps the most important work on the topic, *Al-aḥkām al-sultaniyah* (Principles of Government), includes enforcement of the law and defense and expansion of the realm of Islam, distribution of funds (booty and alms), and the general supervision of the government. Considering that the law such a ruler enforced was the God-given *sharīʿah* and that the territory defended or expanded *(dār al-Islām)* is coterminous with God's order on earth, such political functions were also religious in character. Conversely, the status of Islam as the ideology of the state made the caliph's role as guardian of the faith a political as well as religious one. When the caliph-imam led prayer, he was performing a ceremonial role analogous to functions performed by chiefs of state in the modern world.

At least in theory, the caliph was a limited ruler. He was the chief executive, bound by the *sharīʿah* that he merely enforced, thus providing the basis for classifying the Islamic state as a nomocracy. Unlike the Shīʿī concept of the imam, the Sunnī (and Khārijī) theory ascribed to the caliph no superhuman qualities, sinlessness, or infallibility.

Ideology of Leadership. In Sunnī and Khārijī theory, the caliph was elected by the community, but some jurists legitimized the caliph's designation by his predecessor. They disagreed on the minimum number of electors required and on the qualifications for this role, with some concluding that one was enough, thus undercutting the whole notion of election. Theorists identified various qualifications for the office, such as justice, knowledge, and physical fitness. Sunnī writers generally added descent from the Quraysh tribe that included both Muḥammad's Hashemite clan and the Umayyads; the Khawārij insisted that even an African slave might qualify. There was supposed to be only one caliph at a time, but some authorities recognized that a second caliph might exist under special circumstances.

The initial choice of caliph was to be confirmed by the *bayʿah* (agreement or homage) of the community. Although no one ever specified what individuals were to be involved in this process, it has been portrayed by some modern writers as having ideally constituted the final stage of popular election. In practice, it amounted merely to formal acceptance of whoever had been designated by those in power. [*See* Bayʿah.]

As originally formulated, the theory of the caliphate seems to have approximated a Lockean, mutually binding social contract, with the community ceasing to owe obedience to a caliph who violated the *sharīʿah*. This, together with the principle of election and the Qur'ānic admonition to engage in consultation *(shūrā)*, provides much of the basis for the claim of some modern Muslims that Islam is compatible with democracy. In the medieval period, however, such ideas gradually yielded to those of jurists who gave priority to the fear of chaos *(fitnah)* and of any rejection of the legitimacy of the holder of an office considered to be the keystone of the religio-political order. Muslims were told that an evil ruler, even one who came to power by forcibly overthrowing the legitimate one, must be accepted and indeed may have been sent by God as a punishment for sins.

Legitimation of De Facto Rulers. Beginning in the early ʿAbbāsid period, military commanders in various regions increasingly established their de facto independence while continuing to give formal obeisance to the caliph. By the late ninth century such commanders had become the real rulers in the capital itself. This was true also of the Twelver Shīʿī dynasty, the Būyids (945–1055), for whom the doctrine of the absence of the twelfth imam justified retaining the ʿAbbāsid caliphate, making it easier for the predominantly Sunnī population to tolerate their new rulers.

With the conquest of Baghdad in 1055 by the Sunnī Seljuk Toghril Beg, who was proclaimed *sulṭān* (the one with power), a new distinction emerged between the caliphate and the sultanate *(salṭanah)*. The latter office came to be held by the effective ruler (first at the seat of the caliphate and later in other regions); the former was typically restricted mainly to the role of a ceremonial monarch legitimizing those who held real power.

Whatever their titles, rulers of various parts of the Islamic world often—though with many exceptions, particularly after 1258—valued the legitimation that the caliph could provide. By receiving diplomas of investiture, robes of honor, and other symbols of authority from the caliph and by stamping his name on coins and having it mentioned in the Friday sermon, the real rulers could reassure their Sunnī Muslim subjects that the forms if not the substance of caliphal authority were being maintained.

The Ottoman Claim and Pan-Islam. The Ottoman sultans' serious claim to be caliphs goes back only to the late eighteenth century. It was bolstered by wide dissemination of an apparently baseless and previously unknown story published in France in 1787 to the effect that the ʿAbbāsid Caliph Mutawakkil had turned his family's rights over to the Ottoman Sultan Selim I in 1517. Moreover, in their dealings with Europe at this time the Ottomans found it useful to exploit the age-old confusion about the caliphate as the Islamic counterpart of the papacy and of the Russian ruler's role as head of the Orthodox Church. This confused notion found its first official appearance in the Treaty of Küçhük Kaynarja in 1774, which recognized the Ottomans' loss of the Crimea but provided that the Muslim Crimean Tatars would remain under the religious authority of the Ottoman ruler in his capacity as caliph of the Islamic world.

With the major Sunnī Muslim state having avoided outright colonization by European powers, Muslims—especially in India—increasingly saw the Ottoman sultans in a caliphal role. Some princes in southern India accepted the Ottoman ruler in this capacity in the 1780s, but otherwise the Mughal emperors continued to perform formal caliphal functions in the subcontinent. When the British ended the Mughal Empire in 1857, this created a void for Indian Muslims that the claimants to the caliphate in Istanbul began increasingly to fill, for instance by having their names mentioned in Friday sermons. Indian Muslims began to identify themselves with the Ottomans. Throughout the late nineteenth century this worked to the advantage of British colonial rule in India, for Ottoman rulers who recurrently depended on London's help in stopping Russian expansionism were able to present the British to their coreligionists in India as friends of Islam.

Renewed stress on the claim to the caliphate by Sultan Abdülaziz (r. 1861–1876) came largely in response to the appeals of Muslims outside the empire, especially of refugees from countries that had fallen under non-Muslim rule. Under Sultan Abdülhamid II, who came to the throne in 1876, the claim to the caliphate (written into the constitution of the same year) emerged as a major instrument of the Ottomans' Pan-Islamic policy as well as of their absolutist rule at home. The sultan-caliph sent emissaries throughout the Islamic world to urge unity under his leadership, and his claim to the caliphate received support wherever Muslims found European empires encroaching. Egyptian nationalists such as Muṣṭafā Kāmil supported the caliph in Istanbul as a counterweight to the British occupation of their country. And after the Young Turk Revolution of 1908, the now merely titular caliph remained a useful symbol for the new rulers' continuing Pan-Islamic policies.

Others were suggesting an Arab caliphate to replace that of the Ottomans. In 1881 the English writer Wilfrid Blunt called for a Qurayshī Arab caliphate limited to spiritual matters to be established in Mecca under British protection. There is reason to believe that Blunt saw the Qurayshī caliph as an instrument for the legitimation of colonial rule in India. Demonstrating the beginnings of Arab nationalist feeling, such writers as the Syrian ʿAbd al-Raḥmān al-Kawākibī—who may have been working on behalf of the Egyptian ruling house—called for a Qurayshī Arab caliph to be installed in Mecca as the temporal ruler of the Hejaz but limited to religious functions in the Islamic world as a whole. All of this meshed with the potential claims of the Hashemite *sharīf*s of Mecca, who had long governed the Hejaz under Ottoman overlordship.

The sultan-caliph's proclamation of *jihād* against the Allied Powers in 1914 and Istanbul's subsequent propaganda throughout the Islamic world failed to evoke substantial Pan-Islamic solidarity. But the Khilāfat Movement emerged in India in 1919 to support the authority of an Ottoman dynasty that had by then been reduced to impotence under the enemy occupation of Istanbul at the end of World War I and, after 1922, the control of Mustafa Kemal's nationalist forces. Shīʿīs and even some Hindus joined forces with Sunnīs in this mass movement. [*See* Khilāfat Movement.]

Abolition and Controversy. The Turkish Grand National Assembly began its attack on the Ottoman dynasty in 1922 with the abolition of the sultanate, while leaving a caliph to perform purely spiritual functions. The assembly, which now assigned itself the function of choosing future caliphs from the Ottoman ruling house, deposed Sultan Mehmed VI (Vahidüddin) and installed Abdülmecid as caliph. The way the conservative forces rallied around the new caliph seems to have motivated the nationalists to obliterate this center of opposition. Moreover, the widespread recognition by supporters of the caliphate, both in Turkey and throughout the Islamic world, that this division between spiritual and temporal authority contradicted the Islamic theory of the state further pushed Kemal toward abolishing the office. Finally, the new Turkish leadership resented the protests of Muslims outside the country.

In March 1924, the assembly resolved the matter by abolishing the caliphate and sending Abdülmecid into exile. The former widespread acceptance of the Ottoman claim to the office meant that its abolition shocked many Muslims, but the deposed caliph had to take refuge in Europe when no Muslim country showed willingness to be his host. A few individuals insisted that Abdülmecid was still their caliph, but too many other rulers (and *ʿulamāʾ* who backed them by acquiescing in the decision made in Ankara) aspired to become caliph themselves to allow the Ottoman claim to survive.

King Ḥusayn of the Hejaz (formerly the *sharīf* of Mecca) eagerly sought to become the new caliph. This culminated in his acclamation as the holder of that office during a visit to his son ʿAbd Allāh's British-protected emirate of Transjordan in March 1924. The *bayʿah* was limited to individuals from the Hejaz, Transjordan, and his other son Fayṣal's new kingdom of Iraq. With so many others aspiring to the caliphate and with much of the Islamic world seeing him as a British client who had betrayed the caliph during World War I, Ḥusayn's claims evoked rejection almost everywhere. When a Pilgrimage Congress met in Mecca in July 1924, Ḥusayn failed to get it to legitimate his claims. The quickly ensuing defeat of the Hejaz by the forces of Sultan ʿAbd al-ʿAzīz of Najd put an end to the sharīfian pretensions.

Leading *ʿulamāʾ* in Egypt, particularly Shaykh Muṣṭafā al-Marāghī of al-Azhar University, worked to get their king, Fuʾād, chosen as caliph—a project that the king himself apparently backed. Although initial plans for such a conclave were announced in 1924, opposition from many quarters—including the Wafd and other parties in Egypt—prevented the General Islamic Congress for the Caliphate from meeting in Cairo until two years later. The Congress, in which Muslim countries were unevenly represented, could agree only on the obligation to pick a caliph while admitting to the impossibility of doing so at that time, deferring the matter to another meeting the next year; that meeting never took place. Other Islamic conferences in Mecca in 1926 and Jerusalem in 1931 did not deal with the issue of the caliphate, although Abdülmecid and some of his Indian backers apparently wanted the latter meeting to reaffirm the position of the deposed Ottoman caliph. This possibility aroused the suspicions of the still hopeful King Fuʾād; his aspirations were assumed after 1936 by his successor King Fārūq.

The crisis inspired a series of controversial works on the nature of the caliphate. The most radical idea was that of an al-Azhar-trained Egyptian judge, ʿAlī ʿAbd al-Rāziq, who argued in a book published in 1925 that the caliphate has no basis in Islam. He held that it was coincidental that the Prophet had political as well as spiritual roles, and that the subsequent caliphate did not represent the real consensus (*ijmāʿ*) of the Muslim community because it came to be based on force. ʿAbd al-Rāziq went so far as to assert that there is no necessary relationship between Islam and any particular kind of government, a position that stirred wrath in more traditionalist circles.

In 1922 the Syrian-born Muḥammad Rashīd Riḍā, successor to Muḥammad ʿAbduh as leader of the modernist movement in Egypt, wrote a book condemning what had existed since the Rāshidūn as a grotesque distortion of the true caliphate, but he avoided the kind of hostile reception accorded ʿAbd al-Rāziq. Riḍā stressed the need to work for the restoration of a true caliphate. He proposed that the caliph should perform various functions of an obviously religious nature as well as formally investing rulers, judges, and *muftīs* and engaging in the merely ceremonial supervision of government; he would be elected from an elite group of legal scholars trained by a special institution. This new kind of caliph would preside over the process of updating Islamic law through the exercise of *ijtihād* (independent judgment).

Decreased Salience. Considering the centrality of the caliphate in Islamic political theory, it may seem surprising that its revival eventually ceased to be a major concern, even for many Islamists. The demonstration during the 1920s of the impossibility of agreement on the caliphate seems to have induced Islamists to concentrate on building Islamic orders within the boundaries of existing territorial units. As a case in point, Richard Mitchell (*The Society of the Muslim Brethren*, London, 1969, p. 246) shows that Ḥasan al-Bannāʾ, founder of the Muslim Brotherhood in Egypt, sometimes spoke of the eventual reestablishment of the caliphate, but only vaguely and with little real concern. Al-Bannāʾ even suggested that the title of the chief executive in an Islamic state would not be important. The Indo-Pakistani Islamist Abū al-Aʿlā Mawdūdī advanced the concept of "theodemocracy" and stressed that the *khilāfah* (distinguished from sovereignty in being restricted by divine commands), is vested in all Muslims, who delegate limited authority to their leaders. He thus did not propose a caliph in the usual sense as head of state, although—as Leonard Binder (*Religion and Politics in Pakistan*, Berkeley and Los Angeles, 1963, pp. 161 ff.) documents—a board of experts appointed to advise the authors of the Pakistani constitution took the classical theories of the caliphate into account in 1950 in making proposals relating to the head of state. A lack of concern for the issue is also characteristic of more recent militant groups, although some—notably the Islamic Liberation Party (Ḥizb al-Taḥrīr al-Islāmī) and its Egyptian offshoot, the Jihād Group—have called for reestablishment of the caliphate.

[*See also* Congresses; Pan-Islam; Sultan; Vicegerent.]

BIBLIOGRAPHY

Arnold, Thomas W. *The Caliphate*. Oxford, 1924. Reissued with a concluding chapter by Sylvia G. Haim. London, 1965. History of the institution, and analysis of the theory underlying it.

Berkes, Niyazi. *The Development of Secularism in Turkey*. Montreal,

1964. Thorough study of the emergence of secularism, culminating with the changes made by Mustafa Kemal Atatürk, including the abolition of the sultanate and caliphate.

Enayat, Hamid. *Modern Islamic Political Thought.* Austin, 1982. Analysis of twentieth-century ideas of Muslims, mainly Egyptian and Iranian, about Islam and politics, including much emphasis on the issue of the caliphate.

Gibb, H. A. R. "Constitutional Organization." In *Law in the Middle East,* vol. 1, *Origin and Development of Islamic Law,* edited by Majid Khadduri and Herbert J. Liebesny, pp. 3–27. Washington, D.C., 1955. Concise, authoritative analysis of the theory of the caliphate and the sultanate.

Gibb, H. A. R. *Studies on the Civilization of Islam.* Edited by Stanford J. Shaw and William R. Polk. London, 1962. Reprints of articles, including "Some Considerations on the Sunni Theory of the Caliphate" and "Al-Mawardi's Theory of the Caliphate."

Kedourie, Elie. "Egypt and the Caliphate, 1915–52." In *The Chatham House Version and Other Middle-Eastern Essays,* pp. 177–212. New York, 1970. Thorough study of the aspiration of successive members of the Egyptian ruling family to obtain the caliphate.

Kerr, Malcolm H. *Islamic Reform: The Political and Legal Theories of Muḥammad ʿAbduh and Rashīd Riḍā.* Berkeley and London, 1966. Excellent analysis of such matters as idealism in the classical theory of the caliphate and Rashīd Riḍā's writings on this institution.

Khadduri, Majid. *War and Peace in the Law of Islam.* Baltimore, 1955. Classic work on Islamic principles of international relations, with an introduction that provides an incisive statement on the theory of the state, notably dealing with it in relation to social contract theories.

Kramer, Martin. *Islam Assembled: The Advent of the Muslim Congresses.* New York, 1986. Thorough study of Islamic congresses held after the abolition of the Ottoman caliphate, as well as of earlier proposals, related in large part to the issue of the caliphate.

Landau, Jacob. *The Politics of Pan-Islam: Ideology and Organization.* Oxford, 1990. History of the idea of Islamic unity and attempts to implement it since the late nineteenth century.

Levy, Reuben. *The Social Structure of Islam.* 2d ed. Cambridge, 1962. Broad treatment of Islamic institutions, including the caliphate.

Lewis, Bernard. *The Political Language of Islam.* Chicago and London, 1988. Clear and learned exposition of Islamic political terms.

Minault, Gail. *The Khilafat Movement: Religious Symbolism and Political Mobilization in India.* New York, 1982. The most thorough study of this movement, with useful background material on Indian Muslims vis-à-vis Ottoman claims to the caliphate.

Tyan, Émile. *Institutions du droit public musulman,* vol. 1, *Le califat;* vol. 2, *Sultanat et califat.* Paris, 1954–1956. The most thorough study of the caliphate.

GLENN E. PERRY

CALIPHATE MOVEMENT. *See* Khilāfat Movement.

CALLIGRAPHY AND EPIGRAPHY. The art most cherished by Muslims throughout history has been calligraphy. A saying attributed to the Prophet claims that a person who writes beautifully the Basmalah, the formula "In the name of God the Merciful the Compassionate," will enter paradise. The feeling that the Qur'ān, being God's own word, should be written in a style worthy of its contents has led to the development of different calligraphic styles. The ancient Qur'āns were written in the heavy script called Kufic on vellum in broad format; the letters had neither diacritical marks nor vowel signs. Kufic became the favorite epigraphic style, and its most complicated forms, called floriated, foliated, or plaited Kufic appeared on tombstones, buildings, and utensils. One style called square Kufic is used to this day for decorative purposes (see figure 1).

Nonreligious texts were first written on papyrus, but when the Muslims learned the art of papermaking from the Chinese after 751 CE, numerous styles developed in the cursive hand generally termed *naskh.* The shapes of the letters were standardized by Ibn Muqlah (d. 940) in a refined system of triangles, circles, and semicircles and measured by dots according to the breadth of the reed pen. This system was further developed by Ibn al-Bawwāb (d. c.1020) and reached its apogee in the writing of Yāqūt al-Mustaʿṣimī (d. 1298).

In Iran a "hanging" style prevailed (with a strong tendency to accentuate the writing toward the lower left), influenced by the character of the Persian language. This style also was standardized according to Ibn Muqlah's system around 1400 and was then called *nastaʿlīq.* It is well suited to poetic texts in Persian, Ottoman Turkish, and Urdu. In later times *nastaʿlīq* was "simplified," and the letters were connected in ways that seem illegible to the uninitiated, although strict rules prevail. This style was called *shikastah,* "broken"; it is used to this day in Iran and sometimes in the Indian subcontinent.

Special attention was given to the scripts used in chancelleries such as the large, complicated *tawqīʿ,* the Ottoman *dīvānī,* and the *musalsal* (the "chainlike" script) so that no one would be able to imitate or fake the text of important documents. The Maghribi script, which does not follow the rules of Ibn Muqlah, was restricted to North Africa and Andalusia where writers often used colorful ornamentation of the pages. A similar development can be observed in the Bihari script used in India from the Middle Ages for Qur'ānic texts. These are the basic classical styles of writing that were used through the centuries, with regional variants, wherever Islamic culture prevailed.

FIGURE 1. *Kufic Calligraphy*. The sample reads "Fī sabīl taṭawwur al-khaṭṭ al-ʿarabī" ("For the development of Arabic script"). Artist unknown, Casablanca, c.1960.

The traditionalism of calligraphers was and still is so strong that it seems next to impossible to distinguish between a calligraphic page *(lauḥah)* written by the great Turkish calligrapher Shaykh Hamdullah (d. 1520) and one composed by one of his spiritual heirs Hâfiz Osman (d. 1689) or ʿAzīz Rifāʿī (d. 1934); as in other Islamic arts and sciences, the *silsilah* or chain of transmission that leads back to the founder—or ideally to the Prophet or ʿAlī ibn Abī Ṭālib—is of central importance. Calligraphers still boast of their connections with the earlier masters of the craft. Hence innovative trends developed not so much in copying the Qur'ān or *ḥadīth*s but rather in architectural epigraphy and the decoration of ceramics, metalwork, and the like. Here the inventive power of the artists—almost all anonymous—could show itself from the beginning.

Different types of mirrored script (even fourfold mirroring occurs) are particularly strong in eighteenth- and nineteenth-century Ottoman Turkey and the countries under her influence. To write Qur'ānic texts in circular forms, as one often sees them around the apexes of mosques in Turkey, inspired a number of modern artists to create circular sets of invocations or of the divine names. Such calligrams, which have proliferated throughout the Muslim world during the past two or three centuries, are usually called *tughrā*. The *tughrā* originated in the elaboration of the ruler's handsign that was placed at the top of a document. The true Ottoman *tughrā* is easy to recognize: two oval loops to the left and three vertical strokes are the basic ingredients; these are drawn around the name of the ruling sultan and then decorated according to the taste of the era. In the nineteenth century such *tughrā*s were used on banknotes, postage stamps, and coins; many good calligraphers in both the Ottoman Empire and the Muslim states of India invented fine *tughrā*s for these purposes and thus kept the tradition alive. Later *tughrā*-like writings using the traditional forms were added. These appeared, for example, on title pages of books showing the publisher's name or place. They are often formed from pious invocations, prayer formulas, or saints' blessings; typical is a *tughrā* made for Mawlānā Rūmī in Turkey, which was turned into a fine piece of jewelry. A great many *tughrā*s contain the Basmalah (see figure 2). The term *tughrā* was frequently employed from the nineteenth century for any artistic form of calligraphy, however different it might be from the original style. An increasing interest in meaningful "pseudo-*tughrā*s" is visible in this period, when books on the construction of such forms were published, for instance in India.

The last Mughal emperor, Bahādur Shāh Ẓafar (d. 1862), was not only a fine poet in Urdu but also a skilled calligrapher who produced, as did many of his contemporaries, faces, flowers, and trees formed from sentences. To write an invocation to ʿAlī ibn Abī Ṭālib in the shape of a lion was particularly admired by Shīʿīs because ʿAlī is called Asad Allāh, "God's lion." The art of forming faces and even human figures from letters seems to have developed especially in Turkey, mainly among the Bektāshī Ṣūfīs whose convents were adorned with figures and faces made up from the names of the Panjtan or other important persons. Calligraphers even tried to write entire surahs in animal or flower shapes in both Turkey and India; horses and elephants appear there, and even more common are different kinds of birds, especially for the Basmalah. Falcons and storks are among the most frequently used motifs, but recently a Malaysian artist created a lovely kingfisher from the Basmalah. Somewhat earlier, the perfect semicircular endings of Dīvānī script were used to construct a blessing formula for an Ottoman ruler.

Calligraphy does not consist only of these delightful games with letters. All over the Muslim world artists began to create new or at least less traditional forms of writing. A fine example is Iran, where the masters not only excelled in superb *nastaʿlīq* and even in classical *naskh* (as did Nairīzī, the leading master of the eighteenth century) but also produced a remarkable renaissance of calligraphy in recent decades. Some Persian calligraphy of the late nineteenth century appears to be influenced by Art Nouvcau. Thc classical style of Mīr ʿImād (d. 1615) with its sharp distinction between the thick and thin lines in *nastaʿlīq* is still an unsurpassable

FIGURE 3. *The Basmalah.* Calligraphy by M. Royaee, Iran?, late twentieth century. The style was invented by the artist, developed out of a hybrid *thuluth*.

model, but it was modernized when Mirzā Riẕā Kalhor (d. 1893) wrote somewhat thicker hairlines as an adaptation to reproduction by lithography. ʿImād al-Kuttāb (d. 1936) continued Kalhor's style and deeply influenced the present generation.

Contrary to the classical rule of writing a page with perfectly black or monotone ink, modern Persian calligraphers instead let the ink flow irregularly to achieve a livelier effect; by using different colorful inks they produce calligraphic "paintings" of great beauty. Recent exhibitions of Shams Anwari-Alhosseiny (Cologne) or the new publications of Jalīl Rasūlī clearly show the possibilities of this style, which attracts quite a number of young artists (see figure 4). Other trends range from the "telling" calligraphies of artists like Adharbod to the sculptures of Parvīz Tanāvulī, who uses words like *hīch* "nothing" in various positions in his metalwork. Many approaches are found in Iran, where the art of calligraphy is strongly encouraged. Some modern calligraphers in both Turkey and Pakistan have striven to invent styles that in a certain sense conflict with the classical ideals. In the 1950s in Turkey they used a "flame script" in which the letters are strangely bent; some artists from the Indian subcontinent try to modernize the

FIGURE 2. *Tughrā.* Text taken from surah 6.126 of the Qur'ān. Calligraphy by Zühdü Efendi, Istanbul, AH 1318/1900 CE.

FIGURE 4. *Persian Verse by Khāqānī (d. 1199).* The subject of the passage is the "steed of religion." Calligraphy by Shams Anwari-Alhoseyni, Cologne, 1991.

time-honored forms by introducing weird angles and sharp edges into the letters.

More convincing are attempts to use square Kufic for decorative purposes. This style was often used in the Middle Ages to decorate walls (the Iranian and Central Asian mosques are good examples) because the rectangular shape of glazed tiles lent itself readily to square forms, and Arabic formulas with their comparatively high frequency of tall letters like *alif* and *lām* could be well reproduced in this style. It was used also, though rarely, for book decoration. Recently many leading artists have developed different types of decorative square Kufic; the letters may be written in a square and then cut by diagonals, parts of which are then differently colored. They can be used to form cubes or dodecahedrons; they may appear on ceramics or batik on silk (as in the Iraqi Wasmaa Chorbachi's work); or the artist (e.g., the Iraqi ʿIṣām al-Saʿīd) may use traditional motifs in new techniques such as embossing and color etching. Among the best-known modern calligraphers is Aḥmad Muṣṭafā, an Egyptian living in London, who writes a perfectly classical *naskh-muḥaqqaq* but produces (often in silkscreen technique) fascinating works using mirrors and reflections yielding highly pictorial yet legible color calligrams.

Very different are the works of the Iraqi Hassan Massoudi in Paris, whose most recent publication displays new techniques with what appears to be a dry brush, contrasting one large and artistically shaped word or brief sentence with a background of smaller letters. The artist, who—like several other contemporary calligraphers—was trained in Western arts, often uses brown and blue hues. Some of his large letters remind the spectator of Chinese Arabic calligraphy, whose beauty has only recently been discovered: there the artists produce a style resembling the Chinese script with a large brush, and only at a second look does one realize that the characters are indeed Arabic. This unusual style may well influence some modern artists.

In much modern calligraphy (aside from Qur'ānic manuscripts, which continue to be written in the classical style) the border between calligraphy and painting is often blurred. An exhibition in Karachi in 1975 showed many different approaches to calligraphy in Pakistan alone. Almost every major artist had produced some painting in which calligraphy was used to form a picture or in which calligraphic fragments and pseudocalligraphy appeared—the letters becoming graphic forms devoid of true meaning. Some pictures resembled graffiti on walls; others ventured to combine Mughal architectural structures with a Kufiesque style (as Aslam Kamal put it). The attempts of the Pakistani painter Sadiqain to produce a version of some surah by forming calligraphic pictures has been criticized by both calligraphers and orthodox Muslims. However, one example from this series of paintings is worthy of mention. This is his illustration of the Qur'ānic phrase *kun fa-yakūn,* "Be! and it becomes," in which the round endings of the letter *n* form a spiral nebula out of which the whole universe emerges. The work of the Pakistani artist Guljee also contains some calligraphic pictures and interesting bronze structures; his masterpiece, however, is the *miḥrāb* of the Faisal Mosque in Islamabad, which he shaped like a large book of marble, inscribed in a medieval style of Kufic with parts of surah 55, al-Raḥmān.

FIGURE 5. *Religious Formula.* Calligraphy in the shape of a mosque reading "There is no power and no strength save with God the High the Mighty." Artist unknown, late twentieth century.

Artists have become increasingly interested in using abstract letterforms in their work. Good examples are Nja Mahdoui from Tunis, who does not attempt to write something meaningful but uses letters in isolated and combined forms simply to achieve a fine work of art. Similarly, the Lebanese Ḥusayn Māḍī uses letters in an innovative way, without deeper meaning. Likewise, Wajih Hakleh tries, as his critics claim, to "transcend" pure calligraphy.

Everywhere interest in calligraphy is increasing. Even Bangladesh, Malaysia, and Indonesia, which use scripts other than the Arabic for their languages, seem to be quite interested in turning back to the traditional Islamic features of calligraphy and are producing both modern interpretations of traditional forms and calligraphic paintings. The same holds true in Turkey, where a revival of the calligraphic arts can be observed, largely thanks to the activities of the International Research Center for Islamic Culture and Art (IRCICA) in Istanbul, where competitions in classical calligraphy are held. Many Turks, deprived of the Arabic alphabet since the introduction of the Roman script in 1928, feel that they would like at least to read the beautiful inscriptions on mosques or the tombstones of their ancestors, and so attempts are being made to introduce young people to Arabic letters, and a few young calligraphers may continue the tradition of a country famed for its outstanding calligraphy.

The general interest in the art of writing is visible in the increasing tendency to decorate cards for Muslim festivals such as the two ʿĪd, or announcements of important events with calligraphic text—some of it truly beautiful and some merely well meant. Even UNICEF has added some classical and modern Arabic calligraphic works to the motifs on their holiday cards. Many books printed in Islamic countries have calligraphy of varying quality on their covers, and European or American books on Islamic topics are more often than not decorated with classical or modern calligrams. There are even computer programs offering different styles of Arabic writing. Recently there have appeared computer-generated calligraphy or letter-combinations that, although not "real" calligraphy, show the possibilities of the Arabic script for decorative purposes. These may contribute to further interest in the calligraphic tradition and may perhaps inspire artists to even more innovative experiments.

BIBLIOGRAPHY

Baltacıoğlu, İsmayıl Hakkı. *Türklerde Yazı Sanatı.* Ankara, 1958.
Halem, Hilmann von, ed. *Calligraphy in Modern Art.* Karachi, 1975.
Khatibi, Abdelkebir, and Mohammed Sijelmassi. *The Splendour of Islamic Calligraphy.* London, 1976.
Massoudy, Hassan. *Calligraphie arabe vivante.* Paris, 1981.
Naef, Silvia. *L'art de l'écriture arabe, passé et présent.* Geneva, 1992.
Rasūlī, Jalāl. *Chahār faṣl dar āsār-i Jalāl Rasūlī.* Tehran, 1371/1992.
Safadi, Yasin H. *Islamic Calligraphy.* Boulder, 1978.
Schimmel, Annemarie. *Calligraphy and Islamic Culture.* New York, 1984.
Sicre, Jean-Pierre. *Hassan Massoudy.* Paris, 1991.
Tanāvulī, Parvīz. *Fifteen Years of Bronze Sculpture.* New York, 1977.
Welch, Anthony. *Calligraphy in the Arts of the Muslim World.* Austin, 1979.

ANNEMARIE SCHIMMEL

CAMBODIA. The great Angkor civilization that began in the eighth century and survived until the seventeenth was centered in present-day Cambodia. It was followed by incessant wars with neighboring Thailand, Laos, and Vietnam until Cambodia became a French protectorate in 1863. French rule lasted until 1953, when an independent Cambodia was once again established. However, this was followed by a civil war that ended with the success of the communist Khmer Rouge, who caused countless deaths during their four years of rule. In 1979, with Vietnamese military backing, a new communist-led government was formed. Later, the Paris Conference on Cambodia was held, and the United Nations became involved, a situation that ended with the formation of a coalition government in Phnom Penh and the reinstatement of Prince Norodom Sihanouk as head of state in June 1993.

The Muslim community of Cambodia prior to the victory of the Khmer Rouge in 1975 was essentially composed of Cams (or Chams) from the former kingdom of Campa (Champa). These people had been converted by Arab and Indian merchants and artisans. Large numbers of Cams emigrated to Cambodia in the fifteenth century. Also included in the Muslim community were Malays from present-day Malaysia and Indonesia, who also began to arrive in the fifteenth century, as well as Arabs, emigrants from the Indian subcontinent, and some indigenous converts. Muslims came to live throughout Cambodia, but particularly along the Mekong near the capital Phnom Penh and in Kompot, Tonle Sap, Kompong, and Battambang. They have tended to be employed in trading, agriculture, and fishing.

Cambodian Muslims have primarily been Sunnīs with practices and beliefs similar to other orthodox Southeast Asian Muslims. They have tended to follow religious practices more regularly than their Vietnamese counterparts. Ramaḍān appears to have been respected, but the *ḥajj* was only made by those who could afford it, with as many as eighty pilgrims annually. In 1975 there were between 113 and 120 mosques with some three hundred religious teachers and three hundred preachers. A great many of these teachers were trained in Kelantan, Malaysia, and at Islamic universities in Cairo, India, or Medina. The years from independence to 1975 also saw the formation of Islamic organizations—for example, the Islamic Association in Phnom Penh, which attempted to coordinate all cultural and religious activities, and an Islamic youth group that sought to encourage young people to study at the university.

There were good relations between the Muslim and majority Buddhist communities. During the pre-French period, Muslims played important military and political roles under the kings and held high titles through the centuries. Many Muslims acted as merchants who were also translators for the monarchs in their dealings with Europeans. During the French colonial period Muslims were completely removed from national decision making. However, with the return of independence in 1953 Muslims again were placed in significant posts, including high ranks in the Cambodian military.

The mass murder inflicted on the Cambodian population by the Khmer Rouge after 1975 severely decimated the Muslim population. An untold number were killed, and some twelve to fifteen thousand left the country for nearby refugee camps or settlement overseas. Nearly half the refugees went to Muslim-ruled Malaysia, while others settled in France, Australia, and the United States. Muslims also became part of anticommunist military units based on the Thai-Cambodian border. In 1980, of almost six hundred preachers and religious teachers who had resided in Cambodia in 1975, fewer than forty remained; of nearly 700,000 Muslims prior to 1975, only 150,000 to 190,000 remained. Cambodia's elite were especially targeted by the Khmer Rouge, and this was also true for the Muslim leadership. For example, only one of the country's nine graduates of al-Azhar University survived. During this period most of Cambodia's mosques and Muslim religious books were also destroyed.

The new government allowed the return of religious freedom, and many Muslims moved into important government posts; for example Math Ly or Abdellah Hamzah became vice president of parliament. Ibrahim Athmane was the highest religious authority in the early 1990s. At the same time, the death of so many teachers and other religious leaders has meant a severe weakening of religious education and understanding in the remaining Muslim community. There are major gaps in popular recognition of basic issues in Islamic history, theology, and the international Muslim world.

[*See also* Islam, *article on* Islam in Southeast Asia and the Pacific.]

BIBLIOGRAPHY

Correze, François. "Cambodge: Terre d'Islam." *Sud-est Asie* (March 1981).

Danois, Jacques. *Le temps d'une resurrection*. Paris, 1981.

Phoeur, Mak. "La communauté malaise musulmane au Cambodge." In *Le monde indochinois et la péninsule malaise* (CNRS publication). Paris and Kuala Lumpur, 1990.

Taouti, Seddik. "The Forgotten Muslims of Kampuchea and Viet Nam." *Journal Institute of Muslim Minority Affairs* 4.1–2 (1982): 3–13.

SEDDIK TAOUTI

CAMEROON. The Republic of Cameroon in West Central Africa is a microcosm of African diversity. Inhabited by some 12 million people in 1993, it has a Muslim population of about 21 percent, most of whom live in the northern part of the country. Islam was introduced in this region earlier than the nineteenth century, although it was only after 1806 that it experienced its greatest success there. Islamic expansion was facilitated by the fact that what later became German Cameroon (1884–1916), then French Cameroon and British Cameroon (1916–1960), was located in the Central Sudan belt that had encountered Islam much earlier. The Islamic revolution initiated by Usuman Dan Fodio in 1804 was the catalyst that made northern Cameroon a stronghold of the faith. [*See the biography of Dan Fodio.*]

The greatest carriers of Islam in West Central Africa during the nineteenth century were the Fulani, a pastoral nomadic group from Futa Jalon, Futa Toro, and the Senegal Valley in West Africa who swept through the Sahel at the onset of the seventeenth century and spread their faith among the sedentary peoples. Their conversion method was the *jihād* as well as persuasion (whenever possible) through the work of long-distance merchants, learned men, and, during the nineteenth century and later, the work of organized brotherhoods such as the Qādirīyah and Tijānīyah. The greatest apostle of Islam in northern Cameroon was Modibo Adama (1786–1848), son of Hassan from the Ba family of Gourin on the Faro River, who studied in Bornu. In 1806, Usuman Dan Fodio gave this fiery scholar the authorization to expand Islam into the areas comprising northern Cameroon and northern Chad.

Adama subsequently brought his zeal and his armies to northern Cameroon and made Yola the capital of his Islamic empire, which he named Adamawa after himself; he subdued or drove to the mountains and valleys the indigenous traditionalist population, whom the Fulani called *kirdi* (pagans). Some of the traditionalists converted to Islam in substantial numbers, including the Bamun, who established a sultanate in Foumban with which both the Germans and the French had to contend, especially during the reign of Sultan Njoya (1896–1933). Njoya became a threat to the French occupation, who deposed him in 1923 and exiled him to Yaounde, where he died in 1933.

Adama created a series of chiefdoms (*lamidat*s) under his sons; twenty-one of these units survived until the 1980s. A *lamidat* was run by a political and religious leader known as the *lamido*, who was elected by a council of twelve. A *lamidat* had a feudal structure, including an aristocracy (the Fulani, joined by Arab, Hausa, and Bornuan settlers), the converted *kirdi* locals, and the slaves (*matchoube*). The *matchoube*, who could also be sold, were used by the conquering Fulani in agricultural work and even in the production of objects of art and in metallurgy.

Notwithstanding the rivalries among the *lamidat*s, the Adamawa Islamic empire was flourishing when the Germans arrived during the 1880s. The *lamido*s declared several *jihād*s against them, and in 1888 the *lamido* of Tibati assaulted and defeated a German contingent, forcing it to retreat to Nigeria, and repelled another German occupying force under Captains Morgan and Stelten in 1893. On 24 November 1894 the *lamido* of Rey clashed with German forces under General Passarge. Tibati was finally subdued in 1899, and Rey was occupied in 1901–1902. By 1902 the Germans had finally succeeded in "pacifying" the Islamic country from Ngaoundéré to Maroua.

The Fulani *lamidat*s were left almost alone under the system of indirect rule by both the Germans and the French. Until independence Cameroonian Muslims considered Western education as poison to their children. In some cases, for example, Fulani aristocrats would send their slaves' children rather than their own to Western schools. Resistance to westernization was such that the Germans forbade Christian missionaries from proselytizing in the area. As a result, apart from the few Qur'ānic schools, there were no educational institutions in the north before independence. The economic situation was aggravated by the region's poor soil. Both the Germans and the French concentrated their developmental programs in other parts of the territory. When independence came in 1960 the developmental imbalance in the country was obvious, and most political power was centered in the south, with the differences sharpened by the religious factor. Even during the mid-1980s, while 90 percent of the school-age children attended primary school in the former Centre-South and Littoral provinces, only 31 percent were in school in the north.

What guaranteed Muslim influence in the new Cameroon(s) was the assumption of power by Ahmadou Ahidjo, half-Fulani and a devout Muslim born in Garoua. Ahidjo founded his Union Camerounaise in 1958, combining five small, predominantly Muslim political groups from the north, and became premier that year and later president of Cameroon (1960–1982). Under Ahidjo northern influence was considerable. Northerners protected the regime and the president by heading the Ministry of Defense and by dominating the elite Republican Guard, which was predominantly Muslim. Moreover, during Ahidjo's regime several northern politicians became department ministers, party secretaries-general, judges, and important businessmen. Ahidjo also initiated a bold "affirmative action program" aimed at the underprivileged areas of the country, with the north as the major beneficiary of government developmental programs. With the sudden departure of Ahidjo in 1982, northern influence in the country diminished, particularly after the attempted coups of February and April 1984, in which Ahidjo himself, some of his former northern supporters, and the Republican Guard were implicated.

Although tensions based on religious, social, economic, and political differences between north and south have subsided recently, there is a degree of uneasiness in the country. The fact that the predominantly Muslim north in neighboring Chad toppled a southern-based and non-Muslim regime makes Cameroonian politicians apprehensive about the future. This fear is heightened by the fact that northern Cameroon straddles the Muslim belt, with strong cosmopolitan ties with Sudan, Chad, Nigeria, North Africa, and the Middle East, where Islamic fundamentalist movements are emerging. The Muslim world, in fact, has noted the strength of Islam in the country: Saudi Arabia, as a gesture to Ahidjo's birthplace and to the Islamic community, built the most beautiful and spacious mosque in the country during the 1970s in Garoua.

The yearly pilgrimage of Cameroonian Muslims to Mecca has been going on for centuries, but new communication and transportation systems have made the *ḥajj* easier. Furthermore, the number of Muslims in the country has steadily grown over the years (from 395,000 in former East Cameroon in 1986, to 700,000 in the 1980s, and to an estimated 2.3 million during the early 1990s). While colonization stopped the forceful conversion of Traditionalists, it accelerated Islamic expansion through improvement in communication and transportation and through the enhancement of Islamic society, since administrators (often out of fear) respected Islamic traditions and structures and employed learned Muslim civil servants rather than Traditionalist Africans. The active brotherhoods, which had tended to be more receptive to africanization (including African leadership, tolerance of African traditions, and considerable non-Arab or non-Fulani membership), have been an extremely important vehicle for the spread of Islam both in Cameroon and in other parts of West Central Africa. Active expansion continued after independence, and it appears that, despite the problems, the future of Islam in Cameroon is bright.

BIBLIOGRAPHY

Atterbury, Anson P. *Islam in Africa*. New York, 1889.

Azarya, Victor. *Aristocrats Facing Change: The Fulbe in Guinea, Nigeria, and Cameroon*. Chicago, 1978.

Fisher, Alan G. B., and Humphrey J. Fisher. *Slavery and Muslim Society in Africa*. Garden City, N.Y., 1972.

Holt, P. M., et al., eds. *The Cambridge History of Iran*. Vol. 2. Cambridge, 1970.

Kerekes, Tibor, ed. *The Arab Middle East and Muslim Africa*. New York, 1961.

Kettani, M. Ali. *Muslim Minorities in the World Today*. London, 1986.

Lapidus, Ira. *A History of Islamic Societies*. Cambridge, 1989.

Nimtz, August H., Jr. *Islam and Politics in East Africa*. Minneapolis, 1980.

Njeuma, M. Z. *Fulani Hegemony in Yola (Old Adamawa), 1809–1902*. Buea, Cameroon, 1978.

Stoddard, Philip H., et al., eds. *Change and the Muslim World*. Syracuse, N.Y., 1981.

Tikku, Girdhari L., ed. *Islam and Its Cultural Divergence: Studies in Honor of Gustave E. Von Grunebaum*. Urbana, Ill., 1971.

Trimingham, J. Spencer. *Islam in West Africa*. Oxford, 1959.

Trimingham, J. Spencer. *A History of Islam in West Africa*. London, 1962.

Voll, John Obert. *Islam, Continuity, and Change in the Modern World*. Boulder, 1982.

MARIO J. AZEVEDO

CANADA. Muslim immigration to Canada began in the latter part of the nineteenth century, but the great majority of Canadian Muslims are recent immigrants. For most, emigration from their ancestral lands involved dramatic changes from hegemonic to minoritarian status and from a setting where Muslim religious values are reinforced to a predominantly Christian country that sometimes assumes religious uniformity among its citizens. That context presents particular challenges to Canadians of Muslim heritage.

Most of the early Muslim pioneers came from Turkey

and the territory under Turkish Ottoman rule known as Greater Syria, and some from South Asia. Reportedly there were 13 Muslims in Canada in 1871, 300 to 400 in 1901, and about 1,500 in 1911. Between 1911 and 1931 the size of the Canadian Muslim community declined to 645 owing to the departure of many Turkish immigrants who were classified as enemy aliens during World War I. Additionally, the 1907 government restrictions on the admission of immigrants from Asia reduced Muslim immigration to a trickle. Those able to immigrate to Canada tended to be part of a chain migration of relatives and people from the same villages. The resulting communities were closely knit, primarily Sunnī and "Syrian" (Arab) in origin.

During this period before and immediately after World War II most of the expansion in the Muslim community came from natural increase (births over deaths). After 1951, however, community growth became much more a product of immigration. There were between 2,000 and 3,000 Muslim residents in Canada in 1951. By 1971 this figure had multiplied more than tenfold to 33,370; in 1981, it had tripled to 98,160. Between 1981 and 1991 the Muslim population grew dramatically, rising by 158 percent to 253,260. Nearly eight out of ten Canadian Muslims were born outside Canada (mostly in Asian and African countries), and most entered after 1965. They included a large number of refugees from Lebanon, Iran, Somalia, Afghanistan, and Bosnia.

Most Canadian Muslims are Sunnī. In addition there are various Shīʿī groups, including Ismāʿīlīs and Twelvers. It is estimated that Sunnīs are in the majority (about 70 percent), followed by Ismāʿīlīs (20 percent), with Twelvers and other groups such as the Druze and Aḥmadīs (Qādiānīs) accounting for the balance.

The Muslim population of Canada is ethnically diverse as well. About ninety percent claim a single ethnic origin. Of these more than 82 percent were of Asian and North African descent, including Indo-Pakistanis (numerically the most dominant), followed next by West Asian and North African Arabs and then by Iranians, and Turks, plus a very small percentage of East and Southeast Asians, including Chinese and Filipinos. The remainder (18 percent) represents a wide range of ethnic origins, including European (mostly Balkan but also British and French), African, African-American, Caribbean, "Canadian," and others, reflecting the diversity of worldwide Islam. Of Canada's two official languages, about 30 percent of Canadian Muslims reported English as their mother tongue in 1991, while only 2 percent claimed French. Most reported the language of their country of origin as their mother tongue. The Muslim population's age distribution is relatively youthful. Historically, more Muslim males than females have entered as immigrants; today there are about 120 males per 100 females among Muslims. The average educational background of Canadian Muslims exceeds the national average, especially among males.

Muslim men appear to be well placed in Canadian society, with a large majority falling in the "professional" or "white-collar" occupational category. Prominent Muslims have held positions as provincial cabinet ministers or provincial court judges. Muslim women are much less represented in the professions and, despite their superior educational attainment, they are less well placed occupationally than Canadian women in general. The average employment income of Muslims, especially women, is about 10 percent lower than the income for equivalent Canadians in general.

The great majority of Canadian Muslims live in large urban areas. The province of Ontario is home to 57 percent of Muslims; other provinces with large Muslim concentrations include Quebec (18 percent), Alberta (12 percent), and British Columbia (10 percent).

The Al-Rashid Mosque in Edmonton, Alberta, the first of its kind in Canada and one of the oldest in North America, was completed in 1938. It was constructed through the efforts of a small number of Muslim families, primarily in Alberta and Saskatchewan, with support and funding from non-Muslims as well. Both men and women played important roles in the development of the mosque and its administration. For two decades it was the only mosque in Canada. The original structure is now preserved in a historical park honoring early Canadian pioneers. Mosques are now found in all major Canadian cities; in addition, some Muslim groups hold religious prayers and observances in public buildings. Muslim religious leaders or imams are often brought in from different parts of the Muslim world to attend to the social and spiritual needs of the local community. Other important Muslim institutions include religious and language schools. Community links are reinforced through newsletters, journals, and newspapers.

A number of important religious and charitable institutions have appeared, both local and national. At the national level, the Council of Muslim Communities of Canada (CMCC), founded in 1972, is an important umbrella organization. The CMCC grew out of a commitment to self-help and a perceived need to develop an integrated approach to issues facing the Canadian Muslim community. It is a member of the Federation of Islamic Associations in the United States and Canada. The Canadian Council of Muslim Women, established in 1982, brings women together in a national organization with a focus on women's rights, gender equality, Islamic education, appreciation of Muslim cultural differences, and outreach with women of different religious backgrounds. Another important umbrella organization is the Toronto-based Ismaili National Council for Canada, which coordinates the activities of all branch regional councils.

Other major organizations include the Muslim World League (Canada branch), which has an active office in the Toronto area; the Toronto-based Canadian Muslim Education and Research Institute, which is in the process of developing a resource guide on Islam; and the Muslim Research Foundation, an international organization established in 1985 to enhance global understanding of Muslims and Islam through research and publication. Organizations focusing on international development include the Children of Islamic Nations (COIN), the Ismaili national and regional councils that link with various Aga Khan foundations, and the International Development and Refugee Foundation (IDRF), which emphasizes an Islamic approach to social and economic development. Across Canada organizations of Muslim students are common.

There have been at least three major waves of Muslim immigration to Canada: one beginning at the end of the nineteenth century up through World War II, the second from the postwar era to around 1967, and the third and largest wave from 1967 to the present. Each immigration cohort had distinctive formative experiences in adapting to Canada and made distinctive contributions to Canadian society, and the descendants of each form distinct cohorts. Superimposed on this is the diversity resulting from varied national, cultural and linguistic origins, educational and occupational experiences, and income levels. More recent immigrants have far greater contact with relatives in their ancestral lands and old-country ways. As a result, different cohorts and generations of Canadian Muslims may have differing views on religious observances and practices. Generally speaking, immigrants (who are in the majority) tend to be less accommodating in their conception of Islam than are the Canadian-born Muslims.

Muslim immigrants came to Canada largely from countries where their religion was taken for granted and institutional supports for practicing it were plentiful. The challenge of their new environment has been felt not only by individual Muslims and families but also by the Muslim community as a whole. At one level, the challenge is internal to the community but at another level it is societal in scope. For example, differences in political or ideological attitudes within the community, sometimes glaring and sometimes more nuanced, tend to appear in the context of international crises such as the Gulf War or of newsworthy events, for example, the publication of Salman Rushdie's *Satanic Verses*. During the Gulf War allegations of dangers from "internal terrorism," knowledge that Canada in past wars had detained "enemy" groups, and Canada's position in this war were difficult for Canadian Muslims. This resulted in unfavorable news coverage and actual (if underreported) harassment. Muslim organizations and individuals made representations to the media and government. The federal government organized advisory groups of community leaders and organizations in response. This resulted in increased awareness and somewhat more evenhanded media coverage of Canadian Muslims and their religious practices. For example, Ramaḍān is sometimes given press coverage and even congratulatory front-page headlines.

Nonetheless, popular television and film programming continue to be major sources of distortion and libel regarding Islam and Muslims. In recent years, more immigrants have brought traditional dress codes to Canada, specifically the veil (*ḥijāb*). The visibility of the *ḥijāb* and a common Canadian association of it with female oppression makes it controversial in the larger society, but most who wear it do so without harassment. By contrast, the predominantly African cultural practice of female circumcision (clitoridectomy) has been reported among some recent immigrants (particularly Somalis), and it is highly controversial. Even among Muslims such sharply divergent cultural practices can undermine community unity. [*See* Ḥijāb; Clitoridectomy.]

At a broader societal level, prejudice surfaces intermittently against non-British, non-American, and non-Western European immigrants. In addition, Muslim immigrants represent a region of the world where the geopolitical interests of the West are strong and where there are frequent confrontations between Muslim and foreign interests. Negative images and stereotypes of Muslims and Islam are also encountered in the entertainment media (radio and television), popular literature, and cartoons, as well as the cinema. The Gulf War increased displays of prejudice as Arab and non-Arab members of the Canadian Muslim community were harassed, intimidated, and vandalized, as well as being rumored targets of government internment. Canadian foreign policy in the Middle East and more recently in the Bosnian conflict creates additional difficulties for Canadian Muslims.

The community faces a number of important issues. At the internal level, Canadian Muslims are still grappling with the issue of internal diversity. The issue of diversity is not unknown in many of the countries from which these immigrants came, but it is made more complex in the Canadian environment partly because of their newly acquired minority status and partly because of new national, cultural, and ideological mixture. Although religion bonds people together, apart from religious activities interethnic contacts tend to be limited. A major issue confronting the contemporary Muslim community is how to unite into a coherent whole.

Another issue facing the community concerns the difficulty of practicing the faith in a nonfacilitative, Christian environment. Observing prayer five times a day and dietary restrictions requires immense resistance to pressures from the larger community. Somewhat related is the issue of how to preserve the Islamic cultural heritage while facilitating Muslim integration into the Canadian secular mainstream and, more importantly, how to transmit the heritage effectively to the Canadian-born generation. For parents the marriageability of their children is of primary importance, and pressures toward in-group marriage are strong, particularly among immigrant parents. There tends to be greater control over daughters than sons and greater tolerance for a son's dating and marrying a non-Muslim woman, which contributes to a greater incidence of outmarriage among males and leaves a pool of eligible Muslim females. In 1981 about one-fifth of Muslim husbands and one-tenth of Muslim wives were married to non-Muslims (excluding converts). These figures have implications for the transmission of religious heritage. Studies indicate that where both parents are Muslim, practically all their children are Muslim; where only the father is Muslim, 36 percent of the children are Muslim, and where only the mother is Muslim, 23 percent are. Within each family type, Canadian-born Muslims are less likely to have children who are Muslim.

Concerns regarding the training of children link with the fact that the legacy of Muslim achievement and contributions to Western civilization are not widely known in Canada. This is reflected in school textbooks and in the training of public school teachers. The concern of Muslim groups about children's education has been repeatedly expressed by identifying shortcomings in textbook coverage of Islam and, particularly in Ontario and Quebec, by pressing school boards to broaden the traditional Judeo-Christian perspective to include Islamic values in school programs in moral and religious education.

Gender-related concerns are central for Canadian Muslims, including issues relating to defining propriety in male and female behavior; the tradition of male kin's control over the actions and dress of women and girls, youth, dating, marriage, and possible intermarriage; and the family and public roles of men and women. This continuing interplay of external and internal issues tends to reflect duration of residency as well as ethnic origin and religious identification.

Despite pockets of bigotry and ignorance, there is a tradition of tolerance in Canada. Muslim and non-Muslim activists are working toward improved understanding between faith communities, and Muslim groups have begun to monitor ways in which the larger society misrepresents or distorts Islam, denies Muslims rights, or restricts their ability to practice their faith or transmit it to their children. With respect to the community itself, diversity in interpretation, practice, and cultural tradition presents challenges. As the Canadian Muslim community moves toward the twenty-first century it continues to address issues surrounding adaptation to Canadian society within the framework of Islamic principles.

BIBLIOGRAPHY

Abu-Laban, Baha. *An Olive Branch on the Family Tree: The Arabs in Canada*. Toronto, 1980.

Abu-Laban, Baha, and M. Ibrahim Alladin, eds. *Beyond the Gulf War: Muslims, Arabs, and the West*. Edmonton, Alta., 1991.

Abu-Laban, Sharon McIrvin. "The Co-Existence of Cohorts: Identity and Adaptation among Arab-American Muslims." *Arab Studies Quarterly* 11 (1989): 45–63.

Haddad, Yvonne Yazbeck. "Islam." In *The Canadian Encyclopedia*, 2d ed., vol. 2, pp. 1097–1098. Edmonton, Alta., 1988.

Haddad, Yvonne Yazbeck. "Muslims in Canada: A Preliminary Study." In *Religion and Ethnicity*, edited by Harold Coward and Leslie S. Kawamura, pp. 71–100. Waterloo, Ont., 1978.

Husaini, Zohra. *Muslims in the Canadian Mosaic: Socio-Cultural and Economic Links with Their Countries of Origin*. Edmonton, Alta., 1990.

Rashid, Asma. *The Muslim Canadians: A Profile.* Ottawa, 1985.
Religions in Canada/Statistics Canada. Ottawa, 1993. Census of Canada, 1991, catalogue number 93-319.
Waugh, Earle H., Baha Abu-Laban, and Regula B. Qureshi, eds. *The Muslim Community in North America.* Edmonton, Alta., 1983.
Waugh, Earle H., Sharon McIrvin Abu-Laban, and Regula B. Qureshi, eds. *Muslim Families in North America.* Edmonton, Alta., 1991.

BAHA ABU-LABAN and
SHARON MCIRVIN ABU-LABAN

CAPITALISM AND ISLAM. Debates over Islam's economic implications are even more heated and inconclusive than debates over its social and political implications. Traditional texts and authorities provide countless blueprints for an ideal Muslim family and polity but not for an Islamic economy. The Qur'ān explicitly endorses few economic values beyond private property, commercial honesty, and competition tempered by concern for the disadvantaged. The *ḥadīth* extol the virtues of pious merchants in tones that would be familiar to any reader of *Poor Richard's Almanack.* Yet these adages hardly amount to a business-class creed or an Islamic counterpart to Calvinism. The *sharīʿah* (divine law) lays down firm rules both protecting personal wealth and discouraging excessive profits. However, the more rigid the rules, the more ingenious were the loopholes that judges devised to avoid enforcing them.

During the nineteenth and twentieth centuries, Muslims and Westerners have tried to articulate a clearer set of economic imperatives for Islam that could be either reconciled with or distinguished from competing models of capitalism, socialism, and communism. Premodern texts and practices are malleable enough to lend useful if inadequate support for many of these efforts. By and large, however, Islamic traditions have been most conducive to the development of indigenous capitalism and most hostile to the importation of communism. Sporadic enthusiasm has appeared for nascent theories of Islamic socialism in a few important countries, such as Egypt, Pakistan, Indonesia, and Iran. Yet even the most popular advocates of Islamic socialism are colored by secularist and heterdox reputations that severely limit their appeal to the Muslim mainstream.

Although modern debates over Islamic economics have focused primarily on the relation between religion and capitalism, those debates have moved in three different directions. At first, attention focused on Western arguments that Islam is an obstacle to capitalism. Gradually, Muslim and Western writers converged in viewing Islam as supporting a variety of capitalism. Most recently, Islamic modernists have combined a wide assortment of economic theories and religious programs to portray Islam as a superior alternative to capitalism.

Islam as an Obstacle to Capitalism. Both Orientalists and social scientists have emphasized Islam's supposed incompatibilities with capitalism, but their explanations typically diverge into theological versus institutional analysis. Orientalists tend to characterize Islam as inherently contradictory to capitalism because of basic and unchangeable doctrines, such as fatalism, other worldliness, and disdain for lending money at interest. These polemics often reflect and reinforce crude popular prejudices against Islam by providing them with a patina of pseudoscientific authority.

Social scientists, on the other hand, focus on situational and perhaps temporary tensions between Islam and capitalism. They identify these tensions with particular historical conditions and structures such as feudalism, sultanism, and imperialism. Compared to Orientalists, social scientists are more likely to view conflicts between religion and economics as partial, not all-encompassing, as rooted in malleable institutions and relationships, not in mindless dogmas and dictums. Social scientists tend to think in terms of an adaptive, "historical Islam" rather than a formative, "ethical Islam." "Historical Islam" mirrors predominant cultures and ideologies, whereas "ethical Islam" actively tries to shape them. The former justifies ruling institutions and groups, the latter guides and limits them.

By viewing Islam as less powerful in molding the world, social scientists also portray it as less culpable in retarding capitalism. If Muslims lagged behind others in accumulating private wealth and investing it in more productive enterprises, this was not because of their religion's imagined hostility to economic progress. The most serious obstacle to capitalism was the inhospitable foundation of political, social, and economic institutions that would have stunted entrepreneurs no matter what their degree or brand of piety. Capricious sultans and intriguing concubines, greedy tax farmers and unruly mercenaries, absentee landlords and landless peasants, mosaic societies and frozen classes, unintegrated markets and ungovernable hinterlands, relentless warfare and foreign encroachment—these were the crippling weaknesses of the Muslim world, not the spiritual or moral shortcomings of its creed.

Whereas many social scientists can envision capitalist

revolutions among Muslims who refashion their institutions, most Orientalists cannot. Because social scientists view religion as just one part of a complex Islamic civilization, they can imagine Islam adapting to capitalism and even promoting it in response to pressures from a changing environment. Because Orientalists view Islam as an immutable mentality that affects all other aspects of life, they expect it to distort and defeat capitalist impulses from any source, foreign or domestic.

Islam as a Variety of Capitalism. While Orientalists and social scientists counted and weighed religion's supposed burdens on development, economic historians began to turn the debate in a novel direction. They argued not only that capitalism in the Muslim world was more advanced and widespread than previously assumed, but that Islam itself deserved much of the credit for these achievements. Both Western and Muslim writers described a vibrant merchant capitalism linking the major cities of Asia and Africa in a vast intercontinental network stretching from the Silk Road to the Gold Coast, from the Sahara to the Spice Islands, from the Black Sea to the Cape of Good Hope.

Across city-states and multinational empires, in agrarian kingdoms and maritime principalities, Muslims shared a cosmopolitan culture that was carried not by the soldier or the bureaucrat but by the itinerant trader who often doubled as a mystical missionary. Particularly in non-Arab regions, the *Ṣūfī* merchant became the very embodiment of international Islamic civilization, uniting religion and commerce, town and country, sober mysticism and flexible orthodoxy. In many ways Islam seemed to express the special ethos of a transnational, urban middle class that could most easily adapt to its lunar calendar and devotional rigors, its prudish manners and charitable bent. Muslim traders and preachers helped popularize prophetic traditions exhorting frugality, modesty, and diligence to the point where converting to Islam might have seemed like embracing capitalism as well.

Historians and economists frequently argue that this florescence of international commerce could have promoted industrial revolutions throughout the Islamic world if Muslims had been able to resist the onslaught of European imperialism. From this viewpoint, the decisive inhibitor of capitalist development was not the inherent weakness of Islamic thought or the rigidity of outmoded institutions, but the overpowering force of Western arms and avarice. Indeed, in many countries, Europe's commercial and colonial invasions shattered native crafts and manufacturing. Flooding one region after another with cheap, mass-produced goods, Western traders often deindustrialized the very economies they were integrating into the modern world market.

The sophisticated long-distance trade that for centuries had been both a fountain and a fruit of Islamic civilization could not survive the industrial revolution and the age of imperialism. As long as the power of rival regions was either remote or in check, Islam nourished a distinctive and durable form of international capitalism. However, once Europe's competitive advantages approached global hegemony, the rules and limits of economic development were no longer set by local actors and resources.

Islam as an Alternative to Capitalism. As capitalism became more firmly identified with foreign domination, it lost some of its appeal to Muslims. Rather than asking whether Islam obstructed capitalism, Muslim reformers and nationalists began to see Western economic models as blocking their own paths to independence and prosperity. Instead of stressing those aspects of Islam that had promoted capitalism in the past, they argued that a more authentic and coherent Islamic economics could surpass capitalism in the future.

Efforts to articulate a distinctive Islamic economics are quite recent, taking off during the petroleum boom of the 1970s. Thus far, the most interesting innovations have been not in theories but in structures and practices. The prevailing theoretical tendencies are unmistakably capitalist, stressing the primacy of private property and free enterprise. There is a heightened emphasis on cooperation between the private sector and the state as well as between Muslim firms and governments internationally. There is considerable discussion of economic inequality in the Islamic world and of the need for a more just distribution of wealth both within and between Muslim nations. Moreover, there is a common assertion that ownership of land and natural resources is a public trust that must be safeguarded for the benefit of future generations. Hence, in the Muslim world, as elsewhere, contemporary economic thought is increasingly preoccupied with social harmony, global interdependence, and environmental preservation.

The hallmark of this emerging Islamic capitalism is an impressive array of new institutions that are strikingly multifunctional and multinational. The pivotal role belongs to a few dozen big, state-sponsored Islamic banks that seek to centralize investment and power while sharing risk and profit. To preserve their claim to an Islamic pedigree, these enterprises avoid paying interest at fixed rates. Instead, they generally offer depositors a share in realized gains and losses. Because they ask depositors to accept considerable risk, they often require borrowers to relinquish a degree of managerial control. Although these policies do not alter formal ownership, they nonetheless create a kind of involuntary partnership between depositor, lender, and debtor, who all become joint investors.

The Islamic banks blend the activities of accumulation, appreciation, and speculation in an unusually explicit manner. The prominence of multipurpose banks is not surprising in economies that have large foreign-exchange surpluses but weak capital markets and infrastructures. The overdevelopment of financial institutions might compensate for the underdevelopment of business associations in general, but it creates some peculiar organizational hybrids. Depending on its particular mix of projects and customers, an Islamic bank can combine the roles of an investors' syndicate and a stock market, a mutual fund and a credit union, a commodities exchange and a casino.

The Islamic banks are also distinguished by their mammoth international transactions and their well-publicized political connections. The banks are popular conduits for workers' remittances, pilgrimage expenses, and petrodollars. They are instrumental in recycling capital from oil-producing states to poorer countries with large surpluses of land and labor. Most Islamic banks are openly allied with government agencies, political parties, royal families, social movements, and liberation struggles. These coalitions frequently cut across national borders, projecting a common set of political and ideological conflicts throughout the Muslim world.

Malaysian peasants making installment payments to the Pilgrims' Investment Fund are also subsidizing the ruling party's affirmative-action program for Muslim entrepreneurs. Foreign pilgrims and guest workers in Saudi Arabia use Islamic banks to support families and shops all over Asia and Africa. Oil revenues from banks in the Persian Gulf countries are paying unemployed Egyptians to reclaim Sudanese farmland, financing Turkey's governing alliance of Islamic politicians and business people, arming Muslim fighters in Bosnia, Afghanistan, and the Philippines. The Russian Federation is asking Islamic banks to combat Iranian influence in the newly independent republics of central Asia with loans to import prayer leaders from Egypt, Qur'āns from Pakistan, and teachers from Turkey.

The practice of Islamic economics is more advanced than the theory; its resources and organizations are more crystallized than its goals. Although its proponents insist that Islamic economics is a clear alternative to existing systems, it looks more like a financially driven variety of capitalism with a keen aptitude for building transnational political ties to offset its continued weakness in both local and global markets. Some of the more unconventional Islamic investment companies have suffered mismanagement and corruption, generating sensational stories about bankruptcies, kickbacks, and secret arms deals. In general, however, their impact is conservative and antirevolutionary.

Domestically, the Islamic firms support moderate, right-of-center democrats and modernizing authoritarians against religious radicals and leftists. In the balance of power among Muslim states, they are firmly identified with the mainstream leaders of the Organization of the Islamic Conference. They help to strengthen alliances between Saudi Arabia, Egypt, Turkey, Pakistan, Indonesia, Malaysia, and Nigeria while countering the influence of Iran, Libya, and Iraq. In the global economy, they use their leverage in financial markets to press the advanced industrial countries for concessions in trade, investment, and technology transfer. Nevertheless, they demand not a new world economic order but merely higher standing in a more flexible hierarchy of nations.

[*See also* Trade.]

BIBLIOGRAPHY

Ahmad, Khurshid, ed. *International Conference on Islamic Economics*. Delhi, 1984. Collection of essays by leading theorists of Islamic economics in several countries.

Amin, S. H. *Islamic Banking and Finance: The Experience of Iran*. Tehran, 1986.

Binder, Leonard. *Islamic Liberalism*. Chicago, 1988. Excellent discussion of Islam's possible contributions to democratic and capitalist development.

Coulson, Noel J. *Conflicts and Tensions in Islamic Jurisprudence*. Chicago, 1969.

El-Ashker, Ahmed. *The Islamic Business Enterprise*. London, 1987.

Gran, Peter. *Islamic Roots of Capitalism: Egypt, 1760–1840*. Austin, 1979. Original interpretation of commercial and cultural renaissance in Egypt before the colonial era.

Iqbal, Munawar. *Distributive Justice and Need Fulfillment in an Islamic Economy*. Islamabad, 1986.

Kazarian, Elias, *Islamic versus Traditional Banking: Financial Innovations in Egypt*. Boulder, 1993.

Khan, Shahrukh Rafi. *Profit and Loss Sharing: An Islamic Experiment in Finance and Banking*. New York, 1987.

Rahman, Fazlur. *Islam and Modernity: Transformation of an Intellectual*

Tradition. Chicago, 1982. Excellent analysis of the interaction between "historical Islam" and "ethical Islam."

Rodinson, Maxime. *Islam and Capitalism*. Austin, 1978. The leading critique of Orientalist assumptions that Islam obstructs capitalist development.

Roff, William R., ed. *Islam and the Political Economy of Meaning*. Berkeley, 1987. Collection of essays on religion and economy in the Muslim world by leading social scientists.

Turner, Brian. *Marx and the End of Orientalism*. London, 1978. Marxian assessment of both theological and institutional explanations of Islam's economic ramifications.

Wohlers-Scharf, Traute. *Arab and Islamic Banks: New Business Partners for Developing Countries*. Washington, D.C., 1983.

ROBERT BIANCHI

CAPITULATIONS. Commercial privileges called capitulations were granted by Muslim states, especially the Ottoman and Persian Empires, to Christian European states desiring to carry on trade in what was technically enemy territory. These capitulations set customs rates, established security of life, property, and religion, and set up channels for dealing with problems and legal disputes. As the balance of power shifted toward western Europe, the capitulations were used to obtain advantages and extraterritorial status for European citizens and protégés in Muslim lands, so that in the nineteenth century they became instruments of imperialist exploitation. They were not abolished until well into the twentieth century: in 1914 in the Ottoman Empire, 1928 in Iran, and 1937 in Egypt.

Called *imtiyāzāt* ("privileges") in the Middle Eastern languages, the capitulations were based on the principle of *amān*, the safe-conduct granted by members of the *dār al-Islām* or "abode of Islam" to citizens of non-Muslim countries, the *dār al-ḥarb* where unending war for the faith was legitimate and indeed required. When it would clearly benefit the Muslim community commercially or politically, the state of war could be suspended and truce or safe-conduct extended (for up to a year) to people giving assurances of friendship and good will. Grants of *amān* enabled pilgrims and merchants to travel in safety within the Islamic world. From the twelfth century, the principle of *amān* was joined with that of the treaty to create the new form of capitulations made between states and embodied in an *ahdname* ("covenant"). Still a unilateral concession by a Muslim ruler to a non-Muslim state pledging peace and friendship, the capitulations (the name derives from the headings of the document) extended protection to any citizen of the state and lengthened the period for which it could be obtained to ten years. Capitulations were granted, mainly to Italian city-states, by the Muslim rulers of Spain, the Mamlūks in Egypt, and the Seljuks in Anatolia during the twelfth and thirteenth centuries.

The first Ottoman capitulations were granted in 1352 to Genoa, which was at war with Venice, an ally of the crumbling Byzantine Empire. As the Ottoman state expanded and places having trade relations with Europe came into Ottoman hands over the fourteenth and fifteenth centuries, the Ottomans maintained these relations (e.g., with Venice in Ayasoluk and Balat, with Genoa in Galata, and with Pisa and Florence). These early capitulations set the rates of customs dues for imports and exports and provided for exemption from other fees or dues, ship repairs, aid against pirates, compensation for damages, inheritance, protection of shipwreck victims and their goods, immunity from responsibility for the debts of fellow-countrymen, and just treatment in the courts. A group of foreign merchants in a particular city could constitute itself as a community headed by a consul who received official recognition via an imperial *berat* ("decree") making him the representative of his "nation" and empowering him to settle disputes, supervise affairs, and collect a consulage fee from merchants sailing under his country's flag. The *berat* granted personal immunity and exemption from taxes for the consul and his household and allowed him to call on the Ottoman authorities to enforce his decisions.

The period of Italian dominance of trade yielded in the sixteenth and seventeenth centuries to the growing commercial power of the Atlantic economies. Western nations engaging in distant exploration and commerce sought capitulations of their own to enable them to sail under their own flags and cease paying dues to consuls of other nations. The French had been trading in the Ottoman Empire by virtue of agreements made with the Mamlūk rulers of Egypt that were renewed after the Ottoman conquest in 1517. In 1535, an era of rapprochement between the French and the Ottomans against the Habsburgs, France attempted to obtain new, more extensive capitulations. Although these are often cited as their first capitulations, they were never ratified. In 1569, however, partly to assure French good will in preparation for an attack on Venetian-held Cyprus, the Ottomans granted the French new capitulations based on those of Venice. The English, not to be outdone, sent negotiators to the Ottoman capital in 1580 (secretly via Poland to avoid Habsburg-Venetian interference).

They were favorably received, largely because of their country's opposition to Spain but also because they could supply crucial raw materials like tin and steel along with inexpensive woolen cloth; in return they took home silk, mohair and cotton, dyestuffs, dried fruits, and spices. Capitulations were granted or regranted to England in 1580, 1583, 1601, 1616, 1624, 1643, 1666, and 1675; to France in 1569, 1581, 1597, 1604, 1673, and 1740. Capitulatory privileges were extended to Poland in 1553; to the Dutch, whom both the English and the French had tried to lure to their flags, in 1612; and to Genoa in 1665. Ragusa was recognized as an autonomous tributary state in 1572, ending its need for capitulations. Merchants of nations without capitulations of their own sailed under the flag of one of the capitulatory states.

There ensued a century of English-French competition in the Levant, each nation attempting to entice other nations to sail under its flag (and pay its consulage fees). In 1604 France obtained a clause in its capitulations requiring other nations to sail under its flag; however, the English made themselves so superior as providers of safety on the seas that others preferred their protection. As part of the rivalry, each nation tried to negotiate additional favorable clauses. Detailed regulations on the fair treatment of foreigners in Muslim courts were negotiated by the French in 1569 and included in the English capitulations of 1580. The English in 1601 obtained an article prohibiting exactions by provincial governors that was duplicated by the French in 1604. The English negotiation in 1601 of a 3 percent customs rate in place of the normal 5 percent made other nations rush to the English flag. The French were unable to obtain this rate until 1673, but their capitulations provided for the protection of Christian pilgrims in the Holy Land and gave guarantees against the Barbary pirates.

One important set of clauses established extraterritoriality for capitulatory merchants. Foreigners, except in cases involving Ottoman subjects, were not governed by Ottoman jurisdiction but by their own laws and the regulations established by the trading companies, administered by the consuls. Europeans could make and consume alcoholic beverages within their own quarters and could practice their own religion; importantly, they were not subject to the Muslim laws of inheritance. The consuls' interpreters and servants received freedom from taxation and the right to be judged in the consular court by the English capitulations of 1675.

During this period the English, French, and Dutch were also in competition for the trade of Persia. There, protection was provided by *farmans* ("orders") promulgated by the Ṣafavid shahs. Early Ṣafavid *farmans* provided exemption from taxation, freedom of religion and travel, inheritance rights, recovery of debts, and freedom from interference. It is probable that relations with the Ottoman Empire formed the model for interactions with Persia, and later with China and the Far East. The English in 1600, the Dutch in 1623, and the French in 1665 gained commercial privileges in Persia, and in 1631 Persian merchants were granted comparable privileges in the Netherlands, though none took advantage of them. Treaties of 1708 and 1715 between Persia and France established French trading centers throughout Persia and granted reciprocal privileges to Persian merchants in France.

With the outbreak of the Ottoman-Habsburg war in 1683, relations between the Ottomans and Europeans underwent a change; the capitulations, no longer the gracious gift of a powerful ruler, became bargaining chips in Ottoman negotiations for aid against the Habsburgs. Generous concessions to France (reduction of the Egyptian customs rate from 10 percent to 3 percent, and return to the Catholic Church of sacred sites in Jerusalem) failed to prevent France's joining the Austrian alliance in 1697, and it became the turn of the English to receive more generous terms (a consulate in Egypt and a monopoly of the carrying trade between Egypt and Istanbul). The French privileges of 1740 reflected warming relations with that country; the most extensive to date, they were also binding on subsequent sultans. The increase in French influence permitted by that clause was offset by the extension of separate capitulations to Sweden (1737), Austria (1699 and 1718), Sicily (1740), Denmark (1756), Prussia (1761), Spain (1783), and Russia (1774—not a unilateral capitulation but part of the treaty of Küçük Kaynarja). The Italian cities of Venice and Livorno (Leghorn) also continued to trade in the Ottoman Empire.

By now, the countries of central and eastern Europe were participating in the commercial expansion of the Atlantic states. An exchange of cloth and meat between Ottoman and Germanic territories expanded to other commodities with the Habsburg establishment of consulates, navigation on the Danube, and trade with Persia across the Black Sea. Russians began trading furs for silk in the fifteenth century, and the fur trade grew after the Russian conquest of Kazan in 1552. In Persia fish, caviar, and minerals were important commercial items.

In the eighteenth century trade rivalry among European nations turned into a rush for empire. Imperialism in the Middle East took the form not of outright colonial possession but of economic dominance. By 1781 the Ottoman Empire could be labeled a colony of France; in the second half of the century there was some pressure for a French occupation of Egypt. By the 1774 treaty of Küçük Kaynarja, after a war in which Russia occupied Ottoman Crimea, the Russians gained the right of navigation in the Black Sea and the straits, a right also granted ten years later to the Habsburgs. The treaty of Küçük Kaynarja significantly altered trade relations between Europe and the Middle East. First, as a bilateral treaty, its provisions could not be unilaterally revoked or altered, nor did it have to be renewed by successive sultans. Second, two of its provisions were interpreted to permit a new level of foreign interference with internal conditions in the Ottoman Empire.

The treaty itself allowed Russia to build a church of the Orthodox rite in Beyoğlu, the foreigners' quarter, and to protect it and make representations on its behalf. The Ottoman government promised to take such representations into consideration and to protect the Christian religion generally. Russia construed this limited concession as a right to protect all Orthodox Christians in the Ottoman Empire, to interfere when it deemed their welfare to be at risk, and to be consulted about measures concerning them. France, too, wished to exercise similarly broad prerogatives regarding the Catholics of the empire (Maronites and Uniates of Lebanon, where French priests had been at work since Crusader times) on the basis of clauses in the 1673 capitulations regarding Ottoman protection of its monks. Not to be left out, the English claimed the right to "protect" the Druze of Lebanon and the Jews of Palestine, making these groups their excuse for intervention in Ottoman internal affairs. The natural sympathy of the Europeans for their coreligionists thus became the entering wedge for domination.

Another problem arose out of the clauses protecting the subjects of capitulatory nations from harrassment, exempting them from local jurisdiction and taxation, and granting them a lower customs rate than that paid by Ottoman subjects. These privileges, guaranteed by official *berats*, were extended to the consuls' interpreters and a limited number of local employees. However, consuls began requesting more *berats* for non-Muslim Ottoman subjects, mainly merchants rather than translators. The rights granted to these *beratlıs*, of whom there were many thousands by the nineteenth century, were considered to amount to a change of nationality. The control of the Ottoman state over its own subjects was eroding; in addition, the non-Muslims of the empire gained privileges greater than those of Muslims.

Local governors struggled against the effects of these abuses, imposing monopolies on the sale of commodities, fixing prices, and forbidding access to internal areas of the country. Meanwhile, the state mounted legal barriers to changes of citizenship and collected taxes from property-owners regardless of nationality. Throughout the nineteenth century the Ottomans made efforts to abolish the capitulations, but none succeeded. The treaty of Balta Limanı in 1838 between England and the Ottoman Empire confirmed forever all existing capitulatory privileges and eliminated the monopolies that protected Ottoman manufactures against Western industrial competition.

Two provisions further lessened the Ottoman government's internal control. The first, in the 1838 treaty, abolished the limitations on internal movement by foreigners that had kept part of the trade in Ottoman hands. The opening of Ottoman internal markets to European industrial wares led rapidly to the collapse of Ottoman manufacturing and trade, reducing customs revenues. The second provision, in an imperial *firman* of 1867, permitted foreigners to own property in the Ottoman Empire if they paid Ottoman taxes and obeyed Ottoman law. This opened the door for exploitation by foreign concessionaires. The second half of the century saw the establishment of banks, railroads, port facilities, canals, urban utilities, and mines, all operated by foreign capital. The profits flowed out of the country to enrich the concessionaires.

In Persia, the right to own property had been granted to foreigners from the beginning. The decisive date for the change of the capitulations from benevolent grants to extorted privileges was 1828 in the Treaty of Turcomanchay, after a disastrous defeat by Russia. The important clauses made foreign property immune to Persian inspection and consuls exempt from Persian legal jurisdiction. Special tribunals were set up, as in the Ottoman Empire, to judge cases between foreigners and local subjects. Trials could only take place in the presence of the consul or ambassador, who had final control over the verdict. Similar rights were extended to the British in 1836. Concessions were granted for communications and transportation facilities, mining, banking, fishing, tobacco, and oil.

Trade in Egypt in the nineteenth century was no longer governed by the Mamlūk-Ottoman agreements.

Muḥammad ʿAlī and his successors made independent arrangements with the Europeans that expanded their privileges greatly. The right of foreigners to own land was granted well before 1867. Customs dues were reduced in 1902. Freedom from the poll tax became a complete tax exemption, sometimes even from the land tax. Not only foreigners' homes but also their ships and places of business were inviolate, and foreigners were completely immune from Egyptian law. Attempts to establish a unified court system for cases involving people of different nationalities began in the 1820s, and jurisdiction became a contentious issue.

Throughout the nineteenth century the Ottomans attempted to abolish the capitulations, now embodied in bilateral treaties, but they were unable to obtain the consent of the European powers. The outbreak of World War I finally provided the occasion for their abolition, on 8 September 1914, confirmed by the Treaty of Lausanne in 1923. In the newly independent Arab countries, however, capitulatory provisions were included in the mandates and were only gradually eliminated. The Ottoman abolition of the capitulations inspired the Persians to attempt the same; their first attempts were abortive, but treaties signed with China and Russia in the 1920s lacked extraterritorial provisions. New commercial and judicial codes abolishing capitulatory privileges went into effect on 10 May 1928. The process in Egypt was more difficult, as a British protectorate was declared in 1914 and the Ottoman abolition did not apply; however, the Anglo-Egyptian Treaty of 1936 recommended the speedy abolition of the capitulations, finally achieved in 1937.

[*See also* International Law; International Relations and Diplomacy; Mamlūk State; Ottoman Empire; Ṣafavid Dynasty.]

BIBLIOGRAPHY

Abbott, George F. *Under the Turk in Constantinople*. London, 1920. Account of a seventeenth-century English embassy to Turkey, including the negotiation of the 1675 capitulations.

Bosscha Erdbrink, G. R. *At the Threshold of Felicity: Ottoman-Dutch Relations during the Embassy of Cornelis Calkoen at the Sublime Porte, 1726–1744*. Ankara, 1975. Opens with a short history of Ottoman-Dutch relations prior to 1726.

Charrière, Ernest. *Négociations de la France dans le Levant*. 4 vols. Paris, 1848–1860. Covers the French capitulations.

Grenville, Henry. *Observations sur l'état actuel de l'Empire Ottoman, 1765*. Edited by A. S. Ehrenkreutz. Ann Arbor, 1965. Discusses eighteenth-century commerce and foreign relations.

Hershlag, Zvi Y. *Introduction to the Modern Economic History of the Middle East*. 2d rev. ed. Leiden, 1980. Discusses the economic effect of the capitulations in the nineteenth century.

Hurewitz, J. C. *Diplomacy in the Near and Middle East: A Documentary Record, 1535–1914*. 2 vols. New York, 1972. See for Ottoman and Persian capitulations and treaties with England, France, and Russia.

Khadduri, Majid. *War and Peace in the Law of Islam*. 2d rev. ed. Baltimore, 1955. Explains the concepts of *dār al-ḥarb* and *amān*.

Kurat, Akdes N. *Türk-İngiliz Münasebetlerin Başlangıcı ve Gelişmesi, 1553–1610* (Inception and Growth of Turkish-English Relations, 1553–1610). Ankara, 1953. Includes the text of the English capitulations of 1580 and 1610, together with other correspondence between the English and the Ottomans.

Kurdakul, Necdet. *Osmanlı Devleti'nde Ticaret Antlaşmaları ve Kapitülasyonlar* (Commercial Agreements and Capitulations in the Ottoman State). Istanbul, 1981. The most useful of the recent works; contains Turkish texts of all the French capitulations.

Noradounghian, Gabriel. *Recueil d'actes internationaux de l'Empire Ottoman*. 4 vols. Paris, 1897–1903. Includes capitulations and treaties with all the European nations.

Skilliter, S. A. *William Harborne and the Trade with Turkey, 1578–1582: A Documentary Study of the First Anglo-Ottoman Relations*. London, 1977. Detailed account of the negotiation of the first English capitulations, with correspondence between the English and the Ottomans.

Steensgaard, Niels. "Consuls and Nations in the Levant." *Scandinavian Economic History Review* 15 (1967): 13–55. Compares Venetian, English, and Dutch consular systems.

Susa, Nasim. *The Capitulatory Régime of Turkey: Its History, Origin, and Nature*. Baltimore, 1933. Fulfills its title.

Wansbrough, John, Halil İnalçik, Ann K. S. Lambton, and Gabriel Baer. "Imtiyāzāt." In *Encyclopaedia of Islam*, new ed., vol. 3, pp. 1178–1195. Leiden, 1960–. The most extensive account and the main source for this article; includes a comprehensive bibliography.

Wood, Alfred Cecil. *A History of the Levant Company*. London, 1935. Trade practices and negotiations.

LINDA T. DARLING

CARPETS. The weaving of carpets is one of the most distinctive and characteristic of Islamic art forms, whether manifested in the more familiar pile carpets or the various flat-woven types. Found in a "rug belt" characterized for the most part by a dry and temperate climate, an abundance of marginal grazing land, and nomadic or seminomadic pastoral traditions, the heavy textiles we know as rugs or carpets are woven from Morocco to northern India and western China. Carpets were traditionally woven by and for all levels of Islamic society: court carpets were unique creations made to special order for the palace; commercial carpets were woven for sale in urban workshops; village and nomadic carpets served various domestic needs of their makers and were also made and sold as a source of cash. Because of their social embeddedness, carpets are among the most traditional and unchanging of Islamic art forms; yet because of their popularity in urban and Western markets, carpets are also paradoxically one of the traditional Islamic art forms most subject to influence from outside Islamic society. By the early nineteenth century, the four most important traditions of Islamic carpet weaving were those of Anatolia, Iran, Transcaucasia, and Turkic Central Asia.

Anatolia. The carpets woven in the heartland of the Ottoman Empire, Turkey, constitute the tradition of Islamic carpet-weaving that can be most continually documented since the fourteenth century. Woven in large part for export, by the beginning of the nineteenth century Anatolian carpet production was in decline owing to a shrinking market in Europe. Many local village and nomadic traditions of weaving, largely immune to outside economic pressure, had continued in virtually unbroken form for centuries, but commercial manufactories in west Anatolia in centers such as Ushak were moribund or began to produce machine-made goods in the Western taste for foreign markets. Gradually, in response to growing European and American demand, Anatolian handwoven carpet production increased over the century, largely under a piecework system but also, in the case of larger carpets, in urban weaving factories. Demand for the more traditional village carpets also increased during this century, and the carpets associated with the areas of Milas, Bergama, and the northwestern Anatolian coast, as well as with Mujur, Karapinar, Kirshehir, and Ladik in the west-central Anatolian plain, were produced in ever-increasing numbers. New commercial centers of manufacture, notably in urban Kayseri in central Anatolia, Bandirma in the northwest, and the areas around Gordes and Kula in the west, used the piecework system for the weaving of small *seccade* (Ar., *sajjādah*) or prayer-sized carpets (around 1 by 1.5 meters) for foreign markets; the designs and colors of their products, while reliant on traditional motifs, reflected the demands of the marketplace more than did those of the traditional village carpets. In 1843, the Hereke factory on the Marmara near Istanbul was founded by imperial decree, and in 1891 began producing pile carpets in a variety of traditional and persianized designs. Sometime after 1860 commercial aniline dyestuffs from central Europe flooded Anatolia and quickly replaced the more laborious traditional methods of dyeing wool with vegetal dyestuffs and imported natural indigo. The aniline dyes blighted several generations of Anatolian carpets whose faded purples, jarring oranges, and fugitive reds continued well into the twentieth century, when they were sometimes replaced by harsh but permanent commercial chromium dyes. Another innovation of the later nineteenth century was the introduction of the commercial "wash" process, by which the naturally brilliant hues of traditional carpets were chemically muted or altered. Even the products of village and nomadic weaving in Turkey were often affected by these technical innovations, since the dyeing of wool was often a specialized process done in larger towns, and the weaver had no control over the alteration of a carpet's color once it had been purchased by a middleman.

The fortunes of Anatolian carpet-weaving waxed and waned with taste and economy in the twentieth century. The Turkish war of independence resulted in massive population dislocations around traditional rug-weaving centers in west and central Anatolia; new immigrants, refugees from political turmoil in Transcaucasia and the Balkans, resettled in Anatolia, often bringing their own carpet-weaving traditions with them. The growth of serious carpet-collecting in Europe in the late nineteenth cen-

FIGURE 1. *Contemporary Anatolian Carpet.* The contemporary renaissance of traditionally dyed carpets in traditional designs is exemplified in this example woven in Turkey using a model from northwest Iran. Azeri carpet produced by Woven Legends, Inc., Philadelphia, 213 x 264 cm.

tury and the establishment of the Turkish and Islamic Art Museum in Istanbul in 1908 helped keep alive respect for the great traditions of early nineteenth-century weaving with their strong historical roots. But by the 1960s, most new carpets woven in Turkey were pale shadows of their historical forebears, and the fashion for broadloom carpets in the West had significantly reduced exports.

In the 1970s, an explosion in European collectors' interest in Turkish carpets resulted in skyrocketing prices for old carpets and in attempts by contemporary Turkish carpet-weavers to cater to the growing sophistication in European taste. A remarkable revival of traditional dyeing methods and a concomitant return to traditional carpet designs reflecting examples found in museums were supported by the growth of government-sponsored cooperatives such as the DOBAG project (see figure 2), centered in two traditional west Anatolian weaving areas and soon joined by a host of free-market imitators.

FIGURE 2. *Anatolian Wool Dyeing*. Dyeing of black rug wool using traditional dyestuffs, at the government-sponsored DOBAG cooperative near Ayvacik, northwest Turkey.

Turkish and foreign scholarship produced a flood of books on traditional carpet-weaving; major American and European museums mounted exhibitions of Turkish carpets; and in Istanbul two new museums devoted to pile and flat-woven carpets were opened by the Directorate of Pious Foundations. By the early 1990s the Turkish carpet industry was producing carpets of markedly improved quality in record quantities.

Transcaucasia. Nineteenth- and twentieth-century carpets from the Caucasus find their design roots in the seventeenth century and later, in the large commercial carpets of the south and east Caucasus derived from earlier Persian examples. Local traditions of village weaving seem to have endured through the nineteenth century, resulting in a limited production of small carpets in traditional designs, but the middle to later nineteenth century saw an explosion in production, primarily of *seccade*-sized rugs and other small formats. These small carpets, produced in various locales in widely varying knot density and designs, pose special problems for the carpet historian because of the patchwork of nationalities inhabiting Transcaucasia. Documentary sources indicate that the majority of the weavers were Muslims, while the functions of dyeing and marketing and a good deal of local patronage came from the prosperous Armenian communities in the south Caucasus. Around 1900 production seems to have reached its zenith; Caucasian rugs were inexpensive, they were much in vogue in New England, and they were marketed both in their original colors and in chemically washed versions. Some locales used aniline dyes extensively in their weaving, but others appear to have been virtually untouched by the aniline blight. Nineteenth-century Caucasian rugs became a serious interest of collectors in Britain and the United States around 1900, reaching the latter in vast quantities and marketed by a burgeoning community of immigrant Armenian rug dealers around the country.

After the sovietization of Transcaucasia in the early 1920s, a renewed production of Caucasian carpets in traditional designs was begun under the export-oriented New Economic Policy of the Soviets. These carpets, of high technical quality and woven in impeccably authentic nineteenth-century designs, are as popular among many contemporary collectors as their forebears, despite their use of somewhat harsh and metallic chromium dyes. By the late 1920s, however, carpet production in the Caucasus was in deep decline, and export markets for Soviet goods in the West dried up. By the late twentieth century there was little new carpet production of consequence emerging from the Caucasus, although the collapse of the Soviet Union resulted in a flood of older goods reaching Middle Eastern and European markets. The national governments of Armenia and Azerbaijan have recently promoted the study of older carpets, and museums of carpet history and institutes for carpet design and production exist in both states.

Iran. The mid-eighteenth-century Afghan invasion that brought an end to the Ṣafavid dynasty in Iran also brought about a collapse in the Iranian economy that the emerging nineteenth-century provincial dynasties were unable completely to overcome. The glorious past traditions of urban weaving in Iran were by the middle of the nineteenth century largely in decline, although various village and nomadic weavers continued to produce carpets for their own use. In the later nineteenth century, however, simultaneous with the revival of weaving in Anatolia and Transcaucasia, Iran experienced a remarkable revival in carpet-making that once again brought the Iranian weaving tradition to international prominence. By 1880 merchants from Tabriz, later joined by foreign entrepreneurs, brought about a renaissance in urban rug-weaving in Iran. By adapting the Iranian traditions of weaving large, regularly woven, intricately designed carpets—whose many-plied cotton warps and carefully supervised production made them lie flat and square—to new sizes suitable for the proportions of European and American middleclass living and dining rooms, hallways, foyers, parlors, and bedrooms, the new entrepreneurs quickly created a huge market for Iranian carpets. Companies such as OCM (Oriental Carpet Manufacturers) and Ziegler, based in Britain, controlled urban weaving factories in many Iranian cities and sometimes operated their own design ateliers. Looms were constructed and placed through the piecework system in urban and village homes around the country, and local design workshops produced distinctive regional designs of varying quality. By the early twentieth century the urban looms of Kashan, Tabriz, Kerman, and Mashhad were producing finely woven carpets with intricate designs, while distinctive local products were woven all over the country, with major centers in the Kurdish areas of Bijar and Sanadaj (Sehna), in the Arak district (home of Feraghan and Sarouk carpets), and in Iranian Azerbaijan (site of Heriz and Serab weavings). Stringent government action to discourage the use of aniline dyes was effective in many parts of Iran, although the process of color alteration through "washing" was commonly used in European marketing centers; another phenomenon known as "washing and painting" resulted in the bleaching out of a rug's original colors and the substitution of chromium dyes "painted" on the rug in an entirely different palette. Between the World Wars carpet-weaving in Iran slackened, but after World War II new centers for the production of extremely fine rugs woven in traditional sixteenth- and seventeenth-century designs were established in Isfahan, Qom, and Nayyin (see figure 3). The Pahlavi regime promoted rug-weaving not so much for economic reasons as for its symbolic importance as a national cultural achievement; in the early 1970s a Carpet Museum was established in Tehran. In the meantime, a growing interest on the part of western collectors in traditional village nomadic weaving from Iran resulted in attempts to produce modern carpets in Yalameh and Ardebil that reflected these traditions of design.

The flight of many carpet merchants and their inventories prior to 1978, the large stockpiles of Iranian rugs

FIGURE 3. *Contemporary Iranian Carpet.* The extremely finely knotted contemporary rug production of Iran includes medallion carpets such as this one for sale in the Isfahan bazaar.

in the warehouses of the great European companies, and a porous Iran-Turkey border kept Iranian rugs in Western markets during trade embargo following the Iranian revolution, without much benefit to Iranian weavers or merchants. By the early 1990s, the Iranian government decided to sponsor new efforts to expand carpet exports and invited foreign collectors and dealers to an international conference and trade fair in Tehran in 1992, but the Iranian carpet industry faced serious competition from Iranian-style carpets produced in India, Turkey, Pakistan, China, and Rumania; traditional village and nomadic weaving, meanwhile, had undergone a great decline after the revolution.

Central Asia. The Turkmen peoples of Central Asia have probably woven carpets for well over a millennium, but these carpets appear to have been produced almost entirely for their own consumption; thus examples of Turkmen weaving from before 1800 are both rare and difficult to date precisely. In the early nineteenth century the six major Turkmen rug-weaving tribes—the Salor, Saryk, Yomut, Chaudor, Tekke, and Ersari—saw chaotic change with the expansion of the Russian empire, turmoil in Afghanistan and Iran, and intertribal warfare in Central Asia. The Salor and Saryk tribes were eventually overcome by the more warlike Tekke before the latter were defeated by the Russians in the battle of Gok Tepe in 1881. Traditional Turkmen tribal carpets woven before the middle of the nineteenth century are distinguished by designs and techniques peculiar to each tribe and subtribe and by a variety of genres, including pentagonal camel-trappings, tent-bands, and utilitarian bags peculiar to the nomadic weaving traditions; the predominant dyestuff used in these carpets was madder, giving a variety of reds and red-browns from scarlet to mahogany.

Because of their relative isolation from the forces of modernity and their geographical remoteness from Western markets, Turkmen weavers managed to preserve their traditional weaving practices through most of the nineteenth century, although aniline dyes had made their way into Central Asia by the last two decades of the century. The ascendance of the Tekke resulted in the subordination of the older traditions of the Salor and Saryk; the northern Ersari, who were settled in villages along the Oxus by the nineteenth century, were influenced by the weaving of Iran to the south. At the end of the nineteenth century the opening of a Russian railway into Bukhara led to the first significant appearance of Turkmen rugs in European markets, not surprisingly under the misnomer "Bukhara carpets." Production of carpets continued after sovietization of the Turkmen and Uzbek republics, but with the forced settlement of the formerly nomadic tribes, the many genres of weaving associated with the nomadic tent and tribal festivities quickly disappeared to be replaced by rectangular floor carpets for export made with brilliant and sometimes jarring chromium dyes. Weaving continued on a reduced level of quantity and quality under the Soviets; the reproduction of traditional Turkmen designs in cheap cotton-warped factory rugs made in Pakistan, coupled with the preference of collectors for the older carpets, contributed to the decline of Turkmen weaving by the late twentieth century.

Carpets and Culture. As Islamic nation-states attempt to find living expressions of their cultural identity, as Western museums and collectors expand their

FIGURE 4. *Commercial Weaving*. Commercial rug weaving in the modern Islamic world is often done on steel-pipe vertical looms as seen in this manufactory in Rabat, Morocco.

notions of what art is and what constitutes the legitimate subject of a collector's interest, and as an eclectic and historically aware aesthetic of interior decoration flourishes in the late twentieth century, many parts of the Islamic world are witnessing an increase in rug production, against all predictions made in the early 1970s by historians of carpets. The economic needs of oil-poor third-world Islamic nations, the rising appreciation of Islamic art in the West, and most of all a rising appreciation of national cultural traditions in the Islamic world itself have fueled this phenomenon. How long it will last in the face of economic and social change is still a matter for speculation.

BIBLIOGRAPHY

Brüggemann, Werner, and Harold Böhmer. *Rugs of the Peasants and Nomads of Anatolia*. Munich, 1983. Exhibition catalog with an extensive discussion of more recent Anatolian rug weaving, and a chapter on the reintroduction of traditional dyestuffs.

Denny, Walter B. *Oriental Rugs*. New York, 1979. General introduction to the history and major groups of Islamic carpets.

Eiland, Murray. *Oriental Rugs: A Comprehensive Guide*. Rev. and exp. ed. Boston, 1976. General rug manual with extensive information on nineteenth- and twentieth-century production in the major Islamic weaving areas.

Eiland, Murray. *Chinese and Exotic Rugs*. Boston, 1979. Companion volume to the same author's *Oriental Rugs;* covers peripheral weaving areas from Morocco to China.

Hillmann, Michael C. *Persian Carpets*. Austin, 1984. Discussion of later and contemporary Iranian carpets.

Landreau, Anthony, ed. *Yörük: The Nomadic Weaving Tradition of the Middle East*. Pittsburgh, 1978. Exhibition catalog dealing with nineteenth- and twentieth-century nomadic carpets.

Landreau, Anthony, and W. R. Pickering. *From the Bosporus to Samarkand: Flat-Woven Rugs*. Washington, D.C., 1969. Exhibition catalog focusing on carpets in the various flat-woven techniques.

Mackie, Louise W., and Jon Thompson, eds. *Turkmen: Tribal Carpets and Traditions*. Washington, D.C., 1980. Exhibition catalog, with important contributions by leading scholars on the history, context, and weaving of Turkmen carpets.

Thompson, Jon. *Oriental Carpets from the Tents, Cottages, and Workshops of Asia*. New York, 1988. Fine general introduction to the medium of carpets and their place in traditional and modern Islamic culture.

Wright, Richard. *Rugs and Flatweaves of the Transcaucasus*. Pittsburgh, 1980. Exhibition catalog with commentary on nineteenth- and twentieth-century Caucasian carpets by the leading authority in the field.

WALTER B. DENNY

CASSETTES. Since the 1970s, the "little medium" of the audiocassette has become an important means of communication with a sociopolitical impact reaching far beyond the boundaries of the nation states. This medium differs in significant ways from the "big media," particularly television and radio, which in much of the Islamic world have been a state monopoly pressed into serving national development projects of often repressive governments. Moreover, until recently the big media (which includes cinema) were characterized by centralization of production, distribution, exhibition, and control; one-way transmission of materials; and capital intensiveness, necessitating the existence of highly trained technical and professional infrastructures and equipment. Because of their contribution to monopolization of power, manipulation and homogenization of public opinion, and subversion of traditional and folk ways, these media have been considered negatively and distrusted by large segments of the so-called third and Islamic worlds.

The audiocassette, on the other hand, is potentially a two-way, grassroot medium which is reusable, durable, portable, and inexpensive. The production and distribution of cassettes need not be centralized, and their reception does not depend on a preexisting schedule (as do radio and television broadcasts) or on a special exhibition hall (as do films) or on an expensive playback unit (as do videocassettes). In terms of contents, cassettes can contain polished, studio-recorded productions or impromptu interviews, lectures, sermons, recitations, music and songs, and documentary materials. Tapes can be listened to individually or collectively and in diverse times and locations. Women and ethnic and religious minorities, traditionally shut off from the public sphere, can enter it through listening, retaping, and exchanging of cassettes. Through such activities the receivers of tapes can themselves become transmitters. As such, audiocassettes are not as prone as the big media are to centralized control, and they can be employed as an effective diversifying, participatory medium in support of alternative causes, minority aspirations, or revolutionary ideologies.

For cassettes to act as agents of social change and alternative religious discourse, certain enabling conditions must be present. These include the presence of a repressive and secular government, central hegemonic control of mass media, social and political inequality and turmoil, charismatic religious leaders and speakers, social institutions, such as churches and mosques and underground political groups, which can provide alternatives to the state ideology, traditional economic and social institutions and formations, such as bazaars and labor unions, which can provide financial assistance and networking infrastructure, linkage with expatriate groups, and a population that is orally oriented. The availability in recent years of efficient national and international telephone, low-cost publishing and duplicating, clandestine radio stations, and exile periodicals and radio and television programs abroad has proven to be instrumental in the further relay and propagation of cassettes' messages to and from the nation states.

Two cautionary points must be remembered, however. First, each of these enabling conditions is not sufficient by itself to transform the little medium of audiocassette into one with a mighty social impact. Similar to all social changes, linkage, crossfertilization, and intertextuality among the aforementioned sociopolitical, economic, and technological forces is essential. Second, as illustrated by the cases of Iran and India (below)—in which resurgent Islam and Hindu chauvinism respectively resorted to cassettes—the use of such a potentially democratic, grassroot, "people's" medium does not necessarily guarantee a progressive, democratic, or humane outcome.

Iran. Although audiotapes have been used to record and to listen to religious sermons in such Islamic countries as Afghanistan since the 1950s (Oliver Roy, "The Mujahidin and the Future of Afghanistan," in *The Iranian Revolution: Its Global Impact*, edited by John L. Esposito, Miami, 1990, p. 187), it was the Iranian Revolution of 1979 that catapulted the small medium of audiocassettes into the pantheons of big media in terms of its sociopolitical impact within and beyond national borders. Because in Iran the cassette was so fully and effectively used in support of an Islamist social change, this case deserves elaboration.

In the decade leading up to the revolution, tapes of antishah clandestine radio broadcasts, such as those by the Mujāhidīn-i Khalq organization, provided a link between guerrilla organizations and their sympathizers. But it was the use of audiocassettes by two charismatic leaders that demonstrated that when a number of the enabling conditions are met, audiocassettes can help produce significant social effect and political impact—in fact, an alternative epistemic community sufficiently powerful to topple the powerful Pahlavi regime. The enabling institutions and formations included a network of between 60,000 and 200,000 mullahs with organic ties to the people and to some 90,000 mosques located throughout the country (Tehranian, 1980, pp. 17–18). There were also numerous seminaries (*ḥawzah-yi ilmīyah*), religious councils (*hay'at-i mazhabī*) often sponsored by bazaar merchants and guilds, shrines (*imāmzādah*) and pilgrimage to them organized by the *hay'ats*, performance arenas (*takkīyah*), religious and secular salons (*dawrah*), religious community centers (*ḥusaynīyah*), and colleges and universities. Whether in cities or villages, in these locations religious leaders, scholars, and preachers would lecture, give sermons, pray, recite verses from the Qur'ān, and recount tales of lamentations for the martyrdom of Shīʿī imams (*rawẓah*). Mourning ceremonies and religious processions and passion plays (*taʿziyah*) would also take place at appropriate sites. The established networks of bazaars and guilds throughout the country and the emerging network of antishah leftist and guerrilla organizations provided financial, humanpower, and ideological support that further interlinked and imbricated these disparate institutions and practices. [*See* Bazaar; Guilds; Imāmzādah; Ḥusaynīyah; Taʿziyah.]

During the 1970s, many of the speeches of the Western-educated religious scholar, ʿAlī Sharīʿatī, who combined a revisionist Islamist rereading of Shīʿī ideology with Fanonist liberation ideology, were recorded at Mashhad University and the famous Ḥusaynīyah Irshād in Tehran. Many of the cassettes were subsequently transcribed and published in book form. Both the tapes and the books were clandestinely but widely distributed in Iran and abroad through the aforementioned nexus of institutions and formations. By mid 1970s, the Ayatollah Ruhollah Khomeini began sending from his exile in Iraq increasingly radical antigovernment messages by way of leaflets and cassettes. The tapes were transcribed and distributed by way of similar channels. When in 1978 he was forced into a double exile to France, his access to Western mass media increased greatly as did his taped messages, which were now more resolute and were transmitted by way of telephone lines to banks of cassette recorders in Tehran for duplication and distribution (Sreberny-Mohammadi, 1985, pp. 122–124). In Yazd, Ayatollah Ṣadūqī's house was apparently turned into a major cassette manufacturing center: four or five hours a day, half a dozen phone lines received Khomeini's taped messages from Paris and duplicated them on cassettes at high speed for distribution (Mehdy Naficy, *Klerus, Basar und die iranische Revolution* [Hamburg, 1993], pp. 231–232).

The audiocassette medium proved to be highly suitable for the task of toppling the shah because it met many of the enabling conditions and because of two additional reasons: First, revolutionary speakers, such as Sharīʿatī and Khomeini, turned their lectures and pronouncements into powerfully crafted messages by taking advantage of the intimacy, immediacy, and interactivity of the "live" lecture situation; the narrative structure of Iranian oral and folk traditions; and the rhetorical, symbolic, and performative patterns of religious recitation, mourning and lamentation—so familiar to Iranians, literate or not. Second, the taped messages suited the oral orientation of the transnational electronic news media eager for sensational sound-bites. The political impact of the messages increased vastly when they became the source of news, quoted by Western news organizations, the Persian language programs of Western broadcasting agencies (particularly the BBC), and the antigovernment clandestine radios operating from outside Iran. Each important taped pronouncement from Khomeini or quotation based on it would cause widespread reaction in Iran that would in turn lead to another message, escalating the effect of the previous one. This complex interconnection of forces, media, technologies, and narrative forms turned the traditional local pulpit *(minbar)* into a powerful, interactive, transnational, long-distance, electronic pulpit.

In Iran, both the distribution and the reception of these cassettes defied the pervasive censorship system of the shah's government, turning the exchange of tapes or the mere listening to them into acts of commitment and opposition. Immediately after the revolution, a wide array of religious and revolutionary tapes were distributed by the aforementioned networks and by the newly formed agencies, such as the Reconstruction Crusade, which claimed that in 1983 alone it had distributed 74,789 audiocassettes nationwide along with a profusion of other audiovisual materials (Naficy, 1992, p. 198). In the postrevolution era, for a variety of sociopolitical reasons, the enabling mechanisms were disabled, causing the audiocasstte genie in Iran to be put back in the bottle. However, the exile-produced Iranian pop music from Los Angeles and its wide availability in Iran—despite the official ban—proclaimed yet again a new tact in the long-distance, transnational cassette wars of cultures—this time against the reigning Islamist ideology (Naficy, 1993, pp. 54–58).

India. Audiocassettes containing nationalistic music and political speeches have been instrumental in fomenting or capitalizing on the vast existing religious, linguistic, and nationalistic divisions in India. One recent incident illustrates the manner in which this potentially liberating medium can become a tool of suppression and violence.

Since the 1980s Hindu chauvinists and Muslim militants have engaged in a series of escalating clashes and riots, which culminated in 1992 in the death of over one thousand people and the destruction of the Babri Masjid near Lucknow, a mosque that is said to have been built by the Mughal emperor Babur on the site of a Rama temple that he had destroyed. Before the incident, some Muslim leaders (such as Sayyid Shahābuddīn and Imām al-Bukhārī) had raised the stakes by promoting militancy and confrontation. But it was the inflammatory songs and speeches of firebrand Hindu chauvinists (like Uma Bharati and Sadhvi Ritambhara), distributed by way of videocassettes and audiocassettes that fanned the fires of intolerance and destruction against Muslims. There are deep-rooted mythological and real reasons for the Babri Masjid events, but according to Peter Manuel, who studied the audiocassettes produced during the events leading up to the destruction, they contained a basic recurring message that scapegoated and blamed the Muslims in India for much of the ills of India since its partition in 1948 and for a desire to capture Kashmir and the rest of the country.

On these cassettes, songs and incendiary speeches by male and female speakers repeatedly urged violent action to recapture the mosque, destroy it, and rebuild the temple on its ruins. Some of these cassettes, banned by the government, were the hottest-selling tapes of 1990. Other cassettes were apparently used by Hindus as sparks for Hindu-Muslim sectarian violence in Agra. These recordings, captured by the Agra police, contained Muslim or Hindu slogans (Allāhu Akbar; Jai Shri Ram), blood-curdling screams ("help, help"; "kill, kill"), gunfire, and other sound effects. Street demonstrators or passing cars in the dead of the night played these cassettes at high volume to seed distrust and foment violence in both communities (Manuel, 1993, pp. 250–256).

Afghanistan. Farghanachi Uzbek women and children who were refugees from Afghanistan and living in Karachi, Pakistan, during the Soviet invasion of Afghanistan used audiocassettes in an innovative way that corroborates the capability of this medium to transcend national boundaries and transform the discourse on gender relations—all in the service of Islamic politics and ideologies. During the 1980s these women refugees led a rather traditional life in exile: ensconced within a closed circle of kinship and friendship, frequently visiting each other, wearing either the Afghani veil called *chādarī* or the Saudi Arabian veil called *ḥijāb*. Their communal activities centered around various rites of passage celebrations, religious study, and prayer. During these gatherings they would listen to and discuss one of the numerous cassettes purchased from stores in Pakistan.

Although some cassettes carried folk music and anti-Afghani regime chants, the majority contained stories based on the Qur'ān and the *ḥadīth* that explained the importance of martyrdom and sacrifice in time of *jihād* (war against nonbelievers), particularly the ongoing one against the Soviet invaders and their Afghani collaborators. The stories, taped in Afghanistan during public sermons about the *jihād* were delivered by religious scholars and preachers in Dari that tended to unify the varied linguistic communities of refugees from Afghanistan. Since these cassettes had been taped during public sermons, many of them were dialogic, preserving the live audience-speaker interactions. In them male preachers consistently urged women to participate in this modern *jihād* by following the examples set by women in the early Islamic period. Audrey Shalinsky, who studied these tapes, reports that the stories of the courageous behavior of Muḥammad's womenfolk during the famous battle of Uhud and the vanquishing of the vengeful Hind the liver eater provided ideal role models of mother, wife, and daughter for these displaced women and children (1993, p. 661). Thrust into the extraordinary time of *jihād*, these model women had been able to transcend the boundaries of their traditional roles in order to fight the enemy.

These emotionally charged cassettes were popular with women and children, and to some degree they were successful in their political mission, since they energized some of the listeners to want to return to their homeland—not so much to be reunited with their families (thus fulfilling traditional patterns) as to participate in the on-going *jihād*. Both *jihād* and exile are liminal periods that raise questions about and tend to subvert established identities and traditional social structures.

Uzbekistan. In the former Soviet Union, during the Gorbachev era of *perestroika* (restructuring) and *glasnost* (openness), a shadow information network developed in Uzbekistan that appears to have been a challenge to the official mass media. Audiocassettes were part of this shadow network, which provided songs and speeches asserting Uzbek nationalism and Islamic ideology and culture. There are a few reports of the use of audiocassettes before the Gorbachev era. These indicate that the Ṣūfīs in Uzbekistan, through their network of schools, mosques, and *khānqāh* (Ṣūfī teaching center) extensively used illegally produced "recorded samizdats" and recordings of stories glorifying pre-Communist Turkistan (Alexander Bennigsen and Enders S. Wimbush, *Mystics and Commissars: Sufism in the Soviet Union*, Berkeley, 1985; H. B. Pakovsky, "The Deceivers," *Central Asian Survey* 3.1 [1984]: 124–131; and H. B. Pakovsky, "Chora Batir: A Tartar Admonition to Future Generations," *Studies in Comparative Communism* 19.3–4 [1986]: 253–265). That such an activity, then considered to be criminal and punishable, could be undertaken is an indication of the power of linkage between the small medium of cassette and a religious institution offering itself as an ideological alternative to the state.

During transition to independence, when mass media were still centrally controlled, cassettes containing music, comedy skits, and political and religious discussions became widely available in Uzbekistan cities and villages. They could be heard at home, in the bazaars, or at informal gatherings called *gaps*, causing a lengthy public discussion of the issues the tapes raised. Using the informal networks of distribution, Dadakhan Hasan, a politically active Uzbek singer, became one of the three most respected public figures in Uzbekistan in 1990 (David Tyson, unpublished manuscript, 1992, pp. 16–19). In these cassettes containing nationalist songs interspersed with Islamist commentary, he blamed the social and moral malaise befalling Uzbekistan on Soviet colonialism and urged his listeners to work for political independence through Islamic unity and struggle. In addition to such analysis of a general nature, Hasan's commentaries on specific events (such as the slaughter in June 1990 of hundreds of Uzbeks, apparently at the hands of the Kyrgyz in Osh and Uzgen, Kyrgyzstan) provided an alternative, popular reading to that transmitted by the official mass media. In this case, the relative freedom of expression brought on by political openness allowed a charismatic figure to wed popular music with religiously informed political commentary, producing widely appealing oppositional products.

Indonesia. The case of Indonesia illustrates the intensity of cultural struggle over Islamic legitimacy by means of cassettes and the high cost that individuals can incur in that process. Islam forms the faith of 90 percent of the Indonesian population, yet it is not the official religion of this heterogeneous country. The multifaceted

Islamic revival movement can be broken down into four groups here: traditionalists, radicals, fundamentalists, and revivalists. Each poses a different threat to the state, causing varied governmental responses including coercion, cooptation, establishment of an official Islamic support group, scapegoating of foreign governments, and creation of symbols of legitimacy (Fred von der Mehden, "The Political and Social Challenge of the Islamic Revival in Malaysia and Indonesia," *Muslim World* 76 [July–October 1986]: 219–233). Of these measures, coercion is related to the subject of audiocassettes. In the late 1980s a number of sedition show trials were held in which Muslim preachers, spokespersons, and leaders were charged with fomenting specific violent acts through their writing and speeches which questioned the official ideology of *pancasila* (five principles) and supported an Islamic revolution. Individuals were also charged with publishing and distributing banned and seditious literatures and "inflammatory" sermons and religious speeches. Stiff sentences were requested and handed down in these elaborate trials. For example, in 1985 the prosecution demanded that the accused, Ali Masrun Al Mudafar, a primary school teacher in Surabaya, be given a prison term of twenty years for teaching courses that aimed to undermine and overthrow the state and replace it with an Islamic state. He was further charged with copying the cassettes of speeches by religious figures Amir Biki and Sayrifin Maloko, distributing them free of charge, and broadcasting them over the radio station of the Surabaya Islamic Dakwan College (*Indonesia Report,* April log [25 May 1985]: 47; August log, no. 11 [September 1985]: 34). The reason for the stiff penalty demanded by the prosecutor was partly that the speech that Biki had delivered to a large crowd in Tanjung Priok in September 1984 had caused a street demonstration in which a hundred people had been shot and killed in cold blood by the police. Attempting to prevent further popularization of this inflammatory speech, the court sessions in which the tape was played were held in camera. Maloko himself was charged with subversion and sentenced to ten years in jail (*Indonesia Mirror* 5 [March 1987]: 1).

Even though many tapes of sermons and religious lectures had been in circulation in Indonesia and exported to Malaysia, the Tanjung Priok event forced the governments in both countries to become more sensitive to the power of cassettes. As a result, religious cassettes, even those recorded before the incident, were banned, such as those containing the sermons of the Indonesian Muslim preacher and scholar Abdul Qadir Djaelani. The following excerpt from one of his sermons, entitled "Die As Martyrs," gives an indication of its powerful dialogic form:

> My Muslim brothers, my call to you to die as martyrs is not mere talk. My call comes from the depth of my heart directed to your heart! (Loud shouts of approval) Are you ready to die as martyrs? (Loud shouts of "Yes!") Are you really ready? (Louder shouts) You are not being hypocritical? (Loud shouts of "No!") Are you sincere? (Loud shouts of "Yes!") Then, God willing, we will face this situation gloriously! Let them know, I am ready to die as a martyr now, right now! (Loud shouts) If you want to join me, get ready now, brothers! (Loud shouts of "Ready! Ready!") (*Indonesia Report,* Politics supplement, no. 13 [November 1985]: 2–3.)

In 1985 Djaelani was arrested and tried for subversion, with the prosecutor demanding the death sentence. He was declared guilty and sentenced to eighteen years imprisonment.

Iranian revolutionary and Shīʿī thoughts, particularly those of ʿAlī Sharīʿatī, have penetrated into Indonesia (Fred von der Mehden, *Two Worlds of Islam: Interaction Between Southeast Asia and the Middle East,* Gainesville, 1993, pp. 87–91). Although cassette tapes of his lectures in Persian are not useful because of language differences, his translated books are available. And since many of these are revised transcripts of his speeches, they retain features of the spoken word and of oral narratives.

The use of audiocassettes for transnational propagation of Islamist ideologies and politics has gone beyond the Islamic countries. In North America, some of the cassettes are focused on the politics and societies of that region, such as those containing sermons, speeches, and Qur'ānic recitations delivered by African-American Muslim preachers. These are available in Islamic bookstores. Other cassettes, although produced in the United States, aim to influence the politics of Middle Eastern societies. For example, for a number of years the tapes of sermons and speeches of Shaykh Omar Abdel Rahman (ʿUmar ʿAbd al-Raḥmān), a charismatic Egyptian cleric preaching in New Jersey mosques, were distributed in Egypt. Highly influential from a position in exile, he has been regarded by Egyptian authorities to be the spiritual leader of the Islamic Jihād Organization, which advocates a violent overthrow of the Egyptian government and its replacement with an Islamic state

(*New York Times,* 5 March 1993, p. 1). [*See the biography of Abdel Rahman.*] The broadcast of his taped speeches by the Party of God radio station in Lebanon and by other stations has expanded his influence beyond U.S. mosques and Egyptian borders. However, the shaykh's public utterances came to a halt in 1993 with his arrest on the charge of involvement in the bombing of the World Trade Center building in New York City.

[*See also* Communications Media.]

BIBLIOGRAPHY

Antoun, Richard. *Muslim Preacher in the Modern World: A Jordanian Case Study in Comparative Perspective.* Princeton; 1989. Analysis of the social organization of preachers, their rhetoric, and narratives.

Boyd, Douglas A., et al. *Videocassette Recorders in the Third World.* New York, 1989. Useful analysis of the development and use of videocassettes (which has a bearing on audiocassettes) in the Arab world, Asia, Latin America, and the Caribbean.

Manuel, Peter. *Popular Musics of the Non-Western World: An Introductory Survey.* New York, 1988. Valuable survey of popular musics (including the impact of cassettes) in various non-Western areas, including the Arab and non-Arab Middle East.

Manuel, Peter. *Cassette Culture: Popular Music and Technology in North India.* Chicago, 1993. Detailed discussion of the impact of audiocassettes in forming a popular culture that links music, cinema, and television with capitalist commodification practices.

Mowlana, Hamid. "Technology versus Tradition: Communication in the Iranian Revolution." *Journal of Communication* 29 (Summer 1979): 107–112. Early analysis of the Iranian Revolution from a communication theory standpoint.

Naficy, Hamid. "Islamizing Film Culture in Iran." In *Iran: Political Culture in the Islamic Republic,* edited by Samih K. Farsoun and Mehrdad Mashayekhi, pp. 178–213. London and New York, 1992. Comprehensive analysis of the formation of a new cinema culture in postrevolutionary Iran.

Naficy, Hamid. *The Making of Exile Cultures: Iranian Television in Los Angeles.* Minneapolis, 1993. Theoretical and ethnographic analysis of the place of culture and cultural productions (including audiocassettes) in the formation of exilic identities.

Nelson, Kristina. *The Art of Reciting the Qur'ān.* Austin, 1985. A thorough examination of the various arts of recitation of the Qur'an and their relationship to music.

Shalinsky, Audrey C. "Women's Role in the Afghanistan Jihad." *International Journal of Middle East Studies* 25 (1993): 661–675. Detailed ethnographic study of Afghani women's uses of audiocassettes about the anti-Soviet *jihād.*

Soley, Lawrence C., and John S. Nichols. *Clandestine Radio Broadcasting: A Study of Revolutionary and Counterrevolutionary Electronic Communication.* New York, 1987. Well-documented history of clandestine radio in the world, with sections on Islamic countries.

Sreberny-Mohammadi, Annabelle. "The Power of Tradition: Communication and the Iranian Revolution." Ph.D. diss., Columbia University, 1985. Comprehensive study of the revolution through an examination of the various formal and informal communication systems involved.

Tehranian, Majid. "Communication and Revolution in Iran: The Passing of a Paradigm." *Iranian Studies* 13.1–4 (1980): 5–30. Charts the shift in political and communication discourses from the Pahlavi to the Islamic era.

HAMID NAFICY

CENTRAL ASIAN LITERATURES. Central Asia is understood to include the territories of present Uzbekistan, Kazakhstan, Kyrgyzstan, Tajikistan, and Turkmenistan, the native population of which is Turkic in race and Muslim in religion. The Turkic peoples of Central Asia had a state structure and a rich literary tradition long before the Russian conquest of the region.

The development of a significant literary tradition in Turkic-speaking Central Asia dates back to the ninth and tenth centuries CE. Historically and sociopolitically, we may distinguish three significant periods in the development of literature in Central Asia—the Islamic-imperial, the colonial, and the post-independence periods.

Islamic-Imperial Period. The longest era lasted until the second half of the nineteenth century. During this period numerous literary and poetic works were produced, often under the aegis of the great Turkic Muslim emperors, kings, sultans, and emirs and their courts. Some of the best-known patrons of and contributors to the literature of Central Asia include the Qārakhānids (tenth century); the Timurids (fourteenth through sixteenth centuries) such as Amīr Timur (1336–1405), Ulughbek (1394–1449), and Ḥusayn Bāyqarā (1438–1506); the founder of the Mughal Empire in India, Ẓahīruddīn Muḥammad Bābur (1483–1530); and the late nineteenth-century emir of Khoqand, Umarkhan.

Yūsuf Khāṣṣ Ḥājib was one of the best-known writers of eleventh-century Central Asia. Unfortunately, only one of his works survives, a long didactic poem entitled *Ḳutadghu bilig* (Wisdom of Royal Glory), which is considered one of the oldest monuments of Central Asian Turkic literature.

Aḥmad Yasavī was a Central Asian Turkic Ṣūfī and poet. He was born in the second half of eleventh century near the city of Sayram in Turkistan. *Dīvān-i ḥikmat,* a collection of his didactic character poems written in Central Asian Turki, is still very popular among the peoples of Uzbekistan and Kazakhstan. The oldest surviving manuscript of this work dates from the seventeenth century. Yasavī's poems created a new genre in Central Asian Turkic literature, that of religious folk poetry. In the following centuries many religious poets such as Ṣūfī Allāhyār and Sulaymān Bāqirghanī were influenced by Aḥmad Yasavī.

The best-known poets of the thirteenth and fourteenth centuries whose works have been preserved to modern times are Quṭb, Khvārizmī, and Durbek. Quṭb's *Khusraw va Shīrīn*, Khvārizmī's *Muḥabbatnāmah*, and Durbek's *Yūsuf va Zulaykhā* are still popular among Central Asians, especially Uzbek people. The prose work *Nahjul faradis*, written in the second half of the fourteenth century in Central Asian Turki by an unknown author, consists of four parts. The first part is devoted to the life of Muḥammad, and the second part describes the activities of Caliph Rashīd id-Dīn, ʿAlī, and four imams.

Under the Timurids (fourteenth to sixteenth centuries) Central Asian literature flourished, and a new generation of poets appeared. The poems of Luṭfī, Atāyī, Sakkākī, Gadā'ī, Navā'ī, and Bābur are still read and appreciated by the peoples of Central Asia.

Luṭfī was the great early master of the *ghazāl* genre later perfected by Navā'ī and Bābur. Luṭfī's poetry is more accessible to modern readers because it contains more Turkic words than Arabic and Persian. His works influenced the poetry of his contemporaries Atāyī, Sakkākī, and Gadā'ī, whose poetry was esteemed even during their own lifetimes.

Gadā'ī is one of the most remarkable Central Asian Turkic poets of the fifteenth century. The language of his *dīvān*s (collections of poems) is Turki, the literary language of the Turkic people of Central Asia. Turki was highly developed under the Timurids. Central Asian literary Turki took its classical shape especially in the works of Mīr ʿAlīshīr Navā'ī (1441–1501) and Muḥammad Ẓahīruddīn Bābur (1483–1530).

Navā'ī was an outstanding thinker and poet as well as the great literary patron of his day. He was a statesman and a prominent member of the court of Sultan Ḥusayn Bāyqarā, the Timurid prince who ruled Herat from 1473 to 1506. Navā'ī wrote all his works in Central Asian Turki. His *Hamsa* (Quintet) is comprised of five *dastān*s (long poems): *Ḥayrat al-abrār* (Amazement of the Pious), *Farhād va Shīrīn* (Farhad and Shirin), *Laylī va Majnūn* (Layli and Majnun), *Sabʿa-yi sayyār* (Seven Planets), and *Saddi Iskandarī* (Alexander's Wall). His four *dīvān*s were entitled *Gharā'ib al-sighār* (Curiosities of Childhood), *Nawādir al-shabāb* (Marvels of Youth), *Badā'iʿal-wasaṭ* (Wonders of Middle Age), and *Fawā'id al-kibar* (Advantages of Old Age); they contained more than sixty thousand lines of lyrical verse. He was also the author of a number of scientific treatises and the linguistic work *Judgment on Two Languages*. He exercised great influence on the literatures of Central Asia, Azerbaijan, and Turkey, and his works (numbering more than thirty) also influenced the development of Uzbek literature and language.

Muḥammad Ẓahīruddīn Bābur also made a great contribution to the development of Central Asian literature. Bābur's lyrical poems are colorful. His biographical work *Bāburnāmah* is valuable as the first monument of realistic prose written in Central Asian Turki.

In the sixteenth to nineteenth centuries Central Asian literature developed in the domains of three independent khanates (kingdoms) in their capital cities in Bukhara, Khiva, and Khoqand. The Bukhara khanate existed until 1920. In 1753 it was renamed the Bukhara emirate. In the territory of the khanate where the population spoke mostly in Central Asian Turki and Persian, the literary works were also created mainly in these languages. The most famous poets of the Bukhara khanate were Mujrim Obid, Turdi Faraghi, Sayido Nasafi. Mujrim Obid (late eighteenth–early nineteenth century) was one of the best lyric poets, who wrote *ghazāl*s. Turdi Faraghi lived during the reign of the king Nadir Muhammadshah (governing from 1640) and his sons Abdulaziz (1645) and Subkhanqulikhan (1680). In this period it was difficult for poets to survive in the territory of the khanate; for this reason they left their homeland for the court of the Mughals of India. In the first stage of his creative activity Turdi wrote Ṣūfī poems, and he considered himself as follower of ʿAlīshīr Navā'ī. His poem *Muhammas-i Turki Turdi* is one example. The character and motif of his poems later changed; he began writing poems that expressed social ideas.

In the Khiva khanate the best-known writers were Nishati (sixteenth century), Munis (1778–1844), Agahi (1809–1874), Muhammadniyaz Komil (1825–1899), Avaz Otaroghli (1884–1919). Munis and Agahi were poets as well as historians. Munis began writing a history of Khwārazm titled *Ferdaus ul-lqbal* (The Paradise of Happiness), but he could finish only the introduction and first chapters. Munis's follower, the poet Agahi, finished this excellent work.

The Khoqand khanate for many centuries was the center of poets. Such outstanding poets as Mashrab (seventeenth century), Mahmur (eighteenth century), Gulkhani (1770–1820), Muqimi (1850–1903), Furqat (1859–1909), Zavqi (1853–1921), as well as the many poetesses such as Uwaysi (1780–1846), Nodira (1791–1842), and Anbaratin (1870–1915) were the best in Turkistan of this period.

Colonial and Post-Independence Periods. Little scholarly attention has yet been addressed to literary developments in Central Asia during the period since the imposition of Russian colonial rule in the second half of the nineteenth century and the most recent period leading to the regaining of national sovereignty and independence in 1991. What work was done by former Soviet scholars needs to be critically reviewed from a non-ideological perspective.

The colonial period in Turkistan, beginning with the Russian military invasion and occupation in 1861, marked a dark and tragic era for indigenous literature. From the beginning of their colonial incursion in the region the Russians attempted to make use of literature to further their interests by creating and promoting works that praised Russian culture, political system, and identity. Local poets and writers like Abay, Zhambyl Zhabaev (Kazakh), Aḥmad Dānish (Tajik), Furqat (Uzbek), and others began praising Russians in their works.

Some of Furqat's poems—*Suvorov haqida, Gimnaziia* (Gymnasium), *Vystavka* (Exhibition), and *Rus askarlary ta'rifida* (About Russian Soldiers), praised everything Russian. Archival materials now indicate that whenever Furqat published a poem praising Russians he was rewarded by the Governor-general of Turkistan. This type of antiliterature was produced under the initiative of the editor in chief of the *Türkistan Vilayatynyng Gazeti* and the chief inspector of Turkistan public schools, a Russian named Ostroumov. During the first years after the Russian invasion of Turkistan, Ostroumov and his teacher Il'minsky, a Russian missionary from Kazan, attempted to replace the Arabic script that had been used for more than a thousand years with Cyrillic and to ban Islam; for this purpose the Bible was translated into Uzbek. Although the tsarist rulers of Turkistan did not succeed in implementing these ideas, what they did not do was done by the Bolsheviks.

Eventually Furqat understood the mistake he had made and began to write poetry criticizing the oppressive nature of Russian rule in the Ferghana valley. As a result he was exiled by the Russians and died in Chinese Turkistan.

During the early decades of the twentieth century a new generation of writers, the so-called Ziyalilar (Enlighteners), who were followers of Ismail Bey Gasprinskii and supporters of Jadīdism, emerged, making major contributions to the modern literature of Turkistan. Among them were Mahmudkhodzha Behbudy, Abdurauf Fitrat, Abdulhamid Cholpon, Maghjan Jumabayuli, and Manan Ramiz. [*See* Jadīdism *and the biography of Gasprinskii.*]

In addition to poetry, this period also saw the writing and performance of plays as a new literary and artistic genre in Turkistan. In clear contrast to the nineteenth-century writers and poets who demonstrated their literary skills by praising the beauty of spring or magical moonlight, the Jadīd writers turned their attention to the critique of ideas and social practices. For example, Behbudy's play *Padarkush* (Patricide) written in 1911, and a play by Abdulla Qodiry entitled *Bakhtsyz kuyov* (Unlucky Bridegroom), together with Cholpon's short stories, concentrated on the serious problems families faced in Turkistan following Russian colonial occupation.

Abdurauf Fitrat (1886–1938), one of the early dramatists and an outstanding scholar of the Jadīdi era, both inspired and provided the ideological framework for the indigenous reform movement in Turkistan. Many of Fitrat's plays took the form of historical dramas that depicted actual figures from the early and medieval Islamic periods. His works helped raise national consciousness and feelings of patriotism among the peoples of Turkistan. Some of his best-known plays in this genre include *Abū Muslim* (1918), *Temürning saghanasy* (Timur's Mausoleum, 1919), *Oghizkhan* (1919), *Abul Fayz Khan* (1924), *Isyon'i Vose* (Vose's Uprising, 1927), and others written in either Uzbek or Farsi.

Like Fitrat, many Central Asian writers of this early colonial period were bilingual. Through their efforts to unify the various spoken forms of Turkic they developed the Literary Turki language. Historically and politically, they considered Turkistan to be a single, indivisible state with a common historical and cultural identity. Fitrat played a leading role in this movement and supported the introduction of an array of progressive changes in Turkistan. However, he opposed the imposition of the "proletarian" revolution exported from Russia. Fitrat sought to improve socioeconomic conditions in Turkistan by strengthening its ties with other Turkic and Muslim peoples in the region.

Another new genre, the realistic novel was introduced in Turkistan in the twentieth century by Abdulla Qodiry (1894–1938). Some of his better-known novels in this genre include *Otgan kunlar* (The Bygone Days, 1922), and *Mehrobdan chayon* (Scorpion from the Altar,

1929). He crafted a new method of writing historical novels that differed significantly from the well-known style of Arab writer Jurjī Zaydān, whose aim was to describe the history of Islam through his novels. Abdulla Qodiry's method of writing historical novels more closely resembled that of Walter Scott. The central importance of Abdulla Qodiry's novels lay in their sympathetic rendition of the lives and times of the people of Turkistan before they were robbed of their freedom and independence by Russian colonists. When the Turkistani people read these novels, especially before 1991, they always recalled the long history of their independence and yearned for the return of their freedom. Many other Turkistani novelists like Mukhtar Avezov (Kazakh), and Khydyr Deryaev (Turkmen) followed Abdulla Qodiry's example.

Not surprisingly these writers were much criticized by pro-Soviet authors who accused them of harboring sympathy for the old order. In his satirical writings Abdulla Qodiry criticized everything he considered bad in society, and the Soviets reacted with hostility. His first arrest by the Soviet regime followed the publication of one of his pieces in the satirical magazine *Mushtum* (Fist) in 1926.

By far the most significant contributions to Turkistan's modern literature were made by an author whose entire life and works were dedicated to the realization of the ideals of a democratic and independent Turkistan. This extraordinary writer was Abdulhamid Sulaymon ughli Cholpon (1897–1938). The first collection of his poems, *Uyghonish* (Awakening) was published in 1923. In these poems Cholpon advocated the awakening and resistance of his people against the invaders:

> Oh my heart! why for so long
> Have you become friendly with chains?
> What complaints, what demands have you?
> Why have you become weakened?
>
> . . .
>
> You're alive, not dead
> You are a man, you are a human
> Don't be in chains
> Don't beg
> Because you also are born free!

The last three lines of the above poem by Cholpon have become the motto of the Democratic Party of Uzbekistan (ERK) today.

For Cholpon, as the following verses indicate, the struggle for freedom and independence was the sole reason for living a noble life or dying a glorious death:

> O you widows and helpless ones
> O you bound in chains
> O you beggars for freedom
> Do not beg from them!

Cholpon's patriotism, love of Turkistan, and hatred of the invaders always echoed in the hearts of his readers. His poetry remained a strong source of inspiration and a major symbol of constant struggle for Turkistanis who held the independence and freedom of their homeland as their cherished goal. Only four collections of his poems were published during Cholpon's own lifetime—*Uyghonish* (Awakening), *Buloqlar* (Springs), *Tong sirlary* (Secrets of Dawn), and *Soz* (Musical Instrument). In addition, Cholpon also published part one of his novel *Kecha va kunduz* (Day and Night, 1935) and a number of plays and short stories.

The Communist rulers of Turkistan feared Cholpon, Fitrat, Maghjan, and Abdulla Qodiry because of the appeal their views had among the population at large. The regime attempted to exploit their popularity by encouraging them to write in support of the Soviet colonial system, but these efforts failed.

The classical literary language of Turki was the dominant medium of written expression throughout Central Asia during the fifteenth to late nineteenth centuries. In 1924 the Communist regime split the region into five Soviet republics and instituted a campaign (carried out all over the Soviet Union) of secular education in local indigenous languages. The government supported the writing and publication of works for schools and general readers in these vernaculars, resulting in bodies of Soviet Kazakh, Kirghiz, Tajik, Turkmen, and Uzbek literature.

During the 1930s the literary community in the Soviet Central Asian republics suffered an unprecedented loss in human lives and incurred serious social, cultural, and psychological damage to the community. In 1937–1938 almost all well-known writers and many of their followers and family members were arrested by the Soviets. Special archival materials made available in the period of *glasnost* indicate that many national literary figures of Central Asia (Fitrat, Abdulla Qodiry, Cholpon, and others) were sentenced to death by the Military Group of the Supreme Court of the Ministry of Inner Affairs of the USSR but in fact were shot before sentencing (*Sharq Yulduzi*, Tashkent, No. 6, 1991, p. 90). Numerous honest and talented writers were annihilated and their works removed from public circulation and banned. Despite the concerted efforts of the Soviet rulers to mute the calls for freedom unleashed by these courageous writers, they have continued to inspire a new generation of writers in Turkistan. Today, many carry forward the tradition of pride in the heritage of contemporary Turkistan. They include major literary figures of the present era such as Chingiz Aitmatov (Kirghiz), Olzhas Suleymenov (Kazakh), Erkin Vahidov, Abdullo Oripov (Uzbek), Gulurukhsor Safieva (Tajik), and many others who have resumed the interrupted creative work of their teachers.

The execution of many of the heroes of Turkistani literature during the first decades of Bolshevik rule nonetheless had a chilling effect on literary circles. The decades from 1940 to the 1970s saw the rise of mediocrity as dutiful but unimaginative servants of the invading power—among them Hamza, Ghafur Ghulam, Hamid Alimjan, Yashin, Uyghun (Uzbek), Ayni, Mirzo Tursunzoda, Lahuti (Tajik), Berdi Kerbabaev (Turkmen), and T. Satilghanov (Kirghiz)—eulogized the regime under the banner of "socialist realism" in verses like these:

Joseph Stalin, the whole people say
We saw Lenin in you.
And it is true.
(Ghafur Ghulam)

My elder brother is Russian
If I'll praise [him] in this poem
It will be in good conscience.
(Ghafur Ghulam)

Russia, Russia, the gigantic land.
I am not a guest, I am your son.
(Hamid Alimjan)

These were considered good examples of socialist realism among the ruling circles, and their authors won much praise. The sons and daughters of this land who had suffered so much under the yoke of colonialist oppression found it shameful to label such works literature.

A recurrent theme in Soviet literature was an attack on Islam and its supporters, and this theme became a standard subject for Central Asian pro-Soviet writers. In the 1920s they even founded a literary magazine called *Khudosizlar* (Atheist). Hamza Hakimzada Niyazi (1889–1929) expressed his opposition to Islam not only in his literary works *Maysaraning ishi* (The Tricks of Maysara), *Burungi saylowlar* (Former Elections), and *Boy ila khizmätchi* (Rich and Servant), but also in his political activities; he was stoned to death by a mob.

Even under these difficult circumstances, many talented writers like Mukhtar Avezov (Kazakh) and Aybek (Uzbek) wrote historical novels chronicling their nations' heroic part. Other writers, such as Chingiz Aitmatov (Kirghiz), employed legends and allegories in their novels in order to avoid praising the Soviet reality of this period.

More recently, authors of great skill and genuine talent have offered more truthful approaches to the facts, events, and conditions in contemporary Turkistan. However, the history of Turkistan has continued to inspire new works. The 1970s was a particularly productive period when a number of historical novels were written including A. Yakubov's *Ulughbek hazinasi* (The Treasure of Ulughbek), Pirimqul Qadirov's *Yulduzli tunlar* (Starry Nights) and *Avlodlar davoni* (The Barrier of the Generation), Mirmuhsin's *Me'mor* (The Architect) and Kh. Deryaev's *Qismat* (Destiny). Banned historical novels by Abdulla Qodiry and Mehrobdan Chayon and Cholpon's novel *Kecha va kunduz* (Night and Day) were republished.

During the Soviet period the Central Asian classics were published, but always in shortened form. Until today no full editions have appeared. Even Navā'ī's linguistic work has never been printed in full form in Central Asia, because the writer praised the Prophet and saints. When the Central Asian republics gained independence, authors were allowed to write about their historical past and began more freely to describe the themes of Islam, Sufism, and the Islamic heritage of the country. Abdullo Oripov's *Hadzh daftary* (The Hajj Diary) was the first popular work in this genre.

A country without democracy, and a nation that for years was turned into a labor camp, was referred to only a few years ago by puppets of the ruling circles as the Bakhtlar Vodysy (Valley of Joy). The realities of life during the final years of occupation, however, were described in the works of more objective writers—including Erkin Vahidov, Chingiz Aitmatov, Olzhas Suleymenov, Abdullo Oripov, Muhammad Salih, and A. Sher,—as exemplified in the following poem entitled *Vatan ümidi* (National Hope):

Though my name means Free (Erkin)
I have no freedom, I am a chained prisoner.
I am blindfolded, my heart is full of pain
I have no tongue, I am speechless.
(Erkin Vahidov)

True to the prophetic voices of the national writers, after 130 years real independence came, and it did so with considerable sacrifices and serious economic hardships to the peoples of Central Asia. The end of the twentieth century promises great activity in literature and criticism, with resurgent Islamic influences likely to play a part.

[*See also* Islam, *article on* Islam in Central Asia and the Caucasus.]

BIBLIOGRAPHY

Agaeva, Marina. *Turkmenskaia literatura* (Turkmen Literature). Moscow, 1980.

Allakov, Jora. *Hazirki dövür ve Türkmen edäbiyäti* (Modern Time and Turkmen Literature). Ashgabat, 1982.

Allworth, Edward. *Uzbek Literary Politics*. The Hague, 1964.

Allworth, Edward, ed. *Central Asia: A Century of Russian Rule*. New York, 1967.

Allworth, Edward, ed. *The Nationality Question in Soviet Central Asia*. New York, 1967.

Bacon, Elizabeth E. *Central Asians under Russian Rule: A Study in Culture Change*. Ithaca, N.Y., and London, 1966.

Bombaci, Alessio. "The Turkic Literatures: Introductory Notes on the History and Style." In *Philologiae Turcicae Fundamenta*, vol. 2, pp. 11–71. Wiesbaden, 1965.

Çağatay, Tahir. *Türkistanda Türkçülük ve Halkçılık*. 2 vols. Istanbul, 1951–1954.

Hayit, Baymirza. *Turkestan im XX. Jahrhundert*. Darmstadt, 1956.

Hodizoda, Rasul, Usmon Karimov, and Sadri Sa'diev. *Adabiyoti Tojik* (Tajik Literature). Dushanbe, 1988.

Istoriia Kirghizskoĭ Sovetskoĭ literatury (The History of Kirghiz Soviet Literature). Moscow, 1970.

Istoriia Uzbekskoĭ literatury (The History of Uzbek Literature). 2 vols. Tashkent, 1987.

Istoriia Uzbekskoĭ Sovetskoĭ literatury (The History of Uzbek Soviet Literature). Vol. 1. Tashkent, 1917.

Köprülü, Mehmet Fuat. "Çağatay Edebiyati." In *İslam Ansiklopedisi*, vol. 3. Istanbul, 1963.

Kyrgyz Sovet adabiiatynyn tarykhy (The History of Kirghiz Soviet Literature). 2 vols. Frunze, 1987.

Ocherki istoriĭ Kazakhskoĭ literatury (Outline of the History of Kazakh Literature). Moscow, 1960.

Ozbek adabiyoti tarikhi (The History of Uzbek Literature). Vol. 1. Tashkent, 1990.

Qazaq ädäbietining tarikhy (The History of Kazakh Literature). Vol. 1. Alma-Ata, 1960.

Rustamov, Ergash Rustamovich. *Uzbekskaia poeziia v pervoĭ polovine XV veka* (Uzbek Poetry in the First Half of the Fifteenth Century). Moscow, 1963.

Togan, A. Zeki Velidi. *Bugünkü Türkili (Türkistan) ve Yakın tarihi*. Istanbul, 1942–1947.

Türkmen poeziyasining antologiasi (The Anthology of Turkmen Poetry). Ashgabat, 1958.

KHAYRULLA ISMATULLA

CERAMICS. *See* Pottery and Ceramics.

CHAD. Comprising more than 1,284,000 square kilometers between the northern and southern edges of the central Sahara, Chad lies at the crossroads of the *dār al-Islām* and black Africa. About four-fifths of its territory—the entire area north of the tenth parallel—is under the sway of Islam. Sizable Muslim minorities are also found in many southern towns. Slightly more than half of the country's people (estimated at 4 million in 1978) are Muslims (Chapelle, 1980, p. 149). Numbering approximately 450,000, Arabs are the largest Islamic ethnic community, but they form a distinctive minority in relation to the rest of the Muslim population. For the vast majority of Chadian Muslims Arabic is a foreign language, albeit a sacred one; although Chadian Arabic (Turku) is the lingua franca among northerners, classical Arabic is neither widely spoken nor understood.

The first carriers of Islam into the Chad basin were islamized Berbers (Zeltner, 1992, p. 25). As early as the eleventh century, long before an Arab presence was reported in the area, Islam was firmly anchored among the ruling elites of Kanem and Bornu. Some three centuries later, however, Arabs emerged as the principal vector of the new religion. At the end of the sixteenth century Baguirmi claimed hundreds of converts, as did Waddai a century later. In both states, as in Kanem and Bornu, Islam was at first an urban-based religion confined to the ruling elites, notables, and scholars (*'ulamā'*). By then Islam had long ceased to be the hallmark of Arab elements. A long heritage of intermarriage between Arabs and non-Arabs, coupled with the gradual expansion of Islam among non-Arab communities, resulted in a social landscape in which Arab influences were no longer predominant.

The diffusion of Islam through the rural sectors took much longer. Cattle- and camel-traders, Hausa pilgrims on their way to Mecca, itinerant Qur'ānic teachers, and Ṣūfī orders all played roles in the conversion of rural communities. Although the traders were probably the first to appear, their impact was not as decisive as that of the Hausa pilgrims, the wandering *fuqahā'* (jurists) and *mallamai* (spiritual advisers or clients). By the late nineteenth century many of these itinerants could be seen traveling through the countryside, begging, teaching, trading, and making converts (Works, 1976). Although most belonged to Ṣūfī orders—the Tijānīyah claiming the largest number of devotees after the Qādirīyah and the Sanūsīyah—the spread of the brotherhoods did relatively little to lessen the hold of animism on the rural communities. In contrast with what happened in the cities, rural Islam in Chad remains highly syncretistic and permeated by pre-Islamic beliefs and practices. The phenomenon is nowhere more evident than among the Toubou people of the Tibesti, whose conversion to Islam occurred at a rather late date (late nineteenth century) as a result of their sporadic contacts with the Sanūsīyah (Triaud, 1987). [*See* Tijānīyah; Qādirīyah; Sanūsīyah.]

The significance of the brotherhoods lies in their remarkable adaptability to indigenous power structures, and, with few exceptions, in their unrelenting opposition to colonial rule. This is where the history of the Sanūsīyah merits particular attention (Zeltner, 1988; Triaud, 1987). Besides its sustained resistance to French penetration in the Tibesti, culminating in the bloody battles of Bir Alali (1901) and Ain Galaka (1913), one must stress the psychological impact these encounters had on French attitudes toward the brotherhood. In the minds of many French administrators the Sanūsīyah emerged as the incarnation of evil, the vehicle through which the twin dangers of Pan-Islamism and Pan-Arabism threatened to undermine France's "civilizing mission" in the heart of the continent. While never missing an opportunity to play one brotherhood off against another, the French went to great lengths to make Islam safe for colonial rule by defusing its Pan-Islamic elements and bringing it firmly under the control of the traditional sultans.

Nonetheless, the legacy of conflict between the forces of Islam and France's colonial enterprise is a key factor behind the striking reversal of developmental patterns that has accompanied the intrusion of Western influences. Until the arrival of the French, the Islamic north was far more advanced than the animist south in both the scale and character of its political, economic, commercial, and cultural activities. By the end of the colonial period, however, the now predominantly Christian south—tellingly referred to by the French as *le Tchad utile*, "useful Chad"—had emerged as conspicuously more developed, socially, economically, and politically.

Predictably, the country acceded to independence (1960) under the control of a southern, Sara-dominated government, headed by François Tombalbaye. But if the south inherited the political kingdom, the systematic exclusion of Muslim elements from all positions of authority soon paved the way for the bloody rebellion that broke out at Mangalme in November 1965. Although the immediate cause of the northern rebellion is traceable to the forced collection of taxes at a rate substantially beyond the capabilities of the local taxpayers, for a while Islam provided a powerful unifying bond among otherwise diverse ethnic and regional communities. It also gave Colonel Muʿammar al-Qadhdhāfī a convenient pretext for coming to the assistance of his "Muslim brothers" against the neocolonialist regime of Tombalbaye and his French allies.

In the end France's protracted military involvement on the side of the Chadian government proved utterly ineffective in coming to terms with the roots of the insurgency; the same applies to Tombalbaye's attempt in 1971 to enlist the cooperation of the traditional sultans of Wadai, Kanem, and Baguirmi as a counterweight to the rebel leadership of the Front de Libération National du Tchad (Frolinat), followed by his belated overture to Libya in 1972 that led to the exchange of ambassadors with that state and the severance of diplomatic relations with Israel.

The return of the Frolinat warlord Hissene Habre to Ndjamena in June 1986 brought to a close the long-drawn-out trial of strength between north and south. Habre's victory, however, can hardly be described as emblematic of a triumphant Islam. Although it provided initial social ballast for the rebellion, Islam proved a remarkably feeble counterweight to the divisive forces of ethnicity and regionalism.

Islamic revivalism is now emerging as a powerful source of solidarity among middle- and lower-class Muslim elements in Ndjamena. Echoing the preaching of Ḥasan Ḥusayn, imam of the Grand Mosque, many insist that the only path to salvation is through the *sharīʿah*, the study of the Qur'ān in schools, and the recruitment of educated Muslims into government and the civil service. Islamic fundamentalism has been bolstered by the infiltration of devotees of Ḥasan al-Turābī's National Islamic Front (NIF), operating from the Darfur province in western Sudan, and has become a significant piece on the Chadian chessboard. Its growing appeal among Muslims lies both in the attraction of its ideological worldview and in their conviction that it offers the only viable solution to Chad's endless crisis.

BIBLIOGRAPHY

Chapelle, Jean. *Le peuple Tchadien*. Paris, 1980.

Triaud, Jean-Louis. *Tchad, 1900–1902: Une guerre franco-libyenne oubliée?* Paris, 1987.

Works, John A. *Pilgrims in a Strange Land: Hausa Communities in Chad*. New York, 1976.

Zeltner, Jean-Claude. *Les pays du Tchad dans la tourmente, 1880–1903*. Paris, 1988.

Zeltner, Jean-Claude. "Les Arabes: Propagateurs ou spectateurs de l'Islam au Tchad?" In *L'Islam au Tchad*, edited by Jean-Pierre Magnant, pp. 25–29. Bordeaux, 1992.

René Lemarchand

CHARITABLE ASSOCIATIONS. *See* Muslim Brotherhood; Waqf.

CHILDREN. *See* Family.

CHILDREN'S BOOKS AND CARTOONS. Children's literature goes back centuries in the Islamic world, and is an interesting reflection of developments in Muslim societies generally. The education and entertainment of children play an important role in the socialization process of the young. For the contemporary period, this process is effected through both formal—state and nongovernmental organizations—and informal mechanisms, including children's books, cartoons, and other published materials. Because of its central place in the education of children, the genre has often been employed by the nonspecialist—well-established authors and artists who direct most of their works to an adult audience. Moreover, children's literature provides a fascinating research tool for the social historian, as it reflects general ideological trends and participates in important cultural debates, such as those between secular and religious forces in Muslim society.

It should not be surprising, then, that someone of the stature of the great medieval polymath, Ibn al-Jawzī (d. AH 597/1200 CE), should address his *Laftat al-Kabad ilā Naṣīḥat al-Walad* to his son, Abū al-Qāsim. This edifying work of moral guidance, like other medieval works directed at the education of the child (see, for instance, the same author's *Birr al-Wālidayn*), can be purchased today in a cheap edition on streets and in bookstores in the Arab world, and in Western capitals with large Muslim populations.

Initially, much children's literature in the twentieth-century Muslim world was translated from Western languages. The French detective, Arsène Lupin, transcended his country of birth to become the hero of children in Third World countries. The same was true of the young Belgian reporter, Tin Tin. Mickey Mouse followed a similar trajectory. Although translation from Western languages still occurs, today most children's books and cartoons are indigenous cultural products.

Perhaps the dominant form of children's literature is the illustrated magazine. A varied medium containing both illustrated (e.g., comic strip) and nonillustrated material, the children's magazine may be either more or less secular or religious. The more religiously oriented magazines function almost as spiritual guides rather than sources of light entertainment. Even the secular magazines, however, contain religious material. Verses from the Qur'ān and incidents from the *ḥadīth* are recast and embedded in children's literature.

Children's magazines may be produced by a government's dominant political party. In such cases, the magazine becomes an educational tool largely reflecting official dogma. For example, the Syrian magazine *Al-ṭalīʿī* is published by the Baʿth party. Children's magazines may also be published under the auspices of a governmental agency, such as a ministry or cultural bureau. This is the case, for example, of the Egyptian *Zamzam*, a religiously oriented magazine published by the High Council for Islamic Affairs in Cairo. Then there are, of course, independent children's magazines, such as the Tunisian *Qaws Quzaḥ*.

Although most children's magazines are indigenous productions, they have transnational appeal, with an uncanny ability to cross borders. To take but one example, the most successful children's magazine by all counts (years in production, distribution, quality of color printing, appeal of characters, etc.) is *Mājid*, a weekly produced in the United Arab Emirates. Its editorial board is international, including exiled writers and artists. One can buy *Mājid* in London, Paris, New York—not to mention other world capitals with major Arab and Muslim populations.

Standing alongside the magazine is the children's book. Adventures, mysteries, stories of friendship, historical heroes, and the Prophets: all are designed to attract the child and to excite his or her religious and historical imagination. It is here that one finds contemporary rewritings of stories from the *turāth*, the long-honored Islamic textual tradition that encompasses materials across a range of disciplines: theology, philosophy, geography, history, literature, and lexicography. In this way the philosophical and mystical allegory, *Ḥayy ibn Yaqẓān* (Alive Son of Awake), by the twelfth-century Andalusian philosopher and physician, Ibn Ṭufayl, has become the subject of both a large-format children's book by the late Egyptian poet, Ṣalāḥ ʿAbd al-Ṣabūr, and a serialized comic strip in the Tunisian children's magazine, *Al-ryāḍ*.

The Islamist movement has had a role to play here as well. One finds more and more children's books with a clear religious orientation, such as the recently published series on the Qur'ānic alphabet. Produced in Morocco, these attractive booklets are organized around a letter of the alphabet matched to a Qur'ānic concept. These are then supplemented by verses from the Qur'ān and other edifying stories. The international nature of the Islamist movement also means that a great deal of these children's books and cartoons are produced in various languages, including European ones, and distributed to a linguistically restricted audience (for example, French materials designed for francophone Muslims living in France and Belgium).

The rewriting of the *turāth* for children involves cultural choices and priorities. What text is chosen? How is it recast not only for modern sensibilities but also for the taste of children? The priority given to political issues distinguishes this children's literature from that designed for the Western child. Thus it is that Zakarīyā Tāmir has penned some powerful political allegories designed for children that speak to the plight of the Palestinians. Tāmir is a Syrian writer living in England, and his works transcend geographical boundaries.

The importance of the political should not obscure other prominent elements of children's literature in the Muslim world, primarily the religious. The goal of these materials is generally moral guidance and historical education, rather than theological instruction. Both print and visual media are utilized. For instance, illustrated posters outlining a typical day in the life of a young religious boy are widely distributed.

But it is perhaps the heroes of the electronic media, more than the by now ubiquitous heroes of print media, who will have the last word in children's literature worldwide. Children's stories are now available on cassette, as are television programs designed specifically for the young. Whereas Ibn al-Jawzī had to resort to his famous skills as a religious orator and writer to address his son on proper behavior, contemporary parents may rely on the computer, and the child may learn the rudiments of religious duty through a computer program.

To say that the mass media influence children's books and cartoons is to acknowledge that children's literature has become part of a global culture. Beyond the standard contact with Western cultures, today East Asia seeks young audiences in Muslim lands. The *ḥadīth,* "Seek knowledge even if it is in China," may be updated to reflect the multicultural nature of knowledge daily consumed by children in their own homes.

[*See also* Book Publishing; Communications Media.]

BIBLIOGRAPHY

Douglas, Allen, and Fedwa Malti-Douglas. *Arab Comic Strips: Politics of an Emerging Mass Culture.* Bloomington, 1994. Discusses the enormous production of children's magazines and comic strip albums from Iraq through North Africa to France.

Kīlānī, Najīb al-. *Adab al-Aṭfāl fī Ḍaw' al-Islām.* Beirut, 1986. Committed and programmatic work on children's literature from a Muslim perspective.

Ṭalā'iʿ al-Baʿth. *Adab al-Aṭfāl wa-al-Turāth.* Damascus, n.d. Official publication of the Syrian government containing various studies on priorities for children's literature, from a secular perspective.

FEDWA MALTI-DOUGLAS

CHIRĀGH ʿALĪ (1844–1895), Indian modernist author. Chirāgh ʿAlī came to prominence as a supporter of Sir Sayyid Aḥmad Khān and the Aligarh movement. He came from a Kashmiri family settled in the United Provinces and served the British administration in North India in various judicial and revenue positions. In 1877, thanks to the recommendation of Sir Sayyid, he entered the service of the nizam of Hyderabad. There he rose to the position of Revenue and Political Secretary and was known by the title Nawāb ʿĀzam Yār Jang.

Chirāgh ʿAlī agreed with Sir Sayyid that there could be no conflict between the word of God, as contained in the Qur'ān, and the work of God, as expounded in modern science. His writings are modernist apologetics designed to refute missionary and orientalist criticisms of Islam as incapable of reform. Among his works are *The Proposed Political, Constitutional and Legal Reforms in the Ottoman Empire and Other Mohammedan States* (1883) and *A Critical Exposition of the Popular Jihad* (1885). He also wrote frequently in Sir Sayyid's journal of Muslim social reform, *Tahdhīb al-akhlāq* (The Muslim Reformer), published in Aligarh.

Chirāgh ʿAlī maintained that Islamic religion inculcated no set political or social system and that the schools of Islamic law, as human institutions, were subject to revision. Muslim governments were in no way theocratic, nor did *jihād* imply a forcible expansion of the faith. On the contrary, all the Prophet's wars were defensive in nature. Chirāgh ʿAlī, as a modernist, based his ideas on the teachings of the Qur'ān; all other sources of law, including *ḥadīth,* were subject to interpretation. He was particularly dismissive of the founders of the classical schools of Islamic law, whose writings, he felt, reflected the needs of their times but had little applicability to the modern age.

Chirāgh ʿAlī's writings were influential among Western-educated Muslims of the Aligarh school in the late nineteenth and early twentieth centuries. He championed education for women and was critical of polygamy and divorce. He also argued that slavery was incompatible with the true spirit of Islam. His favorable discussion of political reforms in the Ottoman empire was a factor, albeit a minor one, in the Indian Muslims' growing sympathy for Turkey in the period before World War I.

[*See also* Aligarh *and the biography of Aḥmad Khān*.]

BIBLIOGRAPHY

Ahmad, Aziz. *Islamic Modernism in India and Pakistan, 1857–1964*. London, 1967. Good general guide to intellectual modernism in Indian Islam.

Chirāgh ʿAlī. *The Proposed Political, Constitutional, and Legal Reforms in the Ottoman Empire and Other Mohammedan States*. Bombay, 1883. Chirāgh ʿAlī's main exposition of his reformist ideas.

Hardy, Peter. *The Muslims of British India*. Cambridge, 1972. Short intellectual history of Muslims in nineteenth- and twentieth-century India, in political context.

Saksena, Ram Babu. *A History of Urdu Literature*. Reprint, Lahore, 1975. One of the better guides in English to Urdu authors' lives and works.

Smith, Wilfred Cantwell. *Modern Islam in India*. Rev. ed. Lahore, 1963. Provocative and original Marxist analysis of modernist thought in Indian Islam.

GAIL MINAULT

CHISHTĪYAH. One of the main Ṣūfī brotherhoods of South Asia, Chishtīyah takes its name from the village of Chisht, near Herat in western Afghanistan, where it is said to have originated. Its supposed founder in India, Muʿīnuddīn Chishtī (d. 1236), is a shadowy figure surrounded by many legends. The brotherhood has spread throughout present-day India, Pakistan, and Bangladesh; it is characterized by its extreme enthusiasm for ecstatic listening (*samāʿ*) to music and poetry. In spite of its popular appeal, which by the eighteenth century had brought it more adherents than any other brotherhood in South Asia, the Chishtīyah has now been overtaken in this respect by the rival Qādirīyah. Nonetheless, it has continued to play an important role in harmonizing Islam with indigenous Indian culture, sometimes in ways which have attracted the criticism of Muslim jurists, although it has always claimed to remain within the bounds of Islamic legality.

The golden age of the greatest Chishtī leaders extends from the brotherhood's foundation to the middle of the fourteenth century. They were not academically inclined or sophisticated intellectuals; rather, they insisted on a practical and emotional mysticism in which the close relationship of elder and disciple was particularly stressed. In the thirteenth century the Chishtī masters did not write books at all, but in the fourteenth century records of their successors' conversations were compiled. These are still the most important examples of Indo-Muslim Ṣūfī prose literature and give the modern believer a vivid picture of the medieval teacher in the context of everyday life. They also bear witness to strained relationships with the Suhrawardī brotherhood in Multan (in modern Pakistan), whose leaders were accused by the Chishtīs of excessive formality, self-enrichment, and snobbishness. By contrast, the Chishtīs have portrayed themselves as constantly embracing poverty and avoiding contact with temporal rulers. Some Western scholars have viewed these claims with skepticism.

Chishtī doctrinal simplicity was reinforced by the prolific writer Muḥammad Gīsū Darāz, who died in 1422 at Gulbargā in the Deccan. He upheld the theistic positions of classical Ṣūfī thought and devotionalism as opposed to the innovative and monistic views of Sufism's most influential theorist, Ibn ʿArabī of Murcia (d. 1240). He also defended the controversial Chishtī habit of prostrating oneself in front of one's elder. New perspectives were brought by an important transitional figure, ʿAbd al-Quddūs (1456–1537) of Gangoh in Uttar Pradesh, who was a vigorous advocate of Ibn ʿArabī's doctrines of the "unity of existence" (*waḥdat al-wujūd*) and the "perfect man" (*al-insān al-kāmil*). He departed from his predecessors' insistence on accepting only nonrecurrent gifts rather than permanent grants from rulers, and he adopted Hindu techniques of meditation and breath control. ʿAbd al-Quddūs was also the most fervent defender of the famous Chishtī practice of worshiping upside down while hanging suspended by a rope tied around the ankles.

After a period of decline, the brotherhood was revitalized in the late seventeenth and early eighteenth centuries. Shāh Walī Allāh Dihlawī (1703–1762), the most important Muslim thinker of the eighteenth century, was affiliated to the Chishtīyah, but he belonged to the Naqshbandīyah (which he preferred) and the Qādirīyah as well. He declared that the Chishtīs were best at adapting early Muslim preaching to contemporary conditions.

By the nineteenth century Chishtīs were often hereditary recipients of income at the shrines of their early leaders, living off offerings or the revenue generated by local tenant farmers. Under British rule Chishtī elders were often associated with attempts to reform Islamic institutions, which met with little success, precisely because of the structures of allegiance and authority to which these elders belonged. In the nineteenth century the important Muslim revivalist center of Deoband in Uttar Pradesh was staffed by teachers who were Chishtī in their method of training, although they also claimed to unite the traditions of all the Ṣūfī brotherhoods. They were proud of the early Chishtī masters' alleged aloofness from rulers, but they tried unsuccessfully to eliminate the extravagant observances at the masters' tombs.

During the nineteenth and twentieth centuries the authorities have repeatedly condemned the officers responsible for Muʿīnuddīn Chishtī's shrine, at Ajmer in Rajasthan, for extreme rapacity, corruption, and incompetence. The number of pilgrims coming there on the anniversary of Muʿīnuddīn's death has risen from twenty thousand in 1879 to around one hundred thousand in the 1990s, making it the most important Muslim pilgrimage center in India. At this shrine the Chishtī tradition of distributing free food to the poor is continued, but now much of the food cooked for this purpose is in practice sold. In 1950 the Indian government annexed the lands of the "servants" *(khuddām)* of the shrine, who attend to its ceremonies and pilgrims, and they are now dependent on offerings. At the shrine of Niẓāmuddīn Auliyā', who died at Delhi in 1325, the hereditary custodians claim to be descended from Muḥammad as well as from Niẓāmuddīn's family or disciples. A high-status group, they are noted for their persianized Urdu and refined manners and do not intermarry with people of lower pedigree. Although much of their land has been lost, most of them have income from rents, along with that from pilgrims, to whom they give advice and amulets.

At their shrines the Chishtīs have a flourishing and well-developed musical culture designated by the term *qawwālī*, meaning a group song genre of Hindustani light classical music which presents mystical poetry in Persian, Hindi, and Urdu; it is performed in Ṣūfī assemblies in order to produce religious emotion and ecstasy. In these assemblies particular devotion is expressed toward ʿAlī ibn Abī Ṭālib (d. 661), Muḥammad's cousin and son-in-law, who is seen as the Prophet's first successor in the Chishtī initiatory chain of masters. The performers are hereditary specialists in a close but deferential relationship with their Ṣūfī patrons. Sometimes they elucidate medieval Persian poetry with additional lines in the vernacular, and sometimes their poetry resembles folksong, drawing on Hindi devotional idioms. It is perhaps in this combination of Islamic and regional elements that the greatest achievement of the Chishtīyah is to be recognized.

[*See also* Music; Qādirīyah.]

BIBLIOGRAPHY

Currie, P. M. *The Shrine and Cult of Muʿīn al-Dīn Chishtī of Ajmer*. Delhi, 1989. Rigorously critical historical and anthropological survey.

Digby, S. "ʿAbd Al-Quddus Gangohi (1456–1537 A.D.): The Personality and Attitudes of a Medieval Indian Sufi." *Medieval India* 3 (1975): 1–66. The best study of an individual Chishtī writer.

Gaborieau, Marc. "Les ordres mystiques dans le sous-continent indien: Un point de vue ethnologique." In *Les ordres mystiques dans l'Islam: Cheminements et situation actuelle*, edited by Alexandre Popovic and Gilles Veinstein, pp. 105–134. Paris, 1986.

Gilmartin, David. "Shrines, Succession, and Sources of Moral Authority." In *Moral Conduct and Authority: The Place of* Adab *in South Asian Islam*, edited by Barbara D. Metcalf, pp. 221–240. Berkeley, 1984.

Jeffery, Patricia. *Frogs in a Well: Indian Women in Purdah*. London, 1979. Perceptive anthropological study of the custodians' wives and daughters at the shrine of Niẓāmuddīn Auliyā'.

Metcalf, Barbara D. *Islamic Revival in British India: Deoband, 1860–1900*. Princeton, 1982. Challenging reappraisal of the contribution of traditional Indian Muslim teachers.

Nizami, Khaliq Ahmad. *Some Aspects of Religion and Politics in India during the Thirteenth Century*. 2d ed. Delhi, 1974. Provides a fine survey of early Chishtī organization, practice, and thought, but has a heavily apologetic bias.

Qureshi, Regula B. *Sufi Music of India and Pakistan: Sound, Context, and Meaning in Qawwali*. Cambridge, 1986. Sophisticated ethnomusicological analysis of Chishtī performances.

Troll, Christian W., ed. *Muslim Shrines in India: Their Character, History, and Significance*. Delhi, 1989. Contains sympathetic and detailed descriptions of practices at Chishtī shrines.

JULIAN BALDICK

CHRISTIANITY AND ISLAM. The history of Christian-Muslim relations begins with the biography of the prophet Muḥammad. Muḥammad met Christians and Jews on various occasions. Ibn Isḥāq reports that a Christian uncle of Muḥammad's first wife identified Muḥammad's experience in the cave of Hira as divine revelation. Later, however, Muḥammad disputed with a Christian delegation from Najran about the doctrine of the Incarnation; yet this same delegation had been invited to pray in the Prophet's mosque. This ambivalence is reflected in the Qur'ān and the *ḥadīth*. The Qur'ān tells Muslims that they will find Christians "nearest to them in love" (5.85) but warns them (5.54) not to take Christians or Jews as "close friends" or "protectors" *(awliyā')*. Sometimes the positive and sometimes the negative aspect has received greater emphasis in the history of Muslim relations with Christians.

The earliest Christian reaction to Islam shows ambivalence of a different kind and dates from the time when the early Muslim armies fought the Byzantine army for control of Egypt and Syria. Byzantine polemicists saw Islam as a "Satanic plot" to destroy Christian faith (Gaudeul, 1984, vol. 1, p. 65) and non-Chalcedonian Christians often saw Islam as "the rod of God's anger" "to deliver us from the Byzantines" (Sahas, 1972, p. 23).

The development of *dhimmī* status gave non-Muslims, including Christians, some legal rights as subjects of Islamic government. In fact, relations between Christians and Muslims (especially the Muslim authorities) were generally very good during this period. The Muslim empire originally utilized the existing bureaucracy to administer the empire; the bureaucracy included Christians everywhere, especially in Egypt and Syria. In fact, the first language of Muslim administration in the Umayyad court at Damascus was Greek, not Arabic. Evidence does exist of problems between Christians and Muslims in the general populace, for example, the Coptic uprising in Egypt in 829–830. During this period, Islam inherited the learning of the Hellenistic tradition. The caliph al-Ma'mūn (r. 813–833) founded an academy to translate works of science, philosophy, and medicine from Greek into Arabic. The Bible was one of the few religious works translated. Islam became the heir to the learning of the past and reached creative heights in architecture, science, technology, and philosophy. The concept of legal rights for non-Muslims became an integral principle of Islamic law. Islamic learning and Islamic legal tolerance survived the disintegration of political unity and became important elements of the medieval world.

The Medieval Experience. The ninth century contained the seeds of major changes in the history of Christian-Muslim relations. In the Muslim world there were signs of the breakup of political unity. During periods of instability the rights of non-Muslim minorities were often threatened by popular discontent. This is often the lot of minorities at such times, and the phenomenon is not unique to Islamic history. The various Muslim governments struggling for stability usually sought to protect the legal rights of their minorities. The Byzantine empire was in a state of general decline and, in the eleventh century, had to petition Rome for help, a remarkable confession of weakness following close on the final schism of the Eastern and Western Churches. In the West, however, the same century saw the beginnings of a long struggle toward greater political and social integration, heralded by the Holy Roman Empire of Charlemagne (742–814). Western European history during this period paralleled Muslim history in that both were successions of competing dynasties. Western Europe, however, was struggling toward greater integration and stability, and the Muslim world was evolving toward greater disunity and instability (except for the remarkable period of Ottoman hegemony over the eastern Mediterranean).

These two worlds approached military parity well before they attained any degree of intellectual equality. The Middle Ages was the period of the Crusades and the Reconquista. It was also the time during which Muslim learning was passed on to the Christian West, which had been struggling self-consciously since Charlemagne's reforms to reclaim its own intellectual tradition. The translations of Arabic texts into Latin from the eleventh through the thirteenth centuries played a role in the development of western European civilization similar to that of the earlier translations of Greek texts into Arabic. Christians and Jews studied with Muslims at the universities of Córdoba (968) and Cairo (972), perhaps influencing the later development of western European universities (Paris, 1150; Bologna, 1119). The Middle Ages was a time of contradictions in Christian-Muslim relations: sometimes we find Christians and Muslims studying together, and sometimes we find them opposed to each other on the battlefield. Sometimes the language of interreligious polemic verges on the obscene, and yet Nicholas of Cusa explored the idea of an ultimate unity of all religions, and John of Segovia and George of Trebizond actively campaigned for a Christian-Muslim peace conference. Ibn Ḥazm illustrates the unreliability of the biblical text and Ibn ʿArabī speaks of the presence of God in all religious experience.

Such a complex situation needs to be studied in terms of individual biography and of social history. Some generalities are valid, however. On the intellectual level, Islam played an important role in the development of Western European civilization by passing on both the philosophy of Aristotle and its own scientific, technological, and philosophical tradition. The language of scholarship provided a common vocabulary in which the different traditions could speak to each other. On the other hand, religious tolerance remained a part of Islamic law, although its application varied with social, political, and economic circumstances. Ibn Taymīyah, writing during the time of the combined threat of the Crusades and the Mongol invasions, developed particularly harsh restrictions on the rights of *dhimmīs*. Nonetheless, when the Jews were evicted from Spain in 1492, they went to Muslim lands. The only Christian land to receive many Jews was Italy. Today communities that speak Ladino (Judeo-Spanish) survive only in the eastern Mediterranean lands which were part of the Ottoman Empire. The medieval period may be understood as the interaction of two great civilizations. As it began Islamic civilization was in its prime, and western European civilization was still a child. As the intellectual, technological, and scientific development of western Europe reached its prime, however, Islamic civilization showed definite signs of weakness.

Radical Transformation of the West. Al-Jabartī (1756–1825), the last great Muslim historian of the classical tradition, perceived Napoleon's occupation of Egypt in 1798 as "the beginning of a reversal of the natural order and the corruption or destruction of all things" (Hourani, 1991, p. 51). However, Napoleon did not represent medieval Christendom. He was a child of the French Enlightenment, which believed in reason rather than dogma and exalted not God's law and God's rights but human rights and the ideals of secularism, equality, and democracy. In many ways, contemporary secular civilization challenges both Christianity and Islam as cultural systems and religious faiths. Both religions contain believers who accept that at least some Enlightenment values, albeit first proclaimed outside and even against western institutional religion, represent an authentic development of certain fundamental elements of the Qur'ānic and biblical vision of humanity. Other Christians and Muslims, however, often make common cause against the challenge of secularism and irreligion.

The shift in the West from Christendom to nation began in the late Middle Ages, before the Protestant Reformation. This development meant that the religious dimension of Christian-Muslim relations increasingly became secondary to economic and political national interests. The post-Reformation "wars of religion" focused European attention on internal problems. Islam tended to be viewed by Westerners as just another heresy to be opposed. During the nineteenth and twentieth centuries, rapidly developing science and technology transformed Western society. Modern means of transport and communication welded distant regions and continents into one interdependent global society. International industrial and commercial complexes began to eclipse the power of individual nation states. Greater local and international mobility and the growth of vast conurbations began to erode traditional social and religious structures, resulting in the spread of multiracial, multicultural, and multireligious societies both in terms of geographic area and intensity. Different social and mental structures and perceptions coexist, often in unreconciled tension. Hence, Muslims and Christians live increasingly in mixed societies, sharing a growing awareness of the multiplicity of religions, ideologies, and cultures on many different levels: local, national, and international.

Western political dominance and colonialism. The Industrial Revolution gave increased power to those states where it first took place. It ensured military and technological supremacy to the Western powers whose colonial influence affected most of the Muslim world. In the Peace of Carlowitz (1699), the Ottomans were obliged to yield to increasing European pressure and interference. France, Russia, and Britain benefited from the privileges (capitulations) granted by the Ottoman sultans; these enabled their consuls to interfere in local affairs and to "protect" Christian minority groups [*see* Capitulations]. The European powers supported national revolutions; Greece became independent in 1832, Serbia and Romania in 1878. The Ottoman authorities were either powerless spectators or hidden organizers as some Christian minorities, discontent with *dhimmī* status and encouraged by European powers, became victims of extermination attempts.

Muslims in the Middle East regarded the Christians, with considerable justification, as pawns in the overall plans of the European powers to partition the Ottoman Empire. Following Napoleon's brief incursion into Egypt, European interference increased. The British established a protectorate in Egypt in 1882. Algeria became a French colony in 1830; Tunisia, a French protectorate in 1881. European expansion halted the spread of Islamic states in West Africa. Following a revolt against British interests in 1857, India was placed directly under the British Crown, and repressive measures were directed particularly against the Muslims. In Southeast Asia, British and Dutch colonial rule expanded. World War I resulted in the dismemberment of the Ottoman Empire into the Republic of Turkey (1919) and several smaller Middle Eastern countries under the colonial mandates of Britain and France. Ethnic identity, traditionally strong in this region, played an increasingly important role in the nationalism of the emerging nation-states when the former colonies and mandates gained independence. Muslim nations have played an important role in the movement of nonaligned countries that emerged from the Bandung Conference of 1955. However, Western economic and military supremacy led to continued exploitation, and disadvantaged populations envied the Western way of life, propagated through the mass media.

Colonial policies also affected the religious institutions of Muslim societies. In particular, educational policy effectively marginalized, and so alienated, the traditional religious establishment (*ʿulamāʾ*); today the majority of young people in most Muslim countries receive Western-style educations [*see* Education, *article on* Educational Institutions]. Much the same happened in the sphere of law. The Muslim world felt politically humiliated and threatened by all these developments. Non-Muslims had taken control of Muslim societies and interfered with Islam, the final religion, destined to be successful and dominant (Qurʾān 3.110, 39.74, 21.105). The grievances of Muslims (and other Asians and Africans) against the colonialists reflect the dehumanizing aspect of much European colonialism; the "native" was often considered as being of limited intellectual capacity, inferior dignity, and/or low morality.

The missionary movement and the clash of religious institutions and ideas. Although European churches often lost the support of civil governments and the influence of secular rationalism grew, a vigorous missionary endeavor introduced Christianity into all parts of the world. Missionary preaching, education, and health care could generally depend on the colonial governments' protection, although evangelization was not always encouraged. Fundamentally, however, the missionary movement grew out of a genuine spiritual revival and a commitment to carry the gospel to all people. A number of new missionary institutions were started; for example, Anglican and Protestant Missionary Societies were founded in Britain and the United States during the eighteenth and nineteenth centuries and Catholic missionary orders such as the Society of Missionaries of Africa (the White Fathers), in 1885. Missionary activity among Muslims included the distribution of Bible translations, apologetic-polemical tracts, and public disputations. Karl G. Pfander, a German who worked in India with the Church Missionary Society, translated into Urdu his first book on Islam and Christianity, *Mīzān al-ḥaqq* (Balance of Truth). Muslims in northwestern India felt threatened by his linguistic abilities and his comparisons of the "truth" of Christianity with the "falsity" of Islam. Mawlānā Rahmat Allāh Kayrānawī, published a refutation of Pfander's work, the *Iẓhār al-ḥaqq* (Revelation of Truth), and led Muslim resistance to Christian activities. Later, in a public debate, Rahmat Allāh used the methods of European biblical criticism to refute the fundamentalist approach of his opponents. Still being reprinted, both books circulate as examples of Christian and Muslim apologetics.

By the end of the nineteenth century many missionaries began to abandon this approach; it seemed contrary to the gospel proclamation to love one's neighbor, which was understood to include respect for the dignity of persons and societies. The emphasis was laid on missionary service in education and health care. However, a strong emphasis on conversion in the sense of an institutional change of religious allegiance remained strong among certain groups of Christians and Muslims. On the Catholic side, Cardinal Lavigerie (1825–1892) saw the aim of the Church's mission to be a transformation of individuals and whole cultures and societies by slow impregnation with priority given to a witness of disinterested love and service. Dialogue, meanwhile, must focus on common themes: God's majesty, our creatureliness, our need to repent and to be forgiven. He disapproved of the teaching of Christian dogmas to Muslims and thought the ancient discipline of the Church should be restored: only catechumens, already committed to Christ, should be taught Christian doctrines (Gaudeul, 1984, vol. 1, p. 313).

Islamic Response. Western colonial domination placed enormous stress on Muslims. For centuries, Muslims had faced many challenges, but the sweep of Western civilization proved to be the most serious challenge to Islamic life. The traditional pattern of Islamic life based on the *sharīʿah* was everywhere threatened by what Muslims perceived as the "aggression" of the West: political aggression leading to subjugation, economic aggression leading to poverty, social aggression disrupting family and society, intellectual aggression imposing Western thought and education, and religious aggression. "For, say what we will, Christian missionary work is frequently understood by the peoples of Africa and the East not as the sharing of an inestimable treasure, but as an unwanted imposition from without, inseparably associated with the progress of the colonial powers." (Stephen Neill, *A History of Christian Missions*, Harmondsworth, 1964, p. 250). Muslims often view Western scholars of Islam, usually termed "orientalists," as serving, deliberately or not, the colonial/imperial designs of their home countries. How far this generalization is tenable is a moot point. The question is whether study of a culture and religion by an external observer should be entirely rejected because of a certain inevitable degree of misrepresentation. Christian scholars, on the other hand, have regretted that few, if any, Muslims have attempted to create an Islamic "occidentalism" (Watt, 1991, p. 116). Of course, these Christian scholars intend that such work follow methods of modern, (that is, Western), critical scholarship to balance the work of orientalists and provide Christianity with a much-needed "critique" from without.

The reaction to Western domination has been a struggle to create independent nation-states reflecting the wide variety of Muslim thought. Some emphasize fundamental Islamic faith and practice, with minimal involvement in secular society; others adopt a secular approach and emulate European models. A reformist trend seeks to reconcile Islam with the contemporary world, particularly Western civilization, Christian or otherwise. The West is largely rejected emotionally by Muslims, although Muslim societies usually depend on it economically. These issues have produced a religious revival or resurgence, as the Muslim community seeks to clarify the relationship between Islam and modern national identity. Often the process has been accompanied by revolution. The Islamist trend, powerful in several Muslim nations, advocates the integral implementation of the *sharīʿah*, and some states have declared themselves Islamic republics; this affects Muslim-Christian relations profoundly, as can be seen, for example, in the present situation in Nigeria, Sudan, Egypt, Pakistan, and Malaysia. The creation of the state of Israel in 1948 and the subsequent displacement of the Palestinians have had a profound effect upon Muslim-Christian relations everywhere. Although evangelical Christians often support Zionist policies, many other Christians in the West have been moved by the plight of the Palestinians. Common bonds of language and culture often lead Arab Christians to support Palestinian rights; however, since they share with Jews the experience of *dhimmī* status, they desire more equitable arrangements within a modern democracy.

The Muslim world is searching for effective, modern structures of cohesion and growth for the *ummah* in order to play a decisive role in global affairs. The aims of the Rābiṭat al-ʿĀlam al-Islāmī (Muslim World League), founded in Mecca in 1962, include the propagation (*daʿwah* of Islam in Muslim and non-Muslim countries among Muslims and others. It defends the rights of Muslim minorities in non-Muslim countries and, since 1976, has sponsored the research and publication of the Institute of Muslim Minority Affairs (Jeddah and London). Once the rights of the minorities have been secured in a given country, the second phase of the League's strategy is aimed at transforming the minority into a ruling majority through proselytization. The secretary-general of the League has publicly stated that all the organization's activities wish to proceed in the spirit of dialogue and collaboration with Christians (Nasseef, 1986); the *Journal Institute of Muslim Minority Affairs* has published research on the treatment of Christian minorities in Muslim countries. The Organization of the Islamic Conference (OIC), founded in 1962, set up the Islamic Solidarity Fund in 1974 to support religious, cultural, and charitable work in Muslim communities everywhere. The Islamic Call Society, funded by Libya, was founded in 1970 to spread Islam by propagation and to provide educational and medical services as integral elements of *daʿwah*. These and other organizations have sponsored meetings of Christians and Muslims. [*See* Muslim World League; Organization of the Islamic Conference; Islamic Call Society.] This work also takes place on national and regional levels. The Islamic Foundation in Leicester, United Kingdom, for instance, promotes *daʿwah* among Muslims and non-Muslims through printed and audiovisual media and by training workers "to successfully face the challenge of the West." [*See* Islamic Foundation.]

At least one-third of Muslims today live in minority situations and represent a wide range of understandings of Islam. This situation impresses upon Muslims the need for an intra-Muslim ecumenism and the urgency of developing interreligious ties with other faith communities. The problems of Muslim minorities among Christian majorities cannot be solved without the principle of reciprocity in the freedom of religious expression and movement. Christians and Muslims collaborate on global problems like international trade, economic underdevelopment, hunger, and migration within international and national organizations. No longer can Christian-Muslim relations be perceived in terms of relations between Islam and the West, not least because today the centers of Christianity and Islam have shifted to Africa, Asia, and the Americas. The Vatican II declaration *Nostra Ætate* of 1965 prescribes for members of the Roman Catholic Church "esteem" for Muslim faith and practice and "urges" Christians and Muslims "to strive sincerely for mutual understanding" and "to make common cause of safeguarding and fostering social justice, moral values, peace and freedom." These themes are important elements of contemporary Christian-Muslim dialogue both at the Office for Islam within the Pontifical Council for Dialogue between Religions and in the work of the World Council of Churches (WCC). In 1971 the WCC, representing Anglican, Protestant, and Orthodox Churches, established an Office for Dialogue with People of Living Faiths (DFI). Both the WCC and the Pontifical Council have sponsored many meetings between Christians and Muslims. These central initiatives and offices also occur on regional and national levels; although some politicians seek to replace the Iron Curtain with a "Christian-Muslim Cold War" (an understanding often reflected in the mass media), only determined worldwide efforts to address the divisive issues that have separated Muslims and Christians can make significant headway in achieving reconciliation. Muslim *daʿwah* and Christian mission are being redefined in terms of constructive coexistence, respecting each others' differences and being for one another a source of righteous emulation and challenge.

[*See also* Daʿwah; Dhimmī; Muslim-Christian Dialogue.]

BIBLIOGRAPHY

Ahmad, Khurshid, and David Kerr, eds. "Christian Mission and Islamic Daʿwah." Issue of *International Review of Mission* 65 (1976): 365–460.

"Christian-Muslim Relations into the Twenty-First Century: A Round Table Discussion." *Islam and Christian-Muslim Relations* 3.1 (1992): 5–39.

Courbage, Youssef, and Philippe Fargues. *Chrétiens et Juifs dans l'Islam arabe et turc*. Paris, 1992. Perceptive sociohistorical essay with extensive, relevant demographic information and analysis.

Cragg, Kenneth. *The Arab Christian: A History in the Middle East*. London, 1992. Traces the history of the Arab Christians from its beginning through the birth and growth of Islam to the present, as well as pondering the agenda—and enigma—of the future.

Ellis, Kail C., ed. *The Vatican, Islam, and the Middle East*. Syracuse, N.Y., 1987. Presents a wide spectrum of intellectual and practical insights into contemporary Catholic-Islamic relations, including essays on selected countries of Asia.

Gaudeul, Jean-Marie. *Encounters and Clashes: Islam and Christianity in History*, vol. 1, *A Survey;* vol. 2, *Texts*. Rome, 1984. Detailed analysis of the apologetic, polemical, and irenic efforts and texts placed in their changing historical contexts. Written from a Roman Catholic, post–Vatican II perspective for informed nonspecialists. Most of the selected texts are presented in the original and in translation. Crucial German studies in the field have not been considered.

Hagemann, Ludwig. *Christentum und Islam zwischen Konfrontation und Begegnung*. Altenberge, 1983. Solid survey of the premodern phases.

Hamidullah, Muhammad. *The Muslim Conduct of State* (1935). Reprint, Lahore, 1963.

Hourani, Albert. *Islam in European Thought*. Cambridge, 1991. Masterly critical survey, balancing Edward Said's work.

Islamochristiana, 1975–. Annually published by the Pontificio Istituto di Studie Arabi e d'Islamistica, Rome. Contains a wealth of primary sources and analyses and reports concerning the past and present of Islamic-Christian relations.

Joseph, Suad, and Barbara L. K. Pillsbury, eds. *Muslim-Christian Conflicts: Economic, Political, and Social Origins*. Boulder and Folkestone, 1978. Highlights the need for taking account of the complexity and diversity of the causes of conflict.

Khoury, Adel Theodor, and Ludwig Hagemann. *Christentum und Christen im Denken zeitgenössischer Muslime*. Altenberge, 1986. Based on a wide selection of Arab authors.

Lewis, Bernard. *The Muslim Discovery of Europe*. London and New York, 1982.

Moubarak, Youakim, ed. *Les Musulmans: Consultation islamo-chrétienne entre Muhammad Arkoun, Hasan Askari, Muhammad Hamidullah, Hassan Hanafi, Muhammad Kamel Hussein, Ibrahim Madkour, Seyyed Hossein Nasr, et Youakim Moubarak*. Paris, 1971. Responses by outstanding Muslim scholars to questions regarding the ancient controversies, the present and possible/points of convergence in the future.

Nasseef, Abdullah Omar. "Muslim-Christian Relations: The Muslim Approach." *Journal Institute of Muslim Minority Affairs*, 7.1 (January 1986): 27–31.

Powell, Averil. *Muslims and Missionaries in Pre-Mutiny India*. London, 1992. Pioneering and penetrating study of the momentous Christian-Muslim controversies, placed firmly in the context of Indian-Muslim history.

Sahas, Daniel J. *John of Damascus on Islam: The "Heresy of the Ishmaelites"*. Leiden, 1972. Important study of one of the earliest Christian responses to Islam which also provides much valuable background information.

Said, Edward W. *Orientalism*. New York, 1979. Brilliant and seminal, yet controversial, critical essay.

Schacht, Joseph, and C. E. Bosworth, eds. *The Legacy of Islam*. 2d ed. Oxford, 1974. Especially relevant contributions by Bernard Lewis and Maxime Rodinson.

Southern, Richard W. *Western Views of Islam in the Middle Ages*. Cambridge, Mass., 1962. Classic work on the subject.

Vander Werff, Lyle L. *Christian Mission to Muslims: The Record; Anglican and Reformed Approaches in India and the Near East, 1800–1938*. South Pasadena, Calif., 1977. Thorough historical account from a Protestant insider perspective. Detailed listing of the primary and secondary source material.

Watt, W. Montgomery. *Muslim-Christian Encounters: Perceptions and Misperceptions.* London and New York, 1991. Succinct and brilliant account of central aspects and phases of the historical interaction of the two religions.

BERT F. BREINER and CHRISTIAN W. TROLL

CINEMA. The development of cinema was closely linked to Western industrialization. It was exploited in Europe and the United States as a commercial entertainment for a largely working-class audience, and, even when exported, has remained a secular, commercial entertainment. At the turn of the century, the social and economic conditions in the Islamic world were vastly different from those in Europe and the United States, and it is significant that some of the first contacts between cinema and the Islamic world were through the royal families. In the Ottoman Empire, the first screenings were held in the Sultan's Palace in Istanbul, and in Tehran a cinematograph, acquired on a visit to Paris in 1900 and operated by the court photographer, became a favorite entertainment for members of the Qājār Dynasty. Public screenings came only much later: in 1905 in Tehran and Istanbul, 1908 in Aleppo, and 1909 in Baghdad. Often, in Tehran for example, there was strong initial opposition to such entertainment from religious groups.

Sometimes those responsible for early film showings were local entrepreneurs—Albert Samama, also known as Chikly, in Tunisia, or the Armenian Ardeshir Khan in Iran—who also imported other Western novelties, such as the bicycle, still photography, or the phonograph. Chikly, indeed, is a true pioneer, since he subsequently directed the first Tunisian short film in 1922 and a first feature in 1926. But, as this was an era of colonialism and European domination, many of the early showings were arranged by foreign residents. Thus, in Egypt and Algeria, screenings of the Lumière cinematograph were organized as early as 1896 in those cities with the highest numbers of foreign residents: Cairo and Alexandria, Algiers and Oran. In sub-Saharan Africa it was similarly foreign businessmen who set up first screenings, in Dakar in 1900 and Lagos in 1903. Often local scenes were shot by the Lumière operators to add to the attraction of their programs. In time, screenings for an elite audience—foreign residents and members of a westernized bourgeoisie—came to be supplemented by film shows for a popular audience. A two-tier system of distribution—new imported films in luxurious but expensive air-conditioned cinemas and cheap, low-grade productions shown in poor conditions to the popular audience—remains common in many parts of the Islamic world.

Usually the first film productions, like the first screenings, were the work of foreigners: the Frenchman De Lagarne in Egypt in 1912, the Romanian representative of Pathé, Sigmund Weinberg, in Turkey in 1916, two Dutchmen, Kruger and Heuveldorp, in Indonesia in 1926. Such films were based on foreign models. Thus the Armenian Avans Ohanian's first film—shown in 1930 and one of only four Iranian silent films—was an imitation of a Danish silent comedy, and most Turkish films of the 1920s were adaptations of European stage plays. More authentic national productions usually followed within a few years, but overall film production remained low throughout the silent era of the 1920s. Just thirteen features—including Mohamed Khan's 1930 adaptation of Muḥammad Ḥusayn Haykal's novel, *Zaynab*—were made in Egypt, eight films in Indonesia, a half dozen in Turkey (where production ceased altogether for five years with the advent of Kemal Atatürk's secular republic), three in Syria, one in Lebanon. By contrast, European filmmakers made great use of some parts of the Islamic world as film locations, with more than sixty features shot in North Africa alone before the end of the 1920s.

The coming of sound presented Islamic filmmakers with fresh problems, such as higher production costs and greater technical demands. The employment of foreign directors was therefore common: Italian directors for a number of early Egyptian sound films and an Indian, Ardeshir Irani, for the first Persian-language sound film, shot in Bombay in 1931. Sound also confronted distributors with fresh problems, as differing languages and dialects fragmented previously unified markets. But sound also allowed the possibility of closer links with audiences, through the use of local languages and dialects and, above all, local music and song. Though producers were usually seeking—in an unsophisticated way—to create a popular mass art imbued with national values, they remained very vulnerable to imported films. Far from giving support or offering tariff barriers, governments tended to see cinema simply as a source of tax revenue, at rates usually far higher than in the West. Even a comparatively successful film industry, like that established in Egypt, found it hard to compete with films from the West, especially as these matched the tastes of elite audiences in the major cities, where most cinemas were located.

In most parts of the Islamic world production remained low in the period from 1930 to the end of World War II and beyond. In Tunisia, Chikly's pioneering efforts found little echo, and only two sound features were made in the period before independence in 1966. In Lebanon, where cinema attendance was the highest in the Arab world, only eight features were made between 1930 and 1952, and there was no production at all in Syria or Iraq. Arab cinema became synonymous with Egyptian cinema, as Egyptian producers gradually came to dominate film markets throughout the Arab world. Initial progress was slow, however, though producers showed an early interest in the sound film's potential for films featuring Oriental songs. By the mid-1930s, when the Miṣr studio opened, equipped with imported European facilities and employing staff trained in Europe, output reached twenty-five films in 1945. The bulk of the films—unpretentious love stories with exotic settings and plenty of space for song and dance, bedouin adventure tales, and theatrical melodramas—have little lasting value. But critics are united in praising, as an example of totally independent filmmaking, *The Will/ Al-ʿazīmah* (1939), the first film to look realistically at Egyptian life, directed by Kemal Selim (1913–1945).

Elsewhere in the Middle East progress was more muted. The first five Persian-language feature films shot in Bombay were patriotic films which enjoyed some success with audiences. But the driving force behind them, the actor and director Abdolhossein Sepenta (1907–1969), received no official support and was unable to continue his career on his return to Iran in 1936. Indeed, no further Iranian films were made until 1947. In Turkey, production was more sustained, but remained at under half a dozen films a year until 1948, when changes in taxation made low-budget production profitable. The key figure in the transition from silent to sound cinema was Muhsin Ertuğrul (1892–1979), who joined İpek Film when it was set up in 1928 and directed the first Turkish sound film. Ertuğrul's heavily theatrical style—he was director of the Istanbul Municipal Theater and appeared as an actor in most of his films—set the pattern for younger directors of the period.

In the Far East, filmmaking got under way in Malaysia in the 1930s, but since the films were financed by Chinese producers, written and directed by Indian expatriates, and performed by Malay actors, little cultural authenticity was possible. In Indonesia, film output remained at seven films or less a year until 1939, then swiftly expanded to reach forty-one films in 1941, only to fall back to three or so a year during the Japanese occupation and to dry up completely during the early years of the independence struggle against the Dutch colonizers. It was not until after independence was formalized in 1949 that the industry again began to expand rapidly.

The period after 1945 saw a boom in film production in many parts of the Islamic world. In Egypt, the immediate postwar years were a period of rapid expansion as production levels rose to more than fifty films a year, a total that has been largely maintained into the 1990s. As a result, Egyptian films came to dominate the Arab film market and impose the Egyptian dialect as the "natural" language for Arab films. Most of this output comprised melodramas and farces, with a liberal helping of song and dance, but from the early 1950s, serious writers began to involve themselves in filmmaking and a number of major directors made their appearance. Salah Abou Seif (b. 1915), Youssef Chahine (b. 1926), and Tewfik Saleh (b. 1926), all of whom made strikingly realistic studies of Egyptian lower- and middle-class life, came to dominate Egyptian cinema from the 1950s through the 1980s.

The expansion of cinema in Turkey was even more striking. From just two films in 1947, output rose to thirty-five in the early 1960s, eventually reaching a peak of 298 features in 1972. Some new directors made their reputations: Metin Erksan (b. 1929), Atif Yılmaz (b. 1925), and Lüfti Ö. Akad (b. 1916). But much of this production was mediocre, often derivative of foreign models, and there was even—unique in an Islamic country—a proliferation of pornographic films. But political censorship remained strict, and the charismatic and politically committed actor-director Yılmaz Güney (1937–1984) spent much of his career in jail. Though he ended his life in exile, the films he was able to make in Turkey—such as *Yol* and *Sürü*—gave Güney an international reputation. The economic crisis caused production levels to fall drastically to just sixty-four films by 1980, but Güney's example has been followed in the 1980s and 1990s by two of his collaborators, Zeki Ökten (b. 1941) and Şerif Gören (b. 1944).

Iran experienced a similar upsurge of production

when indigenous production began in 1947. By the mid-1950s, output was around fifteen features, rising to thirty in 1961 and peaking at ninety in 1972, before falling back to just eighteen in 1978. Alongside the conventional commercial production, there emerged in the 1970s a New Iranian Cinema receiving support from the government and the state television service. Among the largely Western-trained directors were Dariush Mehrjui (b. 1940) and Bahram Bayzai (b. 1938), both of whom established an international reputation. This particular organization of cinema ceased, however, with the fall of the shah.

Equally striking has been the growth of production in Indonesia, where production rose from eight features in 1949, the year of independence, to 124 in 1977, staying at more than fifty features a year throughout the 1980s, though falling back in the early 1990s. The backgrounds of the successive generations of directors offer a fascinating reflection of the country's political transformations. The 1950s generation—Usmar Ismail, D. Djajakusuma, and Asrul Sani—studied in Dutch schools, while the 1970s generation comprises both filmmakers trained in Moscow—Wim Umboh (b. 1933), Syumanjaya (b. 1933), and Ami Primyono (b. 1939)—and a younger group coming from Indonesian theater, such as Teguh Karya (b. 1937), Arifin Noer (b. 1941), and Slamet Rahardjo (b. 1949). By contrast, Malaysian cinema, though it experienced a brief growth in the 1950s, has seen its markets continue to be dominated by imported Indonesian films, as government efforts to aid the industry have proved unsuccessful.

At the time of the partition of the Indian subcontinent in 1947, there was no tradition of filmmaking in either West Pakistan or East Pakistan (later to secede as Bangladesh). The all-India movie, which passed two hundred films a year in the 1940s, was a Hindi-language phenomenon, with some Muslim actors, often disguised under Hindi names, but only Hindu filmmakers. Moreover the tight political censorship under British rule had precluded the depiction of religious differences or specifically Muslim viewpoints. From the moment of partition, cinema in the two halves of Pakistan developed separately. Though output levels rose steadily, to peak at a hundred films a year in Pakistan and fifty a year in Bangladesh, most of this production was derivative, even plagiaristic, of Indian models. Few productions have more than local interest, though the great Indian filmmaker, Ritwikkumar Ghatak (1925–1976), did return to his native region of Dhaka to shoot a solitary feature in 1973.

The virtual nationalization of the Egyptian film industry, after the establishment of the General Organization of Egyptian Cinema in 1961, served to give some support to serious filmmaking in Egypt, but was a financial disaster. Perhaps as a result, Egyptian cinema did not experience the kind of renewal common elsewhere in the 1960s, and the one major new filmmaker to emerge, Shadi Abdel-Salam (1930–1986), was never able to create a real career for himself, though his sole feature, *Al-mūmiyah* (1969), was internationally acclaimed. Overall, film production remained at a level of around fifty films a year, and in the 1960s many Egyptian producers moved abroad, particularly to Lebanon, and continued to make "Egyptian" films there. But this did little to foster the emergence of a genuinely Lebanese cinema, and it was not until the 1970s that a number of talented, Western-trained filmmakers, led by Heiny Srour (b. 1945) and Borhan Alawiya (b. 1941), emerged and began to treat the social and political problems of their country in a number of features strongly influenced by documentary techniques.

Though Egypt's nationalized film industry was dissolved in 1972, the Higher Cinema Institute in Cairo has remained in operation. As a result, Egypt is the only Arab country to train its own filmmakers locally. The generation that emerged in the late 1970s and early 1980s, led by Mohamed Khan (b. 1942), has shown itself very aware of the history and style of Egyptian filmmaking. In one of the more remarkable film developments in the Arab world, the so-called New Egyptian Realists have produced a series of films within the commercial structures of the industry which play with the genre conventions of film narrative and star casting.

Though the state film organization eventually proved to be an expensive commercial failure in Egypt, it provided a model for neighboring Arab countries. In Syria, which, like Lebanon, became a site for expatriate Egyptian producers, a state sector was developed alongside the commercial industry. The policy that offered state backing for talented young filmmakers was rewarded with the emergence in the 1980s of two extremely talented newcomers, both born in 1945 and trained in Moscow: Samir Zikra and Mohamed Malass. Another Syrian-born filmmaker to make an international reputation has been the French-trained documentarist, Umar Amiralay (b. 1941), who, after an initial feature-length documentary, has worked largely for television. By contrast, in Iraq, where film production had been sporadic until the 1960s, the General Organization for Cinema, which achieved autonomy in 1964, pursued a policy of funding epic super-productions, some directed by Egyptian veterans such as Tewfik Saleh and Salah Abou Seif, others by Iraqi-born directors, like the British-trained Mohammed Shukry Jamil (b. 1936). Elsewhere in the Middle East, isolated pioneers made their appearance: Toryali Shafaq (b. 1947) in Afghanistan, the Indian-trained Khalid Siddik (b. 1948) in Kuwait, and the Nazareth-born Michel Khleifi (b. 1950), whose work reflects Palestinian values from an exile base in Belgium.

The mid-1960s also saw the emergence of new national cinemas in the Maghrib, though most of the filmmakers were European-trained and the influence of France was all-persuasive. In Algeria the roots of the new cinema lay in the liberation struggle. The nationalized film industry established in the mid-1960s organized first a series of studies of resistance to the French—with notable contributions from Ahmed Rachedi (b. 1938) and especially Mohamed Lakhdar-Hamina (b. 1934)—and then a series on rural reform, beginning with the first feature of Mohamed Bouamari (b. 1945). But already by the late 1970s more distinctive individual voices could be heard—among them Merzak Allouache (b. 1944) and Mahmoud Zemmouri (b. 1946)—and by the mid—1980s the state monopoly had been broken up.

In Tunisia the state had no such clear initial objectives, but there is a strong film culture, evidenced by the biennial film festival, the Journées Cinématographiques de Carthage, in Tunis. Output in Tunisia is largely the work of dedicated individualists such as the self-taught Omar Khlifi (b. 1934) in the 1960s, Abdellatif Ben Ammar (b. 1943) in the 1970s, and Nouri Bouzid (b. 1947) in the 1980s. Output in Morocco shows a similar mix of those, like Souhel Ben Barka (b. 1942), who seek commercial success, and others, among them Moumen Smihi (b. 1945), who are more concerned with formal innovation. But in general, the films of the Maghrib receive more showings at foreign festivals than in local cinemas.

The same problem confronts filmmakers in sub-Saharan Africa, though a few directors have made international reputations, among them the Paris-based Med Hondo (b. 1936) from Mauritania, Souleymane Cissé (b. 1940) from Mali, and Gaston Kaboré (b. 1951) from Burkina Faso. There have been occasional Muslim-inspired films, like the Nigerian Adamu Halilu's *Shehu Uma* (1977), but these have received far less notice and screening than the works of the Marxist Senegalese veteran, Ousmane Sembene (b. 1923), whose *Ceddo* (1976) is an outspoken attack on Islam.

In general, cinema in the Islamic world falls into two categories: mindless commercial production for a limited local audience or Western-influenced "art cinema" destined for foreign film festivals. There have been few attempts to create a genuinely Islamic cinema, though in Turkey a group of filmmakers led by Yücel Çakmaklı (b. 1937), and given some tacit government support, has advocated a return to Islam and national origins. The sole state-backed Islamic cinema developed after the 1979 Revolution in Iran, where attacks on film theaters had formed a key part in the campaign against the shah. Yet the leaders of Iran's Islamic Revolution showed themselves in support of cinema as a positive cultural force, organized through the Farabi Cinema Foundation. After initial interruptions of production, older established filmmakers like Mehrjui and Bayzai were allowed once again to produce freely, fresh opportunities were given to other veterans, like Amir Naderi (b. 1945), and a new generation of directors came to the fore, led by Mohsen Makhmalbaf (b. 1957). Iranian cinema has again found a way to reach its own audiences and reestablish its place at international film festivals.

[*See also* Communications Media.]

BIBLIOGRAPHY

Armes, Roy. *Third World Film Making and the West.* Berkeley and London, 1987. Wide-ranging study of factors governing the emergence and growth of cinema in the Third World.

Barnouw, Erik, and Subrahmanyam Krishnaswamy. *Indian Film.* 2d ed. New York, 1980. Invaluable, pioneering survey.

Diawara, Manthia. *African Cinema: Politics and Culture.* Bloomington, 1992. Wide-ranging survey by a Malian-born academic now teaching in the U.S.

Downing, John D. H., ed. *Film and Politics in the Third World.* New York, 1987. Excellent anthology with articles on African, Arab, Turkish, and Iranian cinema.

Heider, Karl G. *Indonesian Cinema: National Culture on Screen.* Honolulu, 1991. Study of Indonesian cinema as an aspect of national culture, by a U.S. anthropologist.

Issari, Mohammad Ali. *Cinema in Iran, 1900–1979.* Metuchen, N.J., and London, 1989. Meticulous and well-documented history of cinema and its cultural context.

Kabir, Alamgir. *The Cinema in Pakistan.* Dacca, 1969. *Film in Bangladesh.* Dacca, 1979. Two extremely useful general surveys.

Lent, John A. *The Asian Film Industry*. Austin, 1990. Ten essays on Asian national cinemas, with emphasis on contemporary developments.

Malkmus, Lizbeth, and Roy Armes. *Arab and African Film Making*. London and Atlantic Highlands, N.J., 1991. Detailed study of narrative patterns in the cinemas of Africa and the Arab world.

Naficy, Hamid. "The Development of an Islamic Cinema in Iran." *Third World Affairs* (1987): 447–463. Rare example of discussion in English of the implications of a specifically Islamic approach to cinema.

Naficy, Hamid. "Islamizing Film Culture in Iran." In *Iran: Political Culture in the Islamic Republic*, edited by Samih K. Farsoun and Mehrdad Mashayekhi, pp. 178–213. London, 1992. A further examination of the topic.

Pines, Jim, and Paul Willemen, eds. *Questions of Third Cinema*. London, 1989. Essays on theoretical aspects of Third World cinema.

Sadoul, Georges, ed. *The Cinema in the Arab Countries*. Beirut, 1966. Pioneering account of various national cinemas.

ROY ARMES

CIRCUMCISION. The rite of passage of circumcision plays varied roles in Islamic society, depending on gender, ethnic orientation, and modern cultural attitudes. There are differences of opinion among the legal authorities over whether circumcision is *farḍ* (legally obligatory) or *sunnah* (the practice of the Prophet), nor is the motive for the operation always clear. Socially, it is obviously a rite of passage of considerable status significance for young boys when it is performed at ten to twelve years of age, as in some parts of the Arab world, to mark their move to male responsibilities. In the religious sphere, the view that circumcision is necessary for conversion to Islam, as the legist al-Mālik stressed, is still adhered to by many Muslims.

Other sources speak of circumcision within the context of purification; indeed, in the present-day Arab world the rite is called *ṭahārah* (purification) rather than the classical *khitān*. The purification concept probably derives from al-Mālik's *Sunnah of Fiṭrah,* where it is linked with cutting nails, trimming the mustache, and removing hair from the armpits and pubic area. Such notions affirm that circumcision is required of both sexes, as Shāfiʿī (767-820 CE) held. [*See* Purification.] Some Muslims, however, relate the practice to Abraham and thus see it as part of the original law promulgated among their Semitic ancestors, particularly the Jews.

Finally, circumcision is an outward symbol of the religious process of bringing oneself under the discipline of God's requirements, reflecting the inner growth of *ʿaql* (reason) and the submission of base passions to the higher spiritual requisites of true Islam. When interpreted this way, modifying the sexual organs is a physical expression of the acknowledgment of God's hegemony over one's uncontrolled instincts and signals the deeper religious commitment expected of the mature Muslim.

Although the presence of the operation is often regarded by Western writers and many Muslims as evidence of Islamic orthodoxy, it is not universal in the Muslim world: for example, not all Muslims in China practice it, and in many Muslim countries the law is not held binding on females. There is also considerable cultural distinction in the time at which the process is undertaken. In Europe and North America Muslims have adopted the cultural norm of having the operation done to their sons in the hospital immediately after birth, but in the Middle East a separate rite is undertaken sometime between the ages of two and twelve. An Arab proverb perceptively embodies the initiatory meanings: "The Arab is king on his wedding day and his circumcision day." In the Sudan, this proverbial connection influences the activities: the ceremony is referred to as *al-ʿirs* (a wedding); and the young boy is dressed like a girl, wears jewelry and perfume, and is painted with henna to ward off the evil eye. Among the Beja people the boys live together in a special hut along with the individual who performs the operation. In Egypt, barbers often set up circumcision stalls during holy days, such as the Prophet's birthday or the *mawlid*s of saints. Being circumcised during a saint's holy day is held to tie one directly to the *barakah* of the saint, ensuring fertility and blessings later. On such occasions a sheep is also sacrificed. In Morocco, the rite also parallels the wedding rituals and is supervised by the boy's mother; it is customary to dress the boy in a white shift, bathe him, shave his head, and paint his hands with henna the day before the rite. Relatives, neighbors and friends join in eating the sacrificed sheep, and small gifts are brought in his honor.

Among the peoples of Java, where the rite is called *islaman* or sometimes *sunatan,* the wedding motif dominates. It is a time of great celebration and lavish spending, including entertainment by orchestras and traveling dancing troupes, along with massive receptions for the community. Guests bring presents or money. Sometimes groups of boys, usually related, undergo the rite together, and the celebration usually follows the completion of the boys' Islamic studies. The rite itself is performed by a *tjalak* (officially registered operator) who charges for his service and uses a knife called *wesi tawa* ("iron you can't feel"). The initiant is placed on a low bed and his mother steps over him three times, signaling her release of her possessiveness and her dispatch of him to his manly responsibilities. Parallel rites guard against unfit attitudes such as envy or jealousy entering people's hearts, thus undermining the boy's potential in life. This explicit control of negative attitudes at circumcision appears to be exclusive to the Javanese. Because of the expense of the rite, parents often delay it as long as possible, sometimes prompting the boy to campaign for the rite before his parents can afford it. Among the Brunei Malays, the initiation aspect is stressed, but the ceremony is embellished by *dhikr* chanting, thus appropriating the sacrality of Ṣūfī ceremonial life.

In contrast, some countries in Central Africa have distanced themselves from the initiatory meaning of circumcision precisely because of the importance of the rite of passage in traditional African religions. When a tribe is converting to Islam, circumcision is a badge of identity with the new religion, as among the Dagomba; however, the neighboring Nanumba, who do follow a form of Islam, do not circumcise, and indeed regard it as a rite peculiar to the Dagomba. A further development is seen among the Merina of Madagascar, who, though not Muslim, appear to have appropriated some aspects of Muslim circumcision as a means of transferring ancestral power.

The need to take the pain of the operation without flinching is seen by the northern Yemenis as a mark of toughness and manliness. The initiant is surrounded by villagers who cut and toss the foreskin into the milling crowd. The boy finds the skin, is mounted on his mother's shoulder, and proudly displays the severed section to the adulation of the crowd. This emphasis on fortitude occurs in all Islamic societies, but the Yemeni example is unusual in that it highlights virility more than the passage to Islamic maturity.

It is the norm in Islamic cultures that the older circumcised boy is immediately required to join his father and older relatives in public prayer and is restricted from moving freely between the male and female parts of the house. The Islamic character of his changed status is essential. Where the operation is separate from the passage to maturity, as is increasingly the case among urban and middle-class Muslims worldwide, the change in status requires other kinds of celebrations, such as graduation exercises from special classes held by imams to teach the basics of Islam. Since female circumcision is not practiced by the majority of Muslims, and girls too are increasingly given advanced religious training, the differences in the early life-experience of boys and girls are being reduced. Hence Islamic modernity seems to have reduced the contiguity of the physical operation with the change in spiritual status and thus to have made adolescent experience less differentiated by gender.

[*See also* Birth Rites; Puberty Rites; Rites of Passage.]

BIBLIOGRAPHY

Bloch, Maurice. *From Blessing to Violence: History and Ideology in the Circumcision Ritual of the Merina of Madagascar*. Cambridge, 1986.

Broomhall, Marshall. *Islam in China* (1910). New York, 1966.

Eickelman, Dale F. *Moroccan Islam: Tradition and Society in a Pilgrimage Center*. Austin, 1976.

Eickelman, Dale F. "Rites of Passage." In *The Encyclopedia of Religion*, vol. 12, pp. 380–403. New York, 1987.

Geertz, Clifford. *The Religion of Java*. New York, 1960.

Geertz, Hildred. *The Javanese Family: A Study of Kinship and Socialization*. New York, 1961.

Levtzion, Nehemia. *Muslims and Chiefs in West Africa*. Oxford, 1968.

Murray, G. W. *Sons of Ishmael: A Study of the Egyptian Bedouin*. London, 1935.

Trimingham, J. Spencer. *Islam in Ethiopia*. Oxford, 1965.

Trimingham, J. Spencer. *Islam in the Sudan*. Oxford, 1965.

Trimingham, J. Spencer. *The Influence of Islam upon Africa*. 2d ed. London, 1980.

Westermarck, Edward A. *Ritual and Belief in Morocco* (1926). Vol. 2. Reprint, New York, 1968.

EARLE H. WAUGH

CITIZENSHIP. The concept and form of citizenship evolved gradually from the time of the Greek city-state to the formation of nation-states in the nineteenth century. As reflected in the writings of philosophers from Plato and Aristotle to Abbé de Mably and Rousseau, the perception of a subject as a passive member of society was slowly transformed to a citizen as an active member, with certain rights and duties within the community. The modern concept of citizenship within democratic principles allows the citizen to participate in public decisions and imposes various duties, most commonly paying taxes and serving in the military. In modern democracies, then, sovereignty belongs to the citizens of a nation as defined by its laws. Both in concept and in practice, however, in the Western tradition full participation in citizenship was often limited to specific groups. Privileges were granted on the basis of such issues as being born within the limits of a city-state, sex, class, and property ownership.

In Islam, sovereignty belongs to God, and in Islamic history the caliph/sultan ruled over the Islamic community in accordance with *sharīʿah* (Islamic law) based on the Qur'ān and the *sunnah* (the traditions of the prophet Muḥammad). Muslims, as subjects of the ruler, had duties defined by Islamic concepts rather than rights acquired as members of a political community.

In principle, the members of the Islamic community, the *ummah,* were all equal without deference to race, color, or ethnic background. In practice, however, from very early in Islamic history, during the rule of the Umayyad dynasty (661–750 CE), for instance, more than one class of subject emerged. The *mawālī* (singular, *mawlā*), or Muslims who were non-Arabs or not a full member by descent from an Arab tribe, did not receive equal economic and social benefits and were not fully accepted by the Arab aristocracy.

During the rule of the ʿAbbasīd caliphs (750–1258), the practical social order of the Muslim *ummah* was central to the philosophy of the state. Nevertheless, Muslim philosophers and jurists, such as al-Fārābī (d. 950) and al-Māwardī (d. 1058), raised fundamental questions regarding the relations between the ruler and the ruled and their mutual duties. In his *Al-madīnah al-faḍilah* (The Ideas of the Citizens of the Virtuous City), al-Fārābī set the standards by which states should be judged. Later, during the Mamlūk period, one of the most important Muslim philosopher/jurists, Ibn Taymīyah (1263–1328), defined the criteria for "just" rulers and the political and social obligations of the community. In all these expressions, the position of the ruler and the subjects were placed within Islamic principles as interpreted by the *ʿulamā',* the learned men of religion. Also, the membership in the *ummah* recognized no geographical boundaries.

In the Ottoman Empire (c.1300–1918), from the mid-fifteenth century the population was organized into *millet*s, legally recognized religious-communal organizations. The four *millet*s, Greek Orthodox, Armenian, Jewish, and Muslim, were differentiated according to their ecclesiastical affiliations and not according to their ethnic and linguistic differences. With privileges granted by the ruler, the *millet*s under religious leadership assumed a number of social and economic responsibilities. The leaders of the *millet*s thus also had fairly extensive civil authority over the membership, including matters related to internal organization, education, and personal status.

The *millet* system continued long into the nineteenth century—a period of intensive educational, military, and administrative reforms commonly referred to as the Tanzimat (Reorganization) era. With two major reform edicts in 1839 and 1856, the Ottoman government recognized and reaffirmed equality among its subjects and their rights to security of life, honor, and property, preconditions to the modern concept of citizenship. The Ottoman subjects, however, at this time still identified themselves as members of the *millet*s. [*See* Millet; Tanzimat.]

Ideas dealing with equality of Muslim and non-Muslim subjects and the protection of rights in return for specific obligations to the state were clearly expressed by some Muslim intellectuals, such as Rifāʿah Rāfiʿ al-Ṭahṭāwī and Mehmed Sadık Rifat Pasha. Al-Ṭahṭāwī, in *Manāhij al-albāb al-Miṣrīyah fī mabāhij al-ādāb al-ʿaṣrīyah* (Methods for Egyptian Minds on the Joys of Modern Manners), outlined the citizens' duties toward their country (Egypt) as well as their rights. He assigned an active role to the members of the political community. Sadık Rifat Pasha, in his monumental book, *Müntehabat-i Âsar* (Selections of Works), made frequent use of the term *halk,* the people, and discussed the rights of subjects to liberty.

It was during the nineteenth century that various nationalist tendencies emerged in the Ottoman territories. In 1869 the Ottoman government, in its efforts to provide a viable ideology for the unity of the empire and to curb the interference of European powers and Russia in its domestic affairs, issued the law of nationality and naturalization. Article 1 of the law stated that all individuals born to an Ottoman father and mother, or only to an Ottoman father, are Ottoman subjects. Article 2 provided that all individuals born in Ottoman territories to parents of foreign nationality can, at the age of majority, claim Ottoman nationality. Other aspects of the law were in accordance with the principles of international conventions.

This was indeed a landmark in the development of the concept and form of citizenship among Muslims. The law provided a new legal concept regarding the status of Ottoman subjects. Ottomans were no longer merely members of a *millet* but Ottoman nationals. An individual's relation to the state was now more direct, and his or her obligations to it went beyond those to a *millet.* The central government, however, did assume certain social and economic responsibilities which previously fell under the purview of the *millet* administrations. Moreover, by recognizing the right of individuals born in the empire, even to foreign parents, to become Ottoman subjects, the Porte came closer to establishing a modern concept of citizenship related to territorial boundaries of national states.

During the remainder of the nineteenth century, Ottoman intellectuals, notably Namık Kemal (1840–1881), discussed the nature of the political system and the individual's role within it. They recognized certain natural rights for citizens and argued for their preservation. Within the Western liberal political tradition, these writers emphasized "people's will" and the people's rights to exercise sovereignty. At the beginning of the twentieth century, similar arguments were heard among Egyptian intellectuals, the nationalist Young Tunisians, and members of the Young Algerian movement.

From the early decades of the twentieth century, as modern nation-states emerged among Muslim populations, governments defined the rights and duties of their citizens. In Turkey, the National Assembly, established in 1920 during the war of independence by the nationalist government under Mustafa Kemal (later Atatürk), declared that "sovereignty unconditionally belongs to the people," thus establishing de facto a republic before its official declaration in 1923. The deposition of the last Ottoman sultan in 1922 and the abolition of the caliphate in 1924 eliminated any legal basis for a challenge to a people's exercise of political will. The extension of full and equal franchise to women in 1934, permitting them to vote and stand for election and giving them full political rights and duties, allowed all Turkish citizens to become active participants in the political process.

The Anglo-Egyptian Treaty of 1936 recognized Egypt's independence. As other Muslim countries gained their independence—for instance, Indonesia (1945), Transjordan (1946), Libya (1951), Tunisia and Morocco (1956), Algeria (1962)—each country established its own criteria for citizenship, based on its own political ideology, historical experience, and social customs. Although some countries provided their citizens, men and women, Muslim or non-Muslim, with extensive political and social rights (e.g., Egypt, Iraq, and Indonesia), others (e.g., Kuwait and Saudi Arabia) limited the privileges of citizenship. In Kuwait, two classes of citizenship are still in effect: first-class citizens, whose forebears lived in Kuwait before 1922; and second-class citizens, who belong to families that came to Kuwait between 1922 and 1945. Those who arrived after 1945 are not considered for citizenship at all. Also, women who are Kuwaiti citizens are disfranchised. In all instances, however, citizenship in Muslim countries is now defined in specific reference to national boundaries, not in view of general membership within the *ummah*.

BIBLIOGRAPHY

Berkes, Niyazi. *The Development of Secularism in Turkey*. Montreal, 1964. Penetrating study of intellectual currents in late Ottoman and early Turkish history.

Davison, Roderic. *Reform in the Ottoman Empire, 1856–1876*. Princeton, 1963. Detailed study of the Tanzimat reforms.

Hourani, Albert. *Arabic Thought in the Liberal Age, 1798–1939*. London, 1962. Impressive work on Arab intellectual history.

Hourani, Albert. *A History of the Arab Peoples*. Cambridge, 1992. Eloquently written work dealing with the Arab world from the rise of Islam to the present, with very helpful maps.

Keddie, Nikkie R., and Beth Baron, eds. *Women in Middle Eastern History*. New Haven, 1992. Articles dealing with important issues related to Muslim women.

Lapidus, Ira. *A History of Islamic Societies*. Cambridge, 1989. Particularly enlightening on issues dealing with the social history of Muslim peoples.

Lewis, Bernard. *The Emergence of Modern Turkey*. 2d ed. London and New York, 1968. Classic work on modern Turkish history.

Lewis, Bernard. *The Arabs in History*. New ed. Oxford and New York, 1993. Excellent work covering Islamic history and civilization from the days of Muḥammad to modern times.

Mardin, Şerif. *The Genesis of Young Ottoman Thought: A Study in the Modernization of Turkish Political Ideas*. Princeton, 1962. Stands alone, particularly in the discussion of the works of leading Young Ottomans (1856–1876).

Riesenberg, Peter. *Citizenship in the Western Tradition*. Chapel Hill, N.C., and London, 1992. Important survey of Western concepts of citizenship, from Greek antiquity to the French Revolution.

Voll, John Obert. *Islam, Continuity, and Change in the Modern World*. 2d ed. Syracuse, N.Y., 1994. Important work on the influence of Islam in modernizing Muslim societies.

A. ÜNER TURGAY

CLASS. [*This entry comprises two articles. The first explores Islamic concepts of social class; the second considers the application of class analysis to the study of the political and economic structure of modern Islamic societies.*]

Concepts of Class

The notion of class in Islamic civilization differs from the notion of class in modern Western social science. Originally, the word was used to refer to a category of people. In classical Arabic it did not have the connotation of a special income group, and it was used to refer to any group of people with a variety of criteria in mind. The word for social work, *(darajah) ṭabaqah,* appeared in the Qur'ān: "And we have created you into several ranks over other ranks" (6.165). The idea of social inequality and stratification was rationalized in the Qur'ān (43.32): "We have divided among them their livelihood in this world, and raised some in rank over others, so that the one may take the other into his service." It is also said in the Qur'ān (16.71): "God has given preference to some of you over others in regard to livelihood." The Qur'ān accepts the multiplicity of social groups in society, and charity (almsgiving) constitutes one of the five pillars of Islam. Islam rejects neglect of the poor and the orphans, and the *ummah* (Islamic community) as a whole is considered responsible for the improvement of their lot.

Classes existed in Arabia long before the rise of Islam. The tribal aristocracy of Arabia which often coincided with the merchant class enjoyed much of the wealth of society, while the very poor and slaves were located at the bottom of the social hierarchy. The notion of tribal aristocracy was not rejected by Islam, although Muḥammad preached a message reflecting a less-stark social stratification. This explains the humble origins of his early followers who sought equality with the elite of the Quraysh, the tribe of the Prophet. Moreover, the nomadic class was always separate from the rest of the community, although Islam brought a citied life to many of the nomads of Arabia. [*See* Tribe.] Although Islam accepts the principle of inheritance (albeit on the basis of gender inequality, with the woman inheriting half the share of the man), the Qur'ān considers religious devoutness and piety—and not birth within an aristocratic elite—as the only criterion for prestige and honor.

Class conflict is to be avoided from the standpoint of Islam, and the rich are strongly urged to share some of their wealth with the poor. Classlessness in society is incompatible with the provisions of the Qur'ān, and the very notion of the *ummah* implies the unity of all Muslims—regardless of class and ethnic background—under the banner of Islamic solidarity. Some *ḥadīth*s reject pride in one's ancestry, although Muslims continued to place a social emphasis on tribal genealogies. The glorification of Muḥammad's own tribe in Islamic theology and jurisprudence attests to the power of pre-Islamic tribal traditions of prestigious birth. Moreover, Islam did not abolish the institution of slavery; it merely regulated its practice: it was banned in peacetime and legalized in wartime, although Islam encourages the emancipation of slaves.

In practice, the early Islamic rulers, like the rightly guided caliphs, did not try to abolish classes and inequality. Although Muslims sometimes take pride in the egalitarian distribution of spoils by the first rightly guided caliph, Abū Bakr al-Ṣiddīq (r. 632–634), the second rightly guided caliph, ʿUmar ibn al-Khaṭṭāb (r. 634–644), clearly favored the *anṣār* (companions) and the *muhājirūn* (emigrants) in the distribution of spoils (giving each member of the two groups 5,000 dirhams). This practice allowed for the emergence of a privileged class from among the Muslims. The favoritism toward descendants from traditional Arab tribes led to the emergence of a new social group called the *mawālī*, or clients, who attached themselves to established Arab tribes to receive prestige and benefits or to achieve emancipation if they happened to be slaves. Nevertheless, under post-ʿUmar governments the *mawālī* were treated unequally and were subject to the *kharāj* (land tax), from which the Arabs were exempted. [*See* Kharāj.] Furthermore, many Arabs were uncomfortable with the Qur'ānic principle of the equality of all believers regardless of racial or ethnic background and continued to regard African slaves as inferior.

Jews, Christians, and Zoroastrians were tolerated under Islamic rule but only as inferior groups subject to special laws and regulations. A special poll tax was required from them in return for the right to security by the state. [*See* Dhimmī; Jizyah.] Islam—the practice and not the Qur'ān itself—also contributed to the rise of new social groups in society, the most important of which were the *sharīf*s or sayyids who, on claiming (with varying degrees of credibility) descent from the Prophet's family, became entitled to special rights and privileges. [*See* Sharīf; Sayyid.] The status of *ʿulama'* (religions scholars) was so elevated that they emerged as a separate class under the ʿAbbāsid Empire (749–1258) and were often related through intermarriage to the landed and merchant class.

The evolution of classes in Islamic history was not impeded by Islam, because, like Christianity and Judaism, it did not reject on principle the institution of private property. There are some contemporary Muslims, particularly under Gamal Abdel Nasser in Egypt, who tried over the years to argue for the compatibility of Islam and socialism, although the incompatibility of the classless society with Islam can be supported by Qur'ānic citations.

BIBLIOGRAPHY

Batatu, Hanna. *The Old Social Classes and the Revolutionary Movements of Iraq*. Princeton, 1978. Important book on Iraqi social classes, with a brief discussion of the concept of class (pp. 10–11).

Lapidus, Ira. *A History of Islamic Societies*. Cambridge, 1988. General and highly useful history of Islamic societies in and outside of the Middle East, with coverage of the formation of classes in various historical periods.

Levy, Reuben. *The Social Structure of Islam*. 2d ed. Cambridge, 1962. Classic work, and still a valuable source on the social structure of Islamic societies. The first chapter covers "grades of society in Islam."

Sibāʿī, Muṣṭafā al-. *Ishtirākīyat al-Islām* (The Socialism of Islam). Damascus, 1960. Attempts to reconcile Islam with the popular ideas of Nasserist socialism of the 1960s; informative about Islamic socialist tendencies.

AsʿAD ABUKHALIL

Class Analysis

The application of class analysis to Islamic societies has been a subject of considerable controversy, both in academic discussion of the region and in political debates within the Muslim world. With the growing influence of Marxist and, more broadly, sociological thinking within the social sciences, a range of academic work pertinent to Islamic countries, past and present, has been produced. Beyond social science, interpretations derived from class analysis have been diffused throughout the political rhetoric of the region: this applies most especially to the concept of imperialism, seen as a necessary and exploitative emanation of Western society, and to the project, much followed from the 1950s until the late 1980s at least, of a noncapitalist or socialist path of economic and social development.

Class analysis is an approach to the study of society and politics that posits the salience of class in the formation of societies and states, and in the political process, both domestic and international. It is part of the broader approach of political sociology. Class analysis of a Marxist variety sees classes as defined in terms of their relation to production and the ownership of productive forces. It has also taken a Weberian form, with classes defined not only in terms of ownership, but also in terms of skills and education, and with stratification also affected by status, knowledge, and political function. In the class-analysis literature on Islamic societies, it has been the Marxist strand that has predominated. Interpreted in a dogmatic form, by orthodox Marxists as well as by critics, to mean that class and class alone determines the political process, it is not an adequate mechanism for interpreting any society, developed or underdeveloped, Islamic or other: there is no society in which a pure class politics operates, except in brief periods. However, seen as a broad heuristic approach, one that investigates the role of class in social and political change, but seeks to relate it to other forces, including those of ideology, religion, tribe, and community, it has considerable analytic relevance to modern Islamic societies, as to others.

Several major themes can be identified as running through the literature based on class analysis. First, there is an emphasis on the role of class in social and political life and in the explanation of historical change. This has taken as its starting point the pertinence of concepts of class struggle, class formation, and the class character of the state, but has also applied this to broader features of Islamic societies, notably the role of religion: such applications range from the first involvement of urban mercantile and tribal forces in the seventh century to the varied range of contemporary Islamic societies and Islamist movements. Class analysis has also placed particular emphasis on conflicts arising from social considerations, be these urban conflicts, involving workers and trades unions, or rural ones, involving the peasantry. Work produced in this field has, equally, seen anticolonial and other nationalist movements as having a class character. Second, class analysis stresses the formative role in Islamic societies of international economic factors generated by capitalism, particularly those associated with Western economic penetration from the sixteenth century onward—first the incorporation of these societies into a world market, and then colonialism, and subsequent, postcolonial forms of domination. Working in the field of economic history, but more within a framework that locates the modern history of all countries within the expansion of Western industrial society, class analysis seeks to identify the ways in which this external, class-generated penetration of Islamic societies has intersected with local social and ideological systems and transformed their economies.

In addition, however, a class analysis approach would reject as a starting point the very concept of Islamic society or indeed of an Islamic world. In contradistinction to both conventional "Orientalist" approaches, which explain much social and political behavior in terms of Islam, and to Weberian analyses which seek to explain the distinctive path of Middle Eastern history in terms of the tenets of Islam, there is in class analysis a rejection of any necessary connection between religion, in this case, Islam, conceived as a determinant set of values, and social and political practice: although the salience of religious belief and institutions, as molded and interpreted by social forces in any particular situation, is recognized, the terms "Muslim society," "Muslim politics," and analogous formulations are rejected. What this therefore entails, in the denial of any shared Islamic specificity, is a methodological and theoretical universalism: this is not to say that Islamic beliefs are irrelevant to the study of these societies, but only that these beliefs have to be studied in conjunction with other factors, and that these factors can be found in a range of countries across the developing world (see, for example, the work of Rodinson, 1974 and 1979, and Zubaida, 1989). This may be more evident if generalization about what is essentially Muslim is based not just on a narrow range of Middle Eastern societies, but also includes the more populous Islamic countries of Asia, including Indonesia (Taylor and Turton, eds., 1988).

Just as there is nothing that necessarily unites different countries where Islam is the sole or main religion, so there is nothing that necessarily separates them from other societies in comparable social, economic, and political conditions. Issues as diverse as forms of state power and mechanisms of ideological control, democratization and military rule, urbanization and employment, populist movements and peasant resistance, the position of women and the role of law, can all be studied comparatively, as between Islamic and other societies. The question of whether these Islamic societies have anything in common, across time and space, or are in significant respects different from others, is contingent. All societies, irrespective of religion, are part of the overall process of capitalist transformation, state formation, and social change, and the role of religious belief and institutions within this process has to be specified in each case.

Class analysis has therefore sought to provide alternative, materialist accounts of histories conventionally presented in terms of the spread of Islam and of Islamic society. If a considerable body of work has been produced that applies concepts of class to premodern Islamic societies, class analysis has informed the study of the formation of contemporary Islamic societies. Maxime Rodinson in his *Islam and Capitalism* (1974) sought to disentangle the complex questions surrounding the failure of Islamic societies to produce an indigenous capitalist dynamic and to show how the Islamic religion itself, in the sense of the texts and traditions, was a contingent factor in this outcome. Simon Bromley, in his overview of the development of states in the Middle East, distinguishes between the injunctions and influences of religion and the specific forms of state created by tribal and military conquest and, later, by interaction with and subjugation by the West. Roger Owen's analysis of the Ottoman Empire's economy in the nineteenth century placed class relations, and imperialism, at the center of the explanation.

Class analysis of the modern period has, equally, provided explanations of contemporary societies and events. One general set of arguments was advanced by Maxime Rodinson in his *Marxism and the Muslim World* (1979). Here he argued that Marxism could provide an analysis not only of the politics of the Arab states but also of the Islamic religion itself: he stressed the "sociological weighting" that affected the role and shape of all ideologies, including in this weighting the conflict between different social groups for resources and power. This approach is evident in a number of more specific studies of features of modern Islamic society. Beinin and Lockman (1987) have described the central importance of class conflict, including working-class struggle, in the modern history of Egypt, prior to and subsequent to the 1952 revolution. Abrahamian, in his work on Iran between 1941 to 1953 (1982), has equally identified major contributions of the working class movement and more generally of the conflicting classes, interacting with external forces, to the outcome. Outside the Middle East, Lubeck's work on northern Nigeria (1986) charts the intersection of class and religion in a different, Islamic context.

One of the most developed areas of Marxist analysis of Islamic societies has been in regard to the postindependence state and more particularly to the formation of new classes within the parameters of such states. A pioneering work, developed originally with regard to Pakistan, is that of Hamza Alavi (1972), whose theory of the triple alliance underlying the postcolonial state—landowners, military, and bureaucrats—was generalized to other Third World societies, Islamic and non-Islamic. In the Middle East, the consolidation of nationalist military regimes provided the occasion for a large body of work based on class analysis. In regard to Egypt there developed the concept of *al-ṭabaqah al-jadīdah* (the "new class"), whose interests were established by the land redistribution and nationalization of industry under the Nasserite regime: critiques of this were produced by a number of writers, including Anouar Abdel-Malek (1968), Samir Amin (1978), and Mahmoud Hussein (1968). A similar analysis was produced in regard to the regime in Algeria, by Karen Pfeifer (1985). Within the Arab left, the concept of the petty bourgeois regime gained wide currency during the middle 1960s: the defeat by Israel in 1967 was associated with the crisis of such regimes, and the appeal for a politics based not on the Arab states but on mass activity and popular resistance.

Probably the most ambitious attempt to produce a study of a Middle Eastern society using the concept of class, in conjunction with other categories, is that of Hanna Batatu, *The Old Social Classes and the Revolutionary Movement of Iraq* (1978). Batatu took as his starting point the Marxist concept of revolution, as a major social and political upheaval involving classes, and examined the role of different classes—the middle class, with its various subdivisions, the working class, the peasantry—in the overthrow of the monarchy and the creation of a new regime. Batatu examined how these intersected with other loyalties—of family, clan, religion—in contemporary Iraq. As Zubaida (1989) has noted, many of the more creative applications of class to Middle Eastern society have been of a less-rigorous, or orthodox, kind and inclined to use class as one among several variables in political sociology.

As in work produced on other societies, this approach has been as much the context for controversies *within* its overall framework as the provider of a unified analysis. Variations of class analysis have been developed by writers who identify class as an important factor, but see it not as a given but as itself shaped by other political forces, be these the state (Richards and Waterbury, 1990) or ethnic and communal factors (Zubaida). Within the class-analysis approach opinion varied greatly on the character of the nationalist regimes of the 1950s and 1960s, some seeing them as embodying a progressive national bourgeoisie capable of resisting Western domination and introducing some internal change, while others saw them as necessarily limited by their class character and bound, in the end, to capitulate to the West. The issue of imperialism's impact has varied as between those who stress its unequivocally destructive impact, to others which stress the contradictory, destructive and modernizing, impact of Western domination. The literature on Israel and the Palestinians has occasioned extremely wide uses of class analysis: in the period after World War II, Marxists sympathetic to Israel stressed the socialist character of Zionism, in contrast to the more feudal and backward character of the surrounding Arab society; others produced analyses of the Palestinian relation to Israeli society stressing its exploited, class, character. Much Arab nationalist analysis has seen Israel in class terms as the illegitimate product of settler colonialism and of Western imperialism.

Opposition to class analysis has come from a number of sources, academic and political. Within much Western writing on the Middle East, for example, it has been argued that Marxist concepts of class and those derived from it are irrelevant to Islamic societies, in that stratification is based on other considerations of a kind more susceptible to analysis in Weberian terms (descent from the Prophet, possession of knowledge, judicial function, etc.). Equally, it is argued, individuals identify themselves not in relation to a social or economic group but as members of a religious community and, beyond that, by reference to tribe, clan, or region. It has also been argued that the concept of imperialism is without great explanatory force for these countries, since the main axis of their interaction with the outside world has been cultural and religious, and that any project of social or political activity based on historical materialism is irrelevant to the Islamic world. Within Islamic thinking, there has been significant but selective borrowing from Marxism, as in ideas of imperialism or revolution, but many Islamic writers have argued that Marxism, with its atheistic approach, its emphasis on material determination and class conflict, is incompatible with Islam. Islamist movements, although sharing a hostility to Western imperialism and often verbally opposed to what they term capitalism, are equally hostile to Marxism and proffer an economic model that appears to be a variant of capitalism, tempered by religiously-sanctioned redistribution.

[*See also* Communism and Islam; Socialism and Islam.]

BIBLIOGRAPHY

Abdel-Malek, Anouar. *Egypt: Military Society*. New York, 1968. Influential study of the Nasserite regime, based on the concept of the "new class."

Abrahamian, Ervand. *Iran between Two Revolutions*. Princeton, 1982. Comprehensive overview of modern Iranian history, bringing out the role of class factors in the Constitutional and Islamic revolutions.

Alavi, Hamza. "The State in Post-Colonial Societies." *New Left Review* 74 (July–August 1972). Reprinted in *Imperialism and Revolu-*

tion in South Asia, edited by E. Kathleen Gough and Hari P. Sharma, pp. 145–173. New York, 1973. Pioneering work on the postcolonial state, based on the Pakistani case, but of relevance to Islamic and non-Islamic societies alike.

Amin, Samir. *The Arab Nation.* London, 1978. Overview by perhaps the most influential of all Arab Marxists.

Batatu, Hanna. *The Old Social Classes and the Revolutionary Movements of Iraq.* Princeton, 1978. The most ambitious attempt to use the concept of class in relation to a Middle Eastern society, within a broader focus on social revolution and the intersection of class with religious and clan loyalties.

Bayat, Assef. *Workers and Revolution in Iran: A Third World Experience of Workers' Control.* London, 1987. Detailed study of the role of the industrial working class in the Iranian revolution.

Beinin, Joel, and Zachary Lockman. *Workers on the Nile: Nationalism, Communism, Islam, and the Egyptian Working Class, 1882–1954.* Princeton, 1987. Commanding overview of modern Egyptian history, locating it within the context of capitalism and the development of the working and other classes.

Bromley, Simon. *Rethinking Middle East Politics: State, Formation, and Development.* Cambridge, 1994. Survey of the modern Middle East, from a Marxist perspective on state and class formation.

Halliday, Fred. *Arabia without Sultans.* New York, 1975. Overview of social and political upheaval in the Arabian Peninsula and Iran from the end of World War II.

Halliday, Fred, and Hamza, Alavi, eds. *State and Ideology in the Middle East and Pakistan.* London, 1988. Application of class analysis to the Arab world, Turkey, Israel, Iran, and Pakistan.

Hussein, Mahmoud. *Class Struggles in Egypt.* New York, 1968. Forceful critique of the Nasserite regime, from a Marxist perspective.

Keyder, Çağlar. *State and Class in Turkey.* London, 1987. Overview, framed in terms of the process of class formation in modern Turkey, from the Ottoman to the contemporary period.

Lubeck, Paul. *Islam and Urban Labour in Northern Nigeria: The Making of a Muslim Working Class.* Cambridge, 1986.

Owen, Roger. *The Middle East in the World Economy, 1800–1914.* London, 1981.

Pfeifer, Karen. *Agrarian Reform under State Capitalism in Algeria.* Boulder, 1985.

Richards, Alan, and John Waterbury. *A Political Economy of the Middle East: State, Class, and Economic Development.* Boulder, 1990.

Rodinson, Maxime. *Islam and Capitalism.* New York, 1974. Study of the apparent failure of medieval Islamic society to produce a capitalist transformation, arguing against Islamic belief as an explanatory factor.

Rodinson, Maxime. *Marxism and the Muslim World.* London, 1979. Argues for the application of Marxist categories to the histories of Islam and Arab nationalism.

Turner, Bryan S. *Marx and the End of Orientalism.* London, 1978. Critical examination of the works of Marx and Weber as applied to the Middle East, as of their "orientalist" critics.

Taylor, John G., and Andrew Turton, eds. *Southeast Asia.* New York, 1988. Class analyses of Indonesia and Malaysia, often ignored in discussions of the political sociology of Islamic society.

Zubaida, Sami. *Islam, the People, and the State.* London, 1989. Astute sociological study critical of orthodox forms of class analysis, focusing on the Iranian revolution and on the role of classes in the contemporary Middle East. Argues for the role of political forces in shaping classes, and their effectivity.

FRED HALLIDAY

CLITORIDECTOMY, commonly known as female circumcision, has historically been practiced in some areas of the Islamic world. The practice is pre-Islamic in origin and its distribution should be attributed to indigenous cultural norms rather than specifically religious requirements. It is known primarily in a number of African societies, Islamic and non-Islamic, in the area extending eastward from Senegal to the Horn of Africa. The operations referred to collectively as clitoridectomy range from excising only the tip of the clitoris to total excision of the clitoris and labia, and total excision with infibulation. This most severe form of the practice, total excision with infibulation, is referred to commonly as either "pharaonic" or "Sudanese" circumcision and is attested primarily in Sudan, Somalia, Djibouti, and parts of Ethiopia. In those areas where it is practiced, clitoridectomy is not limited to the Muslims. In Egypt, for example, clitoridectomy has a long history among the Coptic population. On the other hand, it is relatively unknown among non-Muslims in Sudan. It is not practiced in Saudi Arabia, Tunisia, Iran, and Turkey, and is practiced unevenly in Java.

The Arabic terminology used to refer to the practice is *khafḍ* or *khitān,* the latter term being used also to refer to male circumcision. There is no mention of it in the Qur'ān, although there is evidence of its existence in the traditions of the Prophet, who condemned the severe forms of the operation as being harmful to women's sexual health and recommended the minor form of the operation (excising only the tip of the clitoris) if it was to be performed. Generally, the schools of Islamic law regard it as a recommended, but not obligatory, practice. Although explicitly religious justifications may be invoked, the rationales given for continuing the practice are generally not expressed in religious terms. The most common justification given is that it is "the custom"; however, numerous other reasons are also given, for example, the control of female sexuality and the preservation of virginity. Failure to perform clitoridectomy is believed by some cultures to result not only in promiscuity and adultery, but also in infant mortality, infertility, and poor general health. In addition, in the cultures where it is practiced, uncircumcised female genitalia are considered to be ugly, and uncircumcised women are considered, for diverse reasons, to be unmarriageable. The practitioners of clitoridectomy are ordinarily women, many of whom are also midwives. Because clitoridectomy is often performed under septic conditions and is associated with a variety of medical complications, better educated parents, especially in urban areas, may seek medical professionals to perform the operation on their daughters under sterile conditions. In some countries where clitoridectomy is widespread, it has been prohibited by law for a number of years (e.g., Egypt and Sudan). In recent decades, clitoridectomy has become a highly politicized issue in the context of human rights and women's rights campaigns to eradicate genital mutilation.

[*See also* Circumcision; Puberty Rites; Rites of Passage.]

BIBLIOGRAPHY

Donzel, E. J. van. "Khafḍ." In *Encyclopaedia of Islam*, new ed., vol. 4, pp. 913–914. Leiden, 1960–.

Giorgis, Belkis Wolde. *Female Circumcision in Africa*. Addis Ababa, 1981. U.N. publication with an extensive annotated bibliography.

Hosken, Fran P. "Female Genital Mutilation and Human Rights." *Feminist Issues* 1 (Summer 1981): 3–23. Outlines human rights arguments.

Saʿdāwī, Nawāl al-. *The Hidden Face of Eve*. Translated by Sherif Hetata. London, 1980. Considered a classic statement on clitoridectomy by an Arab feminist.

Wensinck, A. J. van. "Khitān." In *Encyclopaedia of Islam*, new ed., vol. 5, pp. 20–22. Leiden, 1960–.

PAULA SANDERS

CLOTHING. *See* Dress.

COMMERCIAL LAW. Traditionally the Islamic legal system did not recognize commercial law as a separate body of rules regulating trading activities in a manner distinct from civil law, which governs all other private law relationships. In this regard Islamic law differs from most of the legal systems belonging to the Romano-Germanic family, which recognize commercial law as an autonomous branch of private law. English common law later took the same position as Islamic law in denying the duality of commercial and civil law.

The applicability of *sharīʿah* (Islamic law) to traders and nontraders alike does not mean that it ignored the special needs of commerce or failed to respond positively to situations peculiar to domestic and transnational trade. As the law of a trading nation, *sharīʿah* devised such institutions as the transfer of debt and the concluding of a contract on behalf of an undisclosed principal. These novel institutions were later introduced into other legal systems, probably in response to the same needs of transnational commerce which had given birth to them earlier in Islamic law.

Until the second half of the nineteenth century, the rules of Islamic law were derived directly from the original sources. The rules thus deduced were set forth in the writings of the jurists of the various schools of Islamic law. The judge had to refer to their treatises in order to locate the legal solution to any given case. During the period from 1870 to 1877 the Ottoman Empire, then the major Muslim power, enacted the various chapters of a codification known as the Mecelle (Ar., Majallah). This code, containing systematized sections and articles, improved on the disorderly state of the rules of law in the writings of early jurists—up to that time the only available source of those rules. The Mecelle adhered to the traditional position of Islamic law in rejecting the civil law/commercial law dichotomy.

Previously, in 1850, under the pressure of the need for an expanding trade with the West and in compliance with the wishes of more powerful European nations, the Ottoman Empire had promulgated a Code of Commerce applicable to disputes involving foreign parties. In 1863 a similar Code of Maritime Commerce was enacted. Thus was the autonomy of commercial law introduced into the Islamic legal system. This trend was reinforced when Egypt promulgated a Commercial Code in 1875 to apply to transactions involving foreign parties and another code of general application in 1883. French models were the main source of these Ottoman and Egyptian codes.

In their broad outline, the fundamental principles of *sharīʿah* in the area of contract and business law do not differ much from their counterparts in Western legal systems. The influence of Western systems, particularly the French, which acted on Islamic law since the second half of the nineteenth century, manifested itself more in the process of codification, intended to express legal norms in a clearly written and readily accessible form, than in the substantive content of those norms. Even sections of European codes that were adopted verbatim were not, by and large, different in content from the corresponding rules in Islamic law. Adopting European codes as models was a less-arduous and less time-consuming task than undertaking an original codification of

Islamic law based on the voluminous legal literature and involving updating in some cases to meet the changing needs of the times. Moreover, such a course of action was more likely to meet with the approval of Western powers. The influence of Western-type codification on Islamic law in the nineteenth century, however, was not an abandonment of substantive Islamic law in favor of a different (Western) legal system.

Commercial codes, where they exist, regulate those matters that are peculiar to trading and manufacturing activities. Beyond that specific area, there is a large area of general applicability of which the regulation is left to the civil code, such as contract law and personal and real property law. This explains the importance of the Egyptian Civil Code of 1948 and its influence in surrounding countries.

In the 1930s the need for a revision of the Egyptian Civil Code of 1883, based on the French model, was strongly felt. It was suggested that in reforming the code three sources should be considered: Islamic law, the decisions of Egyptian courts since the promulgation of the old Civil Code, and the various modern Western codes.

The reform entailed years of hard work, to which the contribution of the most prominent twentieth-century Egyptian jurist, the late ʿAbd al-Razzāq al-Sanhūrī (1895–1971), was crucial. The new Civil Code was promulgated in 1948, to go into effect on 15 October 1949, and was heralded as the harbinger of a uniform Arab civil code. The high quality of the new code was readily recognized in other Arab countries. It served as a model for the new civil codes of Syria (1949), Iraq (1951), Libya (1953), Sudan (1971; repealed in 1974), Algeria (1975), Yemen (1979), and Kuwait (1980). The legislative output in all the Gulf States since their accession to independence has been greatly influenced by Egyptian models in all areas, including commercial law. [*See the biography of ʿAbd al-Razzāq al-Sanhūrī.*]

Two institutions crucial to the economic development and growth of Muslim societies in today's global economy are: interest on capital, which is the foundation of the banking sector, and insurance. The status in Islamic law of these two institutions has been clouded by misinformed opinions ventured by some contemporary Muslim jurists. The misguided view that Islamic law prohibits, as *ribā* (lit., "increase"), interest on paper money and that it does not recognize the validity of contracts of insurance has been convincingly refuted to the satisfaction of many, if not most, of the qualified Muslim jurists of our times.

One manifestation of the Muslim countries' concern for promoting their trade relations with the rest of the world is their encouragement of transnational commercial arbitration and conciliation for the resolution of disputes without recourse to the cumbersome and time-consuming judicial process. Many Muslim countries have enacted legislation on the subject and have set up permanent arbitration and conciliation bodies. One example is provided by the Conciliation and Arbitration By-Laws of the French-Arab Chamber of Commerce in Paris. Several Muslim countries are parties to multilateral conventions on commercial arbitration and on the recognition and enforcement of foreign arbitral awards.

[*See also* Capitalism and Islam; Contract Law; Economics, *article on* Economic Theory; Law, *article on* Legal Thought and Jurisprudence.]

BIBLIOGRAPHY

Badr, Gamal M. "The New Egyptian Civil Code and the Unification of the Laws of Arab Countries." *Tulane Law Review* 30 (1955–1956): 299–304. Provides historical background and describes the beginnings of the adoption of the Civil Code of 1948 by other countries.

Badr, Gamal M. "Islamic Law: Its Relations to Other Legal Systems." *American Journal of Comparative Law* 26 (1978): 187–198. Discusses the alleged borrowings by and from Islamic law.

Badr, Gamal M. "Islamic Law and the Challenge of Modern Times." In *Law, Politics, and Personalities in the Middle East: Essays in Honor of Majid Khadduri*, edited by J. P. Piscatori and George Harris, pp. 27–44. Boulder and Washington, D.C., 1987. Provides, *inter alia*, a refutation of the alleged prohibition of interest and nullity of insurance contracts.

Badr, Gamal M. "Interest on Capital in Islamic Law." *American-Arab Affairs* 29 (1989): 86–95. Updates and elaborates on the refutation of the alleged prohibition of interest.

Coulson, Noel J. *Commercial Law in the Gulf States: The Islamic Legal Tradition*. London, 1984. Provides a historical overview and expounds the principles of Islamic law applicable to commercial transactions.

The Laws of Saudi Arabia, the U.A.E., Egypt, and Jordan: A Legal and Investment Guide for American Business. Washington, D.C., n.d.

GAMAL M. BADR

COMMUNICATIONS MEDIA. Communication has been an instrumental and integral part of Islam since its inception as a religio-political movement. Over the centuries Islamic culture and civilization have been influential in the development of three major pillars of human communication: first, a high level of oral communication and culture in which information was produced and transmitted from person to person; second, an unprecedented degree of reproduced books and manuscripts marking an intellectual era of rich scientific, literary, artistic, and linguistic interaction in all branches of knowledge; and third, the first attempt in history to bring oral and written cultures into a unified framework, laying the ground for the scientific revolution that followed in Europe.

The art of oral culture and communication in Islamic societies found its best expression in the Qur'ān (the holy book), the *sunnah* (tradition), and the *ḥadīth* (a record of the acts and sayings of the Prophet and his companions, the *ahl al-bayt*). The Qur'ān is the main source from which Islamic communication practices and precepts are drawn and explained. The *sunnah* of the Prophet, taken from his deeds and judgments and written down, is the standard of conduct alongside the Qur'ān; the *ḥadīths* are the authoritative record of the Prophet's sayings. A *ḥadīth* is credible only when its *isnād* or documentation offers an unbroken series of reliable authorities in oral and written communication. The *ḥadīth* became fundamental to the organization of information and intellectual discourse in Islamic society. Investigation and study of this whole body of communication is called *ʿilm al-ḥadīth.*

Inherent in the Islamic teachings are basic rights of communication, including the rights to know, to read, to write, and to speak. The notion of *ʿilm,* or knowledge, prevails throughout the Qur'ān as the basic tenet of all communication in Islam; an awareness of the concept of *ʿilm* in Islamic society is necessary for understanding the history of communication in Islam. The word *iqra'* (reading) is also important in the Qur'ān. *Iqra'* implicitly conveys the idea of communicating consciously within the Muslim community. At the request of the Prophet, his companions wrote down the Qur'ān in various media of the time to ensure the longevity of its teachings.

The memorization of the Qur'ān is a common act of information and communication that has a long history in Islamic societies; it is still practiced widely in all Muslim countries, serving as an inextricable link between the oral and written modes. The fact that Arabic became the primary language of Islam aided the efficient transmission of ideas throughout the vast Islamic world. With a single religion and a single language, communication became an instrument for the integration of the larger Islamic community, the *ummah.*

Prior to the modern era, the primary centers of communication in the Islamic world were the mosques, especially during the daily and Friday congregations, and the marketplaces and public squares, as well as the religious schools. The mosque served not only for daily prayers but also for spreading news and opinion and as a forum for political decision-making. This form of communication, called *khuṭbah,* was largely based on the Islamic tradition of combining political and religious discourse. For example, during Ramaḍān, theological students and members of the *ʿulamā'* customarily held meetings to present current topics and issues. [*See* Khuṭbah.]

Another important concept in the realm of Islamic communication is *tablīgh,* the notion of the propagation, dissemination, and diffusion of Islamic principles, beliefs, and practices. *Tablīgh,* rooted in the oral and social traditions of the greater Islamic community, established a framework of ethics related to communications and social interactions. [*See* Tablīgh.]

During the later centuries of Islamic history, when the arts of bookmaking and reproduction of manuscripts were widely developed, the oral mode did not lose its significance but remained an inseparable part of culture and communication. The expansion of Islamic states in Asia, Africa, and the Iberian Peninsula, coupled with the introduction of new means of communication, accelerated the process of scientific, commercial, and artistic communication.

Medieval Islamic culture with its scholarly interest in the entire universe provided an intellectual environment that advanced studies in such fields as astronomy, chemistry, geography, history, mathematics, medicine, and philosophy. These studies in turn stimulated a respect for information and knowledge that directed both the domestic and international relations of the Islamic community. Moreover, the unified Islamic civilization took advantage of its pivotal geopolitical position by developing navigation science and communication not only for commerce and trade but also for distributing scholarly and practical knowledge. Written manuscripts and books permeated Islamic society and inspired profound cultural developments.

A group of efficient and intellectual scribes, the *warrāqīn,* served the Islamic community by commenting on and copying manuscripts, often completing more than a hundred pages a day. Under the supervision of the *warrāqīn,* writers and their publishers established an effective system of cooperation within the publication industry. The high demand for books led to the building of numerous private and public libraries.

Between the thirteenth century and the modern era, however, the Islamic world fell short in adopting new communication technologies because of political, economic, and social factors both internal and external. The European invention of the printing press in the mid-fifteenth century heralded the birth of the print culture and a tremendous quantitative jump in the output of information. In the Islamic societies, however, one mode of communication did not supersede another; rather, oral and written communication both continued to develop and came to complement technological forms of communication in the modern era. Hence the growth of communication in the Islamic world was characterized by qualitative progress rather than quantitative jumps.

From the sixteenth to the early nineteenth century, when more or less formalized councils of ministers came into being in Islamic countries such as Iran and Turkey, the official government newswriter occupied an important place. Occasionally the government news—or *akhbār,* as it came to be called—was also read to the public from the stairs of mosques. The official governmental report functioned as a successful medium for disseminating news until the introduction of modern journalism.

Printing presses were introduced into Islamic countries such as Egypt, India, Iran, and Turkey as early as the seventeenth century. During the late eighteenth century and the first half of the nineteenth, the printing press facilitated the establishment of newspapers throughout the Islamic world. This early period of the press was responsible for the importation of modern nationalism and secularism from Europe; it also played an important role in the spread of the nineteenth-century Islamic reform movement as well as the campaign against European colonialism.

The early growth of the modern mass media in the Islamic world was associated first with state intervention in the production and distribution of the press, and second with the influence of both secular and religious leaders who sought to use the press for sociopolitical reforms. Thus, during the last two decades of the nineteenth century, two types of publications emerged in the Islamic world: one journalistic establishment led mainly by the western-trained and educated elites who were promoting European ideas of secularism, liberalism, and modern nationalism, and another pioneered by religious leaders and Islamic reformists such as Sayyid Jamāl al-Dīn al-Afghānī, who was campaigning for a unified Islamic community throughout the Middle East, Asia, and North Africa. Al-Afghānī's influence was strong in most Islamic countries, especially Iran and Egypt; he and his followers published a number of newspapers, including the famous *Al-ʿurwah al-wuthqā,* which was circulated in many countries. By the turn of the century, the new tool of journalism was in widespread use in the Islamic world from Indonesia to North Africa. [*See the biography of Afghānī.*]

The early years of the twentieth century witnessed the great struggle among nationalism, Islamic movements, and imperialism, which was reflected almost continuously in the Islamic media. The press in Egypt, Iran, and Lebanon achieved wide circulation. This was also the period when journalism and modern communications media began to develop and expand in Syria, Iraq, Palestine, Central Asia, and the Indian subcontinent.

With the revolt of the Young Turks against the sultan in 1908, there came a sudden upsurge in the number of newspapers being published in the Arabic-speaking provinces of the Ottoman Empire. Of the three great media of propaganda in the Iranian Constitutional Revolution of 1905–1906—the omnipresent political pamphlets, the secret and revolutionary societies, and the press—it was the last that made the greatest gains. Anticolonial movements and the struggle for independence in India, Indonesia, Morocco, and Algeria led to the growth of the press, political parties, and a number of ideological movements ranging from Islamic radicalism to communist socialism.

The twentieth century thus marked the rise of modern mass communication in the Islamic world. The process of decolonization in a number of Islamic countries in Asia and Africa, coupled with the delineation of economic classes and the recognition of the nation-state system, elevated the communications media to new prominence in which the state played a major role. In the Central Asian republics where Soviet models of media became dominant, Islamic institutions of communication such as mosques and *madrasahs* remained under the control and supervision of the state. In North and West Africa, the communications media of the newly established independent states were developed along the lines of French and English models.

A characteristic of the mass media in the contemporary Islamic world has been the multiplicity of press agencies as well as broadcasting, telecommunications, and cultural industries, which has largely reflected the diversity of ethnic, linguistic, and geographical groups. As a whole, the media in the Islamic world, particularly television, have been strongly influenced by their counterparts in the West. In contrast to the press, which has had a fairly independent, private status, radio and television typically have been operated by centralized, government-supervised institutions.

Among the mass communication media in the Islamic world, the film industry has had the shortest history. The limited development of film and cinema has both technical and cultural roots. In many Islamic societies, films in general and foreign films in particular have been opposed as corrupt and immoral because they promote alien values and their contents conflict with local cultural and religious norms. There is no objection in principle, however, to the technology of film and the legitimate use of it. The barriers have been broken down to a large extent as national and cultural policies have become more selective in the importation of foreign films and as local authorities have encouraged the production of historical, cultural, and educational films.

Because of the lack of production facilities in some Islamic countries and the generally low level of the economy, the media must import much of their equipment. At the same time, the lack of sufficient telecommunications and transportation infrastructure has made distribution both costly and haphazard. For these reasons the media have often relied heavily on outside sources for news and programming. Frequent charges that the media are influenced and even controlled by international agencies, postcolonial ties, and government organizations have stemmed largely from this imbalance in the financing of indigenous news agencies and newsgathering sources, as well as from a lack of comprehensive national communications policies.

The contemporary Islamic media contain ingredients endemic to their regional settings and characteristics that mark them as special products of their social milieu. Certain traits are peculiar to each Islamic region's social and psychological structure. The Middle East and South Asia have the most developed mass communication systems, while the regions of Africa and Central and East Asia require more investment in their systems. However, most Islamic countries fall short in the average number of modern media outlets when compared to the industrialized countries of Europe and North America.

Although population and literacy rates have been increasing in the Islamic world, a comparative study in a number of countries shows that readership numbers have not kept pace. The shortage of paper and machinery has been one reason, and internal political changes in a number of regions has been another. However, the growth of electronic media has been relatively dramatic owing to the spread of modern communication technologies and the use of communication satellites.

Print and electronic media in the Islamic world have helped to concentrate power in the hands of political and economic elites and have contributed to the centralization of modern state apparatus; by contrast, oral modes of communication have remained largely in the hands of traditional and religious groups that have often attempted to decentralize and diffuse the power of the state and establish a counterbalance to authority. Led by traditional authorities such as the *ʿulamāʾ*, the resurgence of Islam and revolutionary movements in the twentieth century points to the potential power of oral media such as the mosque.

One of the most interesting contemporary phenomena in the Islamic world has been the integration of modern communication technologies with the traditional media, a process that has contributed to the legitimation of the centers of power and the acceleration of political and social change. In the 1978–1979 Islamic Revolution in Iran, Ayatollah Ruhollah Khomeini and his followers used such modern means of communication as telephones and cassette tapes along with traditional channels to disseminate their messages throughout the country. In such countries as Indonesia, Malaysia, Pakistan, and Egypt, the use of personal computers and facsimile machines for the diffusion of Islamic ideas has become widespread. Information about Islam has become more accessible to the lay person through databases on the Qur'ān and *ḥadīth*.

In the closing decades of the twentieth century, three important developments have had the most profound impact on the nature and content of information in the Islamic world. The Islamic Revolution in Iran and subsequent political movements in other Islamic countries set the tone for the islamization of the media and created a new ecology of communication in a number of regions. The disintegration of the Soviet Union and the emergence of newly independent states in Islamic regions such as Central Asia contributed to the potential expansion of a greater Islamic communications network. Finally, the growth of national and international telecommunications through satellites has potential to affect the integration of the Islamic regions and political and economic development there. The Islamic world is developing its communications media with a new awareness of global change and, at the same time, a profound sense of history and Islamic identity.

[*See also* Book Publishing; Newspapers and Magazines; Pamphlets and Tracts; Radio and Television.]

BIBLIOGRAPHY

Abu Bakr, Yahya, et al. *Development of Communication in the Arab States: Needs and Priorities*. Paris, 1985.

Kamalipour, Yahya, and Hamid Mowlana, eds. *Mass Media in the Middle East: A Comprehensive Handbook*. Westport, Conn., 1994.

Mowlana, Hamid. "Technology versus Tradition: Communication in the Iranian Revolution." *Journal of Communication* 29 (1979): 107–112.

Mowlana, Hamid. "Mass Media Systems and Communication." In *The Middle East*, edited by Michael Adams, pp. 825–839. New York, 1988.

Mowlana, Hamid. "Communication, Ethics, and the Islamic Tradition." In *Communication Ethics and Global Change*, edited by Thomas W. Cooper et al., pp. 137–146. White Plains, N.Y., 1990.

Nasser, Munir K. *Press, Politics, and Power: Egypt's Heikal and Al-Ahram*. Ames, Iowa, 1979.

Rugh, William. *The Arab Press*. Syracuse, N.Y., 1979.

Sardar, Ziauddin. *Information and the Muslim World*. London, 1988.

Schlesinger, Philip, and Hamid Mowlana, eds. "Islam and Communication." Special issue of *Media, Culture, and Society* 15.1 (January 1993). Collection of essays covering the role of communication media in the Islamic world during classic and modern times.

HAMID MOWLANA

COMMUNISM AND ISLAM. Interaction between communism and Islam can be found in three areas: theories of human society, competing social structures, and political organizations, which claim the theories and structures as their operational goals. In addition to such immediate concerns, there is a more complex, historical narrative encompassing many institutions and social structures called communist or Muslim. In this article, I shall examine the above-mentioned terms and the historical narrative and follow with a review how non-Muslim and noncommunist observers have assessed the relationship between Islam and communism over the past fifty years.

Theories of Human Society. Neither communism nor Islam is only a theory of human society, but each has such a theory. Communist theory of human society began with the work of Karl Marx and was extended by Vladimir Lenin. Marxist-Leninist theory views human history as one of progressive change driven by the tension between the technical requirements of material production at any historical period and the property rights in which those techniques are embedded. Human society, in this theory, has moved from less-effective techniques and less-efficient property rights to greater effectiveness and greater efficiency. The learning curve for all human societies is the same, and the theory predicts a final stage of this process: mechanical mass production in which property rights are vested in society as a whole rather than in individuals. It is held to be legitimate and possibly necessary to effect this final transfer of property rights (from individuals to the society at large) by force; this is the dictatorship of the proletariat. This final stage would be known as communism, hence the name of the theoretical paradigm and also, after 1919, of the parties espousing it.

Islamic theories of human society have developed over a much longer period of time than communist theory and show significantly greater variety. Nevertheless, all Islamic theories are predicated on the belief that there is a constitutive law for human society manifested to human beings in the monotheist Holy Books (Torah, New Testament, and Qur'ān) but only fully known in the Qur'ān as revealed to Muḥammad. This law provides limiting conditions under which social transactions can occur; such transactions are deemed best when voluntary, and generally the limiting conditions are taken to include significant differences in access to wealth and power among human beings as well as rights to private property. Voluntary action by those with wealth and power to share their entitlements are desirable, although in certain cases (the good of the community in Sunnī Islam [*maṣlaḥah*] or the decision of the imam in Shīʿī Islam) authoritative actions to redistribute wealth are acceptable. No predictions exist for secular change in human society, although at some future time human society as presently constituted will end, and all human beings will be subject to divine judgment.

The most profound discontinuity between Marxism-Leninism and classical Islamic doctrine as theories of human society is over the nature of property rights, but significant differences also exist regarding the source of law, the role of law in society, and ultimate ends of society. Lenin's major extension of Marxism was the theory that colonialism formed an integral part of European capitalist development. This claim has been largely accepted by many non-Leninists, although some Islamic activists have argued that the roots of colonialism lie in the nature of European Christianity rather than European capitalism. From this viewpoint, Leninism itself represents an extension of European colonial power rather than a weapon against colonialism.

Islam and Communism as Competing Societies. The major confrontation between communist and Islamic social structures occurred in Central Asia. The independent Muscovite principality of the fifteenth century grew by military confrontation with its Tatar suzerains, and succeeding czarist Russian and Central Asian Islamic states had a long history of conflict. By World War I, the Russian Empire had gained political and military control of largely Muslim Central Asia, although it left the societies basically intact. There was political conflict within these societies (especially the khanates of Bukhara and Khiva) between the traditional religious and political leaders and younger so-called Jadīdī reformers. During the early period of the Soviet Union's history, Communist party leaders allied themselves with sections of the Jadīdī groups to integrate the Central Asians into the new state, the USSR, and defeat all challenges to their new political order. Revolutionary transformation in the 1920s entailed changing the status of women in order to break up patriarchal family structures, which were deemed potential sources of challenge to the new state, as well as investment in industry to create a proletarian work force and social ownership where none had previously existed. Traditional public institutions, such as *waqf* (endowments for the common good), were also seized by the state between 1924 and 1930.

Soviet authorities also set about to construct ethnic identities for the societies of Central Asia. In 1924 the republics of Uzbekistan and Turkmenistan were created. In 1929 Tajikistan became a Soviet republic, and in 1936 the republics of Kazakhstan, Kirghizia, and Azerbaijan entered the union. By 1936 well-defined territorial entities with differentiated standard languages written in Cyrillic (rather than Arabic or Latin) script were in place. The societies of Central Asia were thus detached from other Islamic societies, and until 1991 it was possible to view communism as the political system that had most successfully secularized and industrialized Islamic societies, although the policies of the central government began a process of Russification, which was intensified by the movement of European Soviet citizens into these regions during World War II. The antireligious policies of the Soviet state coupled with relative isolation from historic Islamic centers of learning drastically reduced the number of *ʿulamāʾ* (religious scholars) in Central Asia and tended to transform Islamic identification into a set of customary observances, such as avoidance of pork or alcohol and the practice of circumcision, coupled with ethnicity.

The political impact of the so-called noncapitalist road to socialism had affected various strands of Arab nationalism concerned with building powerful anticolonial movements and postcolonial states, especially the Baʿth party (formed in 1938) of Syria and Iraq, which had a leader who was formerly a member of the Communist party [*see* Baʿth Parties]. After World War II Muslim populations came under control of revolutionary Leninist regimes in China (1949), Yugoslavia (1945), and Albania (1946), and in each case the new governments attempted to redefine the Islamic identity as a form of ethnicity. In the Soviet Union and China, the subordination of the Muslim population to Leninist rule was a side effect of other political and social conflicts; in southeastern Europe it was a fortuitous result of the disposition of forces at the end of World War II. Islamic institutions in these regions were not themselves in competition with Marxist-Leninist parties and often survived in the interstices of society.

The emergence of a Leninist regime in Afghanistan in April 1978 when the People's Democratic Party of Afghanistan (PDPA) seized power appeared to be a reenactment of the drama of Soviet power in the north. The inability of the two factions of the PDPA (Khalq and Parcham) to cohere into a single organization, the small number of party members, and the existence of a society with access to arms and men independent of the state doomed the experiment despite the entry of Soviet armed forces, which began with 50,000 men in 1979 and increased to 120,000 by 1986. The Afghan War hastened the collapse of the Soviet Union in 1991 and has led to the reemergence of independent states with a renewed Muslim identity across Central Asia. [*See also* Afghanistan.]

Competition between Islamic and Communist Organizations. Competition between communist parties and various Islamic institutions and organizations occurred wherever Muslims experienced colonial rule and the social effects of investment (foreign or domestic) in large-scale industrial production. Between the Russian Revolution (1917) and the Seventh Comintern Congress (1935), communist parties generally defined themselves in opposition to established religious hierarchies and were often aggressively atheist. In North Africa, the Middle East, South Asia, and Southeast Asia, the major institutional representation of Islam was the *ʿulamāʾ*. Scholars of Islamic law tended to oppose nascent Leninist organizations on doctrinal grounds discussed above and often issued *fatwā*s (formal legal opinions) condemning communism for abolishing property rights or for atheism; entire collections of such *fatwā*s have been published (for example, ʿAbd al-Ḥalīm Maḥmūd, *Fatāwā ʿan al-shuyūʿīyah*, Cairo, 1976). One of the relatively few social groups over which these two political forces competed was located in the colonial enclave of the Suez Canal Zone, and it was there that Ḥasan al-Bannāʾ formed the Muslim Brotherhood in 1928. During the Great Depression and World War II, Leninist and Islamic organizations increasingly came into conflict in recruiting from the same social strata.

The development of the "united front" concept at the Seventh Comintern Congress coincided with the birth of Islamic parties or similar institutions not controlled by the *ʿulamāʾ*, such as the Muslim Brotherhood in Egypt [*see* Muslim Brotherhood, *article on* Muslim Brotherhood in Egypt]. For both communists and Islamic activists colonialism was the primary enemy, and creating an anticolonial unity was the major political task, setting the stage for real competition for the political audience. After World War II, communists could argue that the Soviet Union proved the success of their ideology, and in countries where communist parties were perceived to be active in the anticolonial movement, they rose to prominence. Soviet recognition of Israel in 1948 often hindered acceptance of the communists as truly nationalist in the Arab world, and in most Muslim communities the Leninist vocabulary regarding equality and social justice remained alien.

In North Africa the communist parties were compromised, probably fatally, to the degree that the French Communist party did not consistently and completely oppose the colonial regimes in Algeria and Tunisia. In March 1956 the French communists voted to support emergency powers for the Guy Mollet government to crush the Algerian revolt; from that point on, Leninism as a contending ideology in North Africa disappeared.

In Egypt small but active groups of Leninists in several different parties (with at most two or three thousand members) engaged in conflict with the much larger Muslim Brotherhood for popular support. Communist influence peaked between 1945 and 1952, and in 1957 the Communist party was dissolved. There were later attempts to reform the Communist party in Egypt that met with little success. The Muslim Brotherhood emerged as a leading contender for popular support in the Arab nationalist state formed after 1952 by the Free Officers, and it provided a model for institutional innovation throughout the Arab Middle East.

Important communist parties existed in Sudan, Iraq, Syria, and Lebanon in the 1950s and 1960s; most were effectively destroyed by repression on the part of Arab nationalist states rather than in competition with Islamic groups. In each country, however, Islamic organizations appear to have appealed successfully to elements of the constituency for radicalism previously associated with the Communist party (notably among the Shīʿīs in Iraq and Lebanon).

An important direct conflict between Leninist and Islamic associations occurred in Iran around the time of the 1979 revolution. Iran's Tudeh (Communist) party had a powerful constituency among oil workers; the religious hierarchy stood in opposition to the shah; and groups of young activists attempted to combine Marxist, Leninist, and Islamic ideas (Fidāʾīyān and Mujāhidīn). An extremely potent revolutionary alternative was created by the Ayatollah Ruhollah Khomeini, who organized the Shīʿī *ʿulamāʾ* against the shah's government and created an institutional and theoretical framework for the transfer of power to the *ʿulamāʾ*, conceptualized in the *wilāyat al-faqīh*. By 1984 the Islamic Republic of Iran was firmly established, and it had routed its internal opposition, including both Marxist and radical Islamic groups. [*See also* Iran; Wilāyat al-Faqīh.]

Direct conflict between Islamic and communist organizations also occurred in Indonesia. The Indonesian Communist party had allied itself with Sukarno during the independence struggle that culminated in 1945, as had several Muslim organizations, notably the Nahdatul Ulama and the Masjumi. By 1959 Sukarno had enhanced his own power by promulgating a national policy known as Nasakom, an acronym for the names of the three major strands of Indonesian politics: nationalist (*nasionalis*), religious (*agama*), and communist (*komunis*). Sukarno attempted to play these three forces against each other, and leaders in each attempted not to lose out to the other two. By 1964 the Indonesia Communist party (PKI) appeared to outsiders to be emerging as a dominant force, although its own leaders were acutely aware of its weakness. In the aftermath of a coup and countercoup on 30 September–1 October 1965, a half-million Indonesian communist militants, sympathizers, and innocent bystanders were massacred, and the most intense conflicts occurred in the highly islamized areas of Indonesia. [*See also* Indonesia; Masjumi; *and* Nahdatul Ulama.]

Islamic societies and even Islamic parties appear at the end of the twentieth century to have greater staying power and a far more promising future than do Marxist-Leninist ones.

Debate among Muslim and Western Intellectuals. The earliest Muslim intellectual to address seriously the issue of communism was a Tatar, Mir Said Sultan Galiev (b. 1880), who was a high-ranking member of the Soviet Communist party from 1920 until 1923 and a specialist on colonialism and nationalism. Sultan Galiev may have been the first to put forward the idea that national independence for colonial peoples had to precede the social revolution. By 1923 Sultan Galiev came to believe that the dictatorship of the proletariat would not change European domination and began to organize opposition to Soviet power, for which he was executed, probably in 1928.

A number of intellectuals in Muslim countries, notably literary figures, were members of communist parties in the 1940s and 1950s. Some, such as the Turkish poet Nâzım Hikmet (1902–1963), or the Egyptian literary critic Maḥmūd Amīn al-ʿĀlim, were lifelong communists. Others, such as the great Iraqi free-verse poet, Badr Shākir al-Sayyāb, quit in great anger. A number of prominent social scientists, of whom the best known is Anouar Abdel-Malek, the author of *Egypt: Military Society* (translated by Charles Lam Markmann, New York, 1968), also share a background of membership in Marxist-Leninist organizations. The relationship of national independence to class conflict figures prominently in the work of these intellectuals.

Communism as an ideological challenge also provoked reaction from a variety of Muslim intellectuals, although in general communism appears in the writing of such figures after the 1920s as simply another species of Western colonialism. In books such as *Social Justice in Islam* (1948; translated by John Hardie, Washington, D.C., 1953), by Sayyid Quṭb, the Egyptian Muslim intellectual who was executed in 1965, communism (like Western capitalism) is devoid of the social and religious content of Islam, but it does not appear as a particularly menacing threat. In addition to orthodox religious criticism of communism, there were also attempts to integrate aspects of Marxism with Islamic orientations. Such attempts were most notable in the activities of the Fidāʾīyān-i Khalq and the Mujāhidīn-i Khalq organizations in Iran prior to and just after the 1979 revolution and in the intellectual activity of ʿAlī Sharīʿatī (d. 1977). Sharīʿatī surpassed the ideas of Sultan Galiev by arguing that the victory against colonialism and an ultimate social revolution against injustice was impossible without a return to the religious roots of cultural identity.

During the cold war (approximately 1947 to 1991) one concern of policymakers in the United States and Europe was how Islamic doctrines and institutions might affect Muslim perceptions of the East-West confrontation. A scholarly literature grew up on Islam and communism. This literature often recapitulated themes about religion, ideology, and social structure already present in the work of Karl Marx, Max Weber, and Emile Durkheim, although it recognized the inherent difficulty of specifying mechanisms linking religion, culture, and social structure. An early contribution was Bernard Lewis's "Communism and Islam" (1954) in which, although doctrinal differences are noted, it is argued that both Islam and communist doctrine claim to derive policies from first principles for all social affairs and thus are properly speaking totalitarian. Other contributors to the debate on the relationship of communism to Islam included Maxime Rodinson ("Rapports entre Islam et Communisme," 1961), who argues in a vein somewhat parallel to Lewis. Leonard Binder argues against Lewis's view in *The Ideological Revolution in the Middle East* (New York, 1964), with a discussion of Islam, nationalism, and communism that is more purely descriptive and contingent. After the Iranian Revolution interest in this subject waned, and it no longer appears as an important controversy, although elements of the debate continue to color attitudes in Europe toward Islamist political movements in the Middle East, South Asia, and Southeast Asia. In arguments by Gilles Kepel, for example, such movements play the transitional role to modern liberalism formerly played by communist parties in western and central Europe (*Les banlieux de l'Islam*, Paris, 1987). With the collapse of both the Soviet Union and Leninism as a vital political movement, the relationship of Islam to communism has ceased to be of any but historical interest. Whether political activists striving to create Islamic states will, as Lewis's argument suggests, recapitulate any of the experiences of the centralized bureaucracies that governed in the name of socialism remains to be seen.

BIBLIOGRAPHY

Abrahamian, Ervand. *Iran Between Two Revolutions.* Princeton, 1982.

Allworth, Edward. *Central Asia: A Century of Russian Rule.* New York, 1967.

Binder, Leonard. *The Ideological Revolution in the Middle East.* New York, 1964.

Botman, Selma. *The Rise of Egyptian Communism, 1939–1970.* Syracuse, N.Y., 1988.

Coulson, Noel J. *A History of Islamic Law.* Edinburgh, 1964.

Gallisot, René. *Mouvement ouvrier: Communisme et nationalismes dans le monde Arabe.* Paris, 1978.

Kepel, Gilles. *Les banlieuex de l'Islam.* Paris, 1987.

Lapidus, Ira, and Edmund Burke, III, eds. *Islam, Politics, and Social Movements.* Berkeley, 1988.

Lewis, Bernard. "Communism and Islam." *The Middle East in Transition,* edited by Walter Laqueur. New York, 1958.

Nove, Alec, and J. A. Newth. *The Soviet Middle East.* London, 1968.

Rodinson, Maxime. *Marxisme et le monde musulman.* Paris, 1972.

ELLIS GOLDBERG

CONGRESSES. Although the sentiment of international Muslim solidarity is intrinsic to the faith of Islam, it took no organized form until modern times. In the course of the twentieth century, modernized communications made it possible to translate vague principles of solidarity into periodic congresses of Muslims from different lands. Some of these congresses have evolved into international Islamic organizations that promote political, economic, and cultural interaction among Muslim peoples and states.

First Initiatives. Muslim reformists were the first to suggest the holding of Islamic congresses, in writings dating from the late nineteenth century. These reformists sought a forum to promote and sanction the internal reform of Islam and also believed that an assembly of influential Muslims would strengthen Islam's ability to resist Western imperialism. The advent of easy and regular steamer transport made it possible to imagine regular gatherings of Muslim thinkers, activists, and notables. As a contemporary observer wrote in 1896, such a congress would "clear Islam of many unjust accusations, and establish its place in the concert of modern civilizations."

A number of émigré intellectuals in Cairo first popularized the idea in the Muslim world. In 1900 one of them, ʿAbd al-Raḥmān al-Kawākibī of Aleppo, published an influential tract entitled *Umm al-Qurā,* which purported to be the secret protocol of an Islamic congress convened in Mecca during the pilgrimage of 1899 (AH 1316). The imaginary congress culminated in a call for a restored Arab caliphate, an idea then in vogue in reformist circles. Support for such a congress also became a staple of the reformist journal *Al-manār* published in Cairo by Muḥammad Rashīd Riḍā of Syrian Tripoli. Kawākibī and Rashīd Riḍā both believed that Mecca during the pilgrimage offered the most appropriate stage for such a congress, but other reformists favored Istanbul or Cairo. The Crimean Tatar reformist Ismāʿīl Gasprali (Gasprinskii) launched the first concrete initiative in Cairo, where he unsuccessfully attempted to convene a "general" Islamic congress in 1907–1908.

Kawākibī's book, Rashīd Riḍā's appeals, and Gasprali's initiative all aroused the suspicion of Ottoman authorities, who believed that a well-attended Islamic congress would fatally undermine the religious authority claimed by the Ottoman sultan-caliph. They feared the possible transformation of any such congress into an electoral college for choosing an Arab caliph who would champion the separation of the Arabic-speaking provinces from the Ottoman Empire. Steadfast Ottoman opposition thwarted all the early initiatives of the reformists and associated the congress idea with political dissidence. In 1911 Rashīd Riḍā wrote that "the Muslims are not yet ready to convene a general Islamic congress for discussion of their interests and how to improve their lot. Intellectuals have repeatedly advocated this step, but no one heard them, noticed them, or showed them any sympathy." [*See the biographies of Kawākibī, Rashīd Riḍā, and Gasprinskii.*]

Early Congresses. The final dismemberment of the Ottoman Empire in World War I removed the Ottoman obstacle and created a void, which a number of Muslim leaders and activists rushed to fill by convening Islamic congresses. In each instance they sought to mark their causes or their ambitions with the stamp of Islamic consensus. Some conveners sought wider Muslim support against non-Muslim enemies; others coveted the title of caliph, which they hoped to secure through the acclaim of a Muslim assembly.

In 1919, Mustafa Kemal Atatürk convened an Islamic congress in Anatolia to mobilize foreign Muslim support for his military campaigns. After his victory, however, Kemal took no further initiatives, and he ultimately severed Turkey from wider Islam by abolishing the caliphate in 1924. During the pilgrimage season of 1924, King Ḥusayn ibn ʿAlī of the Hejaz (Ḥijāz) summoned a "pilgrimage congress" in Mecca to support his own short-lived claim to the caliphate, but he was driven into exile by ʿAbd al-ʿAzīz ibn Saʿūd, who occupied Mecca and convened his own "world" congress during the pilgrimage season of 1926. This congress, which ʿAbd al-ʿAzīz hoped would confer Islamic sanction on his administration of the holy cities, instead leveled many criticisms, and he did not reconvene it. [*See the biographies of Atatürk, Ḥusayn ibn ʿAlī, and Saʿūd (ʿAbd al-ʿAzīz).*]

Also in 1926, the leading clerics of al-Azhar in Cairo summoned a "caliphate congress" to consider the effects of the Turkish abolition of the caliphate. The congress enjoyed the support of Egypt's King Fu'ād, who reputedly coveted the title of caliph, but no decision issued from the gathering. In 1931, Amīn al-Ḥusaynī, *muftī* of Jerusalem, convened a "general" congress of Muslims in Jerusalem to secure foreign Muslim support for the Arab struggle against the British Mandate and Zionism. In 1935, Pan-Islamic activist Shakīb Arslān convened a congress of Europe's Muslims in Geneva to carry the protest against imperialism to the heart of Europe. And in 1938, Abdürräshid Ibragimov, the Volga Tatar Pan-Islamist, convened a "world" congress in Tokyo in a bid to link Japan and Islam in a common struggle against European imperialism.

Each of these early congresses resolved to create a permanent organization and convene additional congresses, but all such efforts were foiled by internal rivalries or by the intervention of the European powers. Each of the early congresses also revolved around political rather than doctrinal matters. Following this precedent, subsequent congresses remained far more concerned with the defense of Islam than with its reform.

The painful partitions of India and Palestine, as well as improvements in air travel, encouraged new initiatives in the 1940s and 1950s. In 1949 Pakistan sponsored the creation of the Karachi-based World Islamic Congress, presided over by the exiled Palestinian leader Amīn al-Ḥusaynī. The organization aimed to promote solidarity between Pakistani and Arab Muslims against India and Israel. Beginning in 1953, many of the leading figures in Islamic activism attended the meetings in Jerusalem of the General Islamic Conference for Jerusalem, which operated under the auspices of the Muslim Brotherhood. It served to organize international Islamic support against Israel and enjoyed the active support of Jordan. These congresses briefly succeeded in creating secretariats and even reconvened at wide intervals before they too became practically defunct. [*See the biography of Ḥusaynī.*]

Obstacle of Arabism. With the progress of decolonization, several Muslim leaders floated new plans for the creation of a permanent organization of independent Muslim states. Pakistan, anxious to secure wider Muslim support against India, took a number of initiatives, especially during a failed 1952 campaign for a conference of Muslim prime ministers. During the Meccan pilgrimage of 1954, an "Islamic congress" assembled the heads of state of Pakistan, Saudi Arabia, and Egypt in Mecca and created a standing organization headquartered in Cairo. The initiative for an organization of Muslims states ran aground, however, as Egypt moved increasingly toward a revolutionary Pan-Arabism under its leader Gamal Abdel Nasser (Jamāl ʿAbd al-Nāṣir). By the mid-1950s Egypt's secular Pan-Arabism had become the dominant ideology in the Arab world. In the name of this ideology Egypt suppressed the Muslim Brotherhood at home and launched a cold war against Saudi Arabia, culminating in Egyptian military intervention in Yemen. [*See* Nasserism *and the biography of Nasser.*]

Saudi Arabia, under siege by Pan-Arab Egypt, responded by developing a rival Pan-Islam around which it rallied other besieged regimes and the Muslim Brotherhood. For this purpose the Saudi government sponsored the establishment in 1962 of the Mecca-based Muslim World League, which built a worldwide network of Muslim clients. The league not only operated among pilgrims but also assembled many congresses of Muslim activists and *ʿulamāʾ* from abroad, especially from among the Muslim Brotherhood. Beginning in 1964, Egypt responded by organizing congresses of Egyptian and foreign *ʿulamāʾ* under the auspices of al-Azhar's Academy of Islamic Researches. These rival bodies then convened a succession of dueling congresses in Mecca and Cairo, each claiming the sole prerogative of defining Islam in such as way as to legitimate Saudi or Egyptian policy. In 1965–1966 Saudi Arabia's King Fayṣal launched a campaign for an Islamic summit conference that would have countered the Arab summits dominated by Egypt; however, Nasser had sufficient influence to thwart the initiative, which he denounced as a foreign-inspired "Islamic pact" designed to defend the interests of Western imperialism. [*See* Muslim World League; *for the biography of Fayṣal, see under Saʿūd.*]

Organization of the Islamic Conference. Israel's 1967 defeat of the combined Arab armies and annexation of East Jerusalem eroded faith in the brand of Pan-Arabism championed by Egypt. They damaged Nasser's standing and inspired a return to Islam, setting the scene for a renewed Saudi initiative. In September

1969, following an arsonist's attack against the al-Aqṣā mosque in Jerusalem, Muslim heads of state set aside their differences and met in Rabat in the first Islamic summit conference. King Fayṣal took this opportunity to press for the creation of a permanent organization of Muslim states. This time the effort succeeded, and in May 1971 the participating states established the Organization of the Islamic Conference (OIC). The new organization, headquartered in Jeddah (pending the restoration of Jerusalem to Islam), adopted its charter in March 1972.

The OIC eventually achieved minor prominence in regional diplomacy, principally through the organization of triennial Islamic summit conferences and annual conferences of the foreign ministers of member states. The OIC's activities fell into three broad categories. First, it extended moral support to Muslim states and movements engaged in conflicts with non-Muslims. Most of these efforts were devoted to the causes of Palestine and Jerusalem, although the OIC supported many other Muslim resistance movements from Afghanistan to the Philippines. Its conferences passed hundreds of resolutions on these issues, although its support for embattled Muslims remained strictly declaratory. Second, the organization offered mediation in disputes and wars between its own members. However, the deep divisions among member states limited the moral force of the OIC's calls for peace, and in any case it lacked armed force for truce supervision or peacekeeping. In practice, the United Nations played a far greater role than the OIC in mediating conflicts between Muslim states. Finally, the OIC sponsored an array of subsidiary and affiliated institutions to promote political, economic, and cultural cooperation among its members. The most influential of these institutions was the Islamic Development Bank, established in December 1973 and formally opened in October 1975. The bank, funded by the wealthier OIC states, financed development projects that promoted cooperation and trade among member states. Yet despite these economic efforts, the amount of trade among member states, as a percentage of their overall trade, continued to decline throughout the 1980s. [*See* Islamic Development Bank.]

The OIC represented the culmination of government efforts to organize Muslim states, but it remained a weak organization, supported largely by Saudi funds and biased in favor of Saudi policies. For this reason, the existence of the OIC did not prevent several of its members from independently organizing international Islamic congresses and organizations. They did so to garner Muslim support for their own policies, often in defiance of Saudi Arabia and the OIC [*See* Organization of the Islamic Conference.]

Impact of Libya and Iran. In September 1969, shortly before the first Islamic summit, Muʿammar al-Qadhdhāfī carried out a coup in Libya and instituted a revolutionary regime based upon his own interpretation of Islam. Qadhdhāfī made it clear that he intended to promote his own leadership of Islam, and the following year he convened a conference that laid the foundations of the Tripoli-based Islamic Call Society (later the World Islamic Call Society). This organization convened frequent conferences in later years and through its far-flung branches did much to disseminate Qadhdhāfī's eclectic vision of Islam beyond Libya's borders. [*See* Islamic Call Society *and the biography of Qadhdhāfī.*]

Iran played an even more important role in stimulating the rapid growth in the variety of Islamic conferences in the 1980s. After the revolution in 1979, and especially after the outbreak of war with Iraq in 1980, Iran conducted a vigorous campaign against Saudi Arabia's claim to organize the consensus of Islam. For a decade Iran virtually ignored the OIC and convened frequent conferences of its own clients and supporters from abroad. Secretariats based in Tehran supported a succession of organizations, including the World Congress of Friday Imams and Prayer Leaders (from 1982), the Conference on Islamic Thought (from 1983), and the International Conference to Support the Islamic Revolution of the People of Palestine (from 1991). Despite their different names, these congress initiatives reassembled many of the same foreign participants, who placed an Islamic stamp of approval on Iran's policies. Iran also convened many extraordinary conferences after the killing of several hundred Iranians in Mecca during the pilgrimage season of 1987, and after Ayatollah Ruhollah Khomeini's edict against the novelist Salman Rushdie in 1989. [*See* Rushdie Affair.]

Saudi Arabia, Egypt, and Iraq were aligned together in opposition to Iran throughout the 1980s and cooperated in convening congresses of those Muslim figures who were prepared to sanction their own policies in the name of Islam. Existing organizations such as Saudi Arabia's Muslim World League and Egypt's Academy of Islamic Researches expanded their cooperation. Saudi Arabia and Egypt also combined with Iraq in 1983 to establish the Baghdad-based Popular Islamic Conference, which mobilized Muslim support for Iraq's war against Iran. (When the Iraqi invasion of Kuwait in 1990 turned Iraq and Saudi Arabia from allies into enemies, both sides simultaneously convened the Popular Islamic Conference in Baghdad and Mecca, where each passed resolutions condemning the other.)

Islamist Congresses. In the 1990s a growing number of semiclandestine Islamist movements came into the open as governments adopted policies of political liberalization. These movements had strengthened their links during the 1980s in little-publicized conferences, often held in Europe. As they began to acquire legitimate standing and even power, they launched their own congress initiatives. In 1990 ʿAbd al-Raḥmān Khalīfah, leader of the Jordanian Muslim Brotherhood, convened a World Islamic Popular Gathering in Amman that was attended by the leading figures of the Muslim Brotherhood worldwide. In 1991 Ḥasan al-Turābī, the Islamist guide of the Sudanese regime, convened a Popular Arab Islamic Conference in Khartoum attended by many of the most notable Islamists. The conference created a permanent secretariat, and Turābī presented the new organization as the populist alternative to the OIC. [*See the biography of Turābī.*]

The plethora of organizations that summoned Islamic congresses and conferences reflected the intensified competition for authority in contemporary Islam. This competition had long pitted states against one another. But as Islam became the common language of protest, congresses increasingly brought together Islamist movements of opposition seeking to help one another in the pursuit of power. Less than a century after Kawākibī's fantasy, a crowded calendar of congresses binds the world of Islam together as never before. It remains uncertain, however, whether these often competing institutions bridge the differences between Muslims or serve to widen them.

[*See also* Daʿwah, *article on* Institutionalization.]

BIBLIOGRAPHY

Dawisha, Adeed, ed. *Islam in Foreign Policy*. Cambridge, 1983. Ten country studies on the general role of Islam in the formulation of foreign policy.

Kramer, Martin. *Islam Assembled: The Advent of the Muslim Congresses*. New York, 1986. Event-by-event account of the development of Islamic congresses, from the first initiatives through World War II, with extensive bibliography.

Landau, Jacob. *The Politics of Pan-Islam: Ideology and Organization*. Oxford, 1990. Detailed survey of the political role of Pan-Islam beginning from the late Ottoman period, with extensive bibliography.

Levtzion, Nehemia. *International Islamic Solidarity and Its Limitations*. Jerusalem, 1979. Includes a survey of the congresses and their sponsoring organizations.

Mattes, Hanspeter. *Die innere und äussere islamische Mission Libyens*. Mainz, 1986. Considers the activities of Libya's Islamic Call Society.

Middle East Contemporary Survey. New York (now Boulder), 1978–. Commencing with volume 5 (1980–1981), each volume of this annual reference work features an essay on current Pan-Islamic activities, including conferences sponsored by the OIC, state-supported Islamic organizations, and Islamist movements.

Moinuddin, Hasan. *The Charter of the Islamic Conference*. Oxford, 1987. Examines the constitutional foundation of the OIC.

Piscatori, J. P. *Islam in a World of Nation-States*. Cambridge, 1986. Considers the tension between Islamic unity and the modern state.

Schulze, Reinhard. *Islamischer Internationalismus im 20. Jahrhundert: Untersuchungen zur Geschichte der Islamischen Weltliga*. Leiden, 1990. Detailed case study of the Mecca-based Muslim World League, preceded by a general account of the development of Islamic congresses.

Martin Kramer

CONSEIL NATIONAL DES FRANÇAIS MUSULMANS. Founded in France in 1989 and governed by the Law on Associations of 1 July 1901, the Conseil National des Français Musulmans (CNFM) was reformed in 1992 and now consists of 190 associations with 14,000 members. Its council includes 40 members, either coopted or presidents of the most important affiliated associations. Its registered office is in Dole in the Jura, its president is Hamaloui Mekachera, and its secretary-general is Soraya Djebbour.

There are approximately 2.5 million French Muslims, most of whom are *harkis* and their children. *Harkis* are Muslim soldiers who fought in the French army during the Algerian war of independence and left Algeria to live in France at the war's end in 1962.

The council acts as a lobby and is generally not directly engaged in politics. Although French Muslims have civil rights equal to those of other French citizens, the council seeks the end of social and economic discrimination against Muslims in France and the full integration of Muslims into French society. It obtains assistance for them in housing, education, and welfare, and it opposes xenophobia, racism, and anti-Semitism. The council militates in favor of "French Islamic institutions" that the government would acknowledge as equal to those of the Catholic, Protestant, and Jewish faiths. To this end, it has asked for the appointment of an imam as an army chaplain and for the reservation of areas within cemeteries for the burial of Muslims.

A branch of the council, the Convention Nationale des Musulmans Français, which is more politically engaged, militates also for national and economic integration and seeks the creation of Islamic colleges and universities directed by French Muslims. Hoping as well for a change in the December 1905 law that has mandated a strict separation of religion from public life, it prefers the less rigid "concordat" system that had prevailed in Alsace-Lorraine since 1918.

It is the Conseil National that had been satisfied by a middle path. At the instigation of the French government, a Conseil Consultatif des Musulmans de France (Consultative Council of Muslims of France) under the presidency of Dr. Dalil Boubaker, the new chancellor of Paris's mosque since the departure for Algeria of Shaykh Haddām Tidjānī, was created in November 1993.

The new chancellor is a French Muslim, deputy chairman of the ʿUlamā' Conference and of the Habous (Religious Endowers) Society from 1987 to 1992. He is the son of the rector of Paris's mosque, Si Hamza Boubaker (1957–1982), and his appointment was denounced by the Fédération Nationale des Musulmans de France (FNMF) as nepotistic (although in reality it is because of his nationality). Indeed the institution of the Consultative Council under Boubaker's aegis has the purpose to promote a "French Islam" and its worship, to oppose all "foreign extremism," and to be a representative structure of Islam and a mediator between the government and the muslims in France.

The CNFM's president, M. Mekachera, is among the twenty-five members, which also includes the leaders of several other organizations, such as the Union des Organisations Islamiques de France (UOIF), Union des Étudiants Islamiques (Muslim Students' Association), Union des Veterans de France de Confession Islamique (French Muslim Veterans' Union), Connaitre l'Islam (Knowledge of Islam), Tablīgh (Faith and Religious Observance), and the rectors of the most important towns. This institution seems to make obsolete the CORIF (Conseil Religieux de l'Islam en France), created in 1990 by the French government. The FNMF has no share in the new council.

[*See also* Fédération Nationale des Musulmans de France; France; Union des Organisations Islamiques de France.]

BIBLIOGRAPHY

Le Rappel (Recalling). National newspaper of French Muslim communities, sold by subscription.

ANNIE KRIEGER-KRYNICKI

CONSENSUS.

In the context of Islamic legal theory, the Arabic term *ijmāʿ* denotes the agreement of a generation of *mujtahids* (those who are qualified to form opinions on religious matters) concerning a particular issue that has arisen since the death of the Prophet. Theoretically, this consensus obtains when such *mujtahids* explicitly state their agreement on a given matter, or when they act uniformly on it, or when such a matter receives their tacit approval. Practically, however, consensus is determined after the fact, when a later generation of scholars looks to the past and finds that a generation or generations of earlier *mujtahids* have universally agreed on a particular question.

As one of the four recognized sources of Sunnī law, consensus functions both as a sanctioning instrument and as a material source of law. Once agreement has been reached on an issue, usually a question of law, that issue becomes epistemologically certain and thus insusceptible to further interpretation. In other words, it is removed, by virtue of the consensus, from the region of probability to that of certainty; and being certain, it can serve as a textual precedent—like the Qur'ān and the *sunnah*—on the basis of which new cases may be solved. The epistemological value attached to consensus renders this instrument so powerful in the realm of doctrine and practice in the community that it can override established practice as well as clear statements of the Qur'ān. For instance, if the community, represented by its *mujtahids*, reaches a consensus that runs counter to a Qur'ānic text, the text is considered to have been superseded by this consensus. The source of such an evaluation is the tradition that states, "my community will never agree in an error."

The notion that the community is infallible has its roots in an old Arabian social and secular concept according to which the common behavior of the tribal group represents an example worthy of being imitated; what the group *(jamāʿah)* decides becomes the norm. During the eighth century, when the geographical schools of law came into being, this concept acquired mild religious connotations but remained largely undefined. It was not until Shāfiʿī, who insisted on grounding all legal deductions in the Qur'ān and the *sunnah* of the Prophet, that consensus was first given a rudimentary but authoritative foundation in the revealed texts. Shāfiʿī's concept of consensus, whose agent is theoretically the entirety of the Muslim community, was reversed by later jurists who insisted that *mujtahid*s were the only persons qualified to form such an authoritative agreement. These jurists, however, still felt compelled to pursue Shāfiʿī's quest to justify consensus on the basis of revelation, even though they largely ignored the arguments he had adduced. Eventually the evidentiary status of consensus *(ḥujjīyat al-ijmāʿ)*, which must rest on conclusive textual proofs, was found in such Qur'ānic verses as 4.115, 2.143, 3.110, 9.16, and 31.15—which generally bid Muslims not to swerve from the path of the Prophet and his community—as well as in numerous Prophetic traditions. Although the latter were related by a single authority *(āḥād)* and thus regarded as probable *(ẓannī)*, they shared one common theme expressed in the dictum mentioned above that the community will never agree on an error. This multiple corroboration assigned these traditions to the *tawātur maʿnawī* type (recurrent traditions that share a single theme); as such they were thought to yield conclusive knowledge requisite for establishing the authoritativeness of consensus.

Another fundamental issue that Muslim jurists debated in some detail was whether consensus is considered settled before or after the demise of the *mujtahid*s who reach it. Some argued that the *mujtahid*s must all be dead for their consensus to become final, since if one or more of them changes his mind, consensus cannot be deemed to have been reached. Other jurists rejected this argument and maintained that the *mujtahid*s are bound by consensus once it is reached, and therefore they would sin should they later depart from it.

In Twelver Shiism, by contrast, consensus in and by itself is neither an infallible sanctioning instrument nor a source of law. When the Twelver jurists reach an agreement on a question of law, the hidden imam is always assumed to partake in that agreement; in fact, it is the posited participation of the imam which alone guarantees the infallibility of consensus. The function of consensus in Twelver Shiism is thus to unveil the infallible opinion of the imam. If and when the imam appears to stipulate the law in person, consensus will be rendered superfluous. This limited function of consensus perhaps explains why it is not necessary, as it is in Sunnism, to obtain the agreement of all qualified jurists in order for consensus to be fully authoritative.

The traditional notion of consensus in Sunnī Islam remained largely unquestioned until the twentieth century, when modern Muslim reformers brought forth a variety of changes to the old concepts. The Egyptian Salafī reformer Muḥammad Rashīd Riḍā (d. 1935) maintained that only the consensus of the Prophet's companions is binding, and this only in matters of worship. The clear texts of the Qur'ān and the *sunnah* that bear upon such matters and that have been subject to the companions' consensus are authoritative, and a departure from the laws of worship instituted throughout the centuries would constitute a sin. But matters of public policy and social morality must be regulated in light of the modern needs faced by the community. Here even the consensus of the companions is not binding. Law governing these matters must be legislated by the qualified legal scholars who are the effective rulers of the community *(ahl al-ḥall wa-al-ʿaqd)* and act on its behalf and in its best interests. Their legislation is the result of a process of consultation *(shūrā)*, and as such it represents the will and consensus of the community. For Rashīd Riḍā, the old concept of consensus is largely irrelevant; it is replaced by a new and more restricted notion that derives its authority from some form of consultative and parliamentary process. [*See* Ahl al-Ḥall wa-al-ʿAqd.]

The ideas of consultation and parliamentarianism have become essential ingredients in nearly all attempts at reformulating a theory of consensus. The Pakistani scholar Kemal Faruki assigns to the community the exclusive right to determine its own affairs as it sees fit. Through an elective process, it vests its authority in learned and trustworthy persons who act on its behalf as a legislative body. This body, though it expresses the will of the community as a totality (and is therefore assured of protection against error), is bound at the same time by the authority of the revealed texts as they have been interpreted by the consensus of previous generations.

[*See also* Law, *article on* Legal Thought and Jurisprudence; *for* mujtahids, *see* Ijtihād.]

BIBLIOGRAPHY

Bernand, Marie. *L'accord unanime de la communauté comme fondement des statuts légaux de l'Islam*. Paris, 1970.

Bravmann, M. M. *The Spiritual Background of Early Islam*. Leiden, 1972.
Faruki, Kemal A. *Ijmaʿ and the Gate of Ijtihad*. Karachi, 1954.
Hallaq, Wael B. "On the Authoritativeness of Sunni Consensus." *International Journal of Middle East Studies* 18 (1986): 427–454.
Mansour, Camille. *L'autorité dans la pensée musulmane*. Paris, 1975.
Sachedina, Abdulaziz. *Islamic Messianism*. New York, 1981.
Schacht, Joseph. *The Origins of Muhammadan Jurisprudence*. Oxford and New York, 1975.
Snouck Hurgronje, Christiaan. *Selected Works*. Edited by G. H. Bousquet and Joseph Schacht. Leiden, 1957.

WAEL B. HALLAQ

CONSTITUTION. Governance in the Islamic Middle East may best be understood as a development from the classical theory of the caliphate *(khilāfah)* and the concept of rule by the "pious sultan," more or less integrated with modern constitutional government.

The ideal model for the Islamic state was the Charter of Medina, a contract between Muḥammad, the prophet and statesman, and his Muslim/Jewish community *(ummah)*. It permitted the coexistence of Muslims and "peoples of the book," (*ahl al-kitāb*, monotheists with a revealed scripture), who enjoyed freedom of worship in return for loyalty and payment of a poll-tax *(jizyah)*.

Abū al-Ḥasan ʿAlī al-Māwardī (d. 1058) was one of the first political philosophers to define the Sunnī concept of the caliphate at a time when it was beginning its decline as a viable institution. His book *Al-aḥkām al-sulṭānīyah* (The Ordinances of Government) proposes that in the Islamic state, sovereignty belongs to God, and his commands, as revealed in the Qur'ān and complemented by the *sunnah* (traditions) are the major bases of Islamic law *(sharīʿah)*. The caliph was a guardian, not a legislator, and was elected after investiture *(bayʿah)* by the *ahl al-ḥall wa-al-ʿaqd* (people with power to loose and bind). The purpose of governance *(wilāyah)* was to enjoin right and forbid wrong, to make possible a life that would safeguard salvation, and to protect and expand the Islamic world, the *dar al-Islām*. [*See* Bayʿah; Ahl al-Ḥall wa-al-ʿAqd; Wilāyah.] Once chosen, the caliph was obeyed out of piety by some, out of fear by others. The Mongol invasion and demise of the ʿAbbāsid caliphate in the thirteenth century gave military commanders (emirs or sultans) power to rule, and autocratic government, whether monarchical or presidential, became legitimized on the model of the "pious sultanate."

Constitutionalism in the Islamic Middle East is a modern phenomenon meant to curb the arbitrary powers of rulers. It arose as economic mismanagement and the growth of Western influence encouraged an elite of landowners and other notables to demand limits on the authority of their rulers.

The first modern contract between a Muslim ruler and his subjects was the *sanad-i ittifāq* (1808), hailed by some as the Turkish "Magna Carta," in which the Ottoman ruling class pledged their loyalty to Sultan Mahmud II in exchange for protection of their status and possessions. It was soon abrogated: subsequent decrees of 1839 and 1856 proclaimed equal rights for Muslims and non-Muslims in response to European pressures, but the sultan remained supreme.

Modern constitutions patterned on Western, often Belgian models were drafted (Ottoman, 1876; Tunis, 1861; Egypt, 1882; and Iran, 1906). They were short-lived or were amended to suit the wishes of an autocratic ruler, a colonial power, or a mandatory government.

Constitutional documents drafted by newly independent states after the end of World War II, whether nationalist, socialist, or traditional, tended to be liberal in nature. They provided for the protection of life and property, the inviolability of the home, and religious freedom, but were also characterized by strong executive power. Autocratic government has been the rule rather than the exception. The monarch or president summons and dismisses parliament and appoints and dismisses ministers. Political parties tend to be weak, sectarian, or cliquish, headed by charismatic leaders. Modernization did not promote the establishment of democratic government. For example, two states with working democracies are Pakistan and Turkey, but in both the military sees itself as the guardian of the political process and intervenes to remove elected officials.

The failure of nationalist, socialist, and secular governments has encouraged the emergence of a revivalist movement that wants to create an Islamic state. Drawing on the teachings of Sayyid Quṭb, Ḥasan al-Bannā', Abū al-Aʿla Mawdūdī, and Ayatollah Ruhollah Khomeini, it demands revolutionary change, including the abolition of western innovations, the overthrow of secular and traditional regimes, and the establishment of a state where sovereignty belongs to God, the *sharīʿah* is the law, and an elected *emir* governs with the aid of a council of experts (shūrā). Islamists do not exclude women from participation in public life, but they maintain that women's primary function as mothers and wives necessarily restricts their sphere of activity.

The Islamic constitution of Shīʿī Iran (1979) gave supreme power to Ayatollah Khomeini, who ruled "in the absence of the Hidden Imam." Subsequently, the *ayatollah al-uzma* (the highest jurisconsult) became the arbiter of the legislative process. Sunnī Islamists, by contrast, tend to follow a republican model, granting a council of *ʿulamāʾ* merely consultative powers. Muhammad Zia ul-Haq of Pakistan and ʿUmar al-Bashir of Sudan, both military men, legitimized their rule by implementing Islamist programs.

The Islamist concept of governance is highly idealistic; it is puritanical and egalitarian, but at the same time totalitarian in character. It assumes that once elected, the emir will not abuse his absolute powers, and that a restoration of early institutions will solve the socioeconomic problems of the Islamic world.

[*See also* Authority and Legitimation.]

BIBLIOGRAPHY

Akhavi, Shahrough. *Religion and Politics in Contemporary Iran.* Albany, N.Y., 1980. Analyzes clergy-state relations to identify the pressures of increasing secularization in society and the response to these pressures by the leaders of religious institutions.

Binder, Leonard. *Religion and Politics in Pakistan.* Berkeley, 1963. Discusses attempts at drafting a constitution for the Islamic state of Pakistan in the early 1950s and lists the views of the Board of Taʿlīmāt-i Islāmīyah on such questions as the qualifications of the head of state, elections, and the separation of powers.

Esposito, John L., ed. *Voices of Resurgent Islam.* New York and Oxford, 1983. Discusses questions of Islamic identity, the pioneers of the Islamic resurgence, and Muslim perspectives on a resurgent Islam.

The Europa World Year Book, 1992. London, 1992. Reference source with historical and political summaries of the countries of the world, including their constitutions.

Kimmens, Andrew C., ed. *Islamic Politics and the Modern World.* New York, 1991. Fifteen contributors discuss such topics as the failure of the secular ideal, islamic revival and radical resurgence, the Salman Rushdie case, and the future of islamic politics.

Piscatori, J. P., ed. *Islam in the Political Process.* Cambridge, 1983. Eleven contributors examine Islamic politics in a number of Muslim states.

Rosenthal, E. I. J. *Political Thought in Medieval Islam.* Cambridge, 1962. *Islam in the Modern National State.* Cambridge, 1965. Discusses the unity of religion and politics in classical Islam and the place of Islam in the nation-state. Although dated in some of its assumptions, the 1965 work is an excellent source on Islam in the post–World War II nation-state.

LUDWIG W. ADAMEC

CONSTITUTIONAL REVOLUTION. The Iranian Constitutional Revolution (1905–1911) was one of two major revolutions in modern Iran that, together with several rebellions, made Iran the most revolutionary Middle Eastern country of the modern era. Iran owed its revolutionary character largely to the country's semicolonial status (much like revolutionary China); the alliance among merchants, *ʿulamāʾ* (religious scholars), and modern intellectuals; and the central role in revolutions of many cities. The particular causes of the 1905–1911 movement included dissatisfaction with the growth of Western power and with economic stagnation, as well as the influence of modern ideas and of the results of the Russo-Japanese war of 1904–1905 and the Russian revolution of 1905.

The immediate cause of revolutionary events was, as is often the case, relatively trivial. In December 1905, the governor of Tehran beat the feet of a sugar merchant accused of raising prices, after which many mullahs and merchants took *basṭ* (sanctuary) in Tehran's royal mosque. After their dispersal, many *ʿulamāʾ* took *basṭ* in a shrine and presented demands to the shah; the crucial one was an undefined "house of justice." The shah dismissed the governor and in principle granted the house of justice in January 1906 but did nothing further. There followed preaching by radical preachers, and a sayyid was killed by an officer; as a result, a great mass of mullahs and others took *basṭ* in Qom in July 1906. A huge crowd of merchants and tradespeople, estimated at twelve to fourteen thousand, took *basṭ* in the British legation in Tehran and began to demand a parliament. In August, Muẓaffar al-Dīn Shah accepted this demand, and the first parliament, or *majlis,* was elected in accordance with a six-class system, which gave more power to the popular-class guilds than they were to enjoy in subsequent parliaments, elected under a nonclass system.

The first Majlis opened in October 1906, and a committee wrote a Fundamental Law, which the shah signed only when he was mortally ill, in December 1906. A longer Supplementary Fundamental Law was signed by the new shah, Muḥammad ʿAlī, in October 1907. Together, these made up the Iranian Constitution that remained, with minor amendments, until the 1979 revolution. It was based largely on the Belgian Constitution of 1830, but on *ʿulamāʾ* insistence it included references to Islam and a provision that a committee of five *mujtahids* would pass on the constitutionality of parliamentary laws. This remained a dead letter. The intent of the parliamentarians was to set up a Western-style constitutional monarchy with power held by parliament and its chosen ministers, but this rarely happened.

There was a flowering of liberal and radical newspapers and societies during the revolutionary period. The new shah brought back a conservative prime minister, the Atabak, and the Majlis majority did not insist on itself making this choice. Those opposed to autocracy comprised several groups: merchants and tradespeople; the *ʿulamāʾ* opposition, led by the liberal sayyid Muḥammad Ḥusayn Ṭabāṭabāʾī and the opportunistic sayyid ʿAbd Allāh Bihbahānī; and liberals and radicals, such as the then-socialist Tabriz deputy Sayyid Ḥasan Taqīzādah. The far left and the shah were both involved in the killing of the Atabak on 31 August 1907, by coincidence the same date as the signing of the Anglo-Russian Treaty dividing Iran into spheres of influence. The introduction of Russo-British cooperation in Iran helped doom the revolution.

The shah, with the aid of the Russian-led Cossack Brigade, staged a successful coup against the Majlis and the opposition in June 1908. Only Tabriz, led by two guerrilla leaders from the popular classes, held out. When Russian troops moved in, in 1909, the guerrillas moved to Gilan, where the constitutionalist movement was also strong. In the south, the Bakhtiārī tribe had its reasons to oppose the shah, and in July 1909, the Bakhtiārīs and the northern revolutionaries converged on Tehran. They deposed the shah and installed his minor son, Aḥmad Shāh, under a regency. Although leftists, including those influenced by Russian social democrats, were strong in the opposition, and in the strong Democrat Party, most power went to a conservative, Bakhtiārī-led cabinet.

Severe financial problems led the government to seek a foreign adviser untied to Britain and Russia, and they brought in an American expert, Morgan Shuster, to reform Iranian finances. Shuster wished to appoint a British subject to head a tax gendarmerie, but the Russians said this violated the Anglo-Russian Treaty, and Britain went along with Russia's position. In November 1911, the Russians issued an ultimatum and sent in troops, and for several years Russia and Britain controlled the government, marking the real end of the revolution, although the constitution and the experience of political participation remained as its legacy.

[*See also* Iran; Majlis; Qājār Dynasty.]

BIBLIOGRAPHY

Bayat, Mangol. *Iran's First Revolution: Shiʿism and the Constitutional Revolution of 1905–1909*. New York, 1991. Questions the usual importance given the *ʿulamāʾ*, and usefully incorporates Russian material, especially on the role of the left.

Browne, Edward G. *The Persian Revolution of 1905–1909*. Cambridge, 1910. The classic work, a partisan prorevolution book written during the revolution; still useful for its translated and summarized primary sources and as a primary source itself of one perspective.

Keddie, Nikki R. *Iran: Religion, Politics, and Society*. London, 1980. Collection of articles, including "Religion and Irreligion in Early Iranian Nationalism" and others discussing the constitutional revolution.

Lambton, Ann K. S., ed. *Qajar Persia: Eleven Studies*. Austin, 1988.

Martin, Vanessa. *Islam and Modernism: The Iranian Revolution of 1906*. London, 1989. The first of three recent comprehensive books on the revolution, readable and strong in its discussion of Shiism and the role of the *ʿulamāʾ*.

Nikki R. Keddie

CONTRACT LAW. Classical Islamic law did not have a comprehensive theory of obligations and contracts. The formation of the law as a distinct discipline, with the rise of *fiqh* treatises after the ninth century and with the common-law jurisprudential accretions through the centuries, meant that a comprehensive system was attempted only in the modern period. This attempt took two forms. Although the theory of obligations and contracts was being presented by some individual authors from Egypt and the Levant (notably Maḥmaṣānī, Chehata [Shiḥātah], and Sanhūrī) in well-constructed treatises, the effective codification of the law of contracts was achieved in most countries of the Islamic world in the late nineteenth and twentieth centuries.

In classical law, the general regulation of a contract can be presented under the twin headings of Qurʾānic injunctions and *fiqh* principles: The first and more straightforward structure of the law of contracts was encompassed by the basic principles adumbrated in some verses of the Qurʾān. The Qurʾānic injunctions require contracts to be entered into and applied in good faith, to be preferably in writing, and to avoid including *ribā* (interest, usury), with the definition of *ribā* remaining ambiguous to date. Second, the classical law of obligations as developed in the jurists' work was elaborated in much more detail, but there is no book of contracts in the great treatises of *fiqh*. Rather, the core model is the contract of sale. This is followed by a number of other, less-important contracts which are discussed, sometimes in minute detail, generally without the clear sense of structure that the modern age requires. The fact that the sale contract appears as a root model is also indicative of the centrality of commerce in classical Islam, and it shows the importance of practice for the formulation of Islamic law.

Apart from the various commentaries one finds in the

fiqh books, contractual models can also be found in the literature of *shurūṭ* (lit., "conditions"). *Shurūṭ* are the legal formulas which judges and legal specialists have followed in the course of their practice and which vary over time and geographical area.

In the nineteenth century a decisive change in legal systems took place with the success of the French Napoleonic Code and its spread in the world with the extension of colonial rule. It was also the occasion for the Muslim tradition, then vested in the Ottoman Empire, to seriously consider the codification of the law of obligations. This resulted in the celebrated *Majallah (Mecelle)*, enacted between 1879 and 1886, which in turn became the model for widespread codification of the law of contracts in the Muslim world. Codification of the Islamic law of obligations then took place in North Africa (Tunisian *Majallah* of 1906, Moroccan Code of 1912) and in the private compilations of the Egyptian Muḥammad Qadrī Bāshā and the Saudi Aḥmad ibn ʿAbd Allāh al-Qārī. In Iran, a similar process was completed in the mid-1930s with the Iranian Civil Code. In other countries of the Muslim world, especially in those countries which were under British or Dutch influence (India, Pakistan, Indonesia), legislation was more piecemeal and tended to be less attentive to the Islamic legacy.

Another major phase of the codification of the law of contracts was completed when the Egyptian Civil Code was passed in 1949, under the guidance of ʿAbd al-Razzāq al-Sanhūrī (d. 1971). The Egyptian Civil Code was the model for Syrian, Kuwaiti, and Libyan contract codes. In Egypt, Sanhūrī was careful to incorporate *fiqh* principles and Egyptian case-law precedents, but the language used by him and his fellow drafters incorporated a comparative element which diluted the more classical terminology of the *Majallah*. Later civil codes (in Jordan, a new code was passed in 1976; in Kuwait, 1980; in the United Arab Emirates, 1985; in the Unified Yemen, 1992) paid more attention to *fiqh* terminology, following the experience of the Iraqi Civil Code of 1953, which appeared as a compromise between Sanhūrī's code and the *Majallah*. There are jurisdictions, such as Saudi Arabia, where a unified civil code has not been passed, and where the law must still be ascertained in the light of the common law represented by classical *fiqh*, but most jurisdictions have preferred the simplicity of an integrated text for the law of obligations and contracts.

Owing to this vast experience, the law of contracts is rich and variegated. A few principles can help set the tone with regard to the general rules of interpretation of contracts, to the requirements of "the contractual session," and to the conditions for a judicial revision of contractual terms.

Article 3 of the *Majallah* specifies that "in matter of contract, intention and meaning have priority over wording and syntax." This establishes the importance of intention over formal expression, and it is derived from a saying ascribed to the Prophet on the basing of acts on intentions. Classical law, however, as Sanhūrī has suggested, "stops at the declared intention and does not go beyond it to the hidden intention. . . . The principal source of interpretation must be found in the expressions and formulas used by the parties in the contract."

Whatever the ultimate importance of formalism and consensualism in the law of contracts, many jurisdictions in the Middle East have introduced the principle of the unity of *majlis al-ʿaqd* ("the contractual session"). A major worry of classical law is the uncertainty of the terms of a contract, and classical jurists have favored the establishment of what amounts to a unit of negotiation for the contract, which is limited in time and place: the *majlis al-ʿaqd*. The theory is complex and elaborate, but it has been described by the Ḥanafī jurist Kāsānī (d. AH 587/1191 CE) as "offer and acceptance in the same session: if the session varies [*ikhtalaf al-majlis*] the contract does not take place" (n.d., vol. 5, p. 136). The term will be found invariably in several modern Muslim jurisdictions, although contracts on future things and variations on the obligations in more complex cases have allowed contemporary requirements to be respected in the present laws of contracts.

Contracts, when valid, are binding. Vices of form and consent are known in Islamic law, but some tenets of the classical theory have been revived in the possibility of revising a contract when some of the obligations have become too onerous on one of the parties. Although these conditions have been strictly limited in the decisions of present-day Arab courts, the principle has been consecrated in several codes, notably in Egypt and Iraq.

[*See also* Commercial Law; Economics, *article on* Economic Theory; *and* Mecelle.]

BIBLIOGRAPHY

Classical *Fiqh* Books of Sales

Kāsānī, Abū Bakr ibn Masʿūd al-. "Kitāb al-buyūʿ" (The Book of Sales). In *Kitāb badāʾiʿ al-ṣanāʾiʿ fī tartīb al-sharāʾiʿ*, vol. 5, pp. 133–310. Beirut, 1974.

Sarakhsī, Muḥammad ibn Aḥmad al-. "Kitāb al-buyūʿ." In *Kitāb al-*

mabsūṭ, vol. 12, pp. 108–219, and vol. 13, pp. 2–199. Beirut, [197–].

Modern Private Compilations of and Commentaries on the Law of Contract

Āl-Kāshif al-Ghiṭā', Muḥammad al-Ḥusayn. *Taḥrīr al-majallah.* 2 vols. Nahaf, 1940–1943.

Qadrī Muḥammad. *Murshid al-ḥayrān ilā maʿrifat aḥwāl al-insān.* Cairo, 1983.

Qārī, Aḥmad ibn ʿAbd Allāh al-. *Majallat al-aḥkām al-sharʿīyah.* Edited, with commentary, by ʿAbd al-Wahhāb I. Abū Sulaymān and Muḥammad I. A. ʿAlī. Jeddah, 1981.

Modern Writings on the Law of Contract

Chehata, Chafik. *Théorie générale de l'obligation en droit musulman hanéfite* (1936). Paris, 1969.

Linant de Bellefonds, Yvon. *Traité de droit musulman comparé.* Vol. 1. Paris, 1965.

Maḥmaṣānī, Ṣubḥī. *Al-naẓarīyah al-ʿāmmah lil-mūjibāt wa-al-ʿuqūd fī al-sharīʿah al-Islāmīyah.* 2 vols. Beirut, 1948.

Rayner, Susan E. *The Theory of Contracts in Islamic Law.* London, 1991.

Sanhūrī, ʿAbd al-Razzāq al-. *Maṣādir al-ḥaqq fī al-fiqh al-Islāmī.* 6 vols. Cairo, 1954–1959.

Sanhūrī, ʿAbd al-Razzāq al-. *Al-wasīṭ fī sharḥ al-qānūn al-madanī.* 12 vols. Cairo, 1952–1970.

The reader may also consult several important modern codes of obligations and contracts, for instance, the Tunisian *Majallah* (1906), the Moroccan Code of Obligations and Contracts (1912), the Egyptian Civil Code (1949), the Jordanian Civil Code (1976), and the Yemeni Civil Code (1992). The Ottoman Civil Code, *Majallat al-aḥkām al-ʿadlīyah* (1879–1886), is available in several English translations, notably by C. A. Hooper, *The Civil Law of Palestine and Trans-Jordan,* 2 vols. (Jerusalem, 1933–1936).

CHIBLI MALLAT

CONVERSION. In one of the first divine revelations recorded in the Qur'ān, the prophet Muḥammed was commanded by God to "arise and warn!" (74.1). This is taken by some Muslim scholars to signal the beginning of public preaching of the message, which until then was presumably done privately among the Prophet's family and intimate friends. Hence, almost from the very outset, Islam was to be a proselytizing faith with a mission to bring its message to all who would listen. In another passage in the Qur'ān Muḥammad was told, "Invite to the way of your Lord with wisdom and beautiful preaching; and argue with them in ways that are best and most gracious" (16.125).

At first, however, most members of the community of Mecca in which Muḥammad lived and to which he brought this message tended to reject it for social, religious, and economic reasons. With his migration to Medina in 622 CE together with his small community of converts, and the acceptance he found there for his message, a strong base was established for the spread of that word and the conversion of most of Arabia. As the message spread through conquest beyond the borders of the Arabian Peninsula, the greater community of new Muslims, at first still largely of Arabian stock, found it difficult to integrate non-Arabian outsiders into its traditional social structure. Acceptance of Islam at that time meant integration into the existing tribal framework of Arabian society. This concept changed slowly under the influence of the very different societies that fell under Muslim sway. Within a relatively short time, as large numbers chose or were forced to join the community, conversion and converts found a place in Islamic society and ideology.

In common English usage, *conversion* means "to turn around, transform, bring over or persuade to a particular view, change or turn from one state to another." This definition, referring to an inner change or transformation, flows from a Christian concept of conversion. It is barely applicable to religious traditions like Judaism and Islam that emphasize the observance of a divine law and of socially validated acts as well as matters of belief. Until modern times when contact with Christian missionaries introduced their concept of conversion, the Arabic lexicon lacked any precise equivalent of this term. This was so, first of all, because in the Islamic tradition entrance into the religious community is viewed less as an inner transformation than as a divinely determined return to *fiṭrah,* the natural disposition or condition in which all humanity is born but which may have been altered by one's parents. Indeed, the Qur'ān states, "Whomsoever it is Allah's will to guide. He expands his bosom to Submission *(Islām)*" (6.126).

The act of becoming a Muslim differs from conversion to Christianity above all because to enter Islam is literally to perform the act of surrender or submission to God and God's will, it also involves *tawbah* ("return, repentance") to the *fiṭrah,* humanity's natural disposition. Hence the word *islām* itself means "submission"; from the same Arabic root come the verbal forms *aslama* and *istaslama,* denoting the act of becoming a *muslim,* literally, "one who submits or surrenders" and professes that surrender by adhering to the Prophet's message.

This act of submission to God consists first and foremost in *tawḥīd* or proclaiming the absolute oneness and uniqueness of God; *shirk,* the cardinal sin in Islam, is the association by comparison of anything with God. In traditional interpretations this includes ascribing to any human being or any aspect of nature powers that belong to God alone. Submission simultaneously involves bearing witness that Muḥammad is the messenger and prophet of God. From these follow the observance of what God commands, as revealed to the prophet Muḥammad (e.g., prayer and almsgiving), and avoidance of what is forbidden (e.g., eating pork and drinking wine). In Muslim tradition this raises the issue of the distinction between *islām* and *īmān,* the latter translated as "faith" or "belief."

When the Prophet was asked, according to several traditions, to clarify the distinction between the two, he said that *islām* consists of "worshiping Allāh, not associating anything with Him, carrying out the prayers, giving the prescribed alms, and fasting during the month of Ramaḍan." These came to be formalized as the Five Pillars of Islam: the confession of faith; prayer preceded by ritual cleansing and involving prescribed actions; almsgiving in a specified amount and manner; fasting during the month of Ramaḍān; and, at least once in a lifetime, pilgrimage to Mecca. But he added to these aspects of *islām, khayrāt* or "good works", saying "to give food (to the hungry), and to greet with peace those one knows and those one does not know." [*See also* Pillars of Islam.]

The standard presentation of *īmān,* on the other hand, came to consist of belief in God, his angels, his revealed books (including the original revelations recorded in the scriptures of the Jews and Christians), his messengers or apostles, the day of resurrection, and fate or destiny. By way of distinction, therefore, *islām* consists of the performance of the Five Pillars, specified acts in a social environment; later *īmān* or faith consists of certain beliefs, as outlined above. This set of beliefs came to be elaborated in several creeds composed during the ninth and tenth centuries CE (third and fourth centuries AH). Whereas *īmān* resides in the heart and may be known only by God, the acts of *islām* should be witnessed by humanity. Muslim scholars have differed over the relationship between *islām* and *īmān,* but one definition in a tenth-century creed states, "There is no faith whatsoever without *islām,* and *islām* could not exist without faith *(īmān)*". [*See* Īmān.]

As the early, rapid conquest of large areas of the Near East and North Africa laid the basis for a vast empire ruled by Muslims, varying approaches were taken toward nonbelievers, first in Arabia and then in the two great empires between which the peninsula was situated. In this early period, the question of conversion depended largely on the attitudes of the military commanders of the various Muslim units. The Sassanian Persian Empire, which ruled over today's Iraq, Iran, and most of Central Asia, was rapidly conquered in its entirety. The adherents of the existing state religion, Zoroastrianism, and its various offshoots were rather rapidly converted to Islam, and it is estimated that Islam became the majority religion by the tenth century. Only small remnants of the once-powerful Zoroastrians and of the Christian and Jewish minorities survive there now. By contrast, in the portions of the Byzantine Empire that were conquered different conditions prevailed in the various provinces. Here the official Greek Orthodox church was challenged by a variety of Eastern Christian churches, and there were widespread Jewish communities as well. The Syro-Palestinian area is said by some Western scholars to have become a majority Muslim area only after the Crusades, and Egypt only somewhat later.

Based on concepts derived from the Qur'ān and the traditions attributed to the Prophet, society in the new Islamic empire came to be divided between two main groups of subjects, the believers and the other peoples of the book—those who possessed sacred scriptures, at first Jews, Christians, and Zoroastrians. These became the so-called "protected peoples" *(dhimmī).* They were guaranteed protection of life and property and the freedom to practice their own religion and administer its laws, but they were subject to certain restrictions, among them the payment of special taxes (largely limited to the *jizyah* or poll-tax) and the observance of sumptuary laws. These were laws governing personal behavior, including the wearing of distinguishing garments, prohibition from riding horses, bearing arms, or building edifices higher than those of Muslims, regulation of public religious practice, and the like. The acceptance of *dhimmah* was thus accompanied by second-class status and formalized acts of degradation; the latter were enforced or ignored depending on the ruler of the time or the power of the Muslim religious authorities in the various Islamic states that arose after the collapse of imperial power. [*See* People of the Book; Dhimmī; Jizyah.]

Although differing in details from one locality to another, the process of conversion has come to be more or less standardized. The act of becoming a Muslim begins with the first of the Five Pillars, the recitation in the presence of witnesses of the *shahādah*, the Confession or Profession of Faith: "I bear witness that there is no god but Allāh, and Muḥammad is the messenger of Allāh." The performance of the other Pillars, also presumably in public, is expected to follow. [*See* Shahādah.] In addition, although not originally mentioned in the Qur'ān, circumcision *(khitān)* came to be seen as an essential requirement for a male convert. The prophetic tradition mentions it as a part of the *fiṭrah*, connecting it with the life of Abraham. In some areas of the world, especially among the uneducated masses, male circumcision came to be recognized as a sign of being a Muslim and indeed to signify the act of entering into Islam. [*See* Circumcision.] Adoption of what came to be considered Muslim names and of specifically Muslim types of dress, especially the modest attire required of women, were also expected in order to differentiate the convert from former coreligionists. Ceasing to eat pork and to drink alcoholic beverages also came to be considered symbolic breaks with the past.

As indicated above, the rate of conversion varied greatly from one area of the empire to another—rapid in some and almost glacial in others. Although the disappearance of pagan religions in areas conquered by Islam has been little investigated, there has been considerable scholarly discussion about the causes for the transformation of once predominantly Christian and Zoroastrian areas, with relatively large Jewish minority communities, into largely Muslim ones. The thoroughness of the process cannot be laid to the use of force or threats of death, although these did occur at times, but rather to a variety of factors. Some of these were economic, often including quite significant differential taxation, certain trade advantages in specific places, and prohibitions against the ownership of land or slaves by non-Muslims. Then there were social motives: intermarriage involving a male *dhimmī* and a Muslim woman, an otherwise forbidden act; the ability to retain high social standing or to rise from a lower one; or the advantages of belonging to the ruling, majority group. Finally there were spiritual reasons such as genuine respect for and attraction to Islamic teachings and practice. The economic and social aspects seemed to dominate during the earlier periods, as Islamic theological and philosophical thought developed sophistication during periods of free intellectual intercourse among scholars of the different faiths in early ʿAbbāsid Baghdad or at the peak of Umayyad rule in Spain. Later, when Ṣūfī ideas and practices spread, these seem to have become very attractive throughout non-Muslim populations of the Islamic realm. One example of this trend may be seen in the circle of Jewish intellectuals around Abraham ben Moses ben Maimon (1186–1237), the grandson of the great Jewish philosopher Maimonides. Although he himself remained a Jew and tried unsuccessfully to introduce Muslim, especially Ṣūfī, practices into Judaism, some of his companions converted to Islam.

There were infrequent instances of forced conversion in various parts of the empire at different times, for instance during the reigns of the mad caliph al-Ḥākim (r. 996–1021) in Egypt and of the fanatical Almohads in Spain and Morocco (1130–1269), when the choice was indeed conversion, exile, or death. Aside from forced conversion, there were relatively large numbers of converts in the face of the stringent enforcement of discriminatory laws during the reigns of certain Mamlūk sultans (1260–1517) in Egypt and Syria, as well as severe persecution under the early Ṣafavid rulers in Iran (1502–1736). These were, however, exceptions. Scholarly opinion now generally holds that Muslims reached majority status in the empire as a whole only by the tenth century, and in certain areas, such as Egypt, as mentioned above, some centuries later.

Since around the middle of the sixteenth century, conversion to Islam has been carried out to a great extent through the activities of traveling merchants, mendicant Ṣūfīs, and Muslim popular preachers, as has been the case in parts of Indonesia and other areas of East Asia and Africa. More recently, other factors have emerged that aid in the spread of Islam. Some of these have resulted from efforts to counter Christian missionary activity, especially in sub-Saharan Africa where Christianity and Islam have engaged in fierce competition for converts. Others flow from the rise of actively proselytizing groups within Islam, such as the Aḥmadīyah sect that has been quite active in Europe and the Americas, leading to activities by other Muslim groups to counter their successes. [*See* Aḥmadīyah.]

An especially impressive development has been the spread of Islam among African-Americans in recent decades. This movement first arose early in the twentieth century and evolved into many subgroups, each following the teachings of a different charismatic leader, and each deviating in important ways from "normative" Islam. These movements generally accepted the idea that Islam was the original religion of their ancestors before they were brought as slaves to America; their thought was permeated by anticolonialism and antiracism that often led to strong antiwhite theories and attitudes. Christianity as a religion has been portrayed as racist, as a "white man's religion," and as an agent of colonialism. Only after the death of Elijah Muhammad, the leader of the Nation of Islam, one of the largest and most important of these movements, did the majority turn toward Sunnī Islam with its teachings of racial harmony. This part of the movement is now accepted in the larger Muslim world and has gained momentum with an active program of prosyletizing. Today Muslims of all groups, Sunnīs as well as remnants of a variety of sects of American origin, make up an important minority within the African-American community. [*See* Nation of Islam.]

The recent large-scale emigration of Muslims from their homelands to Europe and the Americas for economic and political reasons is dramatically changing the demographic distribution of Muslims in majority-Christian areas of western Europe and the United States. This emigration to the West has resulted, among other things, in the establishment of Muslim mosques, schools, and publishing houses where these did not exist previously and has led to considerable missionary activity in those areas. The more than one and a half million Turks in Germany, the several million North Africans and other Muslims in France, and the hundreds of thousands of Pakistanis, Indians, and other Muslims in Britain, are matched by the relatively recent influx of Muslim immigrants to the United States joined with converts to Islam among native-born African-Americans. It is roughly estimated that there are now between three and four million Muslims in the United States, among whom between five hundred thousand and one million are African-Americans.

Contemporary conversionary approaches in the West are generally irenic in tone, tending to stress the fulfillment of the teachings of Judaism and Christianity in the message of Muḥammad. This implies the acceptance of Muḥammad as the last of the line of prophets previously sent by God to those religions—biblical figures such as Abraham, Moses and Jesus, who are revered as prophets in Islam. It also demands recognition of the authenticity of Muḥammad's message as a divine revelation.

BIBLIOGRAPHY

Anawati, Georges C. "Factors and Effects of Arabization and Islamization in Medieval Egypt and Syria." In *Islam and Cultural Change in the Middle Ages*, edited by Speros Vryonis, Jr., pp. 17–41. Wiesbaden, 1975.

Arnold, Thomas W. *The Preaching of Islam: A History of the Propogation of the Muslim Faith*. London, 1913.

Ayalon, David. "Regarding Population Estimates in the Countries of Medieval Islam." *Journal of the Economic and Social History of the Orient* 28 (1985): 1–19.

Brett, Michael. "The Spread of Islam in Egypt and North Africa." In *Northern Africa: Islam and Modernization*, edited by Michael Brett, pp. 1–12. London, 1973.

Bulliet, Richard W. *Conversion to Islam in the Medieval Period: An Essay in Quantitative History*. Cambridge, Mass., 1979.

Dennett, Daniel C. *Conversion and the Poll Tax in Early Islam*. Cambridge, Mass., 1950.

Fattal, Antoine. *Le statut légal des non-musulmans en pays d'Islam*. Beirut, 1958.

Gervers, Michael, and Ramzi Jibran Bikhazi, eds. *Conversion and Continuity: Indigenous Christian Communities in Islamic Lands, Eighth to Eighteenth Centuries*. Toronto, 1990.

Goitein, S. D. *A Mediterranean Society: The Jewish Communities of the Arab World as Portrayed in the Documents of the Cairo Geniza*. 5 vols. Berkeley, 1967–1988.

Kister, M. J. " ʿAn yadin (Qur'an IX/29): An Attempt at Interpretation." *Arabica* 11 (1964): 272–278.

Levtzion, Nehemia, ed. *Conversion to Islam: Papers, 1972–1973*. New York, 1979.

Lewis, Bernard. *The Jews of Islam*. Princeton, 1984.

Little, Donald P. "Coptic Conversion to Islam under the Bahri Mamluks, 692–755/1293–1354." *Bulletin of the School of Oriental and African Studies* 39 (1976): 552–569.

Poliak, Abraham N. "L'arabisation de l'orient sémitique." *Revue des Études Islamiques* 12 (1938): 35–63.

Vryonis, Speros, Jr. *The Decline of Medieval Hellenism in Asia Minor and the Process of Islamization from the Eleventh through the Fifteenth Century*. Berkeley, 1971.

WILLIAM M. BRINNER

CÓRDOBA, CALIPHATE OF.

In AH 138/756 CE, after the fall of the Umayyad dynasty in Damascus, ʿAbd al-Raḥmān I ibn Muʿāwiyah, an Umayyad prince, established himself in Córdoba as ruler of the Iberian Peninsula (al-Andalus). The country thus achieved independence from the ʿAbbāsid caliphate of Baghdad, although the name of the ʿAbbāsid caliph, al-Manṣūr, continued for a time to be mentioned in the Friday prayer; when the name of the Umayyad leader was substituted, the ʿAbbāsid caliph was cursed. The Umayyad rulers in al-Andalus styled themselves as *umarā'* ("princes") until 316/929, and although a number of rebels arose in the name of the ʿAbbāsid caliphs, none presented any real threat, nor did the ʿAbbāsid themselves ever attempt to restore al-Andalus to their sovereignty.

ʿAbd al-Raḥmān III ibn Muḥammad, who had ruled as a prince for sixteen years, proclaimed himself caliph in 316/929 and took the honorific title al-Nāṣir li-dīn Allāh. Several reasons lay behind the decision of ʿAbd al-Raḥmān III to proclaim himself caliph. He struggled initially to reunite and restore peace to the country, which had been prey to various rebels during the reign of his grandfather and predecessor, ʿAbd Allāh. This task accomplished, a new danger emerged—the Fāṭimid caliphate in North Africa. When ʿAbd al-Raḥmān III adopted the title of caliph, he was also posing as defender of the Sunnī community against the Shīʿī Fāṭimids, a role that the weakened ʿAbbāsid caliphate was no longer able to fulfill. Moreover, the Umayyads considered themselves to be the rightful heirs of the caliphate, being descendants of the third "Rightly Guided" caliph, ʿUthmān ibn ʿAffān (d. 656). In his propaganda in North Africa, ʿAbd al-Raḥmān III stated his intention to recover and protect the Muslim holy places, since Mecca had been sacked by sectarian Qarmatians in 317/929.

The Córdoba caliphate, during the tenth century, witnessed the peak of the cultural and artistic flowering of al-Andalus. Following the practice of his forerunners in Syria, ʿAbd al-Raḥmān III built a magnificent palatine city near Córdoba (Madīnat al-Zahrā'), and his son al-Ḥakam II al-Mustanṣir (r. 350–366/961–976), who enlarged the Friday Mosque, was also a well-known bibliophile and patron of the sciences and arts.

The Ummayad caliphate in Córdoba did not last long, however. With the accession of al-Ḥakam's son, Hishām II al-Mu'ayyad, in 366/976, the caliph lost all real power, which now lay in the hands of the capable chamberlain al-Manṣūr ibn Abī ʿĀmir. The only mark of the authority of Hishām II was the appearance of his name on coins and textiles and in the Friday prayer. Al-Manṣūr was succeeded as chamberlain by his son al-Muẓaffar, who maintained the fiction of Hishām II as actual ruler. It was only after al-Muẓaffar's death in 398/1007 that his brother ʿAbd al-Raḥmān attempted to usurp the caliphate, forcing the caliph to appoint him his heir. Subsequent events proved fatal for the Umayyad caliphate. Hishām II fell under the control of the ʿĀmirids, following a similar political pattern in the Muslim East where the Būyids ruled under the nominal authority of the ʿAbbāsid caliph. This led to a succession of ineffectual caliphs reigning amid the political disintegration of the country. The Umayyad caliphate finally collapsed in 407/1016, and several puppet caliphs appeared throughout the tumultuous eleventh century.

[*See also* ʿAbbāsid Caliphate; Umayyad Caliphate.]

BIBLIOGRAPHY

Avila, María Luisa. "La proclamación *(bayʿa)* de Hišām II, año 976 d.C." *Al-qanṭara* 1 (1980): 79–114.

Epalza, Miguel de. "Problemas y reflexiones sobre el califato en al-Andalus." *Revista del Instituto de Estudios Islámicos de Madrid* 21 (1981–1982): 59–73.

Epalza, Miguel de. "Fonction du califat dans la communauté islamique: Cas d'al-Andalus." In *Islam communautaire*, pp. 47–66. Paris, 1984.

Fierro, María Isabel. "Sobre la adopción del título califal por ʿAbd al-Raḥmān III." *Sharq al-Andalus: Estudios Arabes* 6 (1989): 33–42.

Gabrieli, Francesco. "Omayyades d'Espagne et Abbasides." *Studia Islamica* 31 (1970): 93–100.

Turki, Abdel-Majid. "L'engagement politique et la théorie du califat d'Ibn Ḥazm." *Bulletin d'Études Orientales* 30 (1978): 221–251.

Tyan, Émile. "Le califat umayyade d'Espagne." In *Institutions du droit public musulman*, vol. 2, pp. 570–580. Paris, 1956.

MANUELA MARÍN

COSMOLOGY. In Islamic cosmology, the cosmos or the universe *(al-ʿālam)* is defined generally as "everything other than God." This definition, universally accepted in Islam, has its basis in the Qur'ān. It is emphasized repeatedly in the Qur'ān that God is "lord of all the worlds" and that to God belongs "everything in the heavens and the earth" and "what is in between." The sum total of "everything other than God," which constitutes the entire Muslim cosmos, is identified with what the Qur'ān refers to as "all the worlds" and "everything in the heavens and the earth."

The cosmos is also identified with the whole created order *(khalq)* that, according to the Qur'ān, comes into existence through the divine creative command *kun* ("Be!"). For this reason, the term *kawn*, which is etymologically related to the word *kun* and which conveys the meaning of engendered existence, is often used by Muslim cosmologists to refer to the whole cosmos. Consequently, one of the terms used to denote cosmology is *ʿilm al-kawn*, meaning literally "the science of the cosmos."

The above traditional Muslim definition of the cosmos is of great significance to contemporary Muslims as far as their encounter with modern cosmology is concerned. First, in contrast to modern cosmology, which either ignores or rejects altogether the existence and reality of God, and views the cosmos as a completely independent order of reality or even as the one and only reality, Islamic cosmology is theocentric. The idea of the cosmos in Islam is inseparable from the Qur'ānic conception of God.

The most fundamental teaching of the Qur'ān is that

God is the central reality. Although from a certain point of view the cosmos is not God, and there is a fundamental distinction between the two, the cosmos is always defined in relation to this central reality that, in fact, is its metaphysical source and origin as well as its ultimate goal. Indeed, God enters into the definition of the cosmos. And the various cosmological schemes or theories developed by the different schools of Islamic cosmology represent so many ways of looking at the relationship between God and the cosmos. The nature of this relationship is one of the most fundamental issues to have engaged the minds of Muslim cosmologists over the centuries.

Second, in contrast to Islamic cosmology, which deals with all the worlds or the whole cosmos, modern cosmology has in view only a small portion of this cosmos, namely, the physical world. Modern cosmology might have discovered a lot of new facts about the physical universe that were unknown to ancient and medieval cosmologists, and it might have extended the boundaries of that universe far beyond those they had ever known. However, judging by their qualitative contents, the dimensions of the modern cosmos, limited as it were to the physical realm, are far smaller than those of the traditional Muslim cosmos.

Islamic cosmology inquires into the nature and reality of the nonphysical worlds without neglecting the physical world. In fact, it has made important contributions to the development of natural and mathematical studies of the physical cosmos. Clearly, Islamic cosmology covers a far wider domain of rational inquiry than what we find in modern cosmology. As defined by the Brethren of Purity (Ikhwān al-Ṣafā'), a secret brotherhood of philosophers and scientists in tenth- and eleventh-century Islam, which wrote the influential *Rasā'il* (a collection of fifty-two treatises covering almost every branch of medieval philosophy and science), the cosmos is "all the spiritual and material beings who populate the immensity of the skies, who constitute the reign of multiplicity which extends to the spheres, the stars, the elements, their products and to man" (Nasr, 1978, p. 53).

Sources of Islamic Cosmology. For Muslims, the Qur'ān is the most important source of cosmological knowledge. It provides Muslims with knowledge of general cosmological principles that determine the dimensions and boundaries of the Muslim cosmos, both temporally and spatially speaking, and that also serve as a necessary background for the scientific study of that cosmos.

These cosmological principles are either explicitly stated or derived from the metaphysical teachings of the Qur'ān through their application to the cosmic domain. According to the Qur'ān itself, its verses are of two kinds, the *muḥkamāt* (clear) and the *mutashābihāt* (ambiguous). Many cosmological ideas that have been developed in Islam are derived from verses of the second kind. Cosmological meanings contained in such verses have been arrived at primarily through *ta'wīl* (symbolic or esoteric interpretation) that presupposes a deep spiritual insight and the soundness of the faculty of intellectual intuition, as distinct from the faculty of ratiocination or discursive reasoning, on the part of the interpreters, who seek to understand the inner meanings of those verses.

For example, the Qur'ānic metaphysical statement "God is the First and the Last, the Outward and the Inward" (surah 57.3) has immediate implications for the cosmos. To say that God is *al-Awwal* (the First) means that the cosmos has an origin or a beginning. And to say that he is *al-Ākhir* (the Last) means that the cosmos has an end. In other words, the world of multiplicity comes from the One God and returns to the One God. The cosmos therefore has not come into existence by chance or without any ultimate purpose.

On the contrary, it is a purposive world. This fact finds strong support in numerous Qur'ānic verses that state categorically that the whole universe is created in truth and by the truth (*bi-al-ḥaqq*) and not in vain (see, e.g., surahs 16.3 and 21.16). Muslims view the cosmos as being governed by teleological principles. A discussion of these principles has a legitimate and indeed an important place in Islamic cosmology and by extension in the particular sciences, such as the physical and the biological sciences.

If the first pair of the four Divine Names mentioned above, the First and the Last, can be said to have determined the temporal boundaries of the cosmos, then the other pair, the Outward and the Inward, determines its spatial boundaries. How this latter pair of names shapes directly the Muslims' vision of the cosmos is more difficult to see if one were to accept only a logical interpretation of the names. This is because looking at the cosmos through the two names presents two different pictures, one being the reverse of the other.

According to one traditional interpretation, to say that God is the Outward or *al-Ẓāhir* (the Manifested) means that the cosmos is contained or enclosed by God. If the cosmos is divided into its physical and nonphysical parts, then, following the same principle of outwardness, it is the physical world that is enveloped by the nonphysical parts. And to say that God is *al-Bāṭin* (the Hidden) means that the cosmos is a reality that lies outside God and that veils him. If the same relation is now considered between the different parts of the cosmos itself, then it is the physical world that lies outside the spiritual world and that hides the latter.

The two different pictures of the cosmos that result from a consideration of the Divine Names, the Outward and the Inward respectively, might be best represented geometrically by means of two concentric circles. In the first picture, in which God is viewed as the Outward, the inner circle represents the cosmos while the outer circle represents Divine Reality. In the second picture, in which God is viewed as the Inward, we have the reverse. The inner circle now represents Divine Reality whereas the outer circle represents the cosmos. By further considering the hierarchy of existence within both Divine Reality itself and the cosmos, this simple geometric representation can be enlarged to include more concentric circles, each of which represents a particular state of existence. Within this geometric scheme, Muslim cosmologists found a means of integrating elements of pre-Islamic cosmology into the Qur'ānic cosmological perspective.

Allusions to the dimensions of the cosmos are also to be found in those Qur'ānic verses that speak of the seven heavens and the seven earths, of the Divine Throne, *ʿarsh*, and the Divine Footstool, *kursī* (see surahs 20.5 and 2.255), of the cosmic mountain Qaf and of the cosmic tree. Then there are those verses which refer to such complementary pairs as light and darkness, this world and the next world, paradise and hell, the origin and the return, spirit and body, sun and moon, and day and night. All these pairs too allude to the dimensions of the Muslim cosmos. Even the term "Muslim cosmos" itself is derived directly from the Qur'ān. Everything in the cosmos, says the Qur'ān, is a Muslim because it submits willingly or unwillingly to the Will of God as manifested in the laws of the cosmos. Submission to the divine will is precisely what the word Muslim means.

The most popular of all Qur'ānic verses that deal with general cosmological principles are the Throne Verse (2.255) and the Light Verse (24.35). The Light Verse in particular has been commented on by many famous Muslim thinkers, including al-Fārābī (d. 950), Ibn Sīnā (d. 1037), the Ikhwān al-Ṣafā', al-Ghazālī (d. 1111), and Mullā Ṣadrā (d. 1641). In these commentaries are to be found some of the most important cosmological speculations by classical Muslim thinkers, which seek to harmonize pre-Islamic cosmology with cosmological data contained in the Islamic revelation.

For example, the Ikhwān al-Ṣafā' identified the heaven of the fixed stars in the Ptolemaic system of eight concentric spheres with the *kursī* mentioned in the Throne Verse. Further, they equated the *ʿarsh* of the Qur'ān (see also surah 9.129, referring to God as the Lord of the Throne, and surah 69.17, referring to eight angelic bearers of the Divine Throne) with the highest heaven, that is, the ninth and starless heaven that Muslims have added to the Ptolemaic scheme to account for diurnal motion. The Ikhwān called this heaven the *Muḥīṭ* or the outermost sphere, while many other Muslims named it *falak al-aflāk,* meaning the sphere of spheres or the supreme heaven. In their commentary on the Light Verse, the Ikhwān interpreted light *(al-nūr)* as the Universal Intellect, niche *(mishkāt)* as the Universal Soul, glass *(zujājah)* as the prime form *(al-ṣūrah al-ūlā),* a shining star *(kawkab durrī)* as individual form *(al-ṣūrah al-mujarradah),* the blessed olive tree *(shajarah mubārakah zaytūnah)* again as the Universal Soul, and light on light *(nūr ʿalā nūr)* as the light of the intellect over the light of the Soul (see Nasr, 1978, p. 77).

Another revealed datum that has influenced traditional Islamic conceptions of the cosmos refers to Laylat al-miʿrāj, the Prophet's miraculous night journey (see surahs 17.1 and 53.11–18) from the earth to the Divine Throne, an event ever fresh in the memory of every generation of Muslims until our present times, because every year it is celebrated by Muslims all over the world. About the journey itself the Qur'ān tells us very little. We are told only that the Prophet was transported from Mecca to Jerusalem, then taken to the heavens until he reached the farthest Lote tree *(sidrat al-muntahā;* surah 53.14) before being finally brought to the Divine Throne.

Detailed descriptions of the journey are given in the *ḥadīths*. Thanks to this second most important source of knowledge in Islam, we have more information not only about the journey from Mecca to Jerusalem but also about the Prophet's ascension from Jerusalem to the Divine Throne through all the heavens and about the throne itself. There is a description of every heaven through which the Prophet had passed. He was accompanied throughout the journey by the archangel Gabriel, who acted as his guide. The only exception was during the final stage of the journey from the Lote tree to the Divine Throne, when the Prophet alone was given the honor of being transported on a beautiful *rafraf* (narrow piece of silk brocade) (see account given by Jalāl al-Din al-Suyūṭī [d. 1505], translated in A. Jeffery, *Islam: Muhammad and His Religion,* Indianapolis, 1958, pp. 42–46).

The language used to describe the entire journey is largely a symbolic one. The farthest Lote tree symbolizes the outermost region of the universe, and the Prophet's passage through every heaven symbolizes his journey through all states of being in the cosmic hierarchy. The final goal of the journey is to go beyond the cosmos itself, that is, to reach the Divine Presence. Undoubtedly, the Prophet's nocturnal ascension to the Divine Throne has a great significance for Islamic cosmology. On the basis of the data given in both the Qur'ān and the *ḥadīth*s concerning that event, Muslims have been presented with a clear picture of the total dimensions of the cosmos. That event has also taught them the ultimate purpose of cosmology.

The highest goal in the study of the cosmos is to enable oneself to visualize it as a book of symbols that can be meditated on and contemplated for spiritual upliftment or as a prison from which the human soul must escape to attain true freedom. This view concerning the role of the cosmos in man's spiritual journey to God, inspired by the Prophet's *miʿrāj,* was enthusiastically shared by many members of the two main traditions of Islamic cosmology. One is the tradition that is against Greek and other foreign learnings and that relied solely on the Qur'ān and *ḥadīth*s for cosmological knowledge. Religious scholars, such as Abū Muḥammad al-Iṣfahānī (Abū' al-Shaykh, d. 979), the eleventh-century al-Khaṭīb al-Baghdādī, and Jālāl al-Dīn al-Suyūṭī (d. 1505), who can be regarded as among the leading representatives of this tradition but whose cosmological works are little known to the modern world, insisted that, in the study of the cosmos, it is more important to contemplate the cosmos as a book of divine signs than to speculate rationally about it.

The other cosmological tradition, represented mainly by philosophers of various schools and scientists, but also by a number of leading theologians and Ṣūfīs, sought to synthesize cosmological ideas taken from non-Islamic sources and the cosmological teachings of the Qur'ān and *ḥadīth*s. Among many representatives of this tradition, vast knowledge of scientific cosmology was no obstacle to acceptance of a spiritual or metaphysical cosmology in which such ideas as the symbolic interpretation of all natural phenomena, the concept of the interiorization of the cosmos, and a spiritual journey through the universe to what lies beyond it are particularly important. On the contrary, as we find in the "visionary recitals" of Ibn Sīnā (see Corbin, 1980; Nasr, 1978, chap. 15), which were no doubt inspired by the Prophet's *miʿrāj,* they had the spiritual ingenuity of transforming scientific facts drawn from many sciences of the day into cosmic symbols that were to act as guide posts for the traveler on the path of spiritual perfection in his journey through and beyond the cosmos to the Divine Presence.

As a source of cosmology the Qur'ān provides us mainly with knowledge of general principles, but it is much more comprehensive and detailed than all other sacred books of the world in its accounts of cosmogony, cosmography, the qualitative contents of the cosmos, such as the angelic realm, eschatological events, and other cosmic phenomena. However, it is generally the case that concerning all these aspects of the cosmos the Qur'ānic accounts are complemented by those given in the *ḥadīth*s in a more detailed manner. The beginning of cosmological speculation in Islam must be traced back to the commentaries and interpretations of cosmological data contained in these two main sources by the first few generations of Muslims.

There were two main traditions of Islamic cosmology. The indigenous tradition, which was strongly opposed to Greek and other foreign sciences, formulated a cosmology based almost entirely on Islamic sources, namely the Qur'ān, *ḥadīth*s, and transmitted sciences. Seyyed Hossein Nasr, a leading contemporary historian and philosopher of Islamic science, has likened the position of this indigenous cosmology within the total Islamic cosmological tradition to that of Prophetic medicine within the general body of medical knowledge stored within the house of Islam.

The other tradition, which had a far greater impact than the first on the historical and philosophical development of Islamic science, had developed a number of cosmologies that were partly inspired by ideas and theories inherited from pre-Islamic cosmological systems. The most important of these were Hermetic, Pythagorean, and Aristotelian-Ptolemaic cosmologies made available to the Muslims mainly through translations of

Greek sources, Mazdean cosmology from Persia, and certain forms of Indian cosmology. However, all the elements that had been borrowed from these non-Islamic sources were fully integrated into the more universal Qur'ānic cosmological perspective.

Historical Development of Islamic Cosmology. We can identify the historical beginning of Islamic cosmological thought with the first cosmological speculations and utterances on the subject made by some of the most distinguished companions of the Prophet, whom Ḥasan al-Baṣrī (d. 728) referred to as the *ahl al-bāṭin* (people of inwardness), meaning those possessed of an esoteric cast of mind and a sound knowledge in the science of *ta'wīl* of both the Qur'ān and *ḥadīths*, particularly the sacred *ḥadīths* (*ḥadīth qudsī*). Prominent among these companions were ʿAlī ibn Abī Ṭālib, ibn ʿAbbās, Ibn Masʿūd, and Abū Ḥurayrah.

Ibn ʿAbbās, an uncle of the Prophet, told us that he learned from the Prophet the esoteric meaning of the seven heavens and the seven earths mentioned in the Qur'ān. In his commentary on this sacred text, which continues to be widely read in traditional Muslim circles and which is popularly referred to as *tafsīr Ibn ʿAbbās*, he gave many insightful clarifications of the meanings of verses related to cosmology, and also delved into the symbolic meanings of letters of the alphabet which appear at the opening of some chapters of the Qur'ān.

To cite just a few examples, he defined the qualitative contents of the Muslim cosmos through his explanation of the meaning of the Qur'ānic term *ʿālamīn* ("all the worlds"). He explained the nature and number of angelic bearers of the Divine Throne. Then, there is his description in symbolic language of the form of the angel in charge of each of the seven heavens as well as his mention of its name. This shows that from the very beginning of Islamic cosmological thought, there has been a close relationship between cosmology and angelology. Ibn ʿAbbās is also an important early source of a detailed account of the Prophet's *miʿrāj*.

But, without doubt, it was ʿAlī, the Prophet's cousin and son-in-law, the fourth rightly guided caliph of Sunnī Islam and the first imam of Shīʿī Islam, who enjoyed the greatest respect and influence in the domain of both exoteric and esoteric sciences. In what has survived of his sermons, letters, poems, and proverbs, as preserved mainly in the *Nahj al-balāghah* (The Way of Eloquence), a late Shīʿī compilation by Sharīf al-Raḍī (d. 1015), we meet for the first time in Islam a number of technical expressions of an almost philosophical nature as well as tendencies toward an analytical intellectual discourse. Of interest to historians of Islamic cosmology is ʿAlī's reference in one of his poems to man as *al-ʿālam al-ṣaghīr* (microcosm). It was the earliest explicit mention of this important cosmological idea in Islamic sources.

Many traditional sources have also attributed to ʿAlī the origin of several distinctively Islamic arts and sciences, such as the art of *khaṭṭ* (calligraphy) and the science of numerical symbolism of the alphabets (*ʿilm al-jafr*). According to Bel-Mughus al-Maghribī, a sixteenth-century historian of alchemy, ʿAlī also inherited the alchemical art from the Prophet. In Islam, both the science of alphabetical symbolism and alchemy have always had a very close link with cosmology. The cosmological teachings of ʿAlī as inherited and further developed by both his distinguished blood and intellectual descendants must have served as important foundational elements in the early development of Islamic cosmology. His idea of the analogy between the microcosm and the macrocosm, and his use of numerical symbolism for the letters of the Arabic alphabet, found fuller and more systematic exposition in the cosmological writings of the later period, such as those of Ikhwān al-Ṣafā' and Ibn Sīnā.

Among the most distinguished of ʿAlī's early intellectual successors were Ḥasan al-Baṣrī and Jaʿfar al-Ṣādiq (d. 765). Both were Ṣūfīs, but the former, a disciple of ʿAlī who lived long enough to witness the Muslim community of the first three generations, was a Sunnī and the latter the sixth imam of Shiism, although he was revered too by many Sunnīs. From the point of view of the later development of many schools of Islamic cosmology, the alchemical and other esoteric teachings and writings associated with the intellectual circle of Imam Jaʿfar are of particular importance. Jābir ibn Ḥayyān, the greatest alchemist of Islam, also belonged to this circle.

In many alchemical writings attributed to Jābir, in which the author claims to be expounding the teachings of his master, Imān Jaʿfar, we find many cosmological schemes which betray a strong influence of Hermetic, Pythagorean, Aristotelian, and Neoplatonic cosmologies. The Jābirian cosmology is a remarkable synthesis of cosmological and scientific ideas drawn from diverse sources. There is a place in it for the Neoplatonic theory of emanation of the world and depiction of the cosmos as a hierarchy of concentric spheres; a place for the Pythagorean concept of cosmic harmony arising from the qualitative or symbolic properties of numbers; a place for the magic square or the Ming Tang taken from Chinese science thanks to the numerical symbolism inherent in it; and there is a place for Hermetic science of alchemical and astrological symbolisms based on the maxim, "that which is lowest symbolizes that which is highest," in which the sulphur-mercury principle is of fundamental importance. However, the alchemical perspective predominates.

The central idea in Jābirean cosmology which connects the different elements together in a coherent way is the cosmological concept of the balance. The balance is the cosmic principle by means of which the correct proportion of elements is reached. It refers to the harmony of the various tendencies of the Universal Soul that determines and orders the qualities of cosmic existence. In Jābir's cosmological scheme, which he presented as a hierarchy of concentric circles, the Universal Soul exists below the intellect, further above which is the First Cause (God). Below the Universal Soul is the world of substance, which is the principle of the physical cosmos.

Jābirean cosmology exerted a great influence on the cosmological thought of Ikhwān al-Ṣafā' and on Ismāʿīlī and Ṣūfī cosmologies, especially that of Ibn al-ʿArabī (d. 1240). But during the period that separates Jābir from Ikhwān al-Ṣafā' and the flowering of Fāṭimid Ismāʿīlī thought, there emerged another school of Islamic cosmology that was more rational and scientific in its intellectual outlook. This is the Peripatetic school of philosopher-scientists founded by al-Kindī (d. c.873), further developed by al-Fārābī, which reached its greatest height with Ibn Sīnā. Muslim Peripatetic cosmology is based on a synthesis between Aristotelian philosophy as interpreted mainly by the Neoplatonists and the cosmological teachings of Islam.

Al-Kindī argued for a closed and finite cosmos. He also believed in the doctrine of *creatio ex-nihilo*. In contrast, both al-Fārābī and Ibn Sīnā maintained the theory of emanation to explain the existence of the world of multiplicity from the One. The picture of the cosmos associated with this school was the one largely used in Islam by its astronomers. Prior to and parallel to the development of Peripatetic cosmological thought we can refer to the various schools of *kalām* (dialectical theology), especially the Ashʿarīs, who possess what we might call an atomistic cosmology.

Al-Ghazālī, the most well known of the Ashʿarī theologians, criticized severely Peripatetic thought. This criticism helped to pave the way for the emergence of the Illuminationist school of philosophy of Suhrawardī and the mystical philosophy of Ibn al-ʿArabī. Each of these schools developed its own cosmology as well. Ibn al-ʿArabī's cosmology, which constitutes a grand synthesis of all the cosmological ideas that have been developed earlier and those produced by his own creative genius, became the dominant cosmology in many parts of the Islamic world until today. In Iran, Mullā Ṣadrā, while being greatly influenced by Ibn al-ʿArabī's cosmology, attempted to create his own synthesis. Mullā Ṣadrā's contemporaries in the Malay world, such as Ḥamzah Fansūrī and Nūr al-Dīn al-Rānīrī, were busy interpreting and writing Ibn al-ʿArabī's thought in Malay. The cosmological writings of these Malay thinkers continue to be read and discussed.

Many Muslim intellectuals, including scientists, are now interested to know what past Muslim cosmologists have written on the subject of cosmology. Their encounter with modern cosmology has forced them to reexamine Islamic cosmological heritage in a more favorable light.

[*See also* Philosophy; Theology.]

BIBLIOGRAPHY

Bakar, Osman. *Tawhid and Science*. Penang and Kuala Lumpur, 1991. Chapter 5 deals with the atomistic cosmology of the Ashʿarīs.

Chittick, William. *The Sufi Path of Knowledge*. Albany, N.Y., 1989. This book provides a wealth of information on Ṣūfī cosmology as interpreted by Ibn al-ʿArabī.

Corbin, Henry. *Avicenna and the Visionary Recital*. Translated by Willard R. Trask. Irving, Texas, 1980. Contains Ibn Sīnā's three short treatises on symbolic cosmology in which he gives an important place to angels. The most comprehensive work in a Western language on Ibn Sīnā's angelology.

Fakhry, Majid. *A History of Islamic Philosophy*. New York and London, 1983. Although it is a general introductory work on Islamic philosophy, it makes many references to the cosmological ideas of leading Muslim thinkers.

Haq, Syed Nomanul. *Names, Natures, and Things: The Alchemist Jābir ibn Ḥayyān and his Kitāb al-Ahjar (Book of Stones)*. Boston, 1994. A good discussion of some of the principles of Jābirean cosmology.

Heinen, A. M. *Islamic Cosmology: A Study of as-Suyūṭī's al-Hay'a as-sanīyah fi'l-hay'a as-sunnīya*. Beirut and Weisbaden, 1982. A very useful work on the cosmology of religious scholars that is based totally on traditional Islamic sources.

Naguib al-Attas, Syed Muhammad. *The Mysticism of Hamzah Fansuri*. Kuala Lumpur, 1970. It contains a good discussion of the metaphysical cosmology of Fansūrī, the first Malay thinker to write on the subject in the Malay language.

Nasr, Seyyed Hossein. *Islamic Science: An Illustrated Study*. London, 1976. Chapter III provides a good summary of Islamic cosmology and cosmography and clarifies their significance for Islamic science.

Nasr, Seyyed Hossein. *An Introduction to Islamic Cosmological Doctrines*. Boulder, 1978. The first comprehensive work on the subject. Although it was written more than three decades ago, it is still the best work on Islamic cosmology.

Nasr, Seyyed Hossein. "The Cosmos and the Natural Order." In *Islamic Spirituality: Foundations*, edited by Seyyed Hossein Nasr, pp. 345–357. World Spirituality: An Encyclopedic History of the Religious Quest, vol. 19. New York, 1987. An excellent summary of the views of different schools of Islamic cosmology.

Schuon, F. *Dimensions of Islam*. Translated by P. Townsend. London, 1970. Chapter 11 is an excellent discussion of the dimensions of the Muslim cosmos based on revealed data in the Qur'ān and on the teachings of the *ḥadīth*s.

OSMAN BAKAR

CREEDS. *See* ʿAqīdah.

CRIMEA KHANATE. Comprising most of the Crimean peninsula and some of the Desht-i Kipchak (the steppeland north of the peninsula and the Black Sea), the Khanate of Crimea was established in the middle of the fifteenth century by Muslim Tatars and Turks. Muslims had been present in the region from the early thirteenth century, and Muslim institutions including mosques and schools had been built by 1315. Anatolian Turks settled in the peninsula under Seljuk encouragement, and Tatars from the Golden Horde occupied a number of areas that subsequently would become part of the khanate.

The Crimean region played an important role as intermediary between the Tatars of the Golden Horde, the Mamlūk Sultanate in Egypt, the Seljuk state in Anatolia, and the Christian kingdoms of the north (Lithuania, Poland, and Moscow) during the two centuries predating the establishment of the khanate. Religious architecture serves as a good indicator of external Islamic interest in Crimea: the Egyptian Mamlūk Sultan Baybars funded the building of a mosque in the region's first Tatar governmental center, Solhat (Eski Krim), in 1287; a second mosque was built there by the Golden Horde ruler Ozbek Khan in 1314, and the latter building survives today.

The khanate was largely the product of the Giray Tatar clan, especially its fifteenth- and sixteenth-century khans Hadji, Mengli, Sahib, and Selim; it would remain under Giray domination until its collapse in 1774. Although never completely sovereign and independent of the Ottoman sultans, the khanate's political and social institutions developed in their own ways, blending Tatar and steppe traditions with Ottoman bureaucratic and dynastic practices. The former were characterized by decentralized authority, while the Ottoman system was highly centralized.

Tatar institutions included the *kurultay* (the gathering of all clan leaders), whose responsibility included the selection of the khan from among Giray candidates; and the *kalgay* and *nurredin* sultans (first and second "heirs apparent," also expected to be members of the Giray clan). In addition, each of the major clans maintained administrative responsibilities for lands "belonging" to them *(beylik)*; each had a "capital" town where the clan leader *(bey)* resided and in which the *bey*'s own officials administered financial and political affairs. These *bey*s, particularly the *bey* of the Shirin clan, retained much local authority, and their support was essential to the success of Giray policies.

The central government of the khanate consisted of a set of bureaucratic and fiscal offices staffed by servitors *(kapikulu)* of the Girays, a governing council *(divan)*, and judicial offices headed by a chief judge *(kadiasker)* and regional judges (*kadi*s; Ar., *qāḍī*). Law in the khanate combined elements of Tatar customary law (deriving from the Great Yasa of Chinggis Khan) and Ottoman *kanun* law—the former defining social relationships, and the latter establishing fiscal responsibilities.

A third administrative system, outside both central and clan institutions and led by the *muftī* and various Islamic officials, was responsible for the large number of *waqf* lands in the khanate. Finally, dating from 1475 the southern coast of the peninsula was under direct Ottoman control, with local officials appointed from Istanbul. Many of the large towns of the Crimea were situated in this area, which was called the Eyalet-i Kefe.

Crimean economics were based largely on trade: in slaves "harvested" by Tatar forces from the Slavic settlements north of the peninsula, in foodstuffs produced in the fertile lands along the coast and in inland valleys, in fine finished goods produced by Tatar artisans (jewelry, metal, and leatherwork primarily), and in subsidies received from the Ottomans in Istanbul in return for participation in military campaigns. Crimean society was generally prosperous and as a result fairly well developed. Particularly in the Ottoman sector, but also in the peninsular heartland, Jewish and Christian communities played important economic roles (ironically, it was after the Russian conquest that these minorities were removed and replaced by Russian and Ukrainian peasants).

The three major urban areas under the control of the khanate's administration were Gozleve (later Evpatoria), Akmechet (Simferopol), and Bahchesaray. In the last city the Girays maintained their palace, and it was there that most government offices were located. These towns supported an active cultural life reflected in a sophisticated historiographic tradition; the most important chronicles include the *Tevarih desht-i kipchak* and the *Asseb' os-seiiar,* the latter composed by Seïid Muhammed Riza in the mid-eighteenth century. From the early sixteenth century onward an important *medresse (madrasah),* the Zinjirli in Solhat, offered education and training in scholarship that would produce generations of scholars who played important roles in Islamic culture in the khanate and outside. This *medresse* would provide the leadership to Russia's Muslims in the late nineteenth century in their efforts at modernization.

As the result of Russian expansion and development in the eighteenth century and of Crimean and Ottoman decline, the khanate was invaded twice and ultimately collapsed before Russian armies between 1768 and 1774. After a short "experiment" managed by Tsarina Catherine II, the entire peninsula with all its Tatar inhabitants was annexed to the Russian Empire and became the Tavricheskii Oblast'. Refugees from the khanate's ruling classes settled in Istanbul and other Ottoman towns in Bulgaria and Romania; most were ultimately assimilated into the Turkish population.

BIBLIOGRAPHY

Allworth, Edward, ed. *Tatars of the Crimea.* Durham, N.C., 1988.

Bennigsen, Alexandre, et al. *Le Khanat de Crimée dans les Archives du Musée du Palais de Topkapı.* The Hague, 1978.

Fisher, Alan W. *The Russian Annexation of the Crimea, 1772–1783.* Cambridge, 1970.

Fisher, Alan W. *Crimean Tatars.* Stanford, Calif., 1978.

Gökbilgin, Özalp. *1532–1577 yılları arasında Kırım hanlığı'nın siyasî durumu.* Ankara, 1973.

Inalcık, Halil. "Girāy." In *Encyclopaedia of Islam,* new ed., vol. 2, pp. 1112–1114. Leiden, 1960–.

Inalcık, Halil. "Ḳırım." In *Encyclopaedia of Islam,* new ed., vol. 5, pp. 136–143. Leiden, 1960–.

Kellner-Heinkele, Barbara. *Aus den Aufzeichnungen des Sa'id Giray Sulṭān.* Freiburg im Breisgau, 1975.

Lemercier-Quelquejay, Chantal, et al., eds. *Passé turco-tatar, présent soviétique.* Paris, 1986.

Matuz, Josef. *Krimtatarische Urkunden im Reichsarchiv zu Kopenhagen.* Freiburg im Breisgau, 1976.

Muzaffer Ürekli. *Kırım hanlığının kuruluşu ve Osmanlı himâyesinde yükselişi, 1441–1569.* Ankara, 1989.

ALAN FISHER

CRIMINAL LAW. The body of law dealing with wrongs that are punishable by the state with the object of deterrence is known as criminal law. Islamic criminal law recognizes three categories of these wrongs. The first is the *ḥudūd* (plural of *ḥadd* or "limit" set by God), the contravention of which leads to a prescribed and mandatory penalty. The second, *taʿzīr,* comprises those crimes not included among the *ḥudūd* because their punishment is discretionary. The term *taʿzīr* means chastisement and intends the correction or rehabilitation of the culprit; hence, punishment is left to the judge and might vary depending upon who inflicts it and upon whom it is inflicted. The third category, *qiṣāṣ* (retribution), is concerned with crimes against the person such as homicide, infliction of wounds, and battery. Punishment by retribution is set by law, but the victim or his next of kin may waive such retribution by accepting blood money or financial compensation *(diyah)* or by foregoing the right altogether. Because of this waiver, it has been suggested that this crime is in the nature of a private injury, more akin to a tort than to a crime involving a public interest or concern.

Jurists have accorded *ḥudūd* much attention because they are grounded in the Qur'ān and the *ḥadīth,* as is *qiṣāṣ*. *Taʿzīr,* however, because of its discretionary nature, has escaped precise definitions and detailed treatments of the elements of the crimes that it encompasses. It might be said, though, that all acts that violate private or community interests of a public nature are subject to *taʿzīr;* it was left to public authorities to establish rules, within the spirit of the *sharīʿah,* to punish such acts.

Taʿzīr comprised essentially two categories of crimes. The first consisted of either those crimes that did not "measure up" to the strict requirements of *ḥudūd* crimes (although they were of the same nature) or those individual crimes that were not of the sort grouped under *ḥudūd*. Examples of the former are thefts among relatives or thefts of things below a minimum value for a *ḥadd* punishment: attempted robbery, attempted fornication, and lesbian contacts. Examples of the latter type are breach of trust by a testamentary guardian, false testimony, and usury. The second category included those acts that generally caused damage to the public order or public interest or threatened to cause such damage. In the nature of things, the second category, if not kept in check, could result in precautionary measures that might compromise individual rights; therefore, a balance had to be maintained between public order and individual rights. Punishment for *taʿzīr* could range from the exceptional death penalty for espionage and heresy, to flagellation, imprisonment, local banishment, and fines for a variety of crimes. Jurists were careful, though, to limit the flagellation punishment to a level below that of *ḥudūd* punishments.

Qiṣāṣ (talion) encompassed five crimes: murder or intentional killing, quasi-intentional killing or voluntary manslaughter (when a person intends only to beat another but in doing so kills him), involuntary killing, intentional physical injury, and unintentional physical injury. Talion was allowed only in instances of intentional killing and intentional physical injury; even here retribution could be waived by the victim or his family, and monetary compensation *(diyah)* could be exacted instead. In the rest of the *qiṣāṣ* crimes only monetary compensation was exacted. The *diyah* for killing was set by most jurists at one hundred camels or one thousand gold dinars; the *diyah* for physical injuries varied according to the nature of the injury. The law of *qiṣāṣ* was an exception to the principle of individual responsibility for crimes emphasized by Islamic law, because it made the perpetrator's clan *(ʿāqilah)* responsible with him for payment of the *diyah;* correspondingly, the clan of the victim divided up the *diyah* payable for his death in keeping with the legal maxim that liability is proportional to the benefit. In later years when Arabs settled in military camps outside Arabia *(amṣār)*, the *ʿāqilah* became the military unit *(dīwān)* to which the killer or the victim belonged.

In theory all these offenses were to be tried by the *qāḍī*, the representative of the *sharīʿah.* Law books throughout the centuries repeated this theoretical jurisdiction of the *qāḍī*, including the administration of criminal law. But in fact the *qāḍī* must have lost criminal jurisdiction very early in the Islamic centuries. The reasons are several: first, the *sharīʿah* dealt with only a limited number of crimes and their penalties, leaving a host of others ill-defined and lumped under *taʿzīr;* second, the law of evidence in the *sharīʿah,* with its dependence only on trustworthy witnesses *(ʿudūl)* and admissions, and its rejection of circumstantial evidence, was too restrictive to allow for an efficient criminal system; finally, rulers of Islamic empires and states could not leave matters of crime affecting state security in the hands of religious authorities loyal to a body of laws over which they had no control. All these factors gave rise to criminal jurisdictions independent of that of the *qāḍī*, although the latter continued to be involved in matters concerned with homicide and *diyah,* which assumed the character of a tort or a civil claim. As a result the *shurṭah,* (police) assumed the duty of investigating, prosecuting, and sentencing of most crimes with no distinction between one function and the other. The *muḥtasib* (inspector of the marketplace) punished those trade infractions and offenses against morals that were apparent and did not require testimony before a *qāḍī*'s court. In addition, beginning in the early years of the ʿAbbāsid regime in the latter part of the eighth century, a new jurisdiction, called *maẓālim* (Court of grievances) headed by the ruler, vizier, or governor, undertook to repress wrongdoers whom other courts could not control and generally to restrain oppression by officials. All these jurisdictions were not limited by the *sharīʿah,* as the *qāḍī* was. In the main they applied customary law *(ʿurf)* or what political expediency *(siyāsah)* required; often punishments were arbitrary and severe.

The Ottoman sultans who inherited this system attempted to restrain the arbitrary nature of punishments meted out by these extra-*sharīʿah* jurisdictions by issuing regulations *(qānūn)* for secular criminal provisions and procedures. Yet a *qānūnnāme,* or basic law, issued in 1525 for Egypt, a few years after its conquest, seems to indicate that the purpose was to give leeway to non-*sharīʿah* judges to inflict heavy punishments for disputes and feuds that *qāḍīs* could not suppress.

Ottoman Legal Codes. The oldest Ottoman code of criminal and fiscal law is the one attributed to Mehmed II following his conquest of Constantinople in 1453, although some parts of it might have been the product of a later time under Bayezid II (r. 1481–1512), who is credited with a *qānūn* of his own. Of the many *qānūns* compiled in the reign of Sultan Süleyman the Lawgiver *(qānūnī)*, one was a criminal code compiled possibly between 1539 and 1541. It contained all the sections of the earlier criminal codes and a number of other provisions, and it was arranged according to offenses, not according to penalties of fines and strokes. Among the new provisions were those dealing with sodomy, pressing and selling of wine, false testimony, forging of documents, taking of interest, and neglect of prayer or fasting during Ramaḍān (Heyd, 1973, p. 30). The code was sent for enforcement to the *qāḍī* courts of the various districts where all official documents were deposited. The last Ottoman criminal code before the modern era was compiled in the seventeenth century, but it seems to have been privately collected from the previous codes; therefore, it lacked official character.

Although in theory a *qānūn* was valid for only the lifetime of the sultan who issued it, most *qānūns* were reconfirmed under succeeding sultans; *qānūns* issued by previous Muslim rulers whose territories were added to the Ottoman Empire in the sixteenth century were reconfirmed for the provinces until the imperial *qānūn* was finally applied. These *qānūn*s, which contained penal provisions based on *ʿurf* (customary penalties), are exemplified by the penal code of the Dhū al-Qadr Turkomans issued by Süleyman (r. 1520–1566).

Following the previous practice of limiting the jurisdiction of the *qāḍī* in criminal matters, the seventeenth-century code stipulates that the *qāḍī*s "are to carry out the laws of the *sharīʿah* . . . but are ordered to refer matters relating to the order of the realm, the protection and defense of the subjects, and the capital or severe corporal punishment to the representatives of the Sultan, who are the governors in charge of military and serious penal affairs" (Heyd, 1973, p. 209). The issuing of extra-*sharīʿah qānūn*s in the Islamic world was not the exclusive domain of the Ottoman sultans. In addition to the case of Dhū al-Qadr, the Mamlūk dynasty had imposed fines in certain districts in Anatolia for wounds and head injuries, which the Ottomans later confirmed. In the extreme west of the Muslim world, in Morocco, a code paid lip service to the *sharīʿah*. In 1512, a certain Yaḥyā ibn Taʿfūfah, the captain of the Moors in Ṣāfī under Don Manoel of Portugal, set a code for the tribe of Ibn al-Ḥārith that imposed fines for adultery and theft if the *sharīʿah* penalties were not imposed. And in the extreme east, the last great Mughal emperor Aurangzīb ʿĀlamgīr (r. 1658–1707) issued in 1672 a *firmān* (edict) instructing the *qāḍī*s to impose *ḥadd* punishments and the secular authorities to carry out *siyāsah* punishments.

In the Ottoman Empire, the Tanzimat legal reform, following the Hatt-ı Şerif (3 November 1839) and the creation of the Council of Judicial Ordinances, began with the promulgation in May 1840 of a penal code *(ceza kanunnamesi)*. It reiterated the equality of all Ottoman subjects pronounced by the Hatt-ı Şerif and made a conscious effort to put an end to the arbitrary nature of the authority of government agents and corruption. A new code, called *kanun-u cedid* and promulgated in 1851, did not improve matters significantly, and foreigners, in particular, were dissatisfied with the criminal system. During the discussions over the Treaty of Paris following the Crimean War, Grand Vizier ʿAli Pasha asked for the discontinuation of the capitulations, which gave foreign powers extraterritorial rights in the empire, but he was told no consideration would be given to that until Turkish penal and commercial laws were reformed. Therefore, on 9 August 1858 a new criminal code, based on the 1810 French Code, was adopted, marking the empire's first clear rupture with traditional law. It paid lip service to the *sharīʿah* by stating that it was not in opposition to it, and that it merely specified the degrees of *taʿzīr* enunciated by it. It also continued the right given victims or their representatives to sue in *sharīʿah* courts for retribution or for *diyah*. The code was to be administered by a hierarchy of secular *(niẓāmīyah)* courts using laws of procedure adopted from French models. With minor modifications it remained the criminal code of the empire until the beginning of the republic, and the other successor states of the Middle East used it until much later, under the title *Qānūn al-jazāʾ al-ʿUthmānī*.

Modern Legal Codes. In the Turkish republic, Mustafa Kemal Atatürk and his legal advisers, in their attempt to rejuvenate the legal system, looked to Europe for legal models. In civil matters they adopted the Swiss Civil Code, and in criminal matters they followed the Italian Criminal Code of 1889, which in turn had been based on a German model. This new criminal code, introduced in 1926, made clear the new republic's intention to separate religion from politics; Article 163 stipulated that political associations on the basis of religion or religious sentiments could not be formed. (But the years after World War II saw a religious revival whose effect on the orientation of Turkey is still uncertain.) The German code was used for matters of criminal procedure. A conference on the reception of foreign law in Turkey, particularly the Civil Code, concluded that "the foreign legal system . . . may not command universal obedience, but is not unworkable."

A parallel development in legal reform took place in Egypt. Following the Ottoman charter *(firmān)* of 1841, which accorded Muḥammad ʿAlī and his descendents hereditary rights to the governorship of Egypt and gave Egypt virtual autonomy in matters of legislation, rapid steps were taken toward legal reform, particularly after the creation of the Mixed Courts in 1876 to protect "foreign" interests. Long before that, Muḥammad ʿAlī, upon assuming power in 1805, hastened to discard the Ottoman system of administration and to institute in its place his own arrangements. Laws and regulations multiplied and had to be unified in a new code entitled *al-Muntakhabāt* (Selections), which was published in 1829–1830. In the same period, a law entitled *Qānūn al-fallāḥ* (or *al-filāḥah;* the Peasants' Law) was issued to protect the interests of peasants and the state; punishments were specified for such matters as usurpation of land, changing boundaries, thefts of produce, as well as for persons not heeding conscription calls, wrongdoers who breached canals, and notables in the countryside who seduced virgins. The Ottoman Penal Code of 1851 was also applied, after the accession of Saʿīd Pasha in 1854, in a version adapted to Egyptian circumstances, but, crimes and punishments still were not well defined, people were not equal before the law, and criminal responsibility was not limited to the individual perpetrator.

Genuine criminal reform started with the Mixed Courts, but since those courts had limited criminal jurisdiction, substantial reform acquired a momentum only with the establishment of the National Courts and the adoption of the National Penal Code and the Code of Criminal Inquiry in 1883. These codes were adapted from the French codes either directly or by way of the Mixed codes. In 1904 the Criminal Code was amended extensively with elements taken from the Sudanese, Indian, Belgian, and Italian codes. Finally, following the abolition of the foreign capitulations in 1937 and the extension of Egyptian criminal jurisdiction to all residents of Egypt, a new criminal code was promulgated and it remains in force.

The Sudan had been under native sultanates, not Ottoman power, from the sixteenth century until the Anglo-Egyptian condominium. Under British guidance, a penal code, based on the Indian Penal Code of 1860, was introduced for the first time in 1899. In 1925 this code was thoroughly revised into a new code, but the bases of the earlier one remained intact. It differs from the codes of the major Arab countries in that it is based on Anglo-Saxon law, especially in its definitions and examples.

Except for Saudi Arabia and North Yemen, which continued to use traditional Islamic law in penal matters, the following Arab and Islamic countries acquired modern penal codes as set forth in the list below. Each country is followed by the date of its latest code, then by the code from which it was adapted, and finally by the previous legislation in that country.

Algeria: 18 June 1966; French Code; French Code
Iran: 1939; French Code; Code of 1912 and traditional Islamic law
Iraq: 15 September 1969; Proposed Egyptian Code of 1966 and previous legislation; 1918 Baghdad Code and Ottoman Penal Code
Jordan: Law No. 16, 1960; Lebanese Code; Code of 1951 and Ottoman Penal Code
Kuwait: Law No. 16, 1960 as amended by No. 31, 1970; Bahrain Code based on Indian Penal Code of 1860
Lebanon: 1943 enforced 1944; French, Swiss and Italian Codes; Ottoman Penal Code
Libya: 28 November 1953; Italian and Egyptian Codes; Italian Code
Morocco: 26 November 1962; French Code; French and Traditional Islamic
Pakistan: Indian Penal code of 1860; English Law; Traditional Islamic and Tribal Law
Palestine: 1936 Ordinance; Cyprus Code, 1928; Ottoman Penal Code
Syria: 1949 as amended in 1953; Lebanese Code; Ottoman Penal Code

Certain principles well-known in the West characterize the penal codes in these countries. One such principle is the legality principle: there can be no crime or punishment except by law (*nullum crimen nulla poena sine lege*). Another is the nonretroactivity of laws. A third is the principle of territoriality of jurisdiction, with some variations, applied in situations in which only some elements of the crime took place on the territory of the state. A fourth is the principle that certain crimes committed abroad by citizens or noncitizens and affecting vital interests of the state can be tried by the state. A fifth is the principle that the state can try a citizen for a felony or misdemeanor committed abroad if the act is also a crime in the country where it was committed.

The last two decades have witnessed a strong movement to reapply the Islamic law of *ḥadd* and *qiṣāṣ* as a result of an Islamic resurgence. Libya amended its penal code in 1973 so as to introduce the penalties of lapidation for fornication and cutting of the hand for theft; if the stringent proofs required by Islamic law were not met, the provisions of the Penal Code would apply. Similar steps were taken in Pakistan and the Sudan (1983). In Iran, following the revolution of 1978–1979, the Islamic law of *ḥadd* was reintroduced by the Qiṣāṣ Law of 1982; severe punishments are being applied.

[*See also* Capitulations; Ḥudūd; Law, *articles on* Legal Thought and Jurisprudence *and* Modern Legal Reform; Tanzimat.]

BIBLIOGRAPHY

Amin, S. H. *Middle East Legal Systems*. Glasgow, 1985. Survey of legal systems in the Middle East, excluding North African countries. Although a useful book, it should be used with care.

Anderson, J.N.D. "Homicide in Islamic Law." *Bulletin of the School of Oriental and African Studies* 13.4 (1951): 811–828.

Baroody, George M. *Crime and Punishment under Hanbali Law.* Beirut, 1961. Translation with a commentary from *Manār al-sabīl* of Ibrāhīm ibn Muḥammad ibn Salīm ibn Dūyān.

Bassiouni, M. Cherif, ed. *The Islamic Criminal System.* London, 1982. Collection of chapters of varying quality on Islamic criminal law. The best available source on the subject, although a few chapters are apologetic in tone.

Cornelius, A. R. *Law and Judiciary in Pakistan.* Edited by S. M. Haider. Lahore, 1981.

Forte, David F. "Lost, Strayed, or Stolen: Chattle Recovery in Islamic Law." In *Islamic Law and Jurisprudence: Studies in Honor of Farhat J. Ziadeh,* edited by Nicholas Heer, pp. 97–115. Seattle, 1990.

Heyd, Uriel. *Studies in Old Ottoman Criminal Law.* Oxford, 1973. Excellent source for Ottoman criminal law and administration of criminal justice.

Hill, Enid. *Mahkama! Studies in the Egyptian Legal System.* London, 1979. On-the-scene observations of Egypt's legal system.

Liebesny, Herbert J. *The Law of the Near and Middle East.* Albany, N.Y., 1975. Very useful collection of readings, cases, and materials.

Lipstein, Kurt. "Conclusions" to "The Reception of Foreign Law in Turkey." *International Social Science Bulletin* (UNESCO) 9 (1957): 73.

Maḥmaṣānī, Ṣubḥī. *Al-awḍāʿ al-tashrīʿīyah fī al-duwal al-ʿArabīyah.* Beirut, 1957. The first serious survey of legal systems in Arab countries.

Maydani, Riyad. " ʿUqūbāt: Penal Law." In *Law in the Middle East,* edited by Majid Khadduri and Herbert J. Liebesny, pp. 223–235. Washington, D.C., 1955.

Muṣṭafā, Maḥmūd M. *Uṣūl qānūn al-ʿuqūbāt fī al-duwal al-ʿArabīyah.* Cairo, 1970. Comparative approach to criminal law in Arab countries.

Starr, June. *Law as Metaphor: From Islamic Courts to the Palace of Justice.* Albany, N.Y., 1992. Survey of legal developments in Turkey from Ottoman to modern times, and a legal-anthropological study of an area in western Anatolia.

Tyan, Émile. *Histoire de l'organisation judiciare en pays d'Islam.* 2 vols. Paris, 1938–1943.

Ziadeh, Farhat J. " *ʿUrf* and Law in Islam." In *The World of Islam: Studies in Honour of Philip K. Hitti,* edited by James Kritzeck and R. Bayly Winder, pp. 60–67. London, 1959.

Ziadeh, Farhat J. *Lawyers, the Rule of Law, and Liberalism in Modern Egypt.* Stanford, Calif., 1968.

FARHAT J. ZIADEH

CUMHURİYET HALK PARTİSİ. A major political organisation in Turkey for sixty years the Cumhuriyet Halk Partisi (Republican People's Party or CHP) was founded some weeks before the proclamation of the Republic (11 September 1923). After the military coup of 1980, its activities were stopped together with those of other political parties by the junta; it was formally terminated on 16 October 1982 by decision of the National Security Council.

The CHP held dictatorial single-party rule until 1946 and continued in power under a multiparty system until 1950, when it lost in the free general elections. Following the military intervention of 1960, the CHP led several coalition governments (three during 1961–1965 and one in 1974) and again became the major partner in a coalition during 1978–1979. The present SHP (Social Democratic People's Party) and DSP (Democratic Leftist Party) are to some extent heirs to the CHP legacy. Upon the granting of permission to reopen previously banned political parties in 1992, a new CHP was established; however, it is just another pretender to the heritage, rather than being the original resurrected.

The CHP was in many ways a continuation of the Union and Progress (Young Turk) Party that ruled from the last decade of the Ottoman Empire until the defeat in World War I. It had originally grown out of the Defense of Rights Association for Anatolia and Rumelia (DRAAR), created at the Sivas Congress in autumn 1919 against the Greek invasion. Its ideology was that of Ottoman patriotism and Islamism rather than Turkish nationalism. It aimed at preserving the offices of the caliphate and the sultanate, securing the integrity of the Ottoman motherland, and safeguarding national independence. In the absence of a widespread national consciousness, it rallied the people through religion. Indeed, according to the statutes of the association, all Muslim citizens were considered to be its "natural" members.

The DRAAR was transformed into the Grand National Assembly (GNA) early in the war, and a First Group was formed in the assembly to secure party discipline. After the military victory, Mustafa Kemal Pasha Atatürk, the leader of the nationalist struggle, who was both commander-in-chief and the president of the GNA as well as the head of the First Group, reorganized the latter into a political party, utilizing the slogan "Popular Sovereignity"; he called this the People's Party.

The CHP was initially only a parliamentary party, but it soon began to expand into the provinces, purging any potential opponents. (Yet it did not open branches in the eastern provinces with their Kurdish majority until the 1940s.) The party unconditionally obeyed Atatürk's charismatic authority and assimilated his modernization program, which rested on a positivistic worldview and pursued strategies resembling those of enlightened despotisms of eighteenth-century Europe. The abolition of the caliphate in 1924 gave rise to a Kurdish rebellion in the east and initiated virtual one-man rule by Atatürk with the adoption of a Maintenance of Order Act.

Republicanism, populism, nationalism and laicism became the main principles of the CHP in 1927. Four years later two more principles, statism and reformism, were added. Various sociopolitical reforms were carried out under them, ranging from changes in headgear and dress to the adoption of Western laws and the Latin alphabet—all moves in the direction of secularism.

The identification of the party with the state occurred in 1936–1937. The minister of internal affairs became the general secretary of the party, and governors the provincial heads of local CHP organizations. The monopolistic state apparatus could not tolerate the existence of a distinct party structure apart from itself.

Under İsmet İnönü, the second president of the Republic and the CHP, the party underwent an important change. It became a "democratic" opposition party after losing in the freely held general elections of 1950. Thereafter it polled around a third of the votes cast in each election. Beginning in the mid-1960s it became further radicalized and adopted a left-of-center course. The general secretary of the party, Bülent Ecevit, who severely opposed the military coup of 12 March 1971, toppled İsmet İnönü and controlled the party in an extraordinary convention in 1972, advocating a democratic leftist platform. The metamorphosis had already softened the party's previous strict laicism, making concessions to the religious demands of the people. Indeed, in 1974 it even formed a coalition government with the fundamentalist National Salvation Party.

During its last years, CHP suffered difficulties in both preserving the Kemalist legacy and transforming the party along social democratic lines. This dilemma continues to affect its successor parties, whose platforms are only augmented by the addition of an economic liberalism in place of the traditional statism.

[*See also* Kemalism; Turkey; *and the biography of* *Atatürk*.]

BIBLIOGRAPHY

A satisfactory account of the Cumhuriyet Halk Partisi does not yet exist. Among general treatments, Bernard Lewis's *Emergence of Modern Turkey*, 2d ed. (London and New York, 1968), is still unsurpassed. Ezel Kural Shaw and Stanford J. Shaw's *History of the Ottoman Empire and Modern Turkey*, vol. 2, *Reform, Revolution, and Republic: The Rise of Modern Turkey, 1808–1975* (Cambridge and New York, 1977), covers the period, but contains factual and interpretational defects. For the transformation of the political system in the latter half of the 1940s, see Kemal Karpat's *Turkey's Politics: Transition to a Multi-Party System* (Princeton, 1959). In Turkish, my *T.C.'nde Tek-Parti Yönetiminin Kurulması 1923–1931* (Ankara, 1981) deals with the formative years. Hikmet Bila's *CHP Tarihi 1919–1979* (Ankara, 1979), written from a partisan viewpoint, is comprehensive but rather superficial. Two other general works in English that have recently appeared are Feroz Ahmad's *The Making of Modern Turkey* (New York, 1993); and Erik J. Zürcher's *Turkey, A Modern History* (London, 1993).

Other political parties have been better studied in English. As they provide many insights into the history of Cumhuriyet Halk Partisi as well, the following may be consulted: Erik J. Zürcher, *Political Opposition in the Early Turkish Republic: The Progressive Republican Party, 1924–25* (Leiden, 1991); Walter Weiker, *Political Tutelage and Democracy in Turkey: The Free Party and Its Aftermath* (Leiden, 1973); and Daniel Lerner, *The Passing of Traditional Society: Modernizing the Middle East* (Glencoe, Ill., 1958), which includes an overoptimistic evaluation of the Demokrat Parti.

METE TUNÇAY

CUSTOMS. *See* Adat; ʿUrf.

D

DĀʿIYAH. *See* Tablīgh.

DAKWAH. *See* Daʿwah; Malaysia.

DANCE. There is no specific theory of the aesthetic of dance in Islamic civilization; for example, the formalized Indic treatise on dance presented by Bharatanatyasastera has no counterpart in Islamic culture. There has never been any tradition of "Islamic dance" or "Muslim dance" per se. The dance cultures of Islamic peoples are, however, recognizable artistic manifestations, through stylized and disguised in abstractions, of the Islamic tenet of *tawḥīd,* unity of God, humanity, and all existence. Dance as an artform in Islamic culture worldwide adheres to notions of the oneness, peerlessness, and utter transcendence of God. The Islamic ideal of beauty rejects the representation of living forms—either animal or human—and is instead stylized and depersonalized to negate any impression of naturalism. Nonindividuation of content and the repetition of form generate the essence of transcendence in Islamic art.

Tawḥīd is revealed through the geometry and rhythm manifested in arabesque motifs. Thus dance in Islamic culture has tended to comprise a series of design units that are individually pleasing and satisfying. These self-contained parts are harmoniously arranged to form a larger design that is equally satisfying and exuberant in form. The structural characteristic of stylized dance gestures and the symmetrical repetition of dance motifs within a prescribed spatial plan invoke the elaboration of a never-ending arabesque pattern.

Arabesque in Islamic visual art is of two types: the conjunct (*muttaṣil,* "to connect") and the disjunct (*munfaṣil,* "to divide in sections"). A conjunct arabesque resembles a continuum of abstract motifs that are combined in an infinitely circular series. The disjunct or *munfaṣil* comprises a combination of motives in a series of self-contained units, each complete in itself. The absence of iconic forms, the overall arabesque-like floor pattern, the symmetrical repetition of movements in indeterminate succession, and the foliation of dance patterns within self-contained units of dance motifs are among the many elements of the artistic expression of *tawḥīd.*

Dances of Muslim peoples include traditional styles evolved from solo improvisational repertoires, such as the *raqṣ al-baladī* or "dance of the people" (the traditional form of women's solo dance) and the *raqṣ al-sharqī* or "dance of the east"; dances of specific gender groups performed in circular or linear chain formations, such as the *raqṣ al-hawānim* or "dance of the women"; martial or combative dance genres, like the combat dance of Egypt or the *silat* dance of the Malay Archipelago; and the mystical dances of Ṣūfī brotherhoods, such as the *dhikr* sessions of the dervishes of the Mawlawī (Tk., Mevlevî) order.

The solo dances (and to some extent the group dances) feature improvisational creativity: dance steps or even spatial plans are invented by combining and truncating dance motifs and sequences for the pleasure of individual or communal self-expression. Female solo dances are performed only in the home among women as a social pastime. In such intimate social occasions, the audience become spontaneous performers when the *zagharīt,* an ululation or cry of encouragement, is echoed by the spectators; this may also urge participants to prolong the dance. Male solo performance can be performed for a mixed audience who are segregated by gender. Males solo dancers perform energetic movements marked by high skips and stamping that sometimes lead to exhaustion.

Gender-specific group dances are performed by Muslims in the form of chain dances, cluster dances, and linear seated dances. In some of these dances performers hold one another's hands or waists, while some are performed separately in unison. Rhythmical stamping of feet and clapping of hands by rows of dancers who sing repetitive refrains, often repeated to the same melody, characterize gender-specific group dances. Physical contact between male and female dancers is almost nonexistent. In the chain dances, performers advance and retreat from one section of the dance floor in unison to a specific tune or rhythm. Participants are allowed to join or leave the ensemble when a new tune or refrain is introduced. Improvisation in group dances is allowed within the context of the genre being performed; individual performers may deviate a little from the repetitive dance motifs to execute an outburst of improvised solo dance movements before returning to the conventional movements of the group dance. Voluntary and spontaneous substitution of performers may alter or lengthen group dances.

The seated linear dances of the Muslims of Southeast Asia emphasize nonindividuation of content but generate the essence of symmetrical repetition by creating arabesque formations through interlocking hands, bowing heads, and turning torsos. Each performer mirrors another in alternate movements. Only movements of the upper torso and extension of the arms are allowed while the dancers sit crosslegged in a single line. These movements emphasize the harmonious arrangement of self-contained dance motifs, which is equally satisfying when combined as a series of interlocking patterns.

The combat dances of Egypt, Indonesia, and Malaysia emphasize improvisational qualities based on a loose configuration of dance motifs. Movements in each dance motif are meant to attract the attention of the "opponent" by displaying a series of skillful maneuvers, either bare-handed or with weapons such as swords, daggers, spears, or sticks. Acrobatic skills play a significant role in heightening the tension between the "attacker" and the "defender." The combat dances may be performed as solo dances, paired dances, or group dances.

The mystical dances of the Mawlawī order grew out of the *ṭarīqah* (Ṣūfī order) of Mawlānā Jalāl al-Dīn Rūmī. The dance of the "whirling dervishes" arose out of the Ṣūfī practices of *samāᶜ* and *dhikr*, as an expression of joy in achieving of the state of perceiving the mysteries of God. The Mawlawīs are initiated through a covenant of allegiance to the *shaykh* or leader of the society. The *shaykh* leads the initiates in the dance, regulating the tempo and the length of the performance, which consists of *dhikr* sessions involving vocal and instrumental performers, reciters, and dancers.

[*See also* Aesthetic Theory; Mawlawīyah; Tawḥīd.]

BIBLIOGRAPHY

Buonaventura, Wendy. *Serpent of the Nile: Women and Dance in the Arab World*. London, 1989.

Faruqi, Lois Ibsen al-. "Dances of the Muslim Peoples." *Dance Scope* 11.1 (1976): 43–51.

Faruqi, Lois Ibsen al-. "Dance as an Expression of Islamic Culture." *Dance Research Journal* 10.2 (1978): 6–13.

Faruqi, Lois Ibsen al-. *Islam and Art*. Islamabad, 1985.

Friedlander, Ira. *The Whirling Dervishes*. New York, 1975.

Mohd Anis Md Nor. *Randai Dance of Minangkabau Sumatra*. Kuala Lumpur, 1986.

Mohd Anis Md Nor. *Żapin: Folk Dance of the Malay World*. Singapore and New York, 1993.

Nasr, Seyyed Hossein. *Islamic Art and Spirituality*. Ipswich, Suffolk, 1987.

MOHD ANIS MD NOR

DAN FODIO, USUMAN (c. 1754–1817), Nigerian religious leader and reformer. Shaykh ᶜUthmān ibn Muḥammad ibn ᶜUthmān ibn Ṣāliḥ, known to the Hausas as Shehu Usuman Dan Fodio, was born into a family of Muslim Fulani clerics in the Haɓe (Hausa) kingdom of Gobir in present-day northern Nigeria. The family had abandoned the nomadic way of life several generations earlier and was dedicated to the teaching of Sunnī, Mālikī Islam. By the end of the eighteenth century Shehu Usuman Dan Fodio had inspired the Muslim Fulani to begin the *jihād al-qawl* ("preaching jihād") addressed to the Haɓe aristocracy of Gobir and its neighbors. This aristocracy, nominally Muslim, was in the Fulani view polytheistic, given to "mixed Islam," maintaining animist practices while at the same time adopting elements of Islam. Such mixed Islam was common in the aftermath of the collapse of the medieval Islamic empires of the Sahel.

The preaching *jihād*, which extended over several years, demanded the political and cultural surrender of this faintly Muslim, largely animist establishment to the strictly orthodox practice of Sunnī, Mālikī Islam. This the Haɓe refused. In an escalating climate of tension, hostilities broke out between the Muslim Fulani and the Haɓe in 1804. Shehu Usuman, adopting certain precedents from the struggle of the Prophet Muḥammad against the polytheists of Mecca, solemnly elevated this conflict to the status of a "holy war of the sword" that must necessarily follow the "preaching *jihād*" when the latter fails to be effective.

The campaign was conducted not by the Shehu himself, a scholarly and somewhat reclusive mystic, but by his brother Shaykh ʿAbd Allāh ibn Muḥammad, equally scholarly but a hardheaded legalist who proved himself a brilliant field commander. He was unenthusiastic about the Ṣūfī mysticism espoused by his brother Shehu Usuman and more inclined to the strict construction of the *sharīʿah*.

The *jihād* was successful. The "Sokoto caliphate," a centralist Islamic polity to which provincial jihadist emirs owed allegiance, took the place of the hodgepodge of Haɓe principalities that had preceded it. While the Islamic *sharīʿah* cannot be said to have been imposed on this polity with total conformity—much pagan practice did survive—its writ was nevertheless substantial. By the time the British occupied Nigeria early in the twentieth century, there was no doubt that what they took over was a Muslim society governed by *sharīʿah* law.

The *jihād* had two other immediate consequences. First, it transformed Islam from a tolerated minority religion into the official religion of the state. Second, it elevated the Islamic scholars from their previous position as mere advisers of polytheistic rulers who engaged in mixed Islam to a place as the sole custodians of political power and the arbiters of social behavior. The *jihād* also altered the trade patterns of Hausaland by destroying the old centers of trade and setting up new ones.

The significance of the *jihād* for present-day Islam in Nigeria rests more with Shaykh ʿAbd Allāh ibn Muḥammad than with his mystically inclined brother Usuman, who initially inspired the *jihād*. The latter was a Qādirī Ṣūfī given to visions and other liminal experiences greatly revered in his day. With the rise of modern Islamic fundamentalism, while he still enjoys reverence, he has been largely superseded. His brother ʿAbd Allāh, the down-to-earth legalist, whose platform was not mysticism but strict adherence to the letter of the *sharīʿah*, has become the admired exemplar for the present generation of Islamic radicals in northern Nigeria.

[*See also* Nigeria; Sokoto Caliphate.]

BIBLIOGRAPHY

Hiskett, Mervyn. *The Sword of Truth: The Life and Times of the Shehu Usuman Dan Fodio*. London, 1973. The most complete biographical discussion that is readily available.

Martin, B. G. *Muslim Brotherhoods in Nineteenth-Century Africa*. Cambridge, 1976. Helpful introduction in the context of African Muslim movements.

Sulaiman, Ibraheem. *A Revolution in History: The Jihad of Usman Dan Fodio*. London, 1986. Important Muslim interpretation by a prominent Nigerian Islamist scholar.

MERVYN HISKETT

DĀR AL-ḤARB. The concept of *dār al-ḥarb*, or realm of war, comes from the dualistic worldview of the classical Islamic legal tradition. This term denotes the territories bordering the *dār al-Islām* whose leaders are called upon, under threat of invasion, to convert to the Muslim religion. Jurists trace the concept of *dār al-ḥarb* back to the time of the Prophet and cite the messages sent by Islam's founder to the emperors of Persia, Abyssinia, and Byzantium, and to other leaders, summoning them to choose between conversion and war.

Dār al-ḥarb is thus an enemy territory outside the jurisdiction of Islamic law that must be converted to Islamic territory. The inhabitants of *dār al-ḥarb* (*ḥarbī*s or *ahl al-ḥarb*) are defined as those who have refused to convert after being enjoined to do so. This conversion can be effected by means of conquest if the leaders do not submit, but the use of force may be avoided when there is submission. From the moment the leaders of *dār al-ḥarb* accept Islam, this territory is considered as fully part of *dār al-Islām*. Conversely, an Islamic territory taken by infidels becomes *dār al-ḥarb* when the law of the non-Muslims replaces Islamic law. According to certain jurists, the intermediary regions that separate *dār al-Islām* from *dār al-ḥarb*, although they really belong to neither, must be viewed by Muslims as the territory of war, given the security threat these regions pose to the community of the faithful.

The fact that the Islamic worldview includes a space considered to be a place of confrontation and war should not, however, lead to the conclusion that Islamic international law is fundamentally violent and warlike. War is rather an evil that is inevitable given the necessity to repulse aggression, to avoid division of the community, or to contribute to the triumph of divine justice on earth. Thus defensive or offensive *jihād*, which formed the basis for the concept of *dār al-ḥarb*, is practiced according to precise norms and rules that the faithful must in theory respect. These rules provide for distinctions between combatants and noncombatants, the humane treatment of prisoners, food blockades, and indiscriminate use of arms.

The notion of *dār al-ḥarb*, like many other classical concepts of Muslim law, has been affected by historical changes. With the fragmentation of the Muslim world into a multitude of states and the progressive decline of their power, *dār al-ḥarb* has been divested of its significance. Moreover, the inclusion of Muslim countries in the modern international juridical order implies the renunciation of such a concept. However, Islamic international law is seen to be of divine origin and therefore immutable and timeless, so it will never be totally obsolete.

[*See also* Dār al-Islām; Dār al-Ṣulḥ; Jihād.]

BIBLIOGRAPHY

Abel, A. "Dār al-Ḥarb." In *Encyclopaedia of Islam*, new ed., vol. 2, p. 129. Leiden, 1960–.

Māwardī, Abū al-Ḥasan ʿAlī ibn Muḥammad al-. *Les statuts gouvernementaux, ou, Règles de droit public et administratif*. Translated by Edmond Fagnan. Beirut, 1982.

Parvin, Manoucher, and Maurice Sommer. "Dar Al-Islam: The Evolution of Muslim Territoriality and Its Implication for Conflict Resolution in the Middle East." *International Journal of Middle East Studies* 12 (1980): 1–21.

Proctor, J. Harris, ed. *Islam and International Relations*. London, 1965.

MOHAMMAD-REZA DJALILI

Translated from French by Elizabeth Keller

DĀR AL-ISLĀM. An essential part of the doctrine of *jihād* is the division of the world into the "territory of Islam" *(dār al-Islām)* and the "territory of war" *(dār al-ḥarb)*. The Shāfiʿīs have added a third category, the "territory of truce [or treaty] *(dār al-ṣulḥ* or *dār al-ʿahd)*, for enemy territory with whose inhabitants a Muslim government has concluded a truce imposing a tribute on them. The decisive factor for ascertaining whether a region belongs to the *dār al-Islām* is Muslim sovereignty and the application of the *sharīʿah*. If these do not exist in a region occupied by unbelievers, it is to be considered *dār ḥarb*. According to the Ḥanafīs, however, there are further conditions. *Dār al-Islām* becomes *dār al-ḥarb* after conquest by unbelievers, if the laws of the unbelievers are enforced, if the conquered territory is adjacent to *dār al-ḥarb*, and if the lives and goods of Muslims and *dhimmī*s (non-Muslim protected peoples) are not safe. This means that according to the Ḥanafī rules, an Islamic region that has been conquered by unbelievers can remain *dār Islām* as long as the conquerors appoint an Islamic *qāḍī* (judge) to administer Islamic law and as long as Muslims and *dhimmī*s are as secure as they were under Muslim rule.

During the colonial period, debates about the status of a colonized country took place in India. The Indian Sunnī Muslims were chiefly Ḥanafīs, and Ḥanafī theory leaves more room for interpretation than do the other *madhhab*s (schools of law). Before the 1857 Mutiny, the situation in India was somewhat complicated, as there was still a Mughal emperor; however, his rule was only nominal, and actual power was in the hands of the British. In 1803, a *fatwā* had been given by a famous Ḥanafī *ʿālim* to the effect that the northern part of India between Delhi and Calcutta, which was firmly in the hands of the British, was *dār ḥarb* (An English translation of the *fatwā* appears in M. Mujeeb's *The Indian Muslims,* London, 1967, pp. 390–391). Moreover, the Ṭarīqa-yi Muḥammadī and the Farā'iḍī Movement, two religiously motivated groups active during the first half of the nineteenth century, held the same view. This changed during the second half of the nineteenth century. Because the British regarded the Mutiny as the exclusive work of the Muslims, who allegedly wanted to expel the British and restore Muslim rule, they favored the Hindus in the army and in government employment. The Muslim upper and middle classes wanted to safeguard their opportunities for employment by showing that they could be loyal subjects of the British colonial government.

Crucial in this respect was an irenic reinterpretation of the *jihād* doctrine, and in its wake the question of whether India was *dār Islām* or *dār ḥarb*. Interestingly, there appeared to be no linkage between the latter question and the question of whether *jihād* against the British was obligatory. Around 1870 two *fatwā*s were published, both stating that *jihād* against the British was unlawful; however, one proceeded from the assumption that India was *dār ḥarb* and the other from the assumption that it was *dār Islām* (W. W. Hunter, *The Indian Musalmans,* Lahore, 1974, pp. 102–103, 186–187).

In Algeria, by contrast, there was no disagreement about the status of the region: according to Mālikī law, there was no doubt that after the French occupation it had become *dār al-ḥarb*. If any discussion occurred, it revolved around *hijrah,* the obligation to emigrate from occupied territory to *dār al-Islām*.

[*See also* Dār al-Ḥarb; Dār al-Ṣulḥ; Jihād.]

BIBLIOGRAPHY

Khadduri, Majid. *War and Peace in the Law of Islam*. Baltimore, 1955.

Krüger, Hilmar. *Fetwa and Siyar: Zur internationalrechtlichen Gutachtenpraxis der osmanischen Şeyh ül-Islâm vom 17. bis 19. Jahrhundert unter besonderer Berücksichtigung des "Behcet ül-Fetâvâ."* Wiesbaden, 1978.

Kruse, Hans. *Islamische Völkerrechtslehre*. 2d ed. Bochum, 1979.

Peters, Rudolph. "Dār al-Harb, Dār al-Islām und der Kolonialismus." In *XIX. Deutscher Orientalistentag vom 28. September bis 4.*

Oktober 1975 in Freiburg im Breisgau, edited by Wolfgang Voigt, pp. 579–587. Wiesbaden, 1977.

Peters, Rudolph. *Islam and Colonialism: The Doctrine of Jihad in Modern History.* The Hague, 1979.

RUDOLPH PETERS

DĀR AL-ṢULḤ. According to the Shāfiʿī school of law there exists, apart from the territory of Islam *(dār al-Islām)* and the territory of war *(dār al-ḥarb),* a third category called territory of treaty *(dār al-ṣulḥ,* also called *dār al-ʿahd* or *dār al-muwādaʿah).* This is territory whose inhabitants have concluded an armistice with a Muslim government on the condition that they retain the possession of their lands and pay in exchange a certain amount of money or goods to be levied on the land. The other *madhhabs* (schools of law) hold that this kind of territory is either *dār Islām* or *dār ḥarb,* depending on whether sovereignty belongs to the Muslims or not. However, within the Ḥanafī *madhhab,* Muḥammad al-Shaybānī (d. 804) also accepted the existence of territory of truce *(dār al-muwādaʿah)* as a separate category. On the strength of this view, the Ottoman Empire used the concept in its foreign policy. Countries with whom the sultan had concluded a truce were called territories of truce. They could not be attacked, and their inhabitants could not be enslaved or killed. In some modern writings that present the *jihād* doctrine as Muslim international law, *dār al-ṣulḥ* is equated with the territory of friendly nations.

[*See also* Dār al-Ḥarb; Dār al-Islām; Jihād.]

BIBLIOGRAPHY

Krüger, Hilmar. *Fetwa und Siyar: Zur internationalrechtlichen Gutachtenpraxis der osmanischen Şeyh ül-Islâm vom 17. bis 19. Jahrhundert unter besonderer Berücksichtigung des "Behcet ül-Fetâvâ."* Wiesbaden, 1978.

Peters, Rudolph. *Islam and Colonialism: The Doctrine of Jihad in Modern History.* The Hague, 1979.

RUDOLPH PETERS

DAR UL ARQAM. A voluntary, nongovernmental, grass-roots Islamic *daʿwah* movement, Dar ul Arqam was founded in Malaysia in 1968 by Sheikh Imam Ashaari Muhammad At-Tamimi. Its fundamental aim is to revive Islamic religious belief and values and to practice them in a comprehensive way in everyday life. Its first adherents were ten low-income people in Kuala Lumpur whom Sheikh Ashaari guided in the essentials of the Qur'ān and other basics of duty and doctrine. He sought to inculcate in them an awareness of the need to review and reform their individual identities in the context of their inherited religious and cultural values. The emphasis on self-assessment, self-correction, and the formation of an Islamic personality was the essential foundation of the movement.

During its first two years Dar ul Arqam kept a low profile. Its activities took the form of a study group housed at its first center in Datok Keramat, Kuala Lumpur. It was here that the movement was named Dar ul Arqam, in memory of the Prophet's companion, Arqam ibn Abī Arqam, who volunteered his house in Makkah (Mecca) as the early Muslims' first meetingplace.

Dar ul Arqam began to bring its mission to a wider public in its third year, 1970. Shaykh Ashaari's initial propagation was through public Islamic lectures held in private homes as well as in mosques, schools, offices, and universities. These were subsequently augmented by publication of books, magazines, and newspapers, production of audiovisual materials such as video and cassette tapes, exhibitions of the Islamic way of life and the new world of Islam as envisaged by the movement, and the staging of Islamic concerts and cultural shows. The Dar ul Arqam Centre was moved in 1973 to its pioneering Islamic village in Sungei Pencala, 20 kilometers outside Kuala Lumpur.

In 1979 Dar ul Arqam's activities expanded to the international arena through its *daʿwah* missionaries sent overseas. In 1988 Sheikh Ashaari himself undertook intensive missionary programs and diplomatic contacts outside Malaysia. Consequently Dar ul Arqam branches were opened, with largely indigenous membership, in Singapore, Indonesia, Thailand, the Philippines, Brunei, Britain, France, Germany, the United States, Australia, New Zealand, Pakistan, Jordan, Egypt, Uzbekistan, and China. Its membership rose from 70 in 1976 to 6,000 in 1987 and 10,000 in 1993.

This geographical and numerical expansion is due largely to Dar ul Arqam's attempt to present Islam in a harmonious, practical, and exemplary way. It has established forty-eight self-contained Islamic villages all over Malaysia to exhibit the viability of an Islamic sociopolitical and economic system. It has set up 257 schools in Malaysia and eleven abroad with a total enrollment in 1994 of 9,541 students and 696 teachers. It has published four newspapers and fifteen monthly magazines with a total circulation of 928,000 copies per month.

For its publications Dar ul Arqam operates its own computer center and desktop publishing system. The movement also owns recording studios for its electronic media. By 1993 the studios had produced 450 audiocassettes and 500 videocassettes including documentaries, religious talks, *farḍ ʿayn* classes, interviews, general and special *tarbīyah* sessions, dialogues, children's programs, Islamic concerts, and Islamic songs. Dar ul Arqam also runs an advertising agency, a company that provides predictive maintenance services, and a company that provides consultancy services, management courses, and workshops in the area of high technology. It operates an Islamic Medical Centre in Kuala Lumpur, three clinics in regional centers, and small clinics in almost every Dar ul Arqam village, including two specializing in dental treatment.

In Sungei Serai, Hulu Langat, Selangor, Dar ul Arqam in 1991 turned its Islamic village into an Islamic arts training center, the School of Islamic Culture and Arts (MAKSI). The movement is well known for its public presentations of Islamic culture, poetry, and music.

Dar ul Arqam also operates a twenty-acre agricultural complex in Batu Hampar, Perak, where the Al Arqam Centre of Agricultural Training is also situated. It cultivates agricultural land in almost all of its villages, growing a variety of food crops, and it also operates fish farms, poultry farms, and flower nurseries.

In the field of economic development, Dar ul Arqam has produced forty-five brands of foodstuffs, cosmetics, toiletries, and drinking water and owns 417 businesses of various kinds. Abroad, Dar ul Arqam runs businesses and farms in Uzbekistan, Indonesia, China, and Singapore. In August 1993, at Dar ul Arqam's First International Economic Conference held in Chiangmai, Thailand, Sheikh Ashaari declared the establishment of the Al-Arqam Group of Companies. Indicating the movement's more serious involvement in market economy, the group comprises twenty-two sections devoted to a wide range of activities.

Dar ul Arqam's achievements are accomplished independent of external assistance. They are attributable both to the commitment of its members and to an organizational structure resembling that of a nation. The highest leadership is provided by Sheikh Ashaari as the Sheikhul-Arqam or Emir. The founder-leader is supported by a ministerial structure of vice-emirs and their deputies, supplemented by the movement's regional government equivalent to state and local levels. There are also twenty-three Amirs-without-State. Incorporated in this structure are thirteen ministers with the title Amir Shukbah, responsible for sections controlling guidance and education, information, economics and trade, welfare services, Islamic propagation and international relations, agriculture, treasury, health, law, human development, lands and mines, science and technology, and culture and tourism. The "national" officers constitute the Majlis Syuyukh (Ahlul Halli wal Aqdi), which formulates and ensures the execution of the movement's policies. The Majlis is administered by a secretary who is also the deputy chief secretary of the movement.

Dar ul Arqam has exerted noticeable influence on religious, social, and political life of Muslims, particularly in Malaysia and other ASEAN countries. It has offered an exemplary, practical realization of Islam, reflecting the workability of an Islamic system in today's world. It also demonstrates the role of Sufism, in particular Aurad Muhammadiah embraced by the movement, in realizing Islamic teachings through the mobilization of the masses from below.

This has not been done without adverse response from Malaysian Islamic religious authorities. At least three different campaigns have been launched against Dar ul Arqam. Initially the movement was accused of Islamic extremism and of calling Muslims backward to the "age of the camel," isolating its members in its village in Sungei Pencala and ignoring this world for the sake of the hereafter. The movement was then condemned as deviant for practicing the Ṣūfī *tariqat* of the Aurad Muhammadiah. At this stage, the publishing permits of Dar ul Arqam's newspapers and magazines were revoked; some books of Sheikh Ashaari and all Dar ul Arqam's noneconomic activities were banned; the negative image of the movement was heightened through the media, Friday sermons, and other means; and the founder-leader himself was threatened with arrest under the Internal Security Act. At the peak of opposition to the movement, Ashaari left Malaysia in 1988 to spread his movement abroad and he remains an expatriate.

Of late, the movement has been accused of desiring to topple the present Malaysian government and of being "more dangerous than the communists." These allegations relate intimately with the government's fear of Arqam's political potential: its self-reliance and ability to mobilize the masses, the unshaken obedience of its followers to the leadership, and its growing influence among the mainstream political elites in the country. Although some believed that Dar ul Arqam could not be banned legally because, as basically a religious study group, it is not bound by the Malaysian Society Act to register with the Registrar of Societies, the gvernment's National Fatwa Council outlawed the group in August 1994 because it posed "a danger to public order."

Membership in Dar ul Arqam reflects its Ṣūfī origins. Members need not fill out a form nor pay a fee. As long as one upholds the rules of Islam, participates in Dar ul Arqam programs, and sacrifices for the sake of the religion, one automatically becomes a "family member of Abuya" ("father," a title of Sheikh Ashaari), a member of Dar ul Arqam. Members are united by their spiritual practice of the *tariqat* Aurad Muhammadiyah, founded in Mecca by al-Sayyid Muḥammad ibn Abdullāh Al-Suhaymī, a Muslim scholar of Indonesian origin. Sheikh Aṣhaari was initiated into the *tariqat* by his uncle, Lebai Ibrahim, at the age of sixteen and currently serves as the head of the *tariqat*. Dar ul Arqam from the outset has thus been a Ṣūfī movement. The Ṣūfī teacher-disciple bond reinforces obedience to the leadership with systematic spiritual and material practice.

The charisma of Sheikh Ashaari is also important in attracting members of the movement and a factor for unity. Born in 1938 to a religious family in Kampong Pilin, Rembau, Negeri Sembilan, he attended local primary and regional Islamic schools. While still a student, he was appointed as a government Islamic religious teacher, a career he pursued from 1956 to 1976. From 1958 to 1968 he was an active member of the opposition Pan-Malaysian Islamic Party (PAS), holding various leadership responsibilities. He also served for five years on the Information Committee of the Jamiatul Dakwah Islamiah movement, and held the post of Dakwah Chief of the Federal Territory branch of the Malaysian League of Muslim Youth (ABIM). Today Sheikh Ashaari has no personal wealth despite the economic successes of his movement.

The objective of Dar ul Arqam's struggle is to uphold the five basic tenets of the *sharīʿah:* the obligatory *(wajib)*, the commendable *(sunat)*, the permissible *(harus)*, the forbidden *(haram)*, and the detestable *(makruh)*. These must be observed at every level from self to world in both human-God relations *(hablum-minallah)* and interpersonal relations *(hablum-minannas)*. The ultimate aim is to please God; the means of doing so are the reconstruction of one's worldview and the practical realization of authentic values. If this is achieved, one is considered to have complied with the objective of living, to worship God in all activities. Sheikh Ashaari gives five guidelines for making one's activities worship of God: first, the intention behind the affairs is for the sake of God alone; second, the aim of the activities complies with the *sharīʿah;* third, their execution is also within the *sharīʿah;* fourth, their consequences are positive from the Islamic viewpoint; and fifth, the basic tenets of Islam as expressed in the *hablum-minallah* are not neglected.

Dar ul Arqam tries to accomplish this objective through *daʿwah,* first from below at the individual and grass-roots level, and then at the top. Sheikh Ashaari adheres to two main principles: first, *"Change ourselves, then preach to others,"* and second, *"Win people's hearts, not parliamentary seats."* The former reflects Dar ul Arqam's self-correction and self-realization, and the later its grass-roots approach. Sheikh Ashaari himself is convinced that Islam will rise again through *daʿwah* and education, not political activity. He believes a second golden age of Islam will begin in the Far East, in the Malay world.

[*See also* ABIM; Daʿwah, *article on* Modern Practice; Malaysia.]

BIBLIOGRAPHY

25 Years of Darul Arqam: The Struggle of Abuya Syeikh Imam Ashaari Muhammad At-Tamimi. Kuala Lumpur, 1993.

Ashaari Muhammad, Hj. *Huraian Ke Arah Membangun Negara dan Masyarakat Islam*. Kuala Lumpur, 1981.

Ashaari Muhammad, Hj. *Matlamat Perjuangan Menurut Islam*. Kuala Lumpur, 1984.

Ashaari Muhamad, Hj. *Aurad Muhammadiah Pegangan Darul Arqam: Sekaligus Menjawab Tuduhan*. Kuala Lumpur, 1986.

Ashaari Muhammad, Hj. *Inilah Pandanganku*. Kuala Lumpur, 1988.

Ashaari Muhammad, Hj., trans. *Abdul Khaleq Jaafar (This is Our Way)*. Kuala Lumpur, 1989.

Ashaari Muhammad, Hj. *Inilah Sikap Kita*. Kuala Lumpur, 1990.

Muhammad Syukri Salleh. *An Islamic Approach to Rural Development: The Arqam Way*. London, 1992.

MUHAMMAD SYUKRI SALLEH

DARUL ISLAM. Popularly called DI, Darul Islam is the name given to the Islamic insurgent movement in West Java, Indonesia, that challenged the legitimacy and authority of the newly independent Republic of Indonesia between 1948 and 1962. Led by Sukarmadji Maridjan Kartosuwiryo (1905–1962), the Darul Islam's military forces, officially known as the Indonesian Islamic Army (Tentera Islam Indonesia or TII) from its bases in West Java's Sunda highlands sought to give effect to the proclamation (7 August 1949) of the Islamic State of Indonesia (Negara Islam Indonesia) with the charismatic Kartosuwiryo as its head (imam). Acting in loose alliance with armed Islamic dissidents in Aceh led by Daud Beureu'eh and in South Sulawesi led by Kahar Muzakkar, the Darul Islam movement initially enjoyed great support among the villagers and rural Muslim leaders (*kiai* and *ʿulamāʾ*) of West Java. That support fell away, however, as its national resistance to Dutch colonialism in the 1950s became opposition to the independent Indonesian state, and as its military actions turned into wasting rural terrorism. Its lasting legacy was to define for a generation of Indonesian political leaders the need to limit ideologically Islamic opposition to secular nationalism and the pluralist state, and to awaken military leaders to the security problems created by Islamic extremism.

Kartosurwiryo, expelled from medical school in 1927 because of his radical nationalism, became politically active in close association with H. O. S. Tjokroaminoto, the leader of Sarekat Islam (Islamic League). Kartosuwiryo became imbued with Tjokroaminoto's conviction that a truly independent Indonesian state had to be based on Islamic principles. In 1930 Sarekat Islam became a political party, the PSII (Partai Sarekat Islam Indonesia), but was soon replaced as the mainstream of nationalism by the Indonesian Nationalist Party (PNI), whose ideological umbrella covered a broader Indonesian population [*see* Sarekat Islam]. Kartosurwiryo and his followers were dissatisfied with the 1945 compromise on the eve of the declaration of independence, even though most Muslim politicians in the established Nahdatul Ulama and Masjumi parties felt that this settled relations between Islam and the state. This was the "Jakarta Charter" (Piagem Jakarta) by which the orthodox Muslim leadership submitted to a religiously plural state for the sake of national unity in return for the understanding that Muslims would be obligated to follow Islamic law. This was a minimalist Islamic claim on the political system, but one which was never constitutionally incorporated or enacted as law. For Kartosuwiryo and others who by 1945 were operating on the radical fringes of establishment Islamic politics, this was a betrayal. Their unhappiness was sharpened by growing concerns about the influence of the political left in the nationalist ranks. Kartosuwiryo's alternative vision for Indonesia and his demand for a full Islamic state were elaborated in his 1946 ideological tract *Haluan Politik Islam* (A Guide to Islamic Politics). He wrote that only through the creation of the Darul Islam could the well-being and safety of Indonesian Muslims be assured and salvation in the eternal world attained.

Although his own theological credentials and even his knowledge of Arabic have been called into question, Kartosuwiryo founded an Islamic school called the Suffah Institute at Malangbolang, near Garut in West Java. The Suffah Institute was an interesting mix of the tradition of the *pesantren*, the traditional Islamic school, and political indoctrination. In addition to inculcating students with a mystically tinged militant Islam, the Suffah Institute also became a center for military training from which the Hizbullah and Sabilillah armed organizations recruited. Although ideologically distant from the Republic of Indonesia, the Muslim military forces in West Java cooperated with the Indonesian National Army (TNI) in the campaigns against the Dutch. The final political break with the Republic came after the 1948 Renville Agreement, which ceded West Java to occupying Dutch forces during a cease-fire and then to what was considered the Dutch puppet Pasunda state in the shortlived federal Indonesian state. In accordance with the Renville Agreement, the TNI's Siliwangi Division withdrew to Central Java, an act viewed by Kartosuwiryo's forces as betrayal and abandonment. Kartosuwiryo mobilized his supporters under the banner of the Islamic Indonesian State in pursuit of a *jihād* to liberate the land from the Dutch. When the Dutch broke the Renville Agreement in December 1948, the TNI's Siliwangi Division marched back into West Java, where on 25 January 1949 they encountered elements of the TII, and a fire-fight ensued. The ideological and political differences between Kartosurwiryo and the Republic's leaders were now irrevocably translated into an internal war.

At the outbreak of hostilities the DI's military strength was about four thousand men; its political agents operated down to the village level through traditional channels of communication. Large areas of West Java surrounding Bandung, its largest city, paid allegiance to the DI. Although Kartosuwiryo was moved by the ideal of an Islamic state that could be brought into existence in the political chaos of national revolution, more complex motivations stirred many of his followers. The Darul Islam revolt had some of the characteristics of a peasant revolt as well as those of a search for meaning when traditional social structures had broken down. Whatever the cause, however, Kartosuwiryo's Darul Islam forces were no match for the political pressure of the government, which played upon the increasing hardships of life for villagers in DI territory; nor could the DI withstand the military force that the government could bring to bear against it once a military solution was deemed necessary. In the end, the DI was reduced to generalized terrorism, extortion, and rural banditry, becoming not a model of Islamic politics but an armed plague upon the countryside. It lost its appeal to the *kiai* and *ʿulamā'*, who turned to the government for protection. Kartosurwiryo was captured on 2 June 1962. This was followed by the surrender of most of his remaining followers. He was tried for armed revolt by a closed military tribunal in August, and executed by firing squad on 12 September 1962.

[*See also* Indonesia.]

BIBLIOGRAPHY

Boland, B. J. *The Struggle of Islam in Modern Indonesia.* The Hague, 1982. Basic work on Islamic politics in Indonesia which situates the Darul Islam in the full spectrum of Indonesian Muslim political parties and movements.

Dijk, C. van. *Rebellion under the Banner of Islam: The Darul Islam in Indonesia.* The Hague, 1981. Emphasizes the socioeconomic basis of rural rebellion.

Horikoshi, Hiroko. "The Dar ul-Islam Movement in West Java, 1948–1962: An Experience of the Historical Process." *Indonesia* 20 (1975): 59–86.

Jackson, Karl. *Traditional Authority, Islam, and Rebellion: A Study of Indonesian Political Behavior.* Berkeley, 1980. A not fully successful effort to utilize social science survey research techniques to explain differing orientations toward the Darul Islam revolt by West Javanese villagers.

Nieuwenhuijze, C. A. O. van. *Aspects of Islam in Post-Colonial Indonesia.* The Hague and Bandung, 1958. Updates and expands the author's initial survey, "The Darul Islam Movement in West Java," *Pacific Affairs* 13 (1950): 169–183.

Soebardi, S. "Kartosuwiryo and the Darul Islam Rebellion in Indonesia." *Journal of Southeast Asian Studies* 14 (1983): 109–133. Draws on Indonesian language studies, including Pinardi's 1964 biography, *Sekarmadji Maridjan Kartosuwiryo.*

DONALD E. WEATHERBEE

DAʿWAH. [*To explore the dimensions of religious outreach or mission activity in the modern Islamic world, this entry comprises three articles:*

Qur'ānic Concepts
Institutionalization
Modern Usage

The first article surveys issues articulated in the Qur'ān and ḥadīth; *the second describes the development of organizations devoted to Islamic outreach; and the third considers the evolution of the idea in the nineteenth and twentieth centuries. For a related discussion, see* Tablīgh.]

Qur'ānic Concepts

The word *daʿwah* and the verb *daʿā* from which it derives have a range of meanings both in the Qur'ān and in ordinary speech. It can signify, for example, a basic act of invitation, as in a *ḥadīth* that says, in part, "and someone who enters without an invitation [*daʿwah*] enters as a thief." The *ṣāḥib al-daʿwah* ("master of the invitation") is, in this context, nothing more than a "host." But the lexical meanings extend from there to encompass concepts of summoning, calling on, appealing to, invocation, prayer (for and against something or someone), propaganda, missionary activity, and finally legal proceedings and claims. Most nuances displayed by such English renderings are important for differing religious ideas and understandings, some only vaguely represented in the Qur'ān itself.

As would be expected in a revelatory discourse between God and the Prophet, certain amplifications of the concept of *daʿwah* had to await elaboration through historical events. Nevertheless, in modern thought, the Qur'ānic uses of this term retain currency, because for Muslims the Qur'ān preserves its own vitality and immediacy. The meanings of *daʿwah* in any given verse or in any accumulated context reappear frequently in modern literature.

In the Qur'ān (2.186) a basic meaning for *daʿwah*—perhaps its cardinal meaning—is the single act of prayer: "When My servants ask thee about Me, I am indeed close by and answer the prayer [*daʿwah*] of everyone when they pray to Me." *Daʿwah,* therefore, can indicate a certain person's prayer or an entreaty addressed to God; such are the prayers of Moses and Aaron (surah 10.89) or of Abraham, Solomon, or Jonah (asserted in a *ḥadīth* reference to Qur'ānic passages). Prayer can also mean the call to formal prayer rituals, as in a *ḥadīth* that specifies *daʿwah* ("calling to prayer") as an office of the Ethiopian, but it is more commonly an individual's invocation of God for a special purpose, such as the granting of a favor. In fact, many Qur'ānic passages are warnings or admonitions against trying to call on a god other than the One, True God, and a primary lesson in the Qur'ān is that to make a *daʿwah* ("appeal") to other gods is vain either in this life or in the next. Such a *daʿwah* cannot and will not receive an answer; it yields no result, and to persist in it once apprised of its uselessness is a wickedness.

The Qur'ān is thus replete with examples of those who wrongly call on false gods and, naturally, of the correctness of directing a *daʿwah* to the True God, who alone grants the appeal of his servants. Equally, each servant must recognize that God's own *daʿwah*, his summons, requires their response. The ultimate *daʿwah* is that of God himself. This double principle—that God both summons through his *daʿwah* and that he alone answers the *daʿwah* of his servants—results in a sense of the true *daʿwah*, the *daʿwat al-ḥaqq* of surah 13.14: "To Him is the prayer of truth [*daʿwat al-ḥaqq*], and all those they pray to, other than Him, answer them not at all, no more than if they stretched out their hands to reach for water, which reaches them not, for the prayer of the unbelievers is futile."

From examples such as this, the fundamental meaning of the Islamic *daʿwah* emerges. This *daʿwah* is the declaration that there is no god other than the True God (Allāh). The *daʿwah* is Islam, and Islam is the *daʿwah*.

Other, false *daʿwah*s, however, do exist, now as in the past. The Qur'ān, for example, speaks of Satan's *daʿwah* in surah 14.22, where Satan says, "I had no authority over you, but to call upon you, and you answered me; so do not blame me, but blame yourself." The *daʿwah* a true believer issues and responds to must follow closely the lead of those properly appointed to this task. An agent of the *daʿwah* is referred to as a *dāʿī*—the one who makes the call, addresses the appeal, or issues the summons. An important use of *daʿwah* in the Qur'ān is the calling forth of the dead from the earth, as in surah 30.25: "Then when He calls [*daʿā*] you by a single call [*daʿwah*] from the earth, behold you come forth at once." More precisely, the *dāʿī* ("caller") on that august day is the angel Gabriel. The Prophet, too, is said to be *dāʿī Allāh* ("God's summoner") in surahs 33.46 and 46.31–32.

In accord with this, the second duty of a Muslim, besides praying only to the True God, is to answer the *daʿwah* of God's *dāʿī*, Muḥammad, the Prophet. Presumably, other prophets were likewise the *dāʿī*s of God in their time. Surah 14.44 contains a confirmation of this point: on the Day of Reckoning the evildoers will say to God, "If You delay the matter a little, we will accede to Your call [*daʿwah*] and follow the prophets." The concept of *daʿwah* thus passes from God to his representatives on earth. Muḥammad, like the prophets before him, issues his own call, his own *daʿwah*. Each individual prophet calls in some particular way to his own people. This concept appears in several passages regarding the former prophets, such as the account of Noah in surah 71.5–8, which begins, "We sent Noah to his people," continuing with Noah himself complaining, "Oh Lord, I have called [*daʿawtu*] to my people night and day, but my calling only increased them in flight."

The idea of a *daʿwah* aimed at a given community, rather than an isolated individual, is the most obvious message in the passages concerning Noah. Like Noah, Muḥammad summons his people to the true faith; he thus fulfills God's *daʿwah* by instituting his own. Surah 23.73 refers directly to Muḥammad: "Truly you summon them to the straight path." With this affirmation of Muḥammad's mission, the *daʿwah* has become the "straight path" and is more than a simple invocation of the One, True God. Although the opening surah of the Qur'ān, for example, is an invocation addressed to God, and as such the surah itself is called the *daʿwah*, it also contains the message of the "straight path." Surah 10.25 states similarly, "God summons to the abode of peace; and He guides whoever He wants to the straight path." The *daʿwah* is thus equated with the straight path, which is true religion itself.

Opposing connotations of the term *daʿwah*, as outlined above, come together in surah 40.41–43, where the believer addresses his people: "How strange that I call you to salvation and you call me to the Fire." The two *daʿwah*s are in conflict: one is true and the other not; one blasphemes, the other succeeds with a promise of salvation.

These extensions of the notion of each prophet's call lead to an extremely important concept—that of "community" in the sense of "community of believers," no longer merely the people summoned by a single prophet. Although those summoned by a single prophet may not respond to the summons, those who do henceforth constitute the *ummah* ("nation") of Muslims (assuming it is the era of Muḥammad): "Oh you who believe, fear God as He should be, and die not except having become *muslim*" (surah 3.102). The idea of *daʿwah* thus moves one step further. Surah 3.104 continues this idea: "Let there be one nation [*ummah*] of you, calling to the good, enjoining what is right, forbidding what is wrong; those are the ones to prosper." In this verse, the *daʿwah* is an activity of the whole community; it is the command to promote good and fight injustice at large. Surah 3.104 begins to articulate a sense of *daʿwah* as a synonym of *unmah* and of righteousness itself. And it is thus not far from this to the equation of *daʿwah* and *sharīʿah* (the divine law), which, like *daʿwah*, is the "straight path."

Another important indication of this trend is found in surah 57.8: "And the apostle summons you to believe in your Lord; indeed he has made a compact with you, seeing that you are persons of faith." Here the idea of a *mīthāq* (compact or covenant), entered into by the Prophet and the believer as a response to the *daʿwah*, formalizes the *daʿwah*'s communal dimension. The appeal of God transfers into an appeal by the Prophet; whereon Muḥammad, in turn, organizes those who answer him, taking from each a covenant and creating thereby an *ummah* that, ultimately, assumes the responsibility of the *daʿwah* on its own.

The classical concept of *daʿwah* as put forth in the Qur'ān is that *daʿwah* and Islam are so intertwined that one can hardly be separated from the other. It would be wrong, moreover, to conclude that the idea of *daʿwah* grows and develops through stages in the Qur'ān. Rather, the whole complex scope of meaning should be taken together. The *ḥadīth*s, which might have elaborated a particular concept, do not, but instead embellish several themes already stated. In the *ḥadīth* literature, for example, the prayers of the oppressed and the prayer of a Muslim on behalf of a brother are always successful.

There are other views of *daʿwah* that receive their most important amplification beyond the sphere of the Holy Scripture. These are, first, *daʿwah* as a particular cause, either political or religious, within the domain of Islam and between contending Muslim factions; and second, *daʿwah* as the external mission directed broadly toward non-Muslims. It is true that the second notion derives powerful support from surah 16.125, and indeed from the whole Qur'ānic depiction of Muḥammad's mission, but the first notion of *daʿwah* assumed priority in earlier times.

Although *daʿwah* and Islam can be viewed as a single concept, the lexical denotation of *daʿwah* as "a special appeal" or "summons" to or on behalf of a certain cause allowed factional interests to adopt the term for the rights of one party against another. Thus *daʿwah* becomes the instrument by which one Muslim calls another to a specific purpose, such as the Shīʿah or the ʿAbbāsids and their claims in support of a specific imam. The Ismāʿīlīyah developed this concept, institutionalized it, and built out of it an elaborate notion of a cosmic *daʿwah*, arranged in hierarchical order, all members of which call those below to faith in the One, True God above it all. But even the Ismāʿīlī idea of *daʿwah*, though generously amplified by philosophical ideas and other additions, is an amalgamation of Qur'ānic suggestions. The Shīʿah, in fact, claim basically that the *daʿwah* of each iman merely extends and completes the Prophet. Nevertheless, the intensity of special-interest pleading gave rise to the understanding of *daʿwah* as "propaganda" and *dāʿī* as "political agent provovateur."

That sense of the term does not necessarily find support in the Qur'ān, except distantly. For example, unlike the term *tablīgh*, meaning to "fulfill" or "implement" a mission—that is, to cause or bring about a given task, or to convey successfully a specific message—which is an active requirement, *daʿwah* is a passive invitation, a summons, a call, or a prayer. It is perfectly possible, therefore, to speak of the "implementation" of the *daʿwah* that is, *tablīgh al-daʿwah*. [*See* Tablīgh.] The Qur'ān, however, makes it abundantly clear that some persons respond to a *daʿwah* and some do not; some hearken to the call, while some put their fingers in their ears (surah 71.7) and do not hear it. Moreover, surah 16.125 and the verses that follow put the gentlest face on the whole idea of *daʿwah*. In modern apologetics this passagc has, accordingly, become one of the most widely cited Qur'ānic descriptions of *daʿwah* and how it must function. These verses run, in part, as follows: "Call [or invite] to the way of your Lord with wisdom and beautiful preaching and dispute with them in the better manner . . . and if you chastise, chastise even as you have been chastised, but if you show patience that is best."

This is an exhortation to Muḥammad and refers to his own opponents, but it has become a favorite text in support of the external mission of Islam. The missionary *daʿwah* once followed military conquest, but it now bears no direct relationship to that method for the spread of the Islamic domain. Even where conquest occurred in former times, Islam followed slowly through individual conversions, and this concept of *daʿwah* was still applicable. Then, however, the governing powers, politically and economically, were already Muslim before the *daʿwah* commenced. In modern periods, this need not be the case, and hence the *daʿwah* can lead rather than follow, thus placing great stress on the propriety of methods, which is exactly what this verse urges. It is, moreover, a succinct Qur'ānic answer to the charge of forcible conversion and directly rules out all methods of coercion. Thus its importance as a stimulus for missionary activities and also as a tool of interreligious apologetics cannot be underestimated.

Because the Qurānic concept of *daʿwah* is so basic and therefore flexible, the term itself has many uses, each of which can be emphasized without violating the intention of the revelation or deviating widely from the original context. One common theme of modern literature, for example, is the universality of the Islamic *daʿwah:* it was addressed to all peoples, in the past as in the present. If Islam is the religion of God, if Muḥammad is its *dāʿī*, then no person or people is exempt from the reach of its appeal, its *daʿwah*. As another example, a more restricted view sees *daʿwah* as an appeal to true Islam—the Islam of the Prophet—in distinction to the vast elements of innovation that have crept into Islam. Militant Islamic submovements, therefore, employ the idea of *daʿwah* as the original call by Muḥammad to a pure religion. *Daʿwah* is both the call—as in the title of the Muslim Brotherhood's periodical journal—to recreate that Islam and also the separate, individual efforts to preach and practice true Islam in various times and places. The *daʿwah* might thus become a movement in itself. As with other uses of the word, these usages carry a general Qur'ānic resonance in reminding Muslims of Muḥammad's situation and the trials he encountered in issuing and sustaining the first Islamic *daʿwah*.

BIBLIOGRAPHY

There is little, if any, literature specifically on Qur'ānic concepts of *daʿwah* in English, in part because it is seldom considered a separate theme in Qur'ānic studies. For specific verses other than those covered in the article, it is necessary to consult a concordance of the Qur'ān. *Ḥadīth* literature has likewise not been studied for this theme and the standard section of the major *ḥadīth* collections on *daʿwat* refer primarily to uses of the term as meaning "invocation."

For other uses of the term and for the general literature on *daʿwah* as a mission for proselytizing, the following items are useful:

Arnold, Thomas Walker. *The Preaching of Islam: A History of the Propagation of the Muslim Faith*. 2d ed. London, 1913. An older but still classic account of Islamic missionary activity.

Canard, Marius. "Daʿwa." In *Encyclopaedia of Islam*, vol. 2, pp. 168–170. New ed., Leiden, 1960–.

Denny, Frederick Mathewson. "Daʿwah," In *The Encyclopedia of Religion*, edited by Mircea Eliade, vol. 4, pp. 244–245. New York, 1987.

Fārūqī, Ismāʿīl Rājī al-. "On the Nature of the Islamic Daʿwah." In *Christian Mission and Islamic Daʿwah: Proceedings of the Chambesy Dialogue*. London, 1985.

Hamdani, Abbas. "Evolution of the Organizational Structure of the Fatimi Daʿwah." *Arabian Studies* 3 (1976): 85–114. On the Ismāʿīlī *daʿwah* as an institution.

Levtzion, Nehemia, ed. *Conversion to Islam*. New York and London, 1979. A collection of essays on this subject with a particularly valuable and up-to-date bibliogarphy (pp. 247–265) on general as well as regional developments.

Poston, Larry. *Islamic Daʿwah in the West: Muslim Missionary Activity and the Dynamics of Conversion to Islam*. New York and Oxford, 1992. An interesting recent study of *daʿwah* and of the process of conversion to Islam in the West. Includes an important bibliography of works in English.

Sharon, Moshe. *Black Banners from the East*, Jerusalem, 1983. One of several good introductions to the ʿAbbāsid concept of *daʿwah*.

PAUL E. WALKER

Institutionalization

Since the beginning of the twentieth century, modern Islamic *daʿwah* has become a major issue of newly established Islamic institutions and organizations. The Ottoman sultan Abdülhamid II had already included the concept of *daʿwah* in his "imperial ideology," supporting his claim to be the caliph of the Islamic *ummah* ("nation"). ʿAbd al-Raḥmān al-Kawākibī embodied the call to the righteous of (Salafī) Islam into the duties of his fictitious Society for the Edification of the Unitarians (Jamʿīyat Taʿlīm al-Muwaḥḥidīn). But whereas the classical Salafīyah had stressed the concept of *ṭarbiyah* (educating the Muslim believers), independent non-scholarly organizations of the neo-Salafīyah put *daʿwah* into the foreground of their political and cultural activities. During the 1930s in Egypt, two competing organizations, the Muslim Brotherhood (al-Ikhwān al-Muslimūn) and the Association of Young Muslims (Jamʿīyat al-Shubbān al-Muslimīn), not only propagated a temporary withdrawal from society *(hijrah)* but also called on Muslim youth to join the new groups in accordance with the Qur'ān (3.104): "Let there arise out of you a band of people inviting to all that is good, enjoining what is right and forbidding what is wrong. These are the ones to attain felicity." By using this Qur'ānic verse, they tried to legitimate their claim to independent authority in a nation-state community. In a way, *daʿwah* still meant the call to become a member of the only righteous Islamic community within the Muslim *ummah*.

In a different manner, the Society for Teaching and Propagation (Jamāʿat al-Tablīgh wa-al-Daʿwah; more commonly referred to as the Tablīghī Jamāʿat) of the Indian Maulānā Muḥammad Ilyās (1885–1944) had already stressed the necessity of a missionary duty of *daʿwah*. Of Ṣūfī background, the Tablīghī Jamāʿat focused on Muslim communities in the peripheries as well as on neighboring non-Muslims. The large mystical organizations were better able to cover the needs of proselytes in the peripheries than the political associations of the neo-Salafīyah. In West Africa, it was mainly the Sanūsīyah and the Tijānīyah that helped to spread Islam in hitherto non-Muslim territories. Likewise, such sects as the Aḥmadīyah and the Ismāᶜīlīyah used the concept of *daᶜwah* to campaign for proselytes chiefly in communities to which Muslims had migrated but constituted a minority.

Missionary activities of the new Islamic organizations were still marginal and restricted to sporadic activities of several centers of Islamic learning. Thus, during the sessions of the General Islamic Congress of Jerusalem in 1931, Muḥammad Rashīd Riḍā (1865–1935) was able to revive his small Society of Call and Guidance (Jamᶜīyat al-Daᶜwah wa-al-Irshād), which he had founded in 1911 and which he had wanted to become a cornerstone of Ottoman Pan-Islamic activities. Only after the end of World War II did the political tendency to establish transnational Islamic bodies activate the idea of propagating Islam outside the sphere of the *ummah* as well. The short-lived Islamic Conference, established by Saudi Arabia, Egypt, and Pakistan in 1954, demanded that the spread of Islam become a major task of "Islamic work." *Daᶜwah* was now understood to be an integral part of the concept of *waḥdah* (unity): transnational organizations should simultaneously represent the will of the Muslim community to live in a single, at least culturally unified, *ummah* and to work to spread the true teachings of Islam.

During the Arab Cold War (1957–1967), *daᶜwah* work attained greater recognition in Saudi Arabia. Saudi politicians realized the possibility of broadening their political and cultural influence by "promulgating the word of God, promoting the message of Islam and bringing the Moslems back to the orbit of Islam" (Mohammed Ahmad Bashmeel [Bashmīl], *Nationalism in Islam;* Beirut, 1962, p. 92). On 24 October 1961, the Saudi Government opened a new Islamic university in Medina, the task of which was to train Islamic workers for *daᶜwah* in minority communities. In addition, the Muslim World League, founded in May 1962, included *daᶜwah* in its covenant in order "to unify and to spread the Muslims' word."

In the 1960s, Islamic *daᶜwah* was promoted by at least three different types of organizations: interstate or state organizations, such as the Higher Council of Islamic Affairs (al-Majlis al-Aᶜlā lil-Shu'ūn al-Islāmīyah), founded in Cairo in 1960, or the Islamic University in Medina; state-sponsored transnational organizations, such as the Saudi-based Muslim World League; and nongovernmental organizations, such as the Muslim Brotherhood or the Tablīghī Jamāᶜat.

However, the limited influence of transnational organizations was remarkable: in 1965, the Muslim World League had only fifty Islamic workers under contract, whereas the Higher Council of Islamic Affairs disposed of hundreds of students who had been trained at al-Azhar and who continued to work for the *daᶜwah* policy of the university. Obviously, state-sponsored organizations, which claimed nevertheless to be "totally independent," had difficulties in developing a profile of their own in the field of *daᶜwah.* Divergent cultural and political tendencies assembled under the roof of a transnational organization competed for the contents of the true Islamic teaching and thus paralyzed *daᶜwah.* By way of contrast, state organizations or nongovernmental groups like the Muslim Brotherhood possessed a clearer Islamic political program, either in the interest of the government or as a result of a specific ideology.

In the early 1970s, when Islamic politics were becoming a major expression of political and cultural struggle, the *daᶜwah* of the transnational organizations gained greater attention from the Islamic public. In December 1972, the Wahhābī community in Saudi Arabia organized an International Youth Conference for Islamic Daᶜwah, which became the foundation stone of the new Saudi-sponsored World Assembly of Muslim Youth (al-Nadwah al-ᶜĀlamīyah lil-Shabāb al-Islāmī). In May 1972, the Libyan Government inaugurated a new transnational *daᶜwah* organization, the Islamic Call Society (Jamᶜīyat al-Daᶜwah al-Islāmīyah), which during the first ten years of its existence hardly exercised any influence in the field of international *daᶜwah* politics. After having been reorganized in 1982, however, a new suborganization of this society, the World Council for Islamic Call (al-Majlis al-ᶜĀlamī lil-Daᶜwah al-Islāmīyah) became the most important competitor of the Saudi-based Muslim World League and a mouthpiece for Muᶜammar al-Qadhdhāfī's Third Theory.

The simultaneous foundation of the World Assembly of Muslim Youth and the Islamic Call Society demonstrates that the concept of *daᶜwah* was now also applied to the propagation of specific ideological and theological currents that legitimated Saudi and Libyan rule, respectively.

The disappointing effects of international *daᶜwah,* the foundation of new state agencies, and the spontaneous emergence of new radical Islamic political groups stressed the need for coordination and cooperation. In 1973, the Muslim World League accepted volunteers from the Azhar Academy of Islamic Research (Majmaᶜ al-Buḥūth al-Islāmīyah), founded in 1961–1964, in order to fulfill the duties of Islamic work in Africa and

Southeast Asia. In September 1975, the Muslim World League held the Mosque Message Conference, an international *daʿwah* conference, in Mecca. The league proposed the total reorganization of international *daʿwah* activities and the highlighting of mosques as the focal point of *daʿwah*. Accordingly, the World Council of Mosques was established in 1975. Within ten years, the league succeeded in founding several regional branches of this council, which was clearly regarded as a counterweight to the World Council of Churches. Nevertheless, the number of *daʿwah* activists increased only gradually. Although the Muslim World League boasted of cooperating with more than a thousand Islamic organizations all over the world, in 1985 it had only 1,000 Islamic workers under contract (360 in Africa, 473 in Asia, and 167 in Europe and the Americas).

After this reorganization of the institutional field of *daʿwah*, the major transnational Islamic organizations were confronted with new developments resulting from the revolutionary propaganda of the Islamic Republic of Iran. The Iranian leadership had set up an Organization for Islamic Propaganda (Munaẓẓamat-i Iʿlām-i Islāmī) with the rank of a state ministry whose purpose was to win non-Shīʿī Muslims for the Islamic revolution. *Daʿwah* was again aimed more at attracting supporters for a specific political ideology than at recruiting proselytes. Depending on the direct support of the patron regime, political *daʿwah* also followed fluctuations in the government's domestic and foreign policy strategies: in 1982, the Iranian regime began to emphasize its Shīʿī background, thus forcing the propaganda organization to join in this spirit.

From 1982 on, the competition among the major transnational organizations created a new geographical distribution of *daʿwah* activities: the Iranian activists stressed the importance of working among Muslim communities in the Western world; the Muslim World League tried to consolidate its *daʿwah* activities in East Africa, Southeast Asia, Afghanistan, India, and Pakistan; the Libyan Islamic Call Society chiefly intervened in West Africa and in South America. The Cairo-based Higher Council of Islamic Affairs tried to steer clear from this competition and continued to recruit its activists from those parts of the Islamic world that kept traditional contacts with al-Azhar.

In addition to these important *daʿwah* organizations, at least fifteen other bodies and agencies have hoped to gain recognition in the Islamic world by starting independent *daʿwah* activities. Most of the rich Islamic countries established *daʿwah* organizations of their own (e.g., Kuwait's al-Hay'ah al-Khayrīyah al-Islāmīyah al-ʿĀlamīyah or Iraq's Munaẓẓamat al-Mu'tamar al-Islāmī al-Shaʿbī). The resultant social and cultural competition was to be countered by the establishment of a new coordination council. In 1988, seventeen organizations founded the World Islamic Council for Propagation and Relief (al-Majlis al-ʿĀlamī al-Islāmī lil-Daʿwah wa-al-Ighāthah). The Muslim World League had already started to integrate *daʿwah* activities with relief work in 1981. The idea was to direct *daʿwah* to those communities and localities that were affected by natural disaster, unemployment, or poverty. In this way, the *dāʿīs* (agents of *daʿwah*) would demonstrate that Islam also helps to cover the basic needs of humankind and that the Islamic *ummah* is a singular expression of solidarity and humanity.

In general, however, several structural factors constituted a major obstacle to the success of institutionalized *daʿwah:*

First, transnational *daʿwah* was not able to mobilize local forms of Islamic culture, as it had to follow the Salafī tradition, which demanded the abolition of local Islamic cults and cultures. Accordingly, *daʿwah* activists were able to gain influence only among those urban communities that were in a similar social and cultural position. The new Muslim immigrant communities in Europe, for instance, which had lost their traditional cultural bonds, were much more ready to accept the supremacy of one of these bodies than communities in Africa or Southeast Asia.

Second, foreign Muslim activists were scarcely able to penetrate into the local culture of, for instance, the heterogenous ethnic communities of West Africa. Although it was often stated that the Arabic language should be the language of *daʿwah,* communication between the *dāʿīs* and the community was most unlikely in such a case. Likewise, all publications of the transnational organizations were either in Arabic, English, or French. Yet those who were able to speak and read French or English were already connected to an international culture and thus were not predisposed to join the organizational field of Islamic *daʿwah*.

Third, as all the transnational bodies identified *daʿwah* with an increase in the institutionalization of Islamic culture within the scope of their specific ideological tendencies, the success of their work was measured by an increase in membership. Consequently, *daʿwah* was far more able to mobilize already existing institutions, such as small mosques or political communities, which were ready to join a hierarchical, institutional system.

Fourth, because political *daʿwah* favored the patronage of a single regime—be it Saudi Arabia, Iran, or Libya—new members also had to identify with these regimes. However, serious political problems often evolved out of the shifts in state politics.

Whereas al-Azhar or the Muslim World League tried to reduce the political contents of *daʿwah* to a minimum, the Libyan and Iranian organizations, and to a certain extent the Saudi-sponsored World Assembly of Muslim Youth, acted far more politically. Consequently, they seemed to be able to mobilize communities on a specific issue (e.g., the Salman Rushdie affair in 1989), but failed to gain lasting influence, as spontaneous mass mobilization seldom helps to create an institutional basis. Thus, the influence of the Muslim World League in Sudan outlasted all political changes that took place during the years 1983 to 1990, and Libyan influence in Burkina Faso and Mauritania depended on the degree of consensus between the regimes involved.

Institutional *daʿwah* carried out by independent nongovernmental organizations has had different objectives that have helped the organizations to surpass political difficulties. The Aḥmadīyah mission, for instance, was not encumbered with the patronage of a specific regime. Likewise the *daʿwah* of the Tablīghī communities was more successful in Western societies, since hardly anyone imputed to them propaganda in favor of a particular regime. Apparently, the Islamic mission outside Muslim communities is mainly supported by independent, often informal, Islamic groups, whereas the institutionalized *daʿwah* of the large Islamic organizations like the Muslim World League aims principally at integrating Muslim communities whose transnational affiliation is not clear. Thus, in a way, institutionalized *daʿwah* supports the regrouping of the heterogenous Islamic culture.

At an early stage, the Muslim World League had recognized the important role of modern media in the creation of an Islamic *daʿwah* network. In 1984, the league integrated its *daʿwah* apparatus within its Section Six ("media"). In 1977, on the occasion of a *daʿwah* conference in Medina, all delegates had criticized the poor quality of Islamic media. And it was stated that in almost all regions where *daʿwah* was to be carried out, Islamic media were practically nonexistant. In order to solve this problem, the league organized an international media conference in Jakarta in September 1980, during which the delegates passed a Covenant of Islamic Media. The major part of the conference's decisions dealt with institutional questions (e.g., the establishment of a Higher International Council for Islamic Media). It soon became clear, however, that by incorporating *daʿwah* within the field of international or regional media, the delegates were confronted with the question of how to deal with the ideological and theological contents of *daʿwah*. The only common ground was the so-called ideological threats to which the Muslim communities felt exposed. Thus, conference members agreed that media should fight against socialist and atheist ideas, Christian mission, and "pseudo-Islamic groups." Nevertheless, ideas that could have marked the guidelines of the theoretical and practical contents of *daʿwah* were still missing.

It is clear that institutionalizing *daʿwah* has not automatically guaranteed success. On the contrary, the more *daʿwah* has been made a task of the large Islamic organizations, the more it has been paralyzed by institutional hierarchies and neutralized by the divergent Islamic tendencies that these organizations represent. In fact, institutional *daʿwah* continues to be mainly a medium of the patron regimes for the establishment of an informal, but religiously legitimated, foreign policy.

[*See also* Azhar, al-; Communications Media; Islamic Call Society; Muslim World League; Tablīghī Jamāʿat.]

BIBLIOGRAPHY

Draguhn, Werner, ed. *Der Einfluß des Islams auf Politik, Wirtschaft und Gesellschaft in Südostasien*. Hamburg, 1983. Collection of essays on Islam and *daʿwah* activities in Southeast Asia.

Kramer, Martin. *Islam Assembled: The Advent of the Muslim Congresses*. New York, 1986. Excellent introduction to the history of the Muslim Congress movement, 1880 to 1939.

Landau, Jacob. *The Politics of Pan-Islam: Ideology and Organization*. Oxford, 1990. One of the best studies on Pan-Islam to date. The author concentrates on the earlier periods, 1880 to 1939.

Mattes, Hanspeter. *Die innere und äußere Mission Libyens*. Mainz, 1986. Insightful analysis of Libyan missionary activities.

Otayek, René, ed. *Le radicalisme islamique au sud du Sahara: Daʿwa, arabisation et critique de l'Occident*. Paris, 1993. Collection of essays on *daʿwah* activities in Africa.

Piscatori, J. P. *Islam in a World of Nation-States*. Cambridge, 1986. Most useful discussion of the role of Islam in nation-state societies, with many important references to *daʿwah* organizations.

Schulze, Reinhard. *Islamischer Internationalismus im 20. Jahrhundert: Untersuchungen zur Geschichte der Islamischen Weltliga*. Leiden, 1990. Gives a history of Islamic transnationalism and of the Muslim World League.

Sharipova, Raisa M. *Panislamizm Segodnia: Ideologia i praktika Ligi*

Islamskogo Mira. Moscow, 1986. Description and interpretation of the Muslim World League from a political point of view.

REINHARD SCHULZE

Modern Usage

Literally meaning "claim, prayer, invocation," *daᶜwah* has been defined by Frederick M. Denny in the *Encyclopedia of Religion* (New York, 1987, vol. 4, p. 244) as "a religious outreach or mission to exhort people to embrace Islam." The Muslim *daᶜwah* literature generally agrees with this definition. In modern usage, however, *daᶜwah* has acquired meanings other than "mission" and "conversion." Studying modern manifestations of *daᶜwah,* one discerns four obvious trends—political orientation, interiorization, institutional organization, and social-welfare concern.

Political Orientation. *Daᶜwah* was used as a call to establish an alternative political order in the early history of Islam, for instance by the Khawārij and ᶜAbbāsids against the Umayyads and by the Ismāᶜīlīs against the ᶜAbbāsids, but it became gradually divested of this political orientation in later periods. Muslim political theorists generally mentioned *daᶜwah* as one of the duties of a caliph, but this duty was rarely realized in practice. This caliphal doctrine was used rather to redefine *daᶜwah* in terms of preaching and to control *daᶜwah* efforts, particularly to constrain them from seeking political objectives.

The doctrine of *daᶜwah* as a caliphal duty was revived in the nineteenth century by the Ottoman Sultan Abdülhamid II (r. 1876–1909), giving it an entirely new meaning. Instead of referring to preaching and *jihād,* this caliphal duty was now defined to extend the caliph's authority over Muslims in other countries, analogous to the Catholic pope. Although Abdülhamid II used the idea for his own political purposes, it was also readily accepted by the West, largely because, as Thomas Arnold argued in *The Caliphate* (1924), many Western scholars had already compared the caliph with the pope. In addition, some European statesmen and scholars like W. S. Blunt found this doctrine of *daᶜwah* useful in promoting Arab nationalism. Blunt, who believed that Muslims would have a better future if political power were shifted from the Turks to the Arabs, proposed in *The Future of Islam* (1882) that the Ottoman caliph should only be the spiritual head of all Muslims, while executive and administrative powers should be placed in the hands of regional Arab rulers.

In this context *daᶜwah* immediately became a political instrument to propagate Islamic unity. The doctrine of *daᶜwah* as a caliphal function brought Muslims in different territories together under one spiritual head. *Daᶜwah* for the unity of the Muslims was systematically developed by Jamāl al-Dīn al-Afghānī (d. 1897), who founded the Jamᶜīyat al-ᶜUrwat al-Wuthqā (Society of the Reliable Bond), a *daᶜwah* organization promoting Muslim solidarity.

Improved means of communication and news media in the twentieth century increased awareness among Muslim communities, which had remained largely isolated from one another until then. This awareness led to the growth of a sense of solidarity. The political context of democracy and nation-states heightened the importance of attracting large numbers of supporters. The vigorous Christian missionary work of this period was viewed by Muslims as a political threat because it was seen as an effort to increase the number of Christians in Muslim areas. *Daᶜwah* organizations like al-Daᶜwah wa-al-Irshād (Daᶜwah and Guidance), founded by Muḥammad Rashīd Riḍā (d. 1935), were established in response to the perceived threat.

The ideas of nationalism and nation-state also led to the politicization of *daᶜwah.* These ideas called for local self-government and the expulsion of colonial rulers. Since the obvious point of difference between the colonists and the indigenous population was generally religion, the struggle against colonial rule was defined as *daᶜwah* to seek independence from non-Muslim rule and to establish or restore *dār al-Islām.* This interpretation of political action was found convenient because it could be claimed as a religious right from the colonial government, and action against the government could be justified as struggle for religious freedom. Moreover, this *daᶜwah* helped popularize political movements because it provided a broader base for developing national identity in countries of ethnic and linguistic diversity. Finally, national political movements based on such *daᶜwah* could win the sympathy of similar political movements in other Muslim areas.

Daᶜwah as state ideology emerged more clearly in the 1960s under Gamal Abdel Nasser (1918–1970). He established a *daᶜwah* network in the Middle East and Africa with the help of al-Azhar University in order to promote Islam, the Arabic language, and Arab nationalism. Other Muslim states, sensing in the influence of his *daᶜwah* a threat to their national sovereignty, organized their own *daᶜwah* in line with their particular interests.

To combat Arab nationalist *daᶜwah* these Muslim states highlighted the anti-Islamic stance of nationalism and stressed its affiliation with atheism, secularism, and communism. *Daᶜwah* was defined in terms of the revival of pure Islam. This stance was adopted by countries like Saudi Arabia and Libya, which considered *daᶜwah* an important duty of the state and established *daᶜwah* networks throughout the Muslim world.

Saudi Arabia established an Islamic University in Medina in 1961 for the education and training of *daᶜwah* workers. In 1962 the Muslim World League (Rābiṭat al-ᶜĀlam al-Islāmī) was founded to organize various transnational *daᶜwah* activities. The league with its sixty members had as its first goal the fusion of the differing schools of thought in Islamic ideology into one organization. It succeeded very early in bringing together various reformist *daᶜwah* groups in India, Pakistan, Morocco, and Saudi Arabia. With more than twenty-two branches all over the world, the league continued to work independently on the international level even after the foundation of the Organization of the Islamic Conference in 1970. Its activities were extended: Islamic Councils for the five continents were founded in 1974, the World Council of Mosques in 1975, and an Academy for Islamic Law in 1976.

In Egypt a Higher Council for Islamic Affairs, established in 1960, sponsored *daᶜwah* activities. The council sent teachers to various parts of the Muslim world, particularly Africa, and conducted an impressive program of publication. In the 1970s the Muslim World League made an effort to coordinate its *daᶜwah* activities with the governments of Egypt and other countries. A World Assembly of Muslim Youth (WAMY) was formed in 1972. Some countries felt that the league's *daᶜwah* activities and those of its subordinate organizations were guided largely by Saudi interests, and so they founded their own *daᶜwah* organizations. Libya created its Association of Islamic Daᶜwah in 1972, and Iran established the Islamic Information Organization in 1979. [*See* Muslim World League.]

The political orientation of *daᶜwah* has yielded two diametrically opposed results—transnationalism and solidification of the nation-state. First, it has promoted a transnational consciousness of the larger Islamic community *(ummah)* among Muslims. Second, *daᶜwah* organized by a particular state, even on the transnational level, has tended to instill the idea of the nation-state among Muslims, despite the professed objectives of the *daᶜwah* ideologies to the contrary. The emphasis of *daᶜwah* organizations on the islamization of laws and societies also reinforces the concept of the nation-state. *Daᶜwah* groups normally define Muslims as a nation and do not accept other elements of the definition of a modern state; yet their demands for islamization within existing governments amount to acceptance of the idea of territorial boundaries. Further, various Muslim states that support *daᶜwah* activities control these activities as nation-states and reach out to other Muslim states.

Four modes of desirable political operation may be discerned in the modern *daᶜwah* literature: the launching of movements for an alternate political system; lobbying for an Islamic system; infiltration of *daᶜwah* into the current political system; and opposition to political orders seen as un-Islamic. *Daᶜwah* movements have sought to gain the support of some political parties for their objectives; indeed, some parties in Muslim countries have originated from *daᶜwah* movements.

Interiorization. Instead of reaching out to members of other faiths, the modern *daᶜwah* movements work primarily among Muslims. Two factors explain this emphasis. First, the threat of materialism, secularism, and indifference to religion in general and to Islam in particular, have prompted preachers to give disbelief *(kufr)* among Muslims priority. Modern education, science and technology, and modern political systems all pose an immediate threat to religion and its institutions.

Second, *daᶜwah* workers see in the modern governments of Muslim countries a continuity of the Christian and Western rule of the colonial period. Muslim thinkers had developed the conviction during colonial rule that state and governmental institutions were the only instruments that could bring about the revival of Islam. The struggle continues after independence as well, and the result has been not only the politicization of *daᶜwah* but also the preferential targeting of Muslim governments and societies.

The justification for the interiorization of *daᶜwah* is sought in the doctrine of *al-amr bi-al-maᶜrūf,* the Qur'ānic injunction to do good, defined as a distinct duty of the Muslim *ummah.* This duty is understood to aim at all humankind, but in its doctrinal details its scope is generally restricted to Muslims. Another justification is derived from the doctrine of *tartīb al-daᶜwah,* (the order of priority in the spread of *daᶜwah*), an early Islamic doctrine. As explained by Ibn Amīr al-Ḥājj (d. 1474), a Ḥanafī jurist, in *Al-taqrīr wa-al-taḥbīr* (vol. 2, Cairo, 1898, p. 89), this doctrine has reference to Muᶜaᶜdh ibn Jabal's (d. 639) *daᶜwah* that stressed a graded approach in communicating religious duties and doctrines to new converts. Since there were deficient Muslims who needed to be converted to true Islam, the conversion of non-Muslims became secondary in importance.

Saʿīd Ḥawwā in his study of Ḥasan al-Bannā's (d. 1949) educational philosophy (*Fī āfāq al-taʿlīm,* 1980), explains that al-Bannā' defined the priorities of *daʿwah* in the following order: self, home, society, country, government, Muslim *ummah,* and world. It is worth noting that *daʿwah* aims at the non-Muslim world only at the last stage.

Institutional Organization. Throughout the history of Islam, barring the Fāṭimids and Ismāʿīlīs, *daʿwah* was largely an individual and noninstitutionalized activity. In modern times, however, it has become increasingly institutionalized. This concept of *daʿwah* may have arisen in response to the global Christian missionary activities that began to reach the Muslim world in the sixteenth century. The fact that organized *daʿwah* is a recent phenomenon is attested by Thomas Arnold's reference in *The Caliphate* to missionary activities in the Sudan. In the early twentieth century the British government of the Sudan marked out zones of influence for various Christian missionary societies. Muslims in Cairo demanded that some territories should be allotted to the followers of Islam. The government refused because no organized Muslim missionary society existed. Muḥammad Rashīd Riḍā tried to establish a school for training Muslim missionaries in Istanbul but did not succeed until 1910.

The Syrian scholar Wahbah al-Zuḥaylī in *Āthār al-ḥarb fi-al-fiqh al-Islāmī* (Effects of War in Islamic Jurisprudence, Damascus, n.d., p. 55), and the Egyptian writer Muḥammad al-Ghazālī in *Al-ṭarīq min hunā* (The Road Starts Here, 1988, p.80) have also confirmed the absence of institutionalized *daʿwah* in Muslim countries before the twentieth century. Ṣubḥī Ṣāliḥ, a modern Arab historian, discusses the history of the spread of Islam in *Al-nuẓum al-Islāmīyah, nash'atuhā wa-taṭawwuruhā* (The Islamic Organizations, Their Rise and Development, Beirut, 1968) but does not mention such an organization. In fact, al-Ghazālī's and other modern writers' main criticism of past Muslim governments is that they did not pay attention to *daʿwah* on account of their narrow self-interests.

Institutionalized and organized *daʿwah* probably began after 1915. There have been possible parallels with Christian missionary organizations; for example, the World Council of Mosques and the Organization for the Distribution of the Qur'ān are comparable to the World Council of Churches and various Bible societies.

To illustrate the institutionalized aspect of *daʿwah* in modern times, the Daʿwah Academy established in 1985 by the International Islamic University in Islamabad, Pakistan, may be mentioned. The objectives of the academy are to organize programs for the training of imams, community leaders, professionals, and workers; to develop better methods and techniques for *daʿwah* work and the training of imams; to produce and publish literature on *daʿwah* and to develop audio-visual material that is accurate and effective; and to organize orientation courses, symposia, seminars, workshops, and conferences. The academy publishes *daʿwah* literature in several languages in addition to the monthly magazine *Daʿwah. Daʿwah* programs at the Academy are run at both the national and international levels. At the national level it organizes training for imams of the mosques, army officers, medical doctors, engineers, writers, teachers, journalists, and children. It runs correspondence certificate courses on Islamic law, *ḥadīth,* and Islamic general knowledge, and it establishes *daʿwah* libraries in prisons and hospitals. At the international level, the Daʿwah Academy organizes leadership programs and training courses for new Muslims, *daʿwah* workers, and imams in Central Asia. The Academy is coordinating its efforts with twenty-eight other *daʿwah* organizations in various Muslim countries, including the Muslim World League.

Social-Welfare Concerns. Until recently modern Muslim writers on Christian missionary activities strongly criticized the use of educational institutions, hospitals, and other welfare providers by the Christian missions as exploitative. Muṣṭafā Khālidī in *Al-tabshīr wa-al-istiʿmār fi-al-bilād al-ʿArabīyah* (Mission and Colonialism in the Arab World, Beirut, 1964) discusses how educational institutions and hospitals were used by the West to propagate Christianity in order to establish colonial rule. Mawlānā Abū al-Aʿlā Mawdūdī, the founder of Jamāʿat-i Islāmī in Pakistan, responding to a letter by the pope in December 1967, complained that the use of welfare institutions by the Christian missions in the Muslim world not only constituted a form of coercion to convert, but it also defeated the purpose of faith. When a missionary hospital or a school provided its welfare facilities free to converts and charged high fees to Muslims, it forced poor Muslims to convert to Christianity and at the same time contradicted the idea of sincerity in one's faith.

The recent concern for social welfare reflects a different concept of *daʿwah*. Traditionally, as evident in Qārī Ṭayyib's *Uṣūl-i daʿvat-i Islām* (The Principles of the Call to Islam), *daʿwah* meant only the call to spread revealed knowledge; social welfare was beyond its scope. Muslim *daʿwah* organizations began to use welfare facilities for *daʿwah* purposes only recently. The Muslim World League adopted social welfare in its *daʿwah* programs in 1974. It began relief work for Muslims, especially refugees, in 1980, and in 1988 a World Muslim Committee for Daʿwah and Relief was formed. Education and medicine are also the concerns of *daʿwah* movements like WAMY in Saudi Arabia, Jamāʿat Nasr al-Islām and Anṣār al-Islām in Nigeria, ABIM in Malaysia, and Diwan Dawat al-Islam in Indonesia. Muslim *daʿwah* welfare has not, however, been directed to non-Muslims.

BIBLIOGRAPHY

Alūrī, Ādam ʿAbd Allāh al-. *Tārīkh al-daʿwah ilā Allāh bayna al-ams wa-al-yawm* (History of the Call to God between Yesterday and Today). 2d rev. ed. Cairo, 1979. Al-Alūrī, a Nigerian scholar, traces the origin of *daʿwah* to Adam, the first prophet, and defines the term as "a call to save mankind from deviation." He interprets *waʿẓ* (sermon), *irshād* (guidance), *tadhkīr* (reminding), *bishārah tabshīr* (good news), *indhār* (warning), and *ḥisbah* (moral censure) as forms of *daʿwah*, and storytellers as types of *dāʿīs* (preachers). Alūrī's conception of *daʿwah* emerges as a broad term for the message of Islam, including its creeds, rituals, and laws. He cites recently established educational institutions as *daʿwah* movements.

Ghalwash, Aḥmad Aḥmad. *Al-daʿwah al-Islāmīyah: Uṣūluhā wa-wasā'iluhā* (The Islamic Mission: Principles and Problems). Cairo, 1978. Comprehensive treatment of the concept of *daʿwah*, its doctrines, problems, and organization. The author defines *daʿwah* as communication of the teachings of Islam, and argues that non-Muslims are the target of *daʿwah*. In his opinion, *daʿwah* may be performed only by trained persons, and hence training of *daʿwah* workers is essential.

Ghīṭās, Ḥusnī Muḥammad Ibrāhīm. *Al-daʿwah al-Islāmīyah fī ʿAhd Amīr al-Mu'minīn ʿUmar ibn al-Khaṭṭāb* (The Propagation of Islam in ʿUmar ibn al-Khaṭṭāb's Time). Beirut, 1985. Study of the spread of Islam during the rule of the second caliph, with detailed coverage of the doctrines of *daʿwah* as discussed by jurists and commentators on the Qur'ān, and its various stages in early Islamic history. Ghīṭās stresses that *daʿwah*, meaning "call to Islam," is not limited to sermons and preaching.

Jindī, Anwar al-. *Āfāq jadīdah lil-daʿwah al-Islāmīyah fī ʿālam al-Gharb* (New Horizons for Islamic Mission in the Western World). Beirut, 1987. Study of *daʿwah* as a response to various challenges from the West, in which *daʿwah* is defined as a defense: against the Crusades, Christian missionaries, and Orientalists. According to al-Jindī, the target of *daʿwah* is not conversion but a just understanding of Islam by non-Muslims. He emphasizes, however, the need for reform and unity among Muslims themselves.

Qārī Muḥammad Ṭayyib. *Uṣūl-i daʿvat-i Islām* (The Principles of the Call to Islam). Lahore, n.d. The author, an Indian scholar, argues that *daʿwah* is essential to the formation of an Islamic state, but governments in Muslim countries are neglecting this duty. He warns that secularism, that is, the declaration of a state that it does not adhere to any religion, is detrimental to Islam. He stresses that revealed knowledge alone is the subject of *daʿwah;* rational and physical sciences, and sciences not related to divine laws, are beyond the scope of *daʿwah*.

MUHAMMAD KHALID MASUD

DAWLAH. An Arabic term from the root *d-w-l*, meaning to rotate, alternate, take turns, or occur periodically, *dawlah*, in a modern context, refers to the concept of state and is a central concept in the discourse of the contemporary Islamists. In modern Persian a similar word, *dawlat*, sometimes refers to the government, and in that sense, it is interchangeable with another Persian term, *ḥukūmat* (Ar., *ḥukūmah*). In modern Turkish, *devlet* (a derivative from the Arabic) refers only to state, not government. As early as 1837 an official of the Ottoman Empire wrote a memorandum that clearly distinguished between the two meanings of the term in reference to European states and their governments (Lewis, 1988). Hence, in the modern period it would appear that only in Persian is the word susceptible to ambiguity.

In the Qur'ān Allāh is said to "cause the days to alternate" (surah 3.140). In a later chapter, the word is used in the sense of something that is given alternately from one hand to another (surah 59.7). Apparently, there is some evidence for *dawlah* to have been used in the Jāhilīyah (pre-Islamic period) by poets who meant by it "times of success." The first ʿAbbāsid caliph, al-Saffāḥ (r. 749–754), triumphantly declared on his accession: "you have reached our time and Allāh has brought you our *dawlah*" (i.e., "turn/time of success"). His successor, al-Manṣūr (r. 754–775), enthusiastically praised "our *dawlah*." In these uses, the word apparently refers to the dynastic house of the ʿAbbāsid caliphs. It was also applied sometimes in the sense of "victory" in this period (F. Rosenthal, 1960), thus the evidence to equate *dawlah* with dynasty or even more narrowly with the ʿAbbāsid house is inconclusive. Over time, *dawlah* came to connote a "turn of success." The word was also used by the great philosopher al-Kindī (c.801–866) as the equivalent of *mulk*, kingship (F. Rosenthal, 1960). *Dawlah* in the 900s came into use as a sobriquet bestowed on or appropriated by various princes, such as those of the Ḥamdānid (929–1003) and Būyid (932–

1055) houses; hence such titles as Rukn al-Dawlah (Pillar of the State), Sayf al-Dawlah (Sword of the State).

Ibn Khaldūn (d. 1406) preferred to use the terms *mulk* and *siyāsah ʿaqlīyah* (politics or government based on positive law and human reason), but his meaning was close to the modern understanding of *dawlah*. Its definition as a sovereign state with the panoply of statehood did not come until the period of the Ottoman Empire and its confrontation with Christian Europe. During the Qājār and Pahlavi periods in Iran, among the official titles of the shahs was ruler of the *dawlat-i shāhī* and, subsequently, the *dawlat-i shāh-in-shāhī* (the royal or imperial state).

In short, as commercial and diplomatic intercourse quickened between the Middle East and Europe—and ambassadors were exchanged, treaties signed, and economic agreements consummated—the political vocabulary of the region increasingly crystallized. By the mid-nineteenth century the word *dawlah* had taken on the meaning of Weber's celebrated definition of state as a political organization that, based on its juridical sovereignty, monopolizes the means of violence within a given territory. Muslim writers had to deal with this increasing secularization of the political realm (i.e., the separation of religion and state), and the debate continues over the appropriate response. Typically, Islamists are uncomfortable with the term *dawlah* and continue to refer to the Muslims as constituting an *ummah* (community of believers) whose political institution is the *khilāfah* (caliphate) or *imāmah* (imamate). An interesting exception to this is Saʿīd Ḥawwā, leader of the Syrian Muslim Brotherhood, who employed the word *dawlah* in his call for the establishment of *dawlat Allāh* in this world. But note that the translation is the religiously accommodating "kingdom of Allāh", not the laicized "state of Allāh."

In international relations, the period since the Treaty of Westphalia of 1648 has been the era of the nation-state. Thus, territoriality has become a decisive factor of life, with the *ummah* split into a variety of units, each with its own attributes of statehood and government. Muslim reformers have had to take these developments into account. Among the most celebrated attempts to do so is that of Shaykh ʿAlī ʿAbd al-Rāziq (d. 1966), a scholar of al-Azhar, the Islamic world's most famous university and mosque. In 1925, he published a book entitled *Al-Islām wa-uṣūl al-ḥukm (Islam and the Foundations of Rule)*. ʿAbd al-Rāziq scandalized the religious establishment by explicitly rejecting the thesis that Islam was both religion and state. Indeed, he went as far as to say that an Islamic order does not require a caliph ruling on the basis of *sharīʿah* (the divine law). [*See the biography of ʿAbd al-Rāziq.*]

Islamic liberals today, the legatees of ʿAbd al-Rāziq, including the Egyptians Muḥammad ʿImārah, Muḥammad Aḥmad Khalafallāh, Aḥmad Kamāl Abū al-Majd, and Naṣr Ḥāmid Abū Zayd, maintain that the political sphere should be left entirely to the deliberations of the Muslims, in accordance with the saying of the Prophet attributed by three authoritative codices of *ḥadīth*—those of Muslim, Ibn Majāh, and ibn Ḥanbal (780–855)—that "if it is a matter of your religion, then have recourse to me, but if it is a matter of your world, you know better about it [than I do]."

However, the more radical scripturalist or traditionalist tendency among the Islamists differs vocally over this issue. Its spokesmen, such as Bediüzzaman Said Nursî (1873–1960) of Turkey, Sayyid Quṭb (1906–1966) of Egypt, Abu al-Aʿlā al-Mawdūdī (1903–1979) of Pakistan, and Ruhollah al-Musavi Khomeini (1902–1989) of Iran, all condemn the long-term trend of relegating the state to the secular sphere. In doing so, they lament the actual separation of the religious and political realms soon after the "golden age" of Islam (622–661). They maintain that this separation of religion and politics (i.e., religion and the state) had never been intended by the Prophet and his immediate successors. Accordingly, it is their express aim to restore the integration of religion and state, as symbolized by the slogan, *al-islām dīn wa dunyā* [*dawlah*] (Islam is religion and the world [state]). [*See* Nurculuk; *and the biographies of Quṭb, Mawdūdī, and Khomeini.*]

Representative of the thinking of the above four scripturalists and traditionalists is the following statement by Khālid Muḥammad Khālid, an Egyptian who in 1952 had been an ardent supporter of ʿAbd al-Rāziq's anticlerical line but recanted his views in 1981: "We find no religion . . . whose nature demands the establishment of a state as . . . does Islam." Islam may be a religion legislated by Allāh, but "in its human applications it represents a 'social contract' [*sic*] that includes the establishment of an authority that discharges the obligations of this contract and stands guard over its implementation" (1989, pp. 25, 29).

The efforts of contemporary Islamists are ironic, because the great founders of the schools of Islamic law, who lived in the eighth and ninth centuries, never contested the separation of the spheres of religion and state by the ruling caliphs of those times (Zubaida, 1989). If those luminaries had experienced differences with caliphs, these differences were theological in nature, not political. For example, Ibn Ḥanbal quarreled with and was punished by the caliph al-Ma'mūn (r. 813–833) over whether or not the Qur'ān was created or "uncreated." But Ibn Ḥanbal did not suggest that the separation of religion and state that had been effected by al-Ma'mūn's predecessors and maintained by him was wrong or cause for pronouncing unbelief on the ruler. Today's Islamists, who recognize the remarkable contributions of the great legists of the classical/early medieval period as being central to the very identity of Islam, nevertheless are implicitly criticizing these same legists when they declare the rulers of Muslim states today to be infidels.

Radical Islamists today perceive rulers who have slaughtered Muslims (such as Syria's Hafez al-Assad or Iraq's Saddam Hussein) to be apostates. Pro-Western rulers, such as those in Egypt since 1970, are also seen as un- or even anti-Islamic by such radicals. But the radicals additionally believe that rulers who seemingly preside over an Islamic order, such as in Saudi Arabia or Pakistan (between 1979 and 1989) but who in fact have given their blessings to increasing secularization of society, are unbelievers as well. Thus, the radicals entertain as legitimate Islamic states only Sudan (since 1989) and Iran (since 1979).

Yet, the criteria for inclusion in and exclusion from the category of the genuine Islamic state are not unambiguous. For example, even in Iran governmental institutions are based on the notion of separation of powers, a parliament, and popular sovereignty—all legacies of eighteenth century Western history. It is also difficult to imagine a genuine Islamic state whose economic policies are shaped by arrangements that are immune to *sharīʿah* provisions on contracts, loans, ownership, fiduciary responsibilities for joint investments, and international capital flows that are dependent on the exigencies of the capitalist world economy. An authentic Islamic state, as defined by radicals, would also be unable to assume membership in international organizations that operate on the basis of secular international law. It would also be a contradiction to call a nation an exemplary Islamic state if its government's conduct violates a standard canon of the Islamic law of war and peace (such as the doctrine of *amān,* a guarantee of safe conduct for the emissaries of infidels in the lands of the Muslims).

Moderate Islamists, however, explain the apparent borrowing from non-Islamic traditions or deviations from Islamic canons either by reference to established concepts in Islamic experience (for example, the concept of *shūrā* [deliberation] to justify reliance on a Parliament) or by reference to principles in Islamic law that allow Muslims to make adjustments to enhance their life's chances (for example, the doctrine of *istiṣlāḥ/maṣlaḥah mursalah* [deeming something to be good, beneficial, fitting]). The more radical Islamists, however, forthrightly repudiate what they regard as un-Islamic influences on the thinking and conduct of political leaders in their societies.

As can be seen, the concept of state in Islam has evolved over time. Although in theory many Muslims believe that there should be no separation between religion and state, in practice the separation was achieved early in Islamic history. Since Islamists today live in a world of nation-states, a world in which secularization is a fact of life, they cannot escape its portents. Among moderate Islamists, it is an article of faith that Islam has anticipated developments in the modern world either through venerable concepts in the scripture or the actual practice of leaders in Islamic history. They are not alarmed over mechanisms such as constitutions and parliaments. But the radicals among them have condemned both their more moderate colleagues and virtually all national leaders in the Muslim world today for being apostates who have either engineered or acquiesced to the deliberate separation of religion and state. It remains to be seen whether the more radical tendency will supervene in the ongoing conflict over the nature of the state, but that tendency does currently seem to be compelling attention.

Thus, the intellectual odyssey of Shaykh Muḥammad al-Ghazālī (b. 1917), for many years a highly public and visible figure in social discourse in Egypt, can be instructive. Al-Ghazālī, the author of a great number of works and generally considered in the mainstream of Muslim piety in the post–World War II era, has recently adopted an uncompromising stand on apostasy. In July 1992, he issued a *fatwā* which held that the state in Islamic societies today must punish apostates, defined as those who, in his opinion, have "turned their backs" on Islam. The issue is joined in relation to the Qur'ānic verse, "The truth is from your God, so believe or disbelieve as you will" (surah 18.29). Al-Ghazālī has contempt for those who interpret this verse as allowing citizens in Muslim societies to choose not to believe in God or in *sharīʿah.* The verse only applies to the community before its members have embraced Islam, he insists. But once they have recited the credo of faith, prayed, remitted *zakāt* (alms)—in short, once they have adopted the faith—they will never allow a minority to exercise their putative "human rights" (al-Ghazālī's term) by choosing to disbelieve. If anyone disbelieves under such circumstances, then the state must punish him under Islamic law. Unstated in the *fatwā* but well understood by his readers is that apostasy in Islam is a capital offense. The implication is that if the state does not punish apostates, then it would be appropriate for Muslims to replace it with one that would.

If radical Islamists were to take over the currently configured secular Egyptian state at some future time, observers might wonder if al-Ghazālī would go even further and adopt the position embraced by Ayatollah Khomeini in two *fatwā*s that he issued in late 1987 and early 1988. There, Khomeini argued that the state, because it was in his opinion a truly Islamic state, could command its citizens to do anything it deemed essential to protect its interests. By definition this would advance the cause of Islam. Thus, he argued, the state could even order Muslims to suspend prayer and pilgrimage to Mecca (considered two of Islam's most central obligations), if doing so would serve the purpose of maintaining that state from dissolution. Yet, there can be no doubt that jurists in Islamic history would sanction rebellion against a ruler who gave such orders, as that ruler would be guilty of the revocation of two of the five pillars of Islam. After all, it was Ibn Taymīyah (d. 1328) himself, frequently invoked by radical Islamists today to justify pronouncing unbelief on those they believe to be bad Muslims, who issued his famous *fatwā* calling for rebellion against the Mongol rulers of his time for similar offenses.

[*See also* Authority and Legitimation; Ḥukūmah; Imāmah; Nation.]

BIBLIOGRAPHY

Ayubi, Nazih N. *Political Islam*. London and New York, 1991. Wide-ranging discussion of the social aspects of Islam, including a focus on contemporary movements in select Islamic states.

Binder, Leonard. *Islamic Liberalism*. Chicago, 1988. Systematic exposition and analysis of Islamic political theory through the prism of liberalism and its opponents.

Enayat, Hamid. *Modern Islamic Political Thought*. Austin, 1982. Examination of major themes of power, authority, obligation, community, democracy, and others in Islamic discourse.

Ghazālī, Muḥammad al-. "Hādhā Dīnunā" (This is Our Religion). *Al-Shaʿb* (Cairo), 9 July 1992.

Ibn Khaldūn, ʿAbd al-Raḥmān. *The Muqaddimah*. 3 vols. Translated by Franz Rosenthal. New York, 1958. Magnum opus by Islam's most famous social historian, containing his explanation of cyclical historical change.

ʿImārah, Muḥammad. *Al-dawlah al-Islāmīyah bayna al-ʿilmānīyah wa-al-ṣultah al-dīnīyah* (The Islamic State between Secularism and Religious Authority). Cairo, 1988. Vindication of the position of Islamic liberalism on the state, arguing that the Prophet was a religious leader whose political role was contingent rather than absolute.

Khālid, Khālid Muḥammad. *Al-dawlah fī al-Islām* (The State in Islam). 3d ed. Cairo, 1989. Unabashed defense of the argument that Islam is *dīn wa-dawlah*, by an erstwhile Islamic modernist who renounced his earlier views in 1980 for the traditionalist, scripturalist position.

Lewis, Bernard. *The Political Language of Islam*. Chicago and London, 1988. Discussion of key concepts in Islamic discourse on politics, by a well-known Orientalist.

Piscatori, J. P. *Islam in a World of Nation-States*. Cambridge, 1986. Argues that Islamic theories of politics have consistently made an accommodation to the nation-state idea and practice.

Rosenthal, E. I. J. *Islam in the Modern National State*. Cambridge, 1965. Classical scholar's attempt to situate Western concepts of nationalism and nation-state in the context of Islamic history.

Rosenthal, Franz. "Dawla." In *Encyclopaedia of Islam*, new ed., vol. 2, pp. 177–178. Leiden, 1960–. Pithy account of the evolution of the meaning of *dawlah* up to the twelfth–thirteenth centuries of the common era.

Zubaida, Sami. *Islam, the People, and the State*. London, 1989. Contemporary sociologist's critique of the notion that the Islamic resurgence of the post-1967 era is based on a radical break with the assumptions of Western models of politics and the state.

SHAHROUGH AKHAVI

DAWLAH AL-ISLĀMĪYAH, AL-. *See* Islamic State.

DEMOCRACY. Around the middle of the nineteenth century, new ways of thought began to emerge in the Middle East, owing primarily to contact with European industry, communications, and political ideas and institutions. Although the new modes of thought did not represent a break with the Islamic past, there was a modern element in the thought of some Muslim thinkers and officials who learned about Western culture, and who believed that Muslims could increase their strength by adopting Western laws and institutions in a selective fashion. For some writers of this period the principles of social action are rational and change as society changes. Human society, they affirmed, is its own judge and master, and its own interest should reign supreme.

The representative figure of this period is the Egyptian reformer Muḥammad ʿAbduh (1848–1905), who disseminated his ideas through the periodical *Al-manār*. His purpose was to strengthen the moral roots of Islamic society, by returning to the past, but by recognizing and accepting the need for change and by linking that change to the teachings of Islam. ʿAbduh believed that Islam can both adapt to change and also control that change. In short, ʿAbduh asserted that Islam could be the moral basis of a modern, progressive society. Thus ʿAbduh's thought has a traditional Islamic basis, but at the same time it moves in the direction of new ideas about social and political organization.

From about 1900 until the early 1950s, two lines of thought coexisted in the Arab parts of the Middle East. Supporters of the first advocated the principles of secularism and constitutional democracy. A main element in this school was a belief in representative government based on broad political participation. Following the dissolution of the Ottoman state this trend was carried further by leaders of political groups and national liberation movements; it seemed to have reached its logical end with the establishment of quasiconstitutional systems in a number of Arab countries on the model of Western-style democracies. However, experimenting with democracy did not prove a happy experience. Rigged elections, puppet governments, arbitrary arrests, and rubber-stamp parliaments raised serious doubts in many people's minds about the ability of the Arabs to create and tolerate democratic institutions and practices.

Following a second line of thought were those who believed that Islamic law and institutions should be the basis of political and social organization, rejecting the principle that society should be regulated by secular norms. For most of those who subscribed to this view, the ideal was to live in the inherited Islamic world of thought and to preserve the continuity of the Islamic tradition. In many respects, this contrasts with the thought of the advocates of democratic reform, most of whom accepted Islam as a body of principles but believed that the secular norms of nationalism and liberal democracy were best suited for the reorganization of Arab society and politics.

Following the 1948 Palestine war and more specifically with the advent to power of revolutionary regimes in key Arab states (Egypt, Syria, and Iraq), the balance of political ideas tilted decisively in favor of the radicalism of the revolutionary state. The new ways of thought and action were embodied in a form of nationalism that acquired a content of social reform expressed in the idiom of Arab socialism, and a foreign-policy orientation expressed in the language of anticolonialism and positive neutrality. In the 1950s and 1960s, many secularists as well as Islamists were engaged in attempts to prove that Islam and socialism were compatible, and that the pursuit of Arab unity was more important than the pursuit of democracy and pluralism. In North Africa as well as in the Arab East, the principle of Arab unity held first place, on the grounds that socialism, freedom, and the liberation of Palestine could not be achieved except on its basis. This was a position clearly articulated by the representatives of Arab nationalism—Egyptian president Gamal Abdel Nasser (1918–1970), as well as such Baʿthist activists and intellectuals as the Syrian Michel Aflaq (1910–1989), the Palestinian ʿAbd Allāh al-Rīmāwī, and the Jordanian Munīf al-Razzāz.

In the 1970s and 1980s, the unrest generated by war and civil strife in some Arab countries, the failure of Arab governments to stand up to Israel, the rising discontent with socioeconomic performance, and the unchecked growth of the power of the state brought about a change in the scale of political life: there was a broader agenda of grievances, and a larger public for new ideas and rhetoric. The movement for a revival of Islam as the only valid basis for social and political life was perhaps the most significant aspect of this change.

The term "fundamentalist" is too narrow to be applicable to these movements. Fundamentalism has an explanatory value only if it is applied to specific aspects of a political movement or a religious doctrine. Islamic political movements have different, competing, and even conflicting ideas about life in society, and about how Muslims should interact with the outside world. These movements are not monolithic. On the contrary, they are an admixture of diverse religious and political groups, each with its own leadership and organization as well as its own social and political agenda. Not all of them are devoted to absolute truth, and not all are concerned with "essences" and "fundamentals." Indeed, many have specific agendas that are not carved in stone, but rather adapt to changing conditions. [*See* Fundamentalism.]

With the rise of Islamic political movements in the 1970s and 1980s, different writers and activists formulated different ideas about social and political organization. We shall deal in a general way with two of them—the liberal Islamic and the conservative Islamic perspectives—because they are broadly representative of certain attitudes and positions with respect to the notion of democracy; however, the reader should not impose a false unity on the ideas of all those who subscribe to one or the other perspective.

Liberal Islamic View. Advocates of the liberal view were influenced by Muḥammad ʿAbduh. The thrust of this view, essentially ʿAbduh's, is that Islam the religion does not conflict with a secular perspective. In matters of religious doctrine, the role of Islam is to cleanse the soul and guide the believers to their creator. On worldly matters, however, ʿAbduh asserts that Islam's position is a secular one (Muḥammad al-Nuwayhī, "Al-dīn wa-azamat al-tatawwur al-hadari fil-watan al-ʿArabī" [Religion and the Problem of Civilizational Development in the Arab World], *Al-adab,* May 1974, pp. 79–86). Thus, according to ʿAbduh and to those who adopted his view, Islam encourages Muslims to establish their government on the basis of modern reasoning, and on the basis of the rules of government that have been tested and proven by the experience of nations.

Three concepts are central to the liberal Islamic view: *shūrā* (consultation), *al-maṣlaḥah* (public interests), and *ʿadl* (justice). There are disagreements among Muslim scholars with regard to *shūrā,* but in essence they all agree, on the basis of Qur'ānic verses, that God instructed the Prophet to consult with his advisers, even those whose advice had led to defeat in battle. They also agree that good Muslims consult with each other in the course of conducting their affairs. Some observers consider this principle of "mutual consultation" to be a basis for the election of representative leaders and government institutions, as in the case of Western democracies. *Fatwā*s (scholarly opinions), it is further argued, have allowed and will continue to allow different systems of government to legitimize their authority in the name of Islam.

The concept of *al-maṣlaḥah,* though not fully discussed in the writings of liberal Muslim thinkers, means doing what is good for the people and avoiding what is injurious to their interest. A critical issue here is the extent to which the people can be involved in determining what is good and what is not good for them. Theoretically speaking, this can be resolved through "mutual consultation" through the representative organs of the state. But regardless of the extent of consultation, a just rule is a sine qua non for the promotion of public interest. In this regard, Islamic political leaders are considered to be just insofar as they follow policies that are consistent with the public interest as defined through *shūrā,* and insofar as they do not inflict any unnecessary hardship on their people. [*See* Maṣlaḥah.]

Also critical to the emergence and proper functioning of a democratic system is tolerance for pluralism. With respect to this, liberal Islamic thinkers argue that the Qur'ān allows for political and religious diversity. Among the often-cited Qur'ānic verses is 2.256, *lā ikrāha fī al-dīn* ("there is no compulsion in religion"). This is interpreted to indicate the equality of Muslims and non-Muslims in civic rights and duties. There is inequality in matters of faith, but this is something that should be left to God. Human beings are not entitled to pass judgment on other people's religious beliefs. According to the liberals, in dealing with worldly matters the challenge is to enter social transactions and relations on a basis that allows for adaptation to changing conditions. This requires a secular view and a secular way of life. This view and this way of life can be consistent with the religious doctrine of Islam, which is in essence the purest form of worship.

Another liberal view that fits into this category was expounded by the Egyptian thinker Muḥammad ʿImārah. Starting from the assumption that Islam distinguishes between religious matters on the one hand and worldly matters on the other—a distinction which, he says, is not based on separation *(faṣl)* but rather on the distinctiveness *(tamyīz)* of spheres—ʿImārah proceeds to argue that Islam is far from being a theocracy. As far as the lay character of political authority is concerned, ʿImārah says that it is legitimate insofar as it rests on *shūrā,* selection, and public accountability. This does not entail, however, separation of state from religion, because Islam can be realized only through actual practice. ʿImārah's conclusion is that the two spheres of political and religious authority should coexist, but they should not be unified in one structure.

Thus, as far as these two spheres are concerned, distinction and not separation, coexistence and not overlapping, are the framework within which political organization should take place. In this scheme of things, political authority should be vested in the people who are responsible for organizing their political order in accordance with the requirements of their times, but within the framework of the principles of Islam. For ʿImārah, unifying the temporal and religious authorities is not only un-Islamic; it is also tyrannical, primarily because it deprives the people of their right to be involved in the organization of their political life.

Conservative Islamic View. In considering this perspective, we may begin with the Muslim Egyptian thinker Sayyid Quṭb (1906–1966), who was a leading member of the Society of Muslim Brothers and whose writings have become very popular since his execution by the Egyptian authorities in 1966. Quṭb condemns the Arab nation-state systems as un-Islamic and as part of what he calls the modern *jāhilīyah,* a term that originally denoted the period prior to the emergence of Islam in the seventh century. For Quṭb, many prevailing aspects of modern life, including Western institutions and beliefs, are evil and therefore inconsistent with Islam, except for modern science and technology. Quṭb believes in the superiority of the Islamic system. He also believes that the comprehensiveness and universality of Islam make it good for all peoples, regardless of place and time.

On the basis of this belief, Quṭb asserts that the Islamic political order is an eternal system. The foundation of this system rests on three pillars: justice on the part of rulers; obedience on the part of followers; and consultation between leaders and followers. The *sharīʿah* is the source of all rules, both worldly and nonworldly. For Quṭb, a just political and social order based on the Qur'ān and the *sunnah* will lead to the implementation of the *sharīʿah* and will thus fulfill the main goal of Islam, which is the establishment of the Islamic state. Thus the main value is not democracy but the implementation of the *sharīʿah.* Further, the political system that can claim Islamic legitimacy is the one that enforces the *sharīʿah,* whether it is a monarchy, a republic, or any other form of government.

Another representative of this perspective is Ḥasan al-Turābī (b. 1932), a leading contemporary Islamic thinker as well as the primary ideologist of the Sudanese Islamic National Front, the main pillar of the Sudanese government; he argues that any political or social system must be based on *tawḥīd* (unification). The concept of *tawḥīd* means the unification of all Muslims as a fulfilment of the *rabbānīyah* (lordship) of God. *Shūrā* and *tawḥīd* should go hand in hand. *Shūrā* is needed to interpret the *sharīʿah* and to deal with constitutional, legal, social, and economic matters. Al-Turābī distinguishes between the connotations of *shūrā* and those of Western-style democracy. For him *shūrā* represents the ultimate sovereignty of God as embodied in the Qur'ān; democracy, on the other hand, connotes the ultimate sovereignty of the people. [*See* Tawḥīd.]

According to al-Turābī, liberal democratic systems are flawed for two reasons. First, they are based on factional interests and therefore cannot promote real political equality, unity, and freedom. Because wealth, and therefore power, are concentrated in a few hands, ultimate authority lies with a small elite. Second, liberal democracies are based on human reason, and regardless of how much human reason tries to perfect the political and social order, it still suffers from the limitations that God has imposed on humans.

Thus, for al-Turābī, Islam has a unique advantage in that it postulates the divinely-ordained unity of political *shūrā* and *tawḥīd.* This unity guarantees against tyranny because it resolves ideological conflicts and unifies Muslim actions. It also leads to *ʿaqd al-bayʿah* (contract of allegiance) between the people and their ruler. The origin of this *ʿaqd* is *ijmāʿ* (consensus) through political *shūrā.* Al-Turābī believes that by following this course Muslims will be able to create a democratic system free from the flaws of liberal democracies. This system will be able to deliver the Islamic *ummah* from *jāhilīyah,* and will provide through *shūrā* a vehicle of participation and adaptation to change, as well as a mechanism for the realization of true political equality.

These Islamic notions of democracy and life in society are informative not only about the thinkers who articulated them but also about the time when they were presented. One may argue that even though these thinkers influenced the minds of others, none of them produced a comprehensive and sophisticated theory about political and social organization. One may also argue that none of the liberal Islamic thinkers has made a satisfactory effort to make liberal principles applicable in any systematic way to the conditions of Islamic social life.

To some extent, however, one finds in these Islamic ideas the two distinct, though not necessarily conflicting, elements of modernity and tradition that echo the thoughts of nineteenth-century Islamic writers. What is perhaps most significant about them is that they show the point at which certain ideas about political organization have entered contemporary Arab intellectual discourse. They also show the attempts of certain thinkers to restructure Islamic society and politics, either on the basis of an inherited Islamic past, or on the basis of a half-argued theory of liberal norms.

[*See also the biographies of ʿAbduh, Quṭb, and Turābī.*]

BIBLIOGRAPHY

Appleby, R. Scott. "The Dynamics of Religious Fundamentalism." *Headline Series,* no. 301. New York, 1994.

Arkoun, Mohammed. *Rethinking Islam: Common Questions, Uncommon Answers.* Boulder, 1994.

Bulliet, Richard W. "The Future of the Islamic Movement." *Foreign Affairs* 72.5 (November/December 1993): 38–44. The author examines the Islamic movement's role in the PLO-Israeli peace process.

Burgat, François, and William Dowell. *The Islamic Movement in North Africa*. Austin, 1993. The author discusses Islamic groups in North Africa and outlines the main ideas of some of their leading representatives.

Esposito, John L. *The Islamic Threat: Myth or Reality?* New York and Oxford, 1992. Leading expert examines diverse Islamic trends refuting in the process Western notions of a hostile, monolithic Islam.

Haddad, Yvonne Y., John O. Voll, and John L. Esposito, eds. *The Contemporary Islamic Revival: A Critical Survey and Bibliography*. New York, 1991. A well-researched annotated bibliography. Each editor contributes an excellent introductory essay.

Islam, Democracy, the State, and the West: A Round Table with Dr. Hasan Turabi. Tampa, 1993. Presents the text of a lecture given by Turābī, discussions, questions, and a summary by John Voll. The lecture addresses the development of the *sharī'ah*, human rights, and the relationship between state and society.

Keddie, Nikki R. *Iran: Religion, Politics and Society*. London, 1980. Survey of religion, society, and politics in modern Iran.

Mernissi, Fatima. *Islam and Democracy: Fear of the Modern World*. Translated by Mary Jo Lakeland. Reading, Mass., 1992. Focuses on the need of Middle Eastern nations to introduce democratic institutions and the readiness of their peoples to participate in those institutions.

Mortimer, Robert A. "Algeria: The Clash between Islam, Democracy, and the Military." *Current History* 92.570 (January 1993): 37–41. The author examines the political situation in Algeria following the military takeover of January 1992.

Piscatori, James P., ed. *Islam in the Political Process*. Cambridge, 1983.

Zartman, I. William, and William M. Habeeb, eds. *Polity and Society in Contemporary North Africa*. Boulder, 1993. A general survey of the transformations in North Africa since independence with focus on religious, economic, demographic, and political trends.

MUHAMMAD MUSLIH

DEMOKRAT PARTI. Turkey was ruled by the Demokrat Parti (DP) from 1950 until its overthrow by a military coup on 27 May 1960. Its founders, Celâl Bayar (1884–1986), Mehmet Fuat Köprülü (1890–1966), Refik Koraltan (1891–1974), and Adnan Menderes (1899–1961), were all ranking members of the governing Cumhuriyet Halk Partisi (Republican People's Party, CHP). Bayar, a banker in his early life, had played a critical role during the Kemalist period in the liberal, antistatist wing of the party and had served as prime minister in 1937–1938. Köprülü, a historian and Turcologist, had proposed a reformation that would turkify Islam; his proposal, however, was not taken seriously. Koraltan was a bureaucrat, and Menderes a large landowner from the prosperous Aegean region. Together they represented the liberal wing of the CHP; in forming the DP, they responded to the rising bourgeoisie's demand for political and economic liberalization and an end to the state's hegemony over civil society. The Turkish people had also come to hate the single-party regime, which had become increasingly repressive, especially during World War II. The imposition of militant secularism was especially resented by the sullen population. The pressure for political change that came from a victorious America, which encouraged pluralism and a free-market economy, ought not to be discounted either.

The introduction of multiparty politics and the lively competition for votes made Islam a burning issue and forced all parties to reevaluate their religious policy. Between 1945 and the 1950 elections, the CHP abandoned its militant secularism and made concessions to Islamic sentiment. When the Democrats won power in May 1950, they merely accelerated the process, realizing that the overwhelmingly Muslim population had been alienated by state interference in religious life.

The Democrats' first concession was quite dramatic: in June 1950, they lifted the ban on the call to prayer *(ezan)* being made in Arabic and permitted muezzins to sing the *ezan* in either Arabic or Turkish. Most chose Arabic, and the impact of this reform resounded throughout the country. On 5 July they permitted the broadcasting of religious programs over the radio, and the Qur'ān was heard over the airwaves. In October, religious lesson in schools (introduced by the CHP) became virtually obligatory when parents were asked to inform the authorities in writing if they did not want their children to attend such lessons. Few Muslim parents did so.

There was a bipartisan consensus on religious policy as long as the secular reforms of Atatürk were not threatened. In fact, both parties welcomed the Director of Religious Affairs' pronouncement against communism. "Islam," declared Ahmed Hamdi Akseki, "rejects communism absolutely, its ideology in any form and all its practices. Faith and spirit are the most powerful weapons against communism. It is not possible for a genuine believer to reconcile himself to the ideas and practices of communism."

The more liberal atmosphere marked by an emphasis on populist politics also led to the reappearance of a variety of religious orders popular with the masses. Their leaders believed that Islamist political pressure would compel the DP government to reverse some of the major reforms of the republic, notably the Western code of law and the Latin script. In the DP's congress in Konya in 1951, there were demands for the restoration of the fez, the headwear banned in 1925, and the veiling of women. Politics also entered the mosque, and the Friday sermon was often used to denounce the opposition for being anti-Islam. Even Atatürk's busts and statues, found in every village and town, were vandalized.

The CHP, founded by Atatürk and claiming his mantle, blamed the Democrats for failing to protect the Kemalism to which both parties were constitutionally committed. Prime Minister Menderes responded by taking stern measures against the reactionaries. In March 1951 orders were issued to protect Atatürk's statues, and men like Necip Fazıl Kısakürek, who led the Islamic resurgence, were prosecuted. Islamist publications were proscribed. In June 1951 members of the Tijānī order, who were agitating for the restoration of a theocratic monarchy (also a violation of the constitution), were arrested. Their shaykh, Kemal Pilavoğlu, was sentenced to ten years at hard labor. The "Atatürk Bill" passed by the Assembly on 25 July gave the state greater powers to prosecute those who threatened the secular republic. Under this law, the Islamic Democrat Party was dissolved in March 1952, Kısakürek was sent to jail, and Said Nursî (Nurculuk), the leader of the Nurists, was put on trial. Finally, the "Law to protect the Freedom of Conscience" was passed in July 1953 to prevent Islam from being used for political ends. Under this law, when the Nation Party, founded in July 1948 by a right-wing splinter group in the DP, made Islam a part of its political platform, it was dissolved by court order on 27 January 1954. [*See also* Nurculuk*; and the biography of Kısakürek*.]

In the 1954 election, however, all parties exploited religion to attract votes, though with little success. The DP's victory was even more resounding than in 1950, its triumph being based on its economic policies, which initially brought the country prosperity as well as a great sense of dynamism and hope. Only in Kirşehir was Islam's role critical; there the Republican Nation Party, supported by the Bektāshī order, won all seats.

After 1955 the DP too began to exploit Islam more openly. There were two principal reasons for the change. First, the liberal Kemalist wing broke away and formed the Freedom Party, strengthening the right wing. Second, the economy began to stall, leading the Democrats to flout their religious image as a distraction. They cultivated the religious orders because they controlled local voting blocs. More money was spent on mosques, and the Democrats boasted that they had spent 37.5 million liras (over thirteen million dollars) in seven years, while the CHP had spent only 6.5 million liras in their twenty-seven years.

The decline of the DP's vote from 56.6 percent in 1954 to 47.3 percent in 1957 suggests that its religious policy was not paying off. The economic crisis turned voters away, and religious appeal was a poor substitute. Religious activity flourished in 1958, a disastrous year for the economy with the lira devalued by almost four hundred percent. Radio was now allowed to devote more airtime to religious programs, and the Nurists were left free to spread their propaganda.

The Democrats had become identified with the resurgence of Islam. After Menderes survived an airplane crash in London in February 1959, that identification became more explicit; the hand of providence was seen in the escape, described as miraculous. The myth of Menderes's immortality emerged, and it has been suggested that the junta that overthrew him executed Menderes to destroy this myth.

The Demokrat Parti facilitated the Islamic resurgence as any ruling party would have done to survive the challenge of competitive politics. In fact, the resurgence was more the consequence of the mass politics that replaced the politics of elites in 1945. The center of political gravity shifted to the provinces largely untouched by Kemalist reforms or modern secular culture. This was recognized after the fall of the Democrats, and any party that has won power since has had to cope with this element of political life.

[*See also* Turkey.]

BIBLIOGRAPHY

Ahmad, Feroz. *The Turkish Experiment in Democracy, 1950–1975*. London and Boulder, 1977. Contains two interesting chapters on the Demokrat Parti and one on religion and politics.

Karpat, Kemal. *Turkey's Politics: The Transition to a Multi-Party System*. Princeton, 1959. The best study of the 1945–1950 period.

Lewis, Bernard. *The Emergence of Modern Turkey*. 2d ed. London and New York, 1968. Authoritative account of political and intellectual changes in post-Kemalist Turkey, as well as earlier periods.

Sarıbay, Ali Yaşar. "The Democratic Party, 1946–1960." In *Political Parties and Democracy in Turkey*, edited by Metin Heper and Jacob Landau, pp. 119–133. London and New York, 1991. Recent reevaluation of the Demokrat Parti by a Turkish political scientist.

Simpson, Dwight. "Development as a Process: The Menderes Phase in Turkey." *Middle East Journal* 19 (Spring 1965): 141–152.

Toprak, Binnaz. *Islam and Political Development in Turkey*. Leiden, 1981. A book that tries to make sense of this important subject.

FEROZ AHMAD

DEOBANDĪS. The *ʿulamāʾ* associated with the Indo-Pakistani reformist movement centered in the Dār al-ʿUlūm of Deoband are known by the name Deobandīs. The school at Deoband, a country town some ninety miles northeast of Delhi, was founded in 1867. It was a pioneer effort to transmit the religious sciences, specifically the *dars-i niẓāmī* identified with the Lucknow-based *ʿulamāʾ* of Farangī Maḥall, by utilizing institutional forms derived from British schools. The goal of the school was to preserve the teachings of the faith in a period of non-Muslim rule and considerable social change by holding Muslims to a standard of correct practice; central to that goal was the creation of a class of formally trained and popularly supported *ʿulamāʾ*. The school had classrooms, a bureaucratically organized faculty, formal examinations, and an annual convocation. The founders, knowing princely patronage and *waqf* no longer to be dependable sources of financing, created a system of popular contributions utilizing the mail and money orders; donors, many from the *ashrāf* classes involved in government service and trade, were listed in an annual report.

Several men central to the foundation of the school were educated in Delhi in the 1840s and participated in two critically important institutions: the reformist milieu of *ʿulamāʾ* linked to the family of Shāh Walī Allāh and Sayyid Aḥmad Barelwī, and Delhi College, founded by the British to teach both European and "Oriental" subjects through the medium of Urdu rather than in the former court language Persian or the religious languages Sanskrit and Arabic). [*See the biographies of Walī Allāh and Barelwī.*] Among those later active at Deoband were the son and the nephew of a teacher at Delhi College, Maulānā Mamlūk ʿAlī: Muḥammad Yaʿqūb Nanautawī, the first principal or *ṣadr mudarris* (1867–1888) and a revered *murshid* or spiritual guide at the school, and Muḥammad Qāsim Nanautawī (1833–1877), the school's *sarparast* (rector) and also a spiritual guide. Also present in Delhi were Rashīd Aḥmad Gangohī (1829–1905), an early *muhtamim* (chancellor) and a scholar of *ḥadīth* and *fiqh*, and Ḥājjī Imdādullāh (1817–1899), who departed for Mecca after the Mutiny of 1857 and served as the beloved pir of the early Deobandī *ʿulamāʾ*.

Starting with only a dozen students, the school enrolled several hundred by the end of the century; by its first centenary in 1967, it counted a total of 3,795 graduates from throughout India, 3,191 from what was then East and West Pakistan, and 431 from foreign countries. The students, whatever their geographic origin, were united by the use of standard Urdu and shared accommodation in dormitories. The school soon became a metropolitan center, with students coming in the early years from Central Asia, Afghanistan, and all of India; in the twentieth century there have been students from the diaspora populations in East and South Africa, and from Europe and North America as well.

In its six-year course the school emphasized *ḥadīth* and the Ḥanafī legal tradition, using both as a framework to scrutinize customary practices and to enjoin correct observance of ritual and life-cycle events. Students typically sought the personal transformation of sober Sufism with the help of a spiritual guide; multiple initiation into various *silsilah*s was common but occurred at the hands of a single *murshid* or pir. Those tied to Ḥajjī Imdādullāh were primarily Chishtī Sabiri; the influence of the Naqshbandī Mujaddidi was also strong. Hallmarks of Deobandī practice included opposition to *ʿurs* (annual death anniversary celebrations) at the graves of saints, to the so-called *fātiḥah* food offerings for the dead (distributed after reciting the Fātiḥah Chapter of the Qur'ān), and to the elaborate ceremonies associated with birth, marriage, and death often typical of local non-Muslims as well. By emphasizing individual responsibility for correct belief and practice, the Deobandīs provided an alternative to an intercessory religion focused on the Ṣūfī shrines and elaborate customary celebrations.

Deobandīs served as imams, guardians and trustees of mosques and tombs, preachers, writers, and publishers of religious works. Some joined in the public debates that began in response to Christian missionary initiative in the nineteenth century. Many offered *fatwā*s to provide spiritual counsel and guidance on legal matters apart from state institutions. Many were teachers. Among the most celebrated early graduates of the school was the prolific writer and revered spiritual guide Maulānā Ashraf ʿAlī Thānvī (1864–1943). His guide for Muslim girls, the *Bihishtī zevar,* written at the turn of the century, has been widely circulated both in Urdu and in translations into many regional languages.

The Deobandīs from the beginning envisaged a network of schools; the multiple ties of education, Ṣūfī affiliation, and family linked many teachers among them. By the end of the nineteenth century there were more than a dozen schools known as Deobandī from Peshawar to Chittagong to Madras; in the calculations made for the school's centenary, Deobandīs were credited with founding 8,934 schools, both primary and advanced. Among the early schools, and most important down to the present, was the Maẓāhir-i ʿUlūm, founded in nearby Saharanpur; for a time Maulānā Rashīd Aḥmad served as chancellor of that school as well. Today there are Deobandī schools throughout the subcontinent, and the term *Deobandī* still characterizes one of the main divisions *(maslak)* of subcontinental *ʿulamāʾ*.

Originally quiescent politically, individual Deobandīs, if not the school itself, began to act politically in the period before World War I. Maulānā ʿUbaidullāh Sindhī (1872–1944) was one of the first to forge links between the *ʿulamāʾ* and those educated at Aligarh [*see* Aligarh]; during the war he went to Afghanistan to work with German and Turkish agents there. Maulānā Maḥmūdulḥasan (1851–1920), traditionally counted as Deoband's first student and later a celebrated teacher at the school, worked on behalf of the Ottomans in the Hejaz (Ḥijāz), as a result of which he was exiled to Malta. He became known as the "Shaykh al-Hind." As the nationalist movement gained strength, many Deobandīs participated in the organization of the Jamʿīyatul ʿUlamāʾ-i Hind in 1919; the movement allied with the Congress Party but clearly envisaged independence as leading to a federation of religious communities with little common social and political life. As independence approached, most Deobandīs opposed the partition of India and saw Pakistan as the creation of westernized forces and an enforced confinement of Muslim influence. [*See* Jamʿīyatul ʿUlamāʾ-i Hind.] Foremost among the politically active was Maulānā Ḥusain Aḥmad Madanī (1879–1957), who engaged in an exchange with Muhammad Iqbal over the priority of regional and religious identity for statehood. [*See the biography of Iqbal.*] A minority of Deobandīs, led by Maulānā Shabbīr Aḥmad ʿUṣmānī (1887–1949) and including Muftī Muḥammad Shāfiʿ, Maulānā Ihtishāmul Ḥaqq Thānvī, and Maulānā ʿAbdulḥamīd Badāʾūnī (d. 1969), supported the Muslim League's demand for Pakistan; in 1945 in Calcutta they founded the Jamʿīyatul ʿUlamāʾ-i Islām, which continued as a political party in Pakistan. [*See* Jamʿīyatul ʿUlamāʾ-i Islām.] In 1967 Prime Minister Indira Gandhi visited Deoband on its centenary, and a commemorative stamp depicting the school was issued. In the early 1980s the school was torn by factional strife linked to national political affiliation; those associated with the family of the rector, Qārīʾ Muḥammad Ṭayyib Qāsimī, a grandson of Maulānā Muḥammad Qāsim, were ousted. The central school, and Deobandī schools throughout the subcontinent, continue to teach many students. The apolitical strand within the school's teaching has taken shape for many in the widespread, now transnational, movement known since the 1920s as Tablīghī Jamāʿat; the movement has particularly cherished the *ḥadīth*-based writings of Maulānā Muḥammad Zakarīyā Kāndhalavī, long linked to Deoband's sister school, the Maẓāhir-i ʿUlūm.

[*See also* India; Islam, *article on* Islam in South Asia; Pakistan; Tablīghī Jamāʿat.]

BIBLIOGRAPHY

Faruqi, Ziya-ul-Hasan. *The Deoband School and the Demand for Pakistan.* Bombay, 1963. Brief but useful treatment of the role of Deobandīs in support of the Congress movement.

Friedmann, Yohanan. "The Attitude of the *Jamīʿyat ʿUlamaʾ-i Hind* to the Indian National Movement and the Establishment of Pakistan." In *The ʿUlamaʾ in Modern History,* edited by Gabriel Baer, pp. 157–183. Jerusalem, 1971. Detailed treatment of the first major political organization of the *ʿulamāʾ*, primarily Deobandī, which opposed the Pakistan movement. Friedmann notes the parallel opposition of respected Jewish religious leaders to the Zionist movement.

Hardy, Peter. *The Muslims of British India.* Cambridge, 1972. The best overall survey, providing a good context for specific educational and political movements.

Metcalf, Barbara D. *Islamic Revival in British India: Deoband, 1860–1900.* Princeton, 1982. Study of Deoband in its early decades based on institutional records, government records, and writings of the Deobandīs themselves, including biographies, memoirs, diaries, tracts, letters, and *fatwās*. It also includes an overview of other movements of the period: that of the Ahl-i Ḥadīth, the Barelwīs, the Nadwah *ʿulamāʾ*, and Aligarh.

Thānvī, Ashraf ʿAlī. *Perfecting Women: Maulana Ashraf ʿAli Thanawi's Bihishti Zewar.* Translated with commentary by Barbara D. Metcalf. Berkeley, 1990. Partial translation and study of one of the most influential Deobandī texts.

BARBARA D. METCALF

DERVISHES. *See* Sufism.

DESTOUR. At the beginning of the twentieth century an organization known as the Young Tunisians cradled a new sense of Tunisian nationalism. Drawn primarily from the Turkish Mamlūk aristocracy that ruled Tunisia prior to the French protectorate, the French-educated Young Tunisians aspired simply to make Tunisia modern. Anticolonial sentiments grew after World War I, and in 1920 many of those who had belonged to the elite Young Tunisians joined with urban merchants and notables to form a more expressly political organization. As its name suggests, the Destour (Dustūr, or Constitution) party sought a voice in the colonial government through a constitution and duly elected parliament; it did not, however, call for political independence.

Modern secularists of the next generation—including the young lawyer Habib Bourguiba—were initially attracted to the Destour but soon found their energies frustrated by its underlying conservatism. In 1934 they founded the Neo-Destour and rapidly captured the support of a rising middle class and the rural masses, whose hardships during two decades of economic depression had been ignored by both the French and earlier nationalist groups. The Neo-Destour led the drive to independence, and the new government was shaped under its direction in 1957.

Political opposition was not outlawed until 1962, but from the outset the government of independent Tunisia was dominated by a single party. In 1958 the Neo-Destour was restructured to parallel the administrative units at every level of government, and the distinction between state and party became progressively blurred. Through the Neo-Destour and the national organizations it controlled, the government disseminated its message and enacted its programs; in return for their loyalty, the party faithful could expect access to state patronage.

As president and "Supreme Combatant," Bourguiba capitalized on his popularity within the party to promote a program of modernity and progress. With the tacit support of party leadership, he brought the religious establishment under the state's control and introduced broad social reforms. On the economic front, a 1962 commitment to state-led development planning inspired the party to rename itself the Parti Socialiste Destourien (PSD, Destourian Socialist Party). Strong popular resistance, however, forced the program of agricultural cooperatives it had endorsed to be abandoned in 1969.

By this juncture it was apparent that the PSD's hold on society had slipped. From the late 1970s an Islamist movement first known as the Mouvement de la Tendance Islamique (Ar., Ḥarakat al-Ittijāh al-Islāmī; Islamic Tendency Movement; later renamed Ḥizb al-Nahḍah or Renaissance Party) gained popular appeal, and the PSD's efforts to revive its own flagging support were unsuccessful. Its pool of patronage had shrunk, and it had few satisfying answers for those who criticized its pro-Western secularism.

Prime Minister Zine el Abidine Ben Ali (b. 1936) toppled the government of the aging Bourguiba in November 1987, and as a sign of new commitment to republican rule and intent to rejuvenate the party, he rechristened it the Rassemblement Constitutionnel Démocratique (RCD, Democratic Constitutional Rally). When the 1989 legislative elections were opened to opposition parties, however, only Islamists running as independents made an effective showing against the RCD. Ben Ali's government has refused to authorize an Islamist party, and Tunisia continues to operate as a single-party state without benefit of the popular mandate it once could claim.

[*See also* Ḥizb al-Nahḍah; Tunisia.]

BIBLIOGRAPHY

Anderson, Lisa. *The State and Social Transformation in Tunisia and Libya, 1830–1980*. Princeton, 1986.

Moore, Clement Henry. *Tunisia since Independence: The Dynamics of One-Party Government*. Berkeley, 1965.

Rudebeck, Lars. *Party and People: A Study of Political Change in Tunisia*. Stockholm, 1967.

SUSAN WALTZ

DEVIATION.

See Bid'ah.

DEVOTIONAL MUSIC.

The most characteristic sounds of devotional expression in Muslim communities may be the call to prayer *(adhān)* and the recitation of the Qur'ān *(qirā'ah al-Qur'ān)*. Neither of these is considered by Muslims to be music; rather, they are texts that are delivered and sometimes amplified or enhanced using selected musical devices, which are always subordinate to the text.

In Middle Eastern Muslim communities, these sounds are familiar to almost everyone. The call to prayer is heard five times daily, often broadcast over loudspeakers from mosques, but also called out by a *mu'adhdhin* (muezzin) without amplification in such public places as airports or market districts. Qur'ānic recitation permeates life. Many Muslims recite verses to themselves; reciters provide inspiration at public ceremonies, both explicitly religious and more secular; they provide comfort to the bereaved and articulate communal sadness at the deaths of leaders or other misfortunes.

Similar sounds signify Muslim community life worldwide. The Indonesian, Indian, Pakistani, European, and North African communities, for instance, all have their own favorite reciters, many of whose readings are marketed on cassette tapes and compact discs. The sounds of the Qur'ānic texts are heard not only as inspirational but also as beautiful in themselves, melodiously chanted by skilled reciters.

Ṣūfī music—exemplified by the flutes and drums of the Mevlevī dervishes in Turkey and the chanting of men at the Ṣūfī *dhikr*s around the world—forms another important component of Muslim expressive culture. As a means of drawing closer to God, the Ṣūfī *dhikr* or ceremony of remembrance is the quintessential vehicle. Chanting the names of God is a widespread practice with manifestations throughout North Africa and the Middle East, in Pakistan, Indonesia, North America, and Europe. Recordings and scholarship focused on these rituals have brought the attention and ears of outsiders to this repertory. [*See* Sufism, *article on* Ṣūfī Thought and Practice; Dhikr.]

The use of music in devotional expression and to construct the rituals of Muslim holiday celebrations extends beyond Qur'ānic recitation and calls to prayer and beyond the individuals who would readily identify themselves as Ṣūfīs. Its forms are as diverse as the communities themselves. Its practices include elaborate, virtuosic solo singing of supplications, the reciting and singing of religious poetry, and group singing of religious hymns—for instance, songs of pilgrimage to Mecca or other shrines, the *ilahîleri* of Turkish and Balkan communities, and the *indang* of western Sumatra.

The work of anthropologists such as Nancy and Richard Tapper reveals a large domain of expression, neither definitely orthodox nor clearly Ṣūfī, that many participants consider to be Muslim and devotional and in which they partake in a variety of ways. Fazlur Rahman located such practices historically in the domain of popular Islam (*Islam*, 2d ed., Chicago, 1979, chapter 9). Tapper and Tapper argue that they are not merely peripheral but in fact constitute important religious behavior in rituals and daily lives of Muslim communities.

Conservative theologians and historians of religion sometimes claim that these genres and practices of popular devotion are not truly "Islamic"—that they are not canonical. In the strictest sense, they are right. The place of music in Islamic culture has been disputed, as has that of the voices of women in public places. The primary theological authority, the Qur'ān, has yielded no single theological interpretation, and the dispute about the propriety of music is centuries old; it is linked to the larger debate about behaviors obligatory or recommended to Muslims and those that are forbidden or discouraged.

The philosophical support for musical expression proceeds largely from the writings of al-Ghazālī (d. 1111) and Jalāl al-Dīn Rūmī (d. 1273). An unimpeachable Muslim, al-Ghazālī argued that music, properly engaged, actually brought one closer to God. His argument served as the theological foundation for Ṣūfī practices and challenged the more conservative position so strongly that the role of musical performance in Muslim societies has remained contested terrain up to the present day. The propriety of musical practices and devotional practices that seem to be related to music is continually negotiated in different times and places.

Forms of devotional expression outside the domains of Qur'ānic recitation and *dhikr* have rarely been studied, and very little is known about them beyond the boundaries of the communities of practitioners. What is known suggests that Muslim devotional expression includes a wide range of activities, extending from the home and the mosque into public celebrations. As Margaret Kartomi observed in Sumatra, the occasions for performance of Muslim devotional song range "from formal state occasions to intimate personal" ones (1986, p. 29). As such, they overlap, inform, and to some extent construct public culture in Muslim communities.

The diversity of practices is only suggested by the available literature. What is known indicates that forms of musical devotion are highly syncretic. *Gamelan sekati* forms part of the celebration of the Prophet's birthday in Indonesia. Devotional *indang* in western Sumatra involves praise and inspirational singing with drumming and complex body movement performed from a sitting position. *Qawwālī* melodies in Pakistan use classical Indic ragas. The ensemble of Ghulām Farīd Ṣābrī and his brother Maqbūl recently brought *qawwālī* tradition together with musical devices from popular local music and classical performance to create concert performances that were at once "serious and spiritual as well as entertaining" (Qureshi, 1992/93, p. 118). The texts sung by *qawwālī* in India are narrative, didactic, and pluralistic, intended for a pluralistic Indian population. Ways of singing religious songs bear strong links, in terms of musical system and genres, to local song traditions. Local musical and dance practices are typically coupled with concepts of *samā*ᶜ and Islamic religious texts to create locally viable devotional expression.

Supplication is a common genre, exemplified by the

duʿāʾ of the Middle East. This is a prayer text; ideally, it is chanted clearly and emotively by men who have license to improvise melodically on interjections in the prayer such as *Yā rabb!* ("Oh Lord!"). Sayyid al-Naqshabandī was a famous practitioner of this art; his recordings have been broadcast before the breaking of the Ramaḍān fast for decades.

The singing of praise, usually of the prophet Muḥammad, characterizes devotional expression in many, if not most, Muslim communities. Panegyrics are sung throughout the world and are known by a variety of names, including *naʿt, madīḥ,* and *munājāt* in Arabic-speaking communities, *indang* in Indonesia, and *kusama* in Kenya. In West Africa, praise singing lies close to the practices of drumming the chief's name or the name of a potential patron. It has been the subject of contestation, and religious authorities in the Hausa and Fulani communities have variously banned the practice or attempted to direct it toward Muslim saints and Islamic holidays. Praise singing and drumming helps constitute the Damba festival in celebration of the Prophet's birthday in Dagbon, Ghana.

In the Arabic-speaking world, panegyrics often take the form of the sophisticated *qaṣīdah,* a lengthy poem characterized by monorhyme and monometer, or the metrically complex *tawshīḥ,* both the province of accomplished singers such as ʿAlī Maḥmūd (1881–1946). The venues for singing this religious poetry are extensive, from small coffeehouses to the New Cairo Opera House, home to an ensemble of male religious singers who ably perform this repertory to standing ovations and cries for encores.

In more ordinary environments, *maddāḥīn* are common figures. Men or sometimes women, singing in coffeehouses, at saints' days, and by invitation, they perform a panoply of religious songs of varying complexity. Sometimes they adapt the tunes of popular stars to religious lyrics.

Similar religious songs called *ilahî* in Turkish contribute to the repertories of classical and folk music. In Muslim communities of the Balkan peninsula recently, performances of this genre have been adapted to expression of the current political strife. They have helped construct and affirm the identities of Muslim communities.

Many occasions for devotional expression are celebratory. The saints' days, the feasts of Islam, and the nights of Ramaḍān offer venues for expression. Saints'-day celebrations, notably the Prophet's birthday, include recitations of the Qur'ān and singing of religious songs alongside the *dhikr* ceremonies of the Ṣūfīs. These celebrations often take place in public spaces. During the nineteenth century in Egypt, the Prophet's birthday was celebrated in Azbakīyah Garden in the nascent theater district; more recently it is celebrated in the streets surrounding the mosque of Ḥusayn and in many neighborhoods, such as ʿAbdīn and Bāb al-Lūq.

Ramaḍān serves as an occasion for much devotional and related expression, including the perambulations of the *masaḥḥarātī,* a man who walks through his neighborhood after midnight calling out, usually melodically and somewhat poetically, to wake his neighbors in time to eat before the next day's fast begins. Talking-drum orchestras mark the celebration of Ramaḍān among the Yoruba. Praise singing, royal drums and trumpets, and complex call-and-response singing with drum ensembles all form part of the feasts following Ramaḍān in Kano, Nigeria. The venues extend from village celebrations to national radio and television and commercial recording.

Group singing of pilgrimage or other religious songs while en route to Mecca, to a saint's tomb, or to a saint's-day celebration similarly expresses religious commitment or devotion. Saint's-day celebrations involve spectators and listeners. The *qawwālī* rituals that draw large audiences at the shrine of Niẓāmuddin Auliyā in Delhi, described in detail by Qureshi (1986), exemplify these behaviors. On a more modest scale, Elizabeth Fernea's studies of saints' days in Morocco, focused as they are on the behavior of women, also aptly illustrate common behavior.

In Shīʿī communities worldwide, music accompanies commemoration of a slightly different kind: remembering the martyrdom of Ḥusayn occasions performances of religious song and ritual reenactments of his death and the mourning of the community, a ritual called *taʿziyah* by Persian-speakers and by other names in other languages (for instance, *tabut* in Sumatra). [*See* Taʿziyah.]

In a general sense, all these practices are related to the Ṣūfī theology of *samāʿ*, or engaged listening aimed at bringing the listener closer to God. This listening itself constitutes devotional behavior. *Samāʿ* lies at the heart of *dhikr* and forms part of its raison d'être. Importantly, *samāʿ* admits levels of sophistication and the possibility of learning and experience increasing one's ability to attain closeness to God. *Samāʿ* is accessible at some level to the uninitiated and is not restricted to the learned or the committed Ṣūfī. Thus participation extends beyond the Ṣūfī brotherhood into the larger community of Muslims who participate in the celebration of saints' days and religious feasts.

In the twentieth century, devotional expression has found new venues—for example, public contests in which Qur'ānic recitation is judged. In Indonesia, women participate in these events and win prizes. Religious music has found its way into folk festivals such as that in Konya, Turkey. *Qawwālī* performances are heard in films and on commercial recordings.

Not only men but also women and children participate in devotional expression. Many women competently recite the Qur'ān and teach their children to do so. Some have been professional reciters, usually reciting for other women. Women and children characteristically participate in holiday celebrations at which devotional songs are sung—at celebrations welcoming home pilgrims from Mecca, at saints'-day celebrations, or during the long nights of Ramaḍān after the breaking of the day's fast.

Generally the preferred medium of expression is the human voice; indeed, instrumental accompaniment has been occasionally banned. However, in some communities, musical instruments accompany the singing (even in mosques), and professional singers of religious songs have employed instrumental accompaniment for at least a century. Drums of various kinds and flutes are common in religious expression. The frame drums and hourglass drums of the Middle East, the *dholak* on the Indian subcontinent, and the talking drums of West Africa have all taken part in devotional expression. The Arab *qānūn* has accompanied religious song in Egypt, the harmonium in India, and *gamelan sekati* in Indonesia.

Religious singing and supplication is marketed on commercial recordings. Professional singers of less weighty repertories—stars of stage and screen, for instance—have recorded topical religious songs, especially for holidays. Scaled-down *qawwālī* have appeared in Indian films. The accomplished female Lebanese singer, Laure Daccache, became famous for her rendition of "Amint billāh" ("Āmantu bi-Allāh"), which was possibly also her own composition; it has passed into the *turāth,* or heritage, of Arabic religious song. Songs such as Sayyid Darwīsh's "Yā ʿushshāq al-Nabī" (O Lovers of the Prophet) use the language of devotion for a wedding song. This practice is very common, and the boundary of the "devotional" is not always easy to locate. Sayyid Darwīsh composed for musical theater and wrote many popular songs; in his personal life he was hardly a scrupulous Muslim. Yet his upbringing, in Qur'ānic school and under the tutelage of Muslim family members, and his utilization of the aural components of this background, cast him among the *mashāyikh* or learned religious people, the bearers of Muslim law and custom and Arabic literature and poetry. Throughout the twentieth century the *mashāyikh,* popularly represented by figures such as Sayyid Darwīsh, have been invested as the "authentic school" of Egyptian culture. Thus Muslim devotional music moves from the circumscribed *duʿā'* into the larger domain of public culture and Egyptian social identity.

Muslim devotional expression has infused the musical traditions of many communities to the extent that it serves as a conservative force in the maintenance of what is perceived as authentic expressive culture. As noted above, in Egypt the *mashāyikh* are often credited with the transmission of historically Arabic poetry and vocal aesthetics. These distinctly religious songs have passed into the *turāth* or heritage of Arab music, and an ability to sing them, even when displayed by singers of nonreligious popular songs, marks an artist as "authentically Arab" *(aṣīl).* Akin Euba (1971) suggests that Yoruba tradition is similarly kept alive through Muslim song. In many places, as Qureshi writes of Northern India and Pakistan, Muslim devotional expressions form "part of the musical language" of the community (1986, p. 46).

[*See also* Music; Qur'ānic Recitation.]

BIBLIOGRAPHY

Literature

Baily, John. "Qawwali in Bradford: Traditional Music in the Muslim Communities." In *Black Music in Britain: Essays on the Afro-Asian Contribution to Popular Music,* edited by Paul Oliver, pp. 153–165. Milton Keynes, England, 1990.

Besmer, Fremont E. *Kídan Dárán Sállà: Music for the Eve of the Muslim Festivals of ʿĪd al-Fiṭr and ʿĪd al-Kabīr in Kano, Nigeria.* Bloomington, 1974.

Boyd, Alan. "Music in Islam; Lamu, Kenya, a Case Study." In *Discourse in Ethnomusicology,* vol. 2, *A Tribute to Alan P. Merriam,* edited by Caroline Card et al., pp. 83–98. Bloomington, 1981.

Chelkowski, Peter, ed. *Taʿziyeh: Ritual and Drama in Iran.* New York, 1979.

Danielson, Virginia. "Cultural Authenticity in Egyptian Musical Expression: The Repertory of the 'Mashāyikh.' " *Pacific Review of Ethnomusicology* 5 (1989): 49–60.

Danielson, Virginia. " 'Min al-Mashāyikh': A View of Egyptian Musical Tradition." *Asian Music* 22.1 (1990–1991): 113–128.

During, Jean. *Musique et extase: L'audition mystique dans la tradition soufie.* Paris, 1988.

Erlmann, Veit. *Music and the Islamic Reform in the Early Sokoto Empire: Sources, Ideology, Effects*. Stuttgart, 1986.

Euba, Akin, "Islamic Musical Culture among the Yoruba: A Preliminary Survey." In *Essays on Music and History in Africa*, edited by Klaus P. Wachsmann, pp. 171–181. Evanston, Ill., 1971.

Faruqi, Lois Ibsen al-. "Music, Musicians, and Muslim Law." *Asian Music* 17 (1985): 3–36.

Faruqi, Lois Ibsen al-. "Qur'ān Reciters in Competition in Kuala Lumpur." *Ethnomusicology* 31.2 (1987): 221–228.

Fernea, Elizabeth W. *A Street in Marrakech*. 2d ed. Garden City, N.Y., 1980.

Kartomi, Margaret J. "Muslim Music in West Sumatran Culture." *World of Music* 28.3 (1986): 13–32.

Kinney, Sylvia. "Drummers in Dagbon: The Role of the Drummer in the Damba Festival." *Ethnomusicology* 14 (1970): 258–265.

"Musique musulmane." In *Encyclopédie des musiques sacrées*, vol. 1. Paris, 1968.

Neubauer, Eckhard. "Islamic Religious Music." In *New Grove Dictionary of Music and Musicians*, vol. 9, pp. 342–349. Washington, D.C., 1980.

Pacholczyk, Jozef M. "Music and Islam in Indonesia." *World of Music* 28.3 (1986): 3–12.

Qureshi, Regula B. "Indo-Muslim Religious Music: An Overview." *Asian Music* 3.1 (1972): 15–22.

Qureshi, Regula B. *Sufi Music of India and Pakistan: Sound, Context, and Meaning in Qawwali*. Cambirdge, 1986.

Qureshi, Regula B. " 'Muslim Devotional': Popular Religious Music and Muslim Identity under British, Indian, and Pakistani Hegemony." *Asian Music* 24.1 (1992–1993): 111–121.

Tapper, Nancy, and Richard Tapper. "The Birth of the Prophet: Ritual and Gender in Turkish Islam." *Man* 22 (1987): 69–92.

Waugh, Earle H. *The Munshidīn of Egypt: Their World and Their Song*. Columbia, S.C., 1989.

Recordings and Videos

Muslim communities worldwide market and often produce sound recordings of devotional music. These are the best exemplars of current practices and may be obtained by requesting the genres and performers from specialized dealers. The following list is a sample of ethnomusicological recordings that include annotated examples of a variety of traditions and are available in libraries that collect music from around the world. (Some of the LPs listed here may be reissued as compact discs.)

Sound Recordings

Ceremonial Islamic Ritual from Yugoslavia: Zikr of the Rufa'i Brotherhood. Recorded and edited by Bernard Mauguin. (Unesco Collection/Musical Sources) Philips 6586015.

Dikr und madih: islamische Gesänge und Zeremonien/Sudan. Recorded and edited by Artur Simon. Museum für Völkerkunde, Berlin, MC 10, 1980.

Egypte: l'Ordre Chazili 'al-Tariga al-Hamidiyya al-Chaziliyya'. Arion ARN 64211.

Islamic religious chanting from North Yemen. Recorded and edited by Joachen Wenzel and Christian Poche. (Unesco Collection/Musical sources) Philips 6586 040.

Moroccan Sufi Music. Recorded and edited by Philip Schuyler. Lyrichord LLSt 7238.

Moyen-Atlas: Musique sacrée & profane. Recorded and edited by Marc Loopuyt and H. Vuylsteke. (Musiques traditionelles vivantes. V. Musiques populaires) Ocora 558587.

Music of the Waswahili of Lamu, Kenya. 3 vols. Recorded and edited by Alan W. Boyd. Ethnic Folkways FE 4093-95.

Musik från Tunisien. Recorded and edited by Krister Malm and Salah el Mahdi, Caprice CAP 1090.

Syrie, Muezzins d'Alep: chants religieux de l'Islam. Recorded and edited by Christian Poche. Ocora 580038.

Tunisia. Recorded and edited by Alain Daniélou. (Unesco Collection/A Musical Anthology of the Orient) Bärenreiter-Musicaphon BM 30 L 2008.

Turquie: Musique Soufi. (Musiques traditionelles vivantes. II. Musiques rituelles et religieuses) Ocora 558522.

Zikr: Islamic Ritural - Rifa'yya Brotherhood of Aleppo. Recorded by Christian Poche. (Unesco Collection/Musical Sources) Philips 6586 030.

Video Recordings

Aita. Produced by Izza Genini. Icarus/First Run. Focused on a female singer who performs religious music.

Hymns of Praise. Produced by Izza Genini. Icarus/First Run. Focused on a saint's day celebration in Morocco.

Lessons from Gulam: Asian Music in Bradford [England]. Produced by John Baily. Distributed by Documentary Education Resources, Watertown, Mass. Focused on a male singer of *qawwālī*.

Nusrat! Live at Meany Hall. Produced by the University of Washington Ethnomusicology program and available from the University of Washington Press, 1994. A concert of *qawwālī* by Nusrat Fateh Ali Khan.

Saints and Spirits. Produced by Elizabeth Fernea. Directed by Melissa Llewelyn-Davies. Icarus/First Run, 1979. Focused on a saint's day celebration in Morocco with emphasis on the experience of women.

VIRGINIA DANIELSON

DEVOTIONAL POETRY. The creation of religious verse seems to be a latecomer in the Islamic world. An aversion to poetry, especially religious poetry, is palpable in the first centuries of Islam, when it was feared that poetry—criticized in the Qur'ān, (surah 26.226 ff.) and often negatively described in *ḥadīth*—might conflict with the divinely inspired words of the Qur'ān, or that people might think religious verses were divinely inspired. The praise poems by the Prophet's companion Ḥassān ibn Thābit (d. 659) are descriptive and panegyric rather than devotional.

In present-day India and Pakistan and perhaps to a lesser extent in Turkey, Iran, and many of the Arab countries, mystical songs in different languages are heard during religious festivals like the Prophet's birthday or the anniversary of a saint, or in any gathering of devout people; the long, sonorous litanies recited at such occasions often approach real poetry. But only in a milieu somewhat charged with mysticism could something like devotional poetry develop. Thus it is not usually written in classical languages such as the high Arabic of the theologians but rather in the regional vernaculars spoken from West Africa to South Asia.

Ṣūfīs of the ninth century sometimes listened to music and in particular to love songs that might lead them into ecstasy. Many of the early Ṣūfī poems composed in the tenth and eleventh centuries might be sung; they speak in sweet words of the poet's longing for his divine beloved, using imagery of profane love poetry as well as the traditional form of a classical Arabic (or, in Iran, Persian) *ghazal.* Other popular literary forms developed: the Arabs used strophic poems like *zajal* or *muwashshaḥ* in a language not exactly classical; the popular genres of *billīq* and *mawāliyah* are short verses that could be used for both profane and religious purposes. The same holds true for the *dū baytī,* a four-line verse that corresponds roughly to the Persian *rubāʿī.*

Praise of the Prophet, *naʿt,* began to assume all available literary forms from the twelfth century on, from short love verses to longwinded descriptions of his greatness. *Naʿtīyah* poetry remains viable in almost all literatures of the Muslim world to this day, as is apparent in a glance through a Pakistani newspaper during the month of Rabīʿ al-Awwal when the Prophet's birthday is celebrated.

The first major genre entirely confined to devotional expressions was the *mawlūd,* a poem recited on the occasion of the Prophet's birthday on the twelfth day of the third lunar month. *Mawlūd*s were first composed in the early thirteenth century in prose, but these prose versions soon gave way to lengthy poems in the vernaculars. The most famous *mawlūd* (Turkish, *mevlût*) in Turkey is one by Süleyman Çelebi of Bursa (d. 1419) that is recited to this day not only on the Prophet's birthday but also on special occasions such as the fortieth day after a death or the anniversary of one, or in fulfilment of a vow. As performed today in Turkey, it is interspersed with Qur'ānic recitations and prayers; when the actual moment of the Prophet's birth is described, with a swan touching Āminah's back, each participant touches his or her neighbor's back in remembrance of this event.

Muslims in other areas besides Turkey have produced a remarkably large body of *mawlūds.* To recite such a poem opens, as it were, the gates of paradise; Muslims in Nigeria will be as touched by the story as are those in Kenya who listen to a *mawlūd* and feel as if they have entered a heavenly world, purifyed from sin. In recent decades rationalist as well as fundamentalist Muslims have criticized the festive celebration of *mawlūd* and the recitations of marvelous stories that are woven around the luminous appearance of the last messenger of God, when all of nature greeted him who was sent "as a mercy to the worlds" (surah 21.107); yet despite such opposition, it seems impossible for Muslims to give up these pious, poetic songs.

Süleyman Çelebi's *mevlût* was translated into Bosnian, and soon Muslims in the Balkans invented *mawlūd*s in their own languages, as did the Kurds, the Pathans, and most other nations. The name *mawlūd* is applied in some languages, such as Sindhi, not only to long elaborated stories but even more to short devotional poems in which the Prophet's miracles or his wonderful qualities are described. Generally such a short poem is introduced by an important poetic statement that is repeated by a chorus after each line to emphasize the main purpose of the poem. This technique is found in many devotional poems on the folk level.

Another form of devotional poetry seems to have developed almost parallel with the *mawlūd.* This is a kind of narrative ballad that describes in detail the wondrous acts of the Prophet, of the first four caliphs (especially ʿAlī ibn Abī Ṭālib), or, very often, of Ṣūfī pirs. Although such descriptions are known from classical poetry, especially from Persian classical epic, there are many such narratives in vernaculars or varieties close to them. For example, the life of the Prophet was an inspiring topic for many folk poets of Egypt and neighboring countries, and there is no dearth of poems in modern Arabic dialects that tell of major events in the Prophet's life. His marriage with Khadījah, his first wife and the "mother of the faithful," was dear to poets everywhere; it appears in Egypt and Turkey as well as Indo-Pakistan. Perhaps the folk poets' tendency to address Muḥammad as the ideal bridegroom accounts for this type of poetry. Ballads of this kind usually have a basic text that is slightly altered according to the singer's predilections or, as is typical of oral literature, with the passage of time: allusions to contemporary events can be easily inserted into a verse to make the poem more vivid.

One event that has probably been elaborated more in high poetry than on the folk level is the *miʿrājīyah,* which deals with the Prophet's journey through heaven and hell into the immediate presence of God. Other, more human events in the Prophet's life were also the subjects of lengthy poems, many of which use the long *ā* or some other ending as a monorhyme to achieve the form of a rather simple *qaṣīdah.* This form, called *manqabah,* is frequent in Sindhi and exists in Panjabi as well. The poets have favorite themes; two or three are particularly favored: the story of the *ḥannānah,* the sighing palm trunk, and the story of how the Prophet rescued a gazelle are reworked time and again. Other poems deal with an origin legend such as the reason for honey's taste: both in Anatolia and in the Indus Valley one learns that only when the bees hum the blessings over Muḥammad does the honey become sweet.

There are numerous *manāqib* in honor of Ṣūfī saints, especially of ʿAbd al-Qādir al-Jīlānī, the eponym of the most widespread *ṭarīqah.* In such poems the poets may use boundless exaggeration: the first known Sindhi poem in honor of this saint, from the late eighteenth century, enumerates all the countries and cities where the saint's *barakah* is active, and all these names alliterate—a mnemonic device typical of popular poetry.

Similar devices are used in the *sī-ḥarfī* or acrostic poem, a genre well known from antiquity. It occurs frequently in the dervish poetry of Anatolia and Indo-Pakistan. The *sī-ḥarfī,* ("thirty-letter poem") was mainly used for mystic and didactic purposes; the listener was able to follow the sequence of thought by simply keeping in mind the sequence of the alphabet. Among the *sī-ḥarfī* one has become almost proverbial—Sulṭān Bāhū's (d. 1692) Panjabi verse on the letter *alif,* "God is a jasmine bush."

Another form still composed and sung in the Indus valley are *bārahmāsa* poems. This form is originally Indian; it tells the events and feelings in each month of the year as seen through a loving woman's eyes. The months can be the Hindu ones, the Islamic lunar months, or, lately, even the Western months. When the Muslim months are used, the speaker remembers the tragedy of Karbala in Muḥarram, the Prophet's birthday in the third month, ʿAbd al-Qādir's anniversary in the fourth, and the Prophet's heavenly journey in Rajab, and the catalog ends with the happiness of union with the Divine Beloved at the Kaʿbah in Mecca or with the beloved Prophet at his mausoleum in Medina. Other interpretations are possible: in a recent Sindhi *bārahmāsa* poem in the Christian sequence of the months the pious writer even introduces Coca-cola in July instead of the time-honored spiritual wine.

A genre of poems in honor of Medina first appears in the late thirteenth century in Egypt; it became increasingly more important and also more moving the farther the poet lived from the Arabian Peninsula; longing for Medina is reflected to this day in almost every language used by Muslims. Again, the Indo-Pakistani poets in Urdu and Sindhi seem to be the most prolific writers in this field.

The Persians as well as the Ithnā ʿAsharī Shīʿīs of the Indian subcontinent poured out their love and longing for the imams and in particular for Ḥusayn ibn ʿAlī, the martyr of Karbala, in elaborate forms. Allusions to Karbala are frequent in medieval poetry in all Middle Eastern languages, but after the establishment of Twelver Shiism as the state religion in Iran in 1501, the tendency to participate in the imam's suffering by reading or listening to poetry proliferated. In Iran the devotional literature in this field evolved into the *taʿziyah,* dramatic performances of the tragedy at Karbala, in which the poets bring together the most incongruous protagonists; Karbala is perceived as a cosmic event, preordained from eternity, and everyone and everything is somehow involved in it. Thus there is a *taʿziyah* in which the martyr mystic al-Ḥallāj, Mawlānā Rūmī, and his friend Shams-i Tabrīz appear together to evoke the eternal mystical character of Ḥusayn's suffering. Popular songs about Karbala occur in Urdu, Sindhi, and Panjabi, and are enacted in the villages of Muslim India; they often mention not only Ḥusayn but also his elder brother Ḥasan as "the two princes" who were slain in battle, although, historically speaking, Ḥasan predeceased his brother by more than ten years. [*See* Karbala; Taʿziyah.]

The *marthīyah* or elegy as a special genre seems to be a product of the Indian subcontinent. The earliest known *marthīyah* in Dakhni Urdu was written at the Quṭbshāhī court of Golconda in the seventeenth century. When Urdu became the language of literature in northern India around 1700, one of the major poets of Delhi, Mirzā Saudā (d. 1781), composed more than a hundred *marthiyahs* in various forms. The true development, however, occurred at the Shīʿī court of Lucknow, where Anīs (d. 1875) and Dabīr (d. 1874) competed in long, moving poems whose recitations still attract large crowds of Indians and Pakistanis not only in the subcontinent but also in the diaspora, especially in London.

The particular importance of the *marthīyah* lies in its form, the *musaddas,* a six-line stanza with four rhyming lines and two closing lines with a different rhyme. The *musaddas* allowed the poet to extend the poem as much as he wished without becoming tiring, while the traditional *qaṣīdah* with its monorhyme could not keep the listeners' interest awake for more than a hundred lines. The Urdu *marthīyah* in *musaddas* was so popular that the Indian Muslims saw in *musaddas* the ideal form to express religious emotions and moral exhortations. Ḥālī's poem "The Ebb and Flood of Muslim Civilization" (1879) is simply known as "The *Musaddas*"; and Iqbal's religious poems like *Shikwah* (Complaint) and *Jawāb-i Shikwah* (Its Answer), again use the *musaddas* form.

Both the *marthīyah* and the *taᶜziyah* could and still can be used to express the identification of Muslims with the suffering Ḥusayn and his family, and of the Western powers—Britain or America—with the armies of Yazīd, intent on destroying their lives and hopes. Thus the *marthīyah* assumes a highly political character, even though a casual reader may not be aware of this aspect in an apparently religious poem. A simpler form of poetry connected with Karbala is the Bengali *jārīnāmah*, a name derived from *zār*, "complaint."

In addition to the long devotional poems, there are numberless short, singable poems in the Ṣūfī tradition. The Persian *rubāᶜī* was often recited in *samāᶜ* (mystical dance). Short poems in honor of the Prophet appear in Sind, composed by bards called *bhān*.

Popular religious folksongs are attested from the Middle Ages. In the Turkish tradition, Yunus Emre (d. 1321) in Anatolia seems to have been the first to sing of his love of God, his longing, his hope and fear in simple verses. Even though he sometimes used the Arabo-Persian metrical system *ᶜarūẓ*, he chose meters that resemble the Turkish popular syllable-counting meters and can be easily scanned according to stress rather than quantity. The repeated rhyme often consists of a religious formula such as *al-ḥamdu lillāh*—these were also used in the *dhikr* of the dervishes. Yunus's poetry influenced the entire development of Turkish popular mystical literature, and hundreds of poets followed his example. In the Bektāshī order and among the Shīᶜī ᶜAlawīs these forms survived to the nineteenth or even twentieth century. Although Ottoman urban poets did not care much for these products of Anatolia, they remained popular and gained new weight in the Turkish Republic. Sometimes even high-ranking or learned poets turned to such simple, moving verses, among them Ismāᶜīl Hakki Erzerumlu (d. 1785), whose consoling words,

> Let us see what God will do—
> what He does is always good,

still rise to the lips of many modern Turks.

Yunus's deepest influence was visible in the modern Turkish poet Ismail Emre, who composed thousands of verses exactly in the style of previous Bektashī and Ṣūfī poets. An illiterate blacksmith from Adana, he was compelled to sing his verses, which are called *doğuş* ("something that is born") and were transcribed by his friends. Some seemingly unimportant remark or sight would inspire a poem in which he expressed his mystical feelings. Other mystically minded Turkish writers of today composed verses owing to inspiration, but none of them attained the popularity of the "Yeni (new) Yunus Emre." Others, barely known, still sing little poems called *Ramazan manileri* to express their feelings during the month of fasting, or they speak of other religious events in unassuming verses.

Islamic devotional poetry to this day is permeated with the feeling of *waḥdat al-wujūd*, the unity of being, which could easily lead the poets to see that "everything is He," that there is no difference between Pharaoh and Moses or between the martyr mystic Ḥallāj and the judge who condemned him. Such ideas were spread in the Muslim world by the Ṣūfī brotherhoods, and this can explain the remarkable similarity of a Turkish Ṣūfī song and one composed in Sindhi or in Bengali. Everywhere in the eastern Islamic world Ḥallāj appears as the model of the loving Ṣūfī who wants to be killed in order to prove his love—a religious image that permeates even secular poetry in the modern world.

Another aspect of mystical devotional poetry is that it can be easily turned into paradoxes because the poet is aware that he cannot share his experience with the uninitiated, and he can tell the ineffable only by using oxymoron or paradox. During performance, lines of these poems can be changed or verses from other poems inserted, provided they fit the meter; thus the recitation of mystical poetry during *dhikr* is very different from the orderly recitation of classical poetry.

Devotional poetry appears to be very much alive among smaller Islamic sects, and the *ginān* of the Khoja Ismāᶜīlīs is a point in case. The first examples stem from the early fifteenth century, but this genre with its subgenres has remained alive through the centuries. New songs to honor the imam emerge in the community, often with a strange blend of traditional mystical expressions and very modern concepts. Here the evolution of devotional poetry can still be observed. Burushaski, a language of isolated Ismāᶜīlī Hunzas, boasts a large devotional literature that is yet to be studied.

The high literatures of Islam, too, have never ceased

to produce poetry that can be called devotional. Classical poems that were thought to carry a special *barakah* are now available on tape, and it is interesting to see the vitality of Būṣīrī's great poem, the *Burdah*. Translations of this long *qaṣīdah* have been made through the centuries into Persian, Turkish, Urdu, Panjabi, and other languages. The *Burda* is celebrated in the Deccan by inserting Qur'ānic recitation and commentary. In the eighteenth and nineteenth centuries the poem was also enlarged by *takhmīs,* making it into quintuplet verses (two lines from the original poems plus three lines by the later poet). By inserting their own verses into the main body of the *Burdah,* poets in the Arab lands, the Deccan, and West Africa hoped to partake of the *barakah* of this great poem in which veneration of the Prophet resounds so strongly.

Everywhere poets have expressed the same love for the Prophet in their verses, from the Arab poet ʿAbd al-Ghanī al-Nābulusī (d. 1732) or the Indian reformer Shāh Walī Allāh (d. 1762) and his compatriot in the Deccan, Āzād Bilgrāmī (d. 1785), whose powerful *qaṣīdah*s in honor of the Prophet earned him the surname Ḥassān al-Hindī. The last Mughal emperor of Delhi, Bahādur Shāh Ẓafar (d. 1862), wrote *naʿtiyah* poetry in Urdu, and Mirzā Ghālib (d. 1869), the most famous Urdu poet, devoted highly complicated Persian *qaṣīdahs* to the Prophet and to ʿAlī. Some decades later Muḥsin Kakorawī (d. 1905) devoted his entire poetic work to the praise of the Prophet; his *qaṣīdah* "From the area of Kāshī (Benares) a cloud moves toward Matthura" is a masterpiece on two stylistic levels, combining Hindu imagery in pure Hindi with highflown Urdu replete with allusions to the Qur'ān, *ḥadīth,* and traditional eulogies of the prophets. In the poetry of Iqbal (d. 1938) one can find a number of profound Persian and Urdu poems that can be called, without exaggeration, moving devotional poetry. We may also note such modern Arab poets as Ṣalāḥ ʿAbd al-Ṣabūr of Egypt and, finally, the impact of classical religious poetry as sung by Umm Kulthūm upon Muslims through the media of audiotapes, records, and videotapes. The development of new technology is also important for the growth of religious poetry in regional languages in remote areas such as the Hindu Kush, where the radio now broadcasts modern devotional poetry in Khowar and Shina.

[*See also* African Languages and Literatures; Arabic Literature; Persian Literature; Turkish Literature; Urdu Literature; *and* Sufism, *article on* Ṣūfī Thought and Practice.]

BIBLIOGRAPHY

Chelkowski, Peter. *Taʿziyeh: Ritual and Drama in Iran.* New York, 1979.

Emre, İsmail. *Yeni Yunus Emre ve Doğuşları.* 2 vols. in 1. Istanbul, 1950.

Knappert, Jan. *Swahili Islamic Poetry.* 3 vols. Leiden, 1971.

Littmann, Enno, ed. *Aḥmed il-Bedawī: Ein Lied auf den ägyptischen Nationalheiligen.* Wiesbaden, 1950.

Littmann, Enno. *Mohammed im Volksepos.* Copenhagen, 1950.

Littmann, Enno. *Islamisch-arabische Heiligenlieder.* Wiesbaden, 1951.

Schimmel, Annemarie. *As through a Veil: Mystical Poetry in Islam.* New York, 1982. Includes an extensive bibliography.

Schimmel, Annemarie. *And Muhammad Is His Messenger.* Chapel Hill, N.C., 1985.

ANNEMARIE SCHIMMEL

DHIKR. Most commonly associated with Sufism, *dhikr* ("remembrance, reminder, evocation") is both a concept and a meditative practice. It is also a unifying theme across the diversity of cultural forms in Islam, appearing in each form in a distinctive expression. Its specific appearance in Sufism can best be understood against its wider background as a key theme in Islamic cultures.

In poetry, *dhikr* is the remembrance of the lost beloved. The classical ode *(qaṣīdah)* begins with traces of the beloved's campsite *(aṭlāl),* a listing of the stations by which she departed with the women of the tribe *(ẓaʿn),* or her apparition *(ṭayf, khayāl).* Remembrance turns to an idyll evoking the beloved's symbolic analogue, the lost garden. The "Burda" poem of the tribal poet Kaʿb ibn Zuhayr begins with a *dhikr* symbolizing as the lost beloved the pre-Islamic tribal ethos that Kaʿb was giving up by offering his allegiance to Muḥammad. Ḥassān ibn Thābit's elegy on the death of the Prophet begins with a remembrance of Muḥammad as the lost beloved, with his home and mosque in Medina as the traces or *aṭlāl* (I. Isḥāq, *The Life of Muhammad,* translated by A. Guillaume, Oxford, 1955, pp. 597–601, 795–798). Remembrance of the beloved continues through the poetic traditions of the classical Islamic world, particularly in the *ghazal* (love elegy), Ṣūfī poetry, and popular song.

The Qur'ān stresses human forgetfulness, with continual imperatives to remember God, one's own mortality, and the day of judgment *(yawm al-dīn).* The Qur'ān refers to itself and earlier revelations as a *dhikr* or *dhikrā* ("reminder"). Through Qur'ānic recitation and calligraphy, the Qur'ānic text as remembrance is artistically embodied and pervades the sensible particularities of Islamic life. Qur'ānic verses and components of nature (interpreted with Qur'ānic guidance) are signs (*āyahs*) leading their interpreter along the path of remembrance.

The Qur'ān links remembrance to ritual. The five prayers (initiated by the call to prayer) interrupt everyday life and turn the Muslim community toward the focal point of the Kaʿbah. The fasting of Ramaḍān is a reminder both of the condition of those who are hungry and of the compassionate *(al-raḥmān)* through whom sustenance is received. Evening recitations continue the Ramaḍān remembrance. The night of destiny (Laylat al-Qadr) near the end of Ramaḍān is celebrated by a vigil in remembrance of the coming down *(tanzīl)* upon Muḥammad of the spirit *(rūḥ)*. *Zakāt*, contribution to the less fortunate, combines *karam* (generosity) and *dhikr* (remembrance), as the Qur'ānic imperative to remember the orphan, widow, and traveler is institutionalized and placed at the heart of religious obligation.

The pilgrimage to Mecca *(ḥajj)* and the passion play *(taʿziyah)* are culminations of ritual performance of *dhikr*. In the *ḥajj* the pilgrim relives the events of Islamic sacred history—Abraham's sacrifice, Hagar's frantic search for water, and Muḥammad's last sermon on the plain of Arafat—even as the same pilgrim enacts standing before God on the day of judgement. In the intensity of the Shīʿī *ta'ziyah* remembrance of the martyrdom of Ḥusayn, the division between past and present, actors and audience is dissolved. Beyond specific rituals, the life and words of the Prophet serve as a model *(sunnah)* for the Islamic community everywhere, continually recalled through prophetic sayings *(ḥadīth)*, the chain of authorities by which they are related *(isnād)*, and the comprehensive way of life *(sharīʿah)* based on the prophetic model. [*See* Taʿziyah.]

In Sufism, *dhikr* refers both to a divine name or Qur'ānic phrase repeatedly chanted (such as *lā ilāha illā Allāh*, "no god but God"), and to the practice of chanting. *Dhikr* keeps the Ṣūfī from stopping along the mystical ascent and from panic or inappropriate behavior when overcome by various mystical states *(aḥwāl)*. For Abū Ḥāmid al-Ghazālī (d. 1111) *dhikr* polishes the heart, allowing it to serve as a mirror reflecting the divine attributes. In the tradition of Ḥasan of Basra (d. 728), Ghazālī gave particular attention to remembrance of death and the day of judgment. Najm al-Dīn al-Kubrā (d. 1220) writes of *dhikr* sinking down into the heart, as an interior sob or cry of yearning. *Dhikr* ends with *fanā'* (the passing away of the ego-self in union with the divine), at which point, according to many Ṣūfīs, there can be no further *dhikr* because there can be no consciousness of otherness or self. In his *Meccan Illuminations*, Ibn ʿArabī (d. 1240) wrote extensively on the relation of specific *dhikr*s to different religious and psychological types. The combination of *dhikr* with *samāʿ* (ritualized music and dance) leading toward ecstasy *(wajd)* has been a continual source of controversy within Islam. Naqshbandī Ṣūfīs stress a silent *dhikr* *(dhikr khafī)* that can be practiced while one is engaged in the world. The spiritual chain of authority *(isnād)* constitutes another of remembrance, often in the form of memorials *(tadhkirāt)* of one's predecessors.

Visitation *(ziyārah)* to the shrine of a saint (such as Ḥusayn or Zaynab in Cairo, or that of a popular Ṣūfī saint) is a common occasion for remembrance. The pilgrim may recite verbal *dhikr*s, touch the tomb, and receive the blessing *(barakah)* transmitted from the divine through the *walī* (friend of God). Though opposed by the Wahhābī sect of Saudi Arabia, local shrines exist throughout much of the Islamic world, providing accessible occasions for *dhikr* and visitation. [*See* Ziyārah.]

In Naguib Mahfouz's modern story "Zaabalawi" the narrator searches for a famous healer, Shaykh Zaabalawi. The characters he meets mark different stages of his quest. He finally falls into a state of ecstasy, then awakes to find that Zaabalawi had been with him and is gone. The possibility of *dhikr*—of remembering, retrieving, and being healed by one's deeper traditions—is ironically questioned in a modern Islamic world increasingly severed from its roots.

In the "The Doum Tree of Wad Hamid" by the Sudanese author Tayeb Saleh (1968), the doum tree is subtly linked to Qur'ānic tree symbols—the lote tree of the boundary (53.1-18), the tree that succored the virgin Mary, the tree of Jandal, the blessed *(mubārakah)* tree of the light verse (24.35). It embodies the remembrance of the villagers, their common dreams and traditions, and their source of healing. When the tree (threatened by colonialists, nationalists, modernists, and outside preachers) is gone, the old man who speaks for the village says, the community's identity will pass away.

[*See also* Sufism.]

BIBLIOGRAPHY

Böwering, Gerhard. *The Mystical Vision of Existence in Classical Islam.* Berlin, 1980. The thought of Sahl al-Tustarī (d. 896), which relates *dhikr* to the precreative covenant and precreative state of being.

Chittick, William C. "Dhikr." In *Encyclopedia of Religion*, vol. 4, pp. 341–344. New York, 1987. Includes key references to *dhikr* in the Qur'ān and *ḥadīth*.

During, Jean. *Musique et extase: L'audition mystiqiue dans la tradition soufie*. Paris, 1988. Interrelations among poetry, music, *dhikr*, dance, and ecstasy *(wajd)*.

Farīd al-Dīn ʿAṭṭār. *Muslim Saints and Mystics*. Translated and abridged by A. J. Arberry from *Tadhkirāt al-awliyāʾ* (Memorials of the Saints). London, 1966. Superb example of the *tadhkira* genre.

Feldman, Walter. "Musical Genres and Zikir of the Sunni Tarikats of Istanbul." In *The Dervish Lodge*, edited by Raymond Lifchez, pp. 187–202. Berkeley, 1992. Sophisticated examination of liturgy in its musical context.

Gardet, Louis. "La mention du Nom divin dans la mystique musulmane." *Revue Thomiste* 53 (1953): 197–216. Comparisons to *mantra* and other meditation practices.

Ghazālī, Abū Ḥāmid al-. *Revival of the Religious Sciences (Iḥyāʾ ʿulūm ad-dīn)*. See sections translated by Kōjirō Nakamura in *Ghazali on Prayer* (Tokyo, 1973), and T. J. Winter, *The Remembrance of Death and the Afterlife (Kitāb dhikr al-mawt wa mā baʿdahu)* (Cambridge, 1989).

Homerin, Th. Emil. *From Arab Poet to Muslim Saint: Ibn al-Fāriḍ, His Verse and His Shrine*. Charleston, S.C., 1994. Relations between poetry, mystical charisma, *dhikr*, interpretation, hagiography, and the development of a shrine.

Ibn al-ʿArabī. *Bezels of Wisdom (Fuṣūṣ al-ḥikam)*. Translated by R. W. J. Austin. New York, 1980. Ibn ʿArabī's most widely read work, with *dhikr* as both a major theme and a major literary technique.

Ibn al-ʿArabī. *Meccan Openings (Al-futuḥāt al-Makkīyah)*. For two recent selected translations, see: *Les illuminations de la Mecque: Textes choisis/Selected Texts*, translated by Michel Chodkiewicz et al. (Paris, 1989); and *The Sufi Path of Knowledge*, selections with commentary by William C. Chittick (Albany, N.Y., 1989). For the *Futūḥāt*, *Fuṣūṣ*, and other works, see *Muhyiddin Ibn al-ʿArabi*, edited by Stephen Hirtenstein (Oxford, 1993).

Lings, Martin. *A Sufi Saint of the Twentieth Century: Shaikh Aḥmad al-ʿAlawī*. Berkeley, 1971. Includes an illuminating discussion of al-ʿAlawī's practice and teaching of *dhikr*.

Martin, David, "The Return to the One in the Philosophy of Najm ad-Dīn al-Kubrá." In *Neoplatonism and Islamic Thought*, edited by Parviz Morewedge, pp. 221–246. Albany, N.Y., 1992.

Qushayrī, ʿAbd al-Karīm. *Das Sendschreiben al-Qušayrīs über das Sufitum (Al-Risālah al-Qushayrīyah)*. Translated by Richard Gramlich. Wiesbaden, 1989. See as well selections by Barbara von Schlegell in *Principles of Sufism* (Berkeley, 1992).

Ṣāliḥ, Al-Ṭayyib. *The Wedding of Zein and Other Stories*. Translated by Denys Johnson-Davies. London, 1968. Brilliant and accessible evocations of *dhikr* in all aspects of village life.

Sarrāj, Abū Naṣr ʿAbd Allāh al-. *Schlaglichter über das Sufitum (Kitāb al-lumaʿfī al-taṣawwuf)*. Translated by Richard Gramlich. Stuttgart, 1990. Masterwork of early Sufism.

Sells, Michael. *Desert Tracings: Six Classic Arabian Odes*. Middletown, Conn., 1989. Includes five of the more famous *dhikrs* of the beloved in early Arabic poetry.

Stetkevych, Jaroslav. *The Zephyrs of Najd: The Poetics of Nostalgia in the Classical Arabic Nasīb*. Chicago, 1993. Poetic tradition of remembrance and its transformations through the medieval period.

The Traditional World of Islam, 1978. A film series featuring the physical and artistic embodiments of *dhikr* in calligraphy, architecture, village, garden, and city planning, and the relationship of the human to the natural world. See *Man and Nature* and *Patterns of Beauty*.

Zayn al-ʿĀbidīn ʿAlī ibn al-Ḥusayn. *The Psalms of Islam: Al-Ṣaḥīfah al-kāmilah al-Sajjādīyah*. Translated by William C. Chittick. London, 1988. Supplicatory prayers *(duʿaʾ)*, which are closely related to the invocatory prayer of *dhikr*.

MICHAEL A. SELLS

DHIMMĪ. In Islamic law one who is in the covenant of protection *(dhimmah)* with the Muslim power is considered *dhimmī*. In principle, the covenant could be made between Islam and any population of a non-Muslim country conquered by Muslim forces. But in the usual meaning and practice the covenant was made only with scriptuaries, *ahl al-kitāb* ("people of the book"). Besides Jews, Christians, and Sabaeans, the category of *ahl al-kitāb* was often extended to cover Zoroastrians, sometimes members of other faiths were included (e.g., Hindus).

Adult male *dhimmīs* of sound mind were required to pay the special *jizyah* (poll tax) on their incomes as well as the *kharāj* (land tax). In later centuries the *kharāj* was exacted less and ultimately disappeared. Restrictions and regulations in dress, occupation, and residence were often applied to *dhimmīs*. The legal status of *dhimmīs* was in many aspects unequal to that of Muslims. *Dhimmīs* were obliged to comport themselves in a self-effacing and inoffensive manner, and religious publicity and proselytization were forbidden to them. In return for *dhimmī* compliance with the stipulations of the *dhimmah* covenant, Islam offered them security of life and property, defense against enemies, communal self-government, and freedom of religious practice. The *dhimmah* regulations were applied with varying degrees of rigor in different times and places.

In the modern period, the *dhimmī* status has in practice become quite meaningless in most Muslim countries. This is a result of the formation of nation-states throughout the Islamic world and the consequent adoption of Western and quasi-Western legal and political systems. Although Islamic law in most instances played some role in the new order, the *dhimmah* in a traditional sense was usually not represented. Modern conceptions and institutions of nationality and citizenship were more relevant to the nation-state. Former *dhimmīs* became citizens of modern states. In the case of the Jews, most emigrated from those states as a result of the creation of the new Jewish state in 1948.

The concept of *dhimmī* has remained in force intellectually and psychologically in intercommunal relations, though in weakened form. With regard to the Palestine conflict, it has figured prominently in some of the main Arab nationalist and Islamic thought on the subject. In both strains of thought, the pre-Zionist history of Arab-Jewish (or Muslim-Jewish) relations was often portrayed as a positive experience in contrast with the post-Zionist conflict. Many writers called for a return to the *dhimmah* or some modern version thereof as a solution to the conflict. For most conservative Muslim thinkers in the modern period, the *dhimmah* has been an integral part of their version of a reconstituted Islamic society and polity.

[*See also* Jizyah; Kharāj; People of the Book.]

BIBLIOGRAPHY

Stillman, Norman A. *The Jews of Arab Lands in Modern Times*. Philadelphia, 1991. Although mainly on the Jews, gives a good survey of the *dhimmī* situation in the modern period.

Tritton, A. S. *The Caliphs and Their Non-Muslim Subjects: A Critical Study of the Covenant of ʿUmar* (1930). London, 1970. Standard work on the subject, though somewhat dated.

RONALD L. NETTLER

DIETARY RULES. Islamic prescriptions concerning food and drink keep Muslims mindful in their everyday lives of God's will and of their membership in a global community of shared values and obligations, regardless of their social rank. As set forth in the seventh century in the Qur'ān and the *ḥadīths* the rules are based on the categories of pure *(ṭāhir)* and impure *(rijs, najis)* and of lawful *(ḥalāl)* and unlawful *(ḥarām)*. In general they are well known by Muslims, though not always observed. Since the ninth century, jurists have striven to reduce ambiguities in dietary rules and to elaborate on their application to foods and situations not explicitly discussed in the Qur'ān. Although historically related to pre-Islamic Arabian and Jewish dietary rules, the Islamic ones are completely severed from priestly codes of purities and abominations connected with temple worship. Nor are they inherently part of a cosmological scheme of sympathies and antipathies, such as is found in Hellenistic and East Asian religious traditions. In contrast to Hindu dietary rules, Islamic rules do not express caste hierarchies, although they clearly set Muslims apart from non-Muslims.

Basic Rules. The Qur'ān exhorts believers to eat the good, lawful plants and animals that God has provided for them (80.25–32, 2.168, 2.172, 16.14). This general dispensation is subject to several conditions and prohibitions. Plant foods that are especially valued include dates, the vine, olives, pomegranates, and grains (6.99, 6.141, 80.25–32). The preferred flesh is that of domestic cattle, sheep, goats, and camels (6.143–145). Muslims are expressly forbidden from consuming carrion, spurting blood, pork, and food that has been consecrated to any being other than God himself (5.3, 6.145). Date wine *(khamr)* was repudiated gradually after the establishment of the community in Medina; the strongest condemnation (5.90–91) was among the last revelations received by Muḥammad (in 632). Each prohibited substance is declared to be extremely defiling, with wine being further distinguished as an instrument of Satan for sowing discord among the faithful.

The lawfulness of meat is largely determined by how it is obtained. Ritual slaughtering and sacrifice (a form of slaughter qualified by intentionality on sacred occasions) are required for domestic cattle, sheep, goats, and fowl. These must be killed in God's name (6.118, 6.121) by making a fatal incision across the throat. Jurists recommend that camels be slaughtered by stabbing the upper chest. The Qur'ān permits fishing and hunting wild animals as long as the quarry is lawful (5.94–96). It prohibits Muslims from eating anything that has been strangled, beaten, or gored to death, or animals that have died by falling. A creature that has been partly consumed by predatory beasts is also forbidden, unless it has actually been killed by ritual slaughtering or by a trained hunting animal (5.3–4).

Additional dietary rules, based on the Qur'ān and the *ḥadīths*, apply to specific ritual occasions. Thus, during the month of Ramaḍān, every able Muslim is obliged to abstain completely from food and drink during the daylight hours. The same rule applies during the performance of daily and Friday prayers. Pilgrims are prohibited from slaughtering and hunting lawful animals as long as they remain in a sacral state. By contrast, during the two main feasts of the year, following Ramaḍān and the *ḥajj*, the faithful are obliged *not* to fast. *Ḥadīths* also set guidelines for daily hospitality and acceptable table manners—remembering God at mealtime, taking food and drink with the right hand, and not reclining while eating. [*See* Ramaḍān; Ḥajj.]

Developments in *Fiqh*. Muslim jurists have played a significant role in codifying and elaborating the dietary rules of the Qur'ān by using *ḥadīth*s, local Muslim practices, and analogy as their guides. Differences over the rules have arisen among and within their *fiqh* schools. For example, although all schools rejected beheading as a method of ritual slaughter, they differed over details of acceptable slaughtering techniques. Ḥanafīs required cutting the esophagus, trachea, and most of the major blood vessels in the neck; Shafiʿīs called for cutting the esophagus and trachea and recommended severing the two jugular veins; Imāmī Shīʿīs required cutting the two carotids and the two jugulars; and Malikīs said that severing the two jugulars is sufficient. From a legalistic point of view, if the slaughtering is not performed correctly, an otherwise lawful animal becomes carrion, that is, impure and forbidden for human consumption.

The ban on "wine" is another significant area of juristic disputation. The Malikī, Shāfiʿī, and Ḥanbalī schools agreed that *khamr* is a general term for any intoxicating beverage made from dates, grapes, and similar substances. The Ḥanafīs, however, ruled that only a narrow range of beverages can be classed as *khamr:* fermented juice of cooked or uncooked grapes, and uncooked intoxicants obtained from dates and raisins. All schools agreed, however, that consuming *khamr* is unlawful, and that its sale by or to Muslims is forbidden. However, they generally permit medicinal uses in cases of absolute necessity.

The social function of dietary rules in defining Islamic communities and their relation to non-Muslims is evident in the guidelines for deciding who can perform the slaughtering and from whom food can be received. The *fiqh* schools have allowed wide latitude in this regard: meat can be obtained from any rational Muslim, male or female, who is familiar with correct slaughtering procedures. Following guidelines in the Qur'ān (5.5), Muslims usually can also accept meat and other food from Jews, Christians, and other people of the book. Indeed, in accordance with the *ḥadīth,* many hold that if there is doubt about the source of meat, a person need only "mention the name of Allāh over it and eat it" (al-Bukhārī). On the other hand, jurists have forbidden food obtained from known heretics, apostates, idol-worshipers, and atheists.

Transgression of dietary prohibitions temporarily invalidates acts of worship such as prayer, fasting, and pilgrimage. Mere physical contact with pork, carrion, or wine makes a person or object impure, but this can be remedied by simple washing or by physical removal of the offending substance. On the other hand, violating the ban on *khamr* and drunkenness are major crimes requiring legal standards of proof and corporal punishment of forty or eighty lashes. According to one *ḥadīth,* unrepentant violators will be denied the reward of drinking wine in the afterlife.

Contemporary Implications. The dietary rules have acquired new significance in the twentieth century. Although some Muslims have attempted to demonstrate that the rules conform to modern reason and the findings of scientific research, many others have used them in the search for Islamic alternatives to western values, ideologies, and lifestyles. Such reevaluations are occurring in two milieus—among the postcolonial cultures of the traditional Islamic heartland, and among Muslim immigrant communities, especially in the West. Indeed, dietary rules often serve as focal points for islamization movements and individual affirmations of Muslim identity.

Through the centuries, the Islamic ban on intoxicants has been honored in the breach. Wine has been a favorite beverage in royal courts as well as in public taverns; it has been praised in poetry; and some Ṣūfīs, like Rūmī (d. 1273), have used it as a metaphor for transcendence. The Bektāshī order, most popular among Ottoman Janissaries, used wine sacramentally. Jurists periodically decried such practices, but with little success. Sixteenth-century efforts to outlaw coffee as a wine-like beverage in the Hejaz and Egypt failed miserably. Consumption of non-alcoholic intoxicants such as hashish, opium, and qat has become a popular habit among peasants and towndwellers alike in many Muslim countries. Proponents argue that such substances were never explicitly banned in the Qur'ān and *ḥadīth*s; their opponents retort with the *ḥadīth* that proclaims, "Every intoxicant is *khamr,* and every *khamr* is unlawful" (Muslim).

In the modern era some governments in Islamic nation-states have taken strong official stands against alcoholic beverages and narcotics as they move to implement the *sharīʿah.* Usually this means interpreting the ban broadly enough to enforce it against non-Muslims. The Wahhābī authorities of Saudi Arabia outlawed intoxicants to Muslims in 1929 and have prohibited alcohol to foreign residents since 1952. Ad hoc implementations of the *sharīʿah* in Qadhdhafi's Libya (1971) and Nimeiri's Sudan (1983) included official bans on alcohol and, in the case of Sudan, public dumping of millions of dollars worth of liquor as well as the punishment of non-Muslims. It was officially banned in Pakistan and Iran during the early 1980s, and during the early 1990s in Kelantan, a Muslim-majority province in northeast Malaysia.

Muslim countries with secularist regimes, such as Egypt and Turkey, have instituted strict antinarcotics laws but permit controlled import, sale, and consumption of liquor. Consequently, opposition Islamist groups there call for the total eradication of alcohol. In Egypt, outside the political arena, segments of the middle classes have become less forbearing toward relatives and friends who drink. Unlike earlier generations, recent Muslim immigrants to Europe and the United States have made observing the Qur'ānic prohibition a key marker of identity in their host country. Moreover, there are lively debates in these communities about whether Muslims should even work in places where liquor is sold, consumed, or produced—including groceries, restaurants, and vineyards. The liquor ban is also one of the tenets of the Black Muslim movement and its offshoots in the African-American community.

For many immigrants in Europe and the United States during the 1980s and 1990s, the rules of slaughtering and the pork taboo became at least as important as the ban on alcohol. In towns where sizeable Muslim communities have formed, groceries selling lawful meats have opened. Muslims also go to farms where they purchase and slaughter the animals themselves. Otherwise, they feel secure purchasing kosher foods and rely on information garnered from product labels. Yvonne Haddad and Adair Lummis report (*Islamic Values in the United States: A Comparative Study*, New York, 1987, pp. 113–118) that of the American Muslims they surveyed, 93 percent had not consumed pork in the previous six months, some 66 percent had not consumed alcohol, and more than 50 percent had purchased correctly slaughtered meat. In France, Gilles Kepel discovered (*Les banlieues de l'Islam*, Paris, 1987, pp. 34–41) that more than 24 percent of the immigrants he interviewed would not dine in non-Muslim homes because of the dietary restrictions on meat, pork, and alcohol; another 55 percent said they would accept only on the condition that no pork or alcohol be served. If Islamist movements continue to make gains, it is probable that attention to dietary rules will also increase in Muslim majority and minority communities alike.

[*See also* Ḥalāl; Purification.]

BIBLIOGRAPHY

Denny, Frederick Mathewson. *An Introduction to Islam*. 2d ed. New York, 1994. Nuanced treatment of normative and cultural dimensions of Islamic religion in Middle Eastern and Asian contexts, with discussion of dietary practices (pp. 283–285) and annotated bibliography.

Hattox, Ralph S. *Coffee and Coffeehouses: The Origins of a Social Beverage in the Medieval Near East*. Seattle, 1985. Delightful exemplar of social history, with a detailed account of Sunnī legal debates about intoxicating beverages.

Khaṭīb al-Tibrīzī, Muḥammad ibn ʿAbd Allah al-. *Mishkāt al-maṣābīḥ*. Vol. 3. Translated by James Robson. Lahore, 1965–1966. Contains selected *ḥadīth*s dealing with slaughtering, hunting, food, drink, and hospitality.

Qaraḍāwī, Yūsuf al-. *The Lawful and the Prohibited in Islam (Al-ḥalāl wa-al-ḥarām fī al-Islām)*. Translated by Kamal El-Helbawi, M. Moinuddin Siddiqui, and Syed Shukry. Indianapolis, 1960. Popular *fiqh* handbook (now in its twentieth Arabic printing) sponsored by al-Azhar University to introduce Islamic teachings to Muslims and non-Muslims in Europe and America. Dietary rules are discussed in chapter 2. Marred by neglect of ambiguity and variation in *fiqh*.

Rippin, Andrew, and Jan Knappert, eds. and trans. *Textual Sources for the Study of Islam*. Totowa, N.J., 1987. Useful anthology including a selection of *ḥadīth*s on drink from al-Bukhārī (pp. 72–76), and a text dealing with dietary rule variations among the legal schools (pp. 105–108).

JUAN EDUARDO CAMPO

DIHLAWĪ, SHĀH WALĪ ALLĀH. *See* Walī Allāh, Shāh.

DĪN WA-DUNYĀ. *See* Islamic State.

DIPLOMACY. *See* International Relations and Diplomacy.

DIPLOMATIC IMMUNITY. With a long tradition in the customary practices of nations, diplomatic immunity, originally justified on the basis of theories of sovereign representation and exterritoriality, is now accepted as a functional necessity. Customary rules of diplomatic immunity have been codified authoritatively by the Vienna Convention on Diplomatic Relations (1961) and the Vienna Convention on Consular Relations (1963), which have been ratified by most nations. At a minimum diplomatic immunity guarantees the inviolability of diplomats by protecting their persons, property, and premises. The scope of coverage and the extent of immunities accorded often involve intricate legal issues.

Modern diplomatic immunity finds strong support in Islamic historical practices and juridical writings. Medieval Muslim jurists argued that the protections afforded to diplomatic envoys or emissaries is necessitated by *maṣlaḥah* (public welfare) and by the commands of the Prophet. The Prophet sent and received several envoys and is reported to have strictly forbidden their molestation.

An envoy, called *rasūl* or *safīr* in Islamic discourse, performed a variety of functions, including negotiating treaties, attending coronations, conciliating differences, or ransoming captives. According to Islamic law, envoys sent to Islamic territory were entitled to safe conduct without a specific grant of *amān* on presentation of their papers of commission. Their persons and property were immune, and they were exempted from taxation as long as they did not engage in trade. Muslim juridical writings contain elaborate rules regulating the reception of envoys. There is also a wealth of administrative treatises outlining the proper criteria for sending or receiving emissaries.

The Umayyads (661–750) continued the practice of the Prophet in sending and receiving envoys. However, diplomatic intercourse became more significant in the ʿAbbāsid period (749–1258). The Fāṭimids (909–1171) and Mamlūks (1254–1517) increased the practice further by sending envoys to Europe and Central and East Asia.

Largely because of expanding commercial relations, diplomatic representation witnessed a dramatic increase in the sixteenth century. Diplomatic envoys for the most part continued to be sent on a temporary basis with a specific goal in mind. By the end of the sixteenth century, however, several European nations had established resident missions in Ottoman territory. The Ottomans established permanent embassies in Europe in the eighteenth century.

The sixteenth century also witnessed the beginning of the capitulations regimes, which were commercial treaties granting Western nationals certain immunities from the criminal and civil jurisdiction of the host state. By comparison the capitulations granted much broader immunities than those granted by the Vienna Conventions and Muslim nations often considered them humiliating. Separate treaties, such as the Treaty of Küçük Kaynarca (1774), article 27 between Russia and the Ottoman Empire, and the Treaty of Dardanelles (1809), article 7 between Britain and the Ottoman Empire, afforded specific protections to diplomats on a reciprocal basis.

By the 1940s the capitulations had been abolished. Nevertheless, by the 1960s most Muslim nations had acceded to the Vienna Conventions. Muslim nations have maintained a good record in observing diplomatic immunities. Breaches such as the hostage crisis in Iran, which received a great deal of attention, have been infrequent. Nevertheless, the main issue confronting Muslims at the present time is that Islamic law is not entirely consistent with the Vienna Conventions. For example, according to the majority opinion in Islamic law, diplomats are liable for crimes and torts committed in the host state. Muslim nations, to a large extent, resolved the inconsistency by considering themselves bound by the Vienna Conventions regardless.

[*See also* Capitulations; Diplomatic Missions; Hostages; International Law; International Relations and Diplomacy.]

BIBLIOGRAPHY

Bassiouni, M. Cherif. "Protection of Diplomats under Islamic Law." *American Journal of International Law* 74 (1980): 609–633. The only source specifically addressing the subject, but contains certain inaccuracies.

Ghunaimi, Mohammad Talaat al-. *The Muslim Conception of International Law and the Western Approach*. The Hague, 1968. Contains a useful discussion on the history of diplomatic conduct.

Khadduri, Majid. *War and Peace in the Law of Islam*. Baltimore and London, 1955. Remains a useful reference source and contains a section on diplomatic immunity.

Mahmassani, Sobhi. "The Principles of International Law in the Light of Islamic Doctrine." *Hague Recueil (Hague Academy of International Law, Recueil des Cours)* 117 (1966): 201–328. Besides being a very insightful study, it contains a useful section on diplomatic immunity.

Mottahedeh, Roy P. "Iran's Foreign Devils." *Foreign Policy* 38 (Spring 1980): 19–34. Excellent study of the hostage crisis in Iran. Reviews Shīʿī rules on diplomatic immunity and the history of capitulations in Iran.

Shaybānī, Muḥammad ibn al-Ḥasan. *The Islamic Law of Nations: Shaybani's Siyar*. Translated by Majid Khadduri. Baltimore, 1966. One of the very few translations of an Islamic legal text on international law.

KHALED ABOU EL FADL

DIPLOMATIC MISSIONS. An official delegation from one country to another, a diplomatic mission ca be either temporary or permanent. The members of a diplomatic mission have diplomatic status, the most important element of which is diplomatic immunity. Although Muslim and non-Muslim diplomatic missions are virtually identical, they evolved quite separately.

The concept of a diplomatic mission representing one independent ruler to another independent ruler is not entirely compatible with Islamic political theory. The universalist nature of Islam assumes a single *ummah* (community of the faithful) under one law and administered by one government. Theoretically, therefore, no diplomatic missions were needed within the Islamic world, for all were presumably under a single ruler. As for non-Muslim states, the necessity of diplomatic missions was considered to be only temporary, until the whole world came under the dominion of Islam; non-Muslim states were not considered to be moral or political equals of the Islamic state.

In practice, Islamic diplomatic missions, both to other Muslim states and to non-Muslim states, have existed since the time of the Prophet. Muḥammad himself used them to propagate the faith. As the Arab-Islamic empire grew in size and power, the necessity for diplomatic missions grew apace. The caliphs in Damascus and later in Baghdad were in virtually continuous diplomatic communication with neighboring states, particularly with their enemies, the Byzantines and the Franks. The ʿAbbāsid caliph Hārūn al-Rashīd developed extraordinary diplomatic ties with the Holy Roman emperor, Charlemagne, and the two regularly exchanged gifts and dispatched diplomatic missions. In periods of Islamic political decline, diplomatic missions between Muslim rulers also increased.

The basic functions of Islamic diplomatic missions have changed very little over the centuries: negotiating treaties, arbitrating disputes, attending state ceremonies, and also collecting intelligence. *Mufawwaḍah* means "negotiation" in Arabic, and a *mufawwaḍīyah* is a legation, an old form of diplomatic mission. The chief of mission was a *mufawwaḍ* (minister). Another term used for a chief of a diplomatic mission was *rasūl* (messenger).

Historically, the most important role of an Islamic diplomatic mission was probably arbitration. The Arabic for the more contemporary term, "embassy," is *sifārah,* and the chief of mission is a *safīr* (ambassador). Both terms have the connotation of "mediation" or "arbitration," reflecting the greater emphasis in Islamic law on arbitration rather than establishing guilt.

Arbitration was practiced in the Middle East long before the advent of Islam and was simply absorbed into the new religion. The prophet Muḥammad saw himself (and by extension, his successors) as an arbitrator, and the Qur'ān admonishes the faithful, "If you differ, bring it before Allāh and the apostle." (surah 4.59). The same principle was applied to arbitrating between nations.

In the early days of Islam, diplomatic missions were exchanged for the purpose of negotiating or arbitrating a particular issue. Although some missions stayed months or even years in a foreign capital, few were permanent in the contemporary sense. Maintaining permanent diplomatic missions was basically a European practice that developed around the sixteenth century. By the end of the sixteenth century, resident European envoys were accredited to the Ottoman sultan in Constantinople, and by the eighteenth century, Ottoman envoys were resident in Europe.

With increasing European commercial and political penetration in the Muslim world, starting in the eighteenth century, diplomatic relations increased, but not necessarily through the medium of diplomatic missions. With the political decline of the Ottoman Empire, European states established independent ties to the emerging, although not yet technically independent Arab states. Farther east, commercial firms played the role of diplomatic missions. British diplomatic relations with the Ṣafavid Empire in Persia and the Mughals in India, for example, were initially carried out through the British East India Company rather than the Foreign Office. Even after the British Government established more extensive government-to-government relations in the nineteenth century, they were mainly handled by the Colonial Office rather than the Foreign Office.

By the nineteenth century, European colonialism had so permeated the Muslim world that the utility of diplomatic missions had declined measurably. Of particular importance was the capitulations. These were agreements granting special judicial privileges to resident Western nationals engaged in commerce in Muslim countries nominally under the Ottoman Empire. These rights, however, were administered by Western consuls, not through diplomatic missions.

Following World War I, when most Muslim countries had regained at least token independence, resident diplomatic missions again spread throughout the Muslim world. But the war also ended the Ottoman caliphate, and the universalist nature of Islamic political theory no longer represented political reality. Western rules of diplomacy, based on sovereign nation-states, became universally accepted throughout the Muslim world.

Even these practices have not been static, however. After World War II, the previously sharp distinction between diplomatic functions and consular functions virtually disappeared. Today, consular functions, which include granting visas to foreigners wishing to visit one's country, seeking the welfare and protection of one's citizens abroad, and promoting commercial relations, are performed in diplomatic missions, just as traditional diplomatic functions, such as political and economic reporting, are performed in consulates. Depending on the country, consular officials are now regularly granted diplomatic immunity, which was not a traditional practice in the West.

The raising of diplomatic missions to the status of embassies is also virtually universal. Traditionally, missions to less important countries were legations, and the chiefs of mission held the title of minister, whereas the major missions were embassies and the chiefs of mission held the title of ambassador. After World War II, however, because of the sensitivities of the smaller, Third World countries, virtually all countries are now represented by ambassadors, and their missions are designated as embassies.

[*See also* Capitulations; Diplomatic Immunity; International Law; International Relations and Diplomacy.]

BIBLIOGRAPHY

Hitti, Philip K. *History of the Arabs: From the Earliest Times to the Present.* 9th ed. London, 1967. Classic account of Arab history, with many references to diplomatic relations with the West.

Khadduri, Majid, and Herbert J. Liebesny, eds. *Law in the Middle East.* Washington, D.C., 1955. See, in particular, Khadduri's chapter on international law.

Lewis, Bernard. *The Emergence of Modern Turkey.* New York, 1961. Another classic, which includes discussions of Ottoman diplomatic relations.

Shaybānī, Muḥammad ibn al-Ḥasan. *The Islamic Law of Nations: Shaybānī's Siyar.* Translated by Majid Khadduri. Baltimore, 1966.

DAVID E. LONG

DIVINATION. The comprehensive term for divination in the Islamic tradition is *Kihānah,* a term derived from Semitic antiquity. It is connected to all aspects, practical and theoretical, of the art of knowing that which cannot spontaneously be known. Ironic as it may seem, divination remained a subject worthy of the attention of many a serious Islamic thinker despite the fact that a frequently quoted *ḥadīth* had declared that "there is no *kihānah* after the Prophetic Mission."

Ibn Khaldūn (d. 1406) places divination at the lowest rung of prophetic attributes, a divine gift to God's chosen individuals. And while the Qur'ān condemned practices connected with pagan cults, and the institution of the diviners was officially abrogated in Islam, divination continued in various forms and disguises. Many sober sages spoke of "illuminated souls" who were blessed by the knowledge of the occult (*ghayb*); among them were prophets, saints (*walī*), physiognomists, and soothsayers. The knowledge of the unseen or of the future was sometimes revealed in dreams, and the art of the interpretation of dreams (*taʿbīr al-ru'yā*) was elevated to a rank above that of divination, being considered part of prophecy.

Like much in Islamic culture, divination arose out of an innovative blending of Greek, Sanskrit, Pahlavi, and local sources, incorporating under *kihānah* methods pertaining to astrology and magic. Generally divided into the three categories of *firāsah* (physiognomancy), *siḥr* (magic), and *aḥkām al-nujūm* (judicial astrology), divination receives detailed classificatory treatment in the writings of many Muslim encyclopedists, biographers, bibliographers, and historians. Thus under the first category one finds *ʿilm qiyāfat al-āthār/al-bashar* (divination by the observation of footprints/ by morphoscopic and genealogical lines), *ʿilm al-asārīr* (chiromancy), *ʿilm al-aktāf* (omoplatoscopy or divination by the observation of shoulder blades), and so on; under the second, *ʿilm daʿwat al-kawākib* (invocation of celestial bodies), *ʿilm al-khafā'* (making oneself invisible), *ʿilm al-ʿazā'im* (incantations), *ʿilm al-asmā' al-ḥusnā* (science of the beautiful divine names), *ʿilm al-daʿāwā* (science of Islamic personal prayers), and *ʿilm al-saʿbadhah* (conjury); and under the third, *ʿilm al-ikhtiyārāt* (catarchic astrology), *ʿilm al-raml* (geomancy), and *ʿilm al-fa'l* (omens). Here it is interesting to note not only the blending of so many disciplines, but also the imaginative grafting of characteristically Islamic elements onto an eclectic foreign base.

Indeed, a characteristic feature of divination in Islamic culture is its progressive divorce from the primitive oracular traditions, becoming over time a systematic art referred to as one of the sciences, *ʿulūm* (sg., *ʿilm*). This places it on an equal footing with mathematics, astronomy, or medicine, all of which were also called *ʿilm.*

[*See also* Astrology, Geomancy; Magic and Sorcery; Numerology.]

BIBLIOGRAPHY

A comprehensive account of prophecy in Islam is found in Toufic Fahd, *La divination arabe: Études religieuses, sociologiques et folkloriques sur le milieu natif de l'Islam* (Leiden, 1966), based on primary sources. See as well Fahd's article "Kihāna," in the *Encyclopaedia of Islam*, new ed., vol. 5, pp. 99–101 (Leiden, 1960–). Alfred Guillaume's *Prophecy and Divination among the Hebrews and Other Semites* (London, 1938) is a dated but still useful text. Other relevant entries in the new edition of the *Encyclopaedia of Islam* include Charles Pellat's "Anwāʾ" (vol. 1, pp. 523–524); "Djafr" (vol. 2, pp. 375–377), "Ikhtiyārāt" (vol. 3, pp. 1063–1064), "Ḳiyāfa" (vol. 5, pp. 234–235), "Malḥama" (vol. 6, p. 247), "Nīrandj" (vol. 8, pp. 51–52), and "Nudjūm" (vol. 8, pp. 105–108), all by Toufic Fahd. A comprehensive treatment, invaluable for the serious reader, is D. B. Macdonald's "Siḥr," in *E. J. Brill's First Encyclopaedia of Islam*, vol. 7, pp. 409–417 (Leiden, 1987).

S. Nomanul Haq

DIVORCE. *See* Marriage and Divorce.

DĪWĀN. A term of uncertain derivation, used throughout Islamic history to cover a number of institutions and practices, *dīwān* can most inclusively be defined as a collection of a homogeneous body of written materials or an administrative office that produces such a collection.

In the sense of a written body of materials, *dīwān* was, and to a lesser extent still is, used in the literary sphere to denote a collection of poetry (or, sometimes, prose). In the bureaucratic world, it denotes an archival register. In either case, there seems to be at least an indirect association with the Persianate cultural ethos that permeated urban populations and especially scribal milieus since the early caliphate in the Middle Eastern heartland of Islamic civilization. One etymology of the term derives it from the Persian *dīv* ("spirits of evil and of darkness"), supposedly describing bureaucrats. As the differences grew between popular cultural practices and a literature that cultivated the studied emulation of classical Islamic forms, *dīwān* was used more specifically with respect to collections of poetry. The distinction is relatively sharp in Ottoman literature, where a twofold division between *dīwān* poetry and folk poetry is commonly maintained. One can also find the connotation of refinement and urbanity in the use of *dīwān* for a comfortable seat in some Middle Eastern and European languages.

The most common usage of the term, however, has been with respect to certain offices that administered important governmental functions, presumably by extension of the meaning of "account registers" that were called *dīwān* since Caliph ʿUmar ibn al-Khaṭṭāb (r. 634–644).

Although the central administrations of different Islamic states were often called simply *dīwān*, various branches of the government were known as more specifically designated *dīwān*s. In the capacity of central government, a *dīwān* (also given such loftier titles as *dīvān-i aʿlā* or *divan-i hümayun*) would often be headed by the vizier or grand vizier. By a further leap of meaning, the term (usually with the spelling of *dewan* in English) was also used to denote a vizier on the Indian subcontinent since the time of the Mughal Empire. The East India Company, for instance, was appointed *dīwān* of the Province of Bengal.

In terms of the branches of government, there was naturally a great diversity among different states over time and space, and ad hoc arrangements led to the creation or abolition of specific *dīwān*s even under one government. Still, a remarkable continuity can be observed in certain structural features whereby a threefold division was quite characteristic: a *dīwān* of the chancellery (often known as *dīwān al-rasāʾil* or *dīwān al-inshāʾ*); a *dīwān* of finances *(amwāl)*; and a *dīwān* of the military *(jaysh)*. Separate *dīwān*s were commonly set up with specific responsibilities to administer pious foundations, fiefs, various taxes, alms, customs (hence, arguably, the word for customs in some European languages: *douane*, *dogana*, etc.), and so forth. Subbranches of these offices or other administrative bureaus could also be given titles constructed with *dīwān*. Provincial administrations might also have their own local central *dīwān* and divisions into further *dīwān*s that might parallel those at the center. All these might be subjected to inspection by *dīwān*s of control *(zimām)*. Finally, various Islamic governments instituted *dīwān*s of *maẓālim*, which functioned like a court of appeals or complaints and dealt with allegations of abuse of authority and miscarriage of justice. In the sense of tribunal or bureau, *dīwān* survives in the usages of some modern states, but it has been increasingly out of fashion since the nineteenth century along with a good deal of other non-Western modes and terms of governance.

The functioning of the Ottoman *divan-i hümayun* is very well documented. The procedures and hierarchies that governed its functioning and related ceremonies were codified in writing under Mehmed II (r. 1444–

1446, 1451–1481). Since the decisions of the *dīwān*, recorded and kept in *mühimme* registers, are extant from around the mid-sixteenth century, its order of business can be studied in particular detail after that point. The Ottoman *dīwān* would meet every day until sometime before the end of the sixteenth century, when meetings were reduced to only four days a week. It would include, in addition to the viziers, heads of the chancellery and treasury departments and the two top experts in *sharīʿah* (the divine law). Since Mehmed II, the Ottoman sultans did not participate in the meetings of the *dīwān* but might follow the proceedings from behind a grilled window, just as the ʿAbbāsid caliphs followed from behind a curtain. In addition to functioning as some form of cabinet and state council, the Ottoman *dīwān* held hearings on all kinds of cases brought before it by any subject or foreigner with legitimate business. The complaint of a monkey-player whose monkey was killed by the grand vizier's men might be heard on the same day as preparations for war were discussed or Istanbul's firewood shortage was considered.

[*See also* Economics, *article on* Economic Institutions.]

BIBLIOGRAPHY

Balādhurī, Aḥmad ibn Yaḥyā al-. *Futuḥ al-buldān*. Edited by ʿAbd Allāh Anīs al-Ṭabbāʿ and ʿUmar Anīs al-Ṭabbāʿ. Beirut, 1958. Translated by Philip K. Hitti as *The Origins of the Islamic State*. 2 vols. New York, 1968–1969.

"Dīvān." In *İslam Ansiklopedisi*. Istanbul, 1988–.

Dūrī, ʿAbd al-ʿAzīz al-, et al. "Dīwān." In *Encyclopaedia of Islam*, new ed., vol. 2, pp. 323–337. Leiden, 1960–.

Ibn Khaldūn, ʿAbd al-Raḥmān. *Muqaddimat Ibn Khaldūn*. 2d rev. ed. Edited by ʿAlī ʿAbd al-Wāḥid Wāfī. Cairo, 1965. Translated by Franz Rosenthal as *The Muqaddimah*. 3 vols. New York, 1958.

Minorsky, Vladimir, ed. and trans. *Tadhkirat al-Mulūk: A Manual of Ṣafavid Administration (c. 1137/1725)*. London, 1943.

Mumcu, Ahmet. *Divan-ı Hümayun*. Ankara, 1976.

Qalqashandī, Aḥmad ibn ʿAlī al-. *Ṣubḥ al-aʿshā fī ṣināʿat al-anshā*. Edited by Muḥammad Ḥusayn Shams al-Dīn. Beirut, 1987.

Cemal Kafadar

DJIBOUTI. For many centuries the Horn of Africa, in which the Republic of Djibouti forms a small coastal enclave, has provided access for the transmittal of goods and ideas between the Middle East and the African continent. Since the ninth century CE Djibouti has been the point of departure for Islamic missionary activity and for material support of Muslim proselytization and reform in Africa.

In 825 CE missionaries from Arabia introduced Islam into the Horn, which was then ruled by Christian Abyssinia. By the twelfth century merchants and clerics from the Arabian peninsula were proselytizing extensively along the coast, where local clans established small Muslim emirates. From the thirteenth to the seventeenth century these small Muslim states struggled for independence from the Christian Abyssinian rulers and eventually coalesced into three sultanates—Tadjoura, Rahayto, and Bobaad—which survive with symbolic powers in Djibouti today.

Situated on one of the two southern gateways to the Red Sea, Djibouti attracted European attention as early as the sixteenth century. The Portuguese were the first to move into the Red Sea, followed by British and French traders and administrators. During the partition of Africa by European colonial powers, France took possession of the region in 1888 and built up Djibouti's port and town. First known as French Somaliland and later as the French Territory of the Afars and Issas (1967), Djibouti served as a fueling station and military base until independence in 1977. France continues to maintain some four thousand military personnel in the Republic.

Virtually all (1991 estimates range from 94 to 100 percent) of Djibouti's 346,000 people are Sunnī Muslim. Both citydwellers and nomadic pastoralists living in Djibouti's barren countryside share a mystical Muslim tradition. Most follow the Shāfiʿī school of law, and many belong to the Qādirīyah Ṣūfī brotherhood that was well established in the region by the nineteenth century. The Aḥmadīyah and Ṣāliḥīyah also had created a presence in Djibouti by the end of the nineteenth century. The tombs of saintly and learned Muslims in the republic are visited annually by Djiboutian and Somali pilgrims. The highest authority in the Muslim community is the Qāḍī of Djibouti, who is usually of Arab origin. The Qāḍī celebrates marriages, registers divorces and wills, administers properties, and presides over the *sharīʿah* court. The Islamic holy days are legal holidays, and the government observes Ramaḍān with shortened workdays.

Islam, along with a shared language and cultural tradition, has contributed to a strong sense of common identity. Nevertheless, Djiboutians are deeply divided by clan loyalties. The largest kin group is the Somali Issa clan (40 percent of the population), which is concentrated around the capital. Somali Afars (35 percent) living in the countryside are essentially nomadic and ethnically linked to Ethiopian groups. Somali Gadaboursis, Warsangeli, Dulbahante, and Yemeni Arabs make up the balance of the Muslim community. Power-sharing by Issas—who have dominated the highest ranks of government—and Afars, who fill the lower ranks, has been a divisive issue since before independence. Interethnic tensions erupted into violent clashes in 1991, exacerbated by fighting between related groups spilling over from neighboring Somalia and Ethiopia. Since 1991 a simmering insurgency over Afar demands for greater democratization has undermined the government's authority in the north of the country. In June 1992 President Hassan Gouled Aptidon announced a calendar for transition to democracy following a popular referendum on a new constitution that created a multiparty state and an elected legislature.

Despite political frontiers separating it from Somalia and Ethiopia, Djibouti is differentiated neither culturally, ethnically, nor geographically from its neighbors. Djiboutians maintain close contact with Muslim activists in Ethiopia and Somalia along the Dire-Dawa-Djibouti corridor and through their clan ties in northern Somalia.

Djiboutians regularly provide sanctuary to refugees and support for Muslim causes across their borders. Furthermore, contacts with the Middle East and North Africa over the past ten years have helped to energize movements for Islamic renewal and political reform within Djibouti itself, particularly among young people, 70 percent of whom are unemployed. Djiboutians study abroad at centers of Islamic learning. Several Arab countries, including Saudi Arabia and Kuwait, have provided economic assistance to the Muslim community and support Islamic and Arabic-language education. According to the 1992 Annual Report of Imam Muhammad University in Riyadh, the university has established an Arab-Islamic Institute in Djibouti. The Muslim resurgence is increasingly evident in the proliferation of mosques, Qur'ānic schools, and study centers. Groups of reformists with names such as the Islamic Struggle of Djibouti Youth are calling for the establishment of a fully Islamic state in Djibouti and reduction of the European presence in the country.

BIBLIOGRAPHY

Fisher, Humphrey J. "The Western and Central Sudan and East Africa." In *The Cambridge History of Islam*, vol. 2, *The Further Islamic Lands, Islamic Society, and Civilization*, edited by P. M. Holt, Ann K. S. Lambton, and Bernard Lewis, pp. 345–405. Cambridge, 1970. Useful introduction to the Islamic background of the region.

Lewis, I. M. *Peoples of the Horn of Africa: Somali, Afar, and Saho*. London, 1955. Introduction to the ethnography of the region.

Lewis, I. M. *The Modern History of Somaliland*. London, 1965. Introduction to the political and social history of the region. Briefly treats the place of religion in Somali society, the Muslim Brotherhoods, and Muslim resistance to colonial domination.

Lewis, I. M. "Conformity and Contrast in Somali Islam." In *Islam in Tropical Africa*, edited by I. M. Lewis, pp. 253–267. London, 1966. Thought-provoking insights into the structure of Islamic communities in the Horn.

Thompson, Virginia, and Richard Adloff. *Djibouti and the Horn of Africa*. Stanford, Calif., 1968. Overview of Djibouti's history, with an extensive bibliography.

Trimingham, J. Spencer. *Islam in East Africa*. Oxford, 1964.

CHARLOTTE A. QUINN

DRAMA. *For a discussion of religious drama, see* Ta'ziyah.

DRESS. In the Muslim world, dress expresses identity, taste, income, regional patterns of trade, and the religiosity of its wearers. Dress and its use vary with regard to gender, age, marriage status, geographical origin, occupation, and even political sentiment. While the term *Islamic dress* has taken on new meanings in the contemporary period, the dress of Muslims, or the significance of dress in Muslim life extends beyond the indicators of an Islamist or non-Islamist orientation.

Regional variations of dress are significant for its wearers and those from any particular region are better able to recognize nuances of dress than outsiders. For example, Egyptians can readily identify a Sudanese woman in her wrapped diaphanous *thawb*, or a Kuwaiti man in his white tailored *thawb* and distinctive head covering. They may not correctly interpret other markers contained in the length, colors, or patterns of the woman's dress, or in the cut, design, and quality of the male garment specifying town or district of origin, or status. Many young urbanites know little about the variations in rural dress of their own countries, garments that date back more than a generation, or even the antecedents of their own clothing.

Dress may convey Islamic mores, but then again, many Muslims no longer wear traditional clothing, and hold varying views of the modern forms of Islamic dress. Even to those who generally wear Western-style clothing, dress serves as costume on formal occasions, holidays, and at weddings, and fulfills certain requirements during prayer, or on pilgrimage. Dress may also serve as a disguise, intentionally or unintentionally when clothing is displaced through migration, marriage, or trade.

Traditional dress conformed to climactic conditions and to a division between public and private space in the Muslim world. Long and flowing garments have been worn for centuries, not only for reasons of modesty, allowing the wearer to stoop, sit and ride, but also because they are more comfortable in hot and arid climates than tightly fitted garments. Covering protects the skin from sunburn and allows perspiration to remain on the skin, keeping the body moist. Head coverings shield from other elements, for instance, the wind and sand. Berber tribal dress, on the other hand, includes warm woolen garments necessary for the mountains, as in the capes and skirts of the Aït Mgild, Zaian, and Aït Izdeg women, and the knit leggings of the Ounergi men.

The shapes of traditional clothing also reflect the limitations of the loom. Outer wraps were made of one or more rectangular pieces, as were constructed robes (*thawb, jallābīyah, fustān, qufṭān, dishdashah*). Little fabric was wasted, and garments could be fitted through the use of gussets, insets, and a neck slit. Dress styles were modified—widened, narrowed, or otherwise refined when machine sewing was introduced. The use of color and decoration were regionally specific. In Palestine, merchants knew precisely which color thread women needed based on their native village or town. Color indicated marital status in bedouin embroidery, red or orange representing a married woman, while the addition or dominance of blue showed that the wearer was not married. Color preferences and stitch names and styles changed over time, which has complicated the identification of garments. Older, hand-sewn and embroidered garments are now recognized and valued as items of cultural and national identity.

Traditional Standards. Both male and female forms of traditional and contemporary Islamic dress conform to a general understanding of modesty based upon the *ḥadīth*, popular tradition, and traditional forms of costume construction (shape). The body is covered in various degrees depending on whether one is alone, or with a spouse, among friends or relatives of the same sex, or in a mixed setting. Specific areas of the body are regarded as virtue to be protected, or as sexual in nature. Men cover their bodies from their waists to their knees, cover their heads, and wear appropriate outer wear in public. Women cover their bodies from the neckline to the ankle, and their arms to the wrists. The intent of covering the body is to make clear the virtuous character of a woman who otherwise might attract male attention. Thus, a historical aim of Muslim dress has been to delineate acceptable degrees of modesty. Men were considered to lack self-control and were easily stimulated visually, so impeding their view of women's bodies could possibly discourage illicit advances toward women. At the same time, of course, it was understood that men and women should be attracted to one another, and the choosing and wearing of dress within the parameters of modesty might be a part of courtship.

Traditional clothing and modern Islamic dress require that women cover both their hair and neck. Traditional dress forms include an outer concealing layer which may cover the face, as in the *chādur* of Iran, or a specific face mask (*burqu*) worn by bedouin women in Egypt, and by rural and urban women in the Gulf. Historically, the outer wrap was supported on religious grounds by reference to the Qur'ān (4.33). The face veil was more questionable religiously, in fact, women who otherwise covered their face, uncovered it during prayer. As the practice of female seclusion and the harem system ended in certain countries, urban upper- and middle-class women began to appear without the face veil and outer wrap wearing Western-style coats and hats in public instead. Eventually, they went outside without that nod to the past, unless the weather required it. Muslim women who now wear modern fashions based on styles originating in Europe or elsewhere may be quite religious. If wearing pants, or a short skirt, women don long outer skirts over their regular clothing, and wrap fabric around the head and neck in order to modestly assume the positions of prayer.

Transitions in Dress. Dress cannot be categorized merely as traditional or Western, meaning, modern. It is true that except in the rural areas, hand-woven, embroidered "folk-dress" is passing into the category of ceremonial and symbolic dress. Trade and migration affected traditional dress in terms of materials, techniques, prices, and styles. Machine embroidery for the fancy-wear ladies' *thawb* of the Gulf and other garments are now made in India. Notions of modesty varied from area to area along with dress so that in some cases people adopted new garments in spite of their origins or implications.

The transition to "modern" dress was encouraged in some ways by the state itself, which required certain westernized forms of dress for its civil servants and pupils in public schools and universities (pants and jackets in place of men's robes, or hats in place of traditional headgarb). Modern dress, then, became a marker of urbanity and, to some degree, social class affiliation. But this trend was reversed by the adoption of contemporary Islamic dress described below, or in certain cases (as in Libya) where people were paid stipends to don, or re-adopt traditional dress. In other areas the shift from modern to Islamic dress was never mandated, or at least not totally approved, hence, in the Gulf, men wear their own dress, and may or may not wear Western business or leisure clothing abroad. Other Muslims dress in both styles, wearing "oriental" dress at home or for special occasions, but modern clothing for work or school. In a number of areas, brides may, as in the Gulf area, wear an heirloom traditional wedding dress on one night of the wedding festivities and a Western-style bridal gown on another night.

Non-traditional garments reflect the cultural and economic impact of the West. Many Muslim women will not wear clothing with low necklines or backs. However, when the miniskirt and bellbottoms were popular, they were worn in the Muslim world as well, even though they did not accord with notions of modesty. Some women avoid wearing shorts or tight pants. Western-style shoes and stockings have replaced sandals or slippers, except in village settings. Sleeveless garments are worn, but women not wearing Islamic dress, or traditional dress-styles are often harassed by men or young boys in the street. Of course, this behavior is common outside the Muslim world and reveals sexual tensions and notions of female intrusion into public space in many cultures.

Men's clothing also mirrors Western styles in urban areas. Some men wear a modified suit introduced in the 1950s and consisting of a lightweight jacket, fitted, belted, or elasticized at the waist, with short sleeves and a Nehru collar, worn with pants of the same color. Others wear currently fashionable Western suits. In rural areas, men continue to wear traditional dress, or to mix dress styles (jackets worn over *dishdashah*, or *sirwāl*) and to carry weapons and ammunition in public.

Modern Islamic Dress. A particular style of dress for men and women has developed in the Muslim world in the twentieth century, distinct in important ways from both traditional or modern dress. It has been adopted by some members of Muslim communities all over the world.

The female costume, referred to as Islamic dress, *sharʿī*, or improperly, fundamentalist dress, has become far more popular than the male version. It resembles the costume worn by members of the Association of Muslim Women and the women's wing of the Muslim Brotherhood (the Muslim Sisters) from the 1930s onward, consisting of a long skirt and a long-sleeved top, or a long robe, unfitted at the waist (*jilbāb, thawb*) and a head covering draped over the neck and sometimes covering the shoulders (*khimār*). Some women also wear a face veil of plain color (*niqāb*), gloves, and sunglasses. Diaphanous and brightly colored materials are avoided by the more pious who choose plain material and somber colors (black, dark blue, gray, beige, white). Although this costume has been confused with traditional forms of dress, and is claimed by its proponents to be the costume of the Mothers of Believers (the wives of the Prophet), it is distinctly modern. Women sew their own garments, have them made, or buy them ready-made. Some women have adopted the costume at the request of, or in order to please, spouses or relatives, and female covering has been required by the Islamic Republic of Iran. But most Muslim women have voluntarily chosen the *ḥijāb*, as Islamic dress is also called. The numbers of women wearing the *ḥijāb* have increased enormously since the 1970s. Its appearance has provoked dismay and debate, prompting regulations against it (in Turkey, Tunisia, or schools in France, for example) and tolerance for it (in Egyptian, Jordanian, and Syrian universities). In fact, Egyptian university officials have had to intervene to prevent students from requiring that their peers wear the *ḥijāb*. In areas of the Gaza Strip and the West Bank, women have been pelted with eggs or worse for not wearing at least a headscarf.

The male costume incorporates elements of traditional dress, as it includes a long-sleeved tunic and *sirwāl* (baggy pants) or a *jallābīyah* (robe). These garments should be plain in color and weave, cotton being acceptable while silk, as a luxury, is not. The head is often covered, with a prayer cap or another form of traditional head wrapping. A beard is worn, sometimes untrimmed, more often neatly trimmed but covering a portion of the cheeks, unlike the "secular" beard style of other younger men. While the wearer of such a costume would undoubtedly hold Islamist sentiments and profess marked piety, many Islamist men do not in fact wear this sort of dress. Men may have been more reluctant to adopt this dress in areas where the male robe and *sirwāl* are strongly associated with the lower classes.

In addition, the costume and the beard made men vulnerable to identification and arrest at specific points in time. Women, on the other hand, were not identified as activists on the basis of their dress alone, and several regimes decided it would be an ill-thought tactic to pinpoint the *ḥijāb*.

Islamic dress has been regarded with some suspicion both in the West and the Muslim world. Although women involved with the Ikhwān al-Muslimūn (Muslim Brotherhood) wore similar clothing the costume was not at all common during the years that group was suppressed in Egypt. New variants began to be seen during the 1970s, just as small groups of activist and radical Islamists began to emerge. With the Iranian Revolution women's Islamic dress, at first a symbol of opposition, then became a regime policy. It was difficult for some observers in other states to believe that women would willingly adopt Islamic dress, and many thought that stipends were paid to women to wear it to work or school. Various observers, rightly or wrongly, identified the growing use of Islamic dress with the potential for Islamic revolution inspired by the Iranian example. In fact Islamic dress could reflect diverse agendas, ranging from a generalized desire to gradually islamize society, to deep commitment to replace the secular system with an Islamic one as soon as possible.

Women who wear Islamic dress believe themselves to be better Muslims than they were before they adopted the costume. But they may or may not be more pious than other women, or politically active in any way. They also may subscribe to an ideology of gender and gender relations that is more conservative than that of unveiled women, especially in regard to the role of women in the workplace. Nevertheless, they tend to uphold women's rights to education, and to political and social roles. Some women believe their marriage prospects will improve with the adoption of *ḥijāb*, and most claim that the *sharīʿah* requires them to wear it.

Traditional and Ceremonial Dress. While Islamic dress is quite similar from region to region, the traditional dress of Muslim women varies greatly, as does its quality and accompanying jewelry. Many styles are belted or fitted at the waist, like the southern Arabian *quftān*, traditional Moroccan Muslim (and Jewish) urban dresses, bedouin dresses from the northern Sinai and Palestinian dress styles. Others like those from the Egyptian Delta, have a decorated and fitted bodice from which full and unfitted materials flow. The eastern Arabian *thawb* is not fitted at all, though elaborately decorated on filmy chiffon. Sleeve styles vary from long and loose, to short or pointed, and may be tied behind the back to facilitate housework.

In many areas women wore loose, gussetted pants *(sirwāl)* under their clothing. These served as underwear, and in some areas the legs were fitted, embroidered, and meant to be seen. In rural Turkey, the *sirwāl* are patterned and worn with shorter tunics or blouses, while in Pakistan they show under a tunic worn with a neck scarf. Previously, shifts or thin blouses were worn as undergarments and later replaced with knitted, and then sewn, cotton and synthetic underwear.

Traditional garments worn at weddings illustrate family origin, history, and status. The bridal dresses and decoration (including henna applications) of Fez, Sale, or Mecca were so elaborate and heavy they required months of preparation, and the bride could hardly move.

New garments were worn at the ʿĪd al-Fiṭr and at the ʿĪd al-Aḍḥā. Women also wear special clothing for the pilgrimage *(ḥajj)*, travel garments that include the *ʿabāyah* (the outer cover) and the *tarḥah* (headscarf). Bahraini women, for example would bring seven pairs of *sirwāl*, dresses and overdresses and wear a black tulle head scarf trimmed with blue beads *(ghaswah)*. Upon completion of the pilgrimage to Mecca, women cut a small section of their hair.

Men making the pilgrimage wear two seamless lengths of white cloth and a waistband *(bugshah)*. This dress symbolizes the equality of all believers. Men do not cover their heads during prayer while on *hajj* but cut their hair or shave their heads, and trim their nails upon completing their pilgrimage. Indian and Pakistani men often wear a green head cloth at that time.

Men's traditional dress was affected by the introduction of new sorts of jackets worn atop the male robe. The *qunbāz* was adopted in the Fertile Crescent but later gave way to a Western-style jacket worn atop the *thawb* or *dishdashah*. *Sirwāl* were also worn by men under the robe in some areas and a shorter, less full version to the knees can be seen at construction sites around the region. In Lebanon, *sirwāl* were decorated and worn with a shirt and sash, as they were in parts of the Maghrib, where a shorter form made in Tunis was introduced by the Ottomans and worn by members of seamen's guilds along with a decorated jacket. Fishermen of the Alexandrian area also wore *sirwāl*.

Men wearing traditional dress are often assumed to be older, more conservative, or of rural origin, depending on the context in which they appear. However, the wearing of a *thawb*, jacket, and head cloth in Syria or Jordan, for example, may not rule out property ownership, education, or sophistication.

National or Political Symbolism. Some garments have faded from contemporary use but still hold historic and national value, such as the Moroccan bridal headdresses, *abruq* or *sharbīyah*, the mother-of-pearl inlaid, high *qabqab* (or clogs), the Ottoman face veil, the Palestinian *taqṣirah* (embroidered jacket) worn over female dress, and the Lebanese *tantūr*, a tall silver cylinder worn by Druze women on the head, from which a veil fell. Certain items became politically volatile due to historical circumstances. The fez (*ṭarbūsh*) a red brimless hat worn by men, symbolized the Ottoman Empire as well as the status of being an *effendi*, a gentleman, or a white-collar worker, distinguishing one from a peasant. Kemal Atatürk attacked the fez and required Turkish men to adopt a brimmed hat in order to stress Turkey's European and modern outlook, although brimmed hats interfered with prayer. Elsewhere, the fez became associated with the *ancien règime* and disappeared about mid-century. Various political parties adopted uniforms for their youth leagues in the 1930s, including the green shirts of Miṣr Fatāt and blue shirts of the Wafdists, and gray for the Chemises de Fer in Syria. Militarist or nationalist uniforms were adopted by combatants in the Lebanese civil war as well.

Another powerful symbol was the male head cloth, the *kaffīyah*, rooted in tradition, and now expressing antipathy to Zionist policy as well as its more prosaic functions. The Nablus women's association wore the checkered *kaffīyah* in their fund-raising drives in the 1920s. It was worn by the fighters of the 1930s and during the general strike of 1936–1937, and is now worn by anti-Zionist Israelis and fashionable Westerners of both sexes around the neck, as well as Palestinians. In this case, political symbolism crosses religious and national boundaries.

The Israeli state forbade the wearing of the colors of the Palestinian flag, thus promoting the production of items in red, black, green, and white. Traditional Palestinian dresses and embroidery techniques were also worn and made both for income-generating projects and to promote national feeling.

Islamic dress may express opposition to a particular regime, or reflect membership in an Islamist association. It may be an ethnic symbol as well as a political one, as in Malaysia, where Islamic dress clearly designates Malays from Chinese or Indian Malaysians. But the meaning of Islamic dress depends on the context. In France, the headscarf was prohibited in public schools. The Turkish state made the wearing of the headscarf in the public sector illegal, specifically labeling it a political symbol. Women demonstrated in response and have continued to wear the headscarf. Islamic dress was required of female citizens in Iran and thus it represents acquiescence to or fear of the regime. Before the arrests of the FIS (Islamic Salvation Front) in Algeria, some women feared that the party would legally impose the *ḥijāb*, once they achieved a majority, along with other portions of *sharīʿah*.

[*See also* Ḥijāb.]

BIBLIOGRAPHY

Besancenot, Jean. *Costumes of Morocco*. Translated by Caroline Stone. London, 1990. Elaborate handpainted illustrations of dress worn circa 1934, showing rural/urban, Berber/Arab, and Muslim/Jewish contrasts. Text overemphasizes the biblical past, and neglects Pan-Arab, Pan-Islamic, and pan-nomadic features of dress.

Bukhārī, Muḥammad ibn Ismāʿīl al-. *Sahīh al-Bukhārī*. Vols. 1, 2, and 7. Translated by M. M. Khan. Chicago, 1977. *Ḥadīth* collection containing information about dress during prayer, pilgrimage, and shrouding. See "The Book of Dress" in volume 7.

El Guindi, Fadwa. "Veiling *Infitah* with Muslim Ethic." *Social Problems* 28.4 (1981): 465–485. Links the spread of Islamic dress with a reaction to Sadat's Open Door Policy and a quest for a newly relevant Muslim morality in Egypt.

Fenerci Mehmed. *Osmanlı kıyafetleri*, edited by Ilhami Turan. Istanbul, 1986. Text in Turkish accompanies color plates of Ottoman costume dating back to the eighteenth century and representing various occupations, ranks, and regional origins. Source is helpful in investigation of Ottoman features of dress that continue into later periods.

France. Commission des Sciences et Arts d'Egypte. *Descriptions de l'Egypte, ou, Recueils d'observations et des récherches qui ont ete faites en Egypte pendant l'èxpedition de l'armée francaise, publiée par les ordres de Sa Majeste l'empereur Napoleon le Grand*. Paris 1809–1828. 23 vols. Several folio-sized illustrated volumes are bound separately from text and include detailed drawings made by Napoleon's team, of architectural sites, people, implements and dress at the time of the French invasion of Egypt.

Graham-Brown, Sarah. *Images of Women: The Portrayal of Women in Photography of the Middle East, 1860–1950*. New York, 1988. Important photographic documentation. Includes sections on women and nationalism, entertainment, in families, politics, and as objects of the European gaze.

Lane, Edward W. *Manners and Customs of the Modern Egyptians* (1895). The Hague, 1978. Contains information about Muslim clothing in the nineteenth century and detailed semi-mechanical drawings.

Macleod, Arlene Elowe. *Accommodating Protest: Working Women, the New Veiling and Change in Cairo*. New York, 1991. Study of lower middle-class working women in Cairo and the social and economic reasons for their adoption of the *ḥijāb*.

Olson, Emelie A. "Muslim Identity and Secularism in Contemporary Turkey: 'The Headscarf Dispute.' " *Anthropological Quarterly* 58.4 (October 1985): 161–171.

Ross, Heather Colyer. *The Art of Saudi Arabian Costume*. Fribourg, 1981. The most complete illustrated source on Arabian dress, including text, pattern information, photographs, and drawings.

Rugh, Andrea. *Reveal and Conceal: Dress in Contemporary Egypt*. Syracuse, N.Y., 1986. Identifies many dress styles from a wide geographic and social range, with important commentary regarding the significance of dress features.

Scarce, Jennifer. *Women's Costume of the Near and Middle East*. London, 1987. Wide coverage of dress, chronologically and regionally, with an emphasis on the medieval period. Contains photographic reproductions and examples of garments in art.

Stillman, Yedida, and Nancy Micklewright. "Costume in the Middle East." *Middle East Studies Association Bulletin* 26.1 (July 1992). Bibliographic essay on costume studies of the Middle East, many of which focus on premodern periods, while others are concerned with the dress of *ahl al-kitāb* (lit., "peoples of the book").

Weir, Shelagh. *Palestinian Costume*. Austin, 1989. Covers construction, historical origin, social significance, textile and embroidery techniques, and includes photographic illustrations.

Zuhur, Sherifa. *Revealing Reveiling: Islamist Gender Ideology in Contemporary Egypt*. Albany, N.Y., 1992. Historical and current debates over gender issues, and the meaning of Islamic dress according to Islamist theorists, students, working women, and housewives.

SHERIFA ZUHUR

DRUZE. The Druze faith, or *tawḥīd*, grew out of the extremist Ismāʿīlī Shīʿī theology that prevailed in early Fāṭimid Cairo. This system had promised a radical political change within Islam which failed to materialize once the Ismāʿīlīyah gained political power in North Africa, especially in Egypt in 969. People still looked for messianic rule and many came to believe that the caliph al-Ḥākim ibn ʿAmr Allāh (r. 996–1021) was the expected deliverer.

The leading apologist for al-Ḥākim and his divinity was Ḥamzah ibn ʿAlī ibn Aḥmad al-Zūzanī, a Persian Ismāʿīlī theologian. In 1017, a year after Ḥamzah's arrival in Cairo, al-Ḥākim issued a proclamation *(sijill)* in which he revealed himself to be the manifestation of the deity. Ḥamzah pursued the *daʿwah* ("divine call") of the new faith throughout the empire and even beyond, to Damascus and Aleppo, aided in his missionary endeavors by two disciples in particular, Bahā' al-Dīn al-Samūkī and Muḥammad al-Darazī, the latter being generally regarded as having given converts the name by which they became commonly known, Druze.

Even in its earliest stages Druzism was not merely a sect of Islam but a new religion that aimed to establish a millennial world order. Within a year of al-Ḥākim's proclamation, however, a disagreement between Ḥamzah and Darazī arose over who was to exercize the imamate and how converts were to be brought to the faith. Ḥamzah publicly rebuked Darazī, and in 1019 the latter was assassinated and then anathematized by the Druze faith as a heretic. Less than two years later al-Ḥākim disappeared suddenly under mysterious circumstances. His successor, al-Ẓāhir (r. 1021–1035) denied his predecessor's divinity and worked for the destruction of those who believed in the Druze message. Despite persecution, Bahā' al-Dīn continued pursuing the missionary *daʿwah*, gaining new converts and nurturing those who had survived the imperial reprisals, particularly in the remoter regions of Mount Lebanon. During this time he codified the religious teaching of Druzism into six books known as *Al-ḥikmah al-sharīfah* (*The Noble Knowledge*; the so-called Druze canon) containing 111 epistles and *sijill* composed by al-Ḥākim, Ḥamzah, and himself. In 1043 the *daʿwah* was formally ended, and after this no new adherents were admitted to the faith.

Although known to the world as Druze, they are known to themselves as al-Muwaḥḥidūn, or strict Unitarians, believers in absolute monotheism. The tenets of the *tawḥīd* have been held in secret since the closing of the *daʿwah* and shared only by a small number within the community in each succeeding generation initiated into the ranks of the *ʿuqqāl* (the enlightened), which from the earliest days included women. The remainder, known as the *juhhāl* (the ignorant or uninitiated), protected the secrecy and sanctity of their religion through loyalty to one another.

The beliefs and characteristics that set the Druze apart from Muslims are many. Their faith is exclusive and secret rather than universal. They adhere to a belief in the transmigration of souls *(tanāsukh)* which they share in part with the ʿAlawīyah and Yazīdīs. Male circumcision, universal among Muslims, is not ritually practiced among the Druze. Polygamy, while permitted to Muslims, is forbidden to Druze, along with concubinage and temporary marriage *(mutʿah)*. Divorce is not the easy matter it is for a Muslim, and a Druze woman can initiate the proceedings. The so-called five pillars of Islam are not ritually observed or even acknowledged. Toward non-Druze, strict secrecy is required, and to protect oneself and one's family in times of mortal danger a Druze is permitted outwardly to deny the faith—the Shīʿī practice of dissimulation *(taqīyah)*. Unlike the Shīʿīs, however, the Druze place no virtue on martyrdom, and the Islamic concept of predestination does not figure in their theology. Druzism separates itself from Islam irrevocably by declaring that the revelations of al-Ḥākim contain the ultimate truth, not those of the prophet Muḥammad.

After a century of political prominence in Mount Lebanon during the seventeenth century under the Maʿnid dynasty, the Druze split over the succession of the rival Shihāb clan and many fled in the early eighteenth century to the region of southern Syria known thereafter as the Jabal al-Durūz. When the Shihābs converted to Maronite Christianity in the mid-eighteenth century, Druze leadership passed to the Jumblatt (Junblāṭ) family, who were relatively recent arrivals from Aleppo, reputedly of Kurdish stock. Rivalry between the Druze and Maronites flared into open fighting on several occasions in the nineteenth century, particularly in 1860, and subsequent French involvement on behalf of the Maronites resulted in the creation of an autonomous Christian governate *(mutaṣarrifīyah)* which became the basis of an enlarged Lebanon, first under a French mandate in 1920 and then as an independent republic in 1943 in which the Druze counted for only 6.7 percent of the population. The leading Druze political figure from independence until his assassination during the Civil War in 1976 was Kamal Jumblatt. He was succeeded by his son Walīd, who still presides with unquestioned authority over the political interests of the Druze in Lebanon. The political leadership of the Druze in Syria has traditionally been exercised by the al-Aṭrash family. Traditional Druze leadership in Israel has come from the Ṭarīf clan of Julis in Galilee. Since independence, the Druze, alone among the Arabs of the former Palestine mandate, have served in the Israeli military and occasionally been given minor posts in the government and diplomatic service.

Still largely a rural-based community, the Druze are rarely found in communities of their own exceeding 10,000, the exceptions being al-Suwaydā' in Syria and Baʿqlin in Lebanon. They number between 350,000 and 400,000 out of a population of close to 4 million in Lebanon, and in Syria between 400,000 and 450,000 out of a population of over 12 million. A smaller community of 60,000 to 70,000 lives in Israel proper augmented since 1967 by another 15,000 in the occupied Golan Heights. In addition there are some 15,000 to 20,000 Druze in Jordan and perhaps as many as 100,000 living outside the Middle East in the Americas, Australia, and West Africa, giving a total Druze population of slightly over 1 million worldwide. The Druze of Lebanon are found primarily in small towns and villages in the Shūf district on the western slope of Mount Lebanon from the Beirut-Damascus highway south to the Jazzin escarpment. A second concentration is located in the southeast of the country in the Wādī al-Taym district in the western foothills of Mount Hermon around the towns of Hasbayya and Rashayya. A third center is Beirut itself where a small number have permanent residence. In Syria, 80 percent of the Druze are found in the district of al-Suwaydā' (Jabal al-Durūz) south of the Damascus on the Jordanian frontier. A second concentration is located on the eastern slope of Mount Hermon in Damascus province and in the city itself. A third and very historic center is the Jabal al-Aʿlā region west of Aleppo near the Turkish frontier where some 30,000 to 40,000 Druze live in a dozen villages dotted with ruined Byzantine churches (e.g., Qalb Lawzah). The Druze of Israel live primarily in sixteen towns and villages in Galilee (nine of them exclusively Druze) and two major settlements on Mount Carmel southeast of Haifa.

[*See also* Lebanon *and the biography of Jumblatt.*]

BIBLIOGRAPHY

Abu Izzeddin, Nejla M. *The Druzes: A New Study of Their History, Faith, and Society*. Leiden, 1984.

Betts, Robert B. *The Druze*. New Haven, 1988.

Bouron, Narcisse. *Les Druzes: Histoire du Liban et de la montagne haouranaise*. Paris, 1930.

Chasseaud, George Washington. *The Druses of the Lebanon: Their Manners, Customs, and History; with a Translation of Their Religious Code*. London, 1855.

Firro, Kais M. *A History of the Druzes*. Leiden, 1992.

Joumblatt, Kamal. *I Speak for Lebanon*. Translated from French by Michael Pallis. London, 1982.

Layish, Aharon. *Marriage, Divorce, and Succession in the Druze Family*. Leiden, 1982.

Makarem, Sami N. *The Druze Faith*. Delmar, N.Y., 1974.

Najjar, Abdallah. *The Druze: Millennium Scrolls Revealed*. Translated by Fred Massey. [Atlanta,] 1973. Translation of *Madhhab al-Durūz wa-al-tawḥīd* (Cairo, 1965).

Silvestre de Sacy, Antoine I. *Exposé de la religion des Druzes: Tiré des livres religieux de cette secte*. 2 vols. Paris, 1838.

ROBERT BRENTON BETTS

DŪRĪ, ʿABD AL-ʿAZĪZ AL- (b. 1919), Iraqi educator and Arabist social historian. Born in Baghdad, he was educated there and at London University. He taught history at the Higher Teachers' College and the Faculty of Arts, was translation and publications director at the ministry of education, and was dean of Arts and then rector of Baghdad University, ending his working career as professor of history at the University of Jordan in Amman. Al-Dūrī's publications include two studies on the political and financial history of the ʿAbbāsid era, a study of the economic history of Mesopotamia in the tenth century, a study on the origins of Arab historiography, and studies on the history of Arab nationalism, anti-Arab nationalisms *(shuʿūbīyah)* and Arab Socialism.

In addition to his valuable studies on Iraqi history, al-Dūrī has contributed significantly in the field of the socioeconomic history of the Arab world. His suggestion that the emergence of an "Arab Nation," although closely tied to the unity of language, was in many ways molded by a unified, or at least similar, socioeconomic historical pattern, is particularly pioneering. As do most influential Arab nationalists, al-Dūrī regards language as the major factor in forming an Arab identity, thus making Arabism a cultural, rather than an ethnic or regional or religious, matter. Like many Arab nationalists and some cultural Islamists, he tends to subsume Islam into Arabism: Islam unified the Arabs, giving them an intellectual and ideological basis by means of which they formed a state; through the latter they were to spread Islam even further afield, to the extent that to non-Arabs Islam and Arabism became virtually indistinguishable.

Unlike the most influential Arabist, Abū Khaldūn Sāṭiʿ al-Ḥuṣrī, who refused to consider economic interests among the main components in forming a nation, al-Dūrī always has implied that one of the bases of the Arab nation was the emergence of one path in the development of the Arab economy. For example, historically there has been a unified Islamic position toward the ownership (mainly public) of national resources such as land, water, and minerals and a comprehensive system of taxation and tribute with similar features, coinciding with distinct urban development, some improvement of agriculture, and great expansion in trade. This pattern gradually led to the emergence of a semifeudal system of a distinct bureaucratic nature *(iqṭāʿ ʿaskarī)* and the state's crucial role in the economic affairs of the society.

Al-Dūrī emphasizes the social and economic processes through which the various peoples conquered by the Arabian Muslims were arabized in language and culture (as the conquerors and the conquered mingled in various activities in town and country) and how, following the consequent decline in tribalism, one nation, which he defines as an Arab (rather than an Islamic) nation, then emerged. He pays special attention to the "popular classes" and to various social movements (for example, *al-ʿammah, al-ʿayyārūn, al-futūwah*) often overlooked in conventional historical studies.

Al-Dūrī sees the reemergence of Arabist ideas in the nineteenth century as an attempt to revive an earlier cultural heritage that had been abused by non-Arab rulers. The emphasis on Arabic (the language and the culture) as a nationalist link "had its roots in the Arab heritage and historical conscience, and was now being developed as part of the Arabs' self-consciousness vis-à-vis the West," and increasingly expressed in a more comprehensive (Pan-)Arabist fashion. Unlike some other authors, al-Dūrī contends that there is no observable influence or frequent reference to Western national theories in Arabic writings on the subject. Arabist concepts on nationalism are, he believes, authentic but still incomplete: they have not reached the level of forming "a general theory of Arab nationalism"; they have not linked their idea of the Arab nation to any distinct concept of the state; nor have they clarified the groups or classes that "embody the Arabist idea" and, hence, the socioeconomic orientation that the Arabist movement is bound to follow.

[*See also* Arab Nationalism.]

BIBLIOGRAPHY

Dūrī, ʿAbd al-ʿAzīz al-. *Tārīkh al-ʿIrāq al-iqtiṣādī fī al-qarn al-rābiʿ al-Hijrī*. 2d ed. Beirut, 1974. Scholarly study of trade, crafts, agriculture, urban life, and taxation systems in the earlier ʿAbbāsid period.

Dūrī, ʿAbd al-ʿAzīz al-. *Muqaddimah fī al-tārīkh al-iqtiṣādī al-ʿArabī*. Beirut, 1982. Brief introductory study of the economic and social history of the Arab East, from the emergence of Islam to the nineteenth century.

Dūrī, ʿAbd al-ʿAzīz al-. *Al-takwīn al-tārīkhī lil-ummah al-ʿArabīyah*. Beirut, 1984. English translation by Lawrence I. Conrad, *The Historical Formation of the Arab Nation*. London, 1987. Pioneering study of the socioeconomic history of the Arab world (East and West), suggesting that common (or similar) economic patterns have resulted in the development of a shared Arab consciousness.

NAZIH N. AYUBI

DURRĀNĪ DYNASTY. The origin of the Durrānī (also known as Abdālī) Dynasty coincided with the violent death of the Iranian monarch Nādir Shāh Afshār (1747) and the establishment of an independent political entity in a part of Khurasan that by the mid-1800s was known as Afghanistan. The founder of the dynasty was Aḥmad Khān Abdālī (1747–1772), Nādir Shāh's youthful treasury official and a trusted commander of an Afghan (Pashtun) cavalry force.

Upon the murder of Nādir Shāh by his courtiers, Aḥmad Khān escaped with his 4,000-man Afghan cavalry and much of the Shah's portable treasury to Kandahar, his native tribal territory. In a *jirgah* (council) that lasted nine days, the elders of the Abdālī Pashtun tribe selected Aḥmad Khān as their paramount chief, and he became Aḥmad Shāh (king) Abdālī. Supported by his comrades in the Persian army, Uzbek officers, and most Pashtun tribes in the area, Aḥmad Shāh threw off the yoke of foreign domination and launched an ambitious and successful military campaign, ultimately dominating most of the territories of the former Mughal, Ṣafavid, and Shaybānid empires.

Following a dream, Aḥmad Shāh changed his title to Aḥmad Shāh Durr-i Durrān or Durr-i Dowrān (Pearl of Pearls or Pearl of the Age), hence the dynastic and tribal name Durrānī. He was a charismatic leader, a warrior, a poet, a skilled diplomat, and a pious Muslim with strong Ṣūfī ties. The king made Kandahar his capital, built a new city, and organized his court and imperial government following the Persian model he knew best. He also confirmed the land holdings of the Abdālī (now Durrānī) tribe and awarded special privileges to members of his own Sadozai clan. In accordance with the practice of Muslim rulers, Aḥmad Shāh issued coins for circulation in his own name and had his name mentioned as sovereign in the Friday and ʿĪd *khuṭbah*s (sermons).

At Aḥmad Shāh's death (1772) the Durrānī empire stretched from Khurasan to Kashmir and Punjab, and from the Oxus to the Indian Ocean. His principal strategy for empire building was to wage foreign wars of conquest directed essentially toward India. Aḥmad Shāh's repeated successes in military ventures in India increased his reputation and brought him considerable loot with which to maintain a small regular army and keep the continued allegiance of local *khan*s through favors and reward. Aḥmad Shāh's Islamic zeal may have also played an important role in his wars of conquest in India.

Aḥmad Shāh's son Timur Shāh (1772–1793) lost the confidence of local Pashtuns in Kandahar, and so he shifted his capital to Kabul (1775–1776) and barely managed to hold onto his patrimony. The death of Timur Shāh (1793) marked the beginning of the long-term disintegration of the Durrānī empire through internal disorder and European colonial invasions and pressures. Timur Shāh's twenty-three sons from his many wives engaged in bloody fraternal feuds over the royal succession. Eventually the country was plunged into a period of intensified civil war (1818–1826) that ultimately resulted in the shift of dynastic power from the Sadozai clan to the chiefs of the Barakzai (or Muḥammadzai) clan of the Durrānī Pashtuns (1818–1929).

Between 1818 and 1880, the major revenue-producing parts of the Durrānī empire such as Punjab, Kashmir, and Sind were lost to the Sikhs, and Baluchistan to the local independent khans. The rising Qājār Dynasty in Iran had claimed most of Khurasan and repeatedly attacked Herat. Local chieftains held sway in many other areas. Under conditions of multiple power centers and rulers, old feuds were rekindled within the Durrānī tribe as well as between them and the Ghilzai Pashtun. Sectarian and ethnic differences were politicized as various warlords pursued possibilities for furthering personal ambitions to gain the Kabul throne.

Dost Muḥammad, the youngest son of the Sardar Payinda Khan Barakzai, succeeded in his struggle for control of Kabul in 1826. He faced a growing Sikh threat from the east, but it was not until 1834, during a direct Sikh attack on Peshawar, that Dost Muḥammad rose to defend Islam in a *jihād*. Upon his declaring his intentions, the Kabul *ʿulamāʾ* conferred on him the title of *amīr al-muʾminīn* (Commander of the Faithful). This event not only established the potency of the concept of *jihād* against foreign threats but also formally marked the foundation of the dynastic shift to the Barakzai clan when Dost Muḥammad became the Amīr (not Shāh) of Afghanistan (1834–1838).

During the first Anglo-Afghan war (1839–1842) the British installed Shāh Shujāʾ, a former Sadozai monarch (1803–1809), in Kabul. However, upon Britain's military defeat, Amīr Dost Muḥammad resumed the Kabul throne (1842–1863) and received much financial and military aid from Britain. Between 1863 and 1879 Dost Muḥammad's three brothers fought each other over the succession. The intensification of the British and Russian "Great Game" in Central Asia led to the British invasion of Afghanistan. At the end of the Second Anglo-Afghan War (1878–1880), Afghanistan emerged as a buffer state with its present boundaries, demarcated entirely by Britain and Russia. Britain controlled Afghanistan's foreign affairs.

With Britain's assistance, Amīr Dost Muḥammad's grandson Amīr ʿAbd al-Raḥmān (1880–1901), the so-called "Iron Amir," consolidated direct rule across the country. By brutally suppressing tribal and rural leaders and appealing to the Sunni *ʿulamā'*, he created the modern Afghan state. His son Amīr Ḥabīb Allāh (1901–1919) relaxed some of his harsher measures and in 1903 established the first modern school, Ḥabībīyah, and later the first significant newspaper, *Sirāj al-akhbār*. When Ḥabīb Allāh was assassinated, his son Amānullāh took the title of king (1919–1929) and declared Afghanistan's independence from Britain, which was granted after a brief war in 1919. King Amānullāh, impressed by Atatürk's secular experiments, launched a series of liberal constitutional reforms and modernization programs; resistance to these led to a popular *jihād* that forced his abdication and the end of rule by his branch of the Barakzai clan.

Shortly thereafter Muḥammad Nādir Shāh (r. 1929–1933), a member of the Musahiban family (a different branch of the Barakzai clan of the Durrānī), mounted the throne. Following Nādir Shāh's assassination his nineteen-year-old son Muḥammad Zāhir Shāh (r. 1933–1973) became king. From 1933 to 1963 Zāhir Shāh reigned while two of his uncles and a cousin ruled as prime ministers. Concerned primarily with preserving their family's rule, the Musahiban adopted a cautious modernization program based on autocratic domestic and xenophobic foreign policies until 1955. Prince Muḥammad Dā'ūd, prime minister from 1953 to 1963, began a series of five-year plans aimed at expanding education and communications infrastructures, receiving aid from both the USSR and the West. Dā'ūd resigned in 1963 owing to the disfavor of his policies opposing Pakistan and favoring greater dependence on the USSR.

Between 1963 and 1973 the king experimented with democracy, an effort that failed because he did not legalize political parties and allowed interference in politics by his family and friends. The Communist Party and Islamist opposition movements formed during this period and agitated against both the government and each other. In a military coup (1973) assisted by the pro-Soviet Parcham wing of the Communist Party, Muḥammad Dā'ūd overthrew the Durrānī monarchy and declared himself president of the Republic of Afghanistan (1973–1978). Dā'ūd relied heavily on his old royal networks and began to distance himself from the pro-Soviet Communists whom he had earlier protected and nurtured. In an environment of growing discontent, in April 1978, a Communist coup ousted and killed Dā'ūd, thus ending the Durrānī dynasty in Afghanistan.

[*See also* Afghanistan.]

BIBLIOGRAPHY

ʿAbd al-Raḥmān Khān. *The Life of Abdur Rahman, Amir of Afghanistan* (1900). 2 vols. Edited by Sultan Mahomed Khan. Oxford and New York, 1980. Alleged autobiography of the *amīr*, very informative about his views on Afghan society and politics.

Dupree, Louis. *Afghanistan*. Princeton, 1980. Valuable reference on the general history and ethnography of the country.

Elphinstone, Mountstuart. *An Account of the Kingdom of Caubul* (1815). 2 vols. London and New York, 1972. Excellent source on the rise of the Durrānī empire and ethnography of the Pashtun tribes, during the eighteenth and early nineteenth centuries.

Gregorian, Vartan. *The Emergence of Modern Afghanistan: Politics of Reform and Modernization, 1880–1946*. Stanford, Calif., 1969. Superb analysis of state formation in Afghanistan.

Kakar, M. Hasan. *Government and Society in Afghanistan: The Reign of Amir ʿAbd al-Rahman Khan*. Austin and London, 1979. Excellent documentation of the *amīr*'s policies and practices, based on vernacular and Western sources.

Mohan, Lāl. *Life of the Amir Dost Mohammed Khan of Kabul* (1846). 2 vols. Oxford and New York, 1978. Valuable account of the wars of succession and Britain's involvement through the First Anglo-Afghan War.

Poullada, Leon B. *Reform and Rebellion in Afghanistan, 1919–1929: King Amanullah's Failure to Modernize Tribal Society*. Ithaca, N.Y., and London, 1973. Useful but conventional interpretation of King Amānullāh's disastrous attempt at political reform.

Singh, Ganda. *Ahmad Shah Durrani: Father of Modern Afghanistan*. London, 1959. Rich biographical history of a remarkable, but little known Afghan king.

M. NAZIF SHAHRANI

E

ECONOMIC DEVELOPMENT. As Europe's Industrial Revolution got underway, the Islamic world was in the final phase of a protracted decline that began around the twelfth century. The slide had appeared to be over with the rise of the Ottoman Empire, but the Turkish defeats of the seventeenth and eighteenth centuries made it plain that the balance of power now favored the industrializing nations of western Europe. The military failings of the Turks, like those of other Muslim forces, reflected the Islamic world's economic backwardness in regard to the West. At the beginning of the nineteenth century, Muslims remained overwhelmingly illiterate, whereas in large areas of Europe mass education was already more than an ideal. Few Muslims appreciated, and even fewer sought to capitalize on, the scientific discoveries and organizational innovations that were transfiguring production processes, ushering in new commodities, and boosting living standards in the West. Muslim trade with the outside world, even trade within it, was largely under the control of Europeans, whose local representatives came principally from minority groups. The Islamic world featured no major banks, and its public treasuries were too depleted to finance large-scale development projects.

Two centuries later, some Muslim countries are on the World Bank's roster of high-income countries, with many others in the middle-income category. The better-off countries feature well-capitalized local banks that finance both trade and a wide range of investments. Some have rapidly growing and increasingly diverse industries that export heavily to the West. Their private and public sectors operate dams, power facilities, modern transportation and communication networks, agricultural and industrial enterprises, hospitals, and vast education programs. Against these achievements, the Islamic world also contains some impoverished countries. Yet even the poorest countries have undergone profound transformations: in the most populous ones, the share of agriculture within gross domestic product is now below, and in some cases much below, 40 percent.

The economic transformations of the past two centuries have been neither continuous nor free of conflict. Along with periods of feverish reform, there have been times of resistance to institutional change, to integration into the world economy, and to the reallocation of resources.

In the early nineteenth century the Islamic world was rocked by an invasion of mass-produced goods from Europe. The inflow of industrial commodities dealt a severe blow to the profitability of various craft guilds. Some succumbed quickly to the competition. The majority survived, although they lost both market share and political clout. By and large, they reacted to the competition by seeking to strengthen their customary rules through legal codification. They were generally slow to change their production methods and to reorganize. Under the circumstances, the new European technologies were introduced into local economies primarily by entrepreneurs operating outside the traditional craft guilds.

In the second half of the nineteenth century new industries and trading companies were established, first in the major urban centers and then in the hinterland. Although still centers of fine handicrafts, the guilds progressively declined in economic importance. In the process, they started losing their ablest workers. Even some masters joined the exodus, leaving their time-honored marketing districts to open shops in new economic centers or to become workers in nascent factories.

Meanwhile, agriculture became increasingly commercialized, with certain crops cultivated primarily for export to Europe. Largely through the initiative of European trading companies, silk became a major export commodity in Syria, Lebanon, Turkey, and Iran; cotton in Egypt, Syria, and Turkey; wine in Algeria and Tunisia; tobacco in Turkey, Iran, and the Dutch East Indies; rubber in Malaya and the Dutch East Indies; palm oil and groundnuts in Central and West Africa; tea and jute in India; and coffee in Yemen and the Dutch East Indies. An indigenous development of the period was the emergence of the Jaffa orange as a lucrative export commodity in Palestine.

These transformations in the private economy were accompanied by revolutionary changes in the scope and character of government. Until the nineteenth century, the economic functions of Muslim governments went scarcely beyond the enlargement, exploitation, and protection of their revenues and modest efforts at redistribution to preserve social stability. Governments undertook few infrastructural investments, did not engage in economic planning, and left many matters that we now consider essential government functions to the guilds, to local communities, or simply to the discretion of individuals. Their revenue came mainly from direct taxes on land, although at various times and places substantial additional sums were raised from the sale of commercial and artisanal licenses. By the mid-nineteenth century, large regions of the Islamic world, including India, Indonesia, Malaysia, Algeria, and much of sub-Saharan Africa had fallen under European rule. The economies of these regions had thus come to be administered by Europeans. Around this time, in the noncolonized parts of the Islamic world, government activism in the economic sphere was beginning. With Muḥammad ʿAlī's reforms in Egypt (1805–1849) and the Tanzimat in Turkey (1839–1876), independent and semi-independent Muslim governments started promoting new industries; codifying financial, commercial, and administrative procedures; relying increasingly on indirect taxes, including excise taxes, for revenue; and establishing secular schools to train specialists and civil servants. In instituting such reforms, these governments became increasingly centralized.

The nineteenth-century reformers understood that sustained development would require much new infrastructure. They had neither the funds nor the knowhow, however, to undertake major investments on their own, so they borrowed heavily from Western financiers and relied on foreign enterprise. Some of the great infrastructural projects of the period, including the Suez Canal, the Berlin-Baghdad Railway, the ports at Port Said, Beirut, and Haydar Paşa, the gas, water, and power systems of Istanbul, Cairo, Baghdad, Damascus, and other cities, and some of the early irrigation systems in Egypt, were undertaken through borrowed funds and with technical and administrative guidance from foreigners.

The first half of the nineteenth century saw the establishment of private banking firms, mostly British, in major cities of the Islamic world. With government debt rising, several foreign-owned incorporated banks came on the scene in the middle of the century, including the Ottoman Bank, the Bank of Egypt, and the London and Baghdad Association. Shortly thereafter the leading European banks opened their own branches in many places. These banks allowed local government debt to grow enormously, and before long one government after another found itself unable to meet its interest obligations. The standard European response was to put an international commission in charge of the defaulting government's finances. Some countries, such as Turkey and Iran, continued to retain their political independence even as they lost financial autonomy. Others, notably Morocco, Tunisia, and Egypt, endured foreign occupation.

Scant industrial investment took place in the Islamic world until the aftermath of World War I, partly because international treaties precluded local governments from developing industries to compete with foreign enterprises. During World War I, certain local governments found their supplies of industrial commodities cut off, so they began producing domestic substitutes, generally at high cost. After the war, many independent governments as well as some colonial administrations continued promoting nascent local industries, through both subsidies and preferential buying schemes. A highlight of this era of economic nationalism is the opening of the first banks owned and managed by locals: Bank Misr in Egypt and İş Bank in Turkey.

With the onset of the Great Depression, the drive toward self-sufficiency accelerated. Declining world prices for the Islamic world's traditional export products prompted governments facing trade deficits to give their industries high tariff protection. Many Muslim governments were free by this time of treaty restrictions on their tariff policies. In addition to regulating trade, they started to manage consumption patterns and the sectoral allocation of investments. Their efforts coincided with expanding government interventionism in the Soviet Union and in Germany.

As world trade entered a new expansionary phase after World War II, operating the infant industries established to substitute for imports became increasingly costly. Yet most governments went on protecting them through high import barriers.

The most significant economic development of the post–World War II era has been the emergence of oil as an overwhelmingly important source of government revenue and foreign exchange in Saudi Arabia, Kuwait, Qatar, Oman, the United Arab Emirates, Iraq, Iran, Algeria, Libya, Nigeria, Brunei, and Indonesia. All these countries have become major exporters of oil.

The oil industry of the Islamic world had its beginnings in the late nineteenth century in exclusive concessions granted to foreign oil companies in Iran and the Dutch East Indies. Its rise to global prominence came much later, in the mid-twentieth century. In 1940 Muslim countries accounted for 8 percent of the world's oil production. By 1970 their share had surpassed 40 percent.

Prior to the early 1970s, the foreign companies that ran much of the Islamic world's oil industry adhered to common rules with regard to production, marketing, and host country rights. In effect, they acted as a cartel limiting returns to the producing countries. The 1950s and 1960s featured some attempts at nationalization on the part of local governments, but they were generally unsuccessful. Against this background, the Organization of Petroleum Exporting Countries (OPEC) was formed in 1960 to facilitate cooperation among major producers in their dealings with oil companies. In the first decade of its existence, OPEC provided only modest benefits to its members. By 1970, however, its clout was growing as cracks appeared within the cartel of foreign companies. The subsequent decade saw two OPEC-supported jumps in the world price of oil: a quadrupling in 1973–1974 and a further tripling in 1979–1980. Each price hike was triggered by political events in the Middle East. The first occurred when OPEC's sister organization, the Organization of Arab Petroleum Exporting Countries (OAPEC) imposed an oil embargo on certain countries deemed to have supported Israel in the Arab-Israeli War of 1973, including the United States. The second was precipitated by the Iranian Revolution of 1979 and the decision of Iran's new government to slash its oil production.

The price shocks of the 1970s stimulated exploration and production outside of OPEC. Partly as a consequence, OPEC's share of world production fell to 30 percent by 1991, even though it holds about two-thirds of the world's proven reserves. Meanwhile, the price of oil receded to its mid-1970s level. Most analysts attribute the decline not to OPEC as a whole but rather to the efforts of Saudi Arabia, OPEC's leading producer, to preserve the value of its vast reserves by discouraging substitution away from oil in the industrialized West.

The flow of oil revenue to OPEC's Islamic members has served to finance enormous economic development programs. It has allowed these countries to raise their saving and investment rates to unprecedented heights; gain access to advanced technologies; make major improvements in their infrastructures; and offer their populations greatly upgraded and expanded public services. The low-population countries, which have few complementary resources, have gained, in addition, the ability to invest substantial sums in world markets. Most of their investments are in Europe and North America. The oil-poor countries of the Islamic world have benefited in several ways from the boom in the oil-rich countries: higher export earnings, foreign aid, and remittances of guest workers.

Along with many positive economic effects, the oil boom has also had some negative consequences for the oil exporters. The production of other internationally traded commodities, including agricultural goods, has tended to decline. Wage increases have outstripped productivity gains, thus rendering local industrialization unprofitable. Female labor participation rates have fallen, causing fertility rates to rise. With the local investments of all oil exporters concentrated in industries whose demand has suffered from high energy prices—petrochemicals, aluminum refining, dry docks—much established capacity has remained underutilized. Extensive state subsidies to individuals have undermined work effort as well as the incentive to acquire marketable skills.

By the mid-1980s, these adverse effects, together with falling oil revenues, had prompted many oil exporters to seek to diversify their economies and privatize their public enterprises. Such policies were already in place in many of the oil-poor countries, including Malaysia, Turkey, and Egypt. In these countries market-oriented reforms, encompassing also the liberalization of foreign trade, had generally followed balance-of-payments crises. The pro-market drive also drew strength from the emergence of East Asia as an economic powerhouse through export-driven growth policies and from the deepening economic crisis of the Soviet bloc. On the whole, however, liberalization and privatization have proceeded slowly, partly because, in both oil-rich and oil-poor countries, reforms have encountered stiff resistance from civil servants, labor groups, and industrialists long-accustomed to protection. The largest increases in industrial exports have been achieved by Turkey, Tunisia, Malaysia, Indonesia, and Kuwait.

The ownership structure of industry exhibits some variation, although family-owned, small firms are common everywhere. In Turkey, Pakistan, India, and Lebanon, many large enterprises belong to highly diversified private conglomerates; others are state owned. In much of the rest of the Islamic world, including most oil-exporting countries, almost all large enterprises are under state ownership. A few countries allow foreign ownership, but most permit only joint ventures. Inter-Arab joint ventures, both public and private, have become increasingly common since the 1970s.

As the twentieth century draws to a close, the economic achievements of the Islamic world present a decidedly mixed picture. The oil-rich states of Saudi Arabia, Kuwait, the United Arab Emirates, Qatar, Libya, and Brunei have attained per capita incomes that place them among the world's high-income countries. Most of the remaining Arab states fall in the middle-income category, as do four other predominantly Muslim countries, Turkey, Iran, Albania, and Malaysia. Yet six of the eight countries with the largest Muslim populations—India, Indonesia, Pakistan, Bangladesh, Nigeria, and Egypt—are among the world's poorest, as are certain smaller Muslim or semi-Muslim states of Africa and Asia. Life expectancy at birth exceeds sixty-five in Jordan, Lebanon, Turkey, Tunisia, Algeria, Malaysia, the United Arab Emirates, Kuwait, Qatar, and Brunei, whereas it remains below fifty in Afghanistan, Yemen, and several largely Islamic countries of sub-Saharan Africa. Adult literacy stands above 80 percent in Turkey, Lebanon, and Jordan, and above 50 percent in all the other high- and middle-income countries. In the poor countries, by contrast, literacy lies between 20 and 50 percent.

Within individual countries, certain inequalities are very pronounced by global standards. The distributions of wealth and income are highly unequal in most countries because of disparities in land ownership, inequalities in access to education, and in some cases, ineffective redistribution systems. Most of the large countries show huge inequalities between regions and between cities and the countryside. Finally, there are remarkably high inequalities based on age and gender. Where in most parts of the world life expectancy at birth and child survival rates tend to be considerably higher for females than for males, in some parts of the Islamic world, including Bangladesh, India, and Pakistan, they are lower for females. In some countries, males outsrip females in educational attainment, measured in years, by as much as 50 percent, although the gap has been shrinking rapidly.

The ideas, expectations, priorities, and apprehensions that have undergirded the Islamic world's development drive since the nineteenth century have been shaped largely by interactions with the West, although local sensibilities, intellectual traditions, and political conditions have colored every concrete reform. In the second half of the twentieth century, attempts have been made to base the economic transformation of the Islamic world on self-consciously Islamic principles. Some countries, most notably Iran and Pakistan, have tried to eliminate the use of interest and to institute Islamic redistribution schemes. Such efforts have had no major impact on any key indicator of development.

[*See also* Modernization and Development.]

BIBLIOGRAPHY

Askari, Hossein, and John Thomas Cummings. *The Middle East Economies in the 1970s: A Comparative Approach.* New York, 1976. Surveys oil, agriculture, industry, manpower, trade, and government.

Baer, Gabriel. *Egyptian Guilds in Modern Times.* Jerusalem, 1964. Structure, functions, and history of Egypt's guilds.

Furnivall, John S. *Netherlands India: A Study of Plural Economy.* Cambridge, 1939. Detailed treatment of the political economy of colonial Indonesia.

Gelb, Alan, et al. *Oil Windfalls: Blessing or Curse?* New York, 1988. Comparative analysis of the effects of rising oil prices in producing countries; includes case studies of Algeria, Indonesia, and Nigeria.

Hansen, Bent. *The Political Economy of Poverty, Equity, and Growth: Egypt and Turkey.* Oxford, 1991. Covers the period from the 1920s to the 1990s.

Helleiner, Gerald. *Peasant Agriculture, Government, and Economic Growth in Nigeria.* Homewood, Ill., 1966. Provides historical statistics and analysis for 1900–1964, with emphasis on 1945–1964.

Hershlag, Zvi Y. *Introduction to the Modern Economic History of the Middle East,* 2d ed. Leiden, 1980. Covers the nineteenth and twentieth centuries; focuses on industrialization and patterns of trade.

Hershlag, Zvi Y. *The Contemporary Turkish Economy.* London, 1988. Covers the twentieth century, with emphasis on the 1980s.

Hopkins, Anthony G. *An Economic History of West Africa.* London, 1973. Compares colonial administrations, with emphasis on trade, including the slave trade and trans-Saharan trade.

Issawi, Charles, ed. *The Economic History of the Middle East, 1800–1914.* Chicago, 1966. Key reports and essays, including many translated from other languages.

Issawi, Charles, ed. *The Economic History of Iran, 1800–1914.* Chicago, 1971. Includes many contemporary accounts.

Issawi, Charles. *An Economic History of the Middle East and North Africa.* New York, 1982. Best general introduction; covers the period 1800–1980.

Landes, David. *Bankers and Pashas.* Cambridge, Mass., 1958. Informative account of Western banking in the nineteenth-century Middle East.

Lim, Chong-Yah. *Economic Development in Modern Malaya.* New

York, 1967. Emphasizes trade, money, prices, and agricultural development.

Mitchell, Brian R. *International Historical Statistics: Africa and Asia.* New York, 1982. Data on trade, population, production, taxation, and transportation, generally from around 1800.

Papageorgiou, Demetris, Michael Michaely, and Armeane M. Choksi. *Liberalizing Foreign Trade.* 7 vols. Cambridge, Mass., 1991. Includes detailed histories of liberalization attempts in Indonesia, Pakistan, and Turkey.

Richards, Alan, and John Waterbury. *A Political Economy of the Middle East: State, Class, and Economic Development.* Boulder, 1990. Analysis of intergroup conflicts and their consequences for governments and economies.

Stewart, Charles F. *The Economy of Morocco, 1912–1962.* Cambridge, 1964. Broad survey that emphasizes agriculture, mining, manufacturing, and infrastructure.

Tuma, Elias H. *Economic and Political Change in the Middle East.* Palo Alto, Calif., 1987. Covers various dimensions of income distribution, from both historical and comparative perspectives.

TIMUR KURAN and JEFFREY B. NUGENT

ECONOMICS. [*This entry comprises two articles. The first traces the rise and growth of contemporary Islamic economic doctrine; the second surveys the operations of institutions and organizations that play a role in the management of economic activity in the modern Islamic world. For related discussions, see* Economic Development; Modernization and Development.]

Economic Theory

The mid-twentieth century saw the birth of Islamic economics, a doctrine billed as an alternative to neoclassical economics, Marxian economics, and other economic doctrines rooted in Western social thought. Within the span of a few decades, the exponents of Islamic economics, who call themselves Islamic economists, have founded several international institutes, most notably the International Center for Islamic Economics at King Abdulaziz University in Jeddah; launched numerous periodicals, including specialized ones, such as the *Journal of Islamic Banking and Finance;* and published thousands of books in scores of languages.

In the eyes of Islamic economists, three characteristics make Islamic economics *Islamic*. First, it draws inspiration and seeks guidance from the Qur'ān and the *sunnah* (received custom). Second, it considers Islamic civilization a fount of economic perspectives and insights that are lacking in secular philosophical traditions. And third, it aims to rediscover and revive the economic values, priorities, and mores of the earliest Muslim community in seventh-century Arabia.

Islamic economists trace the origins of their doctrine to the beginnings of Islam. However, the notion of an economic doctrine that is distinctly and self-consciously Islamic is a modern development. The classical sources of Islam contain diverse prescriptions that bear on economics, and the religion's early history provides valuable insights into economic behavior and institutions. Yet, not until modern times did Islam produce a separate and independent discipline of economics. Nor did the great philosophers of the premodern Islamic world consider themselves bound on economic matters by Islamic concepts and understandings. Such towering figures as Ibn Taymīyah (1263–1328) and Ibn Khaldūn (1332–1406) wandered freely beyond the confines of previously articulated Islamic thought, even as they tried to ground their novel discoveries, interpretations, and prescriptions in Islamic sources.

The movement to establish a distinctly Islamic economic doctrine was born in India in the decades preceding the country's partition. This was a time when, in fields ranging from dress to economics, growing numbers of Muslims were falling into patterns set by the West. Many Muslim intellectuals saw in this loss of cultural identity a threat to the future of Islamic civilization. As part of a broader response to this threat, they sought to establish distinctly Islamic disciplines, including an economics discipline that Muslims could proudly call their own. The most forceful early promoter of Islamic economics was Sayyid Abūl al-Aʿlā Mawdūdī (1903–1979), who sought to turn Islam into a "complete way of life."

For Mawdūdī, Islamic economics was primarily a vehicle for reasserting the primacy of Islam in the lives of Muslims and only secondarily a vehicle for fundamental economic change. Accordingly, his books and pamphlets on economics are essentially descriptive and prescriptive, outlining, with references to early Muslim practices and to Qur'ānic verses, how a modern Islamic economy would differ from a contemporary capitalist or socialist one. An Islamic system, says Mawdūdī, would differ from socialism in the protection it gives to the market; from capitalism in its emphasis on inculcating market participants with norms of honesty, fairness, brotherhood, and altruism; and from both in its prohibition of interest and its insistence on enforcing Islam's traditional redistribution schemes, most importantly *zakāt* (alms). But Mawdūdī makes no systematic attempt to explain how elements of the Islamic economy would interact with one another. Nor does he give serious thought to matters of feasibility.

Mawdūdī had little exposure to modern economic thought. The same goes for most other early contributors to Islamic economics, whose expertise usually lay in *fiqh* (jurisprudence). The contributors of seminal works include Sayyid Quṭb (1906–1966) of Egypt, who concentrated on matters of economic justice; Muḥammad Bāqir al-Ṣadr (1931–1980) of Iraq, who developed and extended Mawdūdī's contrast between the Islamic economy and the prevailing systems of the modern world; and Maḥmud Ṭāleqāni (1911–1979) of Iran, who produced a tome on ownership. Unlike Mawdūdī and Quṭb, Ṣadr and Ṭāleqāni were Shīʿīs. Probably as a consequence, Sunnī Islamic economists have tended to refrain from honoring and citing their works. Nonetheless, their diagnoses and prescriptions have had a discernible influence on later writings.

Whether by Sunnīs or Shīʿīs, contributions to the first phase of Islamic economics share four characteristics that have carried into the subsequent literature. First, they are all heavily judgmental and normative. They differentiate between right and wrong and between permissible and impermissible. Second, the early contributions reject the notion, which took hold in modern thought with the European Enlightenment, that personal actions motivated by selfishness can produce socially desirable outcomes. Where thinkers as different as Adam Smith and Karl Marx recognized that selfish actions can, and often do, end up serving the social good, Islamic economics has unvaryingly condemned actions taken for purely selfish reasons as morally unacceptable. Islamic economics can be viewed, then, as an attempt to counter a key element of modern social thought by reviving a very old belief pattern—one that is traceable to Aristotle's teachings on the household. The third critical characteristic of the early writings in Islamic economics is a conviction that existing economic systems have failed dismally. And the fourth is an impression that Islamic civilization went into economic decline because Muslims stopped adhering to Islamic norms.

Beginning in the mid-1960s, Islamic economics started attracting researchers steeped in modern economics, including some educated at reputable universities in Western Europe and North America. In the process, it came to feature writings that apply modern analytical techniques, especially the techniques of neoclassical economics, to its core issues. Islamic economics began showing sensitivity, moreover, to theoretical concepts and problems whose origins lie in secular economic philosophies.

The most prolific, wide-ranging, and influential contributors to the second phase of Islamic economics have been Muhammad Nejatullah Siddiqi (b. 1931), an Indian; Mohammad Abdul Mannan (b. 1938), a Bengal-born Pakistani; and Muhammad Umer Chapra (b. 1933), also of Pakistan. The emphasis in the writings of this trio is largely on identifying and promoting behavioral norms to guide Muslims in their economic activities. In keeping with the pattern set by their predecessors, they all reject the notion that individuals are incorrigibly selfish and pragmatic. They insist that, in a society imbued with Islamic teachings and governed by Islamic laws, people will not necessarily behave like the acquisitive *Homo economicus* of neoclassical economics. In a properly Islamic society, say Siddiqi, Mannan, and Chapra, people will be consistently altruistic and principled. They will avoid waste and extravagance, refrain from undertaking socially harmful activities, and be generous toward the needy. Moreover, they will work hard, abstain from destructive competitive behavior, charge fair prices, pay others their due, and avoid activities considered immoral, such as speculation, gambling, and hoarding.

Like most other Islamic economists, Siddiqi, Mannan, and Chapra are convinced that their favored norms provide perfectly clear guidance in every conceivable economic arena. They are convinced, too, that the norms would be equally effective in all Muslim societies, regardless of size, history, level of development, and institutional framework. The critics of Islamic economics have pointed out that the proposed norms leave abundant room for individual judgment and also that any given norm's interpretation can vary systematically across cultures and contexts. They have noted, too, that in practice members of small networks abide more readily by norms of altruism and responsibility than do the members of societies running into the millions.

In countering such charges, Islamic economics appeals only partly to verifiable observations. It relies also on "revelational data," which encompass Qur'ānic verses and, in some views, also the words and deeds of the Prophet and his companions. Even within Islamic circles, however, the lessons embodied in the Qur'ān are sources of disagreement. And renowned scholars question the authenticity of many of the statements and actions attributed to early Muslims. The admissibility of revelational data does not ensure agreement, then, on what is properly Islamic. Still, on issues where Islamic economists present a unified front, as on the feasibility of curbing selfishness, revelational data serve the purpose of shielding some key assertions of Islamic economics from outside criticism.

The priority Mawdūdī gave to the issues of interest and *zakāt* has proved highly durable. These two issues continue to be treated as critical, and every overview of the doctrine gives them both remarkably broad coverage. A striking difference between the early and late phases of Islamic economics lies in the mode of discourse. Especially on interest, expositions have become increasingly mathematical. In particular, a growing number of Islamic economists are using the neoclassical techniques of equilibrium analysis and optimization to demonstrate the practicality and usefulness of Islamic principles. A related development is the use of neoclassical tools to devise Islamic solutions to problems neoclassical economists generally consider unsolvable. Equilibrium models have been developed to show that a ban on interest would eliminate a potent source of capitalist exploitation. Other models demonstrate that, unlike secular redistribution mechanisms, *zakāt* does not have an adverse effect on work effort; the logic here is that *zakāt* is a religious obligation that is performed happily and voluntarily.

By no means is Islamic economics an internally coherent body of thought. Since it approaches issues in piecemeal fashion, some of its prescriptions conflict with one another. Consider profit-and-loss sharing, the favored alternative to interest, whereby borrower and lender divide, according to a predecided ratio, the profits from any investments financed by the loan. In principle, the agreement could give 5 percent of the profits to the borrower and the remaining 95 percent to the lender. Where the borrower is poor and the lender rich, this arrangement would counteract the purpose of *zakāt*, namely, the reduction of inequality. Another such tension is between the prohibition of interest and the commonly expressed view that wages must be prespecified. If fairness requires risk sharing between borrower and lender, it is inconsistent to bar employees from sharing in the risks borne by their employer. Some Islamic economists recognize the existence of inconsistencies among their central prescriptions, but most do not. Consequently, Islamic economics still lacks a general methodology for resolving its inconsistencies.

In addition to inconsistencies, Islamic economics features internal disagreements. Most significantly, it is sharply divided on the limits of individual property rights. Some Islamic economists, including Ṣadr and Quṭb, favor sharp restrictions on the right to accumulate personal assets. They believe that the market process breeds persistent inequalities that are bound to overwhelm the capacity of Islam's traditional redistribution mechanisms. Other thinkers, like Mawdūdī, Ṭāleqāni, Siddiqi, Mannan, and Chapra, display greater faith in the power of schemes like *zakāt*. They favor, moreover, a state that respects the right to own honestly acquired property and that interferes only minimally with market outcomes. At the root of the conflict over property rights are two principles that no Islamic economist rejects, each grounded in the Qur'ān. One is that ownership belongs to God, the other that perfect equality is neither desirable nor necessary. The former principle opens the door to large-scale redistribution, for if all property belongs to God, a state representing the divine will can regulate the distribution of assets however it sees fit. By contrast, the latter principle justifies restrictions on state activism.

The diversity of opinion within Islamic economics has been characterized as a source of convenient flexibility, a trait that permits theoreticians and policy makers to adapt to virtually any exigency without stepping outside Islamic discourse. It did indeed prove useful to the wider Islamic movement when, prior to the Iranian Revolution of 1979, doctrinal controversies on economic matters served the purpose of making Ayatollah Ruhollah Khomeini seem at once an egalitarian redistributionist to the poor and a defender of property rights to the rich.

A small minority within Islamic economics reject the notion that the diversity of Islamic opinion is a sign of strength. The present diversity, they say, is an embarrassing manifestation of intellectual sloppiness and confusion. The leading exponent of the opposing view is the Pakistani economist Syed Nawab Haider Naqvi (b. 1935). To make Islamic economics internally consistent, proposes Naqvi, it should be based on four ethical axioms: unity, equilibrium, free will, and responsibility. The axiomatic approach has the advantage, he maintains, of allowing the derivation of economic prescriptions from fundamental Islamic principles, as opposed to ad hoc reasoning or selective quotings from scripture. Yet Naqvi's axioms do not eliminate the possibility of conflict. An expression of personal free will might violate any number of definitions of social responsibility. Nor are the four axioms free of ambiguity. Even within the confines of Islamic discourse, the notion of responsibility has always admitted widely different interpretations.

Neither individually nor collectively have the works composed under the rubric of Islamic economics laid the foundations of a new general theory, if by this one means a relatively verifiable conception of integrated relationships. It is not a comprehensive formulation of economics, in that it engages only a share of the issues that economists have traditionally worried about. Efforts are under way, though, to introduce Islamic arguments into a widening array of subjects. To this end, various Islamic foundations have invited research proposals in fields not yet touched by Islamic economists, and books have begun to appear in a variety of new fields. The problem is not only one of scope, however. Islamic economics has not developed distinct and coherent methodologies for studying the past, for forming and testing hypotheses, for understanding market dynamics, for exploring how morality changes across time and space, or for linking economics with the rest of human learning. On the whole, Islamic economics has been more successful at explaining what it is not than at specifying what makes it radically different. And it has done better disclosing the flaws of other systems than in demonstrating rigorously that it can do substantially better.

The practical impact of Islamic economics has been limited to banking, redistribution, and moral education, although a few countries, including Iran and Pakistan, have committed themselves to broad Islamic reforms. Even in the countries where Islamic economics is most influential, Muslims who concern themselves with it are outnumbered by those who look for guidance and understanding to secular economic doctrines, approaches, and ideas. Most of the economics departments in the universities of the Muslim world remain under the control of economists who do not characterize their professional identities, research, or courses as distinctly Islamic. Likewise, within government departments, planning agencies, and private organizations, Islamic economics has had little impact on either the language of economic discourse or the choice of economic policies.

[*See also the biographies of Mawdūdī, Quṭb, Ṣadr, and Ṭāleqānī.*]

BIBLIOGRAPHY

Abdul Mannan, Mohammad. *The Making of an Islamic Economic Society: Islamic Dimensions in Economic Analysis*. Cairo, 1984. Utilized as a textbook.

Ahmad, Khurshid, ed. *Studies in Islamic Economics*. Leicester, 1980. Contains important articles on development, consumer behavior, interest, and redistribution.

Behdad, Sohrab. "Property Rights in Contemporary Islamic Economic Thought: A Critical Perspective." *Review of Social Economy* 47 (Summer 1989): 185–211. Focuses on the Shīʿī wing of Islamic economics.

Chapra, Muhammad U. *The Economic System of Islam: A Discussion of Its Goals and Nature*. London, 1970. Influential philosophical exposition.

Choudhury, Masudul Alam. *Islamic Economic Co-operation*. New York, 1989. Attempt to introduce an Islamic perspective into international economics.

Hasanuz Zaman, Syed Muhammad. *Economic Functions of an Islamic State (The Early Experience)*. Leicester, 1991. Spells out the theoretical foundations of Islamic economics through an analysis of the economic institutions of early Islam.

Kuran, Timur. "The Economic System in Contemporary Islamic Thought: Interpretation and Assessment." *International Journal of Middle East Studies* 18 (May 1986): 135–164. Critical overview of Islamic economics.

Kuran, Timur. "On the Notion of Economic Justice in Contemporary Islamic Thought." *International Journal of Middle East Studies* 21 (May 1989): 171–191. Highlights the divisions and inconsistencies in Islamic economics.

Kuran, Timur. "The Economic Impact of Islamic Fundamentalism." In *Fundamentalisms and the State: Remaking Polities, Economies, and Militance*, edited by Martin E. Marty and R. Scott Appleby, pp. 302–341. Chicago, 1993. Addresses the conflicts between the theory and practice of Islamic economics.

Mawdūdī, Sayyid Abū al-Aʿlā. *The Economic Problem of Man and Its Islamic Solution* (1947). Lahore, 1975. Best introduction to Mawdūdī's economic views.

Naqvi, Syed Nawab Haider. *Ethics and Economics: An Islamic Synthesis*. Leicester, 1981.

Philipp, Thomas. "The Idea of Islamic Economics." *Die Welt des Islams* 30 (1990): 117–139. Methodological critique of Islamic economics.

Quṭb, Sayyid. *Social Justice in Islam* (1948). Translated by J. D. Hardie. New York, 1970.

Ṣadr, Muḥammad Bāqir al-. *Iqtiṣādunā: Our Economics* (1961). 4 vols. Tehran, 1982–1984. Ṣadr's masterwork.

Siddiqi, Muhammad N. *The Economic Enterprise in Islam*. Lahore, 1972.

Siddiqi, Muhammad N. *Muslim Economic Thinking: A Survey of Contemporary Literature*. Leicester, 1981. Contains an extensive bibliography of works published up to the late 1970s.

Ṭāleqānī, Sayyid Maḥmud. *Society and Economics in Islam*. Translated by R. Campbell. Berkeley, 1982. Authoritative anthology, which includes a key segment of *Islam and Ownership*, Ṭāleqānī's most famous work.

TIMUR KURAN

Economic Institutions

The last two centuries have seen the emergence of modern government in the Islamic world. An important part of this process has involved the creation of institutions for macroeconomics management. The role of the state in the economy has been formalized, with the introduction of ministries of finance, planning, industry, agriculture, and commerce. At the same time central banks have been created, and a large number of organizations which play some role in the regulation of economic activity, from chambers of commerce to syndicates of workers and trade unions, have emerged. Some of these are mere agents of government, but others enjoy considerable autonomy.

Have the new institutional structures superseded traditional Islamic organizations? Are they mere replicas of Western institutions or have adaptations been made to serve the particular needs of Islamic societies? Do the practices of the new institutions conform with *sharīʿah* ("the divine law"), and are their methods of operation acceptable to the *ʿulamāʾ* ("religious scholars") and the *ummah* (the wider Muslim community)?

Western economics often purports to be universally applicable, reflecting the assumed value-free and culturally independent nature of its methodology. At the policy level experience from many parts of the world indicates that such assumptions are simplistic, if not completely misleading. Yet the universality of economic epistemology is seldom questioned in the West, but it is in the Islamic world, where the subject has its own axioms. The school of Western thought known as institutional economics has perhaps a more relevant approach for dealing with Islamic societies. Its leading advocates, Thorstein Veblen, Wesley Mitchell, and Gunnar Myrdal, did not concern themselves with Islamic societies, though Myrdal, in his classic study, *Asian Drama: An Inquiry into the Poverty of Nations* (London, 1968), demonstrated an awareness of the issues.

Institutionalists believe that the political and social structures of a country influence how its economy works. Other disciplines, including law, sociology, and anthropology, are relevant to economic problems. A neoclassical approach which tries to isolate demand and supply from the market environment in which they operate is not very instructive in Islamic societies. Indeed, excessive abstraction may not be very fruitful in any social context. The institutions involved in economic policy formation or its execution are staffed by people with beliefs and values. Simplistic economic models which assume so-called rational maximizing behavior fail to explain much of what is actually taking place in particular economies, where after all it is social beings who are the economic agents, not impersonal mechanistic forces.

Islamic Financial Administration. There have of course been institutions concerned with the collection of taxation and the disbursement of the proceeds since the time of the Prophet. The Bayt al-Māl is the institution with traditional responsibility for the administration of taxes. Its role and responsibilities with respect to the Muslim community are broadly defined, and there is no exact equivalence in modern societies. One function was that of Bayt al-Māl al-Khāṣṣ, literally, the royal treasury or privy purse. This was concerned with the management of the finances of the caliph (Ar., *khalīfah*), or ruler, including the disbursement of funds to cover his personal expenses. The Bayt al-Māl al-Khāṣṣ was also responsible for the upkeep of palaces, the salaries of the royal guards, gifts to foreign rulers, and the maintenance of the *ḥarīm* (harem, the royal ladies in waiting).

The finances of the Muslim community were administered separately from those of the royal household through the Bayt al-Māl al-Muslim, which was often administered from buildings adjacent to the chief national or provincial mosque, and the work was supervised by the religious authorities. Responsibilities were wide-ranging, from such public works as the construction and maintenance of roads and bridges to social expenditures which were designed to help the poor and needy. The latter was financed with revenue from the *zakāt* (the Islamic taxation on wealth). The ruler could not profit from this, as the proceeds were earmarked for socially worthwhile purposes.

The Bayt al-Māl performed some of the functions of a modern central bank, as it acted as government financier, but it was not concerned with the management of financial intermediation or currency issue. It could undertake most of the essential public financing required in societies where exchange was based either on barter or the use of precious metals, such as silver and gold, as mediums of exchange. The Bayt al-Māl, however, was not involved in deficit financing, which would have been questionable from the *sharīʿah* point of view, as it usually involves the issue of bills bearing *ribā* ("interest"), which is unacceptable under Islamic law. Such limitations were not a constraint in preindustrial economies, but clearly it meant that the ruler and the ruled had fewer economic options than in Western societies. Modern Islamic economists argue that the constraints imposed by the Bayt al-Māl practices and procedures were both desirable and justified. The institutional framework was appropriate for an Islamic society, and its workings reflected Muslim values and aspirations.

Management of Shared Productive Resources. Islam recognizes the private ownership of property; indeed, there are well-defined laws governing the inheritance of property which are clearly set out in the Qur'ān itself. However, there has always been provision for the voluntary transfer of land and other privately owned assets to a *waqf* (charitable trust), and such transfers have been actively encouraged throughout Islamic history. The assets transferred are administered by the *waqf* on behalf of the Muslim community as a whole residing in a particular area or state.

Typically the land transferred was used for the construction of mosques, schools, or health facilities, or other buildings which served the local community. *Waqf* land could also be rented out, and the income used for the payment of teachers salaries and religious scholars. Rental income could be used directly for socially beneficial purposes, including helping the poor and needy. Sharecropping arrangements were sometimes agreed whereby a proportion of the crop would accrue to the tenant and his family, but the rest might go to support sick and disabled Muslims who were unable to work. Hence there was basic social-security provision for the Islamic faithful, independent of family and kinship connections.

In Islam land and other resources represent the bounty of Allāh (God). They are to be used and not squandered. The emphasis is on the productive use of what God has provided. Those concerned with the administration of a *waqf* have a duty to see that *waqf* property is put to good use, and tenants on the property are expected to work effectively. In many contemporary Islamic states responsibility for *waqf* property has been taken over by a government ministry. In Saudi Arabia, for example, there is a Ministry of Pilgrimage and Endowments, which has a deputy minister responsible for *waqf*. In some states this responsibility resides with the Ministry of Religious Affairs, and in others with the Ministry of Justice, where there are specialists in *sharīʿah*. Occasionally, as in Iran under the shah, responsibility for the management of *waqf* lands and property remained with the religious authorities in control of the mosques. This gave the religious leaders considerable economic power, which they resisted giving up even when the Islamic republic was established.

Secular Economic Influences. During the nineteenth century the influence of Western ideas steadily increased throughout the Islamic world, and commercial laws modeled on the British, French, and Dutch equivalents for the most part were introduced in many countries. Government ministries were modernized and restructured, but usually this was associated with an increasing role for the state, as it took on new economic functions. The changes in the organization of government were not challenged by the local Muslim populations on religious grounds. The changes were seen as part of the modernization process and not as secularist trends. The new commercial codes existed in parallel with the *sharīʿah*, and they did not replace them. Often the new laws applied to trade with foreigners as the economies were opened up, and frequently even local business was conducted by foreigners. As far as the mass of the Muslim population was concerned, the new laws were irrelevant; they governed the dealings of the infidel, not their own lives.

The organization of government economic ministries became more formalized as contacts with the industrial powers increased, and many Muslim states became European colonies. State expenditure increased substantially in the nineteenth century, usually outstripping tax revenues, and as a consequence debt finance became a major preoccupation of treasury officials. The Ottoman government in particular incurred substantial debt, not just to European governments but also to private foreign financiers. In some respects its situation was similar to that of contemporary Third World debtor nations, with Ottoman bonds and bills trading far below their face values in international financial markets. This of course raised questions with implications for Islam, as borrowing by issuing interest-bearing bills and bonds means in practice dealing in *ribā*, and profiting from bond price movements may amount to speculation or even gambling. Under Islamic law *gharar* ("speculation") is *ḥarām* ("forbidden").

The Ottoman authorities were under severe pressures from their European creditors and as a consequence were driven to compromise on matters of principle. Under a law passed in 1887 interest was permitted, as long as it did not exceed the principal of the loan. This was a highly dubious interpretation of surah 3.130 of the Qur'ān, which states, "O ye who believe, devour not usury doubled and multiplied." This verse makes no mention of the principle. Some jurists have interpreted it to mean that compound rather than simple interest is *ḥarām*, but both were permitted in the Ottoman Empire by the nineteenth century, although under the 1887 act domestic interest was subject to a ceiling of 9 percent. It is not clear how this figure was arrived at. Modern *fuqahā'* (Islamic jurists) generally regard all interest as *ribā*.

The extent of Western secular influence was most strongly manifest in Egypt, where there were separate courts established for non-Muslim foreigners resident in the country. These courts dealt with both civil and criminal cases and were called to make judgments in commercial cases involving payments defaults and false disclosures by parties involved in trade. The *sharīʿah* law is very clear on such matters, but Islamic *fiqh* ("jurisprudence") was ignored when foreigners were involved. With the 1952 revolution these separate courts were finally abolished as an unacceptable inheritance from the Ottoman "capitulations" that permitted European officials to protect and impose legal sanctions on their own nationals. Egyptian President Gamal Abdel Nasser saw this as an infringement of national sovereignty. Modern Muslims view such practices as a violation of the sovereignty of Islam.

Institutional Development. The expanding role of the state in Islamic economies necessitated the enlargement of government ministries of finance and agriculture and led to the creation of new ministries dealing with planning, industry, petroleum, tourism, and other economically important activities. Modern economies are quite different in their scope and nature from the type of agricultural and trading activity that prevailed at the time of the Prophet more than fourteen hundred years ago. It is only in the past thirty years that Islamic economists have sought to discover how the principles of *sharīʿah* could be applied in such fields as macroeconomics policy, project appraisal, accounting, and national planning.

The introduction of *fiqh* into these new areas has raised many questions. The debate is ongoing and many issues remain to be resolved. *Shūrā* ("consultation") between government and Muslim populations is needed to determine how policy should evolve, and the *ʿulamā'* and increasingly educated Muslim professionals are involved in this process in most Islamic states. Exactly what is *ḥarām* and what is *ḥalāl* (permitted) in modern economies with increasingly sophisticated financial and commercial systems is often far from straightforward.

Macroeconomics policy has Islamic implications, for example, as excessive demand can result in inflationary conditions that can destroy a financial system based on *murābaḥah* (funded trade) and *muḍārabah* (equity participation). It also raises the issue of interest to compensate for inflation that most *fuqahā'* would still regard as *ribā*. Nevertheless excessive constraints on demand can result in an underutilization of capacity, a waste of resources, and unemployment. This can result in *ẓulm,* a term which refers to inequity, injustice, exploitation, oppression, and wrongdoing. In a recession induced by government in the interests of the control of inflation, it is usually the weak and marginal employees who are the first to be dismissed. If the Islamic community or *ummah* suffer from such policies, this is intolerable.

Economic planning is much less in vogue since the collapse of the centrally planned economies of Eastern Europe, but in most Muslim countries there are planning ministries, and national plans are produced to cover each five-year period. In many Muslim countries the plans are a legacy of the nationalistic, and in some cases socialistic, postindependence period. The *ʿulamā'* have often been unhappy with the plans, as there has been little *shūrā* outside government circles. Infrastructure and industrial projects have frequently involved the employment of large numbers of infidels from outside thc Islamic world, and there has been unease concerning the social and cultural impact of these employees.

The new industries have often been a threat to the traditional craft and trading activities which are highly regarded in Islamic societies. The Qur'ān itself has much to say on fair trading practice. Dealing in commodities, as opposed to mere monetary transactions, is regarded as a productive activity, according to surah 2.275: "God hath permitted trade and forbidden usury." The bazaar and souk trading economies have been undermined by the growth of employment in the modern sector, which has benefited from government subsidies, protectionism, and artificial pricing policies. Finance has been made available on generous terms to the modern sector, while the traditional sectors have been starved of funds. This has raised the price of bazaar finance, opening up the whole issue of usury. In such circumstances it is hardly surprising that the bazaar merchants in Iran were among the most fervent supporters of the Islamic revolution, and that the previous career of President Hashemi Rafsanjani himself was as a bazaar merchant.

The Example of Insurance in Islamic Business Institutions. Islamic economic axioms may have had their origins over fourteen hundred years ago, but it would be incorrect to conclude that they are frozen in history and cannot be adapted to changing circumstances. Modern Muslim economists recognize that the needs of business have become more specialized and sophisticated, and such services as insurance coverage are quite reasonably demanded. As the morality and legality of insurance has been a matter for *sharīʿah* scholars, it is interesting to consider how ideas on this type of institution have developed in recent years.

There are several reasons for the *sharīʿah* prohibition regarding conventional insurance. The first relates to the operational practices of the institutions providing insurance, as the money received in premiums is often held in interest-bearing bonds, the maturity of which is designed to match the anticipated liabilities of the insurance company. This applies particularly in the case of endowment policies on a fixed-term basis. The second reason is based on a fundamental objection to all forms of life insurance. Life is the gift of God, not of man, and insurance policies which pay out on death amount to gambling with life. Relatives may benefit, but such a lottery only tempts salary-earners to avoid making proper provision for their families in life. It also undermines the *ummah.* Fellow Muslims have a duty to take care of those in need through almsgiving and *zakāt.* As life insurance eliminates the need for this, it is morally and socially corrupting.

A third objection to insurance contracts is that they involve *gharar,* a wager on risk or a form of speculation or gambling. If insurance is taken out against theft, for example, the payment is made only if the crime actually occurs. This could encourage fraud. Furthermore, there is an element of *jahālah* or uncertainty inherent in the contract. If the good is recovered, then the payment may be less or not made at all. Much will depend on the state of the recovered good, in particular the degree of damage. As this cannot be known in advance at the time of the initial contract, then that contract must be void. The Qur'ān (2.282) stipulates that all contracts should be written down: "O ye who believe, when ye deal with each other in transactions involving future obligations in a fixed period of time, reduce them to writing." Exact terms should be agreed in advance, otherwise one party may be defrauded by the other.

In some modern Muslim nations insurance companies are not permitted to set up premises and solicit for business. Offshore companies from Europe and the Far East handle Saudi Arabian insurance, as no insurance companies are allowed to operate within the kingdom. An Islamically acceptable alternative is available, however, as modern Muslim economists have recognized that there is a need for some types of insurance provision, and only life insurance is completely inadmissible under the *sharīʿah.* There are several *fiqh*s in Islamic jurisprudence which state that insurance conducted under the *takāful* system is permissible providing the following conditions are adhered to.

First, companies offering insurance must be organized on a mutual basis rather than being publicly quoted institutions accountable to shareholders. Second, the aim of such companies should not be to profit from insurance at the expense of the policyholders but rather to share all surplus revenues with the insured. Many leading Western companies are mutual entities rather than being incorporated under company law. The mutual insurance company becomes a type of solidarity fund for the Muslim *ummah,* the participants in which are basically helping each other. Third, risks are shared and thereby reduced for each participant, not actively sought. Fourth, the obligations and liabilities of policyholders should be fixed and written down at the outset. There can be no unlimited liability as with the underwriting syndicates in London which are composed of the Lloyds "names." The implication is that there is a ceiling on what can be covered, and this should be closely related to the value of the goods being insured.

International Islamic Institutions. The Organization of the Islamic Conference is the major intergovernmental institution in which all the Muslim states are represented. Although primarily a political forum, it also serves as an important body for the exchange of economic ideas. The institution became increasingly active in the late 1960s, and it was responsible for the founding of the Islamic Development Bank in 1974. International humanitarian issues affecting Muslims are discussed, and representatives from the Red Crescent, the Islamic equivalent of the Red Cross, have attended some of the meetings. There is a solidarity fund, which disburses grants rather than advancing funds through *murābaḥah* and *muḍārabah,* as is the practice of the Islamic Development Bank. The poorest Muslim countries, such as Bangladesh, Afghanistan and Somalia, have all been beneficiaries of these grants.

At the meetings of the Islamic Conference international issues are discussed at heads-of-state level, but it is the sessions involving finance ministers that are primarily concerned with economic matters. The conference has a distinctive contribution to make on questions, such as Third World debt, which have deeply worried many Muslim states. The cause of the payments difficulties is seen as the *ribā*-based nature of the international financial system, which imposes unfair interest burdens on many developing countries. Swapping debt for equity appears at first sight to be an acceptable solution, as *muḍārabah* funding can replace *ribā* finance. There is some caution over this, however, if it means the transfer of ownership of assets in Muslim debtor nations to the control of infidels.

An Islamic worldview is emerging on the problems facing the international economy, and although there is no definitive agreement on solutions, there is a growing consensus among Muslim economists on the way forward. There are several basic principles in Islam which indicate the type of approach to be taken as far as the Muslim world is concerned. The first is the principle of *tawḥīd* ("divine unity"). This recognizes the continuing involvement of Allāh in all affairs, and it means that Muslims should follow carefully the holy texts. The ultimate aim of development is not material but spiritual, the attainment of *maqāṣid al-sharīʿah,* the goals of Islamic teaching and the law of God. Without this, sociopolitical discontent will intensify. Material prosperity can increase discontent, not reduce it. The real challenge is to create conditions where all members of the *ummah* can realize their human potential by serving Allāh.

The second concept is that of the *khalīfah* ("successor"), that the human being is the viceregent of God on earth. Humans are responsible for the efficient and equitable management of the resources with which God has endowed the world. The believer has a duty to ensure *falāḥ,* the well-being attained by the satisfaction of both the material and spiritual needs of the human personality. This goes beyond the basic-needs approach increasingly stressed by such Western development institutions as the World Bank. The emphasis is on the responsibility of individuals and not merely their requirements in terms of money and possessions. The important matter is to ensure that the members of the *ummah* are in a position to exercise their responsibilities; in other words, the stress is on the need to facilitate, not mere provision.

The third principle is that of justice, *ʿadālah.* Socioeconomic justice does not mean equality of material consumption, as this would at best constitute a mere earthly goal. Rather it means the elimination of exploitation and oppression which prevents the believer from exercising his responsibilities in fulfillment of the will of God. Oppression of the *ummah* in any part of the world is intolerable, whether in Palestine or Bosnia. The strength of feeling on such matters at meetings of the Islamic Conference should not be underestimated.

[*See also* Banks and Banking; Bazaar; Interest; Islamic Development Bank; Organization of the Islamic Conference; *and* Waqf.]

BIBLIOGRAPHY

Ansari, Aqeel. *An Institutional Framework for Capital Formation in an Islamic Economy.* Islamabad, 1981. Considers the role of the family, community, mosque, and state in investment.

Azzam, Abd-al-Rahman. *The Eternal Message of Mohammed.* London, 1979. Includes sections on the Islamic state, international relations, colonialism, and class struggle; the section on social reform deals with economic issues.

Bennabi, Malek. *Islam in History and Society.* Kuala Lumpur, 1991. Analyzes some of the problems facing Muslims in the modern world, stressing spiritual rather than material development.

Chapra, Mohammad Umer. *Islam and the Economic Challenge.* Leicester, 1992. Excellent book that examines the concerns of Muslims on development and suggests a number of ways forward.

Gellner, Ernest. *Post Modernism, Reason, and Religion.* London, 1992. Although not an economics text, this work provides penetrating insights into Islamic social thinking and contrasts this with Western approaches.

Iqbal, Munawar. *Distributive Justice and Need Fulfilment in an Islamic Economy.* Leicester, 1988. Considers issues of poverty, equity, and basic needs in Islamic societies.

Mannan, Mohammed. *Institutional Settings of an Islamic Economic Order: A Comparative Study of Economic Process.* International Centre for Research in Islamic Economics, King Abdul Aziz University, Discussion Paper, no. 8. Jeddah, 1981. Brief but useful discussion of institutional issues.

Pramanik, Ataul Huq. *Poverty, Inequality, and the Role of Some Islamic Economic Institutions.* Islamabad, 1981. Mainly concerned with *zakāt,* but also deals with inheritance issues.

Presley, John, ed. *Directory of Islamic Financial Institutions.* London, 1988. Largely concerned with Islamic banking, but includes an interesting section on the higher religious supervisory board.

Rahman, Afzalur. *Banking and Insurance.* London, 1979. Sets out the Islamic position on risk, uncertainty, and insurance contracts.

Rodinson, Maxime. *Islam and Capitalism.* Middlesex, 1974. Addresses the question of whether there can be an Islamic path for capitalism.

Saleh, Nabil. *Unlawful Gain and Legitimate Profit in Islamic Law.* Cambridge, 1986. Contains a useful section on uncertainty, risk, and speculation.

Sardar, Ziauddin. *Islamic Futures.* London, 1985. Includes an interesting chapter on the Islamic state in the postindustrial age.

Siddiqi, Muhammed Nejatullah. *Insurance in an Islamic Economy.* Leicester, 1985. Explores the Islamic position on insurance in relation to contemporary practice.

Wilson, Rodney. *Islamic Business: Theory and Practice.* London, 1985. Examines the business environment in the Islamic world and deals with issues such as labor relations and insurance.

Rodney Wilson

EDUCATION. [*To explore the dimensions of education in the modern Islamic world, this entry comprises five articles:*

Religious Education
Educational Institutions
Educational Methods
Educational Reform
The Islamization of Knowledge

The introductory article provides an overview of the role and function of religious education in Muslim community life: the four complementary articles provide details on educational practices, theories, and goals in the nineteenth and twentieth centuries.]

Religious Education

Internal political and social movements of the eighteenth, nineteenth, and twentieth centuries within the Muslim world neglected Islamic education and allowed external secular and missionary ideas to turn it into religious education. Variations in worldviews and interpretations of Qur'ānic principles of education resulted in an emphasis on form over essence in the education of Muslims.

Historical accounts of Islamic/Muslim education provide a variety of perspectives on its nature and the function of its traditional institutions. Cultural and political restraints ended Islamic education as a functional system aimed at understanding and appropriating Qur'ānic pedagogical principles and limited it to "religious" knowledge confined to selected men. Islamic education has recently been confused with a subject matter, "religion," or with a moral, social code, *akhlāq*. The primacy of formalized and juridical education over the informal development of Islamic character resulted in curricular and instructional differentiation between class and gender, a separation of "Islamic" and "non-Islamic" knowledge, and a dichotomy between ideal and practice in Muslim education.

Islamic Education and Religious Education. Islamic education, referred to in the Qur'ān (3.110) as the process of shaping character within the Islamic worldview, requires the Muslim family to expose its children and adults to all knowledge as a means of understanding the parameters set in the Qur'ān for a constructive relationship with God, other human beings, and nature. Based on the Qur'ānic dictum, "Read in the name of the Creator . . . who taught (man) by the pen" (96.1–4), which means that to read is to learn and to act as guided by the Book, Islamic education evolved from this kind of comprehensive training in the first Islamic community in Medina (c.623) to a course of study on religion or its inculcation in social mores. What is called "religious education" or "Muslim education" does not reflect the historical process of education in Islam. This process, in the estimate of Waqar Husaini (1981), began to disintegrate at the end of the eleventh century, when science, the humanities, and social sciences were excluded from the curricula. Fazlur Rahman (1982) suggests that it remained functional into the fifteenth century, whereas Dale Eickelman (1985) asserts that it socialized Muslims well into the latter half of the twentieth century.

Religious education differs from Islamic education even though it maintains remnants of the Islamic educational institutions. By separating "revealed" and "human" knowledge, it transformed Qur'ānic principles into formalized legal and moral codes and rituals, creating a dichotomy in Islamic thinking. It also transformed the meaning of the Prophetic dictum "Faqqihhu fī al-dīn" (*Ṣaḥīḥ Muslim*) from teaching within the Islamic worldview to teaching Islam as interpreted by the different *fiqh* (jurisprudence) schools.

The salient features of Islamic education, such as *taḥfīẓ* (oral and aural transmission), are often confused with *talqīn* (the acquisition and dissemination of Qur'ānic principles and spirit). *Talqīn*, as Seyyed Hossein Nasr (1982) asserts, led the field of Islamic education to produce "philosopher-scientists" in various intellectual disciplines. Islamic education's intimate relation to the Qur'ānic revelation and *ḥadīth* (prophetic tradition) does not make it purely religious, nor does it render its other elements exclusively Islamic or absolute. Earlier Muslim intellectuals transformed the form, content, and intent of sciences, education, and arts into Islamic disciplines by integrating intellectual and cultural development within the Islamic worldview. Most contemporary Muslim educators assume Islamic education to be religious indoctrination.

The traditional recitation method of teaching the Qur'ān comes to mind when one thinks about Islamic education, but neither was ever restricted to this method, and Islamic education is not limited to the study of the Qur'ān. The Qur'ān as the foundation of all knowledge guides behavior.

Islamic education has been decentralized, and its

practice has varied. It was reduced to religious education in different regions at different times. This transformation occurred when Islamic philosophy and pedagogy were separated and when strict public moral codes were imposed on women, rendering their public appearance taboo. Concurrently, generations of male religious leaders or jurists emphasized the Qur'ān as either an absolute moral code or a legal law, instead of viewing it as a universal guide for the whole of the community. The principles of Islamic philosophy were idealized, and knowledge was classified by sources and by methods that enhanced the discrepancy between goals and means and the dichotomies between teaching men and women and what is moral (religious/private/informal) and what is rational (juridical/public/formal).

Separation of Philosophy and Pedagogy. Nasr criticizes Muhammad Iqbal (1877–1938) and other "modernist" Islamists for understanding "Greek philosophy through the eyes of its modern Western interpreters" and, hence, separating Islam from philosophy. Fazlur Rahman ("Islam: An Overview," section on "Modernism," in the *Encyclopedia of Religion,* edited by Mircea Eliade, New York, 1987, vol. 7, pp. 318–322) describes Iqbal's accusing "the West of cheating humanity of its basic values with the glittering mirage of its technology" and his strong critique of world Muslim society. For Rahman, Iqbal was a "neofundamentalist" who was reacting to modernism but also "importantly influenced by modernism." Iqbal's (1962) own assertion that the Qur'ān is a book that emphasizes "deed" rather than "idea" is significant to the understanding of the Islamic educational process and its transformation.

To educate in Islam, Iqbal states, means to create a living experience on which religious faith ultimately rests. For Rahman (1982), it means Islamic intellectualism. Though Nasr believes that the Islamic theory of education can be reconstructed within the Qur'ānic philosophy, Iqbal emphasizes that the birth of Islam is the birth of inductive intellect, wherein "to achieve full self-consciousness, Man must finally be thrown back on his own resources."

These diverse views suggest that Muslims, particularly in the past two centuries, not only neglected philosophy, as Nasr suggests, but, as Ismā'īl R. al-Fārūqī (1981) points out, also lost Islam's connection to its pedagogical function and its methods of observation and experimentation. As centers of higher religious learning began formal transmission of "book knowledge" and inculcation in particular interpretations, a dichotomy arose between philosophy, or the ideal, and pedagogy, or the practice. Encouraged by skepticism in modern Western philosophy, this dichotomy widened.

Western-educated Muslim modernists in the nineteenth and twentieth centuries, not aware that the underlying philosophy of Western education differed from that of Islam, were satisfied with teaching courses on religion in the traditional style and neglected to restructure the traditional system. Meanwhile, "traditionalists" emphasized the primacy of Islamic doctrine over *falsafah* (philosophy), creating, in Husaini's words, a schism between them and the modernists and destroying the integrated educational system. Western-educated thinkers who reaffirm the validity of traditional practices (I call them "neotraditionalists") interpret the philosophy of Abū Ḥāmid al-Ghazālī (1058–1111) as the "finally established" Islamic educational theory (Ashraf, 1985) and hold an absolutist perspective of Islamic education. This perspective, discussed elsewhere by this author (1990 and 1991), results, unknowingly, in a dichotomy between the Islamic worldview and its pedagogical process.

Institutions of Islamic Education. Diverse perspectives of Islamic/Muslim education also result in diverse and at times contradictory accounts of its transformation. The *kuttāb* (for primary and Qur'ānic education) and the *madrasah* (for secondary and higher learning) are the most frequent contexts in which Islamic education is discussed. Other places, such as the *ḥalaqah* (study circle in a mosque), *dār al-kutub* (library/bookshop), and private homes play important roles but are rarely recognized, as Munir D. Ahmad ("Muslim Education Prior to the Establishment of Madrasah," *Islamic Studies* [Islamabad] 26.4 [1987]: 321–348) and Salah Hussein Al-Abidi ("The Mosque: Adult Education and Uninterrupted Learning," *Al-Islām al-yawm* [Islam Today, Rabat], 7.7 [1989]: 68–77) indicate, particularly in rural areas that constitute more than 70 percent of the Muslim world and where they might be the only educational institution.

No systematic study of the evolution of the educational process in these situations has been done. There are scattered reports in biographies, books of history and Islamic thought, and encyclopedias, but they typically leave a gap between Ibn Khaldūn's (1332–1406) *Muqaddimah* and the nineteenth-century sources in which Western perspectives dominate. Recent accounts of Islamic education are almost always presented in the contexts of modernization or Muslim revival movements that, Nasr (1987) asserts, Western scholarship overemphasizes even though they did weaken traditional Islam. Fazlur Rahman (1987) was more concerned that these "reformers" integrated science and technology with the "Qur'ānic requirement that man studies the universe" than he was with the transformation from Islamic education into religious education.

Teaching reading and writing in *kuttāb,* according to Ahmad Shalaby (1979), preceded the rise of Islam, but existed on a limited scale. In distinguishing this type from Qur'ānic *kuttāb,* Shalaby notes that several authors have confused the different varieties of this institution and cites Philip Hitti (*The Arabs: A Short History,* Chicago, 1956), Ahmad Amin (*Dhuha al-Islam,* Cairo, 1941), and Ignácz Goldziher. He states that Goldziher ("Education [Muslim]" in the *Encyclopedia of Religion and Ethics,* 1960, vol. 5, pp. 199–207), in his attempt to trace Qur'ānic *kuttāb* back to the early time of Islam, did not distinguish the varieties of *kuttāb.* That Shalaby's account differs from Goldziher's on other matters related to teaching young Muslims suggests differences not only in their perspectives of Islamic education and its institutions but of the problems it has encountered. Though Goldziher relies largely on the same primary sources used by Shalaby, when he says that "modern movements towards reform" (p. 206) were unaffected by Western influence, he does not seem to distinguish between the Islam taught in *kuttāb*s and *madrasah*s and that taught by informal socialization. Thus, he states, "the instruction of the young proceeded mainly on the lines laid down in the older theological writings," suggesting that the problem lies in Muslims' inability to adopt modern technologies. This assessment prevents him from realizing why "religious" content constituted the central curriculum, and in some localities was the only function left for the *kuttāb* when government schools, the Ottomans' Rushdīyah schools, took over the teaching of reading, writing, and other subjects, or why natives resisted modernity (Ahmed, 1988) and gave up even Qur'ānic schools in response to colonial policies (G. W. Leitner, "Indigenous Oriental Education, with Special Reference to India, and, in Particular, to the Panjab," *Asiatic Quarterly Review,* 2d ser., 8, nos. 15 and 16 [1894]: 421–438) and to exploitation of Islam by both colonial and local governments (Harrison, 1990). Similarly, when Rahman (1982) reports on educational reform in the nineteenth century, he confuses the varieties of *kuttāb*s and their relationship to the *madrasah,* stating that in general, primary education given in the *maktab*s or *kuttāb*s was a self-contained unit that did not feed into the higher educational system. Rahman thus contradicts reports by Mohammad Akhlaq Ahmad (1985) and others that *kuttāb*s and mosques played an important role for those continuing their Islamic higher education.

Contradictory accounts also surround the *madrasah.* Shalaby gives a detailed account of the first *madrasah,* established in the eleventh century by Niẓām al-Mulk in Baghdad, and classifies these schools by location, founders and their positions, and the primary sources that cite them. A. L. Tibawi ("Origin and Character of *al-Madrasah,*" *Bulletin of the School of Oriental and African Studies,* 25.2 [1962]: 225–238) concurs with primary Muslim sources such as Ibn Khaldūn in concluding that the main characteristics of these schools varied by region and time, but all were formal residential places of secondary and higher learning, with Arabic as the basic medium of instruction. They relied mainly on dialogue between teacher and disciples. Their curricula covered, in addition to Qur'ānic *talqīn* and Arabic grammar, *tafsīr* (exegesis), *fiqh* (jurisprudence), *ḥadīth, uṣūl al-fiqh* (principles of jurisprudence), *uṣūl al-ḥadīth* (principles of narration), and the biography of the Prophet and *al-Ṣaḥābah* (the Prophet's companions). Classical sciences (astronomy, geography, and medicine) and Arabic *adab* (literature) were also taught, the intensity and depth of instruction depending on the students' mastery of particular subjects and the teachers' strengths. M. A. Ahmad (1985) and other Muslim authors suggest that a similar though less vital educational process still exists in such places of learning. Goldziher, however, does not recognize that what he describes as a "primitive and patriarchal form of instruction still hold[ing] its place" in these institutions is a result of the takeover by technical and military high schools, which left only Islamic subjects to traditionally trained teachers.

In response to colonial policies, these institutions evolved in one of two ways: into traditional, privately sponsored religious schools with some Western orientation or into government-sponsored secular schools with added religion courses. The "traditional" form is represented in the remnants of *kuttāb* and *madrasah.* Famous among them are Deoband in India, al-Niẓāmīyah in Iran, al-Mustanṣirīyah in Baghdad, al-Sulaymānīyah in

Istanbul, al-Nūrīyah in Damascus, al-Azhar in Cairo, al-Qayrawān in Tunis, al-Qarawīyīn in Fez, and Córdoba in Spain. Some of these institutions, such as al-Azhar and Deoband, still grant "Islamic" higher degrees but are weakened by their consideration of religious knowledge as separate from other knowledge.

When modernist elites of the early twentieth century sought reform from outside their society, they created private religious schools (for example, Yâdigâr-ı Hürriyet established in 1908 in Basra, Iraq). Their indiscriminate adoption of Western systems, combined with nationalistic and politicized Islam, emphasized a secular morality in teaching natural and social sciences, which gradually separated Islam from its Qur'ānic base, and favored secondary literary and historical sources of religion.

When the mid-twentieth-century "revivalists" assumed the preservation of Islamic principles by teaching *ʿibādāt* (rituals) and moral codes, courses on religion *(al-daynah)* were added, taking a secondary place in the curriculum in the secular government-sponsored system. At present, overall teaching time in these courses ranges from 32 percent in Saudi elementary schools to 3 percent in Syrian high schools, and their content varies from a watered-down version of *tafsīr, fiqh, ḥadīth,* and Islamic history to *ḥifẓ* (memorization of Qur'ān) and rituals. Further, very few secular universities in the Muslim world offer any such courses on Islam outside the college of Islamic law (Kulliyat al-Sharīʿah).

Education of Women. The imposition of strict public moral codes on women is another indicator of the transformation of Islamic education into religious education; women were forbidden to attend places of learning such as *madrasah*s and mosques, even though women formally and informally transmitted the culture to their offspring as well as to other children and to men and women inside and outside the home in early and medieval Muslim communities (Goldziher). Muslim boys and girls were taught at home and attended formal *kuttāb;* according to Nasr (1987), girls even studied in *madrasah*s when they were first established. No historical accounts mention women as *ʿulamā'* (Islamic scholars), knowledgeable in branches of Qur'ānic sciences such as *tafsīr, kalām* (Islamic philosophy/theology), and *fiqh,* particularly after the formalized higher learning in *madrasah,* although Shalaby notes that many women had established or endowed such institutions. Also, many primary Muslim sources (such as al-Suyuti [d. 1505] and others listed by Goldziher, Nasr, and Shalaby) report that up to the fifteenth century there were outstanding women who memorized and narrated *ḥadīth* to earn them the title of *muḥaddithāt* (female narrators) among their disciples, and some who were well known in Ṣūfī orders.

The assaults on Islamic culture by European Crusaders, Orientalists, and colonial governments, combined with their differentiation between private and public domains, caused Muslim leaders to lose sight of the essence of Islamic education, particularly its informal sector, and take extreme attitudes at the expense of a revival of traditional Islam. These predominantly male leaders, beginning with those of the eighteenth-century Wahhābī puritan movement, propagated the view that as women's primary concern is the home they need a different type of education. "Reformists" such as Muḥammad ʿAbduh (1845–1905) emphasized Islamic ideals of women's higher status in Islam and the obligation of both men and women to seek knowledge; yet, in practice, they did not recognize women's right to access to a thorough knowledge of the Qur'ān as a key to intellectual development.

Revivalists, such as Sayyid Quṭb (1906–1966) and Sayyid Abu al-Aʿlā Mawdūdī (1903–1979), though attempting to restore Islamic education in post–World War II nation-states, used the traditional rationale about women's education and asserted that their "natural" disposition is to transmit culture to the next generation (both boys and girls); but they did not restructure the traditional practices of teaching Islam to allow for this transmission. The primary objectives of women's education in Muḥammad Quṭb's (1961, 1981) curriculum were to prepare them for the biological and emotional aspects of their roles as mothers and housewives. Such objectives further confused and marginalized women's education in Islam.

The post-1969 "islamization" movements leaned toward a politicized Islam and had implications for women's Islamic/religious education. Contrary to their intellectual tradition that culminated in Ismāʿīl al-Fārūqī's (1921–1986) *Islamization of Knowledge* (1982), proponents of these movements emphasized morality, which overshadowed their presumed goal: to restructure the secular system of higher learning in order to address the religious and cultural needs of Muslim societies as part of the new development strategies. The Indonesian and Malay development policies of involving all segments of the population in education and training, reported by Sharom Ahmat and Sharon Siddique (1987), seem to be a first step toward recognizing women's role in social development. Emphasis on morality, however, particularly when women became part of the Malay *madrasahs* (an outgrowth of the *podock* religious training with worldly affairs in sight) of the 1960s and the *dakwa* (Ar., *daʿwah,* call for Islamic orientation) of the 1970s and 1980s, led religious education to take the form of moral dogma. The Indonesian *pesantren* system, which was established in rural areas in the early nineteenth century and spread to urban development in the 1970s and 1980s, maintained an integrated system, and Indonesian women, unlike those in any other Muslim country, occupy a full range of religious leadership roles. [*See* Madrasah; Pesantren.]

Neotraditionalists, like Anis Ahmad (1984), attempted to "liberate Islam from Western cultural colonialism" in the 1980s and gave women's education the form I call "reversed feminism," emphasizing segregated education for different but unequal roles. This trend is flourishing in North American and western European countries, where Muslim males are demanding single-sex schools and, in their private "Islamic/Muslim" schools, are segregating children in the first grade. Curricula in these schools are the same as in public schools except for courses on religion and Arabic language.

Dichotomy of Ideals and Practice. The Organization of the Islamic Conference (OIC), established in 1973, held five world conferences on Muslim education in Mecca (1977), Islamabad (1980), Dhaka (1981), Jakarta (1982), and Cairo (1987). Their recommendations were to "re-classify knowledge into 'revealed' [given to man by God and contained mainly in the Qur'ān and the tradition of the Prophet] and 'acquired' [by man's efforts]" and to teach that "acquired" knowledge from the "Islamic point of view," the process of which is referred to as "Islamization of knowledge" (Ashraf, 1985). The goals, similar to those outlined by al-Fārūqī (1982), to integrate modern sciences and branches of knowledge within the Islamic philosophy, are stated in the Islamic Education Series' seven monographs of which Ashraf is general editor.

A core curriculum (Muhammad Hamid al-Afendi and Nabi Ahmed Baloch, 1980) with a work edited by Syed Muhammad al-Naquib al-Attas (*Aims and Objectives of Islamic Education*, Jeddah, 1979) and other "blueprints" for groundwork and strategies were published in this series, the basic premise of which is that reinterpretation of "all branches of knowledge, particularly social sciences, within the Islamic perspective" is the only way to develop an Islamic curriculum that will alleviate the crisis in Muslim education caused by the dual traditional and secular systems. Yet, because the emphasis was on "revealed" rather than "acquired" knowledge, no action plan was devised either to reconstruct a fresh base for Islamic thought and educational practice in the light of new discoveries and contemporary needs or to alleviate the dichotomy in Muslim thinking that resulted from separating religious and secular knowledge. Nor, despite its urgency in light of new economic developments and the women's emancipation movement, was an action plan chartered for women's education. Instead, the emphasis on different and segregated education resulted only in prescriptive statements, reiterating a perspective on girls' education that has been evolving since the introduction of Western secular education practices. Indeed, although one of the fourteen committees of the World Conferences on Islamic Education was charged with the "teaching of women," no female educator was involved, and the topic was discussed in less than five pages of the seven volumes.

This perspective on women's education in Islam is almost uniform in the countries that adopted segregated education after encountering the European and American systems. In the Indian subcontinent, for example, most girls attending Qur'ānic *kuttāb* not only are denied the opportunity to continue their religious education once they reach puberty but rarely are instructed by their families, as was the practice among learned Muslim families before the British colonization. A similar practice is found in other Muslim countries that interacted with Western educational practices; the emphasis is placed on girls gaining religious knowledge and character in sexually segregated schools (El-Sanabary, 1973); no women teachers are allowed education in religion. Despite their enrollment in *kuttābs* in earlier times, Saudi girls, for example, were not allowed to enroll in religious institutions of higher learning such as Umm al-Qurā in Mecca until 1970–1971, when, according to Mohammed Saad al-Salem ("The Interplay of Tradition and Modernity: A Field Study of Saudi Policy and Educational Development," Ph.D. diss., University of California, Santa Barbara, 1981), only 80 women as compared to 2,210 men were admitted. Thus, girls and young women receive their religious knowledge primarily by observing their elders' practice of local, regional, tribal, or ethnic customary interpretations of Islam;

those who attend public and private schools receive secular knowledge from trained, organized teachers with structured curricula.

In summary, Muslim male educators continue to overlook the dynamics of the role of women as the transmitters, preservers, and transformers of the culture in Muslim societies in the 1980s and 1990s. These educators keep women's religious education peripheral, relegating it to the home. This attitude is only one of many other disparities that have transformed Islamic education, resulting in fragmented educational planning and a lack of balance between religious and secular objectives. This imbalance is primarily the remnant of the colonial and missionary legacies that left the Muslim world in a turmoil even after independence.

[*See also* Women and Islam; Women and Social Reform; *and the biographies of Fārūqī, Iqbal, Nasr, and Rahman.*]

BIBLIOGRAPHY

General Works

Ahmed, Akbar S. *Discovering Islam: Making Sense of Muslim History and Society*. London and New York, 1988. Unique history of Muslim societies' response to world events, by a native Muslim. Chapter 7 gives special treatment to the impact of colonialism on the Muslim rejection of modernity. Chapter 10, on the reconstruction of Muslim thought, is illuminating. The appendix, "Muslim Chronology" (up to 1986), is particularly helpful.

Ashraf, Syed Ali. *New Horizons in Muslim Education*. Cambridge, 1985. Representative of neotraditionalist views on Muslim education. The appendices summarize the recommendations of the four World Conferences on Islamic Education. See also the Islamic Education Series, some volumes of which are cited below.

Eickelman, Dale F. *Knowledge and Power in Morocco: The Education of a Twentieth-Century Notable*. Princeton, 1985. Unprecedented anthropological analysis of the power of knowledge in a Muslim society.

Fārūqī, Ismāʿīl R. al-. *Islamization of Knowledge: General Principles and Workplan*. Washington, D.C., 1982. Essential introduction to the understanding of contemporary trends in Islamic education and thought by an American Muslim scholar.

Iqbal, Muhammad. *The Reconstruction of Religious Thought in Islam* (1934). Reprint, Lahore, 1962. Landmark by the Pakistani poet and scholar, giving his views on reforming Islamic education through the reconstruction of Islamic thought.

Nasr, Seyyed Hossein. *Traditional Islam in the Modern World*. London and New York, 1987. Leading work in deciphering traditional Islam and its contrast to fundamentalism and modernism with respect to Western scholarship.

Quṭb, Muḥammad al-. *Al-tarbīyah al-Islāmīyah*, vol. 2, *Fī al-taṭbīq* (Curriculum of Islamic Education, vol. 2, Application). Reprint, Beirut, 1981. Good representation of revivalists' view of Islamic education, particularly the Muslim Brothers.

Rahman, Fazlur. *Islam and Modernity: Transformation of an Intellectual Tradition*. Chicago and London, 1982. Definitive work for understanding contemporary Islamic intellectualism as the essence of Islamic higher education, and the implications of the method of Qur'ānic interpretation for the development of the intellectual Muslim.

Shalaby, Ahmad. *History of Muslim Education*. Karachi, 1979. Deals with the subject from the beginning of Islam through the fall of the Ayyūbid dynasty in Egypt (1250), covering important issues in the evolution of Muslim education. The bibliography is rich with primary sources in Arabic and English.

Regional Acounts

Ahmad, Mohammad Akhlaq. *Traditional Education among Muslims (A Study of Some Aspects of Modern India)*. Delhi, 1985.

Ahmat, Sharom, and Sharon Siddique, eds. *Muslim Society: Higher Education and Development in Southeast Asia*. Singapore, 1987. Collection of essays surveying historical and contemporary educational issues in the Muslim societies of Indonesia, Malaysia, the Philippines, Singapore, and Thailand.

Barazangi, Nimat Hafez. "The Education of North American Muslim Parents and Children: Conceptual Changes as a Contribution to Islamization of Education." *American Journal of Islamic Social Sciences* 7.3 (1990): 385–402.

Barazangi, Nimat Hafez. "Islamic Education in the United States and Canada: Conception and Practice of the Islamic Belief System." In *The Muslims of America*, edited by Yvonne Y. Haddad, pp. 157–174. New York and Oxford, 1991.

El-Sanabary, Nagat. "A Comparative Study of the Disparities of Educational Opportunities for Girls in the Arab States." Ph.D. diss., University of California, Berkeley, 1973. Rich in data on girls' education.

Harrison, Christopher. *France and Islam in West Africa, 1860–1960*. Reprint, Cambridge, 1990. Chapters 9 and 10, "The French Stake in Islam" and "The 'Rediscovery of Islam,' " are particularly intriguing.

Topical Studies

Afendi, Muhammad Hamid al-, and Nabi Ahmed Baloch, eds. *Curriculum and Teacher Education*. Islamic Education Series. Jeddah, 1980.

Ahmad, Anis. *Muslim Women and Higher Education: A Case for Separate Institutions for Women*. 2d rev. ed. Islamabad, 1984. Provides insights into the neotraditionalists' biased views on women's education.

Fārūqī, Ismāʿīl R. al-. "Islamizing the Social Sciences." In *Social and Natural Sciences: The Islamic Perspectives*, edited by Ismāʿīl R. al-Fārūqī and Abdullah Omar Nasseef, pp. 8–20. Islamic Education Series. Jeddah, 1981.

Husaini, Sayyid Waqqar Ahmed. "Humanistic–Social Sciences Studies in Higher Education: Islamic and International Perspectives." In *Social and Natural Sciences: The Islamic Perspectives*, edited by Ismāʿīl R. al-Fārūqī and Abdullah Omar Nasseef, pp. 148–166. Islamic Education Series. Jeddah, 1981.

Nasr, Seyyed Hossein. "The Teaching of Philosophy." In *Philosophy, Literature, and Fine Arts*, edited by Seyyed Hossein Nasr, pp. 3–21. Islamic Education Series. Jeddah, 1982. Blueprint for the role of philosophy, the arts, and literature in Islamic education.

Nimat Hafez Barazangi

Educational Institutions

As the nineteenth century opened, Islamic societies had highly developed educational institutions—elementary Qur'ān schools (Ar., *kuttāb* or *maktab*) and higher religious schools called *madrasah*s. Less formal education was available from Ṣūfī lodges, literary circles at princely courts, private tutors, and apprenticeships in state bureaus and craftsmen's shops.

After 1800, Western-style schools were introduced to meet new needs. Reforming Muslim rulers created new armies and schools in hopes of warding off the intrusive West and local rivals. Today's state school systems in many Muslim countries grew out of such beginnings. Missionaries and local minority communities also founded private Western-style schools. The new schools became rivals of the Qur'ān schools and *madrasah*s, with a cultural divide separating graduates of the two systems. Conscious and unconscious borrowing has led to considerable convergence of the two systems, but an entirely satisfactory synthesis of Islamic and Western educational institutions remains elusive.

This article discusses five phases of the development of educational institutions in the Islamic world since 1800. In phase one, Islamic schools were unaffected by the West. In phase two, reforming Muslim rulers—and, for different reasons, Western missionaries—set up Western-style schools. In phase three, colonial rulers subordinated schools to their own imperial interests. In phase four, newly independent states unified their school systems and rapidly expanded all levels of schooling. In phase five, Islamists campaigned to islamize education, along with the rest of state and society.

The chronology of these phases varied from place to place, and some countries bypassed a phase or two. The Ottomans entered phase two as early as 1773 by opening a naval engineering school; isolated North Yemen and Saudi Arabia had not yet entered it in 1950. The colonial rule of phase three began before 1800 in the Dutch East Indies and India, but reached Syria and Iraq only after World War I. North Yemen, Saudi Arabia, and Afghanistan skipped the colonial phase. Turkey and Iran won the independence of phase four in the 1920s without having been fully colonized, while the emirates of the lower Gulf did not begin phase four until the British left in 1971.

Phase One: Before Western Intrusion. Qur'ān schools stressed memorization of the Qur'ān, reading, and writing. Often the initial memorization did not mean comprehension, particularly where Arabic was not spoken at home. Teachers taught in homes, mosques, or shops, receiving their pay from pupils' fees or *waqf*s (pious endowments). Although conservative *ʿulamāʾ* might disapprove, girls sometimes attended Qur'ān schools, and a few became Qur'ān reciters or teachers.

Advanced schooling in mosques went back to the seventh century, but the formal *madrasah*—an endowed residential college stressing the *sharīʿah*—took shape only in the eleventh century. The Niẓāmīyah in Baghdad was a renowned prototype. In common usage, distinctions between mosque schools and *madrasah*s disappeared. Subjects seen as closely related to religion were stressed: Qur'ānic exegesis, *ḥadīth,* jurisprudence, theology, Arabic grammar, and logic. There were no formal admissions or graduation ceremonies, no grade levels, written examinations, grades, classrooms, desks, or school diplomas. Barred from the *madrasah,* only a few women pursued higher studies with private tutors.

Al-Azhar in Cairo, the Süleymaniye in Istanbul, Qarawīyīn in Fez, the Zaytūnah in Tunis, and various mosque-*madrasah*s in Mecca, Medina, and Damascus stood out in the Sunnī world of 1800. For Shīʿīs, the *madrasah*s of Najaf (Iraq) were foremost, with others in Isfahan and other Iranian cities.

Phase Two: Western-Style State and Missionary Schools. Defeat in wars with Russia and Napoleon's invasion of Egypt (1798) helped persuade Muslim rulers to reform their armies and military support services along Western lines. This called for a new type of school, and it was easier to bypass the conservative religious schools than to reform them. Phase two thus began a secularizing trend that prevailed until the Islamist challenge of phase five.

Enlisting Europeans as instructors, the Ottomans opened naval engineering and army engineering academies in 1773 and 1793. In 1826 Sultan Mahmud II destroyed the obsolete Janissary corps, a major obstacle to reform. He and his successors opened a bureau to train translators (1821) and schools of medicine (1827), military science (1834), civil administration (1859), and law (1878).

In 1811, Muḥammad (or Mehmed) ʿAlī, the sultan's ambitious vassal in Cairo, destroyed Egypt's obsolete Mamlūk cavalry. Thereafter he rivaled or led Istanbul in military and educational innovations, following his first Western-influenced military school (1816) with schools of engineering (1820), veterinary science (1827), medicine (1827), civil administration (1829), and translation (1836). The school of administration and languages (1868) became a law school. In Tunisia, Aḥmad Bey opened his Bardo military school in 1840.

Three related phenomena (which persist today) accompanied the new schools: importing Western educators, dispatching students to study in the West (small missions first left Egypt in 1809, Iran in 1811, and Istanbul in 1827), and putting new printing presses to work publishing translated Western textbooks.

Recruits from the Qur'ān schools and *madrasah*s proved ill-prepared for higher professional education, so Cairo and Istanbul next began turning Qur'ān schools into state primary schools. Al-Azhar and many other religious schools, however, long eluded serious reform and state control. In the 1860s, ministries of education in Cairo and Istanbul, patterned on the highly centralized French model, laid out blueprints for full state school systems. The Ottomans planned for lower and higher primary, middle, and high schools (*lycées*), capped by higher schools and a university. The French-inspired Galatasary Lycée stood out among eleven Ottoman *lycées* (one of which was for girls) in 1918. Teacher's colleges, founded in Istanbul (1846) and Cairo (1872, Dār al-ʿUlūm), included both Western and Islamic subjects in their curricula.

More isolated from the West and with a weaker state, Iran trailed Egypt and the central Ottoman Empire in military and educational reform. Dār al-Funūn (1851) taught military science, engineering, medicine, and Western languages, but it lacked firm support from the shah. Without an official ministry of education until 1925, other ministries set up their own schools: political science (1899/1900), agriculture (1900/01), arts (1910), and law (1921).

Phase Three: Under Colonial Rule. Colonial rule lasted anywhere from a few years to a century or more, and several Muslim countries escaped it altogether. There were three types of educational institutions under colonial rule: Western-style, unreformed Islamic, and hybrids of the two.

As colonies for European settlement, Algeria, Libya, and Palestine suffered most under colonial rule. In Algeria, over 132 years, the French established primary, secondary, and higher schools (medicine in 1859; law, sciences, and letters in 1879) for the settlers. The University of Algiers brought the higher schools together in 1909. A handful of Muslims submitted to France's "civilizing mission" and assimilated sufficiently to enter this system, but separate "Arab-French" schools were intended for them. Italian rule in Libya (1911–1943) was too brief to leave a comparable educational legacy. Palestine under British rule (1918–1948) was unique, for there most settlers were European Jews. With their own Zionist agenda and Hebrew-language schools, they left state-run schools largely to Palestinian Arabs.

Elsewhere colonial rulers ran Western-style schools mostly for the local population. In Egypt, Syria, and Iraq, these were inherited from indigenous reformers; other colonial regimes mostly started from scratch.

Whether frankly exploitative or conscious of a "white man's burden," colonial regimes put their own interests first. They usually intended for secondary and higher schools to turn out docile government clerks and technicians. In India the British experimented with reformed Muslim *madrasah*s and Hindu Sanskrit schools from the 1780s to the 1830s, when those who wanted to anglicize the courts and administration won out. English-language schools and colleges proliferated thereafter. The universities of Calcutta, Bombay, and Madras opened in 1857 as examining bodies on the model of the University of London.

The Indian "Mutiny" of 1857 haunted Lord Cromer, who administered Egypt for England from 1883 to 1907. He warned that "orientals" with a European education easily turned nationalist if frustrated in aspirations for official posts. He severely restricted enrollments in the elite primary-secondary-higher schools track, imposed school fees few could afford, and developed a curriculum as apolitical and narrowly professional as possible. He did not object to terminal "elementary" (distinguished from the elite "primary") schools for the masses, but these were underfunded and of poor quality in any case.

Cromer squelched Egyptian demands for a university, recommending as a model instead the Muhammadan Anglo-Oriental College (Aligarh University since 1920), founded in India in 1875 by Sayyid Aḥmad Khān. Modeled on the Oxbridge colleges, and with an English headmaster, it turned out officials, lawyers, and teachers—presumably loyal servants of the British Raj. [*See* Aligarh.]

Afraid that the *ʿulamāʾ* might lead mass protests, colonial rulers often left the *madrasah*s alone, starved for funds, overshadowed by state schools, and with dwindling prospects for their graduates. Cromer halfheartedly supported Muḥammad ʿAbduh's effort to reform al-Azhar, but abandoned him when the *ʿulamāʾ* and the palace resisted. In India, a new Azhar-like college at Deoband, which offered a traditional religious education, received no state support.

The colonial age was golden for missionary and minority community schools. Banned from proselytizing Muslims, Catholic and Protestant missionaries either tried to convert Jews and Eastern Christians or emphasized a humanitarian mission of medicine and schools for all. The American University of Beirut (the former Syrian Protestant College), Beirut's Université Saint-Joseph, and Boğaziçi University (formerly Robert College) of Istanbul are legacies of the missionary age. The missionaries also led the way in education for girls, with the first state girls' schools following in Istanbul, Cairo, and Tehran in 1858, 1873, and 1897/98, respectively.

Phase Four: Post-Independence Educational Unification and Expansion. Reacting against colonial policies, newly independent states moved to unify their educational systems by subordinating missionary, minority, and Islamic schools to state control. In Turkey, Mustafa Kemal Atatürk forced national curricula on foreign and minority schools in the 1920s, and Reza Shah nationalized primary and secondary schools in Iran in the 1930s. Syria closed French schools in 1945 during the final struggle for independence. Egypt finally consolidated control over missionary and minority schools as the British left in the 1950s. Exceptionally, the American University in Cairo eluded nationalization (Nasser's daughter and Hosni Mubarak's wife were among its students), as did foreign and communal schools in decentralized Lebanon. Robert College was nationalized and renamed Boğaziçi University.

As for the Islamic schools, Turkey and the Soviet Union simply abolished them. The closing of Istanbul University's faculty of theology (the former Medrese Süleymaniye) in 1933 left Turkey without higher Islamic education until Ankara University added a faculty of theology in 1949. Iranian *madrasah*s survived the Pahlavi regime, but the Qur'ān schools did not. In 1961 Nasser forced al-Azhar into a state university mold, adding colleges of medicine, engineering, and commerce and even a women's college. Indonesia, more diverse culturally, tolerated private Islamic schools and universities alongside its State Islamic Religious Institutes, which trained judges and teachers.

Postindependence Syria switched to Arabic as the language of its medical school, but often vested interests and the need for Western languages as a means of keeping up with world science prevailed over nationalist pressures. In linguistically fragmented India and Nigeria, the English of much advanced schooling unifies the elite but hinders mass access to higher education.

Nationalism, populism, and socialism put free, compulsory, universal schooling on every independent state's agenda, but universality is still an elusive goal. In the 1920s Turkey made all levels of education free, and Iran decreed that only the better-off would have to pay. Egypt made primary school free in 1943—a step toward unification with the inferior "elementary" schools; secondary and higher education became free in 1950 and 1961. Even without questions of quality, the literacy and enrollment rates in Table 1 show the distance yet to be traveled. The gap between male and female enrollments is also a problem: in 1980, 76 percent of Egyptian males were enrolled compared to 63 percent of females, with 78 percent to 56 percent in Turkey, and 95 percent to 55 percent in Iraq.

As Table 1 shows, the Ottomans founded Darülfünun (Istanbul University) in 1900. British-dominated Egypt managed only a small private university in 1908, and had to wait until 1925 for a state university. Tehran followed in 1934. Women entered state higher education in the 1910s in Turkey, 1928 in Egypt, and 1935 in Iran. The Syrian University dates from the French era, the University of Indonesia from the last years of Dutch rule. Gordon Memorial College evolved into the University of Khartoum (1956). In the rush of independence in the 1950s and 1960s, a university seemed almost as important symbolically as a flag.

An interval of some years usually followed before a second state university was founded, with rapid proliferation thereafter in the more populous countries. Ballooning primary and secondary enrollments inexorably increased demand. Quantity overwhelmed quality, financing faltered, standards plunged, and graduates scrambled for government jobs. Educational specialties bore little relation to the job market, and vocational education languished. Iran and Turkey each had twenty-nine universities by 1992; Egypt, with a comparable but more concentrated population and fewer resources, had thirteen. Turkey pioneered adult education programs in the 1920s, and since the 1960s open universities have become popular.

Phase Five: The Challenge of Islamization. Israel's defeat of the Arabs in 1967, the oil price boom following the 1973 War, and Iran's Islamic Revolution (1979) all contributed to the Islamist revival. Though differing

Table 1. *Data on Universities, Literacy, and Enrollment Rates*

Country	First State University	Second State University	No. of State and Private Universities, 1992	Percent Literate, 1990	Percent Enrolled in School, 1990
Turkey	1900	1937	29	81	95
Iran	1934	1947	29	54	
Egypt	1925	1942	13	44	
Syria	1923	1960	4	64	94
Lebanon	1951	none	5	75 (1991)	93 (1991)
Iraq	1957	1963	8	60 (1991)	
Jordan (and West Bank)	1962	1975	6	71 (1989)	
Libya	1955	1973	5	60 (1989)	90 (1989)
Algeria	1909	1965	10	52 (1991)	94 (1991)
Tunisia	1961	1988	5	62	85
Morocco	1959	1963	7	35 (1985)	
Saudi Arabia	1961	1962	7	62	
Kuwait	1966	none	1	71 (1989)	
UAE	1976	none	1	68	
Oman	1986	none	1	20 (1989)	80 (1989)
Yemen	1970	1975 (Aden)	2	38	59
Sudan	1956	1965	7	27 (1991)	50 (1991)
Somalia	1969	none	1	24	50
Nigeria	1960	1961	29	51 (1991)	42 (1991)
Ghana	1961	1961	3	60 (1991)	
Senegal	1957	1990	2	10 (1988)	48 (1988)
Afghanistan	1947	1962	4	29	
Pakistan	1882	1947	22	35 (1991)	
Bangladesh	1921	1953	7	35 (1991)	24 (1991)
India	1857	1857	143	48 (1991)	
Malaysia	1949	1969	7	80 (1989)	96 (1989)
Indonesia	1947	1947	60	85	84

Sources: *The World of Learning 1993* (London, 1992); *The World Almanac and Book of Facts 1993* (New York, 1992). Dates of opening preferred over dates of founding decrees, and dates when acquired university status over founding dates of component colleges or schools. Enrollment ratios are either general or for primary school age only.

widely on specifics, Islamists see current regimes as morally bankrupt and reformed schools as a means of moving toward an ideal Islamic society.

The Islamic Republic of Iran provides the fullest example of a regime's attempt to islamize its educational institutions. Although the Free Islamic University and other new institutions were founded after the revolution, the main task was the overhaul of existing institutions. With minor exceptions, the universities were closed from 1980 to 1983. Professors and school teachers presumed to be enemies of the revolution were fired, and many fled abroad. When the universities reopened, ideological tests were used to screen student applicants and professors. Several universities were renamed for religious leaders. Coeducation at all levels disappeared, and "Islamic dress" became mandatory for females. Required religious courses were emphasized, and there was an attempt to introduce Islamic perspectives into every field of study. With the *ʿulamāʾ* controlling the state, the neglected *madrasahs*—and especially Ayatollah Khomeini's Fayẓīyah Madrasah in Qom—took on a new prominence.

Revolutionary upheaval, war, economic crisis, and runaway population growth inevitably forced the revolutionary regime into pragmatic compromises. To some purists' dismay, English retained a strong place in the curriculum. Now the justification was not only its importance for science and technology, but also its utility in exporting the revolution and making converts to Islam. Acute shortages of teachers, funds, school buildings, and ideologically correct textbooks prompted appeals for emigrés to return, the relaxation of ideological tests, and even the reopening of private schools.

Islamists from Morocco to Indonesia are demanding educational changes similar to Iran's. Since 1980, universities with "Islamic" in their names have opened in Iran, Afghanistan, Pakistan, Bangladesh, Malaysia, and Niger. Very different Islamist regimes in Iran, Pakistan, the Sudan, and Saudi Arabia vie with each other for religious legitimacy. Never having experienced colonialism or coeducation, and fortified by oil wealth and Wahhābī ideology, the Saudis proclaim their brand of Islamism as a model, but their Islamist detractors are unconvinced. In educational institutions and elsewhere, regimes that inherited more complex legacies of indigenous reform, colonial rule, and postindependence nationalism and socialism balance uneasily today between cooption and repression of Islamist challengers.

[*See also* Azhar, al-; International Islamic University at Islamabad; International Islamic University at Kuala Lumpur; Madrasah; Universities; Zaytūnah.]

BIBLIOGRAPHY

Colonna, Fanny. *Instituteurs algériens, 1883–1939*. Paris, 1975. Far broader insights into Algerian education than the specialized title suggests.

Dodge, Bayard. *The American University of Beirut*. Beirut, 1958. Concise survey by a former president of the institution.

Eccel, A. Chris. *Egypt, Islam, and Social Change: Al-Azhar in Conflict and Accommodation*. Berlin, 1984. A mine of information and stimulating interpretation. Despite organizational problems and excessive sociological jargon, the fundamental work in English on al-Azhar.

Findley, Carter V. "Knowledge and Education in the Modern Middle East: A Comparative View." In *The Modern Economic and Social History of the Middle East in Its World Context*, edited by Georges Sabagh, pp. 130–154. Cambridge, 1989. Thoughtful, concise overview.

Heyworth-Dunne, James. *Introduction to the History of Education in Modern Egypt* (1939). London, 1968. Unsurpassed in English on Egyptian education up to the British occupation of 1882.

Ḥusayn, Ṭāhā. *The Stream of Days: A Student at the Azhar*. Translated by Hilary Wayment. 2d ed. London, 1948. Colorful, hostile view of traditional Islamic education by a famous blind writer and reformer.

Lelyveld, David. *Aligarh's First Generation: Muslim Solidarity in British India*. Princeton, 1978.

Matthews, Roderic D., and Matta Akrawi. *Education in Arab Countries of the Near East*. Washington, D.C., 1949. Lacking in historical depth, but still useful for the state of education in Egypt, Syria, Lebanon, Iraq, Transjordan, and Palestine in the 1940s.

Menashri, David. *Education and the Making of Modern Iran*. Ithaca, N.Y., 1992. By far the most thoroughly researched and comprehensive book in English on Iranian education.

Misnad, Sheikha al-. *The Development of Modern Education in the Gulf*. London, 1985. Focuses on Kuwait, Bahrain, and Qatar, and especially useful on the issue of women's education.

Murphy, Lawrence R. *The American University in Cairo, 1919–1987*. Cairo, 1987. Official history.

Qubain, Fahim. *Education and Science in the Arab World*. Baltimore, 1966.

Reid, Donald Malcolm. *Cairo University and the Making of Modern Egypt*. Cambridge, 1990. Education set in social and political context. Also useful for pre-university education.

Szyliowicz, Joseph S. *Education and Modernization in the Middle East*. Ithaca, N.Y., 1973. Historical overview, with emphasis on Turkey, Iran, and Egypt.

Thomas, R. Murray. *A Chronicle of Indonesian Higher Education*. Singapore, 1973.

Tibawi, A. L. *Islamic Education: Its Traditions and Modernization into the Arab National Systems*. London, 1972. Survey by a veteran Palestinian educator.

Waardenburg, Jean-Jacques. *Les universités dans le monde arab actuel*. 2 vols. Paris, 1966. Packed with valuable statistics.

The World of Learning, 1993. London, 1993. Europa Publications' indispensable annual reference volume listing institutions of higher learning.

Donald Malcolm Reid

Educational Methods

Methods are a critical element in realizing the goals of any educational enterprise. They link teachers, students, and content. Curricula may be carefully designed to achieve particular ends, but unless appropriate instructional methods are utilized, the subject matter will not be communicated effectively to the students, the anticipated learning will not take place, and the educational goals will not be achieved. Like all aspects of education, methods are deeply influenced by cultural environments and traditions; thus it is appropriate to consider the educational methods used in traditional Islamic societies.

Inheritance from the Past. Given the central role of the Qur'ān in Islamic civilization, it is natural that Islamic education revolved around the sacred book considered to be the basis of all knowledge. From the time a child began school at the age of six or seven, his major preoccupation was to memorize the Qur'ān as perfectly as possible. The main technique was repetition, in which students learned by imitating the teacher. They would repeat a section of the Qur'ān until it had been committed completely and accurately to memory and then proceed to the next section. The teacher would recite the verse and the students would chant it after him; to aid memorization students would utilize such techniques as rocking back and forth while chanting. The goal of education was to produce students who were good Muslims—that is, students who could recite the Qur'ān accurately; understanding it was not a primary goal.

At the higher levels the focus was also on rote learning, although specific texts and commentaries were studied intensively. The teacher would often dictate passages from a work and then deliver a lecture interpreting them. Students took notes, which they would seek to memorize in order to demonstrate that they had recorded the lesson accurately. Two techniques facilitated the process of committing large quantities of material to memory. First, lessons were repeated aloud until the material was memorized; silent reading was frowned on. Second, many important texts were rewritten in verse form.

The ultimate goal was not to acquire the ability to repeat a text, but to understand it. Students were expected to acquire knowledge first through rote learning but then to learn how to apply what they had memorized creatively to particular issues. Thus students were presumed to learn the argumentative techniques that the authors of the texts had employed. Such methods as discussions and disputations were used in teaching, but these followed well-established patterns and focused on issues that had been debated for generations. At its best this approach produced sharply honed minds, but learning remained a closed process into which new ideas and concepts could not easily be introduced.

Teachers possessed great authority. The Qur'ān gave them the right to administer corporal punishment whenever necessary, and use of the rod was widely regarded as essential if children were to develop suitable character. At the more advanced levels education was highly personalized, because the system was based on the view that knowledge was acquired through contact with learned individuals. A student would select a master and develop a close personal and intellectual relationship with him. The choice of a teacher was usually the single most important decision that a student could make, for one's career was commonly determined by the mentor's reputation. The teacher was responsible for the moral as well as the intellectual development of the student. A psychological distance always remained between them, however, and teachers could and often did punish their disciples severely.

Over time education became more institutionalized, especially at the higher levels, where various kinds of colleges were established; these, however, retained the personal, informal character of earlier institutions. Egypt's famous al-Azhar, for example, possessed no regular schedule, entrance requirements, formal standards, required courses, examinations, or sharp distinction between faculty and students—a teacher in one course could be a student in another.

Some early Arab scholars who studied educational processes advocated the use of different methods and arrangements, especially at the higher levels, but their treatises had only limited impact. The prevailing methods effectively socialized large populations into Islamic beliefs, values, and practices, and Qur'ānic schools using these methods continued to thrive and are today to be found in large numbers throughout the Islamic world.

Creation of Modern Schools. The establishment of modern schools in the nineteenth century did not produce any dramatic change in teaching methods. Two major factors account for this continuity. First, much Western education of the time was also characterized by strict discipline and memorization. Second, the Western powers had no interest in establishing schools that would prepare students to think independently and creatively, especially in the colonies. They developed curricula that were similar to those at home and expected students to master a body of knowledge that would prepare them to be loyal, obedient administrators. The cultivation of intelligence, sensitivity, and awareness was often rigidly suppressed, in Egypt under Lord Cromer. Ministries of education permitted no deviation from strict rules and regulations. A harsh examination system that determined the student's educational position and future prospects reinforced the emphasis on rote learning; students strained to memorize every word in their notebooks in order to pass the dreaded examination that would permit them to continue their academic training.

Even in states that retained their independence, Western influences did not transform traditional patterns. At first large numbers of Europeans were hired to teach in reformist schools, but this was an inefficient arrangement because their lectures had to be translated into the local language. To meet the need for native teachers the Ottomans founded the Darülmuallim in 1848. Its graduates and those of the other teacher-training colleges subsequently opened throughout the region replaced the Europeans, but teaching methods retained their traditional character for two reasons. First, these schools were based on nineteenth-century European models in which lectures and memorization were the norm. Second, since most teachers and students in the new schools were graduates of the religious schools, they tended to maintain traditional patterns.

The major difference between the traditional schools such as al-Azhar and the modern schools, therefore, lay not so much in the methods or in the behavior of teachers but in the bureaucratization and formalization of schooling and in the kinds of knowledge that the new curricula embodied. Although the methods of the latter are usually labeled "Islamic," they were in many ways consonant with Western practices and heavily influenced by the interests and goals of the colonizing power.

Contemporary Methods. The achievement of independence brought little change to these patterns; the character of education remained the same—highly centralized and oriented toward passing examinations—although its size expanded rapidly to meet the pent-up demand for modern schooling. As a result, traditional patterns were reinforced as exploding enrollments at all levels created an ever greater demand for qualified, motivated teachers that could not be met.

Most emerging states had to utilize whatever teaching resources were available, regardless of their qualifications. Hence many teachers, especially at the primary level, have only a secondary education and are poorly prepared in subject matter and teaching methods. Teachers at the secondary level are better trained; most are graduates of teacher-training institutes. They tend to be familiar with the subject matter but usually know little about how to teach effectively, because teacher training remains weak and formalistic. Curricula in the institutes stress theory and abstract subjects; there is little concern with practical preparation or with teaching general and specialized methods of instruction. Moreover, few in-service training programs are available, and so teachers tend to stagnate and to remain at a fixed level of professional development. They remember the body of knowledge that they memorized in school and teach it in the same way until they retire. Most teachers carry out their tasks mechanically and tend to be authoritarian, formalistic, and apathetic, adhering closely to the textual materials, which they either dictate or hand out in condensed form. They have little incentive for innovation, and a national corps of inspectors ensures that the ministry's rules and regulations are scrupulously followed.

Furthermore, teachers tend to regard themselves as authority figures rather than as partners in a learning experience. Students are not expected to ask questions, and certainly not to challenge a teacher's knowledge and authority by raising different points; rather, they are expected to memorize their notes as thoroughly as possible in order to pass the all-important examinations. Even when a teacher assigns a topic for research (a rare event), students are not expected to take the initiative but rather to work within prescribed boundaries by consulting only the sources suggested by the teacher.

When called on to recite or to answer a question, the good student does not present his own ideas but demonstrates his prowess by parroting the proper answer as it appeared, word for word, in the textbook or in the lecture. Often reciters stand at attention while the rest of the class sits quietly. Such behavior is consonant with a cultural environment that emphasizes hierarchy and conformity. Teachers are not expected to be motivators or to prepare students to be creative problem-solvers but to maintain discipline and to socialize students into traditional values of respect for authority and obedience.

Resource constraints further limit the possibility of applying more student-centered methods. The available textbooks are of poor quality; most are merely unadapted translations of Western texts or works produced by authors without any practical experience, and these do little to excite the imagination of the student. Audiovisual materials and other teaching aids are rarely available. Library resources too are very limited, and what is available is usually tightly controlled by librarians who are often legally accountable for each book.

These generalizations apply not only across countries but across subject areas—even those such as science, foreign languages, and vocational training that have received special attention because of their significance for the achievement of national developmental goals. Science continues to be taught in a formalistic manner. Schools at all levels lack adequate laboratory facilities, and what is available is often not utilized properly. Equipment is expensive and scarce, and teachers are usually held personally responsible for every item, so that breakage becomes a catastrophe that the teacher seeks to avoid at any cost. Instead of allowing students to engage in practical work, to solve problems for themselves, the teacher demonstrates his ability by carrying out experiments while the students watch. Even though simple homemade devices can be very effective in science courses, few teachers possess the knowledge or motivation to develop and utilize them.

Foreign-language instruction is another critical area where poor results are commonplace. In most countries every student is required to study at least one foreign language, but few students acquire fluency. Many of the instructors possess only an imperfect knowledge of the language they are teaching. Furthermore, important advances in instructional methods are very rarely encountered in textbooks, teacher manuals, or classrooms.

Vocational and technical education has also been emphasized everywhere, but once again poor teaching methods limit its potential contribution to national development. Vocational schools do not prepare students adequately for industrial occupations because of inadequate facilities and curricula and the difficulty of finding and retaining staff with industrial knowledge. The teaching is theoretical rather than practical, memorization is commonplace, and students spend little if any time working with machinery and tools and acquiring hands-on experience.

Higher Education. Although higher education has been favored by all Islamic states, in this area too the rapid expansion of enrollments has greatly outpaced the available human and physical resources. The result has been that in almost every college facilities are stretched to their utmost, many faculty members are not highly qualified, and student-teacher ratios are too high. Education has become a mass-production process with little interaction between student and teacher. Universities in the richer Arab countries utilize temporary faculty from other states, but this solution creates a divided faculty, many of whom have little interest in the institution or its students.

The drop in quality is evident in all fields, but some—notably the humanities, the arts, and the social sciences—have suffered more than others because enrollments there can be expanded at low cost. To increase the number of students in scientific courses entails expenditures for equipment and the employment of more specialists, whereas in the humanities and social sciences such expenditures can be neglected; the same professor is simply expected to lecture to three or four times as many students as before.

Partly because of the overcrowding that characterizes most universities, mass lectures without questions or discussion have become the common teaching method. Furthermore, these lectures may consist largely of repetitions from notes taken years earlier. Even committed scholars rely on mass lectures. They have few options when facing hundreds or even thousands of poorly prepared students who believe education is synonymous with memorization. In some cases, students come to the university without even the ability to take notes, so faculty members have been known to dictate resumes of their courses for the students to memorize. Under these circumstances there is obviously very limited opportunity for student-faculty interaction or for research activities.

The same patterns severely limit the effectiveness of graduate training. In many countries students pursuing advanced degrees take little formal coursework. They are expected to work independently and to carry out research under the guidance of a senior faculty member. Although this method can produce fine scholars, this seldom happens because of limited student-faculty interaction, resource limitations, and the lack of academic freedom. Thus a vicious cycle is perpetuated.

Prospects for the Future. Throughout the Islamic world one can find exceptions to this sorry state of affairs. There are many teachers who are committed to their students and attempt to make schooling an exciting and stimulating experience. Unfortunately, they are found primarily in the elite schools of urban centers, and even there they struggle against great handicaps. The more remote the area, the worse the facilities and the more traditional the teaching styles.

The problem and its implications are widely recognized. The use of modern teaching methods is usually precluded by poor training, large classes, scarce resources, limited support, high degrees of centralization, rigid examination systems, low morale, and a traditional environment. There is little incentive or opportunity to engage in meaningful teaching or to change the pattern of teacher dominance. Even Turkey, where democratic values prevail, has found it difficult to create a different environment in its schools.

The need to change this situation is by now generally accepted. Many Muslim scholars argue that existing teaching methods are not consonant with a real Qur'ānic approach to education, and pedagogues point out that these patterns do not promote the intellectual and moral development of young people or prepare them to function in modern societies. Nonetheless, the criterion of good teaching remains the number of students who successfully pass the national examinations, the primary purpose of which is to identify those (usually of elite background) who are qualified for further schooling; the majority receive only an elementary education, and the number of functional illiterates remains high.

Many governments are seeking ways to transform these patterns. They accept the need to upgrade teaching staffs, modernize curricula, and improve facilities. Many are turning to modern technologies to improve educational practices. Turkey, for example, has created an "Open University" in which classes are conducted via television. Large numbers of teachers are receiving instruction in subject matter and pedagogical techniques, and it is hoped that thousands of students will be positively affected. Computers are also being emphasized in many countries.

It remains to be seen, however, whether these technologies will contribute to the transformation that is required, or whether they will simply be integrated into the existing educational culture and suffer the fate of other reform projects. Such technologies can play a useful role, but only if a new orientation toward education is accepted within a society. In other words, quality must replace quantity as the major criterion for educational policymakers; political elites must recognize that development requires creative, independent, resourceful citizens capable of critical reasoning and moral judgment, and they must be willing to allocate the necessary resources to create the educational systems that produce such citizens.

BIBLIOGRAPHY

ʿAbd Allāh, ʿAbd al-Raḥmān Ṣāliḥ. *Educational Theory: A Qur'anic Outlook*. Makkah (Mecca), Saudi Arabia, 1982.

Berkey, Jonathan P. *The Transmission of Knowledge in Medieval Cairo*. Princeton, 1992.

Eickelman, Dale F. *Knowledge and Power in Morocco*. Princeton, 1985.

Massialis, Byron G., and Samir Ahmed Jarrar. *Education in the Arab World*. New York, 1983.

Massialis, Byron G., and Samir Ahmed Jarrar. *Arab Education in Transition*. New York, 1991.

Mottahedeh, Roy P. *The Mantle of the Prophet*. New York, 1985.

Szyliowicz, Joseph S. *Education and Modernization in the Middle East*. Ithaca, N.Y., 1973.

Za'rour, George I. "Universities in Arab Countries." PRE Working Paper, no. 62, 1988. Washington, D.C.: World Bank.

JOSEPH S. SZYLIOWICZ

Educational Reform

An understanding of the dynamic relationship among political, social, and educational changes is central to the determination of the nature of educational reform in the Muslim world during the nineteenth and twentieth centuries. Changes in curricular and instructional policies and their implications for intellectual and cultural development are discussed in relation to four major issues.

The Muslim world initially rejected as irrelevant changes introduced from Europe in the early nineteenth century. Changes in technical, military, and vocational training dictated by local rulers and elites did not conform to the traditional educational practices that were the remnants of Islamic education. Comparing these practices with recent changes runs the risk of overstating where and how educational reform has taken place.

Available literature indicates that old practices were not reformed and changes resulted in no significant attitudinal or cultural development. Setting the European utilitarian and the Muslim altruistic modes against each other resulted in centralized state-controlled educational institutions and a complete departure from Islamic education.

The intellectual stagnation that characterized the Muslim world since the early fourteenth century remained despite mass and compulsory schooling in the postcolonial era. Recent reports indicate school and teacher shortages, low educational quality, lack of planning and of curricular and instructional compatibility, and disparity in access to and completion of all types and levels of education between the sexes, between rich and poor, and between rural and urban populations.

Preservation of Islamic Culture. The Islamic world's reaction to Western-introduced changes in education has lacked the intellectual dynamics that once marked its educational system, in which formal and informal teaching and learning took place based on the accomplishments and needs of teachers and pupils. Seyyed Hossein Nasr (1987) discusses the oral transmission that produced some highly knowledgeable, though illiterate, Muslims. Fazlur Rahman (1982) does not mention either these distinctive characteristics or such remaining institutions as the *kuttāb* (place of primary and Qur'ānic education), the *ḥalaqah,* the *majlis* (study circle in a mosque or private home) and the *madrasah* (center of secondary and higher learning). In the Islamic world,

Western educational practices did not produce the same economic, intellectual, and social development that they did in western Europe. Adnan Badran (1989) reports a lacks of cohesion in educational planning, which is inhibited by socioeconomic, technical, or cultural factors. Educational objectives are ambiguous; although the philosophy claims to be rooted in the ideals of Islam, the pedagogical strategies contain both modern methodologies and political, nationalistic rhetoric. The inconclusive, fragmented, and contradictory literature, in both English and Arabic, indicates that educational transformation is an unstable process.

No full account of curricular reform is available despite the many reports on changes in the instructional process and the increased number of schools, universities, and student enrollment. Reports by Albert Hourani (1981 and 1983), Jesse T. Jones (*Education in East Africa*, New York, 1970), UNESCO (1961), and others largely praise the progress of the "reformed and modernized" education system. Recent accounts, however, such as Nasr's, question such conclusions that confuse traditional Islamic reform with fundamentalism and modernity with nationalism. Others, like Stephen P. Heyneman (1971), Ali Mazrui (*The Africans: A Triple Heritage*, Boston and Toronto, 1986), and A. L. Tibawi (1972) expose conflicting purposes and incoherent systems resulting from colonial and missionary educational changes and emphasize problems of imported development strategies and personnel.

These changes were rejected by the local peoples and religious leaders who were suspicious of any new type of formal education, although foreign cultural practices had been integrated during the eighth and ninth centuries. They considered the European educational changes irrelevant, alien, and expressions of colonial exploitation and missionary attempts to christianize the population. These views were not baseless, as missionary education, foreign private, and colonial government-supported school systems attest (*British Parliamentary Records* vol. 137 [1905]).

Changes instituted by the Ottoman ruler Sultan Selim III (r. 1789–1807), considered in the traditional literature on modernization as the precursor to reform, were viewed by Stanford J. Shaw ("Some Aspects of the Aims and Achievements of the Nineteenth-Century Ottoman Reformers" in *Beginnings of Modernization in the Middle East: The Nineteenth Century*, edited by W. R. Polk and R. L. Chambers [Chicago and London, 1968], pp. 29–39) as traditional reforms; old elements remained even when they were superseded. The result was the development of a heavy, complicated, and paralyzing hierarchy that stifled Ottoman educational development.

Sultan Mahmud II's (r. 1808–1839) Tanzimat reform ideology is another example of Ottoman reaction to the military advancement of the French as early as 1789. The impact of this regimented, centralized system on modern bureaucracy in the Muslim world is apparent even now, particularly in the civil service systems: personnel affairs, education, and justice.

Educational objectives shifted from an emphasis on discipline for both children and adults (Eickelman, 1985) to a formalization of the relationship of citizens to the state to meet its economic and political interests. Local governors' policies, led by an eagerness to acquire European technologies to strengthen and modernize the military, weakened the *kuttāb*s and *madrasah*s, often distributing their *waqf* (endowment) among the ruling class and missionary societies to establish private schools. J. Heyworth-Dunne (*An Introduction to the History of Education in Modern Egypt*, new impression [London, 1968]) suggests that the Egyptian Mamlūk Muḥammad ʿAlī's (r. 1806–1841) imposed system is the key to understanding why Egypt's present system is so defective and poorly adapted to the country. Although he established a military school (1816), technical and engineering schools and colleges, and a medical school (1827), they were for men only and staffed by European Christians. He also sent large student missions, all men mainly of ruling and elite families, to study in Europe in 1826. In these European schools, the men were forced to study Turkish, Italian, French, and English. Even when translations were available to aid in the instruction, comprehension problems were not overcome because the men were unprepared. The shortcomings of this instructional system also stemmed, in part, from its neglect of women's education, particularly at the secondary level, and training of teachers for the elementary and the preparatory schools. But, most of all, the system was not coordinated with the traditional practices and appeared to operate as a rival or even as a substitute. New subject matters were divorced from the Qur'ānic study and the sciences of antiquity such as astronomy, geography, and medicine. Above all, Tibawi asserts, the system had little or no direct intellectual purpose; it existed primarily to train the local people to serve colonial and local government interests.

Changing Function of Education. Despite its lack of vitality after the fifteenth century, Lillian Sanderson points out in "Education and Administrative Control in Colonial Sudan and Northern Nigeria" (*African Affairs* 74 [October 1975]: 427–441) that Islamic education achieved its goals: to pass on the customs of the adult community, to teach children the knowledge and skills of the culture that they needed to function effectively, and to instill in them beliefs about the relationship between the seen and the unseen in the universe.

What remained of the Islamic education system became peripheral, reserved for the underprivileged, such as girls and poor rural and urban masses. Primary Islamic education, for example, came to a standstill when Turkish replaced its main language, Arabic, as the medium of instruction in most government schools, as did colonial languages in private schools. Changes, as Gregory Starrett has stated, "transformed people's ideas about religion" and its importance to community development by removing the teaching of Islam as the basis of character formation and making it a new subject called "Religion," without primary status in the curriculum ("Appropriating the Kuttab: The Functionalization of Mass Religious Instruction in Egypt, 1882–1952," paper presented at the Middle East Studies Association Annual Conference, Washington, D.C., 1991).

Changes introduced in the nineteenth century did not meet Islamic cultural needs. The government schools were agents of the colonial policy to control Muslim rulers, administrative management, and agricultural productivity. As described by Leila Ahmad, when enrollments grew, girls were denied places in classrooms and tuition was instituted in secondary schools, making girls' education of low priority (*Women and Gender in Islam*, New Haven and London, 1992).

The English colonial system penetrated the Indian subcontinent, the majority of the Middle East, and many African nations, even though it claimed that it did not interfere in internal affairs (Mazrui). The French colonial system in North and West Africa and in Syria and Lebanon, as W. Bryant Mumford suggests, assimilated the existing system to the point of annihilating it (*Africans Learn to Be French,* New York, 1970). It contributed further to diverting the rural system from traditional Islamic education to superstitious social customs, dogmatic and nationalistic creeds, and passive Ṣūfī orders. And instead of strengthening institutions of higher learning, such as the oldest, the 1,100-year-old al-Qarawīyīn in Fez, Morocco, the colonial government dismantled many old centers.

Similar movements took place in other regions, with varying degrees of interaction with European expatriates and different degrees of emphasis on traditional or modern elements in education depending on the colonizers' policy and the extent of their penetration of native cultures.

Comparing the Two Schemes of Education. A comparison of teaching in the *kuttāb* and the *madrasah* to the colonizers' technical, military, and vocational training or the missionaries' book knowledge is not an accurate indicator of educational reform. What is obvious, however, is that educational practices have changed from informal family-based, formal teacher-centered, and informal decentralized *tarbiyah* (character and intellectual development) to either formal missionary-controlled or state-centralized schooling.

The function of teaching was primarily Qur'ānic *talqīn* (acquisition and dissemination of meaning and spirit), instilling community values while combating illiteracy. Other types of *kuttāb* taught some knowledge of *akhbār* (history), *ḥisāb* (simple arithmetic and reckoning), and elementary Arabic *naḥw* (grammar), reading, and writing. The function of the *madrasah* was to complement the objectives of both *kuttāb*s, as well as the *ḥalaqah*'s advanced *ʿulūm al-Qur'ān* (Qur'ānic sciences), *ʿulūm al-ḥadīth* (sciences of the Prophetic tradition), and their ancillary sciences of Arabic *naḥw* and *adab* (literature). Thus, *ḥikmah* (wisdom), *kalām* (philosophy/theology), *manṭiq* (logic), *ʿilm al-nujūm* (astronomy), music, and *ʿilm al-ṭibb* (medicine) were part of the curriculum even early in the nineteenth century (Ali, 1983). Government and missionary schools, meanwhile, sought to implant European secular and Christian values of agrarian, office, and class bureaucracy (Bennabi, 1969).

Although printed textbooks and notebooks have replaced the *murabbī*'s (teacher or guide) scripted notes and the *lawḥ* (tablet) in the urban schools particularly, book and lecture instruction and memorization of factual information continue to prevail. But they lack the essence of the transmitted oral tradition.

A pupil who used to study under one teacher with whom she or he had a relationship and moved from one subject to the next after showing mastery through oral discussion or by tutoring younger students is now instructed on a mass scale, segregated by sex, and taught different subjects in a school day. The idea of special girls' schools was introduced by the Catholic missionaries. In these schools girls were taught embroidery, home economics, domestic skills, and nursing; they also read the Bible. Boys were taught office skills, agricultural, military, and vocational trades, and some *fiqh* (jurisprudence) to serve government needs. Pupils in these schools, according to M. H. Khan, are tested in material that is irrelevant to their culture so they can be promoted to the next level taught by a new teacher (*History of Muslim Education, vol. 2, 1751–1854 A.D.*, Karachi, 1973). The concept of *tarbiyah* has been reduced to passing on some skills and information to qualify for a job.

These two modes of instruction represent a departure from the Islamic perspective that was instrumental in the evolution of the Islamic civilization. Rahman notes that intellectual stagnation occurred during the thirteenth and fourteenth centuries, when manuals and commentaries dominated, and suggests that the educational process had virtually ceased to function by the late 1500s when the Andalusian Islamic community was dismantled. Eickelman, however, sees the mnemonic devices of Islamic education as a continuation of the socialization process even during and after the colonial period when systems of mass and compulsory schooling were legislated.

The Islamic system was abandoned when the state and colonial governments made decisions for the local peoples, and Muslims lost their scholarly and intellectual initiative. With the exception of scattered individual scholars and artisans during the sixteenth, seventeenth, and eighteenth centuries that Nasr points out, Islamic educational practices fell into abeyance. Attempts to expound the positive attitude of Islam toward science by those Rahman calls "pre-modernist reformers"—Sir Sayyid Aḥmad Khān (1817–1898) and Syed Ameer Ali (d. 1928) of India, Namık Kemal (1840–1888) of Turkey, Jamāl al-Dīn al-Afghānī (1839–1897) and Muḥammad ʿAbduh (1845–1905) of Egypt—resulted instead in complete separation of "Islamic" and "non-Islamic" knowledge. The strategies of nationalist elites such as Maʿrūf al-Raṣāfī (1877–1945) of Iraq, attest to differences in attitude, especially toward the implications of modern science for the traditional worldview and faith. These different attitudes and strategies created further confusion as to how to reintroduce science and technology in the culture. As Bennabi notes, the aspirations of some elites and rulers were not those of the community or the masses, but those of the colonials, missionaries, and romantic Orientalists.

The practical implications of these differences in attitude and of alienated aspirations may be seen in the varied and conflicting responses to modernization and in the present disparity between the ideal and the reality of the Muslim world, particularly in education. Sir Sayyid's call in 1860 for the reinterpretation of the Qur'ān in light of modern experience, for example, failed because his views were not based on the Islamic perspective. He was not able to implement them in the Aligarh Muslim University of India, which he created to integrate religious beliefs with a modern scientific outlook. Islamic education was reduced to religious education and was left to teachers who had little training or support. Other reform ideas, put forth by those who had studied in Europe, had a similar negative results. Though these ideas were supported by elites and rulers, they were opposed by orthodox community leaders who feared they would contaminate the beliefs of the people and were ignored by the masses as irrelevant and providing no practical solutions to the ailing educational practices.

Community Development and Educational Progress. The rival Muslim and European education plans were in place until the second quarter of the twentieth century, when turmoil was the common factor in the social, political, and educational systems until military and political independence from colonialism in the 1950s and 1960s. Elites (who were largely educated either in missionary schools and colleges, or in East and West European and American institutions), Bennabi adds, contributed further to this turmoil by adopting Western ideas of change as the only means for reform without considering the actual needs and the sociopsychological factors of the community.

Postcolonial changes, which almost uniformly used modern educational instructional schemes, also resulted in confusing outcomes. With minor variations in their level of success in achieving the objectives of the ruling class (introducing modern technology as a symbol of progress), the overall picture after almost fifteen years, as A. A. H. El-Koussy (*Survey of Educational Progress in the Arab States, 1960–1965*, Beirut, 1966) describes it, is still an aimless system with no evaluation system or overall direction. His description of the Arab world applies to other Muslim countries as well. Education authorities were working with enthusiasm, but they lacked planning and balance in educational development.

The general uncertainty of objectives prevailed with some exceptions. For example, the goal to return to regional languages (European languages became secondary to Arabic, Persian, or Urdu as the means of instruction in public schools) was achieved on a limited basis. This uncertainty is evident in African countries, especially those in North Africa (Abdelhamid Mansouri, "Algeria between Tradition and Modernity: The Question of language," Ph.D. diss., State University of New York at Albany, 1991), and in Asian countries, particularly in Pakistan where a full transition could not be effected (Taj Ali Koraishy, *How to Reform Educational System in Pakistan and Other Muslim Countries*, Gujranwala, 1972). With the emphasis on nationalistic sentiments, the restoration of Arabic—the language of the Qur'ān—for instruction became an ideal. Meanwhile, the use of regional languages for instruction meant that energy was directed to the translation of European textbooks instead of to writing new, native textbooks.

The rapid increase in the number of schools did not keep up with population growth or with the demand for education. High levels of illiteracy persist (UNESCO, 1990) and, notwithstanding arguments concerning the definition of literacy and the value of oral transmission, the levels and types of education available to women are still inferior to men's (Nagat El-Sanabary, 1992). Educational quality is sacrificed inadvertently in pursuit of universal schooling and mandatory elementary education because of the lack of human and other resources and of coherent regional planning and technical competency (Badran). Intellectual production, Bennabi (1959) laments, is hindered because Muslims value European products and wish to acquire them, without researching the ideas behind these products.

The nature of educational transformation varied among Muslim countries, reflecting on the development model adopted, the post-1969 Muslim world's economic and political polarization, and the role played by oil-rich countries and their international benefactors. For example, the Malaysian government accommodated secularism in its educational program between 1971 and 1980, M. Kamal Hassan (1981) reports, expanding facilities and opportunities for education in science, mathematics, and technology-oriented disciplines along with attempts to equip the young people of all races and both sexes with the knowledge and skills necessary to participate in developing the economy. The relation between tradition and change in the Malaysian context did not arise from the question of cultural change, in which women's place is used as the central discourse as in Saudi Arabia, Iran, and Pakistan. Instead, Muslim religious groups used new discourse to defend the encroachment of Western ideas. By emphasizing the morality question, epitomized in attire and sex segregation, particularly in higher education institutions, they have indirectly restricted intellectual role of women in the development process. Malaysian educational reform did not change the intellectual, attitudinal, and cultural development of the Muslim masses either. As similar movements are spreading in other Muslim communities from Indonesia to North America, one wonders whether there ever was an educational reform.

BIBLIOGRAPHY

General Works

Bennabi, Malek. *Mushkilat al-thaqāfah (The Problem of Educating)*. Arabic translation from the French original, *Le problème des étude*, by ʿAbd al-Ṣabūr Shāhīn. Beirut, 1969. *Islam in History and Society*. Translated from the French original, *Vocation de l'Islam*, by Asma Rashid. Islamabad, 1988. Cairo, 1959. Realistic analysis of the relationship between education and cultural development in the contemporary Muslim world by a native Algerian Muslim scholar.

Eickelman, Dale F. *Knowledge and Power in Morocco: The Education of a Twentieth-Century Notable*. Princeton, 1985. Unprecedented anthropological analysis of the power of knowledge in a Muslim society. Chapter 3 deserves special reading to internalize the Qur'ānic presence in a Muslim intellectual and social development.

Heyneman, Stephen P. *The Conflict over What is to Be Learned in Schools: A History of Curriculum Politics in Africa*. Syracuse, N.Y., 1971.

Hourani, Albert. *Arabic Thought in the Liberal Age, 1798–1939*. Cambridge, 1983. *The Emergence of the Modern Middle East*. Berkeley and Los Angeles, 1981. Considered by Western and Arabic Middle Eastern scholars as classical works on reform and modernization in the region.

Nasr, Seyyed Hossein. *Traditional Islam in the Modern World*. London and New York, 1987. Leading work in deciphering traditional Islam and its contrast to fundamentalism and modernism with respect to Western scholarship. Part 2, "Traditional Islam and Modernism," is particularly illuminating. The notes are rich with primary and secondary sources.

Rahman, Fazlur. *Islam and Modernity: Transformation of an Intellectual Tradition*. Chicago and London, 1982. Definitive work for understanding contemporary Islamic intellectualism as the essence of higher Islamic education, and the implications of the method of Qur'ānic interpretation to the development of the intellectual Muslim.

Tanguiane, Sema. *Literacy and Illiteracy in the World: Situation, Trends, and Prospects*. Paris, 1990.

Tibawi, A. L. *Islamic Education: Its Traditions and Modernizations into the Arab National Systems*. London, 1972. Insightful interpretive work on educational theory in Islam and the implications of the philosophy of modernism on educational systems in the region.

United Nations Educational, Scientific, and Cultural Organization (UNESCO). *Asia, Arab States; Africa: Education and Progress.* Paris, 1961.

Missionary and Colonial Sources

Labaree, Mrs. Benjamin W. "The Heart of the Mohammedan Woman." *Missionary Review of the World* 26.8 (August 1913): 578–582.

"Lebanon and Its Mission Schools." *Church Missionary Intelligencia* 19 (October 1869): 293–306.

Prothero, M. "Recent Educational Changes in India." *Asiatic Quarterly Review,* third series, 16, 31, 32 (July–October 1903): 292–299.

Regional Accounts

Ali, A. K. M. Ayyub. *History of Traditional Islamic Education in Bangladesh (Down to AD 1980).* Dhaka, 1983. Though reporting mainly on Bangladesh, the author presents a sequential development of Muslim education from Islam to 1980 that was very much in place in the entire Indian subcontinent.

Badran, Adnan, ed. *At the Crossroad: Education in the Middle East.* New York, 1989. Collection of essays dealing with various countries in the region, addressing many issues of contemporary education, with emphasis on the role of education in regional development and conflict resolution.

El-Sanabary, Nagat. *Education in the Arab Gulf States and the Arab World.* New York, 1992. Extensive bibliographical guide with 1,775 entries of books, articles, dissertations, and reports covering the period 1959–1989. Important reference source to other Arab countries, even though it covers mainly bibliography concerning the seven Arab Gulf States. The introduction is an especially valuable summary of topics covered in the volume, including Islamic education.

Hassan, M. Kamal. "Education and Family in Modernizing Malaysia." In *Changes and the Muslim World,* edited by Philip H. Stoddard, pp. 65–73. Syracuse, N.Y., 1981.

NIMAT HAFEZ BARAZANGI

The Islamization of Knowledge

Although the phrase "islamization of knowledge" is a recent one, the general impetus behind it is not new. The recurring need to view the approach to knowledge and reality within an Islamic frame is activated whenever Muslim scholars perceive a serious threat to Islam and a need to reemphasize its boundaries. In times of political uncertainty and change this need is the greatest; thus, Shāh Walī Allāh in eighteenth-century India warned of the loss of power and called for a revival in Islamic thought and knowledge. Social and political comment and the radical, first translation of the Qur'ān from Arabic into Urdu, the more popular language, followed, making Islamic thought accessible to a greater number of people than ever before.

In the latter half of the nineteenth century one of the most significant attempts at what could justifiably be termed the islamization of knowledge was made in the famous college (later university) begun by Sir Sayyid Aḥmad Khān in Aligarh. Facing the bleak aftermath of the failed 1857–1858 uprisings against the British, Sir Sayyid sensed a real danger to the Muslims who, insecure, powerless, and vulnerable, now wished to be isolated and to cling to tradition. Rejecting English and Western knowledge, they argued, would allow them to preserve their own identity and, at the same time, express their contempt for the emerging non-Islamic milieu.

Sir Sayyid hoped to benefit Muslim learning with the latest in Western education. His enthusiasm for Western scientific thought and rationalism was unbounded. Victorian clock towers and Islamic architecture, the cricket field and the mosque, Qur'ānic scholars and Cambridge staff combined to produce a remarkable synthesis at Aligarh, which almost by itself produced the first major modern Muslim educational movement. Not all Muslims approved; many traditional religious scholars condemned Sir Sayyid as a *kāfir* (nonbeliever), even a secret Christian convert. In time, Aligarh would provide the lead for the creation of Pakistan. Major modern Muslim figures like Muhammad Iqbal and Mawlānā Mawdūdī found a particularly sympathetic audience in Aligarh students. [*See* Aligarh *and the biographies of Aḥmad Khān, Iqbal, and Mawdūdī.*]

In the Arab world, Muḥammad ʿAbduh and Rashīd Riḍā, based in Cairo, provided an intellectual lead. Their links with al-Azhar, one of the oldest and most respected Islamic universities of the world, further strengthened their position. These Muslims were neither rejecting modern knowledge and education nor simply wanting a return to the past; they were attempting to live in the here and now but in the light of Islam. [*See* Azhar, al-; *and the biographies of ʿAbduh and Rashīd Riḍā.*]

Contemporary Context. Different, yet recognizably similar, perceptions of threat have created the demand for an islamization of knowledge in our times. Contemporary Muslim scholars have argued that although their nations were free from colonial rule, Western intellectual and cultural influences still dominated them. In particular, knowledge itself reflected these influences in the disciplines taught at the university and in the journals published in a European language and sold to the elite. Modern knowledge was clearly devoid of the Qur'ānic concept of human nature and view of the universe. To combat this increasingly powerful trend, it was necessary first to reexamine the major disciplines, economics, anthropology and so on, and then to suggest how best they could reflect authentic Islamic thought. The approach to the discipline more than the discipline itself needed to be cast in a more Islamic frame.

There was reason for alarm. For a few decades after independence, the education available in most Muslim nations was either a shallow imitation of the West (sustaining an often corrupt and self-perpetuating elite) or isolated in traditional religious schools with little or no contact with the outside world. The time was ripe for appraisal.

It is necessary to place this intellectual development in the political context of the 1970s when it first gained strength. That period was one of notable Islamic intellectual and political energy. King Fayṣal of Saudi Arabia mobilized Muslim opinion behind him by his bold support for Islamic causes, support which included the use of OPEC prices as a formidable weapon; General Muhammad Zia ul-Haq declared martial law in Pakistan and launched a movement which would be known as the islamization of Pakistan; Afghanistan was invaded by Soviet troops, and the Afghans declared a "holy war" to liberate their land. Finally, the period culminated in the spectacular overthrow of the shah of Iran by Ayatollah Ruhollah Khomeini and the triumph of his Islamic revolution.

Not surprisingly, this political activity found its counterpart in intellectual endeavor. A fresh confidence and vigor appeared among Muslim scholars, who, in different parts of the world, attempted to reexamine their disciplines in order to recast them in the light of Islam. New Islamic centers and universities provided a natural academic home for their scholarship both in the Muslim world (in Saudi Arabia, the United Arab Emirates, Pakistan, and Malaysia) and in the West (the International Institute of Islamic Thought, formerly in Philadelphia [now Herndon, Virginia] in the United States and, in the United Kingdom, the Islamic Foundation in Leicester and the Islamic Academy in Cambridge).

Developments in communications technology helped to create a global network, facilitating scholarly exchange of ideas. Scholars discovered a thirst for a more Islamic interpretation of knowledge wherever Muslims lived.

The seminal first world conference on Muslim education was held, appropriately, in Makkah (Mecca) in 1977 and generated a series of seminars, conferences and books: educators such as Ali Ashraf wrote of "Islamic education" (1979, 1985), economists such as Khurshid Ahmad of "Islamic economics" (1981), M. N. Siddiqi of "Islamic Banking" (1983), sociologists such as Ilyas Ba-Yunus and Farid Ahmad of "Islamic sociology" (1985), and anthropologists of "Islamic anthropology" (Ahmed 1987). The fact that these scholars came from different countries and represented different disciplines added to the prestige and credibility of the endeavor.

Scholars now grappled seriously with the cluster of ideas that formed around the notion of the islamization of knowledge. One of the most active and committed scholars of his generation, Ismāʿīl al-Fārūqī, a Palestinian settled in the United States, helped to launch the International Institute of Islamic Thought, which became an intellectual powerhouse, providing ideas and publications with a global following; a major program was initiated to examine each main academic discipline in the light of the islamization of knowledge (see Abū Sulaymān, 1989). Tragically, al-Fārūqī was assassinated in 1986 when the first study of the series appeared. In his Foreword to this study, he defined the endeavor:

> This program, conceived and crystallized in a number of symposia on the subject, consists of twelve steps designed to effect the necessary Islamization in the various disciplines of human knowledge. Some of these steps seek to survey and evaluate modern Western accomplishments. Others do the same for the legacy of Muslim learning. The purpose is to reach full mastery of the "state of the art" in each discipline, and to prepare that discipline for re-establishment on Islamic foundations. This implies correction of its prejudices and errors, elimination of its shortcomings, and redress of its methodology and aspirations. (al-Fārūqī, Foreword, in Akbar S. Ahmed, 1987, p. 7).

Al-Fārūqī warned Muslims of the need for rigor and integrity in their own work. He did not wish to replace one kind of dogma by another:

> Islamization does not mean subordination of any body of knowledge to dogmatic principles or arbitrary objectives, but liberation from such shackles. Islam regards all knowledge as critical; i.e., as universal, necessary and rational. It wants to see every claim pass through the tests of internal coherence, correspondence with reality, and enhancement of human life and morality. Consequently, the Islamized discipline which we hope to reach in the future will turn a new page in the history of the human spirit, and bring it closer to the truth. (Ibid.)

Although the intent of islamization and the political context causing its necessity are clear, the actual method is far from resolved. Critics argue that there can no more be an Islamic science of economics, for example, than a Christian, Hindu, or Buddhist one. Precisely, reply the Muslim scholars, the practice of economics is rarely neutral and never free of a moral position. Clearly, there is a Keynesian economics and a Marxist economics.

Islamic Economics. As Western economists reflect the Western capitalist order within which they develop their ideas and socialist economists the communist one, Islamic economics should reflect the core principles of Islam, thereby influencing the very nature of society. This approach would be a departure for those Muslims influenced by either capitalist or communist models. Muslims would emphasize the Qur'ānic notions of *al-ʿadl* (balance) and *al-iḥsān* (compassion). Islamic economists would attempt consciously to create a balanced and compassionate society; thus, for example, individual rights to education, health, and social security would be ensured, since they are simply a restoration of the central notions of Islam: the *tawḥīd* of God, the organic interconnection of life, its high moral purpose, and so on.

For Muslims the starting point is the central concept of *tawḥīd* (God's unity and sovereignty). That God has made the earth for humanity, hence, the good things it produces are theirs to enjoy, is explicit in the holy Qur'ān. Also explicit is humanity's central role in the universe as *khalīfah,* (God's viceregent on earth). From this follows the strong moral imperative to care for one another. "Basic needs" (the current development jargon) are recognized as the right of every human being. Basic needs in the Islamic framework include the rights to education and transport, to found a family, and ensuring self-reliance. Conspicuous consumption is strongly discouraged. Both the Qur'ān and the life of the Prophet, the two major sources of Islamic life, support austerity. The Prophet's saying aptly sums up the position: "My poverty is my pride."

Islamic economics is far from being an intellectual fad or a marginalized eccentricity. It has influenced policy and planning in various countries such as Saudi Arabia and Pakistan, as well as the establishment of university departments to work on numerous economic issues in many Muslim countries; advice has been offered to banking and business concerns. The debate around interest-free banking, that interest itself is *ḥaram* (prohibited), was stimulated by Islamic economics.

Islamic Anthropology. In my discussion of an Islamic anthropology I pointed out the underlying Islamic principles that needed to be identified (Ahmed, 1987, 1988). Islamic anthropology is ideally placed to assist Islamic endeavor, a view supported by Qur'ānic verses and the Prophet's sayings. The Qur'ān tells us: "Say: Travel through the earth and see how God did originate creation" (29.20). Sayings of the Prophet also reflect this sentiment: "Seek knowledge, even unto China." People are asked to contemplate, to think of and marvel at, the multitudinous variety in the heavens and on earth: "And among His signs is the creation of the heavens and the earth, and the variations in your languages and your colours" (surah 30.22).

Islamic anthropology cannot be a passive or neutral science. It must attempt solutions to the major social problems facing humanity in the late twentieth century: drug abuse, alcoholism, AIDS, famine. The Islamic use of the word *jihād,* striving to better the world—incorrectly understood in the Western media as religious war—is apt in this context.

Islam not only encourages commitment, it demands it; it not only strives for moral consensus, it insists on emotional loyalty as well. Islamic ideology has much to say about an entire range of social issues, behavior, and organization. Islam has an intrinsic social side; how a Muslim moves from birth to death, through the rites of passage, how a Muslim eats, walks and talks are all suggested in text and tradition. Muslim sociology for Islam is clearly the manifestation of its theology.

Al-Fārūqī had warned anthropologists:

> Anthropology, like all disciplined pursuit of knowledge, must pull itself out of this narrow vision to which it has been confined by the necessities of European history. It should humanize and universalize itself, and stop looking at the people of the world as if they were specimens in a zoo, each specimen carrying its own habits or "culture" as an autonomous end in itself, or as instruments for Western dominion, or as a vacuum to be filled by Western religion, culture and civilization. It should learn anew the simple but primordial truths of all knowledge that are equally the first truths of Islam, namely, that truth is one, just as God is one and as humankind is one. (Ibid., pp. 8–9)

The intent of Islamic anthropology is not to belittle Western anthropology and its achievements or to annul its past; it seeks to create an additional body of knowledge based on scientific and unbiased information, adding to our understanding. People all over the world today are irreversibly bound together through the power of high technology: computers, videocassettes, and satellite television. In this complex world of ours anthropology can assist, in its own low-key but meaningful way, our understanding of each other and the major contemporary problems we face. This task is the relevance of anthropology in today's world, its special destiny.

However, to validate the assertion that Islamic anthropology is a universal science, Muslim anthropologists first must examine Muslim society from an Islamic perspective and avoid the danger of its idealization, of discussing it as it should be rather than as it is, of whitewashing, of not seeing reality, thereby falling short of accurate analysis. The next challenge is to examine non-Muslim societies. What does Islam have to say about them and what remedies are available to them through the application of Islamic anthropology? Have Muslims themselves solved these problems? These studies must be penetrating and original, for their quality and relevance will determine the importance of Islamic anthropology for non-Muslims.

Future Tasks. Despite the awareness created by the islamization of knowledge exercise, that is, that there are other legitimate ways of examining and confronting knowledge than Western ones, its meaningfulness and permanence will require much work. The label of Islam is no guarantee of islamizing a discipline. There is a danger of reductionism, of rejecting ideas associated with the West as unworthy and unimportant. Indeed, the simplistic understanding of Western economics as amoral and heartless is a dated one. Most economists today are sensitive to humanist welfare and social security considerations in their work.

Perhaps the most serious shortcoming of the quest to islamize the discipline is the failure to establish and develop a wide body of scholarship. There has been excessive reliance on one central intellectual figure at the expense of the development of a school or university; after the death of al-Fārūqī, the vigor of the quest declined. Further, the cause of Muslim scholarship has not been assisted by Muslim governments which aid Islamic centers and colleges and then attempt to use them crudely as political platforms for the projection of their rulers or policies. Too often have the noisy politics of Muslim governments been evident in Muslim educational centers, making the independent work of scholars difficult and preventing the growth of a genuine academic environment. Besides, the power of Western scholarship, the lure of Western universities, and the influence of the Western media remain as strong as ever (Ahmed, 1992).

The quality of Muslim scholarship and the sophistication of its analysis rather than the zeal of its passion and politics will decide the eventual success and influence of the project of the islamization of knowledge. Until then, it will remain a strong if amorphous idea, challenging both Muslim and non-Muslim scholarship and knowledge.

[*See also the biography of Fārūqī.*]

BIBLIOGRAPHY

Abū Sulaymān, ʿAbdul Hamīd, ed. *Islamization of Knowledge: General Principles and Work Plan.* 2d ed., revised and expanded. Herndon, Va., 1989.

Ahmad, Khurshid, ed. *Studies in Islamic Economics.* Jeddah and Leicester, 1981.

Ahmed, Akbar S. *Toward Islamic Anthropology: Definition, Dogma, and Directions.* Foreword by Ismāʿīl R. al-Fārūqī. Lahore, 1987.

Ahmed, Akbar S. *Discovering Islam: Making Sense of Muslim History and Society.* London, 1988.

Ahmed, Akbar S. *Postmodernism and Islam: Predicament and Promise.* London, 1992.

ʿAli, ʿAbdallāh Yūsuf, trans. *The Holy Qurʾān: Text, Translation, and Commentary.* New rev. ed. Brentwood, Md., 1989.

Ashraf, Syed Ali. *New Horizons in Muslim Education.* Cambridge and London, 1985.

Ashraf, Syed Ali, and Syed S. Husain. *Crisis in Muslim Education.* London, 1979.

Ba-Yunus, Ilyas, and Farid Ahmad. *Islamic Sociology: An Introduction.* Cambridge, 1985.

Siddiqi, Muhammad N. *Issues in Islamic Banking: Selected Papers.* Leicester, 1983.

AKBAR S. AHMED

EGYPT. Religion plays a major role in Egypt today. Approximately 90 percent of modern Egypt's estimated 61 million inhabitants are Sunnī Muslim. There are several religious minorities, the largest of which is an indigenous Christian minority constituting the Coptic Church. In 1990, estimates of the Coptic population ranged from 3 million to 7 million, while other Christians included approximately 350,000 followers of the Greek Orthodox Church, 175,000 Eastern and Latin Rite Catholics, and 200,000 Protestants. In addition, an estimated 1,000 Jews remained in Egypt as of 1990. The Jewish population represents a fragment of the community of 80,000 Jews who lived in Egypt before 1948. Broad religious tolerance has been a hallmark of traditional Egyptian culture and freedom of religion is guaranteed by the Egyptian Constitution of 1971, although tensions along religious lines have risen sharply since the 1970s.

The centrality of religion in definining Egypt is deeply rooted historically. By the end of the reign of the second Islamic caliph, ʿUmar ibn ʿAbd al-Khaṭṭāb (r. 634–644), the expanding empire of Islam had succeeded in incorporating the Egyptian provinces of the Byzantine Empire. Ascendent Islam found fertile soil in Egypt. From the time of the pharaohs, demigods in the eyes of their subjects, religion had played a central role in the life of the inhabitants of the Nile Valley. The priests of ancient Egypt, who presided over the cults that defined each province, made up a central part of the ruling class. Persian invaders disrupted these traditional patterns when they defeated the last Egyptian pharoah in 525 BCE. Though religion among the Egyptians took different forms through a succession of foreign conquerors, it always remained a key element of political culture.

The Arab conquest gave this inherited religious bond a distinctive Islamic form. Islam ruled out any version of the old pharaonic claim of rulers to be descendants of the gods and the notion of a closed caste of priests. Instead, the new faith impelled Muslims as a collective body to express their faith by founding a community of believers or *ummah*. The central moral precepts of Islam, expressed in the Qur'ān and the traditions of the Prophet, provided not simply guidance for personal salvation but also the moral basis for a good society on earth. Rulers of Muslim communities were thus impelled to rely not only on men of power but also on men of intellect and faith who could mediate between the timeless revelations of Islam and the exigencies of specific times and places. Power rested with the rulers and their military supporters, but legitimacy derived from the religious scholars or *ʿulamāʾ*, who emerged as the guardians of the legacy and the guarantors of right guidance. In theory, and despite deviations in practice almost from the beginning, only Islamic law (the *sharīʿah*) elaborated by the scholars from the principles of the Qur'ān and the traditions of the prophet Muḥammad could bind the new community while safeguarding its distinctive moral purpose.

The *ʿulamāʾ*, however, were not the only religious leaders in Muslim Egypt. Alongside their austere religion of the mind and the law there arose an Islamic mysticism, Sufism, that shifted emphasis from the mind to the heart and from the law to love. This Islam of the heart evoked a powerful popular response, organized in Ṣūfī orders that coalesced around individual saints. The initial opposition of the *ʿulamāʾ* to the Ṣūfī orders faded into an uneasy compromise as it became clear that persecution did not diminish the appeal of Sufism for the masses.

As the hold of early Muslim empires weakened and local dynasties rose in Egypt, religious leaders retained their importance as a powerful social and spiritual force. The founding of al-Azhar as mosque and university in 970 assured Cairo a secure place in the spiritual and intellectual firmament of Islam. The Ottomans, originating in one of the Turkish principalities of Anatolia, annexed Egypt in 1516–1517 and made it part of the last great Islamic empire. The Ottoman Empire survived until just before the outbreak of World War I, when the British, who had occupied Egypt in 1882, declared the country a protectorate and ended what by then had become nominal Ottoman sovereignty. The Ottoman Empire protected the lands of Islam and expanded their borders whenever possible, creating a diverse, powerful, and inclusive political structure that ruled parts of eastern Europe, western Asia, and most of North Africa for periods ranging from three hundred to six hundred years. The acquisition of Egypt had strategic, financial, and—because of al-Azhar's importance throughout the Muslim world—religious importance to the empire. The Ottomans maintained tight control over this prize through an appointed governor and military corps. Cairo took its place alongside such major Islamic centers as Baghdad, Damascus, Mecca, and Medina in a world empire with Istanbul as its splendid cultural capital.

With time the Ottoman military garrisoned in Egypt put down local roots and entered into alliances not only with wealthy merchants but with the *ʿulamāʾ* as well. Relying on the religious scholars, the Ottomans strengthened the *sharīʿah* and enhanced the study of Arabic. In eighteenth-century Cairo the *ʿulamāʾ* flourished, numbering approximately four thousand out of an estimated adult male population of fifty thousand. From their base in the venerable al-Azhar, the organizing center of a national network of religious education, the Egyptian *ʿulamaʾ* preserved a dense Islamic culture that created a formidable social and moral link between Cairo and the provinces. Moreover, the religious scholars figured prominently in all the political crises experienced by Egypt. Through their control of religious endowments, lawsuits, canonic dues, and inheritances, they held economic resources equal at least to those of the artisans or merchants. Religious leaders acted as intermediaries and occasionally even as protectors who intervened between ordinary Egyptians and their Ottoman rulers.

Napoleon's conquests in Egypt (1798–1801) disrupted this three hundred-year-old order and cast the Egyptian provinces, vulnerable and unprepared, into a global political system dominated by the West. Egyptians encountered the West from a position of great material weakness. In the last stages of Ottoman rule, the Egyptian provinces had entered a period of severe decline. Preoccupied with holding the European territories from which they derived much of their strength, the Ottomans neglected Egypt and the other Arab centers. Local despotisms flourished in the Arab lands, and the economies sank to subsistence levels as imperial linkages weakened. The towns saw little commercial trade and only the most limited artisanal production. The countryside became more vulnerable to nomadic incursions and suffered more than ever from the tax and military exactions of the hard-pressed centers. By the end of the eighteenth century it was clear that the old formulas were everywhere strained, although in Egypt the *ʿulamāʾ* as a corporate body survived as one of the few remaining cohesive elements.

Amid the confusions that followed Napoleon's incursion, the *ʿulamāʾ* played a critical role in bringing to power Muḥammad ʿAlī (1804–1841), the Albanian officer who founded modern Egypt and established the dynasty that held power until 1952. The French invasion had weakened the tie between Egyptians and Ottomans by making it apparent that the Turkish rulers could no longer provide protection against Europeans. The *ʿulamāʾ*, considered the natural leaders of the country, threw their support to Muḥammad ʿAlī on condition that he rule with their consultation. When Muḥammad ʿAlī agreed, they mobilized the population of Cairo to demonstrate against the Ottoman governor, calling successfully on the sultan to ratify the choice of Muḥammad ʿAlī as governor of Egypt. The *ʿulamāʾ* had cleared the way for the man who would set the course of Egyptian history for the next century.

Egypt's energetic new ruler strove to transform a backward country of about two million inhabitants with a subsistence economy into a state powerful enough to counter further assaults from Europe and strong enough to maintain its de facto independence from the Ottoman sultanate. In his drive to strengthen the state and particularly its military arm, Muḥammad ʿAlī launched Egypt's first industrialization effort, borrowing both models and technicians from the West. Exploiting this new strength, Muḥammad ʿAlī projected Egyptian power abroad, involving Egypt in five wars from 1811 to 1828. At home, he sought to discipline the population through new forms of education and social organization that would channel all energies to his dynastic purposes. He weakened or eliminated institutions intermediary between the peasant base and the bureaucracy of his centralized state. In the process he moved against the *ʿulamāʾ*, acting to circumscribe their influence as he consolidated his own power.

The *ʿulamāʾ* never completely recovered the independent economic and political role they had played in the eighteenth century. Yet Muḥammad ʿAlī's successful attempt to reign in the religious establishment did not tell the whole story of Islam in nineteenth-century Egypt. Though weakened, the *ʿulamā* continued to exert from al-Azhar a powerful religious and cultural influence in the countryside and, thanks especially to the reformists among them, on the urban elite, including the new bourgeoisie that emerged in the early decades of the nineteenth century. Had Muḥammad ʿAlī been able to continue his modernization drive unopposed, he probably would have further undercut the role of Islam and the *ʿulamāʾ* in Egyptian national life. Ironically, the intervention of the British arrested that development. [*See* Muḥammad ʿAlī Dynasty.]

Britain had grown alarmed by Egyptian military successes in the Levant and perhaps even more by the creation of the industrial base in Egypt that made them possible. British threats culminated in a dramatic naval show of force in Alexandria, and Muḥammad ʿAlī admitted defeat by signing the Treaty of London in 1840. The Egyptian army was limited in size, war industries were disbanded, and the tariff and monopolies that protected the remaining industries were removed. In these circumstances of containment and imposed weakness, the *ʿulamāʾ* assumed a renewed importance; they provided a reservoir of intellectual, cultural, and religious opposition.

Europe throughout the nineteenth century proceeded to colonize Egypt. Conventional history delineates two fundamental strategies of Egyptian resistance, the first secular nationalist and the second Islamic reformist. In fact, that line should not be drawn too sharply: both strategies drew on an underlying fusion of religion and collective identity. In the battles with the West the masses always felt their strongest solidarity with the *ʿulamāʾ* even when they appeared to speak for the secular interest of the nation, and they responded most dramatically to the calls of political figures when those calls were expressed in Islamic terms. While weaving together diverse patterns of anticolonial sentiment and impulses for modernization and reform, resistance until after World War I remained securely anchored in Islamic structures of thought and civilization. To the present day, the cry that "God is dead" has found little resonance in Egypt.

No figure better captured the energizing thrust of this potent blend of tradition and reforming impulse than the peripatetic Iranian, Jamāl al-Dīn al-Afghānī (1837–1897), who played a large role in the story of Islam in Egypt. Al-Afghānī traversed Iran, India, Turkey, and the Arab world sounding the theme of defensive reform while calling for local and Pan-Islamic revolts. Admired for his classical Islamic learning, al-Afghānī also displayed an impressive familiarity with the social and scientific thought of the West. He argued that reason, science, and liberal ideas of government and social progress were fully compatible with Islam when the message of the faith was properly understood.

Al-Afghānī called on his students, including the Egyptian Shaykh Muḥammad ʿAbduh (1849–1905), to work out interpretations of Islam along these lines. The master's own greatest talents had a more activist thrust. The call for unity al-Afghānī embodied was driven by his conviction that the entire Muslim world, not just its frontiers, lay vulnerable to the power of the West. Deliberately cultivating mystery around his origins and his movements, al-Afghānī made himself a unifying figure, embracing at once Sunnīs, Ṣūfīs, and Shīʿīs. Wherever they could, al-Afghānī and his followers engaged in direct attacks on Western, especially British imperialism. These political confrontations helped legitimate the painful conclusion that successful confrontation of the West would entail almost as much imitation as refusal.

Al-Afghānī's message resonated with particular force in Egypt. Al-Azhar had not remained isolated from modern trends in science and social thought, despite its traditional methods. From the time of Muḥammad ʿAlī its scholars had been sent abroad to study Western sciences. Al-Afghānī made himself a major though controversial intellectual force at al-Azhar. Resistance to the Western threat had become the driving force of Egyptian nineteenth-century history, and al-Azhar became an important center of resistance. [*See* Azhar, al-; *and the biography of Afghānī.*]

None of Muhammad ʿAlī's heirs could match him in ruthless energy, ambition, or vision. With Egypt's industrialization effort stymied, the economy became a huge monoculture cotton farm for Britain's textile factories. The conditions of the masses deteriorated, and the royal government grew more corrupt and inefficient, while the country slipped deeper and deeper into foreign debt. By the time of Khedive Tawfīq (1879–1892) the country had fallen totally under foreign domination. With the foreign ruling elite discredited, the initiative for Egypt's defense passed from the state to broader Egyptian social forces.

The first effort at internal reform arose from an unlikely quarter, the emasculated Egyptian army. The precipitating issue was the blockage of access to the officer corps dominated by a closed Turko-Circassian elite. When Egyptian colonels led by Aḥmad ʿUrābī challenged these restrictions, the government responded by arresting ʿUrābī. The move backfired when the colonels, speaking in the name of the people, broadened their demands to include a constitution, a change of government, and an increase in the overall size of the army to the eighteen thousand men specified in the Treaty of London. Drawing on his traditional religious education, the charismatic young colonel couched his call for reform in terms of Islamic renewal, greatly enhancing his appeal. ʿUrābī became a symbol for a broader campaign that coalesced around the slogan "Egypt for Egyptians." Characteristically, al-Afghānī and his follower Muḥammad ʿAbduh rallied to the ʿUrābists and did their best to bring the *ʿulamāʾ* as a corporate body with them.

Meanwhile, the British Consul persuaded his government that the revolt had produced anarchy in the country. The British and the French dispatched a joint fleet to make a show of force at the port in Alexandria. When riots broke out in the city, the Khedive secretly encouraged the Europeans to shell the city and land forces to destroy the revolution, despite the fact that ʿUrābī had rushed from Cairo and succeeded in restoring order. The British, though not the French, obliged the frightened Khedive and bombarded Alexandria. The forces of ʿUrābī's movement, ten thousand roughly trained men and a rabble of peasants, were crushed in 1882 by an occupying British force of thirty thousand at the Battle of Tel el-Kebir. Al-Afghānī and ʿAbduh were exiled. The era of direct British colonization had begun, to end completely only in 1954.

Returning from exile to a colonial situation dominated by a monarchy imposed by British power, ʿAbduh had little choice but to shift his reformist efforts to the theological, educational, and cultural arenas. The journal he published, *Al-manār,* concentrated on Qur'ānic exegesis and theological explication. Although ʿAbduh had no illusions about the cynical manipulations of the throne and the brutality of the occupier, he also understood that behind their raw power stood the cultural attraction of new principles for organizing society and new kinds of knowledge. An Azhar-trained member of the *ʿulamāʾ*, Abduh taught at al-Azhar, but also at the new college of Dar al-ʿUlūm where a modern curriculum had been developed to prepare functionaries for the state bureaucracies. His modernist project aimed to free religious thought from the shackles of imitation *(taqlīd)* and to open the way to reforms that would express the spiritual power of Islam in terms appropriate to the modern world. [*See* Taqlīd.]

ʿAbduh legitimated this reform program by drawing a careful distinction between the essential spiritual message of Islam and its elaboration in social prescriptions and laws. He explained that the fundamental doctrines of belief in God, of revelation through a line of prophets culminating in Muḥammad, and of moral responsibility had been preserved by a line of pious ancestors *(al-salaf al-ṣāliḥ),* and that these compelling and unchanging principles could be expressed and defended by reason. In contrast, laws and moral injunctions had the status of particular applications of these principles by successive Muslim communities. Naturally, when those circumstances changed, such formulations could be adapted and modified to meet new needs.

ʿAbduh believed that Egypt's situation at the end of the nineteenth century demanded just such restatements. He directed attention first to the modernization of the curriculum and reform of the religious courts. As the senior legal officer or *muftī* of Egypt, he issued progressive legal opinions on the permissibility of Western dress, banking interest, marriage, and divorce.

ʿAbduh intended his compromise with colonial power, and more basically with the westernizing project, to assert Egyptian identity and liberation through the reform of Islam. But the penetration of the West all but overwhelmed his prodigious effort. Having integrated a dependent Egypt into the global economy, the British pressed their effort to remake the country through a web of institutional reforms in the military, the bureaucracy, and the legal and educational systems. From this colonial situation emerged a new Western-oriented elite that wrested control of the national project from Egypt's natural rulers, the *ʿulamāʾ*. The continuities of a reformed Islam, on which ʿAbduh had insisted, faded. [*See the biography of* ʿ*Abduh.*]

In 1919 a second wave of nationalist revolt stirred the country and pushed the secular elites into even greater prominence. Wartime conditions had contributed to the creation of serious food shortages and a staggering rate of inflation. This time nationalist leaders like Saʿd Zaghlūl gave voice to the popular resentment of foreign rule aggravated by these conditions. The rejection of Zaghlūl's request for an Egyptian delegation or *wafd* to the Paris Conference sparked a wave of armed rebellion and strikes that paralyzed the country. Under the pressure of these disturbances, Egypt was declared an independent monarchy in 1922. Egypt's new constitution enshrined liberal nationalist ideas. The Wafd party that Zaghlūl founded included Copts as well as Muslims in its leadership. The country had entered a liberal constitutional era that lasted until the revolution of 1952.

These secularizing events in Egypt coincided with the final destruction at the end of World War I of the overarching Islamic political framework in the Middle East. Events in the Turkish successor state strengthened the hands of secularists in Egypt and throughout the region. Atatürk thwarted imperialist designs on Turkey and launched a development effort under a republican, nationalist, populist, secular, statist, and revolutionary banner; his reforms included abandoning the Arabic script and, even more significantly, abolishing the caliphate.

From the outset, al-Afghānī and ʿAbduh had argued that successful resistance to the West would entail a substantial dose of imitation. In Egypt the followers of ʿAbduh who had responded most to his call to imitate the West now had an influential model that pushed them decisively into the arms of the secular nationalists.

These same ambiguities linking resistance and imitation simultaneously fostered a quite different orientation. Muḥammad Rashīd Riḍā (1865–1935), ʿAbduh's most prominent follower, responded to the pressures of westernization in a strikingly different manner, eventually taking events in Saudi Arabia rather than Turkey for his inspiration. Although Riḍā initially tried to hold onto both aspects of the master's legacy, the deterioration of the faith drove him to increasingly defensive and apologetic strategies. Riḍā drew closer to the conservative Ḥanbalī school of Islamic law and came to believe that the early eighteenth-century Arabian reform movement of Muḥammad ibn ʿAbd al-Wahhāb, which had provided the religious underpinning of the Saudi Arabian state, represented the most viable Islamic alternative to capitulation to the West.

The Wahhābīs called for a return to Ibn Ḥanbal's understanding of Islam that required absolute obedience to the Qur'ān and the *ḥadīth* as interpreted by the responsible *ʿulamā'* of each generation and the rejection of illegitimate innovations. In line with this thinking, Riḍā issued a series of *fatwās* designed to bring existing laws in line with a revised *sharīʿah*. Riḍā noted that the Saudi state that had taken shape on this basis in the early nineteenth century had never succumbed to the colonial onslaught. Like both Afghānī and ʿAbduh, Riḍā, though a reformer, spoke as one of the *ʿulamā'*. While working to contain influences that threatened to undermine the distinctive character of the Muslim community, Riḍā embraced modernist conceptions of instrumental reason and efficiency; above all, he stressed creating new forms of institutional life to reassert Islam's social role under modern conditions. [*See* Wahhābīyah *and the biography of Rashīd Riḍā.*]

In 1928, Rashīd Riḍā's strand of Islamic reform bore its most impressive and lasting fruit when his disciple, the schoolteacher Ḥasan al-Bannā', founded the Muslim Brotherhood. Like his master, al-Bannā' drew on modern institutional and communications strategies to create a durable organization to advance Islamic modernization. Unlike Riḍā, however, his project implied the creation of an Islamist elite by claiming to speak not only for Egypt but also for the world beyond.

The radical character of al-Bannā's project reflected the terrible deterioration of Egypt's material situation. By the late twenties it was clear that Egypt's economy had been colonized. For more than half a century the country had been little more than an exporter of raw cotton to British mills. Direct occupation made effective resistance more difficult as the British tightened the bonds of economic dependency. Control of the Suez Canal by European shareholders continued to bind Egypt to the Western global economic system. Reacting to the Great Depression, the Egyptian private sector, including the large foreign component, moved the country on the path of Western-inspired import substitution and industrialization. The economic and political dimensions of the nation seemed now to be monopolized by the Western-oriented secular elite.

Undoubtedly al-Bannā's immense charisma helped to validate the Muslim Brothers' claim to represent a plausible Islamic alternative, but much more was involved than the personality of one man. Al-Bannā's assessment of Egypt's needs went beyond breaking the bonds of dependency in the political and economic realms: he understood that the most damaging injuries from colonization were internal. Islam's enemies, he warned, had succeeded in entering the social body, attacking and undermining the Islamic community from within and wounding Muslims in mind and soul. The westernized Egyptians who made up the colonial political class became his prime targets.

Ḥasan al-Bannā' cast the Muslim Brothers as the heir of the unified project of resistance—political, economic, and cultural—that had characterized the nineteenth century. It was the brotherhood alone that grasped the possibility for a culturally located mode of resistance. In the face of daunting "internal colonization" the brothers struggled to develop an authentic social ethos consistent with Islam yet compatible with the modern world. They acted on that ethic of "social Islam" in concrete activities and services that reached a large body of Muslims, especially in the urban areas. At the same time, the brothers moved decisively to assume the political responsibilities of resistance, earning enduring appreciation for their role in directly combating British occupation forces in the Canal Zone and the Zionists in Palestine. These militant actions helped solidify the reputation of the brothers abroad and fostered the transnational links to the larger Islamic body that later generated branches of the brotherhood in other parts of the Arab world, most importantly in Syria and Jordan. In Egypt of the 1940s, membership in the Muslim Brothers numbered approximately one million. [*See* Muslim Brotherhood, *article on* Muslim Brotherhood in Egypt; *and the biography of Bannā'.*]

The elaboration of a viable social Islam in Egypt proved to be the Muslim Brothers' most impressive legacy for Egyptian public life. However, from the outset a strand of radicalism, a "political Islam" prone to erupt in violence, threatened to overshadow this achievement. Initially directed at the British and Zionist colonizing agents, the militants gradually turned their weapons against the regime. The central figure in this development was Sayyid Quṭb. The emergence of the new mainstream social Islam created by the Muslim Brothers and Quṭb's radical evolution out of it can only be understood against the backdrop of the relationship between the Free Officers regime and the brotherhood.

Key members of the the young army officers who spearheaded the 1952 Free Officers' coup that became a revolution from above were drawn to the brothers. They knew Ḥasan al-Bannā' personally and shared many of his ideas. When Gamal Abdel Nasser and the young colonels around him first moved to curtail political parties, the brotherhood was exempted. In the critical early days the Muslim Brotherhood supported the military as they moved against the old secular elite. Later, echoing the fate of the traditional *ʿulamā'* at the hands of Muḥammad ʿAlī, Nasser turned against the brothers as he moved to concentrate his own power. The conflict emerged essentially from these power considerations rather than from questions of ideology.

The task of subduing the brothers did not prove easy. On two separate occasions, roughly a decade apart, the regime launched murderous attacks on the brothers. An alleged assassination attempt occurred in 1954 at a time when Nasser was manufacturing incidents to create a climate of general disorder. The regime moved to crush the one remaining organization capable of challenging state power. The brotherhood survived underground, but a decade later it once again became the target of massive repression as the regime moved to consolidate its leftist support. Once again, the brothers were brutally crushed and dispersed.

Within their prison cells and in exile, the Muslim Brothers developed a compelling critique of the Nasserist experience. Egypt in the 1950s and 1960s had drifted from Islam as its mediating device. At the heart of the military regime, they saw a void. The brothers charged that for all the surface movement on economic, political, and foreign-policy issues, the Free Officers had no clear sense of where Egypt was going. The military rulers, the brothers charged, were chasing other people's modernity at the price of their own spiritual and cultural integrity.

Sayyid Quṭb developed his own version of such thinking in the context of terrible personal suffering. Quṭb began his intellectual and moral odyssey from a pro-Western position. As a young man, he found the West and and its modernist project attractive, but a trip to the United States reversed that outlook. Disgusted by the anti-Arab prejudice he encountered and shocked by what he perceived to be the moral turpitude of American cities, Quṭb joined the brotherhood on his return to Egypt.

The brutality of the regime confirmed Quṭb's anti-Western experience and provided the impetus for the elaboration of a new militancy. In outline, Quṭb argued that while there were millions of Muslims in Egypt, the system under which they were forced to live was fundamentally un-Islamic. In *Signposts on the Way*, his most important theoretical statement, Quṭb condemned the Egyptian regime as un-Islamic. Perhaps most significantly, he urged the formation of a vanguard of true believers who would mount militant and armed resistance that alone had a chance to succeed. The regime recognized the direct and dangerous challenge that Quṭb's thought represented: he was executed, and the broad Islamist movement was smashed once again. But by the mid-1960s the regime's effort at modernization had crested. A financial crisis coupled with the devastating defeat by Israel in the 1967 war effectively ended the Nasserist experiment. From these momentous events, many read the message that neither the liberal nor the socialist face of the Western project had much to offer Egyptians. The way had opened for those, whether moderate or radical, who claimed to speak for Islam. [*See* Nasserism *and the biographies of* Nasser *and* Quṭb.]

The death of the defeated Nasser and the succession of Anwar el-Sadat in 1971 paved the way for yet another return of the Muslim Brothers. As Sadat moved his regime to the right on all levels, he turned to the Islamist current to contain the old Nasserists and other elements of the left. Less than five years after Sayyid Quṭb's martyrdom, the Muslim Brothers reemerged to play their most important role in Egyptian public life since the 1940s. There were important differences, of course. No single leader emerged with the stature of Ḥasan al-Bannā'. Equally important, although not initially noticed, the moderate mainstream that returned to civil life was haunted by the shadow of the militants, hardened in concentration camps and inspired by their selective reading of Sayyid Quṭb. The mainstream brothers found themselves caught in a new way between the regime and the violent militants who had emerged from the abused Islamist body.

In this difficult context, the brotherhood assumed something of the role that traditional *ʿulamā'* had once played in speaking for the nation and serving as a reservoir from which a variety of competing strategies emerged. In this sense, the brothers gave rise to both the most moderate and the most militant voices for Islam in the 1980s and 1990s.

The mainstream, under the stable but uninspired leadership of ʿUmar al-Tilimsānī (Omar al-Telmesany), compromised with the Sadat regime and that of Hosni Mubarak. Adopting the conscious strategy of working within the existing order, the brothers took advantage of every opportunity to play as large a role as possible in the emerging civil society. With official Islam diminished by Nasserist authoritarianism and the Ṣūfī orders brought into the same network of control, the brothers constituted a quasi-independent Islamist mainstream that inspired a whole network of Islamist institutions and new forms of Islamist political and social action. Social Islam took on concrete forms.

For a time the compromise with the Sadat regime worked. The brothers threw themselves with genuine commitment into the officially orchestrated de-Nasserization campaign with attacks on socialism and authoritarianism. But when the full implications of Sadat's reorientation became clear in the mid-1970s, especially in the form of the separate peace with Israel in 1979, the tacit alliance came undone. As even the mainstream Brothers saw it, Sadat's break with Arab and Islamic ranks sacrificed Jerusalem and the Palestinians for narrowly conceived Egyptian interests. The United States failed to hold Israel to the Camp David commitment to do something for the Palestinians, and the social gap in Egypt widened under liberalization policies. The Sadat regime's promise of peace and prosperity collapsed, leaving the president isolated and vulnerable. In October 1981 Islamist militants assassinated Sadat as he reviewed a military parade.

Vice President Hosni Mubarak, who was also on the reviewing stand, survived and assumed the presidency in a smooth constitutional transition. Mubarak began with a firm commitment to continue the policies of the Sadat era, including reconciliation with the moderate Muslim Brothers. In some ways Mubarak initially deepened the democratization process that Sadat had tentatively begun. He certainly continued to strengthen the presence of official Islam in public life.

By the end of the first decade of Mubarak's rule the Islamic current in Egypt had assumed an impressive array of forms. Alliances with legitimate political parties gave prominent Islamists seats in parliament, a leading role in the major professional syndicates, and many publishing houses. At the same time, the mosques steadily expanded their functions to include not only religious activities but also medical clinics and social service facilities that offered high-quality services at low prices, attracting middle-class as well as lower middle-class families. But despite these impressive advances of Social Islam, the Islamist radicals cast a threatening shadow.

Militant political Islam, fragmented into small and often violent groups, continued to absorb the regime's energies in increasingly deadly duels. While the broad Islamic current draws support from all social classes, the militants appear to have originated predominantly from the lower middle-class provincials, with their leaders coming from the rural elite. Their roots appear especially strong in those parts of Upper Egypt, such as Minya and Asyut, with large Christian populations. The militants splintered over their assessment of the appropriate target of their violent anger—the regime or society as a whole. They disagreed on strategy, with some militant groups such as the Takfīr wa al-Hijrah urging withdrawal from society to preserve their purity as the vanguard of a genuine Islamic order, and others such as al-Jihād favoring shock attacks and assassinations designed to undermine the Mubarak government and produce the social chaos that would create the opening for a militant takeover. [*See* Takfīr wa al-Hijrah, Jamā'at al-.]

In some ways, the regime's most impressive weapon against the violent Islamist radicals was the moderate brothers. On one hand, the brothers were given increasingly widened scope for their own activities; on the other, they were encouraged by the regime to cooperate in containing more militant elements that might challenge their own leadership. Uninspired leadership prevented moderate brothers from fully exploiting this new opening. In retrospect, the most disappointing aspect of al-Bannā's legacy was the leadership void he left behind. During his lifetime al-Bannā' surrounded himself not with the most talented but with the most loyal, compensating for their limitations with his own impressive abilities. Official repression directed quite consciously against the top leadership cadres worsened the situation.

Not surprisingly, some of the most creative and original minds in the Egyptian Islamist current found the institutional confines of the brotherhood too limiting. As the twentieth century drew to a close, some of the most impressive figures moved out of the brotherhood to play a role as independent Islamist figures, although frequently maintaining loose ties to the brotherhood and always acknowledging the historic role of Ḥasan al-Bannā' and social Islam. Most impressive was the loosely linked group who called themselves the New Islamic Current and brought together such figures as Yūsuf al-Qaraḍāwī, Shaykh Muḥammad al-Ghazālī, Kamāl Abū al-Majd, and Fahmī Huwaydī. At the outset of the Mubarak era, Kamāl Abū al-Majd, on behalf of the group, produced a manifesto that expressed their moderate views, emphasizing commitments to democracy and pluralism. Despite its moderate thrust, the regime blocked the initiative, and the manifesto was not published for a decade. [*See the biography of Ghazālī.*]

In the first decade of Mubarak's rule, however, the New Islamists preserved their presence in Egyptian civil society and attempted to offer enlightened leadership to the rapidly growing Islamist body. They were joined by other prominent independent intellectuals such as the distinguished jurist Ṭāriq al-Bishrī and the diplomat Hussein Amin, who participated actively in rethinking Islam's role in public life. Amin in particular took a sharply rationalist and realist position that went well beyond ʿAbduh. He insisted on fully acknowledging the historical forces that had shaped the religious inheritance and on the necessity, in interpreting Islam today, of taking account of new conditions.

During the Gulf War the New Islamists stepped into the public arena with two statements addressed to the nation, condemning the Iraqi invasion of Kuwait yet calling for an Arab and Islamic diplomatic solution, in opposition to regime support for the American-led military resolution. At moments of grave social tension precipitated by communal strife, key figures from their circle urged religious tolerance and acceptance of Egypt's Christians as full members of the political and social community. With ever greater urgency they addressed their conciliatory message to Egypt's disillusioned young, who, in the deteriorating conditions of the 1990s, appeared to be responding instead to the shriller voices of the most unsubtle heirs of Sayyid Quṭb.

In tracing the history of the relationship between Islam, the Egyptian state, and civil society, it becomes clear that Islam has played a vital yet constantly shifting role in the development of Egyptian public life, particularly with respect to the ongoing need to define a common life for Egyptians. Within this history, prominent Islamist intellectuals and groups have formed and articulated unique and diverse responses to modernism and the influence of the West. This is best evidenced by their creative attempts to mediate modernism so as to appropriate and extend its influence in Egypt under Islamic terms.

BIBLIOGRAPHY

Dessouki, Ali E. Hillal, ed. *Islamic Resurgence in the Arab World*. New York, 1982. Though of uneven quality, the essays usefully place developments in Egypt in the broader Arab context.

Esposito, John L. *The Islamic Threat: Myth or Reality?* New York and Oxford, 1992. Written for a general audience, this authoritative survey of the current scene effectively counters media and scholarly distortions of Islam's role in public life.

Gilsenan, Michael. *Recognizing Islam: Religion and Society in the Modern Arab World*. New York, 1983. Sensitive and probing anthropological study of popular Islam in its full diversity and complexity.

Hourani, Albert. *A History of the Arab Peoples*. Cambridge, Mass., 1991. Brilliant and indispensable history of the Arabs and Islam, with important sections on Egypt, that crowned a lifetime of humanistic scholarship.

Kepel, Gilles. *Muslim Extremism in Egypt: The Prophet and Pharaoh*. Berkeley, 1986. Helpful though one-sided guide to Egypt's radical militants.

Mitchell, Richard P. *The Society of Muslim Brothers*. New York, 1969. Still the most insightful and fairest account of the Brothers' historic role in Egypt and beyond.

Oweiss, Ibrahim M., ed. *The Political Economy of Contemporary Egypt*. Washington, D.C., 1990. Helpful collection sketching the sociopolitical conditions of Egyptian Islamist movements. See in particular the essays by ʿAfāf Luṭfī al-Sayyid Marsot and Moustafa K. El-Sayed.

Sharabi, Hisham. *Neopatriarchy: A Theory of Distorted Change in Arab Society*. New York, 1988. Theoretically eclectic, this influential essay forcefully summarizes and restates negative assessments of the prospects of Islamist political movements in Egypt and elsewhere in the Arab world.

RAYMOND BAKER

ELECTRONIC MEDIA. *See* Radio and Television.

ELIJAH MUHAMMAD (1897–1975), leader of the Black Muslim group, the Nation of Islam, for more than forty years. Born Paul Robert Poole in 1897 on a tenant farm in Sandersville, Georgia, Elijah Muhammad was the seventh of twelve children. He assumed the name Elijah in honor of his grandfather and later chose the last name Muhammad, following the example of his religious guide and mentor, Fard Muhammad (formerly Wallace D. Fard), an enigmatic figure who is believed to be the original founder of the Lost and Found Nation of Islam. In the 1920s, Elijah Muhammad married the former Clara Evans and migrated north to Detroit in search of employment. He changed jobs several times while living in Detroit and, between 1929 and 1931, went on welfare. It is believed that his first meeting with Fard Muhammad took place during this period.

Elijah Muhammad was said to be a follower of Marcus Garvey prior to his encounter with Fard Muhammad. Real or imagined, the fact that his movement embraced theologically grounded black nationalism makes him a fellow traveler. Following the disappearance of Fard Muhammad, Elijah Muhammad became one of the contenders for power within the embryonic Nation of Islam. It is claimed by some scholars that at this time Elijah's life was in jeopardy, and for this and other related reasons, he was on the run between 1935 and 1942. Federal Bureau of Investigation sources obtained under the Freedom of Information Act revealed that in 1941 Muhammad had been jailed in Washington, D.C., where he went by the name of Bogans. He and several dozen members of the Nation of Islam were imprisoned for refusing to register for the draft. During World War II, the Nation of Islam itself was believed by U.S. authorities to be friendly to the Japanese.

During his incarceration, Muhammad embarked on a mission of conversion among prison inmates. He gradually established a prison mission around the country. His most charismatic and powerful jailed convert was Malcolm X. Later known as El-Hajj Malik el-Shabazz, this recruit into the Nation of Islam transformed the manner in which the Black Muslims presented themselves to the press and society at large. As a result of Malcolm X's energetic drive to reach the poor, the jailed, the downtrodden, and the despised black members of the inner cities of America, many young and old African Americans embraced the Nation of Islam. Temples were set up in several U.S. cities, and by 1962 the U.S. media discovered this small but growing religious group.

Elijah Muhammad taught his followers that blacks in the United States were the descendants of the Shabazz tribe of Arabia. He claimed that Fard Muhammad was God himself and that the white people are offspring of the devil, a soulless creature whose existence was made possible by a rebellious black scientist named Yacub. Yacub, according to this story, created the first white man after having discovered a recessive gene and experimenting with sixty thousand people for six hundred years. The philosophy of the Nation of Islam also teaches that the whites of this world have a respite of six thousand years, during which they can do all their evil deeds.

Elijah Muhammad lived to see the transformation of his fledgling organization into one of the most powerful black organizations in the United States. He built a social movement that served as a haven for the underclass, injecting it with a sense of pride, no matter how exaggerated. His success in reforming thousands of black men and women lost to society earned him the respect of some American sociologists. However, it must be stated categorically that Elijah Muhammad's teachings were opposed both by the leaders of the U.S. civil rights movement and by the leaders of the Muslim world. The former opposed his views because of the damage they caused to race relations during a critical period in U.S. history; the latter saw him and the Nation of Islam as a heretical group operating at the outer limits of the Islamic world.

[*See also* Nation of Islam; United States of America; *and the biography of Malcolm X.*]

BIBLIOGRAPHY

El-Amin, Mustafa. *The Religion of Islam and the Nation of Islam: What Is the Difference?* Newark, 1990.

Elijah Muhammad. *Message to the Blackman in America*. Chicago, 1965.

Lincoln, C. Eric. *The Black Muslims in America*. New York, 1961.

Nyang, Sulayman S. "Islam and the American Dream." *Arabia* (London) 15 (November 1982): 24–26.

SULAYMAN S. NYANG

EMBASSIES. *See* Diplomatic Missions.

ENGLAND. *See* Great Britain.

ENNADHA. *See* Ḥizb al-Nahḍah.

ENVER PASHA (1881–1922), Ottoman Turkish general and commander of the Ottoman armies during World War I. Born in Istanbul on 23 November 1881, Enver Pasha graduated from the military academy in 1902 and was posted to Macedonia, where the army was fighting bands of Greek and Bulgarian nationalist guerrillas. Balkan nationalist movements that emerged from the *millet* system had a strong religious component. As a result, early Turkish nationalism was strongly tinged with Islam. In 1906 Enver joined the Committee of Union and Progress (CUP), the leading organization in the Young Turk movement. Following the revolution of July 1908, Enver was promoted by the CUP as a "hero of liberty"; his rank at the time was that of staff major.

The government felt threatened by the charismatic appeal of junior officers like Enver and posted some of them as military attachés to Ottoman diplomatic missions. In 1909 Enver Bey was sent to Berlin, but the outbreak of a counterrevolution in Istanbul in April brought him back to center stage. His role in crushing the insurrection enhanced his popularity. In 1911–1912 he served with distinction in Libya, organizing resistance to the Italian army of occupation. The disastrous defeats of the Balkan wars of 1912–1913 saw him back in the capital; in January 1913 he overthrew the defeatist Kamil Pasha cabinet, which was about to surrender Edirne to the Bulgars, and brought the CUP to power. Enver was at that time a lieutenant colonel.

Enver led the forces that recaptured Edirne from Bulgaria in July 1913, and his prestige soared. When the government needed a young and dynamic war minister to purge and reform the army, Enver was the obvious choice. He was promoted to the rank of general with the title of pasha. He had become a key policymaker in the Committee with pro-German leanings. He was, however, pro-German only because he believed that the German alliance served Ottoman interests. In fact, Istanbul was so entirely dependent on Berlin that Ottoman policy throughout the war was dictated by German strategic needs. Despite the failures of this policy, Enver saw the revolution in Russia as an opportunity to create a new empire embracing the Turkic/Islamic peoples who had been under tsarist rule. This romantic dream failed to materialize. Ottoman armies were defeated on other fronts and forced to sign an armistice with Britain in October 1918. In November Enver and the CUP leaders fled to Germany. Enver went on to Turkistan, where he organized Muslim forces against the Bolsheviks. He was killed in battle in Tajikistan on 4 August 1922.

Nationalist historiography has portrayed Enver Pasha as a Pan-Turanist. Although he may have shared elements of this ideology, his actions suggest that he placed his faith in Ottomanism, which became increasingly Islamist as the non-Muslim nations broke away from Ottoman domination. Moreover, the CUP itself believed in Ottomanism; it married some of its military supporters to Ottoman princesses to link its fortunes to those of the dynasty. Enver married Naciye Sultan, the daughter of Prince Süleyman, a son of Sultan Abdülmecid. Ottomanism within the CUP was strengthened, and as the sultan was also caliph, dynasticism and Islam went hand in hand. Islam was the bond that united the various Muslim ethnic groups in the empire; this is why *jihād* was proclaimed as soon as Istanbul entered the war. Not only would this step unify all Muslim Ottomans, it was also expected to subvert the loyalty of Muslims living under British, French, and Russian rule. Later, when Enver fought the Bolsheviks, he named his force the Army of Islam (İslam Ordusu), though a Turanist might have called it the Turkish Army. Until the creation of the Turkish Republic, Islam remained the dominant ideological strand in the Ottoman Empire.

[*See also* Ottoman Empire; Pan-Turanism; Young Turks.]

BIBLIOGRAPHY

Ahmad, Feroz. *The Young Turks*. Oxford, 1969. Very useful for the years 1908–1914.

Swanson, Glen. "Enver Pasha: The Formative Years." *Middle Eastern Studies* 16 (1980): 193–199. Instructive for Enver's early years.

Trumpener, Ulrich. *Germany and the Ottoman Empire, 1914–1918*. Princeton, 1968. Excellent for the war years though Trumpener's interpretation relies almost entirely on German sources.

Yamauchi, Masayuki. *The Green Crescent under the Red Star: Enver Pasha in Soviet Russia, 1919–1922*. Tokyo, 1991. Yamauchi's introductions to Turkish documents (published in Turkish) provide original accounts of Enver's final years from a variety of sources.

FEROZ AHMAD

EPIGRAPHY. *See* Calligraphy and Epigraphy.

ERBAKAN, NECMETTİN (b. 1926), Turkish political leader. A native of the Black Sea port of Sinop, Necmettin Erbakan spent his childhood in provincial cities where his father served as a judge in criminal courts. He acquired his primary school education in Trabzon, his high school education at Istanbul Lisesi, and his higher education at Istanbul Technical University. He remained at the same institution for his doctoral studies, which he completed in Germany at the Aachen Technische Hochschule. He entered an academic career at Istanbul Technical University and was promoted to full professorship in 1965. In addition to his teaching position, Erbakan played a key role in the establishment of the Gümüş Motor Factory, which produced diesel engines, and served as the factory director between 1956 and 1963. He was also active in the administration of the Turkish Chamber of Commerce and was elected its general-director in 1969, a position that he was able to keep only briefly.

Erbakan left his academic career in 1969 when he was elected to the Grand National Assembly as an independent candidate from Konya. A year later Erbakan founded the Millî Nizam Partisi (MNP or National Order Party). The MNP was a neo-Islamist party that called for a spiritual reawakening combined with technical development programs. It was banned from political activity by the Constitutional Court in 1972 for its violation of legislation forbidding the use of religion for political purposes. The party leadership founded the Millî Selamet Partisi (MSP or National Salvation Party) the same year, with Erbakan as its leader. The MSP's program, like the MNP's, was critical of the republican course of development, which it saw as a failed effort to industrialize and a disastrous project destroying national values in the name of westernization. The MSP ideology emphasized rapid industrialization accompanied by moral and spiritual reconstruction.

The MSP under Erbakan's leadership participated in three coalition governments between 1973 and 1978, with Erbakan acting as deputy prime minister in all three. The party was banned from political activity after the 1980 coup d'état; its leadership was put under custody and tried in military courts, ending in acquittals. With the return to civilian politics in 1983, the defunct MSP was replaced by the Refâh Partisi (RP or Welfare Party), with Erbakan as its leader. The RP ideology has developed into a criticism of capitalism as a Zionist plot and calls for regional cooperation among Muslim countries.

Necmettin Erbakan has been more of a politician than a political thinker. The legitimation of Islamist politics in a secular state and the formulation of an Islamist political program within the limits of parliamentary democracy owe much to his contributions. He has been the major influence in the formulation of the MNP-MSP-RP ideology and has published books and pamphlets explaining the party's views on development, cultural issues, the educational system, foreign policy, and social welfare. However, his and his party's political vision is marginal in Turkish political life, which has been shaped both by the preference of the electorate for center parties and by legal limitations on extremist politics of the left and right.

[*See also* Refâh Partisi; Turkey.]

BIBLIOGRAPHY

Publications by Necmettin Erbakan include: *Millî Görüş* (Istanbul, 1975); *Üç Konferans: İslam ve İlim, İslam'da Kadın, Sanayi Davamız* (Istanbul, 1975); *Türkiye'nin Meseleleri ve Çözümleri* (Ankara, 1991); *Adil Ekonomik Düzen* (Ankara, 1991); and *Erbakan Açıklıyor: Kenan Evren'in Anılarındaki Yanılgılar* (Ankara, 1991).

BINNAZ TOPRAK

ERSOY, MEHMED ÂKİF (1873–1936), Turkish Islamist poet. Born in Istanbul of devout parents, Âkif received a secular education, graduating first in his class (1893) from the Civil School of Veterinary Sciences. He was a gifted linguist in Arabic, Persian and French, but it was through unrivalled mastery in his native Turkish that Âkif was to convey his poetic vision of the ideal Muslim society, based on his study of Islamic doctrine and the Qur'ān. Possessed of conviction and wholehearted commitment, he encapsulated the brooding restlessness of his time—the bitter disillusionment and gloomy introspection of the Muslim world, and especially of the Muslim Turks of the Ottoman Empire. His competent though undistinguished veterinary career (to 1913) was subordinated to his poetic calling, but it nevertheless brought him into close contact with the peoples of the Rumelian, Anatolian, and Arabian provinces, providing valuable insight for his social poetry.

Although publishing from 1893, Âkif was long unable, during a period of strict censorship, to put into print his maturing, poetic, social commentary—instead disseminating it privately. The restoration in 1908 of the 1876 Constitution, however, ushering in the Young Turk era, initiated his literary career proper in verse and prose. Already Âkif was interpreting the crisis of the Ottoman state's struggle for survival, under variform attack from Christendom, on the religious plane as an issue encompassing the entire Muslim world; his writing consequently aimed at an order for Muslim society within the ideal of Islamic unity. His perspective of the disorder in Ottoman society led him to blame not Islam but rather those aspects of the Muslim world created by Muslims and therefore open to correction by them; thus he attributed the failure of education to society's losing sight of the intellectual in Islam. While viewed as conservative, Âkif was so mainly in the sense that he set his revolutionary Islamic thinking within the framework of traditional poetic expression. His magnum opus, the seven-volume *Safahat* (Phases, 1911–1933), transmuted the lives of real people into a stylized social novel in verse form, composed throughout in polished classical prosody and style and displaying a talent for the use of vignette to inveigh against societal ills.

Âkif's pessimism increased during World War I in response to the collaboration by some Ottoman Muslim Arabs with the Christian Powers. His Turkish patriotism shocked into being by the loss of empire, he worked as an educator and preacher in the National

Struggle (1919–1922) toward the foundation of a new Turkish state; but he was distressed by the emergence of a nationalist, secular republic serving its Muslim citizens, rather than his desired Muslim Turkey leading the community of Islam. Disappointed, he settled in Egypt in 1925, where he taught Turkish and wrote little; he was however persuaded, despite misgivings, to translate the Qur'ān into Turkish under commission from the Turkish government. This work he eventually completed but retracted, fearing, in his isolation from events, that it might be misused in the state policy of turkification of the language of worship.

Âkif was not, nor did he wish to be, aloof from the thinking of his day; he challenged the current ideologies of Turkism and so-called Westernism. Yet his strong sense of Turkishness, as in his emphasis on Turkish idiom and vocabulary in composition, manifests itself clearly despite the uncompromising Islamist message of his writing. Few religious and patriotic poets of this century have surpassed Âkif in spiritual depth and nationalist passion, expressed, for example, in the *İstiklâl Marşı* (Independence March), his award-winning poem that was adopted as the Turkish national anthem in 1921.

What endures is the sincerity of the Islamic belief of this Turkish patriot, a man now seen as symbolizing the conjunction of Turkish nationalism and Muslim internationalism. As such, Âkif satisfies the yearning of both learned and unlearned in Turkey in their increasingly defensive reaction against the perceived hostility of the non-Muslim world.

[*See also* Ottoman Empire; Turkey; Young Turks.]

BIBLIOGRAPHY

Ersoy, Mehmed Âkif. *Açıklamalı ve Lûgatçeli Mehmed Âkif Külliyatı*, hazırlayan İsmail Hakkı Şengüler. 10 vols. Istanbul, 1990–1992. Complete works of the poet, with modern Turkish glossary.

Ersoy, Mehmed Âkif. *Safahat*. Prepared by M. Ertuğrul Düzdağ. Istanbul, 1987. Definitive edition of the *Safahat*, which has seen numerous editions and printings. Düzdağ also prepared a critical edition for the specialist (Istanbul, 1987).

İz, Fahir. "Mehmed ʿĀkif." In *Encyclopaedia of Islam*, new ed., vol. 6, pp. 985–986. Leiden, 1960–.

İz, Fahir. "Mehmed Akif Ersoy (1873–1936): A Biography." *Erdem* 4.11 (Mayıs 1988): 311–323. Useful introduction in English, given the paucity of non-Turkish works on Âkif.

Tansel, Fevziye Abdullah. *Mehmed Âkif: Hayatı Eserleri*. 2d ed. Istanbul, 1973. Arguably the best study to date of the poet's life and works.

M. Naim Turfan

ESCHATOLOGY. The study of "last things," eschatology frequently incorporates two separate but related concepts: the afterlife, and the end of the world.

Afterlife. In concepts closely related to ideas from other branches of Near Eastern monotheism, the Qur'ān emphasizes the inevitability of resurrection and judgment and the eternal division of righteous and wicked into heaven and hell. On the day of resurrection (Yawm al-Qiyāmah) humans will stand before God to be judged by their faith in God, their acceptance of God's revelations, and their works. The wicked will be consigned to eternal torment in hell (Jahannam; *nār*, "fire")—an abyss of fire, heat, dryness, and darkness. The righteous will enjoy the pleasures of paradise (Jannah), a magical garden of light (Qur'ān, 3.190–199, 22.19–20, 36.47–57, 37.7–68, 56, 75, 76). The Qur'ān offers sensual descriptions of paradise, including the pleasures of exquisitely delicious food and drink and sexual relations with divine maidens (which many Muslim commentators interpret as metaphorical). Later commentators also provide details of a belief in an intermediate state of the soul (*barzakh*) between death and the resurrection and final judgment. Before the final resurrection and judgment, however, the terrible tribulation of the last days will fall upon the earth.

Day of Judgment. Although the Qur'ān does not specify the time of the day of judgment, it assures its readers that that day is near. It has much to say about the end of the world, especially in its Meccan surahs. The general picture is very similar to that given in the Bible. Great earthquakes will rock the earth, setting mountains in motion (Qur'ān, 99). The sky will split open and heaven will be "stripped off," rolled up like a parchment scroll. The sun will cease to shine, the stars will be scattered and fall down upon the earth. The oceans will boil over. The graves will be opened up, with the earth bringing forth its burdens—the hidden sins, the lost stories, and the dead (82). People will vainly seek to flee from the divine wrath. All will bow, willingly or not, before God. In traditional Islamic thought the day of judgment is a period of great cosmic conflict when the forces of Satan—represented by a false Messiah al-Dajjāl and Gog and Magog (Ya'jūj and Mā'jūj)—come into conflict with the forces of God led by the Mahdi and Jesus.

The "Deceiver" (Dajjāl). An important Islamic eschatological figure is al-Dajjāl, "the deceiver," who is often equated with the Antichrist. In an age of injustice preceding the end of the world, the Deceiver will appear and, for a limited period—sometimes reckoned as forty years, sometimes as forty days—will cause corruption and oppression to sweep over the earth. His appearance is one of the sure signs of the last days. Deceiving many by his false teachings and miracles, he will bring with him supplies of food and water with which he will tempt those who have been suffering. Although the Qur'ān makes no mention of any such person, he is prominent in the *ḥadīth* and later Islamic literature. These ideas seem clearly to be related to Christian apocalyptic legends of the Antichrist.

The Mahdi. The "rightly guided one" also does not appear by name in the Qur'ān. He nonetheless plays a very important eschatological role in various strands of Islam. He is not a savior from sins, in the sense that Christians often attribute to Jesus, nor is he a merely national messiah as conceived in certain varieties of Judaism. Rather, he will come to bring justice and truth to all humanity.

In the first years following the close of Qur'ānic revelation and the death of the Prophet, Islam enjoyed virtually uninterrupted military success. The word *mahdī* was used during this period without messianic significance. By the late seventh century, however, after a period of considerable political turbulence, the term began to be used to refer to a hoped-for ruler who would restore Islam to its original perfection. With the passage of time, humane and just rule seemed an increasingly distant prospect. Thus, particularly following the ʿAbbāsid revolution (750), the figure of the Mahdi took on an ever more eschatological or messianic aura.

Although the Mahdi does occur in Sunnī teaching, he plays a much less significant role there than in Shīʿī belief. His role is particularly important in Twelver Shiism, which has developed the messianic tendencies in Islam to their furthest extent. In 873 the eleventh imam of the Twelver Shīʿīs died, to all appearances leaving no heir. Some of his disciples, however, claimed that he had an infant son who had been hidden for safekeeping. Indeed, between 873 and 941 there were "agents" who claimed to be in contact with the young imam. By this time most Shīʿīs had come to realize that open resistance against the government was futile. These agents promised that at the right time the hidden twelfth imam would emerge and redress the community's wrongs. As the years passed and he did not publicly appear, this figure acquired an ever more obviously messianic character, drawing on elements of other religious traditions to flesh out the image of the eschatological imam. After the elapse of a normal human life span, it began to be felt that the absent twelfth imam was in fact the Mahdi, who was being held in supernatural occultation from which he would someday return in glory to "fill earth with justice as it has been filled with oppression." The intervening time was a test for the faithful. The task of believers was to be faithful, obedient, and alert, watching for the "signs of the times," and evaluating passing events in the light of the apocalyptic prophecies that circulated in the community.

The Mahdi of the Twelvers is thought to reside in Mecca, or at least nearby. It is said that he makes the pilgrimage each year, although he goes unrecognized. Authorities name no year for his return, but many agree that he will disclose himself publicly on ʿĀshūrā', the tenth day of the month of Muḥarram and the anniversary of the martyrdom of the Prophet's grandson Ḥusayn (680 CE). Thus the well-known Shīʿī commemoration of ʿĀshūrā is an expression not merely of sorrow for the death of their beloved martyr, but also of hope for a cessation of suffering and injustice to be effected by a descendant of Ḥusayn. The reappearance of the Mahdi will occur at the Kaʿbah in Mecca. It will be accompanied by spectacular signs such as the rising of the sun in the west and unusual eclipses in the holy month of Ramaḍān. However, the Mahdi will not remain in Mecca. First, he will go to Medina, and from there to Kufa, where he will establish his capital. Ḥusayn, ʿAlī, and the Prophet will also return, with the first two taking especially important roles in the establishment of Islamic rule. The entire world will thereafter accept Islam, willingly or by force. The Mahdi will die some time before the day of resurrection, and his death will be followed by a brief period of turmoil, uncertainty, and temptation.

Both Sunnī and Shīʿī traditions about the Mahdi agree that he will rule the world and bring great wealth, which he will distribute generously; however, his rule will last only a relatively short time. In the Shīʿī view, he will force everyone to accept Shiism. While most Muslims expect him to restore the integrity of the *sharīʿah*, a minority through the years have taught that he would abrogate Islamic law, bringing a new prophetic message in its stead. [*See also* Mahdi; ʿĀshūrā'; Ithnā ʿAsharīyah.]

Second coming of Jesus. As the doctrine of the

Mahdi developed, disagreements occurred over his precise relationship to Jesus. Some Muslim thinkers denied that there will be a Muslim Mahdi, claiming instead that this role will be fulfilled by the second coming of Jesus. Post-Qur'ānic legends had also grown up about the second coming of Christ, which still persist. Some say that Jesus will return as a just judge. One prophecy says that he will descend in Palestine, where he will kill al-Dajjāl; he will then go to Jerusalem, where he will worship and kill both swine and those who disbelieve in him. He will die after a peaceful reign of some forty years and be buried in a spot beside the tomb of Muḥammad in Medina that has been reserved for him.

Modern Significance. Islamic eschatological ideas have exerted an important influence on the development of the modern Middle East. There are several significant examples of the impact of eschatological thought on modern religious, social, and political developments. The origin of the Bābī and Bahā'ī movements in early nineteenth-century Iran was closely tied with Iranian Shīʿī eschatological ideas. Mirzā Ghulām Aḥmad (1835–1908), founder of the Aḥmadīyah movement in Pakistan, claimed to be the Mahdi, drawing ideas not only from Islamic eschatological thought but also from Hinduism and Christianity. Islamic eschatology was fundamental in the founding of the Mahdist state in the Sudan by Muḥammad Aḥmad ibn ʿAbd Allāh (1843–1885), which still influences the Sudan today. On the other hand, many modernist Muslims, influenced by secular western thought, have tended to allegorize traditional eschatological beliefs. [*See* Bābism; Bahā'ī; Aḥmadīyah; Mahdīyah.]

The ideologies of many twentieth-century Islamic fundamentalist movements frequently include a healthy dose of eschatology. The capture of the Grand Mosque at Mecca in 1979 was based in part on Mahdist ideological claims; the ideology of the Iranian revolution was also linked to Shīʿī eschatological thought. The significance of martyrdom among both Shīʿīs and Sunnīs—as manifest in both battle and terrorism—is linked to the Qur'ānic concept that death in the path of God guarantees entry into paradise. There is every indication that eschatological ideas will continue to play an important role in the Islamic world into the twenty-first century.

[*See also* Messianism.]

BIBLIOGRAPHY

Abel, A. "Al-Dadjdjāl." In *Encyclopaedia of Islam,* new ed., vol. 2, pp. 76–77. Leiden, 1960–.

Carra de Vaux, Bernard. "Barzakh." In *Encyclopaedia of Islam,* new ed., vol. 1, pp. 1071–1072. Leiden, 1960–.

Fahd, T. "Nār." In *Encyclopaedia of Islam,* new ed., vol. 7, pp. 957–960. Leiden, 1960–.

Gardet, Louis. "Djahannam." In *Encyclopaedia of Islam,* new ed., vol. 2, pp. 381–382. Leiden, 1960–.

Gardet, Louis. "Djanna." In *Encyclopaedia of Islam,* new ed., vol. 2, pp. 447–452. Leiden, 1960–.

Gardet, Louis. "Ḳiyāma." In *Encyclopaedia of Islam,* new ed., vol. 5, pp. 235–238. Leiden, 1960–.

Jafri, S. Husain M. *Origins and Early Development of Shīʿa Islam.* London, 1979. Detailed study on early Shīʿī ideas of the imam and Mahdi.

Madelung, Wilferd. "Mahdī." In *Encyclopaedia of Islam,* new ed., vol. 5, pp. 1230–1238. Leiden, 1960–.

Meier, Fritz. "The Ultimate Origin and the Hereafter in Islam." In *Islam and Its Cultural Divergence: Studies in Honor of Gustave E. Von Grunebaum,* edited by Girdhari L. Tikku, pp. 96–112. Urbana, Ill., 1971. Good brief summary on the afterlife.

Sachedina, A. A. *Islamic Messianism: The Idea of Mahdī in Twelver Shīʿism.* Albany, N.Y., 1981. Standard study of the Shīʿī interpretation of the Mahdi.

Schimmel, Annemarie. *Mystical Dimensions of Islam.* Chapel Hill, N.C., 1975. Provides insight into Ṣūfī ideas on the afterlife.

Smith, Jane I., and Yvonne Yazbeck Haddad. *The Islamic Understanding of Death and Resurrection.* Albany, N.Y., 1981. Fundamental study on the subject.

Taylor, John B. "Some Aspects of Islamic Eschatology." *Religious Studies* 4 (1968): 57–76. Summary of the basic eschatological ideas.

WILLIAM J. HAMBLIN and DANIEL C. PETERSON

ETHICS. In contemporary Anglo-American discussion, ethics has to do with the study of practical justification. It focuses on describing and evaluating the reasons persons and groups give for judgments they make about right and wrong or good and evil, particularly as those terms relate to human acts, attitudes, and beliefs.

If we proceed from this understanding to a discussion of Islamic tradition, we first note that there is no single analogue for ethics in that tradition. Instead there are several genres of discourse, each with a special set of concerns and roles to play in the development of Islam and each related to the set of interests we associate with ethics.

Among the classical intellectual traditions, for example, *ʿilm al-akhlāq,* the "science of virtue," focuses on concerns about the character of persons. The nature of courage, the practice of wisdom and tolerance, and discussions about the cultivation of such desirable traits are the focus here. Those who write in this vein catalog and describe the predominant ways of acting, feeling, and thinking associated with the ideal of a good person; perhaps the most accessible example of the genre is the *Nasirean Ethics* attributed to the Shīʿī scholar Naṣīr al-Dīn Ṭūsī (d. 1274 CE).

A related form of discourse is indicated by the term *adab*, "letters," used to indicate a variety of types of writing. The unifying theme of *adab* is reflection on the noble ideals that ought to inform the practice of statecraft, medicine, business, and other activities important to society. One prominent form of this genre has a writer presenting wise advice to those who would practice a particular craft. Thus the celebrated Seljuk vizier Niẓām al-Mulk (d. 1092) presents advice to rulers in his *Siyāsat nāmah* or "Rules for Kings." Similarly, a late eighth- or early ninth-century text attributed to one al-Ruhāwī exhorts physicians on the "Way of Behaving Appropriate to Physicians" *(Adab al-ṭabīb)*. Other *adab* writers work in an essay or narrative format, fulfilling the role of pundit for a more general audience: thus al-Jāḥiẓ (d. 868) could write on topics from homosexuality to theological discourse or could provide both entertainment and moral education in collections of stories about famous misers, gluttons, and the like.

One could continue to detail the ways in which various modes of discourse in classical Islam address questions of ethics; for example, the historical writing of al-Ṭabarī (d. 923) or Ibn Khaldūn (d. 1406) might be considered a form of moral discourse. Among the classical disciplines, however, three stand out as essential for any discussion of ethics in Islamic tradition: *falsafah* (philosophy), *kalām* (dialectical theology), and *fiqh* (jurisprudence).

Falsafah, as developed by writers like al-Fārābī (d. 950), Ibn Sīnā (d. 1037), and Ibn Rushd (d. 1198), takes aspects of the Greek philosophical tradition and develops them in relation to Islamic themes. For example, al-Fārābī understands philosophy as a quest for personal excellence, particularly in terms of intellect and moral character. Such a quest is available to anyone who has the requisite intelligence together with enough worldly goods to allow time for contemplation. One tension between *falsafah* and Islamic tradition becomes immediately apparent: practically speaking, philosophy is for an elite group, whereas Islamic revelation confirms the basic equality of human beings before God. Is it possible, then, for the philosopher to reconcile a personal quest for excellence with the message given through prophecy? As al-Fārābī has it, prophecy and *falsafah* are essentially one. The major difference is that the Prophet perceives truth suddenly, by inspiration, while philosophers must gain wisdom through a long and arduous struggle. Further, the Prophet has a special capacity that enables him to put the pure (and abstract) truth sought by philosophers in terms that the mass of humanity can comprehend. It is in this capacity that revealed texts (e.g., the Qur'ān) make use of narratives and poetic discourse rather than philosophic argumentation. Thus revelation is philosophy for the masses, and the prophets become popular examples of obedience to moral law—although the real foundations of morality, as religion, are philosophical rather than revealed.

Kalām begins with a different set of interests and questions. Practitioners of *kalām* focused on clarifying points of doctrine, including the nature of ethical judgment. The Muʿtazilah, perhaps the most influential of the early *kalām* movements, made the discussion of justice a central part of their program. With some variations, they argued as follows. Justice has to do with attributions of praise or blame to agents who perform specific acts. A person who tells the truth usually deserves praise, while one who commits murder deserves blame—from the Muʿtazilī point of view, such judgments are typical of humanity as a whole. The fact of such judgments leaves open an important question, however. How do human beings justify such judgments? According to most Muʿtazilī thinkers, God made the world to be governed by moral law. "He it is who created the heavens and the earth in six days . . . that He might try you, which of you is best in conduct" (Qur'ān, 11.7). It would be unjust for God to impose such a trial unless there is a fair chance for humanity to acquit itself; and so God has given all humanity the ability to discern which acts are blameworthy and which worthy of praise. God has also given humans the capacity to choose which acts to perform. For the Muʿtazilah, the ability to discern is based on a combination of rational reflection and intuition. Human beings, reflecting on the fact of moral judgment, come to understand that it is based on certain "grounds" *(ʿillah)* or basic principles that are "built into" the structure of reality. Prophetic revelation refers to these principles, confirms, extends, and strengthens them.

A contrary position was developed by the Ashʿarīyah. Al-Ashʿarī (d. 935) focused his *kalām* on the notion that nothing happens apart from God's will. Notions of moral intuition and human responsibility are secondary to affirmation of the majesty and power of God. When human beings perform praiseworthy or blameworthy acts, they do so by God's will. Further, the Ashʿarī position is that the only way for human beings to distinguish good and evil is through reading and interpreting revealed texts, in particular the Qur'ān and sound accounts (*ḥadīths*) of Muḥammad's words and deeds.

The Ashʿarīyah emphasized revealed texts in order to establish continuity between their *kalām* and the last of the classical genres to be discussed here: *fiqh,* usually translated "jurisprudence." Literally, the term indicates "comprehension"; in this context, *fiqh* has to do with a concern to comprehend divine guidance. In his famous *Risālah,* al-Shāfiʿī (d. 820) indicates that the concern of *fiqh* is to discern that guidance "whereby no one who takes refuge in it will ever be led astray."

The great contribution of al-Shāfiʿī and other practitioners of *fiqh* lay in their development of a model of reasoning by which human beings could comprehend divine guidance. The theory of *uṣūl al-fiqh* or "the sources of jurisprudence" establishes a hierarchy of revealed texts, together with ways of interpreting and reasoning from the texts. The basic text is the Qur'ān, the "speech" of God. Accounts of the Prophet's exemplary practice *(sunnah)* confirm and extend the Qur'ān. Various modes of reasoning serve to further extend Qur'ān and *sunnah,* especially the use of analogy known as *qiyās.* Other approved types of reasoning include *raʿy* (juristic opinion), *istiḥsān* (juristic preference), and *istiṣlāḥ* (a type of reasoning concerned to balance notions of duty with considerations of the general welfare.) Finally, the judgments of individual scholars are regulated by the notion of ijmāʿ("consensus"), referring either to the consensus of scholars or to the common sense of the Muslim community. [*See* Uṣūl al-Fiqh; Consensus.]

Each of the classical forms of discourse has its modern analogue. The publications of authors like Ṭāhā Ḥusayn and Naguib Mahfouz might be construed as *adab,* for example. Indeed, in some cases Muslim writers see themselves as continuing specific conversations that originated in the classical period. This is clearest in connection with *fiqh,* which for a variety of reasons came to have pride of place among the genres associated with ethical concern. Especially among Sunnī Muslims, the textualist tendencies so important for the Ashʿarīyah and the scholars of *fiqh* became primary. Much Sunnī discourse assumes that judgments about human activity are a matter of discerning God's commands through interpreting the texts and employing the modes of reasoning developed in the classical theory of *uṣūl al-fiqh.* Especially in settings where scholars of *fiqh* participate in a judicial setting (as in most Muslim countries), there is a very strong sense of making judgments informed by precedent or reflecting a conversation between the contemporary scholar and scholars of the past. The *fatwās* or opinions issued on the basis of *uṣūl al-fiqh* by famous al-Azhar jurists like Muḥammad ʿAbduh (d. 1905) and Muḥammad Rashīd Riḍā (d. 1935) have this character, as do many current pronouncements on issues of state policy, medical practice, and the like. Such judgments take place in response to specific cases brought before a scholar, who then makes a judgment concerning the rightness or wrongness of specific courses of action, all the time justifying this judgment in relation to authoritative texts, approved modes of reasoning, and the precedents set by other scholars of *fiqh.* For example, in consideration of the question, "Should Bosnian Muslims emigrate to Islamic territory?" following Austria's annexation of the region in 1908, Rashīd Riḍā's *fatwās* weighed the positions taken in analogous cases by various practitioners of *fiqh* before saying that, in his opinion, any judgment in such a case should reflect on the ability of a group of Muslims to carry out their general obligation to "command good and forbid evil."

At the same time, important Sunnī scholars have argued that the political and social situation of Muslims in the modern world call for reforms not only in forms of government or patterns of investment but also in religious thought. One way to pursue such reform is to revisit relations between *fiqh* and some other classical forms of ethical discourse. Muḥammad ʿAbduh, for example, argued for a new attempt at *kalām,* construed as a way to revisit the ideas of God and human responsibility that undergird *fiqh.* His *Risālat al-tawḥīd* (Theology of Unity) attempts to find a middle way between the Muʿtazilah and Ashʿarīyah on the place of human moral intuition and revealed texts in matters of ethics. For ʿAbduh, moral intuition is sufficient to establish the first principles of morality and also to work out the implications of morality for social and political life. Revelation is necessary to indicate religious obligations, however; and since most human beings require the encouragement provided by "the promise and the threat" associated with the day of judgment as a motive to adhere to moral law, true religion plays an important part in the moral and political life of human societies. In this connection, *fiqh* finds its place as a specifically juridical counterpart to the more general moral concern common among human beings in a particular society. A position similar to ʿAbduh's was developed by the Indian Sayyid Aḥmad Khān (d. 1898). In either case, the revisiting of relations between *kalām* and *fiqh* provides a way of thinking about ethics that is less tied to the Ashʿarī emphasis on the limits of human reason than was characteristic of Sunnī thinking through the centuries.

Among Shīʿī scholars, *fiqh* also assumed first position among the classical genres associated with ethics. In centers of learning like Najaf in Iraq and Qom in Iran, contemporary scholars stress the importance of precedent and legal reasoning in ways that are comparable to those of the Sunnī scholars. The Shīʿī tradition is distinct, however, in regard to *uṣūl al-fiqh,* and even more on the relationships among *fiqh, kalām,* and *falsafah.* In particular, the historic position of Shīʿīs on justice *(al-ʿadl)* has important affinities with Muʿtazilī *kalām,* in which the rational capacities of human beings in matters of moral discernment are emphasized. The related emphasis in *fiqh* on *ʿaql* (reason) as one of the sources by which human beings comprehend divine guidance constitutes an important difference between Shīʿī and Sunnī approaches to ethics. When, under Ṣafavid rule, some Shīʿī scholars (called Akhbārīyah) advocated that the emphasis on *ʿaql* be lessened in favor of the use of textual precedents, the majority (known as Uṣūlīyah) reaffirmed the validity of reason as an independent source of judgment. This historic validation of reason has allowed Shīʿī scholars consistently to construe the relations between religion and ethics in ways similar to that proposed as a reform by Sunnī writers like Muḥammad ʿAbduh and Aḥmad Khān. It has also allowed some Shīʿī scholars to think about matters of ethics in terms of a thoroughgoing teaching on *tawḥīd* (divine unity) as the mode of the Islamic life, in which the concerns of the various classical disciplines are addressed and integrated in holistic fashion. [*See* Akhbārīyah; Uṣūlīyah.]

One of the best contemporary examples of this development is in the thought of the Ayatollah Ruhollah Khomeini (d. 1989). Best known for his lectures on Islamic government and for his leadership of the Iranian Revolution and the Islamic Republic of Iran, Khomeini was also a teacher of *ʿirfān* and *akhlāq* (gnosis and character formation). In various speeches and lectures Khomeini develops an interactive view of the various aspects of an Islamic life. One learns, through reflection and study, that God alone is the source and destiny of all things. Through disciplined and consistent spiritual practice, especially prayer, one comes to hold the notion of God as beneficent and merciful, and especially as "Owner of the Day of Judgment," in a way that fills one's heart and mind. This is the meaning of faith, according to Khomeini; and one who holds the notion of God in this way will find it very hard to commit serious sin. Further, such a person will be motivated to struggle courageously on behalf of justice. Indeed, he or she will be willing to sacrifice life for the cause of God.

Through this teaching Khomeini combines the concerns of various classical disciplines to create a type of "ethical spirituality." The ultimate goal of life, he says, is the development of "truly human" character. Human beings are characterized by their religious/moral capacity. They have the potential to do great things, to develop into virtuous beings; they also have the potential for great sin. The struggle to become virtuous has personal dimensions, as one reflects on one's existence as a creature of God; it has moral and political dimensions, as one struggles to create a just society. Further, the personal and the moral/political interact; in particular, the establishment of a political order governed by Islamic norms is not an end in itself but a way to encourage people to fulfill their potential for virtue through the creation of a social environment that encourages spiritual practice by enforcing the ordinances of Islam.

This contribution of Khomeini and other Shīʿī scholars (for example, Murtaẓā Muṭahharī, d. 1979) to the development of a modern Islamic perspective on ethics is possible, at least in part, because of the way Shīʿī traditions of religious education have kept alive the relationships between *kalām, falsafah, akhlaq,* and *fiqh.* This should not be taken, however, as a denial of similar contributions by Sunnī thinkers. The Egyptian writer Sayyid Quṭb (d. 1965) developed a rather similar way of thinking in his commentary *In the Shade of the Qur'ān;* the many books of the Pakistani writer and activist Abū al-ʿAlā Mawdūdī (d. 1979) also bear consideration in this regard. Indeed, the notion of an ethical or *tawḥīdī* spirituality is common among many of the diverse activist movements that have become prominent in Muslim countries during the 1980s and early 1990s. Deeply involved in an attempt to islamize social and political institutions, such movements are also making contributions to the Islamic tradition of thinking about practical justification, particularly in connection with concrete questions of political, medical, and economic ethics.

[*See also* Philosophy; Theology; *and the biographies of ʿAbduh, Aḥmad Khān, Khomeini, Mawdūdī, Muṭahharī, Quṭb, and Rashīd Riḍā.*]

BIBLIOGRAPHY

Carney, Frederick, ed. "Focus on Islamic Ethics." *Journal of Religious Ethics* 11.2 (1983). Collects five perceptive essays on ethics in classical Islamic disciplines: *fiqh, kalām, falsafah,* mysticism, and exegesis of the Qur'ān.

Carney, Frederick, and John Kelsay, eds. "Focus on Islamic Law and Ethics." *Journal of Religious Ethics* 22.1 (1994). An introduction and three essays on concerns of ethics as reflected in the tradition of *fiqh*.

Enayat, Hamid. *Modern Islamic Political Thought.* Austin, 1982. Outstanding study of trends in contemporary Islamic political writing.

Hourani, George F. *Islamic Rationalism: The Ethics of ʿAbd al-Jabbar.* Oxford, 1971. Groundbreaking study of a late Muʿtazilī thinker.

Hourani, George F. *Reason and Tradition in Islamic Ethics.* Cambridge and New York, 1985. Indispensable collection of essays by one of the leading students of ethics in the Islamic tradition.

Izutsu, Toshihiko. *Ethico-Religious Concepts in the Qur'an.* Montreal, 1966. Important work on key concepts in Qur'ānic ethics, for example *taqwā* and *ẓulm*.

Johnson, James T., and John Kelsay, eds. *Cross, Crescent, and Sword.* Westport, Conn., 1990. This volume and the one following explore the relations between the Euro-American "just war tradition" and the rules governing the use of force in Islamic tradition. Alternatively, see John Kelsay, *Islam and War: A Study in Comparative Ethics* (Louisville, 1993).

Johnson, James T., and John Kelsay, eds. *Just War and Jihad.* Westport, Conn., 1991. See annotation to preceding work.

Khomeini, Ruhollah. *Islam and Revolution: Writings and Declarations of Imam Khomeini.* Translated by Hamid Algar. Berkeley, 1981. An excellent sample of the thinking of the late ayatollah.

Lewis, Bernard. *The Political Language of Islam.* Chicago, 1988. Essays on selected topics related to political thought and practice in Islam.

Rahman, Fazlur. *Health and Medicine in the Islamic Tradition: Change and Identity.* New York, 1989. Well-crafted survey of some important issues connected with medical ethics.

Rajaee, Farhang. *Islamic Values and Worldview: Khomeyni on Man, the State, and International Politics.* Lanham, Md., 1983. Fine study of basic themes in Khomeini's thought.

JOHN KELSAY

ETHIOPIA. Islam has played a significant and at times central role in the political, socioeconomic, and cultural life of Ethiopia throughout the entire history of Islam itself as well as for the last thirteen centuries in Ethiopia. However, particularly in the modern history of Ethiopia, the roles of Islam have nearly always been deeply intermixed with other political and cultural issues and formations such that the distinctive significance of Islam per se is at best difficult to extract. In this respect Islam's place in Ethiopian history differs sharply from its situation in many other countries and regions.

The Ethiopian state of the distant past lay roughly within what are today its northwestern regions. Among the oldest of Christian states, Ethiopia's Coptic Christian political identity was already well established when Islamic rulers made contact with the country in the seventh century. Although these first contacts were characterized by a degree of mutual tolerance, Ethiopia soon became isolated from contact with Europe and the Middle East as a Christian island in an Islamic sea, so rapid was Islam's spread. Muslim rulers in Egypt were in a position to deny Ethiopia's Coptic church access to the see of Alexandria, which provided its spiritual leaders until the 1950s. The price to Ethiopia of this religious lifeline was permission to allow the building of mosques within Ethiopia. Similarly, from the fourteenth century onward the spread of Islam in what is today southern and eastern Ethiopia exposed the vulnerability of what Ethiopian rulers considered to be trade links with the world through Red Sea ports.

Strong Ethiopia rulers, such as Amda Siyon (1313–1344), were able to secure the highland fastnesses of the Amhara kingdom against Muslim advances, aided by divisions among Muslim communities along linguistic and cultural lines. In 1525, however, Ahmad Gran united Muslims in a nearly successful *jihād* to conquer a Christian Ethiopia weakened by decades of internal political instability. Portuguese assistance enabled the kingdom to repel the invaders, and this high tide of Muslim incursion into Ethiopia quickly receded with the leader's death. But the Portuguese subsequently undermined internal Ethiopian political stability through an ultimately futile attempt to convert the Coptic Christian kingdom to Roman Catholicism. Such weakness exposed the kingdom and its dominant Amhara communities to penetration by islamized Oromo peoples from the south and east from the mid-sixteenth to the mid-nineteenth century. Although sometimes frought with conflict, the intermixing of the Amhara and Oromo was often peaceful. Indeed local Amhara leaders often found in the Oromo useful allies in their internecine rivalries, though the cumulative effect of these rivalries was the near eclipse of central government authority between the late eighteenth and the mid-nineteenth centuries.

After 1855 the exertions of Emperors Tewodros and Johannes restored the authority of the monarchy, though the latter died in a battle to repel the incursions of Mahdist forces attacking from Sudan. As king of Shoa, and after Tewodros as emperor, Menelik II (1889–1913) expanded the boundaries of the empire to its present dimensions. His conquests of what is now southern and eastern Ethiopia subjected predominantly islamized peoples, their lands, and their political orders to the authority of an Amhara-dominated Christian imperial central government. The subtleties of Emperor Haile Selassie's rule (1930–1974) and the disestablishment of the Coptic church and attempted land tenure reforms under the government of Mengistu Haile Mariam (1975–1991) did little to change this underlying relationship.

The importance of Islam in twentieth-century Ethiopia has been epitomized by census politics. Ethnic divisions do not neatly follow residence, linguistic, or confessional lines, not least because at elite levels many Oromo responded to incentives established by both Menelik and Haile Selassie to accommodate themselves to their Christian, Amhara-based regimes. However, no twentieth-century regime has permitted a census to attempt to establish the relative size of Ethiopia's religious communities. Verification of best estimates that as many of 40 percent of the population adheres to Islam, perhaps equaling or exceeding the number of Christians, and that Oromo may equal or outnumber Amhara, would have been awkward for the Christian Amhara monarchy. Neither would such information have been welcomed by a Mengistu regime determined to subordinate ethnic affiliation to socialist ideological orthodoxy. The intentions of Mengistu's successors were not yet clear in the early 1990s, nor were those of the government in newly independent Eritrea, notwithstanding its correspondingly large Muslim population.

The importance of Islam in contemporary Ethiopia is matched by the complexities of its position in the life of the country. Although heavily concentrated in the eastern half of the country, important communities are found in the southwest around Jimma, near Gondar in the northwest, and along the boundaries with Sudan both in the north and farther south. Notwithstanding Menelik's conquests, the Italians in both world wars (and the Turks in World War I) failed to destabilize Ethiopia by pitting Islamic peoples against the Christian establishment. A traditional Islamic sultanate based in Awsa in eastern Ethiopia both resisted and collaborated with Haile Selassie's government. Its historically vaguely defined and shifting sphere of influence in the post-Mengistu era has expanded to encompass Afar peoples in both Eritrea and Ethiopia. The EPLF (Eritrean People's Liberation Front) government in Asmara, like its post-Mengistu counterpart in Addis Ababa, has relatively weaker support in Islamic communities than among followers of other religions, though neither regime rests on confessionally based legitimacy. Although a large 1974 Addis Ababa demonstration by Muslims in favor of religious freedom was important in demonstrating the bankruptcy of Haile Selassie's government, Muslims achieved only miniscule representation in Mengistu's government. For a time, however, northern Ethiopia resisted what it regarded as the Islamic and Oromo orientations of the Mengistu government. The significance of Islam in Oromo opposition to the Mengistu regime and potentially its successor has been blurred by the emergence of an Islamic Oromo Liberation Front alongside the Oromo Liberation Front. Despite the political hegemony of Christianity, twentieth-century emperors permitted Islamic courts to adjudicate certain matters of civil law in accord with Islamic law. Yet within Muslim as well as Christian communities, Islamic thought and practice has been tempered by the retention of conflicting preconversion beliefs and practices, such as fear of the "evil eye," even as a number of Ṣūfī orders labor to advance and spread the faith.

BIBLIOGRAPHY

Clapham, Christopher. *Transformation and Continuity in Revolutionary Ethiopia*. London, 1988. Presents a detailed picture of the structure of the Mengistu regime in Ethiopia from its inception in 1974 to its demise in 1991.

Harbeson, John W. *The Ethiopian Transformation: The Quest for the Post-Imperial State*. Boulder, 1988. Places the Mengistu regime in the context of modern Ethiopian political history.

Jones, A. H. M., and Elizabeth Monroe. *A History of Ethiopia*. London, 1938. An enduring and standard history of Ethiopia from the earliest times.

Markakis, John. *Ethiopia: Anatomy of a Traditional Polity*. London 1974. The leading work on the political economy of Ethiopia in the Haile Selassie years.

Rubenson, Sven. *The Survival of Ethiopian Independence*. New York, 1976. The definitive study of Ethiopian domestic and international politics in the early and mid-nineteenth century.

Trimmingham, J. Spencer. *Islam in Ethiopia*. London, 1952. The standard work on the influence of Islam on Ethiopian political and socioeconomic life.

JOHN W. HARBESON

ETHNICITY. The Qur'ān states repeatedly that individuals, not groups, are responsible for what they do, stressing the unity of the Islamic *ummah* (community) in verse after verse and emphasizing the primacy of bonds created through Islam over those based on shared identities of kinship, descent, region, and language—bonds which the medieval Moroccan philosopher Ibn Khaldūn (d. 1406) collectively called *ʿaṣabīyah* ("group cohesiveness").

Muslims say that commitment to Islam supplants ties of ethnicity, the ways in which individuals and groups characterize themselves on the basis of shared language, culture, descent, place of origin, and history. Yet from the first Muslim conquests in seventh-century Arabia, as Muslim armies spread forth from the Arabian Peninsula to peoples who neither spoke Arabic nor could claim Arab descent, such concerns frequently surfaced in practice. Under the Umayyad dynasty (661–750), persons successfully claiming Arab descent obtained economic and political benefits. To the present day, Muslims claiming descent from the prophet Muḥammad, called *sharīf*s in Morocco and sayyids in the Yemen and elsewhere—and such claims are by no means limited to the Arab world—often enjoy religious prestige and legal entitlements. [*See* Sharīf; Sayyid.]

As elsewhere in the world, Muslim notions of ethnicity are cultural constructions. For this reason, it is difficult to find a specific counterpart in Middle Eastern and other languages for the English term *ethnicity*. Ethnicity is an observer's term, for those who assert ethnic ties often regard them as fixed and "natural." Ethnicity is often thought to be a matter of birth, but the exceptions are as frequent as the rule: the social and political significance of ethnic and religious identities alters significantly according to historical and social contexts. For example, take the term *qawm* ("people") in Afghanistan. Depending on context it can mean a tribe or a subdivision of one, a people sharing a common origin or region of residence, or more generally a shared identity of religion and language. Moreover, since the latter half of the twentieth century, the experience of large-scale migration in search of wage labor—Pakistanis to Saudi Arabia, Turks and Kurds to western Germany, and North Africans to France—or as refugees—Afghans to Iran and Western Europe and Bosnian Muslims to Austria and Germany—has had a major impact on changing the significance and political implications of ethnic identity.

In the Arabian Peninsula, claims to ethnic or tribal identity—the two notions are almost indistinguishable in countries such as Saudi Arabia, Oman, Yemen, and the Gulf states—are usually framed in genealogical terms as descending from one of two eponymous ancestors. "Northern" Arabs claim descent from ʿAdnān; "southern" Arabs, including those who speak Semitic languages other than Arabic, claim Qaḥṭān as their ancestor. The possibility for some groups of claiming either ʿAdnān or Qaḥṭān as eponymous ancestors allows for flexibility in making descent claims, although genealogies are considered fixed. Indeed, since the 1960s, groups such as the Sindhi-speaking Shīʿī Liwāṭīyah of coastal Oman have also claimed Arab descent, explaining their "temporary" loss of Arabic (and tribal identity) by centuries of residence on the Indian subcontinent. Ex-slaves (Ar., *khuddām*) attached to tribes and ruling families throughout the Arabian Peninsula, and other groups lacking tribal descent, have traditionally had an inferior social status, as shown by occupation and the lack of intermarriage with other groups, but modern economic conditions are rapidly eroding these distinctions. Visible African descent might suggest slave descent to some traditionalists on the Arabian Peninsula, but it might also imply descent from one of the ruling families in which slave concubines were common in earlier generations.

Contemporary Arab identity suggests how historically and contextually diverse ethnic claims can be. Many Arabs assert that they are a "race," although for centuries populations have mixed and intermarried throughout the Arab world. Although divided politically despite the first claims to Arab unity in the early twentieth century, made as the Ottoman Empire weakened, Arabs are unified by language and culture. Nonetheless, many of the regional dialects of Arabic are mutually unintelligible. For example, Arabs from Saudi Arabia and the Gulf states understand colloquial Moroccan Arabic only with difficulty, and vice-versa. The spread of mass higher education throughout the region since midcentury contributed to widening the appeal of Arab nationalism and Pan-Arabism and of course facilitated communications among Arabs from different regions able to converse in a common "educated" Arabic modeled on classroom and the broadcast media. Still, major differences of dialect and situational identity remain. One is not just Muslim in the Middle East or elsewhere, but also Arab (and there are not only Christian and Muslim Arabs, but also Arabic-speaking Jews in Israel and North Africa), Berber, Nubian, Circassian, Hui, Malay, Sindhi, or Fulani.

Since ethnic and religious considerations are never the sole attribute shared by persons and groups in the Middle East, it is crucial to consider how such social distinctions figure in the overall context of social and personal identity and to not stop at a mosaic-like enumeration of ethnic group, sect, family origin, locality, and occupation. In North Africa, for example, the first Arab invaders came with the advent of Islam in the seventh century, followed by a second, larger wave of bedouin migrations in the eleventh and twelfth centuries. Nonetheless, the peoples of the region claim both Berber and Arab descent, and these claims to ethnic identity are based on language and cultural characteristics. Arabic is the dominant language of the region, and Arab civilization is pervasive, but there are still groups in the mountainous regions and in certain oases, particularly in Morocco and southern Algeria, who retain Berber languages and traditions, and some of these groups, such as traders originally from Morocco's Sus valley, play major roles in urban life elsewhere in the country.

In Morocco, for example, nearly half the population speaks one of the several Berber dialects, although most Moroccan Berbers, especially men, speak Arabic as a second language. The most important dialect (and ethnic) clusters are Shluḥ, spoken in Morocco and Mauritania; Shāwiyah and Kabyle in Algeria; Tamāshek, spoken by the Tuareg of the central Sahara and south of the Niger; Rīfian and Tamazīght, spoken predominantly in Morocco; and Zanāga, in Senegal.

French colonial administrators, first in nineteenth-century Algeria and subsequently in twentieth-century Morocco, sought to nurture the notion that Berber identity was distinct from that of being Arab and Muslim. For reasons of colonial control, the French in Morocco emphasized the real and imagined differences of Berbers, who in the earlier part of the century resided primarily in the mountainous regions and in Morocco's south, from the Arab society of the towns and the agricultural plains. In 1930 the French made a major political miscalculation when they issued the famous Berber Proclamation in Morocco, which legally excluded regions designated as Berber from the jurisdiction of Islamic law courts. The proclamation set off protests throughout Morocco and the Muslim world. This decree was supplemented by policies affecting military recruitment, local administration, and education (Berbers were forbidden to learn Arabic in schools, although most students found the means to do so). Even after Morocco gained its independence from France in 1956, the issue continued to be a delicate one. Some Berber intellectuals would like to see the Berber languages written and taught in schools, although governmental officials in both Morocco and Algeria, which also has a significant Berber population, have discouraged such initiatives for fear of encouraging separatist movements.

In Morocco, the categorizations Arab and Berber are often situational, and persons will stress one or another aspect of their identity depending on context. Identity as Arab and Berber is best thought of as a continuum rather than (as did French colonial officials) as a sharp, mappable distinction. Diverse patterns of occupation, residence, marriage, urban and rural origin, and other factors show that the ethnic distinctions of Arab and Berber in North Africa lack the all-pervasive typification that ethnicity takes in contexts elsewhere, including being Kurdish in northern Iraq or Muslim in Bosnia.

Assertion of an ethnic identity is often a political claim. In Afghanistan, opposition to the Soviet-dominated state which took power in 1978 and to the 1979 Soviet invasion came largely from tribally organized ethnic groups, for whom attachment to Islam served as a common denominator. In Pakistan, especially after the secession of Bangladesh in 1971, the country's ruling Punjabi elite viewed with suspicion the country's other ethnic groups, which include Sindhis, Pashtuns, Muhajirs (Muslim refugees who migrated after 1947 from what is now India), and Baluch. The Pakistani state emphasizes Islam as an identity more important than the common ethnic ties of its minority groups, including the Baluch, who from 1973 to 1977 fought for regional autonomy. The insurgency was unsuccessful, but contributed to a heightened Baluch national consciousness that cut across tribal divisions.

Ethnic stereotyping involves shared notions concerning the motivations and attributes of the members of other ethnic groups and what can be expected of them, as well as those of one's own ethnic group. Ethnic identities, like those of language, sect, nation, and family, can be comprehended only in the context of more general assumptions made in a given society concerning the nature of the social relationships and obligations. Such understandings can be benign, as in most Arab-Berber relations in North Africa, or they can menace the destruction of civil society.

Most modern notions of ethnicity have little to do with the notion of the mappable traits of an earlier generation. Instead, they emphasize how ethnic distinctions are generated, produced, and maintained in society. Ethnic identities are constantly adjusted to changing requirements, even if some advocates of ethnic nationalism maintain that ethnic identities are irreducible and self-evident.

The Kurds are a case in point. How Kurds construct

their ethnic and religious identity, or have the label "Kurd" applied to them by others, indicates the difficulties involved in treating ethnic identities as primordial givens or as locally held aggregations of collective interests.

Kurdistan is a region that crosses several international boundaries. Most Kurds live in Turkey (10 million, perhaps 20 percent of the country's population), although several million live in neighboring Iran and northern Iraq, with smaller numbers in Syria and elsewhere, including western Germany. The number of Kurds is itself a significant issue, with Kurdish spokespersons offering higher figures than those wishing to diminish the political importance of Kurds. For many years, Kurds in Turkey were officially designated as "mountain Turks" who possessed an incomplete command of Turkish. Although other minorities in Turkey had their non-Turkish mother tongues recorded in official censuses, Kurdish was not, and only in recent years has speaking and writing Kurdish become legal. Many Kurds in Turkey are also Alevi (Ar., ʿAlawī) Muslims, a sectarian group looked on with disdain by many Sunnī Turks, so many differ from other Turks not only in terms of language, but also religiosity. The repressive treatment of Kurdish speakers in eastern Anatolia, combined with the region's poverty, has led to their disproportionately high representation in the Turkish migrant community in Germany, estimated to be as large as 2 million.

Identity as Alevi Kurds in Turkey is continually negotiated. From an early age, Alevi children are socialized into seeing themselves as a subordinated people whose religious identity is suppressed by a Sunnī majority, who view them as religiously deviant and backward. The memory of shared injustices and suppression is carried from generation to generation. In contrast, Kurdish-speaking Alevis in western Germany find themselves more free than in Turkey to express themselves as Kurds and as Alevis. Moreover, second generation migrants in Germany often rework their identity as Turks or Kurds in terms learned from European nationalist and ethnic discourse. Ironically, Germans tend to confuse Turks with Greeks, prompting a critical rethinking of identities by workers carrying both national labels. In a similar manner, Sunnī and Alevi Turks in Germany critically rethink their differences as they interact with one another more intensely than they do in Turkey. This has had an impact on improving the situation of Kurds in Turkey.

Contemporary ethnic and religious identities in the new states of Central Asia and the Caucasus merit special consideration. During the Soviet era, Stalin created ethnic identities—"national" identities in the political language of the former Soviet Union—to weaken the possibility of resistance to Soviet domination. Beginning in the nineteenth century, Russian imperial expansion led to the forced migration of the Muslim populations of the region, creating hostility against Russians. Subsequently, those speaking Turkic languages, including the Türkmen, Kazakh, and Kirghiz (whose traditional lifestyles involved pastoralism), and the Uzbeks, primarily agricultural and urban, were considered separate for administrative purposes, as were the Persian-speaking Tajiks. The frequent displacement of populations, heavy Russian immigration to the major towns and to certain regions (such as northern Kazakhstan), and frequent shifts of language policy, including changes of alphabet and the substitution of Russian for the Turkic languages and Persian in schools, served to fragment ethnic identities. The newly independent republics are rapidly reversing this situation. In Azerbaijan, for example, schools are gradually shifting from the Cyrillic to the Latin alphabet and to Azeri Turkish as the language of instruction instead of Russian. Uzbekistan and Kazakhstan have made similar moves. In all cases, the demise of the Soviet Union has led to a growth in ethnic consciousness and ethnic conflicts linked to competing claims over land, water, and other national resources. Because the various ethnic populations often live side-by-side—many Tajiks, for example, live in Uzbekistan, and a significant minority of Uzbeks live in neighboring republics, the possibilities of conflict are enormous. Their right to cultural self-expression has varied considerably in the past and will continue to do so.

The same situation exists in China, where ethnic and religious boundaries can be seen to be cultural and political constructions rather than territorial ones. The attribution of an ethnic, or even a religious, identity to a group or an individual depends on the speaker, the audience, and the context. Such identities are constructed in competition between local communities and the state, classes, and leaders and followers. Not infrequently one answer is given when governments make inquiries, and another when scholars do. Of the fifty-five national minorities listed in China's 1982 census, ten are Muslim by tradition, including the Hui, Uighur, Kazakh, and others, for a total of 15 million, which is probably an underrepresentation. Some groups claim Turkic descent, while others, such as the Hui, consider themselves a mixture of Han, Mongol, and Arab descent.

The decision under post-1949 communist rule to classify the Hui as a national identity rather than a religious one suggests that the authorities regarded ethnic identity as more amenable to control than a religious one. (In a similar manner, Tito's Yugoslavia treated the country's Muslims as a national rather than as a religious identity.) Since the 1980s, China's Muslims have been given limited autonomy. Mosques have been opened and ties restored with Muslim communities elsewhere, so that China's Muslims become increasingly aware of their collective identity and are stressing it more than the complementary identities which they possess. Even if such a shift does not result in demands for greater autonomy, it obliges the central government to take claims for resources and just treatment seriously.

There is a subtle interplay between ethnic and religious identities throughout the Muslim world, but this interplay is not unique to the Muslim world. The intercommunal tensions between Hindus and Muslims in India, a formally secular state, parallel in many respects the interplay of religion and ethnicity between Hindu Tamils and Buddhist Sinhalese in neighboring Sri Lanka. In Malaysia, claims to ethnic identity are inextricably linked to religion and, since the islamization movement of the late 1970s, have led to economic, educational, and legal preferences and entitlements. In neighboring Indonesia, in contrast, the official ideology, the Pancasila, encompasses general principles from several world religions, including Islam, and the government frequently limits the participation of religious organizations in politics. Nonetheless, international corporations and organizations often impute leadership skills to personnel based on ethnic origin. Batak and Ambonese, for example, are sometimes favored over Javanese because of their reputation for being good administrators and for not favoring their relatives.

Ethnic identity is now transregional and transnational. The Yemeni grocer in Brooklyn, New York, might serve as a link for others from his tribe and village in Yemen, and the Turkish factory worker in Germany might facilitate the adjustment for others from his home region or country in adjusting to life in a foreign land. Similarly, in times of ethnic conflict, these transnational times can ease the flow of money and arms across international frontiers.

Some contemporary studies emphasize how ethnicity is embedded in a system of social meanings, an element of social identity among others. Others see ethnicity and sectarianism principally as products of global economic and political circumstances which encourage the formation of such identities, which are then used for obtaining political and economic advantage. Understanding claims to ethnic identity entails attention both to constructed collective meanings and to the economic and political contexts in which such identities are created and sustained. Ethnic distinctions, like those of region, sect, sex, language, and even tribe, are not being erased by modern conditions, as an earlier generation once facilely assumed, but provide the base from which newer social distinctions are created and sustained.

Even when there is a popular consensus or a desire among intellectual and political leaders to facilitate the reshaping of identities and responsibilities, either to mute the importance of divisive ethnic or sectarian identities or to emphasize them, ethnic identities must be taken into consideration. Some governments and political leaders, like their religious counterparts, often seek to ease possible tensions that arise from making such group definitions by officially denying their existence, but it would appear more reasonable to recognize them for what they are and constructively to seek to harness them. Shared notions of community by ethnic group or region often can provide the basis of trust and solidarity necessary for the effective functioning of and participation in modern society. Unfortunately, they can also be used to intimidate and to destroy.

[*See also* ʿAṣabīyah; Tribe.]

BIBLIOGRAPHY

Banuazizi, Ali, and Myron Weiner, eds. *The State, Religion, and Ethnic Politics: Afghanistan, Iran, and Pakistan*. Syracuse, N.Y., 1986. Useful collection, with an especially helpful introduction.

Bennigsen, Alexandre, and S. Enders Wimbush. *Muslims of the Soviet Empire: A Guide*. Bloomington, 1986. Useful gazetteer to ethnic and religious groupings in Central Asia, Russia, and the Caucasus.

Eickelman, Dale F. "Arab Society: Tradition and the Present." In *The Middle East Handbook*, edited by Michael Adams, pp. 765–781. 2d ed. New York, 1988.

Eickelman, Dale F. *The Middle East: An Anthropological Approach*. 2d ed. Englewood Cliffs, N.J., 1989. Offers an overview of factors contributing to social and cultural identity throughout the region, including ethnicity (pp. 207–227).

Eickelman, Dale F., *Russia's Muslim Frontiers: New Directions in Cross-Cultural Analysis*. Bloomington, 1993. Compares ethnic and religious identities in Central Asia and the Muslim Middle East, especially Turkey, Pakistan, and Afghanistan. See especially the chapter by Gene R. Garthwaite comparing tribal, ethnic, and national identities among the Kurds and the Bakhtiyari.

Fuller, Graham E. *Central Asia: The New Geopolitics*. Santa Monica, Calif., 1992. Updates Bennigsen and Wimbush in suggesting possible points of conflict and the regional and external factors contributing to them.

Hussin Mutalib. *Islam and Ethnicity in Malay Politics*. New York and Singapore, 1990. Effective treatment of political ethnicity in one Southeast Asian country.

Newby, L. J. " 'The Pure and True Religion' in China." *Third World Quarterly* 10. 2 (April 1988): 923–947. Succinct survey of Muslim communities in China and changing government attitudes toward them.

Rosen, Lawrence. *Bargaining for Reality: The Construction of Social Relations in a Muslim Community*. Chicago, 1963. See especially pages 133–164 for Arab-Berber and Arab-Jewish relations in Morocco.

Tambiah, Stanley J. "Reflections on Communal Violence in South Asia." *Journal of Asian Studies* 9.4 (November 1990): 741–760. Thoughtful analysis of religious and ethnic violence in Sri Lanka, India, and Pakistan.

Tapper, Richard. "Ethnicity, Order, and Meaning in the Anthropology of Iran and Afghanistan." In *Le fait ethnique en Iran et en Afghanistan*, edited by Jean-Pierre Digard, pp. 21–31. Paris, 1988. Hard to locate, but one of the clearest discussions of ethnicity available for these two countries.

Weekes, Richard V., ed. *Muslim Peoples: A World Ethnographic Survey*. Westport, Conn., 1978. Useful guide, ranging from Muslim communities in sub-Saharan Africa through Southeast Asia.

DALE F. EICKELMAN

EXEGESIS. *See* Tafsīr.

F

FAḌLALLĀH, MUḤAMMAD ḤUSAYN (b. 1935), Lebanese Shīʿī religious scholar and a leader of Ḥizbullāh (Party of God). Born in Najaf, Iraq, into a Shīʿī family from ʿAynātā, a village in southern Lebanon close to Bint Jubayl, Faḍlallāh's father was an *ʿalim* (religious scholar) in the Iraqi shrine and university city, and Faḍlallāh completed all of his studies there. One of his principal teachers was Abol-Qāsem Kho'i (Abū al-Qāsim Khū'ī), whose doctrine and practice rejected direct political participation by the *ʿulamā'* (community of religious scholars). Faḍlallāh cites the influence of his other teacher, Muḥsin al-Ḥakīm, and of his fellow student Muḥammad Bāqir al-Ṣadr, who was two years older. Bāqir al-Ṣadr was politically active in the 1960s, turning the Shīʿī university at Najaf into a center of political and religious opposition to the Iraqi regime, which had at first been favorably inclined toward the Communists, but was soon dominated by the Arab nationalists of the Baʿth party.

In 1964, the young *ʿalim* Faḍlallāh expressed his ideas on the function of a Muslim intellectual: "to bridge the deep divide that exists between youth and religion" because of the public status held by the *ʿulamā'* and the distance between them and young people (1964 interview reprinted in *Manṭiq al-qūwah,* vol. 9, pp. 76–80). When he was appointed in 1966 to the eastern suburb of Beirut, in Nabʿah, an impoverished area, Faḍlallāh established cultural youth clubs as well as free clinics and community centers. The motto of these clubs was "there is no such thing as a stupid or shameful question." In his estimation, these clubs were a great success. In 1972, he also spread his message in his native region, Bint Jubayl, during severe Israeli offensives against the Palestinian bases which were "occupying" area villages, causing a Shīʿī exodus toward Beirut. He finished *The Logic of Force (Manṭiq al-qūwah)* in March 1976. Also in 1976, all of Nabʿah was destroyed by bombs and emptied of its inhabitants by the extremist Maronite militia. Faḍlallāh recounts that he began his book on the present-day requirements of Islam *(Khatawāt)* while the bombs were still falling. He was able to put himself "squarely in the experience of the have-nots," he said in a postscript written in August 1977.

Faḍlallāh was expelled with the other inhabitants and went back to the southern suburban area, which was overflowing with Shīʿī refugees from southern Lebanon. From there he went to Bir al-ʿAbid, making trips to Ghubayrī and to Shīʿah. His entire Lebanese ministry was affected by uninterrupted and ever-increasing violence on all sides, which he suffered along with the poor and defenseless citizens of Lebanon. After the 1978 disappearance of Mūsā al-Ṣadr, the charismatic head of the Ḥarakat al-Maḥrūmīn (Movement of the Disadvantaged) who was abducted and perhaps executed by the Libyans, and after the success of the social, religious, and political movement in Iran from 1978 to 1979, he expounded ideas of revolt inspired by those of Ayatollah Ruhollah Khomeini. Faḍlallāh recognized Khomeini publicly in 1981 and visited him in 1984; in return, Khomeini named him *marjaʿ al-taqlīd* ("source of imitation") in 1986.

In the civil-war configuration of Lebanese politics, Amal—the successor to Ḥarakat al-Maḥrumīn—was pro-Syrian, anti-Palestinian, first and foremost Lebanese, not linked to Khomeini, and disposed to compromise with the Katā'ib (the Phalanges, a Maronite party) and Israel. In the summer of 1982, a coalition of uncompromising activist groups was formed, called the Organization of the Islamic Jihād. Faḍlallāh called them *al-islāmīyūn* (roughly, the "Islamists"). These groups consisted of: Amal Islāmī, formed in 1982 at Baalbek by 300 Iranian Revolutionary Guards who had arrived at the end of 1979 and which increased to 1,500 members in the Syrian-controlled area of Lebanon by the end of 1982; the Sunnī Tawḥīd movement, based in Tripoli, which acquired Palestinian Arafatist elements beginning in 1983; and Ḥizbullāh, in Beirut, which commanded more than 1,000 soldiers. In an open letter in February

1985, the group claimed responsibility for the "first operations of the popular Islamic resistance against Israeli occupation" in 1983. This can be understood to refer principally to the suicide bombings against the American and French barracks of the Multinational Forces in Beirut. Since 1985, Faḍlallāh has been the president of the Lebanese council of Ḥizbullāh and the vice-president of the central council in Teheran of the international Ḥizbullāh.

In the large mosque of the area, and also at the American University in West Beirut (after the virtual Shīʿī annexation of West Beirut in 1984), Faḍlallāh delivered sermons and lectures that were simple, clear, and reflective, yet firm and radical. These had a considerable local influence, and cassettes of them were circulated throughout the world, especially in western Europe. In the spring of 1985, with Ḥizbullāh, Faḍlallāh actively defended Beirut's Palestinian camps, which were beseiged by Amal, acting for Syria. It was thus that the first indirect armed conflict between Iran and Syria, which were nonetheless allied powers, erupted on Lebanese soil. At the end of 1985, and at the beginning of 1986, Ḥizbullāh and its pro-Iranian allies violently rejected the inter-Lebanese agreement drawn up at Damascus in December 1985; in this rejection, Ḥizbullāh followed the example of the Maronite Lebanese Forces and opposed Amal. The agreement was eventually renounced, just as the May 1983 Israeli-Lebanese peace agreement had been.

In the second "war of the (Palestinian) camps" waged after September 1986, Ḥizbullāh was neutral and clashed only with Syrian troops, which were eventually deployed in West Beirut, as they had been before the summer of 1982. There were twenty-six deaths among Ḥizbullāh forces at the end of January 1987, and the Syrian army yielded to the Islamist enclave in the south of West Beirut. At the same time, Faḍlallāh was taking part in two formal scholarly meetings in Tehran and Lausanne. These meetings produced the draft of the Lebanese Islamic Constitution, which was inspired by the model cast by Muḥammad Bāqir al-Ṣadr at Najaf one year before he was murdered by the Iraqi head of state in April 1980. Faḍlallāh had cosigned that proposed constitution. However, at the same time, he revealed in a personal article his anguish and doubts about the Islamic state and the risks of absolute personal power.

Faḍlallāh's political activity and commitment thus seem to stem from his theological reflections. His political commitment seems to engender and nourish his theological reflections. Since 1985, Faḍlallāh has not participated directly in military and political affairs. He did not succeed Shaykh Mūsawī, who was assassinated by Israel in 1991, as operational head of Ḥizbullāh. When, in 1989, Shaykh ʿUbaydallāh was taken hostage by Israel, Faḍlallāh called for the liberation of all of the Lebanese hostages, not only the Western ones. Ḥizbullāh opposed the Ṭa'if accord in October 1989, which proposed constitutional readjustments, but as it was enforced in 1991–1992, Syria left Ḥizbullāh forces free to continue resistance with their light arms against Israeli forces in the Israeli "Security Zone" in the south. Faḍlallāh took part in the August 1992 Lebanese legislative elections, since the new system of confessional secularism, which somewhat favored the Shīʿī community, seemed acceptable to him. He pronounced the Iraqi Shīʿī rebellion of March 1991 to be political and democratic and not religious and sectarian. Predictably, he shared the automatic Iranian opposition to the American-brokered Arab-Israeli negotiations in Madrid in November 1991 and in Washington in 1992, and he took part in the anti-Madrid and anti-Arafat congress in Teheran in October 1992.

Aside from Faḍlallāh's brief commentaries on the Qur'ān, his essays on Sunnī-Shīʿī Muslim ecumenism, and his collections of spiritual poetry, he has been silent about the scientific nature of Orientalism, although he has striven to clothe many of his reflections in historical or psychosociological science. There is, however, nothing new in Faḍlallāh's apologetics, with its concept of a union between missionary Christianity, atheism, Zionism, nationalism, Orientalism, and colonialism. His references to the *Protocols of the Elders of Zion,* a tsarist forgery, as if it were an authentic source also reflects common practice; in a man as educated and cultivated as Faḍlallāh, such uncritical naiveté is disappointing. Ḥizbullāh intentionally reiterated the theme of a "final solution" for the Jews of Israel, a theme that had been expressly eliminated by the Palestine resistance ideology since 1968. The proclaimed Islamism of the Palestinian cause revived and legitimized for Faḍlallāh those anti-Semitic, European National Socialist clichés, which formerly had been so important to Egyptian President Gamal Abdel Nasser and his companions.

As to politics in general and war in particular, Faḍlallāh, like Khomeini, adhered to the *uṣūlī* ("fundamentalist") tradition of modern Shiism that was established at the end of the eighteenth century as an alternative to the great tradition then called *akhbārī* (textual). To be *uṣūlī* is to valorize *ijtihād* in modern circumstances, to give authoritative opinions, advice, and decisions to individuals facing new problems. In the fundamentalist tradition these opinions and authorities are numerous and varied, and each great leader *(marja^c)* has his particular tradition *(taqlīd)*. Faḍlallāh saw *taqīyah* (dissimulation) as a rule governing concrete daily conduct without the supervision of a *marja^c al-taqlīd*. He reproached the Akhbārīs with fixing and even sanctifying the gap between the immutable and ideal norms (*sharī^cah*) of the golden age of the imams and daily life, which has no link with those norms and is guided only by the light of mysticism. [*See* Uṣūlīyah; Akhbārīyah.]

According to Faḍlallāh, the possibility of a violent revolution at an appropriate juncture is not excluded, because of the breach between the intangible ideal of *sharī^cah* and traditional customs and new conditions. In addition Faḍlallāh has sought to emulate the revolutionary examples of ^cAlī and Ḥusayn more than the quietist examples of the subsequent imams. He has even claimed to draw inspiration from the rebellion movements that were crushed by the Shī^cī powers, backed by the *^culamā'* in the name of *taqīyah*. He made such claims as early as the first year of the civil war in Lebanon, in 1976. At the same time, he reproached the Islamic extremists with indulging in impulsive and disorganized actions—"without *taqīyah*" he said. The time of *taqīyah* is the time of education, preparation, and organization in a party which is disciplined and adheres to a firm doctrine. Faḍlallāh describes the Marxist theory of revolution with both sympathy and suspicion, having in mind the Lebanese Communist party and especially the Organization of Lebanese Communist Action (OLCA), a breakaway group close to the Palestinians, in particular to the Popular Democratic Front for the Liberation of Palestine of Nayīf Ḥawātimah. He is distrustful of these groups, preferring to speak of *taghyīr* (change), rather than of *thawrah* (sudden revolution). He speaks highly of the reformist path, and even of reform by parliamentary means in the Western style. At the same time, he favors alliance with the Lebanese Communist party or the OLCA in order to effect the removal of the Lebanese regime. Here again one notes the ambiguity of Faḍlallāh's thought.

This ambiguity was to some extent lessened by the success of the Iranian Revolution. In effect, Faḍlallāh recognized that a general Islamic revolution had begun, and that from then on, not to support it would be *nifāq* (hypocrisy), and no longer only legitimate *taqīyah*. He has stated that even terrorist actions are at least justified as "political *jihād*," if not encouraged.

Nothing that Faḍlallāh has suggested concerning the modernization of *fiqh* (jurisprudence) has gone beyond the level of generalities—certainly seductive to his youthful listeners but lacking concrete revolutionary application. Following the model of Muḥammad Bāqir al-Ṣadr, and not Khomeini, he has particularly emphasized the entire scope of *fiqh*, and its social and political aspects. Thus he intends that the role of *faqīh* (especially that of the *marja^c al-taqlīd*) should go beyond simple director of the individual consciences. He affirms the existence of an Islamic economy, an Islamic social structure, and an Islamic politics, according to certain general principles, which, however, do not establish a specific type of political regime.

More specifically, in the applications of the supposedly modernized *fiqh*, Faḍlallāh rules out the restoration of the caliphate, and is wary of Khomeini's own theory of *wilāyat al-faqīh al-qā'id* (governance of the jurisprudent). It is true that he clearly stated his allegiance to Khomeini, but this allegiance was to his *jihādī* ("struggle movement") rather than to the man himself. Thus, Faḍlallāh excluded the notion that Khomeini was the representative or the forerunner of the imam Mahdi. Rather, Khomeini's legitimacy lay in the reality of his Islamic government, which, Faḍlallāh has said, was truly the first to be established after long centuries of expectation. He has implicitly denied the Islamic character of all other existing regimes in the Muslim world.

Faḍlallāh criticizes the theory of *wilāyat al-faqīh*, which he says can easily lead to autocratic personal power. He emphasizes as preferable the practice of *marja^c īyat al-taqlīd* (authority of the source of imitation), once again following the example of Bāqir al-Ṣadr, whose thoughts had contributed to its establishment and development. Faḍlallāh attempted to keep the *wilāyat al-faqīh* within the framework of the encompassing *marja^cīyah*, which by definition signifies pluralism. Yet he defines *wilāyat al-faqīh* as a function of control over governmental institutions at all levels; it is no longer only a matter of counsel, as with the *marja^cīyah*, but at the same time it is not defined as direct governmental authority. [*See* Wilāyat al-Faqīh; Marja^c al-Taqlīd.]

The Lebanese Islamic Constitution, which Faḍlallāh helped develop, would provide for a *lajnah* (commission) of *wilāyat al-faqīh* to exist alongside the president of the republic, elected for four years, the government, the parliament, and the head of the army (who may be the president). However, this commission would have the power to dismiss the parliament, suspend the government, and demand the president's resignation, as well as nominate and dismiss him. It would be the commission which would put forth the candidates for president. This *lajnah* would be a version of the traditional all-powerful revolutionary councils of the Arab world.

Faḍlallāh's democratic views and his misgivings about the totalitarian *wilayāt al-faqīh,* excluding the *marjaʿ al-taqlīd,* are no longer apparent in this document. The legitimacy of this Lebanese *lajnah* was to be Khomeini, the sole *faqīh qā'id* of all the Muslims in the world. The Lebanese president of this local *lajnah* would be presented simply as Khomeini's representative, designated by him. In this regard, Faḍlallāh finally acknowledged a unique supreme authority *(wilāyah),* as well as delegated, dependent local authorities. The theory of the pluralist *marjaʿīyah* thus collapsed. One should recall that Faḍlallāh had at this same time pondered the question, which he termed "agonizing" of the choice between a sole *wilāyah* for the world or multiple authorities in Muslim countries; the choice was thus between an imperial Muslim state under one single authority or a federation, or better, confederation, of autonomous Islamic states which would meet periodically in a central assembly led by Khomeini. The Lebanese Islamic Constitution adopted the former solution.

Faḍlallāh also addressed the status of non-Muslims in a professed Islamic state. For him, secular individual freedom does not exist. Going against the great Muslim tradition existing in practice as well as theory since the eleventh century, he rejects the fundamental distinction between political and religious power. He opposed his teachers who did not wish to become involved in political activity, in particular his own mentor in Najaf, al-Kho'i. He praised the involvement of Bāqir al-Ṣadr in the Daʿwah party in Iraq, and explains al-Ṣadr's eventual withdrawal and even his refusal to let his disciples be politically active as only a tactical decision of superior wisdom *(taqīyah)* in the face of the all-powerful police strength of Saddam Hussein. Faḍlallāh himself emphasizes the necessity for a well-organized political party in the service of Islam.

One might have expected that his experience in Lebanon, his commendation of coexistence with Christians, his desire for a substantive dialogue, and his desire for an open and humanized *fiqh* would have brought him to discover new solutions. This has not been the case. He has maintained that Christians must renounce political sectarianism. Yet, although he asserts that Muslims should do so as well, in fact the Christians' situation is seen from the perspective of strict Muslim sectarianism. The desired Muslim state is not founded on the legal equality of all people, regardless of their religious and family ties, even though these ties might be taken into account, as in the present-day Lebanese constitution. The same situation applies to the rights of women and the family. Undoubtedly appealing to the new generation of young people, Faḍlallāh, unusual for a *ʿalim,* encourages young women and even mothers to work professionally. In this respect, he is consistent with Iranian practice since 1979. He suggests no new attitude toward mixed marriages, a particular issue in Lebanon, and a concrete element in the Islamic-Christian dialogue he claims to wane. One concession to modernity is a certain understanding of premarital sexual relations. He recommends that, within the framework of a trial, stoning for "crimes of honor" should not result in death. In effect, the *ḥudūd* (Qur'ānic penalties) are in general seen as being the concern of the judicial powers and not the victims themselves.

[*See also* Ḥizbullāh, *article on* Ḥizbullāh in Lebanon; Lebanon; Shīʿī Islam, *article on* Modern Shīʿī Thought; *and the biography of* *Ṣadr.*]

BIBLIOGRAPHY

Works by Muḥammad Ḥusayn Faḍlallāh

Al-Islām wa-manṭiq al-qūwah. 2d ed. Beirut, 1981.

Khaṭawāt ʿalā ṭarīq al-Islām. 3d ed. Beirut, 1982.

Mafāhīm Islāmīyah. 12 vols. 4th ed. Beirut, 1982.

Maʿa al-ḥikmah bi-khaṭṭ al-Islām. Beirut, 1985. Collection of articles published between 1979 and 1981.

Al-muqāwamah al-Islāmīyah. Beirut, 1985.

"ʿAlā ṭarīq ḥarakat al-qūwah fī al-dawlah al-Islāmīyah." *Al-tawḥīd* (March 1986): 85–102.

Secondary Sources

Carré, Olivier. *L'utopie islamique dans l'Orient arabe.* Paris, 1991. See chapter 9, "Khomeinisme libanais: Orgueilleux et déshérités chez Fadlallāh," and chapter 10, "La révolution islamique selon Fadlallāh."

Duran, Khalīd. *Islam und Politischer Extremismus.* Hamburg, 1985.

Kramer, Martin. "Muhammad Husayn Fadlallāh." *Orient,* no. 2 (1985): 147–149.

OLIVIER CARRÉ

Translated from French by Elizabeth Keller

FAITH. *See* Īmān.

FAKHREDDIN, RIZAEDDIN (1859–1936), Volga-Ural Muslim religious scholar and reformist. One of the most prominent Muslims of the Volga-Ural region of the Russian empire, Fakhreddin was born on 17 January 1859 in Kichu Chatï village in Samara *guberniya,* the son of Sayfetdin, the village mullah, and Mähübä, the daughter of Rämkol Maksud, imam of Iske Ishtirak village. It is remarkable that Fakhreddin, an outstanding Islamic scholar, educator, writer, and journalist, was a product of Tatar village *madrasah*s and never attended school in Kazan or Bukhara. He studied first at his father's *madrasah* but at the age of seven went to study at neighboring villages, ultimately spending ten years at Tübän Chïrshïlï studying Islamic theology, jurisprudence, Arabic, Farsi, and Turkish, while also learning Russian on his own. He was an avid reader in all these languages and never missed an opportunity to buy books from the itinerant book merchants who frequented Tatar villages. The library he began to accumulate was further enriched by copies of books he copied by hand.

Upon graduating from the *madrasah* in 1889, Fakhreddin was appointed imam in the village of Ilbäk where, in addition to providing religious guidance to the community, he also taught at the *madrasah.* By the time of this appointment, however, Fakhreddin had already attracted the attention of leading scholars such as Shäkhabäddin Merjani by publishing works including an Arabic grammar (*Kitabä-ät-täs'rïyf;* Kazan, 1887), a text on methodology (*Ät-tökhfät al-Änisiya;* Kazan, 1887), a book of jurisprudence (*Kitabä mokaddimä;* Kazan, 1889), and one on social issues (*Kitabä ig'tiraf;* Kazan, 1889).

In 1891 Fakhreddin left Ilbäk and moved to Ufa, having been elected a *kazi* (Ar., *qāḍī;* judge) and member of the Religious Board of the Muslims (Muftiat). This move launched the "first Ufa period" (1891–1906) of his life, characterized by impressive productivity and breadth in his writings. When Fakhreddin assumed the duties of a *kazi,* the Muftiat had been in existence for more than a hundred years. Its rich archives, however, had never been organized, and he began compiling a systematic catalog of its holdings. He also made copies of those archival materials that interested him most for his personal library. Energized by the wealth of information that surrounded him in the Muftiat archives and by the ongoing discourse concerning the reasons for the backwardness of Muslims of the Russian empire, Fakhreddin entered a most productive period of his life, marked by the publication of literary works and studies on religion, social issues, and pedagogy, as well as contributions to major Muslim newspapers such as *Terjuman, Vaqt,* and *Sharkïy Rus.*

In 1906 Fakhreddin resigned from the Muftiat and moved to Orenburg to become editor of the newspaper *Vaqt,* a leading forum of Muslim reformism, to which he also contributed under the pseudonym Murat. In January 1908 he became the chief editor of the bimonthly journal *Shura,* retaining that position until the end of 1917, when the last of the journal's 240 issues appeared. Fakhreddin chose the name of the journal, meaning "council, forum," and he acknowledged his intention of opening its pages to all those "interested in bringing science and education to their people." Fakhreddin's own contribution to *Shura* amounted to some seven hundred pieces ranging from articles on the history of the Turkic peoples, to essays on the social, cultural, political life of the Tatars, to profiles of famous Western and Muslim thinkers.

Fakhreddin welcomed with hope the February 1917 revolution with its promises of liberty for all but watched with anxiety the coming to power of the Bolsheviks in October 1917. When the first postrevolutionary All-Russian Muslim Congress met in May 1917, Fakhreddin was elected *kazi* in absentia and in January 1918 moved to Ufa to begin his work at the Muftiat. This new assignment inaugurated his "second Ufa period" (1918–1936). In 1922 he was elected *muftī* and as the head of the Religious Board of the Muslims embarked upon the most difficult period of his life, marked by the twin tragedies of personal poverty and imprisonment and the oppression of Muslim communities under the antireligious policies of the Soviet government. He died in Ufa on 11 April 1936, at the age of seventy-seven, leaving a rich legacy as a religious scholar, writer, journalist, and foremost spokesman for the movement of Muslim reformism.

Fakhreddin published some sixty books and seven hundred articles; he left many unpublished works comprising some forty volumes of manuscript on scraps of paper, since during the last years of his life he lived in such poverty that he was forced to sell some of his books in order to buy bread. Many of Fakhreddin's works were so widely read that they were published in ten or twelve editions. Fakhreddin's books fall into the following categories: Islamic history and the history of the Turkic peoples; biographies of famous Muslims; Muslim reformism, education, and curricular reform;

enlightenment, women, and the Muslim family; theology, jurisprudence, the Qur'ān and the *ḥadīth*s; and social and political issues among Russian Muslims.

Fakhreddin's thought developed under three equally important influences—Shaykh Merjani, Ismāʿīl Gasprali (Gasprinskii), and Jamāl al-Afghānī. Like Merjani, he valued the importance of education, science, and the Russian language. Fakhreddin accepted only what was scientifically sound and ethically moral, but he always extended tolerance and respect to other people's ideas. From Gasprali he acquired the idea of the racial and cultural unity of the Turkic peoples, but he rejected political Pan-Turkism while advocating "social unity" for the Turkic peoples. Al-Afghānī's emphasis on the need to reconcile Islam and modernity in order to defend the Islamic world against the encroachments of the West appealed to Fakhreddin, who as a Volga-Ural Muslim had experienced at first hand the meaning of Russian encroachment. [*See the biographies of Gasprinskii and Afghānī.*]

The importance of Fakhreddin's religious writings rests in his emphasis on the integrative capacity of Islam, his restatement of the *sharīʿah* as an all-inclusive concept that integrates the legal and the spiritual into one religious whole, and his advocacy of the codification of Muslim legal practices in Russia. He advocated reform of the Muslim religious administration to enhance the position of the Religious Board and placing the *muftī* under its control. Moreover, he emphasized the importance of having the *muftī* elected by the community on the basis of his competence in religious and secular sciences rather than accepting the nominee of the Russian government. Fakhreddin also considered it necessary that the Muftiat supervise Muslim schools and devise a centralized curriculum for them. His emphasis on *ijtihād* (creative interpretation of dogma) and on education as a weapon against economic backwardness and political encroachment were perhaps Fakhreddin's most enduring legacies to the Muslims of the Russian empire.

BIBLIOGRAPHY

Akkhmer, Sh. *Matbaghachilïq tarikhï*. Kazan, 1909.

Fätkhiev, A. S. *Tatar ädipläre häm galimnäreneng kul'yazmalarï: N. I. Lobachevskiï isemendäge Fänni Kitapkhanä kul'yazmalarïnïng tasvirlamasï*. Kazan, 1960.

Gosmanov, M. *Ütkännän Kilächäkkä*. Kazan, 1990.

Kärimi, F. "Rizaitdin Khäzrät kitü." *Yăngă Vaqt* 2.13 (1918).

Khalikova, Raisa Kh. "125 let so dnia rozhdeniia Rizy Fakhretdinova." *Sovetskaia Tiurkologiia*, no. 2 (1984).

Kharisov, A. I. "Kollektsiia rukopisei Rizaitdina Fakhretdinova v nauchnom arkhive Bashkirskogo filiala ANSSSR." In *Iuzhnoural'skiï arkheograficheskiï sbornik*. Ufa, 1973–.

AZADE-AYŞE RORLICH

FALSAFAH. *See* Philosophy.

FAMILY. The basic social unit of Islamic society is the family. If Islam can be described as the soul of Islamic society, then the family might be seen metaphorically as its body. For thousands of years, the family has been the principal focus of people's emotional, economic, and political identity. Changes in the nineteenth and particularly the twentieth centuries have placed great strains on the unit, yet the family, together with the Islamic faith, retains a central place in the lives of peoples in every social class, in both rural and urban contexts, and in every country classified as Islamic.

"Family" means different things in different societies and in different contexts. In the Western world of the twentieth century, "family" is often understood as the "nuclear family," one or two parents and their children. The Arabic word for family, *ahl* or *ahila*, is a more comprehensive term and may include grandparents, uncles, aunts, and cousins on both sides of the marital connection. In its broadest sense, the family might be perceived as an even larger unit, equal to the *ummah*, or the group of believers in Islam, the Islamic community, or "family" itself.

As early as 3000 BCE in ancient Sumer, the site of the contemporary nation-state of Iraq, evidence is found of a social unit similar to the contemporary Islamic family. This early manifestation, recorded in tablets and on monumental steles, was also a precursor to the family structure of Judaism and Christianity, the other two great monotheistic religions of the Middle East. Proponents of Judaism and Christianity are known in Islam as "people of the book" or *dhimmī*s, those related to Islam through holy scripture and to whom one, as a Muslim, must be tolerant.

This early form of the family was patrilineal, a form of social organization found in perhaps 80 to 90 percent of all human societies. In a patrilineal society, the name of the child and the inheritance pass through the male line; children therefore are known by the names of their fathers. Although all patrilineal families are not equally patriarchal, the linguistic emphasis placed on the male line to an important degree reflects male dominance, both legal and informal, in social relations. The use of the term "patriarch" to refer to the prophets of Judaism and Christianity is an indication of this tendency.

The advent of Islam in the seventh century CE brought changes to the structure of the Arabian family. Although the basic outline of patrilineality was retained, some modifications are evident, particularly in the place of women. The Prophet Muḥammad is often cited as having paid special attention to the plight of the less fortunate in society—women, orphans, slaves—and the revelations recorded in the Qur'ān support this.

First and foremost, the Qur'ān prohibited infanticide, a practice that seems to have reached scandalous proportions in pre-Islamic Arabia, particularly in the case of infant girls. The Qur'ān also recognized women as having legal status as persons with rights and responsibilities. Women have the same religious duties as men, though they may be excused from fasting during Ramaḍān, for example, if they are pregnant or nursing. (Such latitude is clearly given to protect not only the health of the individual woman, but that of the child, either unborn or newly born, and by extension, the health of the family unit itself.) The Qur'ān also gives women the right to accept or reject a marriage partner and the right to divorce in certain cases (the desertion, impotence, or insanity of the husband are most often cited).

In the past, and to a great extent today, the family provided economic and emotional support to its members. An individual, as Halim Barakat points out, "inherited" his or her religious, class, and cultural identity, which was reinforced by the customs and mores of the group. In exchange for the allegiance of its members, the family group served as an employment bureau, insurance agency, child and family counseling service, old people's home, bank, teacher, home for the handicapped (including the mentally ill), and hostel in time of economic need. Men and women both remained members of their natal families for all of their lives, even after marriage. A divorced woman returned to her natal family, which was responsible for her support until remarriage. A divorced man returned to his natal family, and his parents cared for his children. In exchange for these services, the individual members were expected to place the group's survival above their personal desires, especially at the time of marriage, and to uphold the reputation of the family by behaving properly and "maintaining the family honor."

This, of course, was the ideal. In everyday life, ideals are not always realized in practice. Some members have always rebelled and refused to marry the person chosen for them by their family. Some groups did not take in divorced members, sometimes out of poverty, sometimes out of spite. Vengeful fathers did not always pass on to their sons, at the time of maturity, authority over land or shops. Maintaining the family honor sometimes resulted in tragedy. And the care of handicapped and elderly members often put an undue stress upon the younger members of the family.

Yet the institution persisted because it met real needs for people, people for whom no other institution existed. The shift that took place in the West, the assumption of economic and social responsibilities first by the religious hierarchy and then by the secular state, has not occurred in the same manner in Islamic society. Thus for most of its history the family has been an institution that did not merely reproduce itself physically, but reproduced the religious and social values of its members.

The Islamic family unit came under new pressures with the beginning of Western colonial rule in the late eighteenth and early nineteenth centuries. From Egypt to India, Morocco to Indonesia, European immigrants, soldiers, and administrators assumed political control. Local language, culture, economic and social structures were devalued and efforts were made to replace them with Western models. The family unit was not immune to these efforts, but attempted to reject Western incursion. The family unit became first a religious, cultural, and social refuge from colonial domination, and eventually the site of political resistance. This action was strengthened by Western colonial policy, which in most areas left local control intact only in religious affairs and, by inference, Islamic family law, including inheritance. This was crucial for the continuation and support of the family, which in response to the presence of strangers, turned in upon itself. Men, often ridiculed and rejected in the new colonial governmental and economic structures, found their families a sanctuary, a representation of Islamic religious values wherein they were honored. Protection of Muslim women from strangers became more important as well. For example, the all-enveloping *jallābah* with hood and face veil, found in Morocco today, only dates from about 1912, when the French conquered Morocco. Before that time, women as well as men in Morocco wore the *ḥā'ik,* a length of cloth wrapped about the body in various ways. The Qur'ānic school increased in importance as a source of religious instruction even as colonial governments were attempting to limit its influence and elites were attending the secular schools of Christian missionaries.

After 1919, peoples of the Islamic Middle East realized that the independence promised by the Allies was not to be. Organized anticolonial resistance became more serious and militant, as was also the case in India, Indonesia, and other parts of the Islamic world subject to Western European control. The family became the focus of such resistance. Such activity was justified in rhetoric that spoke of maintaining Islamic religion and culture, especially in the family, in the face of a common enemy—Western political and economic power, with its perceived secularist or at least anti-Islamic aims.

Since independence from colonial rule (in the 1950s and 1960s), the family unit has been subject to a variety of economic and political pressures. High rates of unemployment have prompted millions of men and some women to search for work in Europe and the Gulf States. Inflation has also meant that large numbers of women, for the first time, have taken jobs outside their homes. Conflict in Lebanon, Afghanistan, and Iran, as well as Israel/Palestine, has led to family disruption through violent deaths and forced migration. The movement in almost all Islamic countries from rural to urban predominance has further challenged the customary ties of family life. Only in the oil-rich states of the Gulf is it possible for the religious model of the Islamic family to be maintained: father as provider, mother as childbearer and rearer in the home.

Thus the current debate throughout the Islamic world on the place and function of the family is a crucial debate, for it involves not only the suggestion that family responsibilities shall be passed from the family unit to the state, but the definition of basic individual rights: those of women, men, and children. The status of women is not an isolated issue but at the core of the whole debate, for the woman has always been seen as the center of the family unit, the hub around which all its economic, personal, and political activities revolved.

Discussions of *sharīʿah* family law reflect these concerns, as Qur'ānic family law defines relations between men and women through legislation of marriage, divorce, child custody, inheritance, and polygyny (the Qur'ān surah that allows a man to take up to four wives if he can treat them equally). Islamic family law currently operates in most Islamic countries, with the exception of Turkey and Tunisia. But current movements are apparent in Saudi Arabia and Pakistan to stiffen the application of *sharīʿah* family law, and other movements in Algeria and Egypt seek to amend or replace Islamic family law with more secular personal status laws. Both movements underscore the societal awareness of the importance of the family as the base of society, a force for moral and social order, and the mechanism to insure the stability of the next generation. The debate concerns not only the family, but family planning, religious and secular education, and political participation, as well as law, and arguments on both sides use the good of the family as a justification for greater or lesser legal changes. Current popular and widespread Islamic movements also see the family as the rock on which indigenous religious socialization and culture stand. They argue for greater family cohesion in what is perceived as a rapidly changing, unpredictable, and hostile world, where families are being perforce stretched, fragmented, and broken. Khurshid Ahmad, director-general of the Islamic Foundation at the University of Pakistan, says, "We are living in a period of cultural crisis . . . the very foundations of contemporary society are being threatened from within and without. The family, as a basic and most sensitive institution of culture, is being undermined by powerful and destructive forces."

In modern Iran, since the 1979 Islamic revolution, the family has become the platform for the enunciation of the state's goals and ideals, and the subject of government legislation by the Shīʿī *ʿulamāʾ* in many areas of life other than family law—education, leisure activities, literature, politics. The view in Libya, as set down in the 1970s by Colonel Muʿammar al-Qadhdhāfī in his three Green Books, is that "The social bond which binds together each human group, from the family through the tribe to the nation, is the basis for the movement of history." At some level, the family is defined as society, and this formulation, although not stated, leads logically to the family as *ummah,* the community of believers in Islam.

To many observers, the Islamic family seems not to be disintegrating, but rather regrouping and reorganizing in response to contemporary needs. In places where the family unit itself has been dispersed due to war, natural disaster, or economic need, the values and the functions of the family are resurfacing in different forms. Workers abroad group together on the basis of old family ties; young men entering the workforce find jobs in the same factories or businesses as their sisters, cousins, or uncles. For men of elite political groups, family ties continue to be important as political party bases shift. Newcomers to the city make connections through family members. Men on their own in a new place may turn to Islamic religious "brotherhoods," or groups where, as they themselves say, they "feel like one of the family." Women whose husbands are working abroad often form kinlike ties with neighbors.

Through its adaptations and evolution, the Muslim family unit has proven itself to be an interdependent and flexible social institution. For many, it remains the best way to provide for individual needs as well as group survival.

The British historian Lawrence Stone found the English family of past centuries to be a searching, acting, moving institution. The Muslim family, from its sixth-century foundations to its modern expression, might be viewed in the same way, as a structure flexible enough to deal with new pressures and strong enough in its religious and social manifestations to respond to and become part of changing conditions.

[*See also* Family Law; Marriage and Divorce; Polygyny.]

BIBLIOGRAPHY

Ahmad, Kurshid, ed. *Studies in Family Law of Islam*. Karachi, 1968.

Barakat, Halim. "The Arab Family and the Challenge of Social Transformation." In *Women and the Family in the Middle East*, edited by Elizabeth Fernea, pp. 27–48. Syracuse, 1985.

Esposito, John. *Women in Muslim Family Law*. Syracuse, 1982.

Fanon, Frantz. *Studies in a Dying Colonialism*. New York, 1965.

Fernea, Elizabeth, ed. *Women and the Family in the Middle East: New Voices of Change*. Austin, 1985.

Fernea, Elizabeth Warnock, and Basima Qattan Bezirgan, eds. *Middle Eastern Muslim Women Speak*. Austin, 1977. Includes selections from the Qur'ān on the subject of women and the family, pages 7–26.

Gordon, David. *Women of Algeria: An Essay on Change*. Cambridge, Mass., 1968.

Levy, Reuben. *The Social Structure of Islam*. Cambridge, 1957.

Mahdavi, Shireen. "The Position of Women in Shiʿa Iran: Views of the ʿUlama." In *Women and the Family in the Middle East: New Voices of Change*, edited by Elizabeth Fernea, pp. 255–272. Austin, 1985.

Mawdūdī, Sayyid Abū al-Aʿlā. *Purdah and the Status of Women in Islam*. Lahore, 1972.

Minault, Gail, ed. *The Extended Family: Women and Political Participation in India and Pakistan*. Columbia, Mo., 1981.

Mueller, Eric. "Revitalizing Old Ideas: Developments in Middle Eastern Family Law." In *Women and the Family in the Middle East: New Voices of Change*, edited by Elizabeth Fernea, pp. 224–228. Austin, 1985.

Rugh, Andrea. *Family in Contemporary Egypt*. Syracuse, 1984.

Shaltūt, Maḥmūd. *Shaltūt on "The Koran and Women."* Cairo, 1980.

Spectorsky, Susan. *Chapters on Marriage and Divorce: Responses of Ibn Hanbal and Ibn Rahwayh*. Austin, 1993.

Stone, Lawrence. *The Family, Sex and Marriage in England (1500–1800)*. London, 1977.

ELIZABETH WARNOCK FERNEA

FAMILY LAW. Issues of law affecting the family, known as family law, are central to the *sharīʿah*. The Qur'ānic verses which concern themselves with issues of law deal to a great extent with matters affecting the family. Many of the *ḥadīth* concentrate on the same area, and it is therefore no surprise to find that the leading texts of classical Islamic jurists concentrate similarly on the subject of family law. As John Esposito has said it "has enjoyed pride of place within the Shariah" (1982, p. 13). Family law, perhaps more than any other part of the law, is seen as having an eternal value; the rules laid down in the Qur'ān and *sunnah* are viewed as comprehensive; and human intervention in the area is limited to application and adoption of the principles, rather than to innovative reappraisal. In the words of N. J. Coulson, family law is the "stronghold of the Shariah" (1964, p. 161).

At the heart of family law is the creation, the incidents, and the termination of the contract of marriage which, in the language of the Hedaya (the authoritative work used in South Asia, originally compiled in the late twelfth century), "implies a particular contract used for the purpose of legalising generations." The classical jurists do not differ substantially among themselves about the particular attributes of family law, although there are of course many differences of detail. Modern eyes often see Islamic family law as patriarchal and insensitive to the position of the woman, who is not viewed as an equal partner in the relationship. Much occidental criticism has concentrated on the right of polygamy, the power of the husband to terminate unilaterally the relationship, the lack of the wife's similar entitlement, and the rights the husband has over both his wife (as an obedient wife) and as *walī* ("guardian") of his children.

In broad outline, the marriage *(nikāḥ)* is a contract which the groom enters into with the bride or the bride's legal guardian. The guardian can contract his minor daughter in marriage without regard to her consent, although she does have a right, in certain situations, to rescind the contract as soon as she attains puberty. The contract is created by the two "pillars" of offer *(ījāb)* and acceptance *(qabūl)* in the presence of two Muslim male witnesses or one Muslim male and two Muslim female witnesses. The groom contracts to pay his wife a dower *(mahr)* which arises incident to the marriage. Some marriages are considered void *(bāṭil)* and others are irregular *(fāsid)*. Examples of void marriages are marriages with *maḥārim,* for instance, female ascendants and descendants or those related through affinity. In contrast, a *fāsid* marriage is irregular in that, after the required separation of the parties, the particular defect can be removed, at least in theory, and they can then remarry; for example, a *fāsid* marriage occurs when a marriage is entered into in the absence of witnesses. In a *fāsid* relationship, if there has been consummation, then a *mahr* must be paid to the wife, and any children who are born to the couple are deemed to be legitimate. As polygamy is permitted to the maximum of four wives, a fifth marriage would be *fāsid*.

Divorce by the husband is effected by a unilateral pronouncement known as the *ṭalāq* which is a repudiation that cuts off the marital tie. The power to exercise *ṭalāq* belongs to the husband and does not depend on any judicial involvement or consent of the wife. There are a number of different forms of *ṭalāq,* some seen to be more meritorious than others. The most meritorious is the *ṭalāq as-sunna ahsan.* When the wife is free from her menstrual flow, the husband pronounces a *ṭalāq;* he must then refrain from any sexual intercourse for the duration of the *ʿiddah* period, which is a period of three menstrual cycles or three months in the case of women who no longer menstruate. At the end of this time, the marriage is terminated. The wife's right to bring a marriage to an end *(khulʿ)* is very restricted; it involves consent of the husband and consideration paid by the wife. Mālikī law, in particular, gives prominence to the *qāḍī* (judge) who, in certain situations, can separate the parties.

During the marriage, the wife is entitled to maintenance and support which includes food, clothing, and accommodation. This entitlement, however, terminates after the *ʿiddah* period on a divorce, and there is no ongoing entitlement to financial assistance. The entitlement can also be suspended if she is "disobedient," for example, if she refuses to acquiesce in the husband's desire that she not leave the house. Legal adoption of children is not permissible in Islamic law. The mother initially has the entitlement to custody *(hadana)* of a child, but the father acquires custody as soon as the child reaches a certain age. Although each school has different rules, the mother's custody of a child is not extended beyond the age of puberty, by which time, according to all schools, the father has acquired the residual custodial right over the child.

Reforms in Family Law. The emphasis on the preeminent position of the husband and the marked absence of equality within the family between husband and wife were both seen as handicaps by those involved in the drive by some Muslim states toward a process of westernization. Reformers were able to adopt strategems not unknown in the Islamic world. Reforms in the family law area were designed to solve particular perceived problems in an eclectic manner, formally following the jurisprudential principle of *taqlīd* (imitation) and based on the right of the ruler to define and confine the limits of judicial intervention *(siyāsah sharʿīah)*. Thus, differences of detail between the schools have enabled reformers in Ḥanafī countries to adopt the stance taken by jurists of schools other than their own in situations where a change has been seen as desirable. For instance, in 1915, the Ottoman rulers enacted legislation by imperial edict designed to improve the legal status of Muslim wives and provide them with certain rights to petition for divorce. These rights, which were not available in the dominant Ḥanafī law of the Ottoman Empire, were based on Ḥanbalī and Mālikī law and the "weaker" minority Ḥanafī doctrine. Similarly, the criminal law was used to introduce what were seen to be improvements to family law; for instance, in Egypt in 1923 it was made a criminal offense for a registrar to register a marriage when the bride was not above the age of sixteen and the bridegroom not above the age of eighteen. Egypt used procedural devices to restrict further the solemnization of child marriages by precluding the court from hearing any claim arising out of a marriage if the husband had not attained the age of eighteen and the bride the age of sixteen at the time of the litigation, and the courts were barred from considering the question of a disputed marriage unless the marriage had been registered. These early reforms were followed by the adoption of a somewhat more unorthodox approach, namely, *talfīq* ("combining together" the doctrine of one school or jurist with another). This approach allowed reforms viewed as socially desirable to be introduced, while ensuring that there was no significant departure from the *sharīʿah.*

After 1945, however, reforms tended to be based more on the alleged right of a Muslim state, through its rulers, to exercise *ijtihād* (search by independent deduction). Perhaps the most celebrated example of this approach is the abolition of the entitlement of polygamy by Article 18 of the Tunisian Code of Personal Status (1956), based on a reinterpretation of surah 4.3, which states "Marry women of your choice, two or three or four; but if ye fear that ye shall not be able to deal justly [with them], then only one. . . ." The Tunisians equate justice not merely with *nafaqah* ("financial support") but also with love and affection. It is then argued that only the Prophet can treat two wives equally in this way; therefore, in today's conditions the irrebuttable presumption is that a Muslim husband cannot fulfil the requirements laid down in the Qur'ān.

Reforms in other Muslim countries relating to polygamous marriages have not been so dramatic; most countries simply make second marriages dependent on the permission of a court (for example, Syria, 1953; Iraq, 1959) or an arbitration body (for example, Pakistan and Bangladesh, 1961). Similarly, stipulations can be made in the marriage contract that the husband cannot have a co-wife. If he does take a second wife, then the first wife is entitled, for that reason alone, to seek dissolution of the marriage (Jordan, 1976; Morocco, 1958). Indeed, even in the absence of such a stipulation, the Moroccan *qāḍī* may consider whether the second marriage has caused any injury to the first wife. The end result of all these developments has been the enactment of Codes of Family Law in almost all Islamic countries.

Reappraisal of Reforms. Even such limited reforms have been subjected to critical reappraisal in the light of Islamic revivalism. Two examples of this new development illustrate the trend that now appears to be active throughout the Muslim world, the first from Egypt, the second from Pakistan. In Egypt, Law 44 of 1979 was issued by a presidential decree which amended the 1920 and 1929 laws. A pronouncement of *ṭalāq* by the husband is required to be registered, and notification of the *ṭalāq* must be given to the wife. The divorce does not take effect if the notice does not reach her. In the event of a judicial application by the wife for a divorce, which is dealt with by arbitrators, the court is empowered to dissolve the marriage, although the wife must pay compensation. These reforms were far from radical, yet the 1979 law has not survived; in July 1985, the Constitutional Court adjudged it unconstitutional. A new law, Law 100 of 1985, was enacted, which complies more closely with the perceived orthodoxy. For instance, Article 6A in the 1979 law gave a first wife the right to ask for a divorce solely on the basis of a second marriage by her husband. The new Article 11A of Law 100 of 1985 states that a first wife who finds herself in this position must petition a court for a divorce, alleging that she has suffered harm as a result of her husband marrying a second wife; the court must then try to reconcile the parties, and it can grant a divorce only after such endeavors have proved to be unsuccessful. Thus, the attempt in 1979 to introduce a substantial reform which would have given the first wife an automatic right to terminate the marriage in these circumstances has been replaced by a much more limited provision. Islamic tendencies were primarily responsible for the demise of this short-lived 1979 reform.

Perhaps an even more dramatic example of this trend can be seen in Pakistan. The reforming Muslim Family Laws Ordinance 1961, which among other matters imposes restraints on the husband's power to divorce his wife by *ṭalāq* (s 7) and on his right to marry polygamously (s 6), has been subjected to executive, legislative, and judicial attacks of considerable ferocity. The Federal Shariat Court in 1988 ruled that a pronouncement by a husband of a *ṭalāq* which complies with the provisions of Islamic law is not invalid solely on the basis that no notice is given to the chairman of the Union Council as required by section 7 of the Muslim Family Laws Ordinance 1961. This approach has been affirmed in Karachi in a case called *Ashique Hussain* v. *First Additional Judge* (1991; PLD Kar 174) where it was held that the applicant's failure to send the notice of the *ṭalāq* to the chairman under the provisions of section 7 would not be of any consequence so long as the applicant had pronounced *ṭalāq* with an intention to dissolve the marriage. An important development toward the so-called islamicization of the laws in Pakistan has been the introduction in 1985 of Article 2A of the Constitution, which inserts, as a substantive provision, the Objectives Resolution of 1949. This refers to, inter alia, ". . . sovereignty over the entire universe" belonging "to Allāh Almighty alone and the authority which He has delegated to the State of Pakistan, through its people being exercised within the limits prescribed by him" as "a sacred trust." Some have argued that this development undermines all the "non-Islamic" provisions in Pakistan law, including the 1961 ordinance. A number of *sharīʿah* bills have been brought forward, the most recent in April 1991 by Prime Minister Nawaz Sharif. The National Assembly voted to approve the bill, and it was endorsed by the Senate on 28 May 1991.

Is the return to a form of Islamic orthodoxy, which is

illustrated by the Egyptian and Pakistan instances but which occur from Algeria to Malaysia, a passing phase? Or is it an expression from the Islamic world that some of the reforms of the earlier part of the present century have gone too far in the direction of simply aping the West and ignoring completely the aspirations of the Muslim community? The wholesale abandonment of Islamic family law for whatever reason is an approach which no longer commands support. The approach taken at one time by some elements of Muslim opinion not to meddle with the Qur'ān and *sunnah* but to place it entirely on one side and adopt a code of Western inspiration (as in Turkey in 1927) is not likely to be copied. Flirtations with secular radicalism (Somalia, 1975) would appear to be of limited significance on the wider stage. Many of the debates which one associates with discussions on family law in the Western world, such as the rights of unmarried couples, are simply of no consequence in the Islamic world.

It is probable that the mood of Islamic revivalism will involve the continuing dismantling of some aspects of the reform tendencies of the twentieth century. It is, however, highly unlikely that such reforms as those in the field of child marriages, the limitations on polygamy, and the equalization of divorce entitlement between husband and wife will be undermined. Economic considerations could well be as important in this context as religious orthodoxy. More probable to occur in the last years of this century is the continuation of the process whereby Islamic states adopt sympathetic minority opinions of early jurists, or indeed the more acceptable law of another school, as a more accurate reflection of the Islamic ideology of a particular Islamic country.

[*See also* Law; Marriage and Divorce; Polygyny.]

BIBLIOGRAPHY

Anderson, J. N. D. *Law Reform in the Muslim World*. London, 1976. Important description, by one of the most respected commentators on the Islamic world, of trends in the Muslim world up to the mid-1970s. Concentrates on family law reform.

Beck, Lois, and Nikki R. Keddie, eds. *Women in the Muslim World*. Cambridge, Mass., 1978. Includes a valuable essay by Coulson and Hinchcliffe, "Women and Law Reform in Contemporary Islam."

Coulson, Noel J. *A History of Islamic Law*. Edinburgh, 1964. Masterly discussion of the development of Islamic law, with considerable emphasis on family law.

El Alami, Dawoud S. *The Marriage Contract in Islamic Law*. London and New York, 1992. Analysis of marriage law as applied in Egypt and Morocco. Useful for its discussion of Egyptian and Moroccan court decisions.

Esposito, John L. *Women in Muslim Family Law*. Syracuse, N.Y., 1982. Examination of the process, methodology, and extent of modern legal reforms, focusing on Pakistan and Egypt.

Mahmood, Tahir. *Family Law Reform in the Muslim World*. New Delhi, 1972. Useful examination of the pace of reform up to 1970.

Mahmood, Tahir. *Personal Law in Islamic Countries*. New Delhi, 1987. Contains the text of family law statutes from twenty-two countries, together with a helpful comparative overview, and an exceptionally good bibliography at the end of each chapter.

Nasir, Jamal J. *The Islamic Law of Personal Status*. London and New York, 1986. Systematic account of Islamic family law under both *sharīʿah* and modern enactments, particularly in the Arab states.

Pearl, David. *A Textbook on Muslim Personal Law*. 2d ed. London, 1987. Introduction to the main aspects of Islamic family law.

DAVID STEPHEN PEARL

FAMILY PLANNING. High population growth rates over the past forty years coupled with worries about economic and social development have spurred debate on the use of family planning measures by Muslims. In the nineteenth and early twentieth centuries, populations in Muslim countries grew slowly as high birth rates were offset by high mortality rates. Following World War II and continuing today, countries with a majority of Muslim citizens are, generally speaking, characterized by high birth rates, which are falling gradually, and a mortality rate that, although still higher than average, is declining. A variety of factors have combined to decrease the total fertility rate (number of children born), including availability of medical services, widespread community health and sanitation programs, greater literacy, the education of women, migration to urban areas, and employment availability.

Although some Muslim countries have the resources to support a growing population, others with more limited resources fear the impact of population growth on their ability to provide services for their citizens. National family planning programs have been implemented in a number of countries with varying success.

Since the beginning of Islam, the Muslim community has encouraged large families to ensure a strong and vibrant Muslim population. However, religious scholars (*ʿulamāʾ*) assert the religious permissibility of family planning in the *fiqh* (jurisprudence) literature on marriage and family. The Qur'ān makes no mention of family planning measures, but a few *ḥadīth* texts mention *ʿazl (coitus interruptus)*. The *fiqh* discussion centers on the question of the permissibility of *ʿazl,* and schools differ in their response. *ʿAzl* is judged to be *makrūh* (reprehensible), but major variables in determining the permissibility of *ʿazl* is the status of the woman involved (free or slave) and whether she gives her consent to its use. As ʿ*azl* is considered to be detrimental to the woman, depriving her of her right to children (some schools believe it deprives her of sexual satisfaction), it was only permissible with a free woman if she consented to its use. All but the majority of the Shāfiʿī school ruled that the permissibility of ʿ*azl* was contingent upon her consent.

As the jurists were male and ʿ*azl* was controlled by the male partner, this was the only contraceptive method discussed in the *fiqh* literature. Medical texts, however, document that women have utilized a variety of other means of contraception. These methods included infusions, suppositories, sexual techniques, and magic (Hines, 1970).

Contemporary ʿ*ulamā*ʾ tend to resolve the religious permissibility of family planning along the same lines of reasoning as their medieval colleagues. The twentieth century introduced a variety of contraceptive methods whose usage is primarily controlled by women. Accordingly, the majority of ʿ*ulamā*ʾ rule that use of contraceptive methods is permissible for Muslims as long as the husband and the wife agree to it. This position follows the logic of the classical texts in that, although use of contraception may be injurious to the wishes of one spouse, if both agree, then the rights of both are guaranteed.

Less well-educated religious leaders in small towns and villages often hold that family planning is prohibited by Islam. Their reasoning follows a different line, which argues on deterministic grounds. They base their premise on a *ḥadīth* that states: "Marry, have children and multiply that I will be proud of you on Judgment Day." They prohibit family planning on the basis that it opposes the supremacy of the will of God.

Some Muslim scholars, as well as economists and development experts, have challenged Islam's pronatalist policy by questioning whether the traditional way of defining the strength of Islam as proportional to the number of its adherents still applies. Maḥmūd Shaltūt, rector of al-Azhar University during the early part of the regime of Gamal Abdel Nasser, argued for both the permissibility of family planning and the role of the state in implementing family planning programs. Although in early Islam strength was equated with a large population, Shaltūt maintained that in the twentieth century, large populations may weaken rather than strengthen communities. Factors such as poverty, malnutrition, and lessened public morality that are concomitant with large populations in developing areas all make the Muslim community vulnerable to enemies. Shaltūt stated that if family planning would contribute to alleviation of these social ills, it was then permissible in Islam; he implied that the state was responsible for the facilitation of such programs.

Contemporary ʿ*ulamā*ʾ who oppose family planning generally cite reasons having as much to do with politics as religion. The terms used for contraception often indicate political stances. "Birth control" (*taḥdīd al-naṣl*) carries the negative sense of limiting or eliminating progeny; "family planning" (*al-takhṭīṭ al-*ʿ*ā*ʾ*ilī* or *tanẓīm al-usrah*) has a more positive connotation of spacing births in the best interests of all family members. While most ʿ*ulamā*ʾ hold that any family has the option to employ privately family planning measures, at the same time they may oppose government programs that disseminate birth control measures and information. Many see state-sponsored programs as an attempt at coercion.

Some Muslims regard the Western development experts' linkage of population control and economic development as both damaging and fallacious. They postulate that the West seeks to weaken Islam by limiting the size of the Muslim community, and they reject all family planning programs on that basis. Muslim activists or Islamists are among the most vocal opponents of family planning. Islamists in Egypt attack contraceptive use in an attempt to counter the government's two-decade-old family planning program. In 1977 the shaykh (rector) of al-Azhar wrote an essay, "Birth Control is a Refuted Idea," which held that family planning is both unnecessary and counter to Islamic belief. He called for greater human reliance on God for sustenance and for Muslim inventiveness and dedication in the conquest of the desert and better use of resources. Many Islamists hold that use of birth control contributes to greater immorality in the form of premarital sexual activity, adultery, and abortion. These arguments are common in Islamist circles throughout the Muslim world, and are often tied to attempts to restrict greater latitude given to women in personal status laws. All Muslim religious leaders oppose sterilization on religious grounds as it permanently alters what God has created.

[*See also* Abortion; Surrogate Motherhood.]

BIBLIOGRAPHY

Bowen, Donna Lee. "Islam and Family Planning in Morocco." *Maghreb Review* 3.10 (1980): 20–29. Presents views of present-day Moroccan religious leaders on family planning.

Bowen, Donna Lee. "Muslim Juridical Opinions Concerning the Status of Women as Demonstrated by the Case of Azl." *Journal of Near Eastern Studies* 40.4 (1981): 323–328. Presentation of Muslim legal schools' positions on contraceptive use.

Bowen, Donna Lee. "Pragmatic Morality: Islam and Family Planning in Morocco." In *Everyday Life in the Contemporary Middle East*, edited by Donna Lee Bowen and E. A. Early, pp. 91–100. Bloomington, 1993. Presentation and analysis of contemporary Muslim views on family planning.

Hines, Norman E. *Medical History of Contraception* (1936). Boston, 1970. Chapter 6, "The Islamic World and Europe during the Middle Ages," details contraceptive methods used in that period.

Musallam, Basim F. *Sex and Society in Islam: Birth Control before the Nineteenth Century*. Cambridge, 1983. Excellent study of family planning in theory and practice, and the demography of Muslim nations during the medieval and early modern period.

Nazer, Isam R., ed. *Islam and Family Planning*. 2 vols. Beirut, 1974. Collection of articles by Muslim theologians (*ʿulamāʾ*) on all aspects of marriage, family, and family planning. First published in Arabic.

Omran, Abdel Rahim. *Family Planning in the Legacy of Islam*. London and New York, 1992. Comprehensive collection and discussion of Qurʾānic, *ḥadīth*, and jurisprudence references relating to marriage, the family, and family planning.

Shaltūt, Maḥmūd. "Tanẓīm al-Nasl." In *Al-islām: ʿAqīdah wa-sharīʿah*. Cairo, 1966. Controversial reading of Islamic social theory by the politically astute rector of al-Azhar.

Weeks, John R. "The Demography of Islamic Nations." *Population Bulletin* (Washington, D.C.) 43.4 (1988). Handbook on demography and population issues in Islamic countries.

DONNA LEE BOWEN